Collins
gem

Collins
Spanish
Dictionary

Español-Inglés
English-Spanish

HarperCollins Publishers
Westerhill Road
Bishopbriggs
Glasgow
G64 2QT
Great Britain

Seventh Edition/Séptima Edición 2006

© William Collins Sons & Co. Ltd. 1982, 1989
© HarperCollins Publishers 1993, 1998, 2001, 2004, 2006

ISBN-13 978-0-00-722399-2
ISBN-10 0-00-722399-4

Collins Gem® and Bank of English® are registered trademarks of HarperCollins Publishers Limited

www.collins.co.uk

A catalogue record for this book is available from the British Library

Grupo Editorial Random House Mondadori, S.L.
Travessera de Gràcia 47-49, 08021 Barcelona

www.diccionarioscollins.com

ISBN 84-253-4013-6

Typeset by/Fotocomposición Thomas Callan

Printed in Italy by/Impreso en Italia por Legoprint S.P.A.

Acknowledgements
We would like to thank those authors and publishers who kindly gave permission for copyright material to be used in the Collins Word Web. We would also like to thank Times Newspapers Ltd for providing valuable data.

GENERAL EDITOR/
DIRECCIÓN GENERAL
Michela Clari

CONTRIBUTORS/
COLABORADORES
José Martín Galera
Wendy Lee
José María Ruiz Vaca
Cordelia Lilly

EDITORIAL COORDINATION/
COORDINACIÓN EDITORIAL
Joyce Littlejohn
Marianne Davidson
Maree Airlie

SERIES EDITOR/
COLECCIÓN DIRIGIDA POR
Lorna Knight

William Collins' dream of knowledge for all began with the publication of his first book in 1819. A self-educated mill worker, he not only enriched millions of lives, but also founded a flourising publishing house. Today, staying true to this spirit, Collins books are packed with inspiration, innovation, and practical expertise. They place you at the centre of a world of possibility and give you exactly what you need to explore it.

Language is the key to this exploration, and at the heart of Collins Dictionaries is language as it is really used. New words, phrases, and meanings spring up every day, and all of them are captured and analysed by the Collins Word Web. Constantly updated, and with over 2.5 billion entries, this living language resource is unique to our dictionaries.

Words are tools for life. And a Collins Dictionary makes them work for you.

Collins. Do more.

ÍNDICE

CONTENTS

Estamos muy satisfechos de que hayas decidido comprar este diccionario y esperamos que lo disfrutes y que te sirva de gran ayuda ya sea en el colegio, en el trabajo, en tus vacaciones o en casa.

Esta introducción pretende darte algunas indicaciones para ayudarte a sacar el mayor provecho de este diccionario; no sólo de su extenso vocabulario, sino de toda la información que te proporciona cada entrada. Esta te ayudará a leer y comprender – y también a comunicarte y a expresarte – en inglés moderno. Este diccionario comienza con una lista de abreviaturas utilizadas en el texto y con una ilustración de los sonidos representados por los símbolos fonéticos.

EL MANEJO DE TU DICCIONARIO

La amplia información que te ofrece este diccionario aparece presentada en distintas tipografías, con caracteres de diversos tamaños y con distintos símbolos, abreviaturas y paréntesis. Los apartados siguientes explican las reglas y símbolos utilizados.

ENTRADAS

Las palabras que consultas en el diccionario – las entradas – aparecen ordenadas alfabéticamente y en color para una identificación más rápida. La palabra que aparece en la parte superior de cada página es la primera entrada (si aparece en la página izquierda) y la última entrada (si aparece en la página derecha) de la página en cuestión. La información sobre el uso o la forma de determinadas entradas aparece entre paréntesis, detrás de la transcripción fonética, y generalmente en forma abreviada y en cursiva

(p. ej.: (*fam*), (*Com*)). En algunos casos se ha considerado oportuno agrupar palabras de una misma familia (nación, nacionalismo; accept, acceptance) bajo una misma entrada que aparece en color.

Las expresiones de uso corriente en las que aparece una entrada se dan en negrita (p. ej.: hurry: [...] **to be in a ~**).

SÍMBOLOS FONÉTICOS

La transcripción fonética de cada entrada inglesa (que indica su pronunciación) aparece entre corchetes, inmediatamente después de la entrada (p. ej. knife [naif]). En las páginas xv-xviii encontrarás una lista de los símbolos fonéticos utilizados en este diccionario.

TRADUCCIONES

Las traducciones de las entradas aparecen en caracteres normales, y en los casos en los que existen significados o usos diferentes, éstos aparecen separados mediante un punto y coma. A menudo encontrarás también otras palabras en cursiva y entre paréntesis antes de las traducciones. Estas sugieren contextos en los que la entrada podría aparecer (p. ej.: alto (*persona*) o (*sonido*)) o proporcionan sinónimos (p. ej.: mismo (*semejante*)).

PALABRAS CLAVE

Particular relevancia reciben ciertas palabras inglesas y españolas que han sido consideradas palabras 'clave' en cada lengua. Estas pueden, por ejemplo, ser de utilización muy corriente o tener distintos usos (de, haber; get, that). La combinación de triángulos y números te permitirá

distinguir las diferentes categorías gramaticales y los
diferentes significados. Las indicaciones en cursiva y entre
paréntesis proporcionan además importante información
adicional.

FALSOS AMIGOS

Las palabras que se prestan a confusión al traducir han
sido identificadas. En tales entradas existen unas notas
que te ayudaran a evitar errores.

INFORMACIÓN GRAMATICAL

Las categorías gramaticales aparecen en forma abreviada
y en cursiva después de la transcripción fonética de cada
entrada (*vt*, *adv*, *conj*). También se indican la forma
femenina y los plurales irregulares de los sustantivos
del inglés (child, -ren).

We are delighted that you have decided to buy this Spanish dictionary and hope you will enjoy and benefit from using it at school, at home, on holiday or at work.

This introduction gives you a few tips on how to get the most out of your dictionary – not simply from its comprehensive wordlist but also from the information provided in each entry. This will help you to read and understand modern Spanish, as well as communicate and express yourself in the language. This dictionary begins by listing the abbreviations used in the text and illustrating the sounds shown by the phonetic symbols.

USING YOUR DICTIONARY

A wealth of information is presented in the dictionary, using various typefaces, sizes of type, symbols, abbreviations and brackets. The various conventions and symbols used are explained in the following sections.

HEADWORDS

The words you look up in a dictionary – 'headwords' – are listed alphabetically. They are printed in colour for rapid identification. The headwords appearing at the top of each page indicate the first (if it appears on a left-hand page) and last word (if it appears on a right-hand page) dealt with on the page in question.

Information about the usage or form of certain headwords is given in brackets after the phonetic spelling. This usually appears in abbreviated form and in italics (e.g. (*fam*), (*Com*)).

Where appropriate, words related to headwords are grouped in the same entry (nación, nacionalismo; accept, acceptance) and are also in colour. Common expressions in which the headword appears are shown in a different bold roman type (e.g. cola: [...] hacer~).

The phonetic spelling of each headword (indicating its pronunciation) is given in square brackets immediately after the headword (e.g. cohete [ko'ete]). A list of these symbols is given on pages xv-xviii.

TRANSLATIONS
Headword translations are given in ordinary type and, where more than one meaning or usage exists, these are separated by a semi-colon. You will often find other words in italics in brackets before the translations. These offer suggested contexts in which the headword might appear (e.g. fare (on trains, buses) or provide synonyms (e.g. litter (rubbish) o (young animals)). The gender of the Spanish translation also appears in italics immediately following the key element of the translation, except where this is a regular masculine singular noun ending in 'o', or a regular feminine noun ending in 'a'.

KEY WORDS
Special status is given to certain Spanish and English words which are considered as 'key' words in each language. They may, for example, occur very frequently or have several types of usage (e.g. de, haber; get, that). A combination of triangles and numbers helps you to distinguish different

parts of speech and different meanings. Further helpful information is provided in brackets and italics.

FALSE FRIENDS

Words which can be easily confused have been identified in the dictionary. Notes at such entries will help you to avoid these common translation pitfalls.

GRAMMATICAL INFORMATION

Parts of speech are given in abbreviated form in italics after the phonetic spellings of headwords (e.g. *vt*, *adv*, *conj*). Genders of Spanish nouns are indicated as follows: *nm* for a masculine and *nf* for a feminine noun. Feminine and irregular plural forms of nouns are also shown (irlandés, esa; luz (*pl* luces)).

ABREVIATURAS		ABBREVIATIONS
abreviatura	*ab(b)r*	abbreviation
adjetivo, locución adjetiva	*adj*	adjective, adjectival phrase
administración	*Admin*	administration
adverbio, locución adverbial	*adv*	adverb, adverbial phrase
agricultura	*Agr*	agriculture
anatomía	*Anat*	anatomy
Argentina	*Arg*	Argentina
arquitectura	*Arq, Arch*	architecture
el automóvil	*Aut(o)*	the motor car and motoring
aviación, viajes aéreos	*Aviac, Aviat*	flying, air travel
biología	*Bio(l)*	biology
botánica, flores	*Bot*	botany
inglés británico	*BRIT*	British English
Centroamérica	*CAM*	Central America
química	*Chem*	chemistry
comercio, finanzas, banca	*Com(m)*	commerce, finance, banking
informática	*Comput*	computing
conjunción	*conj*	conjunction
construcción	*Constr*	building
compuesto	*cpd*	compound element
Cono Sur	*cs*	Southern Cone
cocina	*Culin*	cookery
economía	*Econ*	economics
eletricidad, electrónica	*Elec*	electricity, electronics
enseñanza, sistema escolar y universitario	*Escol*	schooling, schools and universities
España	*ESP*	Spain
especialmente	*esp*	especially
exclamación, interjección	*excl*	exclamation, interjection
femenino	*f*	feminine
lengua familiar (! vulgar)	*fam(!)*	colloquial usage (! particularly offensive)
ferrocarril	*Ferro*	railways
uso figurado	*fig*	figurative use
fotografía	*Foto*	photography
(verbo inglés) del cual la partícula es inseparable	*fus*	(phrasal verb) where the particle is inseparable
generalmente	*gen*	generally
geografía, geología	*Geo*	geography, geology
geometría	*Geom*	geometry

xii

historia	*Hist*	history
uso familiar	*inf(!)*	colloquial usage
(! vulgar)		(! particularly offensive)
infinitivo	*infin*	infinitive
informática	*Inform*	computing
invariable	*inv*	invariable
irregular	*irreg*	irregular
lo jurídico	*Jur*	law
América Latina	LAM	Latin America
gramática, lingüística	*Ling*	grammar, linguistics
masculino	*m*	masculine
matemáticas	*Mat(h)*	mathematics
masculino/femenino	*m/f*	masculine/feminine
medicina	*Med*	medicine
México	MÉX, MEX	Mexico
lo militar, ejército	*Mil*	military matters
música	*Mús, Mus*	music
substantivo, nombre	*n*	noun
navegación, náutica	*Náut, Naut*	sailing, navigation
sustantivo numérico	*num*	numeral noun
complemento	*obj*	(grammatical) object
	o.s.	oneself
peyorativo	*pey, pej*	derogatory, pejorative
fotografía	*Phot*	photography
fisiología	*Physiol*	physiology
plural	*pl*	plural
política	*Pol*	politics
participio de pasado	*pp*	past participle
preposición	*prep*	preposition
pronombre	*pron*	pronoun
psicología, psiquiatría	*Psico, Psych*	psychology, psychiatry
tiempo pasado	*pt*	past tense
química	*Quím*	chemistry
ferrocarril	*Rail*	railways
religión	*Rel*	religion
Río de la Plata	RPL	River Plate
	sb	somebody
Cono Sur	SC	Southern Cone
enseñanza, sistema escolar	*Scol*	schooling, schools
y universitario		and universities
singular	*sg*	singular
España	SP	Spain
	sth	something

sujeto	su(b)j	(grammatical) subject
subjuntivo	subjun	subjunctive
tauromaquia	Taur	bullfighting
también	tb	also
técnica, tecnología	Tec(h)	technical term, technology
telecomunicaciones	Telec, Tel	telecommunications
imprenta, tipografía	Tip, Typ	typography, printing
televisión	TV	television
universidad	Univ	university
inglés norteamericano	US	American English
verbo	vb	verb
verbo intransitivo	vi	intransitive verb
verbo pronominal	vr	reflexive verb
verbo transitivo	vt	transitive verb
zoología	Zool	zoology
marca registrada	®	registered trademark
indica un equivalente cultural	≈	introduces a cultural equivalent

SPANISH PRONUNCIATION

VOWELS

a	[a]	pata	not as long as *a* in f*a*r. When followed by a consonant in the same syllable (i.e. in a closed syllable), as in *a*mante, the *a* is short, as in b*a*t
e	[e]	me	like *e* in th*ey*. In a closed syllable, as in g*e*nte, the *e* is short as in p*e*t
i	[i]	pino	as in m*ea*n or mach*i*ne
o	[o]	lo	as in l*o*cal. In a closed syllable, as in c*o*ntrol, the *o* is short as in c*o*t
u	[u]	lunes	as in r*u*le. It is silent after q, and in gue, gui, unless marked güe, güi e.g. antigüedad, when it is pronounced like *w* in *w*olf

SEMIVOWELS

i, y	[j]	bien	pronounced like *y* in *y*es
		hielo	
		yunta	
u	[w]	huevo	unstressed *u* between consonant and vowel is pronounced like *w* in *w*ell. See notes on *u* above.
		fuento	
		antigüedad	

DIPHTHONGS

ai, ay	[ai]	baile	as *i* in r*i*de
au	[au]	auto	as *ou* in sh*ou*t
ei, ey	[ei]	buey	as *ey* in gr*ey*
eu	[eu]	deuda	both elements pronounced independently [e] + [u]
oi, oy	[oi]	hoy	as *oy* in t*oy*

CONSONANTS

b	[b,β]	boda	see notes on *v* below
		bomba	
		labor	
c	[k]	caja	*c* before *a, o, u* is pronounced as in *c*at
ce, ci	[θe,θi]	cero	*c* before *e* or *i* is pronounced as in *th*in
		cielo	
ch	[tʃ]	chiste	*ch* is pronounced as *ch* in *ch*air
d	[d,ð]	danés	at the beginning of a phrase or after *l* or *n*, *d* is pronounced as in English. In any other position it is pronounced like *th* in *th*e
		ciudad	

g	[g, ɣ]	gafas paga	g before a, o or u is pronounced as in gap, if at the beginning of a phrase or after n. In other positions the sound is softened
ge, gi	[xe, xi]	gente girar	g before e or i is pronounced similar to ch in Scottish loch
h		haber	h is always silent in Spanish
j	[x]	jugar	j is pronounced similar to ch in Scottish loch
ll	[ʎ]	talle	ll is pronounced like the y in yet or the lli in million
ñ	[ʃ]	niño	ñ is pronounced like the ni in onion
q	[k]	que	q is pronounced as k in king
r, rr	[r, rr]	quitar garra	r is always pronounced in Spanish, unlike the silent r in dancer. rr is trilled, like a Scottish r
s	[s]	quizás isla	s is usually pronounced as in pass, but before b, d, g, l, m or n it is pronounced as in rose
v	[b, β]	vía	v is pronounced something like b. At the beginning of a phrase or after m or n it is pronounced as b in boy. In any other position the sound is softened
z	[θ]	tenaz	z is pronounced as th in thin

f, k, l, m, n, p, t and x are pronounced as in English.

STRESS

The rules of stress in Spanish are as follows:

(a) when a word ends in a vowel or in n or s, the second last syllable is stressed:
    patata, patatas; come, comen
(b) when a word ends in a consonant other than n or s, the stress falls on the last syllable:
    pared, hablar
(c) when the rules set out in (a) and (b) are not applied, an acute accent appears over the stressed vowel:
    común, geografía, inglés

In the phonetic transcription, the symbol ['] precedes the syllable on which the stress falls.

LA PRONUNCIACIÓN INGLESA

VOCALES

	Ejemplo inglés	Explicación
[ɑː]	father	Entre *a* de padre y *o* de noche
[ʌ]	but, come	*a* muy breve
[æ]	man, cat	Con los labios en la posición de *e* en pena y luego se pronuncia el sonido *a* parecido a la *a* de carro
[ə]	father, ago	Vocal neutra parecida a una *e* u *o* casi muda
[əː]	bird, heard	Entre *e* abierta y *o* cerrada, sonido alargado
[ɛ]	get, bed	Como en perro
[ɪ]	it, big	Más breve que en *si*
[iː]	tea, see	Como en *fino*
[ɔ]	hot, wash	Como en *torre*
[ɔː]	saw, all	Como en *por*
[u]	put, book	Sonido breve, más cerrado que *burro*
[uː]	too, you	Sonido largo, como en *uno*

DIPTONGOS

	Ejemplo inglés	Explicación
[aɪ]	fly, high	Como en *fraile*
[au]	how, house	Como en *pausa*
[ɛə]	there, bear	Casi como en *vea*, pero el sonido *a* se mezcla con el indistinto [ə]
[eɪ]	day, obey	*e* cerrada seguida por una *i* débil
[ɪə]	here, hear	Como en *manía*, mezclándose el sonido *a* con el indistinto [ə]
[əu]	go, note	[ə] seguido por una breve *u*
[ɔɪ]	boy, oil	Como en *voy*
[uə]	poor, sure	*u* bastante larga más el sonido indistinto [ə]

CONSONANTES

	Ejemplo inglés	Explicación
[b]	big, lobby	Como en tumban
[d]	mended	Como en conde, andar
[g]	go, get, big	Como en grande, gol
[dʒ]	gin, judge	Como en la *ll* andaluza y en Generalitat (*catalán*)
[ŋ]	sing	Como en vínculo
[h]	house, he	Como la jota hispanoamericana
[j]	young, yes	Como en ya
[k]	come, mock	Como en caña, Escocia
[r]	red, tread	Se pronuncia con la punta de la lengua hacia atrás y sin hacerla vibrar
[s]	sand, yes	Como en casa, sesión
[z]	rose, zebra	Como en desde, mismo
[ʃ]	she, machine	Como en chambre (*francés*), roxo (*portugués*)
[tʃ]	chin, rich	Como en chocolate
[v]	valley	Como *f*, pero se retiran los dientes superiores vibrándolos contra el labio inferior
[w]	water, which	Como la *u* de huevo, puede
[ʒ]	vision	Como en journal (*francés*)
[θ]	think, myth	Como en receta, zapato
[ð]	this, the	Como en hablado, verdad

f, l, m, n, p, t y x iguales que en español.

El signo [*] indica que la r final escrita apenas se pronuncia en inglés británico cuando la palabra siguiente empieza con vocal. El signo ['] indica la sílaba acentuada.

SPANISH VERB TABLES

1 Gerund 2 Imperative 3 Present 4 Preterite 5 Future 6 Present subjunctive 7 Imperfect subjunctive 8 Past participle 9 Imperfect

Etc indicates that the irregular root is used for all persons of the tense, e.g. oír: 6 oiga, oigas, oigamos, oigáis, oigan

agradecer 3 agradezco 6 agradezca *etc*

aprobar 2 aprueba 3 apruebo, apruebas, aprueba, aprueban 6 apruebe, apruebes, apruebe, aprueben

atravesar 2 atraviesa 3 atravieso, atraviesas, atraviesa, atraviesan 6 atraviese, atravieses, atraviese, atraviesen

caber 3 quepo 4 cupe, cupiste, cupo, cupimos, cupisteis, cupieron 5 cabré *etc* 6 quepa *etc* 7 cupiera *etc*

caer 1 cayendo 3 caigo 4 cayó, cayeron 6 caiga *etc* 7 cayera *etc*

cerrar 2 cierra 3 cierro, cierras, cierra, cierran 6 cierre, cierres, cierre, cierren

COMER 1 comiendo 2 come, comed 3 como, comes, come, comemos, coméis, comen 4 comí, comiste, comió, comimos, comisteis, comieron 5 comeré, comerás, comerá, comeremos, comeréis, comerán 6 coma, comas, coma, comamos, comáis, coman 7 comiera, comieras, comiera, comiéramos, comierais, comieran 8 comido 9 comía, comías, comía, comíamos, comíais, comían

conocer 3 conozco 6 conozca *etc*

contar 2 cuenta 3 cuento, cuentas, cuenta, cuentan

cuente, cuentes, cuente, cuenten

dar 3 doy 4 di, diste, dio, dimos, disteis, dieron 7 diera *etc*

decir 2 di 3 digo 4 dije, dijiste, dijo, dijimos, dijisteis, dijeron 5 diré *etc* 6 diga *etc* 7 dijera *etc* 8 dicho

despertar 2 despierta 3 despierto, despiertas, despierta, despiertan 6 despierte, despiertes, despierte, despierten

divertir 1 divirtiendo 2 divierte 3 divierto, diviertes, divierte, divierten 4 divirtió, divirtieron 6 divierta, diviertas, divierta, divirtamos, divirtáis, diviertan 7 divirtiera *etc*

dormir 1 durmiendo 2 duerme 3 duermo, duermes, duerme, duermen 4 durmió, durmieron 6 duerma, duermas, duerma, durmamos, durmáis, duerman 7 durmiera *etc*

empezar 2 empieza 3 empiezo, empiezas, empieza, empiezan 4 empecé 6 empiece, empieces, empiece, empecemos, empecéis, empiecen

entender 2 entiende 3 entiendo, entiendes, entiende, entienden 6 entienda, entiendas, entienda, entiendan

ESTAR 2 está 3 estoy, estás, está, están 4 estuve, estuviste,

estuvo, estuvimos, estuvisteis,
estuvieron 6 esté, estés, esté,
estén 7 estuviera *etc*
HABER 3 he, has, ha, hemos,
han 4 hube, hubiste, hubo,
hubimos, hubisteis, hubieron
5 habré *etc* 6 haya *etc* 7 hubiera
etc
HABLAR 1 hablando 2 habla,
hablad 3 hablo, hablas, habla,
hablamos, habláis, hablan
4 hablé, hablaste, habló,
hablamos, hablasteis,
hablaron 5 hablaré, hablarás,
hablará, hablaremos,
hablaréis, hablarán 6 hable,
hables, hable, hablemos,
habléis, hablen 7 hablara,
hablaras, hablara, habláramos,
hablarais, hablaran 8 hablado
9 hablaba, hablabas, hablaba,
hablábamos, hablabais,
hablaban
hacer 2 haz 3 hago 4 hice,
hiciste, hizo, hicimos,
hicisteis, hicieron 5 haré *etc*
6 haga *etc* 7 hiciera *etc* 8 hecho
instruir 1 instruyendo 2 instruye
3 instruyo, instruyes, instruye,
instruyen 4 instruyó,
instruyeron 6 instruya *etc*
7 instruyera *etc*
ir 1 yendo 2 ve 3 voy, vas, va,
vamos, vais, van 4 fui, fuiste,
fue, fuimos, fuisteis, fueron
6 vaya, vayas, vaya, vayamos,
vayáis, vayan 7 fuera *etc* 9 iba,
ibas, iba, íbamos, ibais, iban
jugar 2 juega 3 juego, juegas,
juega, juegan 4 jugué 6 juegue
etc
leer 1 leyendo 4 leyó, leyeron
7 leyera *etc*
morir 1 muriendo 2 muere
3 muero, mueres, muere,
mueren 4 murió, murieron

6 muera, mueras, muera,
muramos, muráis, mueran
7 muriera *etc* 8 muerto
mover 2 mueve 3 muevo,
mueves, mueve, mueven
6 mueva, muevas, mueva,
muevan
negar 2 niega 3 niego, niegas,
niega, niegan 4 negué
6 niegue, niegues, niegue,
neguemos, neguéis, nieguen
ofrecer 3 ofrezco 6 ofrezca *etc*
oír 1 oyendo 2 oye 3 oigo, oyes,
oye, oyen 4 oyó, oyeron 6 oiga
etc 7 oyera *etc*
oler 2 huele 3 huelo, hueles,
huele, huelen 6 huela, huelas,
huela, huelan
parecer 3 parezco 6 parezca *etc*
pedir 1 pidiendo 2 pide 3 pido,
pides, pide, piden 4 pidió,
pidieron 6 pida *etc* 7 pidiera *etc*
pensar 2 piensa 3 pienso,
piensas, piensa, piensan
6 piense, pienses, piense,
piensen
perder 2 pierde 3 pierdo, pierdes,
pierde, pierden 6 pierda,
pierdas, pierda, pierdan
poder 1 pudiendo 2 puede
3 puedo, puedes, puede,
pueden 4 pude, pudiste, pudo,
pudimos, pudisteis, pudieron
5 podré *etc* 6 pueda, puedas,
pueda, puedan 7 pudiera *etc*
poner 2 pon 3 pongo 4 puse,
pusiste, puso, pusimos,
pusisteis, pusieron 5 pondré *etc*
6 ponga 7 pusiera *etc*
8 puesto
preferir 1 prefiriendo 2 prefiere
3 prefiero, prefieres, prefiere,
prefieren 4 prefirió, prefirieron
6 prefiera, prefieras, prefiera,
prefiramos, prefiráis, prefieran
7 prefiriera *etc*

querer 2 quiere 3 quiero, quieres, quiere, quieren 4 quise, quisiste, quiso, quisimos, quisisteis, quisieron 5 querré *etc* 6 quiera, quieras, quiera, quieran 7 quisiera *etc*

reír 2 ríe 3 río, ríes, ríe, ríen 4 reí, rieron 6 ría, rías, ría, riamos, riáis, rían 7 riera *etc*

repetir 1 repitiendo 2 repite 3 repito, repites, repite, repiten 4 repitió, repitieron 6 repita *etc* 7 repitiera *etc*

rogar 2 ruega 3 ruego, ruegas, ruega, ruegan 4 rogué 6 ruegue, ruegues, ruegue, roguemos, roguéis, rueguen

saber 3 sé 4 supe, supiste, supo, supimos, supisteis, supieron 5 sabré *etc* 6 sepa *etc* 7 supiera *etc*

salir 2 sal 3 salgo 5 saldré *etc* 6 salga *etc*

seguir 1 siguiendo 2 sigue 3 sigo, sigues, sigue, siguen 4 siguió, siguieron 6 siga *etc* 7 siguiera *etc*

sentar 2 sienta 3 siento, sientas, sienta, sientan 6 siente, sientes, siente, sienten

sentir 1 sintiendo 2 siente 3 siento, sientes, siente, sienten 4 sintió, sintieron 6 sienta, sientas, sintamos, sintáis, sientan 7 sintiera *etc*

SER 2 sé 3 soy, eres, es, somos, sois, son 4 fui, fuiste, fue, fuimos, fuisteis, fueron 6 sea *etc* 7 fuera *etc* 9 era, eras, era, éramos, erais, eran

servir 1 sirviendo 2 sirve 3 sirvo, sirves, sirve, sirven 4 sirvió, sirvieron 6 sirva 7 sirviera *etc*

soñar 2 sueña 3 sueño, sueñas, sueña, sueñan 6 sueñe, sueñes, sueñe, sueñen

tener 2 ten 3 tengo, tienes, tiene, tienen 4 tuve, tuviste, tuvo, tuvimos, tuvisteis, tuvieron 5 tendré *etc* 6 tenga *etc* 7 tuviera *etc*

traer 1 trayendo 3 traigo 4 traje, trajiste, trajo, trajimos, trajisteis, trajeron 6 traiga *etc* 7 trajera *etc*

valer 2 vale 3 valgo 5 valdré *etc* 6 valga *etc*

venir 2 ven 3 vengo, vienes, viene, vienen 4 vine, viniste, vino, vinimos, vinisteis, vinieron 5 vendré *etc* 6 venga *etc* 7 viniera *etc*

ver 3 veo 6 vea *etc* 8 visto 9 veía *etc*

vestir 1 vistiendo 2 viste 3 visto, vistes, viste, visten 4 vistió, vistieron 6 vista *etc* 7 vistiera *etc*

VIVIR 1 viviendo 2 vive, vivid 3 vivo, vives, vive, vivimos, vivís, viven 4 viví, viviste, vivió, vivimos, vivisteis, vivieron 5 viviré, vivirás, vivirá, viviremos, viviréis, vivirán 6 viva, vivas, viva, vivamos, viváis, vivan 7 viviera, vivieras, viviera, viviéramos, vivierais, vivieran 8 vivido 9 vivía, vivías, vivía, vivíamos, vivíais, vivían

volver 2 vuelve 3 vuelvo, vuelves, vuelve, vuelven 6 vuelva, vuelvas, vuelva, vuelvan 8 vuelto

VERBOS IRREGULARES EN INGLÉS

PRESENTE	PASADO	PARTICIPIO	PRESENTE	PASADO	PARTICIPIO
arise	arose	arisen	dream	dreamed,	dreamed,
awake	awoke	awoken		dreamt	dreamt
be (am, is, are; being)	was, were	been	drink	drank	drunk
			drive	drove	driven
bear	bore	born(e)	dwell	dwelt	dwelt
beat	beat	beaten	eat	ate	eaten
become	became	become	fall	fell	fallen
begin	began	begun	feed	fed	fed
bend	bent	bent	feel	felt	felt
bet	bet, betted	bet, betted	fight	fought	fought
			find	found	found
bid (at auction, cards)	bid	bid	flee	fled	fled
			fling	flung	flung
bid (say)	bade	bidden	fly	flew	flown
bind	bound	bound	forbid	forbad(e)	forbidden
bite	bit	bitten	forecast	forecast	forecast
bleed	bled	bled	forget	forgot	forgotten
blow	blew	blown	forgive	forgave	forgiven
break	broke	broken	forsake	forsook	forsaken
breed	bred	bred	freeze	froze	frozen
bring	brought	brought	get	got	got, (US) gotten
build	built	built			
burn	burnt, burned	burnt, burned	give	gave	given
			go (goes)	went	gone
burst	burst	burst	grind	ground	ground
buy	bought	bought	grow	grew	grown
can	could	(been able)	hang	hung	hung
cast	cast	cast	hang (suspend)	hanged	hanged
catch	caught	caught	(execute)		
choose	chose	chosen	have	had	had
cling	clung	clung	hear	heard	heard
come	came	come	hide	hid	hidden
cost (be valued at)	cost	cost	hit	hit	hit
			hold	held	held
cost (work out price of)	costed	costed	hurt	hurt	hurt
			keep	kept	kept
creep	crept	crept	kneel	knelt, kneeled	knelt, kneeled
cut	cut	cut			
deal	dealt	dealt	know	knew	known
dig	dug	dug	lay	laid	laid
do (does)	did	done	lead	led	led
draw	drew	drawn	lean	leant,	leant,

PRESENTE	PASADO	PARTICIPIO	PRESENTE	PASADO	PARTICIPIO
	leaned	leaned	shine	shone	shone
leap	leapt,	leapt,	shoot	shot	shot
	leaped	leaped	show	showed	shown
learn	learnt,	learnt,	shrink	shrank	shrunk
	learned	learned	shut	shut	shut
leave	left	left	sing	sang	sung
lend	lent	lent	sink	sank	sunk
let	let	let	sit	sat	sat
lie (lying)	lay	lain	slay	slew	slain
light	lit,	lit,	sleep	slept	slept
	lighted	lighted	slide	slid	slid
lose	lost	lost	sling	slung	slung
make	made	made	slit	slit	slit
may	might	–	smell	smelt,	smelt,
mean	meant	meant		smelled	smelled
meet	met	met	sow	sowed	sown,
mistake	mistook	mistaken			sowed
mow	mowed	mown,	speak	spoke	spoken
		mowed	speed	sped,	sped,
must	(had to)	(had to)		speeded	speeded
pay	paid	paid	spell	spelt,	spelt,
put	put	put		spelled	spelled
quit	quit,	quit,	spend	spent	spent
	quitted	quitted	spill	spilt,	spilt,
read	read	read		spilled	spilled
rid	rid	rid	spin	spun	spun
ride	rode	ridden	spit	spat	spat
ring	rang	rung	spoil	spoiled,	spoiled,
rise	rose	risen		spoilt	spoilt
run	ran	run	spread	spread	spread
saw	sawed	sawed,	spring	sprang	sprung
		sawn	stand	stood	stood
say	said	said	steal	stole	stolen
see	saw	seen	stick	stuck	stuck
seek	sought	sought	sting	stung	stung
sell	sold	sold	stink	stank	stunk
send	sent	sent	stride	strode	stridden
set	set	set	strike	struck	struck
sew	sewed	sewn	strive	strove	striven
shake	shook	shaken	swear	swore	sworn
shear	sheared	shorn,	sweep	swept	swept
		sheared	swell	swelled	swollen,
shed	shed	shed			swelled

PRESENTE	PASADO	PARTICIPIO	PRESENTE	PASADO	PARTICIPIO
swim	swam	swum	wear	wore	worn
swing	swung	swung	weave (on loom)	wove	woven
take	took	taken			
teach	taught	taught	weave (wind)	weaved	weaved
tear	tore	torn	wed	wedded, wed	wedded, wed
tell	told	told			
think	thought	thought	weep	wept	wept
throw	threw	thrown	win	won	won
thrust	thrust	thrust	wind	wound	wound
tread	trod	trodden	wring	wrung	wrung
wake	woke, waked	woken, waked	write	wrote	written

7 (razón): **a 30 céntimos el kilo** at 30 cents a kilo; **a más de 50 km/h** at more than 50 kms per hour

8 (dativo): **se lo di a él** I gave it to him; **vi al policía** I saw the policeman; **se lo compré a él** I bought it from him

9 (tras ciertos verbos): **voy a verle** I'm going to see him; **empezó a trabajar** he started working to to work

10 (+ infin): **al verlo, lo reconocí inmediatamente** when I saw him I recognized him at once; **el camino a recorrer** the distance we etc have to travel; **¡a callar!** keep quiet!; **¡a comer!** let's eat!

PALABRA CLAVE

a [a] (a + el = al) prep **1** (dirección) to; **fueron a Madrid/Grecia** they went to Madrid/Greece; **me voy a casa** I'm going home

2 (distancia): **está a 15 km de aquí** it's 15 kms from here

3 (posición): **estar a la mesa** to be at table; **al lado de** next to, beside; V tb **puerta**

4 (tiempo): **a las 10/a medianoche** at 10/midnight; **a la mañana siguiente** the following morning; **a los pocos días** after a few days; **estamos a 9 de julio** it's the ninth of July; **a los 24 años** at the age of 24; **al año/a la semana** a year/week later

5 (manera): **a la francesa** the French way; **a caballo** on horseback; **a oscuras** in the dark

6 (medio, instrumento): **a lápiz** in pencil; **a mano** by hand; **cocina a gas** gas stove

abad, esa [a'βað, 'ðesa] nm/f abbot/abbess; **abadía** nf abbey

abajo [a'βaxo] adv (situación) (down) below, underneath; (en edificio) downstairs; (dirección) down, downwards; **el piso de ~** the downstairs flat; **la parte de ~** the lower part; **¡~ el gobierno!** down with the government!; **cuesta/río ~** downhill/downstream; **de arriba ~** from top to bottom; **el ~ firmante** the undersigned; **más ~** lower o further down

abalanzarse [aβalan'θarse] vr: **~ sobre** o **contra** to throw o.s. at

abanderado, -a [aβande'raðo] nm/f (portaestandarte) standard bearer; (de un movimiento) champion, leader; (MÉX: esquirol) linesman, assistant referee

abandonado, -a [aβando'naðo, a] adj derelict; (desatendido) abandoned; (desierto) deserted; (descuidado) neglected

abandonar [aβando'nar] vt to leave; (persona) to abandon, desert; (cosa) to abandon, leave behind; (descuidar) to neglect; (renunciar a) to give up; (Inform) to quit; **abandonarse** vr: **~se a** to abandon o.s. to; **abandono** nm (acto) desertion, abandonment; (estado) abandon, neglect; (renuncia) withdrawal, retirement; **ganar por**

abandono to win by default

abanico [aβa'niko] nm fan; (Náut) derrick

abarcar [aβar'kar] vt to include, embrace; (LAM: acaparar) to monopolize

abarrotado, -a [aβarro'taðo, a] adj packed

abarrotar [aβarro'tar] vt (local, estadio, teatro) to fill, pack

abarrotero, -a [aβarro'tero, a] (MÉX) nm/f grocer; **abarrotes** (MÉX) nmpl groceries; **tienda de abarrotes** (MÉX, CAM) grocery store

abastecer [aβaste'θer] vt: ~ **(de)** to supply (with); **abastecimiento** nm supply

abasto [a'βasto] nm supply; **no dar** ~ **a** to be unable to cope with

abatible [aβa'tiβle] adj: **asiento** ~ tip-up seat; (Auto) reclining seat

abatido, -a [aβa'tiðo, a] adj dejected, downcast

abatir [aβa'tir] vt (muro) to demolish; (pájaro) to shoot o bring down; (fig) to depress

abdicar [aβði'kar] vi to abdicate

abdomen [aβ'ðomen] nm abdomen; **abdominales** nmpl (tb: **ejercicios abdominales**) sit-ups

abecedario [aβeθe'ðarjo] nm alphabet

abedul [aβe'ðul] nm birch

abeja [a'βexa] nf bee

abejorro [aβe'xorro] nm bumblebee

abertura [aβer'tura] nf = **apertura**

abeto [a'βeto] nm fir

abierto, -a [a'βjerto, a] pp de **abrir** ▷ adj open

abismal [aβis'mal] adj (fig) vast, enormous

abismo [a'βismo] nm abyss

ablandar [aβlan'dar] vt to soften; **ablandarse** vr to get softer

abocado, -a [aβo'kaðo, a] adj (vino) smooth, pleasant

abochornar [aβotʃor'nar] vt to embarrass

abofetear [aβofete'ar] vt to slap (in the face)

abogado, -a [aβo'ɣaðo, a] nm/f lawyer; (notario) solicitor; (en tribunal) barrister (BRIT), attorney (US); **abogado defensor** defence lawyer o (US) attorney

abogar [aβo'ɣar] vi: ~ **por** to plead for; (fig) to advocate

abolir [aβo'lir] vt to abolish; (cancelar) to cancel

abolladura [aβoʎa'ðura] nf dent

abollar [aβo'ʎar] vt to dent

abombarse [aβom'barse] vr (LAM) to go bad

abominable [aβomi'naβle] adj abominable

abonado, -a [aβo'naðo, a] adj (deuda) paid(-up) ▷ nm/f subscriber

abonar [aβo'nar] vt (deuda) to settle; (terreno) to fertilize; (idea) to endorse; **abonarse** vr to subscribe; **abono** nm payment; fertilizer; subscription

abordar [aβor'ðar] vt (barco) to board; (asunto) to broach

aborigen [aβo'rixen] nmf aborigine

aborrecer [aβorre'θer] vt to hate, loathe

abortar [aβor'tar] vi (malparir) to have a miscarriage; (deliberadamente) to have an abortion; **aborto** nm miscarriage; abortion

abovedado, -a [aβoβe'ðaðo, a] adj vaulted, domed

abrasar [aβra'sar] vt to burn (up); (Agr) to dry up, parch

abrazar [aβra'θar] vt to embrace, hug

abrazo [a'βraθo] nm embrace, hug; **un** ~ (en carta) with best wishes

abrebotellas [aβreβo'teʎas] nm inv bottle opener

abrecartas [aβre'kartas] nm inv letter opener

abrelatas [aβre'latas] nm inv tin (BRIT) o can opener

abreviatura [aβreβja'tura] nf abbreviation

abridor [aβri'ðor] nm bottle opener;

(de latas) tin (BRIT) o can opener

abrigador, a [aβriɣa'ðor, a] (MÉX) adj warm

abrigar [aβri'ɣar] vt (proteger) to shelter; (ropa) to keep warm; (fig) to cherish

abrigo [a'βriɣo] nm (prenda) coat, overcoat; (lugar protegido) shelter

abril [a'βril] nm April

abrillantador [aβriʎanta'ðor] nm polish

abrillantar [aβriʎan'tar] vt to polish

abrir [a'βrir] vt to open (up) ▷ vi to open; **abrirse** vr to open (up); (extenderse) to clear; (cielo) to clear; **-se paso** to find o force a way through

abrochar [aβro'tʃar] vt (con botones) to button (up); (zapato, con broche) to do up

abrupto, -a [a'βrupto, a] adj abrupt; (empinado) steep

absoluto, -a [aβso'luto, a] adj absolute; **en -** adv not at all

absolver [aβsol'βer] vt to absolve; (Jur) to pardon; (: acusado) to acquit

absorbente [aβsor'βente] adj absorbent; (interesante) absorbing

absorber [aβsor'βer] vt to absorb; (embeber) to soak up

absorción [aβsor'θjon] nf absorption; (Com) takeover

abstemio, -a [aβs'temjo, a] adj teetotal

abstención [aβsten'θjon] nf abstention

abstenerse [aβste'nerse] vr: **~ (de)** to abstain o refrain (from)

abstinencia [aβsti'nenθja] nf abstinence; (ayuno) fasting

abstracto, -a [a'βstrakto, a] adj abstract

abstraer [aβstra'er] vt to abstract; **abstraerse** vr to be o become absorbed

abstraído, -a [aβstra'iðo, a] adj absent-minded

absuelto [aβ'swelto] pp de **absolver**

absurdo, -a [aβ'surðo, a] adj absurd

abuchear [aβutʃe'ar] vt to boo

abuelo, -a [a'βwelo, a] nm/f grandfather(-mother); **abuelos** nmpl grandparents

abultado, -a [aβul'taðo, a] adj bulky

abultar [aβul'tar] vi to be bulky

abundancia [aβun'danθja] nf: **una ~** plenty of; **abundante** adj abundant, plentiful

abundar [aβun'dar] vi to abound, be plentiful

aburrido, -a [aβu'rriðo, a] adj (hastiado) bored; (que aburre) boring

aburrimiento [aβurri'mjento] nm boredom, tedium

aburrir [aβu'rrir] vt to bore; **aburrirse** vr to be bored, get bored

abusado, -a [aβu'saðo, a] (MÉX: fam) adj (astuto) sharp, cunning ▷ excl: **¡~!** (inv) look out!, careful!

abusar [aβu'sar] vi to go too far; **~ de** to abuse

abusivo, -a [aβu'siβo, a] adj (precio) exorbitant

abuso [a'βuso] nm abuse

acá [a'ka] adv (lugar) here

acabado, -a [aka'βaðo, a] adj finished, complete; (perfecto) perfect; (agotado) worn out; (fig) masterly ▷ nm finish

acabar [aka'βar] vt (llevar a su fin) to finish, complete; (consumir) to use up; (rematar) to finish off ▷ vi to finish, end; **acabarse** vr to finish, stop; (terminarse) to be over; (agotarse) to run out; **~ con** to put an end to; **~ de llegar** to have just arrived; **~ por hacer** to end (up) by doing; **¡se acabó!** it's all over!; (¡basta!) that's enough!

acabóse [aka'βose] nm: **esto es el ~** this is the last straw

academia [aka'ðemja] nf academy; **academia de idiomas** language school; **académico, -a** adj academic

acalorado, -a [akalo'raðo, a] adj (discusión) heated

acampar [akam'par] vi to camp

acantilado [akanti'laðo] nm cliff

acaparar [akapa'rar] vt to

monopolize; (acumular) to hoard

acariciar [akari'θjar] vt to caress; (esperanza) to cherish

acarrear [akarre'ar] vt to transport; (fig) to cause, result in

acaso [a'kaso] adv perhaps, maybe; **(por) si ~** (just) in case

acatar [aka'tar] vt to respect; (ley) obey

acatarrarse [akata'rrarse] vr to catch a cold

acceder [akθe'ðer] vi: **~ a** (petición etc) to agree to; (tener acceso a) to have access to; (Inform) to access

accesible [akθe'siβle] adj accessible

acceso [ak'θeso] nm access, entry; (camino) access, approach; (Med) attack, fit

accesorio, -a [akθe'sorjo, a] adj, nm accessory

accidentado, -a [akθiðen'taðo, a] adj uneven; (montañoso) hilly; (azaroso) eventful ▷ nm/f accident victim

accidental [akθiðen'tal] adj accidental

accidente [akθi'ðente] nm accident; **accidentes** nmpl (de terreno) unevenness sg; **accidente laboral o de trabajo/de tráfico** industrial/road o traffic accident

acción [ak'θjon] nf action; (acto) action, act; (Com) share; (Jur) action, lawsuit; **accionar** vt to work, operate; (Inform) to drive

accionista [akθjo'nista] nmf shareholder, stockholder

acebo [a'θeβo] nm holly; (árbol) holly tree

acechar [aθe'tʃar] vt to spy on; (aguardar) to lie in wait for; **acecho** nm: **estar al acecho (de)** to lie in wait (for)

aceite [a'θeite] nm oil; **aceite de girasol/oliva** olive/sunflower oil; **aceitera** nf oilcan; **aceitoso, -a** adj oily

aceituna [aθei'tuna] nf olive; **aceituna rellena** stuffed olive

acelerador [aθelera'ðor] nm accelerator

acelerar [aθele'rar] vt to accelerate

acelga [a'θelɣa] nf chard, beet

acento [a'θento] nm accent; (acentuación) stress

acentuar [aθen'twar] vt to accent; to stress; (fig) to accentuate

acepción [aθep'θjon] nf meaning

aceptable [aθep'taβle] adj acceptable

aceptación [aθepta'θjon] nf acceptance; (aprobación) approval

aceptar [aθep'tar] vt to accept; (aprobar) to approve; **~ hacer algo** to agree to do sth

acequia [a'θekja] nf irrigation ditch

acera [a'θera] nf pavement (BRIT), sidewalk (US)

acerca [a'θerka]: **~ de** prep about, concerning

acercar [aθer'kar] vt to bring o move nearer; **acercarse** vr to approach, come near

acero [a'θero] nm steel

acérrimo, -a [a'θerrimo, a] adj (partidario) staunch; (enemigo) bitter

acertado, -a [aθer'taðo, a] adj correct; (apropiado) apt; (sensato) sensible

acertar [aθer'tar] vt (blanco) to hit; (solución) to get right; (adivinar) to guess ▷ vi to get right, be right; **~ a** to manage to; **~ con** to happen o hit on

acertijo [aθer'tixo] nm riddle, puzzle

achacar [atʃa'kar] vt to attribute

achacoso, -a [atʃa'koso, a] adj sickly

achicar [atʃi'kar] vt to reduce; (Náut) to bale out

achicharrar [atʃitʃa'rrar] vt to scorch, burn

achichincle [atʃi'tʃinkle] (MÉX: fam) nmf minion

achicoria [atʃi'korja] nf chicory

achuras [a'tʃuras] (RPL) nfpl offal sg

acicate [aθi'kate] nm spur

acidez [aθiˈðeθ] nf acidity

ácido, -a [ˈaθiðo, a] adj sour, acid ▷ nm acid

acierto etc [aˈθjerto] vb V **acertar** ▷ nm success; (buen paso) wise move; (solución) solution; (habilidad) skill, ability

acitronar [aθitroˈnar] (MÉX: fam) vt to brown

aclamar [aklaˈmar] vt to acclaim; (aplaudir) to applaud

aclaración [aklaraˈθjon] nf clarification, explanation

aclarar [aklaˈrar] vt to clarify, explain; (ropa) to rinse ▷ vi to clear up; **aclararse** vr (explicarse) to understand; **~se la garganta** to clear one's throat

aclimatación [aklimataˈθjon] nf acclimatization

aclimatar [aklimaˈtar] vt to acclimatize; **aclimatarse** vr to become acclimatized

acné [akˈne] nm acne

acobardar [akoβarˈðar] vt to intimidate

acogedor, a [akoxeˈðor, a] adj welcoming; (hospitalario) hospitable

acoger [akoˈxer] vt to welcome; (abrigar) to shelter

acogida [akoˈxiða] nf reception; refuge

acomedido, -a [akomeˈðiðo, a] (MÉX) adj helpful, obliging

acometer [akomeˈter] vt to attack; (emprender) to undertake; **acometida** nf attack, assault

acomodado, -a [akomoˈðaðo, a] adj (persona) well-to-do

acomodador, a [akomoðaˈðor, a] nm/f usher(ette)

acomodar [akomoˈðar] vt to adjust; (alojar) to accommodate; **acomodarse** vr to conform; (instalarse) to install o.s.; (adaptarse) to adapt (to)

acompañar [akompaˈɲar] vt to accompany; (documentos) to enclose

acondicionar [akondiθjoˈnar] vt to

arrange, prepare; (pelo) to condition

aconsejar [akonseˈxar] vt to advise, counsel; **~ a algn hacer** o **que haga algo** to advise sb to do sth

acontecer [akonteˈθer] vi to happen, occur; **acontecimiento** nm event

acopio [aˈkopjo] nm store, stock

acoplar [akoˈplar] vt to fit; (Elec) to connect; (vagones) to couple

acorazado, -a [akoraˈθaðo, a] adj armour-plated, armoured ▷ nm battleship

acordar [akorˈðar] vt (resolver) to agree, resolve; (recordar) to remind; **acordarse** vr to agree; **~ hacer algo** to agree to do sth; **~se (de algo)** to remember (sth); **acorde** adj (Mús) harmonious; **acorde con** (medidas etc) in keeping with ▷ nm chord

acordeón [akordeˈon] nm accordion

acordonado, -a [akordoˈnaðo, a] adj (calle) cordoned-off

acorralar [akorraˈlar] vt to round up, corral

acortar [akorˈtar] vt to shorten; (duración) to cut short; (cantidad) to reduce; **acortarse** vr to become shorter

acosar [akoˈsar] vt to pursue relentlessly; (fig) to hound, pester; **acoso** nm harassment; **acoso sexual** sexual harassment

acostar [akosˈtar] vt (en cama) to put to bed; (en suelo) to lay down; **acostarse** vr to go to bed; to lie down; **~se con algn** to sleep with sb

acostumbrado, -a [akostumˈbraðo, a] adj usual; **~ a** used to

acostumbrar [akostumˈbrar] vt: **~ a algn a algo** to get sb used to sth ▷ vi: **~ (a) hacer** to be in the habit of doing; **acostumbrarse** vr: **~se a** to get used to

acotación [akotaˈθjon] nf marginal note; (Geo) elevation mark; (de límite) boundary mark; (Teatro) stage direction

acotamiento [akotaˈmjento] (MÉX)

nm hard shoulder (BRIT), berm (US)

acre ['akre] *adj* (olor) acrid; (fig) biting
▷ *nm* acre

acreditar [akreði'tar] *vt* (garantizar)
to vouch for, guarantee; (autorizar)
to authorize; (dar prueba de) to prove;
(Com: abonar) to credit; (embajador)
to accredit

acreedor, a [akree'ðor, a] *nm/f*
creditor

acribillar [akriβi'ʎar] *vt*: ~ **a balazos**
to riddle with bullets

acróbata [a'kroβata] *nmf* acrobat

acta ['akta] *nf* certificate; (de
comisión) minutes *pl*, record; **acta
de matrimonio/nacimiento** (MÉX)
marriage/birth certificate; **acta
notarial** affidavit

actitud [akti'tuð] *nf* attitude;
(postura) posture

activar [akti'βar] *vt* to activate;
(acelerar) to speed up

actividad [aktiβi'ðað] *nf* activity

activo, -a [ak'tiβo, a] *adj* active;
(vivo) lively ▷ *nm* (Com) assets *pl*

acto ['akto] *nm* act, action;
(ceremonia) ceremony; (Teatro) act; **en el
~** immediately

actor [ak'tor] *nm* actor; (Jur) plaintiff
▷ *adj*: **parte ~a** prosecution

actriz [ak'triθ] *nf* actress

actuación [aktwa'θjon] *nf* action;
(comportamiento) conduct, behaviour;
(Jur) proceedings *pl*; (desempeño)
performance

actual [ak'twal] *adj* present(-day),
current

⬛ No confundir **actual** con la palabra
inglesa *actual*.

actualidad *nf* present; **actualidades**
nfpl (noticias) news *sg*; **en la
actualidad** at present; (hoy día)
nowadays; **actualizar** [aktwali'θar]
vt = to update, modernize;

actualmente [aktwal'mente] *adv* at
present; (hoy día) nowadays

⬛ No confundir **actualmente** con la
palabra inglesa *actually*.

actuar [ak'twar] *vi* (obrar) to work,
operate; (actor) to act, perform ▷ *vt* to
work, operate; ~ **de** to act as

acuarela [akwa'rela] *nf* watercolour

acuario [a'kwarjo] *nm* aquarium;
(Astrología): **A~** Aquarius

acuático, -a [a'kwatiko, a] *adj*
aquatic

acudir [aku'ðir] *vi* (asistir) to attend;
(ir) to go; ~ **a** (fig) to turn to; ~ **a una
cita** to keep an appointment; ~ **en
ayuda de** to go to the aid of

acuerdo *etc* [a'kwerðo] *vb* V **acordar**
▷ *nm* agreement; **¡de ~!** agreed!; **de
~ con** (persona) in agreement with;
(acción, documento) in accordance with;
estar de ~ to be agreed, agree

acumular [akumu'lar] *vt* to
accumulate, collect

acuñar [aku'nar] *vt* (moneda) to mint;
(frase) to coin

acupuntura [akupun'tura] *nf*
acupuncture

acurrucarse [akurru'karse] *vr* to
crouch; (ovillarse) to curl up

acusación [akusa'θjon] *nf*
accusation

acusar [aku'sar] *vt* to accuse; (revelar)
to reveal; (denunciar) to denounce

acuse [a'kuse] *nm*: ~ **de recibo**
acknowledgement of receipt

acústica [a'kustika] *nf* acoustics *pl*

acústico, -a [a'kustiko, a] *adj*
acoustic

adaptación [aðapta'θjon] *nf*
adaptation

adaptador [aðapta'ðor] *nm* (Elec)
adapter, adaptor; **adaptador
universal** universal adapter o adaptor

adaptar [aðap'tar] *vt* to adapt;
(acomodar) to fit

adecuado, -a [aðe'kwaðo, a] *adj*
(apto) suitable; (oportuno) appropriate

a. de J.C. *abr* (= antes de Jesucristo) B.C.

adelantado, -a [aðelan'taðo, a] *adj*
advanced; (reloj) fast; **pagar por ~** to
pay in advance

adelantamiento [aðelanta'mjento]

nm (Auto) overtaking

adelantar [aðelan'tar] vt to move forward; (avanzar) to advance; (acelerar) to speed up; (Auto) to overtake ▷ vi to go forward, advance; **adelantarse** vr to go forward, advance

adelante [aðe'lante] adv forward(s), ahead ▷ excl come in!; **de hoy en ~** from now on; **más ~** later on; (más allá) further on

adelanto [aðe'lanto] nm advance; (mejora) improvement; (progreso) progress

adelgazar [aðelɣa'θar] vt to thin (down) ▷ vi to get thin; (con régimen) to slim down, lose weight

ademán [aðe'man] nm gesture; **ademanes** nmpl manners

además [aðe'mas] adv besides; (por otra parte) moreover; (también) also; **~ de** besides, in addition to

adentrarse [aðen'trarse] vr: **~ en** to go into, get inside; (penetrar) to penetrate (into)

adentro [a'ðentro] adv inside, in; **mar ~** out at sea; **tierra ~** inland

adepto, -a [a'ðepto, a] nm/f supporter

aderezar [aðere'θar] vt (ensalada) to dress; (comida) to season; **aderezo** nm dressing; seasoning

adeudar [aðeu'ðar] vt to owe

adherirse [aðe'rirse] vr: **~ a** to adhere to; (partido) to join

adhesión [aðe'sjon] nf adhesion; (fig) adherence

adicción [aðik'θjon] nf addiction

adición [aði'θjon] nf addition

adicto, -a [a'ðikto, a] adj: **~ a** addicted to; (dedicado) devoted to ▷ nm/f supporter, follower; (toxicómano) addict

adiestrar [aðjes'trar] vt to train, teach; (conducir) to guide, lead

adinerado, -a [aðine'raðo, a] adj wealthy

adiós [a'ðjos] excl (para despedirse) goodbye!, cheerio!; (al pasar) hello!

aditivo [aði'tiβo] nm additive

adivinanza [aðiβi'nanθa] nf riddle

adivinar [aðiβi'nar] vt to prophesy; (conjeturar) to guess; **adivino, -a** nm/f fortune-teller

adj abr (= adjunto) encl

adjetivo [aðxe'tiβo] nm adjective

adjudicar [aðxuði'kar] vt to award; **adjudicarse** vr: **~se algo** to appropriate sth

adjuntar [aðxun'tar] vt to attach, enclose; **adjunto, -a** adj attached, enclosed ▷ nm/f assistant

administración [aðministra'θjon] nf administration; (dirección) management; **administrador, a** nm/f administrator, manager(ess)

administrar [aðminis'trar] vt to administer; **administrativo, -a** adj administrative

admirable [aðmi'raβle] adj admirable

admiración [aðmira'θjon] nf admiration; (asombro) wonder; (Ling) exclamation mark

admirar [aðmi'rar] vt to admire; (extrañar) to surprise

admisible [aðmi'siβle] adj admissible

admisión [aðmi'sjon] nf admission; (reconocimiento) acceptance

admitir [aðmi'tir] vt to admit; (aceptar) to accept

adobar [aðo'βar] vt (Culin) to season

adobe [a'ðoβe] nm adobe, sun-dried brick

adolecer [aðole'θer] vi: **~ de** to suffer from

adolescente [aðoles'θente] nmf adolescent, teenager

adonde [a'ðonde] conj (to) where

adónde [a'ðonde] adv = **dónde**

adopción [aðop'θjon] nf adoption

adoptar [aðop'tar] vt to adopt

adoptivo, -a [aðop'tiβo, a] adj (padres) adoptive; (hijo) adopted

adoquín [aðo'kin] nm paving stone

adorar [aðo'rar] vt to adore

adornar [aðor'nar] vt to adorn

adorno [a'ðorno] nm ornament; (decoración) decoration

adosado, -a [aðo'saðo, a] adj: **casa adosada** semi-detached house

adosar [aðo'sar] (MÉX) vt (adjuntar) to attach, enclose (with a letter)

adquiero etc vb V **adquirir**

adquirir [aðki'rir] vt to acquire, obtain

adquisición [aðkisi'θjon] nf acquisition

adrede [a'ðreðe] adv on purpose

ADSL nm abr broadband

aduana [a'ðwana] nf customs pl

aduanero, -a [aðwa'nero, a] adj customs cpd ▷ nm/f customs officer

adueñarse [aðwe'narse] vr: **~ de** to take possession of

adular [aðu'lar] vt to flatter

adulterar [aðulte'rar] vt to adulterate

adulterio [aðul'terjo] nm adultery

adúltero, -a [a'ðultero, a] adj adulterous ▷ nm/f adulterer/adulteress

adulto, -a [a'ðulto, a] adj, nm/f adult

adverbio [að'ßerßjo] nm adverb

adversario, -a [aðßer'sarjo, a] nm/f adversary

adversidad [aðßersi'ðað] nf adversity; (contratiempo) setback

adverso, -a [að'ßerso, a] adj adverse

advertencia [aðßer'tenθja] nf warning; (prefacio) preface, foreword

advertir [aðßer'tir] vt to notice; (avisar): **~ a algn de** to warn sb about o of

Adviento [að'ßjento] nm Advent

advierto etc vb V **advertir**

aéreo, -a [a'ereo, a] adj aerial

aerobic [ae'roßik] nm aerobics sg; **aerobics** (MÉX) nmpl aerobics sg

aeromozo, -a [aero'moθo, a] (LAM) nm/f air steward(ess)

aeronáutica [aero'nautika] nf aeronautics sg

aeronave [aero'naße] nm spaceship

aeroplano [aero'plano] nm aeroplane

aeropuerto [aero'pwerto] nm airport

aerosol [aero'sol] nm aerosol

afamado, -a [afa'maðo, a] adj famous

afán [a'fan] nm hard work; (deseo) desire

afanador, a [afana'ðor, a] (MÉX) nm/f (de limpieza) cleaner

afanar [afa'nar] vt to harass; (fam) to pinch

afear [afe'ar] vt to disfigure

afección [afek'θjon] nf (Med) disease

afectado, -a [afek'taðo, a] adj affected

afectar [afek'tar] vt to affect

afectísimo, -a [afek'tisimo, a] adj affectionate; **suyo ~** yours truly

afectivo, -a [afek'tißo, a] adj (problema etc) emotional

afecto [a'fekto] nm affection; **tenerle ~ a algn** to be fond of sb

afectuoso, -a [afek'twoso, a] adj affectionate

afeitar [afei'tar] vt to shave; **afeitarse** vr to shave

afeminado, -a [afemi'naðo, a] adj effeminate

Afganistán [afγanis'tan] nm Afghanistan

afianzar [afjan'θar] vt to strengthen; to secure; **afianzarse** vr to become established

afiche [a'fitʃe] (RPL) nm poster

afición [afi'θjon] nf fondness, liking; **la ~** the fans pl; **pinto por ~** I paint as a hobby; **aficionado, -a** adj keen, enthusiastic; (no profesional) amateur ▷ nm/f enthusiast, fan; amateur; **ser aficionado a algo** to be very keen on o fond of sth

aficionar [afiθjo'nar] vt: **~ a algn a algo** to make sb like sth; **aficionarse** vr: **~se a algo** to grow fond of sth

afilado, -a [afi'laðo, a] adj sharp

afilar [afi'lar] vt to sharpen

afiliarse [afi'ljarse] vr to affiliate

afín [a'fin] adj (parecido) similar; (conexo) related

afinar [afi'nar] vt (Tec) to refine; (Mús) to tune ▷ vi (tocar) to play in tune; (cantar) to sing in tune

afincarse [afin'karse] vr to settle

afinidad [afini'ðað] nf affinity; (parentesco) relationship; **por ~** by marriage

afirmación [afirma'θjon] nf affirmation

afirmar [afir'mar] vt to affirm, state; **afirmativo, -a** adj affirmative

afligir [afli'xir] vt (apenar) to distress

aflojar [aflo'xar] vt to slacken; (desatar) to loosen, undo; (relajar) to relax ▷ vi to drop; (bajar) to go down; **aflojarse** vr to relax

afluente [aflu'ente] adj flowing ▷ nm tributary

afmo, -a abr (= afectísimo(a) suyo(a)) Yours

afónico, -a [a'foniko, a] adj: **estar ~** to have a sore throat; to have lost one's voice

aforo [a'foro] nm (de teatro etc) capacity

afortunado, -a [afortu'naðo, a] adj fortunate, lucky

África ['afrika] nf Africa; **África del Sur** South Africa; **africano, -a** adj, nm/f African

afrontar [afron'tar] vt to confront; (poner cara a cara) to bring face to face

afrutado, -a [afru'taðo, a] adj fruity

after ['after] (pl **~s**) nm after-hours club; **afterhours** [after'aurs] nm inv = **after**

afuera [a'fwera] adv out, outside; **afueras** nfpl outskirts

agachar [aʀa'tʃar] vt to bend, bow; **agacharse** vr to stoop, bend

agalla [a'ʀaʎa] nf (Zool) gill; **tener ~s** (fam) to have guts

agarradera [aʀarra'ðera] (MÉX) nf handle

agarrado, -a [aʀa'rraðo, a] adj mean, stingy

agarrar [aʀa'rrar] vt to grasp, grab; (LAM: tomar) to take, catch; (recoger) to pick up ▷ vi (planta) to take root; **agarrarse** vr to hold on (tightly)

agencia [a'xenθja] nf agency; **agencia de viajes** travel agency; **agencia inmobiliaria** estate (BRIT) or real estate (us) agent's (office)

agenciarse [axen'θjarse] vr to obtain, procure

agenda [a'xenda] nf diary; **~ electrónica** PDA

▌ No confundir **agenda** con la palabra inglesa agenda.

agente [a'xente] nmf agent; (tb: **~ de policía**) policeman/policewoman; **agente de seguros** insurance agent; **agente de tránsito** (MÉX) traffic cop; **agente inmobiliario** estate agent (BRIT), realtor (us)

ágil ['axil] adj agile, nimble; **agilidad** nf agility, nimbleness

agilizar [axili'θar] vt (trámites) to speed up

agiotista [axjo'tista] (MÉX) nmf (usurero) usurer

agitación [axita'θjon] nf (de mano etc) shaking, waving; (de líquido etc) stirring; (fig) agitation

agitado, -a [axi'taðo, a] adj hectic; (viaje) bumpy

agitar [axi'tar] vt to wave, shake; (líquido) to stir; (fig) to stir up, excite; **agitarse** vr to get excited; (inquietarse) to get worried or upset

aglomeración [axlomera'θjon] nf agglomeration; **aglomeración de gente/tráfico** mass of people/traffic jam

aglomerar [axlome'rar] vt to crowd together

agnóstico, -a [aʀ'nostiko, a] adj, nm/f agnostic

agobiar [aʀo'βjar] vt to weigh down; (oprimir) to oppress; (cargar) to burden

agolparse [aʀol'parse] vr to crowd together

agonía [aʀo'nia] nf death throes pl;

(fig) agony, anguish

agonizante [aɣoni'θante] adj dying

agonizar [aɣoni'θar] vi to be dying

agosto [a'ɣosto] nm August

agotado, -a [aɣo'taðo, a] adj (persona) exhausted; (libros) out of print; (acabado) finished; (Com) sold out; **agotador, a** [aɣota'ðor, a] adj exhausting

agotamiento [aɣota'mjento] nm exhaustion

agotar [aɣo'tar] vt to exhaust; (consumir) to drain; (recursos) to use up; deplete; **agotarse** vr to be exhausted; (acabarse) to run out; (libro) to go out of print

agraciado, -a [aɣra'θjaðo, a] adj (atractivo) attractive; (en sorteo etc) lucky

agradable [aɣra'ðaβle] adj pleasant, nice

agradar [aɣra'ðar] vt: **él me agrada** I like him

agradecer [aɣraðe'θer] vt to thank; (favor etc) to be grateful for; **agradecido, -a** adj grateful; **¡muy agradecido!** thanks a lot!; **agradecimiento** nm thanks pl; gratitude

agradezco etc vb **V agradecer**

agrado [a'ɣraðo] nm: **ser de tu** etc **~** to be to your etc liking

agrandar [aɣran'dar] vt to enlarge; (fig) to exaggerate; **agrandarse** vr to get bigger

agrario, -a [a'ɣrarjo, a] adj agrarian, land cpd; (política) agricultural, farming

agravante [aɣra'βante] adj aggravating ▷ nm: **con el ~ de que ...** with the further difficulty that ...

agravar [aɣra'βar] vt (pesar sobre) to make heavier; (irritar) to aggravate; **agravarse** vr to worsen, get worse

agraviar [aɣra'βjar] vt to offend; (ser injusto con) to wrong

agredir [aɣre'ðir] vt to attack

agregado [aɣre'ɣaðo, a] nm/f: **A-** = teacher (who is not head of department)

▷ nm aggregate; (persona) attaché

agregar [aɣre'ɣar] vt to gather; (añadir) to add; (persona) to appoint

agresión [aɣre'sjon] nf aggression

agresivo, -a [aɣre'siβo, a] adj aggressive

agriar [a'ɣrjar] vt to (turn) sour

agrícola [a'ɣrikola] adj farming cpd, agricultural

agricultor, a [aɣrikul'tor, a] nm/f farmer

agricultura [aɣrikul'tura] nf agriculture, farming

agridulce [aɣri'ðulθe] adj bittersweet; (Culin) sweet and sour

agrietarse [aɣrje'tarse] vr to crack; (piel) to chap

agrio, -a [a'ɣrjo, a] adj bitter

agrupación [aɣrupa'θjon] nf group; (acto) grouping

agrupar [aɣru'par] vt to group

agua ['aɣwa] nf water; (Náut) wake; (Arq) slope of a roof; **aguas** nfpl (de piedra) water sg, sparkle sg; (Med) water sg, urine sg; (Náut) waters; **agua bendita/destilada/potable** holy/distilled/drinking water; **agua caliente** hot water; **agua corriente** running water; **agua de colonia** eau de colonia; **agua mineral (con/sin gas)** (sparkling/still) mineral water; **agua oxigenada** hydrogen peroxide; **aguas abajo/arriba** downstream/ upstream; **aguas jurisdiccionales** territorial waters

aguacate [aɣwa'kate] nm avocado (pear)

aguacero [aɣwa'θero] nm (heavy) shower, downpour

aguado, -a [a'ɣwaðo, a] adj watery, watered down

aguafiestas [aɣwa'fjestas] nmf inv spoilsport, killjoy

aguamiel [aɣwa'mjel] (MÉX) nf fermented maguey o agave juice

aguanieve [aɣwa'njeβe] nf sleet

aguantar [aɣwan'tar] vt to bear, put up with; (sostener) to hold up ▷ vi to

last; **aguantarse** vr to restrain o.s.;
aguante nm (paciencia) patience;
(resistencia) endurance
aguar [a'ɣwar] vt to water down
aguardar [aɣwar'ðar] vt to wait for
aguardiente [aɣwar'ðjente] nm
brandy, liquor
aguarrás [aɣwa'rras] nm turpentine
aguaviva [aɣwa'βiβa] (RPL) nf
jellyfish
agudeza [aɣu'ðeθa] nf sharpness;
(ingenio) wit
agudo, -a [a'ɣuðo, a] adj sharp;
(voz) high-pitched, piercing; (dolor,
enfermedad) acute
agüero [a'ɣwero] nm: **buen/mal ~**
good/bad omen
aguijón [aɣi'xon] nm sting; (fig) spur
águila ['aɣila] nf eagle; (fig) genius
aguileño, -a [aɣi'leɲo, a] adj (nariz)
aquiline; (rostro) sharp-featured
aguinaldo [aɣi'naldo] nm Christmas
box
aguja [a'ɣuxa] nf needle; (de reloj)
hand; (Arq) spire; (Tec) firing-pin;
agujas nfpl (Zool) ribs; (Ferro) points
agujerear [aɣuxere'ar] vt to make
holes in
agujero [aɣu'xero] nm hole
agujetas [aɣu'xetas] nfpl stitch sg;
(rigidez) stiffness sg
ahí [a'i] adv there; **de ~ que** so that,
with the result that; **~ llega** here he
comes; **por ~** that way; (allá) over
there; **200 o por ~** 200 or so
ahijado, -a [ai'xaðo, a] nm/f
godson/daughter
ahogar [ao'ɣar] vt to drown; (asfixiar)
to suffocate, smother; (fuego) to put
out; **ahogarse** vr (en el agua) to drown;
(por asfixia) to suffocate
ahogo [a'oɣo] nm breathlessness;
(fig) financial difficulty
ahondar [aon'dar] vt to deepen,
make deeper; (fig) to study thoroughly
▷ vi: **~ en** to study thoroughly
ahora [a'ora] adv now; (hace poco)
a moment ago, just now; (dentro de

poco) in a moment; **~ voy** I'm coming;
~ mismo right now; **~ bien** now then;
por ~ for the present
ahorcar [aor'kar] vt to hang
ahorita [ao'rita] (fam) adv (LAM: en
este momento) right now; (MÉX: hace
poco) just now; (: dentro de poco) in a
minute
ahorrar [ao'rrar] vt (dinero) to save;
(esfuerzos) to save, avoid; **ahorro** nm
(acto) saving; **ahorros** nmpl (dinero)
savings
ahuecar [awe'kar] vt to hollow (out);
(voz) to deepen; **ahuecarse** vr to give
o.s. airs
ahumar [au'mar] vt to smoke, cure;
(llenar de humo) to fill with smoke ▷ vi
to smoke; **ahumarse** vr to fill with
smoke
ahuyentar [aujen'tar] vt to drive off,
frighten off; (fig) to dispel
aire ['aire] nm air; (viento) wind;
(corriente) draught; (Mús) tune;
al ~ libre in the open air; **aire
acondicionado** air conditioning
airear [aire'ar] vt to air; **airearse** vr
to go out for a breath of fresh air;
airoso, -a adj windy; draughty; (fig)
graceful
aislado, -a [ais'laðo, a] adj isolated;
(incomunicado) cut-off; (Elec) insulated
aislar [ais'lar] vt to isolate; (Elec) to
insulate
ajardinado, -a [axarði'naðo, a] adj
landscaped
ajedrez [axe'ðreθ] nm chess
ajeno, -a [a'xeno, a] adj (que
pertenece a otro) somebody else's; **~ a**
foreign to
ajetreado, -a [axetre'aðo, a] adj
busy
ajetreo [axe'treo] nm bustle
ají [a'xi] (cs) nm chil(l)i, red pepper;
(salsa) chil(l)i sauce
ajillo [a'xiʎo] nm: **gambas al ~** garlic
prawns
ajo ['axo] nm garlic
ajuar [a'xwar] nm household

furnishings pl; (de novia) trousseau; (de niño) layette

ajustado, -a [axus'taðo, a] adj (tornillo) tight; (cálculo) right; (ropa) tight(-fitting); (resultado) close

ajustar [axus'tar] vt (adaptar) to adjust; (encajar) to fit; (Tec) to engage; (Imprenta) to make up; (apretar) to tighten; (concertar) to agree (on); (reconciliar) to reconcile; (cuentas, deudas) to settle ▷ vi to fit; **ajustarse** vr: **~se a** (precio etc) to be in keeping with, fit in with; **~ las cuentas a algn** to get even with sb

ajuste [a'xuste] nm adjustment; (Costura) fitting; (acuerdo) compromise; (de cuenta) settlement

al [al] = **a + el**; V **a**

ala ['ala] nf wing; (de sombrero) brim; winger; **ala delta** nf hang-glider

alabanza [ala'βanθa] nf praise

alabar [ala'βar] vt to praise

alacena [ala'θena] nf kitchen cupboard (BRIT) o closet (US)

alacrán [ala'kran] nm scorpion

alambrada [alam'braða] nf wire fence; (red) wire netting

alambre [a'lambre] nm wire; **alambre de púas** barbed wire

alameda [ala'meða] nf (plantío) poplar grove; (lugar de paseo) avenue, boulevard

álamo ['alamo] nm poplar

alarde [a'larðe] nm show, display; **hacer ~ de** to boast of

alargador [alarya'ðor] nm (Elec) extension lead

alargar [alar'yar] vt to lengthen, extend; (paso) to hasten; (brazo) to stretch out; (cuerda) to pay out; (conversación) to spin out; **alargarse** vr to get longer

alarma [a'larma] nf alarm; **alarma de incendios** fire alarm; **alarmar** vt to alarm; **alarmarse** vr to get alarmed; **alarmante** adj alarming

alba ['alβa] nf dawn

albahaca [al'βaka] nf basil

Albania [al'βanja] nf Albania

albañil [alβa'ɲil] nm bricklayer; (cantero) mason

albarán [alβa'ran] nm (Com) delivery note, invoice

albaricoque [alβari'koke] nm apricot

albedrío [alβe'ðrio] nm: **libre ~** free will

alberca [al'βerka] nf reservoir; (MÉx: piscina) swimming pool

albergar [alβer'yar] vt to shelter

albergue etc [al'βerɣe] vb V **albergar** ▷ nm shelter, refuge; **albergue juvenil** youth hostel

albóndiga [al'βondiɣa] nf meatball

albornoz [alβor'noθ] nm (de los árabes) burnous; (para el baño) bathrobe

alborotar [alβoro'tar] vi to make a row ▷ vt to agitate, stir up; **alborotarse** vr to get excited; (mar) to get rough; **alboroto** nm row, uproar

álbum [al'βum] (pl **~s, ~es**) nm album; **álbum de recortes** scrapbook

albur [al'βur] (MÉx) nm (juego de palabras) pun; (doble sentido) double entendre

alcachofa [alka'tʃofa] nf artichoke

alcalde, -esa [al'kalde, esa] nm/f mayor(ess)

alcaldía [alkal'dia] nf mayoralty; (lugar) mayor's office

alcance etc [al'kanθe] vb V **alcanzar** ▷ nm reach; (Com) adverse balance; **al ~ de algn** available to sb

alcancía [alkan'θia] (LAM) nf (para ahorrar) money box; (para colectas) collection box

alcantarilla [alkanta'riʎa] nf (de aguas cloacales) sewer; (en la calle) gutter

alcanzar [alkan'θar] vt (algo: con la mano, el pie) to reach; (alguien: en el camino etc) to catch up (with); (autobús) to catch; (bala) to hit, strike ▷ vi (ser suficiente) to be enough; **~ a hacer** to manage to do

alcaparra [alka'parra] nf caper

alcayata [alka'jata] nf hook

alcázar [al'kaθar] nm fortress; (Náut) quarter-deck

alcoba [al'koβa] nf bedroom

alcohol [al'kol] nm alcohol; **alcohol metílico** methylated spirits pl (BRIT), wood alcohol (US); **alcohólico, -a** adj, nm/f alcoholic; **alcoholímetro** [alko'limetro] nm Breathalyser® (BRIT), drunkometer (US); **alcoholismo** [alko'lismo] nm alcoholism

alcornoque [alkor'noke] nm cork tree; (fam) idiot

aldea [al'dea] nf village; **aldeano, -a** adj village cpd ▷ nm/f villager

aleación [alea'θjon] nf alloy

aleatorio, -a [alea'torjo, a] adj random

aleccionar [alekθjo'nar] vt to instruct; (adiestrar) to train

alegar [ale'ɣar] vt to claim; (Jur) to plead ▷ vi (LAM: discutir) to argue

alegoría [aleɣo'ria] nf allegory

alegrar [ale'ɣrar] vt (causar alegría) to cheer (up); (fuego) to poke; (fiesta) to liven up; **alegrarse** vr (fam) to get merry o tight; **~se de** to be glad about

alegre [a'leɣre] adj happy, cheerful; (fam) merry, tight; (chiste) risqué, blue; **alegría** nf happiness; merriment

alejar [ale'xar] vt to remove; (fig) to estrange; **alejarse** vr to move away

alemán, -ana [ale'man, ana] adj, nm/f German ▷ nm (Ling) German

Alemania [ale'manja] nf Germany

alentador, -a [alenta'ðor, a] adj encouraging

alentar [alen'tar] vt to encourage

alergia [a'lerxja] nf allergy

alero [a'lero] nm (de tejado) eaves pl; (guardabarros) mudguard

alerta [a'lerta] adj, nm alert

aleta [a'leta] nf (de pez) fin; (ala) wing; (de foca, Deporte) flipper; (Auto) mudguard

aletear [alete'ar] vi to flutter

alevín [ale'βin] nm fry, young fish

alevosía [aleβo'sia] nf treachery

alfabeto [alfa'βeto] nm alphabet

alfalfa [al'falfa] nf alfalfa, lucerne

alfarería [alfare'ria] nf pottery; (tienda) pottery shop; **alfarero, -a** nm/f potter

alféizar [al'feiθar] nm window-sill

alférez [al'fereθ] nm (Mil) second lieutenant; (Náut) ensign

alfil [al'fil] nm (Ajedrez) bishop

alfiler [alfi'ler] nm pin; (broche) clip

alfombra [al'fombra] nf carpet; (más pequeña) rug; **alfombrilla** nf rug, mat; (Inform) mouse mat o pad

alforja [al'forxa] nf saddlebag

algas ['alɣas] nfpl seaweed

álgebra ['alxeβra] nf algebra

algo ['alɣo] pron something; anything ▷ adv somewhat, rather; **¿~ más?** anything else?; (en tienda) is that all?; **por ~ será** there must be some reason for it

algodón [alɣo'ðon] nm cotton; (planta) cotton plant; **algodón de azúcar** candy floss (BRIT), cotton candy (US); **algodón hidrófilo** cotton wool (BRIT), absorbent cotton (US)

alguien [al'xjen] pron someone, somebody; (en frases interrogativas) anyone, anybody

alguno, -a [al'ɣuno, a] adj (delante de nm) **algún** some; (después de n): **no tiene talento** ~ he has no talent, he doesn't have any talent ▷ pron (alguien) someone, somebody; **algún que otro libro** some book or other; **algún día iré** I'll go one o some day; **sin interés** ~ without the slightest interest; **~ que otro** an occasional one; **~s piensan** some (people) think

alhaja [a'laxa] nf jewel; (tesoro) precious object, treasure

alhelí [ale'li] nm wallflower, stock

aliado, -a [a'ljaðo, a] adj allied

alianza [a'ljanθa] nf alliance; (anillo) wedding ring

aliar [a'ljar] vt to ally; **aliarse** vr to form an alliance

alias ['aljas] adv alias
alicatado [alika'taðo] (ESP) nm tiling
alicates [ali'kates] nmpl pliers
aliciente [ali'θjente] nm incentive; (atracción) attraction
alienación [aljena'θjon] nf alienation
aliento [a'ljento] nm breath; (respiración) breathing; **sin ~** breathless
aligerar [alixe'rar] vt to lighten; (reducir) to shorten; (aliviar) to alleviate; (mitigar) to ease; (paso) to quicken
alijo [a'lixo] nm consignment
alimaña [ali'maɲa] nf pest
alimentación [alimenta'θjon] nf (comida) food; (acción) feeding; (tienda) grocer's (shop)
alimentar [alimen'tar] vt to feed; (nutrir) to nourish; **alimentarse** vr to feed
alimenticio, -a [alimen'tiθjo, a] adj food cpd; (nutritivo) nourishing, nutritious
alimento [ali'mento] nm food; (nutrición) nourishment
alineación [alinea'θjon] nf alignment; (Deporte) line-up
alinear [aline'ar] vt to align; (Deporte) to select, pick
aliñar [ali'ɲar] vt (Culin) to season; **aliño** nm (Culin) dressing
alioli [ali'oli] nm garlic mayonnaise
alisar [ali'sar] vt to smooth
alistarse [alis'tarse] vr (enlist) to enrol; (inscribirse) to enrol
aliviar [ali'βjar] vt (carga) to lighten; (persona) to relieve; (dolor) to relieve, alleviate
alivio [a'liβjo] nm alleviation, relief
aljibe [al'xiβe] nm cistern
allá [a'ʎa] adv (lugar) there; (por ahí) over there; (tiempo) then; **~ abajo** down there; **más ~** further on; **más ~ de** beyond; **¡~ tú!** that's your problem!; **¡~ voy!** I'm coming!
allanamiento [aʎana'mjento] nm (LAM: de policía) raid; **allanamiento de morada** burglary
allanar [aʎa'nar] vt to flatten, level (out); (igualar) to smooth (out); (fig) to subdue; (Jur) to burgle, break into
allegado, -a [aʎe'xaðo, a] adj near, close ▷ nm/f relation
allí [a'ʎi] adv there; **~ mismo** right there; **por ~** over there; (por ese camino) that way
alma ['alma] nf soul; (persona) person
almacén [alma'θen] nm (depósito) warehouse, store; (Mil) magazine; (cs: de comestibles) grocer's (shop); **grandes almacenes** department store sg; **almacenes** storage
almacenar [almaθe'nar] vt to store, put in storage; (proveerse) to stock up with
almanaque [alma'nake] nm almanac
almeja [al'mexa] nf clam
almendra [al'mendra] nf almond; **almendro** nm almond tree
almíbar [al'miβar] nm syrup
almidón [almi'ðon] nm starch
almirante [almi'rante] nm admiral
almohada [almo'aða] nf pillow; (funda) pillowcase; **almohadilla** nf cushion; (para alfileres) pincushion; (Tec) pad
almohadón [almoa'ðon] nm large pillow; bolster
almorranas [almo'rranas] nfpl piles, haemorrhoids
almorzar [almor'θar] vt: **~ una tortilla** to have an omelette for lunch ▷ vi to (have) lunch
almuerzo etc [al'mwerθo] vb V **almorzar** ▷ nm lunch
alocado, -a [alo'kaðo, a] adj crazy
alojamiento [aloxa'mjento] nm lodging(s) pl; (viviendas) housing
alojar [alo'xar] vt to lodge; **alojarse** vr to lodge, stay
alondra [a'londra] nf lark, skylark
alpargata [alpar'xata] nf rope-soled sandal, espadrille
Alpes ['alpes] nmpl: **los ~** the Alps

alpinismo [alpi'nismo] nm
mountaineering, climbing; **alpinista**
nmf mountaineer, climber
alpiste [al'piste] nm birdseed
alquilar [alki'lar] vt
(propietario: inmuebles) to let, rent
(out); (: coche) to hire out; (: TV) to rent
(out); (alquilador: inmuebles, TV) to rent;
(: coche) to hire; **"se alquila casa"**
"house to let (BRIT) o for rent (US)"
alquiler [alki'ler] nm renting; letting;
hiring; (arriendo) rent; hire charge; **de
~** for hire; **alquiler de automóviles o
coches** car hire
alquimia [al'kimja] nf alchemy
alquitrán [alki'tran] nm tar
alrededor [alreðe'ðor] adv around,
about; **~ de** around, about; **mirar
a su ~** to look (round) about one;
alrededores nmpl surroundings
alta ['alta] nf (certificate of)
discharge
altar [al'tar] nm altar
altavoz [alta'βoθ] nm loudspeaker;
(amplificador) amplifier
alteración [altera'θjon] nf
alteration; (alboroto) disturbance
alterar [alte'rar] vt to alter; to
disturb; **alterarse** vr (persona) to
get upset
altercado [alter'kaðo] nm argument
alternar [alter'nar] vt to alternate
▷ vi to alternate; (turnar) to take turns;
alternarse vr to alternate; to take
turns; **~ con** to mix with; **alternativa**
nf alternative; (elección) choice;
alternativo, -a adj alternative;
(alterno) alternating; **alterno, -a** adj
alternate; (Elec) alternating
Alteza [al'teθa] nf (tratamiento)
Highness
altibajos [alti'βaxos] nmpl ups and
downs
altiplano [alti'plano] nm =
altiplanicie
altisonante [altiso'nante] adj high-
flown, high-sounding
altitud [alti'tuð] nf height; (Aviac,

Geo) altitude
altivo, -a [al'tiβo, a] adj haughty,
arrogant
alto, -a ['alto, a] adj high; (persona)
tall; (sonido) high, sharp; (noble) high,
lofty ▷ nm halt; (Mús) alto; (Geo) hill
▷ adv (de sitio) high; (de sonido) loud,
loudly ▷ excl halt!; **la pared tiene
2 metros de ~** the wall is 2 metres
high; **en alta mar** on the high seas;
en voz alta in a loud voice; **las altas
horas de la noche** the small o wee
hours; **en lo ~ de** at the top of; **pasar
por ~** to overlook; **altoparlante**
[altopar'lante] (LAM) nm loudspeaker
altura [al'tura] nf height; (Náut)
depth; (Geo) latitude; **la pared tiene
1.80 de ~** the wall is 1 metre 80cm high;
a estas ~s at this stage; **a estas ~s del
año** at this time of the year
alubia [a'luβja] nf bean
alucinación [aluθina'θjon] nf
hallucination
alucinar [aluθi'nar] vi to hallucinate
▷ vt to deceive; (fascinar) to fascinate
alud [a'luð] nm avalanche; (fig) flood
aludir [alu'ðir] vi: **~ a** to allude to;
darse por aludido to take the hint
alumbrado [alum'braðo] nm
lighting
alumbrar [alum'brar] vt to light (up)
▷ vi (Med) to give birth
aluminio [alu'minjo] nm aluminium
(BRIT), aluminum (US)
alumno, -a [a'lumno, a] nm/f pupil,
student
alusión [alu'sjon] nf allusion
alusivo, -a [alu'siβo, a] adj allusive
aluvión [alu'βjon] nm alluvium;
(fig) flood
alverja [al'βerxa] (LAM) nf pea
alza ['alθa] nf rise; (Mil) sight
alzamiento [alθa'mjento] nm
(rebelión) rising
alzar [al'θar] vt to lift (up); (precio,
muro) to raise; (cuello de abrigo) to
turn up; (Agr) to gather in; (Imprenta)
to gather; **alzarse** vr to get up,

rise; (*rebelarse*) to revolt; (*Com*) to go
fraudulently bankrupt; (*Jur*) to appeal

ama ['ama] *nf* lady of the house;
(*dueña*) owner; (*institutriz*) governess;
(*madre adoptiva*) foster mother; **ama
de casa** housewife; **ama de llaves**
housekeeper

amabilidad [amaβili'ðað] *nf*
kindness; (*simpatía*) niceness; **amable**
adj kind; nice; **es usted muy amable**
that's very kind of you

amaestrado, -a [amaes'traðo, a]
adj (*animal: en circo etc*) performing

amaestrar [amaes'trar] *vt* to train

amago [a'maɣo] *nm* threat; (*gesto*)
threatening gesture; (*Med*) symptom

amainar [amai'nar] *vi* (*viento*) to
die down

amamantar [amaman'tar] *vt* to
suckle, nurse

amanecer [amane'θer] *vi* to dawn
▷ *nm* dawn; **~ afiebrado** to wake up
with a fever

amanerado, -a [amane'raðo, a]
adj affected

amante [a'mante] *adj*: **~ de** fond of
▷ *nmf* lover

amapola [ama'pola] *nf* poppy

amar [a'mar] *vt* to love

amargado, -a [amar'xaðo, a] *adj*
bitter

amargar [amar'xar] *vt* to make
bitter; (*fig*) to embitter; **amargarse** *vr*
to become embittered

amargo, -a [a'marxo, a] *adj* bitter

amarillento, -a [amari'ʎento, a]
adj yellowish; (*tez*) sallow; **amarillo, -a**
adj, nm yellow

amarrado, -a [ama'rraðo, a]
(*MÉx: fam*) *adj* mean, stingy

amarrar [ama'rrar] *vt* to moor;
(*sujetar*) to tie up

amarras [a'marras] *nfpl*: **soltar ~**
to set sail

amasar [ama'sar] *vt* (*masa*) to knead;
(*mezclar*) to mix, prepare; (*confeccionar*)
to concoct

amateur [ama'ter] *nmf* amateur

amazona [ama'θona] *nf*
horsewoman; **Amazonas** *nm*: **el
Amazonas** the Amazon

ámbar ['ambar] *nm* amber

ambición [ambi'θjon] *nf* ambition;
ambicionar *vt* to aspire to;
ambicioso, -a *adj* ambitious

ambidextro, -a [ambi'ðekstro, a]
adj ambidextrous

ambientación [ambjenta'θjon] *nf*
(*Cine, Teatro etc*) setting; (*Radio*) sound
effects

ambiente [am'bjente] *nm*
atmosphere; (*medio*) environment

ambigüedad [ambixwe'ðað]
nf ambiguity; **ambiguo, -a** *adj*
ambiguous

ámbito ['ambito] *nm* (*campo*) field;
(*fig*) scope

ambos, -as ['ambos, as] *adj pl, pron
pl* both

ambulancia [ambu'lanθja] *nf*
ambulance

ambulante [ambu'lante] *adj*
travelling *cpd*, itinerant

ambulatorio [ambula'torio] *nm*
state health-service clinic

amén [a'men] *excl* amen; **~ de**
besides

amenaza [ame'naθa] *nf* threat;
amenazar *vt* to threaten ▷ *vi*: **amenazar con hacer** to
threaten to do

ameno, -a [a'meno, a] *adj* pleasant

América [a'merika] *nf* America;
América Central/Latina Central/
Latin America; **América del Norte/del
Sur** North/South America; **americana**
nf coat, jacket; *V tb* **americano**;
americano, -a *adj, nm/f* American

ametralladora [ametraʎa'ðora] *nf*
machine gun

amigable [ami'xaβle] *adj* friendly

amígdala [a'mixðala] *nf* tonsil;
amigdalitis *nf* tonsillitis

amigo, -a [a'mixo, a] *adj* friendly
▷ *nm/f* friend; (*amante*) lover; **ser ~ de
algo** to be fond of sth; **ser muy ~s** to be

close friends

aminorar [amino'rar] vt to diminish; (reducir) to reduce; **~ la marcha** to slow down

amistad [amis'tað] nf friendship; **amistades** nfpl (amigos) friends; **amistoso, -a** adj friendly

amnesia [am'nesja] nf amnesia

amnistía [amnis'tia] nf amnesty

amo ['amo] nm owner; (jefe) boss

amolar [amo'lar] (MÉX: fam) vt to ruin, damage

amoldar [amol'dar] vt to mould; (adaptar) to adapt

amonestación [amonesta'θjon] nf warning; **amonestaciones** nfpl (Rel) marriage banns

amonestar [amones'tar] vt to warn; (Rel) to publish the banns of

amontonar [amonto'nar] vt to collect, pile up; **amontonarse** vr to crowd together; (acumularse) to pile up

amor [a'mor] nm love; (amante) lover; **hacer el ~** to make love; **amor propio** self-respect

amoratado, -a [amora'taðo, a] adj purple

amordazar [amorða'θar] vt to muzzle; (fig) to gag

amorfo, -a [a'morfo, a] adj amorphous, shapeless

amoroso, -a [amo'roso, a] adj affectionate, loving

amortiguador [amortigwa'ðor] nm shock absorber; (parachoques) bumper; **amortiguadores** nmpl (Auto) suspension sg

amortiguar [amorti'ɣwar] vt to deaden; (ruido) to muffle; (color) to soften

amotinar [amoti'nar] vt to stir up, incite (to riot); **amotinarse** vr to mutiny

amparar [ampa'rar] vt to protect; **ampararse** vr to seek protection; (de la lluvia etc) to shelter; **amparo** nm help, protection; **al amparo de** under the protection of

amperio [am'perjo] nm ampère, amp

ampliación [amplja'θjon] nf enlargement; (extensión) extension

ampliar [am'pljar] vt to enlarge; to extend

amplificador [amplifika'ðor] nm amplifier

amplificar [amplifi'kar] vt to amplify

amplio, -a [am'pljo, a] adj spacious; (de falda etc) full; (extenso) extensive; (ancho) wide; **amplitud** nf spaciousness; extent; (fig) amplitude

ampolla [am'poʎa] nf blister; (Med) ampoule

amputar [ampu'tar] vt to cut off, amputate

amueblar [amwe'βlar] vt to furnish

anales [a'nales] nmpl annals

analfabetismo [analfaβe'tismo] nm illiteracy; **analfabeto, -a** adj, nm/f illiterate

analgésico [anal'xesiko] nm painkiller, analgesic

análisis [a'nalisis] nm inv analysis

analista [ana'lista] nmf (gen) analyst

analizar [anali'θar] vt to analyse

analógico, -a [ana'loxiko, a] adj (Inform) analog; (reloj) analogue (BRIT), analog (US)

análogo, -a [a'naloxo, a] adj analogous, similar

ananá [ana'na] (RPL) nm pineapple

anarquía [anar'kia] nf anarchy; **anarquista** nmf anarchist

anatomía [anato'mia] nf anatomy

anca ['anka] nf rump, haunch; **ancas** nfpl (fam) behind sg

ancho, -a [an'tʃo, a] adj wide; (falda) full; (fig) liberal ▷ nm width; (Ferro) gauge; **ponerse ~** to get conceited; **estar a sus anchas** to be at one's ease

anchoa [an'tʃoa] nf anchovy

anchura [an'tʃura] nf width; (extensión) wideness

anciano, -a [an'θjano, a] adj old, aged ▷ nm/f old man/woman; elder

ancla ['ankla] nf anchor

Andalucía [andalu'θia] nf
Andalusia; **andaluz, -a** adj, nm/f
Andalusian

andamio [an'damjo] nm
scaffold(ing)

andar [an'dar] vt to go, cover, travel
▷ vi to go, walk, travel; (funcionar) to
go, work; (estar) to be ▷ nm walk,
gait, pace; **andarse** vr to go away;
~ a pie/a caballo/en bicicleta to go
on foot/on horseback/by bicycle; **~
haciendo algo** to be doing sth; **¡anda!**
(sorpresa) go on!; **anda por o en los 40**
he's about 40

andén [an'den] nm (Ferro) platform;
(Náut) quayside; (CAM: de la calle)
pavement (BRIT), sidewalk (US)

Andes ['andes] nmpl: **los ~** the Andes

andinismo [andi'nismo] (LAM) nm
mountaineering, climbing

Andorra [an'dorra] nf Andorra

andrajoso, -a [andra'xoso, a] adj
ragged

anduve etc vb V **andar**

anécdota [a'nekðota] nf anecdote,
story

anegar [ane'xar] vt to flood; (ahogar)
to drown

anemia [a'nemja] nf anaemia

anestesia [anes'tesja] nf (sustancia)
anaesthetic; (proceso) anaesthesia;
anestesia general/local general/
local anaesthetic

anexar [anek'sar] vt to annex;
(documento) to attach; **anexión** nf
annexation; **anexo, -a** adj attached
▷ nm annexe

anfibio, -a [an'fiβjo, a] adj
amphibious ▷ nm amphibian

anfiteatro [anfite'atro] nm
amphitheatre; (Teatro) dress circle

anfitrión, -ona [anfi'trjon, ona]
nm/f host(ess)

ánfora ['anfora] nf (cántaro)
amphora; (MÉX Pol) ballot box

ángel ['anxel] nm angel; **ángel de la
guarda** guardian angel

angina [an'xina] nf (Med)

inflammation of the throat; **tener ~s**
to have tonsillitis; **angina de pecho**
angina

anglicano, -a [angli'kano, a] adj,
nm/f Anglican

anglosajón, -ona [anglosa'xon,
ona] adj Anglo-Saxon

anguila [an'gila] nf eel

angula [an'gula] nf elver, baby eel

ángulo ['angulo] nm angle; (esquina)
corner; (curva) bend

angustia [an'gustja] nf anguish

anhelar [ane'lar] vt to be eager for;
(desear) to long for, desire ▷ vi to pant,
gasp; **anhelo** nm eagerness; desire

anidar [ani'ðar] vi to nest

anillo [a'niʎo] nm ring; **anillo de
boda/compromiso** wedding/
engagement ring

animación [anima'θjon] nf
liveliness; (vitalidad) life; (actividad)
activity; bustle

animado, -a [ani'maðo, a] adj
lively; (vivaz) animated; **animador, a**
nm/f (TV) host(ess), compère; (Deporte)
cheerleader

animal [ani'mal] adj animal; (fig)
stupid ▷ nm animal; (fig) (bestia)
brute

animar [ani'mar] vt (Bio) to animate,
give life to; (fig) to liven up, brighten
up, cheer up; (estimular) to stimulate;
animarse vr to cheer up; to feel
encouraged; (decidirse) to make up
one's mind

ánimo ['animo] nm (alma) soul;
(mente) mind; (valentía) courage ▷ excl
cheer up!

animoso, -a [ani'moso, a] adj brave;
(vivo) lively

aniquilar [aniki'lar] vt to annihilate,
destroy

anís [a'nis] nm aniseed; (licor)
anisette

aniversario [aniβer'sarjo] nm
anniversary

anoche [a'notʃe] adv last night;
antes de ~ the night before last

anochecer [anotʃe'θer] *vi* to get dark ▷*nm* nightfall, dark; **al ~** at nightfall
anodino, -a [ano'ðino, a] *adj* dull, anodyne
anomalía [anoma'lia] *nf* anomaly
anonadado, -a [anona'ðaðo, a] *adj*: **estar ~** to be overwhelmed *o* amazed
anonimato [anoni'mato] *nm* anonymity
anónimo, -a [a'nonimo, a] *adj* anonymous; (*Com*) limited ▷*nm* (*carta anónima*) anonymous letter; (: *maliciosa*) poison-pen letter
anormal [anor'mal] *adj* abnormal
anotación [anota'θjon] *nf* note; annotation
anotar [ano'tar] *vt* to note down; (*comentar*) to annotate
ansia ['ansja] *nf* anxiety; (*añoranza*) yearning; **ansiar** *vt* to long for
ansiedad [ansje'ðað] *nf* anxiety
ansioso, -a [an'sjoso, a] *adj* anxious; (*anhelante*) eager; **~ de** *o* **por algo** greedy for sth
antaño [an'taɲo] *adv* long ago, formerly
Antártico [an'tartiko] *nm*: **el ~** the Antarctic
ante ['ante] *prep* before, in the presence of; (*problema etc*) faced with ▷*nm* (*piel*) suede; **~ todo** above all
anteanoche [antea'notʃe] *adv* the night before last
anteayer [antea'jer] *adv* the day before yesterday
antebrazo [ante'βraθo] *nm* forearm
antecedente [anteθe'ðente] *adj* previous ▷*nm* antecedent; **antecedentes** *nmpl* (*historial*) record *sg*; **antecedentes penales** criminal record
anteceder [anteθe'ðer] *vt* to precede, go before
antecesor, a [anteθe'sor, a] *nm/f* predecessor
antelación [antela'θjon] *nf*: **con ~** in advance
antemano [ante'mano]: **de ~** *adv* beforehand, in advance
antena [an'tena] *nf* antenna; (*de televisión etc*) aerial; **antena parabólica** satellite dish
antenoche [ante'notʃe] (LAM) *adv* the night before last
anteojo [ante'oxo] *nm* eyeglass; **anteojos** *nmpl* (LAM: *gafas*) glasses, spectacles
antepasados [antepa'saðos] *nmpl* ancestors
anteponer [antepo'ner] *vt* to place in front; (*fig*) to prefer
anterior [ante'rjor] *adj* preceding, previous; **anterioridad** *nf*: **con anterioridad a** prior to, before
antes ['antes] *adv* (*con prioridad*) before ▷*prep*: **~ de** before ▷*conj*: **~ de ir/de que te vayas** before going/ before you go; **~ bien** (but) rather; **dos días ~** two days before *o* previously; **no quiso venir ~** she didn't want to come any earlier; **tomo el avión ~ que el barco** I take the plane rather than the boat; **~ de** *o* **que nada** (*en el tiempo*) first of all; (*indicando preferencia*) above all; **~ que yo** before me; **lo ~ posible** as soon as possible; **cuanto ~ mejor** the sooner the better
antibalas [anti'βalas] *adj inv*: **chaleco ~** bullet-proof jacket
antibiótico [anti'βjotiko] *nm* antibiotic
anticaspa [anti'kaspa] *adj inv* anti-dandruff *cpd*
anticipación [antiθipa'θjon] *nf* anticipation; **con 10 minutos de ~** 10 minutes early
anticipado, -a [antiθi'paðo, a] *adj* (*pago*) advance; **por ~** in advance
anticipar [antiθi'par] *vt* to anticipate; (*adelantar*) to bring forward; (*Com*) to advance; **anticiparse** *vr*: **~se a su época** to be ahead of one's time
anticipo [anti'θipo] *nm* (*Com*) advance

anticonceptivo, -a
[antikonθep'tiβo, a] adj, nm
contraceptive

anticongelante [antikonxe'lante]
nm antifreeze

anticuado, -a [anti'kwaðo, a] adj
out-of-date, old-fashioned; (desusado)
obsolete

anticuario [anti'kwarjo] nm
antique dealer

anticuerpo [anti'kwerpo] nm (Med)
antibody

antidepresivo [antiðepre'siβo] nm
antidepressant

antidóping [anti'ðopin] adj
inv: **control ~** drugs test

antídoto [an'tiðoto] nm antidote

antiestético, -a [anties'tetiko, a]
adj unsightly

antifaz [anti'faθ] nm mask; (velo) veil

antiglobalización
[antiɣloβaliθa'θjon] nf anti-
globalization; **antiglobalizador, a** adj
anti-globalization cpd

antiguamente [antixwa'mente]
adv formerly; (hace mucho tiempo)
long ago

antigüedad [antixwe'ðað] nf
antiquity; (artículo) antique; (rango)
seniority

antiguo, -a [an'tixwo, a] adj old,
ancient; (que fue) former

Antillas [an'tiʎas] nfpl: **las ~** the
West Indies

antílope [an'tilope] nm antelope

antinatural [antinatu'ral] adj
unnatural

antipatía [antipa'tia] nf antipathy,
dislike; **antipático, -a** adj
disagreeable, unpleasant

antirrobo [anti'rroβo] adj inv (alarma
etc) anti-theft

antisemita [antise'mita] adj anti-
Semitic ▷ nmf anti-Semite

antiséptico, -a [anti'septiko, a] adj
antiseptic ▷ nm antiseptic

antivirus [anti'birus] nm inv
(Comput) antivirus program

antojarse [anto'xarse] vr (desear): **se
me antoja comprarlo** I have a mind to
buy it; (pensar): **se me antoja que ...** I
have a feeling that ...

antojitos [anto'xitos] (MÉX) nmpl
snacks, nibbles

antojo [an'toxo] nm caprice, whim;
(rosa) birthmark; (lunar) mole

antología [antolo'xia] nf anthology

antorcha [an'tortʃa] nf torch

antro [antro] nm cavern

antropología [antropolo'xia] nf
anthropology

anual [a'nwal] adj annual

anuario [a'nwarjo] nm yearbook

anulación [anula'θjon] nf
annulment; (cancelación) cancellation

anular [anu'lar] vt (contrato) to
annul, cancel; (ley) to revoke, repeal;
(suscripción) to cancel ▷ nm ring finger

anunciar [anun'θjar] vt to
announce; (proclamar) to proclaim; (Com)
to advertise

anuncio [a'nunθjo] nm
announcement; (señal) sign; (Com)
advertisement; (cartel) poster

anzuelo [an'θwelo] nm hook; (para
pescar) fish hook

añadidura [aɲaði'ðura] nf addition,
extra; **por ~** besides, in addition

añadir [aɲa'ðir] vt to add

añejo, -a [a'nexo, a] adj old; (vino)
mellow

añicos [a'ɲikos] nmpl: **hacer ~** to
smash, shatter

año [a'ɲo] nm year; **¡Feliz A~ Nuevo!**
Happy New Year!; **tener 15 ~s** to be 15
(years old); **los ~s 90** the nineties; **el
~ que viene** next year; **año bisiesto/
escolar/fiscal/sabático** leap/school/
tax/sabbatical year

añoranza [aɲo'ranθa] nf nostalgia;
(anhelo) longing

apa [apa] (MÉX) excl goodness me!,
good gracious!

apabullar [apaβu'ʎar] vt to crush,
squash

apacible [apa'θiβle] adj gentle, mild

apaciguar [apaθiˈɣwar] vt to pacify, calm (down)

apadrinar [apaðriˈnar] vt to sponsor, support; (Rel) to be godfather to

apagado, -a [apaˈɣaðo, a] adj (volcán) extinct; (color) dull; (voz) quiet; (sonido) muted, muffled; (persona: apático) listless; **estar ~** (fuego, luz) to be out; (Radio, TV etc) to be off

apagar [apaˈɣar] vt to put out; (Elec, Radio, TV) to turn off; (sonido) to silence, muffle; (sed) to quench

apagón [apaˈɣon] nm blackout; power cut

apalabrar [apalaˈβrar] vt to agree to; (contratar) to engage

apalear [apaleˈar] vt to beat, thrash

apantallar [apantaˈʎar] (MÉX) vt to impress

apañar [apaˈnar] vt to pick up; (asir) to take hold of, grasp; (reparar) to mend, patch up; **apañarse** vr to manage, get along

apapachar [apapaˈtʃar] (MÉX: fam) vt to cuddle, hug

aparador [aparaˈðor] nm sideboard; (MÉX: escaparate) shop window

aparato [apaˈrato] nm apparatus; (máquina) machine; (doméstico) appliance; (boato) ostentation; **aparato digestivo** (Anat) digestive system; **aparatoso, -a** adj showy, ostentatious

aparcamiento [aparkaˈmjento] nm car park (BRIT), parking lot (US)

aparcar [aparˈkar] vt, vi to park

aparear [apareˈar] vt (objetos) to pair, match; (animales) to mate; **aparearse** vr to make a pair; to mate

aparecer [apareˈθer] vi to appear; **aparecerse** vr to appear

aparejador, a [aparexaˈðor, a] nm/f (Arq) master builder

aparejo [apaˈrexo] nm harness, rigging; (de poleas) block and tackle

aparentar [aparenˈtar] vt (edad) to look; (fingir): **~ tristeza** to pretend to be sad

aparente [apaˈrente] adj apparent; (adecuado) suitable

aparezco etc vb V **aparecer**

aparición [apariˈθjon] nf appearance; (de libro) publication; (espectro) apparition

apariencia [apaˈrjenθja] nf (outward) appearance; **en ~** outwardly, seemingly

apartado, -a [aparˈtaðo, a] adj separate; (lejano) remote ▷ nm (tipográfico) paragraph; **apartado de correos** (ESP) post office box; **apartado postal** (LAM) post office box

apartamento [apartaˈmento] nm apartment, flat (BRIT)

apartar [aparˈtar] vt to separate; (quitar) to remove; **apartarse** vr to separate, part; (irse) to move away; to keep away

aparte [aˈparte] adv (separadamente) separately; (además) besides ▷ nm aside; (tipográfico) new paragraph

aparthotel [apartoˈtel] nm serviced apartments

apasionado, -a [apasjoˈnaðo, a] adj passionate

apasionar [apasjoˈnar] vt to excite; **le apasiona el fútbol** she's crazy about football; **apasionarse** vr to get excited

apatía [apaˈtia] nf apathy

apático, -a [aˈpatiko, a] adj apathetic

Apdo abr (= Apartado (de Correos)) PO Box

apeadero [apeaˈðero] nm halt, stop, stopping place

apearse [apeˈarse] vr (jinete) to dismount; (bajarse) to get down o out; (Auto, Ferro) to get off o out

apechugar [apetʃuˈɣar] vr: **~ con algo** to face up to sth

apegarse [apeˈɣarse] vr: **~ a** to become attached to; **apego** nm attachment, devotion

apelar [apeˈlar] vi to appeal; **~ a** (fig) to resort to

apellidar [apeʎi'ðar] vt to call, name; **apellidarse** vr: **se apellida Pérez** her (sur)name's Pérez

apellido [ape'ʎiðo] nm surname

apenar [ape'nar] vt to grieve, trouble; (LAM: avergonzar) to embarrass; **apenarse** vr to grieve; (LAM: avergonzarse) to be embarrassed

apenas [a'penas] adv scarcely, hardly ▷ conj as soon as, no sooner

apéndice [a'pendiθe] nm appendix; **apendicitis** nf appendicitis

aperitivo [aperi'tiβo] nm (bebida) aperitif; (comida) appetizer

apertura [aper'tura] nf opening; (Pol) liberalization

apestar [apes'tar] vt to infect ▷ vi: ~ (a) to stink (of)

apetecer [apete'θer] vt: ¿te apetece un café? do you fancy a (cup of) coffee?; **apetecible** adj desirable; (comida) appetizing

apetito [ape'tito] nm appetite; **apetitoso, -a** adj appetizing; (fig) tempting

apiadarse [apja'ðarse] vr: ~ de to take pity on

ápice ['apiθe] nm whit, iota

apilar [api'lar] vt to pile o heap up

apiñarse [api'narse] vr to crowd o press together

apio ['apjo] nm celery

apisonadora [apisona'ðora] nf steamroller

aplacar [apla'kar] vt to placate

aplastante [aplas'tante] adj overwhelming; (lógica) compelling

aplastar [aplas'tar] vt to squash (flat); (fig) to crush

aplaudir [aplau'ðir] vt to applaud

aplauso [a'plauso] nm applause; (fig) approval, acclaim

aplazamiento [aplaθa'mjento] nm postponement

aplazar [apla'θar] vt to postpone, defer

aplicación [aplika'θjon] nf application; (esfuerzo) effort

aplicado, -a [apli'kaðo, a] adj diligent, hard-working

aplicar [apli'kar] vt (ejecutar) to apply; **aplicarse** vr to apply o.s.

aplique etc [a'plike] vb V **aplicar** ▷ nm wall light

aplomo [a'plomo] nm aplomb, self-assurance

apodar [apo'ðar] vt to nickname

apoderado [apoðe'raðo] nm agent, representative

apoderarse [apoðe'rarse] vr: ~ de to take possession of

apodo [a'poðo] nm nickname

apogeo [apo'xeo] nm peak, summit

apoquinar [apoki'nar] (fam) vt to fork out, cough up

aporrear [aporre'ar] vt to beat (up)

aportar [apor'tar] vt to contribute ▷ vi to reach port; **aportarse** vr (LAM: llegar) to arrive, come

aposta [a'posta] adv deliberately, on purpose

apostar [apos'tar] vt to bet, stake; (tropas etc) to station, post ▷ vi to bet

apóstol [a'postol] nm apostle

apóstrofo [a'postrofo] nm apostrophe

apoyar [apo'jar] vt to lean, rest; (fig) to support, back; **apoyarse** vr: ~ **se en** to lean on; **apoyo** [a'pojo] nm (gen) support; backing, help

apreciable [apre'θjaβle] adj considerable; (fig) esteemed

apreciar [apre'θjar] vt to evaluate, assess; (Com) to appreciate, value; (persona) to respect; (tamaño) to gauge, assess; (detalles) to notice

aprecio [a'preθjo] nm valuation, estimate; (fig) appreciation

aprehender [apreen'der] vt to apprehend, detain

apremio [a'premjo] nm urgency

aprender [apren'der] vt, vi to learn; ~ **algo de memoria** to learn sth (off) by heart

aprendiz, a [apren'diθ, a] nm/f apprentice; (principiante) learner;

aprendizaje nm apprenticeship

aprensión [apren'sjon] nm apprehension, fear; **aprensivo, -a** adj apprehensive

apresar [apre'sar] vt to seize; (capturar) to capture

apresurado, -a [apresu'raðo, a] adj hurried, hasty

apresurar [apresu'rar] vt to hurry, accelerate; **apresurarse** vr to hurry, make haste

apretado, -a [apre'taðo, a] adj tight; (escritura) cramped

apretar [apre'tar] vt to squeeze; (Tec) to tighten; (presionar) to press together, pack ▷ vi to be too tight

apretón [apre'ton] nm squeeze; **apretón de manos** handshake

aprieto [a'prjeto] nm squeeze; (dificultad) difficulty; **estar en un ~** to be in a fix

aprisa [a'prisa] adv quickly, hurriedly

aprisionar [aprisjo'nar] vt to imprison

aprobación [aproβa'θjon] nf approval

aprobar [apro'βar] vt to approve (of); (examen, materia) to pass ▷ vi to pass

apropiado, -a [apro'pjaðo, a] adj suitable

apropiarse [apro'pjarse] vr: **~ de** to appropriate

aprovechado, -a [aproβe'tʃaðo, a] adj industrious, hard-working; (económico) thrifty; (pey) unscrupulous

aprovechar [aproβe'tʃar] vt to use; (explotar) to exploit; (experiencia) to profit from; (oferta, oportunidad) to take advantage of ▷ vi to progress, improve; **aprovecharse** vr: **~se de** to make use of; to take advantage of; **¡que aproveche!** enjoy your meal!

aproximación [aproksima'θjon] nf approximation; (de lotería) consolation prize

aproximar [aproksi'mar] vt to bring nearer; **aproximarse** vr to come near, approach

apruebo etc vb V **aprobar**

aptitud [apti'tuð] nf aptitude

apto, -a [a'pto, a] adj suitable

apuesta [a'pwesta] nf bet, wager

apuesto, -a [a'pwesto, a] adj neat, elegant

apuntar [apun'tar] vt (con arma) to aim at; (con dedo) to point at o to; (anotar) to note (down); (Teatro) to prompt; **apuntarse** vr (Deporte: tanto, victoria) to score; (Escol) to enrol

> No confundir **apuntar** con la palabra inglesa appoint.

apunte [a'punte] nm note

apuñalar [apuɲa'lar] vt to stab

apurado, -a [apu'raðo, a] adj needy; (difícil) difficult; (peligroso) dangerous; (LAM: con prisa) hurried, rushed

apurar [apu'rar] vt (agotar) to drain; (recursos) to use up; (molestar) to annoy; **apurarse** vr (preocuparse) to worry; (LAM: darse prisa) to hurry

apuro [a'puro] nm (aprieto) fix, jam; (escasez) want, hardship; (vergüenza) embarrassment; (LAM: prisa) haste, urgency

aquejado, -a [ake'xaðo, a] adj: **~ de** (Med) afflicted by

aquel, aquella [a'kel, a'keʎa] adj that; **~los(as)** those

aquél, aquélla [a'kel, a'keʎa] pron that (one); **~los(as)** those (ones)

aquello [a'keʎo] pron that, that business

aquí [a'ki] adv (lugar) here; (tiempo) now; **~ arriba** up here; **~ mismo** right here; **~ yace** here lies; **de ~ a siete días** a week from now

ara ['ara] nf: en **~s de** for the sake of

árabe ['araβe] adj, nmf Arab ▷ nm (Ling) Arabic

Arabia [a'raβja] nf Arabia; **Arabia Saudí** o **Saudita** Saudi Arabia

arado [a'raðo] nm plough

Aragón [ara'xon] nm Aragon; **aragonés, -esa** adj, nm/f Aragonese

arancel [aran'θel] nm tariff, duty

arandela [aran'dela] nf (Tec) washer

araña [a'raɲa] nf (Zool) spider; (lámpara) chandelier

arañar [ara'ɲar] vt to scratch

arañazo [ara'naθo] nm scratch

arbitrar [arβi'trar] vt to arbitrate in; (Deporte) to referee ▷ vi to arbitrate

arbitrario, -a [arβi'trarjo, a] adj arbitrary

árbitro ['arβitro] nm arbitrator; (Deporte) referee; (Tenis) umpire

árbol ['arβol] nm (Bot) tree; (Náut) mast; (Tec) axle, shaft; **árbol de Navidad** Christmas tree

arboleda [arβo'leða] nf grove, plantation

arbusto [ar'βusto] nm bush, shrub

arca ['arka] nf chest, box

arcada [ar'kaða] nf arcade; (de puente) arch, span; **arcadas** nfpl (náuseas) retching sg

arcaico, -a [ar'kaiko, a] adj archaic

arce ['arθe] nm maple tree

arcén [ar'θen] nm (de autopista) hard shoulder; (de carretera) verge

archipiélago [artʃi'pjelaɣo] nm archipelago

archivador [artʃiβa'ðor] nm filing cabinet

archivar [artʃi'βar] vt to file (away); **archivo** nm file, archive(s) pl; **archivo adjunto** (Inform) attachment; **archivo de seguridad** (Inform) backup file

arcilla [ar'θiʎa] nf clay

arco ['arko] nm arch; (Mat) arc; (Mil, Mús) bow; **arco iris** rainbow

arder [ar'ðer] vi to burn; **estar que arde** (persona) to fume

ardid [ar'ðið] nm ploy, trick

ardiente [ar'ðjente] adj burning, ardent

ardilla [ar'ðiʎa] nf squirrel

ardor [ar'ðor] nm (calor) heat; (fig) ardour; **ardor de estómago** heartburn

arduo, -a ['arðwo, a] adj arduous

área ['area] nf area; (Deporte) penalty area

arena [a'rena] nf sand; (de una lucha) arena; **arenas movedizas** quicksand

sg; **arenal** [are'nal] nm (terreno arenoso) sandy spot

arenisca [are'niska] nf sandstone; (cascajo) grit

arenoso, -a [are'noso, a] adj sandy

arenque [a'renke] nm herring

arete [a'rete] (MÉX) nm earring

Argel [ar'xel] n Algiers; **Argelia** nf Algeria; **argelino, -a** adj, nm/f Algerian

Argentina [arxen'tina] nf (tb: **la ~**) Argentina

argentino, -a [arxen'tino, a] adj Argentinian; (de plata) silvery ▷ nm/f Argentinian

argolla [ar'ɣoʎa] nf (large) ring

argot [ar'ɣo] (pl **-s**) nm slang

argucia [ar'ɣuθja] nf subtlety, sophistry

argumentar [arɣumen'tar] vt, vi to argue

argumento [arɣu'mento] nm argument; (razonamiento) reasoning; (de novela etc) plot; (Cine, TV) storyline

aria ['arja] nf aria

aridez [ari'ðeθ] nf aridity, dryness

árido, -a ['ariðo, a] adj arid, dry

Aries ['arjes] nm Aries

arisco, -a [a'risko, a] adj surly; (insociable) unsociable

aristócrata [aris'tokrata] nmf aristocrat

arma ['arma] nf arm; **armas** nfpl arms; **arma blanca** blade, knife; **arma de doble filo** double-edged sword; **arma de fuego** firearm; **armas de destrucción masiva** weapons of mass destruction

armada [ar'maða] nf armada; (flota) fleet

armadillo [arma'ðiʎo] nm armadillo

armado, -a [ar'maðo, a] adj armed; (Tec) reinforced

armadura [arma'ðura] nf (Mil) armour; (Tec) framework; (Zool) skeleton; (Física) armature

armamento [arma'mento] nm armament; (Náut) fitting-out

armar [ar'mar] vt (soldado) to arm; (máquina) to assemble; (navío) to fit out; **~la**, **~ un lío** to start a row, kick up a fuss

armario [ar'marjo] nm wardrobe; (de cocina, baño) cupboard; **armario empotrado** built-in cupboard

armatoste [arma'toste] nm (mueble) monstrosity; (máquina) contraption

armazón [arma'θon] nf o m body, chassis; (de mueble etc) frame; (Arq) skeleton

armiño [ar'miɲo] nm stoat; (piel) ermine

armisticio [armis'tiθjo] nm armistice

armonía [armo'nia] nf harmony

armónica [ar'monika] nf harmonica

armonizar [armoni'θar] vt to harmonize; (diferencias) to reconcile

aro ['aro] nm ring; (tejo) quoit; (cs: pendiente) earring

aroma [a'roma] nm aroma, scent; **aromaterapia** n aromatherapy; **aromático, -a** [aro'matiko, a] adj aromatic

arpa ['arpa] nf harp

arpía [ar'pia] nf shrew

arpón [ar'pon] nm harpoon

arqueología [arkeolo'xia] nf archaeology; **arqueólogo, -a** nm/f archaeologist

arquetipo [arke'tipo] nm archetype

arquitecto [arki'tekto] nm architect; **arquitectura** nf architecture

arrabal [arra'βal] nm poor suburb, slum; **arrabales** nmpl (afueras) outskirts

arraigar [arrai'xar] vt to establish ▷ vi to take root

arrancar [arran'kar] vt (sacar) to extract, pull out; (arrebatar) to snatch (away); (Inform) to boot; (fig) to extract ▷ vi (Auto, máquina) to start; (ponerse en marcha) to get going; **~ de** to stem from

arranque etc [a'rranke] vb V **arrancar** ▷ nm sudden start; (Auto)

start; (fig) fit, outburst

arrasar [arra'sar] vt (aplanar) to level, flatten; (destruir) to demolish

arrastrar [arras'trar] vt to drag (along); (fig) to drag down, degrade; (agua, viento) to carry away ▷ vi to drag, trail on the ground; **arrastrarse** vr to crawl; (fig) to grovel; **llevar algo arrastrado** to drag sth along

arrear [arre'ar] vt to drive on, urge on ▷ vi to hurry along

arrebatar [arreβa'tar] vt to snatch (away), seize; (fig) to captivate

arrebato [arre'βato] nm fit of rage, fury; (éxtasis) rapture

arrecife [arre'θife] nm reef

arreglado, -a [arre'xlaðo, a] adj (ordenado) neat, orderly; (moderado) moderate, reasonable

arreglar [arre'xlar] vt (poner orden) to tidy up; (algo roto) to fix, repair; (problema) to solve; **arreglarse** vr to reach an understanding; **arreglárselas** (fam) to get by, manage

arreglo [a'rrexlo] nm settlement; (orden) order; (acuerdo) agreement; (Mús) arrangement, setting

arremangar [arreman'gar] vt to roll up, turn up; **arremangarse** vr to roll up one's sleeves

arremeter [arreme'ter] vi: **~ contra** to attack, rush at

arrendamiento [arrenda'mjento] nm letting; (alquilar) hiring; (contrato) lease; (alquiler) rent; **arrendar** vt to let, lease; to rent; **arrendatario, -a** nm/f tenant

arreos [a'rreos] nmpl (de caballo) harness sg, trappings

arrepentimiento [arrepenti'mjento] nm regret, repentance

arrepentirse [arrepen'tirse] vr to repent; **~ de** to regret

arresto [a'rresto] nm arrest; (Mil) detention; (audacia) boldness, daring; **arresto domiciliario** house arrest

arriar [a'rrjar] vt (velas) to haul down;

(*bandera*) to lower, strike; (*cable*) to pay out

○ **PALABRA CLAVE**

arriba [a'rriβa] *adv* 1 (*posición*) above; **desde arriba** from above; **arriba de todo** at the very top, right on top; **Juan está arriba** Juan is upstairs; **lo arriba mencionado** the aforementioned
2 (*dirección*): **calle arriba** up the street
3 **de arriba abajo** from top to bottom; **mirar a algn de arriba abajo** to look sb up and down
4 **de 5000 euros para arriba** from 5000 euros up(wards)
▷ *adj*: **de arriba: el piso de arriba** the upstairs (BRIT) flat o apartment; **la parte de arriba** the top o upper part
▷ *prep*: **arriba de** (LAM: *por encima de*) above; **arriba de 200 dólares** more than 200 dollars
▷ *excl*: ¡arriba! up!; ¡**manos arriba!** hands up!; ¡**arriba España!** long live Spain!

arribar [arri'βar] *vi* to put into port; (*llegar*) to arrive

arriendo etc [a'rrjendo] *vb* V **arrendar** ▷ *nm* = **arrendamiento**

arriesgado, -a [arrjes'ɣaðo, a] *adj* (*peligroso*) risky; (*audaz*) bold, daring

arriesgar [arrjes'ɣar] *vt* to risk; (*poner en peligro*) to endanger; **arriesgarse** *vr* to take a risk

arrimar [arri'mar] *vt* (*acercar*) to bring close; (*poner de lado*) to set aside; **arrimarse** *vr* to come close o closer; **~se a** to lean on

arrinconar [arrinko'nar] *vt* (*colocar*) to put into a corner; (*enemigo*) to corner; (*fig*) to put to one side; (*abandonar*) to push aside

arroba [a'rroβa] *nf* (*Internet*) at (sign)

arrodillarse [arroði'ʎarse] *vr* to kneel (down)

arrogante [arro'ɣante] *adj* arrogant

arrojar [arro'xar] *vt* to throw, hurl; (*humo*) to emit, give out; (*Com*) to yield, produce; **arrojarse** *vr* to throw o hurl o.s.

arrojo [a'rroxo] *nm* daring

arrollador, -a [arroʎa'ðor, a] *adj* overwhelming

arrollar [arro'ʎar] *vt* (*Auto etc*) to run over, knock down; (*Deporte*) to crush

arropar [arro'par] *vt* to cover, wrap up; **arroparse** *vr* to wrap o.s. up

arroyo [a'rrojo] *nm* stream; (*de la calle*) gutter

arroz [a'rroθ] *nm* rice; **arroz con leche** rice pudding

arruga [a'rruxa] *nf* (*de cara*) wrinkle; (*de vestido*) crease; **arrugar** [arru'ɣar] *vt* to wrinkle; to crease; **arrugarse** *vr* to get creased

arruinar [arrwi'nar] *vt* to ruin, wreck; **arruinarse** *vr* to be ruined, go bankrupt

arsenal [arse'nal] *nm* naval dockyard; (*Mil*) arsenal

arte [ˈarte] *nm* (*gen pl en sg y siempre f en pl*) *nm* art; (*maña*) skill, guile; **artes** *nfpl* (*bellas artes*) arts

artefacto [arte'fakto] *nm* appliance

arteria [ar'terja] *nf* artery

artesanía [artesa'nia] *nf* craftsmanship; (*artículos*) handicrafts pl; **artesano, -a** *nm/f* artisan, craftsman(-woman)

ártico, -a [ˈartiko, a] *adj* Arctic ▷ *nm*: **el Á~** the Arctic

articulación [artikula'θjon] *nf* articulation; (*Med, Tec*) joint

artículo [ar'tikulo] *nm* article; (*cosa*) thing, article; **artículos** *nmpl* (*Com*) goods; **artículos de escritorio** stationery

artífice [ar'tifiθe] *nmf* (*fig*) architect

artificial [artifi'θjal] *adj* artificial

artillería [artiʎe'ria] *nf* artillery

artilugio [arti'luxjo] *nm* gadget

artimaña [arti'maɲa] *nf* trap, snare; (*astucia*) cunning

artista [ar'tista] *nmf* (*pintor*) artist;

painter; (*Teatro*) artist, artiste; **artista de cine** film actor/actress; **artístico, -a** *adj* artistic

artritis [ar'tritis] *nf* arthritis

arveja [ar'βexa] (LAM) *nf* pea

arzobispo [arθo'βispo] *nm* archbishop

as [as] *nm* ace

asa ['asa] *nf* handle; (*fig*) lever

asado [a'saðo] *nm* roast (meat); (LAM: *barbacoa*) barbecue

● **ASADO**
●
● Traditional Latin American
● barbecues, especially in the River
● Plate area, are celebrated in
● the open air around a large grill
● which is used to grill mainly beef
● and various kinds of spicy pork
● sausage. They are usually very
● common during the summer and
● can go on for several days. The
● head cook is nearly always a man.

asador [asa'ðor] *nm* spit

asadura [asa'ðura] *nf* entrails *pl*, offal

asalariado, -a [asala'rjaðo, a] *adj* paid, salaried ▷ *nm/f* wage earner

asaltar [asal'tar] *vt* to attack, assault; (*fig*) to assail; **asalto** *nm* attack, assault; (*Deporte*) round

asamblea [asam'blea] *nf* assembly; (*reunión*) meeting

asar [a'sar] *vt* to roast

ascendencia [asθen'denθja] *nf* ancestry; (LAM: *influencia*) ascendancy; **de ~ francesa** of French origin

ascender [asθen'der] *vi* (*subir*) to ascend, rise; (*ser promovido*) to gain promotion ▷ *vt* to promote; **~ a** to amount to; **ascendiente** *nm* influence ▷ *nmf* ancestor

ascensión [asθen'sjon] *nf* ascent; (*Rel*): **la A~** the Ascension

ascenso [as'θenso] *nm* ascent; (*promoción*) promotion

ascensor [asθen'sor] *nm* lift (BRIT), elevator (US)

asco ['asko] *nm*: **¡qué ~!** how revolting o disgusting; **el ajo me da ~** I hate o loathe garlic; **estar hecho un ~** to be filthy

ascua ['askwa] *nf* ember

aseado, -a [ase'aðo, a] *adj* clean; (*arreglado*) tidy; (*pulcro*) smart

asear [ase'ar] *vt* to clean, wash; to tidy (up)

asediar [ase'ðjar] *vt* (*Mil*) to besiege, lay siege to; (*fig*) to chase, pester; **asedio** *nm* siege; (*Com*) run

asegurado, -a [aseɣu'raðo, a] *adj* insured

asegurador, a [aseɣura'ðor, a] *nm/f* insurer

asegurar [aseɣu'rar] *vt* (*consolidar*) to secure, fasten; (*dar garantía de*) to guarantee; (*preservar*) to safeguard; (*afirmar, dar por cierto*) to assure, affirm; (*tranquilizar*) to reassure; (*tomar un seguro*) to insure; **asegurarse** *vr* to assure o.s., make sure

asemejarse [aseme'xarse] *vr* to be alike; **~ a** to be like, resemble

asentado, -a [asen'taðo, a] *adj* established, settled

asentar [asen'tar] *vt* (*sentar*) to seat, sit down; (*poner*) to place, establish; (*alisar*) to level, smooth down o out; (*anotar*) to note down ▷ *vi* to be suitable, suit

asentir [asen'tir] *vi* to assent, agree; **~ con la cabeza** to nod (one's head)

aseo [a'seo] *nm* cleanliness; **aseos** *nmpl* (*servicios*) toilet *sg* (BRIT), cloakroom *sg* (BRIT), restroom *sg* (US)

aséptico, -a [a'septiko, a] *adj* germ-free, free from infection

asequible [ase'kiβle] *adj* (*precio*) reasonable; (*meta*) attainable; (*persona*) approachable

asesinar [asesi'nar] *vt* to murder; (*Pol*) to assassinate; **asesinato** *nm* murder; assassination

asesino, -a [ase'sino, a] *nm/f*

murderer, killer; (*Pol*) assassin

asesor, a [ase'sor, a] *nm/f* adviser, consultant; **asesorar** [aseso'rar] *vt* (*Jur*) to give legal advice to; (*Com*) to act as consultant to; **asesorarse** *vr*: **asesorarse con** *o* **de** to take advice from, consult; **asesoría** *nf* (*cargo*) consultancy; (*oficina*) consultant's office

asestar [ases'tar] *vt* (*golpe*) to deal, strike

asfalto [as'falto] *nm* asphalt

asfixia [as'fiksja] *nf* asphyxia, suffocation; **asfixiar** [asfik'sjar] *vt* to asphyxiate, suffocate; **asfixiarse** *vr* to be asphyxiated, suffocate

así [a'si] *adv* (*de esta manera*) in this way, like this, thus; (*aunque*) although; (*tan pronto como*) as soon as; **~ que** so; **~ como** as well as; **y todo** even so; **¿no es ~?** isn't it?, didn't you? *etc*; **~ de grande** this big

Asia ['asja] *nf* Asia; **asiático, -a** *adj, nm/f* Asian, Asiatic

asiduo, -a [a'siðwo, a] *adj* assiduous; (*frecuente*) frequent ▷ *nm/f* regular (customer)

asiento [a'sjento] *nm* (*mueble*) seat, chair; (*de coche, en tribunal etc*) seat; (*localidad*) seat, place; (*fundamento*) site; **asiento delantero/trasero** front/back seat

asignación [asixna'θjon] *nf* (*atribución*) assignment; (*reparto*) allocation; (*sueldo*) salary; **asignación (semanal)** pocket money

asignar [asix'nar] *vt* to assign, allocate

asignatura [asixna'tura] *nf* subject; course

asilo [a'silo] *nm* (*refugio*) asylum, refuge; (*establecimiento*) home, institution; **asilo político** political asylum

asimilar [asimi'lar] *vt* to assimilate

asimismo [asi'mismo] *adv* in the same way, likewise

asistencia [asis'tenθja] *nf* audience;

(*Med*) attendance; (*ayuda*) assistance; **asistencia en carretera** roadside assistance; **asistente** *nmf* assistant; **los asistentes** those present; **asistente social** social worker

asistido, -a [asis'tiðo, a] *adj*: **~ por ordenador** computer-assisted

asistir [asis'tir] *vt* to assist, help ▷ *vi*: **~ a** to attend, be present at

asma ['asma] *nf* asthma

asno ['asno] *nm* donkey; (*fig*) ass

asociación [asoθja'θjon] *nf* association; (*Com*) partnership; **asociado, -a** *adj* associate ▷ *nm/f* associate; (*Com*) partner

asociar [aso'θjar] *vt* to associate

asomar [aso'mar] *vt* to show, stick out ▷ *vi* to appear; **asomarse** *vr* to appear, show up; **~ la cabeza por la ventana** to put one's head out of the window

asombrar [asom'brar] *vt* to amaze, astonish; **asombrarse** *vr* (*sorprenderse*) to be amazed; (*asustarse*) to get a fright; **asombro** *nm* amazement, astonishment; (*susto*) fright; **asombroso, -a** *adj* astonishing, amazing

asomo [a'somo] *nm* hint, sign

aspa ['aspa] *nf* (*cruz*) cross; (*de molino*) sail; **en ~** X-shaped

aspaviento [aspa'βjento] *nm* exaggerated display of feeling; (*fam*) fuss

aspecto [as'pekto] *nm* (*apariencia*) look, appearance; (*fig*) aspect

áspero, -a ['aspero, a] *adj* rough; bitter; sour; harsh

aspersión [asper'sjon] *nf* sprinkling

aspiración [aspira'θjon] *nf* breath, inhalation; (*Mús*) short pause; **aspiraciones** *nfpl* (*ambiciones*) aspirations

aspirador [aspira'ðor] *nm* = **aspiradora**

aspiradora [aspira'ðora] *nf* vacuum cleaner, Hoover®

aspirante [aspi'rante] *nmf*

(*candidato*) candidate; (*Deporte*)
contender

aspirar [aspi'rar] *vt* to breathe in
▷ *vi*: **~ a** to aspire to

aspirina [aspi'rina] *nf* aspirin

asqueroso, -a [aske'roso, a] *adj*
disgusting, sickening

asta ['asta] *nf* lance; (*arpón*) spear;
(*mango*) shaft, handle; (*Zool*) horn; **a
media ~** at half mast

asterisco [aste'risko] *nm* asterisk

astilla [as'tiʎa] *nf* splinter; (*pedacito*)
chip; **astillas** *nfpl* (*leña*) firewood *sg*

astillero [asti'ʎero] *nm* shipyard

astro ['astro] *nm* star

astrología [astrolo'xia] *nf* astrology;
astrólogo, -a *nm/f* astrologer

astronauta [astro'nauta] *nmf*
astronaut

astronomía [astrono'mia] *nf*
astronomy

astucia [as'tuθja] *nf* astuteness;
(*ardid*) clever trick

asturiano, -a [astu'rjano, a] *adj,
nm/f* Asturian

astuto, -a [as'tuto, a] *adj* astute;
(*taimado*) cunning

asumir [asu'mir] *vt* to assume

asunción [asun'θjon] *nf*
assumption; (*Rel*): **A~** Assumption

asunto [a'sunto] *nm* (*tema*) matter,
subject; (*negocio*) business

asustar [asus'tar] *vt* to frighten;
asustarse *vr* to be (*o* become)
frightened

atacar [ata'kar] *vt* to attack

atadura [ata'ðura] *nf* bond, tie

atajar [ata'xar] *vt* (*enfermedad, mal*) to
stop ▷ *vi* (*persona*) to take a short cut

atajo [a'taxo] *nm* short cut

atañer [ata'ɲer] *vi*: **~ a** to concern

ataque *etc* [a'take] *vb* V **atacar** ▷ *nm*
attack; **ataque cardíaco** heart attack

atar [a'tar] *vt* to tie, tie up

atardecer [atarðe'θer] *vi* to get dark
▷ *nm* evening; (*crepúsculo*) dusk

atareado, -a [atare'aðo, a] *adj* busy

atascar [atas'kar] *vt* to clog up;
(*obstruir*) to jam; (*fig*) to hinder;
atascarse *vr* to stall; (*cañería*) to get
blocked up; **atasco** *nm* obstruction;
(*Auto*) traffic jam

ataúd [ata'uð] *nm* coffin

ataviar [ata'βjar] *vt* to deck, array

atemorizar [atemori'θar] *vt* to
frighten, scare

Atenas [a'tenas] *n* Athens

atención [aten'θjon] *nf* attention;
(*bondad*) kindness ▷ *excl* (be) careful!,
look out!

atender [aten'der] *vt* to attend to,
look after; (*Tel*) to answer ▷ *vi* to pay
attention

atenerse [ate'nerse] *vr*: **~ a** to abide
by, adhere to

atentado [aten'taðo] *nm* crime,
illegal act; (*asalto*) assault; (*tb*: **~
terrorista**) terrorist attack; **~ contra
la vida de algn** attempt on sb's life;
atentado suicida suicide bombing

atentamente [atenta'mente]
adv: **Le saluda ~** Yours faithfully

atentar [aten'tar] *vi*: **~ a** *o* **contra** to
commit an outrage against

atento, -a [a'tento, a] *adj* attentive,
observant; (*cortés*) polite, thoughtful;
estar ~ a (*explicación*) to pay attention
to

atenuar [ate'nwar] *vt* (*disminuir*) to
lessen, minimize

ateo, -a [a'teo, a] *adj* atheistic
▷ *nm/f* atheist

aterrador, a [aterra'ðor, a] *adj*
frightening

aterrizaje [aterri'θaxe] *nm* landing;
aterrizaje forzoso emergency *o* forced
landing

aterrizar [aterri'θar] *vi* to land

aterrorizar [aterrori'θar] *vt* to
terrify

atesorar [ateso'rar] *vt* to hoard

atestar [ates'tar] *vt* to pack, stuff;
(*Jur*) to attest, testify to

atestiguar [atesti'ɣwar] *vt* to testify

to, bear witness to

atiborrar [atiβo'rrar] vt to fill, stuff;
atiborrarse vr to stuff o.s.

ático ['atiko] nm (desván) attic;
(apartamento) penthouse

atinado, -a [ati'naðo, a] adj
(sensato) wise; (correcto) right, correct

atinar [ati'nar] vi (al disparar): ~ **al
blanco** to hit the target; (fig) to be right

atizar [ati'θar] vt to poke; (horno etc)
to stoke; (fig) to stir up, rouse

atlántico, -a [at'lantiko, a] adj
Atlantic ▷ nm: **el (océano) A~** the
Atlantic (Ocean)

atlas ['atlas] nm inv atlas

atleta [at'leta] nm athlete; **atlético,
-a** adj athletic; **atletismo** nm
athletics sg

atmósfera [at'mosfera] nf
atmosphere

atolladero [atoʎa'ðero] nm (fig)
jam, fix

atómico, -a [a'tomiko, a] adj
atomic

átomo ['atomo] nm atom

atónito, -a [a'tonito, a] adj
astonished, amazed

atontado, -a [aton'taðo, a] adj
stunned; (bobo) silly, daft

atormentar [atormen'tar] vt to
torture; (molestar) to torment; (acosar)
to plague, harass

atornillar [atorni'ʎar] vt to screw
on o down

atosigar [atosi'ɣar] vt to harass,
pester

atracador, a [atraka'ðor, a] nm/f
robber

atracar [atra'kar] vt (Náut) to moor;
(robar) to hold up, rob ▷ vi to moor;
atracarse: **~se (de)** to stuff o.s.
(with)

atracción [atrak'θjon] nf attraction

atraco [a'trako] nm holdup, robbery

atracón [atra'kon] nm: **darse** o
pegarse un ~ (de) (fam) to stuff o.s.
(with)

atractivo, -a [atrak'tiβo, a] adj
attractive ▷ nm appeal

atraer [atra'er] vt to attract

atragantarse [atraɣan'tarse]
vr: **~ (con)** to choke (on); **se me ha
atragantado el chico** I can't stand
the boy

atrancar [atran'kar] vt (puerta) to
bar, bolt

atrapar [atra'par] vt to trap; (resfriado
etc) to catch

atrás [a'tras] adv (movimiento)
back(-wards); (lugar) behind;
(tiempo) previously; **ir hacia ~** to go
back(wards), to go to the rear; **estar ~**
to be behind o at the back

atrasado, -a [atra'saðo, a] adj slow;
(pago) overdue, late; (país) backward

atrasar [atra'sar] vi to be slow;
atrasarse vr to remain behind; (tren)
to be o run late; **atraso** nm slowness;
lateness, delay; (de país) backwardness;
atrasos nmpl (Com) arrears

atravesar [atraβe'sar] vt (cruzar) to
cross (over); (traspasar) to pierce; to go
through; (poner al través) to lay o put
across; **atravesarse** vr to come in
between; (intervenir) to interfere

atravieso etc vb V **atravesar**

atreverse [atre'βerse] vr to dare;
(insolentarse) to be insolent; **atrevido,
-a** daring; insolent; **atrevimiento**
nm daring; insolence

atribución [atriβu'θjon] nf
attribution; **atribuciones** nfpl (Pol)
powers; (Admin) responsibilities

atribuir [atriβu'ir] vt to attribute;
(funciones) to confer

atributo [atri'βuto] nm attribute

atril [a'tril] nm (para libro) lectern;
(Mús) music stand

atropellar [atrope'ʎar] vt (derribar)
to knock over o down; (empujar) to
push (aside); (Auto) to run over, run
down; (agraviar) to insult; **atropello**
nm (Auto) accident; (empujón) push;
(agravio) wrong; (atrocidad) outrage

atroz [a'troθ] adj atrocious, awful

ATS nmf abr (= Ayudante Técnico

Sanitario) nurse

atuendo [a'twendo] *nm* attire

atún [a'tun] *nm* tuna

aturdir [atur'ðir] *vt* to stun; *(de ruido)* to deafen; *(fig)* to dumbfound, bewilder

audacia [au'ðaθja] *nf* boldness, audacity; **audaz** *adj* bold, audacious

audición [auði'θjon] *nf* hearing; *(Teatro)* audition

audiencia [au'ðjenθja] *nf* audience; *(Jur: tribunal)* court

audífono [au'ðifono] *nm (para sordos)* hearing aid

auditor [auði'tor] *nm (Jur)* judge advocate; *(Com)* auditor

auditorio [auði'torjo] *nm* audience; *(sala)* auditorium

auge ['auxe] *nm* boom; *(clímax)* climax

augurar [auɣu'rar] *vt* to predict; *(presagiar)* to portend

augurio [au'ɣurjo] *nm* omen

aula ['aula] *nf* classroom; *(en universidad etc)* lecture room

aullar [au'ʎar] *vi* to howl, yell

aullido [au'ʎiðo] *nm* howl, yell

aumentar [aumen'tar] *vt* to increase; *(precios)* to put up; *(producción)* to step up; *(con microscopio, anteojos)* to magnify ▷ *vi* to increase, be on the increase; **aumentarse** *vr* to increase, be on the increase; **aumento** *nm* increase; rise

aun [a'un] *adv* even; ~ **así** even so; ~ **más** even yet more

aún [a'un] *adv*: ~ **está aquí** he's still here; ~ **no lo sabemos** we don't know yet; **¿no ha venido ~?** hasn't she come yet?

aunque [a'unke] *conj* though, although, even though

aúpa [a'upa] *excl* come on!

auricular [auriku'lar] *nm (Tel)* receiver; **auriculares** *nmpl (cascos)* headphones

aurora [au'rora] *nf* dawn

ausencia [au'senθja] *nf* absence

ausentarse [ausen'tarse] *vr* to go away; *(por poco tiempo)* to go out

ausente [au'sente] *adj* absent

austero, -a [aus'tero, a] *adj* austere

austral [aus'tral] *adj* southern ▷ *nm* monetary unit of Argentina

Australia [aus'tralja] *nf* Australia; **australiano, -a** *adj, nm/f* Australian

Austria ['austrja] *nf* Austria; **austríaco, -a** *adj, nm/f* Austrian

auténtico, -a [au'tentiko, a] *adj* authentic

auto ['auto] *nm (Jur)* edict, decree; *(: orden)* writ; *(Auto)* car; **autos** *nmpl (Jur)* proceedings; *(: acta)* court record *sg*

autoadhesivo [autoaðe'siβo] *adj* self-adhesive; *(sobre)* self-sealing

autobiografía [autoβjoɣra'fia] *nf* autobiography

autobomba [auto'bomba] *(RPL) nf* fire engine

autobronceador [autoβronθea'ðor] *adj* self-tanning

autobús [auto'βus] *nm* bus; **autobús de línea** long-distance coach

autocar [auto'kar] *nm* coach *(BRIT)*, (passenger) bus *(US)*

autóctono, -a [au'toktono, a] *adj* native, indigenous

autodefensa [autoðe'fensa] *nf* self-defence

autodidacta [autoði'ðakta] *adj* self-taught

autoescuela [autoes'kwela] *(ESP) nf* driving school

autógrafo [au'toɣrafo] *nm* autograph

autómata [au'tomata] *nm* automaton

automático, -a [auto'matiko, a] *adj* automatic ▷ *nm* press stud

automóvil [auto'moβil] *nm* (motor) car *(BRIT)*, automobile *(US)*; **automovilismo** *nm (actividad)* motoring; *(Deporte)* motor racing; **automovilista** *nmf* motorist, driver

autonomía [auto'nomja] *nf* autonomy; **autónomo, -a** *(ESP)*, **autonómico, -a** *(ESP) adj (Pol)* autonomous

autopista [auto'pista] nf motorway (BRIT), freeway (US); **autopista de cuota** (ESP) o **peaje** (MÉX) toll (BRIT) o turnpike (US) road

autopsia [au'topsja] nf autopsy, postmortem

autor, a [au'tor, a] nm/f author

autoridad [autori'ðað] nf authority; **autoritario, -a** adj authoritarian

autorización [autoriθa'θjon] nf authorization; **autorizado, -a** adj authorized; (aprobado) approved

autorizar [autori'θar] vt to authorize; (aprobar) to approve

autoservicio [autoser'βiθjo] nm (tienda) self-service shop (BRIT) o store (US); (restaurante) self-service restaurant

autostop [auto'stop] nm hitch-hiking; **hacer~** to hitch-hike; **autostopista** nmf hitch-hiker

autovía [auto'βia] nf ≈ A-road (BRIT), dual carriageway (BRIT), ≈ state highway (US)

auxiliar [auksi'ljar] vt to help ▷ nmf assistant; **auxilio** nm assistance, help; **primeros auxilios** first aid sg

Av abr (= Avenida) Av(e)

aval [a'βal] nm guarantee; (persona) guarantor

avalancha [aβa'lantʃa] nf avalanche

avance [a'βanθe] nm advance; (pago) advance payment; (Cine) trailer

avanzar [aβan'θar] vt, vi to advance

avaricia [aβa'riθja] nf avarice, greed; **avaricioso, -a** adj avaricious, greedy

avaro, -a [a'βaro, a] adj miserly, mean ▷ nm/f miser

Avda abr (= Avenida) Av(e)

AVE ['aβe] nm abr (= Alta Velocidad Española) ≈ bullet train

ave [a'βe] nf bird; **ave de rapiña** bird of prey

avecinarse [aβeθi'narse] vr (tormenta, fig) to be on the way

avellana [aβe'ʎana] nf hazelnut; **avellano** nm hazel tree

avemaría [aβema'ria] nm Hail Mary, Ave Maria

avena [a'βena] nf oats pl

avenida [aβe'niða] nf (calle) avenue

aventajar [aβenta'xar] vt (sobrepasar) to surpass, outstrip

aventón [aβen'ton] (MÉX: fam) nm ride; **dar~a algn** to give sb a ride

aventura [aβen'tura] nf adventure; **aventurero, -a** adj adventurous

avergonzar [aβerɣon'θar] vt to shame; (desconcertar) to embarrass; **avergonzarse** vr to be ashamed; to be embarrassed

avería [aβe'ria] nf (Tec) breakdown, fault

averiado, -a [aβe'rjaðo, a] adj broken down; **"~"** "out of order"

averiguar [aβeri'ɣwar] vt to investigate; (descubrir) to find out, ascertain

avestruz [aβes'truθ] nm ostrich

aviación [aβja'θjon] nf aviation; (fuerzas aéreas) air force

aviador, a [aβja'ðor, a] nm/f aviator, airman(-woman)

ávido, -a ['aβiðo, a] adj avid, eager

avinagrado, -a [aβina'xraðo, a] adj sour, acid

avión [a'βjon] nm aeroplane (BRIT), airplane (US); (ave) martin; **avión de reacción** (jet) (plane)

avioneta [aβjo'neta] nf light aircraft

avisar [aβi'sar] vt (advertir) to warn, notify; (informar) to tell; (aconsejar) to advise, counsel; **aviso** nm warning; (noticia) notice

avispa [a'βispa] nf wasp

avispado, -a [aβis'paðo, a] adj sharp, clever

avivar [aβi'βar] vt to strengthen, intensify

axila [ak'sila] nf armpit

ay [ai] excl (dolor) owl, ouch!; (aflicción) oh!, oh dear!; **¡~ de mí!** poor me!

ayer [a'jer] adv, nm yesterday; **antes de ~** the day before yesterday; **~ mismo** only yesterday

ayote [a'jote] (CAM) nm pumpkin

ayuda [a'juða] *nf* help, assistance
▷ *nm* page; **ayudante** *nmf* assistant,
helper; (*Escol*) assistant; (*Mil*) adjutant

ayudar [aju'ðar] *vt* to help, assist

ayunar [aju'nar] *vi* to fast; **ayunas**
nfpl: **estar en ayunas** to be fasting;
ayuno *nm* fast; fasting

ayuntamiento [ajunta'mjento] *nm*
(*consejo*) town (*o* city) council; (*edificio*)
town (*o* city) hall

azafata [aθa'fata] *nf* air stewardess

azafrán [aθa'fran] *nm* saffron

azahar [aθa'ar] *nm* orange/lemon
blossom

azar [a'θar] *nm* (*casualidad*) chance,
fate; (*desgracia*) misfortune, accident;
por ~ by chance; **al ~** at random

Azores [a'θores] *nfpl*: **las ~** the Azores

azotar [aθo'tar] *vt* to whip, beat;
(*pegar*) to spank; **azote** *nm* (*látigo*)
whip; (*latigazo*) lash, stroke; (*en las
nalgas*) spank; (*calamidad*) calamity

azotea [aθo'tea] *nf* (flat) roof

azteca [aθ'teka] *adj, nmf* Aztec

azúcar [a'θukar] *nm* sugar;
azucarado, -a *adj* sugary, sweet
azucarero, -a [aθuka'rero, a] *adj*
sugar *cpd* ▷ *nm* sugar bowl

azucena [aθu'θena] *nf* white lily

azufre [a'θufre] *nm* sulphur

azul [a'θul] *adj, nm* blue; **azul
celeste/marino** sky/navy blue

azulejo [aθu'lexo] *nm* tile

azuzar [aθu'θar] *vt* to incite, egg on

b

B.A. *abr* (= *Buenos Aires*) B.A.

baba ['baβa] *nf* spittle, saliva; **babear**
vi to drool, slaver

babero [ba'βero] *nm* bib

babor [ba'βor] *nm* port (side)

babosada [baβo'saða] (*MÉX, CAM:
fam*) *nf* drivel; **baboso, -a** [ba'βoso, a]
(*LAM: fam*) *adj* silly

baca ['baka] *nf* (*Auto*) luggage *o*
roof rack

bacalao [baka'lao] *nm* cod(fish)

bache ['batʃe] *nm* pothole, rut; (*fig*)
bad patch

bachillerato [batʃiʎe'rato] *nm* higher
secondary school course

bacinica [baθi'nika] (*LAM*) *nf* potty

bacteria [bak'terja] *nf* bacterium,
germ

Bahama [ba'ama]: **las (Islas) ~** *nfpl*
the Bahamas

bahía [ba'ia] *nf* bay

bailar [bai'lar] *vt, vi* to dance;
bailarín, -ina *nm/f* (ballet) dancer;
baile *nm* dance; (*formal*) ball

baja ['baxa] *nf* drop, fall; (*Mil*)

casualty; **dar de ~** (soldado) to
discharge; (empleado) to dismiss

bajada [ba'xaða] nf descent; (camino)
slope; (de aguas) ebb

bajar [ba'xar] vi to go down, come
down; (temperatura, precios) to drop,
fall ▷ vt (cabeza) to bow; (escalera)
to go down, come down; (precio, voz)
to lower; (llevar abajo) to take down;
bajarse vr (de coche) to get out; (de
autobús, tren) to get off; **~ de** (coche) to
get out of; (autobús, tren) to get off; **~se
algo de Internet** to download sth from
the Internet

bajío [ba'xio] (LAM) nm lowlands pl

bajo, -a ['baxo] adj (mueble, número,
precio) low; (piso) ground; (de estatura)
small, short; (color) pale; (sonido) faint,
soft, low; (voz: en tono) deep; (metal)
base; (humilde) low, humble ▷ adv
(hablar) softly, quietly; (volar) low ▷ prep
under, below, underneath ▷ nm (Mús)
bass; **~ la lluvia** in the rain

bajón [ba'xon] nm fall, drop

bakalao [baka'lao] (ESP: fam) nm
rave (music)

bala ['bala] nf bullet

balacear [balaθe'ar] (MÉX, CAM) vt
to shoot

balance [ba'lanθe] nm (Com) balance;
(: libro) balance sheet; (: cuenta general)
stocktaking

balancear [balanθe'ar] vt to balance
▷ vi to swing (to and fro); (vacilar) to
hesitate; **balancearse** vr to swing (to
and fro), to hesitate

balanza [ba'lanθa] nf scales pl,
balance; **balanza comercial** balance
of trade; **balanza de pagos** balance
of payments

balaustrada [balaus'traða] nf
balustrade; (pasamanos) banisters pl

balazo [ba'laθo] nm (golpe) shot;
(herida) bullet wound

balbucear [balβuθe'ar] vi, vt to
stammer, stutter

balcón [bal'kon] nm balcony

balde ['balde] nm bucket, pail; **de ~**

(for) free, for nothing; **en ~** in vain

baldosa [bal'dosa] nf (azulejo) floor
tile; (grande) flagstone; **baldosín** nm
(small) tile

Baleares [bale'ares] nfpl: **las (Islas) ~**
the Balearic Islands

balero [ba'lero] (LAM) nm (juguete)
cup-and-ball toy

baliza [ba'liθa] nf (Aviac) beacon;
(Náut) buoy

ballena [ba'ʎena] nf whale

ballet [ba'le] (pl **~s**) nm ballet

balneario [balne'arjo] nm spa; (CS: en
la costa) seaside resort

balón [ba'lon] nm ball

baloncesto [balon'θesto] nm
basketball

balonmano [balon'mano] nm
handball

balsa ['balsa] nf raft; (Bot) balsa wood

bálsamo ['balsamo] nm balsam,
balm

baluarte [ba'lwarte] nm bastion,
bulwark

bambú [bam'bu] nm bamboo

banana [ba'nana] (LAM) nf banana;
banano nm (LAM: árbol) banana tree;
(CAM: fruta) banana

banca ['banka] nf (Com) banking

bancario, -a [ban'karjo, a] adj
banking cpd, bank cpd

bancarrota [banka'rrota] nf
bankruptcy; **hacer ~** to go bankrupt

banco ['banko] nm bench; (Escol)
desk; (Com) bank; (Geo) stratum; **banco
de arena** sandbank; **banco de crédito**
credit bank; **banco de datos** databank

banda ['banda] nf band; (pandilla)
gang; (Náut) side, edge; **banda ancha**
broadband; **banda sonora** soundtrack

bandada [ban'daða] nf (de pájaros)
flock; (de peces) shoal

bandazo [ban'daθo] nm: **dar ~s** to
sway from side to side

bandeja [ban'dexa] nf tray

bandera [ban'dera] nf flag

banderilla [bande'riʎa] nf banderilla

bandido [ban'diðo] nm bandit

bando ['bando] nm (edicto) edict, proclamation; (facción) faction; **bandos** nmpl (Rel) banns

bandolera [bando'lera] nf: **llevar en ~** to wear across one's chest

banquero [ban'kero] nm banker

banqueta [ban'keta] nf stool; (MÉX: en calle) pavement (BRIT), sidewalk (US)

banquete [ban'kete] nm banquet; (para convidados) formal dinner; **banquete de boda(s)** wedding reception

banquillo [ban'kiʎo] nm (Jur) dock, prisoner's bench; (banco) bench; (para los pies) footstool

banquina [ban'kina] (RPL) nf hard shoulder (BRIT), berm (US)

bañadera [baɲa'ðera] (RPL) nf bathtub

bañador [baɲa'ðor] (ESP) nm swimming costume (BRIT), bathing suit (US)

bañar [ba'ɲar] vt to bathe, bathe; (objeto) to dip; (de barniz) to coat; **bañarse** vr (en el mar) to bathe, swim; (en la bañera) to have a bath

bañera [ba'ɲera] (ESP) nf bathtub

bañero, -a [ba'ɲero, a] (CS) nm/f lifeguard

bañista [ba'ɲista] nmf bather

baño ['baɲo] nm (en bañera) bath; (en río) dip, swim; (cuarto) bathroom; (bañera) bath(tub); (capa) coating; **darse o tomar un ~** (en bañera) to have o take a bath; (en mar, piscina) to have a swim; **baño María** bain-marie

bar [bar] nm bar

barahúnda [bara'unda] nf uproar, hubbub

baraja [ba'raxa] nf pack of cards; **barajar** vt (naipes) to shuffle; (fig) to jumble up

baranda [ba'randa] nf = **barandilla**

barandilla [baran'diʎa] nf rail, railing

barata [ba'rata] (MÉX) nf (bargain) sale

baratillo [bara'tiʎo] nm (tienda) junkshop; (subasta) bargain sale; (conjunto de cosas) secondhand goods pl

barato, -a [ba'rato, a] adj cheap ▷ adv cheap, cheaply

barba ['barβa] nf (mentón) chin; (pelo) beard

barbacoa [barβa'koa] nf (parrilla) barbecue; (carne) barbecued meat

barbaridad [barβari'ðað] nf barbarity; (acto) barbarism; (atrocidad) outrage; **una ~** (fam) loads; **¡qué ~!** (fam) how awful!

barbarie [bar'βarje] nf barbarism, savagery; (crueldad) barbarity

bárbaro, -a ['barβaro, a] adj barbarous, cruel; (grosero) rough, uncouth ▷ nm/f barbarian ▷ adv: **lo pasamos ~** (fam) we had a great time; **¡qué ~!** (fam) how marvellous!; **un éxito ~** (fam) a terrific success; **es un tipo ~** (fam) he's a great bloke

barbero [bar'βero] nm barber, hairdresser

barbilla [bar'βiʎa] nf chin, tip of the chin

barbudo, -a [bar'βuðo, a] adj bearded

barca ['barka] nf (small) boat; **barcaza** nf barge

Barcelona [barθe'lona] n Barcelona

barco ['barko] nm boat; (grande) ship; **barco de carga/pesca** fishing/cargo boat; **barco de vela** sailing ship

barda ['barða] (MÉX) nf (de madera) fence

baremo [ba'remo] nm (Mat: fag) scale

barítono [ba'ritono] nm baritone

barman ['barman] nm barman

barniz [bar'niθ] nm varnish (en loza) glaze; (fig) veneer; **barnizar** vt to varnish; (loza) to glaze

barómetro [ba'rometro] nm barometer

barquillo [bar'kiʎo] nm cone, cornet

barra ['barra] nf bar, rod; (de un bar, café) bar; (de pan) French stick; (palanca) lever; **barra de labios** lipstick; **barra**

libre free bar

barraca [baˈrraka] nf hut, cabin

barranco [baˈrranko] nm ravine; (fig) difficulty

barrena [baˈrrena] nf drill

barrer [baˈrrer] vt to sweep; (quitar) to sweep away

barrera [baˈrrera] nf barrier

barriada [baˈrrjaða] nf quarter, district

barricada [barriˈkaða] nf barricade

barrida [baˈrriða] nf sweep, sweeping

barriga [baˈrrixa] nf belly; (panza) paunch; **barrigón, -ona** adj potbellied; **barrigudo, -a** adj potbellied

barril [baˈrril] nm barrel, cask

barrio [ˈbarrjo] nm (zona) area, neighborhood (us); (en afueras) suburb; **barrio chino** (ESP) red-light district

barro [ˈbarro] nm (lodo) mud; (objetos) earthenware; (Med) pimple

barroco, -a [baˈrroko, a] adj, nm baroque

barrote [baˈrrote] nm (de ventana) bar

bártola [ˈbartola] nf: **tirarse** o **tumbarse a la ~** to take it easy, be lazy

bártulos [ˈbartulos] nmpl things, belongings

barullo [baˈruʎo] nm row, uproar

basar [baˈsar] vt to base; **basarse** vr: **~se en** to be based on

báscula [ˈbaskula] nf (platform) scales

base [ˈbase] nf base; **a ~ de** on the basis of; (mediante) by means of; **base de datos** (Inform) database

básico, -a [ˈbasiko, a] adj basic

basílica [baˈsilika] nf basilica

básquetbol [ˈbasketbol] nm (LAM) basketball

○ **PALABRA CLAVE**

bastante [basˈtante] adj 1 (suficiente) enough; **bastante dinero** enough o sufficient money; **bastantes libros**

enough books

2 (valor intensivo): **bastante gente** quite a lot of people; **tener bastante calor** to be rather hot

▷ adv: **bastante bueno/malo** quite good/rather bad; **bastante rico** pretty rich; **(lo) bastante inteligente (como) para hacer algo** clever enough o sufficiently clever to do sth

bastar [basˈtar] vi to be enough o sufficient; **bastarse** vr to be self-sufficient; **~ para** to be enough to; **¡basta!** (that's) enough!

bastardo, -a [basˈtarðo, a] adj, nm/f bastard

bastidor [bastiˈðor] nm frame; (de coche) chassis; (Teatro) wing; **entre ~es** (fig) behind the scenes

basto, -a [ˈbasto, a] adj coarse, rough; **bastos** nmpl (Naipes) ≈ clubs

bastón [basˈton] nm stick, staff; (para pasear) walking stick

bastoncillo [bastonˈθiʎo] nm cotton bud

basura [baˈsura] nf rubbish (BRIT), garbage (us) ▷ adj: **comida/televisión ~** junk food/TV

basurero [basuˈrero] nm (hombre) dustman (BRIT), garbage man (us); (lugar) dump; (cubo) (rubbish) bin (BRIT), trash can (us)

bata [ˈbata] nf (gen) dressing gown; (cubretodo) smock, overall; (Med, Tec etc) lab(oratory) coat

batalla [baˈtaʎa] nf battle; **de ~** (fig) for everyday use; **batalla campal** pitched battle

batallón [bataˈʎon] nm battalion

batata [baˈtata] nf sweet potato

batería [bateˈria] nf battery; (Mús) drums; **batería de cocina** kitchen utensils

batido, -a [baˈtiðo, a] adj (camino) beaten, well-trodden ▷ nm (Culin: de leche) milk shake

batidora [batiˈðora] nf beater, mixer; **batidora eléctrica** food mixer, blender

batir [ba'tir] vt to beat, strike; (vencer) to beat, defeat; (revolver) to beat, mix; **batirse** vr to fight; **~ palmas** to applaud

batuta [ba'tuta] nf baton; **llevar la ~** (fig) to be the boss, be in charge

baúl [ba'ul] nm trunk; (Auto) boot (BRIT), trunk (US)

bautismo [bau'tismo] nm baptism, christening

bautizar [bauti'θar] vt to baptize, christen; (fam: diluir) to water down; **bautizo** nm baptism, christening

bayeta [ba'jeta] nf floorcloth

baza ['baθa] nf trick; **meter ~** to butt in

bazar [ba'θar] nm bazaar

bazofia [ba'θofja] nf trash

be [be] nf name of the letter B; **be chica/grande** (MÉX) V/B; **be larga** (LAM) B

beato, -a [be'ato, a] adj blessed; (piadoso) pious

bebé [be'βe] (pl **~s**) nm baby

bebedero [beβe'ðero, a] (MÉX, CS) nm drinking fountain

bebedor, a [beβe'ðor, a] adj hard-drinking

beber [be'βer] vt, vi to drink

bebida [be'βiða] nf drink; **bebido, -a** adj drunk

beca ['beka] nf grant, scholarship; **becario, -a** [be'karjo, a] nm/f scholarship holder, grant holder

bedel [be'ðel] nm (Escol) janitor; (Univ) porter

béisbol ['beisβol] nm baseball

Belén [be'len] nm Bethlehem; **belén** nm (de Navidad) nativity scene, crib

belga ['belɣa] adj, nmf Belgian

Bélgica ['belxika] nf Belgium

bélico, -a ['beliko, a] adj (actitud) warlike

belleza [be'ʎeθa] nf beauty

bello, -a ['beʎo, a] adj beautiful, lovely; **Bellas Artes** Fine Art

bellota [be'ʎota] nf acorn

bemol [be'mol] nm (Mús) flat; **esto tiene ~es** (fam) this is a tough one

bencina [ben'θina] nf (Quím) benzine

bendecir [bende'θir] vt to bless

bendición [bendi'θjon] nf blessing

bendito, -a [ben'dito, a] pp de **bendecir** ▷ adj holy; (afortunado) lucky; (feliz) happy; (sencillo) simple ▷ nm/f simple soul

beneficencia [benefi'θenθja] nf charity

beneficiario, -a [benefi'θjarjo, a] nm/f beneficiary

beneficio [bene'fiθjo] nm (bien) benefit, advantage; (ganancia) profit, gain; **a ~ de algn** in aid of sb; **beneficioso, -a** adj beneficial

benéfico, -a [be'nefiko, a] adj charitable

beneplácito [bene'plaθito] nm approval, consent

benévolo, -a [be'neβolo, a] adj benevolent, kind

benigno, -a [be'niɣno, a] adj kind; (suave) mild; (Med: tumor) benign, non-malignant

berberecho [berβe'retʃo] nm (Zool, Culin) cockle

berenjena [beren'xena] nf aubergine (BRIT), eggplant (US)

Berlín [ber'lin] n Berlin

berlinesa [berli'nesa] (RPL) nf doughnut, donut (US)

bermudas [ber'muðas] nfpl Bermuda shorts

berrido [be'rriðo] nm bellow(ing)

berrinche [be'rrintʃe] (fam) nm temper, tantrum

berro ['berro] nm watercress

berza ['berθa] nf cabbage

besamel [besa'mel] nf (Culin) white sauce, bechamel sauce

besar [be'sar] vt to kiss; (fig: tocar) to graze; **besarse** vr to kiss (one another); **beso** nm kiss

bestia ['bestja] nf beast, animal; (fig) idiot; **bestia de carga** beast of burden; **bestial** adj bestial; (fam) terrific; **bestialidad** nf bestiality; (fam) stupidity

besugo [be'suɣo] *nm* sea bream; (*fam*) idiot

besuquear [besuke'ar] *vt* to cover with kisses; **besuquearse** *vr* to kiss and cuddle

betabel [beta'bel] (*MÉX*) *nm* beetroot (*BRIT*), beet (*US*)

betún [be'tun] *nm* shoe polish; (*Quím*) bitumen

biberón [biβe'ron] *nm* feeding bottle

Biblia ['biβlja] *nf* Bible

bibliografía [biβljoɣra'fia] *nf* bibliography

biblioteca [biβljo'teka] *nf* library; (*mueble*) bookshelves; **biblioteca de consulta** reference library; **bibliotecario, -a** *nm/f* librarian

bicarbonato [bikarβo'nato] *nm* bicarbonate

bicho ['bitʃo] *nm* (*animal*) small animal; (*sabandija*) bug, insect; (*Taur*) bull

bici ['biθi] (*fam*) *nf* bike

bicicleta [biθi'kleta] *nf* bicycle, cycle; **ir en ~** to cycle

bidé [bi'ðe] (*pl ~s*) *nm* bidet

bidón [bi'ðon] *nm* (*de aceite*) drum; (*de gasolina*) can

○ **PALABRA CLAVE**

bien [bjen] *nm* 1 (*bienestar*) good; **te lo digo por tu bien** I'm telling you for your own good; **el bien y el mal** good and evil

2 (*posesión*): **bienes** goods; **bienes de consumo** consumer goods; **bienes inmuebles** *o* **raíces/bienes muebles** real estate *sg* / personal property *sg*

▷ *adv* 1 (*de manera satisfactoria, correcta etc*) well; **trabaja/come bien** she works/eats well; **contestó bien** he answered correctly; **me siento bien** I feel fine; **no me siento bien** I don't feel very well; **se está bien aquí** it's nice here

2 (*frases*): **hiciste bien en llamarme** you were right to call me

3 (*valor intensivo*) very; **un cuarto bien caliente** a nice warm room; **bien se ve que ...** it's quite clear that ...

4 **estar bien: estoy muy bien aquí** I feel very happy here; **está bien que vengan** it's all right for them to come; **¡está bien! lo haré** oh all right, I'll do it

5 (*de buena gana*): **yo bien que iría pero ...** I'd gladly go but ...

▷ *excl*: **¡bien!** (*aprobación*) O.K.!; **¡muy bien!** well done! ▷ *adj inv* (*matiz despectivo*): **gente bien** posh people

▷ *conj* 1 **bien ... bien: bien en coche bien en tren** either by car or by train

2 (*LAM*): **no bien: no bien llegue te llamaré** as soon as I arrive I'll call you

3 **si bien** even though; *V tb* **más**

bienal [bje'nal] *adj* biennial

bienestar [bjenes'tar] *nm* well-being, welfare

bienvenida [bjembe'niða] *nf* welcome; **dar la ~ a algn** to welcome sb

bienvenido [bjembe'niðo] *excl* welcome!

bife ['bife] (*cs*) *nm* steak

bifurcación [bifurka'θjon] *nf* fork

bígamo, -a ['biɣamo, a] *adj* bigamous ▷ *nm/f* bigamist

bigote [bi'ɣote] *nm* moustache; **bigotudo, -a** *adj* with a big moustache

bikini [bi'kini] *nm* bikini; (*Culin*) toasted ham and cheese sandwich

bilingüe [bi'lingwe] *adj* bilingual

billar [bi'ʎar] *nm* billiards *sg*; **billares** *nmpl* (*lugar*) billiard hall; (*sala de juegos*) amusement arcade; **billar americano** pool

billete [bi'ʎete] *nm* ticket; (*de banco*) (bank)note (*BRIT*), bill (*US*); (*carta*) note; **~ de 20 libras** £20 note; **billete de ida y vuelta** return (*BRIT*) *o* round-trip (*US*) ticket; **billete sencillo** *o* **de ida** single (*BRIT*) *o* one-way (*US*) ticket; **billete electrónico** e-ticket

billetera [biʎe'tera] *nf* wallet

billón [bi'ʎon] *nm* billion

bimensual [bimen'swal] *adj* twice monthly

bingo ['bingo] *nm* bingo

biodegradable [bioðeɣra'ðaβle] *adj* biodegradable

biografía [bioɣra'fia] *nf* biography

biología [bjolo'xia] *nf* biology; **biológico, -a** *adj* biological; *(cultivo, producto)* organic; **biólogo, -a** *nm/f* biologist

biombo ['bjombo] *nm* (folding) screen

bioterrorismo [bjoterro'rismo] *nm* bioterrorism

biquini [bi'kini] *nm* o (RPL) f bikini

birlar [bir'lar] (fam) *vt* to pinch

Birmania [bir'manja] *nf* Burma

birome [bi'rome] (RPL) *nf* ballpoint (pen)

birria ['birrja] *nf*: **ser una ~** *(película, libro)* to be rubbish

bis [bis] *excl* encore!

bisabuelo, -a [bisa'βwelo, a] *nm/f* great-grandfather(-mother)

bisagra [bi'saɣra] *nf* hinge

bisiesto [bi'sjesto] *adj*: **año ~** leap year

bisnieto, -a [bis'njeto, a] *nm/f* great-grandson/daughter

bisonte [bi'sonte] *nm* bison

bisté [bis'te] *nm* = **bistec**

bistec [bis'tek] *nm* steak

bisturí [bistu'ri] *nm* scalpel

bisutería [bisute'ria] *nf* imitation o costume jewellery

bit [bit] *nm* (Inform) bit

bizco, -a ['biθko, a] *adj* cross-eyed

bizcocho [biθ'kotʃo] *nm* (Culin) sponge cake

blanca ['blanka] *nf* (Mús) minim; **estar sin ~** (ESP: fam) to be broke; V tb **blanco**

blanco, -a ['blanko, a] *adj* white ▷ *nm/f* white man/woman, white ▷ *nm* (color) white; (en texto) blank; (Mil, fig) target; **en ~** blank; **noche en ~** sleepless night

blandir [blan'dir] *vt* to brandish

blando, -a ['blando, a] *adj* soft; *(tierno)* tender, gentle; *(carácter)* mild; *(fam)* cowardly

blanqueador [blankea'ðor] (MÉX) *nm* bleach

blanquear [blanke'ar] *vt* to whiten; *(fachada)* to whitewash; *(paño)* to bleach ▷ *vi* to turn white

blanquillo [blan'kiʎo] (MÉX, CAM) *nm* egg

blasfemar [blasfe'mar] *vi* to blaspheme, curse

bledo ['bleðo] *nm*: **me importa un ~** I couldn't care less

blindado, -a [blin'daðo, a] *adj* (Mil) armour-plated; (antibala) bullet-proof; **coche** (ESP) o **carro** (LAM) **~** armoured car

bloc [blok] (pl **~s**) *nm* writing pad

blof [blof] (MÉX) *nm* bluff; **blofear** (MÉX) *vi* to bluff

blog [bloɣ] (pl **~s**) *nm* blog

bloque ['bloke] *nm* block; (Pol) bloc

bloquear [bloke'ar] *vt* to blockade; **bloqueo** *nm* blockade; (Com) freezing, blocking; **bloqueo mental** mental block

blusa ['blusa] *nf* blouse

bobada [bo'βaða] *nf* foolish action o foolish statement; **decir ~s** to talk nonsense

bobina [bo'βina] *nf* (Tec) bobbin; (Foto) spool; (Elec) coil

bobo, -a ['boβo, a] *adj* (tonto) daft, silly; (cándido) naïve ▷ *nm/f* fool, idiot ▷ *nm* (Teatro) clown, funny man

boca ['boka] *nf* mouth; (de crustáceo) pincer; (de cañón) muzzle; (entrada) mouth, entrance; **bocas** *nfpl* (de río) mouth *sg*; **~ abajo/arriba** face down/up; **se me hace la ~ ~ agua** my mouth is watering; **boca de incendios** hydrant; **boca del estómago** pit of the stomach; **boca de metro** underground (BRIT) o subway (US) entrance

bocacalle [boka'kaʎe] *nf* (entrance to a) street; **la primera ~** the first

bocadillo | 40

turning o street

bocadillo [boka'ðiʎo] *nm* sandwich

bocado [bo'kaðo] *nm* mouthful, bite; (*de caballo*) bridle

bocajarro [boka'xarro]: **a ~** *adv* (*disparar*) point-blank

bocanada [boka'naða] *nf* (*de vino*) mouthful, swallow; (*de aire*) gust, puff

bocata [bo'kata] (*fam*) *nm* sandwich

bocazas [bo'kaθas] (*fam*) *nm inv* bigmouth

boceto [bo'θeto] *nm* sketch, outline

bochorno [bo'tʃorno] *nm* (*vergüenza*) embarrassment; (*calor*): **hace ~** it's very muggy

bocina [bo'θina] *nf* (*Mús*) trumpet; (*Auto*) horn; (*para hablar*) megaphone

boda [boða] *nf* (*tb*: **~s**) wedding, marriage; (*fiesta*) wedding reception; **bodas de oro/plata** golden/silver wedding *sg*

bodega [bo'ðeɣa] *nf* (*de vino*) (wine) cellar; (*depósito*) storeroom; (*de barco*) hold

bodegón [boðe'ɣon] *nm* (*Arte*) still life

bofetada [bofe'taða] *nf* slap (in the face)

boga [boɣa] *nf*: **en ~** (*fig*) in vogue

Bogotá [boɣo'ta] *n* Bogotá

bohemio, -a [bo'emjo, a] *adj, nm/f* Bohemian

bohío [bo'io] (*CAM*) *nm* shack, hut

boicot [boi'kot] (*pl* **~s**) *nm* boycott; **boicotear** *vt* to boycott

bóiler [ˈboiler] (*MÉX*) *nm* boiler

boina [ˈboina] *nf* beret

bola [ˈbola] *nf* ball; (*canica*) marble; (*Naipes*) (grand) slam; (*betún*) shoe polish; (*mentira*) tale, story; **bolas** *nfpl* (*LAM*: *caza*) bolas *sg*; **bola de billar** billiard ball; **bola de nieve** snowball

boleadoras [bolea'ðoras] *nfpl* bolas *sg*

bolear [bole'ar] (*MÉX*) *vt* (*zapatos*) to polish, shine

bolera [bo'lera] *nf* skittle o bowling alley

bolero, -a [bo'lero] *nm/f* (*limpiabotas*) shoeshine boy/girl

boleta [bo'leta] (*LAM*) *nf* (*de rifa*) ticket; (*cs*: *recibo*) receipt; **boleta de calificaciones** (*MÉX*) report card

boletería [bolete'ria] (*LAM*) *nf* ticket office

boletín [bole'tin] *nm* bulletin; (*periódico*) journal, review; **boletín de noticias** news bulletin

boleto [bo'leto] *nm* (*LAM*) ticket; **boleto de ida y vuelta** (*LAM*) round trip ticket; **boleto electrónico** (*LAM*) e-ticket; **boleto redondo** (*MÉX*) round trip ticket

boli [ˈboli] (*fam*) *nm* Biro®

bolígrafo [bo'liɣrafo] *nm* ball-point pen, Biro®

bolilla [bo'liʎa] (*RPL*) *nf* topic

bolillo [bo'liʎo] (*MÉX*) *nm* (*bread*) roll

bolita [bo'lita] (*cs*) *nf* marble

bolívar [bo'liβar] *nm* monetary unit of Venezuela

Bolivia [bo'liβja] *nf* Bolivia; **boliviano, -a** *adj, nm/f* Bolivian

bollería [boʎe'ria] *nf* cakes *pl* and pastries *pl*

bollo [ˈboʎo] *nm* (*pan*) roll; (*bulto*) bump, lump; (*abolladura*) dent

bolo [ˈbolo] *nm* skittle; (*píldora*) (large) pill; (**juego de**) **bolos** *nmpl* skittles *sg*

bolsa [ˈbolsa] *nf* (*para llevar algo*) bag; (*MÉX, CAM*: *bolsillo*) pocket; (*MÉX*: *de mujer*) handbag; (*Anat*) cavity, sac; (*Com*) stock exchange; (*Minería*) pocket; **de ~** pocket *cpd*; **bolsa de agua caliente** hot water bottle; **bolsa de aire** air pocket; **bolsa de dormir** (*MÉX, RPL*) sleeping bag; **bolsa de la compra** shopping bag; **bolsa de papel/plástico** paper/plastic bag

bolsear [bolse'ar] (*MÉX, CAM*) *vt*: **~ a algn** to pick sb's pocket

bolsillo [bol'siʎo] *nm* pocket; (*cartera*) purse; **de ~** pocket(-size)

bolso [ˈbolso] *nm* (*bolsa*) bag; (*de mujer*) handbag

bomba [ˈbomba] *nf* (*Mil*) bomb; (*Tec*)

pump ▷ adj (fam): **noticia** ~ bombshell
▷ adv (fam): **pasarlo** ~ to have a great
time; **bomba atómica/de efecto
retardado/de humo** atomic/time/
smoke bomb

bombacha [bom'batʃa] (RPL) nf
panties pl

bombardear [bombarðe'ar] vt to
bombard; (Mil) to bomb; **bombardeo**
nm bombardment; bombing

bombazo [bom'baθo] (MÉX) nm
(explosión) explosion; (fam: noticia)
bombshell; (: éxito) smash hit

bombear [bombe'ar] vt (agua) to
pump (out o up)

bombero [bom'bero] nm fireman

bombilla [bom'biʎa] (ESP) nf (light)
bulb

bombita [bom'bita] (RPL) nf (light)
bulb

bombo ['bombo] nm (Mús) bass
drum; (Tec) drum

bombón [bom'bon] nm chocolate;
(MÉX: de caramelo) marshmallow

bombona [bom'bona] (ESP) nf (de
butano, oxígeno) cylinder

bonachón, -ona [bona'tʃon, ona]
adj good-natured, easy-going

bonanza [bo'nanθa] nf (Náut) fair
weather; (fig) bonanza; (Minería) rich
pocket o vein

bondad [bon'dað] nf goodness,
kindness; **tenga la ~ de** (please) be
good enough to

bonito, -a [bo'nito, a] adj pretty;
(agradable) nice ▷ nm (atún) tuna (fish)

bono ['bono] nm voucher; (Finanzas)
bond

bonobús [bono'βus] (ESP) nm bus
pass

bonoloto [bono'loto] nf state-run
weekly lottery

boquerón [boke'ron] nm (pez) (kind
of) anchovy; (agujero) large hole

boquete [bo'kete] nm gap, hole

boquiabierto, -a [bokia'βjerto,
a] adj: **quedarse ~** to be amazed o
flabbergasted

boquilla [bo'kiʎa] nf (para riego)
nozzle; (para cigarro) cigarette holder;
(Mús) mouthpiece

borbotón [borβo'ton] nm: **salir a
borbotones** to gush out

borda ['borða] nf (Náut) (ship's) rail;
tirar algo/caerse por la ~ to throw
sth/fall overboard

bordado [bor'ðaðo] nm embroidery

bordar [bor'ðar] vt to embroider

borde ['borðe] nm edge, border; (de
camino etc) side; (en la costura) hem; **al
~ de** (fig) on the verge o brink of; **ser ~**
(ESP: fam) to be rude; **bordear** vt to
border

bordillo [bor'ðiʎo] nm kerb (BRIT),
curb (US)

bordo ['borðo] nm (Náut) side; **a ~**
on board

borlote [bor'lote] (MÉX) nm row,
uproar

borrachera [borra'tʃera] nf (ebriedad)
drunkenness; (orgía) spree, binge

borracho, -a [bo'rratʃo, a] adj drunk
▷ nm/f (habitual) drunkard, drunk;
(temporal) drunk, drunk man/woman

borrador [borra'ðor] nm (escritura)
first draft, rough sketch; (goma) rubber
(BRIT), eraser

borrar [bo'rrar] vt to erase, rub out

borrasca [bo'rraska] nf storm

borrego, -a [bo'rreγo, a] nm/f
(Zool: joven) (yearling) lamb; (adulto)
sheep ▷ nm (MÉX: fam) false rumour

borrico, -a [bo'rriko, a] nm/f
donkey/she-donkey; (fig) stupid
man/woman

borrón [bo'rron] nm (mancha) stain

borroso, -a [bo'rroso, a] adj vague,
unclear; (escritura) illegible

bosque ['boske] nm wood; (grande)
forest

bostezar [boste'θar] vi to yawn;
bostezo nm yawn

bota ['bota] nf (calzado) boot; (para
vino) leather wine bottle; **botas de
agua** o **goma** Wellingtons

botana [bo'tana] (MÉX) nf snack.

appetizer

botánica [bo'tanika] nf (ciencia)
botany; V tb **botánico**

botánico, -a [bo'taniko, a] adj
botanical ▷ nm/f botanist

botar [bo'tar] vt to throw, hurl; (Náut)
to launch; (LAM: echar) to throw out ▷ vi
(ESP: saltar) to bounce

bote ['bote] nm (salto) bounce;
(golpe) thrust; (ESP: envase) tin,
can; (embarcación) boat; (MÉX,
CAM: pey: cárcel) jail; **de ~ en ~** packed,
jammed full; **bote de la basura** (MÉX)
dustbin (BRIT), trashcan (US); **bote
salvavidas** lifeboat

botella [bo'teʎa] nf bottle; **botellín**
nm small bottle; **botellón**
(ESP: fam) outdoor drinking session

botijo [bo'tixo] nm (earthenware) jug

botín [bo'tin] nm (calzado) half boot;
(polaina) spat; (mil) booty

botiquín [boti'kin] nm (armario)
medicine cabinet; (portátil) first-aid kit

botón [bo'ton] nm button; (Bot) bud
botones [bo'tones] nm inv bellboy
(BRIT), bellhop (US)

bóveda ['boβeða] nf (Arq) vault

boxeador [boksea'ðor] nm boxer

boxeo [bok'seo] nm boxing

boya ['boja] nf (Náut) buoy; (de
caña) float

boyante [bo'jante] adj prosperous

bozal [bo'θal] nm (para caballos)
halter; (de perro) muzzle

bragas ['braxas] nfpl (de mujer)
panties, knickers (BRIT)

bragueta [bra'yeta] nf fly, flies pl

braille [breil] nm braille

brasa ['brasa] nf live hot coal

brasero [bra'sero] nm brazier

brasier [bra'sjer] (MÉX) nm bra

Brasil [bra'sil] nm (tb: **el ~**) Brazil;
brasileño, -a adj, nm/f Brazilian

brassier [bra'sjer] (MÉX) nm V
brasier

bravo, -a ['braβo, a] adj (valiente)
brave; (feroz) ferocious; (salvaje) wild;
(mar etc) rough, stormy ▷ excl bravo!;

bravura nf bravery; ferocity

braza ['braθa] nf fathom; **nadar a ~**
to swim breast-stroke

brazalete [braθa'lete] nm (pulsera)
bracelet; (banda) armband

brazo ['braθo] nm arm; (Zool) foreleg;
(Bot) limb, branch; **luchar a ~ partido**
to fight hand-to-hand; **ir cogidos del ~**
to walk arm in arm

brebaje [bre'βaxe] nm potion

brecha ['bretʃa] nf (hoyo, vacío) gap,
opening; (Mil, fig) breach

brega ['brexa] nf (lucha) struggle;
(trabajo) hard work

breva ['breβa] nf early fig

breve ['breβe] adj short, brief ▷ nf
(Mús) breve; **en ~** (pronto) shortly,
before long; **brevedad** nf brevity,
shortness

bribón, -ona [bri'βon, ona] adj idle,
lazy ▷ nm/f (pícaro) rascal, rogue

bricolaje [briko'laxe] nm do-it-
yourself, DIY

brida ['briða] nf bridle, rein; (Tec)
clamp

bridge [britʃ] nm bridge

brigada [bri'ɣaða] nf (unidad)
brigade; (de trabajadores) squad, gang
▷ nm ≈ staff-sergeant, sergeant-major

brillante [bri'ʎante] adj brilliant
▷ nm diamond

brillar [bri'ʎar] vi to shine; (joyas)
to sparkle

brillo ['briʎo] nm shine; (brillantez)
brilliance; (fig) splendour; **sacar ~ a**
to polish

brincar [brin'kar] vi to skip about,
hop about, jump about

brinco ['brinko] nm jump, leap

brindar [brin'dar] vi: **~ a** o **por** to
drink (a toast) to ▷ vt to offer, present

brindis ['brindis] nm inv toast

brío ['brio] nm spirit, dash

brisa ['brisa] nf breeze

británico, -a [bri'taniko, a] adj
British ▷ nm/f Briton, British person

brizna ['briθna] nf (de hierba, paja)
blade; (de tabaco) leaf

broca ['broka] *nf* (*Tec*) drill, bit

brocha ['brotʃa] *nf* (large) paintbrush; **brocha de afeitar** shaving brush

broche ['brotʃe] *nm* brooch

broma ['broma] *nf* joke; **de o en ~** in fun, as a joke; **broma pesada** practical joke; **bromear** *vi* to joke

bromista [bro'mista] *adj* fond of joking ▷ *nmf* joker, wag

bronca ['bronka] *nf* row; **echar una ~ a algn** to tick sb off

bronce ['bronθe] *nm* bronze; **bronceado, -a** *adj* bronze; (*por el sol*) tanned ▷ *nm* (sun)tan; (*Tec*) bronzing

bronceador [bronθea'ðor] *nm* suntan lotion

broncearse [bronθe'arse] *vr* to get a suntan

bronquio ['bronkjo] *nm* (*Anat*) bronchial tube

bronquitis [bron'kitis] *nf inv* bronchitis

brotar [bro'tar] *vi* (*Bot*) to sprout; (*aguas*) to gush (forth); (*Med*) to break out

brote ['brote] *nm* (*Bot*) shoot; (*Med, fig*) outbreak

bruces ['bruθes]: **de bruces** *adv*: **caer o dar de ~** to fall headlong, fall flat

bruja ['bruxa] *nf* witch; **brujería** *nf* witchcraft

brujo ['bruxo] *nm* wizard, magician

brújula ['bruxula] *nf* compass

bruma ['bruma] *nf* mist

brusco, -a ['brusko, a] *adj* (*súbito*) sudden; (*áspero*) brusque

Bruselas [bru'selas] *n* Brussels

brutal [bru'tal] *adj* brutal; **brutalidad** [brutali'ðað] *nf* brutality

bruto, -a ['bruto, a] *adj* (*idiota*) stupid; (*bestial*) brutish; (*peso*) gross; **en ~** raw, unworked

Bs.As. *abr* (= *Buenos Aires*) B.A.

bucal [bu'kal] *adj* oral; **por vía ~** orally

bucear [buθe'ar] *vi* to dive ▷ *vt* to explore; **buceo** *nm* diving

bucle ['bukle] *nm* curl

budismo [bu'ðismo] *nm* Buddhism

buen [bwen] *adj m V* **bueno**

buenamente [bwena'mente] *adv* (*fácilmente*) easily; (*voluntariamente*) willingly

buenaventura [bwenaβen'tura] *nf* (*suerte*) good luck; (*adivinación*) fortune

buenmozo [bwen'moθo] (*MÉX*) *adj* handsome

○ **PALABRA CLAVE**

bueno, -a ['bweno, a] (*antes de nmsg*: **buen**) *adj* **1** (*excelente etc*) good; **es un libro bueno, es un buen libro** it's a good book; **hace bueno, hace buen tiempo** the weather's fine, it is fine; **el bueno de Paco** good old Paco; **fue muy bueno conmigo** he was very nice o kind to me

2 (*apropiado*): **ser bueno para** to be good for; **creo que vamos por buen camino** I think we're on the right track

3 (*irónico*): **le di un buen rapapolvo** I gave him a good o real ticking off; **¡buen conductor estás hecho!** some o a fine driver you are!; **¡estaría bueno que ...!** a fine thing it would be if ...!

4 (*atractivo, sabroso*): **está bueno este bizcocho** this sponge is delicious; **Carmen está muy buena** Carmen is gorgeous

5 (*saludos*): **¡buen día!, ¡buenos días!** (good) morning!; **¡buenas (tardes)!** (good) afternoon!; (*más tarde*) (good) evening!; **¡buenas noches!** good night!

6 (*otras locuciones*): **estar de buenas** to be in a good mood; **por las buenas o por las malas** by hook or by crook; **de buenas a primeras** all of a sudden ▷ *excl*: **¡bueno!** all right!; **bueno, ¿y qué?** well, so what?

Buenos Aires [bweno'saires] *nm* Buenos Aires

buey [bwei] *nm* ox

búfalo ['bufalo] *nm* buffalo

bufanda [bu'fanda] nf scarf
bufete [bu'fete] nm (despacho de abogado) lawyer's office
bufón [bu'fon] nm clown
buhardilla [buar'ðiʎa] nf attic
búho ['buo] nm owl; (fig) hermit, recluse
buitre ['bwitre] nm vulture
bujía [bu'xia] nf (vela) candle; (Elec) candle (power); (Auto) spark plug
bula ['bula] nf (papal) bull
bulbo ['bulβo] nm bulb
bulevar [bule'βar] nm boulevard
Bulgaria [bul'γarja] nf Bulgaria; **búlgaro, -a** adj, nm/f Bulgarian
bulla ['buʎa] nf (ruido) uproar; (de gente) crowd
bullicio [bu'ʎiθjo] nm (ruido) uproar; (movimiento) bustle
bulto ['bulto] nm (paquete) package; (fardo) bundle; (tamaño) size, bulkiness; (Med) swelling, lump; (silueta) vague shape
buñuelo [bu'nwelo] nm ≈ doughnut (BRIT), ≈ donut (US); (fruta de sartén) fritter
buque ['buke] nm ship, vessel; **buque de guerra** warship
burbuja [bur'βuxa] nf bubble
burdel [bur'ðel] nm brothel
burgués, -esa [bur'γes, esa] adj middle-class, bourgeois; **burguesía** nf middle class, bourgeoisie
burla ['burla] nf (mofa) gibe; (broma) joke; (engaño) trick; **burlar** [bur'lar] vt (engañar) to deceive ▷ vi to joke; **burlarse** vr to joke; **burlarse de** to make fun of
burlón, -ona [bur'lon, ona] adj mocking
buró [bu'ro] (MÉX) nm bedside table
burocracia [buro'kraθja] nf civil service
burrada [bu'rraða] nf: **decir o soltar ~s** to talk nonsense; **hacer ~s** to act stupid; **una ~** (ESP: mucho) a (hell of a) lot
burro, -a ['burro, a] nm/f donkey/

she-donkey; (fig) ass, idiot
bursátil [bur'satil] adj stock-exchange cpd
bus [bus] nm bus
busca ['buska] nf search, hunt ▷ nm (Tel) bleeper; **en ~ de** in search of
buscador [buska'ðor] nm (Internet) search engine
buscar [bus'kar] vt to look for, search for, seek ▷ vi to look, search, seek; **se busca secretaria** secretary wanted
busque etc vb V **buscar**
búsqueda [bus'keða] nf = **busca**
busto ['busto] nm (Anat, Arte) bust
butaca [bu'taka] nf armchair; (de cine, teatro) stall, seat
butano [bu'tano] nm butane (gas)
buzo ['buθo] nm diver
buzón [bu'θon] nm (en puerta) letter box; (en calle) pillar box

C

knight; (*Naipes*) queen; **ir en ~** to ride; caballo de carreras racehorse; caballo de fuerza ovapor horsepower

cabaña [ka'βaɲa] nf (*casita*) hut, cabin

cabecear [kaβeθe'ar] vt, vi to nod

cabecera [kaβe'θera] nf head; (*imprenta*) headline

cabecilla [kaβe'θiλa] nm ringleader

cabellera [kaβe'λera] nf (head of) hair; (*de cometa*) tail

cabello [ka'βeλo] nm (tb: **~s**) hair; cabello de ángel confectionery and pastry filling made of pumpkin and syrup

caber [ka'βer] vi (*entrar*) to fit, go; **caben 3 más** there's room for 3 more

cabestrillo [kaβes'triλo] nm sling

cabeza [ka'βeθa] nf head; (*Pol*) chief, leader; cabeza de ajo bulb of garlic; cabeza de familia head of the household; cabeza rapada skinhead; cabezada nf (*golpe*) butt; **dar cabezadas** to nod; cabezón, -ona adj (*vino*) heady; (*fam*: *persona*) pig-headed

cabida [ka'βiða] nf space

cabina [ka'βina] nf cabin; (*de avión*) cockpit; (*de camión*) cab; cabina telefónica telephone (*BRIT*) box o booth

cabizbajo, -a [kaβiθ'βaxo, a] adj crestfallen, dejected

cable [ka'βle] nm cable

cabo [ka'βo] nm (*de objeto*) end, extremity; (*Mil*) corporal; (*Náut*) rope, cable; (*Geo*) cape; **al ~ de 3 días** after 3 days; **llevar a ~** to carry out

cabra [ka'βra] nf goat

cabré etc vb V **caber**

cabrear [kaβre'ar] (*fam*) vt to bug; **cabrearse** vr (*enfadarse*) to fly off the handle

cabrito [ka'βrito] nm kid

cabrón [ka'βron] nm cuckold; (*fam!*) bastard (*!*)

caca ['kaka] (*fam*) nf pooh

cacahuete [kaka'wete] (*ESP*) nm peanut

C. abr (= centígrado) C; (compañía) Co.

C/ abr (= calle) St

cabal [ka'βal] adj (*exacto*) exact; (*correcto*) right, proper; (*acabado*) finished, complete; cabales nmpl: **no está en sus cabales** she isn't in her right mind

cábalas ['kaβalas] nfpl: **hacer ~** to guess

cabalgar [kaβal'ɣar] vt, vi to ride

cabalgata [kaβal'ɣata] nf procession

caballa [ka'βaλa] nf mackerel

caballería [kaβaλe'ria] nf mount; (*Mil*) cavalry

caballero [kaβa'λero] nm gentleman; (*de la orden de caballería*) knight; (*trato directo*) sir

caballete [kaβa'λete] nm (*Arte*) easel; (*Tec*) trestle

caballito [kaβa'λito] nm (*caballo pequeño*) small horse, pony; caballitos nmpl (*en verbena*) roundabout, merry-go-round

caballo [ka'βaλo] nm horse; (*Ajedrez*)

cacao [ka'kao] *nm* cocoa; (*Bot*) cacao

cacarear [kakare'ar] *vi* (*persona*) to boast; (*gallina*) to crow

cacería [ka0e'ria] *nf* hunt

cacarizo, -a [kaka'riθo, a] (*MÉX*) *adj* pockmarked

cacerola [kaθe'rola] *nf* pan, saucepan

cachalote [katʃa'lote] *nm* (*Zool*) sperm whale

cacharro [ka'tʃarro] *nm* earthenware pot; **cacharros** *nmpl* pots and pans

cachear [katʃe'ar] *vt* to search, frisk

cachemir [katʃe'mir] *nm* cashmere

cachetada [katʃe'taða] (*LAM: fam*) *nf* (*bofetada*) slap

cachete [ka'tʃete] *nm* (*Anat*) cheek; (*ESP: bofetada*) slap (in the face)

cachivache [katʃi'βatʃe] *nm* (*trasto*) piece of junk; **cachivaches** *nmpl* junk *sg*

cacho [ˈkatʃo] *nm* (*small*) bit; (*LAM: cuerno*) horn

cachondeo [katʃon'deo] (*ESP: fam*) *nm* farce, joke

cachondo, -a [ka'tʃondo, a] *adj* (*Zool*) on heat; (*fam: sexualmente*) randy; (*: gracioso*) funny

cachorro, -a [ka'tʃorro, a] *nm/f* (*perro*) pup, puppy; (*león*) cub

cachucha [ka'tʃuka] (*MÉX: fam*) *nf* cap

cacique [ka'θike] *nm* chief, local ruler; (*Pol*) local party boss

cactus [ˈkaktus] *nm inv* cactus

cada [ˈkaða] *adj inv* each; (*antes de número*) every; **~ día** each day, every day; **~ dos días** every other day; **~ uno/a** each one, every one; **~ vez más/menos** more and more/less and less; **~ vez que** whenever, every time (that) ...; **uno de ~ diez** one out of every ten

cadáver [ka'ðaβer] *nm* (*dead*) body, corpse

cadena [ka'ðena] *nf* chain; (*TV*) channel; **trabajo en ~** assembly line work; **cadena montañosa** mountain range; **cadena perpetua** (*Jur*) life

imprisonment

cadera [ka'ðera] *nf* hip

cadete [ka'ðete] *nm* cadet

caducar [kaðu'kar] *vi* to expire; **caduco, -a** *adj* expired; (*persona*) very old

caer [ka'er] *vi* to fall (down); **caerse** *vr* to fall (down); **me cae bien/mal** I get on well with him/I can't stand him; **~ en la cuenta** to realize; **dejar ~** to drop; **su cumpleaños cae en viernes** her birthday falls on a Friday

café [ka'fe] (*pl* **~s**) *nm* (*bebida, planta*) coffee; (*lugar*) café ▷ *adj* (*MÉX: color*) brown, tan; **café con leche** white coffee; **café negro** (*LAM*) black coffee; **café solo** (*ESP*) black coffee

cafetera [kafe'tera] *nf* coffee pot

cafetería [kafete'ria] *nf* (*gen*) café

cafetero, -a [kafe'tero, a] *adj* coffee *cpd*; **ser muy ~** to be a coffee addict

cafishio [ka'fiʃjo] (*cs*) *nm* pimp

cagar [ka'ɣar] (*fam!*) *vt* to bungle, mess up ▷ *vi* to have a shit (!)

caída [ka'iða] *nf* fall; (*declive*) slope; (*disminución*) fall, drop

caído, -a [ka'iðo, a] *adj* drooping

caiga *etc vb* V **caer**

caimán [kai'man] *nm* alligator

caja [ˈkaxa] *nf* box; (*para reloj*) case; (*de ascensor*) shaft; (*Com*) cashbox; (*donde se hacen los pagos*) cashdesk; (*: en supermercado*) checkout, till; **caja de ahorros** savings bank; **caja de cambios** gearbox; **caja de fusibles** fuse box; **caja fuerte** o **de caudales** safe, strongbox

cajero, -a [ka'xero, a] *nm/f* cashier; **cajero automático** cash dispenser

cajetilla [kaxe'tiʎa] *nf* (*de cigarrillos*) packet

cajón [ka'xon] *nm* big box; (*de mueble*) drawer

cajuela [ka'xwela] (*MÉX*) *nf* (*Auto*) boot (*BRIT*), trunk (*US*)

cal [kal] *nf* lime

cala [ˈkala] *nf* (*Geo*) cove, inlet; (*de barco*) hold

calabacín [kalaβa'θin] nm (Bot) baby marrow; (: más pequeño) courgette (BRIT), zucchini (US)

calabacita [kalaβa'θita] (MÉX) nf courgette (BRIT), zucchini (US)

calabaza [kala'βaθa] nf (Bot) pumpkin

calabozo [kala'βoθo] nm (cárcel) prison; (celda) cell

calada [ka'laða] (ESP) nf (de cigarrillo) puff

calado, -a [ka'laðo, a] adj (prenda) lace cpd ▷ nm (Náut) draught

calamar [kala'mar] nm squid no pl

calambre [ka'lambre] nm (Elec) shock

calar [ka'lar] vt to soak, drench; (penetrar) to pierce, penetrate; (comprender) to see through; (vela) to lower; **calarse** vr (Auto) to stall; **~se las gafas** to stick one's glasses on

calavera [kala'βera] nf skull

calcar [kal'kar] vt (reproducir) to trace; (imitar) to copy

calcetín [kalθe'tin] nm sock

calcio ['kalθjo] nm calcium

calcomanía [kalkoma'nia] nf transfer

calculador, a [kalkula'ðor, a] adj (persona) calculating; **calculadora** [kalkula'ðora] nf calculator

calcular [kalku'lar] vt (Mat) to calculate, compute; **~ que ...** to reckon that ...

caldera [kal'dera] nf boiler

calderilla [kalde'riʎa] nf (moneda) small change

caldo ['kaldo] nm stock; (consomé) consommé

calefacción [kalefak'θjon] nf heating; **calefacción central** central heating

calefón [kale'fon] (RPL) nm boiler

calendario [kalen'darjo] nm calendar

calentador [kalenta'ðor] nm heater

calentamiento [kalenta'mjento] nm (Deporte) warm-up

calentamiento global global warming

calentar [kalen'tar] vt to heat (up); **calentarse** vr to heat up, warm up; (fig: discusión etc) to get heated

calentón [kalen'ton] (RPL: fam) adj (sexualmente) horny, randy (BRIT)

calentura [kalen'tura] nf (Med) fever, (high) temperature

calesita [kale'sita] (RPL) nf merry-go-round, carousel

calibre [ka'liβre] nm (de cañón) calibre, bore; (diámetro) diameter; (fig) calibre

calidad [kali'ðað] nf quality; **de ~** quality cpd; **en ~ de** in the capacity of, as

cálido, -a [ka'liðo, a] adj hot; (fig) warm

caliente etc [ka'ljente] vb V **calentar** ▷ adj hot; (fig) fiery; (disputa) heated; (fam: cachondo) randy

calificación [kalifika'θjon] nf qualification; (de alumno) grade, mark

calificado, -a [kalifi'kaðo, a] (LAM) adj (competente) qualified; (obrero) skilled

calificar [kalifi'kar] vt to qualify; (alumno) to grade, mark; **~ de** to describe as

calima [ka'lima] nf (cerca del mar) mist

cáliz ['kaliθ] nm chalice

caliza [ka'liθa] nf limestone

callado, -a [ka'ʎaðo, a] adj quiet

callar [ka'ʎar] vt (asunto delicado) to keep quiet about, say nothing about; (persona, opinión) to silence ▷ vi to keep quiet, be silent; **callarse** vr to keep quiet, be silent; **¡cállate!** be quiet!, shut up!

calle ['kaʎe] nf street; (Deporte) lane; **~ arriba/abajo** up/down the street; **calle de sentido único** one-way street; **calle mayor** (ESP) high (BRIT) o main (US) street; **calle peatonal** pedestrianized o pedestrian street; **calle principal** (LAM) high (BRIT) o main

(US) street; **callejear** vi to wander (about) the streets; **callejero, -a** adj street; the streets; **callejero, -a** adj nm alley, passage; **callejón** nm alley, passage; **callejón** nm alley, passage; **callejón** cul-de-sac; **callejuela** nf side-street, alley

callista [ka'ʎista] nmf chiropodist

callo ['kaʎo] nm callus; (en el pie) corn; **callos** nmpl (Culin) tripe sg

calma ['kalma] nf calm

calmante [kal'mante] nm sedative, tranquillizer

calmar [kal'mar] vt to calm, calm down ▷ vi (tempestad) to abate; (mente etc) to become calm

calor [ka'lor] nm heat; (agradable) warmth; **hace ~** it's hot; **tener ~** to be hot

caloría [kalo'ria] nf calorie

calumnia [ka'lumnja] nf calumny, slander

caluroso, -a [kalu'roso, a] adj hot; (sin exceso) warm; (fig) enthusiastic

calva ['kalβa] nf bald patch; (en bosque) clearing

calvario [kal'βarjo] nm stations pl of the cross

calvicie [kal'βiθje] nf baldness

calvo, -a ['kalβo, a] adj bald; (terreno) bare, barren; (tejido) threadbare

calza ['kalθa] nf wedge, chock

calzada [kal'θaða] nf roadway, highway

calzado, -a [kal'θaðo, a] adj shod ▷ nm footwear

calzador [kalθa'ðor] nm shoehorn

calzar [kal'θar] vt (zapatos etc) to wear; (mueble) to put a wedge under; **calzarse** vr: **~se los zapatos** to put on one's shoes; **¿qué (número) calza?** what size do you take?

calzón [kal'θon] nm (ESP: pantalón corto) shorts; (LAM: ropa interior: de hombre) underpants, pants (BRIT), shorts (US); (: de mujer) panties, knickers (BRIT)

calzoncillos [kalθon'θiʎos] nmpl underpants

cama ['kama] nf bed; **hacer la ~** to make the bed; **cama individual/de matrimonio** single/double bed

camaleón [kamale'on] nm chameleon

cámara ['kamara] nf chamber; (habitación) room; (sala) hall; (Cine) cine camera; (fotográfica) camera; **cámara de aire** (ESP) inner tube; **cámara de comercio** chamber of commerce; **cámara de gas** gas chamber; **cámara digital** digital camera; **cámara frigorífica** cold-storage room

camarada [kama'raða] nmf comrade, companion

camarera [kama'rera] nf (en restaurante) waitress; (en casa, hotel) maid

camarero [kama'rero] nm waiter

camarógrafo, -a [kama'roɣrafo, a] nm/f cameraman/camerawoman

camarón [kama'ron] nm shrimp

camarote [kama'rote] nm cabin

cambiable [kam'bjaβle] adj (variable) changeable, variable; (intercambiable) interchangeable

cambiante [kam'bjante] adj variable

cambiar [kam'bjar] vt to change; (dinero) to exchange ▷ vi to change; **cambiarse** vr (mudarse) to move; (de ropa) to change; **~ de idea** u **opinión** to change one's mind; **~se de ropa** to change one's clothes

cambio ['kambjo] nm change; (trueque) exchange; (Com) rate of exchange; (oficina) bureau de change; (dinero menudo) small change; **a ~ de** in return o exchange for; **en ~** on the other hand; (en lugar de) instead; **cambio climático** climate change; **cambio de divisas** foreign exchange; **cambio de marchas** o **velocidades** gear lever

camelar [kame'lar] vt to sweet-talk

camello [ka'meʎo] nm camel; (fam: traficante) pusher

camerino [kame'rino] nm dressing

room

camilla [ka'miʎa] nf (Med) stretcher

caminar [kami'nar] vi (marchar) to walk, go ▷ vt (recorrer) to cover, travel

caminata [kami'nata] nf long walk; (por el campo) hike

camino [ka'mino] nm way, road; (sendero) track; **a medio ~** halfway (there); **en el ~** on the way, en route; **~ de** on the way to; **Camino de Santiago** Way of St James; **camino particular** private road

○ **CAMINO DE SANTIAGO**
○
○ The **Camino de Santiago** is a
○ medieval pilgrim route stretching
○ from the Pyrenees to Santiago de
○ Compostela in north-west Spain,
○ where tradition has it the body
○ of the Apostle James is buried.
○ Nowadays it is a popular tourist
○ route as well as a religious one.

camión [ka'mjon] nm lorry (BRIT), truck (US); (MÉX: autobús) bus; **camión cisterna** tanker; **camión de la basura** dustcart, refuse lorry; **camión de mudanzas** removal (BRIT) o moving (US) van; **camionero, -a** nm/f lorry o truck driver

camioneta [kamjo'neta] nf van, light truck

camisa [ka'misa] nf shirt; (Bot) skin; **camisa de fuerza** straitjacket

camiseta [kami'seta] nf (prenda) tee-shirt; (ropa interior) vest; (de deportista) top

camisón [kami'son] nm nightdress, nightgown

camorra [ka'morra] nf: **buscar ~** to look for trouble

camote [ka'mote] nm (MÉX, cs: batata) sweet potato, yam; (MÉX: bulbo) tuber, bulb; (cs: fam: enamoramiento) crush

campamento [kampa'mento] nm camp

campana [kam'pana] nf bell; **campanada** nf peal; **campanario** nm belfry

campanilla [kampa'niʎa] nf small bell

campaña [kam'paɲa] nf (Mil, Pol) campaign; **campaña electoral** election campaign

campechano, -a [kampe'tʃano, a] adj (franco) open

campeón, -ona [kampe'on, ona] nm/f champion; **campeonato** nm championship

cámper ['kamper] (LAM) nm o f caravan (BRIT), trailer (US)

campera [kam'pera] (RPL) nf anorak

campesino, -a [kampe'sino, a] adj country cpd, rural; (gente) peasant cpd ▷ nm/f countryman/woman; (agricultor) farmer

campestre [kam'pestre] adj country cpd, rural

camping ['kampin] (pl **~s**) nm camping; (lugar) campsite; **ir** o **estar de ~** to go camping

campo ['kampo] nm (fuera de la ciudad) country, countryside; (Agr, Elec) field; (de fútbol) pitch; (de golf) course; (Mil) camp; **campo de batalla** battlefield; **campo de concentración** concentration camp; **campo de deportes** sports ground, playing field; **campo visual** field of vision, visual field

camuflaje [kamu'flaxe] nm camouflage

cana ['kana] nf white o grey hair; **tener ~s** to be going grey

Canadá [kana'ða] nm Canada; **canadiense** adj, nmf Canadian ▷ nf fur-lined jacket

canal [ka'nal] nm canal; (Geo) channel, strait; (de televisión) channel; (de tejado) gutter; **canal de Panamá** Panama Canal

canaleta [kana'leta] (LAM) nf (de tejado) gutter

canalizar [kanali'θar] vt to channel

canalla [kaˈnaʎa] nf rabble, mob
▷ nm swine

canapé [kanaˈpe] (pl **-s**) nm sofa,
settee; (Culin) canapé

Canarias [kaˈnarjas] nfpl (tb: **las
Islas ~**) the Canary Islands, the
Canaries

canario, -a [kaˈnarjo, a] adj, nm/f
(native) of the Canary Isles ▷ nm (Zool)
canary

canasta [kaˈnasta] nf (round) basket

canasto [kaˈnasto] nm large basket

cancela [kanˈθela] nf gate

cancelación [kanθelaˈθjon] nf
cancellation

cancelar [kanθeˈlar] vt to cancel;
(una deuda) to write off

cáncer [ˈkanθer] nm (Med) cancer; **C~**
(Astrología) Cancer

cancha [ˈkantʃa] nf (de baloncesto)
court; (LAM: campo) pitch; **cancha de
tenis** (LAM) tennis court

canciller [kanθiˈʎer] nm chancellor

canción [kanˈθjon] nf song; **canción
de cuna** lullaby

candado [kanˈdaðo] nm padlock

candente [kanˈdente] adj red-hot;
(fig: tema) burning

candidato, -a [kandiˈðato, a] nm/f
candidate

cándido, -a [ˈkandiðo, a] adj simple;
naive

▌ No confundir **cándido** con la
palabra inglesa **candid**.

candil [kanˈdil] nm oil lamp;
candilejas nfpl (Teatro) footlights

canela [kaˈnela] nf cinnamon

canelones [kaneˈlones] nmpl
cannelloni

cangrejo [kanˈɡrexo] nm crab

canguro [kanˈɡuro] nm kangaroo;
hacer de ~ to babysit

caníbal [kaˈniβal] adj, nmf cannibal

canica [kaˈnika] nf marble

canijo, -a [kaˈnixo, a] adj frail, sickly

canilla [kaˈniʎa] (RPL) nf tap (BRIT),
faucet (US)

canjear [kanxeˈar] vt to exchange

canoa [kaˈnoa] nf canoe

canon [ˈkanon] nm canon; (pensión)
rent; (Com) tax

canonizar [kanoniˈθar] vt to
canonize

canoso, -a [kaˈnoso, a] adj grey-
haired

cansado, -a [kanˈsaðo, a] adj tired,
weary; (tedioso) tedious, boring

cansancio [kanˈsanθjo] nm
tiredness, fatigue

cansar [kanˈsar] vt (fatigar) to tire,
tire out; (aburrir) to bore; (fastidiar) to
bother; **cansarse** vr to tire, get tired;
(aburrirse) to get bored

cantábrico, -a [kanˈtaβriko, a] adj
Cantabrian

cantante [kanˈtante] adj singing
▷ nmf singer

cantar [kanˈtar] vt to sing ▷ vi to
sing; (insecto) to chirp ▷ nm (acción)
singing; (canción) song; (poema) poem

cántaro [ˈkantaro] nm pitcher, jug;
llover a ~s to rain cats and dogs

cante [ˈkante] nm (Mús) Andalusian
folk song; **cante jondo** flamenco
singing

cantera [kanˈtera] nf quarry

cantero [kanˈtero] (RPL) nm (arriate)
border

cantidad [kantiˈðað] nf quantity,
amount; **~ de** lots of

cantimplora [kantimˈplora] nf
(frasco) water bottle, canteen

cantina [kanˈtina] nf canteen; (de
estación) buffet; (LAM: bar) bar

cantinero, -a [kantiˈnero, a] (MÉX)
nm/f barman/barmaid, bartender (US)

canto [ˈkanto] nm singing; (canción)
song; (borde) edge, rim; (de cuchillo)
back; **canto rodado** boulder

cantor, a [kanˈtor, a] nm/f singer

canturrear [kanturreˈar] vi to
sing softly

canuto [kaˈnuto] nm (tubo) small
tube; (fam: droga) joint

caña [ˈkaɲa] nf (Bot: tallo) stem, stalk;
(carrizo) reed; (vaso) tumbler; (de cerveza)

glass of beer; (Anat) shinbone; **caña de azúcar** sugar cane; **caña de pescar** fishing rod

cañada [ka'naða] nf (entre dos montañas) gully, ravine; (camino) cattle track

cáñamo ['kaɲamo] nm hemp

cañería [kaɲe'ria] nf (tubo) pipe

caño ['kaɲo] nm (tubo) tube, pipe; (de albañal) sewer; (Mús) pipe; (de fuente) jet

cañón [ka'ɲon] nm (Mil) cannon; (de fusil) barrel; (Geo) canyon, gorge

caoba [ka'oβa] nf mahogany

caos ['kaos] nm chaos

capa ['kapa] nf cloak, cape; (Geo) layer, stratum; **capa de ozono** ozone layer

capacidad [kapaθi'ðað] nf (medida) capacity; (aptitud) capacity, ability

caparazón [kapara'θon] nm shell

capataz [kapa'taθ] nm foreman

capaz [ka'paθ] adj able, capable; (amplio) capacious, roomy

capellán [kape'ʎan] nm chaplain; (sacerdote) priest

capicúa [kapi'kua] adj inv (número, fecha) reversible

capilla [ka'piʎa] nf chapel

capital [kapi'tal] adj capital ▷ nm (Com) capital ▷ nf (de ciudad) capital; **capital social** share o authorized capital

capitalismo [kapita'lismo] nm capitalism; **capitalista** adj, nmf capitalist

capitán [kapi'tan] nm captain

capítulo [ka'pitulo] nm chapter

capó [ka'po] nm (Auto) bonnet

capón [ka'pon] nm (gallo) capon

capota [ka'pota] nf (de mujer) bonnet; (Auto) hood (BRIT), top (US)

capote [ka'pote] nm (abrigo: de militar) greatcoat; (de torero) cloak

capricho [ka'pritʃo] nm whim, caprice; **caprichoso, -a** adj capricious

Capricornio [kapri'kornjo] nm Capricorn

cápsula ['kapsula] nf capsule

captar [kap'tar] vt (comprender)

to understand; (Radio) to pick up; (atención, apoyo) to attract

captura [kap'tura] nf capture; (Jur) arrest; **capturar** vt to capture; to arrest

capucha [ka'putʃa] nf hood, cowl

capuchón [kapu'tʃon] (ESP) nm (de bolígrafo) cap

capullo [ka'puʎo] nm (Bot) bud; (Zool) cocoon; (fam) idiot

caqui ['kaki] nm khaki

cara ['kara] nf (Anat: de moneda) face; (de disco) side; (descaro) boldness; **~ a** facing; **de ~** opposite, facing; **dar la ~** to face the consequences; **¿~ o cruz?** heads or tails? **¡qué ~ (más dura)!** what a nerve!

Caracas [ka'rakas] n Caracas

caracol [kara'kol] nm (Zool) snail; (concha) (sea) shell

carácter [ka'rakter] (pl **caracteres**) nm character; **tener buen/mal ~** to be good natured/bad tempered

característica [karakte'ristika] nf characteristic

característico, -a [karakte'ristiko, a] adj characteristic

caracterizar [karakteri'θar] vt to characterize, typify

caradura [kara'ðura] nmf: **es un ~** he's got a nerve

carajillo [kara'xiʎo] nm coffee with a dash of brandy

carajo [ka'raxo] (fam!) nm: **¡~!** shit! (!)

caramba [ka'ramba] excl good gracious!

caramelo [kara'melo] nm (dulce) sweet; (azúcar fundida) caramel

caravana [kara'βana] nf caravan; (fig) group; (Auto) tailback

carbón [kar'βon] nm coal; **papel ~** carbon paper

carbono [kar'βono] nm carbon

carburador [karβura'ðor] nm carburettor

carburante [karβu'rante] nm (para motor) fuel

carcajada [karka'xaða] nf (loud)

laugh, guffaw

cárcel ['karθel] nf prison, jail; (Tec) clamp

carcoma [kar'koma] nf woodworm

cardar [kar'ðar] vt (pelo) to backcomb

cardenal [karðe'nal] nm (Rel) cardinal; (Med) bruise

cardíaco, -a [kar'ðiako, a] adj cardiac, heart cpd

cardinal [karði'nal] adj cardinal

cardo ['karðo] nm thistle

carecer [kare'θer] vi: **~ de** to lack, be in need of

carencia [ka'renθja] nf lack; (escasez) shortage; (Med) deficiency

careta [ka'reta] nf mask

carga ['karxa] nf (peso, Elec) load; (de barco) cargo, freight; (Mil) charge; (responsabilidad) duty, obligation

cargado, -a [kar'xaðo, a] adj loaded; (Elec) live; (café, té) strong; (cielo) overcast

cargamento [karxa'mento] nm (acción) loading; (mercancías) load, cargo

cargar [kar'xar] vt (barco, arma) to load; (Elec) to charge; (Com: algo en cuenta) to charge; (Inform) to load ▷ vi (Mil) to charge; (Auto) to load (up); **~ con** to pick up, carry away; (peso: fig) to shoulder, bear; **cargarse** vr (fam: estropear) to break; (: matar) to bump off

cargo ['karxo] nm (puesto) post, office; (responsabilidad) duty, obligation; (Jur) charge; **hacerse ~ de** to take charge of o responsibility for

carguero [kar'xero] nm freighter, cargo boat; (avión) freight plane

Caribe [ka'riβe] nm: **el ~** the Caribbean; **del ~** Caribbean; **caribeño, -a** [kari'βeɲo, a] adj Caribbean

caricatura [karika'tura] nf caricature

caricia [ka'riθja] nf caress

caridad [kari'ðað] nf charity

caries ['karjes] nf inv tooth decay

cariño [ka'riɲo] nm affection, love;

(caricia) caress; (en carta) love ...; **tener ~ a** to be fond of; **cariñoso, -a** adj affectionate

carisma [ka'risma] nm charisma

caritativo, -a [karita'tiβo, a] adj charitable

cariz [ka'riθ] nm: **tener o tomar buen/mal ~** to look good/bad

carmín [kar'min] nm lipstick

carnal [kar'nal] adj carnal; **primo ~** first cousin

carnaval [karna'βal] nm carnival

> ● **CARNAVAL**
>
> ● **Carnaval** is the traditional
> ● period of fun, feasting and
> ● partying which takes place in
> ● the three days before the start
> ● of Lent ("Cuaresma"). Although
> ● in decline during the Franco
> ● years the carnival has grown
> ● in popularity recently in Spain.
> ● Cádiz and Tenerife are particularly
> ● well-known for their flamboyant
> ● celebrations with fancy-dress
> ● parties, parades and firework
> ● displays being the order of the day.

carne ['karne] nf flesh; (Culin) meat; **se me pone la ~ de gallina sólo verlo** I get the creeps just seeing it; **carne de cerdo/cordero/ternera/vaca** pork/lamb/veal/beef; **carne de gallina** (fig) gooseflesh; **carne molida** (LAM) mince (BRIT), ground meat (US); **carne picada** (ESP, RPL) mince (BRIT), ground meat (US)

carné [kar'ne] (ESP) (pl **-s**) nm: **~ de conducir** driving licence (BRIT), driver's license (US); **~ de identidad** identity card; **~ de socio** membership card

carnero [kar'nero] nm sheep, ram; (carne) mutton

carnet [kar'ne] (ESP) (pl **-s**) nm = **carné**

carnicería [karniθe'ria] nf butcher's (shop); (fig: matanza) carnage, slaughter

carnicero, -a [karni'θero, a] *adj* carnivorous ▷ *nm/f* butcher; *(carnívoro)* carnivore

carnívoro, -a [kar'niβoro, a] *adj* carnivorous

caro, -a ['karo, a] *adj* dear; *(Com)* dear, expensive ▷ *adv* dear, dearly

carpa ['karpa] *nf (pez)* carp; *(de circo)* big top; *(LAM: tienda de campaña)* tent

carpeta [kar'peta] *nf* folder, file; **carpeta de anillas** ring binder

carpintería [karpinte'ria] *nf* carpentry, joinery; **carpintero** *nm* carpenter

carraspear [karraspe'ar] *vi* to clear one's throat

carraspera [karras'pera] *nf* hoarseness

carrera [ka'rrera] *nf (acción)* run(ning); *(espacio recorrido)* run; *(competición)* race; *(trayecto)* course; *(profesión)* career; *(licenciatura)* degree; **a la ~** at (full) speed; **carrera de obstáculos** *(Deporte)* steeplechase

carrete [ka'rrete] *nm* reel, spool; *(Tec)* coil

carretera [karre'tera] *nf* (main) road, highway; **carretera de circunvalación** ring road; **carretera nacional** ≈ A road *(BRIT)*, ≈ state highway *(US)*

carretilla [karre'tiʎa] *nf* trolley; *(Agr)* (wheel)barrow

carril [ka'rril] *nm* furrow; *(de autopista)* lane; *(Ferro)* rail; **carril-bici** cycle lane

carrito [ka'rrito] *nm* trolley

carro ['karro] *nm* cart, wagon; *(Mil)* tank; *(LAM: coche)* car; **carro patrulla** *(LAM)* patrol o panda *(BRIT)* car

carrocería [karroθe'ria] *nf* bodywork, coachwork

carroña [ka'rroɲa] *nf* carrion *no pl*

carroza [ka'rroθa] *nf (carruaje)* coach

carrusel [karru'sel] *nm* merry-go-round, roundabout

carta ['karta] *nf* letter; *(Culin)*

menu; *(naipe)* card; *(mapa)* map; *(Jur)* document; **carta certificada/urgente** registered/special-delivery letter

cartabón [karta'βon] *nm* set square

cartel [kar'tel] *nm (anuncio)* poster, placard; *(Escol)* wall chart; *(Com)* cartel; **cartelera** *nf* hoarding, billboard; *(en periódico etc)* entertainments guide; **"en cartelera"** "showing"

cartera [kar'tera] *nf (de bolsillo)* wallet; *(de colegial, cobrador)* satchel; *(de señora)* handbag; *(para documentos)* briefcase; *(Com)* portfolio; **ocupa la ~ de Agricultura** she is Minister of Agriculture

carterista [karte'rista] *nmf* pickpocket

cartero [kar'tero] *nm* postman

cartilla [kar'tiʎa] *nf* primer, first reading book; **cartilla de ahorros** savings book

cartón [kar'ton] *nm* cardboard; **cartón piedra** papier-mâché

cartucho [kar'tutʃo] *nm (Mil)* cartridge

cartulina [kartu'lina] *nf* card

casa ['kasa] *nf* house; *(hogar)* home; *(Com)* firm, company; **en ~** at home; **casa consistorial** town hall; **casa de campo** country house; **casa de huéspedes** boarding house; **casa de socorro** first aid post; **casa rodante** *(CS)* caravan *(BRIT)*, trailer *(US)*

casado, -a [ka'saðo, a] *adj* married ▷ *nm/f* married man/woman

casar [ka'sar] *vt* to marry; *(Jur)* to quash, annul; **casarse** *vr* to marry, get married

cascabel [kaska'βel] *nm* (small) bell

cascada [kas'kaða] *nf* waterfall

cascanueces [kaska'nweθes] *nm inv* nutcrackers *pl*

cascar [kas'kar] *vt* to crack, split, break (open); **cascarse** *vr* to crack, split, break (open)

cáscara ['kaskara] *nf (de huevo, fruta seca)* shell; *(de fruta)* skin; *(de limón)* peel

casco ['kasko] *nm (de bombero,*

soldado) helmet; (*Náut: de barco*) hull; (*Zool: de caballo*) hoof; (*botella*) empty bottle; (*de ciudad*): **el ~ antiguo** the old part; **el ~ urbano** the town centre; **los ~s azules** the UN peace-keeping force, the blue berets

cascote [kas'kote] *nm* rubble

caserío [kase'rio] (*ESP*) *nm* farmhouse; (*casa*) country mansion

casero, -a [ka'sero, a] *adj* (*pan etc*) home-made ⊳*nm* (*propietario*) landlord/lady; **ser muy ~** to be home-loving; **"comida casera"** "home cooking"

caseta [ka'seta] *nf* hut; (*para bañista*) cubicle; (*de feria*) stall

casete [ka'sete] *nm o f* = **cassette**

casi ['kasi] *adv* almost, nearly; **~ nada** hardly anything; **~ nunca** hardly ever, almost never; **~ te caes** you almost fell

casilla [ka'siʎa] *nf* (*casita*) hut, cabin; (*Ajedrez*) square; (*para cartas*) pigeonhole; **casilla de correo** (*CS*) P.O. Box; **casillero** *nm* (*para cartas*) pigeonholes *pl*

casino [ka'sino] *nm* club; (*de juego*) casino

caso ['kaso] *nm* case; **en ~ de** in case of; **en ~ de que ...** in case ...; **el ~ es que ...** the fact is that ...; **en ese/todo ~** in that/any case; **hacer ~ a** to pay attention to; **venir al ~** to be relevant

caspa ['kaspa] *nf* dandruff

cassette [ka'sete] *nm o f* = **casete**

castaña [kas'taɲa] *nf* chestnut

castaño, -a [kas'taɲo, a] *adj* chestnut-(coloured), brown ⊳*nm* chestnut tree

castañuelas [kasta'ɲwelas] *nfpl* castanets

castellano, -a [kaste'ʎano, a] *adj, nm/f* Castilian ⊳*nm* (*Ling*) Castilian, Spanish

castigar [kasti'ɣar] *vt* to punish; (*Deporte*) to penalize; **castigo** *nm* punishment; (*Deporte*) penalty

Castilla [kas'tiʎa] *nf* Castile

castillo [kas'tiʎo] *nm* castle

castizo, -a [kas'tiθo, a] *adj* (*Ling*) pure

casto, -a ['kasto, a] *adj* chaste, pure

castor [kas'tor] *nm* beaver

castrar [kas'trar] *vt* to castrate

casual [ka'swal] *adj* chance, accidental

⚠ No confundir **casual** con la palabra inglesa *casual*.

casualidad *nf* chance, accident; (*combinación de circunstancias*) coincidence; **da la casualidad de que ...** it (just) so happens that ...; **¡qué casualidad!** what a coincidence!

cataclismo [kata'klismo] *nm* cataclysm

catador, a [kata'ðor, a] *nm/f* wine taster

catalán, -ana [kata'lan, ana] *adj, nm/f* Catalan ⊳*nm* (*Ling*) Catalan

catalizador [kataliθa'ðor] *nm* catalyst; (*Auto*) catalytic convertor

catalogar [katalo'ɣar] *vt* to catalogue; **~ a algn (de)** (*fig*) to categorize sb (as)

catálogo [ka'taloɣo] *nm* catalogue

Cataluña [kata'luɲa] *nf* Catalonia

catar [ka'tar] *vt* to taste, sample

catarata [kata'rata] *nf* (*Geo*) waterfall; (*Med*) cataract

catarro [ka'tarro] *nm* catarrh; (*constipado*) cold

catástrofe [ka'tastrofe] *nf* catastrophe

catear [kate'ar] (*fam*) *vt* (*examen, alumno*) to fail

cátedra ['kateðra] *nf* (*Univ*) chair, professorship

catedral [kate'ðral] *nf* cathedral

catedrático, -a [kate'ðratiko, a] *nm/f* professor

categoría [kateɣo'ria] *nf* category; (*rango*) rank, standing; (*calidad*) quality; **de ~** (*hotel*) top-class

cateto, -a [ka'teto, a] (*ESP: pey*) *nm/f* peasant

catolicismo [katoli'θismo] *nm* Catholicism

católico, -a [ka'toliko, a] *adj, nm/f* Catholic

catorce [ka'torθe] *num* fourteen

cauce ['kauθe] *nm* (*de río*) riverbed; (*fig*) channel

caucho ['kautʃo] (ESP) *nm* rubber

caudal [kau'ðal] *nm* (*de río*) volume, flow; (*fortuna*) wealth; (*abundancia*) abundance

caudillo [kau'ðiλo] *nm* leader, chief

causa ['kausa] *nf* cause; (*razón*) reason; (*Jur*) lawsuit, case; **a ~ de** because of; **causar** [kau'sar] *vt* to cause

cautela [kau'tela] *nf* caution, cautiousness; **cauteloso, -a** *adj* cautious, wary

cautivar [kauti'βar] *vt* to capture; (*atraer*) to captivate

cautiverio [kauti'βerjo] *nm* captivity

cautividad [kautiβi'ðað] *nf* = **cautiverio**

cautivo, -a [kau'tiβo, a] *adj, nm/f* captive

cauto, -a ['kauto, a] *adj* cautious, careful

cava ['kaβa] *nm* champagne-type wine

cavar [ka'βar] *vt* to dig

caverna [ka'βerna] *nf* cave, cavern

cavidad [kaβi'ðað] *nf* cavity

cavilar [kaβi'lar] *vt* to ponder

cayendo *etc vb V* **caer**

caza ['kaθa] *nf* (*acción: gen*) hunting; (: *con fusil*) shooting; (*una caza*) hunt, chase; (*de animales*) game ▷ *nm* (*Aviac*) fighter; **ir de ~** to go hunting; **caza mayor** game hunting; **cazador, a** [kaθa'ðor, a] *nm/f* hunter; **cazadora** *nf* jacket; **cazar** [ka'θar] *vt* to hunt; (*perseguir*) to chase; (*prender*) to catch

cazo ['kaθo] *nm* saucepan

cazuela [ka'θwela] *nf* (*vasija*) pan; (*guisado*) casserole

CD *nm abr* (= compact disc) CD

CD-ROM [θeðe'rom] *nm abr* CD-ROM

CE *nf abr* (= Comunidad Europea) EC

cebada [θe'βaða] *nf* barley

cebar [θe'βar] *vt* (*animal*) to fatten (up); (*anzuelo*) to bait; (*Mil, Tec*) to prime

cebo ['θeβo] *nm* (*para animales*) feed, food; (*para peces, fig*) bait; (*de arma*) charge

cebolla [θe'βoλa] *nf* onion; **cebolleta** *nf* spring onion

cebra ['θeβra] *nf* zebra

cecear [θeθe'ar] *vi* to lisp

ceder [θe'ðer] *vt* to hand over, give up, part with ▷ *vi* (*renunciar*) to give in, yield; (*disminuir*) to diminish, decline; (*romperse*) to give way

cedro ['θeðro] *nm* cedar

cédula ['θeðula] *nf* certificate, document; **cédula de identidad** (LAM) identity card; **cédula electoral** (LAM) ballot

cegar [θe'ɣar] *vt* to blind; (*tubería etc*) to block up, stop up ▷ *vi* to go blind; **cegarse** *vr*: **~se (de)** to be blinded (by)

ceguera [θe'ɣera] *nf* blindness

ceja ['θexa] *nf* eyebrow

cejar [θe'xar] *vi* (*fig*) to back down

celada [θe'laða] *nf* ambush, trap

celador, a [θela'ðor, a] *nm/f* (*de edificio*) watchman; (*de museo etc*) attendant

celda ['θelda] *nf* cell

celebración [θeleβra'θjon] *nf* celebration

celebrar [θele'βrar] *vt* to celebrate; (*alabar*) to praise ▷ *vi* to be glad; **celebrarse** *vr* to occur, take place

célebre ['θeleβre] *adj* famous

celebridad [θeleβri'ðað] *nf* fame; (*persona*) celebrity

celeste [θe'leste] *adj* (*azul*) sky-blue

celestial [θeles'tjal] *adj* celestial, heavenly

celo¹ ['θelo] *nm* zeal; (*Rel*) fervour; (*Zool*): **en ~** on heat; **celos** *nmpl* jealousy *sg*; **dar ~s a algn** to make sb jealous; **tener ~s** to be jealous

celo²® ['θelo] *nm* Sellotape®

celofán [θelo'fan] *nm* cellophane

celoso, -a [θe'loso, a] *adj* jealous; (*trabajador*) zealous

celta ['θelta] *adj* Celtic ▷ *nmf* Celt

célula ['θelula] *nf* cell

celulitis [θelu'litis] *nf* cellulite

cementerio [θemen'terjo] *nm* cemetery, graveyard

cemento [θe'mento] *nm* cement; *(hormigón)* concrete; *(LAM: cola)* glue

cena ['θena] *nf* evening meal, dinner; **cenar** [θe'nar] *vt* to have for dinner ▷ *vi* to have dinner

cenicero [θeni'θero] *nm* ashtray

ceniza [θe'niθa] *nf* ash, ashes *pl*

censo ['θenso] *nm* census; **censo electoral** electoral roll

censura [θen'sura] *nf* (*Pol*) censorship; **censurar** [θensu'rar] *vt* (*idea*) to censure; (*cortar: película*) to censor

centella [θen'teʎa] *nf* spark

centenar [θente'nar] *nm* hundred

centenario, -a [θente'narjo, a] *adj* centenary; hundred-year-old ▷ *nm* centenary

centeno [θen'teno] *nm* (*Bot*) rye

centésimo, -a [θen'tesimo, a] *adj* hundredth

centígrado [θen'tiɣraðo] *adj* centigrade

centímetro [θen'timetro] *nm* centimetre (*BRIT*), centimeter (*US*)

céntimo [θen'timo] *nm* cent

centinela [θenti'nela] *nm* sentry, guard

centollo [θen'toʎo] *nm* spider crab

central [θen'tral] *adj* central ▷ *nf* head office; (*Tec*) plant; (*Tel*) exchange; **central eléctrica** power station; **central nuclear** nuclear power station; **central telefónica** telephone exchange

centralita [θentra'lita] *nf* switchboard

centralizar [θentrali'θar] *vt* to centralize

centrar [θen'trar] *vt* to centre

céntrico, -a ['θentriko, a] *adj* central

centrifugar [θentrifu'ɣar] *vt* to spin-dry

centro ['θentro] *nm* centre; **centro comercial** shopping centre; **centro de atención al cliente** call centre; **centro de salud** health centre; **centro escolar** school; **centro juvenil** youth club; **centro turístico** (*lugar muy visitado*) tourist centre; **centro urbano** urban area, city

centroamericano, -a [θentroameri'kano, a] *adj, nm/f* Central American

ceñido, -a [θe'niðo, a] *adj* (*chaqueta, pantalón*) tight(-fitting)

ceñir [θe'nir] *vt* (*rodear*) to encircle, surround; (*ajustar*) to fit (tightly)

ceño ['θeno] *nm* frown, scowl; **fruncir el ~** to frown, knit one's brow

cepillar [θepi'ʎar] *vt* to brush; (*madera*) to plane (down)

cepillo [θe'piʎo] *nm* brush; (*para madera*) plane; **cepillo de dientes** toothbrush

cera ['θera] *nf* wax

cerámica [θe'ramika] *nf* pottery; (*arte*) ceramics

cerca ['θerka] *nf* fence ▷ *adv* near, nearby, close; **~ de** near, close to

cercanías [θerka'nias] *nfpl* (*afueras*) outskirts, suburbs

cercano, -a [θer'kano, a] *adj* close, near

cercar [θer'kar] *vt* to fence in; (*rodear*) to surround

cerco ['θerko] *nm* (*Agr*) enclosure; (*LAM: valla*) fence; (*Mil*) siege

cerdo, -a ['θerðo, a] *nm/f* pig/sow

cereal [θere'al] *nm* cereal; **cereales** *nmpl* cereals, grain *sg*

cerebro [θe'reβro] *nm* brain; (*fig*) brains *pl*

ceremonia [θere'monja] *nf* ceremony; **ceremonioso, -a** *adj* ceremonious

cereza [θe'reθa] *nf* cherry

cerilla [θe'riʎa] *nf* (*fósforo*) match

cerillo [θe'riʎo] *nm* (*MÉX*) match

cero ['θero] *nm* nothing, zero

cerquillo [θer'kiʎo] *nm* (*CAM, RPL*) fringe

fringe (BRIT); bangs pl (US)

cerrado, -a [θeˈrraðo, a] adj closed, shut; (con llave) locked; (cielo) cloudy, overcast; (curva) sharp; (acento) thick, broad

cerradura [θerraˈðura] nf (acción) closing; (mecanismo) lock

cerrajero [θerraˈxero] nm locksmith

cerrar [θeˈrrar] vt to close, shut; (paso, carretera) to close; (grifo) to turn off; (cuenta, negocio) to close ▷ vi to close, shut; (noche) to come down; cerrarse vr to close, shut; ~ con llave to lock; ~ un trato to strike a bargain

cerro [ˈθerro] nm hill

cerrojo [θeˈrroxo] nm (herramienta) bolt; (de puerta) latch

certamen [θerˈtamen] nm competition, contest

certero, -a [θerˈtero, a] adj (gen) accurate

certeza [θerˈteθa] nf certainty

certidumbre [θertiˈðumbre] nf = certeza

certificado, -a [θertifiˈkaðo, a] adj (carta, paquete) registered; (aprobado) certified ▷ nm certificate; certificado médico medical certificate

certificar [θertifiˈkar] vt (asegurar, atestar) to certify

cervatillo [θerβaˈtiʎo] nm fawn

cervecería [θerβeθeˈria] nf (fábrica) brewery; (bar) public house, pub

cerveza [θerˈβeθa] nf beer

cesar [θeˈsar] vi to cease, stop ▷ vt (funcionario) to remove from office

cesárea [θeˈsarea] nf (Med) Caesarean operation o section

cese [ˈθese] nm (de trabajo) dismissal; (de pago) suspension

césped [ˈθespeð] nm grass, lawn

cesta [ˈθesta] nf basket

cesto [ˈθesto] nm (large) basket, hamper

cfr abr (= confróntese) cf.

chabacano, -a [tʃaβaˈkano, a] adj vulgar, coarse

chabola [tʃaˈβola] (ESP) nf shack;

barrio de chabolas shanty town

chacal [tʃaˈkal] nm jackal

chacha [ˈtʃatʃa] (fam) nf maid

cháchara [ˈtʃatʃara] nf chatter; estar de ~ to chatter away

chacra [ˈtʃakra] (CS) nf smallholding

chafa [ˈtʃafa] (MÉX: fam) adj useless, dud

chafar [tʃaˈfar] vt (aplastar) to crush; (plan etc) to ruin

chal [tʃal] nm shawl

chalado, -a [tʃaˈlaðo, a] (fam) adj crazy

chalé [tʃaˈle] (pl ~s) nm villa, = detached house

chaleco [tʃaˈleko] nm waistcoat, vest (US); chaleco de seguridad (Aut) reflective safety vest; chaleco salvavidas life jacket

chalet [tʃaˈle] (pl ~s) nm = chalé

chamaco, -a [tʃaˈmako, a] nm/f (niño) kid

chambear [tʃambeˈar] (MÉX: fam) vi to earn one's living

champán [tʃamˈpan] nm champagne

champiñón [tʃampiˈɲon] nm mushroom

champú [tʃamˈpu] (pl ~es, ~s) nm shampoo

chamuscar [tʃamusˈkar] vt to scorch, sear, singe

chance [ˈtʃanθe] (LAM) nm chance

chancho, -a [ˈtʃantʃo, a] (LAM) nm/f pig

chanchullo [tʃanˈtʃuʎo] (fam) nm fiddle

chandal [tʃanˈdal] nm tracksuit

chantaje [tʃanˈtaxe] nm blackmail

chapa [ˈtʃapa] nf (de metal) plate, sheet; (de madera) board, panel; (RPL Auto) number (BRIT) o license (US) plate; chapado, -a adj: chapado en oro gold-plated

chaparrón [tʃapaˈrron] nm downpour, cloudburst

chaperón [tʃapeˈron] (MÉX) nm: hacer de ~ to play gooseberry;

chaperona (LAM) nf: **hacer de chaperona** to play gooseberry

chapopote [tʃapo'pote] (MÉX) nm tar

chapulín [tʃapu'lin] (MÉX, CAM) nm grasshopper

chapurrear [tʃapurre'ar] vt (idioma) to speak badly

chapuza nf botched job

chapuzón [tʃapu'θon] nm: **darse un ~** to go for a dip

chaqueta [tʃa'keta] nf jacket

chaquetón [tʃake'ton] nm long jacket

charca ['tʃarka] nf pond, pool

charco ['tʃarko] nm pool, puddle

charcutería [tʃarkute'ria] nf (tienda) shop selling chiefly pork meat products; (productos) cooked pork meats pl

charla ['tʃarla] nf talk, chat; (conferencia) lecture; charlar (tʃar'lar) vi to talk, chat; charlatán, -ana [tʃarla'tan, ana] nm/f (hablador) chatterbox; (estafador) trickster

charol [tʃa'rol] nm varnish; (cuero) patent leather

charola [tʃa'rola] (MÉX) nf tray

charro ['tʃarro, a] (MÉX) nm typical Mexican

chasco ['tʃasko] nm (desengaño) disappointment

chasis ['tʃasis] nm inv chassis

chasquido [tʃas'kiðo] nm crack; click

chat [tʃat] nm (Internet) chat room

chatarra [tʃa'tarra] nf scrap (metal)

chatear [tʃate'ar] vi (Internet) to chat

chato, -a ['tʃato, a] adj flat; (nariz) snub

chaucha ['tʃautʃa] (RPL) nf runner (BRIT) o pole (US) bean

chaval, -a [tʃa'βal, a] (ESP) nm/f kid, lad/lass

chavo, -a ['tʃaβo] (MÉX: fam) nm/f guy/girl

checar [tʃe'kar] (MÉX) vt: **~ tarjeta** (al entrar) to clock in o on; (: al salir) to clock off o out

checo, -a ['tʃeko, a] adj, nm/f Czech

▷ nm (Ling) Czech

checoslovaco, -a [tʃekoslo'βako, a] adj, nm/f Czech, Czechoslovak

Checoslovaquia [tʃekoslo'βakja] nf (Hist) Czechoslovakia

cheque ['tʃeke] nm cheque (BRIT), check (US); **cobrar un ~** to cash a cheque; cheque al portador cheque payable to bearer; cheque de viaje traveller's cheque (BRIT), traveler's check (US); cheque en blanco blank cheque

chequeo [tʃe'keo] nm (Med) check-up; (Auto) service

chequera [tʃe'kera] (LAM) nf chequebook (BRIT), checkbook (US)

chévere ['tʃeβere] (LAM: fam) adj great

chícharo ['tʃitʃaro] (MÉX, CAM) nm pea

chichón [tʃi'tʃon] nm bump, lump

chicle ['tʃikle] nm chewing gum

chico, -a ['tʃiko, a] adj small, little ▷ nm/f (niño) child; (muchacho) boy/girl

chiflado, -a [tʃi'flaðo, a] adj crazy

chiflar [tʃi'flar] vt to hiss, boo

chilango, -a [tʃi'laŋgo, a] (MÉX) adj of o from Mexico City

Chile ['tʃile] nm Chile; chileno, -a adj, nm/f Chilean

chile ['tʃile] nm chilli pepper

chillar [tʃi'ʎar] vi (persona) to yell, scream; (animal salvaje) to howl; (cerdo) to squeal

chillido [tʃi'ʎiðo] nm (de persona) yell, scream; (de animal) howl

chimenea [tʃime'nea] nf chimney; (hogar) fireplace

China ['tʃina] nf (tb: **la ~**) China

chinche ['tʃintʃe] nf (insecto) (bed)bug; (Tec) drawing pin (BRIT), thumbtack (US) ▷ nmf nuisance, pest

chincheta [tʃin'tʃeta] nf drawing pin (BRIT), thumbtack (US)

chingada [tʃin'gaða] (MÉX: fam!) nf: **hijo de la ~** bastard

chino, -a ['tʃino, a] adj, nm/f Chinese ▷ nm (Ling) Chinese

chipirón [tʃipi'ron] nm (Zool, Culin)

squid

Chipre ['tʃipre] nf Cyprus; **chipriota**
adj, nmf Cypriot

chiquillo, -a [tʃi'kiʎo, a] nm/f
(fam) kid

chirimoya [tʃiri'moja] nf custard
apple

chiringuito [tʃirin'vito] nm small
open-air bar

chiripa [tʃi'ripa] nf fluke

chirriar [tʃi'rrjar] vi to creak, squeak

chirrido [tʃi'rriðo] nm creak(ing),
squeak(ing)

chisme ['tʃisme] nm (habladurías)
piece of gossip; (fam: objeto)
thingumajig

chismoso, -a [tʃis'moso, a] adj
gossiping ⊳ nm/f gossip

chispa ['tʃispa] nf spark; (fig) sparkle;
(ingenio) wit; (fam) drunkenness

chispear [tʃispe'ar] vi (lloviznar)
to drizzle

chiste ['tʃiste] nm joke, funny story

chistoso, -a [tʃis'toso, a] adj funny,
amusing

chivo, -a ['tʃiβo, a] nm/f (billy-
/nanny-)goat; **chivo expiatorio**
scapegoat

chocante [tʃo'kante] adj startling;
(extraño) odd; (ofensivo) shocking

chocar [tʃo'kar] vi (coches etc) to
collide, crash ⊳ vt to shock; (sorprender)
to startle; **~ con** to collide with; (fig)
to run into, run up against; **¡chócala!**
(fam) put it there!

chochear [tʃotʃe'ar] vi to be senile

chocho, -a ['tʃotʃo, a] adj doddering,
senile; (fig) soft, doting

choclo ['tʃoklo] (cs) nm (grano) sweet
corn; (mazorca) corn on the cob

chocolate [tʃoko'late] adj, nm
chocolate; **chocolatina** nf chocolate

chofer [tʃo'fer] nm = **chófer**

chófer ['tʃofer] nm driver

chollo ['tʃoʎo] (ESP: fam) nm bargain,
snip

choque etc ['tʃoke] vb V chocar ⊳ nm
(impacto) impact; (golpe) jolt; (Auto)

crash; (fig) conflict; **choque frontal**
head-on collision

chorizo [tʃo'riθo] nm hard pork
sausage, (type of) salami

chorrada [tʃo'rraða] (ESP: fam) nf: **¡es
una ~!** that's crap! (!); **decir ~s** to talk
crap (!)

chorrear [tʃorre'ar] vi to gush (out),
spout (out); (gotear) to drip, trickle

chorro ['tʃorro] nm jet; (fig) stream

choza ['tʃoθa] nf hut, shack

chubasco [tʃu'βasko] nm squall

chubasquero [tʃuβas'kero] nm
lightweight raincoat

chuchería [tʃutʃe'ria] nf trinket

chuleta [tʃu'leta] nf chop, cutlet

chulo ['tʃulo] nm (de prostituta) pimp

chupaleta [tʃupa'leta] (MÉX) nf
lollipop

chupar [tʃu'par] vt to suck; (absorber)
to absorb; **chuparse** vr to grow thin

chupete [tʃu'pete] (ESP, CS) nm
dummy (BRIT), pacifier (US)

chupetín [tʃupe'tin] (RPL) nm lollipop

chupito [tʃu'pito] (fam) nm shot

chupón [tʃu'pon] nm (piruleta)
lollipop; (LAM: chupete) dummy (BRIT),
pacifier (US)

churro ['tʃurro] nm (type of) fritter

chusma ['tʃusma] nf rabble, mob

chutar [tʃu'tar] vi to shoot (at goal)

Cía abr (= compañía) Co.

cianuro [θja'nuro] nm cyanide

cibercafé [θiβerka'fe] nm cybercafé

cibernauta [θiβer'nauta] nmf web
surfer, Internet user

ciberterrorista [θiβerterro'rista]
nmf cyberterrorist

cicatriz [θika'triθ] nf scar;
cicatrizarse vr to heal (up), form
a scar

ciclismo [θi'klismo] nm cycling

ciclista [θi'klista] adj cycle cpd ⊳ nmf
cyclist

ciclo ['θiklo] nm cycle; **cicloturismo**
nm touring by bicycle

ciclón [θi'klon] nm cyclone

ciego, -a ['θjevo, a] adj blind ⊳ nm/f

blind man/woman

cielo ['θjelo] nm sky; (Rel) heaven; **¡~s!**
good heavens!

ciempiés [θjem'pjes] nm inv
centipede

cien [θjen] num V **ciento**

ciencia [θjen'θja] nf science; **ciencias**
nfpl (Escol) science sg; ciencia-ficción
nf science fiction

científico, -a [θjen'tifiko, a] adj
scientific ▷ nm/f scientist

ciento ['θjento] num hundred;
pagar a 10 por ~ to pay at 10 per cent;
V tb **cien**

cierre etc ['θjerre] vb V **cerrar** ▷ nm
closing, shutting; (con llave) locking;
(LAM: cremallera) zip (fastener)

cierro etc vb V **cerrar**

cierto, -a ['θjerto, a] adj sure,
certain; (un tal) a certain; (correcto)
right, correct; **por ~** by the way;
~ hombre a certain man; **ciertas
personas** certain o some people; **sí, es
~** yes, that's correct

ciervo ['θjerβo] nm deer; (macho) stag

cifra ['θifra] nf number; (secreta)
code; cifrar [θi'frar] vt to code, write
in code

cigala [θi'ɣala] nf Norway lobster

cigarra [θi'ɣarra] nf cicada

cigarrillo [θiɣa'rriʎo] nm cigarette

cigarro [θi'ɣarro] nm cigarette;
(puro) cigar

cigüeña [θi'ɣweɲa] nf stork

cilíndrico, -a [θi'lindriko, a] adj
cylindrical

cilindro [θi'lindro] nm cylinder

cima ['θima] nf (de montaña) top,
peak; (de árbol) top; (fig) height

cimentar [θimen'tar] vt to lay the
foundations of; (fig: fundar) to found

cimiento [θi'mjento] nm foundation

cincel [θin'θel] nm chisel

cinco ['θinko] num five

cincuenta [θin'kwenta] num fifty

cine ['θine] nm cinema;
cinematográfico, -a
[θinemato'ɣrafiko, a] adj cine-,

film cpd

cínico, -a ['θiniko, a] adj cynical
▷ nm/f cynic

cinismo [θi'nismo] nm cynicism

cinta ['θinta] nf band, strip; (de tela)
ribbon; (película) reel; (de máquina de
escribir) ribbon; cinta adhesiva/
aislante sticky/insulating tape;
cinta de vídeo videotape; cinta
magnetofónica tape; cinta métrica
tape measure

cintura [θin'tura] nf waist

cinturón [θintu'ron] nm belt;
cinturón de seguridad safety belt

ciprés [θi'pres] nm cypress (tree)

circo ['θirko] nm circus

circuito [θir'kwito] nm circuit

circulación [θirkula'θjon] nf
circulation; (Auto) traffic

circular [θirku'lar] adj, nf circular
▷ vi, vt to circulate ▷ vi (conducir) to drive;
"circule por la derecha" "keep (to
the) right"

círculo ['θirkulo] nm circle; círculo
vicioso vicious circle

circunferencia [θirkunfe'renθja] nf
circumference

circunstancia [θirkuns'tanθja] nf
circumstance

cirio ['θirjo] nm (wax) candle

ciruela [θi'rwela] nf plum; ciruela
pasa prune

cirugía [θiru'xia] nf surgery; cirugía
estética o plástica plastic surgery

cirujano [θiru'xano] nm surgeon

cisne ['θisne] nm swan

cisterna [θis'terna] nf cistern, tank

cita ['θita] nf appointment, meeting;
(de novios) date; (referencia) quotation

citación [θita'θjon] nf (Jur) summons
sg

citar [θi'tar] vt (gen) to make an
appointment with; (Jur) to summons;
(un autor, texto) to quote; **citarse** vr: se
~on el cine they arranged to meet
at the cinema

cítricos ['θitrikos] nmpl citrus fruit(s)

ciudad [θju'ðað] nf town; (más

grande) city; **ciudadano, -a** *nm/f* citizen

cívico, -a ['θiβiko, a] *adj* civic

civil [θi'βil] *adj* civil ▷ *nm* (*guardia*) policeman; **civilización** [θiβiliθa'θjon] *nf* civilization; **civilizar** [θiβili'θar] *vt* to civilize

cizaña [θi'θaɲa] *nf* (*fig*) discord

cl. *abr* (= *centilitro*) cl.

clamor [kla'mor] *nm* clamour, protest

clandestino, -a [klandes'tino, a] *adj* clandestine; (*Pol*) underground

clara ['klara] *nf* (*de huevo*) egg white

claraboya [klara'βoja] *nf* skylight

clarear [klare'ar] *vi* (*el día*) to dawn; (*el cielo*) to clear up, brighten up; **clararse** *vr* to be transparent

claridad [klari'ðað] *nf* (*de día*) brightness; (*de estilo*) clarity

clarificar [klarifi'kar] *vt* to clarify

clarinete [klari'nete] *nm* clarinet

claro, -a ['klaro, a] *adj* clear; (*luminoso*) bright; (*color*) light; (*evidente*) clear, evident; (*poco espeso*) thin ▷ *nm* (*en bosque*) clearing ▷ *adv* clearly ▷ *excl*: **¡~ que sí!** of course!; **¡~ que no!** of course not!

clase ['klase] *nf* class; **dar ~(s)** to teach; **clase alta/media/obrera** upper/middle/working class; **clases particulares** private lessons *o* tuition *sg*

clásico, -a ['klasiko, a] *adj* classical

clasificación [klasifika'θjon] *nf* classification; (*Deporte*) league (table)

clasificar [klasifi'kar] *vt* to classify

claustro ['klaustro] *nm* cloister

cláusula ['klausula] *nf* clause

clausura [klau'sura] *nf* closing, closure

clavar [kla'βar] *vt* (*clavo*) to hammer in; (*cuchillo*) to stick, thrust

clave ['klaβe] *nf* key; (*Mús*) clef; **clave de acceso** password; **clave lada** (*MÉX*) dialling (*BRIT*) *o* area (*US*) code

clavel [kla'βel] *nm* carnation

clavícula [kla'βikula] *nf* collar bone

clavija [kla'βixa] *nf* peg, dowel, pin; (*Elec*) plug

clavo ['klaβo] *nm* (*de metal*) nail; (*Bot*) clove

claxon ['klakson] (*pl* **~s**) *nm* horn

clérigo ['kleriɣo] *nm* priest

clero ['klero] *nm* clergy

clicar [kli'kar] *vi* (*Internet*) to click; **~ en el icono** to click on an icon; **~ dos veces** to double-click

cliché [kli'tʃe] *nm* cliché; (*Foto*) negative

cliente, -a ['kljente, a] *nm/f* client, customer; **clientela** [kljen'tela] *nf* clientele, customers *pl*

clima ['klima] *nm* climate; **climatizado, -a** [klimati'θaðo, a] *adj* air-conditioned

clímax ['klimaks] *nm inv* climax

clínica ['klinika] *nf* clinic; (*particular*) private hospital

clip [klip] (*pl* **~s**) *nm* paper clip

clítoris ['klitoris] *nm inv* (*Anat*) clitoris

cloaca [klo'aka] *nf* sewer

clonar [klo'nar] *vt* to clone

cloro ['kloro] *nm* chlorine

clóset ['kloset] (*MÉX*) *nm* cupboard

club [klub] (*pl* **~s** *o* **-es**) *nm* club; **club nocturno** night club

cm *abr* (= *centímetro, centímetros*) cm

coágulo [ko'aɣulo] *nm* clot

coalición [koali'θjon] *nf* coalition

coartada [koar'taða] *nf* alibi

coartar [koar'tar] *vt* to limit, restrict

coba ['koβa] *nf*: **dar ~ a algn** (*adular*) to suck up to sb

cobarde [ko'βarðe] *adj* cowardly ▷ *nm* coward; **cobardía** *nf* cowardice

cobaya [ko'βaja] *nf* guinea pig

cobertizo [koβer'tiθo] *nm* shelter

cobertura [koβer'tura] *nf* cover; **aquí no hay ~** (*Tel*) I can't get a signal

cobija [ko'βixa] (*LAM*) *nf* blanket; **cobijar** [koβi'xar] *vt* (*cubrir*) to cover; (*proteger*) to shelter; **cobijo** *nm* shelter

cobra ['koβra] *nf* cobra

cobrador, a [koβra'ðor, a] *nm/f* (*de*

autobús) conductor/conductress; (*de impuestos*, *gas*) collector

cobrar [ko'βrar] *vt* to cash; (*cheque*) to cash; (*sueldo*) to collect, draw; (*objeto*) to recover; (*precio*) to charge; (*deuda*) to collect ▷ *vi* to be paid; **cóbrese al entregar** cash on delivery; **¿me cobra, por favor?** how much do I owe you?, can I have the bill, please?

cobre ['koβre] *nm* copper; **cobres** *nmpl* (*Mús*) brass instruments

cobro ['koβro] *nm* (*de cheque*) cashing; **presentar al ~** to cash

cocaína [koka'ina] *nf* cocaine

cocción [kok'θjon] *nf* (*Culin*) cooking; (*en agua*) boiling

cocer [ko'θer] *vt*, *vi* to cook; (*en agua*) to boil; (*en horno*) to bake

coche ['kotʃe] *nm* (*Auto*) car (*BRIT*), automobile (*US*); (*de tren*, *de caballos*) coach, carriage; (*para niños*) pram (*BRIT*), baby carriage (*US*); **ir en ~** to drive; **coche celular** police van; **coche de bomberos** fire engine; **coche de carreras** racing car; **coche fúnebre** hearse; **coche-cama** (*pl* **coches-cama**) *nm* (*Ferro*) sleeping car, sleeper

cochera [ko'tʃera] *nf* garage; (*de autobuses*, *trenes*) depot

coche restaurante (*pl* **coches restaurante**) *nm* (*Ferro*) dining car, diner

cochinillo [kotʃi'niʎo] *nm* (*Culin*) suckling pig, sucking pig

cochino, -a [ko'tʃino, a] *adj* filthy, dirty ▷ *nm/f* pig

cocido [ko'θiðo] *nm* stew

cocina [ko'θina] *nf* kitchen; (*aparato*) cooker, stove; (*acto*) cookery; **cocina eléctrica/de gas** electric/gas cooker; **cocina francesa** French cuisine; **cocinar** *vt*, *vi* to cook

cocinero, -a [koθi'nero, a] *nm/f* cook

coco ['koko] *nm* coconut

cocodrilo [koko'ðrilo] *nm* crocodile

cocotero [koko'tero] *nm* coconut palm

cóctel ['koktel] *nm* cocktail; **cóctel molotov** petrol bomb, Molotov cocktail

codazo [ko'ðaθo] *nm*: **dar un ~ a algn** to nudge sb

codicia [ko'ðiθja] *nf* greed; **codiciar** *vt* to covet

código ['koðiɣo] *nm* code; **código civil** common law; **código de barras** bar code; **código de circulación** highway code; **código de la zona** (*LAM*) dialling (*BRIT*) o area (*US*) code; **código postal** postcode

codillo [ko'ðiʎo] *nm* (*Zool*) knee; (*Tec*) elbow (*joint*)

codo ['koðo] *nm* (*Anat*, *de tubo*) elbow; (*Zool*) knee

codorniz [koðor'niθ] *nf* quail

coexistir [koe(k)sis'tir] *vi* to coexist

cofradía [kofra'ðia] *nf* brotherhood, fraternity

cofre ['kofre] *nm* (*de joyas*) case; (*de dinero*) chest

coger [ko'xer] (*ESP*) *vt* to take (hold of); (*objeto caído*) to pick up; (*frutas*) to pick, harvest; (*resfriado*, *ladrón*, *pelota*) to catch ▷ *vi*: **~ por el buen camino** to take the right road; **cogerse** *vr* (*el dedo*) to catch; **~se a algo** to get hold of sth

cogollo [ko'ɣoʎo] *nm* (*de lechuga*) heart

cogote [ko'ɣote] *nm* back o nape of the neck

cohabitar [koaβi'tar] *vi* to live together, cohabit

coherente [koe'rente] *adj* coherent

cohesión [koe'sjon] *nf* cohesion

cohete [ko'ete] *nm* rocket

cohibido, -a [koi'βiðo, a] *adj* (*Psico*) inhibited; (*tímido*) shy

coincidencia [koinθi'ðenθja] *nf* coincidence

coincidir [koinθi'ðir] *vi* (*en idea*) to coincide, agree; (*en lugar*) to coincide

coito ['koito] *nm* intercourse, coitus

coja *etc* *vb* V **coger**

cojear [koxe'ar] *vi* (*persona*) to limp,

hobble; (*mueble*) to wobble, rock

cojera [ko'xera] *nf* limp

cojín [ko'xin] *nm* cushion

cojo, -a etc ['koxo, a] *vb* V **coger**
▷ *adj* (*que no puede andar*) lame,
crippled; (*mueble*) wobbly ▷ *nm/f* lame
person, cripple

cojón [ko'xon] (*fam!*) *nm*: **¡cojones!**
shit! (!); **cojonudo, -a** (*fam*) *adj* great,
fantastic

col [kol] *nf* cabbage; **coles de
Bruselas** Brussels sprouts

cola ['kola] *nf* tail; (*de gente*) queue;
(*lugar*) end, last place; (*para pegar*) glue,
gum; **hacer ~** to queue (up)

colaborador, a [kolaβora'ðor, a]
nm/f collaborator

colaborar [kolaβo'rar] *vi* to
collaborate

colada [ko'laða] (*ESP*) *nf*: **hacer la ~** to
do the washing

colador [kola'ðor] *nm* (*para líquidos*)
strainer; (*para verduras etc*) colander

colapso [ko'lapso] *nm* collapse

colar [ko'lar] *vt* (*líquido*) to strain
off; (*metal*) to cast ▷ *vi* to ooze, seep
(through); **colarse** *vr* to jump the
queue; **~se en** to get into without
paying; (*fiesta*) to gatecrash

colcha ['koltʃa] *nf* bedspread

colchón [kol'tʃon] *nm* mattress;
colchón inflable air bed o mattress

colchoneta [koltʃo'neta] *nf* (*en
gimnasio*) mat; (*de playa*) air bed

colección [kolek'θjon] *nf*
collection; **coleccionar** *vt* to collect;
coleccionista *nmf* collector

colecta [ko'lekta] *nf* collection

colectivo, -a [kolek'tiβo, a] *adj*
collective, joint ▷ *nm* (*ARG: autobús*)
(small) bus

colega [ko'leɣa] *nmf* colleague;
(*ESP: amigo*) mate

colegial, a [kole'xjal, a] *nm/f*
schoolboy(-girl)

colegio [ko'lexjo] *nm* college;
(*escuela*) school; (*de abogados etc*)
association; **colegio electoral** polling

station; **colegio mayor** (*ESP*) hall of
residence

● **COLEGIO**
●
● A **colegio** is normally a private
● primary or secondary school.
● In the state system it means a
● primary school although these
● are also called **escuelas**. State
● secondary schools are called
● **institutos**.

cólera ['kolera] *nf* (*ira*) anger; (*Med*)
cholera

colesterol [koleste'rol] *nm*
cholesterol

coleta [ko'leta] *nf* pigtail

colgante [kol'ɣante] *adj* hanging
▷ *nm* (*joya*) pendant

colgar [kol'ɣar] *vt* to hang (up);
(*ropa*) to hang out ▷ *vi* to hang; (*Tel*)
to hang up

cólico ['koliko] *nm* colic

coliflor [koli'flor] *nf* cauliflower

colilla [ko'liʎa] *nf* cigarette end, butt

colina [ko'lina] *nf* hill

colisión [koli'sjon] *nf* collision;
colisión frontal head-on crash

collar [ko'ʎar] *nm* necklace; (*de
perro*) collar

colmar [kol'mar] *vt* to fill to the brim;
(*fig*) to fulfil, realize

colmena [kol'mena] *nf* beehive

colmillo [kol'miʎo] *nm* (*diente*) eye
tooth; (*de elefante*) tusk; (*de perro*) fang

colmo ['kolmo] *nm*: **¡es el ~!** it's
the limit!

colocación [koloka'θjon] *nf* (*acto*)
placing; (*empleo*) job, position

colocar [kolo'kar] *vt* to place, put,
position; (*dinero*) to invest; (*poner en
empleo*) to find a job for; **colocarse** *vr*
to get a job

Colombia [ko'lombja] *nf* Colombia;
colombiano, -a *adj, nm/f* Colombian

colonia [ko'lonja] *nf* colony; (*agua
de colonia*) cologne; (*MÉX: de casas*)

residential area; **colonia proletaria**
(MÉX) shantytown
colonización [koloniθa'θjon]
nf colonization; **colonizador, a**
[koloniθa'ðor, a] adj colonizing
▷ nm/f colonist, settler
colonizar [koloni'θar] vt to colonize
coloquio [ko'lokjo] nm conversation;
(congreso) conference
color [ko'lor] nm colour
colorado, -a [kolo'raðo, a] adj (rojo)
red; (MÉX: chiste) smutty, rude
colorante [kolo'rante] nm colouring
colorear [kolore'ar] vt to colour
colorete [kolo'rete] nm blusher
colorido [kolo'riðo] nm colouring
columna [ko'lumna] nf column;
(pilar) pillar; (apoyo) support; (tb: ~
vertebral) spine, spinal column; (fig)
backbone
columpiar [kolum'pjar] vt to swing;
columpiarse vr to swing; **columpio**
nm swing
coma ['koma] nf comma ▷ nm (Med)
coma
comadre [ko'maðre] nf (madrina)
godmother; (chismosa) gossip;
comadrona nf midwife
comal [ko'mal] nm (MÉX, CAM) nm
griddle
comandante [koman'dante] nm
commandant
comarca [ko'marka] nf region
comba ['komba] nf (ESP) nf (cuerda)
skipping rope; **saltar a la ~** to skip
combate [kom'bate] nm fight
combatir [komba'tir] vt to fight,
combat
combinación [kombina'θjon] nf
combination; (Quím) compound;
(prenda) slip
combinar [kombi'nar] vt to
combine
combustible [kombus'tiβle] nm fuel
comedia [ko'meðja] nf comedy;
(Teatro) play, drama; **comediante**
[kome'ðjante] nmf (comic) actor/
actress

comedido, -a [kome'ðiðo, a] adj
moderate
comedor, a [kome'ðor, a] nm
(habitación) dining room; (cantina)
canteen
comensal [komen'sal] nmf fellow
guest (o diner)
comentar [komen'tar] vt to
comment on; **comentario**
[komen'tarjo] nm comment,
remark; (literario) commentary;
comentarios nmpl (chismes) gossip sg;
comentarista [komenta'rista] nmf
commentator
comenzar [komen'θar] vt, vi to
begin, start; **~ a hacer algo** to begin o
start doing sth
comer [ko'mer] vt to eat; (Damas,
Ajedrez) to take, capture ▷ vi to eat;
(ESP, MÉX: almorzar) to have lunch;
comerse vr to eat up
comercial [komer'θjal] adj
commercial; (relativo al negocio)
business cpd; **comercializar**
vt (producto) to market; (pey) to
commercialize
comerciante [komer'θjante] nmf
trader, merchant
comerciar [komer'θjar] vi to trade,
do business
comercio [ko'merθjo] nm
commerce, trade; (tienda) shop, store;
(negocio) business; (fig) dealings pl;
comercio electrónico e-commerce;
comercio exterior/interior foreign/
domestic trade
comestible [komes'tiβle] adj
eatable, edible; **comestibles** nmpl
food sg, foodstuffs
cometa [ko'meta] nm comet ▷ nf
kite
cometer [kome'ter] vt to commit
cometido [kome'tiðo] nm task,
assignment
cómic [ko'mik] nm comic
comicios [ko'miθjos] nmpl elections
cómico, -a ['komiko, a] adj
comic(al) ▷ nm/f comedian

comida [ko'miða] nf (alimento) food; (almuerzo, cena) meal; (de mediodía) lunch; **comida basura** junk food; **comida chatarra** (MÉX) junk food

comidilla [komi'ðiʎa] nf: **ser la ~ del barrio** o **pueblo** to be the talk of the town

comienzo etc [ko'mjenθo] vb V **comenzar** ▷ nm beginning, start

comillas [ko'miʎas] nfpl quotation marks

comilona [komi'lona] (fam) nf blow-out

comino [ko'mino] nm: **(no) me importa un ~** I don't give a damn

comisaría [komisa'ria] nf (de policía) police station; (Mil) commissariat

comisario [komi'sarjo] nm (Mil etc) commissary; (Pol) commissar

comisión [komi'sjon] nf commission; **Comisiones Obreras** (ESP) Communist trade union

comité [komi'te] (pl **~s**) nm committee

comitiva [komi'tiβa] nf retinue

como ['komo] adv (tal ~) like; (aproximadamente) about, approximately ▷ conj (ya que, puesto que) as, since; **¡~ no!** of course!; **~ no lo haga hoy** unless he does it today; **~ si** as if; **es tan alto ~ ancho** it's as high as it is wide

cómo ['komo] adv how?, why? ▷ excl what?, I beg your pardon? ▷ nm: **el ~ y el porqué** the whys and wherefores

cómoda ['komoða] nf chest of drawers

comodidad [komoði'ðað] nf comfort

comodín [komo'ðin] nm joker

cómodo, -a ['komoðo, a] adj comfortable; (práctico, de fácil uso) convenient

compact [kom'pakt] (pl **~s**) nm (tb: **~ disc**) compact disk player

compacto, -a [kom'pakto, a] adj compact

compadecer [kompaðe'θer] vt to

pity, be sorry for; **compadecerse** vr: **~se de** to pity, o feel sorry for

compadre [kom'paðre] nm (padrino) godfather; (amigo) friend, pal

compañero, -a [kompa'ɲero, a] nm/f companion; (novio) boy/girlfriend; **compañero de clase** classmate

compañía [kompa'ɲia] nf company; **hacer ~ a algn** to keep sb company

comparación [kompara'θjon] nf comparison; **en ~ con** in comparison with

comparar [kompa'rar] vt to compare

comparecer [kompare'θer] vi to appear (in court)

comparsa [kom'parsa] nmf (Teatro) extra

compartimiento [komparti'mjento] nm (Ferro) compartment

compartir [kompar'tir] vt to share; (dinero, comida etc) to divide (up), share (out)

compás [kom'pas] nm (Mús) beat, rhythm; (Mat) compasses pl; (Náut etc) compass

compasión [kompa'sjon] nf compassion, pity

compasivo, -a [kompa'siβo, a] adj compassionate

compatible [kompa'tiβle] adj compatible

compatriota [kompa'trjota] nmf compatriot, fellow countryman/ woman

compenetrarse [kompene'trarse] vr to be in tune

compensación [kompensa'θjon] nf compensation

compensar [kompen'sar] vt to compensate

competencia [kompe'tenθja] nf (incumbencia) domain, field; (Jur, habilidad) competence; (rivalidad) competition

competente [kompe'tente] adj

competent

competición [kompeti'θjon] nf
competition

competir [kompe'tir] vi to compete

compinche [kom'pintʃe] (LAM) nmf
mate, buddy (US)

complacer [kompla'θer] vt to
please; **complacerse** vr to be pleased

complaciente [kompla'θjente] adj
kind, obliging, helpful

complejo, -a [kom'plexo, a] adj,
nm complex

complementario, -a
[komplemen'tarjo, a] adj
complementary

completar [komple'tar] vt to
complete

completo, -a [kom'pleto, a] adj
complete; (perfecto) perfect; (lleno)
▷ nm full complement

complicado, -a [kompli'kaðo,
a] adj complicated; **estar ~ en** to be
mixed up in

cómplice ['kompliθe] nmf
accomplice

complot [kom'plo(t)] (pl **~s**) nm plot

componer [kompo'ner] vt (Mús,
Literatura, Imprenta) to compose; (algo
roto) to mend, repair; (arreglar) to
arrange; **componerse** vr: **~se de** to
consist of

comportamiento
[komporta'mjento] nm behaviour,
conduct

comportarse [kompor'tarse] vr
to behave

composición [komposi'θjon] nf
composition

compositor, a [komposi'tor, a]
nm/f composer

compostura [kompos'tura] nf
(actitud) composure

compra ['kompra] nf purchase;
hacer la ~ to do the shopping; **ir de ~s**
to go shopping; **comprador, a** nm/f
buyer, purchaser; **comprar** [kom'prar]
vt to buy, purchase

comprender [kompren'der] vt to

understand; (incluir) to comprise,
include

comprensión [kompren'sjon] nf
understanding; **comprensivo, -a** adj
(actitud) understanding

compresa [kom'presa] nf (para
mujer) sanitary towel (BRIT) o napkin
(US)

comprimido, -a [kompri'miðo, a]
adj compressed ▷ nm (Med) pill, tablet

comprimir [kompri'mir] vt to
compress; (Internet) to zip

comprobante [kompro'βante] nm
proof; (Com) voucher; **comprobante de
compra** proof of purchase

comprobar [kompro'βar] vt to
check; (probar) to prove; (Tec) to
check, test

comprometer [komprome'ter]
vt to compromise; (poner en peligro)
to endanger; **comprometerse** vr
(involucrarse) to get involved

compromiso [kompro'miso] nm
(obligación) obligation; (cometido)
commitment; (convenio) agreement;
(apuro) awkward situation

compuesto, -a [kom'pwesto, a]
adj: **~ de** composed of, made up of ▷ nm
compound

computadora [komputa'ðora]
(LAM) nf computer; **computadora
central** mainframe (computer);
computadora personal personal
computer

cómputo ['komputo] nm calculation

comulgar [komul'var] vi to receive
communion

común [ko'mun] adj common
▷ nm: **el ~** the community

comunicación [komunika'θjon] nf
communication; (informe) report

comunicado [komuni'kaðo] nm
announcement; **comunicado de
prensa** press release

comunicar [komuni'kar] vt, vi to
communicate; **comunicarse** vr to
communicate; **está comunicando**
(Tel) the line's engaged (BRIT) o

busy (US); **comunicativo, -a** adj
communicative

comunidad [komuni'ðað] nf
community; **comunidad autónoma**
(ESP) autonomous region; **Comunidad
(Económica) Europea** European
(Economic) Community; **comunidad
de vecinos** residents' association

comunión [komu'njon] nf
communion

comunismo [komu'nismo] nm
communism; **comunista** adj, nmf
communist

○ **PALABRA CLAVE**

con [kon] prep **1** (medio, compañía)
with; **comer con cuchara** to eat with
a spoon; **pasear con algn** to go for a
walk with sb

2 (a pesar de) **con todo, merece
nuestros respetos** all the same, he
deserves our respect

3 (para con): **es muy bueno para con
los niños** he's very good with (the)
children

4 (+ infin): **con llegar a las seis estará
bien** if you come by six it will be fine
▷ conj: **con que: será suficiente con
que le escribas** it will be sufficient if
you write to her

concebir [konθe'βir] vt, vi to
conceive

conceder [konθe'ðer] vt to concede

concejal [konθe'xal, a] nm/f
town councillor

concentración [konθentra'θjon] nf
concentration

concentrar [konθen'trar] vt to
concentrate; **concentrarse** vr to
concentrate

concepto [kon'θepto] nm concept

concernir [konθer'nir] vi to concern;
en lo que concierne a ... as far as ...
is concerned; **en lo que a mí concierne**
as far as I'm concerned

concertar [konθer'tar] vt (Mús)

to harmonize; (acordar: precio) to
agree; (: tratado) to conclude; (trato)
to arrange, fix up; (combinar: esfuerzos)
to coordinate ▷ vi to harmonize,
be in tune

concesión [konθe'sjon] nf
concession

concesionario [konθesjo'narjo] nm
(licensed) dealer, agent

concha ['kontʃa] nf shell

conciencia [kon'θjenθja] nf
conscience; **tomar ~ de** to become
aware of; **tener la ~ tranquila** to have
a clear conscience

concienciar [konθjen'θjar] vt to
make aware; **concienciarse** vr to
become aware

concienzudo, -a [konθjen'θuðo, a]
adj conscientious

concierto etc [kon'θjerto] vb V
concertar ▷ nm concert; (obra)
concerto

conciliar [konθi'ljar] vt to reconcile;
~ el sueño to get to sleep

concilio [kon'θiljo] nm council

conciso, -a [kon'θiso, a] adj concise

concluir [konklu'ir] vt to
conclude; **concluirse** vr to conclude

conclusión [konklu'sjon] nf
conclusion

concordar [konkor'ðar] vt to
reconcile ▷ vi to agree, tally

concordia [kon'korðja] nf harmony

concretar [konkre'tar] vt to
make concrete, make more specific;
concretarse vr to become more
definite

concreto, -a [kon'kreto, a] adj,
nm (LAM: hormigón) concrete; **en ~** (en
resumen) to sum up; (específicamente)
specifically; **no hay nada en ~** there's
nothing definite

concurrido, -a [konku'rriðo, a] adj
(calle) busy; (local, reunión) crowded

concursante [konkur'sante] nmf
competitor

concurso [kon'kurso] nm (de público)
crowd; (Escol, Deporte, competencia)

competition; *(ayuda)* help, cooperation

condal [kon'dal] *adj*: **la Ciudad C~** Barcelona

conde ['konde] *nm* count

condecoración [kondekora'θjon] *nf (Mil)* medal

condena [kon'dena] *nf* sentence; **condenación** [kondena'θjon] *nf* condemnation; *(Rel)* damnation; **condenar** [konde'nar] *vt* to condemn; *(Jur)* to convict; **condenarse** *vr (Rel)* to be damned

condesa [kon'desa] *nf* countess

condición [kondi'θjon] *nf* condition; **a ~ de que ...** on condition that ...; **condicional** *adj* conditional

condimento [kondi'mento] *nm* seasoning

condominio [kondo'minjo] *(LAM) nm* condominium

condón [kon'don] *nm* condom

conducir [kondu'θir] *vt* to lead, direct, conduct; *(coche)* to drive, convey; *(Auto)* to drive ▷ *vi* to drive; *(fig)* to lead; **conducirse** *vr* to behave

conducta [kon'dukta] *nf* conduct, behaviour

conducto [kon'dukto] *nm* pipe, tube; *(fig)* channel

conductor, a [konduk'tor, a] *adj* leading, guiding ▷ *nm (Física)* conductor; *(de vehículo)* driver

conduje *etc vb* V **conducir**

conduzco *etc vb* V **conducir**

conectado, -a [konek'taðo, a] *adj (Inform)* on-line

conectar [konek'tar] *vt* to connect (up); *(enchufar)* plug in

conejillo [kone'xiʎo] *nm*: **~ de Indias** guinea pig

conejo [ko'nexo] *nm* rabbit

conexión [konek'sjon] *nf* connection

confección [konfek'θjon] *nf* preparation; *(industria)* clothing industry

confeccionar [konfekθjo'nar] *vt* to make (up)

conferencia [konfe'renθja] *nf* conference; *(lección)* lecture; *(ESP Tel)* call; **conferencia de prensa** press conference

conferir [konfe'rir] *vt* to award

confesar [konfe'sar] *vt* to confess, admit

confesión [konfe'sjon] *nf* confession

confesionario [konfesjo'narjo] *nm* confessional

confeti [kon'feti] *nm* confetti

confiado, -a [kon'fjaðo, a] *adj (crédulo)* trusting; *(seguro)* confident

confianza [kon'fjanθa] *nf* trust; *(seguridad)* confidence; *(familiaridad)* intimacy, familiarity

confiar [kon'fjar] *vt* to entrust ▷ *vi* to trust; **~ en algn** to trust sb; **~ en que ...** to hope that ...

confidencial [konfiðen'θjal] *adj* confidential

confidente [konfi'ðente] *nmf* confidant/e; *(policial)* informer

configurar [konfiɣu'rar] *vt* to shape, form

confín [kon'fin] *nm* limit; **confines** *nmpl* confines, limits

confirmar [konfir'mar] *vt* to confirm

confiscar [konfis'kar] *vt* to confiscate

confite [kon'fite] *nm* sweet (BRIT), candy (US); **confitería** [konfite'ria] *nf (tienda)* confectioner's (shop)

confitura [konfi'tura] *nf* jam

conflictivo, -a [konflik'tiβo, a] *adj (asunto, propuesta)* controversial; *(país, situación)* troubled

conflicto [kon'flikto] *nm* conflict; *(fig)* clash

confluir [kon'flwir] *vi (ríos)* to meet; *(gente)* to gather

conformar [konfor'mar] *vt* to shape, fashion ▷ *vi* to agree; **conformarse** *vr* to conform; *(resignarse)* to resign o.s.; **~se con algo** to be happy with sth

conforme [kon'forme] *adj*

(*correspondiente*): ~ **con** in line with; (*de acuerdo*): **estar ~s (con algo)** to be in agreement (with sth) ▷ *adv* as ▷ *excl* agreed! ▷ *prep*: ~ **a** in accordance with; **quedarse ~ (con algo)** to be satisfied (with sth)

confortable [konfor'taβle] *adj* comfortable

confortar [konfor'tar] *vt* to comfort

confrontar [konfron'tar] *vt* to confront; (*dos personas*) to bring face to face; (*cotejar*) to compare

confundir [konfun'dir] *vt* (*equivocar*) to mistake, confuse; (*turbar*) to confuse; **confundirse** *vr* (*turbarse*) to get confused; (*equivocarse*) to make a mistake; (*mezclarse*) to mix

confusión [konfu'sjon] *nf* confusion

confuso, -a [kon'fuso, a] *adj* confused

congelado, -a [konxe'laðo, a] *adj* frozen; **congelados** *nmpl* frozen food(s); **congelador** *nm* (*aparato*) freezer, deep freeze

congelar [konxe'lar] *vt* to freeze; **congelarse** *vr* (*sangre, grasa*) to congeal

congeniar [konxe'njar] *vi* to get on (BRIT) o along (US) well

congestión [konxes'tjon] *nf* congestion

congestionar [konxestjo'nar] *vt* to congest

congraciarse [kongra'θjarse] *vr* to ingratiate o.s.

congratular [kongratu'lar] *vt* to congratulate

congregar [kongre'ɣar] *vt* to gather together; **congregarse** *vr* to gather together

congresista [kongre'sista] *nmf* delegate, congressman/woman

congreso [kon'greso] *nm* congress

conjetura [konxe'tura] *nf* guess; **conjeturar** *vt* to guess

conjugar [konxu'ɣar] *vt* to combine, fit together; (*Ling*) to conjugate

conjunción [konxun'θjon] *nf* conjunction

conjunto, -a [kon'xunto, a] *adj* joint, united ▷ *nm* whole; (*Mús*) band; **en ~** as a whole

conmemoración [konmemora'θjon] *nf* commemoration

conmemorar [konmemo'rar] *vt* to commemorate

conmigo [kon'miɣo] *pron* with me

conmoción [konmo'θjon] *nf* shock; (*fig*) upheaval; **conmoción cerebral** (*Med*) concussion

conmovedor, a [konmoβe'ðor, a] *adj* touching, moving; (*emocionante*) exciting

conmover [konmo'βer] *vt* to shake, disturb; (*fig*) to move

conmutador [konmuta'ðor] *nm* switch; (LAM: *centralita*) switchboard; (: *central*) telephone exchange

cono ['kono] *nm* cone; **Cono Sur** Southern Cone

conocedor, a [konoθe'ðor, a] *adj* expert, knowledgeable ▷ *nm/f* expert

conocer [kono'θer] *vt* to know; (*por primera vez*) to meet, get to know; (*entender*) to know about; (*reconocer*) to recognize; **conocerse** *vr* (*una persona*) to know o.s.; (*dos personas*) to get to know each other; **~ a algn de vista** to know sb by sight

conocido, -a [kono'θiðo, a] *adj* (well-)known ▷ *nm/f* acquaintance

conocimiento [konoθi'mjento] *nm* knowledge; (*Med*) consciousness; **conocimientos** *nmpl* (*saber*) knowledge *sg*

conozco *etc vb* V **conocer**

conque ['konke] *conj* and so, so then

conquista [kon'kista] *nf* conquest; **conquistador, a** *adj* conquering ▷ *nm* conqueror; **conquistar** [konkis'tar] *vt* to conquer

consagrar [konsa'ɣrar] *vt* (*Rel*) to consecrate; (*fig*) to devote

consciente [kons'θjente] *adj* conscious

consecución [konseku'θjon] nf
acquisition; (de fin) attainment

consecuencia [konse'kwenθja] nf
consequence, outcome; (coherencia)
consistency

consecuente [konse'kwente] adj
consistent

consecutivo, -a [konseku'tiβo, a]
adj consecutive

conseguir [konse'ɣir] vt to get,
obtain; (objetivo) to attain

consejero, -a [konse'xero, a] nm/f
adviser, consultant; (Pol) councillor

consejo [kon'sexo] nm advice; (Pol)
council; consejo de administración
(Com) board of directors; consejo de
guerra court martial; consejo de
ministros cabinet meeting

consenso [kon'senso] nm consensus

consentimiento [konsenti'mjento]
nm consent

consentir [konsen'tir] vt (permitir,
tolerar) to consent to; (mimar) to
pamper, spoil; (aguantar) to put up with
▷ vi to agree, consent; ~ que algn
haga algo to allow sb to do sth

conserje [kon'serxe] nm caretaker;
(portero) porter

conservación [konserβa'θjon]
nf conservation; (de alimentos, vida)
preservation

conservador, a [konserβa'ðor,
a] adj (Pol) conservative ▷ nm/f
conservative

conservante [konser'βante] nm
preservative

conservar [konser'βar] vt to
conserve, keep; (alimentos, vida) to
preserve; **conservarse** vr to survive

conservas [kon'serβas] nfpl canned
food(s) pl

conservatorio [konserβa'torjo] nm
(Mús) conservatoire, conservatory

considerable [konsiðe'raβle] adj
considerable

consideración [konsiðera'θjon] nf
consideration; (estimación) respect

considerado, -a [konsiðe'raðo, a]

adj (atento) considerate; (respetado)
respected

considerar [konsiðe'rar] vt to
consider

consigna [kon'siɣna] nf (orden)
order, instruction; (para equipajes) left-
luggage office

consigo etc [kon'siɣo] vb V
conseguir ▷ pron (m) with him; (f)
with her; (Vd) with you; (reflexivo)
with o.s.

consiguiendo etc vb V **conseguir**

consiguiente [konsi'ɣjente] adj
consequent; **por ~** and so, therefore,
consequently

consistente [konsis'tente] adj
consistent; (sólido) solid, firm; (válido)
sound

consistir [konsis'tir] vi: ~ **en**
(componerse de) to consist of

consola [kon'sola] nf (mueble)
console table; (de videojuegos)
console

consolación [konsola'θjon] nf
consolation

consolar [konso'lar] vt to console

consolidar [konsoli'ðar] vt to
consolidate

consomé [konso'me] (pl ~**s**) nm
consommé, clear soup

consonante [konso'nante]
adj consonant, harmonious ▷ nf
consonant

consorcio [kon'sorθjo] nm
consortium

conspiración [konspira'θjon] nf
conspiracy

conspirar [konspi'rar] vi to conspire

constancia [kons'tanθja] nf
constancy; **dejar ~ de** to put on record

constante [kons'tante] adj, nf
constant

constar [kons'tar] vi (evidenciarse) to
be clear o evident; ~ **de** to consist of

constipado, -a [konsti'paðo, a]
adj: **estar ~** to have a cold ▷ nm cold
No confundir **constipado** con la
palabra inglesa constipated.

constitución [konstitu'θjon] *nf* constitution

constituir [konstitu'ir] *vt (formar, componer)* to constitute, make up; *(fundar, erigir, ordenar)* to constitute, establish

construcción [konstruk'θjon] *nf* construction, building

constructor, a [konstruk'tor, a] *nm/f* builder

construir [konstru'ir] *vt* to build, construct

construyendo *etc vb* V **construir**

consuelo [kon'swelo] *nm* consolation, solace

cónsul ['konsul] *nm* consul; **consulado** *nm* consulate

consulta [kon'sulta] *nf* consultation; *(Med)* **horas de ~** surgery hours; **consultar** [konsul'tar] *vt* to consult; **consultar algo con algn** to discuss sth with sb; **consultorio** [konsul'torjo] *nm (Med)* surgery

consumición [konsumi'θjon] *nf* consumption; *(bebida)* drink; *(comida)* food; **consumición mínima** cover charge

consumidor, a [konsumi'ðor, a] *nm/f* consumer

consumir [konsu'mir] *vt* to consume; **consumirse** *vr* to be consumed; *(persona)* to waste away

consumismo [konsu'mismo] *nm* consumerism

consumo [kon'sumo] *nm* consumption

contabilidad [kontaβili'ðað] *nf* accounting, book-keeping; *(profesión)* accountancy; **contable** *nmf* accountant

contacto [kon'takto] *nm* contact; *(Auto)* ignition; **estar/ponerse en ~ con algn** to be/to get in touch with sb

contado, -a [kon'taðo, a] *adj:* **~s** *(escasos)* numbered, scarce, few ▷ *nm:* **pagar al ~** to pay (in) cash

contador [konta'ðor] *nm*

(ESP: aparato) meter ▷ *nmf (LAM Com)* accountant

contagiar [konta'xjar] *vt (enfermedad)* to pass on, transmit; *(persona)* to infect; **contagiarse** *vr* to become infected

contagio [kon'taxjo] *nm* infection; **contagioso, -a** *adj* infectious; *(fig)* catching

contaminación [kontamina'θjon] *nf* contamination; *(polución)* pollution

contaminar [kontami'nar] *vt* to contaminate; *(aire, agua)* to pollute

contante [kon'tante] *adj:* **dinero ~ (y sonante)** cash

contar [kon'tar] *vt (páginas, dinero)* to count; *(anécdota, chiste etc)* to tell ▷ *vi* to count; **~ con** to rely on, count on

contemplar [kontem'plar] *vt* to contemplate; *(mirar)* to look at

contemporáneo, -a [kontempo'raneo, a] *adj, nm/f* contemporary

contenedor [kontene'ðor] *nm* container

contener [konte'ner] *vt* to contain, hold; *(retener)* to hold back, contain; **contenerse** *vr* to control o restrain o.s.

contenido, -a [konte'niðo, a] *adj (moderado)* restrained; *(risa etc)* suppressed ▷ *nm* contents *pl*, content

contentar [konten'tar] *vt (satisfacer)* to satisfy; *(complacer)* to please; **contentarse** *vr* to be satisfied

contento, -a [kon'tento, a] *adj (alegre)* pleased; *(feliz)* happy

contestación [kontesta'θjon] *nf* answer, reply

contestador [kontesta'ðor] *nm (tb:* **~ automático)** answering machine

contestar [kontes'tar] *vt* to answer, reply; *(Jur)* to corroborate, confirm
⎮ No confundir **contestar** con la palabra inglesa *contest.*

contexto [kon'te(k)sto] *nm* context

contigo [kon'tiɣo] *pron* with you

contiguo, -a [kon'tiɣwo, a] *adj* adjacent, adjoining

continente [konti'nente] *adj, nm* continent

continuación [kontinwa'θjon] *nf* continuation; **a ~** then, next

continuar [konti'nwar] *vt* to continue, go on with ▷ *vi* to continue, go on; **~ hablando** to continue talking *o* to talk

continuidad [kontinwi'ðað] *nf* continuity

continuo, -a [kon'tinwo, a] *adj* (*sin interrupción*) continuous; (*acción perseverante*) continual

contorno [kon'torno] *nm* outline; (*Geo*) contour; **contornos** *nmpl* neighbourhood *sg*, surrounding area *sg*

contra ['kontra] *prep, adv* against ▷ *nm inv* con ▷ *nf*: **la C~** (*de Nicaragua*) the Contras *pl*

contraataque [kontraa'take] *nm* counter-attack

contrabajo [kontra'βaxo] *nm* double bass

contrabandista [kontraβan'dista] *nmf* smuggler

contrabando [kontra'βando] *nm* (*acción*) smuggling; (*mercancías*) contraband

contracción [kontrak'θjon] *nf* contraction

contracorriente [kontrako'rrjente] *nf* cross-current

contradecir [kontraðe'θir] *vt* to contradict

contradicción [kontraðik'θjon] *nf* contradiction

contradictorio, -a [kontraðik'torjo, a] *adj* contradictory

contraer [kontra'er] *vt* to contract; (*limitar*) to restrict; **contraerse** *vr* to contract; (*limitarse*) to limit o.s.

contraluz [kontra'luθ] *nm* view against the light

contrapartida [kontrapar'tiða] *nf*: **como ~ (de)** in return (for)

contrapelo [kontra'pelo]: **a ~** *adv* the wrong way

contrapeso [kontra'peso] *nm* counterweight

contraportada [kontrapor'taða] *nf* (*de revista*) back cover

contraproducente [kontraproðu'θente] *adj* counterproductive

contrario, -a [kon'trarjo, a] *adj* contrary; (*persona*) opposed; (*sentido, lado*) opposite ▷ *nm/f* enemy, adversary; (*Deporte*) opponent; **al** *o* **por el ~** on the contrary; **de lo ~** otherwise

contrarreloj [kontrarre'lo] *nf* (*tb*: **prueba ~**) time trial

contrarrestar [kontrarres'tar] *vt* to counteract

contrasentido [kontrasen'tiðo] *nm* (*contradicción*) contradiction

contraseña [kontra'seɲa] *nf* (*Inform*) password

contrastar [kontras'tar] *vt, vi* to contrast

contraste [kon'traste] *nm* contrast

contratar [kontra'tar] *vt: firmar un acuerdo para*, to contract for; (*empleados, obreros*) to take on, engage

contratiempo [kontra'tjempo] *nm* setback

contratista [kontra'tista] *nmf* contractor

contrato [kon'trato] *nm* contract

contraventana [kontraβen'tana] *nf* shutter

contribución [kontriβu'θjon] *nf* (*municipal etc*) tax; (*ayuda*) contribution

contribuir [kontriβu'ir] *vt, vi* to contribute; (*Com*) to pay (in taxes)

contribuyente [kontriβu'jente] *nmf* (*Com*) taxpayer; (*que ayuda*) contributor

contrincante [kontrin'kante] *nmf* opponent

control [kon'trol] *nm* control; (*inspección*) inspection, check; **control de pasaportes** passport inspection; **controlador, a** *nm/f* controller; **controlador aéreo** air-traffic controller; **controlar** [kontro'lar] *vt* to control; (*inspeccionar*) to inspect, check

contundente [kontun'dente] *adj* (*instrumento*) blunt; (*argumento, derrota*) overwhelming

contusión [kontu'sjon] *nf* bruise

convalecencia [kombale'θenθja] *nf* convalescence

convalecer [kombale'θer] *vi* to convalesce, get better

convalidar [kombali'ðar] *vt* (*título*) to recognize

convencer [komben'θer] *vt* to convince; **~ a algn (de o para hacer algo)** to persuade sb (to do o sth)

convención [komben'θjon] *nf* convention

conveniente [komben'njente] *adj* suitable; (*útil*) useful

convenio [kom'benjo] *nm* agreement, treaty

convenir [kombe'nir] *vi* (*estar de acuerdo*) to agree; (*venir bien*) to suit, be suitable

   No confundir **convenir** con la palabra inglesa **convene**.

convento [kom'bento] *nm* convent

convenza *etc vb V* **convencer**

convergir [komber'xir] *vi* = **converger**

conversación [kombersa'θjon] *nf* conversation

conversar [komber'sar] *vi* to talk, converse

conversión [komber'sjon] *nf* conversion

convertir [komber'tir] *vt* to convert

convidar [kombi'ðar] *vt* to invite; **~ a algn a una cerveza** to buy sb a beer

convincente [kombin'θente] *adj* convincing

convite [kom'bite] *nm* invitation; (*banquete*) banquet

convivencia [kombi'βenθja] *nf* coexistence, living together

convivir [kombi'βir] *vi* to live together

convocar [kombo'kar] *vt* to summon, call (together)

convocatoria [komboka'torja] *nf* (*de oposiciones, elecciones*) notice; (*de huelga*) call

cónyuge ['konjuxe] *nmf* spouse

coñac [ko'na(k)] (*pl* **-s**) *nm* cognac, brandy

coño ['kopo] (*fam!*) *excl* (*enfado*) shit! (*!*); (*sorpresa*) bloody hell! (*!*)

cool [kul] *adj* (*fam*) cool

cooperación [koopera'θjon] *nf* cooperation

cooperar [koòpe'rar] *vi* to cooperate

cooperativa [koopera'tiβa] *nf* cooperative

coordinadora [koorðina'ðora] *nf* (*comité*) coordinating committee

coordinar [koorði'nar] *vt* to coordinate

copa ['kopa] *nf* cup; (*vaso*) glass; (*bebida*): **tomar una ~** (to have a) drink; (*de árbol*) top; (*de sombrero*) crown; **copas** *nfpl* (*Naipes*) ≈ hearts

copia ['kopja] *nf* copy; **copia de respaldo** *o* **seguridad** (*Inform*) back-up copy; **copiar** *vt* to copy

copla ['kopla] *nf* verse; (*canción*) (popular) song

copo ['kopo] *nm*: **~ de nieve** snowflake; **~s de maíz** cornflakes

coqueta [ko'keta] *adj* flirtatious, coquettish; **coquetear** *vi* to flirt

coraje [ko'raxe] *nm* courage; (*ira*) anger

coral [ko'ral] *adj* choral ▷ *nf* (*Mús*) choir ▷ *nm* (*Zool*) coral

coraza [ko'raθa] *nf* (*armadura*) armour; (*blindaje*) armour-plating

corazón [kora'θon] *nm* heart

corazonada [koraθo'naða] *nf* impulse; (*presentimiento*) hunch

corbata [kor'βata] *nf* tie

corchete [kor'tʃete] *nm* catch, clasp

corcho ['kortʃo] *nm* cork; (*Pesca*) float

cordel [kor'ðel] *nm* cord, line

cordero [kor'ðero] *nm* lamb

cordial [kor'ðjal] *adj* cordial

cordillera [korði'ʎera] nf range (of mountains)

Córdoba ['korðoβa] n Cordova

cordón [kor'ðon] nm (cuerda) cord, string; (de zapatos) lace; (Mil etc) cordon; **cordón umbilical** umbilical cord

cordura [kor'ðura] nf: **con ~** (obrar, hablar) sensibly

corneta [kor'neta] nf bugle

cornisa [kor'nisa] nf (Arq) cornice

coro ['koro] nm chorus; (conjunto de cantores) choir

corona [ko'rona] nf crown; (de flores) garland

coronel [koro'nel] nm colonel

coronilla [koro'niʎa] nf (Anat) crown (of the head)

corporal [korpo'ral] adj corporal, bodily

corpulento, -a [korpu'lento, a] adj (persona) heavily-built

corral [ko'rral] nm farmyard

correa [ko'rrea] nf strap; (cinturón) belt; (de perro) lead, leash; **correa del ventilador** (Auto) fan belt

corrección [korrek'θjon] nf correction; (reprensión) rebuke; **correccional** nm reformatory

correcto, -a [ko'rrekto, a] adj correct; (persona) well-mannered

corredizo, -a [korre'ðiθo, a] adj (puerta etc) sliding

corredor, a [korre'ðor, a] nm (pasillo) corridor; (balcón corrido) gallery; (Com) agent, broker ▷ nm/f (Deporte) runner

corregir [korre'xir] vt (error) to correct; **corregirse** vr to reform

correo [ko'rreo] nm post, mail; (persona) courier; **Correos** nmpl (ESP) Post Office sg; **correo aéreo** airmail; **correo basura** (Inform) spam; **correo electrónico** e-mail, electronic mail; **correo web** webmail

correr [ko'rrer] vt to run; (cortinas) to draw; (cerrojo) to shoot ▷ vi to run; (líquido) to run, flow; **correrse** vr to slide, move; (colores) to run

correspondencia [korrespon'denθja] nf correspondence; (Ferro) connection

corresponder [korrespon'der] vi to correspond; (convenir) to be suitable; (pertenecer) to belong; (concernir) to concern; **corresponderse** vr (por escrito) to correspond; (amarse) to love one another

correspondiente [korrespon'djente] adj corresponding

corresponsal [korrespon'sal] nmf correspondent

corrida [ko'rriða] nf (de toros) bullfight

corrido, -a [ko'rriðo, a] adj (avergonzado) abashed; **un kilo ~ a** good kilo

corriente [ko'rrjente] adj (agua) running; (dinero etc) current; (común) ordinary, normal ▷ nf current ▷ nm current month; **estar al ~ de** to be informed about; **corriente eléctrica** electric current

corrija etc vb V **corregir**

corro ['korro] nm ring, circle (of people)

corromper [korrom'per] vt (madera) to rot; (fig) to corrupt

corrosivo, -a [korro'siβo, a] adj corrosive

corrupción [korrup'θjon] nf rot, decay; (fig) corruption

corsé [kor'se] nm corset

cortacésped [korta'θespeð] nm lawn mower

cortado, -a [kor'taðo, a] adj (gen) cut; (leche) sour; (tímido) shy; (avergonzado) embarrassed ▷ nm coffee (with a little milk)

cortafuegos [korta'fweɣos] nm inv (en el bosque) firebreak, fire lane (US); (Internet) firewall

cortar [kor'tar] vt to cut; (suministro) to cut off; (un pasaje) to cut out ▷ vi to cut; **cortarse** vr (avergonzarse) to become embarrassed; (leche) to turn, curdle; **~se el pelo** to have one's hair cut

cortauñas [korta'uɲas] nm inv nail clippers pl

corte ['korte] nm cut, cutting; (de tela) piece, length ▷ nf: **las C~s** the Spanish Parliament; **corte de luz** power cut; **corte y confección** dressmaking

cortejo [kor'texo] nm entourage; **cortejo fúnebre** funeral procession

cortés [kor'tes] adj courteous, polite

cortesía [korte'sia] nf courtesy

corteza [kor'teθa] nf (de árbol) bark; (de pan) crust

cortijo [kor'tixo] (ESP) nm farm, farmhouse

cortina [kor'tina] nf curtain

corto, -a ['korto, a] adj (breve) short; (tímido) bashful; **~ de luces** not very bright; **~ de vista** short-sighted; **estar ~ de fondos** to be short of funds; **cortocircuito** nm short circuit; **cortometraje** nm (Cine) short

cosa ['kosa] nf thing; **~ de** about; **eso es ~ mía** that's my business

coscorrón [kosko'rron] nm bump on the head

cosecha [ko'setʃa] nf (Agr) harvest; (de vino) vintage; **cosechar** [kose'tʃar] vt to harvest, gather (in)

coser [ko'ser] vt to sew

cosmético, -a [kos'metiko, a] adj, nm cosmetic

cosquillas [kos'kiʎas] nfpl: **hacer ~** to tickle; **tener ~** to be ticklish

costa ['kosta] nf (Geo) coast; **a toda ~** at all costs; **Costa Brava** Costa Brava; **Costa Cantábrica** Cantabrian Coast; **Costa del Sol** Costa del Sol

costado [kos'taðo] nm side

costanera [kosta'nera] (cs) nf promenade, sea front

costar [kos'tar] vt (valer) to cost; **me cuesta hablarle** I find it hard to talk to him

Costa Rica [kosta'rika] nf Costa Rica; **costarricense** adj, nmf Costa Rican; **costarriqueño, -a** adj, nm/f Costa Rican

coste ['koste] nm = **costo**

costear [koste'ar] vt to pay for

costero, -a [kos'tero, a] adj (pueblecito, camino) coastal

costilla [kos'tiʎa] nf rib; (Culin) cutlet

costo ['kosto] nm cost, price; **costo de (la) vida** cost of living; **costoso, -a** adj costly, expensive

costra ['kostra] nf (corteza) crust; (Med) scab

costumbre [kos'tumbre] nf custom, habit

costura [kos'tura] nf sewing, needlework; (zurcido) seam

costurera [kostu'rera] nf dressmaker

costurero [kostu'rero] nm sewing box o case

cotidiano, -a [koti'ðjano, a] adj daily, day to day

cotilla [ko'tiʎa] (ESP: fam) nmf gossip; **cotillear** (ESP) vi to gossip; **cotilleo** (ESP) nm gossip(ing)

cotizar [koti'θar] vt (Com) to quote, price; **cotizarse** vr: **~se a** to sell at, fetch; (Bolsa) to stand at, be quoted at

coto ['koto] nm (terreno cercado) enclosure; (de caza) reserve

cotorra [ko'torra] nf parrot

coyote [ko'jote] nm coyote, prairie wolf

coz [koθ] nf kick

crack [krak] nm (droga) crack

cráneo ['kraneo] nm skull, cranium

cráter ['krater] nm crater

crayón [kra'jon] (MÉX, RPL) nm crayon, chalk

creación [krea'θjon] nf creation

creador, a [krea'ðor, a] adj creative ▷ nm/f creator

crear [kre'ar] vt to create, make

crecer [kre'θer] vi to grow; (precio) to rise

creces ['kreθes]: **con ~** adv amply, fully

crecido, -a [kre'θiðo, a] adj (persona, planta) full-grown; (cantidad) large

crecimiento [kreθi'mjento] nm growth; (aumento) increase

credencial [kreðen'θjal] nf

(LAM: **tarjeta**) *nf* credit card; **credenciales** *nfpl* credentials; **credencial de socio** (LAM) membership card

crédito ['kreðito] *nm* credit

credo ['kreðo] *nm* creed

creencia [kre'enθja] *nf* belief

creer [kre'er] *vt, vi* to think, believe; **creerse** *vr* to believe o.s. (to be); **~ en** to believe in; **creo que sí/no** I think/don't think so; **¡ya lo creo!** I should think so!

creído, -a [kre'iðo, a] *adj* (*engreído*) conceited

crema ['krema] *nf* cream; **crema batida** (LAM) whipped cream; **crema pastelera** (confectioner's) custard

cremallera [krema'ʎera] *nf* zip (fastener)

crepe ['krepe] (ESP) *nf* pancake

cresta ['kresta] *nf* (Geo, Zool) crest

creyendo *etc* *vb* V **creer**

creyente [kre'jente] *nmf* believer

creyó *etc* *vb* V **creer**

crezco *etc* *vb* V **crecer**

cría *etc* ['kria] *vb* V **criar** ▷ *nf* (*de animales*) rearing, breeding; (*animal*) young; V *tb* **crío**

criadero [kria'ðero] *nm* (Zool) breeding place

criado, -a [kri'aðo, a] *nm* servant ▷ *nf* servant, maid

criador [kria'ðor] *nm* breeder

crianza [kri'anθa] *nf* rearing, breeding; (*fig*) breeding

criar [kri'ar] *vt* (*educar*) to bring up; (*producir*) to grow, produce; (*animales*) to breed

criatura [kria'tura] *nf* creature; (*niño*) baby, (small) child

cribar [kri'ßar] *vt* to sieve

crimen ['krimen] *nm* crime

criminal [krimi'nal] *adj, nmf* criminal

crines ['krines] *nfpl* mane

crío, -a ['krio, a] (*fam*) *nm/f* (*niño*) kid

crisis ['krisis] *nf inv* crisis; **crisis nerviosa** nervous breakdown

crismas ['krismas] (ESP) *nm inv* Christmas card

cristal [kris'tal] *nm* crystal; (*de ventana*) glass, pane; (*lente*) lens; ▷ *nm* lens (of the eye)

cristalino, -a *adj* crystalline; (*fig*) clear

cristianismo [kristja'nismo] *nm* Christianity

cristiano, -a [kris'tjano, a] *adj, nm/f* Christian

Cristo ['kristo] *nm* Christ; (*crucifijo*) crucifix

criterio [kri'terjo] *nm* criterion; (*juicio*) judgement

crítica [kri'tika] *nf* criticism; V *tb* **crítico**

criticar [kriti'kar] *vt* to criticize

crítico, -a ['kritiko, a] *adj* critical ▷ *nm/f* critic

Croacia [kro'aθja] *nf* Croatia

cromo ['kromo] *nm* chrome

crónica ['kronika] *nf* chronicle, account

crónico, -a ['kroniko, a] *adj* chronic

cronómetro [kro'nometro] *nm* stopwatch

croqueta [kro'keta] *nf* croquette

cruce *etc* [kru'θe] *vb* V **cruzar** ▷ *nm* (*para peatones*) crossing; (*de carreteras*) crossroads

crucero [kru'θero] *nm* (*viaje*) cruise

crucificar [kruθifi'kar] *vt* to crucify

crucifijo [kruθi'fixo] *nm* crucifix

crucigrama [kruθi'xrama] *nm* crossword (puzzle)

cruda [kru'ða] (MÉX, CAM: *fam*) *nf* hangover

crudo, -a ['kruðo, a] *adj* raw; (*no maduro*) unripe; (*petróleo*) crude; (*rudo, cruel*) cruel ▷ *nm* crude (oil)

cruel [krwel] *adj* cruel; **crueldad** *nf* cruelty

crujiente [kru'xjente] *adj* (*galleta etc*) crunchy

crujir [kru'xir] *vi* (*madera etc*) to creak; (*dedos*) to crack; (*dientes*) to grind; (*nieve, arena*) to crunch

cruz [kruθ] *nf* cross; (*de moneda*) tails *sg*; **cruz gamada** swastika

cruzada [kru'θaða] *nf* crusade

cruzado, -a [kru'θaðo, a] *adj*
crossed ▷ *nm* crusader

cruzar [kru'θar] *vt* to cross; **cruzarse**
vr (*líneas etc*) to cross; (*personas*) to pass
each other

Cruz Roja *nf* Red Cross

cuaderno [kwa'ðerno] *nm*
notebook; (*de escuela*) exercise book;
(*Náut*) logbook

cuadra ['kwaðra] *nf* (*caballeriza*)
stable; (*LAM: entre calles*) block

cuadrado, -a [kwa'ðraðo, a] *adj*
square ▷ *nm* (*Mat*) square

cuadrar [kwa'ðrar] *vt* to square
▷ *vi*: ~ **con** to square with, tally with;
cuadrarse *vr* (*soldado*) to stand to
attention

cuadrilátero [kwaðri'latero]
nm (*Deporte*) boxing ring; (*Geom*)
quadrilateral

cuadrilla [kwa'ðriʎa] *nf* party, group

cuadro ['kwaðro] *nm* square; (*Arte*)
painting; (*Teatro*) scene; (*diagrama*)
chart; (*Deporte, Med*) team; **tela a
~s** checked (*BRIT*) o chequered (*US*)
material

cuajar [kwa'xar] *vt* (*leche*) to curdle;
(*sangre*) to congeal; (*Culin*) to set;
cuajarse *vr* to curdle; to congeal; to
set; (*llenarse*) to fill up

cuajo ['kwaxo] *nm*: **de ~** (*arrancar*) by
the roots; (*cortar*) completely

cual [kwal] *adv* like, as ▷ *pron*: **el** *etc*
~ which; (*persona sujeto*) who; (: *objeto*)
whom ▷ *adj* such as; **cada** ~ each one;
déjalo tal ~ leave it just as it is

cuál [kwal] *pron interr* which (one)

cualesquiera, a [kwales'kjer(a)] *pl de*
cualquier(a)

cualidad [kwali'ðað] *nf* quality

cualquier [kwal'kjer] *adj* V
cualquiera

cualquiera [kwal'kjera] (*pl*
cualesquiera) *adj* (*delante de nm y f*
cualquier) any ▷ *pron* anybody; **un
coche ~ servirá** any car will do; **no es
un hombre ~** he isn't just anybody;
cualquier día/libro any day/book; **eso**

~ **lo sabe hacer** anybody can do that;
es un ~ he's a nobody

cuando ['kwando] *adv* when; (*aún
si*) if, even if ▷ *conj* (*puesto que*) since
▷ *prep*: **yo ... niño ...** when I was a child
...; ~ **no sea así** even if it is not so; ~
más at (the) most; ~ **menos** at least;
~ **no** if not, otherwise; **de ~ en ~** from
time to time

cuándo ['kwando] *adv* when; **¿desde
~?** since when?

cuantía [kwan'tia] *nf* extent

○ **PALABRA CLAVE**

cuanto, -a ['kwanto, a] *adj* **1** (*todo*):
tiene todo cuanto desea he's got
everything he wants; **le daremos
cuantos ejemplares necesite** we'll
give him as many copies as o all the
copies he needs; **cuantos hombres la
ven** all the men who see her
2 *unos cuantos*: **había unos
cuantos periodistas** there were a few
journalists
3 (+ *más*): **cuanto más vino bebes peor
te sentirás** the more wine you drink
the worse you'll feel
▷ *pron*: **tiene cuanto desea** he has
everything he wants; **tome cuanto/
cuantos quiera** take as much/many
as you want
▷ *adv*: **en cuanto**: **en cuanto profesor**
as a teacher; **en cuanto a mí** as for me;
V *tb* **antes**
▷ *conj* **1 cuanto más gana menos
gasta** the more he earns the less
he spends; **cuanto más joven más
confiado** the younger you are the more
trusting you are
2 *en cuanto*: **en cuanto llegue/
llegué** as soon as I arrive/arrived

cuánto, -a ['kwanto, a] *adj*
(*exclamación*) what a lot of; (*interr: sg*)
how much?; (: *pl*) how many? ▷ *pron,
adv* how; (: *interr: sg*) how much?; (: *pl*)
how many?; **¡cuánta gente!** what a

lot of people!; **¿~ cuesta?** how much does it cost?; **¿a ~s estamos?** what's the date?

cuarenta [kwa'renta] num forty

cuarentena [kwaren'tena] nf quarantine

cuaresma [kwa'resma] nf Lent

cuarta ['kwarta] nf (Mat) quarter, fourth; (palmo) span

cuartel [kwar'tel] nm (Mil) barracks pl; **cuartel de bomberos** (RPL) fire station; **cuartel general** headquarters pl

cuarteto [kwar'teto] nm quartet

cuarto, -a ['kwarto, a] adj fourth ▷ nm (Mat) quarter, fourth; (habitación) room; **cuarto de baño** bathroom; **cuarto de estar** living room; **cuarto de hora** quarter (of an) hour; **cuarto de kilo** quarter kilo; **cuartos de final** quarter finals

cuatro ['kwatro] num four

Cuba ['kuβa] nf Cuba

cuba ['kuβa] nf cask, barrel

cubano, -a [ku'βano, a] adj, nm/f Cuban

cubata [ku'βata] nm (fam) large drink (of rum and coke etc)

cubeta [ku'βeta] (ESP, MÉX) nf (balde) bucket, tub

cúbico, -a [ku'βiko, a] adj cubic

cubierta [ku'βjerta] nf cover, covering; (neumático) tyre; (Náut) deck

cubierto, -a [ku'βjerto, a] pp de **cubrir** ▷ adj covered ▷ nm cover; (lugar en la mesa) place; **cubiertos** nmpl cutlery sg; **a ~** under cover

cubilete [kuβi'lete] nm (en juegos) cup

cubito [ku'βito] nm (tb: **~ de hielo**) ice-cube

cubo ['kuβo] nm (Mat) cube; (ESP: balde) bucket, tub; (Tec) drum; **cubo de (la) basura** dustbin (BRIT), trash can (US)

cubrir [ku'βrir] vt to cover; **cubrirse** vr (cielo) to become overcast

cucaracha [kuka'ratʃa] nf cockroach

cuchara [ku'tʃara] nf spoon; (Tec) scoop; **cucharada** nf spoonful; **cucharadita** nf teaspoonful

cucharilla [kutʃa'riʎa] nf teaspoon

cucharón [kutʃa'ron] nm ladle

cuchilla [ku'tʃiʎa] nf (large) knife; (de arma blanca) blade; **cuchilla de afeitar** razor blade

cuchillo [ku'tʃiʎo] nm knife

cuchitril [kutʃi'tril] nm hovel

cuclillas [ku'kliʎas] nfpl: **en ~** squatting

cuco, -a ['kuko, a] adj pretty; (astuto) sharp ▷ nm cuckoo

cucurucho [kuku'rutʃo] nm cornet

cueca ['kweka] nf Chilean national dance

cuello ['kweʎo] nm (Anat) neck; (de vestido, camisa) collar

cuenca ['kwenka] nf (Anat) eye socket; (Geo) bowl, deep valley

cuenco ['kwenko] nm bowl

cuenta etc ['kwenta] vb V **contar** ▷ nf (cálculo) count, counting; (en café, restaurante) bill (BRIT), check (US); (Com) account; (de collar) bead; **a fin de ~s** in the end; **caer en la ~** to catch on; **darse ~ de** to realize; **tener en ~** to bear in mind; **echar ~s** to take stock; **cuenta atrás** countdown; **cuenta corriente/de ahorros** current/savings account; **cuenta de correo (electrónica)** (Inform) email account; **cuentakilómetros** nm inv ≈ milometer; (de velocidad) speedometer

cuento etc ['kwento] vb V **contar** ▷ nm story; **cuento chino** tall story; **cuento de hadas** a fairy tale

cuerda ['kwerða] nf rope; (fina) string; (de reloj) spring; **dar ~ a un reloj** to wind up a clock; **cuerda floja** tightrope; **cuerdas vocales** vocal cords

cuerdo, -a ['kwerðo, a] adj sane; (prudente) wise, sensible

cuerno ['kwerno] nm horn

cuero ['kwero] nm leather; **en ~s** stark naked; **cuero cabelludo** scalp

cuerpo ['kwerpo] nm body

cuervo ['kwerβo] nm crow

cuesta etc ['kwesta] vb V **costar**
▷ nf slope; (en camino etc) hill; **~ arriba/abajo** uphill/downhill; **a ~s** on one's back

cueste etc vb V **costar**

cuestión [kwes'tjon] nf matter, question, issue

cuete ['kwete] adj (MÉX: fam) drunk
▷ nm (LAM: cohete) rocket; (MÉX, RPL: fam: embriaguez) drunkenness; (MÉX: Culin) steak

cueva ['kweβa] nf cave

cuidado [kwi'ðaðo] nm care, carefulness; (preocupación) care, worry
▷ excl carefully, look out!; **eso me tiene sin ~** I'm not worried about that

cuidadoso, -a [kwiða'ðoso, a] adj careful; (preocupado) anxious

cuidar [kwi'ðar] vt (Med) to care for; (ocuparse de) to take care of, look after
▷ vi: **~ de** to take care of, look after; **cuidarse** vr to look after o.s.; **~se de hacer algo** to take care to do sth

culata [ku'lata] nf (de fusil) butt

culebra [ku'leβra] nf snake

culebrón [kule'βron] (fam) nm (TV) soap(-opera)

culo ['kulo] nm bottom, backside; (de vaso, botella) bottom

culpa ['kulpa] nf fault; (Jur) guilt; **por ~ de** because of; **echar la ~ a algn** to blame sb for sth; **tener la ~ (de)** to be to blame (for); **culpable** adj guilty
▷ nmf culprit; **culpar** [kul'par] vt to blame; to accuse

cultivar [kulti'βar] vt to cultivate

cultivo [kul'tiβo] nm (acto) cultivation; (plantas) crop

culto, -a ['kulto, a] adj (que tiene cultura) cultured, educated ▷ nm (homenaje) worship; (religión) cult

cultura [kul'tura] nf culture

culturismo [kultu'rismo] nm body-building

cumbia ['kumbja] nf popular Colombian dance

cumbre ['kumbre] nf summit, top

cumpleaños [kumple'aɲos] nm inv birthday

cumplido, -a [kum'pliðo, a] adj (abundante) plentiful; (cortés) courteous ▷ nm compliment; **visita de ~** courtesy call

cumplidor, a [kumpli'ðor, a] adj reliable

cumplimiento [kumpli'mjento] nm (de un deber) fulfilment; (acabamiento) completion

cumplir [kum'plir] vt (orden) to carry out, obey; (promesa) to carry out, fulfil; (condena) to serve ▷ vi: **~ con** (deber) to carry out, fulfil; **cumplirse** vr (plazo) to expire; **hoy cumple dieciocho años** he is eighteen today

cuna ['kuna] nf cradle, cot

cundir [kun'dir] vi (noticia, rumor, pánico) to spread; (rendir) to go a long way

cuneta [ku'neta] nf ditch

cuña ['kuɲa] nf wedge

cuñado, -a [ku'ɲaðo, a] nm/f brother-/sister-in-law

cuota ['kwota] nf (parte proporcional) share; (cotización) fee, dues pl

cupe etc vb V **caber**

cupiera etc vb V **caber**

cupo ['kupo] vb V **caber** ▷ nm quota

cupón [ku'pon] nm coupon

cúpula ['kupula] nf dome

cura ['kura] nf (curación) cure; (método curativo) treatment ▷ nm priest

curación [kura'θjon] nf (acción) curing

curandero, -a [kuran'dero, a] nm/f quack

curar [ku'rar] vt (Med: herida) to treat, dress; (: enfermo) to cure; (Culin) to salt; (cuero) to tan; **curarse** vr to get well, recover

curiosear [kurjose'ar] vt to glance at, look over ▷ vi to look round, wander round; (explorar) to poke about

curiosidad [kurjosi'ðað] nf curiosity

curioso, -a [ku'rjoso, a] adj curious ▷ nm/f bystander, onlooker

curita [ku'rita] (LAM) nf (sticking) plaster (BRIT), Bandaid® (US)

currante [ku'rrante] (ESP: fam) nmf worker

currar [ku'rrar] (ESP: fam) vi to work

currículo [ku'rrikulo] = **currículum**

currículum [ku'rrikulum] nm curriculum vitae

cursi ['kursi] (fam) adj affected

cursillo [kur'siλo] nm short course

cursiva [kur'siβa] nf italics pl

curso ['kurso] nm course; **en ~** (año) current; (proceso) going on, under way

cursor [kur'sor] nm (Inform) cursor

curul [ku'rul] (MÉX) nm (escaño) seat

curva ['kurβa] nf curve, bend

custodia [kus'toðja] nf safekeeping; custody

cutis ['kutis] nm inv skin, complexion

cutre ['kutre] (ESP: fam) adj (lugar) grotty

cuyo, -a ['kujo, a] pron (de quien) whose; (de que) whose, of which; **en ~ caso** in which case

C.V. abr (= caballos de vapor) H.P.

d

dado, -a ['daðo, a] pp de **dar** ▷ nm die; **dados** nmpl dice; **~ que** given that

daltónico, -a [dal'toniko, a] adj colour-blind

dama ['dama] nf (gen) lady; (Ajedrez) queen; **damas** nfpl (juego) draughts sg; **dama de honor** bridesmaid

damasco [da'masko] (RPL) nm apricot

danés, -esa [da'nes, esa] adj Danish ▷ nm/f Dane

dañar [da'ɲar] vt (objeto) to damage; (persona) to hurt; **dañarse** vr (objeto) to get damaged

dañino, -a [da'ɲino, a] adj harmful

daño ['daɲo] nm (objeto) damage; (persona) harm, injury; **~s y perjuicios** (Jur) damages; **hacer ~ a** to damage; (persona) to hurt, injure; **hacerse ~** to hurt o.s.

○ **PALABRA CLAVE**

dar [dar] vt 1 (gen) to give; (obra de

teatro) to put on; (*film*) to show; (*fiesta*) to hold; **dar algo a algn** to give sb sth o sth to sb; **dar de beber a algn** to give sb a drink

2 (*producir: intereses*) to yield; (*fruta*) to produce

3 (*locuciones + n*): **da gusto escucharle** it's a pleasure to listen to him; V *tb* **paseo**

4 (*+ n: = perífrasis de verbo*): **me da asco** it sickens me

5 (*considerar*): **dar algo por descontado/entendido** to take sth for granted/as read; **dar algo por concluido** to consider sth finished

6 (*hora*): **el reloj dio las 6** the clock struck 6 (o'clock)

7: **me da lo mismo** it's all the same to me; V *tb* **igual, más**

▷ *vi* **1 dar con: dimos con él dos horas más tarde** we came across him two hours later; **al final di con la solución** I eventually came up with the answer

2: **dar en** (*blanco, suelo*) to hit; **el sol me da en la cara** the sun is shining (right) on my face

3: **dar de sí** (*zapatos etc*) to stretch, give

darse *vr* **1**: **darse por vencido** to give up

2 (*ocurrir*): **se han dado muchos casos** there have been a lot of cases

3: **darse a: se ha dado a la bebida** he's taken to drinking

4: **se me dan bien/mal las ciencias** I'm good/bad at science

5: **dárselas de: se las da de experto** he fancies himself o poses as an expert

dardo ['darðo] *nm* dart

dátil ['datil] *nm* date

dato ['dato] *nm* fact, piece of information; **datos personales** personal details

dcha. *abr* (*= derecha*) r.h.

---

d. de C. *abr* (*= después de Cristo*) A.D.

○ **PALABRA CLAVE**

de [de] (*de + el = del*) *prep* **1** (*posesión*) of; **la casa de Isabel/mis padres** Isabel's/my parents' house; **es de ellos** it's theirs

2 (*origen, distancia, con números*) from; **soy de Gijón** I'm from Gijón; **de 8 a 20** from 8 to 20; **salir del cine** to go out of o leave the cinema; **de 2 en 2** 2 by 2, 2 at a time

3 (*valor descriptivo*): **una copa de vino** a glass of wine; **la mesa de la cocina** the kitchen table; **un billete de 10 euros** a 10 euro note; **un niño de tres años** a three-year-old (child); **una máquina de coser** a sewing machine; **ir vestido de gris** to be dressed in grey; **la niña del vestido azul** the girl in the blue dress; **trabaja de profesora** she works as a teacher; **de lado** sideways; **de atrás/delante** rear/front

4 (*hora, tiempo*): **a las 8 de la mañana** at 8 o'clock in the morning; **de día/noche** by day/night; **de hoy en ocho días** a week from now; **de niño era gordo** as a child he was fat

5 (*comparaciones*): **más/menos de cien personas** more/less than a hundred people; **el más caro de la tienda** the most expensive in the shop; **menos/más de lo pensado** less/more than expected

6 (*causa*): **del calor** from the heat

7 (*tema*) about; **clases de inglés** English classes; **¿sabes algo de él?** do you know anything about him?; **un libro de física** a physics book

8 (*adj + de + infin*): **fácil de entender** easy to understand

9 (*oraciones pasivas*): **fue respetado de todos** he was loved by all

10 (*condicional + infin*) if; **de ser posible** if possible; **de no terminarlo hoy** if I *etc* don't finish it today

dé [de] vb V **dar**

debajo [de'βaxo] adv underneath; ~ **de** below, under; **por ~ de** beneath

debate [de'βate] nm debate; **debatir** vt to debate

deber [de'βer] nm duty ▷ vt to owe ▷ vi: **debe (de)** it must, it should; **deberes** nmpl (Escol) homework; **deberse** vr: ~**se a** to be owing o due to; **debo hacerlo** I must do it; **debe de ir** he should go

debido, -a [de'βiðo, a] adj proper, just; ~ **a** due to, because of

débil [ˈdeβil] adj (persona, carácter) weak; (luz) dim; **debilidad** nf weakness; dimness

debilitar [deβili'tar] vt to weaken; **debilitarse** vr to grow weak

débito [ˈdeβito] nm debit; **débito bancario** (LAM) direct debit (BRIT) o billing (US)

debutar [deβu'tar] vi to make one's debut

década [ˈdekaða] nf decade

decadencia [deka'ðenθja] nf (estado) decadence; (proceso) decline, decay

decaído, -a [deka'iðo, a] adj: **estar ~** (abatido) to be down

decano, -a [de'kano, a] nm/f (de universidad etc) dean

decena [de'θena] nf: **una ~** ten (or so)

decente [de'θente] adj decent

decepción [deθep'θjon] nf disappointment

> No confundir **decepción** con la palabra inglesa **deception**.

decepcionar [deθepθjo'nar] vt to disappoint

decidir [deθi'ðir] vt, vi to decide; **decidirse** vr: ~**se a** to make up one's mind to

décimo, -a [ˈdeθimo, a] adj tenth ▷ nm tenth

decir [de'θir] vt to say; (contar) to tell; (hablar) to speak ▷ nm saying; **decirse** vr: **se dice que** it is said that; **es ~** that is (to say); ~ **para sí** to say to o.s.;

querer ~ to mean; **¡dígame!** (Tel) hello!; (en tienda) can I help you?

decisión [deθi'sjon] nf (resolución) decision; (firmeza) decisiveness

decisivo, -a [deθi'siβo, a] adj decisive

declaración [deklara'θjon] nf (manifestación) statement; (de amor) declaration; declaración **fiscal** o **de la renta** income-tax return

declarar [dekla'rar] vt to declare ▷ vi to declare; (Jur) to testify; **declararse** vr to propose

decoración [dekora'θjon] nf decoration

decorado [deko'raðo] nm (Cine, Teatro) scenery, set

decorar [deko'rar] vt to decorate; **decorativo, -a** adj ornamental, decorative

decreto [de'kreto] nm decree

dedal [de'ðal] nm thimble

dedicación [deðika'θjon] nf dedication

dedicar [deði'kar] vt (libro) to dedicate; (tiempo, dinero) to devote; (palabras: decir, consagrar) to dedicate, devote; **dedicatoria** nf (de libro) dedication

dedo [ˈdeðo] nm finger; **hacer ~** (fam) to hitch (a lift); **dedo anular** ring finger; **dedo corazón** middle finger; **dedo (del pie)** toe; **dedo gordo** (de la mano) thumb; (del pie) big toe; **dedo índice** index finger; **dedo meñique** little finger; **dedo pulgar** thumb

deducción [deðuk'θjon] nf deduction

deducir [deðu'θir] vt (concluir) to deduce, infer; (Com) to deduct

defecto [de'fekto] nm defect, flaw; **defectuoso, -a** adj defective, faulty

defender [defen'der] vt to defend; **defenderse** vr (desenvolverse) to get by

defensa [de'fensa] nf defence ▷ nm (Deporte) defender, back; **defensivo, -a** adj defensive; **a la defensiva** on the defensive

defensor, a [defen'sor, a] *adj*
defending ▷ *nm/f* (*abogado defensor*)
defending counsel; (*protector*) protector

deficiencia [defi'θjenθja] *nf*
deficiency

deficiente [defi'θjente] *adj*
(*defectuoso*) defective; ~ **en** lacking o
deficient in; **ser un ~ mental** to be
mentally handicapped

déficit ['defiθit] (*pl* **~s**) *nm* deficit

definición [defini'θjon] *nf* definition

definir [defi'nir] *vt* (*determinar*) to
determine, establish; (*decidir*) to define;
(*aclarar*) to clarify; **definitivo, -a** *adj*
definitive; **en definitiva** definitively;
(*en resumen*) in short

deformación [deforma'θjon] *nf*
(*alteración*) deformation; (*Radio etc*)
distortion

deformar [defor'mar] *vt* (*gen*) to
deform; **deformarse** *vr* to become
deformed; **deforme** *adj* (*informe*)
deformed; (*feo*) ugly; (*malhecho*)
misshapen

defraudar [defrau'ðar] *vt*
(*decepcionar*) to disappoint; (*estafar*)
to defraud

defunción [defun'θjon] *nf* death,
demise

degenerar [dexene'rar] *vi* to
degenerate

degradar [deɣra'ðar] *vt* to debase,
degrade; **degradarse** *vr* to demean
o.s.

degustación [deɣusta'θjon] *nf*
sampling, tasting

dejar [de'xar] *vt* to leave; (*permitir*)
to allow, let; (*abandonar*) to abandon,
forsake; (*beneficios*) to produce, yield
▷ *vi*: ~ **de** (*parar*) to stop; (*no hacer*) to
fail to; ~ **a un lado** to leave o set aside;
~ **entrar/salir** to let in/out; ~ **pasar** to
let through

del [del] (=**de + el**) V **de**

delantal [delan'tal] *nm* apron

delante [de'lante] *adv* in front;
(*enfrente*) opposite; (*adelante*) ahead; ~
de in front of, before

delantera [delan'tera] *nf* (*de vestido,
casa etc*) front part; (*Deporte*) forward
line; **llevar la ~ (a aign)** to be ahead
(of sb)

delantero, -a [delan'tero, a] *adj*
front ▷ *nm* (*Deporte*) forward,
striker

delatar [dela'tar] *vt* to inform on
o against, betray; **delator, a** *nm/f*
informer

delegación [deleɣa'θjon] *nf* (*acción,
delegados*) delegation; (*Com: oficina*)
office, branch; **delegación de policía**
(*MÉX*) police station

delegado, -a [dele'ɣaðo, a] *nm/f*
delegate; (*Com*) agent

delegar [dele'ɣar] *vt* to delegate

deletrear [deletre'ar] *vt* to spell (out)

delfín [del'fin] *nm* dolphin

delgado, -a [del'ɣaðo, a] *adj* thin;
(*persona*) slim, thin; (*tela etc*) light,
delicate

deliberar [deliβe'rar] *vt* to debate,
discuss

delicadeza [delika'ðeθa] *nf* (*gen*)
delicacy; (*refinamiento, sutileza*)
refinement

delicado, -a [deli'kaðo, a] *adj*
(*gen*) delicate; (*sensible*) sensitive;
(*quisquilloso*) touchy

delicia [de'liθja] *nf* delight

delicioso, -a [deli'θjoso, a] *adj*
(*gracioso*) delightful; (*exquisito*)
delicious

delimitar [delimi'tar] *vt* (*función,
responsabilidades*) to define

delincuencia [delin'kwenθja]
nf delinquency; **delincuente** *nmf*
delinquent; (*criminal*) criminal

delineante [deline'ante] *nmf*
draughtsman/woman

delirante [deli'rante] *adj* delirious

delirar [deli'rar] *vi* to be delirious,
rave

delirio [de'lirjo] *nm* (*Med*)
delirium; (*palabras insensatas*)
ravings *pl*

delito [de'lito] *nm* (*gen*) crime;

(infracción) offence

delta ['delta] nm delta

demacrado, -a [dema'kraðo, a] adj: **estar ~** to look pale and drawn, be wasted away

demanda [de'manda] nf (pedido, Com) demand; (petición) request; (Jur) action, lawsuit; **demandar** [deman'dar] vt (gen) to demand; (Jur) to sue, file a lawsuit against

demás [de'mas] adj: **los ~ niños** the other o remaining children ▷ pron: **los/las ~** the others, the rest (of them); **lo ~** the rest (of it)

demasía [dema'sia] nf (exceso) excess, surplus; **comer en ~** to eat to excess

demasiado, -a [dema'sjaðo, a] adj: **~ vino** too much wine ▷ adv (antes de adj, adv) too; **~s libros** too many books; **¡esto es ~!** that's the limit!; **hace ~ calor** it's too hot; **~ despacio** too slowly; **~s** too many

demencia [de'menθja] nf (locura) madness

democracia [demo'kraθja] nf democracy

demócrata [de'mokrata] nmf democrat; **democrático, -a** adj democratic

demoler [demo'ler] vt to demolish; **demolición** nf demolition

demonio [de'monjo] nm devil, demon; **¡~s!** hell!, damn!; **¿cómo ~s?** how the hell?

demora [de'mora] nf delay

demostración [demostra'θjon] nf (Mat) proof; (de afecto) show, display

demostrar [demos'trar] vt (probar) to prove; (mostrar) to show; (manifestar) to demonstrate

den [den] vb V **dar**

denegar [dene'xar] vt (rechazar) to refuse; (Jur) to reject

denominación [denomina'θjon] nf (acto) naming; **Denominación de**

Origen see note

densidad [densi'ðað] nf density; (fig) thickness

denso, -a ['denso, a] adj dense; (espeso, pastoso) thick; (fig) heavy

dentadura [denta'ðura] nf (set of) teeth pl; **dentadura postiza** false teeth pl

dentera [den'tera] nf (grima): **dar ~ a algn** to set sb's teeth on edge

dentífrico, -a [den'tifriko, a] adj dental ▷ nm toothpaste

dentista [den'tista] nmf dentist

dentro ['dentro] adv inside ▷ prep: **~ de**, in, inside, within; **por ~** (on the) inside; **mirar por ~** to look inside; **~ de tres meses** within three months

denuncia [de'nunθja] nf (delación) denunciation; (acusación) accusation; (de accidente) report; **denunciar** vt to report; (delatar) to inform on o against

departamento [departa'mento] nm sección administrativa, department, section; (LAM: apartamento) flat (BRIT), apartment

depender [depen'der] vi: **~ de** to depend on; **depende** it (all) depends

dependienta [depen'djenta] nf saleswoman, shop assistant

dependiente [depen'djente] adj dependent ▷ nm salesman, shop assistant

depilar [depi'lar] vt (con cera) to wax; (cejas) to pluck

deportar [depor'tar] vt to deport

deporte [de'porte] nm sport; **hacer ~** to play sports; **deportista** adj sports cpd ▷ nmf sportsman/woman; **deportivo, -a** adj (club, periódico) sports cpd ▷ nm sports car

depositar [deposi'tar] vt (dinero) to deposit; (mercancías) to put away, store; **depositarse** vr to settle

depósito [de'posito] nm (gen) deposit; (almacén, depósito) store; (de agua, gasolina etc) tank; **depósito de cadáveres** mortuary

depredador, -a [depreða'ðor, a] adj predatory ▷ nm predator

depresión [depre'sjon] nf depression; **depresión nerviosa** nervous breakdown

deprimido, -a [depri'miðo, a] adj depressed

deprimir [depri'mir] vt to depress; **deprimirse** vr (persona) to become depressed

deprisa [de'prisa] adv quickly, hurriedly

depurar [depu'rar] vt to purify; (purgar) to purge

derecha [de'retʃa] nf right(-hand) side; (Pol) right; **a la ~** (estar) on the right; (torcer etc) (to the) right

derecho, -a [de'retʃo, a] adj right, right-hand ▷ nm (privilegio) right; (lado) right(-hand) side; (leyes) law ▷ adv straight, directly; **derechos** nmpl (de aduana) duty sg; (de autor) royalties; **tener ~ a** to have a right to; **derechos de autor** royalties

deriva [de'riβa] nf: **ir o estar a la ~** to drift, be adrift

derivado [deri'βaðo] nm (Com) by-product

derivar [deri'βar] vi to derive; (desviar) to direct ▷ vi to derive, be derived; (Náut) to drift; **derivarse** vr to derive, be derived; to drift

derramamiento [derrama'mjento] nm (dispersión) spilling; **derramamiento de sangre** bloodshed

derramar [derra'mar] vt to spill;

(verter) to pour out; (esparcir) to scatter; **derramarse** vr to pour out

derrame [de'rrame] nm (de líquido) spilling; (de sangre) shedding; (de tubo etc) overflow; (pérdida) leakage; **derrame cerebral** brain haemorrhage

derredor [derre'ðor] adv: **al o en ~ de** around, about

derretir [derre'tir] vt (gen) to melt; (nieve) to thaw; **derretirse** vr to melt

derribar [derri'βar] vt to knock down; (construcción) to demolish; (persona, gobierno, político) to bring down

derrocar [derro'kar] vt (gobierno) to bring down, overthrow

derrochar [derro'tʃar] vt to squander; **derroche** nm (despilfarro) waste, squandering

derrota [de'rrota] nf (Náut) course; (Mil, Deporte etc) defeat, rout; **derrotar** vt (gen) to defeat; **derrotero** (rumbo) course

derrumbar [derrum'bar] vt (edificio) to knock down; **derrumbarse** vr to collapse

des etc vb V **dar**

desabrochar [desaβro'tʃar] vt (botones, broches) to undo, unfasten; **desabrocharse** vr (ropa etc) to come undone

desacato [desa'kato] nm (falta de respeto) disrespect; (Jur) contempt

desacertado, -a [desaθer'taðo, a] adj (equivocado) mistaken; (inoportuno) unwise

desacierto [desa'θjerto] nm mistake, error

desaconsejar [desakonse'xar] vt to advise against

desacreditar [desakreði'tar] vt (desprestigiar) to discredit, bring into disrepute; (denigrar) to run down

desacuerdo [desa'kwerðo] nm disagreement, discord

desafiar [desa'fjar] vt (retar) to challenge; (enfrentarse a) to defy

desafilado, -a [desafi'laðo, a]

adj blunt

desafinado, -a [desafi'naðo, a]
adj: **estar ~** to be out of tune

desafinar [desafi'nar] *vi (al cantar)* to
be o go out of tune

desafío *etc* [desa'fio] *vb* V **desafiar**
▷ *nm (reto)* challenge; *(combate)* duel;
(resistencia) defiance

desafortunado, -a
[desafortu'naðo, a] *adj (desgraciado)*
unfortunate, unlucky

desagradable [desaɣra'ðaβle]
adj (fastidioso, enojoso) unpleasant;
(irritante) disagreeable

desagradar [desaɣra'ðar] *vi*
(disgustar) to displease; *(molestar)* to
bother

desagradecido, -a [desaɣraðe'θiðo,
a] *adj* ungrateful

desagrado [desa'ɣraðo] *nm*
(disgusto) displeasure; *(contrariedad)*
dissatisfaction

desagüe [des'axwe] *nm (de un líquido)*
drainage; *(cañería)* drainpipe; *(salida)*
outlet, drain

desahogar [desao'ɣar] *vt (aliviar)*
to ease, relieve; *(ira)* to vent;
desahogarse *vr (relajarse)* to relax;
(desfogarse) to let off steam

desahogo [desa'oxo] *nm (alivio)*
relief; *(comodidad)* comfort, ease

desahuciar [desau'θjar] *vt (enfermo)*
to give up hope for; *(inquilino)* to evict

desairar [desai'rar] *vt (menospreciar)*
to slight, snub

desalentador, a [desalenta'ðor, a]
adj discouraging

desaliño [desa'liɲo] *nm* slovenliness

desalmado, -a [desal'maðo, a] *adj*
(cruel) cruel, heartless

desalojar [desalo'xar] *vt (expulsar,
echar)* to eject; *(abandonar)* to move out
of ▷ *vi* to move out

desamor [desa'mor] *nm (frialdad)*
indifference; *(odio)* dislike

desamparado, -a [desampa'raðo,
a] *adj (persona)* helpless;
(lugar: expuesto) exposed; *(desierto)*

deserted

desangrar [desan'grar] *vt* to bleed;
(fig: persona) to bleed dry; **desangrarse**
vr to lose a lot of blood

desanimado, -a [desani'maðo,
a] *adj (persona)* downhearted;
(espectáculo, fiesta) dull

desanimar [desani'mar] *vt*
(desalentar) to discourage; *(deprimir)* to
depress; **desanimarse** *vr* to lose heart

desapacible [desapa'θiβle] *adj (gen)*
unpleasant

desaparecer [desapare'θer] *vi (gen)*
to disappear; *(el sol, el luz)* to vanish;
desaparecido, -a *adj* missing;
desaparición *nf* disappearance

desapercibido, -a [desaperθi'βiðo,
a] *adj (desprevenido)* unprepared; **pasar
~** to go unnoticed

desaprensivo, -a [desapren'siβo, a]
adj unscrupulous

desaprobar [desapro'βar] *vt*
(reprobar) to disapprove of; *(condenar)* to
condemn; *(no consentir)* to reject

desaprovechado, -a
[desaproβe'tʃaðo, a] *adj (oportunidad,
tiempo)* wasted; *(estudiante)* slack

desaprovechar [desaproβe'tʃar]
vt to waste

desarmador [desarma'ðor] *(MÉX)*
nm screwdriver

desarmar [desar'mar] *vt (Mil, fig)* to
disarm; *(Tec)* to take apart, dismantle;
desarme *nm* disarmament

desarraigar [desarrai'ɣar] *vt* to
uproot; **desarraigo** *nm* uprooting

desarreglar [desarre'ɣlar] *vt*
(desordenar) to disarrange; *(trastocar)* to
upset, disturb

desarrollar [desarro'ʎar] *vt (gen)* to
develop; **desarrollarse** *vr* to develop;
(ocurrir) to take place; *(Foto)* to develop;
desarrollo *nm* development

desarticular [desartiku'lar] *vt*
(hueso) to dislocate; *(objeto)* to take
apart; *(fig)* to break up

desasosegar [desasose'ɣar] *vt*
(inquietar) to disturb, make uneasy

desasosiego etc [desaso'sjexo] vb
V **desasosegar** ▷ nm (intranquilidad)
uneasiness, restlessness; (ansiedad)
anxiety

desastre [de'sastre] nm disaster;
desastroso, -a adj disastrous

desatar [desa'tar] vt (nudo) to untie;
(paquete) to undo; (separar) to detach;
desatarse vr (zapatos) to come
untied; (tormenta) to break

desatascar [desatas'kar] vt (cañería)
to unblock, clear

desatender [desaten'der] vt no
prestar atención a, to disregard;
(abandonar) to neglect

desatino [desa'tino] nm (idiotez)
foolishness, folly; (error) blunder

desatornillar [desatorni'ʎar] vt to
unscrew

desatrancar [desatran'kar] vt
(puerta) to unbolt; (cañería) to clear,
unblock

desautorizado, -a [desautori'θaðo,
a] adj unauthorized

desautorizar [desautori'θar]
vt (oficial) to deprive of authority;
(informe) to deny

desayunar [desaju'nar] vi to have
breakfast ▷ vt to have for breakfast;
desayuno nm breakfast

desazón [desa'θon] nf anxiety

desbarajuste [desβara'xuste] nm
confusion, disorder

desbaratar [desβara'tar] vt
(deshacer, destruir) to ruin

desbloquear [desβloke'ar] vt
(negociaciones, tráfico) to get going
again; (Com: cuenta) to unfreeze

desbordar [desβor'ðar] vt
(sobrepasar) to go beyond; (exceder)
to exceed; **desbordarse** vr (río) to
overflow; (entusiasmo) to erupt

descabellado, -a [deskaβe'ʎaðo, a]
adj (disparatado) wild, crazy

descafeinado, -a [deskafei'naðo, a]
adj decaffeinated ▷ nm decaffeinated
coffee

descalabro [deska'laβro] nm blow;

(desgracia) misfortune

descalificar [deskalifi'kar] vt to
disqualify; (desacreditar) to discredit

descalzar [deskal'θar] vt (zapato) to
take off; **descalzo, -a** adj barefoot(ed)

descambiar [deskam'bjar] vt to
exchange

descaminado, -a [deskami'naðo,
a] adj (equivocado) on the wrong road;
(fig) misguided

descampado [deskam'paðo] nm
open space

descansado, -a [deskan'saðo, a] adj
(gen) rested; (que tranquiliza) restful

descansar [deskan'sar] vt (gen) to
rest ▷ vi to rest, have a rest; (echarse)
to lie down

descansillo [deskan'siʎo] nm (de
escalera) landing

descanso [des'kanso] nm (reposo)
rest; (alivio) relief; (pausa) break;
(Deporte) interval, half time

descapotable [deskapo'taβle] nm
(tb: **coche ~**) convertible

descarado, -a [deska'raðo, a] adj
shameless; (insolente) cheeky

descarga [des'karxa] nf (Arq, Elec,
Mil) discharge; (Náut) unloading

descargar [deskar'xar] vt to unload;
(golpe) to let fly; **descargarse** vr to
unburden o.s.; **descargarse algo de
Internet** to download sth from the
Internet

descaro [des'karo] nm nerve

descarriar [deska'rrjar] vt
(descaminar) to misdirect; (fig) to lead
astray; **descarriarse** vr (perderse) to
lose one's way; (separarse) to stray;
(pervertirse) to err, go astray

descarrilamiento
[deskarrila'mjento] nm (de tren)
derailment

descarrilar [deskarri'lar] vt to be
derailed

descartar [deskar'tar] vt (rechazar)
to reject; (eliminar) to rule out;
descartarse vr (Naipes) to discard;
-se de to shirk

descendencia [desθen'denθja] nf
(origen) origin, descent; (hijos) offspring

descender [desθen'der] vt
(bajar: escalera) to go down ▷ vi to
descend; (temperatura, nivel) to fall,
drop; **~ de** to be descended from

descendiente [desθen'djente] nmf
descendant

descenso [des'θenso] nm descent;
(de temperatura) drop

descifrar [desθi'frar] vt to decipher;
(mensaje) to decode

descolgar [deskol'ɣar] vt (bajar)
to take down; (teléfono) to pick up;
descolgarse vr to let o.s. down

descolorido, -a [deskolo'riðo, a] adj
faded; (pálido) pale

descompasado, -a
[deskompa'saðo, a] adj (sin
proporción) out of all proportion;
(excesivo) excessive

descomponer [deskompo'ner] vt
(desordenar) to disarrange, disturb; (Tec)
to put out of order; (dividir) to break
down (into parts); (fig) to provoke;
descomponerse vr (corromperse) to
rot, decompose; (LAM Tec) to break
down

descomposición [deskomposi'θjon]
nf (de un objeto) breakdown; (de fruta
etc) decomposition; **descomposición
de vientre** (ESP) stomach upset,
diarrhoea

descompostura [deskompos'tura]
nf (MÉX: avería) breakdown, fault;
(LAM: diarrea) diarrhoea

descomprimir [deskompri'mir]
vt (Internet) to unzip

descompuesto, -a
[deskom'pwesto, a] adj (corrompido)
decomposed; (roto) broken

desconcertado, -a
[deskonθer'taðo, a] adj disconcerted,
bewildered

desconcertar [deskonθer'tar] vt
(confundir) to baffle; (incomodar) to
upset, put out; **desconcertarse** vr
(turbarse) to be upset

desconchado, -a [deskon'tʃaðo, a]
adj (pintura) peeling

desconcierto etc [deskon'θjerto] vb
V **desconcertar** ▷ nm (gen) disorder;
(desorientación) uncertainty; (inquietud)
uneasiness

desconectar [deskonek'tar] vt to
disconnect

desconfianza [deskon'fjanθa] nf
distrust

desconfiar [deskon'fjar] vi to be
distrustful; **~ de** to distrust, suspect

descongelar [deskonxe'lar] vt to
defrost; (Com, Pol) to unfreeze

descongestionar
[deskonxestjo'nar] vt (cabeza, tráfico)
to clear

desconocer [deskono'θer] vt
(ignorar) not to know, be ignorant of

desconocido, -a [deskono'θiðo, a]
adj unknown ▷ nm/f stranger

desconocimiento
[deskonoθi'mjento] nm falta de
conocimientos, ignorance

desconsiderado, -a
[deskonsiðe'raðo, a] adj
inconsiderate; (insensible) thoughtless

desconsuelo etc [deskon'swelo] vb
V **desconsolar** ▷ nm (tristeza) distress;
(desesperación) despair

descontado, -a [deskon'taðo, a]
adj: **dar por ~ (que)** to take (it) for
granted (that)

descontar [deskon'tar] vt (deducir)
to take away, deduct; (rebajar) to
discount

descontento, -a [deskon'tento, a]
adj dissatisfied ▷ nm dissatisfaction,
discontent

descorchar [deskor'tʃar] vt to
uncork

descorrer [desko'rrer] vt (cortinas,
cerrojo) to draw back

descortés [deskor'tes] adj (mal
educado) discourteous; (grosero) rude

descoser [desko'ser] vt to unstitch;
descoserse vr to come apart (at the
seams)

descosido, -a [desko'siðo, a] *adj*
(*Costura*) unstitched

descreído, -a [deskre'iðo, a] *adj*
(*incrédulo*) incredulous; (*falto de fe*)
unbelieving

descremado, -a [deskre'maðo, a]
adj skimmed

describir [deskri'βir] *vt* to describe;
descripción [deskrip'θjon] *nf*
description

descrito [des'krito] *pp de* **describir**

descuartizar [deskwarti'θar] *vt*
(*animal*) to cut up

descubierto, -a [desku'βjerto, a] *pp
de* **descubrir** ▷ *adj* uncovered, bare;
(*persona*) bareheaded ▷ *nm* (*bancario*)
overdraft; **al ~** in the open

descubrimiento [deskuβri'mjento]
nm (*hallazgo*) discovery; (*revelación*)
revelation

descubrir [desku'βrir] *vt* to discover,
find; (*inaugurar*) to unveil; (*vislumbrar*)
to detect; (*revelar*) to reveal, show;
(*destapar*) to uncover; **descubrirse** *vr*
to reveal o.s.; (*quitarse sombrero*) to take
off one's hat; (*confesar*) to confess

descuento *etc* [des'kwento] *vb* V
descontar ▷ *nm* discount

descuidado, -a [deskwi'ðaðo, a]
adj (*sin cuidado*) careless; (*desordenado*)
untidy; (*olvidadizo*) forgetful;
(*dejado*) neglected; (*desprevenido*)
unprepared

descuidar [deskwi'ðar] *vt* (*dejar*)
to neglect; (*olvidar*) to overlook;
descuidarse *vr* (*distraerse*) to be
careless; (*abandonarse*) to let o.s. go;
(*desprevenirse*) to drop one's guard;
¡descuida! don't worry!; **descuido**
nm (*dejadez*) carelessness; (*olvido*)
negligence

○ **PALABRA CLAVE**

desde ['desðe] *prep* 1 (*lugar*) from;
**desde Burgos hasta mi casa hay 30
km** it's 30 km from Burgos to my house
2 (*posición*): **hablaba desde el balcón**

she was speaking from the balcony
3 (*tiempo*: + *adv*, *n*): **desde ahora** from
now on; **desde la boda** since the
wedding; **desde niño** since I *etc* was
a child; **desde 3 años atrás** since 3
years ago
4 (*tiempo*: + *vb*, *fecha*) since; for; **nos
conocemos desde 1992/desde hace
20 años** we've known each other since
1992/for 20 years; **no le veo desde
1997/desde hace 5 años** I haven't seen
him since 1997/for 5 years
5 (*gama*): **desde los más lujosos hasta
los más económicos** from the most
luxurious to the most reasonably
priced
6: **desde luego (que no)** of course
(not)
▷ *conj*: **desde que: desde que
recuerdo** for as long as I can
remember; **desde que llegó no ha
salido** he hasn't been out since he
arrived

desdén [des'ðen] *nm* scorn

desdeñar [desðe'ɲar] *vt* (*despreciar*)
to scorn

desdicha [des'ðitʃa] *nf* (*desgracia*)
misfortune; (*infelicidad*) unhappiness;
desdichado, -a *adj* (*sin suerte*)
unlucky; (*infeliz*) unhappy

desear [dese'ar] *vt* to want, desire,
wish for

desechar [dese'tʃar] *vt* (*basura*) to
throw out o away; (*ideas*) to reject,
discard; **desechos** *nmpl* rubbish *sg*,
waste *sg*

desembalar [desemba'lar] *vt* to
unpack

desembarazar [desembara'θar] *vt*
(*desocupar*) to clear; (*desenredar*) to free;
desembarazarse *vr*: **-se de** to free o.s.
of, get rid of

desembarcar [desembar'kar] *vt*
(*mercancías etc*) to unload ▷ *vi* to
disembark

desembocadura [desembokaˈðura]
nf (*de río*) mouth; (*de calle*) opening

desembocar [desembo'kar] vi (río) to flow into; (fig) to result in

desembolso [desem'bolso] nm payment

desembrollar [desembro'ʎar] vt (madeja) to unravel; (asunto, malentendido) to sort out

desemejanza [deseme'xanθa] nf dissimilarity

desempaquetar [desempake'tar] vt (regalo) to unwrap; (mercancía) to unpack

desempate [desem'pate] nm (Fútbol) replay, play-off; (Tenis) tie-break(er)

desempeñar [desempe'ɲar] vt (cargo) to hold; (papel) to perform; (lo empeñado) to redeem; **~ un papel** (fig) to play (a role)

desempleado, -a [desemple'aðo, a] nm/f unemployed person; **desempleo** nm unemployment

desencadenar [desenkaðe'nar] vt to unchain; (ira) to unleash; **desencadenarse** vr to break loose; (tormenta) to burst; (guerra) to break out

desencajar [desenka'xar] vt (hueso) to dislocate; (mecanismo, pieza) to disconnect, disengage

desencanto [desen'kanto] nm disillusionment

desenchufar [desentʃu'far] vt to unplug

desenfadado, -a [desenfa'ðaðo, a] adj (desenvuelto) uninhibited; (descarado) forward; **desenfado** nm (libertad) freedom; (comportamiento) free and easy manner; (descaro) forwardness

desenfocado, -a [desenfo'kaðo, a] adj (Foto) out of focus

desenfreno [desen'freno] nm wildness; (de las pasiones) lack of self-control

desenganchar [desengan'tʃar] vt (gen) to unhook; (Ferro) to uncouple

desengañar [desenga'ɲar] vt to disillusion; **desengañarse** vr to become disillusioned; **desengaño**

nm disillusionment; (decepción) disappointment

desenlace [desen'laθe] nm outcome

desenmascarar [desenmaska'rar] vt to unmask

desenredar [desenre'ðar] vt (pelo) to untangle; (problema) to sort out

desenroscar [desenros'kar] vt to unscrew

desentenderse [desenten'derse] vr: **~ de** to pretend not to know about; (apartarse) to have nothing to do with

desenterrar [desente'rrar] vt to exhume; (tesoro, fig) to unearth, dig up

desentonar [desento'nar] vi (Mús) to sing (o play) out of tune; (color) to clash

desentrañar [desentra'ɲar] vt (misterio) to unravel

desenvoltura [desenβol'tura] nf ease

desenvolver [desenβol'βer] vt (paquete) to unwrap; (fig) to develop; **desenvolverse** vr (desarrollarse) to unfold, develop; (arreglárselas) to cope

deseo [de'seo] nm desire, wish; **deseoso, -a** adj: **estar deseoso de** to be anxious to

desequilibrado, -a [desekili'βraðo, a] adj unbalanced

desertar [deser'tar] vi to desert

desértico, -a [de'sertiko, a] adj desert cpd

desesperación [desespera'θjon] nf (impaciencia) desperation, despair; (irritación) fury

desesperar [desespe'rar] vt to drive to despair; (exasperar) to drive to distraction ▸ vi: **~ de** to despair of; **desesperarse** vr to despair, lose hope

desestabilizar [desestaβili'θar] vt to destabilize

desestimar [desesti'mar] vt (menospreciar) to have a low opinion of; (rechazar) to reject

desfachatez [desfatʃa'teθ] nf (insolencia) impudence; (descaro) rudeness

desfalco [des'falko] nm embezzlement

desfallecer [desfaʎe'θer] vi (perder las fuerzas) to become weak; (desvanecerse) to faint

desfasado, -a [desfa'saðo, a] adj (anticuado) old-fashioned; **desfase** nm (diferencia) gap

desfavorable [desfaβo'raβle] adj unfavourable

desfigurar [desfiɣu'rar] vt (cara) to disfigure; (cuerpo) to deform

desfiladero [desfila'ðero] nm gorge

desfilar [desfi'lar] vi to parade; **desfile** nm procession; **desfile de modelos** fashion show

desgana [des'ɣana] nf (falta de apetito) loss of appetite; (apatía) unwillingness; **desganado, -a** adj: **estar desganado** (sin apetito) to have no appetite; (sin entusiasmo) to have lost interest

desgarrar [desɣa'rrar] vt to tear (up); (fig) to shatter; **desgarro** nm (en tela) tear; (aflicción) grief

desgastar [desɣas'tar] vt (deteriorar) to wear away o down; (estropear) to spoil; **desgastarse** vr to get worn out; **desgaste** nm wear (and tear)

desglosar [desɣlo'sar] vt (factura) to break down

desgracia [des'ɣraθja] nf misfortune; (accidente) accident; (vergüenza) disgrace; (contratiempo) setback; **por ~** unfortunately; **desgraciado, -a** [desɣra'θjaðo, a] adj (sin suerte) unlucky, unfortunate; (miserable) wretched; (infeliz) miserable

desgravar [desɣra'βar] vt (impuestos) to reduce the tax o duty on

desguace [des'ɣwaθe] (ESP) nm junkyard

deshabitado, -a [desaβi'taðo, a] adj uninhabited

deshacer [desa'θer] vt (casa) to break up; (Tec) to take apart; (enemigo) to defeat; (diluir) to melt; (contrato) to break; (intriga) to solve; **deshacerse**

vr (disolverse) to melt; (despedazarse) to come apart o undone; **~se de** to get rid of; **~se en lágrimas** to burst into tears

deshecho, -a [des'etʃo, a] adj undone; (roto) smashed; (persona): **estar ~** to be shattered

desheredar [desere'ðar] vt to disinherit

deshidratar [desiðra'tar] vt to dehydrate

deshielo [des'jelo] nm thaw

deshonesto, -a [deso'nesto, a] adj indecent

deshonra [des'onra] nf (deshonor) dishonour; (vergüenza) shame

deshora [des'ora]: **a ~** adv at the wrong time

deshuesadero [deswesa'ðero] (MÉX) nm junkyard

deshuesar [deswe'sar] vt (carne) to bone; (fruta) to stone

desierto, -a [de'sjerto, a] adj (casa, calle, negocio) deserted ▷ nm desert

designar [desiɣ'nar] vt (nombrar) to designate; (indicar) to fix

desigual [desi'ɣwal] adj (terreno) uneven; (lucha etc) unequal

desilusión [desilu'sjon] nf disillusionment; (decepción) disappointment; **desilusionar** vt to disillusion; to disappoint; **desilusionarse** vr to become disillusioned

desinfectar [desinfek'tar] vt to disinfect

desinflar [desin'flar] vt to deflate

desintegración [desinteɣra'θjon] nf disintegration

desinterés [desinte'res] nm (desgana) lack of interest; (altruismo) unselfishness

desintoxicarse [desintoksi'karse] vr (drogadicto) to undergo detoxification

desistir [desis'tir] vi (renunciar) to stop, desist

desleal [desle'al] adj (infiel) disloyal; (Com: competencia) unfair; **deslealtad**

nf disloyalty

desligar [desli'ɣar] vt (*desatar*) to untie, undo; (*separar*) to separate; **desligarse** vr (*de un compromiso*) to extricate o.s.

desliz [des'liθ] nm (*fig*) lapse; **deslizar** vt to slip, slide

deslumbrar [deslum'brar] vt to dazzle

desmadrarse [desma'ðrarse] (*fam*) vr (*descontrolarse*) to run wild; (*divertirse*) to let one's hair down; **desmadre** (*fam*) nm (*desorganización*) chaos; (*jaleo*) commotion

desmán [des'man] nm (*exceso*) outrage; (*abuso de poder*) abuse

desmantelar [desmante'lar] vt (*deshacer*) to dismantle; (*casa*) to strip

desmaquillador [desmakiʎa'ðor] nm make-up remover

desmayar [desma'jar] vi to lose heart; **desmayarse** vr (*Med*) to faint; **desmayo** nm (*Med: acto*) faint; (*: estado*) unconsciousness

desmemoriado, -a [desmemo'rjaðo, a] adj forgetful

desmentir [desmen'tir] vt (*contradecir*) to contradict; (*refutar*) to deny

desmenuzar [desmenu'θar] vt (*deshacer*) to crumble; (*carne*) to chop; (*examinar*) to examine closely

desmesurado, -a [desmesu'raðo, a] adj disproportionate

desmontable [desmon'taβle] adj (*que se quita: pieza*) detachable; (*plegable*) collapsible, folding

desmontar [desmon'tar] vt (*deshacer*) to dismantle; (*tierra*) to level ▷ vi to dismount

desmoralizar [desmorali'θar] vt to demoralize

desmoronar [desmoro'nar] vt to wear away, erode; **desmoronarse** vr (*edificio, dique*) to collapse; (*economía*) to decline

desnatado, -a [desna'taðo, a] adj skimmed

desnivel [desni'βel] nm (*de terreno*) unevenness

desnudar [desnu'ðar] vt (*desvestir*) to undress; (*despojar*) to strip; **desnudarse** vr (*desvestirse*) to get undressed; **desnudo, -a** adj naked ▷ nm/f nude; **desnudo de** devoid o bereft of

desnutrición [desnutri'θjon] nf malnutrition; **desnutrido, -a** adj undernourished

desobedecer [desoβeðe'θer] vt, vi to disobey; **desobediencia** nf disobedience

desocupado, -a [desoku'paðo, a] adj at leisure; (*desempleado*) unemployed; (*deshabitado*) empty, vacant

desodorante [desoðo'rante] nm deodorant

desolación [desola'θjon] nf (*de lugar*) desolation; (*fig*) grief

desolar [deso'lar] vt to ruin, lay waste

desorbitado, -a [desorβi'taðo, a] adj (*excesivo: ambición*) boundless; (*deseos*) excessive; (*: precio*) exorbitant

desorden [des'orðen] nm confusion; (*político*) disorder, unrest

desorganización [desorɣaniθa'θjon] nf (*de persona*) disorganization; (*en empresa, oficina*) disorder, chaos

desorientar [desorjen'tar] vt (*extraviar*) to mislead; (*confundir, desconcertar*) to confuse; **desorientarse** vr (*perderse*) to lose one's way

despabilado, -a [despaβi'laðo, a] adj (*despierto*) wide-awake; (*fig*) alert, sharp

despachar [despa'tʃar] vt (*negocio*) to do, complete; (*enviar*) to send, dispatch; (*vender*) to sell, deal in; (*billete*) to issue; (*mandar ir*) to send away

despacho [des'patʃo] nm (*oficina*) office; (*de paquetes*) dispatch; (*venta*) sale; (*comunicación*) message

despacio [des'paθjo] adv slowly

desparpajo [despar'paxo] nm self-confidence; (pey) nerve

desparramar [desparra'mar] vt (esparcir) to scatter; (líquido) to spill

despecho [des'petʃo] nm spite

despectivo, -a [despek'tiβo, a] adj (despreciativo) derogatory; (Ling) pejorative

despedida [despe'ðiða] nf (adiós) farewell; (de obrero) sacking

despedir [despe'ðir] vt (visita) to see off, show out; (empleado) to dismiss; (inquilino) to evict; (objeto) to hurl; (olor etc) to give out o off; despedirse vr: ~se de to say goodbye to

despegar [despe'ɣar] vt to unstick ▷ vi (avión) to take off; despegarse vr to come loose, come unstuck; despego nm detachment

despegue etc [des'peɣe] vb V despegar ▷ nm takeoff

despeinado, -a [despei'naðo, a] adj dishevelled, unkempt

despejado, -a [despe'xaðo, a] adj (lugar) clear, free; (cielo) clear; (persona) wide-awake, bright

despejar [despe'xar] vt (gen) to clear; (misterio) to clear up ▷ vi (el tiempo) to clear; despejarse vr (tiempo, cielo) to clear (up); (misterio) to become clearer; (cabeza) to clear

despensa [des'pensa] nf larder

despeñarse [despe'ɲarse] vr to hurl o.s. down; (coche) to tumble over

desperdicio [desper'ðiθjo] nm (despilfarro) squandering; desperdicios nmpl (basura) rubbish sg (BRIT), garbage sg (US); (residuos) waste sg

desperezarse [despere'θarse] vr to stretch

desperfecto [desper'fekto] nm (deterioro) slight damage; (defecto) flaw, imperfection

despertador [desperta'ðor] nm alarm clock

despertar [desper'tar] nm awakening ▷ vt (persona) to wake up; (recuerdos) to revive; (sentimiento) to arouse ▷ vi to awaken, wake up;

despertarse vr to awaken, wake up

despido etc [des'piðo] vb V despedir ▷ nm dismissal, sacking

despierto, -a etc [des'pjerto, a] vb V despertar ▷ adj awake; (fig) sharp, alert

despilfarro [despil'farro] nm (derroche) squandering; (lujo desmedido) extravagance

despistar [despis'tar] vt to throw off the track o scent; (confundir) to mislead, confuse; despistarse vr to take the wrong road; (confundirse) to become confused

despiste [des'piste] nm absent-mindedness; un ~ a mistake o slip

desplazamiento [desplaθa'mjento] nm displacement

desplazar [despla'θar] vt to move; (Náut) to displace; (Inform) to scroll; (fig) to oust; desplazarse vr (persona) to travel

desplegar [desple'ɣar] vt (tela, papel) to unfold, open out; (bandera) to unfurl; despliegue etc [des'pleɣe] vb V desplegar ▷ nm display

desplomarse [desplo'marse] vr (edificio, gobierno, persona) to collapse

desplumar [desplu'mar] vt (ave) to pluck; (fam: estafar) to fleece

despoblado, -a [despo'βlaðo, a] adj (sin habitantes) uninhabited

despojar [despo'xar] vt (alguien: de sus bienes) to divest of, deprive of; (casa) to strip, leave bare; (alguien: de su cargo) to strip of

despojo [des'poxo] nm (acto) plundering; (objetos) plunder, loot; despojos nmpl (de ave, res) offal sg

desposado, -a [despo'saðo, a] adj, nm/f newly-wed

despreciar [despre'θjar] vt (desdeñar) to despise, scorn; (afrentar) to slight; desprecio nm scorn, contempt; slight

desprender [despren'der] vt (broche) to unfasten; (olor) to give off; desprenderse vr (botón: caerse) to fall off; (broche) to come unfastened; (olor, perfume) to throw off; **~se de algo que ...** to draw from sth that ...

desprendimiento
[desprendi'mjento] nm (gen)
loosening; (generosidad)
disinterestedness; (de tierra, rocas)
landslide; **desprendimiento de retina**
detachment of the retina

despreocupado, -a
[despreoku'paðo, a] adj (sin
preocupación) unworried, nonchalant;
(negligente) careless

despreocuparse [despreoku'parse]
vr not to worry; **~ de** to have no
interest in

desprestigiar [despresti'xjar] vt
(criticar) to run down; (desacreditar) to
discredit

desprevenido, -a [despreβe'niðo,
a] adj (no preparado) unprepared,
unready

desproporcionado, -a
[despropor θjo'naðo, a] adj
disproportionate, out of proportion

desprovisto, -a [despro'βisto, a]
adj: **~ de** devoid of

después [des'pwes] adv afterwards,
later; (próximo paso) next; **~ de comer**
after lunch; **un año ~** a year later; **~ se
debatió el tema** next the matter was
discussed; **~ de corregido el texto**
after the text had been corrected; **~ de
todo** after all

desquiciado, -a [deski'θjaðo, a]
adj deranged

destacar [desta'kar] vt to
emphasize, point up; (Mil) to detach,
detail ▷ vi (resaltarse) to stand
out; (persona) to be outstanding o
exceptional; **destacarse** vr to stand
out; to be outstanding o exceptional

destajo [des'taxo] nm: **trabajar a ~** to
do piecework

destapar [desta'par] vt (botella)
to open; (cacerola) to take the lid off;
(descubrir) to uncover; **destaparse** vr
(revelarse) to reveal one's true character

destartalado, -a [destarta'laðo,

a] adj (desordenado) untidy; (ruinoso)
tumbledown

destello [des'teʎo] nm (de estrella)
twinkle; (de faro) signal light

destemplado, -a [destem'plaðo, a]
adj (Mús) out of tune; (voz) harsh; (Med)
out of sorts; (tiempo) unpleasant, nasty

desteñir [deste'nir] vt to fade ▷ vi to
fade; **desteñirse** vr to fade; **esta tela
no destiñe** this fabric will not run

desternillarse [desterni'ʎarse] vr:
~ de risa to split one's sides laughing

desterrar [deste'rrar] vt (exiliar) to
exile; (fig) to banish, dismiss

destiempo [des'tjempo]: **a ~** adv
out of turn

destierro etc [des'tjerro] vb V
desterrar ▷ nm exile

destilar [desti'lar] vt to distil;
destilería nf distillery

destinar [desti'nar] vt (funcionario)
to appoint, assign; (fondos): **~ (a)** to set
aside (for)

destinatario, -a [destina'tarjo, a]
nm/f addressee

destino [des'tino] nm (suerte)
destiny; (de avión, viajero) destination;
con ~ a Londres (barco) (bound) for
London; (avión, carta) to London

destituir [destitu'ir] vt to dismiss

destornillador [destorniʎa'ðor] nm
screwdriver

destornillar [destorni'ʎar] vt
(tornillo) to unscrew; **destornillarse** vr
to unscrew

destreza [des'treθa] nf (habilidad)
skill; (maña) dexterity

destrozar [destro'θar] vt (romper) to
smash, break (up); (estropear) to ruin;
(nervios) to shatter

destrozo [des'troθo] nm (acción)
destruction; (desastre) smashing;
destrozos nmpl (pedazos) pieces;
(daños) havoc sg

destrucción [destruk'θjon] nf
destruction

destruir [destru'ir] vt to destroy

desuso [des'uso] nm disuse; **caer en**

~ to become obsolete

desvalijar [desbali'xar] vt (persona) to rob; (casa, tienda) to burgle; (coche) to break into

desván [des'βan] nm attic

desvanecer [desβane'θer] vt (disipar) to dispel; (borrar) to blur; **desvanecerse** vr (humo etc) to vanish, disappear; (color) to fade; (recuerdo, sonido) to fade away; (Med) to pass out; (duda) to be dispelled

desvariar [desβa'rjar] vi (enfermo) to be delirious

desvelar [desβe'lar] vt to keep awake; **desvelarse** vr (no poder dormir) to stay awake; (preocuparse) to be vigilant o watchful

desventaja [desβen'taxa] nf disadvantage

desvergonzado, -a [desβerɣon'θaðo, a] adj shameless

desvestir [desβes'tir] vt to undress; **desvestirse** vr to undress

desviación [desβja'θjon] nf deviation; (Auto) diversion, detour

desviar [des'βjar] vt to turn aside; (río) to alter the course of; (navío) to divert, re-route; (conversación) to sidetrack; **desviarse** vr (apartarse del camino) to turn aside; (: barco) to go off course

desvío etc [des'βio] vb V **desviar** ▷ nm (desviación) detour, diversion; (fig) indifference

desvivirse [desβi'βirse] vr: ~ **por** (anhelar) to long for, crave for; (hacer lo posible por) to do one's utmost for

detallar [deta'ʎar] vt to detail

detalle [de'taʎe] nm detail; (gesto) gesture, token; **al ~** in detail; (Com) retail

detallista [deta'ʎista] nmf (Com) retailer

detective [detek'tiβe] nmf detective; **detective privado** private detective

detener [dete'ner] vt (gen) to stop; (Jur) to arrest; (objeto) to keep, detain; (demorarse): **~se** to stop; (demorarse): **~se**

en to delay over, linger over

detenidamente [deteniða'mente] adv (minuciosamente) carefully; (extensamente) at great length

detenido, -a [dete'niðo, a] adj (arrestado) under arrest ▷ nm/f person under arrest, prisoner

detenimiento [deteni'mjento] nm: **con ~** thoroughly; (observar, considerar) carefully

detergente [deter'xente] nm detergent

deteriorar [deterjo'rar] vt to spoil, damage; **deteriorarse** vr to deteriorate; **deterioro** nm deterioration

determinación [determina'θjon] nf (empeño) determination; (decisión) decision; **determinado, -a** adj specific

determinar [determi'nar] vt (plazo) to fix; (precio) to settle; **determinarse** vr to decide

detestar [detes'tar] vt to detest

detractor, a [detrak'tor, a] nm/f slanderer, libeller

detrás [de'tras] adv (tb: **por~**) behind; (atrás) at the back; **~ de** behind

detrimento [detri'mento] nm: **en ~ de** to the detriment of

deuda [ˈdeuða] nf debt; **deuda exterior/pública** foreign/national debt

devaluación [deβalwa'θjon] nf devaluation

devastar [deβas'tar] vt (destruir) to devastate

deveras [de'βeras] (MÉX) nf inv: **un amigo de (a) ~** a true o real friend

devoción [deβo'θjon] nf devotion

devolución [deβolu'θjon] nf (reenvío) return, sending back; (reembolso) repayment; (Jur) devolution

devolver [deβol'βer] vt to return; (lo extraviado, lo prestado) to give back; (carta al correo) to send back; (Com) to repay, refund ▷ vi (vomitar) to be sick

devorar [deβo'rar] vt to devour

devoto, -a [de'βoto, a] *adj* devout
▷ *nm/f* admirer

devuelto *pp de* **devolver**

devuelva *etc vb* V **devolver**

di *etc vb* V **dar; decir**

día ['dia] *nm* day; **¿qué - es?** what's
the date?; **estar/poner a ~** to be/keep
up to date; **el ~ de hoy/de mañana**
today/tomorrow; **al ~ siguiente** (on)
the following day; **vivir al ~** to live from
hand to mouth; **de ~** by day, in daylight;
en pleno ~ in full daylight; Día de la
Independencia Independence Day;
Día de los Muertos (*MÉX*) All Souls'
Day; Día de Reyes Epiphany; **día
feriado** (*LAM*) holiday; **día festivo** (*ESP*)
holiday; **día lectivo** teaching day; **día
libre** day off

diabetes [dja'βetes] *nf* diabetes

diablo ['djaβlo] *nm* devil; **diablura**
nf prank

diadema [dja'ðema] *nf* tiara

diafragma [dja'fraɣma] *nm*
diaphragm

diagnóstico [diax'nostiko] *nm* =
diagnosis

diagonal [djaɣo'nal] *adj* diagonal

diagrama [dja'ɣrama] *nm* diagram

dial [djal] *nm* dial

dialecto [dja'lekto] *nm* dialect

dialogar [djalo'ɣar] *vi*: **~ con** (*Pol*) to
hold talks with

diálogo ['djaloɣo] *nm* dialogue

diamante [dja'mante] *nm* diamond

diana ['djana] *nf* (*Mil*) reveille; (*de
blanco*) centre, bull's-eye

diapositiva [djaposi'tiβa] *nf* (*Foto*)
slide, transparency

diario, -a ['djarjo, a] *adj* daily ▷ *nm*
newspaper; **a ~** daily; **de ~**
everyday

diarrea [dja'rrea] *nf* diarrhoea

dibujar [diβu'xar] *vt* to draw,
sketch; **dibujo** *nm* drawing; **dibujos
animados** cartoons

diccionario [dikθjo'narjo] *nm*
dictionary

dice *etc vb* V **decir**

dicho, -a ['ditʃo, a] *pp de* **decir**
▷ *adj*: **en ~s países** in the
aforementioned countries ▷ *nm*
saying

dichoso, -a [di'tʃoso, a] *adj* happy

diciembre [di'θjembre] *nm*
December

dictado [dik'taðo] *nm* dictation

dictador [dikta'ðor] *nm* dictator;
dictadura *nf* dictatorship

dictar [dik'tar] *vt* (*carta*) to dictate;
(*Jur: sentencia*) to pronounce; (*decreto*) to
issue; (*LAM: clase*) to give

didáctico, -a [di'ðaktiko, a] *adj*
educational

diecinueve [djeθi'nweβe] *num*
nineteen

dieciocho [djeθi'otʃo] *num* eighteen

dieciséis [djeθi'seis] *num* sixteen

diecisiete [djeθi'sjete] *num*
seventeen

diente ['djente] *nm* (*Anat, Tec*) tooth;
(*Zool*) fang; (*: de elefante*) tusk; (*de
ajo*) clove

diera *etc vb* V **dar**

diesel ['disel] *adj*: **motor ~** diesel
engine

diestro, -a ['djestro, a] *adj* (*derecho*)
right; (*hábil*) skilful

dieta ['djeta] *nf* diet; **estar a ~** to be
on a diet

diez [djeθ] *num* ten

diferencia [dife'renθja] *nf*
difference; **a ~ de** unlike; **diferenciar**
vt to differentiate between ▷ *vi* to
differ; **diferenciarse** *vr* to differ, be
different; (*distinguirse*) to distinguish
o.s.

diferente [dife'rente] *adj* different

diferido [dife'riðo] *nm*: **en ~** (*TV etc*)
recorded

difícil [di'fiθil] *adj* difficult

dificultad [difikul'tað] *nf* difficulty;
(*problema*) trouble

dificultar [difikul'tar] *vt* (*complicar*)
to complicate, make difficult; (*estorbar*)
to obstruct

difundir [difun'dir] *vt* (*calor, luz*)
to diffuse; (*Radio, TV*) to broadcast; **~**

una noticia to spread a piece of news; **difundirse** vr to spread (out)

difunto, -a [di'funto, a] adj dead, deceased ▷ nm/f deceased (person)

difusión [difu'sjon] nf (Radio, TV) broadcasting

diga etc vb V **decir**

digerir [dixe'rir] vt to digest; (fig) to absorb; **digestión** nf digestion; **digestivo, -a** adj digestive

digital [dixi'tal] adj digital

dignarse [diɣ'narse] vr to deign to

dignidad [diɣni'ðað] nf dignity

digno, -a ['diɣno, a] adj worthy

digo etc vb V **decir**

dije etc vb V **decir**

dilatar [dila'tar] vt (cuerpo) to dilate; (prolongar) to prolong

dilema [di'lema] nm dilemma

diluir [dilu'ir] vt to dilute

diluvio [di'luβjo] nm deluge, flood

dimensión [dimen'sjon] nf dimension

diminuto, -a [dimi'nuto, a] adj tiny, diminutive

dimitir [dimi'tir] vi to resign

dimos vb V **dar**

Dinamarca [dina'marka] nf Denmark

dinámico, -a [di'namiko, a] adj dynamic

dinamita [dina'mita] nf dynamite

dínamo ['dinamo] nf dynamo

dineral [dine'ral] nm large sum of money, fortune

dinero [di'nero] nm money; **dinero en efectivo** o **metálico** cash; **dinero suelto** (loose) change

dio vb V **dar**

dios [djos] nm god; **¡D~ mío!** (oh,) my God!; **¡por D~!** for heaven's sake!; **diosa** ['djosa] nf goddess

diploma [di'ploma] nm diploma

diplomacia [diplo'maθja] nf diplomacy; (fig) tact

diplomado, -a [diplo'maðo, a] adj qualified

diplomático, -a [diplo'matiko, a]

adj diplomatic ▷ nm/f diplomat

diputación [diputa'θjon] nf (tb: **~ provincial**) ≈ county council

diputado, -a [dipu'taðo, a] nm/f delegate; (Pol) ≈ member of parliament (BRIT) ≈ representative (US)

dique ['dike] nm dyke

diré etc vb V **decir**

dirección [direk'θjon] nf direction; (señas) address; (Auto) steering; (gerencia) management; (Pol) leadership; **dirección única/ prohibida** one-way street/no entry

direccional [direkθjo'nal] (MÉX) nf (Auto) indicator

directa [di'rekta] nf (Auto) top gear

directiva [direk'tiβa] nf (tb: **junta ~**) board of directors

directo, -a [di'rekto, a] adj direct; (Radio, TV) live; **transmitir en ~** to broadcast live

director, a [direk'tor, a] adj leading ▷ nm/f director; (Escol) head(teacher) (BRIT); principal (US); (gerente) manager/ess; (Prensa) editor; **director de cine** film director; **director general** managing director

directorio [direk'torjo] (MÉX) nm (telefónico) phone book

dirigente [diri'xente] nmf (Pol) leader

dirigir [diri'xir] vt (carta) to address; (obra de teatro, film) to direct; (Mús) to conduct; (negocio) to manage; **dirigirse** vr: **~se a** to go towards, make one's way towards; (hablar con) to speak to

dirija etc vb V **dirigir**

disciplina [disθi'plina] nf discipline

discípulo, -a [dis'θipulo, a] nm/f disciple

Discman® ['diskman] nm Discman®

disco ['disko] nm disc; (Deporte) discus; (Tel) dial; (Auto: semáforo) light; (Mús) record; **disco compacto/de larga duración** compact disc/long-playing record; **disco de freno** brake disc; **disco flexible/duro** o rígido (*Inform*) floppy/hard disk

disconforme [diskon'forme] *adj* differing; **estar ~ (con)** to be in disagreement (with)

discordia [dis'korðja] *nf* discord

discoteca [disko'teka] *nf* disco(theque)

discreción [diskre'θjon] *nf* discretion; (*reserva*) prudence; **comer a ~** to eat as much as one wishes

discreto, -a [dis'kreto, a] *adj* discreet

discriminación [diskrimina'θjon] *nf* discrimination

disculpa [dis'kulpa] *nf* excuse; (*pedir perdón*) apology; **pedir ~s a/por** to apologize to/for; **disculpar** *vt* to excuse, pardon; **disculparse** *vr* to excuse o.s.; to apologize

discurso [dis'kurso] *nm* speech

discusión [disku'sjon] *nf* (*diálogo*) discussion; (*riña*) argument

discutir [disku'tir] *vt* (*debatir*) to discuss; (*pelear*) to argue about; (*contradecir*) to argue against ▷ *vi* (*debatir*) to discuss; (*pelearse*) to argue

disecar [dise'kar] *vt* (*conservar*: *animal*) to stuff; (*planta*) to dry

diseñar [dise'nar] *vt, vi* to design

diseño [di'seno] *nm* design

disfraz [dis'fraθ] *nm* (*máscara*) disguise; (*excusa*) pretext; **disfrazar** *vt* to disguise; **disfrazarse** *vr*: **disfrazarse de** to disguise o.s. as

disfrutar [disfru'tar] *vt* to enjoy ▷ *vi* to enjoy o.s.; **~ de** to enjoy, possess

disgustar [disɣus'tar] *vt* (*no gustar*) to displease; (*contrariar, enojar*) to annoy, upset; **disgustarse** *vr* (*enfadarse*) to get upset; (*dos personas*) to fall out

   No confundir **disgustar** con la palabra inglesa *disgust*.

disgusto [dis'ɣusto] *nm* (*contrariedad*) annoyance; (*tristeza*) grief; (*riña*) quarrel

disimular [disimu'lar] *vt* (*ocultar*) to hide, conceal ▷ *vi* to dissemble

dislocarse [dislo'karse] *vr* (*articulación*) to sprain, dislocate

disminución [disminu'θjon] *nf* decrease, reduction

disminuido, -a [dismi'nwiðo, a] *nm/f*: **~ mental/físico** mentally/physically handicapped person

disminuir [disminu'ir] *vt* to decrease, diminish

disolver [disol'βer] *vt* (*gen*) to dissolve; **disolverse** *vr* to dissolve; (*Com*) to go into liquidation

dispar [dis'par] *adj* different

disparar [dispa'rar] *vt, vi* to shoot, fire

disparate [dispa'rate] *nm* (*tontería*) foolish remark; (*error*) blunder; **decir ~s** to talk nonsense

disparo [dis'paro] *nm* shot

dispersar [disper'sar] *vt* to disperse; **dispersarse** *vr* to scatter

disponer [dispo'ner] *vt* (*arreglar*) to arrange; (*ordenar*) to put in order; (*preparar*) to prepare, get ready ▷ *vi*: **~ de** to have, own; **disponerse** *vr*: **~se a** o **para hacer** to prepare to do

disponible [dispo'niβle] *adj* available

disposición [disposi'θjon] *nf* arrangement, disposition; (*voluntad*) willingness; (*Inform*) layout; **a su ~** at your service

dispositivo [disposi'tiβo] *nm* device, mechanism

dispuesto, -a [dis'pwesto, a] *pp de* **disponer** ▷ *adj* (*arreglado*) arranged; (*preparado*) prepared

disputar [dispu'tar] *vt* (*carrera*) to compete in

disquete [dis'kete] *nm* floppy disk, diskette

distancia [dis'tanθja] *nf* distance; **distanciar** [distan'θjar] *vt* to space out; **distanciarse** *vr* to become estranged; **distante** [dis'tante] *adj* distant

diste *vb* V **dar**

disteis *vb* V **dar**

distinción [distin'θjon] nf distinction; (elegancia) elegance; (honor) honour

distinguido, -a [distin'giðo, a] adj distinguished

distinguir [distin'gir] vt to distinguish; (escoger) to single out; **distinguirse** vr to be distinguished

distintivo [distin'tiβo] nm badge; (fig) characteristic

distinto, -a [dis'tinto, a] adj different; (claro) clear

distracción [distrak'θjon] nf distraction; (pasatiempo) hobby, pastime; (olvido) absent-mindedness, distraction

distraer [distra'er] vt (atención) to distract; (divertir) to amuse; (fondos) to embezzle; **distraerse** vr (entretenerse) to amuse o.s.; (perder la concentración) to allow one's attention to wander

distraído, -a [distra'iðo, a] adj (gen) absent-minded; (entretenido) amusing

distribuidor, a [distriβwi'ðor, a] nm/f distributor; **distribuidora** nf (Com) dealer, agent; (Cine) distributor

distribuir [distriβu'ir] vt to distribute

distrito [dis'trito] nm (sector, territorio) region; (barrio) district;
  Distrito Federal (MÉX) Federal District;
  distrito postal postal district

disturbio [dis'turβjo] nm disturbance; (desorden) riot

disuadir [diswa'ðir] vt to dissuade

disuelto [di'swelto] pp de **disolver**

DIU nm abr (= dispositivo intrauterino) IUD

diurno, -a ['djurno, a] adj day cpd

divagar [diβa'xar] vi (desviarse) to digress

diván [di'βan] nm divan

diversidad [diβersi'ðað] nf diversity, variety

diversión [diβer'sjon] nf (gen) entertainment; (actividad) hobby, pastime

diverso, -a [di'βerso, a] adj diverse;

~s libros several books; **diversos** nmpl sundries

divertido, -a [diβer'tiðo, a] adj (chiste) amusing; (fiesta etc) enjoyable

divertir [diβer'tir] vt (entretener, recrear) to amuse; **divertirse** vr (pasarlo bien) to have a good time; (distraerse) to amuse o.s.

dividendos [diβi'ðendos] nmpl (Com) dividends

dividir [diβi'ðir] vt (gen) to divide; (distribuir) to distribute, share out

divierta etc vb V **divertir**

divino, -a [di'βino, a] adj divine

divirtiendo etc vb V **divertir**

divisa [di'βisa] nf (emblema) emblem, badge; **divisas** nfpl foreign exchange sg

divisar [diβi'sar] vt to make out, distinguish

división [diβi'sjon] nf (gen) division; (de partido) split; (de país) partition

divorciar [diβor'θjar] vt to divorce; **divorciarse** vr to get divorced; **divorcio** nm divorce

divulgar [diβul'xar] vt (ideas) to spread; (secreto) to divulge

DNI (ESP) nm abr (= Documento Nacional de Identidad) national identity card

● **DNI**
●
● The **Documento Nacional de Identidad** is a Spanish ID card which must be carried at all times and produced on request for the police. It contains the holder's photo, fingerprints and personal details. It is also known as the **DNI** or "carnet de identidad".

Dña. abr (= doña) Mrs

do [do] nm (Mús) do, C

dobladillo [doβla'ðiλo] nm (de vestido) hem; (de pantalón: inferior) turn-up (BRIT), cuff (US)

doblar [do'βlar] vt to double; (papel) to fold; (caño) to bend; (la esquina) turn, go round; (*film*) to dub ▷ *vi* to turn; (*campana*) to toll; **doblarse** *vr* (*plegarse*) to fold (up), crease; (*encorvarse*) to bend; **~ a la derecha/izquierda** to turn right/left

doble ['doβle] *adj* double; (*de dos aspectos*) dual; (*fig*) two-faced ▷ *nm* double ▷ *nmf* (*Teatro*) double, stand-in; **dobles** *nmpl* (*Deporte*) doubles *sg*; **con ~ sentido** with a double meaning

doce ['doθe] *num* twelve; **docena** *nf* dozen

docente [do'θente] *adj*: **centro/personal ~** teaching establishment/staff

dócil ['doθil] *adj* (*pasivo*) docile; (*obediente*) obedient

doctor, a [dok'tor, a] *nm/f* doctor

doctorado [dokto'raðo] *nm* doctorate

doctrina [dok'trina] *nf* doctrine, teaching

documentación [dokumenta'θjon] *nf* documentation, papers *pl*

documental [dokumen'tal] *adj, nm* documentary

documento [doku'mento] *nm* (*certificado*) document; **documento adjunto** (*Inform*) attachment; **documento nacional de identidad** identity card

dólar ['dolar] *nm* dollar

doler [do'ler] *vt, vi* to hurt; (*fig*) to grieve; **dolerse** *vr* (*de su situación*) to grieve, feel sorry; (*de las desgracias ajenas*) to sympathize; **me duele el brazo** my arm hurts

dolor [do'lor] *nm* pain; (*fig*) grief, sorrow; **dolor de cabeza/estómago/muelas** headache/stomachache/toothache

domar [do'mar] *vt* to tame

domesticar [domesti'kar] *vt* = **domar**

doméstico, -a [do'mestiko, a] *adj* (*vida, servicio*) home; (*tareas*) household; (*animal*) tame, pet

domicilio [domi'θiljo] *nm* home;

servicio a **~** home delivery service; **sin ~ fijo** of no fixed abode; **domicilio particular** private residence

dominante [domi'nante] *adj* dominant; (*persona*) domineering

dominar [domi'nar] *vt* (*gen*) to dominate; (*idiomas*) to be fluent in ▷ *vi* to dominate, prevail

domingo [do'mingo] *nm* Sunday; **Domingo de Ramos/Resurrección** Palm/Easter Sunday

dominio [do'minjo] *nm* (*tierras*) domain; (*autoridad*) power, authority; (*de las pasiones*) grip, hold; (*de idiomas*) command

don [don] *nm* (*talento*) gift; **~ Juan Gómez** Mr Juan Gómez, Juan Gómez Esq (BRIT)

> **DON/DOÑA**
>
> The term **don/doña** often
> abbreviated to **D./Dña** is placed
> before the first name as a mark
> of respect to an older or more
> senior person – eg Don Diego,
> Doña Inés. Although becoming
> rarer in Spain it is still used
> with names and surnames on
> official documents and formal
> correspondence – eg "Sr. D. Pedro
> Rodríguez Hernández", "Sra. Dña.
> Inés Rodríguez Hernández".

dona ['dona] (MÉX) *nf* doughnut, donut (US)

donar [do'nar] *vt* to donate

donativo [dona'tiβo] *nm* donation

donde ['donde] *adv* where ▷ *prep*: **el coche está allí ~ el farol** the car is over there by the lamppost o where the lamppost is; **en ~** where, in which

dónde ['donde] *adv* where?; **¿a vas?** where are you going (to)?; **¿de vienes?** where have you been?; **¿por ~?** where?, whereabouts?

dondequiera [donde'kjera] *adv* anywhere; **por ~** everywhere, all over the place ▷ conj: **~ que** wherever

donut® [do'nut] (ESP) nm doughnut, donut (US)

doña ['doɲa] nf: **~ Alicia** Alicia; **~ Victoria Benito** Mrs Victoria Benito

dorado, -a [do'raðo, a] adj (color) golden; (Tec) gilt

dormir [dor'mir] vt: **~ la siesta** to have an afternoon nap ▷ vi to sleep; **dormirse** vr to fall asleep

dormitorio [dormi'torjo] nm bedroom

dorsal [dor'sal] nm (Deporte) number

dorso ['dorso] nm (de mano) back; (de hoja) other side

dos [dos] num two

dosis ['dosis] nf inv dose, dosage

dotado, -a [do'taðo, a] adj gifted; **~ de** endowed with

dotar [do'tar] vt to endow; **dote** nf dowry; **dotes** nfpl (talentos) gifts

doy [doj] vb V **dar**

drama ['drama] nm drama; **dramaturgo** [drama'turɣo] nm dramatist, playwright

drástico, -a [drastiko, a] adj drastic

drenaje [dre'naxe] nm drainage

droga ['droɣa] nf drug; **drogadicto, -a** [droɣa'ðikto, -a] nm/f drug addict

droguería [droɣe'ria] nf hardware shop (BRIT) o store (US)

ducha ['dutʃa] nf (baño) shower; (Med) douche; **ducharse** vr to take a shower

duda ['duða] nf doubt; **no cabe ~** there is no doubt about it; **dudar** vt, vi to doubt; **dudoso, -a** [du'ðoso, a] adj (incierto) hesitant; (sospechoso) doubtful

duela etc vb V **doler**

duelo ['dwelo] vb V **doler** ▷ nm (combate) duel; (luto) mourning

duende ['dwende] nm imp, goblin

dueño, -a ['dweɲo, a] nm/f (propietario) owner; (de pensión, taberna) landlord/lady; (empresario) employer

duermo etc vb V **dormir**

dulce ['dulθe] adj sweet ▷ adv gently, softly ▷ nm sweet

dulcería [dulθe'ria] (LAM) nf confectioner's (shop)

dulzura [dul'θura] nf sweetness; (ternura) gentleness

dúo ['duo] nm duet

duplicar [dupli'kar] vt (hacer el doble de) to duplicate

duque ['duke] nm duke; **duquesa** nf duchess

duración [dura'θjon] nf (de película, disco etc) length; (de pila etc) life; (curso: de acontecimientos etc) duration

duradero, -a [dura'ðero, a] adj (tela etc) hard-wearing; (fe, paz) lasting

durante [du'rante] prep during

durar [du'rar] vi to last; (recuerdo) to remain

durazno [du'raθno] (LAM) nm (fruta) peach; (árbol) peach tree

durex ['dureks] (MÉX, ARG) nm (tira adhesiva) Sellotape® (BRIT), Scotch tape® (US)

dureza [du'reθa] nf (calidad) hardness

duro, -a ['duro, a] adj hard; (carácter) tough ▷ adv hard ▷ nm (moneda) five-peseta coin o piece

DVD nm abr (= disco de vídeo digital) DVD

e

E abr (=este) E

e [e] conj and

ébano ['eβano] nm ebony

ebrio, -a ['eβrjo, a] adj drunk

ebullición [eβuʎi'θjon] nf boiling

echar [e'tʃar] vt to throw; (agua, vino) to pour (out); (empleado: despedir) to fire, sack; (hojas) to sprout; (cartas) to post; (humo) to emit, give out ⊳ vi: **~ a correr** to run off; **echarse** vr to lie down; **~ llave a** to lock (up); **~ abajo** (gobierno) to overthrow; (edificio) to demolish; **~ mano a** to lay hands on; **~ una mano a algn** (ayudar) to give sb a hand; **~ de menos** to miss; **~se atrás** (fig) to back out

eclesiástico, -a [ekle'sjastiko, a] adj ecclesiastical

eco ['eko] nm echo; **tener ~** to catch on

ecología [ekolo'ɣia] nf ecology; **ecológico, -a** adj (producto, método) environmentally-friendly; (agricultura) organic; **ecologista** adj ecological, environmental ⊳ nmf

environmentalist

economía [ekono'mia] nf (sistema) economy; (carrera) economics

económico, -a [eko'nomiko, a] adj (barato) cheap, economical; (ahorrativo) thrifty; (Com: año etc) financial; (: situación) economic

economista [ekono'mista] nmf economist

Ecuador [ekwa'ðor] nm Ecuador; **ecuador** nm (Geo) equator

ecuatoriano, -a [ekwato'rjano, a] adj, nm/f Ecuadorian

ecuestre [e'kwestre] adj equestrian

edad [e'ðað] nf age; **¿qué ~ tienes?** how old are you?; **tiene ocho años de ~** he's eight (years old); **de ~ mediana/ avanzada** middle-aged/advanced in years; **la E~ Media** the Middle Ages

edición [eði'θjon] nf (acto) publication; (ejemplar) edition

edificar [eðifi'kar] vt, vi to build

edificio [eði'fiθjo] nm building; (fig) edifice, structure

Edimburgo [eðim'burɣo] nm Edinburgh

editar [eði'tar] vt (publicar) to publish; (preparar textos) to edit

editor, a [eði'tor, a] nm/f (que publica) publisher; (redactor) editor ⊳ adj publishing cpd; **editorial** adj editorial ⊳ nm leading article, editorial; **casa editorial** publisher

edredón [eðre'ðon] nm duvet

educación [eðuka'θjon] nf education; (crianza) upbringing; (modales) (good) manners pl

educado, -a [eðu'kaðo, a] adj: **bien/ mal ~** well/badly behaved

educar [eðu'kar] vt to educate; (criar) to bring up; (voz) to train

EE. UU. nmpl abr (=Estados Unidos) US(A)

efectivamente [efectiβa'mente] adv (como respuesta) exactly, precisely; (verdaderamente) really; (de hecho) in fact

efectivo, -a [efek'tiβo, a] adj effective; (real) actual, real ⊳ nm: **pagar**

en ~ to pay (in) cash; **hacer ~ un cheque** to cash a cheque

efecto [e'fekto] *nm* effect, result; **efectos** *nmpl* (*efectos personales*) effects; (*bienes*) goods; (*Com*) assets; **en ~** in fact; (*respuesta*) exactly, indeed; **efecto invernadero** greenhouse effect; **efectos especiales/ secundarios/sonoros** special/side/ sound effects

efectuar [efek'twar] *vt* to carry out; (*viaje*) to make

eficacia [efi'kaθja] *nf* (*de persona*) efficiency; (*de medicamento etc*) effectiveness

eficaz [efi'kaθ] *adj* (*persona*) efficient; (*acción*) effective

eficiente [efi'θjente] *adj* efficient

egipcio, -a [e'xipθjo, a] *adj, nm/f* Egyptian

Egipto [e'xipto] *nm* Egypt

egoísmo [eɣo'ismo] *nm* egoism

egoísta [eɣo'ista] *adj* egotistical, selfish ▷ *nmf* egoist

Eire ['eire] *nm* Eire

ej. *abr* (= *ejemplo*) eg

eje ['exe] *nm* (*Geo, Mat*) axis; (*de rueda*) axle; (*de máquina*) shaft, spindle

ejecución [exeku'θjon] *nf* execution; (*cumplimiento*) carrying out; (*Mús*) performance; (*Jur: embargo de deudor*) attachment

ejecutar [exeku'tar] *vt* to execute, carry out; (*matar*) to execute; (*cumplir*) to fulfil; (*Mús*) to perform; (*Jur: embargar*) to attach, distrain (on)

ejecutivo, -a [exeku'tiβo, a] *adj* executive; **el (poder) ~** the executive (power)

ejemplar [exem'plar] *adj* exemplary ▷ *nm* example; (*Zool*) specimen; (*de libro*) copy; (*de periódico*) number, issue

ejemplo [e'xemplo] *nm* example; **por ~** for example

ejercer [exer'θer] *vt* to exercise; (*influencia*) to exert; (*un oficio*) to practise ▷ *vi* (*practicar*) **~ (de)** to practise (as)

ejercicio [exer'θiθjo] *nm* exercise; (*período*) tenure; **hacer ~** to take exercise; **ejercicio comercial** financial year

ejército [e'xerθito] *nm* army; **entrar en el ~** to join the army, join up; **ejército del aire/de tierra** Air Force/Army

ejote [e'xote] (*MÉX*) *nm* green bean

○ **PALABRA CLAVE**

el [el] (*f* **la**, *pl* **los, las**, *neutro* **lo**) *art def* 1 the: **el libro/la mesa/los estudiantes** the book/table/students
2 (*con n abstracto: no se traduce*): **el amor/la juventud** love/youth
3 (*posesión: se traduce a menudo por adj posesivo*): **romperse el brazo** to break one's arm; **levantó la mano** he put his hand up; **se puso el sombrero** she put her hat on
4 (*valor descriptivo*): **tener la boca grande/los ojos azules** to have a big mouth/blue eyes
5 (*con días*) on; **me iré el viernes** I'll leave on Friday; **los domingos suelo ir a nadar** on Sundays I generally go swimming
6 (*lo +adj*): **lo difícil/caro** what is difficult/expensive; (*cuán*) **no se da cuenta de lo pesado que es** he doesn't realise how boring he is
▷ *pron demos* 1: **mi libro y el de usted** my book and yours; **las de Pepe son mejores** Pepe's are better; **no la(s) blanca(s) sino la(s) gris(es)** not the white one(s) but the grey one(s)
2: **lo de: lo de ayer** what happened yesterday; **lo de las facturas** that business about the invoices
▷ *pron relativo* 1 (*indef*): **el que: el (los) que quiera(n) que se vaya(n)** anyone who wants to can leave; **llévese el que más le guste** take the one you like best
2 (*def*): **el que: el que compré ayer** the one I bought yesterday; **los que se van** those who leave

3: lo que: lo que pienso yo/más me gusta what I think/like most
▷ conj: **el que: el que lo diga** the fact that he says so; **el que sea tan vago me molesta** his being so lazy bothers me
▷ excl: **¡el susto que me diste!** what a fright you gave me!
▷ pron personal **1** (persona: m) him; (: f) her; (: pl) them; **lo/las veo** I can see him/them
2 (animal, cosa: sg) it; (: pl) them; **lo** (o **la) veo** I can see it; **los** (o **las) veo** I can see them
3 (como sustituto de frase): **lo: no lo sabía** I didn't know; **ya lo entiendo** I understand now

él [el] pron (persona) he; (cosa) it; (después de prep: persona) him; (: cosa) it; **de ~** his
elaborar [elaβo'rar] vt (producto) to make, manufacture; (preparar) to prepare; (madera, metal etc) to work; (proyecto etc) to work on o out
elástico, -a [e'lastiko, a] adj elastic; (flexible) flexible ▷ nm elastic; (un elástico) elastic band
elección [elek'θjon] nf election; (selección) choice, selection; **elecciones generales** general election sg
electorado [elekto'raðo] nm electorate, voters pl
electricidad [elektriθi'ðað] nf electricity
electricista [elektri'θista] nmf electrician
eléctrico, -a [e'lektriko, a] adj electric
electro... [elektro] prefijo electro...; **electrocardiograma** nm electrocardiogram; **electrocutar** vt to electrocute; **electrodo** nm electrode; **electrodomésticos** nmpl (electrical) household appliances
electrónica [elek'tronika] nf electronics sg
electrónico, -a [elek'troniko, a] adj

electronic
elefante [ele'fante] nm elephant
elegancia [ele'ɣanθja] nf elegance, grace; (estilo) stylishness
elegante [ele'ɣante] adj elegant, graceful; (estiloso) stylish, fashionable
elegir [ele'xir] vt (escoger) to choose, select; (optar) to opt for; (presidente) to elect
elemental [elemen'tal] adj (claro, obvio) elementary; (fundamental) elemental, fundamental
elemento [ele'mento] nm element; (fig) ingredient; **elementos** nmpl elements, rudiments
elevación [eleβa'θjon] nf elevation; (acto) raising, lifting; (de precios) rise; (Geo etc) height, altitude
elevar [ele'βar] vt to raise, lift (up); (precio) to put up; **elevarse** vr (edificio) to rise; (precios) to go up
eligiendo etc vb V **elegir**
elija etc vb V **elegir**
eliminar [elimi'nar] vt to eliminate, remove
eliminatoria [elimina'torja] nf heat, preliminary (round)
élite ['elite] nf elite
ella ['eʎa] pron (persona) she; (cosa) it; (después de prep: persona) her; (: cosa) it; **de ~** hers
ellas ['eʎas] pron (personas y cosas) they; (después de prep) them; **de ~** theirs
ello ['eʎo] pron it
ellos ['eʎos] pron they; (después de prep) them; **de ~** theirs
elogiar [elo'xjar] vt to praise; **elogio** nm praise
elote [e'lote] (MÉX) nm corn on the cob
eludir [elu'ðir] vt to avoid
email [i'mel] nm email; (dirección) email address; **mandar un ~ a algn** to email sb, send sb an email
embajada [emba'xaða] nf embassy
embajador, a [embaxa'ðor, a] nm/f ambassador/ambassadress
embalar [emba'lar] vt to parcel, wrap (up); **embalarse** vr to go fast

embalse [em'balse] nm (presa) dam; (lago) reservoir

embarazada [embara'θaða] adj pregnant ▷ nf pregnant woman ▮ No confundir **embarazada** con la palabra inglesa embarrassed.

embarazo [emba'raθo] nm (de mujer) pregnancy; (impedimento) obstacle, obstruction; (timidez) embarrassment; **embarazoso, -a** adj awkward, embarrassing

embarcación [embarka'θjon] nf (barco) boat, craft; (acto) embarkation, boarding

embarcadero [embarka'ðero] nm pier, landing stage

embarcar [embar'kar] vt (cargamento) to ship, stow; (persona) to embark, put on board; **embarcarse** vr to embark, go on board

embargar [embar'ɣar] vt (Jur) to seize, impound

embargo [em'barɣo] nm (Jur) seizure; (Com, Pol) embargo

embargue etc vb V **embargar**

embarque etc [em'barke] vb V **embarcar** ▷ nm shipment, loading

embellecer [embeʎe'θer] vt to embellish, beautify

embestida [embes'tiða] nf attack, onslaught; (carga) charge

embestir [embes'tir] vt to attack, assault; to charge, attack ▷ vi to attack

emblema [em'blema] nm emblem

embobado, -a [embo'βaðo, a] adj (atontado) stunned, bewildered

embolia [em'bolja] nf (Med) clot

émbolo ['embolo] nm (Auto) piston

emborrachar [emborra'tʃar] vt to make drunk, intoxicate; **emborracharse** vr to get drunk

emboscada [embos'kaða] nf ambush

embotar [embo'tar] vt to blunt, dull

embotellamiento [emboteʎa'mjento] nm (Auto) traffic jam

embotellar [embote'ʎar] vt to bottle

embrague [em'braɣe] nm (tb: **pedal de -**) clutch

embrión [em'brjon] nm embryo

embrollo [em'broʎo] nm (enredo) muddle, confusion; (aprieto) fix, jam

embrujado, -a [embru'xaðo, a] adj bewitched; **casa embrujada** haunted house

embrutecer [embrute'θer] vt (atontar) to stupefy

embudo [em'buðo] nm funnel

embuste [em'buste] nm (mentira) lie; **embustero, -a** adj lying, deceitful ▷ nm/f (mentiroso) liar

embutido [embu'tiðo] nm (Culin) sausage; (Tec) inlay

emergencia [emer'xenθja] nf emergency; (surgimiento) emergence

emerger [emer'xer] vi to emerge, appear

emigración [emiɣra'θjon] nf emigration; (de pájaros) migration

emigrar [emi'ɣrar] vi (personas) to emigrate; (pájaros) to migrate

eminente [emi'nente] adj eminent, distinguished; (elevado) high

emisión [emi'sjon] nf (acto) emission; (Com etc) issue; (Radio, TV: acto) broadcasting; (: programa) broadcast, programme (BRIT), program (US)

emisora [emi'sora] nf radio o broadcasting station

emitir [emi'tir] vt (olor etc) to emit, give off; (moneda etc) to issue; (opinión) to express; (Radio) to broadcast

emoción [emo'θjon] nf emotion; (excitación) excitement; (sentimiento) feeling

emocionante [emoθjo'nante] adj (excitante) exciting, thrilling

emocionar [emoθjo'nar] vt (excitar) to excite, thrill; (conmover) to move, touch; (impresionar) to impress

emoticón [emoti'kon], **emoticono** [emoti'kono] nm smiley

emotivo, -a [emo'tiβo, a] adj emotional

empacho [em'patʃo] nm (Med) indigestion; (fig) embarrassment

empalagoso, -a [empala'ɣoso, a] adj cloying; (fig) tiresome

empalmar [empal'mar] vt to join, connect ▷ vi (dos caminos) to meet, join; **empalme** nm joint, connection; junction; (de trenes) connection

empanada [empa'naða] nf pie, pasty

empañarse [empa'narse] vr (cristales etc) to steam up

empapar [empa'par] vt (mojar) to soak, saturate; (absorber) to soak up, absorb; **empaparse** vr: **~se de** to soak up

empapelar [empape'lar] vt (paredes) to paper

empaquetar [empake'tar] vt to pack, parcel up

empastar [empas'tar] vt (embadurnar) to paste; (diente) to fill

empaste [em'paste] nm (de diente) filling

empatar [empa'tar] vi to draw, tie; **~on a dos** they drew two-all; **empate** nm draw, tie

empecé etc vb V **empezar**

empedernido, -a [empeðer'niðo, a] adj hard, heartless; (fumador) inveterate

empeine [em'peine] nm (de pie, zapato) instep

empeñado, -a [empe'naðo, a] adj (persona) determined; (objeto) pawned

empeñar [empe'nar] vt (objeto) to pawn, pledge; (persona) to compel; **empeñarse** vr (endeudarse) to get into debt; **~se en** to be set on, be determined to

empeño [em'peno] nm (determinación, insistencia) determination, insistence; **casa de ~** pawnshop

empeorar [empeo'rar] vt to make worse, worsen ▷ vi to get worse, deteriorate

empezar [empe'θar] vt, vi to begin, start

empiece etc vb V **empezar**

empiezo etc vb V **empezar**

emplasto [em'plasto] nm (Med) plaster

emplazar [empla'θar] vt (ubicar) to site, place, locate; (Jur) to summons; (convocar) to summon

empleado, -a [emple'aðo, a] nm/f (gen) employee; (de banco etc) clerk

emplear [emple'ar] vt (usar) to use, employ; (dar trabajo a) to employ; **emplearse** vr (conseguir trabajo) to be employed; (ocuparse) to occupy o.s.

empleo [em'pleo] nm (puesto) job; (puestos: colectivamente) employment; (uso) use, employment

empollar [empo'ʎar] vt, vi to swot (up); **empollón, -ona** nm/f (ESP: fam) swot

emporio [em'porjo] (LAM) nm (gran almacén) department store

empotrado, -a [empo'traðo, a] adj (armario etc) built-in

emprender [empren'der] vt (empezar) to begin, embark on; (acometer) to tackle, take on

empresa [em'presa] nf (de espíritu etc) enterprise; (Com) company, firm; **empresariales** nfpl business studies; **empresario, -a** nm/f (Com) businessman(-woman)

empujar [empu'xar] vt to push, shove

empujón [empu'xon] nm push, shove

empuñar [empu'nar] vt (asir) to grasp, take (firm) hold of

○ **PALABRA CLAVE**

en [en] prep **1** (posición) in; (: sobre) on; **está en el cajón** it's in the drawer; **en Argentina/La Paz** in Argentina/La Paz; **en la oficina/el colegio** at the office/school; **está en el suelo/quinto piso** it's on the floor/the fifth floor **2** (dirección) into; **entró en el aula** she went into the classroom; **meter algo en el bolso** to put sth into one's bag

3 (*tiempo*) in; on; **en 1605/3 semanas/invierno** in 1605/3 weeks/winter; **en (el mes de) enero** in (the month of) January; **en aquella ocasión/época** on that occasion/at that time

4 (*precio*) for; **lo vendió en 20 dólares** he sold it for 20 dollars

5 (*diferencia*) by; **reducir/aumentar en una tercera parte/un 20 por ciento** to reduce/increase by a third/20 per cent

6 (*manera*): **en avión/autobús** by plane/bus; **escrito en inglés** written in English

7 (*después de vb que indica gastar etc*) on; **han cobrado demasiado en dietas** they've charged too much to expenses; **se le va la mitad del sueldo en comida** he spends half his salary on food

8 (*tema, ocupación*): **experto en la materia** expert on the subject; **trabaja en la construcción** he works in the building industry

9 (*adj + en + infin*): **lento en reaccionar** slow to react

enaguas [e'naɣwas] *nfpl* petticoat *sg*, underskirt *sg*

enajenación [enaxena'θjon] *nf* (*Psico: tb:* **~ mental**) mental derangement

enamorado, -a [enamo'raðo, a] *adj* in love ▷ *nm/f* lover; **estar ~ (de)** to be in love (with)

enamorar [enamo'rar] *vt* to win the love of; **enamorarse** *vr:* **~se de algn** to fall in love with sb

enano, -a [e'nano, a] *adj* tiny ▷ *nm/f* dwarf

encabezamiento [enkaβeθa'mjento] *nm* (*de carta*) heading; (*de periódico*) headline

encabezar [enkaβe'θar] *vt* (*movimiento, revolución*) to lead, head; (*lista*) to head, be at the top of; (*carta*) to

put a heading to

encadenar [enkaðe'nar] *vt* to chain (together); (*poner grilletes a*) to shackle

encajar [enka'xar] *vt* (*ajustar*): **~ (en)** to fit (into); (*fam: golpe*) to take ▷ *vi* to fit (well); (*fig: corresponder a*) to match

encaje [en'kaxe] *nm* (*labor*) lace

encallar [enka'ʎar] *vi* (*Náut*) to run aground

encaminar [enkami'nar] *vt* to direct, send

encantado, -a [enkan'taðo, a] *adj* (*hechizado*) bewitched; (*muy contento*) delighted; **¡~!** how do you do, pleased to meet you

encantador, -a [enkanta'ðor, a] *adj* charming, lovely ▷ *nm/f* magician, enchanter/enchantress

encantar [enkan'tar] *vt* (*agradar*) to charm, delight; (*hechizar*) to bewitch, cast a spell on; **me encanta eso** I love that; **encanto** *nm* (*hechizo*) spell, charm; (*fig*) charm, delight

encarcelar [enkarθe'lar] *vt* to imprison, jail

encarecer [enkare'θer] *vt* to put up the price of; **encarecerse** *vr* to get dearer

encargado, -a [enkar'ɣaðo, a] *adj* in charge ▷ *nm/f* agent, representative; (*responsable*) person in charge

encargar [enkar'ɣar] *vt* to entrust; (*recomendar*) to urge, recommend; **encargarse** *vr:* **~se de** to look after, take charge of; **~ algo a algn** to put sb in charge of sth; **~ a algn que haga algo** to ask sb to do sth

encargo [en'karɣo] *nm* (*tarea*) assignment, job; (*responsabilidad*) responsibility; (*Com*) order

encariñarse [enkari'ɲarse] *vr:* **~ con** to grow fond of, get attached to

encarnación [enkarna'θjon] *nf* incarnation, embodiment

encarrilar [enkarri'lar] *vt* (*tren*) to put back on the rails; (*fig*) to correct, put on the right track

encasillar [enkasiˈʎar] vt (fig) to pigeonhole; (actor) to typecast

encendedor [enθendeˈðor] nm lighter

encender [enθenˈder] vt (con fuego) to light; (luz, radio) to put on, switch on; (avivar: pasión) to inflame; **encenderse** vr to catch fire; (excitarse) to get excited; (de cólera) to flare up; (el rostro) to blush

encendido [enθenˈðiðo] nm (Auto) ignition

encerado [enθeˈraðo] nm (Escol) blackboard

encerrar [enθeˈrrar] vt (confinar) to shut in, shut up; (comprender, incluir) to include, contain

encharcado, -a [entʃarˈkaðo, a] adj (terreno) flooded

encharcarse [entʃarˈkarse] vr to get flooded

enchufado, -a [entʃuˈfaðo, a] (fam) nm/f well-connected person

enchufar [entʃuˈfar] vt (Elec) to plug in; (Tec) to connect, fit together; **enchufe** nm (Elec: clavija) plug; (: toma) socket; (de dos tubos) joint, connection; (fam: influencia) contact, connection; (: puesto) cushy job

encía [enˈθia] nf gum

encienda etc vb V **encender**

encierro etc [enˈθjerro] vb V **encerrar** ⊳ nm shutting in, shutting up; (calabozo) prison

encima [enˈθima] adv (sobre) above, over; (además) besides; **~ de** (en on, on top of; (sobre) above, over; (además de) besides, on top of; **por ~ de** over; **¿llevas dinero ~?** have you (got) any money on you?; **se me vino ~** it took me by surprise

encina [enˈθina] nf holm oak

encinta [enˈθinta] adj pregnant

enclenque [enˈklenke] adj weak, sickly

encoger [enkoˈxer] vt to shrink, contract; **encogerse** vr to shrink, contract; (fig) to cringe; **~se de**

hombros to shrug one's shoulders

encomendar [enkomenˈdar] vt to entrust, commend; **encomendarse** vr: **~se a** to put one's trust in

encomienda etc [enkoˈmjenda] vb V **encomendar** ⊳ nf (encargo) charge, commission; (elogio) tribute; **encomienda postal** (LAM) package

encontrar [enkonˈtrar] vt (hallar) to find; (inesperadamente) to meet, run into; **encontrarse** vr to meet (each other); (situarse) to be (situated); **~se con** to meet; **~se bien (de salud)** to feel well

encrucijada [enkruθiˈxaða] nf crossroads sg

encuadernación [enkwaðernaˈθjon] nf binding

encuadrar [enkwaˈðrar] vt (retrato) to frame; (ajustar) to fit, insert; (contener) to contain

encubrir [enkuˈβrir] vt (ocultar) to hide, conceal; (criminal) to harbour, shelter

encuentro etc [enˈkwentro] vb V **encontrar** ⊳ nm (de personas) meeting; (Auto etc) collision, crash; (Deporte) match, game; (Mil) encounter

encuerado, -a (MÉX) [enkweˈraðo, a] adj nude, naked

encuesta [enˈkwesta] nf inquiry, investigation; (sondeo) (public) opinion poll

encumbrar [enkumˈbrar] vt (persona) to exalt

endeble [enˈdeβle] adj (persona) weak; (argumento, excusa, persona) weak

endemoniado, -a [endemoˈnjaðo, a] adj possessed (of the devil); (travieso) devilish

enderezar [endereˈθar] vt (poner derecho) to straighten (out); (: verticalmente) to set upright; (situación) to straighten o sort out; (dirigir) to direct; **enderezarse** vr (persona sentada) to straighten up

endeudarse [endeuˈðarse] vr to get into debt

endiablado, -a [endja'βlaðo, a] *adj* devilish, diabolical; (*travieso*) mischievous

endilgar [endil'ɣar] (*fam*) *vt*: **~le algo a algn** to lumber sb with sth

endiñar [endi'ɲar] (*ESP: fam*) *vt* (*bofetón*) to land, belt

endosar [endo'sar] *vt* (*cheque etc*) to endorse

endulzar [endul'θar] *vt* to sweeten; (*suavizar*) to soften

endurecer [endure'θer] *vt* to harden; **endurecerse** *vr* to harden, grow hard

enema [e'nema] *nm* (*Med*) enema

enemigo, -a [ene'miɣo, a] *adj* enemy, hostile ▷ *nm/f* enemy

enemistad [enemis'tað] *nf* enmity

enemistar [enemis'tar] *vt* to make enemies of, cause a rift between; **enemistarse** *vr* to become enemies; (*amigos*) to fall out

energía [ener'xia] *nf* (*vigor*) energy, drive; (*empuje*) push; (*Tec, Elec*) energy, power; **energía eólica** wind power; **energía solar** solar energy o power

enérgico, -a [e'nerxiko, a] *adj* (*gen*) energetic; (*voz, modales*) forceful

energúmeno, -a [ener'xumeno, a] (*fam*) *nm/f* (*fig*) madman(-woman)

enero [e'nero] *nm* January

enfadado, -a [enfa'ðaðo, a] *adj* angry, annoyed

enfadar [enfa'ðar] *vt* to anger, annoy; **enfadarse** *vr* to get angry o annoyed

enfado [en'faðo] *nm* (*enojo*) anger, annoyance; (*disgusto*) trouble, bother

énfasis [ˈenfasis] *nm* emphasis, stress

enfático, -a [en'fatiko, a] *adj* emphatic

enfermar [enfer'mar] *vt* to make ill ▷ *vi* to fall ill, be taken ill

enfermedad [enferme'ðað] *nf* illness; **enfermedad venérea** venereal disease

enfermera [enfer'mera] *nf* nurse

enfermería [enferme'ria] *nf* infirmary; (*de colegio etc*) sick bay

enfermero [enfer'mero] *nm* (male) nurse

enfermizo, -a [enfer'miθo, a] *adj* (*persona*) sickly, unhealthy; (*fig*) unhealthy

enfermo, -a [en'fermo, a] *adj* ill, sick ▷ *nm/f* invalid, sick person; (*en hospital*) patient; **caer o ponerse ~** to fall ill

enfocar [enfo'kar] *vt* (*foto etc*) to focus; (*problema etc*) to approach

enfoque [en'foke] *vb* V **enfocar** ▷ *nm* focus

enfrentar [enfren'tar] *vt* (*peligro*) to face (up to), confront; (*oponer*) to bring face to face; **enfrentarse** *vr* (*dos personas*) to face o confront each other; (*Deporte: dos equipos*) to meet; **~se a o con** to face up to, confront

enfrente [en'frente] *adv* opposite; **la casa de ~** the house opposite, the house across the street; **~ de** opposite, facing

enfriamiento [enfria'mjento] *nm* chilling, refrigeration; (*Med*) cold, chill

enfriar [enfri'ar] *vt* (*alimentos*) to cool, chill; (*algo caliente*) to cool down; **enfriarse** *vr* to cool down; (*Med*) to catch a chill; (*amistad*) to cool

enfurecer [enfure'θer] *vt* to enrage, madden; **enfurecerse** *vr* to become furious, fly into a rage; (*mar*) to get rough

enganchar [engan'tʃar] *vt* to hook; (*dos vagones*) to hitch up; (*Tec*) to couple, connect; (*Mil*) to recruit; **engancharse** *vr* (*Mil*) to enlist, join up

enganche [en'gantʃe] *nm* hook; (*ESP Tec*) coupling, connection; (*acto*) hooking (up); (*Mil*) recruitment, enlistment; (*MÉX: depósito*) deposit

engañar [enga'ɲar] *vt* to deceive; (*estafar*) to cheat, swindle; **engañarse** *vr* (*equivocarse*) to be wrong; (*disimular la verdad*) to deceive o.s.

engaño [en'gaɲo] *nm* deceit;

(*estafa*) trick, swindle; (*error*) mistake, misunderstanding; (*ilusión*) delusion; **engañoso, -a** *adj* (*tramposo*) crooked; (*mentiroso*) dishonest, deceitful; (*aspecto*) deceptive; (*consejo*) misleading

engatusar [engatu'sar] (*fam*) *vt* to coax

engendro [en'xendro] *nm* (*Bio*) foetus; (*fig*) monstrosity

englobar [englo'βar] *vt* to include, comprise

engordar [engor'ðar] *vt* to fatten ▷ *vi* to get fat, put on weight

engorroso, -a [engo'rroso, a] *adj* bothersome, trying

engranaje [engra'naxe] *nm* (*Auto*) gear

engrasar [engra'sar] *vt* (*Tec: poner grasa*) to grease; (: *lubricar*) to lubricate, oil; (*manchar*) to make greasy

engreído, -a [engre'iðo, a] *adj* vain, conceited

enhebrar [ene'βrar] *vt* to thread

enhorabuena [enora'βwena] *excl* ¡~! congratulations! ▷ *nf*: **dar la ~ a** to congratulate

enigma [e'niɣma] *nm* enigma; (*problema*) puzzle; (*misterio*) mystery

enjambre [en'xambre] *nm* swarm

enjaular [enxau'lar] *vt* (*put in a cage*; (*fam*) to jail, lock up

enjuagar [enxwa'ɣar] *vt* (*ropa*) to rinse (out)

enjuague *etc* [en'xwaxe] *vb* V **enjuagar** ▷ *nm* (*Med*) mouthwash; (*de ropa*) rinse, rinsing

enlace [en'laθe] *nm* link, connection; (*relación*) relationship; (*tb*: **~ matrimonial**) marriage; (*de carretera, trenes*) connection; **enlace sindical** shop steward

enlatado, -a [enla'taðo, a] *adj* (*alimentos, productos*) tinned, canned

enlazar [enla'θar] *vt* (*unir con lazos*) to bind together; (*atar*) to tie; (*conectar*) to link, connect; (*LAM: caballo*) to lasso

enloquecer [enloke'θer] *vt* to drive

mad ▷ *vi* to go mad

enmarañar [enmara'nar] *vt* (*enredar*) to tangle (up), entangle; (*complicar*) to complicate; (*confundir*) to confuse

enmarcar [enmar'kar] *vt* (*cuadro*) to frame

enmascarar [enmaska'rar] *vt* to mask; **enmascararse** *vr* to put on a mask

enmendar [enmen'dar] *vt* to emend, correct; (*constitución etc*) to amend; (*comportamiento*) to reform; **enmendarse** *vr* to reform, mend one's ways; **enmienda** *nf* correction; amendment; reform

enmudecer [enmuðe'θer] *vi* (*perder el habla*) to fall silent; (*guardar silencio*) to remain silent

ennoblecer [ennoβle'θer] *vt* to ennoble

enojado, -a [eno'xaðo, a] (*LAM*) *adj* angry

enojar [eno'xar] *vt* (*encolerizar*) to anger; (*disgustar*) to annoy, upset; **enojarse** *vr* to get angry; to get annoyed

enojo [e'noxo] *nm* (*cólera*) anger; (*irritación*) annoyance

enorme [e'norme] *adj* enormous, huge; (*fig*) monstrous

enredadera [enreða'ðera] *nf* (*Bot*) creeper, climbing plant

enredar [enre'ðar] *vt* (*cables, hilos etc*) to tangle (up), entangle; (*situación*) to complicate, confuse; (*meter cizaña*) to sow discord among o between; (*implicar*) to embroil, implicate; **enredarse** *vr* to get entangled, get tangled (up); (*situación*) to get complicated; (*persona*) to get embroiled; (*LAM: fam*) to meddle

enredo [en'reðo] *nm* (*maraña*) tangle; (*confusión*) mix-up, confusion; (*intriga*) intrigue

enriquecer [enrike'θer] *vt* to make rich, enrich; **enriquecerse** *vr* to get rich

enrojecer [enroxe'θer] vt to redden
▷ vi (persona) to blush; **enrojecerse**
vr to blush

enrollar [enro'ʎar] vt to roll (up),
wind (up)

ensalada [ensa'laða] nf salad;
ensaladilla (rusa) nf Russian salad

ensanchar [ensan'tʃar] vt (hacer
más ancho) to widen; (agrandar) to
enlarge, expand; (Costura) to let out;
ensancharse vr to widen, expand

ensayar [ensa'jar] vt to test, try
(out); (Teatro) to rehearse

ensayo [en'sajo] nm test, trial;
(Quím) experiment; (Teatro) rehearsal;
(Deporte) try; (Escol, Literatura) essay

enseguida [ense'βiða] adv at once,
right away

ensenada [ense'naða] nf inlet, cove

enseñanza [ense'nanθa] nf
(educación) education; (acción)
teaching; (doctrina) teaching, doctrine;
enseñanza (de) primaria/secundaria
elementary/secondary education

enseñar [ense'nar] vt (educar) to
teach; (mostrar, señalar) to show

enseres [en'seres] nmpl belongings

ensuciar [ensu'θjar] vt (manchar) to
dirty, soil; (fig) to defile; **ensuciarse** vr
to get dirty; (bebé) to dirty one's nappy

entablar [enta'βlar] vt (recubrir) to
board (up); (Ajedrez, Damas) to set up;
(conversación) to strike up; (Jur) to file
▷ vi to draw

ente ['ente] nm (organización) body,
organization; (fam: persona) odd
character

entender [enten'der] vt (comprender)
to understand; (darse cuenta) to realize
▷ vi to understand; (creer) to think,
believe; **entenderse** vr (comprenderse)
to be understood; (ponerse de acuerdo)
to agree, reach an agreement; **~ de**
to know all about; **~ algo de** to know
a little about; **~ en** to deal with, have
to do with; **~ mal** to misunderstand;
~se con algn (llevarse bien) to get on
along with sb; **~se mal** (dos personas) to

get on badly

entendido, -a [enten'diðo, a] adj
(comprendido) understood; (hábil)
skilled; (inteligente) knowledgeable
▷ nm/f (experto) expert ▷ excl agreed!;
entendimiento nm (comprensión)
understanding; (inteligencia) mind,
intellect; (juicio) judgement

enterado, -a [ente'raðo, a] adj well-
informed; **estar ~ de** to know about,
be aware of

enteramente [entera'mente] adv
entirely, completely

enterar [ente'rar] vt (informar) to
inform, tell; **enterarse** vr to find out,
get to know

enterito [ente'rito] (RPL) nm boiler
suit (BRIT), overalls (US)

entero, -a [en'tero, a] adj (total)
whole, entire; (fig: honesto) honest;
(: firme) firm, resolute ▷ nm
(Com: punto) point

enterrar [ente'rrar] vt to bury

entidad [enti'ðað] nf (empresa) firm,
company; (organismo) body; (sociedad)
society; (Filosofía) entity

entiendo etc vb V **entender**

entierro [en'tjerro] nm (acción)
burial; (funeral) funeral

entonación [entona'θjon] nf (Ling)
intonation

entonar [ento'nar] vt (canción) to
intone; (colores) to tone; (Med) to tone
up ▷ vi to be in tune

entonces [en'tonθes] adv then,
at that time; **desde ~** since then; **en
aquel ~** at that time; **(pues) ~** and so

entornar [entor'nar] vt (puerta,
ventana) to half-close, leave ajar; (los
ojos) to screw up

entorpecer [entorpe'θer] vt
(entendimiento) to dull; (impedir) to
obstruct, hinder; (: tránsito) to slow
down, delay

entrada [en'traða] nf (acción) entry,
access; (sitio) entrance, way in; (Inform)
input; (Com) receipts pl, takings pl;
(Culin) starter; (Deporte) innings sg;

(*Teatro*) house, audience; (*billete*) ticket; **~s y salidas** (*Com*) income and expenditure; **de ~** from the outset; **entrada de aire** (*Tec*) air intake o inlet

entrado, -a [en'traðo, a] *adj*: **~ en años** elderly; **una vez ~ el verano** in the summer(time), when summer comes

entramparse [entram'parse] *vr* to get into debt

entrante [en'trante] *adj* next, coming; **mes/año ~** next month/year; **entrantes** *nmpl* starters

entraña [en'traɲa] *nf* (*fig: centro*) heart, core; (*raíz*) root; **entrañas** *nfpl* (*Anat*) entrails; (*fig*) heart *sg*; **entrañable** *adj* close, intimate; **entrañar** *vt* to entail

entrar [en'trar] *vt* (*introducir*) to bring in; (*Inform*) to input ▷ *vi* (*meterse*) to go in, come in, enter; (*comenzar*): **~ diciendo** to begin by saying; **hacer ~** to show in; **me entró sed/sueño** I started to feel thirsty/sleepy; **no me entra** I can't get the hang of it

entre ['entre] *prep* (*dos*) between; (*más de dos*) among(st)

entreabrir [entrea'ßrir] *vt* to half-open, open halfway

entrecejo [entre'θexo] *nm*: **fruncir el ~** to frown

entredicho [entre'ðitʃo] *nm* (*Jur*) injunction; **poner en ~** to cast doubt on; **estar en ~** to be in doubt

entrega [en'treɣa] *nf* (*de mercancías*) delivery; (*de novela etc*) instalment; **entregar** [entre'ɣar] *vt* (*dar*) to hand (over), deliver; **entregarse** *vr* (*rendirse*) to surrender, give in, submit; (*dedicarse*) to devote o.s.

entremeses [entre'meses] *nmpl* hors d'œuvres

entremeter [entreme'ter] *vt* to insert, put in; **entremeterse** *vr* to meddle, interfere; **entremetido, -a** *adj* meddling, interfering

entremezclar [entremeθ'klar] *vt* to intermingle; **entremezclarse** *vr* to intermingle

entrenador, a [entrena'ðor, a] *nm/f* trainer, coach

entrenarse [entre'narse] *vr* to train

entrepierna [entre'pjerna] *nf* crotch

entresuelo [entre'swelo] *nm* mezzanine

entretanto [entre'tanto] *adv* meanwhile, meantime

entretecho [entre'tetʃo] (cs) *nm* attic

entretejer [entrete'xer] *vt* to interweave

entretener [entrete'ner] *vt* (*divertir*) to entertain, amuse; (*detener*) to hold up, delay; **entretenerse** *vr* (*divertirse*) to amuse o.s.; (*retrasarse*) to delay, linger; **entretenido, -a** *adj* entertaining, amusing; **entretenimiento** *nm* entertainment, amusement

entrever [entre'ßer] *vt* to glimpse, catch a glimpse of

entrevista [entre'ßista] *nf* interview; **entrevistar** *vt* to interview; **entrevistarse** *vr* to have an interview

entristecer [entriste'θer] *vt* to sadden, grieve; **entristecerse** *vr* to grow sad

entrometerse [entrome'terse] *vr*: **~ (en)** to interfere (in o with)

entumecer [entume'θer] *vt* to numb, benumb; **entumecerse** *vr* (*por el frío*) to go o become numb

enturbiar [entur'βjar] *vt* (*el agua*) to make cloudy; (*fig*) to confuse; **enturbiarse** *vr* (*oscurecerse*) to become cloudy; (*fig*) to get confused, become obscure

entusiasmar [entusjas'mar] *vt* to excite, fill with enthusiasm; (*gustar mucho*) to delight; **entusiasmarse** *vr*: **~se con o por** to get enthusiastic o excited about

entusiasmo [entu'sjasmo] *nm* enthusiasm; (*excitación*) excitement

entusiasta [entu'sjasta] *adj*
enthusiastic ▷ *nmf* enthusiast

enumerar [enume'rar] *vt* to
enumerate

envainar [embai'nar] *vt* to sheathe

envalentonar [embalento'nar] *vt*
to give courage to; **envalentonarse** *vr*
(*pey: jactarse*) to boast, brag

envasar [emba'sar] *vt* (*empaquetar*)
to pack, wrap; (*enfrascar*) to bottle;
(*enlatar*) to can; (*embolsar*) to pocket

envase [em'base] *nm* (*en paquete*)
packing, wrapping; (*en botella*)
bottling; (*en lata*) canning; (*recipiente*)
container; (*paquete*) package; (*botella*)
bottle; (*lata*) tin (*BRIT*), can

envejecer [embexe'θer] *vt* to make
old, age ▷ *vi* (*volverse viejo*) to grow old;
(*parecer viejo*) to age

envenenar [embene'nar] *vt* to
poison; (*fig*) to embitter

envergadura [emberɣa'ðura] *nf*
(*fig*) scope, compass

enviar [em'bjar] *vt* to send; **~ un
mensaje a algn** (*por movil*) to text sb, to
send sb a text message

enviciarse [embi'θjarse] *vr*: **~ (con)**
to get addicted to

envidia [em'biðja] *nf* envy; **tener
~ a** to envy, be jealous of; **envidiar**
vt to envy

envío [em'bio] *nm* (*acción*) sending;
(*de mercancías*) consignment; (*de dinero*)
remittance

enviudar [embju'ðar] *vi* to be
widowed

envoltura [embol'tura] *nf* (*cobertura*)
cover; (*embalaje*) wrapper, wrapping;
envoltorio *nm* package

envolver [embol'βer] *vt* to wrap (up);
(*cubrir*) to cover; (*enemigo*) to surround;
(*implicar*) to involve, implicate

envuelto [em'bwelto] *pp de*
envolver

enyesar [enje'sar] *vt* (*pared*) to
plaster; (*Med*) to put in plaster

enzarzarse [enθar'θarse] *vr*: **~ en**
(*pelea*) to get mixed up in; (*disputa*) to

get involved in

épica ['epika] *nf* epic

epidemia [epi'ðemja] *nf* epidemic

epilepsia [epi'lepsja] *nf* epilepsy

episodio [epi'soðjo] *nm* episode

época ['epoka] *nf* period, time; (*Hist*)
age, epoch; **hacer ~** to be epoch-
making

equilibrar [ekili'βrar] *vt* to balance;
equilibrio *nm* balance, equilibrium;
mantener/perder el equilibrio to
keep/lose one's balance; **equilibrista**
nmf (*funámbulo*) tightrope walker;
(*acróbata*) acrobat

equipaje [eki'paxe] *nm* luggage;
(*avíos*): **hacer el ~** to pack; **equipaje de
mano** hand luggage

equipar [eki'par] *vt* (*proveer*) to equip

equipararse [ekipa'rarse] *vr*: **~ con**
to be on a level with

equipo [e'kipo] *nm* (*conjunto de
cosas*) equipment; (*Deporte*) team; (*de
obreros*) shift

equis ['ekis] *nf inv* (the letter) X

equitación [ekita'θjon] *nf* horse
riding

equivalente [ekiβa'lente] *adj*, *nm*
equivalent

equivaler [ekiβa'ler] *vi* to be
equivalent o equal

equivocación [ekiβoka'θjon] *nf*
mistake, error

equivocado, -a [ekiβo'kaðo, a] *adj*
wrong, mistaken

equivocarse [ekiβo'karse] *vr* to be
wrong, make a mistake; **~ de camino**
to take the wrong road

era ['era] *vb* V **ser** ▷ *nf* era, age

erais *vb* V **ser**

éramos *vb* V **ser**

eran *vb* V **ser**

eras *vb* V **ser**

erección [erek'θjon] *nf* erection

eres *vb* V **ser**

erigir [eri'xir] *vt* to erect, build;
erigirse *vr*: **~se en** to set o.s. up as

erizo [e'riθo] *nm* (*Zool*) hedgehog;
erizo de mar sea-urchin

ermita [er'mita] nf hermitage;
ermitaño, -a [ermi'taɲo, a] nm/f
hermit

erosión [ero'sjon] nf erosion

erosionar [erosjo'nar] vt to erode

erótico, -a [e'rotiko, a] adj erotic;
erotismo nm eroticism

errante [e'rrante] adj wandering,
errant

erróneo, -a [e'rroneo, a] adj
(equivocado) wrong, mistaken

error [e'rror] nm error, mistake;
(Inform) bug; **error de imprenta**
misprint

eructar [eruk'tar] vt to belch, burp

erudito, -a [eru'ðito, a] adj erudite,
learned

erupción [erup'θjon] nf eruption;
(Med) rash

es vb V **ser**

esa ['esa] (pl ~s) adj demos V **ese**

ésa ['esa] (pl ~s) pron V **ése**

esbelto, -a [es'βelto, a] adj slim,
slender

esbozo [es'βoθo] nm sketch, outline

escabeche [eska'βetʃe] nm brine; (de
aceitunas etc) pickle; **en ~** pickled

escabullirse [eskaβu'ʎirse] vr to slip
away, to clear out

escafandra [eska'fandra] nf (buzo)
diving suit; (escafandra espacial)
space suit

escala [es'kala] nf (proporción, Mús)
scale; (de mano) ladder; (Aviac) stopover;
hacer ~ en to stop o call in at

escalafón [eskala'fon] nm (escala de
salarios) salary scale, wage scale

escalar [eska'lar] vt to climb, scale

escalera [eska'lera] nf stairs pl,
staircase; (escala) ladder; (Naipes) run;
escalera de caracol spiral staircase;
escalera de incendios fire escape;
escalera mecánica escalator

escalfar [eskal'far] vt (huevos) to
poach

escalinata [eskali'nata] nf staircase

escalofriante [eskalo'frjante] adj
chilling

escalofrío [eskalo'frio] nm (Med)
chill; **escalofríos** nmpl (fig) shivers

escalón [eska'lon] nm step, stair; (de
escalera) rung

escalope [eska'lope] nm (Culin)
escalope

escama [es'kama] nf (de pez,
serpiente) scale; (de jabón) flake; (fig)
resentment

escampar [eskam'par] vb impers to
stop raining

escandalizar [eskandali'θar] vt to
scandalize, shock; **escandalizarse**
vr to be shocked; (ofenderse) to be
offended

escándalo [es'kandalo] nm scandal;
(alboroto, tumulto) row, uproar;
escandaloso, -a adj scandalous,
shocking

escandinavo, -a [eskandi'naβo, a]
adj, nm/f Scandinavian

escanear [eskane'ar] vt to scan

escaño [es'kaɲo] nm bench; (Pol) seat

escapar [eska'par] vi (gen) to escape,
run away; (Deporte) to break away;
escaparse vr to escape, get away;
(agua, gas) to leak (out)

escaparate [eskapa'rate] nm shop
window

escape [es'kape] nm (de agua, gas)
leak; (de motor) exhaust

escarabajo [eskara'βaxo] nm beetle

escaramuza [eskara'muθa] nf
skirmish

escarbar [eskar'βar] vt (tierra) to
scratch

escarceos [eskar'θeos] nmpl: **en mis
~ con la política ...** in my dealings
with politics ...; **escarceos amorosos**
love affairs

escarcha [es'kartʃa] nf frost;
escarchado, -a [eskar'tʃaðo, a] adj
(Culin: fruta) crystallized

escarlatina [eskarla'tina] nf scarlet
fever

escarmentar [eskarmen'tar] vt to
punish severely ▷ vi to learn one's
lesson

escarmiento etc [eskar'mjento] vb
V escarmentar ▷ nm (ejemplo) lesson;
(castigo) punishment

escarola [eska'rola] nf endive

escarpado, -a [eskar'paðo, a] adj
(pendiente) sheer, steep; (rocas) craggy

escasear [eskase'ar] vi to be scarce

escasez [eska'seθ] nf (falta) shortage,
scarcity; (pobreza) poverty

escaso, -a [es'kaso, a] adj (poco)
scarce; (raro) rare; (ralo) thin, sparse;
(limitado) limited

escatimar [eskati'mar] vt to skimp
(on), be sparing with

escayola [eska'jola] nf plaster

escena [es'θena] nf scene; escenario
[esθe'narjo] nm (Teatro) stage; (Cine)
set; (fig) scene

No confundir **escenario** con la
palabra inglesa *scenery*.

escenografía nf set design

escéptico, -a [es'θeptiko, a] adj
sceptical ▷ nm/f sceptic

esclarecer [esklare'θer] vt (misterio,
problema) to shed light on

esclavitud [esklaβi'tuð] nf slavery

esclavizar [esklaβi'θar] vt to enslave

esclavo, -a [es'klaβo, a] nm/f slave

escoba [es'koβa] nf broom; escobilla
nf brush

escocer [esko'θer] vt to burn, sting;
escocerse vr to chafe, get chafed

escocés, -esa [esko'θes, esa] adj
Scottish ▷ nm/f Scotsman(-woman),
Scot

Escocia [es'koθja] nf Scotland

escoger [esko'xer] vt to choose,
pick, select; escogido, -a adj chosen,
selected

escolar [esko'lar] adj school cpd
▷ nm/f schoolboy(-girl), pupil

escollo [es'koλo] nm (obstáculo) pitfall

escolta [es'kolta] nf escort; escoltar
vt to escort

escombros [es'kombros] nmpl
(basura) rubbish sg; (restos) debris sg

esconder [eskon'der] vt to hide,
conceal; esconderse vr to hide;

escondidas (LAM) nfpl: a escondidas
secretly; escondite nm hiding place;
(ESP: juego) hide-and-seek; escondrijo
nm hiding place, hideout

escopeta [esko'peta] nf shotgun

escoria [es'korja] nf (de alto horno)
slag; (fig) scum, dregs pl

Escorpio [es'korpjo] nm Scorpio

escorpión [eskor'pjon] nm scorpion

escotado, -a [esko'taðo, a] adj
low-cut

escote [es'kote] nm (de vestido) low
neck; pagar a ~ to share the expenses

escotilla [esko'tiʎa] nf (Náut)
hatch(way)

escozor [esko'θor] nm (dolor)
sting(ing)

escribir [eskri'βir] vt, vi to write; ~ a
máquina to type; ¿cómo se escribe?
how do you spell it?

escrito, -a [es'krito, a] pp de
escribir ▷ nm (documento) document;
(manuscrito) text, manuscript; por ~
in writing

escritor, a [eskri'tor, a] nm/f writer

escritorio [eskri'torjo] nm desk

escritura [eskri'tura] nf (acción)
writing; (caligrafía) (hand)writing;
(Jur: documento) deed

escrúpulo [es'krupulo] nm scruple;
(minuciosidad) scrupulousness;
escrupuloso, -a adj scrupulous

escrutinio [eskru'tinjo] nm (examen
atento) scrutiny; (Pol: recuento de votos)
count(ing)

escuadra [es'kwaðra] nf (Mil etc)
squad; (Náut) squadron; (flota: de coches
etc) fleet; escuadrilla nf (de aviones)
squadron; (LAM: de obreros) gang

escuadrón [eskwa'ðron] nm
squadron

escuálido, -a [es'kwaliðo, a] adj
skinny, scraggy; (sucio) squalid

escuchar [esku'tʃar] vt to listen to
▷ vi to listen

escudo [es'kuðo] nm shield

escuela [es'kwela] nf school; escuela

de artes y oficios (ESP) ≈ technical college; **escuela de choferes** (LAM) driving school; **escuela de manejo** (MÉX) driving school

escueto, -a [es'kweto, a] adj plain; (estilo) simple

escuincle, -a [es'kwinkle, a] (MÉX: fam) nm/f kid

esculpir [eskul'pir] vt to sculpt; (grabar) to engrave; (tallar) to carve; **escultor, a** nm/f sculptor(-tress); **escultura** nf sculpture

escupidera [eskupi'ðera] nf spittoon

escupir [esku'pir] vt, vi to spit (out)

escurreplatos [eskurre'platos] (ESP) nm inv draining board (BRIT), drainboard (US)

escurridero [eskurri'ðero] (LAM) nm draining board (BRIT), drainboard (US)

escurridizo, -a [eskurri'ðiθo, a] adj slippery

escurridor [eskurri'ðor] nm colander

escurrir [esku'rrir] vt (ropa) to wring out; (verduras, platos) to drain ▷ vi (líquidos) to drip; **escurrirse** vr (secarse) to drain; (resbalarse) to slip, slide; (escaparse) to slip away

ese ['ese] (f esa, pl esos, esas) adj demos (sg) that; (pl) those

ése ['ese] (f ésa, pl ésos, ésas) pron (sg) that (one); (pl) those (ones); ~ ... **éste** ... the former ... the latter ...; **no me vengas con ésas** don't give me any more of that nonsense

esencia [e'senθja] nf essence; **esencial** adj essential

esfera [es'fera] nf sphere; (de reloj) face; **esférico, -a** adj spherical

esforzarse [esfor'θarse] vr to exert o.s., make an effort

esfuerzo etc [es'fwerθo] vb V esforzarse ▷ nm effort

esfumarse [esfu'marse] vr (apoyo, esperanzas) to fade away

esgrima [es'γrima] nf fencing

esguince [es'γinθe] nm (Med) sprain

eslabón [esla'βon] nm link

eslip [ez'lip] nm pants pl (BRIT), briefs pl

eslovaco, -a [eslo'βako, a] adj, nm/f Slovak, Slovakian ▷ nm (Ling) Slovak, Slovakian

Eslovaquia [eslo'βakja] nf Slovakia

esmalte [es'malte] nm enamel; **esmalte de uñas** nail varnish o polish

esmeralda [esme'ralda] nf emerald

esmerarse [esme'rarse] vr (aplicarse) to take great pains, exercise great care; (afanarse) to work hard

esmero [es'mero] nm (great) care

esnob [es'noβ] (pl ~s) adj (persona) snobbish ▷ nm/f snob

eso ['eso] pron that, that thing o matter; ~ **de su coche** that business about his car; ~ **de ir al cine** all that about going to the cinema; **a ~ de las cinco** at about five o'clock; **en ~** thereupon, at that point; ~ **es** that's it; **¡~ sí que es vida!** now that's real living!; **por ~ te lo dije** that's why I told you; **y ~ que llovía** in spite of the fact it was raining

esos adj demos V **ese**

ésos pron V **ése**

espabilar etc [espaβi'lar] = **despabilar** etc

espacial [espa'θjal] adj (del espacio) space cpd

espaciar [espa'θjar] vt to space (out)

espacio [es'paθjo] nm space; (Mús) interval; (Radio, TV) programme (BRIT), program (US); **el ~** space; **espacio aéreo/exterior** air/outer space; **espacioso, -a** adj spacious, roomy

espada [es'paða] nf sword; **espadas** nfpl (Naipes) spades

espaguetis [espa'yetis] nmpl spaghetti sg

espalda [es'palda] nf (gen) back; **espaldas** nfpl (hombros) shoulders; **a ~s de algn** behind sb's back; **estar de ~** to have one's back turned; **tenderse de ~** to lie (down) on one's back; **volver la ~ a algn** to cold-shoulder sb

espantajo [espan'taxo] nm = **espantapájaros**

espantapájaros [espanta'paxaros] nm inv scarecrow

espantar [espan'tar] vt (asustar) to frighten, scare; (ahuyentar) to frighten off; (asombrar) to horrify, appal; **espantarse** vr to get frightened o scared; to be appalled

espanto [es'panto] nm (susto) fright; (terror) terror; (asombro) astonishment; **espantoso, -a** adj frightening; terrifying; astonishing

España [es'paɲa] nf Spain; **español, a** adj Spanish ▷ nm/f Spaniard ▷ nm (Ling) Spanish

esparadrapo [espara'ðrapo] nm (sticking) plaster (BRIT), adhesive tape (US)

esparcir [espar'θir] vt to spread; (diseminar) to scatter; **esparcirse** vr to spread (out), to scatter; (divertirse) to enjoy o.s.

espárrago [es'parraxo] nm asparagus

esparto [es'parto] nm esparto (grass)

espasmo [es'pasmo] nm spasm

espátula [es'patula] nf spatula

especia [es'peθja] nf spice

especial [espe'θjal] adj special; **especialidad** nf speciality (BRIT), specialty (US)

especie [es'peθje] nf (Bio) species; (clase) kind, sort; **en ~** in kind

especificar [espeθifi'kar] vt to specify; **específico, -a** adj specific

espécimen [es'peθimen] nm (pl **especímenes**) nm specimen

espectáculo [espek'takulo] nm (gen) spectacle; (Teatro etc) show

espectador, a [espekta'ðor, a] nm/f spectator

especular [espeku'lar] vt, vi to speculate

espejismo [espe'xismo] nm mirage

espejo [es'pexo] nm mirror; **(espejo) retrovisor** rear-view mirror

espeluznante [espeluθ'nante] adj horrifying, hair-raising

espera [es'pera] nf (pausa, intervalo) wait; (Jur: plazo) respite; **en ~ de** waiting for; (con expectativa) expecting

esperanza [espe'ranθa] nf (confianza) hope; (expectativa) expectation; **hay pocas ~s de que venga** there is little prospect of his coming; **esperanza de vida** life expectancy

esperar [espe'rar] vt (aguardar) to wait for; (tener expectativa) to expect; (desear) to hope for ▷ vi to wait; to expect; to hope; **hacer ~ a algn** to keep sb waiting; **~ un bebé** to be expecting (a baby)

esperma [es'perma] nf sperm

espeso, -a [es'peso, a] adj thick; **espesor** nm thickness

espía [es'pia] nmf spy; **espiar** vt (observar) to spy on

espiga [es'pixa] nf (Bot: de trigo etc) ear

espigón [espi'xon] nm (Bot) ear; (Náut) breakwater

espina [es'pina] nf thorn; (de pez) bone; **espina dorsal** (Anat) spine

espinaca [espi'naka] nf spinach

espinazo [espi'naθo] nm spine, backbone

espinilla [espi'niʎa] nf (Anat: tibia) shin(bone); (grano) blackhead

espinoso, -a [espi'noso, a] adj (planta) thorny, prickly; (asunto) difficult

espionaje [espjo'naxe] nm spying, espionage

espiral [espi'ral] adj, nf spiral

espirar [espi'rar] vt to breathe out, exhale

espiritista [espiri'tista] adj, nmf spiritualist

espíritu [es'piritu] nm spirit; **Espíritu Santo** Holy Ghost o Spirit; **espiritual** adj spiritual

espléndido, -a [es'plendiðo, a] adj (magnífico) magnificent, splendid; (generoso) generous

esplendor [esplen'dor] nm
splendour

espolvorear [espolβore'ar] vt to
dust, sprinkle

esponja [es'ponxa] nf sponge; (fig)
sponger; **esponjoso, -a** adj spongy

espontaneidad [espontanei'ðað]
nf spontaneity; **espontáneo, -a** adj
spontaneous

esposa [es'posa] nf wife; **esposas**
nfpl handcuffs; **esposar** vt to
handcuff

esposo [es'poso] nm husband

espray [es'prai] nm spray

espuela [es'pwela] nf spur

espuma [es'puma] nf foam; (de
cerveza) froth, head; (de jabón) lather;
espuma de afeitar shaving foam;
espumadera nf (utensilio) skimmer;
espumoso, -a adj frothy, foamy; (vino)
sparkling

esqueleto [eske'leto] nm skeleton

esquema [es'kema] nm (diagrama)
diagram; (dibujo) plan; (Filosofía)
schema

esquí [es'ki] (pl **~s**) nm (objeto) ski;
(Deporte) skiing; **esquí acuático** water-
skiing; **esquiar** vi to ski

esquilar [eski'lar] vt to shear

esquimal [eski'mal] adj, nmf Eskimo

esquina [es'kina] nf corner;
esquinazo [eski'naθo] nm: **dar
esquinazo a algn** (ESP) to give sb the slip

esquirol [eski'rol] (ESP) nm
strikebreaker, scab

esquivar [eski'βar] vt to avoid

esta ['esta] adj demos V **este²**

está vb V **estar**

ésta pron V **éste**

estabilidad [estaβili'ðað] nf
stability; **estable** adj stable

establecer [estaβle'θer] vt to
establish; **establecerse** vr to
establish o.s.; (echar raíces) to settle
(down); **establecimiento** nm
establishment

establo [es'taβlo] nm (Agr) stable

estaca [es'taka] nf stake, post; (de

tienda de campaña) peg

estacada [esta'kaða] nf (cerca) fence,
fencing; (palenque) stockade

estación [esta'θjon] nf station;
(del año) season; **estación balnearia**
seaside resort; **estación de autobuses**
bus station; **estación de servicio**
service station

estacionamiento
[estaθjona'mjento] nm (Auto)
parking; (Mil) stationing

estacionar [estaθjo'nar] vt (Auto) to
park; (Mil) to station

estadía [esta'ðia] (LAM) nf stay

estadio [es'taðjo] nm (fase) stage,
phase; (Deporte) stadium

estadista [esta'ðista] nm (Pol)
statesman; (Mat) statistician

estadística [esta'ðistika] nf figure,
statistic; (ciencia) statistics sg

estado [es'taðo] nm (Pol: condición)
state; **estar en** ~ to be pregnant;
estado civil marital status; **estado
de ánimo** state of mind; **estado
de cuenta** bank statement; **estado de
sitio** state of siege; **estado mayor**
staff; **Estados Unidos** United States
(of America)

estadounidense [estaðouni'ðense]
adj United States cpd, American ▷ nmf
American

estafa [es'tafa] nf swindle, trick;
estafar vt to swindle, defraud

estáis vb V **estar**

estallar [esta'ʎar] vi to burst; (bomba)
to explode, go off; (epidemia, guerra,
rebelión) to break out; ~ **en llanto**
to burst into tears; **estallido** nm
explosion; (fig) outbreak

estampa [es'tampa] nf print,
engraving; **estampado, -a**
[estam'paðo, a] adj print ▷ nm
(impresión: acción) printing; (: efecto)
print; (marca) stamping

estampar [estam'par] vt (imprimir)
to print; (marcar) to stamp; (metal) to
engrave; (poner sello en) to stamp; (fig)
to stamp, imprint

estampida [estam'piða] *nf*
stampede

estampido [estam'piðo] *nm* bang,
report

estampilla [estam'piʎa] (LAM) *nf*
(postage) stamp

están *vb* V **estar**

estancado, -a [estan'kaðo, a] *adj*
stagnant

estancar [estan'kar] *vt* (aguas)
to hold up, hold back; (Com) to
monopolize; (fig) to block, hold up;
estancarse *vr* to stagnate

estancia [estan'θja] *nf* (ESP,
MÉX: permanencia) stay; (sala)
room; (RPL: de ganado) farm, ranch;
estanciero (RPL) *nm* farmer, rancher

estanco, -a [estan'ko, a] *adj*
watertight ▷ *nm* tobacconist's (shop),
cigar store (US)

○ **ESTANCO**

  ● Cigarettes, tobacco, postage
  ● stamps and official forms are all
  ● sold under state monopoly in
  ● shops called **estancos**. Although
  ● tobacco products can also be
  ● bought in bars and quioscos they
  ● are generally more expensive.

estándar [es'tandar] *adj, nm*
standard

estandarte [estan'darte] *nm*
banner, standard

estanque [es'tanke] *nm* (lago) pool,
pond; (Agr) reservoir

estanquero, -a [estan'kero, a] *nm/f*
tobacconist

estante [es'tante] *nm* (armario)
rack, stand; (biblioteca) bookcase;
(anaquel) shelf; **estantería** *nf* shelving,
shelves *pl*

estaño [es'taɲo] *nm* tin

estar [es'tar] *vi* **1** (posición) to be; **está
en la plaza** it's in the square; **¿está**

Juan? is Juan in?; **estamos a 30 km de
Junín** we're 30 kms from Junín

2 (+ adj: estado) to be; **estar enfermo** to
be ill; **está muy elegante** he's looking
very smart; **¿cómo estás?** how are
you keeping?

3 (+ gerundio) to be; **estoy leyendo**
I'm reading

4 (uso pasivo): **está condenado a
muerte** he's been condemned to
death; **está envasado en ...** it's
packed in ...

5 (con fechas): **¿a cuántos estamos?**
what's the date today?; **estamos a 5 de
mayo** it's the 5th of May

6 (locuciones): **¿estamos?** (¿de acuerdo?)
okay?; (¿listo?) ready?

7 : **estar de: estar de vacaciones/
viaje** to be on holiday/away o on a
trip; **está de camarero** he's working
as a waiter

8 : **estar para: está para salir** he's
about to leave; **no estoy para bromas**
I'm not in the mood for jokes

9 : **estar por** (propuesta etc) to be in
favour of; (persona etc) to support, side
with; **está por limpiar** it still has to
be cleaned

10 : **estar sin: estar sin dinero** to have
no money; **está sin terminar** it isn't
finished yet

estarse *vr*: **se estuvo en la cama
toda la tarde** he stayed in bed all
afternoon

estas ['estas] *adj demos* V **este²**

éstas *pron* V **éste**

estatal [esta'tal] *adj* state *cpd*

estático, -a [es'tatiko, a] *adj* static

estatua [es'tatwa] *nf* statue

estatura [esta'tura] *nf* stature,
height

este¹ ['este] *nm* east

este² ['este] (*f* **esta**, *pl* **estos**)
adj demos (sg) this; (pl) these

éste *etc vb* V **estar**

éste ['este] (**ésta**, *pl* **éstos, éstas**)
pron (sg) this (one); (pl) these (ones);

ése ... ~ ... the former ... the latter ...

estén *etc vb* V **estar**

estepa [es'tepa] *nf (Geo)* steppe

estera [es'tera] *nf* mat(ting)

estéreo [es'tereo] *adj inv, nm* stereo; **estereotipo** *nm* stereotype

estéril [es'teril] *adj* sterile, barren; *(fig)* vain, futile; **esterilizar** *vt* to sterilize

esterlina [ester'lina] *adj*: **libra ~** pound sterling

estés *etc vb* V **estar**

estética [es'tetika] *nf* aesthetics *sg*

estético, -a [es'tetiko, a] *adj* aesthetic

estiércol [es'tjerkol] *nm* dung, manure

estigma [es'tiɣma] *nm* stigma

estilo [es'tilo] *nm* style; *(Tec)* stylus; *(Natación)* stroke; **algo por el ~** something along those lines

estima [es'tima] *nf* esteem, respect; **estimación** [estima'θjon] *nf (evaluación)* estimation; *(aprecio, afecto)* esteem, regard; **estimado, -a** *adj* esteemed; **E~ señor** Dear Sir

estimar [esti'mar] *vt (evaluar)* to estimate; *(valorar)* to value; *(apreciar)* to esteem, respect; *(pensar, considerar)* to think, reckon

estimulante [estimu'lante] *adj* stimulating ▷ *nm* stimulant

estimular [estimu'lar] *vt* to stimulate; *(excitar)* to excite

estímulo [es'timulo] *nm* stimulus; *(ánimo)* encouragement

estirar [esti'rar] *vt* to stretch; *(dinero, suma etc)* to stretch out; **estirarse** *vr* to stretch

estirón [esti'ron] *nm* pull, tug; *(crecimiento)* spurt, sudden growth; **dar o pegar un ~** *(fam: niño)* to shoot up *(inf)*

estirpe [es'tirpe] *nf* stock, lineage

estival [esti'βal] *adj* summer *cpd*

esto ['esto] *pron* this, this thing o matter; **~ de la boda** this business about the wedding

Estocolmo [esto'kolmo] *nm* Stockholm

estofado [esto'faðo] *nm* stew

estómago [es'tomaɣo] *nm* stomach; **tener ~** to be thick-skinned

estorbar [estor'βar] *vt* to hinder, obstruct; *(molestar)* to bother, disturb ▷ *vi* to be in the way; **estorbo** *nm (molestia)* bother, nuisance; *(obstáculo)* hindrance, obstacle

estornudar [estornu'ðar] *vi* to sneeze

estos ['estos] *adj demos* V **este²**

éstos *pron* V **éste**

estoy *vb* V **estar**

estrado [es'traðo] *nm* platform

estrafalario, -a [estrafa'larjo, a] *adj* odd, eccentric

estrago [es'traɣo] *nm* ruin, destruction; **hacer ~s en** to wreak havoc among

estragón [estra'ɣon] *nm* tarragon

estrambótico, -a [estram'botiko, a] *adj (persona)* eccentric; *(peinado, ropa)* outlandish

estrangular [estraŋɡu'lar] *vt (persona)* to strangle; *(Med)* to strangulate

estratagema [estrata'xema] *nf (Mil)* stratagem; *(astucia)* cunning

estrategia [estra'texja] *nf* strategy; **estratégico, -a** *adj* strategic

estrato [es'trato] *nm* stratum, layer

estrechar [estre'tʃar] *vt (reducir)* to narrow; *(Costura)* to take in; *(abrazar)* to hug, embrace; **estrecharse** *vr (reducirse)* to narrow, grow narrow; *(abrazarse)* to embrace; **~ la mano** to shake hands

estrechez [estre'tʃeθ] *nf* narrowness; *(de ropa)* tightness; **estrecheces** *nfpl (dificultades económicas)* financial difficulties

estrecho, -a [es'tretʃo, a] *adj* narrow; *(apretado)* tight; *(íntimo)* close, intimate; *(miserable)* mean ▷ *nm* strait; **~ de miras** narrow-minded

estrella [es'treʎa] *nf* star; **estrella de mar** *(Zool)* starfish; **estrella fugaz** shooting star

estrellar [estre'ʎar] vt (hacer añicos) to smash (to pieces); (huevos) to fry; **estrellarse** vr to smash (to pieces); (chocarse) to crash; (fracasar) to fail

estremecer [estreme'θer] vt to shake; **estremecerse** vr to shake, tremble

estrenar [estre'nar] vt (vestido) to wear for the first time; (casa) to move into; (película, obra de teatro) to première; **estrenarse** vr (persona) to make one's début; **estreno** nm (Cine etc) première

estreñido, -a [estre'ɲiðo, a] adj constipated

estreñimiento [estreɲi'mjento] nm constipation

estrepitoso, -a [estrepi'toso, a] adj noisy; (fiesta) rowdy

estría [es'tria] nf groove

estribar [estri'βar] vi: **- en** to lie on

estribillo [estri'βiʎo] nm (Literatura) refrain; (Mús) chorus

estribo [es'triβo] nm (de jinete) stirrup; (de coche, tren) step; (de puente) support; (Geo) spur; **perder los ~s** to fly off the handle

estribor [estri'βor] nm (Náut) starboard

estricto, -a [es'trikto, a] adj (riguroso) strict; (severo) severe

estridente [estri'ðente] adj (color) loud; (voz) raucous

estropajo [estro'paxo] nm scourer

estropear [estrope'ar] vt to spoil; (dañar) to damage; **estropearse** vr (objeto) to get damaged; (persona, piel) to be ruined

estructura [estruk'tura] nf structure

estrujar [estru'xar] vt (apretar) to squeeze; (aplastar) to crush; (fig) to drain, bleed

estuario [es'twarjo] nm estuary

estuche [es'tutʃe] nm box, case

estudiante [estu'ðjante] nmf student; **estudiantil** adj student cpd

estudiar [estu'ðjar] vt to study

estudio [es'tuðjo] nm study; (Cine, Arte, Radio) studio; **estudios** nmpl studies; (erudición) learning sg; **estudioso, -a** adj studious

estufa [es'tufa] nf heater, fire

estupefaciente [estupefa'θjente] nm drug, narcotic

estupefacto, -a [estupe'fakto, a] adj speechless, thunderstruck

estupendo, -a [estu'pendo, a] adj wonderful, terrific; (fam) great; **¡~!** that's great!, fantastic!

estupidez [estupi'ðeθ] nf (torpeza) stupidity; (acto) stupid thing (to do)

estúpido, -a [es'tupiðo, a] adj stupid, silly

estuve etc vb v **estar**

ETA ['eta] (ESP) nf abr (= Euskadi ta Askatasuna) ETA

etapa [e'tapa] nf (de viaje) stage; (Deporte) leg; (parada) stopping place; (fase) stage, phase

etarra [e'tarra] nmf member of ETA

etc. abr (= etcétera) etc

etcétera [et'θetera] adv etcetera

eternidad [eterni'ðað] nf eternity; **eterno, -a** adj eternal, everlasting

ética ['etika] nf ethics pl

ético, -a [e'tiko, a] adj ethical

etiqueta [eti'keta] nf (modales) etiquette; (rótulo) label, tag

Eucaristía [eukaris'tia] nf Eucharist

euforia [eu'forja] nf euphoria

euro ['euro] nm (moneda) euro

eurodiputado, -a [euroðipu'taðo, a] nm/f Euro MP, MEP

Europa [eu'ropa] nf Europe; **europeo, -a** adj, nm/f European

Euskadi [eus'kaði] nm the Basque Country o Provinces pl

euskera [eus'kera] nm (Ling) Basque

evacuación [eβakwa'θjon] nf evacuation

evacuar [eβa'kwar] vt to evacuate

evadir [eβa'ðir] vt to evade, avoid; **evadirse** vr to escape

evaluar [eβa'lwar] vt to evaluate

evangelio [eβan'xeljo] nm gospel

evaporar [eβapo'rar] vt to evaporate; **evaporarse** vr to vanish

evasión [eβa'sjon] nf escape, flight; (fig) evasion; **evasión de capitales** flight of capital

evasiva [eβa'siβa] nf (pretexto) excuse

evento [e'βento] nm event

eventual [eβen'twal] adj possible, conditional (upon circumstances); (trabajador) casual, temporary

No confundir **eventual** con la palabra inglesa **eventual**.

evidencia [eβi'ðenθja] nf evidence, proof

evidente [eβi'ðente] adj obvious, clear, evident

evitar [eβi'tar] vt (evadir) to avoid; (impedir) to prevent; **~ hacer algo** to avoid doing sth

evocar [eβo'kar] vt to evoke, call forth

evolución [eβolu'θjon] nf (desarrollo) evolution, development; (cambio) change; (Mil) manoeuvre; **evolucionar** vi to evolve; to manoeuvre

ex [eks] adj ex-; **el ~ ministro** the former minister, the ex-minister

exactitud [eksakti'tuð] nf exactness; (precisión) accuracy; (puntualidad) punctuality; **exacto, -a** adj exact; accurate; punctual; **¡exacto!** exactly!

exageración [eksaxera'θjon] nf exaggeration

exagerar [eksaxe'rar] vt, vi to exaggerate

exaltar [eksal'tar] vt to exalt, glorify; **exaltarse** vr (excitarse) to get excited o worked up

examen [ek'samen] nm examination; **examen de conducir** driving test; **examen de ingreso** entrance examination

examinar [eksami'nar] vt to examine; **examinarse** vr to be examined, take an examination

excavadora [ekskaβa'ðora] nf excavator

excavar [ekska'βar] vt to excavate

excedencia [eksθe'ðenθja] nf: **estar en ~** to be on leave; **pedir o solicitar la ~** to ask for leave

excedente [eksθe'ðente] adj, nm excess, surplus

exceder [eksθe'ðer] vt to exceed, surpass; **excederse** vr (extralimitarse) to go too far

excelencia [eksθe'lenθja] nf excellence; **su E~** his Excellency; **excelente** adj excellent

excéntrico, -a [eks'θentriko, a] adj, nm/f eccentric

excepción [eksθep'θjon] nf exception; **a ~ de** with the exception of, except for; **excepcional** adj exceptional

excepto [eks'θepto] adv excepting, except (for)

exceptuar [eksθep'twar] vt to except, exclude

excesivo, -a [eksθe'siβo, a] adj excessive

exceso [eks'θeso] nm (gen) excess; (Com) surplus; **exceso de equipaje/peso** excess luggage/weight; **exceso de velocidad** speeding

excitado, -a [eksθi'taðo, a] adj excited; (emociones) aroused

excitar [eksθi'tar] vt to excite; (incitar) to urge; **excitarse** vr to get excited

exclamación [eksklama'θjon] nf exclamation

exclamar [ekskla'mar] vi to exclaim

excluir [eksklu'ir] vt to exclude; (dejar fuera) to shut out; (descartar) to reject

exclusiva [eksklu'siβa] nf (Prensa) exclusive, scoop; (Com) sole right

exclusivo, -a [eksklu'siβo, a] adj exclusive; **derecho ~** sole o exclusive right

Excmo. abr = **excelentísmo**

excomulgar [ekskomul'ɣar] vt (Rel) to excommunicate

excomunión [ekskomu'njon] nf excommunication

excursión [ekskur'sjon] nf
excursion, outing; **excursionista** nmf
(turista) sightseer

excusa [eks'kusa] nf excuse;
(disculpa) apology; **excusar**
[eksku'sar] vt to excuse

exhaustivo, -a [eksaus'tiβo, a] adj
(análisis) thorough; (estudio) exhaustive

exhausto, -a [ek'sausto, a] adj
exhausted

exhibición [eksiβi'θjon] nf
exhibition, display, show

exhibir [eksi'βir] vt to exhibit,
display, show

exigencia [eksi'xenθja] nf
demand, requirement; **exigente** adj
demanding

exigir [eksi'xir] vt (gen) to demand,
require; **~ el pago** to demand payment

exiliado, -a [eksi'ljaðo, a] adj exiled
▷ nm/f exile

exilio [ek'siljo] nm exile

eximir [eksi'mir] vt to exempt

existencia [eksis'tenθja] nf
existence; **existencias** nfpl stock(s) pl

existir [eksis'tir] vi to exist, be

éxito ['eksito] nm (triunfo) success;
(Mús etc) hit; **tener ~** to be successful

   No confundir **éxito** con la palabra
   inglesa exit.

exorbitante [eksorβi'tante] adj
(precio) exorbitant; (cantidad) excessive

exótico, -a [ek'sotiko, a] adj exotic

expandir [ekspan'dir] vt to expand

expansión [ekspan'sjon] nf
expansion

expansivo, -a [ekspan'siβo, a]
adj: **onda expansiva** shock wave

expatriarse [ekspa'trjarse] vr to
emigrate; (Pol) to go into exile

expectativa [ekspekta'tiβa] nf
(espera) expectation; (perspectiva)
prospect

expedición [ekspeði'θjon] nf
(excursión) expedition

expediente [ekspe'ðjente] nm
expedient; (Jur: procedimiento) action,
proceedings pl; (: papeles) dossier,

file, record

expedir [ekspe'ðir] vt (despachar) to
send, forward; (pasaporte) to issue

expensas [eks'pensas] nfpl: **a ~ de** at
the expense of

experiencia [ekspe'rjenθja] nf
experience

experimentado, -a
[eksperimen'taðo, a] adj experienced

experimentar [eksperimen'tar] vt
(en laboratorio) to experiment with;
(probar) to test, try out; (notar, observar)
to experience; (deterioro, pérdida) to
suffer; **experimento** nm experiment

experto, -a [eks'perto, a] adj expert,
skilled ▷ nm/f expert

expirar [ekspi'rar] vi to expire

explanada [ekspla'naða] nf (llano)
plain

explayarse [ekspla'jarse] vr (en
discurso) to speak at length; **~ con algn**
to confide in sb

explicación [eksplika'θjon] nf
explanation

explicar [ekspli'kar] vt to explain;
explicarse vr to explain (o.s.)

explícito, -a [eks'pliθito, a] adj
explicit

explique etc vb V **explicar**

explorador, a [eksplora'ðor, a] nm/f
(pionero) explorer; (Mil) scout ▷ nm
(Med) probe; (Tec) (radar) scanner

explorar [eksplo'rar] vt to explore;
(Med) to probe; (radar) to scan

explosión [eksplo'sjon] nf
explosion; **explosivo, -a** adj explosive

explotación [eksplota'θjon] nf
exploitation; (de planta etc) running

explotar [eksplo'tar] vt to exploit to
run, operate ▷ vi to explode

exponer [ekspo'ner] vt to expose;
(cuadro) to display; (vida) to risk;
(idea) to explain; **exponerse** vr: **~se
a (hacer)** algo to run the risk of
(doing) sth

exportación [eksporta'θjon] nf
(acción) export; (mercancías) exports pl

exportar [ekspor'tar] vt to export

exposición [ekspo'θjon] *nf* (gen)
exposure; (de arte) show, exhibition;
(explicación) explanation; (declaración)
account, statement

expresamente [ekspresa'mente]
adv (decir) clearly; (a propósito) expressly

expresar [ekspre'sar] *vt* to express;
expresión *nf* expression

expresivo, -a [ekspre'siβo, a] *adj*
(persona, gesto, palabras) expressive;
(cariñoso) affectionate

expreso, -a [eks'preso, a] *pp de*
expresar ▷ *adj* (explícito) express;
(claro) specific, clear; (tren) fast
▷ *adv*: **enviar** to send by express
(delivery)

express [eks'pres] (LAM) *adv*: **enviar**
algo ~ to send sth special delivery

exprimidor [eksprimi'ðor] *nm*
squeezer

exprimir [ekspri'mir] *vt* (fruta) to
squeeze; (zumo) to squeeze out

expuesto, -a [eks'pwesto, a] *pp de*
exponer ▷ *adj* exposed; (cuadro etc) on
show, on display

expulsar [ekspul'sar] *vt* (echar) to
eject, throw out; (alumno) to expel;
(despedir) to sack, fire; (Deporte) to
send off; **expulsión** *nf* expulsion;
sending-off

exquisito, -a [ekski'sito, a] *adj*
exquisite; (comida) delicious

éxtasis ['ekstasis] *nm* ecstasy

extender [eksten'der] *vt* to extend;
(los brazos) to stretch out, hold out;
(mapa, tela) to spread (out), open (out);
(mantequilla) to spread; (certificado)
to issue; (cheque, recibo) to make out;
(documento) to draw up; **extenderse**
vr (gen) to extend; (persona: en el suelo)
to stretch out; (epidemia) to spread;
extendido, -a *adj* (abierto) spread out,
open; (brazos) outstretched; (costumbre)
widespread

extensión [eksten'sjon] *nf* (de
terreno, mar) expanse, stretch;
(de tiempo) length, duration; (Tel)
extension; **en toda la ~ de la palabra**

in every sense of the word

extenso, -a [eks'tenso, a] *adj*
extensive

exterior [ekste'rjor] *adj* (de fuera)
external; (afuera) outside, exterior;
(apariencia) outward; (deuda, relaciones)
foreign ▷ *nm* (gen) exterior, outside;
(aspecto) outward appearance;
(Deporte) wing(er); (países extranjeros)
abroad; **en el** ~ abroad; **al** ~ outwardly,
on the surface

exterminar [ekstermi'nar] *vt* to
exterminate

externo, -a [eks'terno, a] *adj*
(exterior) external, outside; (superficial)
outward ▷ *nm/f* day pupil

extinguir [ekstin'gir] *vt* (fuego) to
extinguish, put out; (raza, población) to
wipe out; **extinguirse** *vr* (fuego) to go
out; (Bio) to die out, become extinct

extintor [ekstin'tor] *nm* (fire)
extinguisher

extirpar [ekstir'par] *vt* (Med) to
remove (surgically)

extra ['ekstra] *adj inv* (tiempo) extra;
(chocolate, vino) good-quality ▷ *nmf*
extra ▷ *nm* extra; (bono) bonus

extracción [ekstrak'θjon] *nf*
extraction; (en lotería) draw

extracto [eks'trakto] *nm* extract

extradición [ekstraði'θjon] *nf*
extradition

extraer [ekstra'er] *vt* to extract,
take out

extraescolar [ekstraesko'lar]
adj: **actividad** ~ extracurricular activity

extranjero, -a [ekstran'xero, a] *adj*
foreign ▷ *nm/f* foreigner ▷ *nm* foreign
countries *pl*; **en el** ~ abroad

> No confundir **extranjero** con la
> palabra inglesa *stranger*.

extrañar [ekstra'ɲar] *vt* (sorprender)
to find strange o odd; (echar de menos) to
miss; **extrañarse** *vr* (sorprenderse) to
be amazed, be surprised; **me extraña**
I'm surprised

extraño, -a [eks'traɲo, a] *adj*
(extranjero) foreign; (raro, sorprendente)

strange, odd

extraordinario, -a
[ekstraorˈðiˈnarjo, a] *adj*
extraordinary; (*edición, número*) special
▷ *nm* (*de periódico*) special edition;
horas extraordinarias overtime *sg*

extrarradio [ekstraˈrraðjo] *nm*
suburbs

extravagante [ekstraβaˈɣante]
adj (*excéntrico*) eccentric; (*estrafalario*)
outlandish

extraviado, -a [ekstraˈβjaðo, a] *adj*
lost, missing

extraviar [ekstraˈβjar] *vt*
(*persona: desorientar*) to mislead,
misdirect; (*perder*) to lose, misplace;
extraviarse *vr* to lose one's way,
get lost

extremar [ekstreˈmar] *vt* to carry
to extremes

extremaunción [ekstremaunˈθjon]
nf extreme unction

extremidad [ekstremiˈðað] *nf*
(*punta*) extremity; **extremidades** *nfpl*
(*Anat*) extremities

extremo, -a [eksˈtremo, a] *adj*
extreme; (*último*) last ▷ *nm* end; (*límite,
grado sumo*) extreme; **en último ~** as
a last resort

extrovertido, -a [ekstroβerˈtiðo, a]
adj, nm/f extrovert

exuberante [eksuβeˈrante] *adj*
exuberant; (*fig*) luxuriant, lush

eyacular [ejakuˈlar] *vt, vi* to
ejaculate

---

adj, nm/f extrovert

exuberante [eksuβeˈrante] *adj*
exuberant; (*fig*) luxuriant, lush

eyacular [ejakuˈlar] *vt, vi* to
ejaculate

o lose one's way, get lost

extremar [ekstreˈmar] *vt* to carry
to extremes

extremaunción [ekstremaunˈθjon]
nf extreme unction

extremidad [ekstremiˈðað] *nf*
(*punta*) extremity; **extremidades** *nfpl*
(*Anat*) extremities

extremo, -a [eksˈtremo, a] *adj*
extreme; (*último*) last ▷ *nm* end; (*límite,
grado sumo*) extreme; **en último ~** as
a last resort

extrovertido, -a [ekstroβerˈtiðo, a]

f

fa [fa] *nm* (*Mús*) fa, F

fabada [fa'βaða] *nf* bean and sausage stew

fábrica ['faβrika] *nf* factory; **marca de ~** trademark; **precio de ~** factory price

 No confundir **fábrica** con la palabra inglesa *fabric*.

fabricación [faβrika'θjon] *nf* (*manufactura*) manufacture; (*producción*) production; **de ~ casera** home-made; **fabricación en serie** mass production

fabricante [faβri'kante] *nmf* manufacturer

fabricar [faβri'kar] *vt* (*manufacturar*) to manufacture, make; (*construir*) to build; (*cuento*) to fabricate, devise

fábula ['faβula] *nf* (*cuento*) fable; (*chisme*) rumour; (*mentira*) fib

fabuloso, -a [faβu'loso, a] *adj* (*oportunidad, tiempo*) fabulous, great

facción [fak'θjon] *nf* (*Pol*) faction; **facciones** *nfpl* (*de rostro*) features

faceta [fa'θeta] *nf* facet

facha ['fatʃa] (*fam*) *nf* (*aspecto*) look; (*cara*) face

fachada [fa'tʃaða] *nf* (*Arq*) façade, front

fácil ['faθil] *adj* (*simple*) easy; (*probable*) likely

facilidad [faθili'ðað] *nf* (*capacidad*) ease; (*sencillez*) simplicity; (*de palabra*) fluency; **facilidades** *nfpl* facilities; **facilidades de pago** credit facilities

facilitar [faθili'tar] *vt* (*hacer fácil*) to make easy; (*proporcionar*) to provide

factor [fak'tor] *nm* factor

factura [fak'tura] *nf* (*cuenta*) bill; **facturación** *nf* (*de equipaje*) check-in; **facturar** *vt* (*Com*) to invoice, charge for; (*equipaje*) to check in

facultad [fakul'tað] *nf* (*aptitud, Escol etc*) faculty; (*poder*) power

faena [fa'ena] *nf* (*trabajo*) work; (*quehacer*) task, job

faisán [fai'san] *nm* pheasant

faja ['faxa] *nf* (*para la cintura*) sash; (*de mujer*) corset; (*de tierra*) strip

fajo ['faxo] *nm* (*de papeles*) bundle; (*de billetes*) wad

falda ['falda] *nf* (*prenda de vestir*) skirt; **falda pantalón** culottes *pl*, split skirt

falla ['faʎa] *nf* (*defecto*) fault, flaw; **falla humana** (*LAM*) human error

fallar [fa'ʎar] *vt* (*Jur*) to pronounce sentence on ▸ *vi* (*memoria*) to fail; (*motor*) to miss

Fallas ['faʎas] *nfpl* Valencian celebration of the feast of St Joseph

- **FALLAS**

- In the week of 19 March (the feast of San José), Valencia honours its patron saint with a spectacular fiesta called **Las Fallas**. The **Fallas** are huge papier-mâché, cardboard and wooden sculptures which are built by competing teams throughout the year. They represent politicians and well-known public figures and are thrown onto

● bonfires and set alight once a jury
● has judged them – only the best
● sculpture escapes the flames.

fallecer [faʎe'θer] vi to pass away,
die; **fallecimiento** nm decease,
demise

fallido, -a [fa'ʎiðo, a] adj (gen)
frustrated, unsuccessful

fallo ['faʎo] nm (Jur) verdict, ruling;
(fracaso) failure; **fallo cardíaco** heart
failure; **fallo humano** (ESP) human
error

falsificar [falsifi'kar] vt (firma etc) to
forge; (moneda) to counterfeit

falso, -a ['falso, a] adj false;
(documento, moneda etc) fake; **en ~**
falsely

falta ['falta] nf (defecto) fault, flaw;
(privación) lack, want; (ausencia)
absence; (carencia) shortage;
(equivocación) mistake; (Deporte) foul;
echar en ~ to miss; **hacer ~** to
be necessary to do sth; **me hace
~ una pluma** I need a pen; **falta de
educación** bad manners pl; **falta de
ortografía** spelling mistake

faltar [fal'tar] vi (escasear) to be
lacking, be wanting; (ausentarse) to
be absent, be missing; **faltan 2 horas
para llegar** there are 2 hours to go
till arrival; **~ al respeto a algn** to be
disrespectful to sb; **¡no faltaba
más!** (no hay de qué) don't mention it

fama ['fama] nf (renombre) fame;
(reputación) reputation

familia [fa'milja] nf family; **familia
numerosa** large family; **familia
política** in-laws pl

familiar [fami'ljar] adj (relativo a la
familia) family cpd; (conocido, informal)
familiar ▷ nm relative, relation

famoso, -a [fa'moso, a] adj
(renombrado) famous

fan [fan] (pl ~s) nmf fan

fanático, -a [fa'natiko, a] adj
fanatical ▷ nm/f fanatic; (Cine,
Deporte) fan

fanfarrón, -ona [fanfa'rron, ona]
adj boastful

fango ['fango] nm mud

fantasía [fanta'sia] nf fantasy;
imagination; **joyas de ~** imitation
jewellery sg

fantasma [fan'tasma] nm (espectro)
ghost, apparition; (fanfarrón) show-off

fantástico, -a [fan'tastiko, a] adj
fantastic

farmacéutico, -a [farma'θeutiko,
a] adj pharmaceutical ▷ nm/f
chemist (BRIT), pharmacist

farmacia [far'maθja] nf (chemist's
(shop) (BRIT), pharmacy; **farmacia de
guardia** all-night chemist

fármaco ['farmako] nm drug

faro ['faro] nm (Náut: torre)
lighthouse; (Auto) headlamp;
faros antiniebla fog lamps; **faros
delanteros/traseros** headlights/rear
lights

farol [fa'rol] nm lantern, lamp

farola [fa'rola] nf street lamp (BRIT)
o light (US)

farra ['farra] (LAM: fam) nf party; **ir de
~** to go on a binge

farsa ['farsa] nf (gen) farce

farsante [far'sante] nmf fraud, fake

fascículo [fas'θikulo] nm (de revista)
part, instalment

fascinar [fasθi'nar] vt (gen) to
fascinate

fascismo [fas'θismo] nm fascism;
fascista adj, nmf fascist

fase ['fase] nf phase

fashion ['faʃon] adj (fam) trendy

fastidiar [fasti'ðjar] vt (molestar)
to annoy, bother; (estropear) to spoil;
fastidiarse vr; **¡que se fastidie!** (fam)
he'll just have to put up with it!

fastidio [fas'tiðjo] nm (molestia)
annoyance; **fastidioso, -a** adj
(molesto) annoying

fatal [fa'tal] adj (gen) fatal;
(desgraciado) ill-fated; (fam: malo,
pésimo) awful; **fatalidad** nf (destino)
fate; (mala suerte) misfortune

fatiga [fa'tiɣa] nf (cansancio) fatigue, weariness

fatigar [fati'ɣar] vt to tire, weary

fatigoso, -a [fati'ɣoso, a] adj (cansador) tiring

fauna ['fauna] nf fauna

favor [fa'ɓor] nm favour; **estar a ~ de** to be in favour of; **haga el ~ de ...** would you be so good as to ...; kindly ...; **por ~** please; **favorable** adj favourable

favorecer [faɓore'θer] vt to favour; (vestido etc) to become, flatter; **este peinado le favorece** this hairstyle suits him

favorito, -a [faɓo'rito, a] adj, nm/f favourite

fax [faks] nm inv fax; **mandar por ~ to fax**

fe [fe] nf (Rel) faith; (documento) certificate; **actuar con buena/mala ~** to act in good/bad faith

febrero [fe'ɓrero] nm February

fecha ['fetʃa] nf date; **con ~ adelantada** postdated; **en ~ próxima** soon; **hasta la ~** to date, so far; **poner ~ to date; fecha de caducidad** (de producto alimenticio) sell-by date; (de contrato etc) expiry date; **fecha de nacimiento** date of birth; **fecha límite** o **tope** deadline

fecundo, -a [fe'kundo, a] adj (fértil) fertile; (fig) prolific; (productivo) productive

federación [feðera'θjon] nf federation

felicidad [feliθi'ðað] nf happiness; **¡~es!** (deseos) best wishes, congratulations!; (en cumpleaños) happy birthday!

felicitación [feliθita'θjon] nf (tarjeta) greeting(s) card

felicitar [feliθi'tar] vt to congratulate

feliz [fe'liθ] adj happy

felpudo [fel'puðo] nm doormat

femenino, -a [feme'nino, a] adj, nm feminine

feminista [femi'nista] adj, nmf feminist

fenómeno [fe'nomeno] nm phenomenon; (fig) freak, accident ▷ adj great ▷ excl great!, marvellous!; **fenomenal** adj → **fenómeno**

feo, -a ['feo, a] adj (gen) ugly; (desagradable) bad, nasty

féretro ['feretro] nm (ataúd) coffin; (sarcófago) bier

feria ['ferja] nf (gen) fair; (descanso) holiday, rest day; (MÉX: cambio) small o loose change; (CS: mercado) village market

feriado [fe'rjaðo] (LAM) nm holiday

fermentar [fermen'tar] vi to ferment

feroz [fe'roθ] adj (cruel) cruel; (salvaje) fierce

férreo, -a ['ferreo, a] adj iron

ferretería [ferrete'ria] nf (tienda) ironmonger's (shop) (BRIT), hardware store (US)

ferrocarril [ferroka'rril] nm railway

ferroviario, -a [ferro'βjarjo, a] adj rail cpd

ferry ['ferri] (pl ~s o **ferries**) nm ferry

fértil ['fertil] adj (productivo) fertile; (rico) rich; **fertilidad** nf (gen) fertility; (productividad) fruitfulness

fervor [fer'ɓor] nm fervour

festejar [feste'xar] vt (celebrar) to celebrate

festejo [fes'texo] nm celebration; **festejos** nmpl (fiestas) festivals

festín [fes'tin] nm feast, banquet

festival [festi'βal] nm festival

festividad [festiβi'ðað] nf festivity

festivo, -a [fes'tiβo, a] adj (de fiesta) festive; (Cine, Literatura) humorous; **día ~** holiday

feto ['feto] nm foetus

fiable ['fjaβle] adj (persona) trustworthy; (máquina) reliable

fiambre ['fjambre] nm cold meat

fiambrera [fjam'brera] nf (para almuerzo) lunch box

fianza ['fjanθa] nf surety; (Jur): **libertad bajo ~** release on bail

fiar [fi'ar] vt (salir garante de) to guarantee; (vender a crédito) to sell on credit ▷ vi to trust; **fiarse** vr to trust (in), rely on; **~ a** (secreto) to confide (to); **~se de algn** to rely on sb

fibra ['fiβra] nf fibre; **fibra óptica** optical fibre

ficción [fik'θjon] nf fiction

ficha ['fit∫a] nf (Tel) token; (en juegos) counter, marker; (tarjeta) (index) card; **fichaje** nm (Deporte) signing; **fichar** vt (archivar) to file, index; (Deporte) to sign; **estar fichado** to have a record; **fichero** nm box file; (Inform) file

ficticio, -a [fik'tiθjo, a] adj (imaginario) fictitious; (falso) fabricated

fidelidad [fiðeli'ðað] nf (lealtad) fidelity, loyalty; **alta ~** high fidelity, hi-fi

fideos [fi'ðeos] nmpl noodles

fiebre ['fjeβre] nf (Med) fever; (fig) fever, excitement; **tener ~** to have a temperature; **fiebre aftosa** foot-and-mouth disease

fiel [fjel] adj (leal) faithful, loyal; (fiable) reliable; (exacto) accurate, faithful ▷ nm: **los ~es** the faithful

fieltro ['fjeltro] nm felt

fiera ['fjera] nf (animal feroz) wild animal o beast; (fig) dragon; V tb **fiero**

fiero, -a ['fjero, a] adj (cruel) cruel; (feroz) fierce; (duro) harsh

fierro ['fjerro] nm (LAM) nm (hierro) iron

fiesta ['fjesta] nf party; (de pueblo) festival; (vacaciones: tb: **~s**) holiday sg; **fiesta mayor** annual festival; **fiesta patria** (LAM) independence day

Fiestas can be official public holidays or holidays set by each autonomous region, many of which coincide with religious festivals. There are also many **fiestas** all over Spain for a local patron saint or the Virgin Mary. These often last several days and

can include religious processions, carnival parades, bullfights and dancing.

figura [fi'γura] nf (gen) figure; (forma, imagen) shape, form; (Naipes) face card

figurar [fiγu'rar] vt (representar) to represent; (fingir) to figure ▷ vi to figure; **figurarse** vr (imaginarse) to imagine; (suponer) to suppose

fijador [fixa'ðor] nm (Foto etc) fixative; (de pelo) gel

fijar [fi'xar] vt (gen) to fix; (estampilla) to affix, stick (on); **fijarse** vr: **~se en** to notice

fijo, -a ['fixo, a] adj (gen) fixed; (firme) firm; (permanente) permanent ▷ adv: **mirar ~** to stare

fila ['fila] nf row; (Mil) rank; **ponerse en ~** to line up, get into line; **fila india** single file

filatelia [fila'telja] nf philately, stamp collecting

filete [fi'lete] nm (de carne) fillet steak; (de pescado) fillet

filiación [filja'θjon] nf (Pol) affiliation

filial [fi'ljal] adj filial ▷ nf subsidiary

Filipinas [fili'pinas] nfpl: **las (Islas) ~** the Philippines; **filipino, -a** adj, nm/f Philippine

filmar [fil'mar] vt to film, shoot

filo ['filo] nm (gen) edge; **sacar ~ a** to sharpen; **al ~ del mediodía** at about midday; **de doble ~** double-edged

filología [filolo'γia] nf philology; **filología inglesa** (Univ) English Studies

filón [fi'lon] nm (Minería) vein, lode; (fig) goldmine

filosofía [filoso'fia] nf philosophy; **filósofo, -a** nm/f philosopher

filtrar [fil'trar] vt, vi to filter, strain; **filtrarse** vr to filter; **filtro** nm (Tec, utensilio) filter

fin [fin] nm end; (objetivo) aim, purpose; **al y al cabo** when all's said and done; **a ~ de** in order to; **por ~** finally; **en ~** in short; **fin de semana**

weekend

final [fi'nal] *adj* final ▷ *nm* end, conclusion ▷ *nf* final; **al ~** in the end; **a ~es de** at the end of; **finalidad** *nf* (*propósito*) purpose, intention; **finalista** *nmf* finalist; **finalizar** *vt* to end, (*Inform*) to log out o off ▷ *vi* to end, come to an end

financiar [finan'θjar] *vt* to finance; **financiero, -a** *adj* financial ▷ *nm/f* financier

finca ['finka] *nf* (*casa de campo*) country house; (*ESP: bien inmueble*) property, land; (*LAM: granja*) farm

finde ['finde] *nm abr* (*fam: fin de semana*) weekend

fingir [fin'xir] *vt* (*simular*) to simulate, feign ▷ *vi* (*aparentar*) to pretend

finlandés, -esa [finlan'des, esa] *adj* Finnish ▷ *nm/f* Finn ▷ *nm* (*Ling*) Finnish

Finlandia [fin'landja] *nf* Finland

fino, -a ['fino, a] *adj* fine; (*delgado*) slender; (*de buenas maneras*) polite, refined; (*jerez*) fino, dry

firma ['firma] *nf* signature; (*Com*) firm, company

firmamento [firma'mento] *nm* firmament

firmar [fir'mar] *vt* to sign

firme ['firme] *adj* firm; (*estable*) stable; (*sólido*) solid; (*constante*) steady; (*decidido*) resolute ▷ *nm* road (surface); **firmeza** *nf* firmness; (*constancia*) steadiness; (*solidez*) solidity

fiscal [fis'kal] *adj* fiscal ▷ *nmf* public prosecutor; **año ~** tax o fiscal year

fisgonear [fisɣone'ar] *vt* to poke one's nose into ▷ *vi* to pry, spy

física ['fisika] *nf* physics sg; *vt tb* **físico**

físico, -a ['fisiko, a] *adj* physical ▷ *nm* physique ▷ *nm/f* physicist

fisura [fi'sura] *nf* crack; (*Med*) fracture

flác(c)ido, -a [fla'(k)θiðo, a] *adj* flabby

flaco, -a ['flako, a] *adj* (*muy delgado*) skinny, thin; (*débil*) weak, feeble

flagrante [fla'ɣrante] *adj* flagrant

flama ['flama] (*MÉX*) *nf* flame; **flamable** (*MÉX*) *adj* flammable

flamante [fla'mante] (*fam*) *adj* brilliant; (*nuevo*) brand-new

flamenco, -a [fla'menko, a] *adj* (*de Flandes*) Flemish; (*baile, música*) flamenco ▷ *nm* (*baile, música*) flamenco; (*Zool*) flamingo

flamingo [fla'mingo] (*MÉX*) *nm* flamingo

flan [flan] *nm* creme caramel

▌ No confundir **flan** con la palabra ~ inglesa *flan*.

flash [flaʃ] (*pl ~ o ~es*) *nm* (*Foto*) flash

flauta ['flauta] *nf* (*Mús*) flute

flecha ['fletʃa] *nf* arrow

flechazo [fle'tʃaθo] *nm* love at first sight

fleco ['fleko] *nm* fringe

flema ['flema] *nm* phlegm

flequillo [fle'kiʎo] *nm* (*pelo*) fringe

flexible [flek'siβle] *adj* flexible

flexión [flek'sjon] *nf* press-up

flexo ['flekso] *nm* adjustable table-lamp

flirtear [flirte'ar] *vi* to flirt

flojera [flo'xera] (*LAM: fam*) *nf*: **me da ~** I can't be bothered

flojo, -a ['floxo, a] *adj* (*gen*) loose; (*sin fuerzas*) limp; (*débil*) weak

flor [flor] *nf* flower; **a ~ de** on the surface of; **flora** *nf* flora; **florecer** *vi* (*Bot*) to flower, bloom; (*fig*) to flourish; **florería** (*LAM*) *nf* florist's (shop); **florero** *nm* vase; **floristería** *nf* florist's (shop)

flota ['flota] *nf* fleet

flotador [flota'ðor] *nm* (*gen*) float; (*para nadar*) rubber ring

flotar [flo'tar] *vi* (*gen*) to float; **flote** *nm*: **a flote** afloat; **salir a flote** (*fig*) to get back on one's feet

fluidez [flui'ðeθ] *nf* fluidity; (*fig*) fluency

fluido, -a ['fluiðo, a] *adj, nm* fluid

fluir [flu'ir] *vi* to flow

flujo ['fluxo] *nm* flow; **flujo y reflujo** ebb and flow

flúor ['fluor] nm fluoride

fluorescente [flwores'θente] adj
fluorescent ▷ nm fluorescent light

fluvial [flu'βial] adj (navegación,
cuenca) fluvial, river cpd

fobia ['fobja] nf phobia; **fobia a las
alturas** fear of heights

foca ['foka] nf seal

foco ['foko] nm focus; (Elec) floodlight;
(Méx: bombilla) (light) bulb

fofo, -a ['fofo, a] adj soft, spongy;
(carnes) flabby

fogata [fo'xata] nf bonfire

fogón [fo'xon] nm (de cocina) ring,
burner

folio ['foljo] nm folio, page

follaje [fo'ʎaxe] nm foliage

folleto [fo'ʎeto] nm (Pol) pamphlet

follón [fo'ʎon] (ESP: fam) nm (lío)
mess; (conmoción) fuss; **armar un ~** to
kick up a row

fomentar [fomen'tar] vt (Med) to
foment

fonda ['fonda] nf inn

fondo ['fondo] nm (de mar) bottom;
(de coche, sala) back; (Arte etc)
background; (reserva) fund; **fondos**
nmpl (Com) funds, resources; **una
investigación a ~** a thorough
investigation; **en el ~** at bottom,
deep down

fonobuzón [fonoβu'θon] nm voice
mail

fontanería [fontane'ria] nf
plumbing; **fontanero, -a** nm/f
plumber

footing ['futin] nm jogging; **hacer ~**
to jog, go jogging

forastero, -a [foras'tero, a] nm/f
stranger

forcejear [forθexe'ar] vi (luchar) to
struggle

forense [fo'rense] nmf pathologist

forma ['forma] nf (figura) form,
shape; (Med) fitness; (método) way,
means; **las ~s** the conventions; **estar
en ~** to be fit; **de ~ que ...** so that ...; **de
todas ~s** in any case

formación [forma'θjon] nf (gen)
formation; (educación) education;
formación profesional vocational
training

formal [for'mal] adj (gen) formal;
(fig: serio) serious; (: de fiar) reliable;
formalidad nf formality; seriousness;
formalizar vr (Jur) to formalize;
(situación) to put in order, regularize;
formalizarse vr (situación) to be put in
order, be regularized

formar [for'mar] vt (componer) to
form, shape; (constituir) to make up,
constitute; (Escol) to train, educate;
formarse vr (Escol) to be trained,
educated; (cobrar forma) to form, take
form; (desarrollarse) to develop

formatear [formate'ar] vt to format

formato [for'mato] nm format

formidable [formi'ðaβle] adj
(temible) formidable; (estupendo)
tremendous

fórmula ['formula] nf formula

formulario [formu'larjo] nm form

fornido, -a [for'niðo, a] adj well-
built

foro ['foro] nm (Pol, Inform etc) forum

forrar [fo'rrar] vt (abrigo) to line;
(libro) to cover; **forro** nm (de cuaderno)
cover; (Costura) lining; (de sillón)
upholstery; **forro polar** fleece

fortalecer [fortale'θer] vt to
strengthen

fortaleza [forta'leθa] nf (Mil)
fortress, stronghold; (fuerza) strength;
(determinación) resolution

fortuito, -a [for'twito, a] adj
accidental

fortuna [for'tuna] nf (suerte) fortune,
(good) luck; (riqueza) fortune, wealth

forzar [for'θar] vt (puerta) to force
(open); (compeler) to compel

forzoso, -a [for'θoso, a] adj
necessary

fosa ['fosa] nf (sepultura) grave; (en
tierra) pit; **fosas nasales** nostrils

fósforo ['fosforo] nm (Quím)
phosphorus; (cerilla) match

fósil ['fosil] nm fossil

foso ['foso] nm ditch; (Teatro) pit; (Auto) inspection pit

foto ['foto] nf photo, snap(shot); **sacar una ~** to take a photo o picture; **foto (de) carné** passport(-size) photo

fotocopia [foto'kopja] nf photocopy; **fotocopiadora** nf photocopier; **fotocopiar** vt to photocopy

fotografía [fotoɣra'fia] nf (Arte) photography; (una fotografía) photograph; **fotografiar** vt to photograph

fotógrafo, -a [fo'toɣrafo, a] nm/f photographer

fotomatón [fotoma'ton] nm photo booth

FP (ESP) nf abr (= Formación Profesional) vocational courses for 14-to 18-year-olds

fracasar [fraka'sar] vi (gen) to fail

fracaso [fra'kaso] nm failure

fracción [frak'θjon] nf fraction

fractura [frak'tura] nf fracture, break

fragancia [fra'ɣanθja] nf (olor) fragrance, perfume

frágil ['fraxil] adj (débil) fragile; (Com) breakable

fragmento [fraɣ'mento] nm (pedazo) fragment

fraile ['fraile] nm (Rel) friar; (: monje) monk

frambuesa [fram'bwesa] nf raspberry

francés, -esa [fran'θes, esa] adj French ▷ nm/f Frenchman(-woman) ▷ nm (Ling) French

Francia [franθja] nf France

franco, -a ['franko, a] adj (cándido) frank, open; (Com: exento) free ▷ nm (moneda) franc

francotirador, a [frankotira'ðor, a] nm/f sniper

franela [fra'nela] nf flannel

franja ['franxa] nf fringe

franquear [franke'ar] vt (camino) to clear; (carta, paquete postal) to frank, stamp; (obstáculo) to overcome

franqueo [fran'keo] nm postage

franqueza [fran'keθa] nf (candor) frankness

frasco ['frasko] nm bottle, flask

frase ['frase] nf sentence; **frase hecha** set phrase; (pey) stock phrase

fraterno, -a [fra'terno, a] adj brotherly, fraternal

fraude ['frauðe] nm (cualidad) dishonesty; (acto) fraud

frazada [fra'saða] (LAM) nf blanket

frecuencia [fre'kwenθja] nf frequency; **con ~** frequently, often

frecuentar [frekwen'tar] vt to frequent

frecuente [fre'kwente] adj (gen) frequent

fregadero [freɣa'ðero] nm (kitchen) sink

fregar [fre'ɣar] vt (frotar) to scrub; (platos) to wash (up); (LAM: fam: fastidiar) to annoy; (: malograr) to screw up

fregona [fre'ɣona] nf mop

freír [fre'ir] vt to fry

frenar [fre'nar] vt to brake; (fig) to check

frenazo [fre'naθo] nm: **dar un ~** to brake sharply

frenesí [frene'si] nm frenzy

freno ['freno] nm (Tec, Auto) brake; (de cabalgadura) bit; (fig) check; **freno de mano** handbrake

frente ['frente] nm (Arq, Pol) front; (de objeto) front part ▷ nf forehead, brow; **~ a** in front of; (en situación opuesta de) opposite; **al ~ de** (fig) at the head of; **chocar de ~** to crash head-on; **hacer ~ a** to face up to

fresa ['fresa] (ESP) nf strawberry

fresco, -a ['fresko, a] adj (nuevo) fresh; (frío) cool; (descarado) cheeky ▷ nm (aire) fresh air; (Arte) fresco; (LAM: jugo) fruit drink ▷ nm/f (fam): **ser un ~** to have a nerve; **tomar el ~** to get some fresh air; **frescura** nf freshness; (descaro) cheek, nerve

frialdad [frial'daθ] nf (gen) coldness; (indiferencia) indifference

frigidez [frixi'ðeθ] nf frigidity

frigorífico [friɣo'rifiko] nm
refrigerator

frijol [fri'xol] nm kidney bean

frío, -a etc ['frio, a] vb V **freír** ▷ adj
cold; (indiferente) indifferent ▷ nm
indifference; **hace ~** it's cold; **tener ~**
to be cold

frito, -a ['frito, a] adj fried; **me trae
~ ese hombre** I'm sick and tired of that
man; **fritos** nmpl fried food

frívolo, -a ['friβolo, a] adj frivolous

frontal [fron'tal] adj frontal; **choque
~** head-on collision

frontera [fron'tera] nf frontier;
fronterizo, -a adj frontier cpd;
(contiguo) bordering

frontón [fron'ton] nm (Deporte:
cancha) pelota court; (: juego) pelota

frotar [fro'tar] vt to rub; **frotarse**
vr: **~se las manos** to rub one's hands

fructífero, -a [fruk'tifero, a] adj
fruitful

fruncir [frun'θir] vt to pucker;
(Costura) to pleat; **~ el ceño** to knit
one's brow

frustrar [frus'trar] vt to frustrate

fruta ['fruta] nf fruit; **frutería** nf
fruit shop; **frutero, -a** adj fruit cpd
▷ nm/f fruiterer ▷ nm fruit bowl

frutilla [fru'tiʎa] (cs) nf strawberry

fruto ['fruto] nm fruit; (fig: resultado)
result; (: beneficio) benefit; **frutos secos**
nuts and dried fruit pl

fucsia ['fuksja] nf fuchsia

fue [fwe] vb V **ser**; **ir**

fuego ['fweɣo] nm (gen) fire; **a ~ lento**
on a low heat; **¿tienes ~?** have you (got)
a light?; **fuego amigo** friendly fire;
fuegos artificiales fireworks

fuente ['fwente] nf fountain;
(manantial: fig) spring; (origen) source;
(plato) large dish

fuera etc ['fwera] vb V **ser**; **ir** ▷ adv
out(side); (en otra parte) away; (excepto,
salvo) except, save ▷ prep: **~ de** outside;
(fig) besides; **~ de sí** beside o.s.; **por ~**
(on the) outside

fuera-borda ['fwera'βorða] nm
speedboat

fuerte ['fwerte] adj strong; (golpe)
hard; (ruido) loud; (comida) rich; (lluvia)
heavy; (dolor) intense ▷ adv strongly;
hard; loud(ly)

fuerza etc ['fwerθa] vb V **forzar** ▷ nf
(fortaleza) strength; (Tec, Elec) power;
(coacción) force; (Mil, Pol) force; **a ~ de**
by dint of; **cobrar ~s** to recover one's
strength; **tener ~s para** to have the
strength to; **a la ~** forcibly, by force;
por ~ of necessity; **fuerza de voluntad**
willpower; **fuerzas aéreas** air force sg;
fuerzas armadas armed forces

fuga ['fuɣa] nf (huida) flight, escape;
(de gas etc) leak

fugarse [fu'ɣarse] vr to flee, escape

fugaz [fu'ɣaθ] adj fleeting

fugitivo, -a [fuxi'tiβo, a] adj, nm/f
fugitive

fui [fwi] vb V **ser**; **ir**

fulano, -a [fu'lano, a] nm/f so-and-
so, what's-his-name/what's-her-name

fulminante [fulmi'nante] adj
(fig: mirada) fierce; (Med: enfermedad,
ataque) sudden; (fam: éxito, golpe)
sudden

fumador, a [fuma'ðor, a] nm/f
smoker

fumar [fu'mar] vt, vi to smoke; **~ en
pipa** to smoke a pipe

función [fun'θjon] nf function; (en
trabajo) duties pl; (espectáculo) show;
entrar en funciones to take up one's
duties

funcionar [funθjo'nar] vi (gen)
to function; (máquina) to work; **"no
funciona"** "out of order"

funcionario, -a [funθjo'narjo, a]
nm/f civil servant

funda ['funda] nf (gen) cover; (de
almohada) pillowcase

fundación [funda'θjon] nf
foundation

fundamental [fundamen'tal] adj
fundamental, basic

fundamento [funda'mento] nm

(base) foundation

fundar [fun'dar] *vt* to found; **fundarse** *vr:* **~ se en** to be founded on

fundición [fundi'θjon] *nf* fusing; *(fábrica)* foundry

fundir [fun'dir] *vt (gen)* to fuse; *(metal)* to smelt, melt down; *(nieve etc)* to melt; *(Com)* to merge; *(estatua)* to cast; **fundirse** *vr (colores etc)* to merge, blend; *(unirse)* to fuse together; *(Elec: fusible, lámpara etc)* to fuse, blow; *(nieve etc)* to melt

fúnebre ['funeβre] *adj* funeral *cpd*, funereal

funeral [fune'ral] *nm* funeral; **funeraria** *nf* undertaker's

funicular [funiku'lar] *nm (tren)* funicular; *(teleférico)* cable car

furgón [fur'xon] *nm* wagon; **furgoneta** *nf (Auto, Com)* (transit) van *(BRIT)*, pick-up (truck) *(US)*

furia ['furja] *nf (ira)* fury; *(violencia)* violence; **furioso, -a** *adj (iracundo)* furious; *(violento)* violent

furtivo, -a [fur'tiβo, a] *adj* furtive ▷ *nm* poacher

fusible [fu'siβle] *nm* fuse

fusil [fu'sil] *nm* rifle; **fusilar** *vt* to shoot

fusión [fu'sjon] *nf (gen)* melting; *(unión)* fusion; *(Com)* merger

fútbol ['futβol] *nm* football *(BRIT)*, soccer *(US)*; **fútbol americano** American football *(BRIT)*, football *(US)*; **fútbol sala** indoor football *(BRIT)* o soccer *(US)*; **futbolín** *nm* table football; **futbolista** *nmf* footballer

futuro, -a [fu'turo, a] *adj, nm* future

g

gabardina [gaβar'ðina] *nf* raincoat, gabardine

gabinete [gaβi'nete] *nm (Pol)* cabinet; *(estudio)* study; *(de abogados etc)* office

gachas ['gatʃas] *nfpl* porridge *sg*

gafas ['gafas] *nfpl* glasses; **gafas de sol** sunglasses

gafe [gafe] *(ESP)* *nmf* jinx

gaita ['gaita] *nf* bagpipes *pl*

gajes ['gaxes] *nmpl:* **~ del oficio** occupational hazards

gajo ['gaxo] *nm (de naranja)* segment

gala ['gala] *nf (traje de etiqueta)* full dress; **galas** *nfpl (ropa)* finery *sg;* **estar de ~** to be in one's best clothes; **hacer ~ de** to display

galápago [ga'lapaxo] *nm (Zool)* turtle

galardón [galar'ðon] *nm* award, prize

galaxia [ga'laksja] *nf* galaxy

galera [ga'lera] *nf (nave)* galley; *(carro)* wagon; *(Imprenta)* galley

galería [gale'ria] *nf (gen)* gallery;

(balcón) veranda(h); (pasillo) corridor;
galería comercial shopping mall
Gales ['gales] nm (tb: **País de ~**)
Wales; **galés, -esa** adj Welsh ▷ nm/f
Welshman(-woman) ▷ nm (Ling)
Welsh
galgo, -a ['galɣo, a] nm/f greyhound
gallego, -a [ga'ʎeɣo, a] adj, nm/f
Galician
galleta [ga'ʎeta] nf biscuit (BRIT),
cookie (US)
gallina [ga'ʎina] nf hen ▷ nm
(fam: cobarde) chicken; **gallinero** nm
henhouse; (Teatro) top gallery
gallo ['gaʎo] nm cock, rooster
galopar [galo'par] vi to gallop
gama ['gama] nf (fig) range
gamba ['gamba] nf prawn (BRIT),
shrimp (US)
gamberro, -a [gam'berro, a] (ESP)
nm/f hooligan, lout
gamuza [ga'muθa] nf chamois
gana ['gana] nf (deseo) longing,
wish; (apetito) appetite; (voluntad)
will; (añoranza) longing; **de buena ~**
willingly; **de mala ~** reluctantly; **me
da ~s de** I feel like, I want to; **no me
da la ~** I don't feel like it, I want to;
tener ~s de to feel like
ganadería [ganaðe'ria] nf (ganado)
livestock; (ganado vacuno) cattle pl; (cría,
comercio) cattle raising
ganadero, -a [gana'ðero, a] (ESP)
nm/f (hacendado) rancher
ganado [ga'naðo] nm livestock;
ganado porcino pigs pl
ganador, a [gana'ðor, a] adj
winning ▷ nm/f winner
ganancia [ga'nanθja] nf (lo ganado)
gain; (aumento) increase; (beneficio)
profit; **ganancias** nfpl (ingresos)
earnings; (beneficios) profit sg,
winnings
ganar [ga'nar] vt (obtener) to get,
obtain; (sacar ventaja) to gain; (salario
etc) to earn; (Deporte, premio) to win;
(derrotar a) to beat; (alcanzar) to reach
▷ vi (Deporte) to win; **ganarse** vr: **~se**

la vida to earn one's living
ganchillo [gan'tʃiʎo] nm crochet
gancho ['gantʃo] nm (gen) hook;
(colgador) hanger
gandul, a [gan'dul, a] adj, nm/f
good-for-nothing, layabout
ganga ['ganga] nf bargain
gangrena [gan'grena] nf gangrene
ganso, -a ['ganso, a] nm/f (Zool)
goose; (fam) idiot
ganzúa [gan'θua] nf skeleton key
garabato [gara'βato] nm (escritura)
scrawl, scribble
garaje [ga'raxe] nm garage
garantía [garan'tia] nf guarantee
garantizar [garanti'θar] vt to
guarantee
garbanzo [gar'βanθo] nm chickpea
(BRIT), garbanzo (US)
garfio ['garfjo] nm grappling iron
garganta [gar'ɣanta] nf (Anat)
throat; (de botella) neck; **gargantilla**
nf necklace
gárgaras ['garɣaras] nfpl: **hacer ~**
to gargle
gargarear [garɣare'ar] (LAM) vi to
gargle
garita [ga'rita] nf cabin, hut; (Mil)
sentry box
garra ['garra] nf (de gato, Tec) claw; (de
ave) talon; (fam: mano) hand, paw
garrafa [ga'rrafa] nf carafe, decanter
garrapata [garra'pata] nf tick
gas [gas] nm gas; **gases**
lacrimógenos tear gas sg
gasa ['gasa] nf gauze
gaseosa [gase'osa] nf lemonade
gaseoso, -a [gase'oso, a] adj gassy,
fizzy
gasoil [ga'soil] nm diesel (oil)
gasóleo [ga'soleo] nm = **gasoil**
gasolina [gaso'lina] nf petrol (BRIT),
gas(oline) (US); **gasolinera** nf petrol
(BRIT) o gas (US) station
gastado, -a [gas'taðo, a] adj (dinero)
spent; (ropa) worn out; (usado: frase
etc) trite
gastar [gas'tar] vt (dinero, tiempo) to

spend; (*fuerzas*) to use up; (*desperdiciar*) to waste; (*llevar*) to wear; **gastarse** vr to wear out; (*estropearse*) to waste; **~ en** to spend on; **~ bromas** to crack jokes; **¿qué número gastas?** what size (shoe) do you take?

gasto ['gasto] nm (*desembolso*) expenditure, spending; (*consumo, uso*) use; **gastos** nmpl (*desembolsos*) expenses; (*cargos*) charges, costs

gastronomía [gastrono'mia] nf gastronomy

gatear [gate'ar] vi (*andar a gatas*) to go on all fours

gatillo [ga'tiʎo] nm (*de arma de fuego*) trigger; (*de dentista*) forceps

gato, -a ['gato, a] nm/f cat ▷ nm (*Tec*) jack; **andar a gatas** to go on all fours

gaucho ['gautʃo] nm gaucho

○ **GAUCHO**
○
○ **Gauchos** are the herdsmen or
○ riders of the Southern Cone plains.
○ Although popularly associated
○ with Argentine folklore, **gauchos**
○ belong equally to the cattle-
○ raising areas of Southern Brazil
○ and Uruguay. **Gauchos'** traditions
○ and clothing reflect their mixed
○ ancestry and cultural roots. Their
○ baggy trousers are Arabic in
○ origin, while the horse and guitar
○ are inherited from the Spanish
○ conquistadors; the poncho, maté
○ and **boleadoras** (strips of leather
○ weighted at either end with
○ stones) form part of the Indian
○ tradition.

gaviota [ga'βjota] nf seagull

gay [ge] adj inv, nm gay, homosexual

gazpacho [gaθ'patʃo] nm gazpacho

gel [xel] nm: **~ de baño/ducha** bath/shower gel

gelatina [xela'tina] nf jelly; (*polvos etc*) gelatine

gema ['xema] nf gem

gemelo, -a [xe'melo, a] adj, nm/f twin; **gemelos** nmpl (*de camisa*) cufflinks; (*prismáticos*) field glasses, binoculars

gemido [xe'miðo] nm (*quejido*) moan, groan; (*aullido*) howl

Géminis ['xeminis] nm Gemini

gemir [xe'mir] vi (*quejarse*) to moan, groan; (*aullar*) to howl

generación [xenera'θjon] nf generation

general [xene'ral] adj general ▷ nm general; **por lo o en ~** in general; **Generalitat** nf Catalan parliament; **generalizar** vt to generalize; **generalizarse** vr to become generalized, spread

generar [xene'rar] vt to generate

género ['xenero] nm (*clase*) kind, sort; (*tipo*) type; (*Bio*) genus; (*Ling*) gender; (*Com*) material; **género humano** human race

generosidad [xenerosi'ðað] nf generosity; **generoso, -a** adj generous

genial [xe'njal] adj inspired; (*idea*) brilliant; (*estupendo*) wonderful

genio ['xenjo] nm (*carácter*) nature, disposition; (*humor*) temper; (*facultad creadora*) genius; **de mal ~** bad-tempered

genital [xeni'tal] adj genital; **genitales** nmpl genitals

genoma [xe'noma] nm genome

gente ['xente] nf (*personas*) people pl; (*parientes*) relatives pl

gentil [xen'til] adj (*elegante*) graceful; (*encantador*) charming

▌ No confundir **gentil** con la palabra inglesa *gentle*.

genuino, -a [xe'nwino, a] adj genuine

geografía [xeoɣra'fia] nf geography

geología [xeolo'xia] nf geology

geometría [xeome'tria] nf geometry

gerente [xe'rente] nmf (*supervisor*) manager; (*jefe*) director

geriatría [xeria'tria] nf (Med)
geriatrics sg

germen ['xermen] nm germ

gesticular [xestiku'lar] vi to
gesticulate; (hacer muecas) to grimace;
gesticulación nf gesticulation;
(mueca) grimace

gestión [xes'tjon] nf management;
(diligencia, acción) negotiation

gesto ['xesto] nm (mueca) grimace;
(ademán) gesture

Gibraltar [xiβral'tar] nm Gibraltar;
gibraltareño, -a adj, nm/f
Gibraltarian

gigante [xi'xante] adj, nmf giant;
gigantesco, -a adj gigantic

gilipollas [xili'poʎas] (fam) adj inv
daft ▷ nmf inv wally

gimnasia [xim'nasja] nf gymnastics
pl; **gimnasio** nm gymnasium;
gimnasta nmf gymnast

ginebra [xi'neβra] nf gin

ginecólogo, -a [xine'koloɣo, a]
nm/f gynaecologist

gira ['xira] nf tour, trip

girar [xi'rar] vt (dar la vuelta) to
turn (around); (: rápidamente) to
(Com: giro postal) to draw; (: letra de
cambio) to issue ▷ vi to turn (round);
(rápido) to spin

girasol [xira'sol] nm sunflower

giratorio, -a [xira'torjo, a] adj
revolving

giro ['xiro] nm (movimiento) turn,
revolution; (Ling) expression; (Com)
draft; **giro bancario/postal** bank
draft/money order

gis [xis] (Méx) nm chalk

gitano, -a [xi'tano, a] adj, nm/f
gypsy

glacial [gla'θjal] adj icy, freezing

glaciar [gla'θjar] nm glacier

glándula ['glandula] nf gland

global [glo'βal] adj global;
globalización nf globalization

globo ['gloβo] nm (esfera) globe,
sphere; (aerostato, juguete) balloon

glóbulo ['gloβulo] nm globule; (Anat)
corpuscle

gloria ['glorja] nf glory

glorieta [glo'rjeta] nf (de jardín)
bower, arbour; (plazoleta) roundabout
(BRIT), traffic circle (US)

glorioso, -a [glo'rjoso, a] adj
glorious

glotón, -ona [glo'ton, ona] adj
gluttonous, greedy ▷ nm/f glutton

glucosa [glu'kosa] nf glucose

gobernador, a [goβerna'ðor, a]
adj governing ▷ nm/f governor;
gobernante adj governing

gobernar [goβer'nar] vt (dirigir) to
guide, direct; (Pol) to rule, govern ▷ vi
to govern; (Náut) to steer

gobierno etc [go'βjerno] vb V
gobernar ▷ nm (Pol) government;
(dirección) guidance, direction; (Náut)
steering

goce etc [goθe] vb V **gozar** ▷ nm
enjoyment

gol [gol] nm goal

golf [golf] nm golf

golfa ['golfa] (fam!) nf (mujer) slut,
whore

golfo, -a ['golfo, a] nm (Geo) gulf
▷ nm/f (fam: niño) urchin; (gamberro)
lout

golondrina [golon'drina] nf
swallow

golosina [golo'sina] nf (dulce) sweet;
goloso, -a adj sweet-toothed

golpe ['golpe] nm blow; (de puño)
punch; (de mano) smack; (de remo)
stroke; (Pol: de Estado) coup; (fig)
clash; **no dar ~** to be bone idle; **de un ~** one blow;
de ~ suddenly; **golpe (de estado)**
(d'état); **golpear** vt, vi to strike, knock;
(asestar) to beat; (de puño) to punch;
(golpetear) to tap

goma ['goma] nf (caucho) rubber;
(elástico) elastic; (una goma) elastic
band; **goma de borrar** eraser, rubber
(BRIT); **goma espuma** foam rubber

gomina [go'mina] nf hair gel

gomita [go'mita] (RPL) nf rubber
band

gordo, -a ['gorðo, a] adj (gen) fat;
(fam) enormous; **el (premio) ~** (en
lotería) first prize

gorila [go'rila] nm gorilla

gorra ['gorra] nf cap; (de bebé) bonnet;
(militar) bearskin; **entrar de ~** (fam) to
gatecrash; **ir de ~** to sponge

gorrión [go'rrjon] nm sparrow

gorro ['gorro] nm (gen) cap; (de bebé,
mujer) bonnet

gorrón, -ona [go'rron, ona]
nm/f scrounger; **gorronear** (fam) vi
to scrounge

gota ['gota] nf (gen) drop; (de sudor)
bead; (Med) gout; **gotear** vi to drip;
(lloviznar) to drizzle; **gotera** nf leak

gozar [go'θar] vi to enjoy o.s.; **~ de**
(disfrutar) to enjoy; (poseer) to possess

gr. abr (= gramo, gramos) g

grabación [graβa'θjon] nf recording

grabado [gra'βaðo] nm print,
engraving

grabadora [graβa'ðora] nf tape-
recorder; **grabadora de CD/DVD**
CD/DVD writer

grabar [gra'βar] vt to engrave; (discos,
cintas) to record

gracia ['graθja] nf (encanto) grace,
gracefulness; (humor) humour, wit;
¡(muchas) ~s! thanks (very much)!;
~s a thanks to; **dar las ~s a algn por
algo** to thank sb for sth; **tener ~** (chiste
etc) to be funny; **no me hace ~** I am
not keen; **gracioso, -a** adj (divertido)
funny, amusing; (cómico) comical
▷ nm/f (Teatro) comic character

grada ['graða] nf (de escalera) step;
(de anfiteatro) tier, row; **gradas** nfpl
(Deporte: de estadio) terraces

grado ['graðo] nm degree; (de aceite,
vino) grade; (grada) step; (Mil) rank; **de
buen ~** willingly; **grado centígrado/
Fahrenheit** degree centigrade/
Fahrenheit

graduación [graðwa'θjon] nf
(del alcohol) proof, strength; (Escol)
graduation; (Mil) rank

gradual [gra'ðwal] adj gradual

graduar [gra'ðwar] vt (gen) to
graduate; (Mil) to commission;
graduarse vr to graduate; **~se la
vista** to have one's eyes tested

gráfica ['grafika] nf graph

gráfico, -a ['grafiko, a] adj graphic
▷ nm diagram; **gráficos** nmpl (Inform)
graphics

grajo ['graxo] nm rook

gramática [gra'matika] nf grammar

gramo ['gramo] nm gramme (BRIT),
gram (US)

gran [gran] adj V **grande**

grana ['grana] nf (color, tela) scarlet

granada [gra'naða] nf pomegranate;
(Mil) grenade

granate [gra'nate] adj deep red

Gran Bretaña [-bre'taɲa] nf Great
Britain

grande ['grande] (antes de nmsg **gran**)
adj (de tamaño) big, large; (alto) tall;
(distinguido) great; (impresionante) grand
▷ nm grandee

granel [gra'nel] **a ~** adv (Com) in bulk

granero [gra'nero] nm granary, barn

granito [gra'nito] nm (Agr) small
grain; (roca) granite

granizado [grani'θaðo] nm iced
drink

granizar [grani'θar] vi to hail;
granizo nm hail

granja ['granxa] nf (gen) farm;
granjero, -a nm/f farmer

grano ['grano] nm grain; (semilla)
seed; (de café) bean; (Med) pimple, spot

granuja [gra'nuxa] nmf rogue;
(golfillo) urchin

grapa ['grapa] nf staple; (Tec) clamp;
grapadora nf stapler

grasa ['grasa] nf (gen) grease; (de
cocinar) fat, lard; (sebo) suet; (mugre)
filth; **grasiento, -a** adj greasy; (de
aceite) oily; **graso, -a** adj (leche, queso,
carne) fatty; (pelo, piel) greasy

gratinar [grati'nar] vt to cook au
gratin

gratis ['gratis] adv free

grato, -a ['grato, a] adj (agradable)

pleasant, agreeable

gratuito, -a [gra'twito, a] *adj*
(gratis) free; *(sin razón)* gratuitous

grave ['graβe] *adj* heavy; *(serio)* grave,
serious; **gravedad** *nf* gravity

Grecia ['greθja] *nf* Greece

gremio ['gremjo] *nm* trade, industry

griego, -a ['grjeβo, a] *adj, nm/f* Greek

grieta ['grjeta] *nf* crack

grifo ['grifo] *(ESP)* *nm* tap *(BRIT)*,
faucet *(US)*

grillo ['griʎo] *nm* *(Zool)* cricket

gripa ['gripa] *(MÉX)* *nf* flu, influenza

gripe ['gripe] *nf* flu, influenza; **gripe
aviar** bird flu

gris [gris] *adj (color)* grey

gritar [gri'tar] *vt, vi* to shout, yell;
grito *nm* shout, yell; *(de horror)* scream

grosella [gro'seʎa] *nf (red)*currant

grosero, -a [gro'sero, a] *adj (poco
cortés)* rude, bad-mannered; *(ordinario)*
vulgar, crude

grosor [gro'sor] *nm* thickness

grúa ['grua] *nf (Tec)* crane; *(de petróleo)*
derrick

grueso, -a ['grweso, a] *adj* thick;
(persona) stout ⊳ *nm* bulk; **el ~ de**
the bulk of

grulla ['gruʎa] *nf* crane

grumo ['grumo] *nm* clot, lump

gruñido [gru'niðo] *nm* grunt; *(de
persona)* grumble

gruñir [gru'nir] *vi (animal)* to growl;
(persona) to grumble

grupo ['grupo] *nm* group; *(Tec)* unit,
set; **grupo de presión** pressure group;
grupo sanguíneo blood group

gruta ['gruta] *nf* grotto

guacho, -a ['gwatʃo, a] *(cs)* *nm/f*
homeless child

guajolote [gwaxo'lote] *(MÉX)* *nm*
turkey

guante ['gwante] *nm* glove; **guantes
de goma** rubber gloves; **guantera** *nf*
glove compartment

guapo, -a ['gwapo, a] *adj* good-
looking, attractive; *(elegante)* smart

guarda ['gwarða] *nmf (persona)*

guard, keeper ⊳ *nf (acto)* guarding;
(custodia) custody; **guarda jurado**
(armed) security guard; **guardabarros**
nm inv mudguard *(BRIT)*, fender *(US)*;
guardabosques *nm inv* gamekeeper;
guardacostas *nm inv* coastguard
vessel ⊳ *nmf* guardian, protector;
guardaespaldas *nmf inv* bodyguard;
guardameta *nmf* goalkeeper;
guardar *vt (gen)* to keep; *(vigilar)* to
guard, watch over; *(dinero: ahorrar)* to
save; **guardarse** *vr (preservarse)* to
protect o.s.; *(evitar)* to avoid; **guardar
cama** to stay in bed; **guardarropa** *nm*
(armario) wardrobe; *(en establecimiento
público)* cloakroom

guardería [gwarðe'ria] *nf* nursery

guardia ['gwarðja] *nf (Mil)* guard;
(cuidado) care, custody ⊳ *nmf* guard;
(policía) policeman(-woman); **estar de
~** to be on guard; **montar ~** to mount
guard; **Guardia Civil** Civil Guard

guardián, -ana [gwar'ðjan, ana]
nm/f (gen) guardian, keeper

guarida [gwa'riða] *nf (de animal)* den,
lair; *(refugio)* refuge

guarnición [gwarni'θjon] *nf (de
vestimenta)* trimming; *(de piedra)*
mount; *(Culin)* garnish; *(arneses)*
harness; *(Mil)* garrison

guarro, -a ['gwarro, a] *nm/f* pig

guasa ['gwasa] *nf* joke; **guasón, -ona**
adj (bromista) joking ⊳ *nm/f* wit; joker

Guatemala [gwate'mala] *nf*
Guatemala

guay [gwai] *(fam)* *adj* super, great

güero, -a ['gwero, a] *(MÉX)* *adj*
blond(e)

guerra ['gerra] *nf* war; **dar ~** to
annoy; **guerra civil** civil war; **guerra
fría** cold war; **guerrero, -a** *adj*
fighting; *(carácter)* warlike ⊳ *nm/f*
warrior

guerrilla [ge'rriʎa] *nf* guerrilla
warfare; *(tropas)* guerrilla band o group

guía *etc* ['gia] *vb V* **guiar** ⊳ *nmf*
(persona) guide; *(nf: libro)* guidebook;
guía telefónica telephone directory;

guía turística tourist guide
guiar [gi'ar] *vt* to guide, direct; *(Auto)* to steer; **guiarse** *vr*: **~se por** to be guided by
guinda ['ginda] *nf* morello cherry
guindilla [gin'diʎa] *nf* chilli pepper
guiñar [gi'ɲar] *vt* to wink
guión [gi'on] *nm* (Ling) hyphen, dash; *(Cine)* script; **guionista** *nmf* scriptwriter
guiri ['giri] *(esp: fam, pey)* *nmf* foreigner
guirnalda [gir'nalda] *nf* garland
guisado [gi'saðo] *nm* stew
guisante [gi'sante] *nm* pea
guisar [gi'sar] *vt, vi* to cook; **guiso** *nm* cooked dish
guitarra [gi'tarra] *nf* guitar
gula ['gula] *nf* gluttony, greed
gusano [gu'sano] *nm* worm; *(lombriz)* earthworm
gustar [gus'tar] *vt* to taste, sample ▷ *vi* to please, be pleasing; **~ de algo** to like o enjoy sth; **me gustan las uvas** I like grapes; **le gusta nadar** she likes o enjoys swimming
gusto ['gusto] *nm* (sentido, sabor) taste; *(placer)* pleasure; **tiene ~ a menta** it tastes of mint; **tener buen ~** to have good taste; **coger el o tomar ~ a algo** to take a liking to sth; **sentirse a ~** to feel at ease; **mucho ~ (en conocerle)** pleased to meet you; **el ~ es mío** the pleasure is mine; **con ~** willingly, gladly

h

ha *vb* V **haber**
haba ['aβa] *nf* bean
Habana [a'βana] *nf*: **la ~** Havana
habano [a'βano] *nm* Havana cigar
habéis *vb* V **haber**

○ **PALABRA CLAVE**

haber [a'βer] *vb aux* **1** *(tiempos compuestos)* to have; **había comido** I had eaten; **antes/después de haberlo visto** before seeing/after seeing o having seen it
2: **¡haberlo dicho antes!** you should have said so before!
3: **haber de**: **he de hacerlo** I have to do it; **ha de llegar mañana** it should arrive tomorrow
▷ *vb impers* **1** *(existencia: sg)* there is; *(: pl)* there are; **hay un hermano/dos hermanos** there is one brother/there are two brothers; **¿cuánto hay de aquí a Sucre?** how far is it from here to Sucre?
2 *(obligación)*: **hay que hacer algo**

something must be done; **hay que apuntarlo para acordarse** you have to write it down to remember

3: **¡hay que ver!** well I never!

4: **¡no hay de o por** (LAM) **qué!** don't mention it!, not at all!

5: **¿qué hay?** (*¿qué pasa?*) what's up?, what's the matter?; (*¿qué tal?*) how's it going?

▷ *vt*: **he aquí unas sugerencias** here are some suggestions; **no hay cintas blancas pero sí las hay rojas** there aren't any white ribbons but there are some red ones

▷ *nm* (*en cuenta*) credit side; **haberes** *nmpl* assets; **¿cuánto tengo en el haber?** how much do I have in my account?; **tiene varias novelas en su haber** he has several novels to his credit

haberse *vr*: **habérselas con algn** to have it out with sb

habichuela [aβiˈtʃwela] *nf* kidney bean

hábil [ˈaβil] *adj* (*listo*) clever, smart; (*capaz*) fit, capable; (*experto*) expert; **día ~** working day; **habilidad** *nf* skill, ability

habitación [aβitaˈθjon] *nf* (*cuarto*) room; (Bio: *morada*) habitat; **habitación doble** *o* **de matrimonio** double room; **habitación individual** *o* **sencilla** single room

habitante [aβiˈtante] *nm/f* inhabitant

habitar [aβiˈtar] *vt* (*residir en*) to inhabit; (*ocupar*) to occupy ▷ *vi* to live

hábito [ˈaβito] *nm* habit

habitual [aβiˈtwal] *adj* usual

habituar [aβiˈtwar] *vt* to accustom; **habituarse** *vr*: **~se a** to get used to

habla [ˈaβla] *nf* (*capacidad de hablar*) speech; (*idioma*) language; (*dialecto*) dialect; **perder la ~** to become speechless; **de ~ francesa** French-speaking; **estar al ~** to be in contact; (Tel) to be on the line; **¡González al ~!** (Tel) González speaking!

hablador, -ora [aβlaˈðor, a] *adj*

talkative ▷ *nm/f* chatterbox

habladuría [aβlaðuˈria] *nf* rumour; **habladurías** *nfpl* gossip *sg*

hablante [aˈβlante] *adj* speaking ▷ *nmf* speaker

hablar [aˈβlar] *vt* to speak, talk ▷ *vi* to speak; **hablarse** *vr* to speak to each other; **~ con** to speak to; **~ de** to speak of *o* about; **¡ni ~!** it's out of the question!; **"se habla inglés"** "English spoken here"

habré *etc* [aˈβre] *vb V* **haber**

hacendado [aθenˈdaðo] (LAM) *nm* rancher, farmer

hacendoso, -a [aθenˈdoso, a] *adj* industrious

○ **PALABRA CLAVE**

hacer [aˈθer] *vt* **1** (*fabricar, producir*) to make; (*construir*) to build; **hacer una película/un ruido** to make a film/noise; **el guisado lo hice yo** I made *o* cooked the stew

2 (*ejecutar: trabajo etc*) to do; **hacer la colada** to do the washing; **hacer la comida** to do the cooking; **¿qué haces?** what are you doing?; **hacer el malo** *o* **el papel del malo** (Teatro) to play the villain

3 (*estudios, algunos deportes*) to do; **hacer español/economics** to do *o* study Spanish/economics; **hacer yoga/gimnasia** to do yoga/go to gym

4 (*transformar, incidir en*): **esto lo hará más difícil** this will make it more difficult; **salir te hará sentir mejor** going out will make you feel better

5 (*cálculo*): **2 y 2 hacen 4** 2 and 2 make 4; **éste hace 100** this makes 100

6 (+ *sub*): **esto hará que ganemos** this will make us win; **harás que no quiera venir** you'll stop him wanting to come

7 (*como sustituto de vb*) to do; **él bebió y yo hice lo mismo** he drank and I did likewise

8 **no hace más que criticar** all he does is criticize

▷ *vb semi-aux* (*directo*): **hacer +infin: les hice venir** I made o had them come; **hacer trabajar a los demás** to get others to work

▷ *vi* **1 haz como que no lo sabes** act as if you don't know

2 (*ser apropiado*): **si os hace** if it's alright with you

3 hacer de: hacer de Otelo to play Othello

▷ *vb impers* **1 hace calor/frío** it's hot/cold; V tb **bueno, sol, tiempo**

2 (*tiempo*): **hace 3 años** 3 years ago; **hace un mes que voy/no voy** I've been going/I haven't been for a month

3 ¿cómo has hecho para llegar tan rápido? how did you manage to get here so quickly?

hacerse *vr* **1** (*volverse*) to become; **se hicieron amigos** they became friends

2 (*acostumbrarse*): **hacerse a** to get used to

3 se hace con huevos y leche it's made out of eggs and milk; **eso no se hace** that's not done

4 (*obtener*): **hacerse de** o **con algo** to get hold of sth

5 (*fingirse*): **hacerse el sueco** to turn a deaf ear

hacha ['atʃa] *nf* axe; (*antorcha*) torch

hachís [a'tʃis] *nm* hashish

hacia ['aθja] *prep* (*en dirección de*) towards; (*cerca de*) near; (*actitud*) towards; **~ adelante/atrás** forwards/backwards; **~ arriba/abajo** up(wards)/down(wards); **~ mediodía/las cinco** about noon/five

hacienda [a'θjenda] *nf* (*propiedad*) property; (*finca*) farm; (*LAM: rancho*) ranch; (**Ministerio de) H~** Exchequer (*BRIT*), Treasury Department (*US*); **hacienda pública** public finance

hada ['aða] *nf* fairy

hago *etc vb* V **hacer**

Haití [ai'ti] *nm* Haiti

halagar [ala'ɣar] *vt* to flatter

halago [a'laɣo] *nm* flattery

halcón [al'kon] *nm* falcon, hawk

hallar [a'ʎar] *vt* (*gen*) to find; (*descubrir*) to discover; (*toparse con*) to run into; **hallarse** *vr* (*estar*) to be (situated)

halterofilia [altero'filja] *nf* weightlifting

hamaca [a'maka] *nf* hammock

hambre ['ambre] *nf* hunger; (*plaga*) famine; (*deseo*) longing; **tener ~** to be hungry; **¡me hambre de ~!** I'm hungry!; **hambriento, -a** *adj* hungry, starving

hamburguesa [ambur'ɣesa] *nf* hamburger; **hamburguesería** *nf* burger bar

han *vb* V **haber**

harapos [a'rapos] *nmpl* rags

haré *vb* V **hacer**

harina [a'rina] *nf* flour; **harina de maíz** cornflour (*BRIT*), cornstarch (*US*); **harina de trigo** wheat flour

hartar [ar'tar] *vt* to satiate, glut; (*fig*) to tire, sicken; **hartarse** *vr* (*de comida*) to fill o.s., gorge o.s.; (*cansarse*): **~se (de)** to get fed up (with); **harto, -a** *adj* (*lleno*) full; (*cansado*) fed up ▷ *adv* (*bastante*) enough; (*muy*) very; **estar harto de hacer algo/de algn** to be fed up of doing sth/with sb

has *vb* V **haber**

hasta ['asta] *adv* even ▷ *prep* (*alcanzando a*) as far as; up to; down to; (*de tiempo: a tal hora*) till, until; (*antes de*) before ▷ *conj*: **~ que ...** until; **~ luego/el sábado** see you soon/on Saturday; **~ ahora** (*al despedirse*) see you in a minute; **~ pronto** see you soon

hay *vb* V **haber**

Haya ['aja] *nf*: **la ~** The Hague

haya *etc* ['aja] *vb* V **haber** ▷ *nf* beech tree

haz [aθ] *vb* V **hacer** ▷ *nm* (*de luz*) beam

hazaña [a'θaɲa] *nf* feat, exploit

hazmerreír [aθmerre'ir] *nm inv* laughing stock

he *vb* V **haber**

hebilla [e'βiʎa] *nf* buckle, clasp

hebra ['eβra] *nf* thread; (*Bot: fibra*)

fibre, grain

hebreo, -a [e'βreo, a] adj, nm/f Hebrew ▷ nm (Ling) Hebrew

hechicero [etʃi'θero] vt to cast a spell on, bewitch

hechizo [e'tʃiθo] nm witchcraft, magic; (acto de magia) spell, charm

hecho, -a ['etʃo, a] pp de **hacer** ▷ adj (carne) done; (Costura) ready-to-wear ▷ nm deed, act; (dato) fact; (cuestión) matter; (suceso) event ▷ excl agreed!, done!; **de ~** in fact, as a matter of fact; **el ~ es que ...** the fact is that ...; **¡bien ~!** well done!

hechura [e'tʃura] nf (forma) form, shape; (de persona) build

hectárea [ek'tarea] nf hectare

helada [e'laða] nf frost

heladera [ela'ðera] (LAM) nf (refrigerador) refrigerator

helado, -a [e'laðo, a] adj frozen; (glacial) icy; (fig) chilly, cold ▷ nm ice cream

helar [e'lar] vt to freeze, ice (up); (dejar atónito) to amaze; (desalentar) to discourage ▷ vi to freeze; **helarse** vr to freeze

helecho [e'letʃo] nm fern

hélice ['eliθe] nf (Tec) propeller

helicóptero [eli'koptero] nm helicopter

hembra ['embra] nf (Bot, Zool) female; (mujer) woman; (Tec) nut

hemorragia [emo'rraxja] nf haemorrhage

hemorroides [emo'rroiðes] nfpl haemorrhoids, piles

hemos vb V **haber**

heno ['eno] nm hay

heredar [ere'ðar] vt to inherit; **heredero, -a** nm/f heir(ess)

hereje [e'rexe] nm/f heretic

herencia [e'renθja] nf inheritance

herida [e'riða] nf wound, injury; V tb **herido**

herido, -a [e'riðo, a] adj injured, wounded ▷ nm/f casualty

herir [e'rir] vt to wound, injure; (fig)

to offend

hermanastro, -a [erma'nastro, a] nm/f stepbrother/sister

hermandad [erman'daθ] nf brotherhood

hermano, -a [er'mano, a] nm/f brother/sister; **hermano**(-a) gemelo(-a), twin brother/sister; **hermano**(-a) político(-a), brother-in-law/sister-in-law

hermético, -a [er'metiko, a] adj hermetic; (fig) watertight

hermoso, -a [er'moso, a] adj beautiful, lovely; (estupendo) splendid; (guapo) handsome; **hermosura** nf beauty

hernia ['ernja] nf hernia; **hernia discal** slipped disc

héroe ['eroe] nm hero

heroína [ero'ina] nf (mujer) heroine; (droga) heroin

herradura [erra'ðura] nf horseshoe

herramienta [erra'mjenta] nf tool

herrero [e'rrero] nm blacksmith

hervidero [erβi'ðero] nm (fig) swarm; (Pol etc) hotbed

hervir [er'βir] vi to boil; (burbujear) to bubble; **~ a fuego lento** to simmer; **hervor** nm boiling; (fig) ardour, fervour

heterosexual [eterosek'swal] adj heterosexual

hice etc vb V **hacer**

hidratante [iðra'tante] adj: **crema ~** moisturizing cream, moisturizer; **hidratar** vt (piel) to moisturize; **hidrato** nm hydrate; **hidratos de carbono** carbohydrates

hidráulico, -a [i'ðrauliko, a] adj hydraulic

hidro... [iðro] prefijo hydro..., water-...; **hidroeléctrico, -a** adj hydroelectric; **hidrógeno** nm hydrogen

hiedra ['jeðra] nf ivy

hiel [jel] nf gall, bile; (fig) bitterness

hiela etc vb V **helar**

hielo ['jelo] nm (gen) ice; (escarcha)

frost; (fig) coldness, reserve
hiena ['jena] nf hyena
hierba ['jerβa] nf (pasto) grass; (Culin, Med: planta) herb; **mala ~** weed; (fig) evil influence; **hierbabuena** nf mint
hierro ['jerro] nm (metal) iron; (objeto) iron object
hígado ['iɣaðo] nm liver
higiene [i'xjene] nf hygiene; **higiénico, -a** adj hygienic
higo ['iɣo] nm fig; **higo seco** dried fig; **higuera** nf fig tree
hijastro, -a [i'xastro, a] nm/f stepson/daughter
hijo, -a ['ixo, a] nm/f son/daughter, child; **hijos** nmpl children, sons and daughters; **hijo adoptivo** adopted child; **hijo de papá/mamá** daddy's/mummy's boy; **hijo de puta** (fam!) bastard (!), son of a bitch (!); **hijo/a político/a** son-/daughter-in-law
hilera [i'lera] nf row, file
hilo ['ilo] nm thread; (Bot) fibre; (metal) wire; (de agua) trickle, thin stream
hilvanar [ilβa'nar] vt (Costura) to tack (BRIT), baste (US); (fig) to do hurriedly
himno ['imno] nm hymn; **himno nacional** national anthem
hincapié [inka'pje] nm: **hacer ~ en** to emphasize
hincar [in'kar] vt to drive (in), thrust (in)
hincha ['intʃa] (fam) nmf fan
hinchado, -a [in'tʃaðo, a] adj (gen) swollen; (persona) pompous
hinchar [in'tʃar] vt (gen) to swell; (inflar) to blow up, inflate; (fig) to exaggerate; **hincharse** vr (inflarse) to swell up; (fam: de comer) to stuff o.s.; **hinchazón** nf (Med) swelling; (altivez) arrogance
hinojo [i'noxo] nm fennel
hipermercado [ipermer'kaðo] nm hypermarket, superstore
hípico, -a ['ipiko, a] adj horse cpd
hipnotismo [ipno'tismo] nm hypnotism; **hipnotizar** vt to hypnotize

hipo ['ipo] nm hiccups pl
hipocresía [ipokre'sia] nf hypocrisy; **hipócrita** adj hypocritical ▷ nmf hypocrite
hipódromo [i'poðromo] nm racetrack
hipopótamo [ipo'potamo] nm hippopotamus
hipoteca [ipo'teka] nf mortgage
hipótesis [i'potesis] nf inv hypothesis
hispánico, -a [is'paniko, a] adj Hispanic
hispano, -a [is'pano, a] adj Hispanic, Spanish, Hispano- ▷ nm/f Spaniard; **Hispanoamérica** nf Latin America; **hispanoamericano, -a** adj, nm/f Latin American
histeria [is'terja] nf hysteria
historia [is'torja] nf history; (cuento) story, tale; **historias** nfpl (chismes) gossip sg; **dejarse de ~s** to come to the point; **pasar a la ~** to go down in history; **historiador, a** nm/f historian; historical nm (profesional) curriculum vitae, C.V.; (Med) case history; **histórico, -a** adj historical; (memorable) historic
historieta [isto'rjeta] nf tale, anecdote; (dibujos) comic strip
hito ['ito] nm (fig) landmark
hizo vb V **hacer**
hocico [o'θiko] nm snout
hockey ['xokei] nm hockey; **hockey sobre hielo/patines** ice/roller hockey
hogar [o'ɣar] nm fireplace, hearth; (casa) home; (vida familiar) home life; **hogareño, -a** adj home cpd; (persona) home-loving
hoguera [o'ɣera] nf bonfire
hoja ['oxa] nf (gen) leaf; (de flor) petal; (de papel) sheet; (página) page; **hoja de afeitar** (LAM) razor blade; **hoja electrónica** o **de cálculo** spreadsheet; **hoja informativa** leaflet, handout
hojalata [oxa'lata] nf tin(plate)
hojaldre [o'xaldre] nm (Culin) puff

pastry

hojear [oxe'ar] vt to leaf through, turn the pages of

hojuela [o'xwela] (MÉX) nf flake

hola ['ola] excl hello!

holá [o'la] (RPL) excl hello!

Holanda [o'landa] nf Holland; **holandés, -esa** adj Dutch ▷ nm/f Dutchman(-woman) ▷ nm (Ling) Dutch

holgado, -a [ol'ɣaðo, a] adj (ropa) loose, baggy; (rico) comfortable

holgar [ol'ɣar] vi (descansar) to rest; (sobrar) to be superfluous

holgazán, -ana [olɣa'θan, ana] adj idle, lazy ▷ nm/f loafer

hollín [o'ʎin] nm soot

hombre ['ombre] nm (gen) man; (raza humana): **el ~** man(kind) ▷ excl: **¡sí ~!** (claro) of course!; (para énfasis) man, old boy; **hombre de negocios** businessman; **hombre de pro** honest man; **hombre-rana** frogman

hombrera [om'brera] nf shoulder strap

hombro ['ombro] nm shoulder

homenaje [ome'naxe] nm (gen) homage; (tributo) tribute

homicida [omi'θiða] adj homicidal ▷ nm/f murderer; **homicidio** nm murder, homicide

homologar [omolo'ðar] vt (Com: productos, tamaños) to standardize

homólogo, -a [o'moloxo, a] nm/f: **su** etc ~ his etc counterpart o opposite number

homosexual [omosek'swal] adj, nmf homosexual

honda ['onda] (cs) nf catapult

hondo, -a ['ondo, a] adj deep; **lo ~** the depth(s) pl, the bottom; **hondonada** nf hollow, depression; (cañón) ravine

Honduras [on'duras] nf Honduras

hondureño, -a [ondu'reɲo, a] adj, nm/f Honduran

honestidad [onesti'ðað] nf purity,

chastity; (decencia) decency; **honesto, -a** adj chaste; decent; honest; (justo) just

hongo ['ongo] nm (Bot: gen) fungus; (: comestible) mushroom; (: venenoso) toadstool

honor [o'nor] nm (gen) honour; **en ~ a la verdad** to be fair; **honorable** adj honourable

honorario, -a [ono'rarjo, a] adj honorary; **honorarios** nmpl fees

honra ['onra] nf (gen) honour; (renombre) good name; **honradez** nf honesty; (de persona) integrity; **honrado, -a** adj honest, upright; **honrar** [on'rar] vt to honour

hora ['ora] nf (una hora) hour; (tiempo) time; **¿qué ~ es?** what time is it?; **¿a qué ~?** at what time?; **media ~** half an hour; **a la ~ de recreo** at playtime; **a primera ~** first thing (in the morning); **a última ~** at the last moment; **¡a buena o altas ~s** in the small hours; **¡a buena ~!** about time too!; **pedir ~** to make an appointment; **dar la ~** to strike the hour; **horas de oficina/trabajo** office/working hours; **horas de visita** visiting times; **horas extras** o **extraordinarias** overtime sg; **horas pico** (LAM) rush o peak hours; **horas punta** (ESP) rush hours

horario, -a [o'rarjo, a] adj hourly, hour cpd ▷ nm timetable; **horario comercial** business hours pl

horca ['orka] nf gallows sg

horcajadas [orka'xaðas]: **a ~** adv astride

horchata [or'tʃata] nf cold drink made from tiger nuts and water, tiger nut milk

horizontal [oriθon'tal] adj horizontal

horizonte [ori'θonte] nm horizon

horma ['orma] nf mould

hormiga [or'miɣa] nf ant; **hormigas** nfpl (Med) pins and needles

hormigón [ormi'ɣon] nm concrete; **hormigón armado/pretensado** reinforced/prestressed concrete;

hormigonera nf cement mixer

hormigueo [ormi'ɣeo] nm (comezón) itch

hormona [or'mona] nf hormone

hornillo [or'niʎo] nm (cocina) portable stove; **hornillo de gas** nm gas ring

horno ['orno] nm (Culin) oven; (Tec) furnace; **alto ~** blast furnace

horóscopo [o'roskopo] nm horoscope

horquilla [or'kiʎa] nf hairpin; (Agr) pitchfork

horrendo, -a [o'rrendo, a] adj horrendous, frightful

horrible [o'rriβle] adj horrible, dreadful

horripilante [orripi'lante] adj hair-raising, horrifying

horror [o'rror] nm horror, dread; (atrocidad) atrocity; **¡qué ~!** (fam) how awful!; **horrorizar** vt to horrify, frighten; **horrorizarse** vr to be horrified; **horroroso, -a** adj horrifying, ghastly

hortaliza [orta'liθa] nf vegetable

hortelano, -a [orte'lano, a] nm/f (market) gardener

hortera [or'tera] (fam) adj tacky

hospedar [ospe'ðar] vt to put up; **hospedarse** vr to stay, lodge

hospital [ospi'tal] nm hospital

hospitalario, -a [ospita'larjo, a] adj (acogedor) hospitable; **hospitalidad** nf hospitality

hostal [os'tal] nm small hotel

hostelería [ostele'ria] nf hotel business o trade

hostia ['ostja] nf (Rel) host, consecrated wafer; (fam!: golpe) whack, punch ▷ excl (fam!): **¡~(s)!** damn!

hostil [os'til] adj hostile

hotdog [ot'dog] (LAM) nm hot dog

hotel [o'tel] nm hotel; **hotelero, -a** adj hotel cpd ▷ nm/f hotelier

● **HOTEL**
●
● In Spain you can choose from
● the following categories of
● accommodation, in descending
● order of quality and price: **hotel**
● (from 5 stars to 1), **hostal, pensión,**
● **casa de huéspedes, fonda.** The
● State also runs luxury hotels called
● **paradores,** which are usually sited
● in places of particular historical
● interest and are often historic
● buildings themselves.

hoy [oi] adv (este día) today; (la actualidad) now(adays) ▷ nm present time; **~ (en) día** now(adays)

hoyo ['ojo] nm hole, pit

hoz [oθ] nf sickle

hube etc vb V **haber**

hucha ['utʃa] nf money box

hueco, -a ['weko, a] adj (vacío) hollow, empty; (resonante) booming ▷ nm hollow, cavity

huelga etc ['welxa] vb V **holgar** ▷ nf strike; **declararse en ~** to go on strike, come out on strike; **huelga de hambre** hunger strike; **huelga general** general strike

huelguista [wel'xista] nmf striker

huella ['weʎa] nf (pisada) tread; (marca del paso) footprint, footstep; (: de animal, máquina) track; **huella dactilar** fingerprint

huelo etc vb V **oler**

huérfano, -a ['werfano, a] adj orphan(ed) ▷ nm/f orphan

huerta ['werta] nf market garden; (en Murcia y Valencia) irrigated region

huerto ['werto] nm kitchen garden; (de árboles frutales) orchard

hueso ['weso] nm (Anat) bone; (de fruta) stone

huésped, -a ['wespeð] nmf guest

hueva ['weβa] nf roe

huevera [we'βera] nf eggcup

huevo ['weβo] nm egg; **huevo a la copa** (cs) soft-boiled egg; **huevo duro/escalfado** hard-boiled/poached egg; **huevo estrellado** (LAM) fried egg; **huevo frito** (ESP) fried egg; **huevo**

pasado por agua soft-boiled egg;
huevos revueltos scrambled eggs;
huevo tibio (*MÉX*) soft-boiled egg

huida [u'iða] *nf* escape, flight

huir [u'ir] *vi* (*escapar*) to flee, escape;
(*evitar*) to avoid

hule ['ule] *nm* oilskin; (*MÉX: goma*)
rubber

hulera [u'lera] (*MÉX*) *nf* catapult

humanidad [umani'ðað] *nf*
(*género humano*) man(kind); (*cualidad*)
humanity

humanitario, -a [umani'tarjo, a] *adj* humanitarian

humano, -a [u'mano, a] *adj* (*gen*)
human; (*humanitario*) humane ▷ *nm*
human; **ser ~** human being

humareda [uma'reða] *nf* cloud
of smoke

humedad [ume'ðað] *nf* (*de clima*)
humidity; (*de pared etc*) dampness; **a
prueba de ~** damp-proof; **humedecer**
vt to moisten, wet; **humedecerse** *vr*
to get wet

húmedo, -a ['umeðo, a] *adj* (*mojado*)
damp, wet; (*tiempo etc*) humid

humilde [u'milde] *adj* humble,
modest

humillación [umiʎa'θjon] *nf*
humiliation; **humillante** *adj*
humiliating

humillar [umi'ʎar] *vt* to humiliate

humo ['umo] *nm* (*de fuego*) smoke;
(*gas nocivo*) fumes *pl*; (*vapor*) steam,
vapour; **humos** *nmpl* (*fig*) conceit *sg*

humor [u'mor] *nm* (*disposición*)
mood, temper; (*lo que divierte*) humour;
de buen/mal ~ in a good/bad mood;
humorista *nmf* comic; **humorístico,
-a** *adj* funny, humorous

hundimiento [undi'mjento] *nm*
(*gen*) sinking; (*colapso*) collapse

hundir [un'dir] *vt* to sink; (*edificio,
plan*) to ruin, destroy; **hundirse** *vr* to
sink, collapse

húngaro, -a ['ungaro, a] *adj, nm/f*
Hungarian

Hungría [un'gria] *nf* Hungary

huracán [ura'kan] *nm* hurricane

huraño, -a [u'raɲo, a] *adj* (*antisocial*)
unsociable

hurgar [ur'ɣar] *vt* to poke, jab;
(*remover*) to stir (up); **hurgarse** *vr*: **~se
(las narices)** to pick one's nose

hurón, -ona [u'ron, ona] *nm* (*Zool*)
ferret

hurtadillas [urta'ðiʎas]: **a ~** *adv*
stealthily, on the sly

hurtar [ur'tar] *vt* to steal; **hurto** *nm*
theft, stealing

husmear [usme'ar] *vt* (*oler*) to sniff
out, scent; (*fam*) to pry into

huyo *etc vb* V **huir**

I

iba etc vb V **ir**

ibérico, -a [i'βeriko, a] adj Iberian

iberoamericano, -a [iβeroameri'kano, a] adj, nm/f Latin American

Ibiza [i'βiθa] nf Ibiza

iceberg [iθe'βer] nm iceberg

icono [i'kono] nm ikon, icon

ida ['iða] nf going, departure; **~ y vuelta** round trip, return

idea [i'ðea] nf idea; **no tengo la menor ~** I haven't a clue

ideal [iðe'al] adj, nm ideal; **idealista** nmf idealist; **idealizar** vt to idealize

ídem ['iðem] pron ditto

idéntico, -a [i'ðentiko, a] adj identical

identidad [iðenti'ðað] nf identity

identificación [iðentifika'θjon] nf identification

identificar [iðentifi'kar] vt to identify; **identificarse** vr: **~se con** to identify with

ideología [iðeolo'xia] nf ideology

idilio [i'ðiljo] nm love-affair

idioma [i'ðjoma] nm (gen) language
No confundir **idioma** con la palabra inglesa *idiom*.

idiota [i'ðjota] adj idiotic ▷ nmf idiot

ídolo ['iðolo] nm (tb fig) idol

idóneo, -a [i'ðoneo, a] adj suitable

iglesia [i'ɣlesja] nf church

ignorante [iɣno'rante] adj ignorant, uninformed ▷ nmf ignoramus

ignorar [iɣno'rar] vt not to know, be ignorant of; (no hacer caso a) to ignore

igual [i'ɣwal] adj (gen) equal; (similar) like, similar; (mismo) (the) same; (constante) constant; (temperatura) even ▷ nmf equal; **~ que** like, the same as; **me da es ~** I don't care; **son ~es** they're the same; **al ~ que** (prep, conj) like, just like

igualar [iɣwa'lar] vt (gen) to equalize, make equal; (allanar, nivelar) to level (off), even (out); **igualarse** vr (platos de balanza) to balance out

igualdad [iɣwal'dað] nf equality; (similaridad) sameness; (uniformidad) uniformity

igualmente [iɣwal'mente] adv equally; (también) also, likewise ▷ excl the same to you!

ilegal [ile'ɣal] adj illegal

ilegítimo, -a [ile'xitimo, a] adj illegitimate

ileso, -a [i'leso, a] adj unhurt

ilimitado, -a [ilimi'taðo, a] adj unlimited

iluminación [ilumina'θjon] nf illumination; (alumbrado) lighting

iluminar [ilumi'nar] vt to illuminate, light (up); (fig) to enlighten

ilusión [ilu'sjon] nf illusion; (quimera) delusion; (esperanza) hope; **hacerse ilusiones** to build up one's hopes; **ilusionado, -a** adj excited; **ilusionar** vi: **le ilusiona ir de vacaciones** he's looking forward to going on holiday; **ilusionarse** vr: **ilusionarse (con)** to get excited (about)

iluso, -a [i'luso, a] adj easily deceived ▷ nm/f dreamer

ilustración [ilustra'θjon] nf
illustration; (saber) learning, erudition;
la I~ the Enlightenment; **ilustrado, -a**
adj illustrated; learned

ilustrar [ilus'trar] vt to illustrate;
(instruir) to instruct; (explicar) to
explain, make clear

ilustre [i'lustre] adj famous,
illustrious

imagen [i'maxen] nf (gen) image;
(dibujo) picture

imaginación [imaxina'θjon] nf
imagination

imaginar [imaxi'nar] vt (gen) to
imagine; (idear) to think up; (suponer) to
suppose; **imaginarse** vr to imagine;
imaginario, -a adj imaginary;
imaginativo, -a adj imaginative

imán [i'man] nm magnet

imbécil [im'beθil] nmf imbecile, idiot

imitación [imita'θjon] nf imitation;
de ~ imitation cpd

imitar [imi'tar] vt to imitate;
(parodiar, remedar) to mimic, ape

impaciente [impa'θjente] adj
impatient; (nervioso) anxious

impacto [im'pakto] nm impact

impar [im'par] adj odd

imparcial [impar'θjal] adj impartial,
fair

impecable [impe'kaβle] adj
impeccable

impedimento [impeði'mento] nm
impediment, obstacle

impedir [impe'ðir] vt (obstruir) to
impede, obstruct; (estorbar) to prevent;
~ a algn hacer o **que algn haga algo**
to prevent sb (from) doing sth, stop
sb doing sth

imperativo, -a [impera'tiβo, a] adj
(urgente, Ling) imperative

imperdible [imper'ðiβle] nm
safety pin

imperdonable [imperðo'naβle] adj
unforgivable, inexcusable

imperfecto, -a [imper'fekto, a] adj
imperfect

imperio [im'perjo] nm empire;
(autoridad) rule, authority; (fig) pride,
haughtiness

impermeable [imperme'aβle] adj
waterproof ▷ nm raincoat, mac (BRIT)

impersonal [imperso'nal] adj
impersonal

impertinente [imperti'nente] adj
impertinent

ímpetu ['impetu] nm (impulso)
impetus, impulse; (impetuosidad)
impetuosity; (violencia) violence

implantar [implan'tar] vt to
introduce

implemento [imple'mento] nm (LAM)
nm tool, implement

implicar [impli'kar] vt to involve;
(entrañar) to imply

implícito, -a [im'pliθito, a] adj
(tácito) implicit; (sobreentendido)
implied

imponente [impo'nente] adj
(impresionante) impressive, imposing;
(solemne) grand

imponer [impo'ner] vt (gen) to
impose; (exigir) to exact; **imponerse**
vr to assert o.s.; (prevalecer) to prevail;
imponible adj (Com) taxable

impopular [impopu'lar] adj
unpopular

importación [importa'θjon]
nf (acto) importing; (mercancías)
imports pl

importancia [impor'tanθja] nf
importance; (valor) value, magnitude;
(extensión) size, magnitude; **no
tiene ~** it's nothing; **importante** adj
important; valuable, significant

importar [impor'tar] vt (del
extranjero) to import; (costar) to amount
to ▷ vi to be important, matter; **me
importa un rábano** I couldn't care
less; **no importa** it doesn't matter;
¿le importa que fume? do you mind
if I smoke?

importe [im'porte] nm (total)
amount; (valor) value

imposible [impo'siβle] adj (gen)
impossible; (insoportable) unbearable,

intolerable

imposición [imposi'θjon] nf
imposition; (Com: impuesto) tax;
(: inversión) deposit

impostor, a [impos'tor, a] nm/f
impostor

impotencia [impo'tenθja] nf
impotence; **impotente** adj impotent

impreciso, -a [impre'θiso, a] adj
imprecise, vague

impregnar [impreɣ'nar] vt to
impregnate; **impregnarse** vr to
become impregnated

imprenta [im'prenta] nf (acto)
printing; (aparato) press; (casa)
printer's; (letra) print

imprescindible [impresθin'dible]
adj essential, vital

impresión [impre'sjon] nf (gen)
impression; (Imprenta) printing;
(edición) edition; (Foto) print; (marca)
imprint; **impresión digital** fingerprint

impresionante [impresjo'nante]
adj impressive; (tremendo) tremendous;
(maravilloso) great, marvellous

impresionar [impresjo'nar] vt
(conmover) to move; (afectar) to impress,
strike; (película fotográfica) to expose;
impresionarse vr to be impressed;
(conmoverse) to be moved

impreso, -a [im'preso, a] pp de
imprimir ▷ adj printed; **impresos**
nmpl printed matter; **impresora** nf
printer

imprevisto, -a [impre'βisto, a]
adj (gen) unforeseen; (inesperado)
unexpected

imprimir [impri'mir] vt to imprint,
impress, stamp; (textos) to print;
(Inform) to output, print out

improbable [impro'βaβle] adj
improbable; (inverosímil) unlikely

impropio, -a [im'propjo, a] adj
improper

improvisado, -a [improβi'saðo, a]
adj improvised

improvisar [improβi'sar] vt to
improvise

improviso, -a [impro'βiso, a] adj: **de**
~ unexpectedly, suddenly

imprudencia [impru'ðenθja] nf
imprudence; (indiscreción) indiscretion;
(descuido) carelessness; **imprudente**
adj unwise, imprudent; (indiscreto)
indiscreet

impuesto, -a [im'pwesto, a] adj
imposed ▷ nm tax; **impuesto al valor
agregado** o **añadido** (LAM) value added
tax (BRIT) = sales tax (US); **impuesto
sobre el valor añadido** (ESP) value
added tax (BRIT) = sales tax (US)

impulsar [impul'sar] vt to drive;
(promover) to promote, stimulate

impulsivo, -a [impul'siβo, a] adj
impulsive; **impulso** nm impulse;
(fuerza, empuje) thrust, drive;
(fig: sentimiento) urge, impulse

impureza [impu'reθa] nf impurity;
impuro, -a adj impure

inaccesible [inakθe'siβle] adj
inaccessible

inaceptable [inaθep'taβle] adj
unacceptable

inactivo, -a [inak'tiβo, a] adj
inactive

inadecuado, -a [inaðe'kwaðo, a]
adj (insuficiente) inadequate; (inapto)
unsuitable

inadvertido, -a [inaðβer'tiðo, a] adj
(no visto) unnoticed

inaguantable [inaɣwan'taβle] adj
unbearable

inanimado, -a [inani'maðo, a] adj
inanimate

inaudito, -a [inau'ðito, a] adj
unheard-of

inauguración [inauɣura'θjon] nf
inauguration; opening

inaugurar [inauɣu'rar] vt to
inaugurate; (exposición) to open

inca [in̄ka] nmf Inca

incalculable [inkalku'laβle] adj
incalculable

incandescente [inkandes'θente]
adj incandescent

incansable [inkan'saβle] adj

tireless, untiring

incapacidad [inkapaθi'ðað] *nf* incapacity; (*incompetencia*) incompetence; **incapacidad física/mental** physical/mental disability

incapacitar [inkapaθi'tar] *vt* (*inhabilitar*) to incapacitate, render unfit; (*descalificar*) to disqualify

incapaz [inka'paθ] *adj* incapable

incautarse [inkau'tarse] *vr*: **~ de** to seize, confiscate

incauto, -a [in'kauto, a] *adj* (*imprudente*) incautious, unwary

incendiar [inθen'djar] *vt* to set fire to; (*fig*) to inflame; **incendiarse** *vr* to catch fire; **incendiario, -a** [inθen'djarjo, a] *adj* incendiary

incendio [in'θendjo] *nm* fire

incentivo [inθen'tiβo] *nm* incentive

incertidumbre [inθerti'ðumbre] *nf* (*inseguridad*) uncertainty; (*duda*) doubt

incesante [inθe'sante] *adj* incessant

incesto [in'θesto] *nm* incest

incidencia [inθi'ðenθja] *nf* (*Mat*) incidence

incidente [inθi'ðente] *nm* incident

incidir [inθi'ðir] *vi* (*influir*) to influence; (*afectar*) to affect

incienso [in'θjenso] *nm* incense

incierto, -a [in'θjerto, a] *adj* uncertain

incineración [inθinera'θjon] *nf* incineration; (*de cadáveres*) cremation

incinerar [inθine'rar] *vt* to burn; (*cadáveres*) to cremate

incisión [inθi'sjon] *nf* incision

incisivo, -a [inθi'siβo, a] *adj* sharp, cutting; (*fig*) incisive

incitar [inθi'tar] *vt* to incite, rouse

inclemencia [inkle'menθja] *nf* (*severidad*) harshness, severity; (*del tiempo*) inclemency

inclinación [inklina'θjon] *nf* (*gen*) inclination; (*de tierras*) slope, incline; (*de cabeza*) nod, bow; (*fig*) leaning, bent

inclinar [inkli'nar] *vt* to incline; (*cabeza*) to nod, bow ▷ *vi* to lean, slope; **inclinarse** *vr* to bow; (*encorvarse*) to

stoop; **~se a** (*parecerse a*) to take after, resemble; **~se ante** to bow down to; **me inclino a pensar que ...** I'm inclined to think that ...

incluir [inklu'ir] *vt* to include; (*incorporar*) to incorporate; (*meter*) to enclose

inclusive [inklu'siβe] *adv* inclusive ▷ *prep* including

incluso [in'kluso] *adv* even

incógnita [in'koɣnita] *nf* (*Mat*) unknown quantity

incógnito [in'koɣnito] *nm*: **de ~** incognito

incoherente [inkoe'rente] *adj* incoherent

incoloro, -a [inko'loro, a] *adj* colourless

incomodar [inkomo'ðar] *vt* to inconvenience; (*molestar*) to bother, trouble; (*fastidiar*) to annoy

incomodidad [inkomoði'ðað] *nf* inconvenience; (*fastidio, enojo*) annoyance; (*de vivienda*) discomfort

incómodo, -a [in'komoðo, a] *adj* (*inconfortable*) uncomfortable; (*molesto*) annoying; (*inconveniente*) inconvenient

incomparable [inkompa'raβle] *adj* incomparable

incompatible [inkompa'tiβle] *adj* incompatible

incompetente [inkompe'tente] *adj* incompetent

incompleto, -a [inkom'pleto, a] *adj* incomplete, unfinished

incomprensible [inkompren'siβle] *adj* incomprehensible

incomunicado, -a [inkomuni'kaðo, a] *adj* (*aislado*) cut off, isolated; (*confinado*) in solitary confinement

incondicional [inkondiθjo'nal] *adj* unconditional; (*apoyo*) wholehearted; (*partidario*) staunch

inconfundible [inkonfun'diβle] *adj* unmistakable

incongruente [inkon'grwente] *adj* incongruous

inconsciente [inkons'θjente] *adj*

unconscious; thoughtless

inconsecuente [inkonse'kwente]
adj inconsistent

inconstante [inkons'tante] adj
inconstant

incontable [inkon'taβle] adj
countless, innumerable

inconveniencia [inkombe'njenθeja]
nf unsuitability, inappropriateness;
(descortesía) impoliteness;

inconveniente adj unsuitable;
impolite ▷ nm obstacle; (desventaja)
disadvantage; **el inconveniente es
que ...** the trouble is that ...

incordiar [inkor'ðjar] (fam) vt to
bug, annoy

incorporar [inkorpo'rar] vt to
incorporate; **incorporarse** vr to sit
up; **~se a** to join

incorrecto, -a [inko'rrekto,
a] adj (gen) incorrect, wrong;
(comportamiento) bad-mannered

incorregible [inkorre'xiβle] adj
incorrigible

incrédulo, -a [in'kreðulo, a] adj
incredulous, unbelieving; sceptical

increíble [inkre'iβle] adj incredible

incremento [inkre'mento] nm
increment; (aumento) rise, increase

increpar [inkre'par] vt to reprimand

incruento, -a [in'krwento, a] adj
bloodless

incrustar [inkrus'tar] vt to incrust;
(piedras: en joya) to inlay

incubar [inku'βar] vt to incubate

inculcar [inkul'kar] vt to inculcate

inculto, -a [in'kulto, a] adj (persona)
uneducated; (grosero) uncouth ▷ nm/f
ignoramus

incumplimiento
[inkumpli'mjento] nm non-
fulfilment; **incumplimiento de
contrato** breach of contract

incurrir [inku'rrir] vi: **~ en** to incur;
(crimen) to commit

indagar [inda'var] vt to investigate;
to search; (averiguar) to ascertain

indecente [inde'θente] adj indecent,

improper; (lascivo) obscene

indeciso, -a [inde'θiso, a] adj (por
decidir) undecided; (vacilante) hesitant

indefenso, -a [inde'fenso, a] adj
defenceless

indefinido, -a [indefi'niðo, a] adj
indefinite; (vago) vague, undefined

indemne [in'demne] adj (objeto)
undamaged; (persona) unharmed,
unhurt

indemnizar [indemni'θar] vt to
indemnify; (compensar) to compensate

independencia [indepen'denθja] nf
independence

independiente [indepen'djente]
adj (libre) independent; (autónomo)
self-sufficient

indeterminado, -a
[indetermi'naðo, a] adj indefinite;
(desconocido) indeterminate

India ['indja] nf: **la ~** India

indicación [indika'θjon] nf
indication; (señal) sign; (sugerencia)
suggestion, hint

indicado, -a [indi'kaðo, a] adj
(momento, método) right; (tratamiento)
appropriate; (solución) likely

indicador [indika'ðor] nm indicator;
(Tec) gauge, meter

indicar [indi'kar] vt (mostrar) to
indicate, show; (termómetro etc) to
read, register; (señalar) to point to

índice ['indiθe] nm index; (catálogo)
catalogue; (Anat) index finger,
forefinger; **índice de materias** table
of contents

indicio [in'diθjo] nm indication, sign;
(en pesquisa etc) clue

indiferencia [indife'renθja] nf
indifference; (apatía) apathy;
indiferente adj indifferent

indígena [in'dixena] adj indigenous,
native ▷ nmf native

indigestión [indixes'tjon] nf
indigestion

indigesto, -a [indi'xesto, a] adj
(alimento) indigestible; (fig) turgid

indignación [indixna'θjon] nf

indignation
indignar [indiɣ'nar] vt to anger, make indignant; **indignarse** vr: **~se por** to get indignant about
indigno, -a [in'diɣno, a] adj (despreciable) low, contemptible; (inmerecido) unworthy
indio, -a ['indjo, a] adj, nm/f Indian
indirecta [indi'rekta] nf insinuation, innuendo; (sugerencia) hint
indirecto, -a [indi'rekto, a] adj indirect
indiscreción [indiskre'θjon] nf (imprudencia) indiscretion; (irreflexión) tactlessness; (acto) gaffe, faux pas
indiscreto, -a [indis'kreto, a] adj indiscreet
indiscutible [indisku'tiβle] adj indisputable, unquestionable
indispensable [indispen'saβle] adj indispensable, essential
indispuesto, -a [indis'pwesto, a] adj (enfermo) unwell, indisposed
indistinto, -a [indis'tinto, a] adj indistinct; (vago) vague
individual [indiβi'ðwal] adj individual; (habitación) single ▷ nm (Deporte) singles sg
individuo, -a [indi'βiðwo, a] adj, nm individual
índole ['indole] nf (naturaleza) nature; (clase) sort, kind
inducir [indu'θir] vt to induce; (inferir) to infer; (persuadir) to persuade
indudable [indu'ðaβle] adj undoubted; (incuestionable) unquestionable
indultar [indul'tar] vt (perdonar) to pardon, reprieve; (librar de pago) to exempt; **indulto** nm pardon; exemption
industria [in'dustrja] nf industry; (habilidad) skill; **industrial** adj industrial ▷ nm industrialist
inédito, -a [in'eðito, a] adj (texto) unpublished; (nuevo) new
ineficaz [inefi'kaθ] adj (inútil) ineffective; (ineficiente) inefficient

ineludible [inelu'ðiβle] adj inescapable, unavoidable
ineptitud [inepti'tuð] nf ineptitude, incompetence; **inepto, -a** adj inept, incompetent
inequívoco, -a [ine'kiβoko, a] adj unequivocal; (inconfundible) unmistakable
inercia [in'erθja] nf inertia; (pasividad) passivity
inerte [in'erte] adj inert; (inmóvil) motionless
inesperado, -a [inespe'raðo, a] adj unexpected, unforeseen
inestable [ines'taβle] adj unstable
inevitable [ineβi'taβle] adj inevitable
inexacto, -a [inek'sakto, a] adj inaccurate; (falso) untrue
inexperto, -a [inek'sperto, a] adj (novato) inexperienced
infalible [infa'liβle] adj infallible; (plan) foolproof
infame [in'fame] adj infamous; (horrible) dreadful; **infamia** nf infamy; (deshonra) disgrace
infancia [in'fanθja] nf infancy, childhood
infantería [infante'ria] nf infantry
infantil [infan'til] adj (pueril, aniñado) infantile; (cándido) childlike; (literatura, ropa etc) children's
infarto [in'farto] nm (tb: **~ de miocardio**) heart attack
infatigable [infati'ɣaβle] adj tireless, untiring
infección [infek'θjon] nf infection; **infeccioso, -a** adj infectious
infectar [infek'tar] vt to infect; **infectarse** vr to become infected
infeliz [infe'liθ] adj unhappy, wretched ▷ nmf wretch
inferior [infe'rjor] adj inferior; (situación) lower ▷ nmf inferior, subordinate
inferir [infe'rir] vt (deducir) to infer, deduce; (causar) to cause
infidelidad [infiðeli'ðað] nf (gen)

infidelity, unfaithfulness

infiel [in'fjel] *adj* unfaithful, disloyal; (erróneo) inaccurate ▷ *nmf* infidel, unbeliever

infierno [in'fjerno] *nm* hell

infiltrarse [infil'trarse] *vr:* ~ **en** to infiltrate in(to); (persona) to work one's way in(to)

ínfimo, -a [i'infimo, a] *adj* (más bajo) lowest; (despreciable) vile, mean

infinidad [infini'ðað] *nf* infinity; (abundancia) great quantity

infinito, -a [infi'nito, a] *adj, nm* infinite

inflación [infla'θjon] *nf* (hinchazón) swelling; (monetaria) inflation; (fig) conceit

inflamable [infla'maβle] *adj* flammable

inflamar [infla'mar] *vt* (Med: fig) to inflame; **inflamarse** *vr* to catch fire; to become inflamed

inflar [in'flar] *vt* (hinchar) to inflate, blow up; (fig) to exaggerate; **inflarse** *vr* to swell (up); (fig) to get conceited

inflexible [inflek'siβle] *adj* inflexible; (fig) unbending

influencia [influ'enθja] *nf* influence

influir [influ'ir] *vi* to influence

influjo [in'fluxo] *nm* influence

influya *etc vb* **V influir**

influyente [influ'jente] *adj* influential

información [informa'θjon] *nf* information; (noticias) news *sg*; (Jur) inquiry; **I~** (oficina) Information Office; (mostrador) Information Desk; (Tel) Directory Enquiries

informal [infor'mal] *adj* (gen) informal

informar [infor'mar] *vt* (gen) to inform; (revelar) to reveal, make known ▷ *vi* (Jur) to plead; (denunciar) to inform; (dar cuenta de) to report on; **informarse** *vr* to find out; ~**se de** to inquire into

informática [infor'matika] *nf* computer science, information technology

informe [in'forme] *adj* shapeless ▷ *nm* report

infracción [infrak'θjon] *nf* infraction, infringement

infravalorar [infraβalo'rar] *vt* to undervalue, underestimate

infringir [infrin'xir] *vt* to infringe, contravene

infundado, -a [infun'daðo, a] *adj* groundless, unfounded

infundir [infun'dir] *vt* to infuse, instil

infusión [infu'sjon] *nf* infusion; **infusión de manzanilla** camomile tea

ingeniería [inxenje'ria] *nf* engineering; **ingeniería genética** genetic engineering; **ingeniero, -a** *nm/f* engineer; **ingeniero civil** o **de caminos** civil engineer

ingenio [in'xenjo] *nm* (talento) talent; (agudeza) wit; (habilidad) ingenuity, inventiveness; **ingenio azucarero** (LAM) sugar refinery; **ingenioso, -a** [inxe'njoso, a] *adj* ingenious, clever; (divertido) witty; **ingenuo, -a** *adj* ingenuous

ingerir [inxe'rir] *vt* to ingest (tragar) to swallow; (consumir) to consume

Inglaterra [ingla'terra] *nf* England

ingle ['ingle] *nf* groin

inglés, -esa [in'gles, esa] *adj* English ▷ *nm/f* Englishman(-woman) ▷ *nm* (Ling) English

ingrato, -a [in'grato, a] *adj* (gen) ungrateful

ingrediente [ingre'ðjente] *nm* ingredient

ingresar [ingre'sar] *vt* (dinero) to deposit ▷ *vi* to come in; ~ **en el hospital** to go into hospital

ingreso [in'greso] *nm* (entrada) entry; (en hospital etc) admission; **ingresos** *nmpl* (dinero) income *sg*; (Com) takings *pl*

inhabitable [inaβi'taβle] *adj* uninhabitable

inhalar [ina'lar] *vt* to inhale

inhibir [ini'βir] *vt* to inhibit

inhóspito, -a [i'nospito, a] *adj* (*región, paisaje*) inhospitable

inhumano, -a [inu'mano, a] *adj* inhuman

inicial [ini'θjal] *adj, nf* initial

iniciar [ini'θjar] *vt* (*persona*) to initiate; (*empezar*) to begin, commence; (*conversación*) to start up

iniciativa [iniθja'tiβa] *nf* initiative; **iniciativa privada** private enterprise

ininterrumpido, -a [ininterrum'piðo, a] *adj* uninterrupted

injertar [inxer'tar] *vt* to graft; **injerto** *nm* graft

injuria [in'xurja] *nf* (*agravio, ofensa*) offence; (*insulto*) insult

> No confundir **injuria** con la palabra inglesa *injury*.

injusticia [inxus'tiθja] *nf* injustice

injusto, -a [in'xusto, a] *adj* unjust, unfair

inmadurez [inmaðu'reθ] *nf* immaturity

inmediaciones [inmeðja'θjones] *nfpl* neighbourhood *sg*, environs

inmediato, -a [inme'ðjato, a] *adj* immediate; (*contiguo*) adjoining; (*rápido*) prompt; (*próximo*) neighbouring, next; **de ~** immediately

inmejorable [inmexo'raβle] *adj* unsurpassable; (*precio*) unbeatable

inmenso, -a [in'menso, a] *adj* immense, huge

inmigración [inmiɣra'θjon] *nf* immigration

inmobiliaria [inmoβi'ljarja] *nf* estate agency

inmolar [inmo'lar] *vt* to immolate, sacrifice

inmoral [inmo'ral] *adj* immoral

inmortal [inmor'tal] *adj* immortal; **inmortalizar** *vt* to immortalize

inmóvil [in'moβil] *adj* immobile

inmueble [in'mweβle] *adj*: **bienes ~s** real estate, landed property ▷ *nm* property

inmundo, -a [in'mundo, a] *adj* filthy

inmune [in'mune] *adj*: **~ (a)** (*Med*) immune (to)

inmunidad [inmuni'ðað] *nf* immunity

inmutarse [inmu'tarse] *vr* to turn pale; **no se inmutó** he didn't turn a hair

innato, -a [in'nato, a] *adj* innate

innecesario, -a [inneθe'sarjo, a] *adj* unnecessary

innovación [innoβa'θjon] *nf* innovation

innovar [inno'βar] *vt* to introduce

inocencia [ino'θenθja] *nf* innocence

inocentada [inoθen'taða] *nf* practical joke

inocente [ino'θente] *adj* (*ingenuo*) naive, innocent; (*inculpable*) innocent; (*sin malicia*) harmless ▷ *nmf* simpleton; **el día de los (Santos) I~s** ≈ April Fools' Day

---

● **DÍA DE LOS (SANTOS)**
● **INOCENTES**
●
● The 28th December, **el día de los**
● **(Santos) Inocentes**, is when
● the Church commemorates the
● story of Herod's slaughter of the
● innocent children of Judaea.
● On this day Spaniards play
● **inocentadas** (practical jokes) on
● each other, much like our April
● Fool's Day pranks.

---

inodoro [ino'ðoro] *nm* toilet, lavatory (BRIT)

inofensivo, -a [inofen'siβo, a] *adj* inoffensive, harmless

inolvidable [inolβi'ðaβle] *adj* unforgettable

inoportuno, -a [inopor'tuno, a] *adj* untimely; (*molesto*) inconvenient

inoxidable [inoksi'ðaβle] *adj*: **acero ~** stainless steel

inquietar [inkje'tar] *vt* to worry, trouble; **inquietarse** *vr* to worry, get upset; **inquieto, -a** *adj* anxious,

worried; **inquietud** nf anxiety, worry
inquilino, -a [iŋki'lino, a] nm/f
tenant
insaciable [insa'θjaβle] adj
insatiable
inscribir [inskri'βir] vt to inscribe; ~
a algn en (lista) to put sb on; (censo) to
register sb on
inscripción [inskrip'θjon] nf
inscription; (Escol etc) enrolment; (en
censo) registration
insecticida [insekti'θiða] nm
insecticide
insecto [in'sekto] nm insect
inseguridad [inseɣuri'ðað] nf
insecurity; **inseguridad ciudadana**
lack of safety in the streets
inseguro, -a [inse'ɣuro, a] adj
insecure; (inconstante) unsteady;
(incierto) uncertain
insensato, -a [insen'sato, a] adj
foolish, stupid
insensible [insen'siβle] adj
(gen) insensitive; (movimiento)
imperceptible; (sin sentir) numb
insertar [inser'tar] vt to insert
inservible [inser'βiβle] adj useless
insignia [in'siɣnja] nf (señal
distintiva) badge; (estandarte) flag
insignificante [insiɣnifi'kante] adj
insignificant
insinuar [insi'nwar] vt to insinuate,
imply
insípido, -a [in'sipiðo, a] adj insipid
insistir [insis'tir] vi to insist; ~ **en
algo** to insist on sth; (enfatizar) to
stress sth
insolación [insola'θjon] nf (Med)
sunstroke
insolente [inso'lente] adj insolent
insólito, -a [in'solito, a] adj unusual
insoluble [inso'luβle] adj insoluble
insomnio [in'somnjo] nm insomnia
insonorizado, -a [insonori'θaðo, a]
adj (cuarto etc) soundproof
insoportable [insopor'taβle] adj
unbearable
inspección [inspek'θjon] nf

inspection, check; **inspeccionar**
vt (examinar) to inspect, examine;
(controlar) to check
inspector, a [inspek'tor, a] nm/f
inspector
inspiración [inspira'θjon] nf
inspiration
inspirar [inspi'rar] vt to inspire;
(Med) to inhale; **inspirarse** vr: ~**se en**
to be inspired by
instalación [instala'θjon] nf (equipo)
fittings pl, equipment; **instalación
eléctrica** wiring
instalar [insta'lar] vt (establecer)
to instal; (erguir) to set up, erect;
instalarse vr to establish o.s.; (en una
vivienda) to move into
instancia [ins'tanθja] nf (Jur)
petition; (ruego) request; **en última ~**
as a last resort
instantáneo, -a [instan'taneo,
a] adj instantaneous; **café ~** instant
coffee
instante [ins'tante] nm instant,
moment; **al ~** right now
instar [ins'tar] vt to press, urge
instaurar [instau'rar] vt (costumbre)
to establish; (normas, sistema) to bring
in, introduce; (gobierno) to instal
instigar [insti'ɣar] vt to instigate
instinto [ins'tinto] nm instinct; **por
~** instinctively
institución [institu'θjon] nf
institution, establishment
instituir [institu'ir] vt to establish;
(fundar) to found; **instituto** nm (gen)
institute; (ESP Escol) ≈ comprehensive
(BRIT) o high (US) school
institutriz [institu'triθ] nf
governess
instrucción [instruk'θjon] nf
instruction
instruir [instru'ir] vt (gen) to
instruct; (enseñar) to teach, educate
instrumento [instru'mento] nm
(gen) instrument; (herramienta) tool,
implement
insubordinarse [insuβorði'narse] vr

vr to rebel

insuficiente [insufiˈθjente] adj (gen) insufficient; (Escol: calificación) unsatisfactory

insular [insuˈlar] adj insular

insultar [insulˈtar] vt to insult; **insulto** nm insult

insuperable [insupeˈraβle] adj (excelente) unsurpassable; (problema etc) insurmountable

insurrección [insurrekˈθjon] nf insurrection, rebellion

intachable [intaˈtʃaβle] adj irreproachable

intacto, -a [inˈtakto, a] adj intact

integral [inteˈɣral] adj integral; (completo) complete; **pan ~** wholemeal (BRIT) o wholewheat (US) bread

integrar [inteˈɣrar] vt to make up, compose; (Mat: fig) to integrate

integridad [inteɣriˈðað] nf wholeness; (carácter) integrity; **íntegro, -a** adj whole, entire; (honrado) honest

intelectual [intelekˈtwal] adj, nmf intellectual

inteligencia [inteliˈxenθja] nf intelligence; (ingenio) ability; **inteligente** adj intelligent

intemperie [intemˈperje] nf: **a la ~** out in the open, exposed to the elements

intención [intenˈθjon] nf (gen) intention, purpose; **con segundas intenciones** maliciously; **con ~** deliberately

intencionado, -a [intenθjoˈnaðo, a] adj deliberate; **mal ~** ill-disposed, hostile

intensidad [intensiˈðað] nf (gen) intensity; (Elec, Tec) strength; **llover con ~** to rain hard

intenso, -a [inˈtenso, a] adj intense; (sentimiento) profound, deep

intentar [intenˈtar] vt (tratar) to try, attempt; **intento** nm attempt

interactivo, -a [interakˈtiβo, a] adj (Inform) interactive

intercalar [interkaˈlar] vt to insert

intercambio [interˈkambjo] nm exchange, swap

interceder [interθeˈðer] vi to intercede

interceptar [interθepˈtar] vt to intercept

interés [inteˈres] nm (gen) interest; (parte) share, part; (pey) self-interest; **intereses creados** vested interests

interesado, -a [intereˈsaðo, a] adj interested; (prejuiciado) prejudiced; (pey) mercenary, self-seeking

interesante [intereˈsante] adj interesting

interesar [intereˈsar] vt, vi to interest, be of interest to; **interesarse** vr: **~se en o por** to take an interest in

interferir [interfeˈrir] vt to interfere with; (Tel) to jam ▷ vi to interfere

interfón [interˈfon] (MÉX) nm entry phone

interino, -a [inteˈrino, a] adj temporary ▷ nm/f temporary holder of a post; (Med) locum; (Escol) supply teacher

interior [inteˈrjor] adj inner, inside; (Com) domestic, internal ▷ nm interior, inside; (fig) soul, mind; **Ministerio del I~** = Home Office (BRIT) = Department of the Interior (US); **interiorista** (ESP) nmf interior designer

interjección [interxekˈθjon] nf interjection

interlocutor, a [interlokuˈtor, a] nm/f speaker

intermedio, -a [interˈmeðjo, a] adj intermediate ▷ nm interval

interminable [intermiˈnaβle] adj endless

intermitente [intermiˈtente] adj intermittent ▷ nm (Auto) indicator

internacional [internaθjoˈnal] adj international

internado [interˈnaðo] nm boarding school

internar [interˈnar] vt to intern; (en

un manicomio) to commit; **internarse**
vr (penetrar) to penetrate

internauta [inter'nauta] nmf web
surfer, Internet user

Internet, internet [inter'net] nm
of Internet

interno, -a [in'terno, a] adj internal,
interior; (Pol etc) domestic ▷ nm/f
(alumno) boarder

interponer [interpo'ner] vt to
interpose, put in; **interponerse** vr to
intervene

interpretación [interpreta'θjon] nf
interpretation

interpretar [interpre'tar] vt to
interpret; (Teatro, Mús) to perform,
play; **intérprete** nmf (Ling) interpreter,
translator; (Mús, Teatro) performer,
artist(e)

interrogación [interroɣa'θjon] nf
interrogation; (Ling: tb: **signo de ~**)
question mark

interrogar [interro'ɣar] vt to
interrogate, question

interrumpir [interrum'pir] vt to
interrupt

interrupción [interrup'θjon] nf
interruption

interruptor [interrup'tor] nm (Elec)
switch

intersección [intersek'θjon] nf
intersection

interurbano, -a [interur'βano,
a] adj: **llamada interurbana** long-
distance call

intervalo [inter'βalo] nm interval;
(descanso) break

intervenir [interβe'nir] vt (controlar)
to control, supervise; (Med) to operate
on ▷ vi (participar) to take part,
participate; (mediar) to intervene

interventor, a [interβen'tor, a]
nm/f inspector; (Com) auditor

intestino [intes'tino] nm (Med)
intestine

intimar [inti'mar] vi to become
friendly

intimidad [intimi'ðað] nf intimacy;

(familiaridad) familiarity; (vida privada)
private life; (Jur) privacy

íntimo, -a ['intimo, a] adj intimate

intolerable [intole'raβle] adj
intolerable, unbearable

intoxicación [intoksika'θjon] nf
poisoning; **intoxicación alimenticia**
food poisoning

intranet [intra'net] nf intranet

intranquilo, -a [intran'kilo, a] adj
worried

intransitable [intransi'taβle] adj
impassable

intrépido, -a [in'trepiðo, a] adj
intrepid

intriga [in'triɣa] nf intrigue; (plan)
plot; **intrigar** vt, vi to intrigue

intrínseco, -a [in'trinseko, a] adj
intrinsic

introducción [introðuk'θjon] nf
introduction

introducir [introðu'θir] vt (gen)
to introduce; (moneda etc) to insert;
(Inform) to input, enter

intromisión [intromi'sjon] nf
interference, meddling

introvertido, -a [introβer'tiðo, a]
adj, nm/f introvert

intruso, -a [in'truso, a] adj intrusive
▷ nm/f intruder

intuición [intwi'θjon] nf intuition

inundación [inunda'θjon] nf
flood(ing); **inundar** vt to flood; (fig) to
swamp, inundate

inusitado, -a [inusi'taðo, a] adj
unusual, rare

inútil [in'util] adj useless; (esfuerzo)
vain, fruitless

inutilizar [inutili'θar] vt to make o
render useless

invadir [imba'ðir] vt to invade

inválido, -a [im'baliðo, a] adj
invalid ▷ nm/f invalid

invasión [imba'sjon] nf invasion

invasor, a [imba'sor, a] adj invading
▷ nm/f invader

invención [imben'θjon] nf invention

inventar [imben'tar] vt to invent

inventario [imben'tarjo] nm inventory

invento [im'bento] nm invention

inventor, a [imben'tor, a] nm/f inventor

invernadero [imberna'ðero] nm greenhouse

inverosímil [imbero'simil] adj implausible

inversión [imber'sjon] nf (Com) investment

inverso, -a [im'berso, a] adj inverse, opposite; **en el orden ~** in reverse order; **a la inversa** inversely, the other way round

inversor, a [imber'sor, a] nm/f (Com) investor

invertir [imber'tir] vt (Com) to invest; (volcar) to turn upside down; (tiempo etc) to spend

investigación [imbestiɣa'θjon] nf investigation; (Escol) research; **investigación y desarrollo** research and development

investigar [imbesti'ɣar] vt to investigate; (Escol) to do research into

invierno [im'bjerno] nm winter

invisible [imbi'siβle] adj invisible

invitado, -a [imbi'taðo, a] nm/f guest

invitar [imbi'tar] vt to invite; (incitar) to entice; (pagar) to buy, pay for

invocar [imbo'kar] vt to invoke, call on

involucrar [imbolu'krar] vt: **~ en** to involve in; **involucrarse** vr (persona) **~se en** to get mixed up in

involuntario, -a [imbolun'tarjo, a] adj (movimiento, gesto) involuntary; (error) unintentional

inyección [injek'θjon] nf injection

inyectar [injek'tar] vt to inject

iPod® ['ipoð] (pl **~s**) nm iPod®

○ PALABRA CLAVE

ir [ir] vi **1** to go; (a pie) to walk; (viajar)

to travel; **ir caminando** to walk; **fui en tren** I went o travelled by train; **¡(ahora) voy!** (I'm just) coming!

2: **ir (a) por**: **ir (a) por el médico** to fetch the doctor

3 (progresar: persona, cosa) to go; **el trabajo va muy bien** work is going very well; **¿cómo te va?** how are things going?; **me va muy bien** I'm getting on very well; **le fue fatal** it went awfully badly for him

4 (funcionar): **el coche no va muy bien** the car isn't running very well

5: **te va estupendamente ese color** that colour suits you fantastically well

6 (locuciones): **¿vino?** - **¡qué va!** did he come? - of course not!; **vamos, no llores** come on, don't cry; **¡vaya coche!** what a car!, that's some car!

7: **no vaya a ser**: **tienes que correr, no vaya a ser que pierdas el tren** you'll have to run so as not to miss the train

8 (+ pp): **iba vestido muy bien** he was very well dressed

9: **ni me** etc **va ni me** etc **viene** I etc don't care

▷ vb aux **1** ir a: **voy/iba a hacerlo hoy** I am/was going to do it today

2 (+ gerundio): **iba anocheciendo** it was getting dark; **todo se me iba aclarando** everything was gradually becoming clearer to me

3 (+ pp: = pasivo): **van vendidos 300 ejemplares** 300 copies have been sold so far

irse vr **1**: **¿por dónde se va al zoológico?** which is the way to the zoo?

2 (marcharse) to leave; **ya se habrán ido** they must already have left o gone

ira ['ira] nf anger, rage

Irak [i'rak] nm = **Iraq**

Irán [i'ran] nm Iran; **iraní** adj, nmf Iranian

Iraq [i'rak] nm Iraq; **iraquí** adj, nmf Iraqi

iris ['iris] nm inv (tb: **arco ~**) rainbow; (Anat) iris

Irlanda [ir'landa] nf Ireland; **irlandés, -esa** adj Irish ▷ nm/f Irishman(-woman); **los irlandeses** the Irish

ironía [iro'nia] nf irony; **irónico, -a** adj ironic(al)

IRPF nm abr (= Impuesto sobre la Renta de las Personas Físicas) (personal) income tax

irreal [irre'al] adj unreal

irregular [irrexu'lar] adj (gen) irregular; (situación) abnormal

irremediable [irreme'ðjaβle] adj irremediable; (vicio) incurable

irreparable [irrepa'raβle] adj (daños) irreparable; (pérdida) irrecoverable

irrespetuoso, -a [irrespe'twoso, a] adj disrespectful

irresponsable [irrespon'saβle] adj irresponsible

irreversible [irreβer'sible] adj irreversible

irrigar [irri'ɣar] vt to irrigate

irrisorio, -a [irri'sorjo, a] adj derisory, ridiculous

irritar [irri'tar] vt to irritate, annoy

irrupción [irrup'θjon] nf irruption; (invasión) invasion

isla ['isla] nf island

Islam [is'lam] nm Islam; **las enseñanzas del ~** the teachings of Islam; **islámico, -a** adj Islamic

islandés, -esa [islan'des, esa] adj Icelandic ▷ nm/f Icelander

Islandia [is'landja] nf Iceland

isleño, -a [is'leɲo, a] adj island cpd ▷ nm/f islander

Israel [isra'el] nm Israel; **israelí** adj, nmf Israeli

istmo ['istmo] nm isthmus

Italia [i'talja] nf Italy; **italiano, -a** adj, nm/f Italian

itinerario [itine'rarjo] nm itinerary, route

ITV (ESP) nf abr (= inspección técnica de vehículos) roadworthiness test, ≈

MOT (BRIT)

IVA ['iβa] nm abr (= impuesto sobre el valor añadido) VAT

izar [i'θar] vt to hoist

izdo, -a abr (= izquierdo, a) l

izquierda [iθ'kjerda] nf left; (Pol) left (wing); **a la ~** (= estar) on the left; (torcer etc) (to the) left

izquierdo, -a [iθ'kjerðo, a] adj left

j

jabalí [xaβa'li] nm wild boar

jabalina [xaβa'lina] nf javelin

jabón [xa'βon] nm soap

jaca ['xaka] nf pony

jacal [xa'kal] (MÉX) nm shack

jacinto [xa'θinto] nm hyacinth

jactarse [xak'tarse] vr to boast, brag

jadear [xaðe'ar] vi to pant, gasp for breath

jaguar [xa'ɣwar] nm jaguar

jaiba ['xaiβa] (LAM) nf crab

jalar [xa'lar] (LAM) vt to pull

jalea [xa'lea] nf jelly

jaleo [xa'leo] nm racket, uproar; **armar un ~** to kick up a racket

jalón [xa'lon] (LAM) nm tug

jamás [xa'mas] adv never

jamón [xa'mon] nm ham; **jamón dulce** o **de York** cooked ham; **jamón serrano** cured ham

Japón [xa'pon] nm Japan; **japonés, -esa** adj, nm/f Japanese ▷ nm (Ling) Japanese

jaque ['xake] nm (Ajedrez) check; **jaque mate** checkmate

jaqueca [xa'keka] nf (very bad) headache, migraine

jarabe [xa'raβe] nm syrup

jardín [xar'ðin] nm garden; **jardín infantil** o **de infancia** nursery (school); **jardinería** nf gardening; **jardinero, -a** nm/f gardener

jarra ['xarra] nf jar; (jarro) jug

jarro ['xarro] nm jug

jarrón [xa'rron] nm vase

jaula ['xaula] nf cage

jauría [xau'ria] nf pack of hounds

jazmín [xaθ'min] nm jasmine

J.C. abr (= Jesucristo) J.C.

jeans [jins, dʒins] (LAM) nmpl jeans, denims; **unos ~** a pair of jeans

jefatura [xefa'tura] nf (tb: **~ de policía**) police headquarters sg

jefe, -a ['xefe, a] nm/f (gen) chief, head; (patrón) boss; **jefe de cocina** chef; **jefe de estación** stationmaster; **jefe de Estado** head of state; **jefe de estudios** (Escol) director of studies; **jefe de gobierno** head of government

jengibre [xen'xiβre] nm ginger

jeque ['xeke] nm sheik

jerárquico, -a [xe'rarkiko, a] adj hierarchic(al)

jerez [xe'reθ] nm sherry

jerga ['xerɣa] nf jargon

jeringa [xe'ringa] nf syringe; (LAM: molestia) annoyance, bother; **jeringuilla** nf syringe

jeroglífico [xero'xlifiko] nm hieroglyphic

jersey [xer'sei] (pl **~s**) nm jersey, pullover, jumper

Jerusalén [xerusa'len] n Jerusalem

Jesucristo [xesu'kristo] nm Jesus Christ

jesuita [xe'swita] adj, nm Jesuit

Jesús [xe'sus] nm Jesus; **¡~!** good heavens!; (al estornudar) bless you!

jinete [xi'nete] nmf horseman(-woman), rider

jipijapa [xipi'xapa] (LAM) nm straw hat

jirafa [xi'rafa] nf giraffe

jirón [xi'ron] nm rag, shred

jitomate [xito'mate] (MÉX) nm tomato

joder [xo'ðer] (fam!) vt, vi to fuck (!)

jogging ['joxin] (RPL) nm tracksuit (BRIT), sweat suit (US)

jornada [xor'naða] nf (viaje de un día) day's journey; (camino o viaje entero) journey; (día de trabajo) working day

jornal [xor'nal] nm (day's) wage; **jornalero** nm (day) labourer

joroba [xo'roβa] nf hump, hunched back; **jorobado, -a** adj hunchbacked ▷ nm/f hunchback

jota ['xota] nf (the letter) J; (danza) Aragonese dance; **no saber ni ~** to have no idea

joven ['xoβen] (pl **jóvenes**) adj young ▷ nm young man, youth ▷ nf young woman, girl

joya ['xoja] nf jewel, gem; (fig: persona) gem; **joyas de fantasía** costume o imitation jewellery; **joyería** nf (joyas) jewellery; (tienda) jeweller's (shop); **joyero** nm (persona) jeweller; (caja) jewel case

juanete [xwa'nete] nm (del pie) bunion

jubilación [xuβila'θjon] nf (retiro) retirement

jubilado, -a [xuβi'laðo, a] adj retired ▷ nm/f pensioner (BRIT), senior citizen

jubilar [xuβi'lar] vt to pension off, retire; (fam) to discard; **jubilarse** vr to retire

júbilo ['xuβilo] nm joy, rejoicing; **jubiloso, -a** adj jubilant

judía [xu'ðia] (ESP) nf (Culin) bean; **judía blanca/verde** haricot/French bean; V tb **judío**

judicial [xuði'θjal] adj judicial

judío, -a [xu'ðio, a] adj Jewish ▷ nm/f Jew(ess)

judo ['juðo] nm judo

juego etc ['xweɣo] vb V **jugar** ▷ nm (gen) play; (pasatiempo, partido) game; (en casino) gambling; (conjunto) set; **fuera de ~** (Deporte: persona) offside;

(: pelota) out of play; **juego de palabras** pun, play on words; **Juegos Olímpicos** Olympic Games

juerga ['xwerɣa] (ESP: fam) nf binge; (fiesta) party; **ir de ~** to go out on a binge

jueves ['xweβes] nm inv Thursday

juez [xweθ] nmf judge; **juez de instrucción** examining magistrate; **juez de línea** linesman; **juez de salida** starter

jugada [xu'ɣaða] nf play; **buena ~** good move o shot o stroke etc

jugador, a [xuɣa'ðor, a] nm/f player; (en casino) gambler

jugar [xu'ɣar] vt, vi to play; (en casino) to gamble; (apostar) to bet; **~ al fútbol** to play football

juglar [xu'ɣlar] nm minstrel

jugo ['xuɣo] nm (Bot) juice; (fig) essence, substance; **jugo de naranja** (LAM) orange juice; **jugoso, -a** adj juicy; (fig) substantial, important

juguete [xu'ɣete] nm toy; **juguetear** vi to play; **juguetería** nf toyshop

juguetón, -ona [xuɣe'ton, ona] adj playful

juicio ['xwiθjo] nm judgement; (razón) sanity, reason; (opinión) opinion

julio ['xuljo] nm July

jumper ['dʒumper] (LAM) nm pinafore dress (BRIT), jumper (US)

junco ['xunko] nm rush, reed

jungla ['xungla] nf jungle

junio ['xunjo] nm June

junta ['xunta] nf (asamblea) meeting, assembly; (comité, consejo) council, committee; (Com, Finanzas) board; (Tec) joint; **junta directiva** board of directors

juntar [xun'tar] vt to join, unite; (maquinaria) to assemble, put together; (dinero) to collect; **juntarse** vr to join, meet; (reunirse: personas) to meet, assemble; (arrimarse) to approach, draw closer; **~se con algn** to join sb

junto, -a ['xunto, a] adj joined; (unido) united; (anexo) near, close;

(contiguo, próximo) next, adjacent
▷ adv: **todo ~** all at once; **~s** together;
~ a near (to), next to; **~ con** (together)
with

jurado [xu'raðo] nm (Jur: individuo)
juror; (: grupo) jury; (de concurso: grupo)
panel (of judges); (: individuo) member
of a panel

juramento [xura'mento] nm oath;
(maldición) oath, curse; **prestar ~** to
take the oath; **tomar ~ a** to swear in,
administer the oath to

jurar [xu'rar] vt, vi to swear; **~ en
falso** to commit perjury; **tenérsela
jurada a algn** to have it in for sb

jurídico, -a [xu'riðiko, a] adj legal

jurisdicción [xurisðik'θjon]
nf (poder, autoridad) jurisdiction;
(territorio) district

justamente [xusta'mente] adv
justly, fairly; (precisamente) just, exactly

justicia [xus'tiθja] nf justice;
(equidad) fairness, justice

justificación [xustifika'θjon] nf
justification; **justificar** vt to justify

justo, -a ['xusto, a] adj (equitativo)
just, fair, right; (preciso) exact, correct;
(ajustado) tight ▷ adv (precisamente)
exactly, precisely; (LAM: apenas a tiempo)
just in time

juvenil [xuβe'nil] adj youthful

juventud [xuβen'tuð] nf
(adolescencia) youth; (jóvenes) young
people pl

juzgado [xuθ'γaðo] nm tribunal;
(Jur) court

juzgar [xuθ'γar] vt to judge; **a ~ por
...** to judge by ..., judging by ...

K

kárate ['karate] nm karate

kg abr (= kilogramo) kg

kilo ['kilo] nm kilo; **kilogramo**
nm kilogramme; **kilometraje** nm
distance in kilometres ≈ mileage;
kilómetro nm kilometre; **kilovatio**
nm kilowatt

kiosco ['kjosko] nm = **quiosco**

kleenex® ['kli'neks] nm paper
handkerchief, tissue

Kosovo [ko'soβo] nm Kosovo

km abr (= kilómetro) km

kv abr (= kilovatio) kw

I *abr* (= litro) l

la [la] *art def* the ▷ *pron* her; (Ud.) you; (cosa) it ▷ *nm* (Mús) la; **~ del sombrero rojo** the girl in the red hat; V tb **el**

laberinto [laβe'rinto] *nm* labyrinth

labio ['laβjo] *nm* lip

labor [la'βor] *nf* labour; (Agr) farm work; (tarea) job, task; (Costura) needlework; **labores domésticas** o **del hogar** household chores; **laborable** *adj* workable; **día laborable** working day; **laboral** *adj* (accidente) at work; (jornada) working

laboratorio [laβora'torjo] *nm* laboratory

laborista [laβo'rista] *adj*: **Partido L~** Labour Party

labrador, a [laβra'ðor, a] *adj* farming *cpd* ▷ *nm/f* farmer

labranza [la'βranθa] *nf* (Agr) cultivation

labrar [la'βrar] *vt* (gen) to work; (madera etc) to carve; (fig) to cause, bring about

laca ['laka] *nf* lacquer

lacio, -a ['laθjo, a] *adj* (pelo) straight

lacón [la'kon] *nm* shoulder of pork

lactancia [lak'tanθja] *nf* lactation

lácteo, -a ['lakteo, a] *adj*: **productos ~s** dairy products

ladear [laðe'ar] *vt* to tip, tilt ▷ *vi* to tilt; **ladearse** *vr* to lean

ladera [la'ðera] *nf* slope

lado ['laðo] *nm* (gen) side; (fig) protection; (Mil) flank; **al ~ de** beside; **poner de ~** to put on its side; **poner a un ~** to put aside; **por todos ~s** on all sides, all round (BRIT)

ladrar [la'ðrar] *vi* to bark; **ladrido** *nm* bark, barking

ladrillo [la'ðriʎo] *nm* (gen) brick; (azulejo) tile

ladrón, -ona [la'ðron, ona] *nm/f* thief

lagartija [laɣar'tixa] *nf* (Zool) (small) lizard

lagarto [la'ɣarto] *nm* (Zool) lizard

lago ['laɣo] *nm* lake

lágrima ['laɣrima] *nf* tear

laguna [la'ɣuna] *nf* (lago) lagoon; (hueco) gap

lamentable [lamen'taβle] *adj* lamentable, regrettable; (miserable) pitiful

lamentar [lamen'tar] *vt* (sentir) to regret; (deplorar) to lament; **lamentarse** *vr* to lament; **lo lamento mucho** I'm very sorry

lamer [la'mer] *vt* to lick

lámina ['lamina] *nf* (plancha delgada) sheet; (para estampar, estampa) plate

lámpara ['lampara] *nf* lamp; **lámpara de alcohol/gas** spirit/gas lamp; **lámpara de pie** standard lamp

lana ['lana] *nf* wool

lancha ['lantʃa] *nf* launch; **lancha motora** motorboat, speedboat

langosta [lan'gosta] *nf* (crustáceo) lobster; (: de río) crayfish; **langostino** *nm* Dublin Bay prawn

lanza ['lanθa] *nf* (arma) lance, spear

lanzamiento [lanθa'mjento] *nm* (gen) throwing; (Náut, Com) launch, launching; **lanzamiento de peso** putting the shot

lanzar [lan'θar] vt (gen) to throw; (Deporte: pelota) to bowl; (Náut, Com) to launch; (Jur) to evict; **lanzarse** vr to throw o.s.

lapa ['lapa] nf limpet

lapicero [lapi'θero] (CAM) nm (boligrafo) ballpoint pen, Biro®

lápida ['lapiða] nf stone; **lápida mortuoria** headstone

lápiz ['lapiθ] nm pencil; **lápiz de color** coloured pencil; **lápiz de labios** lipstick; **lápiz de ojos** eyebrow pencil

largar [lar'ɣar] vt (soltar) to release; (aflojar) to loosen; (lanzar) to launch; (fam) to let fly; (velas) to unfurl; (LAM: lanzar) to throw; **largarse** vr (fam) to beat it; **~se a** (CS: empezar) to start to

largo, -a ['larɣo, a] adj (longitud) long; (tiempo) lengthy; (fig) generous ▷ nm length; (Mús) largo; **dos años ~s** two long years; **tiene 9 metros de ~** it is 9 metres long; **a la larga** in the long run; **a lo ~ de** along; (tiempo) all through, throughout

▌ No confundir **largo** con la palabra inglesa large.

largometraje nm feature film

laringe [la'rinxe] nf larynx; **laringitis** nf laryngitis

las [las] art def the ▷ pron them; **~ que cantan** the ones o women o girls who sing; V tb **el**

lasaña [la'saɲa] nf lasagne, lasagna

láser ['laser] nm laser

lástima ['lastima] nf (pena) pity; **dar ~** to be pitiful; **es una ~ que ...** it's a pity that ...; **¡qué ~!** what a pity!; **está hecha una ~** she looks pitiful

lastimar [lasti'mar] vt (herir) to wound; (ofender) to offend; **lastimarse** vr to hurt o.s.

lata ['lata] nf (metal) tin; (caja) tin (BRIT), can; (fam) nuisance; **en ~** tinned (BRIT), canned; **dar la ~** to be a nuisance

latente [la'tente] adj latent

lateral [late'ral] adj side cpd, lateral ▷ nm (Teatro) wings

latido [la'tiðo] nm (de corazón) beat

latifundio [lati'fundjo] nm large estate

latigazo [lati'ɣaθo] nm (golpe) lash; (sonido) crack

látigo ['latiɣo] nm whip

latín [la'tin] nm Latin

latino, -a [la'tino, a] adj Latin; **latinoamericano, -a** adj, nm/f Latin-American

latir [la'tir] vi (corazón, pulso) to beat

latitud [lati'tuð] nf (Geo) latitude

latón [la'ton] nm brass

laurel [lau'rel] nm (Bot) laurel; (Culin) bay

lava ['laβa] nf lava

lavabo [la'βaβo] nm (pila) washbasin; (tb: **~s**) toilet

lavado [la'βaðo] nm washing; (de ropa) laundry; (Arte) wash; **lavado de cerebro** brainwashing; **lavado en seco** dry-cleaning

lavadora [laβa'ðora] nf washing machine

lavanda [la'βanda] nf lavender

lavandería [laβande'ria] nf laundry; (automática) launderette

lavaplatos [laβa'platos] nm inv dishwasher

lavar [la'βar] vt to wash; (borrar) to wipe away; **lavarse** vr to wash o.s.; **~se las manos** to wash one's hands; **~se los dientes** to brush one's teeth; **~ y marcar** (pelo) to shampoo and set; **~ en seco** to dry-clean; **~ los platos** to wash the dishes

lavarropas [laβa'rropas] (RPL) nm inv washing machine

lavavajillas [laβaβa'xiʎas] nm inv dishwasher

laxante [lak'sante] nm laxative

lazarillo [laθa'riʎo] nm (tb: **perro ~**) guide dog

lazo ['laθo] nm knot; (lazada) bow; (para animales) lasso; (trampa) snare;

(vínculo) tie

le [le] *pron (directo)* him (*o* her); (: *usted*) you; (*indirecto*) to him (*o* her *o* it); (: *usted*) to you

leal [le'al] *adj* loyal; **lealtad** *nf* loyalty

lección [lek'θjon] *nf* lesson

leche ['letʃe] *nf* milk; **tiene mala ~** (*fam!*) he's a swine (!); **leche condensada** condensed milk; **leche desnatada** skimmed milk

lecho ['letʃo] *nm (cama: de río)* bed; (*Geo*) layer

lechón [le'tʃon] *nm* sucking (*BRIT*) *o* suckling (*US*) pig

lechoso, -a [le'tʃoso, a] *adj* milky

lechuga [le'tʃuɣa] *nf* lettuce

lechuza [le'tʃuθa] *nf* owl

lector, a [lek'tor, a] *nm/f* reader ▷ *nm:* **~ de discos compactos** CD player

lectura [lek'tura] *nf* reading

leer [le'er] *vt* to read

legado [le'ɣaðo] *nm (don)* bequest; (*herencia*) legacy; (*enviado*) legate

legajo [le'ɣaxo] *nm* file

legal [le'ɣal] *adj (gen)* legal; (*persona*) trustworthy; **legalizar** [leɣali'θar] *vt* to legalize; (*documento*) to authenticate

legaña [le'ɣaɲa] *nf* sleep (*in eyes*)

legión [le'xjon] *nf* legion; **legionario, -a** *adj* legionary ▷ *nm* legionnaire

legislación [lexisla'θjon] *nf* legislation

legislar [lexis'lar] *vi* to legislate

legislatura [lexisla'tura] *nf (Pol)* period of office

legítimo, -a [le'xitimo, a] *adj (genuino)* authentic; (*legal*) legitimate

legua ['leɣwa] *nf* league

legumbres [le'ɣumbres] *nfpl* pulses

leído, -a [le'iðo, a] *adj* well-read

lejanía [lexa'nia] *nf* distance; **lejano, -a** *adj* far-off; (*en el tiempo*) distant; (*fig*) remote

lejía [le'xia] *nf* bleach

lejos ['lexos] *adv* far, far away; **a lo ~** in the distance; **de** *o* **desde ~** from afar; **~ de** far from

lema ['lema] *nm* motto; (*Pol*) slogan

lencería [lenθe'ria] *nf* linen, drapery

lengua ['lengwa] *nf* tongue; (*Ling*) language; **morderse la ~** to hold one's tongue

lenguado [len'gwaðo] *nm* sole

lenguaje [len'gwaxe] *nm* language; **lenguaje de programación** program(m)ing language

lengüeta [len'gweta] *nf (Anat)* epiglottis; (*zapatos*) tongue; (*Mús*) reed

lente ['lente] *nf* lens; (*lupa*) magnifying glass; **lentes** *nfpl* lenses ▷ *nmpl* (*LAM: gafas*) glasses; **lentes bifocales/de sol** (*LAM*) bifocals/sunglasses; **lentes de contacto** contact lenses

lenteja [len'texa] *nf* lentil; **lentejuela** *nf* sequin

lentilla [len'tiʎa] *nf* contact lens

lentitud [lenti'tuð] *nf* slowness; **con ~** slowly

lento, -a ['lento, a] *adj* slow

leña ['leɲa] *nf* firewood; **leñador, a** *nm/f* woodcutter

leño ['leɲo] *nm (trozo de árbol)* log; (*madero*) timber; (*fig*) blockhead

Leo ['leo] *nm* Leo

león [le'on] *nm* lion; **león marino** sea lion

leopardo [leo'parðo] *nm* leopard

leotardos [leo'tarðos] *nmpl* tights

lepra ['lepra] *nf* leprosy; **leproso, -a** *nm/f* leper

les [les] *pron (directo)* them; (: *ustedes*) you; (*indirecto*) to them; (: *ustedes*) to you

lesbiana [les'βjana] *adj, nf* lesbian

lesión [le'sjon] *nf* wound, lesion; (*Deporte*) injury; **lesionado, -a** *adj* injured ▷ *nm/f* injured person

letal [le'tal] *adj* lethal

letanía [leta'nia] *nf* litany

letra ['letra] *nf* letter; (*escritura*) handwriting; (*Mús*) lyrics *pl*; **letra de cambio** bill of exchange; **letra de imprenta** print; **letrado, -a** *adj* learned ▷ *nm/f* lawyer; **letrero**

(cartel) sign; (etiqueta) label

letrina [le'trina] nf latrine

leucemia [leu'θemja] nf leukaemia

levadura [leβa'ðura] nf (para el pan) yeast; (de cerveza) brewer's yeast

levantar [leβan'tar] vt (gen) to raise; (del suelo) to pick up; (hacia arriba) to lift (up); (plan) to make, draw up; (mesa) to clear; (campamento) to strike; (fig) to cheer up, hearten; **levantarse** vr to get up; (enderezarse) to straighten up; (rebelarse) to rebel; **el ánimo** to cheer up

levante [le'βante] nm east coast; **el L**~ region of Spain extending from Castellón to Murcia

levar [le'βar] vt to weigh

leve ['leβe] adj light; (fig) trivial

levita [le'βita] nf frock coat

léxico ['leksiko] nm (vocabulario) vocabulary

ley [lei] nf (gen) law; (metal) standard

leyenda [le'jenda] nf legend

leyó etc vb V **leer**

liar [li'ar] vt to tie (up); (unir) to bind; (envolver) to wrap (up); (enredar) to confuse; (cigarrillo) to roll; **liarse** vr (fam) to get involved; **se a palos** to get involved in a fight

Líbano ['liβano] nm: **el** ~ the Lebanon

libélula [li'βelula] nf dragonfly

liberación [liβera'θjon] nf liberation; (de la cárcel) release

liberal [liβe'ral] adj, nmf liberal

liberar [liβe'rar] vt to liberate

libertad [liβer'tað] nf liberty, freedom; **libertad bajo fianza** bail; **libertad bajo palabra** parole; **libertad condicional** probation; **libertad de culto/de prensa/de comercio** freedom of worship/of the press/of trade

libertar [liβer'tar] vt (preso) to set free; (de una obligación) to release; (eximir) to exempt

libertino, -a [liβer'tino, a] adj permissive ▷ nm/f permissive person

libra ['liβra] nf pound; **L**~ (Astrología)

Libra; **libra esterlina** pound sterling

libramiento [liβra'mjento] (MÉX) nm ring road (BRIT), beltway (US)

librar [li'βrar] vt (de peligro) to save; (batalla) to wage, fight; (de impuestos) to exempt; (cheque) to make out; (Jur) to exempt; **librarse** vr: **~se de** to escape from, free o.s. from

libre ['liβre] adj free; (lugar) unoccupied; (asiento) vacant; (de deudas) free of debts; ~ **de impuestos** free of tax; **tiro** ~ free kick; **los 100 metros** ~**s** the 100 metres free-style (race); **al aire** ~ in the open air

librería [liβre'ria] nf (tienda) bookshop

> No confundir **librería** con la palabra inglesa library.

librero, -a nm/f bookseller

libreta [li'βreta] nf notebook

libro ['liβro] nm book; **libro de bolsillo** paperback; **libro de texto** textbook; **libro electrónico** e-book

Lic. abr = **licenciado, a**

licencia [li'θenθja] nf (gen) licence; (permiso) permission; **licencia de caza** game licence; **licencia por enfermedad** (MÉX, RPL) sick leave; **licenciado, -a** adj licensed ▷ nm/f graduate; **licenciar** vt (empleado) to dismiss; (permitir) to permit, allow; (soldado) to discharge; (estudiante) to confer a degree upon; **licenciarse** vr: **licenciarse en Derecho** to graduate in law

lícito, -a ['liθito, a] adj (legal) lawful; (justo) fair, just; (permisible) permissible

licor [li'kor] nm spirits pl (BRIT), liquor (US); (de frutas etc) liqueur

licuadora [likwa'ðora] nf blender

líder ['liðer] nmf leader; **liderato** nm leadership; **liderazgo** nm leadership

lidia ['liðja] nf bullfighting; (una lidia) bullfight; **toros de** ~ fighting bulls;

lidiar vt, vi to fight

liebre ['ljeβre] nf hare

lienzo ['ljenθo] nm linen; (Arte) canvas; (Arq) wall

liga ['liɣa] nf (de medias) garter, suspender; (LAM: goma) rubber band; (confederación) league

ligadura [liɣa'ðura] nf bond, tie; (Med, Mús) ligature

ligamento [liɣa'mento] nm ligament

ligar [li'ɣar] vt (atar) to tie; (unir) to join; (Med) to bind up; (Mús) to slur ▷ vi to mix, blend; (fam): (**él) liga mucho** he pulls a lot of women; **ligarse** vr to commit o.s.

ligero, -a [li'xero, a] adj (de peso) light; (tela) thin; (rápido) swift, quick; (ágil) agile, nimble; (de importancia) slight; (de carácter) flippant, superficial ▷ adv: **a la ligera** superficially

liguero [li'ɣero] nm suspender (BRIT) o garter (US) belt

lija ['lixa] nf (Zool) dogfish; (tb: **papel de ~**) sandpaper

lila ['lila] nf lilac

lima ['lima] nf file; (Bot) lime; **lima de uñas** nailfile; **limar** vt to file

limitación [limita'θjon] nf limitation, limit

limitar [limi'tar] vt to limit; (reducir) to reduce, cut down ▷ vi: **~ con** to border on; **limitarse** vr: **~se a** to limit o.s. to

límite ['limite] nm (gen) limit; (fin) end; (frontera) border; **límite de velocidad** speed limit

limítrofe [li'mitrofe] adj neighbouring

limón [li'mon] nm lemon ▷ adj: **amarillo ~** lemon-yellow; **limonada** nf lemonade

limosna [li'mosna] nf alms pl; **vivir de ~** to live on charity

limpiador [limpja'ðor] (MÉX) nm = **limpiaparabrisas**

limpiaparabrisas [limpjapara'brisas] nm inv windscreen (BRIT) o windshield (US) wiper

limpiar [lim'pjar] vt to clean; (con trapo) to wipe; (quitar) to wipe away;

(zapatos) to shine, polish; (fig) to clean up

limpieza [lim'pjeθa] nf (estado) cleanliness; (acto) cleaning; (: de las calles) cleansing; (: de zapatos) polishing; (habilidad) skill; (fig: Policía) clean-up; (pureza) purity; (Mil): **operación de ~** mopping-up operation; **limpieza en seco** dry cleaning

limpio, -a ['limpjo, a] adj clean; (moralmente) pure; (Com) clear, net; (fam) honest ▷ adv: **jugar ~** to play fair; **pasar a** (ESP) **o en** (LAM) **~** to make a clean copy of

lince ['linθe] nm lynx

linchar [lin'tʃar] vt to lynch

lindar [lin'dar] vi to adjoin; **~ con** to border on

lindo, -a ['lindo, a] adj pretty, lovely ▷ adv: **nos divertimos de lo ~** we had a marvellous time; **canta muy ~** (LAM) he sings beautifully

línea ['linea] nf (gen) line; **en ~** (Inform) on line; **línea aérea** airline; **línea de meta** goal line; (en carrera) finishing line; **línea discontinua** (Auto) broken line; **línea recta** straight line

lingote [lin'gote] nm ingot

lingüista [lin'gwista] nmf linguist; **lingüística** nf linguistics sg

lino ['lino] nm linen; (Bot) flax

linterna [lin'terna] nf torch (BRIT), flashlight (US)

lío ['lio] nm bundle; (fam) fuss; (desorden) muddle, mess; **armar un ~** to make a fuss

liquen ['liken] nm lichen

liquidación [likiða'θjon] nf liquidation; **venta de ~** clearance sale

liquidar [liki'ðar] vt (mercancías) to liquidate; (deudas) to pay off; (empresa) to wind up

líquido, -a ['likiðo, a] adj liquid; (ganancia) net ▷ nm liquid; **líquido imponible** net taxable income

lira ['lira] nf (Mús) lyre; (moneda) lira

lírico, -a ['liriko, a] adj lyrical

lirio ['lirjo] nm (Bot) iris

lirón [li'ron] nm (Zool) dormouse; (fig) sleepyhead

Lisboa [lis'βoa] n Lisbon

lisiar [li'sjar] vt to maim

liso, -a ['liso, a] adj (terreno) flat; (cabello) straight; (superficie) even; (tela) plain

lista ['lista] nf list; (de alumnos) school register; (de libros) catalogue; (de platos) menu; (de precios) price list; **pasar ~** to call the roll; **tela de ~s** striped material; **lista de espera** waiting list; **lista de precios** price list; **listín** nm (tb: **listín telefónico o de teléfonos**) telephone directory

listo, -a ['listo, a] adj (perspicaz) smart, clever; (preparado) ready

listón [lis'ton] nm (de madera, metal) strip

litera [li'tera] nf (en barco, tren) berth; (en dormitorio) bunk, bunk bed

literal [lite'ral] adj literal

literario, -a [lite'rarjo, a] adj literary

literato, -a [lite'rato, a] adj literary ▷ nm/f writer

literatura [litera'tura] nf literature

litigio [li'tixjo] nm (Jur) lawsuit; (fig): **en ~ con** in dispute with

litografía [litogra'fia] nf lithography; (una litografía) lithograph

litoral [lito'ral] adj coastal ▷ nm coast, seaboard

litro ['litro] nm litre

lívido, -a ['liβiðo, a] adj livid

llaga ['ʎaxa] nf wound

llama ['ʎama] nf flame; (Zool) llama

llamada [ʎa'maða] nf call; **llamada a cobro revertido** reverse-charge (BRIT) o collect (US) call; **llamada al orden** call to order; **llamada de atención** warning; **llamada local** (LAM) local call; **llamada metropolitana** (ESP) local call; **llamada por cobrar** (MÉX) reverse-charge (BRIT) o collect (US) call

llamamiento [ʎama'mjento] nm call

llamar [ʎa'mar] vt to call; (atención) to

attract ▷ vi (por teléfono) to phone; (a la puerta) to knock o (ring); (por señas) to beckon; (Mil) to call up; **llamarse** vr to be called, be named; **¿cómo se llama (usted)?** what's your name?

llamativo, -a [ʎama'tiβo, a] adj showy; (color) loud

llano, -a ['ʎano, a] adj (superficie) flat; (persona) straightforward; (estilo) clear ▷ nm plain, flat ground

llanta ['ʎanta] nf (ESP) (wheel) rim; **llanta (de goma)** (LAM: neumático) tyre; (: cámara) inner (tube); **llanta de repuesto** (LAM) spare tyre

llanto ['ʎanto] nm weeping

llanura [ʎa'nura] nf plain

llave ['ʎaβe] nf key; (del agua) tap; (Mecánica) spanner; (de la luz) switch; (Mús) key; **echar la ~ a** to lock up; **llave de contacto** (ESP Auto) ignition key; **llave de encendido** (LAM Auto) ignition key; **llave de paso** stopcock; **llave inglesa** monkey wrench; **llave maestra** master key; **llavero** nm keyring

llegada [ʎe'xaða] nf arrival

llegar [ʎe'xar] vi to arrive; (alcanzar) to reach; (bastar) to be enough; **llegarse** vr: **~se a** to approach; **~ a** to manage to, succeed in; **~ a saber** to find out; **~ a ser** to become; **~ a las manos de** to come into the hands of

llenar [ʎe'nar] vt to fill; (espacio) to cover; (formulario) to fill in o up; (fig) to heap

lleno, -a ['ʎeno, a] adj full, filled; (repleto) full up ▷ nm (Teatro) full house; **dar de ~ contra un muro** to hit a wall head-on

llevadero, -a [ʎeβa'ðero, a] adj bearable, tolerable

llevar [ʎe'βar] vt to take; (ropa) to wear; (cargar) to carry; (quitar) to take away; (en coche) to drive; (transportar) to transport; (traer: dinero) to carry; (conducir) to lead; (Mat) to carry ▷ vi (suj: camino etc): **~ a** to lead to; **llevarse** vr to carry off, take away; **llevamos**

dos días aquí we have been here for two days; **él me lleva 2 años** he's 2 years older than me; **~ los libros** (Com) to keep the books; **~se bien** to get on well (together)

llorar [ʎoˈrar] vt, vi to cry, weep; **~ de risa** to cry with laughter

llorón, -ona [ʎoˈron, ona] adj tearful ▷ nm/f cry-baby

lloroso, -a [ʎoˈroso, a] adj (gen) weeping, tearful; (triste) sad, sorrowful

llover [ʎoˈβer] vi to rain

llovizna [ʎoˈβiθna] nf drizzle; **lloviznar** vi to drizzle

llueve etc vb V **llover**

lluvia [ˈʎuβja] nf rain; **lluvia radioactiva** (radioactive) fallout; **lluvioso, -a** adj rainy

lo [lo] art def: **~ bel~** the beautiful, what is beautiful, that which is beautiful ▷ pron (persona) him; (cosa) it; **~ que sea** whatever; V tb **el**

loable [loˈaβle] adj praiseworthy

lobo [ˈloβo] nm wolf; **lobo de mar** (fig) sea dog

lóbulo [ˈloβulo] nm lobe

local [loˈkal] adj local ▷ nm place, site; (oficinas) premises pl; **localidad** (barrio) locality; (lugar) location; (Teatro) seat, ticket; **localizar** vt (ubicar) to locate, find; (restringir) to localize; (situar) to place

loción [loˈθjon] nf lotion

loco, -a [ˈloko, a] adj mad ▷ nm/f lunatic, mad person; **estar ~ con o por algo/por algn** to be mad about sth/sb

locomotora [lokomoˈtora] nf engine, locomotive

locuaz [loˈkwaθ] adj loquacious

locución [lokuˈθjon] nf expression

locura [loˈkura] nf madness; (acto) crazy act

locutor, a [lokuˈtor, a] nm/f (Radio) announcer; (comentarista) commentator; (TV) newsreader

locutorio [lokuˈtorjo] nm (en telefónica) telephone booth

lodo [ˈloðo] nm mud

lógica [ˈloxika] nf logic

lógico, -a [ˈloxiko, a] adj logical

login [ˈloxin] nm login

logística [loˈxistika] nf logistics sg

logotipo [loɣoˈtipo] nm logo

logrado, -a [loˈɣraðo, a] adj (interpretación, reproducción) polished, excellent

lograr [loˈɣrar] vt to achieve; (obtener) to get, obtain; **~ hacer** to manage to do; **~ que algn venga** to manage to get sb to come

logro [ˈloɣro] nm achievement, success

lóker [ˈloker] (LAM) nm locker

loma [ˈloma] nf hillock (BRIT), small hill

lombriz [lomˈbriθ] nf worm

lomo [ˈlomo] nm (de animal) back; (Culin: de cerdo) pork loin; (: de vaca) rib steak; (de libro) spine

lona [ˈlona] nf canvas

loncha [ˈlontʃa] nf = **lonja**

lonchería [lontʃeˈria] (LAM) nf snack bar, diner (us)

Londres [ˈlondres] n London

longaniza [longaˈniθa] nf pork sausage

longitud [lonxiˈtuð] nf length; (Geo) longitude; **tener 3 metros de ~** to be 3 metres long; **longitud de onda** wavelength

lonja [ˈlonxa] nf slice; (de tocino) rasher; **lonja de pescado** fish market

loro [ˈloro] nm parrot

los [los] art def the ▷ pron them; (ustedes) you; **mis libros y ~ tuyos** my books and yours; V tb **el**

losa [ˈlosa] nf stone

lote [ˈlote] nm portion; (Com) lot

lotería [loteˈria] nf lottery; (juego) lotto

LOTERÍA

Millions of pounds are spent on lotteries each year in Spain, two of which are state-run: the

Lotería Primitiva and the **Lotería Nacional**, with money raised going directly to the government. One of the most famous lotteries is run by the wealthy and influential society for the blind, "la ONCE".

loza ['loθa] nf crockery

lubina [lu'βina] nf sea bass

lubricante [luβri'kante] nm lubricant

lubricar [luβri'kar] vt to lubricate

lucha ['lutʃa] nf fight, struggle; **lucha de clases** class struggle; **lucha libre** wrestling; **luchar** vi to fight

lúcido, -a [lu'θiðo, a] adj (persona) lucid; (mente) logical; (idea) crystal-clear

luciérnaga [lu'θjernaxa] nf glow-worm

lucir [lu'θir] vt to illuminate, light (up); (ostentar) to show off ▷ vi (brillar) to shine; **lucirse** vr (irónico) to make a fool of o.s.

lucro ['lukro] nm profit, gain

lúdico, -a ['luðiko, a] adj (aspecto, actividad) play cpd

luego ['lweɣo] adv (después) next; (más tarde) later, afterwards

lugar [lu'ɣar] nm place; (sitio) spot; **en primer ~** in the first place, firstly; **en ~ de** instead of; **hacer ~** to make room; **fuera de ~** out of place; **sin ~ a dudas** without doubt, undoubtedly; **dar ~ a** to give rise to; **tener ~** to take place; **yo en su ~** if I were him; **lugar común** commonplace

lúgubre ['luɣuβre] adj mournful

lujo ['luxo] nm luxury; (fig) profusion, abundance; **de ~** luxury cpd, de luxe; **lujoso, -a** adj luxurious

lujuria [lu'xurja] nf lust

lumbre ['lumbre] nf fire; (para cigarrillo) light

luminoso, -a [lumi'noso, a] adj luminous, shining

luna ['luna] nf moon; (de un espejo) glass; (de gafas) lens; (fig) crescent; **estar en la ~** to have one's head in the clouds; **luna de miel** honeymoon; **luna llena/nueva** full/new moon

lunar [lu'nar] adj lunar ▷ nm (Anat) mole; **tela de ~es** spotted material

lunes ['lunes] nm inv Monday

lupa ['lupa] nf magnifying glass

lustre ['lustre] nm polish; (fig) lustre; **dar ~ a** to polish

luto ['luto] nm mourning; **llevar el o vestirse de ~** to be in mourning

Luxemburgo [luksem'burxo] nm Luxembourg

luz [luθ] (pl **luces**) nf light; **dar a ~ un niño** to give birth to a child; **sacar a la ~** to bring to light; **dar o encender** (ESP) o **prender** (LAM)/**apagar la ~** to switch the light on/off; **tener pocas luces** to be dim o stupid; **traje de luces** bullfighter's costume; **luces de tráfico** traffic lights; **luz de freno** brake light; **luz roja/verde** red/green light

m

nature, character; **una ~** a piece of wood

madrastra [ma'ðrastra] nf stepmother

madre ['maðre] adj mother cpd ▷ nf mother; (de niño etc) dregs pl; **madre política/soltera** mother-in-law/unmarried mother

Madrid [ma'ðrið] n Madrid

madriguera [maðri'ɣera] nf burrow

madrileño, -a [maðri'leɲo, a] adj of o from Madrid ▷ nm/f native of Madrid

madrina [ma'ðrina] nf godmother; (Arq) prop, shore; (Tec) brace; (de boda) bridesmaid

madrugada [maðru'ɣaða] nf early morning; (alba) dawn, daybreak

madrugador, a [maðruɣa'ðor, a] adj early-rising

madrugar [maðru'ɣar] vi to get up early; (fig) to get ahead

madurar [maðu'rar] vt, vi (fruta) to ripen; (fig) to mature; **madurez** nf ripeness; maturity; **maduro, -a** adj ripe; mature

maestra nf V **maestro**

maestría [maes'tria] nf mastery; (habilidad) skill, expertise

maestro, -a [ma'estro, a] adj masterly; (principal) main ▷ nm/f master/mistress; (profesor) teacher ▷ nm (autoridad) authority; (Mús) maestro; (experto) master; **maestro albañil** master mason

magdalena [maɣða'lena] nf fairy cake

magia ['maxja] nf magic; **mágico, -a** adj magic(al) ▷ nm/f magician

magisterio [maxis'terjo] nm (enseñanza) teaching; (profesión) teaching profession; (maestros) teachers pl

magistrado [maxis'traðo] nm magistrate

magistral [maxis'tral] adj magisterial; (fig) masterly

magnate [maɣ'nate] nm magnate, tycoon

---

m abr (= metro) m; (= minuto) m

macana [ma'kana] (MÉX) nf truncheon (BRIT), billy club (US)

macarrones [maka'rrones] nmpl macaroni sg

macedonia [maθe'ðonja] nf (tb: ~ **de frutas**) fruit salad

maceta [ma'θeta] nf (de flores) pot of flowers; (para plantas) flowerpot

machacar [matʃa'kar] vt to crush, pound ▷ vi (insistir) to go on, keep on

machete [ma'tʃete] nm machete, (large) knife

machetear [matʃete'ar] (MÉX) vt to swot (BRIT), grind away (US)

machismo [ma'tʃismo] nm male chauvinism; **machista** adj, nm sexist

macho ['matʃo] adj male; (fig) virile ▷ nm male; (fig) he-man

macizo, -a [ma'θiθo, a] adj (grande) massive; (fuerte, sólido) solid ▷ nm mass, chunk

madeja [ma'ðexa] nf (de lana) skein, hank; (de pelo) mass, mop

madera [ma'ðera] nf wood; (fig)

magnético, -a [maɣˈnetiko, a] *adj* magnetic

magnetofón [maɣnetoˈfon] *nm* tape recorder

magnetófono [maɣneˈtofono] *nm* = **magnetofón**

magnífico, -a [maɣˈnifiko, a] *adj* splendid, magnificent

magnitud [maɣniˈtuð] *nf* magnitude

mago, -a [ˈmaɣo, a] *nm/f* magician; **los Reyes M~s** the Three Wise Men

magro, -a [ˈmaɣro, a] *adj* (*carne*) lean

mahonesa [maoˈnesa] *nf* mayonnaise

maître [ˈmetre] *nm* head waiter

maíz [maˈiθ] *nm* maize (BRIT), corn (US); sweet corn

majestad [maxesˈtað] *nf* majesty

majo, -a [ˈmaxo, a] *adj* nice; (*guapo*) attractive, good-looking; (*elegante*) smart

mal [mal] *adv* badly; (*equivocadamente*) wrongly ▷ *adj* = **malo** ▷ *nm* evil; (*desgracia*) misfortune; (*daño*) harm, damage; (*Med*) illness; **~ que bien** rightly or wrongly; **ir de ~ en peor** to get worse and worse

malabarista [malaβaˈrista] *nmf* juggler

malaria [maˈlarja] *nf* malaria

malcriado, -a [malˈkrjaðo, a] *adj* spoiled

maldad [malˈdað] *nf* evil, wickedness

maldecir [maldeˈθir] *vt* to curse

maldición [maldiˈθjon] *nf* curse

maldito, -a [malˈdito, a] *adj* (*condenado*) damned; (*perverso*) wicked; **¡~ sea!** damn it!

malecón [maleˈkon] (LAM) *nm* sea front, promenade

maleducado, -a [maleðuˈkaðo, a] *adj* bad-mannered, rude

malentendido [malentenˈdiðo] *nm* misunderstanding

malestar [malesˈtar] *nm* (*gen*) discomfort; (*fig: inquietud*) uneasiness; (*Pol*) unrest

maleta [maˈleta] *nf* case, suitcase; (*Auto*) boot (BRIT), trunk (US); **hacer las ~s** to pack; **maletero** *nm* (*Auto*) boot (BRIT), trunk (US); **maletín** *nm* small case, bag

maleza [maˈleθa] *nf* (*malas hierbas*) weeds *pl*; (*arbustos*) thicket

malgastar [malɣasˈtar] *vt* (*tiempo*, *dinero*) to waste; (*salud*) to ruin

malhechor, a [maleˈtʃor, a] *nm/f* delinquent

malhumorado, -a [malumoˈraðo, a] *adj* bad-tempered

malicia [maˈliθja] *nf* (*maldad*) wickedness; (*astucia*) slyness, guile; (*mala intención*) malice, spite; (*carácter travieso*) mischievousness

maligno, -a [maˈliɣno, a] *adj* evil; (*malévolo*) malicious; (*Med*) malignant

malla [ˈmaʎa] *nf* mesh; (*de baño*) swimsuit; (*de ballet, gimnasia*) leotard; **mallas** *nfpl* tights; **malla de alambre** wire mesh

Mallorca [maˈʎorka] *nf* Majorca

malo, -a [ˈmalo, a] *adj* bad, false ▷ *nm/f* villain; **estar ~** to be ill

malograr [maloˈɣrar] *vt* to spoil; (*plan*) to upset; (*ocasión*) to waste

malparado, -a [malpaˈraðo, a] *adj*: **salir ~** to come off badly

malpensado, -a [malpenˈsaðo, a] *adj* nasty

malteada [malteˈaða] (LAM) *nf* milkshake

maltratar [maltraˈtar] *vt* to ill-treat, mistreat

malvado, -a [malˈβaðo, a] *adj* evil, villainous

Malvinas [malˈβinas] *nfpl* (*tb*: **Islas ~**) Falklands, Falkland Islands

mama [ˈmama] *nf* (*de animal*) teat; (*de mujer*) breast

mamá [maˈma] (*pl* **~s**) (*fam*) *nf* mum, mummy

mamar [maˈmar] *vt, vi* to suck

mamarracho [mamaˈrratʃo] *nm* sight, mess

mameluco [mameluko] (RPL) nm
dungarees pl (BRIT), overalls pl (US)

mamífero [ma'mifero] nm mammal

mampara [mam'para] nf (entre
habitaciones) partition; (biombo) screen

mampostería [mamposte'ria] nf
masonry

manada [ma'naða] nf (Zool) herd;
(: de leones) pride; (: de lobos) pack

manantial [manan'tjal] nm spring

mancha ['mantʃa] nf stain, mark;
(Zool) patch; **manchar** vt (gen) to
stain, mark; (ensuciar) to soil, dirty

manchego, -a [man'tʃeɣo, a] adj of
o from La Mancha

manco, -a ['manko, a] adj (de un
brazo) one-armed; (de una mano) one-
handed; (fig) defective, faulty

mancuernas [man'kwernas] (MÉX)
nfpl cufflinks

mandado [man'daðo] (LAM) nm
errand

mandamiento [manda'mjento]
nm (orden) order, command; (Rel)
commandment

mandar [man'dar] vt (ordenar) to
order; (dirigir) to lead, command;
(enviar) to send; (pedir) to order, ask for
▷ vi to be in charge; (pey) to be bossy;
¡mande? (MÉX: ¿cómo dice?) pardon?,
excuse me?; **~ hacer un traje** to make
a suit made

mandarina [manda'rina] (ESP) nf
tangerine, mandarin (orange)

mandato [man'dato] nm (orden)
order; (Pol: período) term of office;
(: territorio) mandate

mandíbula [man'diβula] nf jaw

mandil [man'dil] nm apron

mando ['mando] nm (Mil) command;
(de país) rule; (el primer lugar) lead; (Tec)
term of office; (Tec) control; **~ a la
izquierda** left-hand drive; **mando a
distancia** remote control

mandón, -ona [man'don, ona] adj
bossy, domineering

manejar [mane'xar] vt to manage;
(máquina) to work, operate; (caballo

etc) to handle; (casa) to run, manage;
(LAM: coche) to drive; **manejarse**
vr (comportarse) to act, behave;
(arreglárselas) to manage; **manejo**
nm (de bicicleta) handling; (de negocio)
management, running; (LAM Auto)
driving; (facilidad de trato) ease,
confidence; **manejos** nmpl (intrigas)
intrigues

manera [ma'nera] nf way, manner,
fashion; **maneras** nfpl (modales)
manners; **su ~ de ser** the way he
is; (aire) his manner; **de ninguna
~** no way, by no means; **de otra ~**
otherwise; **de todas ~s** at any rate; **no
hay ~ de persuadirle** there's no way of
convincing him

manga ['manga] nf (de camisa) sleeve;
(de riego) hose

mango ['mango] nm handle; (Bot)
mango

manguera [man'gera] nf hose

maní [ma'ni] (LAM) nm peanut

manía [ma'nia] nf (Med) mania;
(fig: moda) rage, craze; (disgusto) dislike;
(malicia) spite; **coger ~ a algn** to take a
dislike to sb; **tener ~ a algn** to dislike
sb; **maníaco, -a** adj(pl) ▷ nm/f
maniac

maniático, -a [ma'njatiko, a] adj
maniac(al) ▷ nm/f maniac

manicomio [mani'komjo] nm
mental hospital (BRIT), insane asylum
(US)

manifestación [manifesta'θjon] nf
(declaración) statement, declaration;
(de emoción) show, display; (Pol: desfile)
demonstration; (: concentración) mass
meeting

manifestar [manifes'tar] vt to
show, manifest; (declarar) to state,
declare; **manifiesto, -a** adj clear,
manifest ▷ nm manifesto

manillar [mani'ʎar] nm handlebars pl

maniobra [ma'njoβra] nf
manoeuvre; **maniobras** nfpl (Mil)
manoeuvres; **maniobrar** vt to
manoeuvre

manipulación [manipula'θjon] *nf* manipulation

manipular [manipu'lar] *vt* to manipulate; (*manejar*) to handle

maniquí [mani'ki] *nm* dummy ▷*nmf* model

manivela [mani'βela] *nf* crank

manjar [man'xar] *nm* (*tasty*) dish

mano ['mano] *nf* hand; (*Zool*) foot, paw; (*de pintura*) coat; (*serie*) lot, series; **a ~** by hand; **a ~ derecha/izquierda** on the right(-hand side)/left(-hand side); **de primera ~** (at) first hand; **de segunda ~** (at) second hand; **robo a ~ armada** armed robbery; **estrechar la ~ a algn** to shake sb's hand; **mano de obra** labour, manpower; **manos libres** *adj inv* (*teléfono, dispositivo*) hands-free ▷*nm inv* hands-free kit

manojo [ma'noxo] *nm* handful, bunch; (*de llaves*) bunch

manopla [ma'nopla] *nf* mitten

manosear [manose'ar] *vt* (*tocar*) to handle, touch; (*desordenar*) to mess up, rumple; (*insistir en*) to overwork; (*LAM: acariciar*) to caress, fondle

manotazo [mano'taðo] *nm* slap, smack

mansalva [man'salβa]: **a ~** *adv* indiscriminately

mansión [man'sjon] *nf* mansion

manso, -a ['manso, a] *adj* gentle, mild; (*animal*) tame

manta ['manta] (*ESP*) *nf* blanket

manteca [man'teka] *nf* fat; (*CS: mantequilla*) butter; **manteca de cerdo** lard

mantecado [mante'kaðo] (*ESP*) *nm* Christmas sweet made from flour, almonds and lard

mantel [man'tel] *nm* tablecloth

mantendré *etc vb* V **mantener**

mantener [mante'ner] *vt* to support, maintain; (*alimentar*) to sustain; (*conservar*) to keep; (*Tec*) to maintain, service; **mantenerse** *vr* (*seguir de pie*) to be still standing; (*no ceder*) to hold one's ground;

(*subsistir*) to sustain o.s., keep going; **mantenimiento** *nm* maintenance; sustenance; (*sustento*) support

mantequilla [mante'kiʎa] *nf* butter

mantilla [man'tiʎa] *nf* mantilla; **mantillas** *nfpl* (*de bebé*) baby clothes

manto ['manto] *nm* (*capa*) cloak; (*de ceremonia*) robe, gown

mantuve *etc vb* V **mantener**

manual [ma'nwal] *adj* manual ▷*nm* manual, handbook

manuscrito, -a [manus'krito, a] *adj* handwritten ▷*nm* manuscript

manutención [manuten'θjon] *nf* maintenance; (*sustento*) support

manzana [man'θana] *nf* apple; (*Arq*) block (of houses)

manzanilla [manθa'niʎa] *nf* (*planta*) camomile; (*infusión*) camomile tea

manzano [man'θano] *nm* apple tree

maña ['maɲa] *nf* (*gen*) skill, dexterity; (*pey*) guile; (*destreza*) trick, knack

mañana [ma'ɲana] *adv* tomorrow ▷*nm* future ▷*nf* morning; **de o por la ~** in the morning; **¡hasta ~!** see you tomorrow!; **~ por la ~** tomorrow morning

mapa ['mapa] *nm* map

maple ['maple] (*LAM*) *nm* maple

maqueta [ma'keta] *nf* (*scale*) model

maquiladora [makila'ðora] (*MÉX*) *nf* (*Com*) bonded assembly plant

maquillaje [maki'ʎaxe] *nm* make-up; (*acto*) making up

maquillar [maki'ʎar] *vt* to make up; **maquillarse** *vr* to put on (some) make-up

máquina ['makina] *nf* machine; (*de tren*) locomotive, engine; (*Foto*) camera; (*fig*) machinery; **escrito a ~** typewritten; **máquina de coser** sewing machine; **máquina de escribir** typewriter; **máquina fotográfica** camera

maquinaria [maki'narja] *nf* (*máquinas*) machinery; (*mecanismo*) mechanism, works *pl*

maquinilla [maki'niʎa] (*ESP*) *nf*

(tb: ~ **de afeitar**) razor

maquinista [maki'nista] nmf (de tren) engine driver; (Tec) operator; (Náut) engineer

mar [mar] nm o f sea; ~ **adentro** out at sea; **en alta** ~ on the high seas; **la** ~ **de** (fam) lots of; **el Mar Negro/Báltico** the Black/Baltic Sea

maraña [ma'raɲa] nf (maleza) thicket; (confusión) tangle

maravilla [mara'βiʎa] nf marvel, wonder; (Bot) marigold; **maravillar** vt to astonish, amaze; **maravillarse** vr to be astonished, be amazed; **maravilloso, -a** adj wonderful, marvellous

marca ['marka] nf (gen) mark; (sello) stamp; (Com) make, brand; **de** ~ excellent, outstanding; **marca de fábrica** trademark; **marca registrada** registered trademark

marcado, -a [mar'kaðo, a] adj marked, strong

marcador [marka'ðor] nm (Deporte) scoreboard; (: persona) scorer

marcapasos [marka'pasos] nm inv pacemaker

marcar [mar'kar] vt (gen) to mark; (número de teléfono) to dial; (gol) to score; (números) to record, keep a tally of; (pelo) to set ▷ vi (Deporte) to score; (Tel) to dial

marcha ['martʃa] nf march; (Tec) running, working; (Auto) gear; (velocidad) speed; (fig) progress; (dirección) course; **poner en** ~ to put into gear; (fig) to set in motion, get going; **dar** ~ **atrás** to reverse, put into reverse; **estar en** ~ to be under way, be in motion

marchar [mar'tʃar] vi (ir) to go; (funcionar) to work, go; **marcharse** vr to go (away), leave

marchitar [martʃi'tar] vt to wither, dry up; **marchitarse** vr (Bot) to wither; (fig) to fade away; **marchito, -a** adj withered, faded; (fig) in decline

marciano, -a [mar'θjano, a] adj,

nm/f Martian

marco ['marko] nm frame; (moneda) mark; (fig) framework

marea [ma'rea] nf tide; **marea negra** oil slick

marear [mare'ar] vt (fig) to annoy, upset; (Med): ~ **a algn** to make sb feel sick; **marearse** vr (tener náuseas) to feel sick; (desvanecerse) to feel faint; (aturdirse) to feel dizzy; (fam: emborracharse) to get tipsy

maremoto [mare'moto] nm tidal wave

mareo [ma'reo] nm (náusea) sick feeling; (en viaje) travel sickness; (aturdimiento) dizziness; (fam: lata) nuisance

marfil [mar'fil] nm ivory

margarina [marva'rina] nf margarine

margarita [marva'rita] nf (Bot) daisy; (Tip) daisywheel

margen ['marxen] nm (borde) edge, border; (fig) margin, space ▷ nf (de río etc) bank; **dar** ~ **para** to give an opportunity for; **mantenerse al** ~ to keep out (of things)

marginar [marxi'nar] vt (socialmente) to marginalize, ostracize

mariachi [ma'rjatʃi] nm (persona) mariachi musician; (grupo) mariachi band

● **MARIACHI**

●

● Mariachi music is the musical style
● most characteristic of Mexico.
● From the state of Jalisco in the 19th
● century, this music spread rapidly
● throughout the country, until each
● region had its own particular style
● of the Mariachi "sound". A Mariachi
● band can be made up of several
● singers, up to eight violins, two
● trumpets, guitars, a "vihuela" (an
● old form of guitar), and a harp. The
● dance associated with this music
● is called the "zapateado".

marica [ma'rika] (fam) nm
sissy

maricón [mari'kon] (fam) nm
queer

marido [ma'riðo] nm husband

marihuana [mari'wana] nf
marijuana, cannabis

marina [ma'rina] nf navy; **marina
mercante** merchant navy

marinero, -a [mari'nero, a] adj sea
cpd ▷ nm sailor, seaman

marino, -a [ma'rino, a] adj sea cpd,
marine ▷ nm sailor

marioneta [marjo'neta] nf
puppet

mariposa [mari'posa] nf
butterfly

mariquita [mari'kita] nf ladybird
(BRIT), ladybug (US)

marisco [ma'risko] (ESP) nm shellfish
· inv, seafood; **mariscos** (LAM) nmpl =
marisco

marítimo, -a [ma'ritimo, a] adj sea
cpd, maritime

mármol [marmol] nm marble

marqués, -esa [mar'kes, esa] nm/f
marquis/marchioness

marrón [ma'rron] adj brown

marroquí [marro'ki] adj, nmf
Moroccan ▷ nm Morocco (leather)

Marruecos [ma'rrwekos] nm
Morocco

martes ['martes] nm inv Tuesday; **~ y
trece** = Friday 13th

martillo [mar'tiʎo] nm hammer

mártir ['martir] nmf martyr;
martirio nm martyrdom; (fig) torture,
torment

marxismo [mark'sismo] nm
Marxism

marzo ['marθo] nm March

○ **PALABRA CLAVE**

más [mas] adj, adv 1: **más (que** o **de)**
(comprar) more (than), ... + er (than); **más
grande/inteligente** bigger/
more intelligent; **trabaja más (que
yo)** he works more (than me); V tb **cada**
2 (superl): **el más** the most, ... + est; **el
más grande/inteligente (de)** the
biggest/most intelligent (in)
3 (negativo): **no tengo más dinero** I
haven't got any more money; **no viene
más por aquí** he doesn't come round
here any more
4 (adicional): **no le veo más solución
que ...** I see no other solution than to
...; **¿quién más?** anybody else?
5 (+ adj: valor intensivo): **¡qué perro
más sucio!** what a filthy dog!; **¡es más
tonto!** he's so stupid!
6 (locuciones): **más o menos** more or
less; **los más** most people; **es más**
furthermore; **más bien** rather;
¡qué más da! what does it matter!;
V tb **no**
7: **por más: por más que te esfuerces**
no matter how hard you try; **por más
que ...** much as I should
like to ...
8: **de más: veo que aquí estoy de más**
I can see I'm not needed here; **tenemos
uno de más** we've got one extra
▷ prep: **2 más 2 son 4** 2 and 2 are 4; **4
más 2 plus 2 are 4**
▷ nm inv: **este trabajo tiene sus más
y sus menos** this job's got its good
points and its bad points

mas [mas] conj but

masa ['masa] nf (mezcla) dough;
(volumen) volume, mass; (Física) mass;
en ~ en masse; **las ~s** (Pol) the masses

masacre [ma'sakre] nf massacre

masaje [ma'saxe] nm massage

máscara ['maskara] nf mask;
máscara antigás/de oxígeno
gas/oxygen mask; **mascarilla** nf (de

belleza, Med) mask

masculino, -a [masˈkulino, a] adj masculine; (Bio) male

masía [maˈsia] nf farmhouse

masivo, -a [maˈsiβo, a] adj mass cpd

masoquista [masoˈkista] nmf masochist

máster ['master] (ESP) nm master

masticar [mastiˈkar] vt to chew

mástil [ˈmastil] nm (de navío) mast; (de guitarra) neck

mastín [masˈtin] nm mastiff

masturbarse [masturˈβarse] vr to masturbate

mata [ˈmata] nf (arbusto) bush, shrub; (de hierba) tuft

matadero [mataˈðero] nm slaughterhouse, abattoir

matamoscas [mataˈmoskas] nm inv (pala) fly swat

matanza [maˈtanθa] nf slaughter

matar [maˈtar] vt, vi to kill; **matarse** vr (suicidarse) to kill o.s., commit suicide; (morir) to be o get killed; **~ el hambre** to stave off hunger

matasellos [mataˈseʎos] nm inv postmark

mate [ˈmate] adj matt ⊳ nm (en ajedrez) (check)mate; (LAM: hierba) maté; (: vasija) gourd

matemáticas [mateˈmatikas] nfpl mathematics; **matemático, -a** adj mathematical ⊳ nm/f mathematician

materia [maˈterja] nf (gen) matter; (Tec) material; (Escol) subject; **en ~ de** on the subject of; **materia prima** raw material; **material** adj material ⊳ nm material; (Tec) equipment; **materialista** adj materialist(ic); **materialmente** adv materially; (fig) absolutely

maternal [materˈnal] adj motherly, maternal

maternidad [materniˈðað] nf motherhood, maternity; **materno, -a** adj maternal; (lengua) mother cpd

matinal [matiˈnal] adj morning cpd

matiz [maˈtiθ] nm shade; **matizar** vt

(variar) to vary; (Arte) to blend; **matizar de** to tinge with

matón [maˈton] nm bully

matorral [matoˈrral] nm thicket

matrícula [maˈtrikula] nf (registro) register; (Auto) registration number; (: placa) number plate; **matrícula de honor** (Univ) top marks in a subject at university with the right to free registration the following year; **matricular** vt to register, enrol

matrimonio [matriˈmonjo] nm (pareja) (married) couple; (unión) marriage

matriz [maˈtriθ] nf (Anat) womb; (Tec) mould

matrona [maˈtrona] nf (persona de edad) matron; (comadrona) midwife

matufia [maˈtufja] (RPL: fam) nf put-up job

maullar [mauˈʎar] vi to mew, miaow

maxilar [maksiˈlar] nm jaw(bone)

máxima [ˈmaksima] nf maxim

máximo, -a [ˈmaksimo, a] adj maximum; (más alto) highest; (más grande) greatest ⊳ nm maximum; **como ~** at most

mayo [ˈmajo] nm May

mayonesa [majoˈnesa] nf mayonnaise

mayor [maˈjor] adj main, chief; (adulto) adult; (de edad avanzada) elderly; (Mús) major; (compar: de tamaño) bigger; (superl: de tamaño) biggest; (: de edad) older; (superl: de edad) oldest ⊳ nm (adulto) adult; **mayores** nmpl (antepasados) ancestors; **al por ~** wholesale; **mayor de edad** adult

mayoral [majoˈral] nm foreman

mayordomo [majorˈðomo] nm butler

mayoría [majoˈria] nf majority, greater part

mayorista [majoˈrista] nmf wholesaler

mayoritario, -a [majoriˈtarjo, a] adj majority cpd

mayúscula [maˈjuskula] nf capital

letter

mazapán [maθa'pan] *nm* marzipan

mazo ['maθo] *nm* (*martillo*) mallet; (*de flores*) bunch; (*Deporte*) bat

me [me] *pron* (*directo*) me; (*indirecto*) (to) me; (*reflexivo*) (to) myself; **¡dá~lo!** give it to me!

mear [me'ar] (*fam*) *vi* to pee, piss (*!*)

mecánica [me'kanika] *nf* (*Escol*) mechanics *sg*; (*mecanismo*) mechanism; V tb **mecánico**

mecánico, -a [me'kaniko, a] *adj* mechanical ▷ *nm/f* mechanic

mecanismo [meka'nismo] *nm* mechanism; (*marcha*) gear

mecanografía [mekanoɣra'fia] *nf* typewriting; **mecanógrafo, -a** *nm/f* typist

mecate [me'kate] (MÉX, CAM) *nm* rope

mecedora [meθe'ðora] *nf* rocking chair

mecer [me'θer] *vt* (*cuna*) to rock; **mecerse** *vr* to rock; (*rama*) to sway

mecha ['metʃa] *nf* (*de vela*) wick; (*de bomba*) fuse

mechero [me'tʃero] *nm* (*cigarette*) lighter

mechón [me'tʃon] *nm* (*gen*) tuft; (*de pelo*) lock

medalla [me'ðaʎa] *nf* medal

media ['meðja] *nf* stocking; (LAM: *calcetín*) sock; (*promedio*) average

mediado, -a [me'ðjaðo, a] *adj* half-full; (*trabajo*) half-completed; **a ~s de** in the middle of, halfway through

mediano, -a [me'ðjano, a] *adj* (*regular*) medium, average; (*mediocre*) mediocre

medianoche [meðja'notʃe] *nf* midnight

mediante [me'ðjante] *adv* by (means of), through

mediar [me'ðjar] *vi* (*interceder*) to mediate, intervene

medicamento [meðika'mento] *nm* medicine, drug

medicina [meði'θina] *nf* medicine

médico, -a ['meðiko, a] *adj* medical

▷ *nm/f* doctor

medida [me'ðiða] *nf* measure; (*medición*) measurement; (*prudencia*) moderation, prudence; **en cierta/gran ~** up to a point/to a great extent; **un traje a la ~** a made-to-measure suit; **~ de cuello** collar size; **a ~ de** in proportion to; (*de acuerdo con*) in keeping with; **a ~ que** (*conforme*) as; **medidor** (LAM) *nm* meter

medio, -a ['meðjo, a] *adj* half (a); (*punto*) middle, middle; (*promedio*) average ▷ *adv* half ▷ *nm* (*centro*) middle, centre; (*promedio*) average; (*método*) means, way; (*ambiente*) environment; **medios** *nmpl* means, resources; **~ litro** half a litre; **las tres y media** half past three; **a ~ terminar** half finished; **pagar a medias** to share the cost; **medio ambiente** environment; **medio de transporte** means of transport; **Medio Oriente** Middle East; **medios de comunicación** media; **medioambiental** *adj* (*política, efectos*) environmental

mediocre [me'ðjokre] *adj* mediocre

mediodía [meðjo'ðia] *nm* midday, noon

medir [me'ðir] *vt, vi* (*gen*) to measure

meditar [meði'tar] *vt* to ponder, think over, meditate on; (*planear*) to think out

mediterráneo, -a [meðite'rraneo, a] *adj* Mediterranean ▷ *nm*: **el M~** the Mediterranean

médula ['meðula] *nf* (Anat) marrow; **médula espinal** spinal cord

medusa [me'ðusa] (ESP) *nf* jellyfish

megáfono [me'ɣafono] *nm* megaphone

megapíxel [meɣa'piksel] (*pl* **megapíxeles** or **~es**) *nm* megapixel

mejilla [me'xiʎa] *nf* cheek

mejillón [mexi'ʎon] *nm* mussel

mejor [me'xor] *adj, adv* (*compar*) better; (*superl*) best; **a lo ~** probably; (*quizá*) maybe; **~ dicho** rather; **tanto ~**

so much the better

mejora [me'xora] nf improvement; **mejorar** vt to improve, make better ⊳ vi to improve, get better ⊳ **mejorarse** vr to improve, get better

melancólico, -a [melan'koliko, a] adj (triste) sad, melancholy; (soñador) dreamy

melena [me'lena] nf (de persona) long hair; (Zool) mane

mellizo, -a [me'ʎiθo, a] adj, nm/f twin

melocotón [meloko'ton] (ESP) nm peach

melodía [melo'ðia] nf melody, tune

melodrama [melo'ðrama] nm melodrama; **melodramático, -a** adj melodramatic

melón [me'lon] nm melon

membrete [mem'brete] nm letterhead

membrillo [mem'briʎo] nm quince; **(carne de) ~** quince jelly

memoria [me'morja] nf (gen) memory; **memorias** nfpl (de autor) memoirs; **memorizar** vt to memorize

menaje [me'naxe] nm (tb: **artículos de ~**) household items

mencionar [menθjo'nar] vt to mention

mendigo, -a [men'diɣo, a] nm/f beggar

menear [mene'ar] vt to move; **menearse** vr to shake; (balancearse) to sway; (moverse) to move; (fig) to get a move on

menestra [me'nestra] nf (tb: **~ de verduras**) vegetable stew

menopausia [meno'pausja] nf menopause

menor [me'nor] adj (más pequeño: compar) smaller; (: superl) smallest; (más joven: compar) younger; (: superl) youngest; (Mús) minor ⊳ nmf (joven) young person, juvenile; **no tengo la ~ idea** I haven't the faintest idea; **al por ~** retail; **menor de edad** person under age

Menorca [me'norka] nf Minorca

○ **PALABRA CLAVE**

menos [menos] adj 1: **menos (que o de:** compar: cantidad) less (than); (: número) fewer (than); **con menos entusiasmo** with less enthusiasm; **menos gente** fewer people; V tb **cada**

2 (superl): **es el que menos culpa tiene** he is the least to blame

⊳ adv 1 (compar): **menos (que o de)** less (than); **me gusta menos que el otro** I like it less than the other one

2 (superl): **es el menos listo (de su clase)** he's the least bright in his class; **de todas ellas es la que menos me agrada** out of all of them she's the one I like least

3 (locuciones): **no quiero verle y menos visitarle** I don't want to see him, let alone visit him; **tenemos siete de menos** we're seven short; **(por) lo menos** at (the very) least; **¡menos mal!** thank goodness!

⊳ prep except; (cifras) minus; **todos menos él** everyone except (for) him; **5 menos 2 5** minus 2

⊳ conj: **a menos que: a menos que venga mañana** unless he comes tomorrow

menospreciar [menospre'θjar] vt to underrate, undervalue; (despreciar) to scorn, despise

mensaje [men'saxe] nm message; **enviar un ~ a algn** (por móvil) to text sb, send sb a text message; **mensaje de texto** text message; **mensajero, -a** nm/f messenger

menso, -a ['menso, a] (MÉX: fam) adj stupid

menstruación [menstrua'θjon] nf menstruation

mensual [men'swal] adj monthly; **100 euros ~es** 100 euros a month; **mensualidad** nf (salario) monthly salary; (Com) monthly payment, monthly instalment

menta ['menta] nf mint

mental [men'tal] adj mental; **mentalidad** nf mentality; **mentalizar** vt (sensibilizar) to make aware; (convencer) to convince; (padres) to prepare (mentally); **mentalizarse** vr (concienciarse) to become aware; **mentalizarse de** to get used to the idea (of); **mentalizarse de que ...** (convencerse) to get it into one's head that ...

mente ['mente] nf mind

mentir [men'tir] vi to lie

mentira [men'tira] nf (una mentira) lie; (acto) lying; (invención) fiction; **parece mentira que ...** it seems incredible that ..., I can't believe that ...; **mentiroso, -a** [menti'roso, a] adj lying ⊳ nm/f liar

menú [me'nu] (pl **-s**) nm menu; **menú del día** set menu; **menú turístico** tourist menu

menudencias [menu'ðenθjas] (LAM) nfpl giblets

menudo, -a [me'nuðo, a] adj (pequeño) small, tiny; (sin importancia) petty, insignificant; **¡~ negocio!** (fam) some deal!; **a ~** often, frequently

meñique [me'ɲike] nm little finger

mercadillo [merka'ðiʎo] (ESP) nm flea market

mercado [mer'kaðo] nm market; **mercado de pulgas** (LAM) flea market

mercancía [merkan'θia] nf commodity; **mercancías** nfpl goods, merchandise sg

mercenario, -a [merθe'narjo, a] adj, nm mercenary

mercería [merθe'ria] nf haberdashery (BRIT), notions pl (US); (tienda) haberdasher's (BRIT), notions store (US)

mercurio [mer'kurjo] nm mercury

merecer [mere'θer] vt to deserve, merit ⊳ vi to be deserving, be worthy; **merece la pena** it's worthwhile;

merecido, -a adj (well) deserved; **llevar su merecido** to get one's deserts

merendar [meren'dar] vt to have for tea ⊳ vi to have tea; (en el campo) to have a picnic; **merendero** nm open-air cafe

merengue [me'renge] nm meringue

meridiano [meri'ðjano] nm (Geo) meridian

merienda [me'rjenda] nf (light) tea, afternoon snack; (de campo) picnic

mérito ['merito] nm merit; (valor) worth, value

merluza [mer'luθa] nf hake

mermelada [merme'laða] nf jam

mero, -a ['mero, a] adj mere; (MÉX, CAM: fam) very

merodear [meroðe'ar] vi: **~ por** to prowl about

mes [mes] nm month

mesa ['mesa] nf table; (de trabajo) desk; (Geo) plateau; **poner/quitar la ~** to lay/clear the table; **mesa electoral** officials in charge of a polling station; **mesa redonda** (reunión) round table; **mesero, -a** (LAM) nm/f waiter/waitress

meseta [me'seta] nf (Geo) plateau, tableland

mesilla [me'siʎa] nf (tb: **~ de noche**) bedside table

mesón [me'son] nm inn

mestizo, -a [mes'tiθo, a] adj half-caste, of mixed race ⊳ nm/f half-caste

meta ['meta] nf goal; (de carrera) finish

metabolismo [metaβo'lismo] nm metabolism

metáfora [me'tafora] nf metaphor

metal [me'tal] nm (materia) metal; (Mús) brass; **metálico, -a** adj metallic; (de metal) metal ⊳ nm (dinero contante) cash

meteorología [meteorolo'xia] nf meteorology

meter [me'ter] vt (colocar) to put, place; (introducir) to put in, insert; (involucrar) to involve; (causar) to make,

cause; **meterse** vr: **~se en** to go into,
enter; (fig) to interfere in, meddle
in; **~se a** to start; **~se a escritor** to
become a writer; **~se con uno** to
provoke sb, pick a quarrel with sb
meticuloso, -a [metiku'loso, a] adj
meticulous, thorough
metódico, -a [me'toðiko, a] adj
methodical
método ['metoðo] nm method
metralleta [metra'ʎeta] nf sub-
machine-gun
métrico, -a [me'triko, a] adj metric
metro ['metro] nm metre; (tren)
underground (BRIT), subway (US)
metrosexual [metrosek'swal] adj,
nm metrosexual
mexicano, -a [mexi'kano, a] adj,
nm/f Mexican
México ['mexiko] nm Mexico;
Ciudad de ~ Mexico City
mezcla [ˈmeθkla] nf mixture;
mezcladora (MÉX) nf (tb: **mezcladora
de cemento**) cement mixer; **mezclar**
vt to mix (up); **mezclarse** vr to mix,
mingle; **mezclarse en** to get mixed up
in, get involved in
mezquino, -a [meθ'kino, a] adj
mean
mezquita [meθ'kita] nf mosque
mg. abr (= miligramo) mg
mi [mi] adj pos my ▷ nm (Mús) E
mí [mi] pron me; myself
mía pron V **mío**
michelín [mitʃe'lin] (fam) nm, (de
grasa) spare tyre
microbio [mi'kroβjo] nm microbe
micrófono [mi'krofono] nm
microphone
microondas [mikro'ondas] nm inv
(tb: **horno ~**) microwave (oven)
microscopio [mikro'skopjo] nm
microscope
miedo ['mjeðo] nm fear; (nerviosismo)
apprehension, nervousness; **tener ~** to
be afraid; **de ~** wonderful, marvellous;
hace un frío de ~ (fam) it's terribly cold;
miedoso, -a adj fearful, timid

miel [mjel] nf honey
miembro ['mjembro] nm limb;
(socio) member; **miembro viril** penis
mientras ['mjentras] conj while;
(duración) as long as ▷ adv meanwhile;
~ tanto meanwhile
miércoles ['mjerkoles] nm inv
Wednesday
mierda ['mjerða] (fam!) nf shit (!)
miga ['miɣa] nf crumb; (fig: meollo)
essence; **hacer buenas ~s** (fam) to
get on well
mil [mil] num thousand; **dos ~ libras**
two thousand pounds
milagro [mi'laɣro] nm miracle;
milagroso, -a adj miraculous
milésima [mi'lesima] nf (de segundo)
thousandth
mili ['mili] (ESP: fam) nf: **hacer la ~** to
do one's military service
milímetro [mi'limetro] nm
millimetre
militante [mili'tante] adj militant
militar [mili'tar] adj military ▷ nm/f
soldier ▷ vi (Mil) to serve; (en un
partido) to be a member
milla ['miʎa] nf mile
millar [mi'ʎar] nm thousand
millón [mi'ʎon] num million;
millonario, -a nm/f millionaire
milusos [mi'lusos] (MÉX) nm inv
odd-job man
mimar [mi'mar] vt to spoil, pamper
mimbre ['mimbre] nm wicker
mímica ['mimika] nf (para
comunicarse) sign language; (imitación)
mimicry
mimo ['mimo] nm (caricia) caress; (de
niño) spoiling; (Teatro) mime; (: actor)
mime artist
mina ['mina] nf mine
mineral [mine'ral] adj mineral ▷ nm
(Geo) mineral; (mena) ore
minero, -a [mi'nero, a] adj mining
cpd ▷ nm/f miner
miniatura [minja'tura] adj inv, nf
miniature
minidisco [mini'disko] nm

MiniDisc®

minifalda [mini'falda] nf miniskirt

mínimo, -a ['minimo, a] adj, nm minimum

minino, -a [mi'nino, a] (fam) nm/f puss, pussy

ministerio [minis'terjo] nm Ministry; **Ministerio de Hacienda/de Asuntos Exteriores** Treasury (BRIT), Treasury Department (US)/Foreign Office (BRIT), State Department (US)

ministro, -a [mi'nistro, a] nm/f minister

minoría [mino'ria] nf minority

minúscula [mi'nuskula] nf small letter

minúsculo, -a [mi'nuskulo, a] adj tiny, minute

minusválido, -a [minus'βalido, a] adj (physically) handicapped ▷ nm/f (physically) handicapped person

minuta [mi'nuta] nf (de comida) menu

minutero [minu'tero] nm minute hand

minuto [mi'nuto] nm minute

mío, -a ['mio, a] pron: **el ~/la mía** mine; **un amigo ~** a friend of mine; **lo ~** what is mine

miope [mi'ope] adj short-sighted

mira ['mira] nf (de arma) sight(s) (pl); (fig) aim, intention

mirada [mi'raða] nf look, glance; (expresión) look, expression; **clavar la ~ en** to stare at; **echar una ~ a** to glance at

mirado, -a [mi'raðo, a] adj (sensato) sensible; (considerado) considerate; **bien/mal ~** (estimado) well/not well thought of; **bien ~ ...** all things considered ...

mirador [mira'ðor] nm viewpoint, vantage point

mirar [mi'rar] vt to look at; (observar) to watch; (considerar) to consider, think over; (vigilar, cuidar) to watch, look after ▷ vi to look; (Arq) to face; **mirarse** vr (dos personas) to look at each other; **~**

bien/mal to think highly of/have a poor opinion of; **~se al espejo** to look at o.s. in the mirror

mirilla [mi'riʎa] nf spyhole, peephole

mirlo ['mirlo] nm blackbird

misa ['misa] nf mass

miserable [mise'raβle] adj (avaro) mean, stingy; (nimio) miserable, paltry; (lugar) squalid; (fam) vile, despicable ▷ nmf (malvado) rogue

miseria [mi'serja] nf (pobreza) poverty; (tacañería) meanness, stinginess; (condiciones) squalor; **una ~** a pittance

misericordia [miseri'korðja] nf (compasión) compassion, pity; (piedad) mercy

misil [mi'sil] nm missile

misión [mi'sjon] nf mission; **misionero, -a** nm/f missionary

mismo, -a ['mismo, a] adj (semejante) same; (después de pron) -self; (para énfasis) very ▷ adv: **aquí/hoy ~** right here/this very day; **ahora ~** right now ▷ conj: **lo que** just like o as; **el ~ traje** the same suit; **en ese ~ momento** at that very moment; **vino el ~ ministro** the minister himself came; **yo ~ lo vi** I saw it myself; **lo ~** the same (thing); **da lo ~** it's all the same; **quedamos en las mismas** we're no further forward; **por lo ~** for the same reason

misterio [mis'terjo] nm mystery; **misterioso, -a** adj mysterious

mitad [mi'tað] nf (medio) half; (centro) middle; **a ~ de precio** (at) half-price; **en o a ~ del camino** halfway along the road; **cortar por la ~** to cut through the middle

mitin ['mitin] (pl **mítines**) nm meeting

mito ['mito] nm myth

mixto, -a ['miksto, a] adj mixed

mm. abr (= milímetro) mm

ml. abr (= mililitro) ml

mm. abr (= milímetro) mm

mobiliario [moβi'ljarjo] nm furniture

mochila [mo'tʃila] nf rucksack (BRIT), back-pack

moco ['moko] nm mucus; **mocos** nmpl (fam) snot; **limpiarse los ~s de la nariz** (fam) to wipe one's nose

moda ['moða] nf fashion; (estilo) style; **a la o de ~** in fashion, fashionable; **pasado de ~** out of fashion

modales [mo'ðales] nmpl manners

modelar [moðe'lar] vt to model

modelo [mo'ðelo] adj inv, nmf model

módem ['moðem] nm (Inform) modem

moderado, -a [moðe'raðo, a] adj moderate

moderar [moðe'rar] vt to moderate; (violencia) to restrain, control; (velocidad) to reduce; **moderarse** vr to restrain o.s., control o.s.

modernizar [moðerni'θar] vt to modernize

moderno, -a [mo'ðerno, a] adj modern; (actual) present-day

modestia [mo'ðestja] nf modesty; **modesto, -a** adj modest

modificar [moðifi'kar] vt to modify

modisto, -a [mo'ðisto, a] nm/f (diseñador) couturier, designer; (que confecciona) dressmaker

modo ['moðo] nm way, manner; (Mús) mode; **modos** nmpl manners; **de ningún ~** in no way; **de todos ~s** at any rate; **modo de empleo** directions pl (for use)

mofarse [mo'farse] vr: **~ de** to mock, scoff at

mofle ['mofle] (MÉX, CAM) nm silencer (BRIT), muffler (US)

mogollón [moɣo'ʎon] (ESP: fam) adv a hell of a lot

moho ['moo] nm mould, mildew; (en metal) rust

mojar [mo'xar] vt to wet; (humedecer) to damp(en), moisten; (calar) to soak; **mojarse** vr to get wet

molcajete [molka'xete] (MÉX) nm mortar

molde ['molde] nm mould; (Costura)

pattern; (fig) model; **moldeado** nm soft perm; **moldear** vt to mould

mole ['mole] nf mass, bulk; (edificio) pile

moler [mo'ler] vt to grind, crush

molestar [moles'tar] vt to bother; (fastidiar) to annoy; (incomodar) to inconvenience, put out ▷ vi to be a nuisance; **molestarse** vr to bother; (incomodarse) to go to trouble; (ofenderse) to take offence; **¿(no) te molesta si ...?** do you mind if ...?

  No confundir **molestar** con la palabra inglesa **molest**.

molestia [mo'lestja] nf bother, trouble; (incomodidad) inconvenience; (Med) discomfort; **es una ~** it's a nuisance; **molesto, -a** adj (que fastidia) annoying; (incómodo) inconvenient; (inquieto) uncomfortable, ill at ease; (enfadado) annoyed

molido, -a [mo'liðo, a] adj: **estar ~** (fig) to be exhausted o dead beat

molinillo [moli'niʎo] nm hand mill; **molinillo de café** coffee grinder

molino [mo'lino] nm (edificio) mill; (máquina) grinder

momentáneo, -a [momen'taneo, a] adj momentary

momento [mo'mento] nm moment; **de ~** at o for the moment

momia ['momja] nf mummy

monarca [mo'narka] nmf monarch, ruler; **monarquía** nf monarchy

monasterio [monas'terjo] nm monastery

mondar [mon'dar] vt to peel; **mondarse** vr (ESP): **~se de risa** (fam) to split one's sides laughing

mondongo [mon'dongo] (LAM) nm tripe

moneda [mo'neða] nf (tipo de dinero) currency, money; (pieza) coin; **una ~ de 2 euros** a 2 euro piece; **monedero** nm purse

monitor, a [moni'tor, a] nm/f instructor, coach ▷ nm (TV) set; (Inform) monitor

monja ['monxa] nf nun

monje ['monxe] nm monk

mono, -a ['mono, a] adj (bonito) lovely, pretty; (gracioso) nice, charming ▷ nm/f monkey, ape ▷ nm dungarees pl; (overoles) overalls pl

monopatín [monopa'tin] nm skateboard

monopolio [mono'poljo] nm monopoly; **monopolizar** vt to monopolize

monótono, -a [mo'notono, a] adj monotonous

monstruo ['monstrwo] nm monster ▷ adj inv fantastic; **monstruoso, -a** adj monstrous

montaje [mon'taxe] nm assembly; (Teatro) décor; (Cine) montage

montaña [mon'tana] nf (monte) mountain; (sierra) mountains pl, mountainous area; **montaña rusa** roller coaster; **montañero, -a** nm/f mountaineer; **montañismo** nm mountaineering

montar [mon'tar] vt (subir a) to mount, get on; (Tec) to assemble, put together; (negocio) to set up; (arma) to cock; (colocar) to lift on to; (Culin) to beat ▷ vi to mount, get on; (sobresalir) to overlap; ~ **en bicicleta** to ride a bicycle; ~ **en cólera** to get angry; ~ **a caballo** to ride, go horseriding

monte ['monte] nm (montaña) mountain; (bosque) woodland; (área sin cultivar) wild area, wild country; **monte de piedad** pawnshop

montón [mon'ton] nm heap, pile; (fig): **un ~ de** heaps o lots of

monumento [monu'mento] nm monument

moño ['mono] nm bun

moqueta [mo'keta] nf fitted carpet

mora ['mora] nf blackberry; V tb **moro**

morado, -a [mo'raðo, a] adj purple, violet ▷ nm bruise

moral [mo'ral] adj moral ▷ nf (ética) ethics pl; (moralidad) morals pl,

morality; (ánimo) morale

moraleja [mora'lexa] nf moral

morboso, -a [mor'βoso, a] adj morbid

morcilla [mor'θiʎa] nf blood sausage = black pudding (BRIT)

mordaza [mor'ðaθa] nf (para la boca) gag; (Tec) clamp

morder [mor'ðer] vt to bite; (fig: consumir) to eat away, eat into; **mordisco** nm bite

moreno, -a [mo'reno, a] adj (color) (dark) brown; (de tez) dark; (de pelo moreno) dark-haired; (negro) black

morfina [mor'fina] nf morphine

moribundo, -a [mori'βundo, a] adj dying

morir [mo'rir] vi to die; (fuego) to die down; (luz) to go out; **morirse** vr to die; (fig) to be dying; **murió en un accidente** he was killed in an accident; **~se por algo** to be dying for sth

moro, -a ['moro, a] adj Moorish ▷ nm/f Moor

moroso, -a [mo'roso, a] nm/f bad debtor, defaulter

morralla [mo'raʎa] nf (MÉX) (cambio) small o loose change

morro ['moro] nm (Zool) snout, nose; (Auto, Aviac) nose

morsa ['morsa] nf walrus

mortadela [morta'ðela] nf mortadella

mortal [mor'tal] adj mortal; (golpe) deadly; **mortalidad** nf mortality

mortero [mor'tero] nm mortar

mosca ['moska] nf fly

Moscú [mos'ku] n Moscow

mosquearse [moske'arse] (fam) vr (enojarse) to get cross; (ofenderse) to take offence

mosquitero [moski'tero] nm mosquito net

mosquito [mos'kito] nm mosquito

mostaza [mos'taθa] nf mustard

mosto ['mosto] nm (unfermented)

grape juice

mostrador [mostra'ðor] nm (de tienda) counter; (de café) bar

mostrar [mos'trar] vt to show; (exhibir) to display, exhibit; (explicar) to explain; **mostrarse** vr: **~se amable** to be kind; to prove to be kind; **no se muestra muy inteligente** he doesn't seem (to be) very intelligent

mota ['mota] nf speck, tiny piece; (en diseño) dot

mote ['mote] nm nickname

motín [mo'tin] nm (del pueblo) revolt, rising; (del ejército) mutiny

motivar [moti'βar] vt (causar) to cause, motivate; (explicar) to explain, justify; **motivo** nm motive, reason

moto ['moto] (fam) nf = **motocicleta**

motocicleta [motoθi'kleta] nf motorbike (BRIT), motorcycle

motoneta [moto'neta] (CS) nf scooter

motor [mo'tor] nm motor, engine; **motor a chorro o de reacción/de explosión** jet engine/internal combustion engine

motora [mo'tora] nf motorboat

movedizo, -a adj V **arena**

mover [mo'βer] vt to move; (cabeza) to shake; (accionar) to drive; (fig) to cause, provoke; **moverse** vr to move; (fig) to get a move on

móvil ['moβil] adj mobile; (pieza de máquina) moving; (mueble) movable ▷ nm (motivo) motive; (teléfono) mobile

movimiento [moβi'mjento] nm movement; (Tec) motion; (actividad) activity

mozo, -a ['moθo, a] adj (joven) young ▷ nm/f youth, young man/girl; (cs: mesero) waiter/waitress

MP3 nm nm MP3; **reproductor (de) ~** MP3 player

mucama [mu'kama] (RPL) nf maid

muchacho, -a [mu'tʃatʃo, a] nm/f (niño) boy/girl; (criado) servant; (criada)

maid

muchedumbre [mutʃe'ðumbre] nf crowd

○ **PALABRA CLAVE**

mucho, -a ['mutʃo, a] adj 1 (cantidad) a lot of, much; (número) lots of, a lot of, many; **mucho dinero** a lot of money; **hace mucho calor** it's very hot; **muchas amigas** lots o a lot of friends

2 (sg: grande): **ésta es mucha casa para él** this house is much too big for him

▷ pron: **tengo mucho que hacer** I've got a lot to do; **muchos dicen que ...** a lot of people say that ...; V tb **tener**

▷ adv 1 **me gusta mucho** I like it a lot; **lo siento mucho** I'm very sorry; **come mucho** he eats a lot; **¿te vas a quedar mucho?** are you going to be staying long?

2 (respuesta) very; **¿estás cansado? - ¡mucho!** are you tired? - very!

3 (locuciones): **como mucho** at (the) most; **con mucho: el mejor con mucho** by far the best; **ni mucho menos: no es rico ni mucho menos** he's far from being rich

4: **por mucho que: por mucho que le creas** no matter how o however much you believe her

muda ['muða] nf change of clothes

mudanza [mu'ðanθa] nf (de casa) move

mudar [mu'ðar] vt to change; (Zool) to shed ▷ vi to change; **mudarse** vr (ropa) to change; **~se de casa** to move house

mudo, -a ['muðo, a] adj dumb; (callado, Cine) silent

mueble ['mweβle] nm piece of furniture; **muebles** nmpl furniture sg

mueca ['mweka] nf face, grimace; **hacer ~s a** to make faces at

muela ['mwela] nf back tooth; **muela del juicio** wisdom tooth

muelle ['mweʎe] nm spring; (Náut) wharf; (malecón) pier

muero etc vb V **morir**

muerte ['mwerte] nf death; (homicidio) murder; **dar ~ a** to kill

muerto, -a ['mwerto, a] pp de **morir** ▷ adj dead ▷ nm/f dead man/woman; (difunto) deceased; (cadáver) corpse; **estar ~ de cansancio** to be dead tired; **Día de los Muertos** (MÉX) All Souls' Day

● **DÍA DE LOS MUERTOS**
●
● All Souls' Day (or "Day of the Dead")
● in Mexico coincides with All
● Saints' Day, which is celebrated
● in the Catholic countries of Latin
● America on November 1st and
● 2nd. All Souls' Day is actually
● a celebration which begins
● in the evening of October 31st
● and continues until November
● 2nd. It is a combination of the
● Catholic tradition of honouring
● the Christian saints and martyrs,
● and the ancient Mexican or Aztec
● traditions, in which death was not
● something sinister. For this reason
● all the dead are honoured by
● bringing offerings of food, flowers
● and candles to the cemetery.

muestra ['mwestra] nf (señal) indication, sign; (demostración) demonstration; (prueba) proof; (estadística) sample; (modelo) model, pattern; (testimonio) token

muestro etc vb V **mostrar**

muevo etc vb V **mover**

mugir [mu'xir] vi (vaca) to moo

mugre ['muɣre] nf dirt, filth

mujer [mu'xer] nf woman; (esposa) wife; **mujeriego** nm womanizer

mula ['mula] nf mule

muleta [mu'leta] nf (para andar) crutch; (Taur) stick with red cape attached

multa ['multa] nf fine; **poner una ~ a** to fine; **multar** vt to fine

multicines [multi'θines] nmpl multiscreen cinema sg

multinacional [multinaθjo'nal] nf multinational

múltiple ['multiple] adj multiple; (pl) many, numerous

multiplicar [multipli'kar] vt (Mat) to multiply; (fig) to increase; **multiplicarse** vr (Bio) to multiply; (fig) to be everywhere at once

multitud [multi'tuð] nf (muchedumbre) crowd; **~ de** lots of

mundial [mun'djal] adj world-wide, universal; (guerra, récord) world cpd

mundo ['mundo] nm world; **todo el ~** everybody; **tener ~** to be experienced, know one's way around

munición [muni'θjon] nf ammunition

municipal [muniθi'pal] adj municipal, local

municipio [muni'θipjo] nm (ayuntamiento) town council, corporation; (territorio administrativo) town, municipality

muñeca [mu'neka] nf (Anat) wrist; (juguete) doll

muñeco [mu'neko] nm (figura) figure; (marioneta) puppet; (fig) puppet, pawn

mural [mu'ral] adj mural, wall cpd ▷ nm mural

muralla [mu'raʎa] nf (city) wall(s) (pl)

murciélago [mur'θjelaxo] nm bat

murmullo [mur'muʎo] nm murmur(ing); (cuchicheo) whispering

murmurar [murmu'rar] vi to murmur, whisper; (cotillear) to gossip

muro ['muro] nm wall

muscular [musku'lar] adj muscular

músculo ['muskulo] nm muscle

museo [mu'seo] nm museum; **museo de arte** art gallery

musgo ['musxo] nm moss

música ['musika] nf music; V tb **músico**

músico, -a ['musiko, a] adj musical

▷ *nm/f* musician

muslo ['muslo] *nm* thigh

musulmán, -ana [musul'man, ana] *nm/f* Moslem

mutación [muta'θjon] *nf* (Bio) mutation; (*cambio*) (sudden) change

mutilar [muti'lar] *vt* to mutilate; (*a una persona*) to maim

mutuo, -a ['mutwo, a] *adj* mutual

muy [mwi] *adv* very; (*demasiado*) too; **M~ Señor mío** Dear Sir; **~ de noche** very late at night; **eso es ~ de él** that's just like him

N *abr* (= *norte*) N

nabo ['naβo] *nm* turnip

nacer [na'θer] *vi* to be born; (*de huevo*) to hatch; (*vegetal*) to sprout; (*río*) to rise; **nací en Barcelona** I was born in Barcelona; **nacido, -a** *adj* born; **recién nacido** newborn; **nacimiento** *nm* birth; (*de Navidad*) Nativity; (*de río*) source

nación [na'θjon] *nf* nation; **nacional** *adj* national; **nacionalismo** *nm* nationalism

nada ['naða] *pron* nothing ▷ *adv* not at all, in no way; **no decir ~** to say nothing, not to say anything; **~ más** nothing else; **de ~** don't mention it

nadador, a [naða'ðor, a] *nm/f* swimmer

nadar [na'ðar] *vi* to swim

nadie ['naðje] *pron* nobody, no-one; **~ habló** nobody spoke; **no había ~** there was nobody there, there wasn't anybody there

nado ['naðo] **a nado** *adv*: **pasar a ~** to swim across

nafta ['nafta] (RPL) nf petrol (BRIT), gas (US)

naipe ['naipe] nm (playing) card; **naipes** nmpl cards

nalgas ['nalɣas] nfpl buttocks

nalguear [nalɣe'ar] (MÉX, CAM) vt to spank

nana ['nana] (ESP) nf lullaby

naranja [na'ranxa] adj inv, nf orange; **media ~** (fam) better half; **naranjada** nf orangeade; **naranjo** nm orange tree

narciso [nar'θiso] nm narcissus

narcótico, -a [nar'kotiko, a] adj, nm narcotic; **narcotizar** vt to drug; **narcotráfico** nm drug trafficking o running

nariz [na'riθ] nf nose; **nariz chata/ respingona** snub/turned-up nose

narración [narra'θjon] nf narration

narrar [na'rrar] vt to narrate, recount; **narrativa** nf narrative

nata ['nata] nf cream; **nata montada** whipped cream

natación [nata'θjon] nf swimming

natal [na'tal] adj: **ciudad ~** home town; **natalidad** nf birth rate

natillas [na'tiʎas] nfpl custard sg

nativo, -a [na'tiβo, a] adj, nm/f native

natural [natu'ral] adj natural; (fruta etc) fresh ▷ nmf native ▷ nm (disposición) nature

naturaleza [natura'leθa] nf nature; (género) nature, kind; **naturaleza muerta** still life

naturalmente [natural'mente] adv (de modo natural) in a natural way; **¡~!** of course!

naufragar [naufra'ɣar] vi to sink; **naufragio** nm shipwreck

nauseabundo, -a [nausea'βundo, a] adj nauseating, sickening

náuseas ['nauseas] nfpl nausea sg; **me da ~** it makes me feel sick

náutico, -a ['nautiko, a] adj nautical

navaja [na'βaxa] nf knife; (de barbero, peluquero) razor

naval [na'βal] adj naval

Navarra [na'βarra] n Navarre

nave ['naβe] nf (barco) ship, vessel; (Arq) nave; **nave espacial** spaceship; **nave industrial** factory premises pl

navegador [naβexa'ðor] nm (Inform) browser

navegante [naβe'xante] nmf navigator

navegar [naβe'xar] vi (barco) to sail; (avión) to fly; **~ por Internet** to surf the Net

Navidad [naβi'ðað] nf Christmas; **Navidades** nfpl Christmas time; **¡Feliz ~!** Merry Christmas!; **navideño, -a** adj Christmas cpd

nazca etc vb V **nacer**

nazi ['naθi] adj, nmf Nazi

NE abr (= nord(d)este) NE

neblina [ne'βlina] nf mist

necesario, -a [neθe'sarjo, a] adj necessary

neceser [neθe'ser] nm toilet bag; (bolsa grande) holdall

necesidad [neθesi'ðað] nf need; (lo inevitable) necessity; (miseria) poverty; **en caso de ~** in case of need o emergency; **hacer sus ~es** to relieve o.s.

necesitado, -a [neθesi'taðo, a] adj needy, poor; **~ de** in need of

necesitar [neθesi'tar] vt to need, require

necio, -a ['neθjo, a] adj foolish

nectarina [nekta'rina] nf nectarine

nefasto, -a [ne'fasto, a] adj ill-fated, unlucky

negación [neɣa'θjon] nf negation; (rechazo) refusal, denial

negar [ne'ɣar] vt (renegar, rechazar) to refuse; (prohibir) to refuse, deny; (desmentir) to deny; **negarse** vr: **~se a** to refuse to

negativa [neɣa'tiβa] nf negative; (rechazo) refusal, denial

negativo, -a [neɣa'tiβo, a] adj, nm negative

negociante [neɣo'θjante] nmf businessman/woman

negociar [neɣo'θjar] vt, vi to negotiate; **~ en** to deal or trade in

negocio [ne'ɣoθjo] nm (Com) business; (asunto) affair, business; (operación comercial) deal, business, transaction; (lugar) place of business; **negocios** nmpl business sg; **hacer ~** to do business

negra ['neɣra] nf (Mús) crotchet; V tb **negro**

negro, -a ['neɣro, a] adj black; (suerte) awful ▷ nm black ▷ nm/f black man/woman

nene, -a ['nene, a] nm/f baby, small child

neón [ne'on] nm: **luces/lámpara de ~** neon lights/lamp

neoyorquino, -a [neojor'kino, a] adj (of) New York

nervio ['nerβjo] nm nerve; **nerviosismo** nm nervousness, nerves pl; **nervioso, -a** adj nervous

neto, -a ['neto, a] adj net

neumático, -a [neu'matiko, a] adj pneumatic ▷ nm (ESP) tyre (BRIT), tire (US); **neumático de recambio** spare tyre

neurólogo, -a [neu'roloɣo, a] nm/f neurologist

neurona [neu'rona] nf nerve cell

neutral [neu'tral] adj neutral; **neutralizar** vt to neutralize; (contrarrestar) to counteract

neutro, -a ['neutro, a] adj (Bio, Ling) neuter

neutrón [neu'tron] nm neutron

nevada [ne'βaða] nf snowstorm; (caída de nieve) snowfall

nevar [ne'βar] vi to snow

nevera [ne'βera] (ESP) nf refrigerator (BRIT), icebox (US)

nevería [neβe'ria] (MÉX) nf ice-cream parlour

nexo ['nekso] nm link, connection

ni [ni] conj nor, neither; (tb: **~ siquiera**) not ... even; **~ aunque que** not even if; **~ blanco ~ negro** neither white

nor black

Nicaragua [nika'raɣwa] nf Nicaragua; **nicaragüense** adj, nmf Nicaraguan

nicho ['nitʃo] nm niche

nicotina [niko'tina] nf nicotine

nido ['niðo] nm nest

niebla ['njeβla] nf fog; (neblina) mist

niego etc vb V **negar**

nieto, -a ['njeto, a] nm/f grandson/ daughter; **nietos** nmpl grandchildren

nieve etc ['njeβe] vb V **nevar** ▷ nf snow; (MÉX: helado) ice cream

NIF nm abr (= Número de Identificación Fiscal) personal identification number used for financial and tax purposes

ninfa ['ninfa] nf nymph

ningún adj V **ninguno**

ninguno, -a [nin'guno, a] (adj **ningún**) pron (nadie) nobody; (ni uno) none, not one; (no ... ninguno) neither; **de ninguna manera** by no means, not at all

niña ['nina] nf (Anat) pupil; V tb **niño**

niñera [ni'nera] nf nursemaid, nanny

niñez [ni'neθ] nf childhood; (infancia) infancy

niño, -a ['nino, a] adj (joven) young; (inmaduro) immature ▷ nm/f child, boy/girl

nipón, -ona [ni'pon, ona] adj, nm/f Japanese

níquel ['nikel] nm nickel

níspero ['nispero] nm medlar

nítido, -a [ni'tiðo, a] adj clear, sharp

nitrato [ni'trato] nm nitrate

nitrógeno [ni'troxeno] nm nitrogen

nivel [ni'βel] nm (Geo) level; (norma) level, standard; (altura) height; **nivel de aceite** oil level; **nivel de aire** spirit level; **nivel de vida** standard of living; **nivelar** vt to level out; (fig) to even up; (Com) to balance

no [no] adv no; not; (con verbo) not ▷ excl no!; **~ tengo nada** I don't have anything, I have nothing; **~ es el mío** it's not mine; **ahora ~** not now; **¿~ lo sabes?** don't you know?; **~ mucho** not much; **~ bien termine, lo entregaré** as soon as I finish, I'll hand it over; **~ más: ayer ~ más** just yesterday; **¡pase ~ más!** come in!; **¡a que ~ lo sabes!** I bet you don't know!; **¡cómo ~!** of course!; **la ~ intervención** non-intervention

noble [ˈnoβle] *adj, nmf* noble; **nobleza** *nf* nobility

noche [ˈnotʃe] *nf* night, night-time; (*la tarde*) evening; **de ~, por la ~** at night; **es de ~** it's dark; **Noche de San Juan** *see note*

○ **NOCHE DE SAN JUAN**
○
○ The **Noche de San Juan** on the
○ 24th June is a **fiesta** coinciding
○ with the summer solstice and
○ which has taken the place of
○ other ancient pagan festivals.
○ Traditionally fire plays a major
○ part in these festivities with
○ celebrations and dancing taking
○ place around bonfires in towns
○ and villages across the country.

nochebuena [notʃeˈβwena] *nf* Christmas Eve

○ **NOCHEBUENA**
○
○ Traditional Christmas
○ celebrations in Spanish-speaking
○ countries mainly take place
○ on the night of **Nochebuena**,
○ Christmas Eve. Families gather
○ together for a large meal and the
○ more religiously inclined attend
○ Midnight Mass. While presents are
○ traditionally given by **los Reyes
○ Magos** on the 6th January, more
○ and more people are exchanging
○ gifts on Christmas Eve.

nochevieja [notʃeˈβjexa] *nf* New Year's Eve

nocivo, -a [noˈθiβo, a] *adj* harmful

noctámbulo, -a [nokˈtambulo, a]

nm/f sleepwalker

nocturno, -a [nokˈturno, a] *adj* (*de la noche*) nocturnal, night *cpd*; (*de la tarde*) evening *cpd* ▷ *nm* nocturne

nogal [noˈɣal] *nm* walnut tree

nómada [ˈnomaða] *adj* nomadic ▷ *nmf* nomad

nombrar [nomˈbrar] *vt* (*designar*) to name; (*mencionar*) to mention; (*dar puesto a*) to appoint

nombre [ˈnombre] *nm* name; (*sustantivo*) noun; **~ y apellidos** name in full; **poner ~ a** to call, name; **nombre común/propio** common/proper noun; **nombre de pila/de soltera** Christian/maiden name

nómina [ˈnomina] *nf* (*lista*) payroll; (*hoja*) payslip

nominal [nomiˈnal] *adj* nominal

nominar [nomiˈnar] *vt* to nominate

nominativo, -a [nominaˈtiβo, a] *adj* (*Com*): **cheque ~ a X** cheque made out to X

nordeste [norˈðeste] *adj* north-east, north-eastern, north-easterly ▷ *nm* north-east

nórdico, -a [ˈnorðiko, a] *adj* Nordic

noreste [noˈreste] *adj*, *nm* = **nordeste**

noria [ˈnorja] *nf* (*Agr*) waterwheel; (*de carnaval*) big (BRIT) o Ferris (US) wheel

norma [ˈnorma] *nf* rule (of thumb)

normal [norˈmal] *adj* (*corriente*) normal; (*habitual*) usual, natural; **normalizarse** *vr* to return to normal; **normalmente** *adv* normally

normativa [normaˈtiβa] *nf* (set of) rules *pl*, regulations *pl*

noroeste [noroˈeste] *adj* north-west, north-western, north-westerly ▷ *nm* north-west

norte [ˈnorte] *adj* north, northern, northerly ▷ *nm* north; (*fig*) guide

norteamericano, -a [norteameriˈkano, a] *adj, nm/f* (North) American

Noruega [noˈrweɣa] *nf* Norway

noruego, -a [noˈrweɣo, a] *adj, nm/f* Norwegian

nos [nos] *pron* (*directo*) us; (*indirecto*) us; to us; for us; from us; (*reflexivo*) (to) ourselves; (*recíproco*) (to) each other; **levantamos a las 7** we get up at 7

nosotros, -as [no'sotros, as] *pron* (*sujeto*) we; (*después de prep*) us

nostalgia [nos'talxja] *nf* nostalgia

nota ['nota] *nf* note; (*Escol*) mark

notable [no'taβle] *adj* notable; (*Escol*) outstanding

notar [no'tar] *vt* to notice; note; **notarse** *vr* to be obvious; **se nota que** ... one observes that ...

notario [no'tarjo] *nm* notary

noticia [no'tiθja] *nf* (*información*) piece of news; **las ~s** the news *sg*; **tener ~s de algn** to hear from sb
> No confundir **noticia** con la palabra inglesa *notice*.

noticiero [noti'θjero] (*LAM*) *nm* news bulletin

notificar [notifi'kar] *vt* to notify, inform

notorio, -a [no'torjo, a] *adj* (*público*) well-known; (*evidente*) obvious

novato, -a [no'βato, a] *adj* inexperienced ▷ *nm/f* beginner, novice

novecientos, -as [noβe'θjentos, as] *num* nine hundred

novedad [noβe'ðað] *nf* (*calidad de nuevo*) newness; (*noticia*) piece of news; (*cambio*) change, (new) development

novel [no'βel] *adj* new; (*inexperto*) inexperienced ▷ *nmf* beginner

novela [no'βela] *nf* novel

noveno, -a [no'βeno, a] *adj* ninth

noventa [no'βenta] *num* ninety

novia *nf* V **novio**

novicio, -a [no'βiθjo, a] *nm/f* novice

noviembre [no'βjembre] *nm* November

novillada [noβi'ʎaða] *nf* (*Taur*) bullfight with young bulls; **novillero** *nm* novice bullfighter; **novillo** *nm* young bull, bullock; **hacer novillos** (*fam*) to play truant

novio, -a ['noβjo, a] *nm/f* boyfriend/girlfriend; (*prometido*) fiancé/fiancée; (*recién casado*) bridegroom/bride; **los ~s** the newly-weds

nube ['nuβe] *nf* cloud

nublado, -a [nu'βlaðo, a] *adj* cloudy; **nublarse** *vr* to grow dark

nubosidad [nuβosi'ðað] *nf* cloudiness; **había mucha ~** it was very cloudy

nuca ['nuka] *nf* nape of the neck

nuclear [nukle'ar] *adj* nuclear

núcleo ['nukleo] *nm* (*centro*) core; (*Física*) nucleus; **núcleo urbano** city centre

nudillo [nu'ðiʎo] *nm* knuckle

nudista [nu'ðista] *adj* nudist

nudo ['nuðo] *nm* knot; (*de carreteras*) junction

nuera ['nwera] *nf* daughter-in-law

nuestro, -a ['nwestro, a] *adj pos* our ▷ *pron* ours; **~ padre** our father; **un amigo ~** a friend of ours; **es el ~** it's ours

Nueva York [-jɔrk] *n* New York

Nueva Zelanda [-θe'landa] *nf* New Zealand

nueve ['nweβe] *num* nine

nuevo, -a ['nweβo, a] *adj* (*gen*) new; **de ~** again

nuez [nweθ] *nf* walnut; (*Anat*) Adam's apple; **nuez moscada** nutmeg

nulo, -a ['nulo, a] *adj* (*inepto, torpe*) useless; (*inválido*) (null and) void; (*Deporte*) drawn, tied

núm. *abr* (= *número*) no.

numerar [nume'rar] *vt* to number

número ['numero] *nm* (*gen*) number; (*tamaño: de zapato*) size; (*ejemplar: de diario*) number, issue; **sin ~** numberless, unnumbered; **número atrasado** back number; **número de matrícula/teléfono** registration/telephone number; **número impar/par** odd/even number; **número romano** Roman numeral

numeroso, -a [nume'roso, a] *adj* numerous

nunca ['nunka] *adv* (*jamás*) never; **~**

lo pensé I never thought it; **no viene
~** he never comes; **~ más** never again;
más que ~ more than ever
nupcias ['nupθjas] *nfpl* wedding
sg, nuptials
nutria ['nutrja] *nf* otter
nutrición [nutri'θjon] *nf* nutrition
nutrir [nu'trir] *vt (alimentar)* to
nourish; *(dar de comer)* to feed; *(fig)*
to strengthen; **nutritivo, -a** *adj*
nourishing, nutritious
nylon [ni'lon] *nm* nylon

ñango, -a ['nango, a] *(MÉX) adj* puny
ñapa ['napa] *(LAM) nf* extra
ñata ['nata] *(LAM: fam) nf* nose; V
tb **ñato**
ñato, -a ['nato, a] *(LAM) adj* snub-
nosed
ñoñería [nope'ria] *nf* insipidness
ñoño, -a ['nono, a] *adj (fam: tonto)*
silly, stupid; *(soso)* insipid; *(persona)*
spineless; *(ESP: película, novela)*
sentimental

O, o [o]

O abr (= _oeste_) W

o [o] _conj_ or

oasis [o'asis] _nm inv_ oasis

obcecarse [oβθe'karse] _vr_ to get o become stubborn

obedecer [oβeðe'θer] _vt_ to obey; **obediente** _adj_ obedient

obertura [oβer'tura] _nf_ overture

obeso, -a [o'βeso, a] _adj_ obese

obispo [o'βispo] _nm_ bishop

obituario [oβi'twarjo] (LAM) _nm_ obituary

objetar [oβxe'tar] _vt, vi_ to object

objetivo, -a [oβxe'tiβo, a] _adj, nm_ objective

objeto [oβ'xeto] _nm_ (_cosa_) object; (_fin_) aim

objetor, a [oβxe'tor, a] _nm/f_ objector

obligación [oβliɣa'θjon] _nf_ obligation; (Com) bond

obligar [oβli'ɣar] _vt_ to force; **obligarse** _vr_ to bind o.s.; **obligatorio, -a** _adj_ compulsory, obligatory

oboe [o'βoe] _nm_ oboe

obra ['oβra] _nf_ work; (Arq) construction, building; (Teatro) play; **por ~ de** thanks to (the efforts of); **obra maestra** masterpiece; **obras públicas** public works; **obrar** _vt_ to work; (_tener efecto_) to have an effect on ⊳ _vi_ to act, behave; (_tener efecto_) to have an effect; **la obra está en su poder** the letter is in his/her possession

obrero, -a [o'βrero, a] _adj_ (_clase_) working; (_movimiento_) labour _cpd_ ⊳ _nm/f_ (_gen_) worker; (_sin oficio_) labourer

obsceno, -a [oβs'θeno, a] _adj_ obscene

obscu... = **oscu...**

obsequiar [oβse'kjar] _vt_ (_ofrecer_) to present with; (_agasajar_) to make a fuss of, lavish attention on; **obsequio** _nm_ (_regalo_) gift; (_cortesía_) courtesy, attention

observación [oβserβa'θjon] _nf_ observation; (_reflexión_) remark

observador, a [oβserβa'ðor, a] _nm/f_ observer

observar [oβser'βar] _vt_ to observe; (_anotar_) to notice; **observarse** _vr_ to keep to, observe

obsesión [oβse'sjon] _nf_ obsession; **obsesivo, -a** _adj_ obsessive

obstáculo [oβs'takulo] _nm_ obstacle; (_impedimento_) hindrance, drawback

obstante [oβs'tante]: **no ~** _adv_ nevertheless

obstinado, -a [oβsti'naðo, a] _adj_ obstinate, stubborn

obstinarse [oβsti'narse] _vr_ to be obstinate; **~ en** to persist in

obstruir [oβstru'ir] _vt_ to obstruct

obtener [oβte'ner] _vt_ (_gen_) to obtain; (_premio_) to win

obturador [oβtura'ðor] _nm_ (Foto) shutter

obvio, -a ['oββjo, a] _adj_ obvious

oca ['oka] _nf_ (_animal_) goose; (_juego_) = snakes and ladders

ocasión [oka'sjon] _nf_ (_oportunidad_) opportunity, chance; (_momento_) occasion, time; (_causa_) cause; **de ~**

secondhand; **ocasionar** vt to cause

ocaso [o'kaso] nm (fig) decline

occidente [okθi'ðente] nm west

OCDE nf abr (= Organización de Cooperación y Desarrollo Económico) OECD

océano [o'θeano] nm ocean; **Océano Índico** Indian Ocean

ochenta [o'tʃenta] num eighty

ocho [o'tʃo] num eight; **dentro de ~ días** within a week

ocio [o'θjo] nm (tiempo) leisure; (pey) idleness

octavilla [okta'viʎa] nf leaflet, pamphlet

octavo, -a [ok'taβo, a] adj eighth

octubre [ok'tuβre] nm October

oculista [oku'lista] nmf oculist

ocultar [okul'tar] vt (esconder) to hide; (callar) to conceal; **oculto, -a** adj hidden; (fig) secret

ocupación [okupa'θjon] nf occupation

ocupado, -a [oku'paðo, a] adj (persona) busy; (plaza) occupied, taken; (teléfono) engaged; **ocupar** vt (gen) to occupy; **ocuparse** vr: **ocuparse de o en** (gen) to concern o.s. with; (cuidar) to look after

ocurrencia [oku'rrenθja] nf (idea) bright idea

ocurrir [oku'rrir] vi to happen; **ocurrirse** vr: **se me ocurrió que ...** it occurred to me that ...

odiar [o'ðjar] vt to hate; **odio** nm hate, hatred; **odioso, -a** adj (gen) hateful; (malo) nasty

odontólogo, -a [oðon'toloxo, a] nm/f dentist, dental surgeon

oeste [o'este] nm west; **una película del ~** a western

ofender [ofen'der] vt (agraviar) to offend; (insultar) to insult; **ofenderse** vr to take offence; **ofensa** nf offence; **ofensiva** nf offensive; **ofensivo, -a** adj offensive

oferta [o'ferta] nf offer; (propuesta) proposal; **la ~ y la demanda** supply

and demand; **artículos en ~** goods on offer

oficial [ofi'θjal] adj official ▷ nm (Mil) officer

oficina [ofi'θina] nf office; **oficina de correos** post office; **oficina de información** information bureau; **oficina de turismo** tourist office; **oficinista** nmf clerk

oficio [o'fiθjo] nm (profesión) profession; (puesto) post; (Rel) service; **ser del ~** to be an old hand; **tener mucho ~** to have a lot of experience; **oficio de difuntos** funeral service

ofimática [ofi'matika] nf office automation

ofrecer [ofre'θer] vt (dar) to offer; (proponer) to propose; **ofrecerse** vr (persona) to offer o.s., volunteer; (situación) to present itself; **¿qué se le ofrece?, ¿se le ofrece algo?** what can I do for you?, can I get you anything?

ofrecimiento [ofreθi'mjento] nm offer

oftalmólogo, -a [oftal'moloxo, a] nm/f ophthalmologist

oída [o'iða] nf: **de ~s** by hearsay

oído [o'iðo] nm (Anat) ear; (sentido) hearing

oigo etc vb V **oír**

oír [o'ir] vt (gen) to hear; (atender a) to listen to; **¡oiga!** listen!; **~ misa** to attend mass

OIT nf abr (= Organización Internacional del Trabajo) ILO

ojal [o'xal] nm buttonhole

ojalá [oxa'la] excl if only (it were so!), some hope! ▷ conj if only ...!, would that ...!; **~ (que) venga hoy** I hope he comes today

ojeada [oxe'aða] nf glance

ojera [o'xera] nf: **tener ~s** to have bags under one's eyes

ojo ['oxo] nm eye; (de puente) span; (de cerradura) keyhole; **¡ojo!** careful!; **tener ~ para** to have an eye for; **ojo de buey** porthole

okey ['okei] (LAM) excl O.K.

okupa [o'kupa] (ESP: fam) nmf squatter

ola ['ola] nf wave

olé [o'le] excl bravo!, olé!

oleada [ole'aða] nf big wave, swell; (fig) wave

oleaje [ole'axe] nm swell

óleo ['oleo] nm oil; **oleoducto** nm (oil) pipeline

oler [o'ler] vt (gen) to smell; (inquirir) to pry into; (fig: sospechar) to sniff out ▷ vi to smell; **~ a** to smell of

olfatear [olfate'ar] vt to smell; (inquirir) to pry into; **olfato** nm sense of smell

olimpiada [olim'piaða] nf: **las O~s** the Olympics; **olímpico, -a** [o'limpiko, a] adj Olympic

oliva [o'liβa] nf (aceituna) olive; **aceite de ~** olive oil; **olivo** nm olive tree

olla ['oʎa] nf (gen; comida) stew; **olla exprés o a presión** (ESP) pressure cooker; **olla podrida** type of Spanish stew

olmo ['olmo] nm elm (tree)

olor [o'lor] nm smell; **oloroso, -a** adj scented

olvidar [olβi'ðar] vt to forget; (omitir) to omit; **olvidarse** vr (fig) to forget o.s.; **se me olvidó** I forgot

olvido [ol'βiðo] nm oblivion; (despiste) forgetfulness

ombligo [om'bliɣo] nm navel

omelette [ome'lete] (LAM) nf omelet(te)

omisión [omi'sjon] nf (abstención) omission; (descuido) neglect

omiso, -a [o'miso, a] adj: **hacer caso ~ de** to ignore, pass over

omitir [omi'tir] vt to omit

omnipotente [omnipo'tente] adj omnipotent

omóplato [o'moplato] nm shoulder blade

OMS nf abr (= Organización Mundial de la Salud) WHO

once ['onθe] num eleven; **onces** (CS) nfpl tea break sg

onda ['onda] nf wave; **onda corta/larga/media** short/long/medium wave; **ondear** vt, vi to wave; (tener ondas) to be wavy; (agua) to ripple

ondulación [ondula'θjon] nf undulation; **ondulado, -a** adj wavy

ONG nf abr (= organización no gubernamental) NGO

ONU ['onu] nf abr (= Organización de las Naciones Unidas) UNO

opaco, -a [o'pako, a] adj opaque

opción [op'θjon] nf (gen) option; (derecho) right, option

OPEP ['opep] nf abr (= Organización de Países Exportadores de Petróleo) OPEC

ópera ['opera] nf opera; **ópera bufa o cómica** comic opera

operación [opera'θjon] nf (gen) operation; (Com) transaction, deal

operador, a [opera'ðor, a] nm/f operator; (Cine: de proyección) projectionist; (: de rodaje) cameraman

operar [ope'rar] vt (producir) to produce, bring about; (Med) to operate on ▷ vi (Com) to operate, deal; **operarse** vr to occur; (Med) to have an operation

opereta [ope'reta] nf operetta

opinar [opi'nar] vt to think ▷ vi to give one's opinion; **opinión** nf (creencia) belief; (criterio) opinion

opio ['opjo] nm opium

oponer [opo'ner] vt (resistencia) to put up, offer; **oponerse** vr (objetar) to object; (estar frente a frente) to be opposed; (dos personas) to oppose each other; **~ A a B** to set A against B; **me opongo a pensar que ...** I refuse to believe o think that ...

oportunidad [oportuni'ðað] nf (ocasión) opportunity; (posibilidad) chance

oportuno, -a [opor'tuno, a] adj (en su tiempo) opportune, timely; (respuesta) suitable; **en el momento ~** at the right moment

oposición [oposi'θjon] nf opposition; **oposiciones** nfpl (Escol) public examinations

opositor, a [oposi'tor, a] nm/f (adversario) opponent; (candidato): **~ (a)** candidate (for)

opresión [opre'sjon] nf oppression; **opresor, a** nm/f oppressor

oprimir [opri'mir] vt to squeeze; (fig) to oppress

optar [op'tar] vi (elegir) to choose; **~ por** to opt for; **optativo, -a** adj optional

óptico, -a ['optiko, a] adj optic(al) ▷nm/f optician; **óptica** nf optician's (shop); **desde esta óptica** from this point of view

optimismo [opti'mismo] nm optimism; **optimista** nmf optimist

opuesto, -a [o'pwesto, a] adj (contrario) opposite; (antagónico) opposing

oración [ora'θjon] nf (Rel) prayer; (Ling) sentence

orador, a [ora'ðor, a] nm/f (conferenciante) speaker, orator

oral [o'ral] adj oral

orangután [orangu'tan] nm orangutan

orar [o'rar] vi to pray

oratoria [ora'torja] nf oratory

órbita ['orβita] nf orbit

orden ['orðen] nm (gen) order ▷nf (gen) order; (Inform) command; **en ~ de prioridad** in order of priority; **orden del día** agenda

ordenado, -a [orðe'naðo, a] adj (metódico) methodical; (arreglado) orderly

ordenador [orðena'ðor] nm computer; **ordenador central** mainframe computer

ordenar [orðe'nar] vt (mandar) to order; (poner orden) to put in order, arrange; **ordenarse** vr (Rel) to be ordained

ordeñar [orðe'ɲar] vt to milk

ordinario, -a [orði'narjo, a] adj (común) ordinary, usual; (vulgar) vulgar, common

orégano [o'reɣano] nm oregano

oreja [o'rexa] nf ear; (Mecánica) lug, flange

orfanato [orfa'nato] nm orphanage

orfebrería [orfeβre'ria] nf gold/ silver work

orgánico, -a [or'ɣaniko, a] adj organic

organismo [orɣa'nismo] nm (Bio) organism; (Pol) organization

organización [orɣaniθa'θjon] nf organization; **organizar** vt to organize

órgano ['orɣano] nm organ

orgasmo [or'ɣasmo] nm orgasm

orgía [or'xia] nf orgy

orgullo [or'ɣuʎo] nm pride; **orgulloso, -a** adj (gen) proud; (altanero) haughty

orientación [orjenta'θjon] nf (posición) position; (dirección) direction

oriental [orjen'tal] adj eastern; (del Extremo Oriente) oriental

orientar [orjen'tar] vt (situar) to orientate; (señalar) to point; (dirigir) to direct; (guiar) to guide; **orientarse** vr to get one's bearings

oriente [o'rjente] nm east; **el O~ Medio** the Middle East; **el Próximo/ Extremo O~** the Near/Far East

origen [o'rixen] nm origin

original [orixi'nal] adj (nuevo) original; (extraño) odd, strange; **originalidad** nf originality

originar [orixi'nar] vt to start, cause; **originarse** vr to originate; **originario, -a** adj original; **originario de** native of

orilla [o'riʎa] nf (borde) border; (de río) bank; (de bosque, tela) edge; (de mar) shore

orina [o'rina] nf urine; **orinal** nm (chamber) pot; **orinar** vi to urinate; **orinarse** vr to wet o.s.

oro ['oro] nm gold; **oros** nmpl (Naipes) hearts

orquesta [or'kesta] nf orchestra; **orquesta sinfónica** symphony orchestra

orquídea [or'kiðea] nf orchid

ortiga [or'tixa] nf nettle

ortodoxo, -a [orto'ðokso, a] adj orthodox

ortografía [ortoɣra'fia] nf spelling

ortopedia [orto'peðja] nf orthopaedics sg; **ortopédico, -a** adj orthopaedic

oruga [o'ruxa] nf caterpillar

orzuelo [or'θwelo] nm stye

os [os] pron (gen) you; (a vosotros) to you

osa ['osa] nf (she-)bear; **Osa Mayor/ Menor** Great/Little Bear

osadía [osa'ðia] nf daring

osar [o'sar] vi to dare

oscilación [osθila'θjon] nf (movimiento) oscillation; (fluctuación) fluctuation

oscilar [osθi'lar] vi to oscillate; to fluctuate

oscurecer [oskure'θer] vt to darken
▷ vi to grow dark; **oscurecerse** vr to grow o get dark

oscuridad [oskuri'ðað] nf obscurity; (tinieblas) darkness

oscuro, -a [os'kuro, a] adj dark; (fig) obscure; **a oscuras** in the dark

óseo, -a [o'seo, a] adj bone cpd

oso ['oso] nm bear; **oso de peluche** teddy bear; **oso hormiguero** anteater

ostentar [osten'tar] vt (gen) to show; (pey) to flaunt, show off; (poseer) to have, possess

ostión [os'tjon] (MÉX) nm = **ostra**

ostra ['ostra] nf oyster

OTAN ['otan] nf abr (= Organización del Tratado del Atlántico Norte) NATO

otitis [o'titis] nf earache

otoñal [oto'ɲal] adj autumnal

otoño [o'toɲo] nm autumn

otorgar [otor'xar] vt (conceder) to concede; (dar) to grant

otorrino, -a [oto'rrino, a], **otorrinolaringólogo, -a** [otorrinolarin'ɣolovo, a] nm/f ear,

nose and throat specialist

otro, -a ['otro, a] adj 1 (distinto: sg) another; (: pl) other; **con otros amigos** with other o different friends
2 (adicional): **tráigame otro café (más), por favor** can I have another coffee please; **otros diez días más** another ten days
▷ pron 1 **el otro** the other one; **(los) otros** (the) others; **de otro** somebody else's; **que lo haga otro** let somebody else do it
2 (recíproco): **se odian (la) una a (la) otra** they hate one another o each other
3: **otro tanto**: **comer otro tanto** to eat the same o as much again; **recibió una decena de telegramas y otras tantas llamadas** he got about ten telegrams and as many calls

ovación [oβa'θjon] nf ovation

oval [o'βal] adj oval; **ovalado, -a** adj oval; **óvalo** nm oval

ovario [o'βarjo] nm ovary

oveja [o'βexa] nf sheep

overol [oβe'rol] (LAM) nm overalls pl

ovillo [o'βiʎo] nm (de lana) ball of wool

OVNI ['oβni] nm abr (= objeto volante no identificado) UFO

ovulación [oβula'θjon] nf ovulation; **óvulo** nm ovum

oxidación [oksiða'θjon] nf rusting

oxidar [oksi'ðar] vt to rust; **oxidarse** vr to go rusty

óxido [o'ksiðo] nm oxide

oxigenado, -a [oksixe'naðo, a] adj (Quím) oxygenated; (pelo) bleached

oxígeno [o'ksixeno] nm oxygen

oyente [o'jente] nmf listener

oyes etc vb V **oír**

ozono [o'θono] nm ozone

P

pabellón [paβeˈʎon] nm bell tent; (Arq) pavilion; (de hospital etc) block, section; (bandera) flag

pacer [paˈθer] vi to graze

paciencia [paˈθjenθja] nf patience

paciente [paˈθjente] adj, nmf patient

pacificación [paθifikaˈθjon] nf pacification

pacífico, -a [paˈθifiko, a] adj (persona) peaceable; (existencia) peaceful; **el (Océano) P~** the Pacific (Ocean)

pacifista [paθiˈfista] nmf pacifist

pacotilla [pakoˈtiʎa] nf: **de ~** (actor, escritor) third-rate

pactar [pakˈtar] vt to agree to o on ▷ vi to come to an agreement

pacto [ˈpakto] nm (tratado) pact; (acuerdo) agreement

padecer [paðeˈθer] vt (sufrir) to suffer; (soportar) to endure, put up with; **padecimiento** nm suffering

padrastro [paˈðrastro] nm stepfather

padre [ˈpaðre] nm father ▷ adj (fam): **un éxito ~** a tremendous success; **padres** nmpl parents; **padre político** father-in-law

padrino [paˈðrino] nm (Rel) godfather; (tb: **~ de boda**) best man; (fig) sponsor, patron; **padrinos** nmpl godparents

padrón [paˈðron] nm (censo) census, roll

padrote [paˈðrote] nm (MÉX: fam) pimp

paella [paˈeʎa] nf paella, dish of rice with meat, shellfish etc

paga [ˈpaxa] nf (pago) payment; (sueldo) pay, wages pl

pagano, -a [paˈxano, a] adj, nm/f pagan, heathen

pagar [paˈxar] vt to pay; (las compras, crimen) to pay for; (fig: favor) to repay ▷ vi to pay; **~ al contado/a plazos** to pay (in) cash/in instalments

pagaré [paxaˈre] nm I.O.U.

página [ˈpaxina] nf page; **página de inicio** (Inform) home page; **página web** (Inform) web page

pago [ˈpaxo] nm (dinero) payment; **en ~ de** in return for; **pago anticipado/a cuenta/contra reembolso/en especie** advance payment/payment on account/cash on delivery/payment in kind

pág(s). abr (= página(s)) p(p).

pague etc vb V **pagar**

país [paˈis] nm (gen) country; (región) land; **los P~es Bajos** the Low Countries; **el P~ Vasco** the Basque Country

paisaje [paiˈsaxe] nm landscape, scenery

paisano, -a [paiˈsano, a] adj of the same country ▷ nm/f (compatriota) fellow countryman/woman; **vestir de ~** (soldado) to be in civvies; (guardia) to be in plain clothes

paja [ˈpaxa] nf straw; (fig) rubbish (BRIT), trash (US)

pajarita [paxaˈrita] nf (corbata) bow tie

pájaro ['paxaro] nm bird; **pájaro carpintero** woodpecker

pajita [pa'xita] nf (drinking) straw

pala ['pala] nf spade, shovel; (raqueta etc) bat; (: de tenis) racquet; (Culin) slice; **pala mecánica** power shovel

palabra [pa'laβra] nf word; (facultad) (power of) speech; (derecho de hablar) right to speak; **tomar la ~** (en mitin) to take the floor

palabrota [pala'brota] nf swearword

palacio [pa'laθjo] nm palace; (mansión) mansion, large house; **palacio de justicia** courthouse; **palacio municipal** town o city hall

paladar [pala'ðar] nm palate; **paladear** vt to taste

palanca [pa'lanka] nf lever; (fig) pull, influence

palangana [palan'gana] nf washbasin

palco ['palko] nm box

Palestina [pales'tina] nf Palestine; **palestino, -a** nm/f Palestinian

paleta [pa'leta] nf (de pintor) palette; (de albañil) trowel; (de ping-pong) bat; (MÉX, CAM: helado) ice lolly (BRIT), Popsicle® (US)

palidecer [paliðe'θer] vi to turn pale; **palidez** nf paleness; **pálido, -a** adj pale

palillo [pa'liʎo] nm (mondadientes) toothpick; (para comer) chopstick

palito [pa'lito] (RPL) nm (helado) ice lolly (BRIT), Popsicle® (US)

paliza [pa'liθa] nf beating, thrashing

palma ['palma] nf (Anat) palm; (árbol) palm tree; **batir** o **dar ~s** to clap, applaud; **palmada** nf slap; **palmadas** nfpl clapping sg, applause sg

palmar [pal'mar] (fam) vi (tb: **~la**) to die, kick the bucket

palmear [palme'ar] vi to clap

palmera [pal'mera] nf (Bot) palm tree

palmo ['palmo] nm (medida) span; (fig) small amount; **~ a ~** inch by inch

palo ['palo] nm stick; (poste) post; (de tienda de campaña) pole; (mango) handle, shaft; (golpe) blow, hit; (de golf) club; (de béisbol) bat; (Náut) mast; (Naipes) suit

paloma [pa'loma] nf dove, pigeon

palomitas [palo'mitas] nfpl popcorn sg

palpar [pal'par] vt to touch, feel

palpitar [palpi'tar] vi to palpitate; (latir) to beat

palta ['palta] (CS) nf avocado

paludismo [palu'ðismo] nm malaria

pamela [pa'mela] nf picture hat, sun hat

pampa ['pampa] nf pampas, prairie

pan [pan] nm bread; (una barra) loaf; **pan integral** wholemeal (BRIT) o wholewheat (US) bread; **pan rallado** breadcrumbs pl; **pan tostado** (MÉX: tostada) toast

pana ['pana] nf corduroy

panadería [panaðe'ria] nf baker's (shop); **panadero, -a** nm/f baker

Panamá [pana'ma] nm Panama; **panameño, -a** adj Panamanian

pancarta [pan'karta] nf placard, banner

panceta [pan'θeta] (ESP, RPL) nf bacon

pancho [pan'tʃo] (RPL) nm hot dog

pancito [pan'θito] nm (bread) roll

panda ['panda] nm (Zool) panda

pandereta [pande'reta] nf tambourine

pandilla [pan'diʎa] nf set, group; (de criminales) gang; (pey: camarilla) clique

panecillo [pane'θiʎo] (ESP) nm (bread) roll

panel [pa'nel] nm panel; **panel solar** solar panel

panfleto [pan'fleto] nm pamphlet

pánico ['paniko] nm panic

panorama [pano'rama] nm panorama; (vista) view

panqueque [pan'keke] (LAM) nm pancake

pantalla [pan'taʎa] nf (de cine) screen; (de lámpara) lampshade

pantalón [panta'lon] nm trousers; **pantalones** nmpl trousers; **pantalones cortes** shorts

pantano [pan'tano] nm (ciénaga) marsh, swamp; (depósito de agua) reservoir; (fig) jam, difficulty

panteón [pante'on] nm (monumento) pantheon

pantera [pan'tera] nf panther

pantimedias [panti'meðjas] (MÉX) nfpl = **pantis**

pantis ['pantis] nmpl tights (BRIT), pantyhose (US)

pantomima [panto'mima] nf pantomime

pantorrilla [panto'rriʎa] nf calf (of the leg)

pants [pants] (MÉX) nmpl tracksuit (BRIT), sweat suit (US)

pantufla [pan'tufla] nf slipper

panty(s) ['panti(s)] nm(pl) tights (BRIT), pantyhose (US)

panza ['panθa] nf belly, paunch

pañal [pa'ɲal] nm nappy (BRIT), diaper (US); **pañales** nmpl (fig) early stages, infancy sg

paño ['paɲo] nm (tela) cloth; (pedazo de tela) (piece of) cloth; (trapo) duster, rag; **paños menores** underclothes

pañuelo [pa'ɲwelo] nm handkerchief, hanky; (fam: para la cabeza) (head)scarf

papa ['papa] nf (LAM) potato ▷ nm: **el P-** the Pope ▷ nf (LAM: patata) potato; **papas fritas** (LAM) French fries, chips (BRIT); (de bolsa) crisps (BRIT), potato chips (US)

papá [pa'pa] (fam) nm dad(dy), pa (US)

papada [pa'paða] nf double chin

papagayo [papa'gaʝo] nm parrot

papalote [papa'lote] (MÉX, CAM) nm kite

papanatas [papa'natas] (fam) nm inv simpleton

papaya [pa'paʝa] nf papaya

papear [pape'ar] (fam) vt, vi to scoff

papel [pa'pel] nm (material) paper; (hoja de papel) sheet of paper; (Teatro: fig) role; **papel de aluminio** aluminium (BRIT)

o aluminum (US) foil; **papel de arroz/envolver/fumar** rice/wrapping/cigarette paper; **papel de estaño** o **plata** tinfoil; **papel de lija** sandpaper; **papel higiénico** toilet paper; **papel moneda** paper money; **papel secante** blotting paper

papeleo [pape'leo] nm red tape

papelera [pape'lera] nf wastepaper basket; (en la calle) litter bin; **papelera (de reciclaje)** (Inform) wastebasket

papelería [papele'ria] nf stationer's (shop)

papeleta [pape'leta] (ESP) nf (Pol) ballot paper

paperas [pa'peras] nfpl mumps sg

papilla [pa'piʎa] nf (de bebé) baby food

paquete [pa'kete] nm (de cigarrillos etc) packet; (Correos etc) parcel

par [par] adj (igual) like, equal; (Mat) even ▷ nm (de guantes) pair; (de veces) couple; (Pol) peer; (Golf, Com) par; **abrir de par en -** to open wide

para ['para] prep for; **no es - comer** it's not for eating; **decir - sí** to say to o.s.; **¿- qué lo quieres?** what do you want it for?; **se casaron - separarse otra vez** they married only to separate again; **lo tendré - mañana** I'll have it (for) tomorrow; **ir - casa** to go home, head for home; **- profesor es muy estúpido** he's very stupid for a teacher; **¿quién es usted - gritar así?** who are you to shout like that?; **tengo bastante - vivir** I have enough to live on; Vt b **con**

parabién [para'βjen] nm congratulations pl

parábola [pa'raβola] nf parable; (Mat) parabola; **parabólica** nf (tb: **antena parabólica**) satellite dish

parabrisas [para'βrisas] nm inv windscreen (BRIT), windshield (US)

paracaídas [paraka'iðas] nm inv parachute; **paracaidista** nmf parachutist; (Mil) paratrooper

parachoques [para'tʃokes] nm inv

(Auto) bumper; (Mecánica etc) shock absorber

parada [pa'raða] nf stop; (acto) stopping; (de industria) shutdown, stoppage; (lugar) stopping place; **parada de autobús** bus stop; **parada de taxis** taxi stand o rank (BRIT)

paradero [para'ðero] nm stopping-place; (situación) whereabouts

parado, -a [pa'raðo, a] adj (persona) motionless, standing still; (fábrica) closed, at a standstill; (coche) stopped; (LAM: de pie) standing (up); (ESP: sin empleo) unemployed, idle

paradoja [para'ðoxa] nf paradox

parador [para'ðor] nm parador, state-run hotel

paragolpes [para'golpes] (RPL) nm inv (Auto) bumper, fender (US)

paraguas [pa'raɣwas] nm inv umbrella

Paraguay [paraɣ'wai] nm Paraguay; **paraguayo, -a** adj, nm/f Paraguayan

paraíso [para'iso] nm paradise, heaven

paraje [pa'raxe] nm place, spot

paralelo, -a [para'lelo, a] adj parallel

parálisis [pa'ralisis] nf inv paralysis; **paralítico, -a** adj, nm/f paralytic

paralizar [parali'θar] vt to paralyse; **paralizarse** vr to become paralysed; (fig) to come to a standstill

páramo ['paramo] nm bleak plateau

paranoico, -a [para'noiko, a] nm/f paranoiac

parapente [para'pente] nm (deporte) paragliding; (aparato) paraglider

parapléjico, -a [para'plexiko, a] adj, nm/f paraplegic

parar [pa'rar] vt to stop; (golpe) to ward off ▷ vi to stop; **pararse** vr to stop; (LAM: ponerse de pie) to stand up; **ha parado de llover** it has stopped raining; **van a ir a ~ a comisaría** they're going to end up in a police station; **~se** to pay attention to

pararrayos [para'rajos] nm inv

lightning conductor

parásito, -a [pa'rasito, a] nm/f parasite

parcela [par'θela] nf plot, piece of ground

parche ['partʃe] nm (gen) patch

parchís [par'tʃis] nm ludo

parcial [par'θjal] adj (pago) part-; (eclipse) partial; (Jur) prejudiced, biased; (Pol) partisan

parecer [pare'θer] nm (opinión) opinion, view; (aspecto) looks pl ▷ vi (tener apariencia) to seem, look; (asemejarse) to look o seem like; (aparecer, llegar) to appear; **parecerse** vr to look alike, resemble each other; **al ~** apparently; **según parece** evidently, apparently; **~se a** to look like, resemble; **me parece que** I think (that), it seems to me that

parecido, -a [pare'θiðo, a] adj similar ▷ nm similarity, likeness, resemblance; **bien ~** good-looking, nice-looking

pared [pa'reð] nf wall

pareja [pa'rexa] nf (par) pair; (dos personas) couple; (otro: de un par) other one (of a pair); (persona) partner

parentesco [paren'tesko] nm relationship

paréntesis [pa'rentesis] nm inv parenthesis; (en escrito) bracket

parezco etc vb V **parecer**

pariente [pa'rjente] nmf relative, relation

> No confundir **pariente** con la palabra inglesa parent.

parir [pa'rir] vt to give birth to ▷ vi (mujer) to give birth, have a baby

París [pa'ris] n París

parka ['parka] (LAM) nm anorak

parking ['parkin] nm car park (BRIT), parking lot (US)

parlamentar [parlamen'tar] vi to parley

parlamentario, -a [parlamen'tarjo, a] adj parliamentary ▷ nm/f member of parliament

parlamento [parla'mento] nm parliament

parlanchín, -ina [parlan'tʃin, ina] adj indiscreet ▷ nm/f chatterbox

parlar [par'lar] vi to chatter (away)

paro ['paro] nm (huelga) stoppage (of work), strike; (ESP: desempleo) unemployment; (: subsidio) unemployment benefit; **estar en ~** (ESP) to be unemployed; **paro cardíaco** cardiac arrest

parodia [pa'roðja] nf parody; **parodiar** vt to parody

parpadear [parpaðe'ar] vi (ojos) to blink; (luz) to flicker

párpado ['parpaðo] nm eyelid

parque ['parke] nm (lugar verde) park; (MÉX: munición) ammunition; **parque de atracciones** fairground; **parque de bomberos** (ESP) fire station; **parque infantil/temático/zoológico** playground/theme park/zoo

parqué [par'ke] nm parquet (flooring)

parquímetro [par'kimetro] nm parking meter

parra ['parra] nf (grape)vine

párrafo ['parrafo] nm paragraph; **echar un ~** (fam) to have a chat

parranda [pa'rranda] (fam) nf spree, binge

parrilla [pa'rriʎa] nf (Culin) grill; (de coche) grille; **(carne a la) ~** barbecue; **parrillada** nf barbecue

párroco ['parroko] nm parish priest

parroquia [pa'rrokja] nf parish; (iglesia) parish church; (Com) clientele, customers pl; **parroquiano, -a** nm/f parishioner; (Com) client, customer

parte ['parte] nm message; (informe) report ▷ nf (lado, cara) side; (de reparto) share; (Jur) party: **en alguna ~ de Europa** somewhere in Europe; **en o por todas ~s** everywhere; **en gran ~** to a large extent; **la mayor ~ de los españoles** most Spaniards; **de un tiempo a esta ~** for some time past; **de ~ de algn** on sb's behalf; **¿de**

~ de quién? (Tel) who is speaking?; **por ~ de** on the part of; **yo por mi ~** I for my part; **por otra ~** on the other hand; **dar ~** to inform; **tomar ~** to take part; **parte meteorológico** weather forecast o report

participación [partiθipa'θjon] nf (acto) participation, taking part; (parte, Com) share; (de lotería) shared prize; (aviso) notice, notification

participante [partiθi'pante] nmf participant

participar [partiθi'par] vt to notify, inform ▷ vi to take part, participate

partícipe [par'tiθipe] nmf participant

particular [partiku'lar] adj (especial) particular, special; (individual, personal) private, personal ▷ nm (punto, asunto) particular, point; (individuo) individual; **tiene coche ~** he has a car of his own

partida [par'tiða] nf (salida) departure; (Com) entry, item; (juego) game; (grupo de personas) band, group; **mala ~** dirty trick; **partida de nacimiento/matrimonio/defunción** (ESP) birth/marriage/death certificate

partidario, -a [parti'ðarjo, a] adj partisan ▷ nm/f supporter, follower

partido [par'tiðo] nm (Pol) party; (Deporte) game, match; **sacar ~ de** to profit o benefit from; **tomar ~** to take sides

partir [par'tir] vt (dividir) to split, divide; (compartir, distribuir) to share (out), distribute; (romper) to break open, split open; (rebanada) to cut (off) ▷ vi (ponerse en camino) to set off o out; (comenzar) to start (off o out); **partirse** vr to crack o split o break (in two etc); **a ~ de** (starting) from

partitura [parti'tura] nf (Mús) score

parto ['parto] nm birth; (fig) product, creation; **estar de ~** to be in labour

parvulario [parβu'larjo] (ESP) nm nursery school, kindergarten

pasa ['pasa] nf raisin; **pasa de Corinto** currant

pasacintas [pasa'θintas] (LAM) nm cassette player

pasada nf ver **pasado**

pasadizo [pasa'ðiθo] nm (pasillo) passage, corridor; (callejuela) alley

pasado, -a [pa'saðo, a] adj past; (malo: comida, fruta) bad; (muy cocido) overdone; (anticuado) out of date ▷ nm past; ~ **mañana** the day after tomorrow; **el mes** ~ last month

pasador [pasa'ðor] nm (cerrojo) bolt; (de pelo) hair slide; (horquilla) grip

pasaje [pa'saxe] nm (precio) fare; (los pasajeros) passengers pl; (pasillo) passageway

pasajero, -a [pasa'xero, a] adj passing; (situación, estado) temporary; (amor, enfermedad) brief ▷ nm/f passenger

pasamontañas [pasamon'taɲas] nm inv balaclava helmet

pasaporte [pasa'porte] nm passport

pasar [pa'sar] vt to pass; (tiempo) to spend; (desgracias) to suffer, endure; (noticia) to give, pass on; (río) to cross; (barrera) to pass through; (falta) to overlook, tolerate; (contrincante) to surpass, do better than; (coche) to overtake; (Cine) to show; (enfermedad) to give, infect with ▷ vi (gen) to pass; (terminarse) to be over; (ocurrir) to happen; **pasarse** vr (flores) to fade; (comida) to go bad o off; (fig) to overdo it, go too far; ~ **de** to go beyond, exceed; ~ **por** (Auto) to fetch; **lo bien/mal** to have a good/bad time; **¡pase!** come in!; **hacer** ~ to show in; **lo que pasa es que ...** the thing is ...; **~se al enemigo** to go over to the enemy; **se me pasó** I forgot; **no se le pasa nada** he misses nothing; **pase lo que pase** come what may; **¿qué pasa?** what's going on?, what's up?; **¿qué te pasa?** what's wrong?

pasarela [pasa'rela] nf footbridge; (en barco) gangway

pasatiempo [pasa'tjempo] nm pastime, hobby

Pascua ['paskwa] nf (en Semana Santa) Easter; **Pascuas** nfpl Christmas (time); **¡felices ~s!** Merry Christmas!

pase ['pase] nm pass; (Cine) performance, showing

pasear [pase'ar] vt to take for a walk; (exhibir) to parade, show off ▷ vi to walk, go for a walk; **pasearse** vr to walk, go for a walk; ~ **en coche** to go for a drive; **paseo** nm (avenida) avenue; (distancia corta) walk, stroll; **dar un o ir de paseo** to go for a walk; **paseo marítimo** (ESP) promenade

pasillo [pa'siʎo] nm passage, corridor

pasión [pa'sjon] nf passion

pasivo, -a [pa'siβo, a] adj passive; (inactivo) inactive ▷ nm (Com) liabilities pl, debts pl

pasmoso, -a [pas'moso, a] adj amazing, astonishing

paso, -a ['paso, a] adj dried ▷ nm step; (modo de andar) walk; (huella) footprint; (rapidez) speed, pace, rate; (camino accesible) way through, passage; (cruce) crossing; (pasaje) passing, passage; (Geo) pass; (estrecho) strait; **a ese** ~ (fig) at that rate; **salir al** ~ **de** a o to waylay; **estar de** ~ to be passing through; **prohibido el** ~ no entry; **ceda el** ~ give way; **paso a nivel** (Ferro) level-crossing; **paso (de) cebra** (ESP) zebra crossing; **paso de peatones** pedestrian crossing; **paso elevado** flyover

pasota [pa'sota] (ESP: fam) adj, nmf ≈ dropout; **ser un** ~ to be a bit of a dropout; (ser indiferente) not to care about anything

pasta ['pasta] nf paste; (Culin: masa) dough; (: de bizcochos etc) pastry; (fam) dough; **pastas** nfpl (bizcochos) pastries, small cakes; (fideos, espaguetis etc) pasta; **pasta dentífrica o de dientes** toothpaste

pastar [pas'tar] vt, vi to graze

pastel [pas'tel] nm (dulce) cake; (Arte)

pastel; **pastel de carne** meat pie; **pastelería** *nf* cake shop

pastilla [pas'tiʎa] *nf (de jabón, chocolate)* bar; *(píldora)* tablet, pill

pasto ['pasto] *nm (hierba)* grass; *(lugar)* pasture, field; **pastor, a** [pas'tor, a] *nm/f* shepherd/ess ▷ *nm (Rel)* clergyman, minister; **pastor alemán** Alsatian

pata ['pata] *nf (pierna)* leg; *(pie)* foot; *(de muebles)* leg; **~s arriba** upside down; **metedura de ~** *(fam)* gaffe; **meter la ~** *(fam)* to put one's foot in it; **tener buena/mala ~** to be lucky/unlucky; **pata de cabra** *(Tec)* crowbar; **patada** *nf (en el suelo)* stamp

patata [pa'tata] *nf* potato; **patatas fritas** chips, French fries; *(de bolsa)* crisps

paté [pa'te] *nm* pâté

patente [pa'tente] *adj* obvious, evident; *(Com)* patent ▷ *nf* patent

paternal [pater'nal] *adj* fatherly; **paterno, a** *adj* paternal

patético, -a [pa'tetiko, a] *adj* pathetic, moving

patilla [pa'tiʎa] *nf (de gafas)* side(piece); **patillas** *nfpl* sideburns

patín [pa'tin] *nm* skate; *(de trineo)* runner; **patín de ruedas** roller skate; **patinaje** *nm* skating; **patinar** *vi* to skate; *(resbalarse)* to skid, slip; *(fam)* to slip up, blunder

patineta [pati'neta] *nf (MÉX: patinete)* scooter; *(cs: monopatín)* skateboard

patinete [pati'nete] *nm* scooter

patio ['patjo] *nm (de casa)* patio, courtyard; **patio de recreo** playground

pato ['pato] *nm* duck; **pagar el ~** *(fam)* to take the blame, carry the can

patoso, -a [pa'toso, a] *(fam) adj* clumsy

patotero [pato'tero] *(cs) nm* hooligan, lout

patraña [pa'traɲa] *nf* story, fib

patria ['patrja] *nf* native land, mother country

patrimonio [patri'monjo] *nm*

inheritance; *(fig)* heritage

patriota [pa'trjota] *nmf* patriot

patrocinar [patroθi'nar] *vt* to sponsor

patrón, -ona [pa'tron, ona] *nm/f (jefe)* boss, chief, master(mistress); *(propietario)* landlord/lady; *(Rel)* patron saint ▷ *nm (Tec, Costura)* pattern

patronato [patro'nato] *nm* sponsorship; *(acto)* patronage; *(fundación benéfica)* trust, foundation

patrulla [pa'truʎa] *nf* patrol

pausa ['pausa] *nf* pause, break

pauta ['pauta] *nf* line, guide line

pava ['paβa] *(RPL) nf* kettle

pavimento [paβi'mento] *nm (de losa)* pavement, paving

pavo ['paβo] *nm* turkey; **pavo real** peacock

payaso, -a [pa'jaso, a] *nm/f* clown

payo, -a ['pajo, a] *nm/f* non-gipsy

paz [paθ] *nf* peace; *(tranquilidad)* peacefulness, tranquillity; **hacer las paces** to make peace; *(fig)* to make up; **¡déjame en ~!** leave me alone!

PC *nm* PC, personal computer

P.D. *abr (= posdata)* P.S., p.s.

peaje [pe'axe] *nm* toll

peatón [pea'ton] *nm* pedestrian; **peatonal** *adj* pedestrian

peca ['peka] *nf* freckle

pecado [pe'kaðo] *nm* sin; **pecador, a** *adj* sinful ▷ *nm/f* sinner

pecaminoso, -a [pekami'noso, a] *adj* sinful

pecar [pe'kar] *vi (Rel)* to sin; **peca de generoso** he is generous to a fault

pecera [pe'θera] *nf* fish tank; *(redonda)* goldfish bowl

pecho ['petʃo] *nm (Anat)* chest; *(de mujer)* breast; **dar el ~ a** to breast-feed; **tomar algo a ~** to take sth to heart

pechuga [pe'tʃuɣa] *nf* breast

peculiar [peku'ljar] *adj* special, peculiar; *(característico)* typical, characteristic

pedal [pe'ðal] *nm* pedal; **pedalear** *vi* to pedal

pedante [pe'ðante] adj pedantic
▷ nmf pedant

pedazo [pe'ðaθo] nm piece, bit;
hacerse ~s to smash, shatter

pediatra [pe'ðjatra] nmf
paediatrician

pedido [pe'ðiðo] nm (Com) order;
(petición) request

pedir [pe'ðir] vt to ask for, request;
(comida, Com: mandar) to order;
(necesitar) to need, demand, require
▷ vi to ask; **me pidió que cerrara la
puerta** he asked me to shut the door;
¿cuánto piden por el coche? how
much are they asking for the car?

pedo ['peðo] (fam!) nm fart

pega ['peɣa] nf snag; **poner ~s (a)** to
complain (about)

pegadizo, -a [peɣa'ðiθo, a] adj
(Mús) catchy

pegajoso, -a [peɣa'xoso, a] adj
sticky, adhesive

pegamento [peɣa'mento] nm
gum, glue

pegar [pe'ɣar] vt (papel, sellos) to
stick (on); (cartel) to stick up; (coser)
to sew (on); (unir: partes) to join, fix
together; (Comput) to paste; (Med) to
give, infect with; (dar: golpe) to give,
deal ▷ vi (adherirse) to stick, adhere; (ir
juntos: colores) to match, go together;
(golpear) to hit; (quemar: el sol) to strike
hot, burn; **pegarse** vr (gen) to stick;
(dos personas) to hit each other, fight;
(fam): **~ un grito** to let out a yell; **~ un
salto** to jump (with fright); **~ en** to
touch; **~se un tiro** to shoot o.s.

pegatina [peɣa'tina] nf sticker

pegote [pe'ɣote] (fam) nm eyesore,
sight

peinado [pei'naðo] nm hairstyle

peinar [pei'nar] vt to comb; (hacer
estilo) to style; **peinarse** vr to comb
one's hair

peine ['peine] nm comb; **peineta** nf
ornamental comb

p.ej. abr (= por ejemplo) e.g.

Pekín [pe'kin] n Pekin(g)

pelado, -a [pe'laðo, a] adj (fruta,
patata etc) peeled; (cabeza) shorn;
(campo, fig) bare; (fam: sin dinero) broke

pelar [pe'lar] vt (fruta, patatas etc) to
peel; (cortar el pelo a) to cut the hair of;
(quitar la piel: animal) to skin; **pelarse** vr
(la piel) to peel off; **voy a ~me** I'm going
to get my hair cut

peldaño [pel'daɲo] nm step

pelea [pe'lea] nf (lucha) fight;
(discusión) quarrel, row; **peleado, -a**
[pele'aðo, a] adj: **estar peleado (con
algn)** to have fallen out (with sb);
pelear [pe'lear] vi to fight; **pelearse**
vr to fight; (reñirse) to fall out, quarrel

pelela [pe'lela] (cs) nf potty

peletería [pelete'ria] nf furrier's,
fur shop

pelícano [pe'likano] nm pelican

película [pe'likula] nf film; (cobertura
ligera) thin covering; (Foto: rollo) roll
o reel of film; **película de dibujos
(animados)/del oeste** cartoon/
western

peligro [pe'liɣro] nm danger; (riesgo)
risk; **correr ~ de** to run the risk of;
peligroso, -a adj dangerous; risky

pelirrojo, -a [peli'rroxo, a] adj red-
haired, red-headed ▷ nm/f redhead

pellejo [pe'ʎexo] nm (de animal)
skin, hide

pellizcar [peʎiθ'kar] vt to pinch, nip

pelma ['pelma], **pelmazo** [pel'maθo] nmf (in
the neck)

pelmazo [pel'maθo] (fam) nm =
pelma

pelo ['pelo] nm (cabellos) hair;
(de barba, bigote) whisker; (de
animal: pellejo) hair, fur, coat; **venir al
~** to be exactly what one needs; **un
hombre de ~ en pecho** a brave man;
por los ~s by the skin of one's teeth; **no
tener ~ s en la lengua** to be outspoken,
not to mince one's words; **con ~ y
señales** in minute detail; **tomar el ~ a
algn** to pull sb's leg

pelota [pe'lota] nf ball; **en ~** stark
naked; **hacer la ~ (a algn)** (ESP: fam) to

creep (to sb); **pelota vasca** pelota

pelotón [pelo'ton] nm (Mil) squad, detachment

peluca [pe'luka] nf wig

peluche [pe'lutʃe] nm: **oso/muñeco de ~** teddy bear/soft toy

peludo, -a [pe'luðo, a] adj hairy, shaggy

peluquería [peluke'ria] nf hairdresser's; **peluquero, -a** nm/f hairdresser

pelusa [pe'lusa] nf (Bot) down; (en tela) fluff

pena ['pena] nf (congoja) grief, sadness; (remordimiento) regret; (dificultad) trouble; (dolor) pain; (Jur) sentence; **merecer o valer la ~** to be worthwhile; **a duras ~s** with great difficulty; **¡qué ~!** what a shame!; **pena capital** capital punishment; **pena de muerte** death penalty

penal [pe'nal] adj penal ▷ nm (cárcel) prison

penalidad [penali'ðað] nf (problema, dificultad) trouble, hardship; (Jur) penalty, punishment; **penalidades** nfpl trouble sg, hardship sg

penalti [pe'nalti] nm = **penalty**

penalty [pe'nalti] (pl **~s o penalties**) nm penalty (kick)

pendiente [pen'djente] adj pending, unsettled ▷ nm earring ▷ nf hill, slope

pene ['pene] nm penis

penetrante [pene'trante] adj (herida) deep; (persona, arma) sharp; (sonido) penetrating, piercing; (mirada) searching; (viento, ironía) biting

penetrar [pene'trar] vt to penetrate, pierce; (entender) to grasp ▷ vi to penetrate, go in; (entrar) to enter, go in; (líquido) to soak in; (fig) to pierce

penicilina [peniθi'lina] nf penicillin

península [pe'ninsula] nf peninsula; **peninsular** adj peninsular

penique [pe'nike] nm penny

penitencia [peni'tenθja] nf penance

penoso, -a [pe'noso, a] adj (lamentable) distressing; (difícil)

arduous, difficult

pensador, a [pensa'ðor, a] nm/f thinker

pensamiento [pensa'mjento] nm thought; (mente) mind; (idea) idea

pensar [pen'sar] vt to think; (considerar) to think over, think out; (proponerse) to intend, plan; (imaginarse) to think up, invent ▷ vi to think; **~ en** to aim at, aspire to; **pensativo, -a** adj thoughtful, pensive

pensión [pen'sjon] nf (casa) boarding o guest house; (dinero) pension; (cama y comida) board and lodging; **media ~** half-board; **pensión completa** full board; **pensionista** nmf (jubilado) (old-age) pensioner; (huésped) lodger

penúltimo, -a [pe'nultimo, a] adj penultimate, last but one

penumbra [pe'numbra] nf half-light

peña ['pena] nf (roca) rock; (cuesta) cliff, crag; (grupo) stone, circle; (LAM: club) folk club

peñasco [pe'nasko] nm large rock, boulder

peñón [pe'non] nm wall of rock; **el P~** the Rock (of Gibraltar)

peón [pe'on] nm labourer; (LAM Agr) farm labourer, farmhand; (Ajedrez) pawn

peonza [pe'onθa] nf spinning top

peor [pe'or] adj (comparativo) worse; (superlativo) worst ▷ adv worse; worst; **de mal en ~** to go from bad to worse

pepinillo [pepi'niʎo] nm gherkin

pepino [pe'pino] nm cucumber; **(no) me importa un ~** I don't care one bit

pepita [pe'pita] nf (Bot) pip; (Minería) nugget

pepito [pe'pito] (ESP) nm (tb: **~ de ternera**) steak sandwich

pequeño, -a [pe'keno, a] adj small, little

pera ['pera] nf pear; **peral** nm pear tree

percance [per'kanθe] nm setback, misfortune

percatarse [perka'tarse] vr: **~ de** to

notice, take note of
percebe [per'θeβe] nm barnacle
percepción [perθep'θjon] nf (vista)
perception; (idea) notion, idea
percha ['pertʃa] nf (coat)hanger;
(ganchos) coat hooks pl; (de ave) perch
percibir [perθi'βir] vt to perceive,
notice; (Com) to earn, get
percusión [perku'sjon] nf
percussion
perdedor, a [perðe'ðor, a] adj losing
▷ nm/f loser
perder [per'ðer] vt to lose; (tiempo,
palabras) to waste; (oportunidad) to
lose, miss; (tren) to miss ▷ vi to lose;
perderse vr (extraviarse) to get lost;
(desaparecer) to disappear, be lost; (la
vista) to view; (arruinarse) to be ruined; **echar a
~** (comida) to spoil, ruin; (oportunidad)
to waste
pérdida ['perðiða] nf loss; (de tiempo)
waste; **pérdidas** nfpl (Com) losses
perdido, -a [per'ðiðo, a] adj lost
perdiz [per'ðiθ] nf partridge
perdón [per'ðon] nm (disculpa)
pardon, forgiveness; (clemencia) mercy;
¡~! sorry!, I beg your pardon!; **perdonar**
vt to pardon, forgive; (la vida) to spare;
(excusar) to exempt, excuse; **¡perdone
(usted)!** sorry!, I beg your pardon!
perecedero, -a [pereθe'ðero, a] adj
perishable
perecer [pere'θer] vi to perish, die
peregrinación [perexrina'θjon] nf
(Rel) pilgrimage
peregrino, -a [pere'ɣrino, a] adj
(idea) strange, absurd ▷ nm/f pilgrim
perejil [pere'xil] nm parsley
perenne [pe'renne] adj everlasting,
perennial
pereza [pe'reθa] nf laziness, idleness;
perezoso, -a adj lazy, idle
perfección [perfek'θjon] nf
perfection; **perfeccionar** vt to
perfect; (mejorar) to improve; (acabar) to
complete, finish
perfecto, -a [per'fekto, a] adj
perfect; (total) complete

perfil [per'fil] nm profile; (contorno)
silhouette, outline; (Arq) (cross)
section; **perfiles** nmpl features
perforación [perfora'θjon] nf
perforation; (con taladro) drilling;
perforadora nf punch
perforar [perfo'rar] vt to perforate;
(agujero) to drill, bore; (papel) to punch a
hole in ▷ vi to drill, bore
perfume [per'fume] nm perfume,
scent
periferia [peri'ferja] nf periphery; (de
ciudad) outskirts pl
periférico [peri'feriko] (LAM) nm ring
road (BRIT), beltway (US)
perilla [pe'riʎa] nf (barba) goatee;
(LAM: de puerta) doorknob, door handle
perímetro [pe'rimetro] nm
perimeter
periódico, -a [pe'rjoðiko, a] adj
periodic(al) ▷ nm newspaper
periodismo [perjo'ðismo] nm
journalism; **periodista** nmf journalist
periodo [pe'rjoðo] nm period
período [pe'rioðo] nm = **periodo**
periquito [peri'kito] nm budgerigar,
budgie
perito, -a [pe'rito, a] adj (experto)
expert; (diestro) skilled, skilful
▷ nm/f expert; skilled worker; (técnico)
technician
perjudicar [perxuði'kar] vt (gen)
to damage, harm; **perjudicial** adj
damaging, harmful; (en detrimento)
detrimental; **perjuicio** nm damage,
harm
perjurar [perxu'rar] vi to commit
perjury
perla ['perla] nf pearl; **me viene de ~s**
it suits me fine
permanecer [permane'θer] vi
(quedarse) to stay, remain; (seguir) to
continue to be
permanente [perma'nente] adj
permanent, constant ▷ nf perm wave
permiso [per'miso] nm permission;
(licencia) permit, licence; **con ~** excuse
me; **estar de ~** (Mil) to be on leave;

permiso de conducir driving licence (BRIT); driver's license (US); **permiso por enfermedad** (LAM) sick leave

permitir [permi'tir] vt to permit, allow

pernera [per'nera] nf trouser leg

pero ['pero] conj but; (aún) yet ▷ nm (defecto) flaw, defect; (reparo) objection

perpendicular [perpendiku'lar] adj perpendicular

perpetuo, -a [per'petwo, a] adj perpetual

perplejo, -a [per'plexo, a] adj perplexed, bewildered

perra ['perra] nf (Zool) bitch; **estar sin una ~** (ESP: fam) to be flat broke

perrera [pe'rrera] nf kennel

perrito [pe'rrito] nm (tb: **~ caliente**) hot dog

perro ['perro] nm dog

persa ['persa] adj, nmf Persian

persecución [perseku'θjon] nf pursuit, chase; (Rel, Pol) persecution

perseguir [perse'xir] vt to pursue, hunt; (cortejar) to chase after; (molestar) to pester, annoy; (Rel, Pol) to persecute

persiana [per'sjana] nf (Venetian) blind

persistente [persis'tente] adj persistent

persistir [persis'tir] vi to persist

persona [per'sona] nf person; **persona mayor** elderly person

personaje [perso'naxe] nm important person, celebrity; (Teatro etc) character

personal [perso'nal] adj (particular) personal; (para una persona) single, for one person ▷ nm personnel, staff; **personalidad** nf personality

personarse [perso'narse] vr to appear in person

personificar [personifi'kar] vt to personify

perspectiva [perspek'tiβa] nf perspective; (vista, panorama) view, panorama; (posibilidad futura) outlook, prospect

persuadir [perswa'ðir] vt (gen) to persuade; (convencer) to convince; **persuadirse** vr to become convinced; **persuasión** nf persuasion

pertenecer [pertene'θer] vi to belong; (fig) to concern; **perteneciente** adj: **perteneciente a** belonging to; **pertenencia** nf ownership; **pertenencias** nfpl (bienes) possessions, property sg

pertenezca etc vb V **pertenecer**

pértiga ['pertixa] nf: **salto de ~** pole vault

pertinente [perti'nente] adj relevant, pertinent; (apropiado) appropriate; **~ a** concerning, relevant to

perturbación [perturβa'θjon] nf (Pol) disturbance; (Med) upset, disturbance

Perú [pe'ru] nm Peru; **peruano, -a** adj, nm/f Peruvian

perversión [perβer'sjon] nf perversion; **perverso, -a** adj perverse; (depravado) depraved

pervertido, -a [perβer'tiðo, a] adj perverted ▷ nm/f pervert

pervertir [perβer'tir] vt to pervert, corrupt

pesa ['pesa] nf weight; (Deporte) shot

pesadez [pesa'ðeθ] nf (peso) heaviness; (lentitud) slowness; (aburrimiento) tediousness

pesadilla [pesa'ðiʎa] nf nightmare, bad dream

pesado, -a [pe'saðo, a] adj heavy; (lento) slow; (difícil, duro) tough, hard; (aburrido) boring, tedious; (tiempo) sultry

pésame ['pesame] nm expression of condolence, message of sympathy; **dar el ~** to express one's condolences

pesar [pe'sar] vt to weigh ▷ vi to weigh; (ser pesado) to weigh a lot, be heavy; (fig: opinión) to carry weight; **no pesa mucho** it's not very heavy ▷ nm (arrepentimiento) regret; (pena) grief, sorrow; **a ~ de o pese a (que)** in spite of, despite

pesca ['peska] nf (acto) fishing; (lo pescado) catch; **ir de ~** to go fishing

pescadería [peskaðe'ria] nf fish shop, fishmonger's (BRIT)

pescadilla [peska'ðiʎa] nf whiting

pescado [pes'kaðo] nm fish

pescador, a [peska'ðor, a] nm/f fisherman/woman

pescar [pes'kar] vt (tomar) to catch; (intentar tomar) to fish for; (conseguir: trabajo) to manage to get ▷ vi to fish, go fishing

pesebre [pe'seβre] nm manger

peseta [pe'seta] nf (Hist) peseta

pesimista [pesi'mista] adj pessimistic ▷ nmf pessimist

pésimo, -a ['pesimo, a] adj awful, dreadful

peso ['peso] nm weight; (balanza) scales pl; (moneda) peso; **vender al ~** to sell by weight; **peso bruto/neto** gross/net weight; **peso pesado/ pluma** heavyweight/featherweight

pesquero, -a [pes'kero, a] adj fishing cpd

pestaña [pes'taɲa] nf (Anat) eyelash; (borde) rim

peste ['peste] nf plague; (mal olor) stink, stench

pesticida [pesti'θiða] nm pesticide

pestillo [pes'tiʎo] nm (cerrojo) bolt; (picaporte) door handle

petaca [pe'taka] nf (de cigarros) cigarette case; (de pipa) tobacco pouch; (MÉX: maleta) suitcase

pétalo ['petalo] nm petal

petardo [pe'tarðo] nm firework, firecracker

petición [peti'θjon] nf (pedido) request, plea; (memorial) petition; (Jur) plea

peto ['peto] (ESP) nm dungarees pl, overalls pl (US)

petróleo [pe'troleo] nm oil, petroleum; **petrolero, -a** adj petroleum cpd ▷ nm (oil) tanker

peyorativo, -a [pejora'tiβo, a] adj pejorative

pez [peθ] nm fish; **pez espada** swordfish

pezón [pe'θon] nm teat, nipple

pezuña [pe'θuɲa] nf hoof

pianista [pja'nista] nmf pianist

piano ['pjano] nm piano

piar [pjar] vi to cheep

pibe, -a ['piβe, a] (RPL) nm/f boy/girl

picadero [pika'ðero] nm riding school

picadillo [pika'ðiʎo] nm mince, minced meat

picado, -a [pi'kaðo, a] adj pricked, punctured; (Culin) minced, chopped; (mar) choppy; (diente) bad; (tabaco) cut; (enfadado) cross

picador [pika'ðor] nm (Taur) picador; (minero) faceworker

picadura [pika'ðura] nf (pinchazo) puncture; (de abeja) sting; (de mosquito) bite; (tabaco picado) cut tobacco

picante [pi'kante] adj hot; (comentario, chiste) racy, spicy

picaporte [pika'porte] nm (manija) doorhandle; (pestillo) latch

picar [pi'kar] vt (agujerear, perforar) to prick, puncture; (abeja) to sting; (mosquito, serpiente) to bite; (Culin) to mince, chop; (incitar) to incite, goad; (dañar, irritar) to annoy, bother; (quemar: lengua) to burn, sting ▷ vi (pez) to bite, take the bait; (sol) to burn, scorch; (abeja, Med) to sting; (mosquito) to bite; **picarse** vr (agriarse) to turn sour, go off; (ofenderse) to take offence

picardía [pikar'ðia] nf villainy; (astucia) slyness, craftiness; (una picardía) dirty trick; (palabra) rude/bad word o expression

pícaro, -a ['pikaro, a] adj (malicioso) villainous; (travieso) mischievous ▷ nm (astuto) crafty sort; (sinvergüenza) rascal, scoundrel

pichi ['pitʃi] (ESP) nm pinafore dress (BRIT), jumper (US)

pichón [pi'tʃon] nm young pigeon

pico ['piko] nm (de ave) beak; (punta)

sharp point; (Tec) pick, pickaxe; (Geo) peak, summit; **y ~ and a bit; las seis y ~ six and a bit**

picor [pi'kor] nm itch

picoso, -a [pi'koso, a] (MÉX) adj (comida) hot

picudo, -a [pi'kuðo, a] adj pointed, with a point

pidió etc vb V **pedir**

pido etc vb V **pedir**

pie [pje] (pl **~s**) nm foot; (fig: motivo) motive, basis; (: fundamento) foothold; **ir a ~** to go on foot, walk; **estar de ~** to be standing (up); **ponerse de ~** to stand up; **de ~s a cabeza** from top to bottom; **al ~ de la letra** (citar) literally, verbatim; (copiar) exactly, word for word; **en ~ de guerra** on a war footing; **dar ~ a** to give cause for; **hacer ~** (en el agua) to touch (the) bottom

piedad [pje'ðað] nf (lástima) pity, compassion; (clemencia) mercy; (devoción) piety, devotion

piedra ['pjeðra] nf stone; (roca) rock; (de mechero) flint; (Meteorología) hailstone; **piedra preciosa** precious stone

piel [pjel] nf (Anat) skin; (Zool) skin, hide, fur; (cuero) leather; (Bot) skin, peel

pienso etc vb V **pensar**

pierdo etc vb V **perder**

pierna ['pjerna] nf leg

pieza ['pjeθa] nf piece; (habitación) room; **pieza de recambio o repuesto** spare (part)

pigmeo, -a [pix'meo, a] adj, nm/f pigmy

pijama [pi'xama] nm pyjamas pl (BRIT), pajamas pl (US)

pila ['pila] nf (Elec) battery; (montón) heap, pile; (lavabo) sink

píldora ['pildora] nf pill; **la ~ (anticonceptiva)** the (contraceptive) pill

pileta [pi'leta] (RPL) nf (fregadero) (kitchen) sink; (piscina) swimming pool

pillar [pi'ʎar] vt (saquear) to pillage, plunder; (fam: coger) to catch; (: agarrar)

to grasp, seize; (: entender) to grasp, catch on to; **pillarse** vr: **~se un dedo con la puerta** to catch one's finger in the door

pillo, -a ['piʎo, a] adj villainous; (astuto) sly, crafty ▷ nm/f rascal, rogue, scoundrel

piloto [pi'loto] nm pilot; (de aparato) (pilot) light; (Auto: luz) tail o rear light; (: conductor) driver; **piloto automático** automatic pilot

pimentón [pimen'ton] nm paprika

pimienta [pi'mjenta] nf pepper

pimiento [pi'mjento] nm pepper, pimiento

pin [pin] (pl **~s**) nm badge

pinacoteca [pinako'teka] nf art gallery

pinar [pi'nar] nm pine forest (BRIT), pine grove (US)

pincel [pin'θel] nm paintbrush

pinchadiscos [pintʃa'ðiskos] (ESP) nmf inv disc-jockey, DJ

pinchar [pin'tʃar] vt (perforar) to prick, pierce; (neumático) to puncture; (fig: incitar) to prod; (Inform) to click

pinchazo [pin'tʃaθo] nm (perforación) prick; (de neumático) puncture; (fig) prod

pincho ['pintʃo] nm savoury (snack); **pincho de tortilla** small slice of omelette; **pincho moruno** shish kebab

ping-pong ['piŋ'pon] nm table tennis

pingüino [piŋ'gwino] nm penguin

pino ['pino] nm pine (tree)

pinta ['pinta] nf spot; (de líquidos) spot, drop; (aspecto) appearance, look(s) (pl); (pintado, -a adj spotted; (de colores) colourful; **pintadas** nfpl graffiti sg

pintalabios [pinta'laβjos] nm inv lipstick

pintar [pin'tar] vt to paint ▷ vi to paint; (fam) to count, be important; **pintarse** vr to put on make-up

pintor, a [pin'tor, a] nm/f painter

pintoresco, -a [pinto'resko, a] adj picturesque

pintura [pin'tura] *nf* painting; **pintura al óleo** oil painting

pinza [pin'θa] *nf* (Zool) claw; (para colgar ropa) clothes peg; (Tec) pincers *pl*; **pinzas** *nfpl* (para depilar etc) tweezers *pl*

piña ['piɲa] *nf* (de pino) pine cone; (fruta) pineapple; (fig) group

piñata [pi'ɲata] *nf* container hung up at parties to be beaten with sticks until sweets or presents fall out

● **PIÑATA**

● **Piñata** is a very popular party
● game in Mexico. The **piñata** itself
● is a hollow figure made of papier
● maché or, traditionally, from
● adobe, in the shape of an object,
● a star, a person or an animal. It is
● filled with either sweets and toys,
● or fruit and yam beans. The game
● consists of hanging the **piñata**
● from the ceiling, and beating it
● with a stick, blindfolded, until it
● breaks and the presents fall out

piñón [pi'ɲon] *nm* (fruto) pine nut; (Tec) pinion

pío, -a ['pio, a] *adj* (devoto) pious, devout; (misericordioso) merciful

piojo ['pjoxo] *nm* louse

pipa ['pipa] *nf* pipe; **pipas** *nfpl* (Bot) (edible) sunflower seeds

pipí [pi'pi] (fam) *nm*: **hacer ~** to have a wee(-wee) (BRIT), have to go (wee-wee) (US)

pique [pi'ke] *nm* (resentimiento) pique, resentment; (rivalidad) rivalry, competition; **irse a ~** to sink; (esperanza, familia) to be ruined

piqueta [pi'keta] *nf* pick(axe)

piquete [pi'kete] *nm* (Mil) squad, party; (de obreros) picket; (MÉX: de insecto) bite; **piquetear** (LAM) *vt* to picket

pirado, -a [pi'raðo, a] (fam) *adj* round the bend ▷ *nm/f* nutter

piragua [pi'raɣwa] *nf* canoe; **piragüismo** *nm* canoeing

pirámide [pi'ramiðe] *nf* pyramid

pirata [pi'rata] *adj, nm* pirate; **pirata informático** hacker

Pirineo(s) [piri'neo(s)] *nm(pl)* Pyrenees *pl*

pirómano, -a [pi'romano, a] *nm/f* (Med, Jur) arsonist

piropo [pi'ropo] *nm* compliment, (piece of) flattery

pirueta [pi'rweta] *nf* pirouette

piruleta [piru'leta] (ESP) *nf* lollipop

pis [pis] (fam) *nm* pee, piss; **hacer ~** to have a pee; (para niños) to wee-wee

pisada [pi'saða] *nf* (paso) footstep; (huella) footprint

pisar [pi'sar] *vt* (caminar sobre) to walk on, tread on; (apretar con el pie) to press; (fig) to trample on, walk all over ▷ *vi* to tread, step, walk

piscina [pis'θina] *nf* swimming pool

Piscis ['pisθis] *nm* Pisces

piso ['piso] *nm* (suelo, planta) floor; (ESP: apartamento) flat (BRIT), apartment; **primer ~** (ESP) first floor; (LAM: planta baja) ground floor

pisotear [pisote'ar] *vt* to trample on o underfoot

pista ['pista] *nf* track, trail; (indicio) clue; **pista de aterrizaje** runway; **pista de baile** dance floor; **pista de hielo** ice rink; **pista de tenis** (ESP) tennis court

pistola [pis'tola] *nf* pistol; (Tec) spray-gun

pistón [pis'ton] *nm* (Tec) piston; (Mús) key

pitar [pi'tar] *vt* (silbato) to blow; (rechiflar) to whistle at, boo ▷ *vi* to whistle; (Auto) to sound o toot one's horn; (LAM: fumar) to smoke

pitillo [pi'tiʎo] *nm* cigarette

pito ['pito] *nm* whistle; (de coche) horn

pitón [pi'ton] *nm* (Zool) python

pitonisa [pito'nisa] *nf* fortune-teller

pitorreo [pito'rreo] *nm* joke; **estar de ~** to be joking

píxel ['piksel] (pl **pixels** or **~es**) *nm*

pixel

piyama [pi'jama] (LAM) nm pyjamas pl (BRIT), pajamas pl (US)

pizarra [pi'θarra] nf (piedra) slate; (ESP: encerado) blackboard; **pizarra blanca** whiteboard; **pizarra interactiva** interactive whiteboard

pizarrón [piθa'rron] (LAM) nm blackboard

pizca ['piθka] nf pinch, spot; (fig) spot, speck; **ni ~** not a bit

placa ['plaka] nf plate; (distintivo) badge, insignia; **placa de matrícula** (LAM) number plate

placard [pla'kar] (RPL) nm cupboard

placer [pla'θer] nm pleasure ▷ vt to please

plaga ['plaɣa] nf pest; (Med) plague; (abundancia) abundance

plagio ['plaxjo] nm plagiarism

plan [plan] nm (esquema, proyecto) plan; (idea, intento) idea, intention; **tener un ~** (fam) to have a date; **tener un ~** (fam) to have an affair; **en ~ económico** (fam) on the cheap; **vamos en ~ de turismo** we're going as tourists; **si te pones en ese ~ …** if that's your attitude …

plana ['plana] nf sheet (of paper), page; (Tec) trowel; **en primera ~** on the front page

plancha ['plantʃa] nf (para planchar) iron; (rótulo) plate, sheet; (Náut) gangway; **a la ~** (Culin) grilled; **planchar** vt to iron ▷ vi to do the ironing

planear [plane'ar] vt to plan ▷ vi to glide

planeta [pla'neta] nm planet

plano, -a ['plano, a] adj flat, level, even ▷ nm (Mat, Tec) plane; (Foto) shot; (Arq) plan; (Geo) map; (de ciudad) map, street plan; **primer ~** close-up

planta ['planta] nf (Bot, Tec) plant; (Anat) sole of the foot, foot; (piso) floor; (LAM: personal) staff; **planta baja** ground floor

plantar [plan'tar] vt (Bot) to plant;

(levantar) to erect, set up; **plantarse** vr to stand firm; **~ a algn en la calle** to throw sb out; **dejar plantado a algn** (fam) to stand sb up

plantear [plante'ar] vt (problema) to pose; (dificultad) to raise

plantilla [plan'tiʎa] nf (de zapato) insole; (personal) personnel; **ser de ~** (ESP) to be on the staff

plantón [plan'ton] nm (Mil) guard, sentry; (fam) long wait; **dar (un) ~ a algn** to stand sb up

plasta ['plasta] (ESP: fam) adj inv boring ▷ nmf bore

plástico, -a ['plastiko, a] adj plastic ▷ nm plastic

Plastilina ['plasti'lina] nf Plasticine®

plata ['plata] nf (metal) silver; (cosas hechas de plata) silverware; (cs: dinero) cash, dough

plataforma [plata'forma] nf platform; **plataforma de lanzamiento/perforación** launch(ing) pad/drilling rig

plátano ['platano] nm (fruta) banana; (árbol) plane tree; banana tree

platea [pla'tea] nf (Teatro) pit

plática [pla'tika] nf talk, chat; **platicar** vi to talk, chat

platillo [pla'tiʎo] nm saucer; **platillos** nmpl (Mús) cymbals; **platillo volante** flying saucer

platino [pla'tino] nm platinum; **platinos** nmpl (Auto) contact points

plato ['plato] nm plate, dish; (parte de comida) course; (comida) dish; **primer ~** first course; **plato combinado** set main course (served on one plate); **plato fuerte** main course

playa ['plaja] nf beach; (costa) seaside; **playa de estacionamiento** (cs) car park (BRIT), parking lot (US)

playera [pla'jera] nf (MÉX: camiseta) T-shirt; **playeras** nfpl (zapatos) canvas shoes

plaza [pla'θa] nf square; (mercado) market(place); (sitio) room, space; (de *vehículo)* seat, place; *(colocación)* post, job; **plaza de toros** bullring

plazo ['plaθo] *nm (lapso de tiempo)* time, period; *(fecha de vencimiento)* expiry date; *(pago parcial)* instalment; **a corto/largo ~** short-/long-term; **comprar algo a ~s** to buy sth on hire purchase *(BRIT)* o on time *(US)*

plazoleta [plaθo'leta] *nf* small square

plebeyo, -a [ple'βejo, a] *adj* plebeian; *(pey)* coarse, common

plegable [ple'xaβle] *adj* collapsible; *(silla)* folding

pleito ['pleito] *nm (Jur)* lawsuit, case; *(fig)* dispute, feud

plenitud [pleni'tuð] *nf* plenitude, fullness; *(abundancia)* abundance

pleno, -a ['pleno, a] *adj* full; *(completo)* complete ▷ *nm* plenum; **en ~ día** in broad daylight; **en ~ verano** at the height of summer; **en plena cara** full in the face

pliego *etc* ['pljexo] *vb* V **plegar**
▷ *nm (hoja)* sheet (of paper); *(carta)* sealed letter/document; **pliego de condiciones** details *pl*, specifications *pl*

pliegue *etc* ['pljexe] *vb* V **plegar** ▷ *nm* fold, crease; *(de vestido)* pleat

plomería [plome'ria] *(LAM) nf* plumbing; **plomero** *(LAM) nm* plumber

plomo ['plomo] *nm (metal)* lead; *(Elec)* fuse; **sin ~** unleaded

pluma ['pluma] *nf* feather; *(para escribir)*: **~ (estilográfica)** ink pen; **~ fuente** *(LAM)* fountain pen

plumero [plu'mero] *nm (para el polvo)* feather duster

plumón [plu'mon] *nm (de ave)* down

plural [plu'ral] *adj* plural

pluriempleo [pluriem'pleo] *nm* having more than one job

plus [plus] *nm* bonus

población [poβla'θjon] *nf* population; *(pueblo, ciudad)* town, city

poblado, -a [po'βlaðo, a] *adj* inhabited ▷ *nm (aldea)* village; *(pueblo*

(small) town; **densamente ~** densely populated

poblador, a [poβla'ðor, a] *nm/f* settler, colonist

pobre ['poβre] *adj* poor ▷ *nmf* poor person; **pobreza** *nf* poverty

pocilga [po'θilxa] *nf* pigsty

○ **PALABRA CLAVE**

poco, -a ['poko, a] *adj* 1 *(sg)* little, not much; **poco tiempo** little o not much time; **de poco interés** of little interest, not very interesting; **poca cosa** not much
2 *(pl)* few, not many; **unos pocos** a few, some; **pocos niños comen lo que les conviene** few children eat what they should
▷ *adv* 1 little, not much; **cuesta poco** it doesn't cost much
2 *(+ adj: negativo, antónimo)*: **poco amable/inteligente** not very nice/intelligent
3: **por poco me caigo** I almost fell
4: **a poco: a poco de haberse casado** shortly after getting married
5: **poco a poco** little by little
▷ *nm* a little, a bit; **un poco triste/de dinero** a little sad/money

podar [po'ðar] *vt* to prune

○ **PALABRA CLAVE**

poder [po'ðer] *vi* 1 *(tener capacidad)* can, be able to; **no puedo hacerlo** I can't do it, I'm unable to do it
2 *(tener permiso)* can, may, be allowed to; **¿se puede?** may I o we)?; **puedes irte ahora** you may go now; **no se puede fumar en este hospital** smoking is not allowed in this hospital
3 *(tener posibilidad)* may, might, could; **puede llegar mañana** he may o might arrive tomorrow; **pudiste haberte hecho daño** you might o could have

hurt yourself; **¡podías habérmelo dicho antes!** you might have told me before!

4: **puede ser** perhaps; **puede ser que lo sepa Tomás** Tomás may o might know

5: **¡no puedo más!** I've had enough!; **es tonto a más no poder** he's as stupid as they come

6: **poder con: no puedo con este crío** this kid's too much for me
▷ *nm* power; **detentar** o **ocupar** o **estar en el poder** to be in power; **poder adquisitivo/ejecutivo/ legislativo/judicial** purchasing/executive/ legislative power; **poder judicial** judiciary

poderoso, -a [poðeˈroso, a] *adj (político, país)* powerful

podio [ˈpoðjo] *nm (Deporte)* podium

podium [ˈpoðjum] = **podio**

podrido, -a [poˈðriðo, a] *adj* rotten, bad; *(fig)* rotten, corrupt

podrir [poˈðrir] = **pudrir**

poema [poˈema] *nm* poem

poesía [poeˈsia] *nf* poetry

poeta [poˈeta] *nmf* poet; **poético, -a** *adj* poetic(al)

poetisa [poeˈtisa] *nf (woman)* poet

póker [ˈpoker] *nm* poker

polaco, -a [poˈlako, a] *adj* Polish
▷ *nm/f* Pole

polar [poˈlar] *adj* polar

polea [poˈlea] *nf* pulley

polémica [poˈlemika] *nf* polemics *sg; (una polémica)* controversy, polemic

polen [ˈpolen] *nm* pollen

policía [poliˈθia] *nmf* policeman/ woman ▷ *nf* police; **policíaco, -a** *adj* police *cpd;* **novela policíaca** detective story; **policial** *adj* police *cpd*

polideportivo [poliðeporˈtiβo] *nm* sports centre o complex

polígono [poˈliɣono] *nm (Mat)* polygon; **polígono industrial** (ESP) industrial estate

polilla [poˈliʎa] *nf* moth

polio [ˈpoljo] *nf* polio

política [poˈlitika] *nf* politics *sg; (económica, agraria etc)* policy; V *tb* **político**

político, -a [poˈlitiko, a] *adj* political; *(discreto)* tactful; *(de familia)* ...-in-law ▷ *nm/f* politician; **padre ~** father-in-law

póliza [ˈpoliθa] *nf* certificate, voucher; *(impuesto)* tax stamp; **póliza de seguro(s)** insurance policy

polizón [poliˈθon] *nm* stowaway

pollera [poˈʎera] *(cs) nf* skirt

pollo [ˈpoʎo] *nm* chicken

polo [ˈpolo] *nm (Geo, Elec)* pole; *(helado)* ice lolly *(BRIT)*, Popsicle® *(US); (Deporte)* polo-neck; *(suéter)* polo-neck; **polo Norte/Sur** North/South Pole

Polonia [poˈlonja] *nf* Poland

poltrona [polˈtrona] *nf* easy chair

polución [poluˈθjon] *nf* pollution

polvera [polˈβera] *nf* powder compact

polvo [ˈpolβo] *nm* dust; *(Quím, Culin, Med)* powder; **polvos** *nmpl (maquillaje)* powder *sg;* **en ~** powdered; **quitar el ~ to** dust; **estar hecho ~** *(fam)* to be worn out o exhausted; **polvos de talco** talcum powder *sg*

pólvora [ˈpolβora] *nf* gunpowder

polvoriento, -a [polβoˈrjento, a] *adj (superficie)* dusty; *(sustancia)* powdery

pomada [poˈmaða] *nf* cream, ointment

pomelo [poˈmelo] *nm* grapefruit

pómez [ˈpomeθ] *nf:* **piedra ~** pumice stone

pomo [ˈpomo] *nm* doorknob

pompa [ˈpompa] *nf (burbuja)* bubble; *(bomba)* pump; *(esplendor)* pomp, splendour

pómulo [ˈpomulo] *nm* cheekbone

pon [pon] *vb* V **poner**

ponchadura [pontʃaˈðura] *(MÉX) nf* puncture *(BRIT)*, flat *(US);* **ponchar** *(MÉX) vt (llanta)* to puncture

ponche ['pontʃe] nm punch

poncho ['pontʃo] nm poncho

pondré etc vb V **poner**

○ **PALABRA CLAVE**

poner [po'ner] vt 1 (colocar) to put; (telegrama) to send; (obra de teatro) to put on; (película) to show; **ponlo más fuerte** turn it up; **¿qué ponen en el Excelsior?** what's on at the Excelsior?

2 (tienda) to open; (instalar: gas etc) to put in; (radio, TV) to switch o turn on

3 (suponer): **pongamos que ...** let's suppose that ...

4 (contribuir): **el gobierno ha puesto otro millón** the government has contributed another million

5 (Tel): **póngame con el Sr. López** can you put me through to Mr. López

6: **poner de: le han puesto de director general** they've appointed him general manager

7 (+ adj) to make; **me estás poniendo nerviosa** you're making me nervous

8 (dar nombre): **al hijo le pusieron Diego** they called their son Diego

▷ vi (gallina) to lay

ponerse vr 1 (colocarse): **se puso a mi lado** he came and stood beside me; **tú ponte en esa silla** you go and sit on that chair

2 (vestido, cosméticos) to put on; **¿por qué no te pones el vestido nuevo?** why don't you put on o wear your new dress?

3 (+ adj) to turn; to get; become; **se puso muy serio** he got very serious; **después de lavarla la tela se puso azul** after washing it the material turned blue

4: **ponerse a: se puso a llorar** he started to cry; **tienes que ponerte a estudiar** you must get down to studying

pongo etc vb V **poner**

poniente [po'njente] nm (occidente) west; (viento) west wind

pontífice [pon'tifiðe] nm pope, pontiff

popa ['popa] nf stern

popote [po'pote] (MÉX) nm straw

popular [popu'lar] adj popular; (cultura) of the people, folk cpd; **popularidad** nf popularity

○ **PALABRA CLAVE**

por [por] prep 1 (objetivo) for; **luchar por la patria** to fight for one's country

2 (+ infin): **por no llegar tarde** so as not to arrive late; **por citar unos ejemplos** to give a few examples

3 (causa) out of, because of; **por escasez de fondos** through o for lack of funds

4 (tiempo): **por la mañana/noche** in the morning/at night; **se queda por una semana** she's staying (for) a week

5 (lugar): **pasar por Madrid** to pass through Madrid; **ir a Guayaquil por Quito** to go to Guayaquil via Quito; **caminar por la calle** to walk along the street; V tb **todo**

6 (cambio, precio): **te doy uno nuevo por el que tienes** I'll give you a new one (in return) for the one you've got

7 (valor distributivo): **6 euros por hora/cabeza** 6 euros an o per hour/a o per head

8 (modo, medio) by; **por correo/avión** by post/air; **entrar por la entrada principal** to go in through the main entrance

9: **10 por 10 son 100** 10 times 10 is 100

10 (en lugar de): **vino él por su jefe** he came instead of his boss

11: **por mí que revienten** as far as I'm concerned they can drop dead

12: **¿por qué?** why?; **¿por qué no?** why not?

porcelana [porθe'lana] nf porcelain;

(china) china

porcentaje [porθen'taxe] nm
percentage

porción [por'θjon] nf (parte) portion,
share; (cantidad) quantity, amount

porfiar [por'fjar] vi to persist, insist;
(disputar) to argue stubbornly

pormenor [porme'nor] nm detail,
particular

pornografía [pornoɣra'fia] nf
pornography

poro ['poro] nm pore

pororó [poro'ro] (RPL) nm popcorn

poroso, -a [po'roso, a] adj porous

poroto [po'roto] (cs) nm bean

porque ['porke] conj (a causa de)
because; (ya que) since; (con el fin de) so
that, in order that

porqué [por'ke] nm reason, cause

porquería [porke'ria] nf (suciedad)
filth, dirt; (acción) dirty trick; (objeto)
small thing, trifle; (fig) rubbish

porra ['porra] (ESP) nf (arma) stick,
club

porrazo [po'raθo] nm blow, bump

porro ['porro] (fam) nm (droga) joint
(fam)

porrón [po'rron] nm glass wine jar with
a long spout

portaaviones [porta'a(β)βjones] nm
inv aircraft carrier

portada [por'taða] nf (de revista)
cover

portador, a [porta'ðor, a] nm/f
carrier, bearer; (Com) bearer, payee

portaequipajes [portaeki'paxes]
nm inv (Auto: maletero) boot; (: baca)
luggage rack

portafolio [porta'foljo] (LAM) nm
briefcase

portal [por'tal] nm (entrada)
vestibule, hall; (portada) porch,
doorway; (puerta de entrada) main door;
(Internet) portal; **portales** nmpl (LAM)
arcade sg

portamaletas [portama'letas]
nm inv (Auto: maletero) boot; (: baca)
roof rack

portarse [por'tarse] vr to behave,
conduct o.s.

portátil [por'tatil] adj portable

portavoz [porta'βoθ] nmf
spokesman/woman

portazo [por'taθo] nm: **dar un ~** to
slam the door

porte [por'te] nm (Com) transport;
(precio) transport charges pl

portentoso, -a [porten'toso, a] adj
marvellous, extraordinary

porteño, -a [por'teɲo, a] adj of o
from Buenos Aires

portería [porte'ria] nf (oficina)
porter's office; (Deporte) goal

portero, -a [por'tero, a] nm/f porter;
(conserje) caretaker; (ujier) doorman;
(Deporte) goalkeeper; **portero
automático** (ESP) entry phone

pórtico [por'tiko] nm (patio) portico,
porch; (fig) gateway; (arcada) arcade

portorriqueño, -a [portorri'keɲo,
a] adj Puerto Rican

Portugal [portu'ɣal] nm Portugal;
portugués, -esa adj, nm/f Portuguese
▷ nm (Ling) Portuguese

porvenir [porβe'nir] nm future

pos [pos] prep: **en ~ de** after, in
pursuit of

posaderas [posa'ðeras] nfpl
backside sg, buttocks

posar [po'sar] vt (en el suelo) to lay
down, put down; (la mano) to place,
put gently ▷ vi (modelo) to sit, pose;
posarse vr to settle; (pájaro) to perch;
(avión) to land, come down

posavasos [posa'basos] nm inv
coaster; (para cerveza) beermat

posdata [pos'ðata] nf postscript

pose ['pose] nf pose

poseedor, a [posee'ðor, a] nm/f
owner, possessor; (de récord, puesto)
holder

poseer [pose'er] vt to possess, own;
(ventaja) to enjoy; (récord, puesto)
to hold

posesivo, -a [pose'siβo, a] adj
possessive

posibilidad [posiβili'ðað] nf possibility; (oportunidad) chance; **posibilitar** vt to make possible; (hacer realizable) to make feasible

posible [po'siβle] adj possible; (realizable) feasible; **de ser ~** if possible; **en lo ~** as far as possible

posición [posi'θjon] nf position; (rango social) status

positivo, -a [posi'tiβo, a] adj positive

poso ['poso] nm sediment; (heces) dregs pl

posponer [pospo'ner] vt (relegar) to put behind/below; (aplazar) to postpone

posta ['posta] nf: **a ~** deliberately, on purpose

postal [pos'tal] adj postal ▷ nf postcard

poste ['poste] nm (de telégrafos etc) post, pole; (columna) pillar

póster ['poster] (pl **~es, ~s**) nm poster

posterior [poste'rjor] adj back, rear; (siguiente) following, subsequent; (más tarde) later

postgrado [post'graðo] nm = **posgrado**

postizo, -a [pos'tiθo, a] adj false, artificial ▷ nm hairpiece

postre ['postre] nm sweet, dessert

póstumo, -a ['postumo, a] adj posthumous

postura [pos'tura] nf (del cuerpo) posture, position; (fig) attitude, position

potable [po'taβle] adj drinkable; **agua ~** drinking water

potaje [po'taxe] nm thick vegetable soup

potencia [po'tenθja] nf power; **potencial** [poten'θjal] adj, nm potential

potente [po'tente] adj powerful

potro, -a ['potro, a] nm/f (Zool) colt/ filly ▷ nm (de gimnasia) vaulting horse

pozo ['poθo] nm well; (de río) deep pool; (de mina) shaft

PP (ESP) nm abr = **Partido Popular**

práctica ['praktika] nf practice; (método) method; (arte, capacidad) skill; **en la ~** in practice

practicable [prakti'kaβle] adj practicable; (camino) passable

practicante [prakti'kante] nmf (Med: ayudante de doctor) medical assistant; (: enfermero) nurse; (quien practica algo) practitioner ▷ adj practising

practicar [prakti'kar] vt to practise; (Deporte) to play; (realizar) to carry out, perform

práctico, -a ['praktiko, a] adj practical; (instruido: persona) skilled, expert

practique etc vb V **practicar**

pradera [pra'ðera] nf meadow; (US etc) prairie

prado ['praðo] nm (campo) meadow, field; (pastizal) pasture

Praga ['praxa] n Prague

pragmático, -a [prax'matiko, a] adj pragmatic

precario, -a [pre'karjo, a] adj precarious

precaución [prekau'θjon] nf (medida preventiva) preventive measure, precaution; (prudencia) caution, wariness

precedente [preθe'ðente] adj preceding; (anterior) former ▷ nm precedent

preceder [preθe'ðer] vt, vi to precede, go before, come before

precepto [pre'θepto] nm precept

precinto [pre'θinto] nm (tb: ~ **de garantía**) seal

precio ['preθjo] nm price; (costo) cost; (valor) value, worth; (de viaje) fare; **precio al contado/de coste/de oportunidad** cash/cost/bargain price; **precio por menor** retail price; **precio de ocasión** bargain price; **precio de venta al público** retail price; **precio tope** top price

preciosidad [preθjosi'ðað] nf (valor)

(high) value, (great) worth; (*encanto*) charm; (*cosa bonita*) beautiful thing; **es una ~** it's lovely, it's really beautiful

precioso, -a [pre'θjoso, a] *adj* precious; (*de mucho valor*) valuable; (*fam*) lovely, beautiful

precipicio [preθi'piθjo] *nm* cliff, precipice; (*fig*) abyss

precipitación [preθipita'θjon] *nf* haste; (*lluvia*) rainfall

precipitado, -a [preθipi'taðo, a] *adj* (*conducta*) hasty, rash; (*salida*) hasty, sudden

precipitar [preθipi'tar] *vt* (*arrojar*) to hurl down, throw; (*apresurar*) to hasten; (*acelerar*) to speed up, accelerate; **precipitarse** *vr* to throw o.s.; (*apresurarse*) to rush; (*actuar sin pensar*) to act rashly

precisamente [preθisa'mente] *adv* precisely; (*exactamente*) precisely, exactly

precisar [preθi'sar] *vt* (*necesitar*) to need, require; (*fijar*) to determine exactly, fix; (*especificar*) to specify

precisión [preθi'sjon] *nf* (*exactitud*) precision

preciso, -a [pre'θiso, a] *adj* (*exacto*) precise; (*necesario*) necessary, essential

preconcebido, -a [prekonθe'βiðo, a] *adj* preconceived

precoz [pre'koθ] *adj* (*persona*) precocious; (*calvicie etc*) premature

predecir [preðe'θir] *vt* to predict, forecast

predestinado, -a [preðesti'naðo, a] *adj* predestined

predicar [preði'kar] *vt, vi* to preach

predicción [preðik'θjon] *nf* prediction

predilecto, -a [preði'lekto, a] *adj* favourite

predisposición [preðisposi'θjon] *nf* inclination; prejudice, bias

predominar [preðomi'nar] *vt* to dominate ▷ *vi* to predominate; (*prevalecer*) to prevail; **predominio** *nm* predominance; prevalence

preescolar [pre(e)sko'lar] *adj* preschool

prefabricado, -a [prefaβri'kaðo, a] *adj* prefabricated

prefacio [pre'faθjo] *nm* preface

preferencia [prefe'renθja] *nf* preference; **de ~** preferably, for preference

preferible [prefe'riβle] *adj* preferable

preferir [prefe'rir] *vt* to prefer

prefiero *etc vb* V **preferir**

prefijo [pre'fixo] *nm* (*Tel*) (dialling) code

pregunta [pre'γunta] *nf* question; **hacer una ~** to ask a question; **preguntas frecuentes** FAQs, frequently asked questions

preguntar [preγun'tar] *vt* to ask; (*cuestionar*) to question ▷ *vi* to ask; **preguntarse** *vr* to wonder; **preguntar por algn** to ask for sb; **preguntón, -ona** [preγun'ton, ona] *adj* inquisitive

prehistórico, -a [preis'toriko, a] *adj* prehistoric

prejuicio [pre'xwiθjo] *nm* (*acto*) prejudgement; (*idea preconcebida*) preconception; (*parcialidad*) prejudice, bias

preludio [pre'luðjo] *nm* prelude

prematuro, -a [prema'turo, a] *adj* premature

premeditar [premeði'tar] *vt* to premeditate

premiar [pre'mjar] *vt* to reward; (*en un concurso*) to give a prize to

premio ['premjo] *nm* reward; prize; (*Com*) premium

prenatal [prena'tal] *adj* antenatal, prenatal

prenda ['prenda] *nf* (*ropa*) garment, article of clothing; (*garantía*) pledge; **prendas** *nfpl* (*talentos*) talents, gifts

prender [pren'der] *vt* (*captar*) to catch, capture; (*detener*) to arrest; (*Costura*) to pin, attach; (*sujetar*) to fasten ▷ *vi* to catch; (*arraigar*) to take root; **prenderse** *vr* (*encenderse*) to catch fire

prendido, -a [pren'diðo, a] (LAM) adj
(luz etc) on

prensa ['prensa] nf press; **la ~** the
press

preñado, -a [pre'naðo, a] adj
pregnant; **~ de** pregnant with, full of

preocupación [preokupa'θjon] nf
worry, concern; (ansiedad) anxiety

preocupado, -a [preoku'paðo,
a] adj worried, concerned; (ansioso)
anxious

preocupar [preoku'par] vt to worry;
preocuparse vr to worry; **~se de algo**
(hacerse cargo) to take care of sth

preparación [prepara'θjon] nf
(acto) preparation; (estado) readiness;
(entrenamiento) training

preparado, -a [prepa'raðo, a] adj
(dispuesto) prepared; (Culin) ready (to
serve) ▷ nm preparation

preparar [prepa'rar] vt (disponer)
to prepare, get ready; (Tec: tratar) to
prepare, process; (entrenar) to teach,
train; **prepararse** vr: **~se a o para**
to prepare to o for, get ready to o for;
preparativo, -a adj preparatory,
preliminary; **preparativos** nmpl
preparations; **preparatoria** (MÉX) nf
sixth-form college (BRIT), senior high
school (us)

presa ['presa] nf (cosa apresada) catch;
(víctima) victim; (de animal) prey; (de
agua) dam

presagiar [presa'xjar] vt to presage,
forebode; **presagio** nm omen

prescindir [presθin'dir] vi: **~ de**
(privarse de) to do o go without;
(descartar) to dispense with

prescribir [preskri'βir] vt to
prescribe

presencia [pre'senθja] nf presence;
presenciar vt to be present at; (asistir
a) to attend; (ver) to see, witness

presentación [presenta'θjon]
nf presentation; (introducción)
introduction

presentador, a [presenta'ðor, a]

nm/f presenter, compère

presentar [presen'tar] vt to present;
(ofrecer) to offer; (mostrar) to show,
display; (a una persona) to introduce;
presentarse vr (llegar inesperadamente)
to appear, turn up; (ofrecerse: como
candidato) to run, stand; (aparecer) to
show, appear; (solicitar empleo) to apply

presente [pre'sente] adj present
▷ nm present; **hacer ~** to state, declare;
tener ~ to remember, bear in mind

presentimiento [presenti'mjento]
nm premonition, presentiment

presentir [presen'tir] vt to have a
premonition of

preservación [preserβa'θjon] nf
protection, preservation

preservar [preser'βar] vt to protect,
preserve; **preservativo** nm sheath,
condom

presidencia [presi'ðenθja] nf
presidency; (de comité) chairmanship

presidente [presi'ðente] nmf
president; (de comité) chairman/
woman

presidir [presi'ðir] vt (dirigir) to
preside at, preside over; (: comité)
to take the chair at; (dominar) to
dominate, rule ▷ vi to preside; to take
the chair

presión [pre'sjon] nf pressure;
presión atmosférica atmospheric
o air pressure; **presionar** vt to
press; (fig) to press, put pressure on
▷ vi: **presionar para** to press for

preso, -a ['preso, a] nm/f prisoner;
tomar o **llevar a algn** to arrest sb,
take sb prisoner

prestación [presta'θjon] nf service;
(subsidio) benefit; **prestaciones** nfpl
(Tec, Auto) performance features

prestado, -a [pres'taðo, a] adj on
loan; **pedir ~** to borrow

prestamista [presta'mista] nmf
moneylender

préstamo ['prestamo] nm loan;
préstamo hipotecario mortgage

prestar [pres'tar] vt to lend, loan;

(atención) to pay; (ayuda) to give

prestigio [pres'tixjo] nm prestige;
prestigioso, -a adj (honorable)
prestigious; (famoso, renombrado)
renowned, famous

presumido, -a [presu'miðo, a] adj
(persona) vain

presumir [presu'mir] vt to presume
▷ vi (tener aires) to be conceited;
presunto, -a adj (supuesto) supposed,
presumed; (así llamado) so-called;
presuntuoso, -a adj conceited,
presumptuous

presupuesto [presu'pwesto] pp de
presuponer ▷ nm (Finanzas) budget;
(estimación: de costo) estimate

pretencioso, -a [preten'θjoso, a]
adj pretentious

pretender [preten'der] vt (intentar)
to try to, seek to; (reivindicar) to claim;
(buscar) to seek, try for; (cortejar) to
woo, court; **~ que** to expect that
> No confundir **pretender** con la
> palabra inglesa pretend.
pretendiente nmf (amante) suitor;
(al trono) pretender; **pretensión** f
(aspiración) aspiration; (reivindicación)
claim; (orgullo) pretension

pretexto [pre'teksto] nm pretext;
(excusa) excuse

prevención [preβen'θjon] nf
prevention; (precaución) precaution

prevenido, -a [preβe'niðo, a] adj
prepared, ready; (cauteloso) cautious

prevenir [preβe'nir] vt (impedir) to
prevent; (predisponer) to prejudice,
bias; (avisar) to warn; (preparar) to
prepare, get ready; **prevenirse** vr to
get ready, prepare; **~se contra** to take
precautions against; **preventivo, -a**
adj preventive, precautionary

prever [pre'βer] vt to foresee

previo, -a [pre'βjo, a] adj (anterior)
previous; (preliminar) preliminary
▷ prep: **~ acuerdo de los otros** subject
to the agreement of the others

previsión [preβi'sjon] nf (perspicacia)
foresight; (predicción) forecast;

previsto, -a adj anticipated, forecast

prima ['prima] nf (Com) bonus; (de
seguro) premium; V tb **primo**

primario, -a [pri'marjo, a] adj
primary

primavera [prima'βera] nf spring(-
time)

primera [pri'mera] nf (Auto) first
gear; (Ferro: tb: **~ clase**) first class; **de ~**
(fam) first-class, first-rate

primero, -a [pri'mero, a] (adj **primer**)
first; (principal) prime adv first; (más
bien) sooner, rather; **primera plana**
front page

primitivo, -a [primi'tiβo, a] adj
primitive; (original) original

primo, -a ['primo, a] adj prime
▷ nm/f cousin; (fam) fool, idiot;
materias primas raw materials;
primo hermano first cousin

primogénito, -a [primo'xenito, a]
adj first-born

primoroso, -a [primo'roso, a] adj
exquisite, delicate

princesa [prin'θesa] nf princess

principal [prinθi'pal] adj principal,
main ▷ nm (jefe) chief, principal

príncipe ['prinθipe] nm prince

principiante [prinθi'pjante] nmf
beginner

principio [prin'θipjo] nm (comienzo)
beginning, start; (origen) origin;
(primera etapa) rudiment, basic idea;
(moral) principle; **desde el ~** from the
first; **en un ~** at first; **a ~s de** at the
beginning of

pringue ['pringe] nm (grasa) grease,
fat, dripping

prioridad [priori'ðað] nf priority

prisa ['prisa] nf (apresuramiento) hurry,
haste; (rapidez) speed; (urgencia) (sense
of) urgency; **a o de ~** quickly; **correr
~** to be urgent; **darse ~** to hurry up;
tener ~ to be in a hurry

prisión [pri'sjon] nf (cárcel) prison;
(período de cárcel) imprisonment;
prisionero, -a nm/f prisoner

prismáticos [pris'matikos] nmpl

binoculars

privado, -a [pri'βaðo, a] *adj* private

privar [pri'βar] *vt* to deprive; **privativo, -a** *adj* exclusive

privilegiar [priβile'xjar] *vt* to grant a privilege to; (*favorecer*) to favour

privilegio [priβi'lexjo] *nm* privilege; (*concesión*) concession

pro [pro] *nm o f* profit, advantage ▷ *prep*: **asociación ~ ciegos** association for the blind ▷ *prefijo*: **~ americano** pro-American; **en ~ de** on behalf of, for; **los ~s y los contras** the pros and cons

proa ['proa] *nf* bow, prow; **de ~** *cpd*, fore

probabilidad [proβaβili'ðað] *nf* probability, likelihood; (*oportunidad, posibilidad*) chance, prospect; **probable** *adj* probable, likely

probador [proβa'ðor] *nm* (*en tienda*) fitting room

probar [pro'βar] *vt* (*demostrar*) to prove; (*someter a prueba*) to test, try out; (*ropa*) to try on; (*comida*) to taste ▷ *vi* to try; **~se un traje** to try on a suit

probeta [pro'βeta] *nf* test tube

problema [pro'βlema] *nm* problem

procedente [proθe'ðente] *adj* (*razonable*) reasonable; (*conforme a derecho*) proper, fitting; **~ de** coming from, originating in

proceder [proθe'ðer] *vi* (*avanzar*) to proceed; (*actuar*) to act; (*ser correcto*) to be right (and proper), be fitting ▷ *nm* (*comportamiento*) behaviour, conduct; **~ de** to come from, originate in; **procedimiento** *nm* procedure; (*proceso*) process; (*método*) means *pl*, method

procesador [proθesa'ðor] *nm* processor; **procesador de textos** word processor

procesar [proθe'sar] *vt* to try, put on trial

procesión [proθe'sjon] *nf* procession

proceso [pro'θeso] *nm* process; (*Jur*) trial

proclamar [prokla'mar] *vt* to proclaim

procrear [prokre'ar] *vt, vi* to procreate

procurador, a [prokura'ðor, a] *nm/f* attorney

procurar [proku'rar] *vt* (*intentar*) to try, endeavour; (*conseguir*) to get, obtain; (*asegurar*) to secure; (*producir*) to produce

prodigio [pro'ðixjo] *nm* prodigy; (*milagro*) wonder, marvel; **prodigioso, -a** *adj* prodigious, marvellous

pródigo, -a ['proðiɣo, a] *adj*: **hijo ~** prodigal son

producción [proðuk'θjon] *nf* (*gen*) production; (*producto*) output; **producción en serie** mass production

producir [proðu'θir] *vt* to produce; (*causar*) to cause, bring about; **producirse** *vr* (*cambio*) to come about; (*accidente*) to take place; (*problema etc*) to arise; (*hacerse*) to be produced, be made; (*estallar*) to break out

productividad [proðuktiβi'ðað] *nf* productivity; **productivo, -a** *adj* productive; (*provechoso*) profitable

producto [pro'ðukto] *nm* product

productor, a [proðuk'tor, a] *adj* productive, producing ▷ *nm/f* producer

proeza [pro'eθa] *nf* exploit, feat

profano, -a [pro'fano, a] *adj* profane ▷ *nm/f* layman/woman

profecía [profe'θia] *nf* prophecy

profesión [profe'sjon] *nf* profession; (*en formulario*) occupation; **profesional** *adj* professional

profesor, a [profe'sor, a] *nm/f* teacher; **profesorado** *nm* teaching profession

profeta [pro'feta] *nmf* prophet

prófugo, -a ['profuɣo, a] *nm/f* fugitive; (*Mil: desertor*) deserter

profundidad [profundi'ðað] *nf* depth; **profundizar** *vi*: **profundizar en** to go deeply into; **profundo, -a** *adj* deep; (*misterio, pensador*) profound

progenitor [proxeni'tor] nm
ancestor; **progenitores** nmpl (padres)
parents

programa [pro'xrama] nm
programme (BRIT), program (US);
programa de estudios curriculum,
syllabus; **programación** nf
programming; **programador, a**
nm/f programmer; **programar** vt to
program

progresar [proxre'sar] vi to
progress, make progress; **progresista**
adj, nmf progressive; **progresivo,
-a** adj progressive; (gradual) gradual;
(continuo) continuous; **progreso** nm
progress

prohibición [proiβi'θjon] nf
prohibition, ban

prohibir [proi'βir] vt to prohibit, ban,
forbid; **prohibido o se prohibe fumar**
no smoking; **"prohibido el paso"**
"no entry"

prójimo, -a ['proximo, a] nm/f
fellow man; (vecino) neighbour

prólogo ['proloxo] nm prologue

prolongar [prolon'xar] vt to extend;
(reunión etc) to prolong; (calle, tubo)
to extend

promedio [pro'meðjo] nm average;
(de distancia) middle, mid-point

promesa [pro'mesa] nf promise

prometer [prome'ter] vt to promise
▷ vi to show promise; **prometerse** vr
(novios) to get engaged; **prometido,
-a** adj promised; engaged ▷ nm/f
fiancé/fiancée

prominente [promi'nente] adj
prominent

promoción [promo'θjon] nf
promotion

promotor [promo'tor] nm promoter;
(instigador) instigator

promover [promo'βer] vt to
promote; (causar) to cause; (instigar) to
instigate, stir up

promulgar [promul'xar] vt to
promulgate; (anunciar) to proclaim

pronombre [pro'nombre] nm
pronoun

pronosticar [pronosti'kar] vt to
predict, foretell, forecast; **pronóstico**
nm prediction, forecast; **pronóstico
del tiempo** weather forecast

pronto, -a ['pronto, a] adj (rápido)
prompt, quick; (preparado) ready ▷ adv
quickly, promptly; (en seguida) at once,
right away; (dentro de poco) soon;
(temprano) early ▷ nm: **tiene unos
~s muy malos** he gets ratty all of a
sudden (inf); **de ~** suddenly; **por lo ~**
meanwhile, for the present

pronunciación [pronunθja'θjon] nf
pronunciation

pronunciar [pronun'θjar] vt to
pronounce; (discurso) to make, deliver;
pronunciarse vr to revolt, rebel;
(declararse) to declare o.s.

propagación [propaxa'θjon] nf
propagation

propaganda [propa'xanda] nf (Pol)
propaganda; (Com) advertising

propenso, -a [pro'penso, a] adj
inclined to; **ser ~ a** to be inclined to,
have a tendency to

propicio, -a [pro'piθjo, a] adj
favourable, propitious

propiedad [propje'ðað] nf property;
(posesión) possession, ownership;
propiedad particular private property

propietario, -a [propje'tarjo, a]
nm/f owner, proprietor

propina [pro'pina] nf tip

propio, -a ['propjo, a] adj own,
of one's own; (característico)
characteristic, typical; (debido) proper;
(mismo) selfsame, very; **el ~ ministro**
the minister himself; **¿tienes casa
propia?** have you a house of your own?

proponer [propo'ner] vt to propose,
put forward; (problema) to pose;
proponerse vr to propose, intend

proporción [propor'θjon] nf
proportion; (Mat) ratio; **proporciones**
nfpl (dimensiones) dimensions;
(fig) size sg; **proporcionado,
-a** adj proportionate; (regular)

medium, middling; (*justo*) just right;
proporcionar vt (*dar*) to give, supply,
provide
proposición [proposi'θjon] nf
proposition; (*propuesta*) proposal
propósito [pro'posito] nm purpose;
(*intento*) aim, intention ▷ adv: a ~
by the way, incidentally; (*a posta*) on
purpose, deliberately; **a ~ de** about,
with regard to
propuesta [pro'pwesta] vb V
proponer ▷ nf proposal
propulsar [propul'sar] vt to drive,
propel; (*fig*) to promote, encourage;
propulsión nf propulsion; **propulsión
a chorro** o **por reacción** jet propulsion
prórroga ['prorroɣa] nf extension;
(*Jur*) stay; (*Com*) deferment; (*Deporte*)
extra time; **prorrogar** vt (*período*) to
extend; (*decisión*) to defer, postpone
prosa ['prosa] nf prose
proseguir [prose'ɣir] vt to continue,
carry on ▷ vi to continue, go on
prospecto [pros'pekto] nm
prospectus
prosperar [prospe'rar] vi to prosper,
thrive, flourish; **prosperidad** nf
prosperity; (*éxito*) success; **próspero,
-a** adj prosperous, flourishing; (*que
tiene éxito*) successful
próstíbulo [pros'tiβulo] nm brothel
(*BRIT*), house of prostitution (*US*)
prostitución [prostitu'θjon] nf
prostitution
prostituir [prosti'twir] vt to
prostitute; **prostituirse** vr to
prostitute o.s., become a prostitute
prostituta [prosti'tuta] nf
prostitute
protagonista [protaɣo'nista] nmf
protagonist
protección [protek'θjon] nf
protection
protector, a [protek'tor, a] adj
protective, protecting ▷ nm/f
protector
proteger [prote'xer] vt to protect;
protegido, -a nm/f protégé/protégée

proteína [prote'ina] nf protein
protesta [pro'testa] nf protest;
(*declaración*) protestation
protestante [protes'tante] adj
Protestant
protestar [protes'tar] vt to protest,
declare ▷ vi to protest
protocolo [proto'kolo] nm protocol
prototipo [proto'tipo] nm prototype
provecho [pro'βetʃo] nm advantage,
benefit; (*Finanzas*) profit; **¡buen ~!** bon
appétit!; **en ~ de** to the benefit of;
sacar ~ de to benefit from, profit by
provenir [proβe'nir] vi: **~ de** to come
o stem from
proverbio [pro'βerβjo] nm proverb
providencia [proβi'ðenθja] nf
providence
provincia [pro'βinθja] nf province
provisión [proβi'sjon] nf provision;
(*abastecimiento*) provision, supply;
(*medida*) measure, step
provisional [proβisjo'nal] adj
provisional
provocar [proβo'kar] vt to provoke;
(*alentar*) to tempt, invite; (*causar*)
to bring about, lead to; (*promover*)
to promote; (*estimular*) to rouse,
stimulate; **¿te provoca un café?** (CAM)
would you like a coffee?; **provocativo,
-a** adj provocative
proxeneta [prokse'neta] nm pimp
próximamente [proksima'mente]
adv shortly, soon
proximidad [proksimi'ðað] nf
closeness, proximity; **próximo, -a**
adj near, close; (*vecino*) neighbouring;
(*siguiente*) next
proyectar [projek'tar] vt (*objeto*) to
hurl, throw; (*luz*) to cast, shed; (*Cine*) to
screen, show; (*planear*) to plan
proyectil [projek'til] nm projectile,
missile
proyecto [pro'jekto] nm plan;
(*estimación de costo*) detailed estimate
proyector [projek'tor] nm (*Cine*)
projector
prudencia [pru'ðenθja] nf (*sabiduría*)

wisdom; (cuidado) care; **prudente** adj
sensible, wise; (conductor) careful

prueba etc ['prweβa] vb V **probar** ▷ nf
proof; (ensayo) test, trial; (degustación)
tasting, sampling; (de ropa) fitting; **a
~ on trial; a ~** waterproof against; **a ~ de
agua/fuego** waterproof/fireproof;
someter a ~ to put to the test

psico... [siko] prefijo psycho...;
psicología nf psychology;
psicológico, -a adj psychological;
psicólogo, -a nm/f psychologist;
psicópata nmf psychopath; **psicosis**
nf inv psychosis

psiquiatra [si'kjatra] nmf
psychiatrist; **psiquiátrico, -a** adj
psychiatric

PSOE [pe'soe] (ESP) nm abr = **Partido
Socialista Obrero Español**

púa ['pua] nf (Bot, Zool) prickle, spine;
(para guitarra) plectrum (BRIT), pick
(US); **alambre de ~** barbed wire

pubertad [puβer'tað] nf puberty

publicación [puβlika'θjon] nf
publication

publicar [puβli'kar] vt (editar) to
publish; (hacer público) to publicize;
(divulgar) to make public, divulge

publicidad [puβliθi'ðað] nf
publicity; (Com: propaganda)
advertising; **publicitario, -a** adj
publicity cpd; advertising cpd

público, -a ['puβliko, a] adj public
▷ nm public; (Teatro etc) audience

puchero [pu'tʃero] nm (Culin: guiso)
stew; (: olla) cooking pot; **hacer ~s**
to pout

pucho ['putʃo] (cs: fam) nm cigarette,
fag (BRIT)

pude etc vb V **poder**

pudiente [pu'ðjente] adj (rico)
wealthy, well-to-do

pudiera etc vb V **poder**

pudor [pu'ðor] nm modesty

pudrir [pu'ðrir] vt to rot; **pudrirse** vr
to rot, decay

pueblo ['pweβlo] nm people; (nación)
nation; (aldea) village

puedo etc vb V **poder**

puente ['pwente] nm bridge; **hacer ~**
(fam) to take extra days off work between 2
public holidays; to take a long weekend;
puente aéreo shuttle service; **puente
colgante** suspension bridge; **puente
levadizo** drawbridge

● **HACER PUENTE**
●
● When a public holiday in Spain
● falls on a Tuesday or Thursday it is
● common practice for employers
● to make the Monday or Friday
● a holiday as well and to give
● everyone a four-day weekend. This
● is known as **hacer puente**. When
● a named public holiday such as the
● **Día de la Constitución** falls on a
● Tuesday or Thursday, people refer
● to the whole holiday period as e.g.
● the **puente de la Constitución**.

puerco, -a ['pwerko, a] nm/f pig/
sow ▷ adj (sucio) dirty, filthy; (obsceno)
disgusting; **puerco espín** porcupine

pueril [pwe'ril] adj childish

puerro ['pwerro] nm leek

puerta ['pwerta] nf door; (de jardín)
gate; (portal) doorway; (Tip) gateway;
(portería) goal; **a la ~** at the door;
cerrada behind closed doors; **puerta
giratoria** revolving door

puerto ['pwerto] nm port; (paso)
pass; (fig) haven, refuge

Puerto Rico [pwerto'riko] nm
Puerto Rico; **puertorriqueño, -a** adj,
nm/f Puerto Rican

pues [pwes] adv (entonces) then;
(bueno) well, well then; (así que)
so ▷ conj (ya que) since; **¡~ sí!** yes!,
certainly!

puesta ['pwesta] nf (apuesta) bet,
stake; **puesta al día** updating; **puesta
a punto** fine tuning; **puesta de sol**
sunset; **puesta en marcha** starting

puesto, -a ['pwesto, a] pp de **poner**
▷ adj: **tener algo ~** to have sth on, be

wearing sth ▷ *nm* (lugar, posición) place; (trabajo) post, job; (Com) stall ▷ *conj*: **~ que** since, as

púgil ['puxil] *nm* boxer

pulga ['pulɣa] *nf* flea

pulgada [pul'ɣaða] *nf* inch

pulgar [pul'xar] *nm* thumb

pulir [pu'lir] *vt* to polish; (alisar) to smooth; (fig) to polish up, touch up

pulmón [pul'mon] *nm* lung; **pulmonía** *nf* pneumonia

pulpa ['pulpa] *nf* pulp; (de fruta) flesh, soft part

pulpería [pulpe'ria] (LAM) *nf* (tienda) small grocery store

púlpito ['pulpito] *nm* pulpit

pulpo ['pulpo] *nm* octopus

pulque ['pulke] *nm* pulque

> PULQUE
>
> **Pulque** is a thick, white, alcoholic
> drink which is very popular in
> Mexico. In ancient times it was
> considered sacred by the Aztecs.
> It is produced by fermenting the
> juice of the **maguey**, a Mexican
> cactus similar to the agave. It can
> be drunk by itself or mixed with
> fruit or vegetable juice.

pulsación [pulsa'θjon] *nf* beat; **pulsaciones** pulse rate

pulsar [pul'sar] *vt* (tecla) to touch, tap; (Mús) to play; (botón) to press, push ▷ *vi* to pulsate; (latir) to beat, throb

pulsera [pul'sera] *nf* bracelet

pulso ['pulso] *nm* (Anat) pulse; (fuerza) strength; (firmeza) steadiness, steady hand

pulverizador [pulβeriθa'ðor] *nm* spray, spray gun

pulverizar [pulβeri'θar] *vt* to pulverize; (líquido) to spray

puna ['puna] (CAM) *nf* mountain sickness

punta ['punta] *nf* point, tip; (extremo) end; (fig) touch, trace; **horas ~** peak o

rush hours; **sacar ~ a** to sharpen

puntada [pun'taða] *nf* (Costura) stitch

puntal [pun'tal] *nm* prop, support

puntapié [punta'pje] *nm* kick

puntería [punte'ria] *nf* (de arma) aim, aiming; (destreza) marksmanship

puntero, -a [pun'tero, a] *adj* leading ▷ *nm* (palo) pointer

puntiagudo, -a [puntja'ɣuðo, a] *adj* sharp, pointed

puntilla [pun'tiʎa] *nf* (encaje) lace edging o trim; **(andar) de ~s** (to walk) on tiptoe

punto ['punto] *nm* (gen) point; (señal diminuta) spot, dot; (Costura, Med) stitch; (lugar) spot, place; (momento) point, moment; **a ~** ready; **estar a ~ de** to be on the point of o about to; **en ~** on the dot; **hasta cierto ~** to some extent; **hacer ~** (ESP: tejer) to knit; **dos ~s** (Ling) colon; **punto de interrogación** question mark; **punto de vista** point of view, viewpoint; **punto final** full stop (BRIT), period (US); **punto muerto** dead center; (Auto) neutral (gear); **punto y aparte** (en dictado) full stop, new paragraph; **punto y coma** semicolon

puntocom [punto'kom] *adj inv, nf inv* dotcom

puntuación [puntwa'θjon] *nf* punctuation; (puntos: en examen) mark(s) (pl); (Deporte) score

puntual [pun'twal] *adj* (a tiempo) punctual; (exacto) exact, accurate; **puntualidad** *nf* punctuality; exactness, accuracy

puntuar [pun'twar] *vi* (Deporte) to score, count

punzante [pun'θante] *adj* (dolor) shooting, sharp; (herramienta) sharp

puñado [pu'ɲaðo] *nm* handful

puñal [pu'ɲal] *nm* dagger; **puñalada** *nf* stab

puñetazo [puɲe'taθo] *nm* punch

puño ['puɲo] *nm* (Anat) fist; (cantidad) fistful, handful; (Costura) cuff; (de herramienta) handle

pupila [pu'pila] *nf* pupil

pupitre [pu'pitre] *nm* desk

puré [pu're] *nm* purée; (*sopa*) (thick) soup; **puré de papas** (LAM) mashed potatoes; **puré de patatas** (ESP) mashed potatoes

purga ['purɣa] *nf* purge; **purgante** *adj, nm* purgative

purgatorio [purɣa'torjo] *nm* purgatory

purificar [purifi'kar] *vt* to purify; (*refinar*) to refine

puritano, -a [puri'tano, a] *adj* (*actitud*) puritanical; (*iglesia, tradición*) puritan ▷ *nm/f* puritan

puro, -a ['puro, a] *adj* pure; (*verdad*) simple, plain ▷ *nm* cigar

púrpura ['purpura] *nf* purple

pus [pus] *nm* pus

puse *etc* *vb* V **poder**

pusiera *etc* *vb* V **poder**

puta ['puta] (*fam!*) *nf* whore, prostitute

putrefacción [putrefak'θjon] *nf* rotting, putrefaction

PVP *nm abr* (= *precio de venta al público*) RRP

pyme, PYME ['pime] *nf abr* (= *Pequeña y Mediana Empresa*) SME

q

○ PALABRA CLAVE

que [ke] *conj* **1** (*con oración subordinada: muchas veces no se traduce*) that; **dijo que vendría** he said (that) he would come; **espero que lo encuentres** I hope (that) you find it; V *tb* **el**

2 (*en oración independiente*): **¡que entre!** send him in; **¡que aproveche!** enjoy your meal!; **¡que se mejore tu padre!** I hope your father gets better

3 (*enfático*): **¿me quieres? – ¡que sí!** do you love me? – of course!

4 (*consecutivo: muchas veces no se traduce*) that; **es tan grande que no lo puedo levantar** it's so big (that) I can't lift it

5 (*comparaciones*) than; **yo que tú/él** if I were you/him; V *tb* **más, menos, mismo**

6 (*valor disyuntivo*): **que le guste o no** whether he likes it or not; **que venga o que no venga** whether he comes or not

7 (*porque*): **no puedo, que tengo que quedarme en casa** I can't, I've got to stay in
▷ *pron* **1** (*cosa*) that, which; (+ *prep*) which; **el sombrero que te compraste** the hat (that o which) you bought; **la cama en que dormí** the bed (that o which) I slept in
2 (*persona*: *suj*) that, who; (: *objeto*) that, whom; **el amigo que me acompañó al museo** the friend that o who went to the museum with me; **la chica que invité** the girl (that o whom) I invited

qué [ke] *adj* what?, which? ▷ *pron* what?; **¡~ divertido!** how funny!; **¿~ edad tienes?** how old are you?; **¿de ~ me hablas?** what are you saying to me?; **¿~ tal?** how are you?, how are things?; **¿~ hay (de nuevo)?** what's new?

quebrado, -a [ke'βraðo, a] *adj* (*roto*) broken ▷ *nm/f* bankrupt ▷ *nm* (*Mat*) fraction

quebrantar [keβran'tar] *vt* (*infringir*) to violate, transgress

quebrar [ke'βrar] *vt* to break, smash ▷ *vi* to go bankrupt

quedar [ke'ðar] *vi* to stay, remain; (*encontrarse*: *sitio*) to be; (*haber aún*) to remain, be left; **quedarse** *vr* to remain, stay (behind); **~se (con) algo** to keep sth; **~ en** (*acordar*) to agree on/to; **~ en nada** to come to nothing; **~ por hacer** to be still to be done; **~ ciego/mudo** to be left blind/dumb; **no te queda bien ese vestido** that dress doesn't suit you; **eso queda muy lejos** that's a long way (away); **quedamos a las seis** we agreed to meet at six

quedo, -a [ke'ðo, a] *adj* still ▷ *adv* softly, gently

quehacer [kea'θer] *nm* task, job; **quehaceres (domésticos)** *nmpl* household chores

queja ['kexa] *nf* complaint; **quejarse** *vr* (*enfermo*) to moan, groan; (*protestar*) to complain; **quejarse de que** to

complain (about the fact) that; **quejido** *nm* moan

quemado, -a [ke'maðo, a] *adj* burnt

quemadura [kema'ðura] *nf* burn, scald

quemar [ke'mar] *vt* to burn; (*fig*: *malgastar*) to burn up, squander ▷ *vi* to be burning hot; **quemarse** *vr* (*consumirse*) to burn (up); (*del sol*) to get sunburnt

quemarropa [kema'rropa]: **a ~** *adv* point-blank

quepo *etc vb* V **caber**

querella [ke'reʎa] *nf* (*Jur*) charge; (*disputa*) dispute

⚪ **PALABRA CLAVE**

querer [ke'rer] *vt* **1** (*desear*) to want; **quiero más dinero** I want more money; **quisiera o querría un té** I'd like a tea; **sin querer** unintentionally; **quiero ayudar/que vayas** I want to help/you to go
2 (*preguntas*: *para pedir algo*): **¿quiere abrir la ventana?** could you open the window?; **¿quieres echarme una mano?** can you give me a hand?
3 (*amar*) to love; (*tener cariño a*) to be fond of; **te quiero** I love you; **quiere mucho a sus hijos** he's very fond of his children
4 **le pedí que me dejara ir pero no quiso** I asked him to let me go but he refused

querido, -a [ke'riðo, a] *adj* dear ▷ *nm/f* darling; (*amante*) lover

queso ['keso] *nm* cheese; **queso crema** (LAM) cream cheese; **queso de untar** (ESP) cream cheese; **queso manchego** sheep's milk cheese made in La Mancha; **queso rallado** grated cheese

quicio ['kiθjo] *nm* hinge; **sacar a algn de ~** to get on sb's nerves

quiebra ['kjeβra] *nf* break, split; (*Com*) bankruptcy; (*Econ*) slump

quiebro ['kjeβro] *nm* (*del cuerpo*)

swerve

quien [kjen] *pron* who; **hay ~ piensa que** there are those who think that; **no hay ~ lo haga** no-one will do it

quién [kjen] *pron* who, whom; **¿~ es?** who's there?

quienquiera [kjen'kjera] (*pl* **quienesquiera**) *pron* whoever

quiero *etc vb* V **querer**

quieto, -a ['kjeto, a] *adj* still; (*carácter*) placid

▌ No confundir **quieto** con la palabra inglesa *quiet*.

quietud *nf* stillness

quilate [ki'late] *nm* carat

químico, -a ['kimiko, a] *adj* chemical ▷ *nm/f* chemist ▷ *nf* chemistry

quincalla [kin'kaʎa] *nf* hardware, ironmongery (*BRIT*)

quince ['kinθe] *num* fifteen; **~ días** a fortnight; **quinceañero, -a** *nm/f* teenager; **quincena** *nf* fortnight; (*pago*) fortnightly pay; **quincenal** *adj* fortnightly

quiniela [ki'njela] *nf* football pools *pl*; **quinielas** *nfpl* (*impreso*) pools coupon *sg*

quinientos, -as [ki'njentos, as] *adj, num* five hundred

quinto, -a ['kinto, a] *adj* fifth ▷ *nf* country house; (*Mil*) call-up, draft

quiosco ['kjosko] *nm* (*de música*) bandstand; (*de periódicos*) news stand

quirófano [ki'rofano] *nm* operating theatre

quirúrgico, -a [ki'rurxiko, a] *adj* surgical

quise *etc vb* V **querer**

quisiera *etc vb* V **querer**

quisquilloso, -a [kiski'ʎoso, a] *adj* (*susceptible*) touchy; (*meticuloso*) pernickety

quiste ['kiste] *nm* cyst

quitaesmalte [kitaes'malte] *nm* nail-polish remover

quitamanchas [kita'mantʃas] *nm inv* stain remover

quitanieves [kita'njeβes] *nm inv* snowplough (*BRIT*), snowplow (*US*)

quitar [ki'tar] *vt* to remove, take away; (*ropa*) to take off; (*dolor*) to relieve; **¡quita de ahí!** get away!; **quitarse** *vr* to withdraw; (*ropa*) to take off; **se quitó el sombrero** he took off his hat

Quito ['kito] *n* Quito

quizá(s) [ki'θa(s)] *adv* perhaps, maybe

r

rábano [ˈraβano] nm radish; **me importa un ~** I don't give a damn

rabia [ˈraβja] nf (Med) rabies sg; (ira) fury, rage; **rabiar** vi to have rabies; to rage, be furious; **rabiar por algo** to long for sth

rabieta [raˈβjeta] nf tantrum, fit of temper

rabino [raˈβino] nm rabbi

rabioso, -a [raˈβjoso, a] adj rabid; (fig) furious

rabo [ˈraβo] nm tail

racha [ˈratʃa] nf gust of wind; **buena/ mala ~** spell of good/bad luck

racial [raˈθjal] adj racial, race cpd

racimo [raˈθimo] nm bunch

ración [raˈθjon] nf portion; **raciones** nfpl rations

racional [raθjoˈnal] adj (razonable) reasonable; (lógico) rational

racionar [raθjoˈnar] vt to ration (out)

racismo [raˈθismo] nm racism; **racista** adj, nm racist

radar [raˈðar] nm radar

radiador [raðjaˈðor] nm radiator

radiante [raˈðjante] adj radiant

radical [raðiˈkal] adj, nmf radical

radicar [raðiˈkar] vi: **~ en** (dificultad, problema) to lie in; (solución) to consist in

radio [ˈraðjo] nf radio; (aparato) radio (set) ▷ nm (Mat) radius; (Quím) radium; **radiactividad** nf radioactivity; **radioactivo, -a** adj radioactive; **radiografía** nf X-ray; **radioterapia** nf radiotherapy; **radioyente** nmf listener

ráfaga [ˈrafaxa] nf gust; (de luz) flash; (de tiros) burst

raíz [raˈiθ] nf root; **a ~ de** as a result of; **raíz cuadrada** square root

raja [ˈraxa] nf (de melón etc) slice; (grieta) crack; **rajar** vt to split; (fam) to slash; **rajarse** vr to split, crack; **rajarse de** to back out of

rajatabla [raxaˈtaβla]: **a ~** adv (estrictamente) strictly, to the letter

rallador [raʎaˈðor] nm grater

rallar [raˈʎar] vt to grate

rama [ˈrama] nf branch; **ramaje** nm branches pl, foliage; **ramal** nm (de cuerda) strand; (Ferro) branch line (BRIT); (Auto) branch (road) (BRIT)

rambla [ˈrambla] nf (avenida) avenue

ramo [ˈramo] nm branch; (sección) department, section

rampa [ˈrampa] nf ramp; **rampa de acceso** entrance ramp

rana [ˈrana] nf frog; **salto de ~** leapfrog

ranchero [ranˈtʃero] nm (MÉX) (hacendado) rancher; smallholder

rancho [ˈrantʃo] nm (grande) ranch; (pequeño) small farm

rancio, -a [ˈranθjo, a] adj (comestibles) rancid; (vino) aged, mellow; (fig) ancient

rango [ˈrango] nm rank, standing

ranura [raˈnura] nf groove; (de teléfono etc) slot

rapar [raˈpar] vt to shave; (los cabellos) to crop

rapaz [raˈpaθ] (nf **~a**) nmf young

boy/girl ▷ adj (Zool) predatory

rape ['rape] nm (pez) monkfish; **al ~** cropped

rapé [ra'pe] nm snuff

rapidez [rapi'ðeθ] nf speed, rapidity;

rápido, -a [ˈrapiðo] adj fast, quick ▷ adv quickly ▷ nm (Ferro) express; **rápidos** nmpl rapids

rapiña [ra'piɲa] nm robbery; **ave de ~** bird of prey

raptar [rap'tar] vt to kidnap; **rapto** nm kidnapping; (impulso) sudden impulse; (éxtasis) ecstasy, rapture

raqueta [ra'keta] nf racquet

raquítico, -a [ra'kitiko, a] adj stunted; (fig) poor, inadequate

rareza [ra'reθa] nf rarity; (fig) eccentricity

raro, -a ['raro, a] adj (poco común) rare; (extraño) odd, strange; (excepcional) remarkable

ras [ras] nm: **a ~ de** level with; **a ~ de tierra** at ground level

rasar [ra'sar] vt (igualar) to level

rascacielos [raska'θjelos] nm inv skyscraper

rascar [ras'kar] vt (con las uñas etc) to scratch; (raspar) to scrape; **rascarse** vr to scratch (o.s.)

rasgar [ras'xar] vt to tear, rip (up)

rasgo ['rasxo] nm (con pluma) stroke; **rasgos** nmpl (facciones) features, characteristics; **a grandes ~s** in outline, broadly

rasguño [ras'xuɲo] nm scratch

raso, -a ['raso, a] adj (liso) flat, level; (a baja altura) very low ▷ nm satin; **cielo ~** clear sky

raspadura [raspa'ðura] nf (acto) scrape, scraping; (marca) scratch; **raspaduras** nfpl (de papel etc) scrapings

raspar [ras'par] vt to scrape; (arañar) to scratch; (limar) to file

rastra ['rastra] nf (Agr) rake; **a ~s** by dragging; (fig) unwillingly

rastrear [rastre'ar] vt (seguir) to track

rastrero, -a [ras'trero, a] adj (Bot,

Zool) creeping; (fig) despicable, mean

rastrillo [ras'triʎo] nm rake

rastro ['rastro] nm (Agr) rake; (pista) track, trail; (vestigio) trace; **el R~** (ESP) the Madrid fleamarket

rasurado [rasu'raðo] (MÉX) nm shaving; **rasuradora** [rasura'ðora] (MÉX) nf electric shaver; **rasurar** [rasu'rar] (MÉX) vt to shave; **rasurarse** vr to shave

rata ['rata] nf rat

ratear [rate'ar] vt (robar) to steal

ratero, -a [ra'tero, a] adj light-fingered ▷ nm/f (carterista) pickpocket; (ladrón) petty thief

rato ['rato] nm while, short time; **a ~s** from time to time; **hay para ~** there's still a long way to go; **al poco ~** soon afterwards; **pasar el ~** to kill time; **pasar un buen/mal ~** to have a good/rough time; **en mis ~s libres** in my spare time

ratón [ra'ton] nm mouse; **ratonera** [rato'nera] nf mousetrap

raudal [rau'ðal] nm torrent; **a ~es** in abundance

raya ['raja] nf line; (marca) scratch; (en tela) stripe; (de pelo) parting; (límite) boundary; (pez) ray; (puntuación) dash; **a ~s** striped; **pasarse de la ~** to go too far; **tener a ~** to keep in check; **rayar** [ra'jar] vt to line; to scratch; (subrayar) to underline ▷ vi: **rayar en o con** to border on

rayo ['rajo] nm (del sol) ray, beam; (de luz) shaft; (en una tormenta) (flash of) lightning; **rayos X** X-rays

raza ['raθa] nf race; **raza humana** human race

razón [ra'θon] nf reason; (justicia) right, justice; (razonamiento) reasoning; (motivo) reason, motive; (Mat) ratio; **a ~ de 10 cada día** at the rate of 10 a day; **en ~ de** with regard to; **dar ~ a algn** to agree that sb is right; **tener ~** to be right; **razón de ser** raison d'être; **razón directa/inversa** direct/inverse proportion; **razonable**

adj reasonable; (*justo, moderado*) fair; **razonamiento** *nm* (*juicio*) judg(e)ment; (*argumento*) reasoning; **razonar** *vt, vi* to reason, argue

re [re] *nm* (*Mús*) D

reacción [reak'θjon] *nf* reaction; **avión a ~** jet plane; **reacción en cadena** chain reaction; **reaccionar** *vi* to react

reacio, -a [re'aθjo, a] *adj* stubborn

reactivar [reakti'βar] *vt* to revitalize

reactor [reak'tor] *nm* reactor

real [re'al] *adj* real; (*del rey, fig*) royal

realidad [reali'ðað] *nf* reality, fact; (*verdad*) truth

realista [rea'lista] *nmf* realist

realización [realiθa'θjon] *nf* fulfilment

realizador, a [realiθa'ðor, a] *nm/f* film-maker

realizar [reali'θar] *vt* (*objetivo*) to achieve; (*plan*) to carry out; (*viaje*) to make, undertake; **realizarse** *vr* to come about, come true

realmente [real'mente] *adv* really, actually

realzar [real'θar] *vt* to enhance; (*acentuar*) to highlight

reanimar [reani'mar] *vt* to revive; (*alentar*) to encourage; **reanimarse** *vr* to revive

reanudar [reanu'ðar] *vt* (*renovar*) to renew; (*historia, viaje*) to resume

reaparición [reapari'θjon] *nf* reappearance

rearme [re'arme] *nm* rearmament

rebaja [re'βaxa] *nf* (*Com*) reduction; (: *descuento*) discount; **rebajas** *nfpl* (*Com*) sale; **rebajar** *vt* (*bajar*) to lower; (*reducir*) to reduce; (*disminuir*) to lessen; (*humillar*) to humble

rebanada [reβa'naða] *nf* slice

rebañar [reβa'ɲar] *vt* (*comida*) to scrape up; (*plato*) to scrape clean

rebaño [re'βaɲo] *nm* herd; (*de ovejas*) flock

rebatir [reβa'tir] *vt* to refute

rebeca [re'βeka] *nf* cardigan

rebelarse [reβe'larse] *vr* to rebel, revolt

rebelde [re'βelde] *adj* rebellious; (*niño*) unruly ▷ *nmf* rebel; **rebeldía** *nf* rebelliousness; (*desobediencia*) disobedience

rebelión [reβe'ljon] *nf* rebellion

reblandecer [reβlande'θer] *vt* to soften

rebobinar [reβoβi'nar] *vt* (*cinta, película de video*) to rewind

rebosante [reβo'sante] *adj* overflowing

rebosar [reβo'sar] *vi* (*líquido, recipiente*) to overflow; (*abundar*) to abound, be plentiful

rebotar [reβo'tar] *vt* to bounce; (*rechazar*) to repel ▷ *vi* (*pelota*) to bounce; (*bala*) to ricochet; **rebote** *nm* rebound; **de rebote** on the rebound

rebozado, -a [reβo'θaðo, a] *adj* fried in batter o breadcrumbs

rebozar [reβo'θar] *vt* to wrap up; (*Culin*) to fry in batter o breadcrumbs

rebuscado, -a [reβus'kaðo, a] *adj* (*amanerado*) affected; (*palabra*) recherché; (*idea*) far-fetched

rebuscar [reβus'kar] *vi* ~ (**en/por**) to search carefully (in/for)

recado [re'kaðo] *nm* (*mensaje*) message; (*encargo*) errand; **tomar un ~** (*Tel*) to take a message

recaer [reka'er] *vi* to relapse; ~ **en** to fall to o on; (*criminal etc*) to fall back into, relapse into; **recaída** *nf* relapse

recalcar [rekal'kar] *vt* (*fig*) to stress, emphasize

recalentar [rekalen'tar] *vt* (*volver a calentar*) to reheat; (*calentar demasiado*) to overheat

recámara [re'kamara] (*MÉX*) *nf* bedroom

recambio [re'kambjo] *nm* spare; (*de pluma*) refill

recapacitar [rekapaθi'tar] *vi* to reflect

recargado, -a [rekar'ɣaðo, a] *adj* overloaded

recargar [rekar'ɣar] vt to overload;
(*batería*) to recharge; **~ el saldo de** (*Tel*)
to top up; **recargo** nm surcharge;
(*aumento*) increase

recatado, -a [reka'taðo, a] adj
(*modesto*) modest, demure; (*prudente*)
cautious

recaudación [rekauða'θjon] nf
(*acción*) collection; (*cantidad*) takings pl;
(*en deporte*) gate; **recaudador, a** nm/f
tax collector

recelar [reθe'lar] vt: **~ que ...**
(*sospechar*) to suspect that ...; (*temer*) to
fear that ... ▷ vi: **~ de** to distrust; **recelo**
nm distrust, suspicion

recepción [reθep'θjon] nf reception;
recepcionista nmf receptionist

receptor, a [reθep'tor, a] nm/f
recipient ▷ nm (*Tel*) receiver

recesión [reθe'sjon] nf (*Com*)
recession

receta [re'θeta] nf (*Culin*) recipe; (*Med*)
prescription

> No confundir **receta** con la palabra
> inglesa *receipt*.

rechazar [retʃa'θar] vt to reject;
(*oferta*) to turn down; (*ataque*) to repel

rechazo [re'tʃaθo] nm rejection

rechinar [retʃi'nar] vi to creak;
(*dientes*) to grind

rechistar [retʃis'tar] vi: **sin ~** without
a murmur

rechoncho, -a [re'tʃontʃo, a] (*fam*)
adj thickset (BRIT), heavy-set (US)

rechupete [retʃu'pete]: **de ~** adj
(*comida*) delicious, scrumptious

recibidor [reθiβi'ðor] nm entrance
hall

recibimiento [reθiβi'mjento] nm
reception, welcome

recibir [reθi'βir] vt to receive; (*dar
la bienvenida*) to welcome ▷ vi to
entertain; **recibirse** vr: **~ de** to
qualify as; **recibo** nm receipt

reciclable [reθi'klaβle] adj recyclable

reciclar [reθi'klar] vt to recycle

recién [re'θjen] adv recently, newly;
los ~ casados the newly-weds; **el ~
llegado** the newcomer; **el ~ nacido** the

newborn child

reciente [re'θjente] adj recent;
(*fresco*) fresh

recinto [re'θinto] nm enclosure;
(*área*) area, place

recio, -a ['reθjo, a] adj strong, tough;
(*voz*) loud ▷ adv hard, loud(ly)

recipiente [reθi'pjente] nm
receptacle

recíproco, -a [re'θiproko, a] adj
reciprocal

recital [reθi'tal] nm (*Mús*) recital;
(*Literatura*) reading

recitar [reθi'tar] vt to recite

reclamación [reklama'θjon] nf
claim, demand; (*queja*) complaint

reclamar [rekla'mar] vt to claim,
demand ▷ vi: **~ contra** to complain
about; **reclamo** nm (*anuncio*)
advertisement; (*tentación*) attraction

reclinar [rekli'nar] vt to recline, lean;
reclinarse vr to lean back

reclusión [reklu'sjon] nf (*prisión*)
prison; (*refugio*) seclusion

recluta [re'kluta] nmf recruit ▷ nf
recruitment; **reclutar** vt (*datos*)
to collect; (*dinero*) to collect up;
reclutamiento nm recruitment

recobrar [reko'βrar] vt (*salud*)
to recover; (*rescatar*) to get back;
recobrarse vr to recover

recodo [re'koðo] nm (*de río, camino*)
bend

recogedor [rekoxe'ðor] nm dustpan

recoger [reko'xer] vt to collect;
(*Agr*) to harvest; (*levantar*) to pick up;
(*juntar*) to gather; (*pasar a buscar*)
to come for, get; (*dar asilo*) to give
shelter to; (*faldas*) to gather up; (*pelo*)
to put up; **recogerse** vr (*retirarse*) to
retire; **recogido, -a** adj (*lugar*) quiet,
secluded; (*pequeño*) small ▷ nf (*Correos*)
collection; (*Agr*) harvest

recolección [rekolek'θjon] nf (*Agr*)
harvesting; (*colecta*) collection

recomendación [rekomenda'θjon]
nf (*sugerencia*) suggestion,
recommendation; (*referencia*) reference

recomendar [rekomenˈdar] vt to suggest, recommend; (confiar) to entrust

recompensa [rekomˈpensa] nf reward, recompense; **recompensar** vt to reward, recompense

reconciliación [rekonθiljaˈθjon] nf reconciliation

reconciliar [rekonθiˈljar] vt to reconcile; **reconciliarse** vr to become reconciled

recóndito, -a [reˈkondito, a] adj (lugar) hidden, secret

reconocer [rekonoˈθer] vt to recognize; (registrar) to search; (Med) to examine; **reconocido, -a** adj recognized; (agradecido) grateful; **reconocimiento** nm recognition; search; examination; gratitude; (confesión) admission

reconquista [rekonˈkista] nf reconquest; **la R~** the Reconquest (of Spain)

reconstituyente [rekonstituˈjente] nm tonic

reconstruir [rekonstruˈir] vt to reconstruct

reconversión [rekonβerˈsjon] nf (reestructuración) restructuring; **reconversión industrial** industrial rationalization

recopilación [rekopilaˈθjon] nf (resumen) summary; (compilación) compilation; **recopilar** vt to compile

récord [ˈrekorð] (pl **-s**) adj inv, nm record

recordar [rekorˈðar] vt (acordarse de) to remember; (acordar a otro) to remind ▷ vi to remember

   No confundir **recordar** con la palabra inglesa **record**.

recorrer [rekoˈrrer] vt (país) to cross, travel through; (distancia) to cover; (registrar) to search; (repasar) to look over; **recorrido** nm run, journey; **tren de largo recorrido** main-line train

recortar [rekorˈtar] vt to cut out; **recorte** nm (acción, de prensa) cutting; (de telas, chapas) trimming; **recorte presupuestario** budget cut

recostar [rekosˈtar] vt to lean; **recostarse** vr to lie down

recoveco [rekoˈβeko] nm (de camino, río etc) bend; (en casa) cubby hole

recreación [rekreaˈθjon] nf recreation

recrear [rekreˈar] vt (entretener) to entertain; (volver a crear) to recreate; **recreativo, -a** adj recreational; **recreo** nm recreation; (Escol) break, playtime

recriminar [rekrimiˈnar] vt to reproach ▷ vi to recriminate; **recriminarse** vr to reproach each other

recrudecer [rekruðeˈθer] vt, vi to worsen; **recrudecerse** vr to worsen

recta [ˈrekta] nf straight line

rectángulo, -a [rekˈtanɡulo, a] adj rectangular ▷ nm rectangle

rectificar [rektifiˈkar] vt to rectify; (volverse recto) to straighten ▷ vi to correct o.s.

rectitud [rektiˈtuð] nf straightness

recto, -a [ˈrekto, a] adj straight; (persona) honest, upright; **siga todo ~** go straight on ▷ nm rectum

rector, -a [rekˈtor, a] adj governing

recuadro [reˈkwaðro] nm box; (Tip) inset

recubrir [rekuˈβrir] vt: **~ (con)** (pintura, crema) to cover (with)

recuento [reˈkwento] nm inventory; **hacer el ~ de** to count o reckon up

recuerdo [reˈkwerðo] nm souvenir; **recuerdos** nmpl (memorias) memories; **¡~s a tu madre!** give my regards to your mother!

recular [rekuˈlar] vi to back down

recuperación [rekuperaˈθjon] nf recovery

recuperar [rekupeˈrar] vt to recover; (tiempo) to make up; **recuperarse** vr to recuperate

recurrir [rekuˈrrir] vi (Jur) to appeal; **~ a** to resort to; (persona) to turn to;

recurso nm resort; (medios) means pl, resources pl; (Jur) appeal

red [reδ] nf net, mesh; (Ferro etc) network; (trampa) trap; **la R~** (Internet) the Net

redacción [reδak'θjon] nf (acción) editing; (personal) editorial staff; (Escol) essay, composition

redactar [reδak'tar] vt to draw up, draft; (periódico) to edit

redactor, a [reδak'tor, a] nm/f editor

redada [re'δaδa] nf (de policía) raid, round-up

rededor [reδe'δor] nm: **al o en ~** around, round about

redoblar [reδo'βlar] vt to redouble ▷ vi (tambor) to roll

redonda [re'δonda] nf: **a la ~** around, round about

redondear [reδonde'ar] vt to round, round off

redondel [reδon'del] nm (círculo) circle; (Taur) bullring, arena

redondo, -a [re'δondo, a] adj (circular) round; (completo) complete

reducción [reδuk'θjon] nf reduction

reducido, -a [reδu'θiδo, a] adj reduced; (limitado) limited; (pequeño) small

reducir [reδu'θir] vt to reduce; to limit; **reducirse** vr to diminish

redundancia [reδun'danθja] nf redundancy

reembolsar [re(e)mbol'sar] vt (persona) to reimburse; (dinero) to repay, pay back; (depósito) to refund; **reembolso** nm reimbursement; refund

reemplazar [re(e)mpla'θar] vt to replace; **reemplazo** nm replacement; **de reemplazo** (Mil) reserve

reencuentro [re(e)n'kwentro] nm reunion

reescribible [reeskri'βiβle] adj rewritable

refacción [refak'θjon] (Méx) nf spare (part)

referencia [refe'renθja] nf reference; **con ~ a** with reference to

referéndum [refe'rendum] (pl ~s) nm referendum

referente [refe'rente] adj: **~ a** concerning, relating to

réferi ['referi] (Lam) nmf referee

referir [refe'rir] vt (contar) to tell, recount; (relacionar) to refer, relate; **referirse** vr: **~se a** to refer to

refilón [refi'lon]: **de ~** adv obliquely

refinado, -a [refi'naδo, a] adj refined

refinar [refi'nar] vt to refine; **refinería** nf refinery

reflejar [refle'xar] vt to reflect; **reflejo, -a** adj reflected; (movimiento) reflex ▷ nm reflection; (Anat) reflex

reflexión [reflek'sjon] nf reflection; **reflexionar** vt to reflect on ▷ vi to reflect; (detenerse) to pause (to think)

reflexivo, -a [reflek'siβo, a] adj thoughtful; (Ling) reflexive

reforma [re'forma] nf reform; (Arq etc) repair; **reforma agraria** agrarian reform

reformar [refor'mar] vt to reform; (modificar) to change, alter; (Arq) to repair; **reformarse** vr to mend one's ways

reformatorio [reforma'torjo] nm reformatory

reforzar [refor'θar] vt to strengthen; (Arq) to reinforce; (fig) to encourage

refractario, -a [refrak'tarjo, a] adj (Tec) heat-resistant

refrán [re'fran] nm proverb, saying

refregar [refre'xar] vt to scrub

refrescante [refres'kante] adj refreshing, cooling

refrescar [refres'kar] vt to refresh ▷ vi to cool down; **refrescarse** vr to get cooler; (tomar aire fresco) to go out for a breath of fresh air; (beber) to have a drink

refresco [re'fresko] nm soft drink, cool drink; **"~s"** "refreshments"

refriega [re'frjexa] nf scuffle, brawl

refrigeración [refrixera'θjon] nf refrigeration; (de sala) air-conditioning

refrigerador [refrixera'ðor] nm refrigerator (BRIT), icebox (US)

refrigerar [refrixe'rar] vt to refrigerate; (sala) to air-condition

refuerzo [re'fwerθo] nm reinforcement; (Tec) support

refugiado, -a [refu'xjaðo, a] nm/f refugee

refugiarse [refu'xjarse] vr to take refuge, shelter

refugio [re'fuxjo] nm refuge; (protección) shelter

refunfuñar [refunfu'ɲar] vi to grunt, growl; (quejarse) to grumble

regadera [rega'ðera] nf watering can

regadío [rega'ðio] nm irrigated land

regalado, -a [rega'laðo, a] adj comfortable, luxurious; (gratis) free, for nothing

regalar [rexa'lar] vt (dar) to give (as a present); (entregar) to give away; (mimar) to pamper, make a fuss of

regaliz [rexa'liθ] nm liquorice

regalo [re'xalo] nm (obsequio) gift, present; (gusto) pleasure

regañadientes [rexaɲa'ðjentes]: **a ~** adv reluctantly

regañar [rexa'ɲar] vt to scold ▷ vi to grumble; **regañón, -ona** adj nagging

regar [re'xar] vt to water, irrigate; (fig) to scatter, sprinkle

regatear [rexate'ar] vt (Com) to bargain over; (escatimar) to be mean with ▷ vi to bargain, haggle; (Deporte) to dribble; **regateo** nm bargaining; (del cuerpo) swerve, dodge

regazo [re'xaθo] nm lap

regenerar [rexene'rar] vt to regenerate

régimen ['reximen] (pl **regímenes**) nm regime; (Med) diet

regimiento [rexi'mjento] nm regiment

regio, -a ['rexjo, a] adj royal, regal; (fig: suntuoso) splendid; (cs: fam) great, terrific

región [re'xjon] nf region

regir [re'xir] vt to govern, rule; (dirigir) to manage, run ▷ vi to apply, be in force

registrar [rexis'trar] vt (buscar) to search; (: en cajón) to look through; (inspeccionar) to inspect; (anotar) to register, record; (Inform) to log; **registrarse** vr to register; (ocurrir) to happen

registro [re'xistro] nm (acto) registration; (Mús, libro) register; (inspección) inspection, search; **registro civil** registry office

regla ['rexla] nf (ley) rule, regulation; (de medir) ruler, rule; (Med: período) period; **en ~** in order

reglamentación [rexlamenta'θjon] nf (acto) regulation; (lista) rules pl

reglamentar [rexlamen'tar] vt to regulate; **reglamentario, -a** adj statutory; **reglamento** nm rules pl, regulations pl

regocijarse [rexoθi'xarse] vr (alegrarse) to rejoice; **regocijo** nm joy, happiness

regrabadora [reɣraβa'ðora] nf rewriter; **regrabadora de DVD** DVD rewriter

regresar [rexre'sar] vi to come back, go back, return; **regreso** nm return

reguero [re'xero] nm (de sangre etc) trickle; (de humo) trail

regulador [rexula'ðor] nm regulator; (de radio etc) knob, control

regular [rexu'lar] adj regular; (normal) normal, usual; (común) ordinary; (organizado) regular, orderly; (mediano) average; (fam) not bad, so-so ▷ adv so-so, alright ▷ vt (controlar) to control, regulate; (Tec) to adjust; **por lo ~** as a rule; **regularidad** nf regularity; **regularizar** vt to regularize

rehabilitación [reaβilita'θjon] nf rehabilitation; (Arq) restoration

rehabilitar [reaβili'tar] vt to rehabilitate; (Arq) to restore; (reintegrar) to reinstate

rehacer [rea'θer] vt (reparar) to mend, repair; (volver a hacer) to redo, repeat; **rehacerse** vr (Med) to recover

rehén [re'en] nm hostage

rehuir [reu'ir] vt to avoid, shun

rehusar [reu'sar] vt, vi to refuse

reina ['reina] nf queen; **reinado** nm reign

reinar [rei'nar] vi to reign

reincidir [reinθi'ðir] vi to relapse

reincorporarse [reinkorpo'rarse] vr: **~ a** to rejoin

reino ['reino] nm kingdom; **reino animal/vegetal** animal/plant kingdom; **el Reino Unido** the United Kingdom

reintegrar [reinte'γrar] vt (reconstruir) to reconstruct; (persona) to reinstate; (dinero) to refund, pay back; **reintegrarse** vr: **~se a** to return to

reír [re'ir] vi to laugh; **reírse** vr to laugh; **~se de** to laugh at

reiterar [reite'rar] vt to reiterate

reivindicación [reiβindika'θjon] nf (demanda) claim, demand; (justificación) vindication

reivindicar [reiβindi'kar] vt to claim

reja ['rexa] nf (de ventana) grille, bars pl; (en la calle) grating

rejilla [re'xiʎa] nf grating, grille; (muebles) wickerwork; (de ventilación) vent; (de coche etc) luggage rack

rejoneador [rexonea'ðor] nm mounted bullfighter

rejuvenecer [rexuβene'θer] vt, vi to rejuvenate

relación [rela'θjon] nf relation, relationship; (Mat) ratio; (narración) report; **con ~ a, en ~ con** in relation to; **relaciones públicas** public relations; **relacionar** vt to relate, connect; **relacionarse** vr to be connected, be linked

relajación [relaxa'θjon] nf relaxation

relajar [rela'xar] vt to relax; **relajarse** vr to relax

relamerse [rela'merse] vr to lick one's lips

relámpago [re'lampaɣo] nm flash of lightning; **visita ~** lightning visit

relatar [rela'tar] vt to tell, relate

relativo, -a [rela'tiβo, a] adj relative; **en lo ~ a** concerning

relato [re'lato] nm (narración) story, tale

relegar [rele'ɣar] vt to relegate

relevante [rele'βante] adj eminent, outstanding

relevar [rele'βar] vt (sustituir) to relieve; **relevarse** vr to relay; **~ a algn de un cargo** to relieve sb of his post

relevo [re'leβo] nm relief; **carrera de ~s** relay race

relieve [re'ljeβe] nm (Arte, Tec) relief; (fig) prominence, importance; **bajo ~** bas-relief

religión [reli'xjon] nf religion; **religioso, -a** adj religious ▷ nm/f monk/nun

relinchar [relin'tʃar] vi to neigh

reliquia [re'likja] nf relic; **reliquia de familia** heirloom

rellano [re'ʎano] nm (Arq) landing

rellenar [reʎe'nar] vt (llenar) to fill up; (Culin) to stuff; (Costura) to pad; **relleno, -a** adj full up; stuffed ▷ nm stuffing; (de tapicería) padding

reloj [re'lo(x)] nm clock; **poner el ~ (en hora)** to set one's watch (o the clock); **reloj (de pulsera)** wristwatch; **reloj despertador** alarm (clock); **reloj digital** digital watch; **relojero, -a** nm/f clockmaker; watchmaker

reluciente [relu'θjente] adj brilliant, shining

relucir [relu'θir] vi to shine; (fig) to excel

remachar [rema'tʃar] vt to rivet; (fig) to hammer home, drive home; **remache** nm rivet

remangar [reman'gar] vt to roll up

remanso [re'manso] nm pool

remar [re'mar] vi to row

rematado, -a [rema'taðo, a] adj complete, utter

rematar [rema'tar] vt to finish off; (Com) to sell off cheap ▷ vi to end, finish off; (Deporte) to shoot

remate [re'mate] nm end, finish; (punta) tip; (Deporte) shot; (Arq) top; **de o para ~** to crown it all (BRIT), to top it off

remedar [reme'ðar] vt to imitate

remediar [reme'ðjar] vt to remedy; (subsanar) to make good, repair; (evitar) to avoid

remedio [re'meðjo] nm remedy; (alivio) relief, help; (Jur) recourse, remedy; **poner ~ a** to correct, stop; **no tener más ~** to have no alternative; **¡qué ~!** there's no choice!; **sin ~** hopeless

remendar [remen'dar] vt to repair; (con parche) to patch

remiendo [re'mjendo] nm mend; (con parche) patch; (cosido) darn

remilgado, -a [remil'xaðo, a] adj prim; (afectado) affected

remilgo [re'milxo] nm primness; (afectación) affectation

remiso, -a [re'miso, a] adj slack, slow

remite [re'mite] nm (en sobre) name and address of sender

remitir [remi'tir] vt to remit, send ▷ vi to slacken; (en carta): **remite: X** sender: X; **remitente** nmf sender

remo [ˈremo] nm (de barco) oar; (Deporte) rowing

remojar [remo'xar] vt to steep, soak; (galleta etc) to dip, dunk

remojo [re'moxo] nm: **dejar la ropa en ~** to leave clothes to soak

remolacha [remo'latʃa] nf beet, beetroot

remolcador [remolka'ðor] nm (Náut) tug; (Auto) breakdown lorry

remolcar [remol'kar] vt to tow

remolino [remo'lino] nm eddy; (de agua) whirlpool; (de viento) whirlwind; (de gente) crowd

remolque [re'molke] nm tow, towing; (cuerda) towrope; **llevar a ~** to tow

remontar [remon'tar] vt to mend;

remontarse vr to soar; **~se a** (Com) to amount to; **~ el vuelo** to soar

remorder [remor'ðer] vt to distress, disturb; **~le la conciencia a algn** to have a guilty conscience; **remordimiento** nm remorse

remoto, -a [re'moto, a] adj remote

remover [remo'βer] vt to stir; (tierra) to turn over; (objetos) to move round

remuneración [remunera'θjon] nf remuneration

remunerar [remune'rar] vt to remunerate; (premiar) to reward

renacer [rena'θer] vi to be reborn; (fig) to revive; **renacimiento** nm rebirth; **el Renacimiento** the Renaissance

renacuajo [rena'kwaxo] nm (Zool) tadpole

renal [re'nal] adj renal, kidney cpd

rencilla [ren'θiʎa] nf quarrel

rencor [ren'kor] nm rancour, bitterness; **rencoroso, -a** adj spiteful

rendición [rendi'θjon] nf surrender

rendido, -a [ren'diðo, a] adj (sumiso) submissive; (cansado) worn-out, exhausted

rendija [ren'dixa] nf (hendedura) crack, cleft

rendimiento [rendi'mjento] nm (producción) output; (Tec, Com) efficiency

rendir [ren'dir] vt (vencer) to defeat; (producir) to produce; (dar beneficio) to yield; (agotar) to exhaust ▷ vi to pay; **rendirse** vr (someterse) to surrender; (cansarse) to wear o.s. out; **~ homenaje o culto a** to pay homage to

renegar [rene'xar] vi (renunciar) to renounce; (blasfemar) to blaspheme; (quejarse) to complain

RENFE [ˈrenfe] nf abr (= Red Nacional de los Ferrocarriles Españoles)

renglón [ren'glon] nm (línea) line; (Com) item, article; **a ~ seguido** immediately after

renombre [re'nombre] nm renown

renovación [renoβa'θjon] nf (de

contrato) renewal; (*Arq*) renovation

renovar [reno'βar] *vt* to renew; (*Arq*) to renovate

renta ['renta] *nf* (*ingresos*) income; (*beneficio*) profit; (*alquiler*) rent; **renta vitalicia** annuity; **rentable** *adj* profitable

renuncia [re'nunθja] *nf* resignation; **renunciar** [renun'θjar] *vt* to renounce; (*tabaco, alcohol etc*): **renunciar a** to give up; (*oferta, oportunidad*) to turn down; (*puesto*) to resign ▷ *vi* to resign

reñido, -a [re'ɲiðo, a] *adj* (*batalla*) bitter, hard-fought; **estar ~ con algn** to be on bad terms with sb

reñir [re'ɲir] *vt* (*regañar*) to scold ▷ *vi* (*estar peleado*) to quarrel, fall out; (*combatir*) to fight

reo ['reo] *nmf* culprit, offender; (*acusado*) accused, defendant

reojo [re'oxo]: **de ~** *adv* out of the corner of one's eye

reparación [repara'θjon] *nf* (*acto*) mending, repairing; (*Tec*) repair; (*fig*) amends *pl*, reparation

reparar [repa'rar] *vt* to repair; (*fig*) to make amends for; (*observar*) to observe ▷ *vi*: **~ en** (*darse cuenta de*) to notice; (*prestar atención a*) to pay attention to

reparo [re'paro] *nm* (*advertencia*) observation; (*duda*) doubt; (*dificultad*) difficulty; **poner ~s (a)** to raise objections (to)

repartidor, a [reparti'ðor, a] *nm/f* distributor

repartir [repar'tir] *vt* to distribute, share out; (*Correos*) to deliver; **reparto** *nm* distribution; delivery; (*Teatro, Cine*) cast; (*CAM: urbanización*) housing estate (*BRIT*), real estate development (*US*)

repasar [repa'sar] *vt* (*Escol*) to revise; (*Mecánica*) to check, overhaul; (*Costura*) to mend; **repaso** *nm* revision; overhaul, checkup; mending

repecho [re'petʃo] *nm* steep incline

repelente [repe'lente] *adj* repellent, repulsive

repeler [repe'ler] *vt* to repel

repente [re'pente]: **de ~** *adv* suddenly

repentino, -a [repen'tino, a] *adj* sudden

repercusión [reperku'sjon] *nf* repercussion

repercutir [reperku'tir] *vi* (*objeto*) to rebound; (*sonido*) to echo; **~ en** (*fig*) to have repercussions on

repertorio [reper'torjo] *nm* list; (*Teatro*) repertoire

repetición [repeti'θjon] *nf* repetition

repetir [repe'tir] *vt* to repeat; (*plato*) to have a second helping of ▷ *vi* to repeat; (*sabor*) to come back; **repetirse** *vr* (*volver sobre un tema*) to repeat o.s.

repetitivo, -a [repeti'tiβo, a] *adj* repetitive, repetitious

repique [re'pike] *nm* pealing, ringing; **repiqueteo** *nm* pealing; (*de tambor*) drumming

repisa [re'pisa] *nf* ledge, shelf; (*de ventana*) windowsill; **la ~ de la chimenea** the mantelpiece

repito *etc vb* V **repetir**

replantearse [replante'arse] *vr*: **~ un problema** to reconsider a problem

repleto, -a [re'pleto, a] *adj* replete, full up

réplica ['replika] *nf* answer; (*Arte*) replica

replicar [repli'kar] *vi* to answer; (*objetar*) to argue, answer back

repliegue [re'pljexe] *nm* (*Mil*) withdrawal

repoblación [repoβla'θjon] *nf* repopulation; (*de río*) restocking; **repoblación forestal** reafforestation

repoblar [repo'βlar] *vt* to repopulate; (*con árboles*) to reafforest

repollito [repo'ʎito] (*cs*) *nm*: **~s de Bruselas** (Brussels) sprouts

repollo [re'poʎo] *nm* cabbage

reponer [repo'ner] *vt* to replace, put back; (*Teatro*) to revive; **reponerse** *vr* to recover; **~ que ...** to reply that ...

reportaje [repor'taxe] *nm* report,

article

reportero, -a [repor'tero, a] nm/f reporter

reposacabezas [reposaka'βeθas] nm inv headrest

reposar [repo'sar] vi to rest, repose

reposera [repo'sera] (RPL) nf deck chair

reposición [reposi'θjon] nf replacement; (Cine) remake

reposo [re'poso] nm rest

repostar [repos'tar] vt to replenish; (Auto) to fill up (with petrol BRIT) o gasoline (US))

repostería [reposte'ria] nf confectioner's (shop)

represa [re'presa] nf dam; (lago artificial) lake, pool

represalia [repre'salja] nf reprisal

representación [representa'θjon] nf representation; (Teatro) performance; **representante** nmf representative; performer

representar [represen'tar] vt to represent; (Teatro) to perform; (edad) to look; **representarse** vr to imagine; **representativo, -a** adj representative

represión [repre'sjon] nf repression

reprimenda [repri'menda] nf reprimand, rebuke

reprimir [repri'mir] vt to repress

reprobar [repro'βar] vt to censure, reprove

reprochar [repro'tʃar] vt to reproach; **reproche** nm reproach

reproducción [reproðuk'θjon] nf reproduction

reproducir [reproðu'θir] vt to reproduce; **reproducirse** vr to breed; (situación) to recur

reproductor, a [reproðuk'tor, a] adj reproductive ▷ nm player; **reproductor de CD** CD player

reptil [rep'til] nm reptile

república [re'puβlika] nf republic; **República Dominicana** Dominican Republic; **republicano, -a** adj, nm republican

repudiar [repu'ðjar] vt to repudiate; (fe) to renounce

repuesto [re'pwesto] nm (pieza de recambio) spare (part); (abastecimiento) supply; **rueda de ~** spare wheel

repugnancia [repuɣ'nanθja] nf repugnance; **repugnante** adj repugnant, repulsive

repugnar [repuɣ'nar] vt to disgust

repulsa [re'pulsa] nf rebuff

repulsión [repul'sjon] nf repulsion, aversion; **repulsivo, -a** adj repulsive

reputación [reputa'θjon] nf reputation

requerir [reke'rir] vt (pedir) to ask, request; (exigir) to require; (llamar) to send for, summon

requesón [reke'son] nm cottage cheese

requete... [re'kete] prefijo extremely

réquiem ['rekjem] (pl ~s) nm requiem

requisito [reki'sito] nm requirement, requisite

res [res] nf beast, animal

resaca [re'saka] nf (de mar) undertow, undercurrent; (fam) hangover

resaltar [resal'tar] vt to project, stick out; (fig) to stand out

resarcir [resar'θir] vt to compensate; **resarcirse** vr to make up for

resbaladero [resβala'ðero] (MÉX) nm slide

resbaladizo, -a [resβala'ðiθo, a] adj slippery

resbalar [resβa'lar] vi to slip, slide; (fig) to slip (up); **resbalarse** vr to slip, slide; to slip (up); **resbalón** nm (acción) slip

rescatar [reska'tar] vt (salvar) to save, rescue; (objeto) to get back, recover; (cautivos) to ransom

rescate [res'kate] nm rescue; (de objeto) recovery; **pagar un ~** to pay a ransom

rescindir [resθin'dir] vt to rescind

rescisión [resθi'sjon] nf cancellation

resecar [rese'kar] vt to dry

thoroughly; (Med) to cut out, remove; **resecarse** vr to dry up

reseco, -a [re'seko, a] adj very dry; (fig) skinny

resentido, -a [resen'tiðo, a] adj resentful

resentimiento [resenti'mjento] nm resentment, bitterness

resentirse [resen'tirse] vr (debilitarse: persona) to suffer; **~ de** (consecuencias) to feel the effects of; **~ de (o por) algo** to resent sth, be bitter about sth

reseña [re'seɲa] nf (cuenta) account; (informe) report; (Literatura) review

reseñar [rese'ɲar] vt to describe; (Literatura) to review

reserva [re'serβa] nf reserve; (reservación) reservation

reservado, -a [reser'βaðo, a] adj reserved; (retraído) cold, distant ▷ nm private room

reservar [reser'βar] vt (guardar) to keep; (habitación, entrada) to reserve; **reservarse** vr to save o.s.; (callar) to keep to o.s.

resfriado [resfri'aðo] nm cold; **resfriarse** vr to cool; (Med) to catch a cold

resguardar [resɣwar'ðar] vt to protect, shield; **resguardarse** vr: **~se de** to guard against; **resguardo** nm defence; (vale) voucher; (recibo) receipt, slip

residencia [resi'ðenθja] nf residence; **residencia de ancianos** residential home, old people's home; **residencia universitaria** hall of residence; **residencial** nf (urbanización) housing estate

residente [resi'ðente] adj, nmf resident

residir [resi'ðir] vi to reside, live; **~ en** to reside in, lie in

residuo [re'siðwo] nm residue

resignación [resiɣna'θjon] nf resignation; **resignarse** vr: **resignarse a o con** to resign o.s. to, be resigned to

resina [re'sina] nf resin

resistencia [resis'tenθja] nf (dureza) endurance, strength; (oposición, Elec) resistance; **resistente** adj strong, hardy; resistant

resistir [resis'tir] vt (soportar) to bear; (oponerse a) to resist, oppose; (aguantar) to put up with ▷ vi to resist; (aguantar) to last, endure; **resistirse** vr: **~se a** to refuse to, resist

resoluto, -a [reso'luto, a] adj resolute

resolver [resol'βer] vt to resolve; (solucionar) to solve, resolve; (decidir) to decide, settle; **resolverse** vr to make up one's mind

resonar [reso'nar] vi to ring, echo

resoplar [reso'plar] vi to snort; **resoplido** nm heavy breathing

resorte [re'sorte] nm spring; (fig) lever

resortera [resor'tera] (MÉX) nf catapult

respaldar [respal'dar] vt to back (up), support; **respaldarse** vr to lean back; **~se con o en** (fig) to take one's stand on; **respaldo** nm (de sillón) back; (fig) support, backing

respectivo, -a [respek'tiβo, a] adj respective; **en lo ~ a** with regard to

respecto [res'pekto] nm: **al ~** on this matter; **con ~ a, ~ de** with regard to, in relation to

respetable [respe'taβle] adj respectable

respetar [respe'tar] vt to respect; **respeto** nm respect; (acatamiento) deference; **respetos** nmpl respects; **respetuoso, -a** adj respectful

respingo [res'pingo] nm start, jump

respiración [respira'θjon] nf breathing; (Med) respiration; (ventilación) ventilation; **respiración asistida** artificial respiration (by machine)

respirar [respi'rar] vi to breathe; **respiratorio, -a** adj respiratory; **respiro** nm breathing; (fig: descanso) respite

resplandecer [resplande'θer]
vi to shine; **resplandeciente** adj
resplendent, shining; **resplandor**
nm brilliance, brightness; (de luz,
fuego) blaze

responder [respon'der] vt to answer
▷ vi to answer; (fig) to respond; (pey) to
answer back; **~ de o por** to answer for;
respondón, -ona adj cheeky

responsabilidad [responsaβili'ðað]
nf responsibility

responsabilizarse
[responsaβili'θarse] vr to make o.s.
responsible, take charge

responsable [respon'saβle] adj
responsible

respuesta [res'pwesta] nf answer,
reply

resquebrajar [reskeβra'xar] vt to
crack, split; **resquebrajarse** vr to
crack, split

resquicio [res'kiθjo] nm chink;
(hendedura) crack

resta ['resta] nf (Mat) remainder

restablecer [restaβle'θer] vt to
re-establish, restore; **restablecerse**
vr to recover

restante [res'tante] adj remaining;
lo ~ the remainder

restar [res'tar] vt (Mat) to subtract;
(fig) to take away ▷ vi to remain, be left

restauración [restaura'θjon] nf
restoration

restaurante [restau'rante] nm
restaurant

restaurar [restau'rar] vt to restore

restituir [restitu'ir] vt (devolver) to
return, give back; (rehabilitar) to restore

resto ['resto] nm (residuo) rest,
remainder; (apuesta) stake; **restos**
nmpl remains

restorán [resto'ran] nm (Lam)
restaurant

restregar [restre'xar] vt to scrub, rub

restricción [restrik'θjon] nf
restriction

restringir [restrin'xir] vt to restrict,

limit

resucitar [resuθi'tar] vt, vi to
resuscitate, revive

resuelto, -a [re'swelto, a] pp de
resolver ▷ adj resolute,
determined

resultado [resul'taðo] nm result;
(conclusión) outcome; **resultante** adj
resulting, resultant

resultar [resul'tar] vi (ser) to be;
(llegar a ser) to turn out to be; (salir bien)
to turn out well; (Com) to amount to;
~ de to stem from; **me resulta difícil
hacerlo** it's difficult for me to do it

resumen [re'sumen] (pl **resúmenes**)
nm summary, résumé; **en ~** in short

resumir [resu'mir] vt to sum
up; (cortar) to abridge, cut down;
(condensar) to summarize

> No confundir **resumir** con la
> palabra inglesa **resume**.

resurgir [resur'xir] vi (reaparecer)
to reappear

resurrección [resurre(k)'θjon] nf
resurrection

retablo [re'taβlo] nm altarpiece

retaguardia [reta'ɣwarðja] nf
rearguard

retahíla [reta'ila] nf series, string

retal [re'tal] nm remnant

retar [re'tar] vt to challenge; (desafiar)
to defy, dare

retazo [re'taθo] nm snippet (BRIT),
fragment

retención [reten'θjon] nf (tráfico)
hold-up; **retención fiscal** deduction
for tax purposes

retener [rete'ner] vt (intereses) to
withhold

reticente [reti'θente] adj (tono)
insinuating; (postura) reluctant; **ser ~ a
hacer algo** to be reluctant o unwilling
to do sth

retina [re'tina] nf retina

retintín [retin'tin] nm jangle, jingle

retirada [reti'raða] nf (Mil, refugio)
retreat; (de dinero) withdrawal; (de
embajador) recall; **retirado, -a** adj
(lugar) remote; (vida) quiet; (jubilado)

retired

retirar [reti'rar] vt to withdraw; (*quitar*) to remove; (*jubilar*) to retire, pension off; **retirarse** vr to retreat, withdraw; to retire; (*acostarse*) to retire, go to bed; **retiro** nm retreat; retirement; (*pago*) pension

reto ['reto] nm dare, challenge

retocar [reto'kar] vt (*fotografía*) to touch up, retouch

retoño [re'toɲo] nm sprout, shoot; (*fig*) offspring, child

retoque [re'toke] nm retouching

retorcer [retor'θer] vt to twist; (*manos, lavado*) to wring; **retorcerse** vr to become twisted; (*mover el cuerpo*) to writhe

retorcido, -a [retor'θiðo, a] adj (*persona*) devious

retorcijón [retorθi'xon] (LAM) nm (tb: ~ **de tripas**) stomach cramp

retórica [re'torika] nf rhetoric; (*pey*) affectedness

retorno [re'torno] nm return

retortijón [retorti'xon] (ESP) nm (tb: ~ **de tripas**) stomach cramp

retozar [reto'θar] vi (*juguetear*) to frolic, romp; (*saltar*) to gambol

retracción [retrak'θjon] nf retraction

retraerse [retra'erse] vr to retreat, withdraw; **retraído, -a** adj shy, retiring; **retraimiento** nm retirement; (*timidez*) shyness

retransmisión [retransmi'sjon] nf repeat (broadcast)

retransmitir [retransmi'tir] vt (*mensaje*) to relay; (*TV etc*) to repeat, retransmit; (: *en vivo*) to broadcast live

retrasado, -a [retra'saðo, a] adj late; (*Med*) mentally retarded; (*país etc*) backward, underdeveloped

retrasar [retra'sar] vt (*demorar*) to postpone, put off; (*retardar*) to slow down ▷ vi (*atrasarse*) to be late; (*reloj*) to be slow; (*producción*) to fall (off); (*quedarse atrás*) to lag behind; **retrasarse** vr to be late; to be slow; to

fall (off); to lag behind

retraso [re'traso] nm (*demora*) delay; (*lentitud*) slowness; (*tardanza*) lateness; (*atraso*) backwardness; **retrasos** nmpl (*Finanzas*) arrears; **llegar con** ~ to arrive late; **retraso mental** mental deficiency

retratar [retra'tar] vt (*Arte*) to paint the portrait of; (*fotografía*) to photograph; (*fig*) to depict, describe; **retrato** nm portrait; (*fig*) likeness; **retrato-robot** (ESP) nm Identikit®

retrete [re'trete] nm toilet

retribuir [retri'βwir] vt (*recompensar*) to reward; (*pagar*) to pay

retro... ['retro] prefijo retro...

retroceder [retroθe'ðer] vi (*echarse atrás*) to move back(wards); (*fig*) to back down

retroceso [retro'θeso] nm backward movement; (*Med*) relapse; (*fig*) backing down

retrospectivo, -a [retrospek'tiβo, a] adj retrospective

retrovisor [retroβi'sor] nm (tb: **espejo** ~) rear-view mirror

retumbar [retum'bar] vi to echo, resound

reúma [re'uma], **reuma** ['reuma] nm rheumatism

reunión [reu'njon] nf (*asamblea*) meeting; (*fiesta*) party

reunir [reu'nir] vt (*juntar*) to reunite, join (together); (*recoger*) to gather (together); (*personas*) to get together; (*cualidades*) to combine; **reunirse** vr (*personas: en asamblea*) to meet, gather

revalidar [reβali'ðar] vt (*ratificar*) to confirm, ratify

revalorizar [reβalori'θar] vt to revalue, reassess

revancha [re'βantʃa] nf revenge

revelación [reβela'θjon] nf revelation

revelado [reβe'laðo] nm developing

revelar [reβe'lar] vt to reveal; (*Foto*) to develop

reventa [re'βenta] nf (de

entradas: para concierto) touting

reventar [reβen'tar] vt to burst, explode

reventón [reβen'ton] nm (Auto) blow-out (BRIT), flat (US)

reverencia [reβe'renθja] nf reverence; **reverenciar** vt to revere

reverendo, -a [reβe'rendo, a] adj reverend

reverente [reβe'rente] adj reverent

reversa [re'βersa] nf (MÉX, CAM) reverse (gear)

reversible [reβer'siβle] adj (prenda) reversible

reverso [re'βerso] nm back, other side; (de moneda) reverse

revertir [reβer'tir] vi to revert

revés [re'βes] nm back, wrong side; (fig) reverse, setback; (Deporte) backhand; **al ~** the wrong way round; (de arriba abajo) upside down; (ropa) inside out; **volver algo del ~** to turn sth round; (ropa) to turn sth inside out

revisar [reβi'sar] vt (examinar) to check; (texto etc) to revise; **revisión** nf revision; **revisión salarial** wage review

revisor, a [reβi'sor, a] nm/f inspector; (Ferro) ticket collector

revista [re'βista] nf magazine, review; (Teatro) revue; (inspección) inspection; **pasar ~ a** to review, inspect; **revista del corazón** magazine featuring celebrity gossip and real-life romance stories

revivir [reβi'βir] vi to revive

revolcarse [reβol'karse] vr to roll about

revoltijo [reβol'tixo] nm mess, jumble

revoltoso, -a [reβol'toso, a] adj (travieso) naughty, unruly

revolución [reβolu'θjon] nf revolution; **revolucionario, -a** adj, nm/f revolutionary

revolver [reβol'βer] vt (desordenar) to disturb, mess up; (mover) to move about ▷ vi: **~ en** to go through;

rummage (about) in; **revolverse** vr (volver contra) to turn on o against

revólver [re'βolβer] nm revolver

revuelo [re'βwelo] nm fluttering; (fig) commotion

revuelta [re'βwelta] nf (motín) revolt; (agitación) commotion

revuelto, -a [re'βwelto, a] pp de **revolver** ▷ adj (mezclado) mixed-up, in disorder

rey [rei] nm king; **Día de R~es** Twelfth Night; **los R~es Magos** the Three Wise Men, the Magi

● **REYES MAGOS**
●
● On the night before the 6th
● January (the Epiphany), children
● go to bed expecting **los Reyes**
● **Magos** (the Three Wise Men) to
● bring them presents. Twelfth
● Night processions, known as
● **cabalgatas**, take place that
● evening when 3 people dressed
● as **los Reyes Magos** arrive in the
● town by land or sea to the delight
● of the children.

reyerta [re'jerta] nf quarrel, brawl

rezagado, -a [reθa'xaðo, a] nm/f straggler

rezar [re'θar] vi to pray; **~ con** (fam) to concern, have to do with; **rezo** nm prayer

rezumar [reθu'mar] vt to ooze

ría ['ria] nf estuary

riada [ri'aða] nf flood

ribera [ri'βera] nf (de río) bank; (: área) riverside

ribete [ri'βete] nm (de vestido) border; (fig) addition

ricino [ri'θino] nm: **aceite de ~** castor oil

rico, -a ['riko, a] adj rich; (adinerado) wealthy, rich; (lujoso) luxurious; (comida) delicious; (niño) lovely, cute ▷ nm/f rich person

ridiculez [riðiku'leθ] nf absurdity

ridiculizar [riðikuli'θar] vt to ridicule

ridículo, -a [ri'ðikulo, a] adj ridiculous; **hacer el ~** to make a fool of o.s.; **poner a algn en ~** to make a fool of sb

riego ['rjeɣo] nm (aspersión) watering; (irrigación) irrigation; **riego sanguíneo** blood flow o circulation

riel [rjel] nm rail

rienda ['rjenda] nf rein; **dar ~ suelta a** to give free rein to

riesgo ['rjesɣo] nm risk; **correr el ~ de** to run the risk of

rifa ['rifa] nf (lotería) raffle; **rifar** vt to raffle

rifle ['rifle] nm rifle

rigidez [rixi'ðeθ] nf rigidity, stiffness; (fig) strictness; **rígido, -a** adj rigid, stiff; strict, inflexible

rigor [ri'ɣor] nm strictness, rigour; (inclemencia) harshness; **de ~** de rigueur, essential; **riguroso, -a** adj rigorous; harsh; (severo) severe

rimar [ri'mar] vi to rhyme

rimbombante [rimbom'bante] adj pompous

rímel ['rimel] nm mascara

rímmel ['rimel] nm = **rímel**

rin [rin] (MÉX) nm (wheel) rim

rincón [rin'kon] nm corner (inside)

rinoceronte [rinoθe'ronte] nm rhinoceros

riña ['riɲa] nf (disputa) argument; (pelea) brawl

riñón [ri'ɲon] nm kidney

río etc ['rio] vb V **reír** ▷ nm river; (fig) torrent, stream; **río abajo/arriba** downstream/upstream; **Río de la Plata** River Plate

rioja [ri'oxa] nm (vino) rioja wine

rioplatense [riopla'tense] adj of o from the River Plate region

riqueza [ri'keθa] nf wealth, riches pl; (cualidad) richness

risa ['risa] nf laughter; (una risa) laugh; **¡qué ~!** what a laugh!

risco ['risko] nm crag, cliff

ristra ['ristra] nf string

risueño, -a [ri'sweɲo, a] adj (sonriente) smiling; (contento) cheerful

ritmo ['ritmo] nm rhythm; **a ~ lento** slowly; **trabajar a ~ lento** to go slow; **ritmo cardíaco** heart rate

rito ['rito] nm rite

ritual [ri'twal] adj, nm ritual

rival [ri'βal] adj, nmf rival; **rivalidad** nf rivalry; **rivalizar** vi: **rivalizar con** to rival, vie with

rizado, -a [ri'θaðo, a] adj curly ▷ nm curls pl

rizar [ri'θar] vt to curl; **rizarse** vr (pelo) to curl; (agua) to ripple; **rizo** nm curl; ripple

RNE nf abr = **Radio Nacional de España**

robar [ro'βar] vt to rob; (objeto) to steal; (casa etc) to break into; (Naipes) to draw

roble ['roβle] nm oak; **robledal** nm oakwood

robo ['roβo] nm robbery, theft

robot [ro'βot] nm robot; **robot (de cocina)** (ESP) food processor

robustecer [roβuste'θer] vt to strengthen

robusto, -a [ro'βusto, a] adj robust, strong

roca ['roka] nf rock

roce ['roθe] nm (caricia) brush; (Tec) friction; (en la piel) graze; **tener ~ con** to be in close contact with

rociar [ro'θjar] vt to spray

rocín [ro'θin] nm nag, hack

rocío [ro'θio] nm dew

rocola [ro'kola] (LAM) nf jukebox

rocoso, -a [ro'koso, a] adj rocky

rodaballo [roða'βaʎo] nm turbot

rodaja [ro'ðaxa] nf slice

rodaje [ro'ðaxe] nm (Cine) shooting, filming; (Auto): **en ~** running in

rodar [ro'ðar] vt (vehículo) to wheel (along); (escalera) to roll down; (viajar por) to travel (over) ▷ vi to roll; (coche) to go, run; (Cine) to shoot, film

rodear [roðe'ar] vt to surround ▷ vi

to go round; **rodearse** vr: **~se de amigos** to surround o.s. with friends

rodeo [ro'ðeo] nm (ruta indirecta) detour; (evasión) evasion; (Deporte) rodeo; **hablar sin ~s** to come to the point, speak plainly

rodilla [ro'ðiʎa] nf knee; **de ~s** kneeling; **ponerse de ~s** to kneel (down)

rodillo [ro'ðiʎo] nm roller; (Culin) rolling-pin

roedor, a [roe'ðor, a] adj gnawing ▷ nm rodent

roer [ro'er] vt (masticar) to gnaw; (corroer, fig) to corrode

rogar [ro'ɣar] vt, vi (pedir) to ask for; (suplicar) to beg, plead; **se ruega no fumar** please do not smoke

rojizo, -a [ro'xiθo, a] adj reddish

rojo, -a ['roxo, a] adj, nm red; **al ~ vivo** red-hot

rol [rol] nm list, roll; (papel) role

rollito [ro'ʎito] nm (tb: **~ de primavera**) spring roll

rollizo, -a [ro'ʎiθo, a] adj (objeto) cylindrical; (persona) plump

rollo ['roʎo] nm roll; (de cuerda) coil; (madera) log; (Esp: fam) bore; **¡qué ~!** (Esp: fam) what a carry-on!

Roma ['roma] n Rome

romance [ro'manθe] nm (amoroso) romance; (Literatura) ballad

romano, -a [ro'mano, a] adj, nm/f Roman; **a la romana** in batter

romanticismo [romanti'θismo] nm romanticism

romántico, -a [ro'mantiko, a] adj romantic

rombo ['rombo] nm (Geom) rhombus

romería [rome'ria] nf (Rel) pilgrimage; (excursión) trip, outing

○ rural festival which accompanies
○ the pilgrimage. People come from
○ all over to attend, bringing their
○ own food and drink, and spend the
○ day in celebration.

romero, -a [ro'mero, a] nm/f pilgrim ▷ nm rosemary

romo, -a ['romo, a] adj blunt; (fig) dull

rompecabezas [rompeka'βeθas] nm inv riddle, puzzle; (juego) jigsaw (puzzle)

rompehuelgas [rompe'welɣas] (LAM) nm inv strikebreaker, scab

rompeolas [rompe'olas] nm inv breakwater

romper [rom'per] vt to break; (hacer pedazos) to smash; (papel, tela etc) to tear, rip ▷ vi (olas) to break; (sol, diente) to break through; **romperse** vr to break up; **~ un contrato** to break a contract; **~ a** (empezar a) to start (suddenly) to; **~ a llorar** to burst into tears; **~ con algn** to fall out with sb

ron [ron] nm rum

roncar [ron'kar] vi to snore

ronco, -a ['ronko, a] adj (afónico) hoarse; (áspero) raucous

ronda ['ronda] nf (gen) round; (patrulla) patrol; **rondar** vt to patrol ▷ vi to patrol; (fig) to prowl round

ronquido [ron'kiðo] nm snore, snoring

ronronear [ronrone'ar] vi to purr

roña ['roɲa] nf (Veterinaria) mange; (mugre) dirt, grime; (óxido) rust

roñoso, -a [ro'ɲoso, a] adj (mugriento) filthy; (tacaño) mean

ropa ['ropa] nf clothes pl, clothing; **ropa blanca** linen; **ropa de cama** bed linen; **ropa de color** coloureds pl; **ropa interior** underwear; **ropa sucia** dirty washing; **ropaje** nm gown, robes pl

ropero [ro'pero] nm linen cupboard; (guardarropa) wardrobe

rosa ['rosa] adj pink ▷ nf rose

rosado, -a [ro'saðo, a] adj pink

▷ *nm* rosé

rosal [ro'sal] *nm* rosebush

rosario [ro'sarjo] *nm* (Rel) rosary;
rezar el ~ to say the rosary

rosca ['roska] *nf* (de tornillo) thread;
(de humo) coil, spiral; (pan, postre) ring-
shaped roll/pastry

rosetón [rose'ton] *nm* rosette; (Arq)
rose window

rosquilla [ros'kiʎa] *nf* doughnut-
shaped fritter

rostro ['rostro] *nm* (cara) face

rotativo, -a [rota'tiβo, a] *adj* rotary

roto, -a ['roto, a] *pp de* **romper** ▷ *adj*
broken

rotonda [ro'tonda] *nf* roundabout

rótula ['rotula] *nf* kneecap; (Tec) ball-
and-socket joint

rotulador [rotula'ðor] *nm* felt-tip
pen

rótulo ['rotulo] *nm* heading; title;
label; (letrero) sign

rotundamente [rotunda'mente]
adv (negar) flatly; (responder, afirmar)
emphatically; **rotundo, -a** *adj* round;
(enfático) emphatic

rotura [ro'tura] *nf* (acto) breaking;
(Med) fracture

rozadura [roθa'ðura] *nf* abrasion,
graze

rozar [ro'θar] *vt* (frotar) to rub;
(arañar) to scratch; (tocar ligeramente)
to shave, touch lightly; **rozarse** *vr* to
rub (together); **~se con** (fam) to rub
shoulders with

rte. *abr* (= *remite, remitente*) sender

RTVE *nf abr* = **Radiotelevisión
Española**

rubí [ru'βi] *nm* ruby; (de reloj) jewel

rubio, -a ['ruβjo, a] *adj* fair-haired,
blond(e) ▷ *nm/f* blond/blonde;
tabaco ~ Virginia tobacco

rubor [ru'βor] *nm* (sonrojo) blush;
(timidez) bashfulness; **ruborizarse**
vr to blush

rúbrica ['ruβrika] *nf* (de la firma)
flourish; **rubricar** *vt* (firmar) to sign
with a flourish; (concluir) to sign

and seal

rudimentario, -a [ruðimen'tarjo,
a] *adj* rudimentary

rudo, -a ['ruðo, a] *adj* (sin pulir)
unpolished; (grosero) coarse; (violento)
violent; (sencillo) simple

rueda ['rweða] *nf* wheel; (círculo)
ring, circle; (rodaja) slice, round; **rueda
de auxilio** (RPL) spare tyre; **rueda
delantera/trasera/de repuesto**
front/back/spare wheel; **rueda de
prensa** press conference; **rueda
gigante** (LAM) big (BRIT) o Ferris (US)
wheel

ruedo ['rweðo] *nm* (círculo) circle;
(Taur) arena, bullring

ruego etc ['rwexo] *vb* V **rogar** ▷ *nm*
request

rugby ['ruxβi] *nm* rugby

rugido [ru'xiðo] *nm* roar

rugir [ru'xir] *vi* to roar

rugoso, -a [ru'xoso, a] *adj* (arrugado)
wrinkled; (áspero) rough; (desigual)
ridged

ruido ['rwiðo] *nm* noise; (sonido)
sound; (alboroto) racket, row;
(escándalo) commotion, rumpus;
ruidoso, -a *adj* noisy, loud; (fig)
sensational

ruin [rwin] *adj* contemptible, mean

ruina ['rwina] *nf* ruin; (colapso)
collapse; (de persona) ruin, downfall

ruinoso, -a [rwi'noso, a] *adj*
ruinous; (destartalado) dilapidated,
tumbledown; (Com) disastrous

ruiseñor [rwise'nor] *nm* nightingale

rulero [ru'lero] (RPL) *nm* roller

ruleta [ru'leta] *nf* roulette

rulo ['rulo] *nm* (para el pelo) curler

Rumanía [ruma'nia] *nf* Rumania

rumba ['rumba] *nf* rumba

rumbo ['rumbo] *nm* (ruta) route,
direction; (ángulo de dirección) course,
bearing; (fig) course of events; **ir con ~
a** to be heading for

rumiante [ru'mjante] *nm* ruminant

rumiar [ru'mjar] *vt* to chew; (fig) to
chew over ▷ *vi* to chew the cud

rumor [ruˈmor] nm (ruido sordo) low
sound; (murmuración) murmur, buzz;
rumorearse vr: **se rumorea que ...** it
is rumoured that ...
rupestre [ruˈpestre] adj rock cpd
ruptura [rupˈtura] nf rupture
rural [ruˈral] adj rural
Rusia [ˈrusja] nf Russia; **ruso, -a** adj,
nm/f Russian
rústico, -a [ˈrustiko, a] adj rustic;
(ordinario) coarse, uncouth ▷ nm/f
yokel
ruta [ˈruta] nf route
rutina [ruˈtina] nf routine

S

S abr (= santo, a) St; (= sur) S
s. abr (= siglo) C.; (= siguiente) foll
S.A. abr (= Sociedad Anónima) Ltd. (BRIT),
Inc. (US)
sábado [ˈsaβaðo] nm Saturday
sábana [ˈsaβana] nf sheet
sabañón [saβaˈɲon] nm chilblain
saber [saˈβer] vt to know; (llegar
a conocer) to find out, learn; (tener
capacidad de) to know how to
▷ vi: **~ a** to taste of, taste like ▷ nm
knowledge, learning; **a ~** namely;
¿sabes conducir/nadar? can you
drive/swim?; **¿sabes francés?** do you
speak French?; **~ de memoria** to know
by heart; **hacer ~ algo a algn** to inform
sb of sth, let sb know sth
sabiduría [saβiðuˈria] nf
(conocimientos) wisdom; (instrucción)
learning
sabiendas [saˈβjendas]: **a ~** adv
knowingly
sabio, -a [ˈsaβjo, a] adj (docto)
learned; (prudente) wise, sensible
sabor [saˈβor] nm taste, flavour;

saborear [saβoˈrear] vt to taste, savour; (fig) to relish

sabotaje [saβoˈtaxe] nm sabotage

sabré etc vb V **saber**

sabroso, -a [saˈβroso, a] adj tasty; (fig: fam) racy, salty

sacacorchos [sakaˈkortʃos] nm inv corkscrew

sacapuntas [sakaˈpuntas] nm inv pencil sharpener

sacar [saˈkar] vt to take out; (fig: extraer) to get (out); (quitar) to remove, get out; (hacer salir) to bring out; (conclusión) to draw; (novela etc) to publish, bring out; (ropa) to take off; (obra) to make; (premio) to receive; (entradas) to get; (Tenis) to serve; ~ **adelante** (niño) to bring up; (negocio) to carry on, go on with; ~ **a algn a bailar** to get sb up to dance; ~ **una foto** to take a photo; ~ **la lengua** to stick out one's tongue; ~ **buenas/malas notas** to get good/bad marks

sacarina [sakaˈrina] nf saccharin(e)

sacerdote [saθerˈðote] nm priest

saciar [saˈθjar] vt (hambre, sed) to satisfy; **saciarse** vr (de comida) to get full up

saco [ˈsako] nm bag; (grande) sack; (su contenido) bagful; (LAM: chaqueta) jacket; **saco de dormir** sleeping bag

sacramento [sakraˈmento] nm sacrament

sacrificar [sakrifiˈkar] vt to sacrifice; **sacrificio** nm sacrifice

sacristía [sakrisˈtia] nf sacristy

sacudida [sakuˈðiða] nf (agitación) shake, shaking; (sacudimiento) jolt, bump; **sacudida eléctrica** electric shock

sacudir [sakuˈðir] vt to shake; (golpear) to hit

Sagitario [saxiˈtarjo] nm Sagittarius

sagrado, -a [saˈɣraðo, a] adj sacred, holy

Sáhara [ˈsaara] nm: **el ~** the Sahara (desert)

sal [sal] vb V **salir** ▷ nf salt; **sales de**

baño bath salts

sala [ˈsala] nf room; (tb: ~ **de estar**) living room; (Teatro) house, auditorium; (de hospital) ward; **sala de espera** waiting room; **sala de estar** living room; **sala de fiestas** dance hall

salado, -a [saˈlaðo, a] adj salty; (fig) witty, amusing; **agua salada** salt water

salar [saˈlar] vt to salt, add salt to

salario [saˈlarjo] nm wage, pay

salchicha [salˈtʃitʃa] nf (pork) sausage; **salchichón** nm (salami-type) sausage

saldo [ˈsaldo] nm (pago) settlement; (de una cuenta) balance; (lo restante) remnant(s) (pl), remainder; (de móvil) credit; **saldos** nmpl (en tienda) sale

saldré etc vb V **salir**

salero [saˈlero] nm salt cellar

salgo etc vb V **salir**

salida [saˈliða] nf (puerta etc) exit, way out; (acto) leaving, going out; (de tren, Aviac) departure; (Tec) output, production; (fig) way out; (Com) opening; (Geo, válvula) outlet; (de gas) leak; **calle sin ~** cul-de-sac; **salida de baño** (RPL) bathrobe; **salida de emergencia/incendios** emergency exit/fire escape

◯ PALABRA CLAVE

salir [saˈlir] vi 1 (partir: tb: **salir de**) to leave; **Juan ha salido** Juan is out; **salió de la cocina** he came out of the kitchen

2 (aparecer) to appear; (disco, libro) to come out; **anoche salió en la tele** she appeared o was on TV last night; **salió en todos los periódicos** it was in all the papers

3 (resultar): **la muchacha nos salió muy trabajadora** the girl turned out to be a very hard worker; **la comida te ha salido exquisita** the food was delicious; **sale muy caro** it's very expensive

4: salirle a uno algo: la entrevista que hice me salió bien/mal the interview I did went o turned out well/badly

5: salir adelante: no sé como haré para salir adelante I don't know how I'll get by

salirse vr (líquido) to spill; (animal) to escape

saliva [sa'liβa] nf saliva

salmo ['salmo] nm psalm

salmón [sal'mon] nm salmon

salmonete [salmo'nete] nm red mullet

salón [sa'lon] nm (de casa) living room, lounge; (muebles) lounge suite; **salón de baile** dance hall; **salón de belleza** beauty parlour

salpicadera [salpika'ðera] (MÉX) nf mudguard (BRIT), fender (US)

salpicadero [salpika'ðero] nm (Auto) dashboard

salpicar [salpi'kar] vt (rociar) to sprinkle, spatter; (esparcir) to scatter

salpicón [salpi'kon] nm (tb: ~ **de marisco**) seafood salad

salsa ['salsa] nf sauce; (con carne asada) gravy; (fig) spice

saltamontes [salta'montes] nm inv grasshopper

saltar [sal'tar] vt to jump (over), leap (over); (dejar de lado) to skip, miss out ▷ vi to jump, leap; (pelota) to bounce; (al aire) to fly up; (quebrarse) to break; (al agua) to dive; (fig) to explode, blow up

salto ['salto] nm jump, leap; (al agua) dive; **salto de agua** waterfall; **salto de altura/longitud** high/long jump

salud [sa'luð] nf health; **¡(a su) ~!** cheers!, good health!; **saludable** adj (de buena salud) healthy; (provechoso) good, beneficial

saludar [salu'ðar] vt to greet; (Mil) to salute; **saludo** nm greeting; **"saludos"** (en carta) "best wishes", "regards"

salvación [salβa'θjon] nf salvation;

(rescate) rescue

salvado [sal'βaðo] nm bran

salvaje [sal'βaxe] adj wild; (tribu) savage

salvamanteles [salβaman'teles] nm inv table mat

salvamento [salβa'mento] nm rescue

salvapantallas [salβapan'taʎas] nm inv screen saver

salvar [sal'βar] vt (rescatar) to save, rescue; (resolver) to overcome, resolve; (cubrir distancias) to cover, travel; (hacer excepción) to except, exclude; (barco) to salvage

salvavidas [salβa'βiðas] adj inv: **bote/chaleco ~** lifeboat/life jacket

salvo, -a ['salβo, a] adj safe ▷ adv except (for), save; **a ~** out of danger; **~ que** unless

san [san] adj saint; **S~ Juan** St John

sanar [sa'nar] vt (herida) to heal; (persona) to cure ▷ vi (persona) to get well, recover; (herida) to heal

sanatorio [sana'torjo] nm sanatorium

sanción [san'θjon] nf sanction

sancochado, -a [sanko'tʃaðo, a] (MÉX) adj (Culin) underdone, rare

sandalia [san'dalja] nf sandal

sandía [san'dia] nf watermelon

sandwich ['sandwitʃ] (pl **~s, ~es**) nm sandwich

sanfermines [sanfer'mines] nmpl festivities in celebration of San Fermín (Pamplona)

SANFERMINES

The **Sanfermines** is a week-long festival in Pamplona made famous by Ernest Hemingway. From the 7th July, the feast of "San Fermín", crowds of mainly young people take to the streets drinking, singing and dancing. Early in the morning bulls are released along the narrow streets leading

to the bullring, and young men
risk serious injury to show their
bravery by running out in front
of them, a custom which is also
typical of many Spanish villages.

sangrar [san'grar] vt, vi to bleed;
sangre nf blood

sangría [san'gria] nf sangria,
sweetened drink of red wine with fruit

sangriento, -a [san'grjento, a]
adj bloody

sanguíneo, -a [san'gineo, a] adj
blood cpd

sanidad [sani'ðað] nf (tb: ~ pública)
public health

San Isidro [sani'siðro] nm patron
saint of Madrid

SAN ISIDRO

San Isidro is the patron saint of
Madrid, and gives his name to
the week-long festivities which
take place around the 15th May.
Originally an 18th-century trade
fair, the **San Isidro** celebrations
now include music, dance, a
famous **romería**, theatre and
bullfighting.

sanitario, -a [sani'tarjo, a] adj
health cpd; **sanitarios** nmpl toilets
(BRIT), washroom (US)

sano, -a ['sano, a] adj healthy; (sin
daños) sound; (comida) wholesome;
(entero) whole, intact; **~ y salvo** safe
and sound

> No confundir **sano** con la palabra
> inglesa sane.

Santiago [san'tjaɣo] nm: **~ (de Chile)**
Santiago

santiamén [santja'men] nm: **en un ~**
in no time at all

santidad [santi'ðað] nf holiness,
sanctity

santiguarse [santi'ɣwarse] vr to
make the sign of the cross

santo, -a ['santo, a] adj holy; (fig)
wonderful, miraculous ▷ nm/f saint
▷ nm saint's day; **~ y seña** password

santuario [san'twarjo] nm
sanctuary, shrine

sapo ['sapo] nm toad

saque ['sake] nm (Tenis) service,
serve; (Fútbol) throw-in; **saque de
esquina** corner (kick)

saquear [sake'ar] vt (Mil) to sack;
(robar) to loot, plunder; (fig) to ransack

sarampión [saram'pjon] nm
measles sg

sarcástico, -a [sar'kastiko, a] adj
sarcastic

sardina [sar'ðina] nf sardine

sargento [sar'xento] nm sergeant

sarmiento [sar'mjento] nm (Bot)
vine shoot

sarna ['sarna] nf itch; (Med) scabies

sarpullido [sarpu'ʎiðo] nm (Med)
rash

sarro ['sarro] nm (en dientes) tartar,
plaque

sartén [sar'ten] nf frying pan

sastre ['sastre] nm tailor; **sastrería**
nf (arte) tailoring; (tienda) tailor's
(shop)

Satanás [sata'nas] nm Satan

satélite [sa'telite] nm satellite

sátira ['satira] nf satire

satisfacción [satisfak'θjon] nf
satisfaction

satisfacer [satisfa'θer] vt to satisfy;
(gastos) to meet; (pérdida) to make
good; **satisfacerse** vr to satisfy o.s.,
be satisfied; (vengarse) to take revenge;
satisfecho, -a adj satisfied; (contento)
content(ed), happy; (tb: **satisfecho de
sí mismo**) self-satisfied, smug

saturar [satu'rar] vt to saturate;
saturarse vr (mercado, aeropuerto) to
reach saturation point

sauce ['sauθe] nm willow; **sauce
llorón** weeping willow

sauna ['sauna] nf sauna

savia ['saβja] nf sap

saxofón [sakso'fon] nm saxophone

sazonar | 252

sazonar [saθo'nar] vt to ripen; (Culin) to flavour, season

scooter [e'skuter] (ESP) nf scooter

Scotch® [skotʃ] (LAM) nm Sellotape® (BRIT), Scotch tape® (US)

SE abr (= sudeste) SE

○ PALABRA CLAVE

se [se] pron 1 (reflexivo: sg: m) himself; (: pl) themselves; (: f) herself; (: pl) yourselves; (: cosa) itself; (: de Vd) yourself; (: de Vds) yourselves; **se está preparando** she's preparing herself

2 (con complemento indirecto) to him; to her; to them; to it; to you; **a usted se lo dije ayer** I told you yesterday; **se compró un sombrero** he bought himself a hat; **se rompió la pierna** he broke his leg

3 (uso recíproco) each other, one another; **se miraron (el uno al otro)** they looked at each other o one another

4 (en oraciones pasivas): **se han vendido muchos libros** a lot of books have been sold

5 (impers): **se dice que ...** people say that ..., it is said that ...; **allí se come muy bien** the food there is very good, you can eat very well there

sé etc [se] vb V **saber**; **ser**

sea etc vb V **ser**

sebo [seβo] nm fat, grease

secador [seka'ðor] nm: **~ de pelo** hair-dryer

secadora [seka'ðora] nf tumble dryer

secar [se'kar] vt to dry; **secarse** vr to dry (off); (río, planta) to dry up

sección [sek'θjon] nf section

seco, -a [seko, a] adj dry; (carácter) cold; (respuesta) sharp, curt; **parar en ~** to stop dead; **decir algo a secas** to say sth curtly

secretaría [sekreta'ria] nf secretariat

secretario, -a [sekre'tarjo, a] nm/f

secretary

secreto, -a [se'kreto, a] adj (persona) secretive ▷ nm secret; (calidad) secrecy

secta ['sekta] nf sect

sector [sek'tor] nm sector

secuela [se'kwela] nf consequence

secuencia [se'kwenθja] nf sequence

secuestrar [sekwes'trar] vt to kidnap; (bienes) to seize, confiscate; **secuestro** nm kidnapping; seizure, confiscation

secundario, -a [sekun'darjo, a] adj secondary

sed [seð] nf thirst; **tener ~** to be thirsty

seda ['seða] nf silk

sedal [se'ðal] nm fishing line

sedán [se'ðan] (LAM) nm saloon (BRIT), sedan (US)

sedante [se'ðante] nm sedative

sede ['seðe] nf (de gobierno) seat; (de compañía) headquarters pl; **Santa S~** Holy See

sedentario, -a [seðen'tarjo, a] adj sedentary

sediento, -a [se'ðjento, a] adj thirsty

sedimento [seði'mento] nm sediment

seducción [seðuk'θjon] nf seduction

seducir [seðu'θir] vt to seduce; (cautivar) to charm, fascinate; (atraer) to attract; **seductor, a** adj seductive; charming, fascinating; attractive ▷ nm/f seducer

segar [se'ɣar] vt (mies) to reap, cut; (hierba) to mow, cut

seglar [se'ɣlar] adj secular, lay

seguida [se'ɣiða] nf: **en ~** at once, right away

seguido, -a [se'ɣiðo, a] adj (continuo) continuous, unbroken; (recto) straight ▷ adv (directo) straight (on); (después) after; (LAM: a menudo) often; **-s** consecutive, successive; **5 días ~s** 5 days running, 5 days in a row

seguir [se'ɣir] vt to follow; (venir

después) to follow on, come after; (*proseguir*) to continue; (*perseguir*) to chase, pursue ▷ *vi* (*gen*) to follow; (*continuar*) to continue, carry o go on; **seguirse** *vr* to follow; **sigo sin comprender** I still don't understand; **sigue lloviendo** it's still raining

según [se'xun] *prep* according to ▷ *adv*: **¿irás? – –** are you going? – it all depends ▷ *conj* as; **~ caminamos** while we walk

segundo, -a [se'xundo, a] *adj* second ▷ *nm* second ▷ *nf* second meaning; **de segunda mano** second-hand; **segunda (clase)** second class; **segunda (marcha)** (*Auto*) second (gear)

seguramente [sexura'mente] *adv* surely; (*con certeza*) for sure, with certainty

seguridad [sexuri'ðað] *nf* safety; (*del estado, de casa etc*) security; (*certidumbre*) certainty; (*confianza*) confidence; (*estabilidad*) stability; **seguridad social** social security

seguro, -a [se'xuro, a] *adj* (*cierto*) sure, certain; (*fiel*) trustworthy; (*libre de peligro*) safe; (*bien defendido, firme*) secure ▷ *adv* for sure, certainly ▷ *nm* (*Com*) insurance; **seguro contra terceros/a todo riesgo** third party/comprehensive insurance; **seguros sociales** social security *sg*

seis [seis] *num* six

seísmo [se'ismo] *nm* tremor, earthquake

selección [selek'θjon] *nf* selection; **seleccionar** *vt* to pick, choose, select

selectividad [selektiβi'ðað] (*ESP*) *nf* university entrance examination

selecto, -a [se'lekto, a] *adj* select, choice; (*escogido*) selected

sellar [se'ʎar] *vt* (*documento oficial*) to seal; (*pasaporte, visado*) to stamp

sello [se'ʎo] *nm* stamp; (*precinto*) seal

selva ['selβa] *nf* (*bosque*) forest, woods *pl*; (*jungla*) jungle

semáforo [se'maforo] *nm* (*Auto*)

traffic lights *pl*; (*Ferro*) signal

semana [se'mana] *nf* week; **entre ~** during the week; **Semana Santa** Holy Week; **semanal** *adj* weekly; **semanario** *nm* weekly magazine

● **SEMANA SANTA**
●
● In Spain celebrations for **Semana**
● **Santa** (Holy Week) are often
● spectacular. "Viernes Santo,"
● "Sábado Santo" and "Domingo de
● Resurrección" (Good Friday, Holy
● Saturday, Easter Sunday) are all
● national public holidays, with
● additional days being given as
● local holidays. There are fabulous
● **procesiones** all over the country,
● with members of "cofradías"
● (brotherhoods) dressing in hooded
● robes and parading their "pasos"
● (religious floats and sculptures)
● through the streets. Seville has
● the most famous Holy Week
● processions.

sembrar [sem'brar] *vt* to sow; (*objetos*) to sprinkle, scatter about; (*noticias etc*) to spread

semejante [seme'xante] *adj* (*parecido*) similar ▷ *nm* fellow man, fellow creature; **~s** alike, similar; **nunca hizo cosa ~** he never did any such thing; **semejanza** *nf* similarity, resemblance

semejar [seme'xar] *vi* to seem like, resemble; **semejarse** *vr* to look alike, be similar

semen ['semen] *nm* semen

semestral [semes'tral] *adj* half-yearly, bi-annual

semicírculo [semi'θirkulo] *nm* semicircle

semidesnatado, -a [semiðesna'taðo, a] *adj* semi-skimmed

semifinal [semifi'nal] *nf* semifinal

semilla [se'miʎa] *nf* seed

seminario [semi'narjo] nm (Rel) seminary; (Escol) seminar

sémola ['semola] nf semolina

senado [se'naðo] nm senate; **senador, a** nm/f senator

sencillez [senθi'λeθ] nf simplicity; (de persona) naturalness; **sencillo, -a** adj simple; natural, unaffected

senda ['senda] nf path, track

senderismo [sende'rismo] nm hiking

sendero [sen'dero] nm path, track

sendos, -as ['sendos, as] adj pl: **les dio ~ golpes** he hit both of them

senil [se'nil] adj senile

seno ['seno] nm (Anat) bosom, bust; (fig) bosom; **~s** breasts

sensación [sensa'θjon] nf sensation; (sentido) sense; (sentimiento) feeling; **sensacional** adj sensational

sensato, -a [sen'sato, a] adj sensible

sensible [sen'sible] adj sensitive; (apreciable) perceptible, appreciable; (pérdida) considerable

| No confundir **sensible** con la palabra inglesa *sensible*.

sensiblero, -a adj sentimental

sensitivo, -a [sensi'tiβo, a] adj sense cpd

sensorial [senso'rjal] adj sensory

sensual [sen'swal] adj sensual

sentada [sen'taða] nf sitting; (protesta) sit-in

sentado, -a [sen'taðo, a] adj: **estar ~** to sit, be sitting (down); **dar por ~** to take for granted, assume

sentar [sen'tar] vt to sit, seat; (fig) to establish ▷ vi (vestido) to suit; (alimento): **~ bien/mal a** to agree/ disagree with; **sentarse** vr (persona) to sit, sit down; (los depósitos) to settle

sentencia [sen'tenθja] nf (máxima) maxim, saying; (Jur) sentence; **sentenciar** vt to sentence

sentido, -a [sen'tiðo, a] adj (pérdida) regrettable; (carácter) sensitive ▷ nm sense; (sentimiento) feeling; (significado) sense, meaning; (dirección) direction;

mi más ~ pésame my deepest sympathy; **tener ~** to make sense; **sentido común** common sense; **sentido del humor** sense of humour; **sentido único** one-way (street)

sentimental [sentimen'tal] adj sentimental; **vida ~** love life

sentimiento [senti'mjento] nm feeling

sentir [sen'tir] vt to feel; (percibir) to perceive, sense; (lamentar) to regret, be sorry for ▷ vi (tener la sensación) to feel; (lamentarse) to feel sorry; **~se bien/mal** to feel well/ill; **lo siento** I'm sorry

seña ['sena] nf sign; (Mil) password; **señas** nfpl (dirección) address sg; **señas personales** personal description sg

señal [se'nal] nf sign; (síntoma) symptom; (Ferro, Tel) signal; (marca) mark; (Com) deposit; **en ~ de** as a token o sign of; **señalar** vt to mark; (indicar) to point out, indicate

señor [se'nor] nm (hombre) man; (caballero) gentleman; (dueño) owner, master; (trato: antes de nombre propio) Mr; (: hablando directamente) sir; **muy ~ mío** Dear Sir; **el ~ alcalde/presidente** the mayor/president

señora [se'nora] nf (dama) lady; (trato: antes de nombre propio) Mrs; (: hablando directamente) madam; (esposa) wife; **Nuestra S~** Our Lady

señorita [seno'rita] nf (con nombre y/o apellido) Miss; (mujer joven) young lady

señorito [seno'rito] nm young gentleman; (pey) rich kid

sepa etc vb V **saber**

separación [separa'θjon] nf separation; (división) division; (hueco) gap

separar [sepa'rar] vt to separate; (dividir) to divide; **separarse** vr (parte) to come away; (partes) to come apart; (persona) to leave, go away; (matrimonio) to separate; **separatismo** nm separatism

sepia ['sepja] nf cuttlefish

septentrional [septentrjo'nal] adj northern

septiembre [sep'tjembre] nm September

séptimo, -a ['septimo, a] adj, nm seventh

sepulcral [sepul'kral] adj (fig: silencio, atmósfera) deadly; **sepulcro** nm tomb, grave

sepultar [sepul'tar] vt to bury; **sepultura** nf (acto) burial; (tumba) grave, tomb

sequía [se'kia] nf drought

séquito ['sekito] nm (de rey etc) retinue; (seguidores) followers pl

O PALABRA CLAVE

ser [ser] vi **1** (descripción) to be; **es médica/muy alta** she's a doctor/very tall; **la familia es de Cuzco** his (o her etc) family is from Cuzco; **soy Ana** (Tel) Ana speaking o here
2 (propiedad): **es de Joaquín** it's Joaquín's, it belongs to Joaquín
3 (horas, fechas, números): **es la una** it's one o'clock; **son las seis y media** it's half-past six; **es el 1 de junio** it's the first of June; **somos/son seis** there are six of us/them
4 (en oraciones pasivas): **ha sido descubierto ya** it's already been discovered
5 es de esperar que ... it is to be hoped o I etc hope that ...
6 (locuciones con ser): **o sea** that is to say; **sea él sea su hermana** either him or his sister
7. a no ser por él ... but for him ...
8. a no ser que: a no ser que tenga uno ya unless he's got one already
▷ nm being; **ser humano** human being

sereno, -a [se'reno, a] adj (persona) calm, unruffled; (el tiempo) fine, settled; (ambiente) calm, peaceful ▷ nm night watchman

serial [ser'jal] nm serial

serie ['serje] nf series; (cadena) sequence, succession; **fuera de ~** out of order; (fig) special, out of the ordinary; **fabricación en ~** mass production

seriedad [serje'ðað] nf seriousness; (formalidad) reliability; **serio, -a** adj serious; reliable, dependable; grave, serious; **en serio** adv seriously

serigrafía [serixra'fia] nf silk-screen printing

sermón [ser'mon] nm (Rel) sermon

seropositivo, -a [seroposi'tiβo] adj HIV positive

serpentear [serpente'ar] vi to wriggle; (camino, río) to wind, snake

serpentina [serpen'tina] nf streamer

serpiente [ser'pjente] nf snake; **serpiente de cascabel** rattlesnake

serranía [serra'nia] nf mountainous area

serrar [se'rrar] vt = **aserrar**

serrín [se'rrin] nm sawdust

serrucho [se'rrut∫o] nm saw

service [ser'βis] (RPL) nm (Auto) service

servicio [ser'βiθjo] nm service; (LAM Auto) service; **servicios** nmpl (ESP) toilet(s); **servicio incluido** service charge included; **servicio militar** military service

servidumbre [serβi'ðumbre] nf (sujeción) servitude; (criados) servants pl, staff

servil [ser'βil] adj servile

servilleta [serβi'ʎeta] nf serviette, napkin

servir [ser'βir] vt to serve ▷ vi to serve; (tener utilidad) to be of use, be useful; **servirse** vr to serve o.s.; **~se de algo** to make use of sth, use sth; **sírvase pasar** please come in

sesenta [se'senta] num sixty

sesión [se'sjon] nf (Pol) session, sitting; (Cine) showing

seso ['seso] nm brain; **sesudo, -a** adj sensible, wise

seta ['seta] nf mushroom; **seta venenosa** toadstool

setecientos, -as [sete'θjentos, as] adj, num seven hundred

setenta [se'tenta] num seventy

seto ['seto] nm hedge

severo, -a [se'βero, a] adj severe

Sevilla [se'βiʎa] n Seville; **sevillano, -a** adj of o from Seville ▷ nm/f native o inhabitant of Seville

sexo ['sekso] nm sex

sexto, -a ['seksto, a] adj, nm sixth

sexual [sek'swal] adj sexual; **vida ~** sex life

si [si] conj if ▷ nm (Mús) B; **me pregunto ~ ...** I wonder if o whether ...

sí [si] adv yes ▷ nm consent ▷ pron (uso impersonal) oneself; (sg: m) himself; (: f) herself; (: de cosa) itself; (de usted) yourself; (pl) themselves; (de ustedes) yourselves; (recíproco) each other; **él no quiere pero yo ~** he doesn't want to but I do; **ella ~ vendrá** she will certainly come, she is sure to come; **claro que ~** of course; **creo que ~** I think so

siamés, -esa [sja'mes, esa] adj, nm/f Siamese

SIDA ['siða] nm abr (= Síndrome de Inmunodeficiencia Adquirida) AIDS

siderúrgico, -a [siðe'ruːxico, a] adj iron and steel ▷ nm steel cpd

sidra ['siðra] nf cider

siembra ['sjembra] nf sowing

siempre ['sjempre] adv always; (todo el tiempo) all the time; **~ que** (cada vez) whenever; (dado que) provided that; **como ~** as usual; **para ~** for ever

sien [sjen] nf temple

siento etc ['sjento] vb V **sentar; sentir**

sierra ['sjerra] nf (Tec) saw; (cadena de montañas) mountain range

siervo, -a ['sjerβo, a] nm/f slave

siesta ['sjesta] nf siesta, nap; **echar la ~** to have an afternoon nap o a siesta

siete ['sjete] num seven

sifón [si'fon] nm syphon

sigla ['siɣla] nf abbreviation; acronym

siglo ['siɣlo] nm century; (fig) age

significado [siɣnifi'kaðo] nm (de palabra etc) meaning

significar [siɣnifi'kar] vt to mean, signify; (notificar) to make known, express

signo ['siɣno] nm sign; **signo de admiración** o **exclamación** exclamation mark; **signo de interrogación** question mark

sigo etc vb V **seguir**

siguiente [si'ɣjente] adj next, following

siguió etc vb V **seguir**

sílaba ['silaβa] nf syllable

silbar [sil'βar] vt, vi to whistle; **silbato** nm whistle; **silbido** nm whistle, whistling

silenciador [silenθja'ðor] nm silencer

silenciar [silen'θjar] vt (persona) to silence; (escándalo) to hush up; **silencio** nm silence, quiet; **silencioso, -a** adj silent, quiet

silla ['siʎa] nf (asiento) chair; (tb: **~ de montar**) saddle; **silla de ruedas** wheelchair

sillón [si'ʎon] nm armchair, easy chair

silueta [si'lweta] nf silhouette; (de edificio) outline; (figura) figure

silvestre [sil'βestre] adj wild

simbólico, -a [sim'boliko, a] adj symbolic(al)

simbolizar [simboli'θar] vt to symbolize

símbolo ['simbolo] nm symbol

similar [simi'lar] adj similar

simio ['simjo] nm ape

simpatía [simpa'tia] nf liking; (afecto) affection; (amabilidad) kindness; **simpático, -a** adj nice, pleasant; kind

▌ No confundir **simpático** con la palabra inglesa sympathetic.

simpatizante [simpati'θante] nmf sympathizer

simpatizar [simpati'θar] *vi*: **~ con** to get on well with

simple ['simple] *adj* simple; *(elemental)* simple, easy; *(mero)* mere; *(puro)* pure, sheer ▷ *nmf* simpleton; **simpleza** *nf* simpleness; *(necedad)* silly thing; **simplificar** *vt* to simplify

simposio [sim'posjo] *nm* symposium

simular [simu'lar] *vt* to simulate

simultáneo, -a [simul'taneo, a] *adj* simultaneous

sin [sin] *prep* without; **la ropa está ~ lavar** the clothes are unwashed; **~ que** without; **~ embargo** however, still

sinagoga [sina'ɣoɣa] *nf* synagogue

sinceridad [sinθeri'ðað] *nf* sincerity; **sincero, -a** *adj* sincere

sincronizar [sinkroni'θar] *vt* to synchronize

sindical [sindi'kal] *adj* union *cpd*, trade-union *cpd*; **sindicalista** *adj, nmf* trade unionist

sindicato [sindi'kato] *nm* *(de trabajadores)* trade(s) union; *(de negociantes)* syndicate

síndrome ['sindrome] *nm* *(Med)* syndrome; **síndrome de abstinencia** *(Med)* withdrawal symptoms; **síndrome de la clase turista** *(Med)* economy-class syndrome

sinfín [sin'fin] *nm*: **un ~ de** a great many, no end of

sinfonía [sinfo'nia] *nf* symphony

singular [singu'lar] *adj* singular; *(fig)* outstanding, exceptional; *(raro)* peculiar, odd

siniestro, -a [si'njestro, a] *adj* sinister ▷ *nm* *(accidente)* accident

sinnúmero [sin'numero] *nm* = **sinfín**

sino ['sino] *nm* fate, destiny ▷ *conj* *(pero)* but; *(salvo)* except, save

sinónimo, -a [si'nonimo, a] *adj* synonymous ▷ *nm* synonym

síntesis ['sintesis] *nf* synthesis; **sintético, -a** *adj* synthetic

sintió *vb* V **sentir**

síntoma ['sintoma] *nm* symptom

sintonía [sinto'nia] *nf* *(Radio, Mús: de programa)* tuning; **sintonizar** *vt* *(Radio: emisora)* to tune (in)

sinvergüenza [simber'ɣwenθa] *nmf* rogue, scoundrel; **¡es un ~!** he's got a nerve!

siquiera [si'kjera] *conj* even if, even though ▷ *adv* at least; **ni ~** not even

Siria ['sirja] *nf* Syria

sirviente, -a [sir'βjente, a] *nm/f* servant

sirvo *etc vb* V **servir**

sistema [sis'tema] *nm* system; *(método)* method; **sistema educativo** education system; **sistemático, -a** *adj* systematic

SISTEMA EDUCATIVO

The reform of the Spanish **sistema educativo** (education system) begun in the early 90s has replaced the courses **EGB**, **BUP** and **COU** with the following: "Primaria" a compulsory 6 years; "Secundaria" a compulsory 4 years and "Bachillerato" an optional 2-year secondary school course, essential for those wishing to go on to higher education.

sitiar [si'tjar] *vt* to besiege, lay siege to

sitio ['sitjo] *nm* *(lugar)* place; *(espacio)* room, space; *(Mil)* siege; **sitio de taxis** *(MÉX: parada)* taxi stand o rank *(BRIT)*; **sitio web** *(Inform)* website

situación [sitwa'θjon] *nf* situation, position; *(estatus)* position, standing

situado, -a [si'twaðo] *adj* situated, placed

situar [si'twar] *vt* to place, put; *(edificio)* to locate, situate

slip [slip] *nm* pants *pl*, briefs *pl*

smoking ['smokin, es'mokin] *(pl* **~s)** *nm* dinner jacket *(BRIT)*, tuxedo *(US)*

▌ No confundir **smoking** con la palabra inglesa *smoking*.

SMS nm (mensaje) text message, SMS message

snob [es'nob] = **esnob**

SO abr (= suroeste) SW

sobaco [so'βako] nm armpit

sobar [so'βar] vt (ropa) to rumple; (comida) to play around with

soberanía [soβera'nia] nf sovereignty; **soberano, -a** adj sovereign; (fig) supreme ⊳ nm/f sovereign

soberbia [so'βerβja] nf pride; haughtiness, arrogance; magnificence

soberbio, -a [so'βerβjo, a] adj (orgulloso) proud; (altivo) arrogant; (estupendo) magnificent, superb

sobornar [soβor'nar] vt to bribe; **soborno** nm bribe

sobra ['soβra] nf excess, surplus; **sobras** nfpl left-overs, scraps; **de** ~ surplus, extra; **tengo de** ~ I've more than enough; **sobrado, -a** adj (más que suficiente) more than enough; (superfluo) excessive; **sobrante** adj remaining, extra ⊳ nm surplus, remainder

sobrar [so'βrar] vt to exceed, surpass ⊳ vi (tener de más) to be more than enough; (quedar) to remain, be left (over)

sobrasada [soβra'saða] nf pork sausage spread

sobre ['soβre] prep (gen) on; (encima) on (top of); (por encima de, arriba de) over, above; (más que) more than; (además) in addition to, besides; (alrededor de) about ⊳ nm envelope; ~ **todo** above all

sobrecama [soβre'kama] nf bedspread

sobrecargar [soβrekar'ɣar] vt (camión) to overload; (Com) to surcharge

sobredosis [soβre'ðosis] nf inv overdose

sobreentender [soβreenten'der] vt to deduce, infer; **sobreentenderse** vr: **se sobreentiende que ...** it is

implied that ...

sobrehumano, -a [soβreu'mano, a] adj superhuman

sobrellevar [soβreʎe'βar] vt to bear, endure

sobremesa [soβre'mesa] nf: **durante la** ~ after dinner

sobrenatural [soβrenatu'ral] adj supernatural

sobrenombre [soβre'nombre] nm nickname

sobrepasar [soβrepa'sar] vt to exceed, surpass

sobreponerse [soβrepo'nerse] vr: ~ **a** to overcome

sobresaliente [soβresa'ljente] adj outstanding, excellent

sobresalir [soβresa'lir] vi to project, jut out; (fig) to stand out, excel

sobresaltar [soβresal'tar] vt (asustar) to scare, frighten; (sobrecoger) to startle; **sobresalto** nm (movimiento) start; (susto) scare; (turbación) sudden shock

sobretodo [soβre'toðo] nm overcoat

sobrevenir [soβreβe'nir] vi (ocurrir) to happen (unexpectedly); (resultar) to follow, ensue

sobrevivir [soβreβi'βir] vi to survive

sobrevolar [soβreβo'lar] vt to fly over

sobriedad [soβrje'ðað] nf sobriety, soberness; (moderación) moderation, restraint

sobrino, -a [so'βrino, a] nm/f nephew/niece

sobrio, -a ['soβrjo, a] adj sober; (moderado) moderate, restrained

socarrón, -ona [soka'tron, ona] adj (sarcástico) sarcastic, ironic(al)

socavón [soka'βon] nm (hoyo) hole

sociable [so'θjaβle] adj (persona) sociable, friendly; (animal) social

social [so'θjal] adj social; (Com) company cpd

socialdemócrata [soθjalde'mokrata] nmf social democrat

socialista [soθja'lista] adj, nm socialist

socializar [soθjali'θar] vt to socialize

sociedad [soθje'ðað] nf society; (Com) company; **sociedad anónima** limited company; **sociedad de consumo** consumer society

socio, -a ['soθjo, a] nm/f (miembro) member; (Com) partner

sociología [soθjolo'xia] nf sociology; **sociólogo, -a** nm/f sociologist

socorrer [soko'rrer] vt to help; **socorrista** nm/f first aider; (en piscina, playa) lifeguard; **socorro** nm (ayuda) help, aid; (Mil) relief; **¡socorro!** help!

soda ['soða] nf (sosa) soda; (bebida) soda (water)

sofá [so'fa] (pl ~s) nm sofa, settee; **sofá-cama** nm studio couch; sofa bed

sofocar [sofo'kar] vt to suffocate; (apagar) to smother, put out; **sofocarse** vr to suffocate; (fig) to blush, feel embarrassed; **sofoco** nm suffocation; embarrassment

sofreír [sofre'ir] vt (Culin) to fry lightly

soga ['soxa] nf rope

sois etc vb V **ser**

soja ['soxa] nf soya

sol [sol] nm sun; (luz) sunshine, sunlight; (Mús) G; **hace** ~ it's sunny

solamente [sola'mente] adv only, just

solapa [so'lapa] nf (de chaqueta) lapel; (de libro) jacket

solapado, -a [sola'paðo, a] adj (intenciones) underhand; (gestos, movimiento) sly

solar [so'lar] adj solar, sun cpd

soldado [sol'daðo] nm soldier; **soldado raso** private

soldador [solda'ðor] nm soldering iron; (persona) welder

soldar [sol'dar] vt to solder, weld

soleado, -a [sole'aðo, a] adj sunny

soledad [sole'ðað] nf solitude; (estado infeliz) loneliness

solemne [so'lemne] adj solemn

soler [so'ler] vi to be in the habit of, be

accustomed to; **suele salir a las ocho** she usually goes out at eight o'clock

solfeo [sol'feo] nm solfa

solicitar [soliθi'tar] vt (permiso) to ask for, seek; (puesto) to apply for; (votos) to canvass for; (atención) to attract

solícito, -a [so'liθito, a] adj (diligente) diligent; (cuidadoso) careful; **solicitud** nf (calidad) great care; (petición) request; (a un puesto) application

solidaridad [soliðari'ðað] nf solidarity; **solidario, -a** (participación) joint, common; (compromiso) mutually binding

sólido, -a ['soliðo, a] adj solid

soliloquio [soli'lokjo] nm soliloquy

solista [so'lista] nm/f soloist

solitario, -a [soli'tarjo, a] adj (persona) lonely, solitary; (lugar) lonely, desolate ▷ nm/f (recluso) recluse; (en la sociedad) loner ▷ nm solitaire

sollozar [soλo'θar] vi to sob; **sollozo** nm sob

solo, -a ['solo, a] adj (único) single, sole; (sin compañía) alone; (solitario) lonely; **hay una sola dificultad** there is just one difficulty; **a solas** alone, by oneself

sólo ['solo] adv only, just

solomillo [solo'miλo] nm sirloin

soltar [sol'tar] vt (dejar ir) to let go of; (desprender) to unfasten, loosen; (librar) to release, set free; (risa etc) to let out

soltero, -a [sol'tero, a] adj single, unmarried ▷ nm bachelor/single woman; **solterón, -ona** nm/f old bachelor/spinster

soltura [sol'tura] nf looseness, slackness; (de los miembros) agility, ease of movement; (en el hablar) fluency, ease

soluble [so'luβle] adj (Quím) soluble; (problema) solvable; ~ **en agua** soluble in water

solución [solu'θjon] nf solution; **solucionar** vt (problema) to solve;

(asunto) to settle, resolve

solventar [solβen'tar] vt *(pagar)* to settle, pay; *(resolver)* to resolve; **solvente** adj *(Econ: empresa, persona)* solvent

sombra ['sombra] nf shadow; *(como protección)* shade; **sombras** nfpl *(oscuridad)* darkness sg, shadows; **tener buena/mala** ~ to be lucky/unlucky

sombrero [som'brero] nm hat

sombrilla [som'briʎa] nf parasol, sunshade

sombrío, -a [som'brio, a] adj *(oscuro)* dark; *(triste)* sombre, sad; *(persona)* gloomy

someter [some'ter] vt *(país)* to conquer; *(persona)* to subject to one's will; *(informe)* to present, submit; **someterse** vr to give in, yield, submit; ~ **a** to subject to

somier [so'mjer] *(pl* **~s**) n spring mattress

somnífero [som'nifero] nm sleeping pill

somos vb V **ser**

son [son] vb V **ser** ▷ nm sound

sonaja [so'naxa] *(MÉX)* nf = **sonajero**

sonajero [sona'xero] nm *(baby's)* rattle

sonambulismo [sonambu'lismo] nm sleepwalking; **sonámbulo, -a** nm/f sleepwalker

sonar [so'nar] vt to ring ▷ vi to sound; *(hacer ruido)* to make a noise; *(pronunciarse)* to be sounded, be pronounced; *(ser conocido)* to sound familiar; *(campana)* to ring; *(reloj)* to strike, chime; **sonarse** vr: ~**se (las narices)** to blow one's nose; **me suena ese nombre** that name rings a bell

sonda ['sonda] nf *(Náut)* sounding; *(Tec)* bore, drill; *(Med)* probe

sondear [sonde'ar] vt to sound; to bore (into), drill; to probe, sound; *(fig)* to sound out; **sondeo** nm sounding, boring, drilling; *(fig)* poll, enquiry

sonido [so'niðo] nm sound

sonoro, -a [so'noro, a] adj sonorous;

(resonante) loud, resonant

sonreír [sonre'ir] vi to smile; **sonreírse** vr to smile; **sonriente** adj smiling; **sonrisa** nf smile

sonrojarse [sonro'xarse] vr to blush, go red; **sonrojo** nm blush

soñador, a [soɲa'ðor, a] nm/f dreamer

soñar [so'ɲar] vt, vi to dream; ~ **con** to dream about of

soñoliento, -a [soɲo'ljento, a] adj sleepy, drowsy

sopa ['sopa] nf soup

soplar [so'plar] vt *(polvo)* to blow away, blow off; *(inflar)* to blow up; *(vela)* to blow out ▷ vi to blow; **soplo** nm blow, puff; *(de viento)* puff, gust

soplón, -ona [so'plon, ona] *(fam)* nm/f *(niño)* telltale; *(de policía)* grass *(fam)*

soporífero [sopo'rifero] nm sleeping pill

soportable [sopor'taβle] adj bearable

soportar [sopor'tar] vt to bear, carry; *(fig)* to bear, put up with

> ▌ No confundir **soportar** con la palabra inglesa support.

soporte nm support; *(fig)* pillar, support

soprano [so'prano] nf soprano

sorber [sor'βer] vt *(chupar)* to sip; *(absorber)* to soak up, absorb

sorbete [sor'βete] nm iced fruit drink

sorbo ['sorβo] nm *(trago: grande)* gulp, swallow; *(: pequeño)* sip

sordera [sor'ðera] nf deafness

sórdido, -a ['sorðiðo, a] adj dirty, squalid

sordo, -a ['sorðo, a] adj *(persona)* deaf ▷ nm/f deaf person; **sordomudo, -a** adj deaf and dumb

sorna ['sorna] nf sarcastic tone

soroche [so'rotʃe] *(CAM)* nm mountain sickness

sorprendente [sorpren'dente] adj surprising

sorprender [sorpren'der] vt to

surprise; **sorpresa** nf surprise
sortear [sorte'ar] vt to draw lots
for; (rifar) to raffle; (dificultad) to avoid;
sorteo nm (en lotería) draw; (rifa) raffle
sortija [sor'tixa] nf ring; (rizo)
ringlet, curl
sosegado, -a [sose'xaðo, a] adj
quiet, calm
sosiego [so'sjeɣo] nm quiet(ness),
calm(ness)
soso, -a ['soso, a] adj (Culin)
tasteless; (aburrido) dull, uninteresting
sospecha [sos'petʃa] nf suspicion;
sospechar vt to suspect;
sospechoso, -a adj suspicious;
(testimonio, opinión) suspect ▷ nm/f
suspect
sostén [sos'ten] nm (apoyo)
support; (sujetador) bra; (alimentación)
sustenance, food
sostener [soste'ner] vt to support;
(mantener) to keep up, maintain;
(alimentar) to sustain, keep going;
sostenerse vr to support o.s.; (seguir)
to continue, remain; **sostenido, -a** adj
continuous, sustained; (prolongado)
prolonged
sotana [so'tana] nf (Rel) cassock
sótano ['sotano] nm basement
soy [soi] vb V **ser**
soya ['soja] (LAM) nf soya (BRIT),
soy (US)
Sr. abr (= Señor) Mr
Sra. abr (= Señora) Mrs
Sres. abr (= Señores) Messrs
Srta. abr (= Señorita) Miss
Sta. abr (= Santa) St
Sto. abr (= Santo) St
su [su] pron (de él) his; (de ella) her; (de
una cosa) its; (de ellos, ellas) their; (de
usted, ustedes) your
suave ['swaβe] adj gentle; (superficie)
smooth; (trabajo) easy; (música, voz)
soft, sweet; **suavidad** nf gentleness;
smoothness; softness, sweetness;
suavizante nm (de ropa) softener;
(del pelo) conditioner; **suavizar** vt to
soften; (quitar la aspereza) to smooth

(out)
subasta [su'βasta] nf auction;
subastar vt to auction (off)
subcampeón, -ona [suβkampe'on,
ona] nm/f runner-up
subconsciente [suβkon'sθjente]
adj, nm subconscious
subdesarrollado, -a
[suβðesarro'λaðo, a] adj
underdeveloped
subdesarrollo [suβðesa'rroλo] nm
underdevelopment
subdirector, a [suβðirek'tor, a]
nm/f assistant director
súbdito, -a ['suβðito, a] nm/f
subject
subestimar [suβesti'mar] vt to
underestimate, underrate
subida [su'βiða] nf (de montaña etc)
ascent, climb; (de precio) rise, increase;
(pendiente) slope, hill
subir [su'βir] vt (objeto) to raise,
lift up; (cuesta, calle) to go up; (colina,
montaña) to climb; (precio) to raise, put
up ▷ vi to go up, come up; (a un coche)
to get in; (a un autobús, tren o avión) to
get on, board; (precio) to rise, go up;
(río, marea) to rise; **subirse** vr to get
up, climb
súbito, -a ['suβito, a] adj (repentino)
sudden; (imprevisto) unexpected
subjetivo, -a [suβxe'tiβo, a] adj
subjective
sublevar [suβle'βar] vt to rouse to
revolt; **sublevarse** vr to revolt, rise
sublime [su'βlime] adj sublime
submarinismo [suβmari'nismo]
nm scuba diving
submarino, -a [suβma'rino, a] adj
underwater ▷ nm submarine
subnormal [suβnor'mal] adj
subnormal ▷ nmf subnormal person
subordinado, -a [suβorði'naðo, a]
adj, nm/f subordinate
subrayar [suβra'jar] vt to underline
subsanar [suβsa'nar] vt to rectify
subsidio [suβ'siðjo] nm (ayuda) aid,
financial help; (subvención) subsidy,

grant; (de enfermedad, paro etc) benefit, allowance

subsistencia [suβsis'tenθja] nf subsistence

subsistir [suβsis'tir] vi to subsist; (sobrevivir) to survive, endure

subte ['suβte] (RPL) nm underground (BRIT), subway (US)

subterráneo, -a [suβte'rraneo, a] adj underground, subterranean ▷ nm underpass, underground passage

subtítulo [suβ'titulo] nm (Cine) subtitle

suburbio [su'βurβjo] nm (barrio) slum quarter

subvención [suββen'θjon] nf (Econ) subsidy, grant; **subvencionar** vt to subsidize

sucedáneo, -a [suθe'ðaneo, a] adj substitute ▷ nm substitute (food)

suceder [suθe'ðer] vt, vi to happen; (seguir) to succeed, follow; **lo que sucede es que ...** the fact is that ...; **sucesión** nf succession; (serie) sequence, series

sucesivamente [suθesiβa'mente] adv: **y así ~** and so on

sucesivo, -a [suθe'siβo, a] adj successive, following; **en lo ~** in future, from now on

suceso [su'θeso] nm (hecho) event, happening; (incidente) incident

No confundir **suceso** con la palabra inglesa success.

suciedad [suθje'ðað] nf (estado) dirtiness; (mugre) dirt, filth

sucio, -a ['suθjo, a] adj dirty

suculento, -a [suku'lento, a] adj succulent

sucumbir [sukum'bir] vi to succumb

sucursal [sukur'sal] nf branch (office)

sudadera [suða'ðera] nf sweatshirt

Sudáfrica [suð'afrika] nf South Africa

Sudamérica [suða'merika] nf South America; **sudamericano, -a** adj, nm/f South American

sudar [su'ðar] vt, vi to sweat

sudeste [su'ðeste] nm south-east

sudoeste [suðo'este] nm south-west

sudor [su'ðor] nm sweat; **sudoroso, -a** adj sweaty, sweating

Suecia ['sweθja] nf Sweden; **sueco, -a** adj Swedish ▷ nm/f Swede

suegro, -a ['sweɣro, a] nm/f father-/mother-in-law

suela ['swela] nf sole

sueldo ['sweldo] nm pay, wage(s) (pl)

suele etc vb V **soler**

suelo ['swelo] nm (tierra) ground; (de casa) floor

suelto, -a ['swelto, a] adj loose; (libre) free; (separado) detached; (ágil) quick, agile ▷ nm (loose) change, small change

sueñito [swe'ɲito] (LAM) nm nap

sueño etc [swe'ɲo] vb V **soñar** ▷ nm sleep; (somnolencia) sleepiness, drowsiness; (lo soñado, fig) dream; **tener ~** to be sleepy

suero ['swero] nm (Med) serum; (de leche) whey

suerte ['swerte] nf (fortuna) luck; (azar) chance; (destino) fate, destiny; (especie) sort, kind; **tener ~** to be lucky

suéter ['sweter] nm sweater

suficiente [sufi'θjente] adj enough, sufficient ▷ nm (Escol) pass

sufragio [su'fraxjo] nm (voto) vote; (derecho de voto) suffrage

sufrido, -a [su'friðo, a] adj (persona) tough; (paciente) long-suffering, patient

sufrimiento [sufri'mjento] nm (dolor) suffering

sufrir [su'frir] vt (padecer) to suffer; (soportar) to bear, put up with; (apoyar) to hold up, support ▷ vi to suffer

sugerencia [suxe'renθja] nf suggestion

sugerir [suxe'rir] vt to suggest; (sutilmente) to hint

sugestión [suxes'tjon] nf suggestion; (sutil) hint; **sugestionar** vt to influence

sugestivo, -a [suxes'tiβo, a] *adj* stimulating; (*fascinante*) fascinating

suicida [sui'θiða] *adj* suicidal ▷ *nmf* suicidal person; (*muerto*) suicide, person who has committed suicide; **suicidarse** *vr* to commit suicide, kill o.s.; **suicidio** *nm* suicide

Suiza ['swiθa] *nf* Switzerland; **suizo, -a** *adj, nm/f* Swiss

sujeción [suxe'θjon] *nf* subjection

sujetador [suxeta'ðor] *nm* (*sostén*) bra

sujetar [suxe'tar] *vt* (*fijar*) to fasten; (*detener*) to hold down; **sujetarse** *vr* to subject o.s.; **sujeto, -a** *adj* fastened, secure ▷ *nm* subject; (*individuo*) individual; **sujeto a** subject to

suma ['suma] *nf* (*cantidad*) total, sum; (*de dinero*) sum; (*acto*) adding (up), addition; **en ~** in short

sumamente [suma'mente] *adv* extremely, exceedingly

sumar [su'mar] *vt* to add (up) ▷ *vi* to add up

sumergir [sumer'xir] *vt* to submerge; (*hundir*) to sink

suministrar [sumini'strar] *vt* to supply, provide; **suministro** *nm* supply; (*acto*) supplying, providing

sumir [su'mir] *vt* to sink, submerge; (*fig*) to plunge

sumiso, -a [su'miso, a] *adj* submissive, docile

sumo, -a ['sumo, a] *adj* great, extreme; (*autoridad*) highest, supreme

suntuoso, -a [sun'twoso, a] *adj* sumptuous, magnificent

supe *etc vb* V **saber**

super... *pref* prefijo super..., over...

superbueno, -a [super'bweno, a] *adj* great, fantastic

súper ['super] *nf* (*gasolina*) four-star (petrol)

superar [supe'rar] *vt* (*sobreponerse a*) to overcome; (*rebasar*) to surpass, do better than; (*pasar*) to go beyond; **superarse** *vr* to excel o.s.

superficial [superfi'θjal] *adj*

superficial; (*medida*) surface *cpd*, of the surface

superficie [super'fiθje] *nf* surface; (*área*) area

superfluo, -a [su'perflwo, a] *adj* superfluous

superior [supe'rjor] *adj* (*piso, clase*) upper; (*temperatura, número, nivel*) higher; (*mejor: calidad, producto*) superior, better ▷ *nmf* superior; **superioridad** *nf* superiority

supermercado [supermer'kaðo] *nm* supermarket

superponer [superpo'ner] *vt* to superimpose

superstición [supersti'θjon] *nf* superstition; **supersticioso, -a** *adj* superstitious

supervisar [superβi'sar] *vt* to supervise

supervivencia [superβi'βenθja] *nf* survival

superviviente [superβi'βjente] *adj* surviving

supiera *etc vb* V **saber**

suplantar [suplan'tar] *vt* to supplant

suplemento [suple'mento] *nm* supplement

suplente [su'plente] *adj, nm* substitute

supletorio, -a [suple'torjo, a] *adj* supplementary ▷ *nm* supplement; **teléfono ~** extension

súplica ['suplika] *nf* request; (*Jur*) petition

suplicar [supli'kar] *vt* (*cosa*) to beg (for), plead for; (*persona*) to beg, plead with

suplicio [su'pliθjo] *nm* torture

suplir [su'plir] *vt* (*compensar*) to make good, make up for; (*reemplazar*) to replace, substitute for; ▷ *vi*: **~ a** to take the place of, substitute for

supo *etc vb* V **saber**

suponer [supo'ner] *vt* to suppose; **suposición** *nf* supposition

suprimir [supri'mir] *vt* to suppress;

(*derecho, costumbre*) to abolish; (*palabra etc*) to delete; (*restricción*) to cancel; **supuesto, -a** [su'pwesto, a] *pp de* **suponer** ▷ *adj* (*hipotético*) supposed ▷ *nm* assumption, hypothesis; **~ que** since; **por ~** of course

sur [sur] *nm* south

surcar [sur'kar] *vt* to plough; **surco** *nm* (*en metal, disco*) groove; (*Agr*) furrow

surgir [sur'xir] *vi* to arise, emerge; (*dificultad*) to come up, crop up

suroeste [suro'este] *nm* south-west

surtido, -a [sur'tiðo, a] *adj* mixed, assorted ▷ *nm* (*selección*) selection, assortment; (*abastecimiento*) supply, stock; **surtidor** *nm* (*tb:* **surtidor de gasolina**) petrol pump (BRIT), gas pump (US)

surtir [sur'tir] *vt* to supply, provide ▷ *vi* to spout, spurt

susceptible [susθep'tiβle] *adj* susceptible; (*sensible*) sensitive; **~ de** capable of

suscitar [susθi'tar] *vt* to cause, provoke; (*interés, sospechas*) to arouse

suscribir [suskri'βir] *vt* (*firmar*) to sign; (*respaldar*) to subscribe to, endorse; **suscribirse** *vr* to subscribe; **suscripción** *nf* subscription

susodicho, -a [suso'ðitʃo, a] *adj* above-mentioned

suspender [suspen'der] *vt* (*objeto*) to hang (up), suspend; (*trabajo*) to stop, suspend; (*Escol*) to fail; (*interrumpir*) to adjourn; (*atrasar*) to postpone

suspense [sus'pense] (ESP) *nm* suspense; **película/novela de ~** thriller

suspensión [suspen'sjon] *nf* suspension; (*fig*) stoppage, suspension

suspenso, -a [sus'penso, a] *adj* hanging, suspended; (ESP *Escol*) failed ▷ *nm* (ESP *Escol*) fail; **película o novela de ~** (LAM) thriller; **quedar o estar en ~** to be pending

suspicaz [suspi'kaθ] *adj* suspicious, distrustful

suspirar [suspi'rar] *vi* to sigh;

suspiro *nm* sigh

sustancia [sus'tanθja] *nf* substance

sustento [sus'tento] *nm* support; (*alimento*) sustenance, food

sustituir [sustitu'ir] *vt* to substitute, replace; **sustituto, -a** *nm/f* substitute, replacement

susto ['susto] *nm* fright, scare

sustraer [sustra'er] *vt* to remove, take away; (*Mat*) to subtract

susurrar [susu'rrar] *vi* to whisper; **susurro** *nm* whisper

sutil [su'til] *adj* (*aroma, diferencia*) subtle; (*tenue*) thin; (*inteligencia, persona*) sharp

suyo, -a ['sujo, a] (*con artículo o después del verbo* **ser**) *adj* (*de él*) his; (*de ella*) hers; (*de ellos, ellas*) theirs; (*de Ud, Uds*) yours; **un amigo ~** a friend of his (o hers o theirs o yours)

t

tabú [ta'βu] nm taboo

taburete [taβu'rete] nm stool

tacaño, -a [ta'kaɲo, a] adj mean

tacha ['tatʃa] nf flaw; (Tec) stud; **tachar** vt (borrar) to cross out; **tachar de** to accuse of

tacho ['tatʃo] (cs) nm (balde) bucket; **tacho de la basura** rubbish bin (BRIT), trash can (US)

taco ['tako] nm (Billar) cue; (de billetes) book; (cs: de zapato) heel; (tarugo) peg; (palabrota) swear word

tacón [ta'kon] nm heel; **de ~ alto** high-heeled

táctica ['taktika] nf tactics pl

táctico, -a ['taktiko, a] adj tactical

tacto ['takto] nm touch; (fig) tact

tajada [ta'xaða] nf slice

tajante [ta'xante] adj sharp

tajo ['taxo] nm (corte) cut; (Geo) cleft

tal [tal] adj such ▷ pron (persona) someone, such a one; (cosa) something, such a thing ▷ adv: **~ como** (igual) just as ▷ conj: **con ~ de que** provided that; **~ cual** (como es) just as it is; **~ vez** perhaps; **~ como** such as; **~ para cual** (dos iguales) two of a kind; **¿qué ~?** how are things?; **¿qué ~ te gusta?** how do you like it?

taladrar [tala'ðrar] vt to drill; **taladro** nm drill

talante [ta'lante] nm (humor) mood; (voluntad) will, willingness

talar [ta'lar] vt to fell, cut down; (devastar) to devastate

talco ['talko] nm (polvos) talcum powder

talento [ta'lento] nm talent; (capacidad) ability

TALGO ['talɣo] (ESP) nm abr (= tren articulado ligero Goicoechea-Oriol) ≈ HST (BRIT)

talismán [talis'man] nm talisman

talla ['taʎa] nf (estatura, fig, Arte) height, stature; (palo) measuring rod; (Arte) carving; (medida) size

tallar [ta'ʎar] vt (madera) to carve;

Tabacalera [taβaka'lera] nf Spanish state tobacco monopoly

tabaco [ta'βako] nm tobacco; (ESP: fam) cigarettes pl

tabaquería [tabake'ria] (LAM) nf tobacconist's (shop) (BRIT), smoke shop (US); **tabaquero, -a** (LAM) nm/f tobacconist

taberna [ta'βerna] nf bar, pub (BRIT)

tabique [ta'βike] nm partition (wall)

tabla ['taβla] nf (de madera) plank; (estante) shelf; (de vestido) pleat; (Arte) panel; **tablas** nfpl: **estar o quedar en ~s** to draw; **tablado** nm (plataforma) platform; (Teatro) stage

tablao [ta'βlao] nm (tb: **~ flamenco**) flamenco show

tablero [ta'βlero] nm (de madera) plank, board; (de ajedrez, damas) board; **tablero de mandos** (LAM Auto) dashboard

tableta [ta'βleta] nf (Med) tablet; (de chocolate) bar

tablón [ta'βlon] nm (de suelo) plank; (de techo) beam; **tablón de anuncios**

(metal etc) to engrave; (medir) to measure

tallarines [taʎa'rines] nmpl noodles

talle ['taʎe] nm (Anat) waist; (fig) appearance

taller [ta'ʎer] nm (Tec) workshop; (de artista) studio

tallo ['taʎo] nm (de planta) stem; (de hierba) blade; (brote) shoot

talón [ta'lon] nm (Anat) heel; (Com) counterfoil; (cheque) cheque (BRIT), check (US)

talonario [talo'narjo] nm (de cheques) chequebook (BRIT), checkbook (US); (de recibos) receipt book

tamaño, -a [ta'maɲo, a] adj (tan grande) such a big; (tan pequeño) such a small ▷ nm size; **de ~ natural** full-size

tamarindo [tama'rindo] nm tamarind

tambalearse [tambale'arse] vr (persona) to stagger; (vehículo) to sway

también [tam'bjen] adv (igualmente) also, too, as well; (además) besides

tambor [tam'bor] nm drum; (Anat) eardrum; **tambor del freno** brake drum

tamizar [tami'θar] vt to sieve

tampoco [tam'poko] adv nor, neither; **yo ~ lo compré** I didn't buy it either

tampón [tam'pon] nm tampon

tan [tan] adv **~ es así que ...** so much so that ...

tanda ['tanda] nf (gen) series; (turno) shift

tangente [tan'xente] nf tangent

tangerina [tanxe'rina] (LAM) nf tangerine

tangible [tan'xiβle] adj tangible

tanque ['tanke] nm (cisterna, Mil) tank; (Auto) tanker

tantear [tante'ar] vt (calcular) to reckon (up); (medir) to take the measure of; (probar) to test, try out; (tomar la medida: persona) to take the measurements of; (situación) to weigh up; (persona: opinión) to sound out ▷ vi

(Deporte) to score; **tanteo** nm (cálculo) (rough) calculation; (prueba) test, trial; (Deporte) scoring

tanto, -a ['tanto, a] adj (cantidad) so much, as much ▷ adv (cantidad) so much, as much; (tiempo) so long, as long ▷ conj: **en ~ que** while ▷ nm (suma) certain amount; (proporción) so much; (punto) point; (gol) goal; **un ~ perezoso** somewhat lazy ▷ pron: **cada uno paga ~** each one pays so much; **~s** so many, as many; **20 y ~s** 20-odd; **hasta ~ (que)** until such time as; **~ tú como yo** both you and I, **~ como eso** as much as that; **~ más ... cuanto que** all the more ... because; **~ mejor/peor** so much the better/the worse; **~ si viene como si va** whether he comes or whether he goes; **~ es así que** so much so that; **por (lo) ~** therefore; **entre ~** meanwhile; **estar al ~** to be up to date; **me he vuelto ronco de o con ~ hablar** I have become hoarse with so much talking; **a ~s de agosto** on such and such a day in August

tapa ['tapa] nf (de caja, olla) lid; (de botella) top; (de libro) cover; (comida) snack

tapadera [tapa'ðera] nf lid, cover

tapar [ta'par] vt (cubrir) to cover; (envolver) to wrap o cover up; (la vista) to obstruct; (persona, falta) to conceal; (MÉX, CAM: diente) to fill; **taparse** vr to wrap o.s. up

taparrabo [tapa'rraβo] nm loincloth

tapete [ta'pete] nm table cover

tapia ['tapja] nf (garden) wall

tapicería [tapiθe'ria] nf tapestry; (para muebles) upholstery; (tienda) upholsterer's (shop)

tapiz [ta'piθ] nm (alfombra) carpet; (tela tejida) tapestry; **tapizar** vt (muebles) to upholster

tapón [ta'pon] nm (de botella) top; (de lavabo) plug; **tapón de rosca** screw-top

taquigrafía [takiɣra'fia] nf shorthand; **taquígrafo, -a** nm/f shorthand writer, stenographer

taquilla [ta'kiʎa] nf (donde se compra) booking office; (suma recogida) takings pl

tarántula [ta'rantula] nf tarantula

tararear [tarare'ar] vi to hum

tardar [tar'ðar] vi (tomar tiempo) to take a long time; (llegar tarde) to be late; (demorar) to delay; **¿tarda mucho el tren?** does the train take (very) long?; **a más ~** at the latest; **no tardes en venir** come soon

tarde ['tarðe] adv late ▷ nf (de día) afternoon; (al anochecer) evening; **de ~ en ~** from time to time; **¡buenas ~s!** good afternoon!; **a o por la ~** in the afternoon; in the evening

tardío, -a [tar'ðio, a] adj (retrasado) late; (lento) slow (to arrive)

tarea [ta'rea] nf task; (faena) chore; (Escol) homework

tarifa [ta'rifa] nf (lista de precios) price list; (precio) tariff

tarima [ta'rima] nf (plataforma) platform

tarjeta [tar'xeta] nf card; **tarjeta de crédito/de Navidad/postal/ telefónica** credit card/Christmas card/postcard/phonecard; **tarjeta de embarque** boarding pass; **tarjeta de memoria** memory card; **tarjeta prepago** top-up card; **tarjeta SIM** SIM card

tarro ['tarro] nm jar, pot

tarta ['tarta] nf (pastel) cake; (de base dura) tart

tartamudear [tartamuðe'ar] vi to stammer; **tartamudo, -a** adj stammering ▷ nm/f stammerer

tártaro, -a ['tartaro, a] adj: **salsa tártara** tartar(e) sauce

tasa ['tasa] nf (precio) (fixed) price, rate; (valoración) valuation; (medida, norma) measure, standard; **tasa de cambio/interés** exchange/interest rate; **tasas de aeropuerto** airport tax; **tasas universitarias** university fees

tasar [ta'sar] vt (arreglar el precio) to fix a price for; (valorar) to value, assess

tasca ['taska] (fam) nf pub

tatarabuelo, -a [tatara'βwelo, a] nm/f great-great-grandfather/mother

tatuaje [ta'twaxe] nm (dibujo) tattoo; (acto) tattooing

tatuar [ta'twar] vt to tattoo

taurino, -a [tau'rino, a] adj bullfighting cpd

Tauro ['tauro] nm Taurus

tauromaquia [tauro'makja] nf tauromachy, (art of) bullfighting

taxi ['taksi] nm taxi; **taxista** [tak'sista] nmf taxi driver

taza ['taθa] nf cup; (de retrete) bowl; **~ para café** coffee cup; **taza de café** cup of coffee; **tazón** nm (taza grande) mug, large cup; (de fuente) basin

te [te] pron (complemento de objeto) you; (complemento indirecto) (to) you; (reflexivo) (to) yourself; **¿~ duele mucho el brazo?** does your arm hurt a lot?; **~ equivocas** you're wrong; **¡cálma~!** calm down!

té [te] nm tea

teatral [tea'tral] adj theatre cpd; (fig) theatrical

teatro [te'atro] nm theatre; (Literatura) plays pl, drama

tebeo [te'βeo] nm comic

techo ['tetʃo] nm (externo) roof; (interno) ceiling; **techo corredizo** sunroof

tecla ['tekla] nf key; **teclado** nm keyboard; **teclear** vi (Mús) to strum; (con los dedos) to tap ▷ vt (Inform) to key in

técnica ['teknika] nf technique; (tecnología) technology; V tb **técnico**

técnico, -a ['tekniko, a] adj technical ▷ nm/f technician; (experto) expert

tecnología [teknolo'xia] nf technology; **tecnológico, -a** adj technological

tecolote [teko'lote] (méx) nm owl

tedioso, -a [te'ðjoso, a] adj boring, tedious

teja ['texa] nf tile; (Bot) lime (tree);

tejado nm (tiled) roof

tejemaneje [texema'nexe] nm (lío) fuss; (intriga) intrigue

tejer [te'xer] vt to weave; (hacer punto) to knit; (fig) to fabricate; **tejido** nm (tela) material, fabric; (telaraña) web; (Anat) tissue

tel [tel] abr (= teléfono) tel

tela ['tela] nf (tejido) material; (telaraña) web; (en líquido) skin; **telar** nm (máquina) loom

telaraña [tela'raɲa] nf cobweb

tele ['tele] (fam) nf telly (BRIT), tube (US)

tele... ['tele] prefijo tele...; **telebasura** nf trashTV; **telecomunicación** nf telecommunication; **telediario** nm television news; **teledirigido, -a** adj remote-controlled

teleférico [tele'feriko] nm (de esquí) ski-lift

telefonear [telefone'ar] vi to telephone

telefónico, -a [tele'foniko, a] adj telephone cpd

telefonillo [telefo'niʎo] nm (de puerta) intercom

telefonista [telefo'nista] nmf telephonist

teléfono [te'lefono] nm (tele)phone; **estar hablando al ~** to be on the phone; **llamar a algn por ~** to ring sb (up) o phone sb (up); **teléfono celular** (LAM) mobile phone; **teléfono con cámara** camera phone; **teléfono inalámbrico** cordless phone; **teléfono móvil** (ESP) mobile phone

telégrafo [te'leɣrafo] nm telegraph

telegrama [tele'ɣrama] nm telegram

tele: **telenovela** nf soap (opera); **teleobjetivo** nm telephoto lens; **telepatía** nf telepathy; **telepático, -a** adj telepathic; **telerrealidad** nf reality TV; **telescopio** nm telescope; **telesilla** nm chairlift; **telespectador, a** nm/f viewer; **telesquí** nm ski-lift; **teletarjeta** nf phonecard; **teletipo** nm

teletype; **teletrabajador, a** nm/f teleworker; **teletrabajo** nm teleworking; **televentas** nfpl telesales

televidente [teleβi'ðente] nmf viewer

televisar [teleβi'sar] vt to televise

televisión [teleβi'sjon] nf television; **televisión digital** digital television

televisor [teleβi'sor] nm television set

télex ['teleks] nm inv telex

telón [te'lon] nm curtain; **telón de acero** (Pol) iron curtain; **telón de fondo** backcloth, background

tema ['tema] nm (asunto) subject, topic; (Mús) theme; **temático, -a** adj thematic

temblar [tem'blar] vi to shake, tremble; (por frío) to shiver; **temblor** nm trembling; (de tierra) earthquake; **tembloroso, -a** adj trembling

temer [te'mer] vt to fear ▷ vi to be afraid; **temo que llegue tarde** I am afraid he may be late

temible [te'miβle] adj fearsome

temor [te'mor] nm (miedo) fear; (duda) suspicion

témpano ['tempano] nm (tb: ~ de hielo) ice-floe

temperamento [tempera'mento] nm temperament

temperatura [tempera'tura] nf temperature

tempestad [tempes'tað] nf storm

templado, -a [tem'plaðo, a] adj (moderado) moderate; (frugal) frugal; (agua) lukewarm; (clima) mild; (Mús) well-tuned; **templanza** nf moderation; mildness

templar [tem'plar] vt (moderar) to moderate; (furia) to restrain; (calor) to reduce; (afinar) to tune (up); (acero) to temper; (tuerca) to tighten up; **temple** nm (ajuste) tempering; (afinación) tuning; (pintura) tempera

templo ['templo] nm (iglesia) church; (pagano etc) temple

temporada [tempo'raða] nf time, period; (estación) season

temporal [tempo'ral] adj (no permanente) temporary ▷ nm storm

temprano, -a [tem'prano, a] adj early; (demasiado pronto) too soon, too early

ten vb V **tener**

tenaces [te'naθes] adj pl V **tenaz**

tenaz [te'naθ] adj (material) tough; (persona) tenacious; (creencia, resistencia) stubborn

tenaza(s) [te'naθa(s)] nf(pl) (Med) forceps; (Tec) pliers; (Zool) pincers

tendedero [tende'ðero] nm (para ropa) drying place; (cuerda) clothes line

tendencia [ten'denθja] nf tendency; **tener ~ a** to tend to, have a tendency to

tender [ten'der] vt (extender) to spread out; (colgar) to hang out; (vía férrea, cable) to lay; (estirar) to stretch ▷ vi: **~ a** to tend to, have a tendency towards; **tenderse** vr to lie down; **~ la cama/mesa** (LAM) to make the bed/lay (BRIT) o set (US) the table

tenderete [tende'rete] nm (puesto) stall; (exposición) display of goods

tendero, -a [ten'dero, a] nm/f shopkeeper

tendón [ten'don] nm tendon

tendré etc vb V **tener**

tenebroso, -a [tene'βroso, a] adj (oscuro) dark; (fig) gloomy

tenedor [tene'ðor] nm (Culin) fork

tenencia [te'nenθja] nf (de casa) tenancy; (de oficio) tenure; (de propiedad) possession

○ **PALABRA CLAVE**

tener [te'ner] vt 1 (poseer, gen) to have; (en la mano) to hold; **¿tienes un boli?** have you got a pen?; **va a tener un niño** she's going to have a baby; **¡ten** (o **tenga)!, ¡aquí tienes** (o **tiene)!** here you are!

2 (edad, medidas) to be; **tiene 7 años** she's 7 (years old); **tiene 15 cm de largo**

it's 15 cm long; V **calor; hambre** etc

3 (considerar): **lo tengo por brillante** I consider him to be brilliant; **tener en mucho a** to think very highly of sb

4 (+ pp: = pretérito): **tengo terminada ya la mitad del trabajo** I've done half the work already

5: **tener que hacer algo** to have to do sth; **tengo que acabar este trabajo hoy** I have to finish this job today

6: **¿qué tienes, estás enfermo?** what's the matter with you, are you ill?

tenerse vr 1 **tenerse en pie** to stand up

2 **tenerse por** to think o.s.

tengo etc vb V **tener**

tenia ['tenja] nf tapeworm

teniente [te'njente] nm (rango) lieutenant; (ayudante) deputy

tenis ['tenis] nm tennis; **tenis de mesa** table tennis; **tenista** nmf tennis player

tenor [te'nor] nm (sentido) meaning; (Mús) tenor; **a ~ de** on the lines of

tensar [ten'sar] vt to tighten; (arco) to draw

tensión [ten'sjon] nf tension; (Tec) stress; **tener la ~ alta** to have high blood pressure; **tensión arterial** blood pressure

tenso, -a ['tenso, a] adj tense

tentación [tenta'θjon] nf temptation

tentáculo [ten'takulo] nm tentacle

tentador, a [tenta'ðor, a] adj tempting

tentar [ten'tar] vt (seducir) to tempt; (atraer) to attract

tentempié [tentem'pje] nm snack

tenue ['tenwe] adj (delgado) thin, slender; (neblina) light; (lazo, vínculo) slight

teñir [te'nir] vt to dye; (fig) to tinge; **teñirse** vr to dye; **~se el pelo** to dye one's hair

teología [teolo'xia] nf theology

teoría [teo'ria] nf theory; **en ~** in

theory; **teórico, -a** adj theoretic(al)
▷ nm/f theoretician, theorist; **teorizar**
vi to theorize

terapéutica [tera'peutika], adj therapeutic

terapia [te'rapja] nf therapy

tercer adj V **tercero**

tercermundista [terθermun'dista]
adj Third World cpd

tercero, -a [ter'θero, a] (delante de
nmsg: **tercer**) adj third ▷ nm (Jur)
third party

terceto [ter'θeto] nm trio

terciar [ter'θjar] vi (participar) to
take part; (hacer de árbitro) to mediate;
terciario, -a adj tertiary

tercio [ter'θjo] nm third

terciopelo [terθjo'pelo] nm velvet

terco, -a [ter'ko, a] adj obstinate

tergal® [ter'xal] nm type of polyester

tergiversar [terxiβer'sar] vt to
distort

termal [ter'mal] adj thermal

termas [termas] nfpl hot springs

térmico, -a [ter'miko, a] adj
thermal

terminal [termi'nal] adj, nm, nf
terminal

terminante [termi'nante] adj
(final) final, definitive; (tajante)
categorical; **terminantemente**
adv: **terminantemente prohibido**
strictly forbidden

terminar [termi'nar] vt (completar)
to complete, finish; (concluir) to end
▷ vi (llegar a su fin) to end; (parar) to
stop; (acabar) to finish; **terminarse** vr
to come to an end; **~ por hacer algo** to
end up (by) doing sth

término [termino] nm end,
conclusion; (parada) terminus; (límite)
boundary; **en último ~** (a fin de cuentas)
in the last analysis; (como último
recurso) as a last resort; **término medio**
average; (fig) middle way

termómetro [ter'mometro] nm
thermometer

termo(s)® ['termo(s)] nm Thermos®

termostato [termo'stato] nm
thermostat

ternero, -a [ter'nero, a] nm/f
(animal) calf ▷ nf (carne) veal

ternura [ter'nura] nf (trato)
tenderness; (palabra) endearment;
(cariño) fondness

terrado [te'raðo] nm terrace

terraplén [terra'plen] nm
embankment

terrateniente [terrate'njente] nmf
landowner

terraza [te'raθa] nf (balcón) balcony;
(tejado) (flat) roof; (Agr) terrace

terremoto [terre'moto] nm
earthquake

terrenal [terre'nal] adj earthly

terreno [te'reno] nm (tierra) land;
(parcela) plot; (suelo) soil; (fig) field; **un ~**
a piece of land

terrestre [te'restre] adj terrestrial;
(ruta) land cpd

terrible [te'rriβle] adj terrible, awful

territorio [terri'torjo] nm territory

terrón [te'rron] nm (de azúcar) lump;
(de tierra) clod, lump

terror [te'rror] nm terror; **terrorífico,
-a** adj terrifying; **terrorista** adj,
terrorist; **terrorista suicida** suicide
bomber

terso, -a ['terso, a] adj (liso) smooth;
(pulido) polished

tertulia [ter'tulja] nf (reunión
informal) social gathering; (grupo)
group, circle

tesis ['tesis] nf inv thesis

tesón [te'son] nm (firmeza) firmness;
(tenacidad) tenacity

tesorero, -a [teso'rero, a] nm/f
treasurer

tesoro [te'soro] nm treasure; (Com,
Pol) treasury

testamento [testa'mento] nm will

testarudo, -a [testa'ruðo, a] adj
stubborn

testículo [tes'tikulo] nm testicle

testificar [testifi'kar] vt to testify;
(fig) to attest ▷ vi to give evidence

testigo [tes'tiɣo] nmf witness;
testigo de cargo/descargo witness
for the prosecution/defence; **testigo
ocular** eye witness

testimonio [testi'monjo] nm
testimony

teta ['teta] nf (de biberón) teat;
(Anat: fam) breast

tétanos ['tetanos] nm tetanus

tetera [te'tera] nf teapot

tétrico, -a ['tetriko, a] adj gloomy,
dismal

textil [teks'til] adj textile

texto ['teksto] nm text; **textual** adj
textual

textura [teks'tura] nf (de tejido)
texture

tez [teθ] nf (cutis) complexion

ti [ti] pron you; (reflexivo) yourself

tía ['tia] nf (pariente) aunt; (fam)
chick, bird

tibio, -a ['tiβjo, a] adj lukewarm

tiburón [tiβu'ron] nm shark

tic [tik] nm (ruido) click; (de reloj) tick;
(Med): **~ nervioso** nervous tic

tictac [tik'tak] nm (de reloj) tick tock

tiempo ['tjempo] nm time; (época,
período) age, period; (Meteorología)
weather; (Ling) tense; (Deporte) half; **a ~**
in time; **a uno al mismo ~** at the same
time; **al poco ~** very soon (after); **se
quedó poco ~** he didn't stay very long;
hace poco ~ not long ago; **mucho ~** a
long time; **de ~ en ~** from time to time;
hace buen/mal ~ the weather is fine/
bad; **estar a ~** to be in time; **hace ~**
some time ago; **hacer ~** to while away
the time; **motor de 2 ~s** two-stroke
engine; **primer ~** first half

tienda ['tjenda] nf shop, store;
tienda de abarrotes (MÉX, CAM)
grocer's (BRIT), grocery store
(US); **tienda de alimentación** o
comestibles grocer's (BRIT), grocery
store (US); **tienda de campaña** tent

tienes etc vb V **tener**

tienta etc ['tjenta] vb V **tentar**
▷ nf: **andar a ~s** to grope one's way

along

tiento etc ['tjento] vb V **tentar** ▷ nm
(tacto) touch; (precaución) wariness

tierno, -a ['tjerno, a] adj (blando)
tender; (fresco) fresh; (amable) sweet

tierra ['tjerra] nf earth; (suelo) soil;
(mundo) earth, world; (país) country,
land; **~ adentro** inland

tieso, -a ['tjeso, a] adj (rígido) rigid;
(duro) stiff; (fam: orgulloso) conceited

tiesto ['tjesto] nm flowerpot

tifón [ti'fon] nm typhoon

tifus ['tifus] nm typhus

tigre ['tiɣre] nm tiger

tijera [ti'xera] nf scissors pl; (Zool)
claw; **tijeras** nfpl scissors; (para
plantas) shears

tila ['tila] nf lime blossom tea

tildar [til'dar] vt: **~ de** to brand as

tilde ['tilde] nf (Tip) tilde

tilín [ti'lin] nm tinkle

timar [ti'mar] vt (estafar) to swindle

timbal [tim'bal] nm small drum

timbre ['timbre] nm (sello) stamp;
(campanilla) bell; (tono) timbre; (Com)
stamp duty

timidez [timi'ðeθ] nf shyness;
tímido, -a adj shy

timo ['timo] nm swindle

timón [ti'mon] nm helm, rudder;
timonel nm helmsman

tímpano ['timpano] nm (Anat)
eardrum; (Mús) small drum

tina ['tina] nf (tb: baño) bath (tub);
tinaja nf large jar

tinieblas [ti'njeβlas] nfpl darkness
sg; (sombras) shadows

tino ['tino] nm (habilidad) skill; (juicio)
insight

tinta ['tinta] nf ink; (Tec) dye; (Arte)
colour

tinte ['tinte] nm dye

tintero [tin'tero] nm inkwell

tinto ['tinto] nm red wine

tintorería [tintore'ria] nf dry
cleaner's

tío ['tio] nm (pariente) uncle;
(fam: individuo) bloke (BRIT), guy

tiovivo [tio'βiβo] nm merry-go-round

típico, -a ['tipiko, a] adj typical

tipo ['tipo] nm (clase) type, kind; (hombre) fellow; (Anat: de hombre) build; (: de mujer) figure; (Imprenta) type; **tipo bancario/de descuento/de interés/ de cambio** bank/discount/interest/ exchange rate

tipografía [tipoɣra'fia] nf printing cpd

tíquet ['tiket] (pl **~s**) nm ticket; (en tienda) cash slip

tiquismiquis [tikis'mikis] nm inv fussy person ▷nmpl (querellas) squabbling sg; (escrúpulos) silly scruples

tira ['tira] nf strip; (fig) abundance; **tira y afloja** give and take

tirabuzón [tiraβu'θon] nm (rizo) curl

tirachinas [tira'tʃinas] nm inv catapult

tirada [ti'raða] nf (acto) cast, throw; (serie) series; (Tip) printing, edition; **de una ~** at one go

tirado, -a [ti'raðo, a] adj (barato) dirt-cheap; (fam: fácil) very easy

tirador [tira'ðor] nm (mango) handle

tirano, -a [ti'rano, a] adj tyrannical ▷nm/f tyrant

tirante [ti'rante] adj (cuerda etc) tight, taut; (relaciones) strained ▷nm (Arq) brace; (Tec) stay; **tirantes** nmpl (de pantalón) braces (BRIT), suspenders (US); **tirantez** nf tightness; (fig) tension

tirar [ti'rar] vt to throw; (dejar caer) to drop; (volcar) to upset; (derribar) to knock down o over; (desechar) to throw out o away; (dinero) to squander; (imprimir) to print ▷vi (disparar) to shoot; (de la puerta etc) to pull; (fam: andar) to go; (tender a, buscar realizar) to tend to; (Deporte) to shoot; **tirarse** vr to throw o.s.; **~ abajo** to bring down, destroy; **tira más a su padre** he takes more after his father; **ir tirando** to manage

tirita [ti'rita] nf (sticking) plaster

(BRIT), Bandaid® (US)

tiritar [tiri'tar] vi to shiver

tiro ['tiro] nm (lanzamiento) throw; (disparo) shot; (Deporte) shot; (Golf, Tenis) drive; (alcance) range; **caballo de ~** cart-horse; **tiro al blanco** target practice

tirón [ti'ron] nm (sacudida) pull, tug; **de un ~** in one go, all at once

tiroteo [tiro'teo] nm exchange of shots, shooting

tisis ['tisis] nf inv consumption, tuberculosis

títere ['titere] nm puppet

titubear [tituβe'ar] vi to stagger; to stammer; (fig) to hesitate; **titubeo** nm staggering; stammering; hesitation

titulado, -a [titu'laðo, a] adj (libro) entitled; (persona) titled

titular [titu'lar] adj titular ▷nmf holder ▷nm headline ▷vt to title; **titularse** vr to be entitled; **título** nm title; (de diario) headline; (certificado) professional qualification; (universitario) (university) degree; **a título de** in the capacity of

tiza ['tiθa] nf chalk

toalla [to'aʎa] nf towel

tobillo [to'βiʎo] nm ankle

tobogán [toβo'ɣan] nm (montaña rusa) roller-coaster; (de niños) chute, slide

tocadiscos [toka'ðiskos] nm inv record player

tocado, -a [to'kaðo, a] adj (fam) touched ▷nm headdress

tocador [toka'ðor] nm (mueble) dressing table; (cuarto) boudoir; (fam) ladies' toilet (BRIT) o room (US)

tocar [to'kar] vt to touch; (Mús) to play; (referirse a) to allude to; (timbre) to ring ▷vi (corresponder a) to knock (on o at the door); (ser de turno) to fall to, be the turn of; (ser hora) to be time for; **tocarse** vr (cubrirse la cabeza) to cover one's head; (tener contacto) to touch (each other); **por lo que a mí me toca** as far as I'm concerned; **te toca a ti** it's your turn

tocayo, -a [to'kajo, a] *nm/f* namesake

tocino [to'θino] *nm* bacon

todavía [toða'βia] *adv* (*aun*) even; (*aún*) still, yet; **~ más** yet more; **~ no** not yet

○ **PALABRA CLAVE**

todo, -a ['toðo, a] *adj* 1 (*con artículo sg*) all; **toda la carne** all the meat; **toda la noche** the whole night; **todo el libro** the whole book; **toda una botella** a whole bottle; **todo lo contrario** quite the opposite; **está toda sucia** she's all dirty; **por todo el país** throughout the whole country

2 (*con artículo pl*) all; every; **todos los libros** all the books; **todas las noches** every night; **todos los que quieran salir** all those who want to leave

▷ *pron* 1 everything, all; **todos** everyone, everybody; **lo sabemos todo** we know everything; **todos querían más tiempo** everybody *o* everyone wanted more time; **nos marchamos todos** all of us left

2: **con todo: con todo él me sigue gustando** even so I still like him ▷ *adv* all; **vaya todo seguido** keep straight on *o* ahead

▷ *nm*: **como un todo** as a whole; **del todo: no me agrada del todo** I don't entirely like it

todopoderoso, -a [toðopoðe'roso, a] *adj* all powerful; (*Rel*) almighty

todoterreno [toðote'rreno] *sm inv* four-wheel drive, SUV (ESP US)

toga ['toɣa] *nf* toga; (*Escol*) gown

Tokio ['tokjo] *n* Tokyo

toldo ['toldo] *nm* (*para el sol*) sunshade (BRIT), parasol; (*tienda*) marquee

tolerancia [tole'ranθja] *nf* tolerance; **tolerante** *adj* (*sociedad*) liberal; (*persona*) open-minded

tolerar [tole'rar] *vt* to tolerate; (*resistir*) to endure

toma ['toma] *nf* (*acto*) taking; (*Med*) dose; **toma de corriente** socket; **toma de tierra** earth (wire); **tomacorriente** (LAM) *nm* socket

tomar [to'mar] *vt* to take; (*aspecto*) to take on; (*beber*) to drink ▷ *vi* to take; (LAM: *beber*) to drink; **tomarse** *vr* to take; **~se por** to consider o.s. to be; **~ a bien/mal** to take well/badly; **~ en serio** to take seriously; **~ el pelo a algn** to pull sb's leg; **~la con algn** to pick a quarrel with sb; **¡tome!** here you are!; **~ el sol** to sunbathe

tomate [to'mate] *nm* tomato

tomillo [to'miʎo] *nm* thyme

tomo ['tomo] *nm* (*libro*) volume

ton [ton] *abr* = **tonelada** ▷ *nm*: **sin ~ ni son** without rhyme or reason

tonalidad [tonali'ðað] *nf* tone

tonel [to'nel] *nm* barrel

tonelada [tone'laða] *nf* ton; **tonelaje** *nm* tonnage

tónica ['tonika] *nf* (*Mús*) tonic; (*fig*) keynote

tónico, -a ['toniko, a] *adj* tonic ▷ *nm* (*Med*) tonic

tono ['tono] *nm* tone; **fuera de ~** inappropriate

tontería [tonte'ria] *nf* (*estupidez*) foolishness; (*cosa*) stupid thing; (*acto*) foolish act; **tonterías** *nfpl* (*disparates*) rubbish *sg*, nonsense *sg*

tonto, -a ['tonto, a] *adj* stupid, silly ▷ *nm/f* fool

topar [to'par] *vi*: **~ contra** *o* **en** to run into; **~ con** to run up against

tope ['tope] *adj* maximum ▷ *nm* (*fin*) end; (*límite*) limit; (*Ferro*) buffer; (*Auto*) bumper; **al ~** end to end

tópico, -a ['topiko, a] *adj* topical ▷ *nm* platitude

topo ['topo] *nm* (*Zool*) mole; (*fig*) blunderer

toque *etc* ['toke] *vb* = **tocar** ▷ *nm* touch; (*Mús*) beat; (*de campana*) peal; **dar un ~ a** to warn; **toque de queda**

curfew

toqué *etc vb* V **tocar**

toquetear [tokete'ar] *vt* to finger

toquilla [to'kiʎa] *nf* (*pañuelo*) headscarf; (*chal*) shawl

tórax ['toraks] *nm* thorax

torbellino [torβe'ʎino] *nm* whirlwind; (*fig*) whirl

torcedura [torθe'ðura] *nf* twist; (*Med*) sprain

torcer [tor'θer] *vt* to twist; (*la esquina*) to turn; (*Med*) to sprain ▷ *vi* (*desviar*) to turn off; **torcerse** *vr* (*ladearse*) to bend; (*desviarse*) to go astray; (*fracasar*) to go wrong; **torcido, -a** *adj* twisted; (*fig*) crooked ▷ *nm* curl

tordo, -a ['torðo, a] *adj* dappled ▷ *nm* thrush

torear [tore'ar] *vt* (*fig: evadir*) to avoid; (*jugar con*) to tease ▷ *vi* to fight bulls; **toreo** *nm* bullfighting; **torero, -a** *nm/f* bullfighter

tormenta [tor'menta] *nf* storm; (*fig: confusión*) turmoil

tormento [tor'mento] *nm* torture; (*fig*) anguish

tornar [tor'nar] *vt* (*devolver*) to return, give back; (*transformar*) to transform ▷ *vi* to go back

tornasolado, -a [tornaso'laðo, a] *adj* (*brillante*) iridescent; (*reluciente*) shimmering

torneo [tor'neo] *nm* tournament

tornillo [tor'niʎo] *nm* screw

torniquete [torni'kete] *nm* (*Med*) tourniquet

torno ['torno] *nm* (*Tec*) winch; (*tambor*) drum; **en ~** around, about

toro ['toro] *nm* bull; (*fam*) he-man; **los ~s** bullfighting

toronja [to'ronxa] *nf* grapefruit

torpe ['torpe] *adj* (*poco hábil*) clumsy, awkward; (*necio*) dim; (*lento*) slow

torpedo [tor'peðo] *nm* torpedo

torpeza [tor'peθa] *nf* (*falta de agilidad*) clumsiness; (*lentitud*) slowness; (*error*) mistake

torre ['torre] *nf* tower; (*de petróleo*) derrick

torrefacto, -a [torre'fakto, a] *adj* roasted

torrente [to'rrente] *nm* torrent

torrija [to'rrixa] *nf* French toast

torsión [tor'sjon] *nf* twisting

torso ['torso] *nm* torso

torta ['torta] *nf* cake; (*fam*) slap

tortícolis [tor'tikolis] *nm inv* stiff neck

tortilla [tor'tiʎa] *nf* omelette; (*lam: de maíz*) maize pancake; **tortilla de papas** (*lam*) potato omelette; **tortilla de patatas** (*esp*) potato omelette; **tortilla francesa** (*esp*) plain omelette

tórtola ['tortola] *nf* turtledove

tortuga [tor'tuɣa] *nf* tortoise

tortuoso, -a [tor'twoso, a] *adj* winding

tortura [tor'tura] *nf* torture; **torturar** *vt* to torture

tos [tos] *nf* cough; **tos ferina** whooping cough

toser [to'ser] *vi* to cough

tostada [tos'taða] *nf* piece of toast; **tostado, -a** *adj* toasted; (*por el sol*) dark brown; (*piel*) tanned

tostador [tosta'ðor] (*esp*) *nm* toaster; **tostadora** (*lam*) *nf* = **tostador**

tostar [tos'tar] *vt* to toast; (*café*) to roast; (*persona*) to tan; **tostarse** *vr* to get brown

total [to'tal] *adj* total ▷ *adv* in short; (*al fin y al cabo*) when all is said and done ▷ *nm* total; **en ~** in all; **~ que ...** to cut (*brit*) o make (*us*) a long story short ...

totalidad [totali'ðað] *nf* whole

totalitario, -a [totali'tarjo, a] *adj* totalitarian

tóxico, -a ['toksiko, a] *adj* toxic ▷ *nm* poison; **toxicómano, -a** *nm/f* drug addict

toxina [to'ksina] *nf* toxin

tozudo, -a [to'θuðo, a] *adj* obstinate

trabajador, -a [traβaxa'ðor, a] *adj* hard-working ▷ *nm/f* worker;

trabajador autónomo o **por cuenta propia** self-employed person

trabajar [traβa'xar] vt to work; (Agr) to till; (empeñarse en) to work at; (convencer) to persuade ▷ vi to work; (esforzarse) to strive; **trabajo** nm work; (tarea) task; (Pol) labour; (fig) effort: **tomarse el trabajo de** to take the trouble to; **trabajo a destajo** piecework; **trabajo en equipo** teamwork; **trabajo por turnos** shift work; **trabajos forzados** hard labour sg

trabalenguas [traβa'lenÉ£was] nm inv tongue twister

tracción [trak'Î¸jon] nf traction; **tracción delantera/trasera** front-wheel/rear-wheel drive

tractor [trak'tor] nm tractor

tradición [traÎ'Î¸jon] nf tradition; **tradicional** adj traditional

traducción [traÎuk'Î¸jon] nf translation

traducir [traÎu'Î¸ir] vt to translate; **traductor, a** nm/f translator

traer [tra'er] vt to bring; (llevar) to carry; (llevar puesto) to wear; (incluir) to carry; (causar) to cause; **traerse** vr: **~se algo** to be up to sth

traficar [trafi'kar] vi to trade

tráfico ['trafiko] nm (Com) trade; (Auto) traffic

tragaluz [traÉ£a'luÎ¸] nm skylight

tragamonedas [traÉ£amo'neÎas] (LAM) nf inv slot machine

tragaperras [traÉ£a'perras] (ESP) nf inv slot machine

tragar [tra'É£ar] vt to swallow; (devorar) to devour, bolt down; **tragarse** vr to swallow

tragedia [tra'xeÎja] nf tragedy; **trágico, -a** adj tragic

trago ['traÉ£o] nm (líquido) drink; (bocado) gulp; (fam: de bebida) swig; (desgracia) blow: **echar un ~** to have a drink

traición [trai'Î¸jon] nf treachery; (Jur) treason; (una traición) act of treachery;

traicionar vt to betray

traidor, a [trai'Îor, a] adj treacherous ▷ nm/f traitor

traigo etc vb V **traer**

traje ['traxe] vb V **traer** ▷ nm (de hombre) suit; (de mujer) dress; (vestido típico) costume; **traje de baño/chaqueta** swimsuit/suit; **traje de etiqueta** dress suit; **traje de luces** bullfighter's costume

trajera etc vb V **traer**

trajín [tra'xin] nm (fam: movimiento) bustle; **trajinar** vi (moverse) to bustle about

trama ['trama] nf (intriga) plot; (de tejido) weft (BRIT), woof (US); **tramar** vt to plot; (Tec) to weave

tramitar [trami'tar] vt (asunto) to transact; (negociar) to negotiate

trámite ['tramite] nm (paso) step; (Jur) transaction; **trámites** nmpl (burocracia) procedure sg; (Jur) proceedings

tramo ['tramo] nm (de tierra) plot; (de escalera) flight; (de vía) section

trampa ['trampa] nf (trap; (en el suelo) trapdoor; (truco) trick; (engaño) fiddle; **trampear** vt, vi to cheat

trampolín [trampo'lin] nm (de piscina etc) diving board

tramposo, -a [tram'poso, a] adj crooked, cheating ▷ nm/f crook, cheat

tranca ['tranka] nf (palo) stick; (de puerta, ventana) bar; **trancar** vt to bar

trance ['tranÎ¸e] nm (momento difícil) difficult moment o juncture; (estado hipnotizado) trance

tranquilidad [trankili'Îað] nf (calma) calmness, stillness; (paz) peacefulness

tranquilizar [trankili'Î¸ar] vt (calmar) to calm (down); (asegurar) to reassure; **tranquilizarse** vr to calm down; **tranquilo, -a** adj (calmado) calm; (apacible) peaceful; (mar) calm; (mente) untroubled

transacción [transak'Î¸jon] nf transaction

transbordador [transβorða'ðor]
nm ferry

transbordo [trans'βorðo] nm
transfer; **hacer** ~ to change (trains etc)

transcurrir [transku'rrir] vi (tiempo)
to pass; (hecho) to take place

transcurso [trans'kurso] nm: ~ **del**
tiempo lapse (of time)

transeúnte [transe'unte] nmf
passer-by

transferencia [transfe'renθja] nf
transference; (Com) transfer

transferir [transfe'rir] vt to transfer

transformador [transforma'ðor]
nm (Elec) transformer

transformar [transfor'mar] vt to
transform; (convertir) to convert

transfusión [transfu'sjon] nf
transfusion

transgénico, -a [trans'xeniko, a]
adj genetically modified, GM

transición [transi'θjon] nf transition

transigir [transi'xir] vi to
compromise, make concessions

transitar [transi'tar] vi to go (from
place to place); **tránsito** nm transit;
(Auto) traffic; **transitorio, -a** adj
transitory

transmisión [transmi'sjon] nf (Tec)
transmission; (transferencia) transfer;
transmisión exterior/en directo
outside/live broadcast

transmitir [transmi'tir] vt to
transmit; (Radio, TV) to broadcast

transparencia [transpa'renθja]
nf transparency; (claridad) clearness,
clarity; (foto) slide

transparentar [transparen'tar]
vt to reveal ▷ vi to be transparent;
transparente adj transparent;
(claro) clear

transpirar [transpi'rar] vi to perspire

transportar [transpor'tar] vt to
transport; (llevar) to carry; **transporte**
nm (Com) haulage

transversal [transβer'sal] adj
transverse, cross

tranvía [tram'bia] nm tram

trapeador [trapea'ðor] (LAM) nm
mop; **trapear** (LAM) vt to mop

trapecio [tra'peθjo] nm trapeze;
trapecista nmf trapeze artist

trapero, -a [tra'pero, a] nm/f
ragman

trapicheo [trapi'tʃeo] (fam) nm
scheme, fiddle

trapo ['trapo] nm (tela) rag; (de
cocina) cloth

tráquea ['trakea] nf windpipe

traqueteo [trake'teo] nm rattling

tras [tras] prep (detrás) behind;
(después) after

trasatlántico [trasat'lantiko] nm
(barco) (cabin) cruiser

trascendencia [trasθen'denθja] nf
(importancia) importance; (Filosofía)
transcendence

trascendental [trasθenden'tal] adj
important; (Filosofía) transcendental

trasero, -a [tra'sero, a] adj back,
rear ▷ nm (Anat) bottom

trasfondo [tras'fondo] nm
background

trasgredir [trasɣre'ðir] vt to
contravene

trashumante [trasu'mante] adj
(animales) migrating

trasladar [trasla'ðar] vt to move;
(persona) to transfer; (postergar) to
postpone; (copiar) to copy; **trasladarse**
vr (mudarse) to move; **traslado** nm
move; (mudanza) move, removal

traslucir [traslu'θir] vt to show

trasluz [tras'luθ] nm reflected light;
al ~ against o up to the light

trasnochador, a [trasnotʃa'ðor, a]
nm/f night owl

trasnochar [trasno'tʃar] vi (acostarse
tarde) to stay up late

traspapelar [traspape'lar] vt
(documento, carta) to mislay, misplace

traspasar [traspa'sar] vt (suj: bala
etc) to pierce, go through; (propiedad)
to sell, transfer; (calle) to cross over;
(límites) to go beyond; (ley) to break;
traspaso nm (venta) transfer, sale

traspatio [tras'patjo] (LAM) nm backyard

traspié [tras'pje] nm (tropezón) trip; (error) blunder

trasplantar [trasplan'tar] vt to transplant

traste ['traste] nm (Mús) fret; **dar al ~ con algo** to ruin sth

trastero [tras'tero] nm storage room

trastienda [tras'tjenda] nf back of shop

trasto ['trasto] nm (pey) (cosa) piece of junk; (persona) dead loss

trastornado, -a [trastor'naðo, a] adj (loco) mad, crazy

trastornar [trastor'nar] vt (fig: planes) to disrupt; (: nervios) to shatter; (: persona) to drive crazy; **trastornarse** vr (volverse loco) to go mad o crazy; **trastorno** nm (acto) overturning; (confusión) confusion

tratable [tra'taβle] adj friendly

tratado [tra'taðo] nm (Pol) treaty; (Com) agreement

tratamiento [trata'mjento] nm treatment; **tratamiento de textos** (Inform) word processing cpd

tratar [tra'tar] vt (ocuparse de) to treat; (manejar, Tec) to handle; (Med) to treat; (dirigirse a: persona) to address ▷ vi: **~ de** (hablar sobre) to deal with, be about; (intentar) to try to; **tratarse** vr to treat each other; **~ con** (Com) to trade in; (negociar) to negotiate with; (tener contactos) to have dealings with; **¿de qué se trata?** what's it about?; **trato** nm dealings pl; (relaciones) relationship; (comportamiento) manner; (Com) agreement

trauma ['trauma] nm trauma

través [tra'βes] nm (fig) reverse; **al ~** across, crossways; **a ~ de** across; (sobre) over; (por) through

travesaño [traβe'saɲo] nm (Arq) crossbeam; (Deporte) crossbar

travesía [traβe'sia] nf (calle) cross-street; (Náut) crossing

travesura [traβe'sura] nf (broma)

prank; (ingenio) wit

travieso, -a [tra'βjeso, a] adj (niño) naughty

trayecto [tra'jekto] nm (ruta) road, way; (viaje) journey; (tramo) stretch; **trayectoria** nf trajectory; (fig) path

traza ['traβa] nf (aspecto) looks pl; (señal) sign; **trazado, -a** adj: **bien trazado** shapely, well-formed ▷ nm (Arq) plan, design; (fig) outline

trazar [tra'θar] vt (Arq) to plan; (Arte) to sketch; (fig) to trace; (plan) to draw up; **trazo** nm (línea) line; (bosquejo) sketch

trébol ['treβol] nm (Bot) clover

trece ['treθe] num thirteen

trecho ['tretʃo] nm (distancia) distance; (tiempo) while

tregua ['trexwa] nf (Mil) truce; (fig) respite

treinta ['treinta] num thirty

tremendo, -a [tre'mendo, a] adj (terrible) terrible; (imponente: cosa) imposing; (fam: fabuloso) tremendous

tren [tren] nm train; **tren de aterrizaje** undercarriage; **tren de cercanías** suburban train

trenca ['trenka] nf duffel coat

trenza ['trenθa] nf (de pelo) plait (BRIT), braid (US)

trepadora [trepa'ðora] nf (Bot) climber

trepar [tre'par] vt, vi to climb

tres [tres] num three

tresillo [tre'siʎo] nm three-piece suite; (Mús) triplet

treta ['treta] nf trick

triángulo ['trjangulo] nm triangle

tribu ['triβu] nf tribe

tribuna [tri'βuna] nf (plataforma) platform; (Deporte) (grand)stand

tribunal [triβu'nal] nm (Jur) court; (comisión, fig) tribunal; **~ popular** jury

tributo [tri'βuto] nm (Com) tax

trigal [tri'xal] nm wheat field

trigo ['trixo] nm wheat

trigueño, -a [tri'xeɲo, a] adj (pelo) corn-coloured

trillar [tri'ʎar] vt (Agr) to thresh

trimestral [trimes'tral] adj quarterly; (Escol) termly

trimestre [tri'mestre] nm (Escol) term

trinar [tri'nar] vi (pájaros) to sing; (rabiar) to fume, be angry

trinchar [trin'tʃar] vt to carve

trinchera [trin'tʃera] nf (fosa) trench

trineo [tri'neo] nm sledge

trinidad [trini'ðað] nf trio; (Rel): **la T~** the Trinity

tripa ['tripa] nf (Anat) intestine; (fam: tb: **~s**) insides pl

triple ['triple] adj triple

triplicado, -a [tripli'kaðo, a] adj: **por ~** in triplicate

tripulación [tripula'θjon] nf crew

tripulante [tripu'lante] nmf crewman/woman

tripular [tripu'lar] vt (barco) to man; (Auto) to drive

triquiñuela [triki'nwela] nf trick

tris [tris] nm inv crack

triste ['triste] adj sad; (lamentable) sorry, miserable; **tristeza** nf (aflicción) sadness; (melancolía) melancholy

triturar [tritu'rar] vt (moler) to grind; (mascar) to chew

triunfar [trjun'far] vi (tener éxito) to triumph; (ganar) to win; **triunfo** nm triumph

trivial [tri'βjal] adj trivial

triza ['triθa] nf: **hacer ~s** to smash to bits; (papel) to tear to shreds

trocear [troθe'ar] vt (carne, manzana) to cut up, cut into pieces

trocha ['trotʃa] nf short cut

trofeo [tro'feo] nm (premio) trophy; (éxito) success

tromba ['tromba] nf downpour

trombón [trom'bon] nm trombone

trombosis [trom'bosis] nf inv thrombosis

trompa ['trompa] nf horn; (trompo) humming top; (hocico) snout; (fam): **cogerse una ~** to get tight

trompazo [trom'paθo] nm bump, bang

trompeta [trom'peta] nf trumpet; (clarín) bugle

trompicón [trompi'kon]: **a trompicones** adv in fits and starts

trompo ['trompo] nm spinning top

trompón [trom'pon] nm bump

tronar [tro'nar] vt (MÉX, CAM: fusilar) to shoot; (MÉX: examen) to flunk ▷ vi to thunder; (fig) to rage

tronchar [tron'tʃar] vt (árbol) to chop down; (fig: vida) to cut short; (: esperanza) to shatter; (persona) to tire out; **troncharse** vr to fall down

tronco ['tronko] nm (de árbol, Anat) trunk

trono ['trono] nm throne

tropa ['tropa] nf (Mil) troop; (soldados) soldiers pl

tropezar [trope'θar] vi to trip, stumble; (errar) to slip up; **~ con** to run into; (topar con) to bump into; **tropezón** nm trip; (fig) blunder

tropical [tropi'kal] adj tropical

trópico ['tropiko] nm tropic

tropiezo [tro'pjeθo] vb V **tropezar** ▷ nm (error) slip, blunder; (desgracia) misfortune; (obstáculo) snag

trotamundos [trota'mundos] nm inv globetrotter

trotar [tro'tar] vi to trot; **trote** nm trot; (fam) travelling; **de mucho trote** hard-wearing

trozar [tro'θar] vt (LAM) to cut up, cut into pieces

trozo ['troθo] nm bit, piece

trucha ['trutʃa] nf trout

truco ['truko] nm (habilidad) knack; (engaño) trick

trueno ['trweno] nm thunder; (estampido) bang

trueque etc ['tweke] vb V **trocar** ▷ nm exchange; (Com) barter

trufa ['trufa] nf (Bot) truffle

truhán, -ana [tru'an, ana] nm/f rogue

truncar [trun'kar] vt (cortar) to truncate; (fig: la vida etc) to cut short; (: el desarrollo) to stunt

tu [tu] adj your

tú [tu] pron you

tubérculo [tu'βerkulo] nm (Bot) tuber

tuberculosis [tuβerku'losis] nf inv tuberculosis

tubería [tuβe'ria] nf pipes pl; (conducto) pipeline

tubo ['tuβo] nm tube, pipe; tubo de ensayo test tube; tubo de escape exhaust (pipe)

tuerca ['twerka] nf nut

tuerto, -a ['twerto, a] adj blind in one eye ▷ nm/f one-eyed person

tuerza etc vb V torcer

tuétano ['twetano] nm marrow; (Bot) pith

tufo ['tufo] nm (hedor) stench

tul [tul] nm tulle

tulipán [tuli'pan] nm tulip

tullido, -a [tu'ʎiðo, a] adj crippled

tumba ['tumba] nf (sepultura) tomb

tumbar [tum'bar] vt to knock down; tumbarse vr (echarse) to lie down; (extenderse) to stretch out

tumbo ['tumbo] nm: dar ~s to stagger

tumbona [tum'bona] nf (butaca) easy chair; (de playa) deckchair (BRIT), beach chair (US)

tumor [tu'mor] nm tumour

tumulto [tu'multo] nm turmoil

tuna ['tuna] nf (Mús) student music group; V tb tuno

○ TUNA
○
○ A tuna is a musical group made
○ up of university students or
○ former students who dress up
○ in costumes from the "Edad de
○ Oro", the Spanish Golden Age.
○ These groups go through the
○ town playing their guitars, lutes
○ and tambourines and serenade
○ the young ladies in the halls of
○ residence or make impromptu
○ appearances at weddings or
○ parties singing traditional
○ Spanish songs for a few coins.

tunante [tu'nante] nmf rascal

tunear [tune'ar] vt (Auto) to style, mod (inf)

túnel ['tunel] nm tunnel

tuning ['tunin] nm (Auto) car styling, modding (inf)

tuno, -a ['tuno, a] nm/f (fam) rogue ▷ nm member of student music group

tupido, -a [tu'piðo, a] adj (denso) dense; (tela) close-woven

turbante [tur'βante] nm turban

turbar [tur'βar] vt (molestar) to disturb; (incomodar) to upset

turbina [tur'βina] nf turbine

turbio, -a [tur'βjo, a] adj cloudy; (tema etc) confused

turbulencia [turβu'lenθja] nf turbulence; (fig) restlessness

turbulento, -a adj turbulent; (fig: intranquilo) restless; (: ruidoso) noisy

turco, -a ['turko, a] adj Turkish ▷ nm/f Turk

turismo [tu'rismo] nm tourism; (coche) car; turista nmf tourist; turístico, -a adj tourist cpd

turnar [tur'nar] vi to take (it in) turns; turnarse vr to take (it in) turns; turno nm (de trabajo) shift; (en juegos etc) turn

turquesa [tur'kesa] nf turquoise

Turquía [tur'kia] nf Turkey

turrón [tu'rron] nm (dulce) nougat

tutear [tute'ar] vt to address as familiar "tú"; tutearse vr to be on familiar terms

tutela [tu'tela] nf (legal) guardianship; tutelar adj tutelary ▷ vt to protect

tutor, -a [tu'tor, a] nm/f (legal) guardian; (Escol) tutor

tuve etc vb V tener

tuviera etc vb V tener

tuyo, -a [tujo, a] adj yours, of yours ▷ pron yours; un amigo ~ a friend of yours; los ~s (fam) your relations o family

TV nf abr (= televisión) TV

TVE nf abr = Televisión Española

u

u [u] *conj* or

ubicar [uβi'kar] *vt* to place, situate; (LAM: *encontrar*) to find; **ubicarse** *vr* (LAM: *encontrarse*) to lie, be located

ubre ['uβre] *nf* udder

UCI *nf abr* (= *Unidad de Cuidados Intensivos*) ICU

Ud(s) *abr* = **usted(es)**

UE *nf abr* (= *Unión Europea*) EU

ufanarse [ufa'narse] *vr* to boast; **ufano, -a** *adj* (*arrogante*) arrogant; (*presumido*) conceited

UGT (ESP) *nf abr* = **Unión General de Trabajadores**

úlcera ['ulθera] *nf* ulcer

ulterior [ulte'rjor] *adj* (*más allá*) farther, further; (*subsecuente, siguiente*) subsequent

últimamente [ultima'mente] *adv* (*recientemente*) lately, recently

ultimar [ulti'mar] *vt* to finish; (*finalizar*) to finalize; (LAM: *matar*) to kill

ultimátum [ulti'matum] (*pl* **-s**) *nm* ultimatum

último, -a ['ultimo, a] *adj* last; (*más reciente*) latest, most recent; (*más bajo*) bottom; (*más alto*) top; **en las últimas** on one's last legs; **por ~** finally

ultra ['ultra] *adj* ultra ▷ *nmf* extreme right-winger

ultraje [ul'traxe] *nm* outrage; insult

ultramar [ultra'mar] *nm*: **de o en ~** abroad, overseas

ultramarinos [ultrama'rinos] *nmpl* groceries; **tienda de ~** grocer's (shop)

ultranza [ul'tranθa]: **a ~** *adv* (*a todo trance*) at all costs; (*completo*) outright

umbral [um'bral] *nm* (*gen*) threshold

○ **PALABRA CLAVE**

un, una [un, 'una] *art indef* a; (*antes de vocal*) an; **una mujer/naranja** a woman/an orange
▷ *adj*: **unos** (o **unas**): **hay unos regalos para ti** there are some presents for you; **hay unas cervezas en la nevera** there are some beers in the fridge

unánime [u'nanime] *adj* unanimous; **unanimidad** *nf* unanimity

undécimo, -a [un'deθimo, a] *adj* eleventh

ungir [un'xir] *vt* to anoint

ungüento [un'gwento] *nm* ointment

único, -a ['uniko, a] *adj* only, sole; (*sin par*) unique

unidad [uni'ðað] *nf* unity; (Com, Tec etc) unit

unido, -a [u'niðo, a] *adj* joined, linked; (*fig*) united

unificar [unifi'kar] *vt* to unite, unify

uniformar [unifor'mar] *vt* to make uniform, level up; (*persona*) to put into uniform

uniforme [uni'forme] *adj* uniform, equal; (*superficie*) even ▷ *nm* uniform

unilateral [unilate'ral] *adj* unilateral

unión [u'njon] *nf* union; (*acto*) uniting, joining; (*unidad*) unity; (Tec) joint; **Unión Europea** European Union

unir [u'nir] *vt* (*juntar*) to join, unite;

(*atar*) to tie, fasten; (*combinar*) to combine; **unirse** to join together, unite; (*empresas*) to merge

unísono [u'nisono] *nm*: **al ~** in unison

universal [uniβer'sal] *adj* universal; (*mundial*) world cpd

universidad [uniβersi'ðað] *nf* university

universitario, -a [uniβersi'tarjo, a] *adj* university cpd ⊳ *nm/f* (*profesor*) lecturer; (*estudiante*) (university) student; (*graduado*) graduate

universo [uni'βerso] *nm* universe

○ **PALABRA CLAVE**

uno, -a ['uno, a] *adj* one; **unos pocos** a few; **unos cien** about a hundred
⊳ *pron* 1 one; **quiero sólo uno** I only want one; **uno de ellos** one of them
2 (*alguien*) somebody, someone; **conozco a uno que se te parece** I know somebody o someone who looks like you; **uno mismo** oneself; **unos querían quedarse** some (people) wanted to stay
3 (los) **unos ... (los) otros ...** some ... others
⊳ *nf* one; **es la una** it's one o'clock
⊳ *nm* (number) one

untar [un'tar] *vt* (*mantequilla*) to spread; (*engrasar*) to grease, oil

uña ['uɲa] *nf* (*Anat*) nail; (*garra*) claw; (*casco*) hoof; (*arrancaclavos*) claw

uranio [u'ranjo] *nm* uranium

urbanización [urβaniθa'θjon] *nf* (*barrio, colonia*) housing estate

urbanizar [urβani'θar] *vt* (*zona*) to develop, urbanize

urbano, -a [ur'βano, a] *adj* (*de ciudad*) urban; (*cortés*) courteous, polite

urbe ['urβe] *nf* large city

urdir [ur'ðir] *vt* to warp; (*complot*) to plot, contrive

urgencia [ur'xenθja] *nf* urgency; (*prisa*) haste, rush; (*emergencia*) emergency; **servicios de ~** emergency services; **"U~s"** "Casualty"; **urgente** *adj* urgent

urgir [ur'xir] *vi* to be urgent; **me urge** I'm in a hurry for it

urinario, -a [uri'narjo, a] *adj* urinary ⊳ *nm* urinal

urna ['urna] *nf* urn; (*Pol*) ballot box

urraca [u'rraka] *nf* magpie

URSS [urs] *nf* (*Hist*): **la URSS** the USSR

Uruguay [uru'ɣwai] *nm* (tb: **el ~**) Uruguay; **uruguayo, -a** *adj, nm/f* Uruguayan

usado, -a [u'saðo, a] *adj* used; (*de segunda mano*) secondhand

usar [u'sar] *vt* to use; (*ropa*) to wear; (*tener costumbre*) to be in the habit of; **usarse** *vr* to be used; **uso** *nm* use; wear; (*costumbre*) usage, custom; (*moda*) fashion; **al uso** in keeping with custom; **al uso de** in the style of; **de uso externo** (*Med*) for external use

usted [us'teð] *pron* (sg) you sg; (pl): **-es** you pl

usual [u'swal] *adj* usual

usuario, -a [u'swarjo, a] *nm/f* user

usura [u'sura] *nf* usury; **usurero, -a** *nm/f* usurer

usurpar [usur'par] *vt* to usurp

utensilio [uten'siljo] *nm* tool; (*Culin*) utensil

útero ['utero] *nm* uterus, womb

útil ['util] *adj* useful ⊳ *nm* tool; **utilidad** *nf* usefulness; (*Com*) profit; **utilizar** *vt* to use, utilize

utopía [uto'pia] *nf* Utopia; **utópico, -a** *adj* Utopian

uva ['uβa] *nf* grape

● ● ● **LAS UVAS**
●
● In Spain **Las uvas** play a big part on
● New Year's Eve (**Nochevieja**), when
● on the stroke of midnight people
● gather at home, in restaurants or
● in the **plaza mayor** and eat a grape
● for each stroke of the clock of the
● **Puerta del Sol** in Madrid. It is said
● to bring luck for the following year.

V

v abr (= voltio) v

va vb V **ir**

vaca ['baka] nf (animal) cow; **carne de ~** beef

vacaciones [baka'θjones] nfpl holidays

vacante [ba'kante] adj vacant, empty ▷ nf vacancy

vaciar [ba'θjar] vt to empty out; (ahuecar) to hollow out; (moldear) to cast; **vaciarse** vr to empty

vacilar [baθi'lar] vi to be unsteady; (al hablar) to falter; (dudar) to hesitate, waver; (memoria) to fail

vacío, -a [ba'θio, a] adj empty; (puesto) vacant; (desocupado) idle; (vano) vain ▷ nm emptiness; (Física) vacuum; (un vacío) (empty) space

vacuna [ba'kuna] nf vaccine; **vacunar** vt to vaccinate

vacuno, -a [ba'kuno, a] adj cow cpd; **ganado ~** cattle

vadear [baðe'ar] vt (río) to ford; **vado** nm ford

vagabundo, -a [baxa'βundo, a] adj wandering ▷ nm tramp

vagancia [ba'xanθja] nf (pereza) idleness, laziness

vagar [ba'xar] vi to wander; (no hacer nada) to idle

vagina [ba'xina] nf vagina

vago, -a ['baxo, a] adj vague; (perezoso) lazy ▷ nm/f (vagabundo) tramp; (flojo) lazybones sg, idler

vagón [ba'xon] nm (Ferro: de pasajeros) carriage; (: de mercancías) wagon

vaho ['bao] nm (vapor) vapour, steam; (respiración) breath

vaina ['baina] nf sheath

vainilla [bai'niʎa] nf vanilla

vais vb V **ir**

vaivén [bai'βen] nm to-and-fro movement; (de tránsito) coming and going; **vaivenes** nmpl (fig) ups and downs

vajilla [ba'xiʎa] nf crockery, dishes pl; (juego) service, set

valdré etc vb V **valer**

vale ['bale] nm voucher; (recibo) receipt; (pagaré) IOU

valedero, -a [bale'ðero, a] adj valid

valenciano, -a [balen'θjano, a] adj Valencian

valentía [balen'tia] nf courage, bravery

valer [ba'ler] vt to be worth; (Mat) to equal; (costar) to cost ▷ vi (ser útil) to be useful; (ser válido) to be valid; **valerse** vr to take care of oneself; **~se de** to make use of, take advantage of; **~ la pena** to be worthwhile; **¿vale?** (ESP) OK?; **más vale que nos vayamos** we'd better go; **¡eso a mí no me vale!** (MÉX: fam: no importar) I couldn't care less about that

valeroso, -a [bale'roso, a] adj brave, valiant

valgo etc vb V **valer**

valía [ba'lia] nf worth, value

validar [bali'ðar] vt to validate; **validez** nf validity; **válido, -a** adj valid

valiente [ba'ljente] adj brave, valiant

▷ nm hero

valija [ba'lixa] (cs) nf (suit)case

valioso, -a [ba'ljoso, a] adj valuable

valla ['baʎa] nf fence; (Deporte) hurdle; **valla publicitaria** hoarding; **vallar** vt to fence in

valle ['baʎe] nm valley

valor [ba'lor] nm value, worth; (precio) price; (valentía) valour, courage; (importancia) importance; **valores** nmpl (Com) securities; **valorar** vt to value

vals [bals] nm inv waltz

válvula ['balβula] nf valve

vamos vb V **ir**

vampiro, -resa [bam'piro, 'resa] nm/f vampire

van vb V **ir**

vanguardia [ban'gwardja] nf vanguard; (Arte etc) avant-garde

vanidad [bani'ðað] nf vanity; **vanidoso, -a** adj vain, conceited

vano, -a ['bano, a] adj vain

vapor [ba'por] nm vapour; (vaho) steam; **al ~** (Culin) steamed; **vapor de agua** water vapour; **vaporizador** nm atomizer; **vaporizar** vt to vaporize; **vaporoso, -a** adj vaporous

vaquero, -a [ba'kero, a] adj cattle cpd ▷ nm cowboy; **vaqueros** nmpl (pantalones) jeans

vaquilla [ba'kiʎa] nf (Zool) heifer

vara ['bara] nf stick; (Tec) rod

variable [ba'rjaβle] adj, nf variable

variación [barja'θjon] nf variation

variar [bar'jar] vt to vary; (modificar) to modify; (cambiar de posición) to switch around ▷ vi to vary

varicela [bari'θela] nf chickenpox

varices [ba'riθes] nfpl varicose veins

variedad [barje'ðað] nf variety

varilla [ba'riʎa] nf stick; (Bot) twig; (Tec) rod; (de rueda) spoke

vario, -a ['barjo, a] adj varied; **~s** various, several

varita [ba'rita] nf (tb: **~ mágica**) magic wand

varón [ba'ron] nm male, man; **varonil**

adj manly, virile

Varsovia [bar'soβja] n Warsaw

vas vb V **ir**

vasco, -a ['basko, a] adj, nm/f Basque; **vascongado, -a** [baskon'gaðo, a] adj Basque; **las Vascongadas** the Basque Country

vaselina [base'lina] nf Vaseline®

vasija [ba'sixa] nf container, vessel

vaso ['baso] nm glass, tumbler; (Anat) vessel

> ▎No confundir **vaso** con la palabra inglesa vase.

vástago ['bastaɣo] nm (Bot) shoot; (Tec) rod; (fig) offspring

vasto, -a ['basto, a] adj vast, huge

Vaticano [bati'kano] nm: **el ~** the Vatican

vatio ['batjo] nm (Elec) watt

vaya etc vb V **ir**

Vd(s) abr = **usted(es)**

ve [be] vb V **ir**; **ver**

vecindad [beθin'dað] nf neighbourhood; (habitantes) residents pl

vecindario [beθin'darjo] nm neighbourhood; residents pl

vecino, -a [be'θino, a] adj neighbouring ▷ nm/f neighbour; (residente) resident

veda ['beða] nf prohibition; **vedar** [be'ðar] vt (prohibir) to ban, prohibit; (impedir) to stop, prevent

vegetación [bexeta'θjon] nf vegetation

vegetal [bexe'tal] adj, nm vegetable

vegetariano, -a [bexeta'rjano, a] adj, nm/f vegetarian

vehículo [be'ikulo] nm vehicle; (Med) carrier

veía etc vb V **ver**

veinte ['beinte] num twenty

vejar [be'xar] vt (irritar) to annoy, vex; (humillar) to humiliate

vejez [be'xeθ] nf old age

vejiga [be'xiɣa] nf (Anat) bladder

vela ['bela] nf (de cera) candle; (Náut) sail; (insomnio) sleeplessness; (vigilia) vigil; (Mil) sentry duty; **estar a dos ~s** (fam: sin dinero) to be skint

velado, -a [be'laðo, a] adj veiled; (sonido) muffled; (Foto) blurred ▷ nf soirée

velar [be'lar] vt (vigilar) to keep watch over ▷ vi to stay awake; **~ por** to watch over, look after

velatorio [bela'torjo] nm (funeral) wake

velero [be'lero] nm (Náut) sailing ship; (Aviac) glider

veleta [be'leta] nf weather vane

veliz [be'lis] (MÉX) nm (suit)case

vello [ˈbeʎo] nm down, fuzz

velo [ˈbelo] nm veil

velocidad [beloθiˈðað] nf speed; (Tec, Auto) gear

velocímetro [beloˈθimetro] nm speedometer

velorio [beˈlorjo] (LAM) nm (funeral) wake

veloz [beˈloθ] adj fast

ven vb V **venir**

vena [ˈbena] nf vein

venado [beˈnaðo] nm deer

vencedor, a [benθeˈðor, a] adj victorious ▷ nm/f victor, winner

vencer [benˈθer] vt (dominar) to defeat, beat; (derrotar) to vanquish; (superar, controlar) to overcome, master ▷ vi (triunfar) to win (through), triumph; (plazo) to expire; **vencido, -a** adj (derrotado) defeated, beaten; (Com) due ▷ adv: **pagar vencido** to pay in arrears

venda [ˈbenda] nf bandage; **vendaje** nm bandage, dressing; **vendar** vt to bandage; **vendar los ojos** to blindfold

vendaval [bendaˈβal] nm (viento) gale

vendedor, a [bendeˈðor, a] nm/f seller

vender [benˈder] vt to sell; **venderse** vr (estar a la venta) to be on sale; **~ al contado/al por mayor/al por menor** to sell for cash/wholesale/retail; **"se vende"** "for sale"

vendimia [benˈdimja] nf grape harvest

vendré etc vb V **venir**

veneno [beˈneno] nm poison; (de serpiente) venom; **venenoso, -a** adj poisonous; venomous

venerable [beneˈraβle] adj venerable; **venerar** vt (respetar) to revere; (adorar) to worship

venéreo, -a [beˈnereo, a] adj: **enfermedad venérea** venereal disease

venezolano, -a [beneθoˈlano, a] adj Venezuelan

Venezuela [beneˈθwela] nf Venezuela

venganza [benˈganθa] nf vengeance, revenge; **vengar** vt to avenge; **vengarse** vr to take revenge; **vengativo, -a** adj (persona) vindictive

vengo etc vb V **venir**

venia [ˈbenja] nf (perdón) pardon; (permiso) consent

venial [beˈnjal] adj venial

venida [beˈniða] nf (llegada) arrival; (regreso) return

venidero, -a [beniˈðero, a] adj coming, future

venir [beˈnir] vi to come; (llegar) to arrive; (ocurrir) to happen; (fig): **~ de** to stem from; **~ bien/mal** to be suitable/unsuitable; **el año que viene** next year; **~se abajo** to collapse

venta [ˈbenta] nf (Com) sale; **"en ~"** "for sale"; **estar a la o en ~** to be (up) for sale o on the market; **venta a domicilio** door-to-door selling; **venta a plazos** hire purchase; **venta al contado/al por mayor/al por menor** cash sale/wholesale/retail

ventaja [benˈtaxa] nf advantage; **ventajoso, -a** adj advantageous

ventana [benˈtana] nf window; **ventanilla** nf (de taquilla) window (of booking office etc)

ventilación [bentilaˈθjon] nf ventilation; (corriente) draught

ventilador [bentilaˈðor] nm fan

ventilar [benti'lar] vt to ventilate; (para secar) to put out to dry; (asunto) to air, discuss

ventisca [ben'tiska] nf blizzard

ventrílocuo, -a [ben'trilokwo, a] nm/f ventriloquist

ventura [ben'tura] nf (felicidad) happiness; (buena suerte) luck; (destino) fortune; **a la (buena) ~** at random; **venturoso, -a** adj happy; (afortunado) lucky, fortunate

veo etc vb V **ver**

ver [ber] vt to see; (mirar) to look at, watch; (entender) to understand; (investigar) to look into ⊳ vi to see; to understand; **verse** vr (encontrarse) to meet; (dejarse ver) to be seen; (hallarse: en un apuro) to find o.s., be; **(vamos) a ~** let's see; **no tener nada que ~ con** to have nothing to do with; **a mi modo de ~** as I see it; **ya ~emos** we'll see

vera ['bera] nf edge, verge; (de río) bank

veranear [berane'ar] vi to spend the summer; **veraneo** nm summer holiday; **veraniego, -a** adj summer cpd

verano [be'rano] nm summer

veras ['beras] nfpl truth sg; **de ~** really, truly

verbal [ber'βal] adj verbal

verbena [ber'βena] nf (baile) open-air dance

verbo ['berβo] nm verb

verdad [ber'ðað] nf truth; (fiabilidad) reliability; **de ~** real, proper; **a decir ~** to tell the truth; **verdadero, -a** adj (veraz) true, truthful; (fiable) reliable; (fig) real

verde ['berðe] adj green; (chiste) blue, dirty ⊳ nm green; **viejo ~** dirty old man; **verdear** vi to turn green; **verdor** nm greenness

verdugo [ber'ðuɣo] nm executioner

verdulero, -a [berðu'lero, a] nm/f greengrocer

verduras [ber'ðuras] nfpl (Culin) greens

vereda [be'reða] nf path; (cs: acera) pavement (BRIT), sidewalk (US)

veredicto [bere'ðikto] nm verdict

vergonzoso, -a [berɣon'θoso, a] adj shameful; (tímido) timid, bashful

vergüenza [ber'xwenθa] nf shame, sense of shame; (timidez) bashfulness; (pudor) modesty; **me da ~** I'm ashamed

verídico, -a [be'riðiko, a] adj true, truthful

verificar [berifi'kar] vt to check; (corroborar) to verify; (llevar a cabo) to carry out; **verificarse** vr (predicción) to prove to be true

verja ['berxa] nf (cancela) iron gate; (valla) iron railings pl; (de ventana) grille

vermut [ber'mut] (pl ~s) nm vermouth

verosímil [bero'simil] adj likely, probable; (relato) credible

verruga [be'rruxa] nf wart

versátil [ber'satil] adj versatile

versión [ber'sjon] nf version

verso ['berso] nm verse; **un ~** a line of poetry

vértebra ['berteβra] nf vertebra

verter [ber'ter] vt (líquido: adrede) to empty, pour (out); (: sin querer) to spill; (basura) to dump ⊳ vi to flow

vertical [berti'kal] adj vertical

vértice ['bertiθe] nm vertex, apex

vertidos [ber'tiðos] nmpl waste sg

vertiente [ber'tjente] nf slope; (fig) aspect

vértigo ['bertiɣo] nm vertigo; (mareo) dizziness

vesícula [be'sikula] nf blister

vespino® [bes'pino] nm o f moped

vestíbulo [bes'tiβulo] nm hall; (de teatro) foyer

vestido [bes'tiðo] nm (ropa) clothes pl, clothing; (de mujer) dress, frock ⊳ pp de **vestir**; **~ de azul/marinero** dressed in blue/as a sailor

vestidor [besti'ðor] (MÉX) nm (Deporte) changing (BRIT) o locker (US) room

vestimenta [besti'menta] nf
clothing

vestir [bes'tir] vt (poner: ropa) to put
on; (llevar: ropa) to wear; (proveer de ropa
a) to clothe; (sastre) to make clothes for
▷ vi to dress; (verse bien) to look good;
vestirse vr to get dressed, dress o.s.

vestuario [bes'twarjo] nm clothes
pl, wardrobe; (Teatro: cuarto) dressing
room; (Deporte) changing (BRIT) o locker
(US) room

vetar [be'tar] vt to veto

veterano, -a [bete'rano, a] adj,
nm veteran

veterinaria [beteri'narja] nf
veterinary science; V tb **veterinario**

veterinario, -a [beteri'narjo, a]
nm/f vet(erinary surgeon)

veto ['beto] nm veto

vez [beθ] nf (gen: turno) turn; **a la ~
que** at the same time as; **a su ~** in its
turn; **otra ~** again; **una ~** once; **de una
~** in one go; **de una ~ para siempre**
once and for all; **en ~ de** instead of;
a o algunas veces sometimes; **una
y otra ~** repeatedly; **de ~ en cuando**
from time to time; **7 veces 9** 7 times
9; **hacer las veces de** to stand in for;
tal ~ perhaps

vía ['bia] nf track, route; (Ferro) line;
(fig) way; (Anat) passage, tube ▷ prep
via, by way of; **por ~ judicial** by legal
means; **en ~s de** in the process of; **vía
aérea** airway; **Vía Láctea** Milky Way;
vía pública public road o thoroughfare

viable ['bjaβle] adj (solución, plan,
alternativa) feasible

viaducto [bja'ðukto] nm viaduct

viajante [bja'xante] nm commercial
traveller

viajar [bja'xar] vi to travel; **viaje** nm
journey; (gira) tour; (Náut) voyage;
estar de viaje to be on a trip; **viaje
de ida y vuelta** round trip; **viaje
de novios** honeymoon; **viajero,
-a** adj travelling; (Zool) migratory
▷ nm/f (quien viaja) traveller; (pasajero)
passenger

víbora ['biβora] nf (Zool) viper;
(: (MÉX: venenoso) poisonous snake

vibración [biβra'θjon] nf vibration

vibrar [bi'βrar] vt, vi to vibrate

vicepresidente [biθepresi'ðente]
nm/f vice-president

viceversa [biθe'βersa] adv vice versa

vicio ['biθjo] nm vice; (mala costumbre)
bad habit; **vicioso, -a** adj (muy malo)
vicious; (corrompido) depraved ▷ nm/f
depraved person

víctima ['biktima] nf victim

victoria [bik'torja] nf victory;
victorioso, -a adj victorious

vid [bið] nf vine

vida ['biða] nf (gen) life; (duración)
lifetime; **de por ~** for life; **en la o mi
~** never; **estar con ~** to be still alive;
ganarse la ~ to earn one's living

vídeo ['biðeo] nm video ▷ adj
inv: **película de ~** video film;
videocámara nf camcorder;
videocasete nm video cassette;
videotape; **videoclub** nm video
club; **videojuego** nm video game;
videollamada nf video call;
videoteléfono nf videophone

vidrio ['biðrjo] nm glass

vieira ['bjeira] nf scallop

viejo, -a ['bjexo, a] adj old ▷ nm/f
old man/woman; **hacerse ~** to get old

Viena ['bjena] n Vienna

vienes etc vb V **venir**

vienés, -esa [bje'nes, esa] adj
Viennese

viento ['bjento] nm wind; **hacer ~**
to be windy

vientre ['bjentre] nm belly; (matriz)
womb

viernes ['bjernes] nm inv Friday;
Viernes Santo Good Friday

Vietnam [bjet'nam] nm Vietnam;
vietnamita adj Vietnamese

viga ['biɣa] nf beam, rafter; (de metal)
girder

vigencia [bi'xenθja] nf validity;
estar en ~ to be in force; **vigente** adj
valid, in force; (imperante) prevailing

vigésimo, -a [bi'xesimo, a] *adj* twentieth

vigía [bi'xia] *nm* look-out

vigilancia [bixi'lanθja] *nf*: **tener a algn bajo ~** to keep watch on sb

vigilar [bixi'lar] *vt* to watch over ▷ *vi* (*gen*) to be vigilant; (*hacer guardia*) to keep watch; **~ por** to take care of

vigilia [vi'xilja] *nf* wakefulness, being awake; (*Rel*) fast

vigor [bi'yor] *nm* vigour, vitality; **en ~** in force; **entrar/poner en ~** to come/put into effect; **vigoroso, -a** *adj* vigorous

VIH *nm abr* (= *virus de la inmunodeficiencia humana*) HIV; **VIH negativo/positivo** HIV-negative/-positive

vil [bil] *adj* vile, low

villa ['biλa] *nf* (*casa*) villa; (*pueblo*) small town; (*municipalidad*) municipality

villancico [biλan'θiko] *nm* (Christmas) carol

vilo ['bilo]: **en ~** *adv* in the air, suspended; (*fig*) on tenterhooks, in suspense

vinagre [bi'naɣre] *nm* vinegar

vinagreta [bina'ɣreta] *nf* vinaigrette, French dressing

vinculación [binkula'θjon] *nf* (*lazo*) link, bond; (*acción*) linking

vincular [binku'lar] *vt* to link, bind; **vínculo** *nm* link, bond

vine *etc vb V* **venir**

vinicultura [binikul'tura] *nf* wine growing

viniera *etc vb V* **venir**

vino ['bino] *vb V* **venir** ▷ *nm* wine; **vino blanco/tinto** white/red wine

viña ['biɲa] *nf* vineyard; **viñedo** *nm* vineyard

viola ['bjola] *nf* viola

violación [bjola'θjon] *nf* violation; (*sexual*) rape

violar [bjo'lar] *vt* to violate; (*sexualmente*) to rape

violencia [bjo'lenθja] *nf* violence,

force; (*incomodidad*) embarrassment; (*acto injusto*) unjust act; **violentar** *vt* to force; (*casa*) to break into; (*agredir*) to assault; (*violar*) to violate; **violento, -a** *adj* violent; (*furioso*) furious; (*situación*) embarrassing; (*acto*) forced, unnatural

violeta [bjo'leta] *nf* violet

violín [bjo'lin] *nm* violin

violón [bjo'lon] *nm* double bass

virar [bi'rar] *vi* to change direction

virgen [birxen] *adj*, *nf* virgin

Virgo ['birɣo] *nm* Virgo

viril [bi'ril] *adj* virile; **virilidad** *nf* virility

virtud [bir'tuð] *nf* virtue; **en ~ de** by virtue of; **virtuoso, -a** *adj* virtuous ▷ *nm/f* virtuoso

viruela [bi'rwela] *nf* smallpox

virulento, -a [biru'lento, a] *adj* virulent

virus ['birus] *nm inv* virus

visa ['bisa] (*LAM*) *nf* = **visado**

visado [bi'saðo] (*ESP*) *nm* visa

víscera ['bisθera] *nf* (*Anat*, *Zool*) gut, bowel; **vísceras** *nfpl* entrails

visceral [bisθe'ral] *adj* (*odio*) intense; **reacción ~** gut reaction

visera [bi'sera] *nf* visor

visibilidad [bisiβili'ðað] *nf* visibility; **visible** *adj* visible; (*fig*) obvious

visillos [bi'siλos] *nmpl* lace curtains

visión [bi'sjon] *nf* (*Anat*) vision; (*eye*)sight; (*fantasía*) vision, fantasy

visita [bi'sita] *nf* call, visit; (*persona*) visitor; **hacer una ~** to pay a visit; **visitar** [bisi'tar] *vt* to visit, call on

visón [bi'son] *nm* mink

visor [bi'sor] *nm* (*Foto*) viewfinder

víspera ['bispera] *nf*: **la ~ de ...** the day before ...

vista ['bista] *nf* sight, vision; (*capacidad de ver*) (eye)sight; (*mirada*) look(s) (*pl*); **a primera ~** at first glance; **hacer la ~ gorda** to turn a blind eye; **volver la ~** to look back; **está a la ~ que** it's obvious that; **en ~ de** in view of; **en ~ de que** in view of the fact that; **¡hasta la ~!** so long!, see you!; **con ~s**

a with a view to; **vistazo** nm glance; **dar** o **echar un vistazo a** to glance at

visto, -a ['bisto, a] pp de **ver** ▷ vb V tb **vestir** ▷ adj seen; (considerado) considered ▷ nm: **~ bueno** approval; **por lo ~** apparently; **está ~ que** it's clear that; **está bien/mal ~** it's acceptable/unacceptable; **~ que** since, considering that

vistoso, -a [bis'toso, a] adj colourful

visual [bi'swal] adj visual

vital [bi'tal] adj life cpd, living cpd; (fig) vital; (persona) lively, vivacious; **vitalicio, -a** [bita'liθjo, a] adj for life; **vitalidad** [bitali'ðað] nf (de persona, negocio) energy; (de ciudad) liveliness

vitamina [bita'mina] nf vitamin

vitorear [bitore'ar] vt to cheer, acclaim

vitrina [bi'trina] nf show case; (LAM: escaparate) shop window

viudo, -a ['bjuðo, a] nm/f widower/widow

viva ['biβa] excl hurrah!; **¡~ el rey!** long live the king!

vivaracho, -a [biβa'ratʃo, a] adj jaunty, lively; (ojos) bright, twinkling

vivaz [bi'βaθ] adj lively

víveres ['biβeres] nmpl provisions

vivero [bi'βero] nm (para plantas) nursery; (para peces) fish farm; (fig) hotbed

viveza [bi'βeθa] nf liveliness; (agudeza: mental) sharpness

vivienda [bi'βjenda] nf housing; (una vivienda) house; (piso) flat (BRIT), apartment (US)

viviente [bi'βjente] adj living

vivir [bi'βir] vt, vi to live ▷ nm life, living

vivo, -a ['biβo, a] adj living, alive; (fig: descripción) vivid; (persona: astuto) smart, clever; **en ~** (transmisión etc) live

vocablo [bo'kaβlo] nm (palabra) word; (término) term

vocabulario [bokaβu'larjo] nm vocabulary

vocación [boka'θjon] nf vocation

vocacional (LAM) nf ≈ technical college

vocal [bo'kal] adj vocal ▷ nf vowel; **vocalizar** vt to vocalize

vocero [bo'θero] (LAM) nmf spokesman/woman

voces ['boθes] pl de **voz**

vodka [boð'ka] nm o f vodka

vol abr = **volumen**

volado [bo'laðo] (MÉX) adv in a rush, hastily

volador, a [bola'ðor, a] adj flying

volandas [bo'landas]: **en ~** adv in the air

volante [bo'lante] adj flying ▷ nm (de coche) steering wheel; (de reloj) balance

volar [bo'lar] vt (edificio) to blow up ▷ vi to fly

volátil [bo'latil] adj volatile

volcán [bol'kan] nm volcano; **volcánico, -a** adj volcanic

volcar [bol'kar] vt to upset, overturn; (tumbar, derribar) to knock over; (vaciar) to empty out ▷ vi to overturn; **volcarse** vr to tip over

voleibol [bolei'βol] nm volleyball

volqué etc vb V **volcar**

voltaje [bol'taxe] nm voltage

voltear [bolte'ar] vt to turn over; (volcar) to turn upside down

voltereta [bolte'reta] nf somersault

voltio [bol'tjo] nm volt

voluble [bo'luβle] adj fickle

volumen [bo'lumen] (pl **volúmenes**) nm volume; **voluminoso, -a** adj voluminous; (enorme) massive

voluntad [bolun'tað] nf will; (resolución) willpower; (deseo) desire, wish

voluntario, -a [bolun'tarjo, a] adj voluntary ▷ nm/f volunteer

volver [bol'βer] vt (gen) to turn; (dar vuelta a) to turn (over); (voltear) to turn round, turn upside down; (poner al revés) to turn inside out; (devolver) to return ▷ vi to return, go back, come back; **volverse** vr to turn round; **~ a**

espalda to turn one's back; **~ triste** *etc*
a algn to make sb sad *etc*; **~ a hacer**
to do again; **~ en sí** to come to; **~se**
insoportable/muy caro to get o
become unbearable/very expensive;
~se loco to go mad

vomitar [bomi'tar] *vt*, *vi* to vomit;
vómito *nm* vomit

voraz [bo'raθ] *adj* voracious

vos [bos] (*LAM*) *pron* you

vosotros, -as [bo'sotros, as] (*ESP*)
pron you; (*reflexivo*): **entre/para ~**
among/for yourselves

votación [bota'θjon] *nf* (*acto*) voting;
(*voto*) vote

votar [bo'tar] *vi* to vote: **voto** *nm*
vote; (*promesa*) vow; **votos** *nmpl*
(good) wishes

voy *vb* V **ir**

voz [boθ] *nf* voice; (*grito*) shout;
(*rumor*) rumour; (*Ling*) word; **dar voces**
to shout, yell; **de viva ~** verbally; **en ~**
alta aloud; **en ~ baja** in a low voice, in
a whisper; **voz de mando** command

vuelco ['bwelko] *vb* V **volcar** ⊳ *nm*
spill, overturning

vuelo ['bwelo] *vb* V **volar** ⊳ *nm*
flight; (*encaje*) lace, frill; **coger al ~** to
catch in flight; **vuelo chárter/regular**
charter/scheduled flight; **vuelo libre**
(*Deporte*) hang-gliding

vuelque *etc vb* V **volcar**

vuelta ['bwelta] *nf* (*gen*) turn; (*curva*)
bend, curve; (*regreso*) return; (*revolución*)
revolution; (*de circuito*) lap; (*de papel,
tela*) reverse; (*cambio*) change; **a la ~**
on one's return; **a la ~ (de la esquina)**
round the corner; **a ~ de correo** by
return of post; **dar ~s** (*cabeza*) to spin;
dar(se) la ~ (*volverse*) to turn round;
dar ~s a una idea to turn over an idea
(in one's head); **estar de ~** to be back;
dar una ~ to go for a walk; (*en coche*) to
go for a drive; **vuelta ciclista** (*Deporte*)
(cycle) tour

vuelto ['bwelto] *pp de* **volver**

vuelvo *etc vb* V **volver**

vuestro, -a ['bwestro, a] *adj pos*

your; **un amigo ~** a friend of yours
⊳ *pron*: **el ~/la vuestra, los ~s/las**
vuestras yours

vulgar [bul'ɣar] *adj* (*ordinario*)
vulgar; (*común*) common; **vulgaridad**
nf commonness; (*acto*) vulgarity;
(*expresión*) coarse expression

vulnerable [bulne'raβle] *adj*
vulnerable

vulnerar [bulne'rar] *vt* (*ley, acuerdo*)
to violate, breach; (*derechos, intimidad*)
to violate; (*reputación*) to damage

W X

walkie-talkie ['wɔlki-'tɔlki] (*pl* **~s**) *nm* walkie-talkie

Walkman® ['wɔlkman] *nm* Walkman®

wáter ['bater] *nm* (*taza*) toilet; (*LAM: lugar*) toilet (*BRIT*), rest room (*US*)

web [web] *nm o f* (*página*) website; (*red*) (World Wide) Web; **webcam** *nf* webcam; **webmaster** *nmf* webmaster; **website** *nm* website

western ['western] (*pl* **~s**) *nm* western

whisky ['wiski] *nm* whisky, whiskey

windsurf ['winsurf] *nm* windsurfing; **hacer ~** to go windsurfing

xenofobia [kseno'foβja] *nf* xenophobia

xilófono [ksi'lofono] *nm* xylophone

xocoyote, -a [ksoko'yote, a] (*MÉX*) *nm/f* baby of the family, youngest child

yuca ['juka] *nf* *(alimento)* cassava, manioc root
Yugoslavia [juɣos'laβja] *nf* *(Hist)* Yugoslavia
yugular [juɣu'lar] *adj* jugular
yunque ['junke] *nm* anvil
yuyo ['jujo] *(RPL)* *nm* *(mala hierba)* weed

y [i] *conj* and
ya [ja] *adv* *(gen)* already; *(ahora)* now; *(en seguida)* at once; *(pronto)* soon ▷ *excl* all right! ▷ *conj* *(ahora que)* now that; **~ lo sé** I know; **~ que ...** since; **¡~ está bien!** that's (quite) enough!; **¡~ voy!** coming!
yacaré [jaka're] *(cs)* *nm* cayman
yacer [ja'θer] *vi* to lie
yacimiento [jaθi'mjento] *nm* *(de mineral)* deposit; *(arqueológico)* site
yanqui ['janki] *adj, nmf* Yankee
yate ['jate] *nm* yacht
yazco *etc vb* V **yacer**
yedra ['jeðra] *nf* ivy
yegua ['jeɣwa] *nf* mare
yema ['jema] *nf* *(del huevo)* yolk; *(Bot)* leaf bud; *(fig)* best part; **yema del dedo** fingertip
yerno ['jerno] *nm* son-in-law
yeso ['jeso] *nm* plaster
yo [jo] *pron* I; **soy ~** it's me
yodo ['joðo] *nm* iodine
yoga ['joɣa] *nm* yoga
yogur(t) [jo'ɣur(t)] *nm* yoghurt

Z

zafar [θa'far] vt (*soltar*) to untie; (*superficie*) to clear; **zafarse** vr (*escaparse*) to escape; (*Tec*) to slip off

zafiro [θa'firo] nm sapphire

zaga ['θaxa] nf: **a la ~** behind

zaguán [θa'ɣwan] nm hallway

zalamero, -a [θala'mero, a] adj flattering; (*cobista*) suave

zamarra [θa'marra] nf (*chaqueta*) sheepskin jacket

zambullirse [θambu'ʎirse] vr to dive

zampar [θam'par] vt to gobble down

zanahoria [θana'orja] nf carrot

zancadilla [θanka'ðiʎa] nf trip

zanco ['θanko] nm stilt

zanja ['θanxa] nf (*surco*) ditch; **zanjar** vt (*resolver*) to resolve

zapata [θa'pata] nf (*Mecánica*) shoe

zapatería [θapate'ria] nf (*oficio*) shoemaking; (*tienda*) shoe shop; (*fábrica*) shoe factory; **zapatero, -a** nm/f shoemaker

zapatilla [θapa'tiʎa] nf slipper; **zapatilla de deporte** training shoe

zapato [θa'pato] nm shoe

zapping ['θapin] nm channel-hopping; **hacer ~** to channel-hop

zar [θar] nm tsar, czar

zarandear [θaranðe'ar] (*fam*) vt to shake vigorously

zarpa ['θarpa] nf (*garra*) claw

zarpar [θar'par] vi to weigh anchor

zarza ['θarθa] nf (*Bot*) bramble; **zarzamora** nf blackberry

zarzuela [θar'θwela] nf Spanish light opera

zigzag [θix'θax] nm zigzag

zinc [θink] nm zinc

zíper ['θiper] (*MÉX, CAM*) nm zip (fastener) (*BRIT*), zipper (*US*)

zócalo ['θokalo] nm (*Arq*) plinth, base; (*de pared*) skirting board (*BRIT*), baseboard (*US*); (*MÉX: plaza*) main o public square

zoclo ['θoklo] (*MÉX*) nm skirting board (*BRIT*), baseboard (*US*)

zodíaco [θo'ðiako] nm zodiac

zona ['θona] nf zone; **zona fronteriza** border area; **zona roja** (*LAM*) red-light district

zonzo, -a (*LAM: fam*) ['θonθo, a] adj silly ▷ nm/f fool

zoo ['θoo] nm zoo

zoología [θoolo'xia] nf zoology; **zoológico, -a** adj zoological ▷ nm (*tb*: **parque zoológico**) zoo; **zoólogo, -a** nm/f zoologist

zoom [θum] nm zoom lens

zopilote [θopi'lote] (*MÉX, CAM*) nm buzzard

zoquete [θo'kete] nm (*fam*) blockhead

zorro, -a ['θorro, a] adj crafty ▷ nm/f fox/vixen

zozobrar [θoθo'βrar] vi (*hundirse*) to capsize; (*fig*) to fail

zueco ['θweko] nm clog

zumbar [θum'bar] vt (*golpear*) to hit ▷ vi to buzz; **zumbido** nm buzzing

zumo ['θumo] nm juice

zurcir [θur'θir] vt (*coser*) to darn

zurdo, -a ['θurðo, a] adj left-handed

zurrar [θu'rrar] (*fam*) vt to wallop

A [eɪ] n (*Mus*) la m

○ **KEYWORD**

a [ə] (*before vowel or silent h: an*) indef art
1 un(a): **a book** un libro; **an apple**
una manzana; **she's a doctor** (ella)
es médica
2 (*instead of the number "one"*) un(a); **a**
year ago hace un año; **a hundred/**
thousand etc **pounds** cien/mil etc
libras
3 (*in expressing ratios, prices etc*): **3 a**
day/week 3 al día/a la semana; **10 km**
an hour 10 km por hora; **£5 a person** £5
por persona; **30 p a kilo** 30 p el kilo

A2 (*BRIT: Scol*) n segunda parte de los
"A levels"

A.A. n abbr (*BRIT: = Automobile*
Association) ≈ RACE m (*SP*), (= Alcoholics
Anonymous) Alcohólicos Anónimos

A.A.A. (*US*) n abbr (= *American*
Automobile Association) ≈ RACE m (*SP*)

aback [ə'bæk] adv: **to be taken ~**

quedar desconcertado
abandon [ə'bændən] vt abandonar;
(*give up*) renunciar a
abattoir ['æbətwɑ:*] (*BRIT*) n
matadero
abbey ['æbɪ] n abadía
abbreviation [əˌbri:vɪ'eɪʃən] n (*short*
form) abreviatura
abdomen ['æbdəmən] n abdomen m
abduct [æb'dʌkt] vt raptar,
secuestrar
abide [ə'baɪd] vt: **I can't ~ it/him**
no lo/le puedo ver; **abide by** vt fus
atenerse a
ability [ə'bɪlɪtɪ] n habilidad f,
capacidad f; (*talent*) talento
able ['eɪbl] adj capaz; (*skilled*) hábil; **to**
be ~ to do sth poder hacer algo
abnormal [æb'nɔ:məl] adj anormal
aboard [ə'bɔ:d] adv a bordo ▷ prep
a bordo de
abolish [ə'bɔlɪʃ] vt suprimir, abolir
abolition [æbəʊ'lɪʃən] n supresión
f, abolición f
abort [ə'bɔ:t] vt, vi abortar; **abortion**
[ə'bɔ:ʃən] n aborto; **to have an**
abortion abortar, hacerse abortar

○ **KEYWORD**

about [ə'baut] adv **1** (*approximately*)
más o menos, aproximadamente;
about a hundred/thousand etc
unos(unas) cien/mil etc; **it takes**
about 10 hours se tarda unas or más
o menos 10 horas; **at about 2 o'clock**
sobre las dos; **I've just about finished**
casi he terminado
2 (*referring to place*) por todas partes;
to leave things lying about dejar las
cosas (tiradas) por ahí; **to run about**
correr por todas partes; **to walk about**
pasearse, ir y venir
3: **to be about to do sth** estar a punto
de hacer algo
▷ prep **1** (*relating to*) de, sobre, acerca
de; **a book about London** un libro
sobre or acerca de Londres; **what is it**

about? ¿de qué se trata?; **we talked about it** hablamos de eso or ello; **what** or **how about doing this?** ¿qué tal si hacemos esto?

2 (referring to place) por; **to walk about the town** caminar por la ciudad

above [əˈbʌv] adv encima, por encima, arriba ▷ prep encima de las; (greater than: in number) más de; (: in rank) superior; **mentioned ~** susodicho; **~ all** sobre todo

abroad [əˈbrɔːd] adv (to be) en el extranjero; (to go) al extranjero

abrupt [əˈbrʌpt] adj (sudden) brusco; (curt) áspero

abscess [ˈæbsɪs] n absceso

absence [ˈæbsəns] n ausencia

absent [ˈæbsənt] adj ausente; **absent-minded** adj distraído

absolute [ˈæbsəluːt] adj absoluto; **absolutely** [-ˈluːtlɪ] adv (totally) totalmente; (certainly!) ¡por supuesto (que sí)!

absorb [əbˈzɔːb] vt absorber; **to be ~ed in a book** estar absorto en un libro; **absorbent cotton** (US) n algodón m hidrófilo; **absorbing** adj absorbente

abstain [əbˈsteɪn] vi: **to ~ (from)** abstenerse de

abstract [ˈæbstrækt] adj abstracto

absurd [əbˈsɜːd] adj absurdo

abundance [əˈbʌndəns] n abundancia

abundant [əˈbʌndənt] adj abundante

abuse [n əˈbjuːs, vb əˈbjuːz] n (insults) insultos mpl, injurias fpl; (ill-treatment) malos tratos mpl; (misuse) abuso ▷ vt insultar; maltratar; abusar de; **abusive** adj ofensivo

abysmal [əˈbɪzməl] adj pésimo; (failure) garrafal; (ignorance) supino

academic [ækəˈdemɪk] adj académico, universitario; (pej: issue) puramente teórico ▷ n estudioso/a, profesor(a) m/f universitario/a; **academic year** n (Univ) año m

académico; (Scol) año m escolar

academy [əˈkædəmɪ] n (learned body) academia; (school) instituto, colegio; **~ of music** conservatorio

accelerate [ækˈseləreɪt] vt, vi acelerar; **acceleration** [ækseləˈreɪʃən] n aceleración f; **accelerator** (BRIT) n acelerador m

accent [ˈæksent] n acento; (fig) énfasis m

accept [əkˈsept] vt aceptar; (responsibility, blame) admitir; **acceptable** adj aceptable; **acceptance** n aceptación f

access [ˈækses] n acceso; **to have ~ to** tener libre acceso a; **accessible** [-ˈsesəbl] adj (place, person) accesible; (knowledge etc) asequible

accessory [ækˈsesərɪ] n accesorio; (Law): **~ to** cómplice de

accident [ˈæksɪdənt] n accidente m; (chance event) casualidad f; **by ~** (unintentionally) sin querer; (by chance) por casualidad; **accidental** [-ˈdentl] adj accidental, fortuito; **accidentally** [-ˈdentəlɪ] adv sin querer; por casualidad; **Accident and Emergency Department** n (BRIT) Urgencias fpl; **accident insurance** n seguro contra accidentes

acclaim [əˈkleɪm] vt aclamar, aplaudir ▷ n aclamación f, aplausos mpl

accommodate [əˈkɒmədeɪt] vt (person) alojar, hospedar; (: car, hotel etc) tener cabida para; (oblige, help) complacer

accommodation [əkɒməˈdeɪʃən] (US **accommodations**) n alojamiento

accompaniment [əˈkʌmpənɪmənt] n acompañamiento

accompany [əˈkʌmpənɪ] vt acompañar

accomplice [əˈkʌmplɪs] n cómplice mf

accomplish [əˈkʌmplɪʃ] vt (finish) concluir; (achieve) lograr; **accomplishment** n (skill: gen pl)

talento; (completion) realización f
accord [ə'kɔːd] n acuerdo
▷ vt conceder; **of his own ~**
espontáneamente; **accordance**
n: **in accordance with** de acuerdo
con; **according ▷ according to** prep
según; (in accordance with) conforme
a; **accordingly** adv (appropriately)
de acuerdo con esto; (as a result) en
consecuencia
account [ə'kaunt] n (Comm)
cuenta; (report) informe m; **accounts**
npl (Comm) cuentas fpl; **of no ~** de
ninguna importancia; **on ~** a cuenta;
on no ~ bajo ningún concepto; **on ~
of** a causa de, por motivo de; **to take
into ~, take ~ of** tener en cuenta;
account for vt fus (explain) explicar;
(represent) representar; **accountable**
adj: **accountable (to)** responsable
(ante); **accountant** n contable mf,
contador(a) m/f; **account number** n
(at bank etc) número de cuenta
accumulate [ə'kjuːmjuleɪt] vt
acumular ▷ vi acumularse
accuracy ['ækjurəsɪ] n (of total)
exactitud f; (of description etc)
precisión f
accurate ['ækjurɪt] adj (total) exacto;
(description) preciso; (person) cuidadoso;
(device) de precisión; **accurately** adv
con precisión
accusation [ækju'zeɪʃən] n
acusación f
accuse [ə'kjuːz] vt: **to ~ sb (of sth)**
acusar a algn (de algo); **accused** n
(Law) acusado/a
accustomed [ə'kʌstəmd] adj: **~ to**
acostumbrado a
ace [eɪs] n as m
ache [eɪk] n dolor m ▷ vi doler; **my
head ~s** me duele la cabeza
achieve [ə'tʃiːv] vt (aim, result)
alcanzar; (success) lograr, conseguir;
achievement n (completion)
realización f; (success) éxito
acid ['æsɪd] adj ácido; (taste) agrio ▷ n
(Chem, inf: LSD) ácido

acknowledge [ək'nɔlɪdʒ] vt
(letter: also: **~ receipt of**) acusar recibo
de; (fact, situation, person) reconocer;
acknowledgement n acuse m de
recibo
acne ['æknɪ] n acné m
acorn ['eɪkɔːn] n bellota
acoustic [ə'kuːstɪk] adj acústico
acquaintance [ə'kweɪntəns] n
(person) conocido/a; (with person,
subject) conocimiento
acquire [ə'kwaɪə*] vt adquirir;
acquisition [ækwɪ'zɪʃən] n
adquisición f
acquit [ə'kwɪt] vt absolver, exculpar;
to ~ o.s. well salir con éxito
acre ['eɪkə*] n acre m
acronym ['ækrənɪm] n siglas fpl
across [ə'krɔs] prep (on the other side
of) al otro lado de, del otro lado de;
(crosswise) a través de ▷ adv de un lado
a otro, de una parte a otra; a través,
través; (measurement): **the road is 10m
~** la carretera tiene 10m de ancho; **to
run/swim ~** atravesar corriendo/
nadando; **~ from** enfrente de
acrylic [ə'krɪlɪk] adj acrílico ▷ n
acrílica
act [ækt] n acto, acción f; (of play)
acto; (in music hall etc) número; (Law)
decreto, ley f ▷ vi (behave)
comportarse; (have effect: drug,
chemical) hacer efecto; (Theatre) actuar;
(pretend) fingir; (take action) obrar ▷ vt
(part) hacer el papel de; **in the ~ of:**
catch sb in the ~ of ... pillar a algn en
el momento en que ...; **to ~ as** actuar
o hacer de; **act up**(inf) vi (person)
portarse mal; **acting** adj suplente
▷ n (activity) actuación f; (profession)
profesión f de actor
action ['ækʃən] n acción f, acto;
(Mil) acción f, batalla; (Law) proceso,
demanda; **out of ~** (person) fuera de
combate; (thing) estropeado; **to take ~**
tomar medidas; **action replay** n (TV)
repetición f
activate ['æktɪveɪt] vt activar

active ['æktɪv] *adj* activo, enérgico; (*volcano*) en actividad; **actively** *adv* activamente; (*discourage, dislike*) enérgicamente

activist ['æktɪvɪst] *n* activista *m/f*

activity [-'tɪvɪtɪ] *n* actividad *f*; **activity holiday** *n* vacaciones con actividades organizadas

actor ['æktə*] *n* actor *m*, actriz *f*

actress ['æktrɪs] *n* actriz *f*

actual ['æktjuəl] *adj* verdadero, real; (*emphatic use*) propiamente dicho
> Be careful not to translate **actual** by the Spanish word *actual*.

actually ['æktjuəlɪ] *adv* realmente, en realidad; (*even*) incluso
> Be careful not to translate **actually** by the Spanish word *actualmente*.

acupuncture ['ækjupʌnktʃə*] *n* acupuntura

acute [ə'kju:t] *adj* agudo

ad [æd] *n abbr* = **advertisement**

A.D. *adv abbr* (= *anno Domini*) DC

adamant ['ædəmənt] *adj* firme, inflexible

adapt [ə'dæpt] *vt* adaptar ▷ *vi*: **to ~ (to)** adaptarse (a), ajustarse (a); **adapter** (*US* **adaptor**) *n* (*Elec*) adaptador *m*; (*for several plugs*) ladrón *m*

add [æd] *vt* añadir, agregar; **add up** *vt* (*figures*) sumar ▷ *vi* (*fig*): **it doesn't add up** no tiene sentido; **add up to** *vt fus* (*Math*) sumar, ascender a; (*fig*: *mean*) querer decir, venir a ser

addict ['ædɪkt] *n* adicto/a; (*enthusiast*) entusiasta *mf*; **addicted** [ə'dɪktɪd] *adj*: **to be addicted to** ser adicto a, ser fanático de; **addiction** [ə'dɪkʃən] *n* (*to drugs etc*) adicción *f*; **addictive** [ə'dɪktɪv] *adj* que causa adicción

addition [ə'dɪʃən] *n* (*adding up*) adición *f*; (*thing added*) añadidura, añadido; **in ~** además, por añadidura; **in ~ to** además de; **additional** *adj* adicional

additive ['ædɪtɪv] *n* aditivo

address [ə'drɛs] *n* dirección *f*, señas

fpl; (*speech*) discurso ▷ *vt* (*letter*) dirigir; (*speak to*) dirigirse a, dirigir la palabra a; (*problem*) tratar; **address book** *n* agenda (de direcciones)

adequate ['ædɪkwɪt] *adj* (*satisfactory*) adecuado; (*enough*) suficiente

adhere [əd'hɪə*] *vi*: **to ~ to** (*stick to*) pegarse a; (*fig*: *abide by*) observar; (: *belief etc*) ser partidario de

adhesive [əd'hi:zɪv] *n* adhesivo; **adhesive tape** *n* (*BRIT*) cinta adhesiva; (*us Med*) esparadrapo

adjacent [ə'dʒeɪsənt] *adj*: **~ to** contiguo a, inmediato a

adjective ['ædʒɛktɪv] *n* adjetivo

adjoining [ə'dʒɔɪnɪŋ] *adj* contiguo, vecino

adjourn [ə'dʒə:n] *vt* aplazar ▷ *vi* suspenderse

adjust [ə'dʒʌst] *vt* (*change*) modificar; (*clothing*) arreglar; (*machine*) ajustar ▷ *vi*: **to ~ (to)** adaptarse (a); **adjustable** *adj* ajustable; **adjustment** *n* adaptación *f*; (*to machine, prices*) ajuste *m*

administer [əd'mɪnɪstə*] *vt* administrar; **administration** [-'treɪʃən] *n* (*management*) administración *f*; (*government*) gobierno; **administrative** [-trətɪv] *adj* administrativo

administrator [əd'mɪnɪstreɪtə*] *n* administrador(a) *m/f*

admiral ['ædmərəl] *n* almirante *m*

admiration [ædmə'reɪʃən] *n* admiración *f*

admire [əd'maɪə*] *vt* admirar; **admirer** *n* (*fan*) admirador(a) *m/f*

admission [əd'mɪʃən] *n* (*to university, club*) ingreso; (*entry fee*) entrada; (*confession*) confesión *f*

admit [əd'mɪt] *vt* (*confess*) confesar; (*permit to enter*) dejar entrar, dar entrada a; (*club, organization*) admitir; (*accept: defeat*) reconocer; **to be ~ted to hospital** ingresar en el hospital; **admit to** *vt fus* confesarse

culpable de; **admittance** n entrada;
admittedly adv es cierto or verdad
que

adolescent [ædəuˈlɛsnt] adj, n
adolescente mf

adopt [əˈdɔpt] vt adoptar; **adopted**
adj adoptivo; **adoption** [əˈdɔpʃən] n
adopción f

adore [əˈdɔ:*] vt adorar

adorn [əˈdɔ:n] vt adornar

Adriatic [eɪdrɪˈætɪk] n: **the ~ (Sea)** el
(Mar) Adriático

adrift [əˈdrɪft] adv a la deriva

adult [ˈædʌlt] n adulto/a ▷ adj
(grown-up) adulto; (for adults)
para adultos; **adult education** n
educación f para adultos

adultery [əˈdʌltəri] n adulterio

advance [ədˈvɑ:ns] n (gen)
adelanto, progreso; (money) anticipo,
préstamo; (Mil) avance m ▷ vt (money)
anticipar; (theory, idea) proponer
(para la discusión) ▷ vi avanzar,
adelantarse; **to make ~s (to sb)**
hacer proposiciones (a algn); **in ~** por
adelantado; **advanced** adj avanzado;
(Scol: studies) adelantado

advantage [ədˈvɑ:ntɪdʒ] n (also
Tennis) ventaja; **to take ~ of** (person)
aprovecharse de; (opportunity)
aprovechar

advent [ˈædvɛnt] n advenimiento;
A~ Adviento

adventure [ədˈvɛntʃə*] n aventura;
adventurous [-tʃərəs] adj atrevido;
aventurero

adverb [ˈædvə:b] n adverbio

adversary [ˈædvəsəri] n adversario,
contrario

adverse [ˈædvə:s] adj adverso,
contrario

advert [ˈædvə:t] (BRIT) n abbr =
advertisement

advertise [ˈædvətaɪz] vi (in newspaper
etc) anunciar, hacer publicidad; **to ~
for** (staff, accommodation etc) buscar

por medio de anuncios ▷ vt anunciar;
advertisement [ədˈvə:tismənt]
n (Comm) anuncio; **advertiser**
n anunciante m; **advertising** n
publicidad f, anuncios mpl; (industry)
industria publicitaria

advice [ədˈvaɪs] n consejo, consejos
mpl; (notification) aviso; **a piece of ~** un
consejo; **to take legal ~** consultar con
un abogado

advisable [ədˈvaɪzəbl] adj
aconsejable, conveniente

advise [ədˈvaɪz] vt aconsejar;
(inform): **to ~ sb of sth** informar a algn
de algo; **to ~ sb against sth/doing sth**
desaconsejar algo a algn/aconsejar
a algn que no haga algo; **adviser**,
advisor n consejero/a; (consultant)
asesor/a m/f; **advisory** adj consultivo

advocate [vb ˈædvəkeɪt, n -kɪt] vt
abogar por ▷ n (lawyer) abogado;
(supporter): **~ of** defensor/a m/f de

Aegean [i:ˈdʒi:ən] n: **the ~ (Sea)** el
(Mar) Egeo

aerial [ˈɛərɪəl] n antena ▷ adj aéreo

aerobics [ɛəˈrəubɪks] n aerobic m

aeroplane [ˈɛərəpleɪn] (BRIT) n
avión m

aerosol [ˈɛərəsɔl] n aerosol m

affair [əˈfɛə*] n asunto; (also: **love ~**)
aventura (amorosa)

affect [əˈfɛkt] vt (influence) afectar,
influir en; (afflict, concern) afectar;
(move) conmover; **affected** adj
afectado; **affection** n afecto, cariño;
affectionate adj afectuoso, cariñoso

afflict [əˈflɪkt] vt afligir

affluent [ˈæfluənt] adj (wealthy)
acomodado; **the ~ society** la sociedad
opulenta

afford [əˈfɔ:d] vt (provide)
proporcionar; **can we ~ (to buy)
it?** ¿tenemos bastante dinero para
comprarlo?; **affordable** adj asequible

Afghanistan [æfˈɡænɪstæn] n
Afganistán m

afraid [əˈfreɪd] adj: **to be ~ of** (person)
tener miedo a; (thing) tener miedo de;

to be ~ to tener miedo de, temer; **I am ~ that** me temo que; **I am ~ not/so** lo siento, pero no/es así

Africa ['æfrɪkə] n África; **African** adj, n africano/a m/f; **African-American** adj, n afroamericano/a m/f

after ['ɑːftə*] prep (time) después de; (place, order) detrás de, tras ▷ adv después ▷ conj después (de) que; **what/who are you ~?** ¿qué/a quién busca usted?; **~ having done/he left** después de haber hecho/después de que se marchó; **to name sb ~ sb** llamar a algn por algn; **it's twenty ~ eight** (us) son las ocho y veinte; **to ask ~ sb** preguntar por algn; **~ all** después de todo, al fin y al cabo; **~ you!** ¡pase usted!; **after-effects** npl consecuencias fpl, efectos mpl; **aftermath** n consecuencias fpl, resultados mpl; **afternoon** n tarde f; **after-shave (lotion)** n afeitado m; **aftersun (lotion/cream)** n loción f/crema para después del sol, aftersun m; **afterwards** (us **afterward**) adv después, más tarde

again [ə'gɛn] adv otra vez, de nuevo; **to do sth ~** volver a hacer algo; **~ and ~** una y otra vez

against [ə'gɛnst] prep (in opposition to) en contra de; (leaning on, touching) contra, junto a

age [eɪdʒ] n edad f; (period) época ▷ vi envejecer(se) ▷ vt envejecer; **she is 20 years of ~** tiene 20 años; **to come of ~** llegar a la mayoría de edad; **it's been ~s since I saw you** hace siglos que no te veo; **~d 10** de 10 años de edad; **age group** n: **to be in the same age group** tener la misma edad; **age limit** n edad f mínima (or máxima)

agency ['eɪdʒənsɪ] n agencia

agenda [ə'dʒɛndə] n orden m del día

Be careful not to translate **agenda** by the Spanish word agenda.

agent ['eɪdʒənt] n agente mf; (Comm: holding concession) representante mf, delegado/a; (Chem,

fig) agente m

aggravate ['æɡrəveɪt] vt (situation) agravar; (person) irritar

aggression [ə'ɡrɛʃən] n agresión f

aggressive [ə'ɡrɛsɪv] adj (belligerent) agresivo; (assertive) enérgico

agile ['ædʒaɪl] adj ágil

agitated ['ædʒɪteɪtɪd] adj agitado

AGM n abbr (= annual general meeting) asamblea anual

ago [ə'ɡəʊ] adv: **2 days ~** hace 2 días; **not long ~** hace poco; **how long ~?** ¿hace cuánto tiempo?

agony ['æɡənɪ] n (pain) dolor m agudo; (distress) angustia; **to be in ~** retorcerse de dolor

agree [ə'ɡriː] vt (price, date) acordar, quedar en ▷ vi (have same opinion): **to ~ (with/that)** estar de acuerdo (con/que); (correspond) coincidir, concordar; (consent) acceder; **to ~ with** (person) estar de acuerdo con, ponerse de acuerdo con; (: food) sentar bien a; (Ling) concordar con; **to ~ to sth/to do sth** consentir en algo/aceptar hacer algo; **to ~ that** (admit) estar de acuerdo en que; **agreeable** adj (pleasant) agradable; (person) simpático; (willing) de acuerdo, conforme; **agreed** adj (time, place) convenido; **agreement** n acuerdo; (contract) contrato; **in agreement** de acuerdo, conforme

agricultural [æɡrɪ'kʌltʃərəl] adj agrícola

agriculture ['æɡrɪkʌltʃə*] n agricultura

ahead [ə'hɛd] adv (in front) delante; (into the future): **she had no time to think** no tenía tiempo de hacer planes para el futuro; **~ of** delante de; (in advance of) antes de; **~ of time** antes de la hora; **go right** or **straight ~** (direction) siga adelante; (permission) hazlo (or hágalo)

aid [eɪd] n ayuda, auxilio; (device) aparato ▷ vt ayudar, auxiliar; **in ~ of** a beneficio de

aide [eɪd] n (person, also Mil) ayudante

mf

AIDS [eɪdz] *n abbr* (= acquired immune deficiency syndrome) SIDA *m*

ailing ['eɪlɪŋ] *adj* (person, economy) enfermizo

ailment ['eɪlmənt] *n* enfermedad *f*, achaque *m*

aim [eɪm] *vt* (gun, camera) apuntar; (missile, remark) dirigir; (blow) asestar ▷ *vi* (also: **take ~**) apuntar ▷ *n* (in shooting: skill) puntería *f*; (objective) propósito, meta; **to ~ at** (with weapon) apuntar a; (objective) aspirar a, pretender; **to ~ to do** tener la intención de hacer

ain't [eɪnt] (inf) = **am not; aren't; isn't**

air [εə*] *n* aire *m*; (appearance) aspecto ▷ *cpd* aéreo; **to throw sth into the ~** (ball etc) lanzar algo al aire; **by ~** (travel) en avión; **to be on the ~** (Radio, TV) estar en antena; **airbag** *n* airbag *m inv*; **airbed** (BRIT) *n* colchón *m* neumático; **airborne** *adj* (in the air) en el aire; **as soon as the plane was airborne** tan pronto como el avión estuvo en el aire; **air-conditioned** *adj* climatizado; **air conditioning** *n* aire acondicionado; **aircraft** *n inv* avión *m*; **airfield** *n* campo de aviación; **Air Force** *n* fuerzas *fpl* aéreas, aviación *f*; **air hostess** (BRIT) *n* azafata; **airing cupboard** *n* (BRIT) armario *m* para oreo; **airlift** *n* puente *m* aéreo; **airline** *n* línea aérea; **airliner** *n* avión *m* de pasajeros; **airmail** *n*: **by airmail** por avión; **airplane** (US) *n* avión *m*; **airport** *n* aeropuerto; **air raid** *n* ataque *m* aéreo; **airsick** *adj*: **to be airsick** marearse (en avión); **airspace** *n* espacio aéreo; **airstrip** *n* pista de aterrizaje; **air terminal** *n* terminal *f*; **airtight** *adj* hermético; **air-traffic controller** *n* controlador(a) *m/f*(aérea)*; **airy** *adj* (room) bien ventilado; (fig: manner) desenfadado

aisle [aɪl] *n* (of church) nave *f*; (of theatre, supermarket) pasillo; **aisle seat**

n (on plane) asiento de pasillo

ajar [ə'dʒɑː*] *adj* entreabierto

à la carte [ælæ'kɑːt] *adv* a la carta

alarm [ə'lɑːm] *n* (anxiety) inquietud *f* ▷ *vt* asustar, inquietar; **alarm call** *n* (in hotel etc) alarma; **alarm clock** *n* despertador *m*; **alarmed** *adj* (person) alarmado, asustado; (house, car etc) con alarma; **alarming** *adj* alarmante

Albania [æl'beɪnɪə] *n* Albania

albeit [ɔːl'biːɪt] *conj* aunque

album ['ælbəm] *n* álbum *m*; (L.P.) elepé *m*

alcohol ['ælkəhɒl] *n* alcohol *m*; **alcohol-free** *adj* sin alcohol; **alcoholic** [-'hɒlɪk] *adj*, *n* alcohólico/a *m/f*

alcove ['ælkəʊv] *n* nicho, hueco

ale [eɪl] *n* cerveza

alert [ə'lɜːt] *adj* (attentive) atento; (to danger, opportunity) alerta ▷ *n* alerta *m*, alarma *f* ▷ *vt* poner sobre aviso; **to be on the ~** (also Mil) estar alerta or sobre aviso

algebra ['ældʒɪbrə] *n* álgebra

Algeria [æl'dʒɪərɪə] *n* Argelia

alias ['eɪlɪæs] *adv* alias, conocido por ▷ *n* (of criminal) apodo; (of writer) seudónimo

alibi ['ælɪbaɪ] *n* coartada

alien ['eɪlɪən] *n* (foreigner) extranjero/a; (extraterrestrial) extraterrestre *mf* ▷ *adj*: **~ to** ajeno a; **alienate** *vt* enajenar, alejar

alight [ə'laɪt] *adj* ardiendo; (eyes) brillante ▷ *vi* (person) apearse, bajar; (bird) posarse

align [ə'laɪn] *vt* alinear

alike [ə'laɪk] *adj* semejantes, iguales ▷ *adv* igualmente, del mismo modo; **to look ~** parecerse

alive [ə'laɪv] *adj* vivo; (lively) alegre

○ **KEYWORD**

all [ɔːl] *adj* (sg) todo/a; (pl) todos/as; **all day** todo el día; **all night** toda la noche; **all men** todos los hombres;

all five came vinieron los cinco; **all the books** todos los libros; **all his life** toda su vida
▷ *pron* **1** todo; **I ate it all, I ate all of it** me lo comí todo; **all of us went** fuimos todos; **all the boys went** fueron todos los chicos; **is that all?** ¿eso es todo?, ¿algo más?; (*in shop*) ¿algo más?, ¿alguna cosa más?
2 (*in phrases*): **above all** sobre todo; por encima de todo; **after all** después de todo; **at all: not at all** (*in answer to question*) en absoluto; (*in answer to thanks*) ¡de nada!, ¡no hay de qué!; **I'm not at all tired** no estoy nada cansado/a; **anything at all will do** cualquier cosa viene bien; **all in all** al fin de cuentas
▷ *adv*: **above all** estar completamente solo/a; **it's not as hard as all that** no es tan difícil como lo pintas; **all the more/the better** tanto más/mejor; **all but** casi; **the score is 2 all** están empatados a 2

Allah ['ælə] *n* Alá *m*
allegation [ælɪ'ɡeɪʃən] *n* alegato *m*
alleged [ə'ledʒd] *adj* supuesto, presunto; **allegedly** *adv* supuestamente, según se afirma
allegiance [ə'liːdʒəns] *n* lealtad *f*
allergic [ə'lɜːdʒɪk] *adj*: **~ to** alérgico a
allergy ['ælədʒɪ] *n* alergia *f*
alleviate [ə'liːvɪeɪt] *vt* aliviar
alley ['ælɪ] *n* callejuela
alliance [ə'laɪəns] *n* alianza *f*
allied ['ælaɪd] *adj* aliado
alligator ['ælɪɡeɪtə*] *n* (*Zool*) caimán *m*
all-in (*BRIT*) ['ɔːlɪn] *adj, adv* (*charge*) todo incluido
allocate ['æləkeɪt] *vt* (*money etc*) asignar
allot [ə'lɒt] *vt* asignar
all-out ['ɔːlaut] *adj* (*effort etc*) supremo
allow [ə'lau] *vt* permitir, dejar; (*a claim*) admitir; (*sum, time etc*)

dar, conceder; (*concede*): **to ~ that** reconocer que; **to ~ sb to do** permitir a algn hacer; **he is ~ed to ...** se le permite ...; **allow for** *vt fus* tener en cuenta;
allowance *n* subvención *f*; (*welfare payment*) subsidio, pensión *f*; (*pocket money*) dinero de bolsillo; (*tax allowance*) desgravación *f*; **to make allowances for** (*person*) disculpar a; (*thing*) tener en cuenta
all right *adv* bien; (*as answer*) ¡conforme!, ¡está bien!
ally ['ælaɪ] *n* aliado *m* ▷ *vt*: **to ~ o.s. with** aliarse con
almighty [ɔːl'maɪtɪ] *adj* todopoderoso; (*row etc*) imponente
almond ['ɑːmənd] *n* almendra
almost ['ɔːlməust] *adv* casi
alone [ə'ləun] *adj, adv* solo; **to leave sb ~** dejar a algn en paz; **to leave sth ~** no tocar algo, dejar algo sin tocar; **let ~ ...** y mucho menos ...
along [ə'lɒŋ] *prep* a lo largo de, por ▷ *adv*: **is he coming ~ with us?** ¿viene con nosotros?; **he was limping ~** iba cojeando; **~ with** junto con; **all ~** (*all the time*) desde el principio; **alongside** *prep* al lado de ▷ *adv* al lado
aloof [ə'luːf] *adj* reservado ▷ *adv*: **to stand ~** mantenerse apartado
aloud [ə'laud] *adv* en voz alta
alphabet ['ælfəbet] *n* alfabeto
Alps [ælps] *npl*: **the ~** los Alpes
already [ɔːl'redɪ] *adv* ya
alright [ɔːl'raɪt] (*BRIT*) *adv* = **all right**
also ['ɔːlsəu] *adv* también, además
altar ['ɒltə*] *n* altar *m*
alter ['ɒltə*] *vt* cambiar, modificar ▷ *vi* cambiar; **alteration** [ɒltə'reɪʃən] *n* cambio; (*to clothes*) arreglo; (*to building*) arreglos *mpl*
alternate [*adj* ɒl'tɜːnɪt, *vb* 'ɒltɜːneɪt] *adj* (*actions etc*) alternativo; (*events*) alterno; (*us*) = **alternative** ▷ *vi*: **to ~ (with)** alternar (con); **~ days** un día sí y otro no
alternative [ɒl'tɜːnətɪv] *adj* alternativo ▷ *n* alternativa; **~**

medicine medicina alternativa; **alternatively** adv: **alternatively one could ...** por otra parte se podría ...

although [ɔːlˈðəu] conj aunque

altitude [ˈæltɪtjuːd] n altura

altogether [ɔːltəˈgeðə*] adv completamente, del todo; (on the whole) en total, en conjunto

aluminium [æljuˈmɪnɪəm] (BRIT), **aluminum** [əˈluːmɪnəm] (US) n aluminio

always [ˈɔːlweɪz] adv siempre

Alzheimer's (disease) [ˈæltshaɪməz-] n enfermedad f de Alzheimer

am [æm] vb see **be**

amalgamate [əˈmælgəmeɪt] vi amalgamarse ⊳ vt amalgamar, unir

amass [əˈmæs] vt amontonar, acumular

amateur [ˈæmətə*] n aficionado/a, amateur mf

amaze [əˈmeɪz] vt asombrar, pasmar; **to be ~d (at)** quedar pasmado (de); **amazed** adj asombrado; **amazement** n asombro, sorpresa; **amazing** adj extraordinario; (fantastic) increíble

Amazon [ˈæməzən] n (Geo) Amazonas m

ambassador [æmˈbæsədə*] n embajador(a) m/f

amber [ˈæmbə*] n ámbar m; **at ~** (BRIT Aut) en el amarillo

ambiguous [æmˈbɪgjuəs] adj ambiguo

ambition [æmˈbɪʃən] n ambición f; **ambitious** [-ʃəs] adj ambicioso

ambulance [ˈæmbjuləns] n ambulancia

ambush [ˈæmbuʃ] n emboscada ⊳ vt tender una emboscada a

amen [ɑːˈmɛn] excl amén

amend [əˈmɛnd] vt enmendar; **to make ~s** dar cumplida satisfacción; **amendment** n enmienda

amenities [əˈmiːnɪtɪz] npl comodidades fpl

America [əˈmɛrɪkə] n (USA)

Estados mpl Unidos; **American** adj, n norteamericano/a; estadounidense mf. **American football** n (BRIT) fútbol m americano

amicable [ˈæmɪkəbl] adj amistoso, amigable

amid(st) [əˈmɪd(st)] prep entre, en medio de

ammunition [æmjuˈnɪʃən] n municiones fpl

amnesty [ˈæmnɪstɪ] n amnistía

among(st) [əˈmʌŋ(st)] prep entre, en medio de

amount [əˈmaunt] n (gen) cantidad f; (of bill etc) suma, importe m ⊳ vi: **to ~ to** sumar; (be same as) equivaler a, significar

amp(ère) [ˈæmp(ɛə*)] n amperio

ample [ˈæmpl] adj (large) grande; (abundant) abundante; (enough) bastante, suficiente

amplifier [ˈæmplɪfaɪə*] n amplificador m

amputate [ˈæmpjuteɪt] vt amputar

Amtrak [ˈæmtræk] (US) n empresa nacional de ferrocarriles de los EEUU

amuse [əˈmjuːz] vt divertir; (distract) distraer, entretener; **amusement** n diversión f; (pastime) pasatiempo; (laughter) risa; **amusement arcade** n salón m de juegos; **amusement park** n parque m de atracciones

amusing [əˈmjuːzɪŋ] adj divertido

an [æn] indef art see **a**

anaemia [əˈniːmɪə] (US **anemia**) n anemia

anaemic [əˈniːmɪk] (US **anemic**) adj anémico; (fig) soso, insípido

anaesthetic [ænɪsˈθetɪk] (US **anesthetic**) n anestesia

analog(ue) [ˈænəlɒg] adj (computer, watch) analógico

analogy [əˈnælədʒɪ] n analogía

analyse [ˈænəlaɪz] (US **analyze**) vt analizar; **analysis** [əˈnæləsɪs] (pl **analyses**) n análisis m inv; **analyst** [-lɪst] n (political analyst, psychoanalyst) analista mf

analyze ['ænəlaɪz] (US) vt = **analyse**

anarchy ['ænəkɪ] n anarquía, desorden m

anatomy [ə'nætəmɪ] n anatomía

ancestor ['ænsɪstə*] n antepasado

anchor ['æŋkə*] n ancla, áncora ⊳ vi (also: **to drop ~**) anclar ⊳ vt anclar; **to weigh ~** levar anclas

anchovy ['æntʃəvɪ] n anchoa

ancient ['eɪnʃənt] adj antiguo

and [ænd] conj y; (before i-, hi- + consonant) e; **men ~ women** hombres y mujeres; **father ~ son** padre e hijo; **trees ~ grass** árboles y hierba; **~ so on** etcétera, y así sucesivamente; **try ~ come** procura venir; **he talked ~ talked** habló sin parar; **better ~ better** cada vez mejor

Andes ['ændiːz] npl: **the ~** los Andes

Andorra [æn'dɔːrə] n Andorra

anemia etc [ə'niːmɪə] (US) = **anaemia** etc

anesthetic [ænɪs'θetɪk] (US) = **anaesthetic**

angel ['eɪndʒəl] n ángel m

anger ['æŋɡə*] n cólera

angina [æn'dʒaɪnə] n angina (del pecho)

angle ['æŋɡl] n ángulo; **from their ~** desde su punto de vista

angler ['æŋɡlə*] n pescador(a) m/f (de caña)

Anglican ['æŋɡlɪkən] adj, n anglicano/a m/f

angling ['æŋɡlɪŋ] n pesca con caña

angrily ['æŋɡrɪlɪ] adv coléricamente, airadamente

angry ['æŋɡrɪ] adj enfadado, airado; (wound) inflamado; **to be ~ with sb/at sth** estar enfadado con algn/por algo; **to get ~** enfadarse, enojarse

anguish ['æŋɡwɪʃ] n (physical) tormentos mpl; (mental) angustia

animal ['ænɪməl] n animal m; (pej: person) bestia ⊳ adj animal

animated ['ænɪmeɪtɪd] adj animado

animation [ænɪ'meɪʃən] n animación f

aniseed ['ænɪsiːd] n anís m

ankle ['æŋkl] n tobillo

annex [n 'æneks, vb æ'neks] n (BRIT: also: **~e:** building) edificio anexo ⊳ vt (territory) anexionar

anniversary [ænɪ'vəːsərɪ] n aniversario

announce [ə'nauns] vt anunciar; **announcement** n anuncio; (official) declaración f; **announcer** n (Radio) locutor(a) m/f; (TV) presentador(a) m/f

annoy [ə'nɔɪ] vt molestar, fastidiar; **don't get ~ed!** ¡no se enfade!; **annoying** adj molesto, fastidioso; (person) pesado

annual ['ænjuəl] adj anual ⊳ n (Bot) anual m; (book) anuario; **annually** adv anualmente, cada año

annum ['ænəm] n see **per**

anonymous [ə'nɒnɪməs] adj anónimo

anorak ['ænəræk] n anorak m

anorexia [ænə'reksɪə] n (Med: also: **~ nervosa**) anorexia

anorexic [ænə'reksɪk] adj, n anoréxico/a m/f

another [ə'nʌðə*] adj (one more, a different one) otro ⊳ pron otro; see **one**

answer ['ɑːnsə*] n contestación f, respuesta; (to problem) solución f ⊳ vi contestar, responder ⊳ vt (reply to) contestar a, responder a; (problem) resolver; (prayer) escuchar; **in ~ to your letter** contestando or en contestación a su carta; **to ~ the phone** contestar or coger el teléfono; **to ~ the bell** or **the door** acudir a la puerta; **answer back** vi replicar, ser respondón/ona; **answerphone** n (esp BRIT) contestador m (automático)

ant [ænt] n hormiga

Antarctic [ænt'ɑːktɪk] n: **the ~** el Antártico

antelope ['æntɪləup] n antílope m

antenatal ['æntɪ'neɪtl] adj antenatal, prenatal

antenna [æn'tenə, pl -niː] (pl **antennae**) n antena

anthem ['ænθəm] n: **national ~** himno nacional

anthology [æn'θɒlədʒɪ] n antología

anthrax ['ænθræks] n ántrax m

anthropology [ænθrə'pɒlədʒɪ] n antropología

anti [æntɪ] prefix anti; **antibiotic** [-baɪ'ɒtɪk] n antibiótico; **antibody** ['æntɪbɒdɪ] n anticuerpo

anticipate [æn'tɪsɪpeɪt] vt prever; (expect) esperar, contar con; (look forward to) esperar con ilusión; (do first) anticiparse a, adelantarse a; **anticipation** [-'peɪʃən] n (expectation) previsión f; (eagerness) ilusión f, expectación f

anticlimax [æntɪ'klaɪmæks] n decepción f

anticlockwise [æntɪ'klɒkwaɪz] (BRIT) adv en dirección contraria a la de las agujas del reloj

antics ['æntɪks] npl gracias fpl

anti: antidote ['æntɪdəʊt] n antídoto; **antifreeze** ['æntɪfriːz] n anticongelante m; **antihistamine** [-'hɪstəmiːn] n antihistamínico; **antiperspirant** ['æntɪpəːspɪrənt] n antitranspirante m

antique [æn'tiːk] n antigüedad f ▷ adj antiguo; **antique shop** n tienda de antigüedades

antiseptic [æntɪ'septɪk] adj, n antiséptico

antisocial [æntɪ'səʊʃəl] adj antisocial

antivirus [æntɪ'vaɪərəs] adj (program, software) antivirus inv

antlers ['æntləz] npl cuernas fpl, cornamenta sg

anxiety [æŋ'zaɪətɪ] n inquietud f, (Med) ansiedad f; **~ to do** deseo de hacer

anxious ['æŋkʃəs] adj inquieto, preocupado; (worrying) preocupante; (keen): **to be ~ to do** tener muchas

ganas de hacer

○ **KEYWORD**

any ['enɪ] adj ₁ (in questions etc) algún/alguna; **have you any butter/ children?** ¿tienes mantequilla/ hijos?; **if there are any tickets left** si quedan billetes, si queda algún billete

₂ (with negative): **I haven't any money/ books** no tengo dinero/libros

₃ (no matter which) cualquier; **any excuse will do** valdrá or servirá cualquier excusa; **choose any book you like** escoge el libro que quieras

₄ (in phrases): **in any case** de todas formas, en cualquier caso; **any day now** cualquier día (de estos); **at any moment** en cualquier momento, de un momento a otro; **at any rate** en todo caso; **any time: come (at) any time** ven cuando quieras; **he might come (at) any time** podría llegar de un momento a otro

▷ pron ₁ (in questions etc): **have you got any?** ¿tienes alguno(s)/a(s)?; **can any of you sing?** ¿sabe cantar alguno de vosotros/ustedes?

₂ (with negative): **I haven't any (of them)** no tengo ninguno

₃ (no matter which one(s)): **take any of those books (you like)** toma el libro que quieras de ésos

▷ adv ₁ (in questions etc): **do you want any more soup/sandwiches?** ¿quieres más sopa/bocadillos?; **are you feeling any better?** ¿te sientes algo mejor?

₂ (with negative): **I can't hear him any more** ya no le oigo; **don't wait any longer** no esperes más

any: anybody pron cualquiera; (in interrogative sentences) alguien; (in negative sentences): **I don't see anybody** no veo a nadie; **if anybody should phone ...** si llama alguien

...; **anyhow** adv (at any rate) de todos modos, de todas formas; (haphazard): **do it anyhow you like** hazlo como quieras; **she leaves things just anyhow** deja las cosas como quiera or de cualquier modo; **I shall go anyhow** de todos modos iré; **anyone** pron = **anybody**; **anything** pron (in questions etc) algo, alguna cosa; (with negative) nada; **can you see anything?** ¿ves algo?; **if anything happens to me ...** si algo me ocurre ...; (no matter what): **you can say anything you like** puedes decir lo que quieras; **anything will do** vale todo or cualquier cosa; **he'll eat anything** come de todo or lo que sea; **anytime** adv (at any moment) en cualquier momento, de un momento a otro; (whenever): no importa cuándo, cuando quiera; **anyway** adv (at any rate) de todos modos, de todas formas; **I shall go anyway** iré de todos modos; (besides): **anyway, I couldn't come even if I wanted to** además, no podría venir aunque quisiera; **why are you phoning, anyway?** ¿entonces, por qué llamas?, ¿por qué llamas, pues?; **anywhere** adv (in questions etc): **can you see him anywhere?** ¿le ves por algún lado?; **are you going anywhere?** ¿vas a algún sitio?; (with negative): **I can't see him anywhere** no le veo por ninguna parte; **anywhere in the world** (no matter where) en cualquier parte del mundo); **put the books down anywhere** deja los libros donde quieras

apart [əˈpɑːt] adv (aside) aparte; (situation): **~ (from)** separado (de); (movement): **to pull ~** separar; **10 miles ~** separados 10 su 10 millas; **to take ~** desmontar; **~ from** prep aparte de

apartment [əˈpɑːtmənt] n (US) piso (SP), departamento (LAM), apartamento; (room) cuarto; **apartment building** (US) n edificio de apartamentos

apathy [ˈæpəθɪ] n apatía

indiferencia

ape [eɪp] n mono ▷ vt imitar, remedar

aperitif [əˈperɪtɪf] n aperitivo

aperture [ˈæpətjʊə*] n rendija, resquicio; (Phot) abertura

APEX [ˈeɪpeks] n abbr (= Advanced Purchase Excursion Fare) tarifa f APEX

apologize [əˈpɒlədʒaɪz] vi: **to ~ (for sth to sb)** disculparse (con algn de algo)

apology [əˈpɒlədʒɪ] n disculpa, excusa

   Be careful not to translate **apology** by the Spanish word apología.

apostrophe [əˈpɒstrəfɪ] n apóstrofo

appal [əˈpɔːl] (US **appall**) vt horrorizar, espantar; **appalling** adj espantoso; (awful) pésimo

apparatus [æpəˈreɪtəs] n (equipment) equipo; (organization) aparato; (in gymnasium) aparatos mpl

apparent [əˈpærənt] adj aparente; (obvious) evidente; **apparently** adv por lo visto, al parecer

appeal [əˈpiːl] vi (Law) apelar ▷ n (Law) apelación f; (request) llamamiento; (plea) petición f; (charm) atractivo; **to ~ for** reclamar; **to ~ to** (be attractive to) atraer; **it doesn't ~ to me** no me atrae, no me llama la atención; **appealing** adj (attractive) atractivo

appear [əˈpɪə*] vi aparecer, presentarse; (Law) comparecer; (publication) salir (a luz), publicarse; (seem) parecer; **to ~ on TV/in "Hamlet"** salir por la tele/hacer un papel en "Hamlet"; **it would ~ that** parecería que; **appearance** n aparición f; (look) apariencia, aspecto

appendices [əˈpendɪsiːz] npl of **appendix**

appendicitis [əpendɪˈsaɪtɪs] n apendicitis f

appendix [əˈpendɪks] (pl **appendices**) n apéndice m

appetite [ˈæpɪtaɪt] n apetito; (fig) deseo, anhelo

appetizer [ˈæpɪtaɪzə*] n (drink) aperitivo m; (food) tapas fpl (SP)

applaud [əˈplɔːd] vt, vi aplaudir

applause [əˈplɔːz] n aplausos mpl

apple [ˈæpl] n manzana f; **apple pie** n pastel m de manzana, pay m de manzana (LAM)

appliance [əˈplaɪəns] n aparato

applicable [əˈplɪkəbl] adj (relevant): **to be ~ (to)** referirse a

applicant [ˈæplɪkənt] n candidato/ a; solicitante m/f

application [æplɪˈkeɪʃən] n aplicación f; (for a job etc) solicitud f, petición f; **application form** n solicitud f

apply [əˈplaɪ] vt (paint etc) poner; (law etc: put into practice) poner en vigor ▷ vi: **to ~ to** (ask) dirigirse a; (be applicable) ser aplicable a; **to ~ for** (permit, grant, job) solicitar; **to ~ o.s. to** aplicarse a, dedicarse a

appoint [əˈpɔɪnt] vt (to post) nombrar a

> Be careful not to translate **appoint** by the Spanish word apuntar.

appointment n (with client) cita; (act) nombramiento m; (post) puesto; (at hairdresser etc): **to have an appointment** tener hora; **to make an appointment (with sb)** citarse (con algn)

appraisal [əˈpreɪzl] n valoración f

appreciate [əˈpriːʃieɪt] vt apreciar, tener en mucho; (be grateful for) agradecer; (be aware) comprender ▷ vi (Comm) aumentar(se) en valor

appreciation [-ˈeɪʃən] n apreciación f; (gratitude) reconocimiento, agradecimiento; (Comm) aumento en valor

apprehension [æprɪˈhenʃən] n (fear) aprensión f

apprehensive [æprɪˈhensɪv] adj aprensivo

apprentice [əˈprentɪs] n aprendiz(a) m/f

approach [əˈprəʊtʃ] vi acercarse

▷ vt acercarse a; (ask, apply to) dirigirse a; (situation, problem) abordar ▷ n acercamiento; (access) acceso; (to problem, situation): **~ (to)** actitud f (ante)

appropriate [adj əˈprəʊprɪət, vb əˈprəʊprɪeɪt] adj apropiado, conveniente ▷ vt (take) apropiarse de

approval [əˈpruːvəl] n aprobación f, visto bueno; (permission) consentimiento; **on ~** (Comm) a prueba

approve [əˈpruːv] vt aprobar; **approve of** vt fus (thing) aprobar; (person): **they don't approve of her** (ella) no les parece bien

approximate [əˈprɒksɪmɪt] adj aproximado; **approximately** adv aproximadamente, más o menos

Apr. abbr (= April) abr

apricot [ˈeɪprɪkɒt] n albaricoque m, chabacano (MEX), damasco (RPL)

April [ˈeɪprəl] n abril m; **April Fools' Day** n el primero de abril, ≈ día m de los Inocentes (28 December)

apron [ˈeɪprən] n delantal m

apt [æpt] adj acertado, apropiado; (likely): **~ to** propenso a hacer

aquarium [əˈkweərɪəm] n acuario

Aquarius [əˈkweərɪəs] n Acuario

Arab [ˈærəb] adj, n árabe mf

Arabia [əˈreɪbɪə] n Arabia; **Arabian** adj árabe; **Arabic** [ˈærəbɪk] adj árabe; (numerals) arábigo ▷ n árabe m

arbitrary [ˈɑːbɪtrərɪ] adj arbitrario

arbitration [ɑːbɪˈtreɪʃən] n arbitraje m

arc [ɑːk] n arco

arcade [ɑːˈkeɪd] n (round a square) soportales mpl; (shopping mall) galería comercial

arch [ɑːtʃ] n arco; (of foot) arco del pie ▷ vt arquear

archaeology [ɑːkɪˈɒlədʒɪ] (US **archeology**) n arqueología

archbishop [ɑːtʃˈbɪʃəp] n arzobispo

archeology [ɑːkɪˈɒlədʒɪ] (US) = **archaeology**

architect [ˈɑːkɪtekt] n arquitecto/a;

architectural [ɑːkɪˈtɛktʃərəl] adj arquitectónico; **architecture** n arquitectura

archive [ˈɑːkaɪv] n (often pl: also Comput) archivo

Arctic [ˈɑːktɪk] adj ártico ▷ n: **the ~ el** Ártico

are [ɑː*] vb see **be**

area [ˈɛərɪə] n área, región f; (part of place) zona; (Math etc) área, superficie f; (in room: e.g. dining area) parte f; (of knowledge, experience) campo; **area code** (us) n (Tel) prefijo

arena [əˈriːnə] n estadio; (of circus) pista

aren't [ɑːnt] = **are not**

Argentina [ɑːdʒənˈtiːnə] n Argentina; **Argentinian** [-ˈtɪnɪən] adj, n argentino a m/f

arguably [ˈɑːgjʊəblɪ] adv posiblemente

argue [ˈɑːgjuː] vi (quarrel) discutir, pelearse; (reason) razonar, argumentar; **to ~ that** sostener que

argument [ˈɑːgjʊmənt] n discusión f, pelea; (reasons) argumento

Aries [ˈɛərɪz] n Aries m

arise [əˈraɪz] (pt **arose**, pp **arisen**) vi surgir, presentarse

arithmetic [əˈrɪθmətɪk] n aritmética

arm [ɑːm] n brazo ▷ vt armar; **arms** npl armas fpl; **~ in ~** cogidos del brazo; **armchair** [ˈɑːmtʃɛə*] n sillón m, butaca

armed [ɑːmd] adj armado; **armed robbery** n robo a mano armada

armour [ˈɑːmə*] n (us **armor**) n armadura; (Mil: tanks) blindaje m

armpit [ˈɑːmpɪt] n sobaco, axila

armrest [ˈɑːmrɛst] n apoyabrazos m inv

army [ˈɑːmɪ] n ejército; (fig) multitud f

A road (BRIT) ≈ carretera f nacional

aroma [əˈrəumə] n aroma m, fragancia; **aromatherapy** n aromaterapia

arose [əˈrəuz] pt of **arise**

around [əˈraund] adv alrededor; (in the area) **there is no one else ~** no hay nadie más por aquí ▷ prep alrededor de

arouse [əˈrauz] vt despertar; (anger) provocar

arrange [əˈreɪndʒ] vt arreglar, ordenar; (organize) organizar; **to ~ to do sth** quedar en hacer algo; **arrangement** n arreglo; (agreement) acuerdo; **arrangements** npl (preparations) preparativos mpl

array [əˈreɪ] n: **~ of** (things) serie f de; (people) conjunto de

arrears [əˈrɪəz] npl atrasos mpl; **to be in ~ with one's rent** estar retrasado en el pago del alquiler

arrest [əˈrɛst] vt detener; (sb's attention) llamar ▷ n detención f; **under ~** detenido

arrival [əˈraɪvəl] n llegada; **new ~** recién llegado/a; (baby) recién nacido

arrive [əˈraɪv] vi llegar; (baby) nacer; **arrive at** vt fus (decision, solution) llegar a

arrogance [ˈærəgəns] n arrogancia, prepotencia (LAM)

arrogant [ˈærəgənt] adj arrogante

arrow [ˈærəu] n flecha

arse [ɑːs] (BRIT: infl) n culo, trasero

arson [ˈɑːsn] n incendio premeditado

art [ɑːt] n arte m; (skill) destreza; **art college** n escuela f de Bellas Artes

artery [ˈɑːtərɪ] n arteria

art gallery n pinacoteca; (saleroom) galería de arte

arthritis [ɑːˈθraɪtɪs] n artritis f

artichoke [ˈɑːtɪtʃəuk] n alcachofa; **Jerusalem ~** aguaturma

article [ˈɑːtɪkl] n artículo

articulate [adj ɑːˈtɪkjulɪt, vb ɑːˈtɪkjuleɪt] adj claro, bien expresado ▷ vt expresar

artificial [ɑːtɪˈfɪʃəl] adj artificial; (affected) afectado

artist [ˈɑːtɪst] n artista mf; (Mus) intérprete mf; **artistic** [ɑːˈtɪstɪk] adj

artístico
art school n escuela de bellas artes

○ KEYWORD

as [æz] conj 1 (referring to time) cuando, mientras; a medida que; **as the years went by** con el paso de los años; **he came in as I was leaving** entró cuando me marchaba; **as from tomorrow** desde or a partir de mañana
2 (in comparisons): **as big as** tan grande como; **twice as big as** el doble de grande que; **as much money/many books as** tanto dinero/tantos libros como; **as soon as** en cuanto
3 (since, because) como, ya que; **he left early as he had to be home by 10** se fue temprano ya que tenía que estar en casa a las 10
4 (referring to manner, way): **do as you wish** haz lo que quieras; **as she said** como dijo; **he gave it to me as a present** me lo dio de regalo
5 (in the capacity of): **he works as a barman** trabaja de barman; **as chairman of the company, he ...** como presidente de la compañía ...
6 (concerning): **as for or to that** por or en lo que respecta a eso
7: **as if or though** como si; **he looked as if he was ill** parecía como si estuviera enfermo, tenía aspecto de enfermo; *see also* **long; such; well**

a.s.a.p. abbr (= as soon as possible) cuanto antes
asbestos [æz'bɛstəs] n asbesto, amianto
ascent [ə'sɛnt] n subida; (slope) cuesta, pendiente f
ash [æʃ] n ceniza; (tree) fresno
ashamed [ə'ʃeɪmd] adj avergonzado, apenado (LAM); **to be ~ of** avergonzarse de
ashore [ə'ʃɔː*] adv en tierra; (swim etc) a tierra

ashtray ['æʃtreɪ] n cenicero
Ash Wednesday n miércoles m de Ceniza
Asia ['eɪʃə] n Asia; **Asian** adj, n asiático/a m/f
aside [ə'saɪd] adv a un lado ▷ n aparte m
ask [ɑːsk] vt (question) preguntar; (invite) invitar; **to ~ sb sth/to do sth** preguntar algo a algn/pedir a algn que haga algo; **to ~ sb about sth** preguntar algo a algn; **to ~ (sb) a question** hacer una pregunta a algn; **to ~ sb out to dinner** invitar a cenar a algn; **ask for** vt fus pedir; (trouble) buscar
asleep [ə'sliːp] adj dormido; **to fall ~** dormirse, quedarse dormido
asparagus [əs'pærəgəs] n (plant) espárrago; (food) espárragos mpl
aspect ['æspɛkt] n aspecto, apariencia; (direction in which a building etc faces) orientación f
aspirations [æspɪ'reɪʃənz] npl aspiraciones fpl; (ambition) ambición f
aspire [əs'paɪə*] vi: **to ~ to** aspirar a, ambicionar
aspirin ['æsprɪn] n aspirina
ass [æs] n asno, burro; (inf: idiot) imbécil mf; (us: infl) culo, trasero
assassin [ə'sæsɪn] n asesino/a; **assassinate** vt asesinar
assault [ə'sɔːlt] n asalto; (Law) agresión f ▷ vt asaltar, atacar; (sexually) violar
assemble [ə'sɛmbl] vt reunir, juntar; (Tech) montar ▷ vi reunirse, juntarse
assembly [ə'sɛmblɪ] n reunión f, asamblea; (parliament) parlamento; (construction) montaje m
assert [ə'sɜːt] vt afirmar; (authority) hacer valer; **assertion** [-ʃən] n afirmación f
assess [ə'sɛs] vt valorar, calcular; (tax, damages) fijar; (for tax) gravar; **assessment** n valoración f; (for tax) gravamen m
asset ['æsɛt] n ventaja; **assets** npl (Comm) activo; (property, funds)

fondos *mpl*

assign [ə'saɪn] *vt*: **to ~ (to)** *(date)* fijar (para); *(task)* asignar a; *(resources)* destinar a; **assignment** *n* tarea

assist [ə'sɪst] *vt* ayudar; **assistance** *n* ayuda, auxilio; **assistant** *n* ayudante *mf*; (BRIT: *also*: **shop assistant**) dependiente/a *m/f*

associate [*adj*, *n* ə'səʊʃɪɪt, *vb* ə'səʊʃɪeɪt] *adj* asociado ▷ *n* (*at work*) colega *mf* ▷ *vt* asociar; (*ideas*) relacionar ▷ *vi*: **to ~ with sb** tratar con algn

association [əsəʊsɪ'eɪʃən] *n* asociación *f*

assorted [ə'sɔːtɪd] *adj* surtido, variado

assortment [ə'sɔːtmənt] *n* (*of shapes, colours*) surtido; (*of books*) colección *f*; (*of people*) mezcla

assume [ə'sjuːm] *vt* suponer; (*responsibilities*) asumir; (*attitude*) adoptar, tomar

assumption [ə'sʌmpʃən] *n* suposición *f*, presunción *f*; (*of power etc*) toma

assurance [ə'ʃʊərəns] *n* garantía, promesa; (*confidence*) confianza, aplomo; (*insurance*) seguro

assure [ə'ʃʊə*] *vt* asegurar

asterisk ['æstərɪsk] *n* asterisco

asthma ['æsmə] *n* asma

astonish [ə'stɒnɪʃ] *vt* asombrar, pasmar; **astonished** *adj* estupefacto, pasmado; **to be astonished (at)** asombrarse (de); **astonishing** *adj* asombroso, pasmoso; **I find it astonishing that ...** me asombra or pasma que ...; **astonishment** *n* asombro, sorpresa

astound [ə'staʊnd] *vt* asombrar, pasmar

astray [ə'streɪ] *adv*: **to go ~** extraviarse; **to lead ~** (*morally*) llevar por mal camino

astrology [æs'trɒlədʒɪ] *n* astrología

astronaut ['æstrənɔːt] *n* astronauta *mf*

astronomer [əs'trɒnəmə*] *n* astrónomo/a

astronomical [æstrə'nɒmɪkəl] *adj* astronómico

astronomy [æs'trɒnəmɪ] *n* astronomía

astute [əs'tjuːt] *adj* astuto

asylum [ə'saɪləm] *n* (*refuge*) asilo; (*mental hospital*) manicomio

○ **KEYWORD**

at [æt] *prep* **1** (*referring to position*) en; (*direction*) a; **at the top** en lo alto; **at home/school** en casa/la escuela; **to look at sth/sb** mirar algo/a algn

2 (*referring to time*): **at 4 o'clock** a las 4; **at night** de noche; **at Christmas** en Navidad; **at times** a veces

3 (*referring to rates, speed etc*): **at £1 a kilo** a una libra el kilo; **two at a time** de dos en dos; **at 50 km/h** a 50 km/h

4 (*referring to manner*): **at a stroke** de un golpe; **at peace** en paz

5 (*referring to activity*): **to be at work** estar trabajando; (*in the office etc*) estar en el trabajo; **to play at cowboys** jugar a los vaqueros; **to be good at sth** ser bueno en algo

6 (*referring to cause*): **shocked/surprised/annoyed at sth** asombrado/sorprendido/fastidiado por algo; **I went at his suggestion** fui a instancias suyas

7 (*symbol*) arroba

ate [eɪt] *pt of* **eat**

atheist ['eɪθɪɪst] *n* ateo/a

Athens ['æθɪnz] *n* Atenas

athlete ['æθliːt] *n* atleta *mf*

athletic [æθ'letɪk] *adj* atlético; **athletics** *n* atletismo

Atlantic [ət'læntɪk] *adj* atlántico ▷ *n*: **the ~ (Ocean)** el (Océano) Atlántico

atlas ['ætləs] *n* atlas *m inv*

A.T.M. *n abbr* (= *automated telling*

machine) cajero automático

atmosphere [ˈætməsfɪə*] *n*
atmósfera; (*of place*) ambiente *m*

atom [ˈætəm] *n* átomo; **atomic**
[əˈtɒmɪk] *adj* atómico; **atom(ic)
bomb** *n* bomba atómica

A to Z® *n* (*map*) callejero

atrocity [əˈtrɒsɪtɪ] *n* atrocidad *f*

attach [əˈtætʃ] *vt* (*fasten*) atar;
(*join*) unir, sujetar; (*document,
letter*) adjuntar; (*importance etc*)
dar, conceder; **to be ~ed to sb/sth**
(*to like*) tener cariño a algn/algo;
attachment *n* (*tool*) accesorio;
(*Comput*) archivo, documento adjunto;
(*love*): **attachment (to)** apego (a)

attack [əˈtæk] *vt* (*Mil*) atacar;
(*criminal*) agredir, asaltar; (*criticize*)
criticar; (*task*) emprender ▷ *n* ataque
m, asalto; (*on sb's life*) atentado;
(*fig*: *criticism*) crítica; (*of illness*) ataque
m; **heart ~** infarto (de miocardio);
attacker *n* agresor(a) *m/f*, asaltante
mf

attain [əˈteɪn] *vt* (*also*: **~ to**) alcanzar;
(*achieve*) lograr, conseguir

attempt [əˈtempt] *n* tentativa,
intento; (*attack*) atentado ▷ *vt*
intentar

attend [əˈtend] *vt* asistir a; (*patient*)
atender; **attend to** *vt fus* ocuparse
de; (*customer, patient*) atender a;
attendance *n* asistencia, presencia;
(*people present*) concurrencia;
attendant *n* ayudante *mf*; (*in garage
etc*) encargado *m* ▷ *adj* (*dangers*)
concomitante

attention [əˈtenʃən] *n* atención
f; (*care*) atenciones *fpl* ▷ *excl* (*Mil*)
¡firme(s)!; **for the ~ of ...** (*Admin*)
atención ...

attic [ˈætɪk] *n* desván *m*

attitude [ˈætɪtjuːd] *n* actitud *f*;
(*disposition*) disposición *f*

attorney [əˈtɜːnɪ] *n* (*lawyer*)
abogado *m*; **Attorney General** *n*
(*BRIT*) ≈ Presidente *m* del Consejo del
Poder Judicial (*SP*); (*US*) ≈ ministro

de Justicia

attract [əˈtrækt] *vt* atraer; (*sb's
attention*) llamar; **attraction**
[əˈtrækʃən] *n* encanto; (*gen
pl*: *amusements*) diversiones *fpl*;
(*Physics*) atracción *f*; (*fig*: *towards sb,
sth*) atractivo; **attractive** *adj* guapo;
(*interesting*) atrayente

attribute [*n* ˈætrɪbjuːt, *vb* əˈtrɪbjuːt]
n atributo ▷ *vt*: **to ~ sth to** atribuir
algo a

aubergine [ˈəʊbəʒiːn] (*BRIT*) *n*
berenjena; (*colour*) morado

auburn [ˈɔːbən] *adj* color castaño
rojizo

auction [ˈɔːkʃən] *n* (*also*: **sale by ~**)
subasta ▷ *vt* subastar

audible [ˈɔːdɪbl] *adj* audible, que se
puede oír

audience [ˈɔːdɪəns] *n* público; (*Radio*)
radioescuchas *mpl*; (*TV*)
telespectadores *mpl*; (*interview*)
audiencia

audit [ˈɔːdɪt] *vt* revisar, intervenir

audition [ɔːˈdɪʃən] *n* audición *f*

auditor [ˈɔːdɪtə*] *n* interventor(a)
m/f, censor(a) *m/f* de cuentas

auditorium [ɔːdɪˈtɔːrɪəm] *n*
auditorio

Aug. *abbr* (= *August*) ag

August [ˈɔːgəst] *n* agosto

aunt [ɑːnt] *n* tía; **auntie**, **aunty**
n diminutive of **aunt**

au pair [ˈəʊˈpeə*] *n* (*also*: **~ girl**)
(chica) au pair *f*

aura [ˈɔːrə] *n* aura; (*atmosphere*)
ambiente *m*

austerity [ɔˈstɛrɪtɪ] *n* austeridad *f*

Australia [ɔˈstreɪlɪə] *n* Australia;
Australian *adj*, *n* australiano/a *m/f*

Austria [ˈɔstrɪə] *n* Austria; **Austrian**
adj, *n* austríaco/a *m/f*

authentic [ɔːˈθentɪk] *adj* auténtico

author [ˈɔːθə*] *n* autor(a) *m/f*

authority [ɔːˈθɒrɪtɪ] *n* autoridad *f*;
(*official permission*) autorización *f*; **the
authorities** *npl* las autoridades

authorize [ˈɔːθəraɪz] *vt* autorizar

auto [ˈɔːtəu] (us) n coche m (sp), carro (LAM), automóvil m

auto: autobiography [ɔːtəbaɪˈɒgrəfɪ] n autobiografía; **autograph** [ˈɔːtəgrɑːf] n autógrafo ⊳ vt (photo etc) dedicar; (programme) firmar; **automatic** [ɔːtəˈmætɪk] adj automático ⊳ n (gun) pistola automática; (car) coche m automático; **automatically** adv automáticamente; **automobile** [ˈɔːtəməbiːl] n coche m (sp), carro (LAM), automóvil m; **autonomous** [ɔːˈtɒnəməs] adj autónomo; **autonomy** [ɔːˈtɒnəmɪ] n autonomía

autumn [ˈɔːtəm] n otoño

auxiliary [ɔːgˈzɪlɪərɪ] adj, n auxiliar mf

avail [əˈveɪl] vt: **to ~ o.s. of** aprovechar(se) de ⊳ n: **to no ~** en vano, sin resultado

availability [əveɪləˈbɪlɪtɪ] n disponibilidad f

available [əˈveɪləbl] adj disponible; (unoccupied) libre; (person: unattached) soltero y sin compromiso

avalanche [ˈævəlɑːnʃ] n alud m, avalancha

Ave. abbr = **avenue**

avenue [ˈævənjuː] n avenida; (fig) camino

average [ˈævərɪdʒ] n promedio, término medio ⊳ adj medio, de término medio; (ordinary) regular, corriente ⊳ vt sacar un promedio de; **on ~** por regla general

avert [əˈvɜːt] vt prevenir; (blow) desviar; (one's eyes) apartar

avid [ˈævɪd] adj ávido

avocado [ævəˈkɑːdəu] n (also BRIT: **~ pear**) aguacate m, palta (sc)

avoid [əˈvɔɪd] vt evitar, eludir

await [əˈweɪt] vt esperar, aguardar

awake [əˈweɪk] (pt **awoke**, pp **awoken** or **awaked**) adj despierto ⊳ vt despertar ⊳ vi despertarse; **to be ~** estar despierto

award [əˈwɔːd] n premio;

(Law: damages) indemnización f ⊳ vt otorgar, conceder; (Law: damages) adjudicar

aware [əˈweə⁎] adj: **~ (of)** consciente (de); **to become ~ of/that** (realize) darse cuenta de/de que; (learn) enterarse de/de que; **awareness** n conciencia; (knowledge) conocimiento

away [əˈweɪ] adv fuera; (movement): **she went ~** se marchó; **far ~** lejos; **two kilometres ~** a dos kilómetros de distancia; **two hours ~ by car** a dos horas en coche; **the holiday was two weeks ~** faltaban dos semanas para las vacaciones; **he's ~ for a week** estará ausente una semana; **to take ~ (from)** quitar (a); (subtract) substraer (de); **to work/pedal ~** seguir trabajando/pedaleando; **to fade ~** (colour) desvanecerse; (sound) apagarse

awe [ɔː] n admiración f respetuosa; **awesome** [ˈɔːsəm] (us) adj (excellent) formidable

awful [ˈɔːfəl] adj horroroso; (quantity): **an ~ lot (of)** cantidad (de); **awfully** adv (very) terriblemente

awkward [ˈɔːkwəd] adj desmañado, torpe; (shape) incómodo; (embarrassing) delicado, difícil

awoke [əˈwəuk] pt of **awake**

awoken [əˈwəukən] pp of **awake**

axe [æks] (us **ax**) n hacha ⊳ vt (project) cortar; (jobs) reducir

axle [ˈæksl] n eje m, árbol m

ay(e) [aɪ] excl sí

azalea [əˈzeɪlɪə] n azalea

b

B [bi:] n (Mus) si m

B.A. abbr = **Bachelor of Arts**

baby ['beɪbɪ] n bebé mf; (us: inf: darling) mi amor; **baby carriage** (us) n cochecito; **baby-sit** vi hacer de canguro; **baby-sitter** n canguro/a; **baby wipe** n toallita húmeda (para bebés)

bachelor ['bætʃələ*] n soltero; **B~ of Arts/Science** licenciado/a en Filosofía y Letras/Ciencias

back [bæk] n (of person) espalda; (of animal) lomo; (of hand) dorso; (as opposed to front) parte f de atrás; (of chair) respaldo; (of page) reverso; (of book) final m; (Football) defensa m; (of crowd): **the ones at the ~** los del fondo ▷ vt (candidate: also: **~ up**) respaldar, apoyar; (horse: at races) apostar a; (car) dar marcha atrás a or con ▷ vi (car etc) ir (or salir or entrar) marcha atrás ▷ adj (payment, rent) atrasado; (seats, wheels) de atrás ▷ adv (not forward) (hacia) atrás; (returned): **he's ~** está de vuelta, ha vuelto; **he ran ~** volvió corriendo;

(restitution): **throw the ball ~** devuelve la pelota; **can I have it ~?** ¿me lo devuelve?; (again): **he called ~** llamó de nuevo; **back down** vi echarse atrás; **back out** vi (of promise) volverse atrás; **back up** vt (person) apoyar, respaldar; (theory) defender; (Comput) hacer una copia preventiva or de reserva; **backache** n dolor m de espalda; **backbencher** (BRIT) n miembro del parlamento sin cargo relevante; **backbone** n columna vertebral; **back door** n puerta f trasera; **backfire** vi (Aut) petardear; (plans) fallar, salir mal; **backgammon** n backgammon m; **background** n fondo m; (of events) antecedentes mpl; (basic knowledge) bases fpl; (experience) conocimientos mpl, educación f; **family background** origen m, antecedentes mpl; **backing** n (fig) apoyo, respaldo; **backlog** n: **backlog of work** trabajo atrasado; **backpack** n mochila; **backpacker** n mochilero/a; **backslash** n pleca, barra inversa; **backstage** adv entre bastidores; **backstroke** n espalda; **backup** adj suplementario; (Comput) de reserva ▷ n (support) apoyo; (also: **backup file**) copia preventiva or de reserva; **backward** adj (movement) hacia atrás; (person, country) atrasado; **backwards** adv hacia atrás; (read a list) al revés; (fall) de espaldas; **backyard** n traspatio

bacon ['beɪkən] n tocino, beicon m

bacteria [bæk'tɪərɪə] npl bacterias fpl

bad [bæd] adj malo; (mistake, accident) grave; (food) podrido, pasado; **his ~ leg** su pierna lisiada; **to go ~** (food) pasarse

badge [bædʒ] n insignia; (policeman's) chapa, placa

badger ['bædʒə*] n tejón m

badly ['bædlɪ] adv mal; **to reflect ~ on sb** influir negativamente en la reputación de algn; **~ wounded** gravemente herido; **he needs it ~** le hace gran falta; **to be ~ off (for money)** andar mal de dinero

bad-mannered ['bæd'mænəd] adj

mal educado

badminton ['bædmɪntən] n bádminton m

bad-tempered ['bæd'tempəd] adj de mal genio or carácter; (temporarily) de mal humor

bag [bæg] n bolsa; (handbag) bolso; (satchel) mochila; (case) maleta; **~s of** (inf) un montón de; **baggage** n equipaje m; **baggage allowance** n límite m de equipaje; **baggage reclaim** n recogida de equipajes; **baggy** adj amplio; **bagpipes** npl gaita

bail [beɪl] n fianza ▷ vt (prisoner: gen: grant bail to) poner en libertad bajo fianza; (boat: also: ~ **out**) achicar; **on ~** (prisoner) bajo fianza; **to ~ sb out** obtener la libertad de algn bajo fianza

bait [beɪt] n cebo ▷ vt poner cebo en; (tease) tomar el pelo a

bake [beɪk] vt cocer (al horno) ▷ vi cocerse; **baked beans** npl judías fpl en salsa de tomate; **baked potato** n patata al horno; **baker** n panadero/a; **bakery** n panadería; (for cakes) pastelería; **baking** n (act) amasar m; (batch) hornada; **baking powder** n levadura (en polvo)

balance ['bæləns] n equilibrio; (Comm: sum) balance m; (remainder) resto; (scales) balanza ▷ vt equilibrar; (budget) nivelar; (account) saldar; (make equal) equilibrar; **~ of trade/ payments** balanza de comercio/ pagos; **balanced** adj (personality, diet) equilibrado; (report) objetivo; **balance sheet** n balance m

balcony ['bælkənɪ] n balcón m; (closed) galería; (in theatre) anfiteatro

bald [bɔːld] adj calvo; (tyre) liso

Balearics [bælɪ'ærɪks] npl: **the ~** las Baleares

ball [bɔːl] n pelota; (football) balón m; (of wool, string) ovillo; (dance) baile m; **to play ~** (fig) cooperar

ballerina [bælə'riːnə] n bailarina

ballet ['bæleɪ] n ballet m; **ballet dancer** n bailarín/ina m/f

balloon [bə'luːn] n globo

ballot ['bælət] n votación f

ballpoint (pen) ['bɔːlpɔɪnt-] n bolígrafo

ballroom ['bɔːlrum] n salón m de baile

Baltic ['bɔːltɪk] n: **the ~ (Sea)** el (Mar) Báltico

bamboo [bæm'buː] n bambú m

ban [bæn] n prohibición f, proscripción f ▷ vt prohibir, proscribir

banana [bə'nɑːnə] n (LAM) plátano, banano (CAM)

band [bænd] n grupo; (strip) faja, tira; (stripe) lista; (Mus: jazz) orquesta; (: rock) grupo; (Mil) banda

bandage ['bændɪdʒ] n venda, vendaje m ▷ vt vendar

Band-Aid® ['bændeɪd] (US) n tirita

bandit ['bændɪt] n bandido

bang [bæŋ] n (of gun, exhaust) estallido, detonación f; (of door) portazo; (blow) golpe m ▷ vt (door) cerrar de golpe; (one's head) golpear ▷ vi estallar; (door) cerrar de golpe

Bangladesh [bɑːŋglə'deʃ] n Bangladesh m

bangle ['bæŋgl] n brazalete m, ajorca

bangs [bæŋz] (US) npl flequillo

banish ['bænɪʃ] vt desterrar

banister(s) ['bænɪstə(z)] n(pl) barandilla, pasamanos m inv

banjo ['bændʒəu] (pl **~es** or **~s**) n banjo

bank [bæŋk] n (Comm) banco; (of river, lake) ribera, orilla; (of earth) terraplén m ▷ vi (Aviat) ladearse; **bank on** vt fus contar con; **bank account** n cuenta de banco; **bank balance** n saldo; **bank card** n tarjeta bancaria; **bank charges** npl comisión fsg; **banker** n banquero; **bank holiday** n (BRIT) día m festivo or de fiesta; **banking** n banca; **bank manager** n director(a) m/f (de sucursal) de banco; **banknote**

billete *m* de banco

bankrupt ['bæŋkrʌpt] *adj* quebrado, insolvente; **to go ~** hacer bancarrota; **to be ~** estar en quiebra; **bankruptcy** *n* quiebra

bank statement *n* balance *m* or detalle *m* de cuenta

banner ['bænə*] *n* pancarta

bannister(s) ['bænɪstə(z)] *n(pl)* = **banister(s)**

banquet ['bæŋkwɪt] *n* banquete *m*

baptism ['bæptɪzəm] *n* bautismo; (*act*) bautizo

baptize [bæp'taɪz] *vt* bautizar

bar [bɑ:*] *n* (*pub*) bar *m*; (*counter*) mostrador *m*; (*rod*) barra; (*of window, cage*) reja; (*of soap*) pastilla; (*of chocolate*) tableta; (*fig: hindrance*) obstáculo; (*prohibition*) proscripción *f*; (*Mus*) barra ▷ *vt* (*road*) obstruir; (*person*) excluir; (*activity*) prohibir; **the B~** (*Law*) la abogacía; **behind ~s** entre rejas; **~ none** sin excepción

barbaric [bɑ:'bærɪk] *adj* bárbaro

barbecue ['bɑ:bɪkju:] *n* barbacoa

barbed wire ['bɑ:bd-] *n* alambre *m* de púas

barber ['bɑ:bə*] *n* peluquero, barbero; **barber's (shop)** (*us* **barber (shop)**) *n* peluquería

bar code *n* código de barras

bare [bɛə*] *adj* desnudo; (*trees*) sin hojas; (*necessities etc*) básico ▷ *vt* desnudar; (*teeth*) enseñar; **barefoot**

adj, adv descalzo; **barely** *adv* apenas

bargain ['bɑ:gɪn] *n* pacto, negocio; (*good buy*) ganga ▷ *vi* negociar; (*haggle*) regatear; **into the ~** además, por añadidura; **bargain for** *vt fus*: **he got more than he bargained for** le resultó peor de lo que esperaba

barge [bɑ:dʒ] *n* barcaza; **barge in** *vi* irrumpir; (*interrupt: conversation*) interrumpir

bark [bɑ:k] *n* (*of tree*) corteza; (*of dog*) ladrido ▷ *vi* ladrar

barley ['bɑ:lɪ] *n* cebada

barmaid ['bɑ:meɪd] *n* camarera

barman ['bɑ:mən] (*irreg*) *n* camarero, barman *m*

barn [bɑ:n] *n* granero

barometer [bə'rɒmɪtə*] *n* barómetro

baron ['bærən] *n* barón *m*; (*press baron etc*) magnate *m*; **baroness** *n* baronesa

barracks ['bærəks] *npl* cuartel *m*

barrage ['bærɑ:ʒ] *n* (*Mil*) descarga, bombardeo; (*dam*) presa; (*of criticism*) lluvia, aluvión *m*

barrel ['bærəl] *n* barril *m*; (*of gun*) cañón *m*

barren ['bærən] *adj* estéril

barrette [bə'ret] (*us*) *n* pasador *m* (*LAM, SP*), broche *m* (*MEX*)

barricade [bærɪ'keɪd] *n* barricada

barrier ['bærɪə*] *n* barrera

barring ['bɑ:rɪŋ] *prep* excepto, salvo

barrister ['bærɪstə*] (*BRIT*) *n* abogado/a

barrow ['bærəu] *n* (*cart*) carretilla (de mano)

bartender ['bɑ:tendə*] (*us*) *n* camarero, barman *m*

base [beɪs] *n* base *f* ▷ *vt*: **to ~ sth on** basar or fundar algo en ▷ *adj* bajo, infame

baseball ['beɪsbɔ:l] *n* béisbol *m*; **baseball cap** *n* gorra *f* de béisbol

basement ['beɪsmənt] *n* sótano

bases¹ ['beɪsɪz] *npl of* **basis**

bases² ['beɪsɪz] *npl of* **base**

bash [bæʃ] (*inf*) *vt* golpear

basic ['beɪsɪk] adj básico; **basically** adv fundamentalmente, en el fondo; (simply) sencillamente; **basics** npl: **the basics** los fundamentos

basil ['bæzl] n albahaca

basin ['beɪsn] n cuenco, tazón m; (Geo) cuenca; (also: **~ wash~**) lavabo

basis ['beɪsɪs] (pl **bases**) n base f; **on a part-time/trial ~** a tiempo parcial/a prueba

basket ['bɑ:skɪt] n cesta, cesto; canasta; **basketball** n baloncesto

bass [beɪs] n (Mus: instrument) bajo; (double bass) contrabajo; (singer) bajo

bastard ['bɑ:stəd] n bastardo; (inf!) hijo de puta (!)

bat [bæt] n (Zool) murciélago; (for ball games) palo; (BRIT: for table tennis) pala ▷ vt: **he didn't ~ an eyelid** ni pestañeó

batch [bætʃ] n (of bread) hornada; (of letters etc) lote m

bath [bɑ:θ, pl bɑ:ðz] n (action) baño; (bathtub) bañera (SP), tina (LAM), bañadera (RPL) ▷ vt bañar; **to have a ~** bañarse, tomar un baño; see also **baths**

bathe [beɪð] vi bañarse ▷ vt (wound) lavar

bathing ['beɪðɪŋ] n el bañarse; **bathing costume** (us **bathing suit**) n traje m de baño

bath: bathrobe n (man's) batín m; (woman's) bata; **bathroom** n (cuarto m de) baño; **baths** [bɑ:ðz] npl (also: **swimming baths**) piscina; **bath towel** n toalla de baño; **bathtub** n bañera

baton ['bætən] n (Mus) batuta; (Athletics) testigo; (weapon) porra

batter ['bætə*] vt maltratar; (rain etc) azotar ▷ n masa (para rebozar); **battered** adj (hat, pan) estropeado

battery ['bætərɪ] n (Aut) batería; (of torch) pila; **battery farming** n cría intensiva

battle ['bætl] n batalla; (fig) lucha ▷ vi luchar; **battlefield** n campo m de batalla

bay [beɪ] n (Geo) bahía; **B~ of Biscay**

= mar Cantábrico; **to hold sb at ~** mantener a algn a raya

bazaar [bə'zɑ:*] n bazar m; (fete) venta con fines benéficos

B, **& B**. n abbr = **bed and breakfast**; (place) pensión f; (terms) cama y desayuno

BBC n abbr (= British Broadcasting Corporation) cadena de radio y televisión estatal británica

B.C. adv abbr (= before Christ) a. de C.

○ **KEYWORD**

be [bi:] (pt **was**, **were**, pp **been**) aux vb 1 (with present participle: forming continuous tenses): **what are you doing?** ¿qué estás haciendo?, ¿qué haces?; **they're coming tomorrow** vienen mañana; **I've been waiting for you for hours** llevo horas esperándote

2 (with pp: forming passives) ser (but often replaced by active or reflexive constructions): **to be murdered** ser asesinado; **the box had been opened** habían abierto la caja; **the thief was nowhere to be seen** no se veía al ladrón por ninguna parte

3 (in tag questions): **it was fun, wasn't it?** fue divertido, ¿no? or ¿verdad?; **he's good-looking, isn't he?** es guapo, ¿no te parece?; **she's back again, is she?** entonces, ¿ha vuelto?

4 (+to +infin): **the house is to be sold** (necessity) hay que vender la casa; (future) van a vender la casa; **he's not to open it** no tiene que abrirlo ▷ vb +complement 1 (with noun or num complement, but see also 3, 4, 5 and impers vb below) ser; **I'm English** soy inglés/esa; **she's tall/pretty** es alta/bonita; **he's young** es joven; **be careful/good/quiet** ten cuidado/

2 (with adj complement: expressing permanent or inherent quality) ser; (: expressing state seen as temporary or reversible) estar; **I'm English** soy inglés/esa; **she's tall/pretty** es alta/bonita; **he's young** es joven; **be careful/good/quiet** ten cuidado/

2 **and 2 are 4** y 2 son 4

pórtate bien/cállate; **I'm tired** estoy cansado/a; **it's dirty** está sucio/a

3 (of health) estar; **how are you?** ¿cómo estás?; **he's very ill** está muy enfermo; **I'm better now** ya estoy mejor

4 (of age) tener; **how old are you?** ¿cuántos años tienes?; **I'm sixteen (years old)** tengo dieciséis años

5 (cost) costar; ser; **how much was the meal?** ¿cuánto fue or costó la comida?; **that'll be £5.75, please** son £5.75, por favor; **this shirt is £17** esta camisa cuesta £17

▷ vi **1** (exist, occur etc) existir, haber; **the best singer that ever was** el mejor cantante que existió jamás; **is there a God?** ¿hay un Dios?, ¿existe Dios?; **be that as it may** sea como sea; **so be it** así sea

2 (referring to place) estar; **I won't be here tomorrow** no estaré aquí mañana

3 (referring to movement): **where have you been?** ¿dónde has estado?

▷ impers vb **1** (referring to time): **it's 5 o'clock** son las 5; **it's the 28th of April** estamos a 28 de abril

2 (referring to distance): **it's 10 km to the village** el pueblo está a 10 km

3 (referring to the weather): **it's too hot/cold** hace demasiado calor/frío; **it's windy today** hace viento hoy

4 (emphatic): **it's me** soy yo; **it was Maria who paid the bill** fue María la que pagó la cuenta

beach [biːtʃ] n playa ▷ vt varar

beacon ['biːkən] n (lighthouse) faro; (marker) guía

bead [biːd] n cuenta; (of sweat etc) gota; **beads** npl (necklace) collar m

beak [biːk] n pico

beam [biːm] n (Arch) viga, travesaño; (of light) rayo, haz m de luz ▷ vi brillar; (smile) sonreír

bean [biːn] n judía; **runner/broad ~** habichuela/haba; **coffee ~** grano de café; **beansprouts** npl brotes

---

315 | **bed**

mpl de soja

bear [bɛə*] (pt **bore**, pp **borne**) n oso ▷ vt (weight etc) llevar; (cost) pagar; (responsibility) tener; (endure) soportar, aguantar; (children) parir, tener; (fruit) dar ▷ vi: **to ~ right/left** torcer a la derecha/izquierda

beard [bɪəd] n barba

bearer ['bɛərə*] n portador(a) m/f

bearing ['bɛərɪŋ] n porte m, comportamiento; (connection) relación f

beast [biːst] n bestia; (inf) bruto, salvaje m

beat [biːt] (pt ~, pp **beaten**) n (of heart) latido; (Mus) ritmo, compás m; (of policeman) ronda ▷ vt pegar, golpear; (eggs) batir; (defeat: opponent) vencer, derrotar; (: record) sobrepasar ▷ vi (heart) latir; (drum) redoblar; (rain, wind) azotar; **off the ~en track** aislado; **to ~ it** (inf) largarse; **beat up** vt (attack) dar una paliza a; **beating** n paliza

beautiful ['bjuːtɪful] adj precioso, hermoso, bello; **beautifully** adv maravillosamente

beauty ['bjuːtɪ] n belleza; **beauty parlour** (us **beauty parlor**) n salón m de belleza; **beauty salon** n salón m de belleza; **beauty spot** n (Tourism) lugar m pintoresco

beaver ['biːvə*] n castor m

became [bɪ'keɪm] pt of **become**

because [bɪ'kɒz] conj porque; **~ of** debido a, a causa de

beckon ['bɛkən] vt (also: **~ to**) llamar con señas

become [bɪ'kʌm] (pt **became**, pp **~**) vt (suit) favorecer, sentar bien a (+ n); hacerse, llegar a ser; (+ adj) ponerse, volverse; **to ~ fat** engordar

bed [bɛd] n cama; (of flowers) macizo; (of coal, clay) capa; (of river) lecho; (of sea) fondo; **to go to ~** acostarse; **bed and breakfast** n (place) pensión f; (terms) cama y desayuno; **bedclothes** npl ropa de cama; **bedding** n ropa de cama; **bed linen** n (BRIT) ropa f de cama

BED AND BREAKFAST

Se llama **bed and breakfast** a una forma de alojamiento, en el campo o la ciudad, que ofrece cama y desayuno a precios inferiores a los de un hotel. El servicio se suele anunciar con carteles en los que a menudo se usa únicamente la abreviatura **B. & B.**

bed: **bedroom** n dormitorio; **bedside** n: **at the bedside of** a la cabecera de; **bedside lamp** n lámpara de noche; **bedside table** n mesilla de noche; **bedsit(ter)** (BRIT) n cuarto de alquiler; **bedspread** n cubrecama m, colcha; **bedtime** n hora de acostarse

bee [biː] n abeja

beech [biːtʃ] n haya

beef [biːf] n carne f de vaca; **roast ~** rosbif m; **beefburger** n hamburguesa; **Beefeater** n alabardero de la Torre de Londres

been [biːn] pp of **be**

beer [bɪə*] n cerveza; **beer garden** n (BRIT) terraza f de verano, jardín m (de un bar)

beet [biːt] (US) n (also: **red ~**) remolacha

beetle ['biːtl] n escarabajo

beetroot ['biːtruːt] (BRIT) n remolacha

before [bɪ'fɔː*] prep (of time) antes de; (of space) delante de ▷ conj antes (de) que ▷ adv antes, anteriormente; delante, adelante; **~ going** antes de marcharse; **~ she goes** antes de que se vaya; **the week ~** la semana anterior; **I've never seen it ~** no lo he visto nunca; **beforehand** adv de antemano, con anticipación

beg [beg] vi pedir limosna ▷ vt pedir, rogar; (entreat) suplicar; **to ~ sb to do sth** rogar a algn que haga algo; see also **pardon**

began [bɪ'gæn] pt of **begin**

beggar ['begə*] n mendigo/a

begin [bɪ'gɪn] (pt **began**, pp **begun**) vt, vi empezar, comenzar; **to ~ doing** or **to do sth** empezar a hacer algo; **beginner** n principiante mf; **beginning** mf, principio, comienzo

begun [bɪ'gʌn] pp of **begin**

behalf [bɪ'hɑːf] n: **on ~ of** en nombre de, por; (for benefit of) en beneficio de; **on my/his ~** por mí/él

behave [bɪ'heɪv] vi (person) portarse, comportarse; (well: also: **~ o.s.**) portarse bien; **behaviour** (US **behavior**) n comportamiento, conducta

behind [bɪ'haɪnd] prep detrás de; (supporting): **to be ~ sb** apoyar a algn ▷ adv detrás, por detrás, atrás ▷ n trasero; **to be ~ (schedule)** ir retrasado; **~ the scenes** (fig) entre bastidores

beige [beɪʒ] adj color beige

Beijing ['beɪ'dʒɪŋ] n Pekín m

being ['biːɪŋ] n ser m; (existence): **in ~** existente; **to come into ~** aparecer

belated [bɪ'leɪtɪd] adj atrasado, tardío

belch [beltʃ] vi eructar ▷ vt (gen: belch out: smoke etc) arrojar

Belgian ['beldʒən] adj, n belga mf

Belgium ['beldʒəm] n Bélgica

belief [bɪ'liːf] n opinión f; (faith) fe f

believe [bɪ'liːv] vt, vi creer; **to ~ in** creer en; **believer** n partidario/a; (Rel) creyente mf, fiel mf

bell [bel] n campana; (small) campanilla; (on door) timbre m

bellboy ['belbɔɪ] (BRIT) n botones m inv

bellhop ['belhɔp] (US) n = **bellboy**

bellow ['beləu] vi bramar; (person) rugir

bell pepper n (esp US) pimiento, pimentón m (LAM)

belly ['belɪ] n barriga, panza; **belly button** (inf) n ombligo

belong [bɪ'lɔŋ] vi: **to ~ to** pertenecer

a; (club etc) ser socio de; **this book ~s here** este libro va aquí; **belongings** npl pertenencias fpl

beloved [bɪ'lʌvɪd] adj querido/a

below [bɪ'ləʊ] prep bajo, debajo de; (less than) inferior a ▷ adv abajo, (por) debajo; **see** ~ véase más abajo

belt [belt] n cinturón m; (Tech) correa, cinta ▷ vt (thrash) pegar con correa; **beltway** (us) n (Aut) carretera de circunvalación

bemused [bɪ'mjuːzd] adj perplejo

bench [bentʃ] n banco; (BRIT Pol): **the Government/Opposition ~es** (los asientos de) los miembros del Gobierno/de la Oposición; **the B~** (Law: judges) magistratura

bend [bend] (pt, pp **bent**) vt doblar ▷ vi inclinarse ▷ n (in road, river) curva; (in pipe) codo; **bend down** vi inclinarse, doblarse; **bend over** vi inclinarse

beneath [bɪ'niːθ] prep bajo, debajo de; (unworthy) indigno de ▷ adv abajo, (por) debajo

beneficial [benɪ'fɪʃəl] adj beneficioso

benefit ['benɪfɪt] n beneficio; (allowance of money) subsidio ▷ vt beneficiar ▷ vi: **he'll ~ from it** le sacará provecho

benign [bɪ'naɪn] adj benigno; (smile) afable

bent [bent] pt, pp de **bend** ▷ n inclinación f ▷ adj: **to be ~ on** estar empeñado en

bereaved [bɪ'riːvd] npl: **the ~s** los íntimos de una persona afligidos por su muerte

beret ['bereɪ] n boina

Berlin [bəː'lɪn] n Berlín

Bermuda [bə'mjuːdə] n las Bermudas

berry ['berɪ] n baya

berth [bəːθ] n (bed) litera; (cabin) camarote m; (for ship) amarradero ▷ vi atracar, amarrar

beside [bɪ'saɪd] prep junto a, al lado de; **to be ~ o.s. with anger** estar fuera

de sí; **that's ~ the point** eso no tiene nada que ver; **besides** adv además ▷ prep además de

best [best] adj (el/la) mejor ▷ adv (lo) mejor; **the ~ part of** (quantity) la mayor parte de; **at ~** en el mejor de los casos; **to make the ~ of sth** sacar el mejor partido de algo; **to do one's ~** hacer todo lo posible; **to the ~ of my knowledge** que yo sepa; **to the ~ of my ability** como mejor puedo; **best-before date** n fecha de consumo preferente; **best man** (irreg) n padrino de boda; **bestseller** n éxito de librería, bestseller m

bet [bet] (pt, pp ~ or ~ted) n apuesta ▷ vt: **to ~ money on** apostar dinero por ▷ vi apostar; **to ~ sb** apostar algo a algn

betray [bɪ'treɪ] vt traicionar; (trust) faltar a

better ['betə*] adj, adv mejor ▷ vt superar ▷ n: **to get the ~ of sb** quedar por encima de algn; **you had ~ do it** más vale que lo hagas; **he thought ~ of it** cambió de parecer; **to get ~** (Med) mejorar(se)

betting ['betɪŋ] n juego, el apostar; **betting shop** (BRIT) n agencia de apuestas

between [bɪ'twiːn] prep entre ▷ adv (time) mientras tanto; (place) en medio

beverage ['bevərɪdʒ] n bebida

beware [bɪ'weə*] vi: **to ~ (of)** tener cuidado (con); **"~ of the dog"** "perro peligroso"

bewildered [bɪ'wɪldəd] adj aturdido, perplejo

beyond [bɪ'jɒnd] prep más allá de; (past: understanding) fuera de; (after: date) después de, más allá de; (above) superior a ▷ adv (in space) más allá; (in time) posteriormente; **~ doubt** fuera de toda duda; **~ repair** irreparable

bias ['baɪəs] n (prejudice) prejuicio, pasión f; (preference) predisposición f; **bias(s)ed** adj parcial

bib [bɪb] n babero
Bible ['baɪbl] n Biblia
bicarbonate of soda [baɪ'kɑ:bənɪt-] n bicarbonato sódico
biceps ['baɪseps] n bíceps m
bicycle ['baɪsɪkl] n bicicleta; **bicycle pump** n bomba de bicicleta
bid [bɪd] (pt **bade** or ~, pp **bidden** or ~) n oferta, postura; (in tender) licitación f; (attempt) tentativa, conato ▷ vi hacer una oferta ▷ vt (offer) ofrecer; **to ~ sb good day** dar a algn los buenos días; **bidder** n: **the highest bidder** el mejor postor
bidet ['biːdeɪ] n bidet m
big [bɪɡ] adj grande; (brother, sister) mayor; **bigheaded** adj engreído; **big toe** n dedo gordo (del pie)
bike [baɪk] n bici f; **bike lane** n carril-bici m
bikini [bɪ'kiːnɪ] n bikini m
bilateral [baɪ'lætərl] adj (agreement) bilateral
bilingual [baɪ'lɪŋɡwəl] adj bilingüe
bill [bɪl] n cuenta; (invoice) factura; (Pol) proyecto de ley; (us: banknote) billete m; (of bird) pico; (of show) programa m; **"post no ~s"** "prohibido fijar carteles"; **to fit** or **fill the ~** (fig) cumplir con los requisitos; **billboard** (us) n cartelera; **billfold** ['bɪlfəʊld] (us) n cartera
billiards ['bɪljədz] n billar m
billion ['bɪljən] n (BRIT) billón m (millón de millones); (us) mil millones mpl
bin [bɪn] n (for rubbish) cubo or bote m (MEX) or tacho (SC) de la basura; (container) recipiente m
bind [baɪnd] (pt, pp **bound**) vt atar; (book) encuadernar; (oblige) obligar ▷ n (inf: nuisance) lata
binge [bɪndʒ] (inf) n: **to go on a ~** ir de juerga
bingo ['bɪŋɡəʊ] n bingo m
binoculars [bɪ'nɒkjʊlaz] npl prismáticos mpl
bio... ['baɪəʊ] prefix: **biochemistry** n

bioquímica; **biodegradable** [baɪəʊdɪ'ɡreɪdəbl] adj biodegradable; **biography** [baɪ'ɒɡrəfɪ] n biografía; **biological** adj biológico; **biology** [baɪ'ɒlədʒɪ] n biología; **biometric** [baɪə'metrɪk] adj biométrico
Biro® ['baɪərəʊ] n boli m
birch [bɜːtʃ] n (tree) abedul m
bird [bɜːd] n ave f, pájaro; (BRIT: inf) chica; **bird flu** n gripe f aviar; **bird of prey** n ave f de presa; **birdwatching** n: **he likes to go birdwatching on Sundays** los domingos le gusta ver pájaros
birth [bɜːθ] n nacimiento; **to give ~ to** parir, dar a luz; **birth certificate** n partida de nacimiento; **birth control** n (policy) control m de natalidad; (methods) métodos mpl anticonceptivos; **birthday** n cumpleaños m inv ▷ cpd (cake, card etc) de cumpleaños; **birthmark** n antojo, marca de nacimiento; **birthplace** n lugar m de nacimiento
biscuit ['bɪskɪt] (BRIT) n galleta
bishop ['bɪʃəp] n obispo; (Chess) alfil m
bistro ['biːstrəʊ] n café-bar m
bit [bɪt] pt of **bite** ▷ n trozo, pedazo, pedacito; (Comput) bit m, bitio; (for horse) freno, bocado; **a ~ of** un poco de; **a ~ mad** un poco loco; **~ by ~** poco a poco
bitch [bɪtʃ] n perra; (infl: woman) zorra (!)
bite [baɪt] (pt **bit**, pp **bitten**) vt, vi morder; (insect etc) picar ▷ n (insect bite) picadura; (mouthful) bocado; **to ~ one's nails** comerse las uñas; **let's have a ~ (to eat)** (inf) vamos a comer algo
bitten ['bɪtn] pp of **bite**
bitter ['bɪtə*] adj amargo; (wind) cortante, penetrante; (battle) encarnizado ▷ n (BRIT: beer) cerveza típica británica a base de lúpulos
bizarre [bɪ'zɑ:*] adj raro, extraño
black [blæk] adj negro; (tea, coffee) solo ▷ n color m negro; (person): **B~**

negro/a ▷ vt (BRIT Industry) boicotear;
to give sb a ~ eye ponerle a algn
el ojo morado; **~ and blue** (bruised)
amoratado; **to be in the ~** (bank
account) estar en números negros;
black out vi (faint) desmayarse;
blackberry n zarzamora; **blackbird**
n mirlo; **blackboard** n pizarra; **black
coffee** n café m solo; **blackcurrant**
n grosella negra; **black ice** n hielo
invisible en la carretera; **blackmail**
n chantaje m ▷ vt chantajear; **black
market** n mercado negro; **blackout**
n (Mil) oscurecimiento; (power cut)
apagón m; (TV, Radio) interrupción f de
programas; (fainting) desvanecimiento;
black pepper n pimienta f negra;
black pudding n morcilla; **Black Sea**
n: **the Black Sea** el Mar Negro
bladder ['blædə*] n vejiga
blade [bleɪd] n hoja; (of propeller)
paleta; **a ~ of grass** una brizna de
hierba
blame [bleɪm] n culpa ▷ vt: **to ~ sb
for sth** echar a algn la culpa de algo; **to
be to ~ (for)** tener la culpa de (de)
bland [blænd] adj (music, taste) soso
blank [blæŋk] adj en blanco; (look) sin
expresión ▷ n (of memory): **my mind is
a ~** no puedo recordar nada; (on form)
blanco, espacio en blanco; (cartridge)
cartucho sin bala or de fogueo
blanket ['blæŋkɪt] n manta (SP),
cobija (LAM); (of snow) capa; (of fog)
manto
blast [blɑːst] n (of wind) ráfaga, soplo;
(of explosive) explosión f ▷ vt (blow
up) volar
blatant ['bleɪtənt] adj descarado
blaze [bleɪz] n (fire) fuego; (fig: of
colour) despliegue m; (: of glory)
esplendor m ▷ vi arder en llamas; (fig)
brillar ▷ vt: **to ~ a trail** (fig) abrir un
camino; **in a ~ of publicity** con gran
publicidad
blazer ['bleɪzə*] n chaqueta de uniforme
de colegial o de socio de club
bleach [bliːtʃ] n (also: **household ~**)

lejía ▷ vt blanquear; **bleachers**
npl (Sport) gradas fpl al sol
bleak [bliːk] adj (countryside) desierto;
(prospect) poco prometedor(a);
(weather) crudo; (smile) triste
bled [bled] pt, pp of **bleed**
bleed [bliːd] (pt, pp **bled**) vt, vi
sangrar; **my nose is ~ing** me está
sangrando la nariz
blemish ['blemɪʃ] n marca, mancha;
(on reputation) tacha
blend [blend] n mezcla ▷ vt mezclar;
(colours etc) combinar, mezclar ▷ vi
(colours etc: also: **~ in**) combinarse,
mezclarse; **blender** n (Culin) batidora
bless [bles] (pt, pp **~ed** or **blest**) vt
bendecir; **~ you!** (after sneeze) ¡Jesús!;
blessing n (approval) aprobación f;
(godsend) don m del cielo, bendición f;
(advantage) beneficio, ventaja
blew [bluː] pt of **blow**
blight [blaɪt] n (hopes etc) frustrar,
arruinar
blind [blaɪnd] adj ciego; (fig): **~ (to)**
ciego (a) ▷ n (for window) persiana ▷ vt
cegar; (dazzle) deslumbrar; (deceive): **to
~ sb to ...** cegar a algn a ...; **the blind**
npl los ciegos; **blind alley** n callejón
m sin salida; **blindfold** n venda ▷ adv
con los ojos vendados ▷ vt vendar
los ojos a
blink [blɪŋk] vi parpadear, pestañear;
(light) oscilar
bliss [blɪs] n felicidad f
blister ['blɪstə*] n ampolla ▷ vi
(paint) ampollarse
blizzard ['blɪzəd] n ventisca
bloated ['bləʊtɪd] adj hinchado;
(person: full) ahíto
blob [blɒb] n (drop) gota; (indistinct
object) bulto
block [blɒk] n bloque m; (in pipes)
obstáculo; (of buildings) manzana
(SP), cuadra (LAM) ▷ vt obstruir,
cerrar; (progress) estorbar; **~ of flats**
(BRIT) bloque m de pisos; **mental ~**
bloqueo mental; **block up** vt tapar,
obstruir; (pipe) atascar; **blockade**

blog | ['blɒɡ] *n* bloqueo ▷ *vt* bloquear; **blockage** *n* estorbo, obstrucción *f*; **blockbuster** *n* (*book*) bestseller *m*; (*film*) éxito de público; **block capitals** *npl* mayúsculas *fpl*; **block letters** *npl* mayúsculas *fpl*

blog [blɒɡ] *n* blog *m*

bloke [bləʊk] (BRIT: *inf*) *n* tipo, tío

blond(e) [blɒnd] *adj*, *n* rubio/a *m/f*

blood [blʌd] *n* sangre *f*; **blood donor** *n* donante *mf* de sangre; **blood group** *n* grupo sanguíneo; **blood poisoning** *n* envenenamiento de la sangre; **blood pressure** *n* presión *f* sanguínea; **bloodshed** *n* derramamiento de sangre; **bloodshot** *adj* inyectado en sangre; **bloodstream** *n* corriente *f* sanguínea; **blood test** *n* análisis *m* inv de sangre; **blood transfusion** *n* transfusión *f* de sangre; **blood type** *n* grupo sanguíneo; **blood vessel** *n* vaso sanguíneo; **bloody** *adj* sangriento; (*BRIT*: *inf!*): **this bloody …** este condenado o puñetero …; **bloody strong/good** (*BRIT*: *inf!*) terriblemente fuerte/bueno

bloom [bluːm] *n* flor *f* ▷ *vi* florecer

blossom ['blɒsəm] *n* flor *f* ▷ *vi* florecer

blot [blɒt] *n* borrón *m*; (*fig*) mancha ▷ *vt* (*stain*) manchar

blouse [blaʊz] *n* blusa

blow [bləʊ] (*pt* **blew**, *pp* **blown**) *n* golpe *m*; (*with sword*) espadazo ▷ *vi* soplar; (*dust, sand etc*) volar; (*fuse*) fundirse ▷ *vt* (*wind*) llevarse; (*fuse*) quemar; (*instrument*) tocar; **to ~ one's nose** sonarse; **blow away** *vt* llevarse, arrancar; **blow out** *vi* apagarse; **blow up** *vi* estallar ▷ *vt* volar; (*tyre*) inflar; (*Phot*) ampliar; **blow-dry** *n* moldeado (con secador)

blown [bləʊn] *pp of* **blow**

blue [bluː] *adj* (*depressed*) deprimido; **~ film/joke** película/chiste *m* verde; **out of the ~** (*fig*) de repente; **bluebell** *n* campanilla, campánula

azul; **blueberry** *n* arándano; **blue cheese** *n* queso azul; **blues** *npl*: **the blues** (*Mus*) el blues; **to have the blues** estar triste; **bluetit** *n* herrerillo *m* (común)

bluff [blʌf] *vi* tirarse un farol, farolear ▷ *n* farol *m*; **to call sb's ~** coger a algn la palabra

blunder ['blʌndə*] *n* patinazo, metedura de pata ▷ *vi* cometer un error, meter la pata

blunt [blʌnt] *adj* (*pencil*) despuntado; (*knife*) desafilado, romo; (*person*) franco, directo

blur [blɜː*] *n* (*shape*): **to become a ~** hacerse borroso ▷ *vt* (*vision*) enturbiar; (*distinction*) borrar; **blurred** *adj* borroso

blush [blʌʃ] *vi* ruborizarse, ponerse colorado ▷ *n* rubor *m*; **blusher** *n* colorete *m*

board [bɔːd] *n* (*cardboard*) cartón *m*; (*wooden*) tabla, tablero; (*on wall*) tablón *m*; (*for chess etc*) tablero; (*committee*) junta, consejo; (*in firm*) mesa or junta directiva; (*Naut, Aviat*): **on ~** a bordo ▷ *vt* (*ship*) embarcarse en; (*train*) subir a; **full ~** (*BRIT*) pensión completa; **half ~** (*BRIT*) media pensión; **to go by the ~** (*fig*) ser abandonado or olvidado; **board game** *n* juego de tablero; **boarding card** (*BRIT*) *n* tarjeta de embarque; **boarding pass** (*US*) *n* = **boarding card**; **boarding school** *n* internado; **board room** *n* sala de juntas

boast [bəʊst] *vi*: **to ~ (about or of)** alardear (de)

boat [bəʊt] *n* barco, buque *m*; (*small*) barca, bote *m*

bob [bɒb] *vi* (*also*: **~ up and down**) menearse, balancearse

bobby pin ['bɒbɪ-] (*US*) *n* horquilla

body ['bɒdɪ] *n* cuerpo; (*corpse*) cadáver *m*; (*of car*) caja, carrocería; (*fig*: *group*) grupo; (*: organization*) organismo; **body-building** *n* culturismo; **bodyguard** *n* guardaespaldas *m inv*; **bodywork** *n* carrocería

bog [bɒg] n pantano, ciénaga ▷ vt: **to get ~ged down** (fig) empantanarse, atascarse

bogus ['bəʊgəs] adj falso, fraudulento

boil [bɔɪl] vt (water) hervir; (eggs) pasar por agua, cocer ▷ vi hervir; (fig: with anger) estar furioso; (: with heat) asfixiarse ▷ n (Med) furúnculo, divieso; **to come to the ~, to come to a ~** (us) comenzar a hervir; **to ~ down to** (fig) reducirse a; **boil over** vi salirse, rebosar; (anger etc) llegar al colmo; **boiled egg** n (soft) huevo tibio (MEX) or pasado por agua ora la copa (sc); (hard) huevo duro; **boiled potatoes** npl patatas fpl (SP) or papas fpl (LAM) cocidas; **boiler** n caldera; **boiling** ['bɔɪlɪŋ] adj: **I'm boiling (hot)** (inf) estoy asado; **boiling point** n punto de ebullición

bold [bəʊld] adj valiente, audaz; (pej) descarado; (colour) llamativo

Bolivia [bə'lɪvɪə] n Bolivia; **Bolivian** adj, n boliviano/a m/f

bollard ['bɒlɑd] (BRIT) n (Aut) poste m

bolt [bəʊlt] n (lock) cerrojo; (with nut) perno, tornillo ▷ adv: **~ upright** rígido, erguido ▷ vt (door) echar el cerrojo a; (also: **~ together**) sujetar con tornillos; (food) engullir ▷ vi fugarse; (horse) desbocarse

bomb [bɒm] n bomba ▷ vt bombardear; **bombard** [bɒm'bɑːd] vt bombardear; (fig) asediar; **bomber** n (Aviat) bombardero; **bomb scare** n amenaza de bomba

bond [bɒnd] n (promise) fianza; (Finance) bono; (link) vínculo, lazo; (Comm): **in ~** en depósito bajo fianza; **bonds** npl (chains) cadenas fpl

bone [bəʊn] n hueso; (of fish) espina ▷ vt deshuesar; quitar las espinas a

bonfire ['bɒnfaɪə*] n hoguera, fogata

bonnet ['bɒnɪt] n gorra; (BRIT: of car) capó m

bonus ['bəʊnəs] n (payment) paga extraordinaria, plus m; (fig) bendición f

boo [buː] excl ¡uh! ▷ vt abuchear,

rechiflar

book [bʊk] n libro; (of tickets) taco; (of stamps etc) librito ▷ vt (ticket) sacar; (seat, room) reservar; **books** npl (Comm) cuentas fpl, contabilidad f; **book in** vi (at hotel) registrarse; **book up** vt: **to be booked up** (hotel) estar completo; **bookcase** n librería, estante m para libros; **booking** n reserva; **booking office** n (BRIT Rail) despacho de billetes (SP) or boletos (LAM); (Theatre) taquilla (SP), boletería (LAM); **bookkeeping** n contabilidad f; **booklet** n folleto; **bookmaker** n corredor m de apuestas; **bookmark** n (also Comput) marcador; **bookseller** n librero; **bookshelf** n estante m (para libros); **bookshop, book store** n librería

boom [buːm] n (noise) trueno, estampido; (in prices etc) alza rápida; (Econ, in population) boom m ▷ vi (cannon) hacer gran estruendo, retumbar; (Econ) estar en alza

boost [buːst] n estímulo, empuje m ▷ vt estimular, empujar

boot [buːt] n bota; (BRIT: of car) maleta, maletero SP or LAM; (~ to start a computer) arrancar; **to ~** (in addition) además, por añadidura

booth [buːð] n (telephone booth, voting booth) cabina

booze [buːz] (inf) n bebida

border ['bɔːdə*] n borde m, margen m; (of a country) frontera; (for flowers) arriate m ▷ vt (road) bordear; (another country: also: **~ on**) lindar con; **borderline** n: **on the borderline** en el límite

bore [bɔː*] pt of **bear** ▷ vt (hole) hacer un agujero en; (well) perforar; (person) aburrir ▷ n (person) pelmazo, pesado; (of gun) calibre m; **bored** adj aburrido; **he's bored to tears** or **to death** or **stiff** está aburrido como una ostra, está muerto de aburrimiento; **boredom** n aburrimiento

boring ['bɔːrɪŋ] adj aburrido

born [bɔːn] adj: **to be ~** nacer; **I was ~**

in 1960 nací en 1960

borne [bɔ:n] pp of **bear**

borough ['bʌrə] n municipio

borrow ['bɒrəʊ] vt: **to ~ sth (from sb)** tomar algo prestado (a algn)

Bosnia(-Herzegovina) ['bɒznɪə(hɜːtsəgəʊvɪ:nə)] n Bosnia(-Herzegovina)

Bosnian ['bɒznɪən] adj, n bosnio/a

bosom ['bʊzəm] n pecho

boss [bɒs] n jefe m ▷ vt (also: **~ about or around**) mangonear; **bossy** adj mandón/ona

both [bəʊθ] adj, pron ambos/as, los dos(las dos); **~ of us went, we ~ went** fuimos los dos, ambos fuimos ▷ adv: **~ A and B** tanto A como B

bother ['bɒðə] vt (worry) preocupar; (disturb) molestar, fastidiar ▷ vi (also: **~ o.s.**) molestarse ▷ n (trouble) dificultad f; (nuisance) molestia, lata; **to ~ doing** tomarse la molestia de hacer

bottle ['bɒtl] n botella; (small) frasco; (baby's) biberón m ▷ vt embotellar; **bottle bank** n contenedor m de vidrio; **bottle-opener** n abrebotellas m inv

bottom ['bɒtəm] n (of box, sea) fondo; (buttocks) trasero, culo; (of page) pie m; (of list) final m; (of class) último/a ▷ adj (lowest) más bajo; (last) último

bought [bɔ:t] pt, pp of **buy**

boulder ['bəʊldə] n canto rodado

bounce [baʊns] vi (ball) (re)botar; (cheque) ser rechazado ▷ vt hacer (re)botar ▷ n (rebound) (re)bote m; **bouncer** (inf) n gorila m (que echa a los alborotadores de un bar, club etc)

bound [baʊnd] pt, pp of **bind** ▷ n (leap) salto; (gen pl: limit) límite m ▷ vi (leap) saltar ▷ vt (border) rodear ▷ adj: **~ by** rodeado de; **to ~ to do sth** (obliged) tener el deber de hacer algo; **he's ~ to come** es seguro que vendrá; **out of ~s** prohibido el paso; **~ for** con destino a

boundary ['baʊndrɪ] n límite m

bouquet [bukeɪ] n (of flowers) ramo

bourbon ['bʊəbən] (us) n (also: ~

whiskey) whisky m americano, bourbon m

bout [baʊt] n (of malaria etc) ataque m; (of activity) período; (Boxing etc) combate m, encuentro

boutique [bu:'ti:k] n boutique f, tienda de ropa

bow¹ [bəʊ] n (knot) lazo; (weapon, Mus) arco

bow² [baʊ] n (of the head) reverencia; (Naut: also: **~s**) proa ▷ vi inclinarse, hacer una reverencia

bowels [baʊəlz] npl intestinos mpl, vientre m; (fig) entrañas fpl

bowl [bəʊl] n tazón m, cuenco; (ball) bola f ▷ vi (Cricket) arrojar la pelota; see also **bowls**; **bowler** n (Cricket) lanzador m (de la pelota); (BRIT: also: **bowler hat**) hongo, bombín m; **bowling** n (game) bochas fpl, bolos mpl; **bowling alley** n bolera; **bowling green** n pista para bochas; **bowls** n juego de las bochas, bolos mpl

bow tie [bəʊ-] n corbata de lazo, pajarita

box [bɒks] n (also: **cardboard ~**) caja, cajón m; (Theatre) palco ▷ vt encajonar ▷ vi (Sport) boxear; **boxer** ['bɒksə] n (person) boxeador m; **boxer shorts** ['bɒksəʃɔ:ts] pl n bóxers; **a pair of boxer shorts** unos bóxers; **boxing** ['bɒksɪŋ] n (Sport) boxeo; **Boxing Day** (BRIT) n día en que se dan los aguinaldos, 26 de diciembre; **boxing gloves** npl guantes mpl de boxeo; **boxing ring** n ring m, cuadrilátero; **box office** n taquilla (sp), boletería (LAM)

boy [bɔɪ] n (young) niño; (older) muchacho, chico; (son) hijo; **boy band** n boy band (grupo musical de chicos

boycott ['bɔɪkɒt] n boicot m ▷ vt boicotear

boyfriend ['bɔɪfrend] n novio

bra [brɑː] n sostén m, sujetador m

brace [breɪs] n (BRIT: also: **~s: on teeth**) corrector m, aparato; (tool) berbiquí m ▷ vt (knees, shoulders) tensionar; **braces** npl (BRIT) tirantes mpl; **to ~ o.s.** (fig) prepararse

bracelet ['breɪslɪt] n pulsera, brazalete m

bracket ['brækɪt] n (Tech) soporte m, puntal m; (group) clase f, categoría f; (also: **brace ~**) soporte m, abrazadera; (also: **round ~**) paréntesis m inv; (also: **square ~**) corchete n ▷ vt (word etc) poner entre paréntesis

brag [bræg] vi jactarse

braid [breɪd] n (trimming) galón m; (of hair) trenza

brain [breɪn] n cerebro; **brains** npl sesos mpl; **she's got ~s** es muy lista

braise [breɪz] vt cocer a fuego lento

brake [breɪk] n (on vehicle) freno ▷ vt, vi frenar; **brake light** n luz f de frenado

bran [bræn] n salvado

branch [brɑːntʃ] n rama; (Comm) sucursal f; **branch off** vi: **a small road branches off to the right** hay una carretera pequeña que sale hacia la derecha; **branch out** vi (fig) extenderse

brand [brænd] n (fig: type) tipo ▷ vt (cattle) marcar con hierro candente; **brand name** n marca; **brand-new** adj flamante, completamente nuevo

brandy ['brændɪ] n coñac m

brash [bræʃ] adj (cheeky) descarado

brass [brɑːs] n latón m; **the ~** (Mus) los cobres; **brass band** n banda de metal

brat [bræt] n (pej) mocoso/a

brave [breɪv] adj valiente, valeroso ▷ vt (face up to) desafiar; **bravery** n valor m, valentía

brawl [brɔːl] n pelea, reyerta

Brazil [brə'zɪl] n (el) Brasil; **Brazilian** adj, n brasileño/a m/f

breach [briːtʃ] vt abrir brecha en ▷ n (gap) brecha; (breaking): **~ of contract** infracción f de contrato; **~ of the peace** perturbación f del órden público

bread [bred] n pan m; **breadbin** n panera; **breadbox** (us) n panera; **breadcrumbs** npl migajas fpl; (Culin) pan rallado

breadth [bretθ] n anchura; (fig) amplitud f

break [breɪk] (pt **broke**, pp **broken**) vt romper; (promise) faltar a; (law) violar, infringir; (record) batir ▷ vi romperse, quebrarse; (storm) estallar; (weather) cambiar; (dawn) despuntar; (news etc) darse a conocer ▷ n (gap) abertura; (fracture) fractura; (time) intervalo; (: at school) (período de) recreo; (chance) oportunidad f; **to ~ the news to sb** comunicar la noticia a algn; **break down** vt (figures, data) analizar, descomponer ▷ vi (machine) estropearse; (Aut) averiarse; (person) romper a llorar; (talks) fracasar; **break in** vt (horse etc) domar ▷ vi (burglar) forzar una entrada; (interrupt) interrumpir; **break into** vt fus (house) forzar; **break off** vi (speaker) pararse, detenerse; (branch) partir; **break out** vi estallar; (prisoner) escaparse; **to break out in spots** salirle a algn granos; **break up** vi (ship) hacerse pedazos; (crowd, meeting) disolverse; (marriage) deshacerse; (Scol) terminar (el curso); (line) cortarse ▷ vt (rocks etc) partir; (journey) partir; (fight etc) acabar con; **the line's** or **you're breaking up** se corta; **breakdown** n (Aut) avería; (in communications) interrupción f; (Med: also: **nervous breakdown**) colapso, crisis f nerviosa; (of marriage, talks) fracaso; (of statistics) análisis m inv; **breakdown truck, breakdown van** n (camión m) grúa

breakfast ['brekfəst] n desayuno

break: break-in n robo con allanamiento de morada; **breakthrough** n (also fig) avance m

breast [brest] n (of woman) pecho, seno; (chest) pecho; (of bird) pechuga; **breast-feed** (pt, pp **breast-fed**) vt, vi amamantar, criar a los pechos; **breaststroke** n braza (de pecho)

breath [breθ] n aliento, respiración f; **to take a deep ~** respirar hondo; **out of ~** sin aliento, sofocado

Breathalyser ['breθəlaɪzə*'] (BRIT)
n alcoholímetro

breathe [bri:ð] vt, vi respirar;
breathe in vt, vi aspirar; **breathe
out** vt, vi espirar; **breathing** n
respiración f

breath: breathless adj sin aliento,
jadeante; **breathtaking** adj
imponente, pasmoso; **breath test** n
prueba de la alcoholemia

bred [bred] pt, pp of **breed**

breed [bri:d] (pt, pp **bred**) vt criar ⊳ vi
reproducirse, procrear ⊳ n (Zool) raza,
casta; (type) tipo

breeze [bri:z] n brisa

breezy ['bri:zɪ] adj de mucho viento,
ventoso; (person) despreocupado

brew [bru:] vt (tea) hacer; (beer)
elaborar ⊳ vi (fig: trouble) prepararse;
(storm) amenazar; **brewery** n fábrica
de cerveza, cervecería f

bribe [braɪb] n soborno ⊳ vt
sobornar, cohechar; **bribery** n
soborno, cohecho

bric-a-brac ['brɪkəbræk] n inv
baratijas fpl

brick [brɪk] n ladrillo; **bricklayer** n
albañil m

bride [braɪd] n novia; **bridegroom** n
novio; **bridesmaid** n dama de honor

bridge [brɪdʒ] n puente m; (Naut)
puente m de mando; (of nose) caballete
m; (Cards) bridge m ⊳ vt (fig): **to ~ a gap**
llenar un vacío

bridle ['braɪdl] n brida, freno

brief [bri:f] adj breve, corto; n (Law)
escrito; (task) cometido, encargo
⊳ vt informar; **briefs** npl (for men)
calzoncillos mpl; (for women) bragas fpl;
briefcase n cartera (SP), portafolio
(LAM); **briefing** n (Press) informe m;
briefly adv (glance) fugazmente; (say)
en pocas palabras

brigadier [brɪgə'dɪə*] n general m
de brigada

bright [braɪt] adj brillante; (room)
luminoso; (day) de sol; (person: clever)
listo, inteligente; (: lively) alegre;

(colour) vivo; (future) prometedor(a)

brilliant ['brɪljənt] adj brillante; (inf)
fenomenal

brim [brɪm] n borde m; (of hat) ala

brine [braɪn] n (Culin) salmuera

bring [brɪŋ] (pt, pp **brought**) vt (thing,
person: with you) traer; (: to sb) llevar,
conducir; (trouble, satisfaction) causar;
bring about vt ocasionar, producir;
bring back vt volver a traer; (return)
devolver; **bring down** vt (government,
plane) derribar; (price) rebajar; **bring
in** vt (harvest) recoger; (person) hacer
entrar o pasar; (object) traer; (Pol: bill,
law) presentar; (produce: income)
producir, rendir; (: person) causar;
bring on vt (illness,
attack) producir, causar; (player,
substitute) sacar (de la reserva), hacer
salir; **bring out** vt sacar; (book etc)
publicar; (meaning) subrayar; **bring
up** vt subir; (person) educar, criar;
(question) sacar a colación; (food: vomit)
devolver, vomitar

brink [brɪŋk] n borde m

brisk [brɪsk] adj (abrupt: tone) brusco;
(person) enérgico, vigoroso; (pace)
rápido; (trade) activo

bristle ['brɪsl] n cerda ⊳ vi: **to ~ in
anger** temblar de rabia

Brit [brɪt] n abbr (inf: = British person)
británico/a

Britain ['brɪtən] n (also: **Great ~**)
Gran Bretaña

British ['brɪtɪʃ] adj británico
⊳ npl: **the ~** los británicos; **British Isles**
npl: **the British Isles** las Islas Británicas

Briton ['brɪtən] n británico/a

brittle ['brɪtl] adj quebradizo, frágil

broad [brɔ:d] adj ancho; (range)
amplio; (smile) abierto; (general: outlines
etc) general; (accent) cerrado; **in ~
daylight** en pleno día; **broadband** n
banda ancha; **broad bean** n haba;
broadcast (pt, pp ~) n emisión f
⊳ vt (Radio) emitir; (TV) transmitir
⊳ vi emitir; transmitir; **broaden** vt
ampliar ⊳ vi ensancharse; **to broaden
one's mind** hacer más tolerante o

align; broadly adv en general; **broad-minded** adj tolerante, liberal

broccoli ['brɒkəlɪ] n brécol m

brochure ['brəʊʃʊə*] n folleto

broil [brɔɪl] vt (Culin) asar a la parrilla

broiler ['brɔɪlə*] n (grill) parrilla

broke [brəʊk] pt of **break** ▷ adj (inf) pelado, sin blanca

broken ['brəʊkən] pp of **break** ▷ adj roto; (machine: also: **~ down**) averiado; **~ leg** pierna rota; **in ~ English** en un inglés imperfecto

broker ['brəʊkə*] n agente mf, bolsista mf; (insurance broker) agente de seguros

bronchitis [brɒŋ'kaɪtɪs] n bronquitis f

bronze [brɒnz] n bronce m

brooch [brəʊtʃ] n prendedor m, broche m

brood [bruːd] n camada, cría ▷ vi (person) dejarse obsesionar

broom [brum] n escoba; (Bot) retama

Bros. abbr (= Brothers) Hnos

broth [brɒθ] n caldo

brothel ['brɒθəl] n burdel m

brother ['brʌðə*] n hermano; **brother-in-law** n cuñado

brought [brɔːt] pt, pp of **bring**

brow [braʊ] n (forehead) frente m; (eyebrow) ceja; (of hill) cumbre f

brown [braʊn] adj (colour) marrón; (hair) castaño; (tanned) moreno, bronceado ▷ n (colour) color m marrón or pardo ▷ vt (Culin) dorar; **brown bread** n pan integral

Brownie ['braʊnɪ] n niña exploradora

brown rice n arroz m integral

brown sugar n azúcar m terciado

browse [braʊz] vi (through book) hojear; (in shop) mirar; **browser** n (Comput) navegador m

bruise [bruːz] n cardenal m (sp), moretón m ▷ vt magullar

brunette [bruː'nɛt] n morena

brush [brʌʃ] n cepillo; (for painting, shaving etc) brocha; (artist's) pincel m;

(with police etc) roce m ▷ vt (sweep) barrer; (groom) cepillar; (also: **~ against**) rozar al pasar

Brussels ['brʌslz] n Bruselas

Brussels sprout n col f de Bruselas

brutal ['bruːtl] adj brutal

B.Sc. abbr (= Bachelor of Science) licenciado en Ciencias

BSE n abbr (= bovine spongiform encephalopathy) encefalopatía espongiforme bovina

bubble ['bʌbl] n burbuja ▷ vi burbujear, borbotar; **bubble bath** n espuma del baño; **bubble gum** n chicle m de globo; **bubblejet printer** ['bʌbldʒɛt-] n impresora de inyección por burbujas

buck [bʌk] n (rabbit) conejo macho; (deer) gamo; (us: inf) dólar m ▷ vi corcovear; **to pass the ~ (to sb)** echar (a algn) el muerto

bucket ['bʌkɪt] n cubo, balde m

buckle ['bʌkl] n hebilla ▷ vt abrochar con hebilla ▷ vi combarse

bud [bʌd] n (of plant) brote m, yema; (of flower) capullo ▷ vi brotar, echar brotes

Buddhism ['bʊdɪzm] n Budismo

Buddhist ['bʊdɪst] adj, n budista m/f

buddy ['bʌdɪ] (us) n compañero, compinche m

budge [bʌdʒ] vt mover; (fig) hacer ceder ▷ vi moverse, ceder

budgerigar ['bʌdʒərɪgɑː*] n periquito

budget ['bʌdʒɪt] n presupuesto ▷ vi: **to ~ for sth** presupuestar algo

budgie ['bʌdʒɪ] n = **budgerigar**

buff [bʌf] adj (colour) color de ante ▷ n (inf: enthusiast) entusiasta mf

buffalo ['bʌfələʊ] (pl **~ or ~es**) n (BRIT) búfalo; (us: bison) bisonte m

buffer ['bʌfə*] n (Comput) memoria intermedia; (Rail) tope m

buffet[1] ['bʌfɪt] vt golpear

buffet[2] ['bʊfeɪ] n (BRIT: in station) bar m, cafetería; (food) buffet m; **buffet car** (BRIT) n (Rail) coche-comedor m

bug [bʌg] n (esp us: insect) bicho, sabandija; (Comput) error m; (germ) microbio, bacilo; (spy device) micrófono oculto ▷ vt (inf: annoy) fastidiar; (room) poner micrófono oculto en

buggy ['bʌgɪ] n cochecito de niño

build [bɪld] (pt, pp **built**) n (of person) tipo ▷ vt construir, edificar; **build up** vt (morale, forces, production) acrecentar; (stocks) acumular; **builder** n (contractor) contratista mf; **building** n construcción f; (structure) edificio; **building site** n obra; **building society** (BRIT) n sociedad f inmobiliaria

built [bɪlt] pt, pp of **build**; **built-in** adj (cupboard) empotrado; (device) interior, incorporado; **built-up** adj (area) urbanizado

bulb [bʌlb] n (Bot) bulbo; (Elec) bombilla, foco (MEX), bujía (CAM), bombita (RPL)

Bulgaria [bʌl'gɛərɪə] n Bulgaria; **Bulgarian** adj, n búlgaro/a m/f

bulge [bʌldʒ] n bulto, protuberancia ▷ vi bombearse, pandearse; (pocket etc): **to ~ (with)** rebosar (de)

bulimia [bə'lɪmɪə] n bulimia

bulimic [bju:'lɪmɪk] adj, n bulímico/a m/f

bulk [bʌlk] n masa, mole f; **in ~** (Comm) a granel; **the ~ of** la mayor parte de; **bulky** adj voluminoso, abultado

bull [bul] n toro; (male elephant, whale) macho

bulldozer ['buldəuzə*] n bulldozer m

bullet ['bulɪt] n bala

bulletin ['bulɪtɪn] n anuncio, parte m; (journal) boletín m; **bulletin board** n (US) tablón m de anuncios; (Comput) tablero de noticias

bullfight ['bulfaɪt] n corrida de toros; **bullfighter** n torero; **bullfighting** n los toros m, el toreo

bully ['bulɪ] n valentón m, matón m ▷ vt intimidar, tiranizar

bum [bʌm] n (inf: backside) culo; (esp US: tramp) vagabundo

bumblebee ['bʌmblbi:] n abejorro

bump [bʌmp] n (blow) tope m, choque m; (jolt) sacudida; (on road etc) bache m; (on head etc) chichón m ▷ vb (strike) chocar contra; **bump into** vt fus chocar contra, tropezar con; (person) topar con; **bumper** n (Aut) parachoques m ▷ adj: **bumper crop** or **harvest** cosecha abundante; **bumpy** adj (road) lleno de baches

bun [bʌn] n (BRIT: cake) pastel m; (US: bread) bollo; (of hair) moño

bunch [bʌntʃ] n (of flowers) ramo; (of keys) manojo; (of bananas) piña; (of people) grupo; (pej) pandilla; **bunches** npl (in hair) coletas fpl

bundle ['bʌndl] n bulto, fardo; (of sticks) haz m; (of papers) legajo ▷ vt (also: **~ up**) atar, envolver; **to ~ sth/sb into** meter algo/a algn precipitadamente

bungalow ['bʌngələu] n bungalow m, chalé m

bungee jumping ['bʌndʒi:'dʒʌmpɪŋ] n puenting m, banyi m

bunion ['bʌnjən] n juanete m

bunk [bʌnk] n litera; **bunk beds** npl literas fpl

bunker ['bʌnkə*] n (coal store) carbonera; (Mil) refugio; (Golf) bunker m

bunny ['bʌnɪ] n (inf: also: **~ rabbit**) conejito

buoy [bɔɪ] n boya; **buoyant** adj (ship) capaz de flotar; (economy) boyante; (person) optimista

burden ['bə:dn] n carga ▷ vt cargar

bureau [bjuə'rəu] (pl **~x**) n (BRIT: writing desk) escritorio, buró m; (US: chest of drawers) cómoda; (office) oficina, agencia

bureaucracy [bjuə'rɔkrəsɪ] n burocracia

bureaucrat ['bjuərəkræt] n burócrata m/f

bureau de change [-də'ʃɑ:ʒ] (pl **bureaux de change**) n caja f de cambio

bureaux ['bjuərəuz] npl of **bureau**

burger ['bə:gə*] n hamburguesa

burglar ['bə:glə*] n ladrón/ona m/f;
burglar alarm n alarma f antirrobo;
burglary n robo con allanamiento,
robo de una casa

burial ['bɛrɪəl] n entierro

burn [bə:n] (pt, pp ~ed o ~t) vt
quemar; (house) incendiar ▷ vi
quemarse, arder; incendiarse; (sting)
escocer ▷ n quemadura; **burn down**
vt incendiar; **burn out** vt (writer
etc): **to b.o. out** agotarse; **burning**
adj (building etc) en llamas;
(hot: sand etc) abrasador(a); (ambition)
ardiente

Burns' Night [bə:nz-] n ver recuadro

burnt [bə:nt] pt, pp of **burn**

burp [bə:p] (inf) n eructo ▷ vi eructar

burrow ['bʌrəu] n madriguera ▷ vi
hacer una madriguera; (rummage)
hurgar

burst [bə:st] (pt, pp ~) vt reventar;
(river: banks etc) romper ▷ vi
reventarse; (tyre) pincharse ▷ n (of
gunfire) ráfaga; (also: ~ **pipe**) reventón
m; **a ~ of energy/speed/enthusiasm**
una explosión de energía/un
ímpetu de velocidad/un arranque
de entusiasmo; **to ~ into flames**

estallar en llamas; **to ~ into tears**
deshacerse en lágrimas; **to ~ out
laughing** soltar la carcajada; **to ~
open** abrirse de golpe; **to be ~ing with**
(container) estar lleno a rebosar de;
(: person) reventar por; **burst into**
vt fus (room etc) irrumpir en

bury ['bɛrɪ] vt enterrar; (body)
enterrar, sepultar

bus [bʌs] (pl ~es) n autobús m; **bus
conductor** n cobrador(a) m/f

bush [buʃ] n arbusto; (scrub land)
monte m; **to beat about the ~**
andar(se) con rodeos

business ['bɪznɪs] n (matter) asunto;
(trading) comercio, negocios mpl; (firm)
empresa, casa; (occupation) oficio;
to be away on ~ estar en viaje de
negocios; **it's my ~ to ...** me toca or
corresponde ...; **it's none of my ~** yo no
tengo nada que ver; **he means ~** habla
en serio; **business class** n (Aer) clase f
preferente; **businesslike** adj eficiente;
businessman (irreg) n hombre m de
negocios; **business trip** n viaje m de
negocios; **businesswoman** (irreg) n
mujer f de negocios

busker ['bʌskə*] (BRIT) n músico/a
ambulante

bus: bus pass n bonobús; **bus shelter**
n parada cubierta; **bus station** n
estación f de autobuses; **bus-stop** n
parada de autobús

bust [bʌst] (Anat) (Anat) pecho; (sculpture)
busto ▷ adj (inf: broken) roto,
estropeado; **to go ~** quebrar

bustling ['bʌslɪŋ] adj (town)
animado, bullicioso

busy ['bɪzɪ] adj ocupado, atareado;
(shop, street) concurrido, animado;
(Tel: line) comunicando; **to ~ o.s.
with** ocuparse en; **busy signal** (us) n
(Tel) señal f de comunicando

○ **KEYWORD**

but [bʌt] conj ¹ pero; **he's not very
bright, but he's hard-working** no es

muy inteligente, pero es trabajador **2** (in direct contradiction) sino; **he's not English but French** no es inglés sino francés; **he didn't sing but he shouted** no cantó sino que gritó **3** (showing disagreement, surprise etc): **but that's far too expensive!** ¡pero eso es carísimo!; **but it does work!** ¡(pero) sí que funciona! ▷ prep (apart from, except) menos, salvo; **we've had nothing but trouble** no hemos tenido más que problemas; **no-one but him can do it** nadie más que él puede hacerlo; **who but a lunatic would do such a thing?** ¡sólo un loco haría una cosa así!; **but for you/your help** si no fuera por ti/tu ayuda; **anything but that** cualquier cosa menos eso ▷ adv (just, only): **she's but a child** no es más que una niña; **had I but known** si lo hubiera sabido; **I can but try** al menos lo puedo intentar; **it's all but finished** está casi acabado

butcher ['butʃə*] n carnicero ▷ vt hacer una carnicería con; (cattle etc) matar; **butcher's (shop)** n carnicería **butler** ['bʌtlə*] n mayordomo **butt** [bʌt] n (barrel) tonel m; (of gun) culata; (of cigarette) colilla; (BRIT: fig: target) blanco ▷ vt dar cabezadas contra, top(et)ar **butter** ['bʌtə*] n mantequilla ▷ vt untar con mantequilla; **buttercup** n botón m de oro **butterfly** ['bʌtəflaɪ] n mariposa; (Swimming: also: ~ **stroke**) braza de mariposa **buttocks** ['bʌtəks] npl nalgas fpl **button** ['bʌtn] n botón m; (us) placa, chapa ▷ vt (also: ~ **up**) abotonar, abrochar ▷ vi abrocharse **buy** [baɪ] (pt, pp **bought**) vt comprar ▷ n compra; **to ~ sb sth/sth from sb** comprarle algo a algn; **to ~ sb a drink** invitar a algn a tomar algo; **buy out** vt

(partner) comprar la parte de; **buy up** vt (property) acaparar; (stock) comprar todas las existencias de; **buyer** n comprador(a) m/f

buzz [bʌz] n zumbido; (inf: phone call) llamada (por teléfono) ▷ vi zumbar; **buzzer** n timbre m

○ **KEYWORD**

by [baɪ] prep **1** (referring to cause, agent) por; de; **killed by lightning** muerto por un relámpago; **a painting by Picasso** un cuadro de Picasso **2** (referring to method, manner, means): **by bus/car/train** en autobús/coche/ tren; **to pay by cheque** pagar con un cheque; **by moonlight/candlelight** a la luz de la luna/una vela; **by saving hard he ...** ahorrando ... **3** (via, through) por; **we came by Dover** vinimos por Dover **4** (close to, past): **the house by the river** la casa junto al río; **she rushed by me** pasó a mi lado corriendo a una exhalación; **I go by the post office every day** paso por delante de Correos todos los días **5** (time: not later than) antes de; **by daylight** de día; **by 4 o'clock** para las cuatro; **by this time tomorrow** mañana a estas horas; **by the time I got here it was too late** cuando llegué ya era demasiado tarde **6** (amount): **by the metre/kilo** por metro/kilo; **paid by the hour** pagado por hora **7** (Math, measure): **to divide/multiply by 3** dividir/multiplicar por 3; **a room 3 metres by 4** una habitación de 3 metros por 4; **it's broader by a metre** es un metro más ancho **8** (according to) según, de acuerdo con; **it's 3 o'clock by my watch** según mi reloj, son las tres; **it's all right by me** por mí, está bien **9**: **(all) by oneself** etc todo solo; **he did it (all) by himself** lo hizo él solo;

he was standing (all) by himself in a corner estaba de pie solo en un rincón **10: by the way** a propósito, por cierto; **this wasn't my idea, by the way** pues, no fue idea mía ▷ *adv* **1** *see* **go; pass** *etc* **2: by and by** finalmente; **they'll come back by and by** acabarán volviendo; **by and large** en líneas generales, en general

bye(-bye) ['baɪ('baɪ)] *excl* adiós, hasta luego

by-election (BRIT) *n* elección *f* parcial

bypass ['baɪpɑ:s] *n* carretera de circunvalación; (Med) (operación *f* de) by-pass *f* ▷ *vt* evitar

byte [baɪt] *n* (Comput) byte *m*, octeto

C

C [si:] *n* (Mus) do *m*
cab [kæb] *n* taxi *m*; (of truck) cabina
cabaret ['kæbəreɪ] *n* cabaret *m*
cabbage ['kæbɪdʒ] *n* col *f*, berza
cabin ['kæbɪn] *n* cabaña; (on ship) camarote *m*; (on plane) cabina; **cabin crew** *n* tripulación *f* de cabina
cabinet ['kæbɪnɪt] *n* (Pol) consejo de ministros; (furniture) armario; (also: **display ~**) vitrina; **cabinet minister** *n* ministro/a (del gabinete)
cable ['keɪbl] *n* cable *m* ▷ *vt* cablegrafiar; **cable car** *n* teleférico; **cable television** *n* televisión *f* por cable
cactus ['kæktəs] (*pl* **cacti**) *n* cacto
café ['kæfeɪ] *n* café *m*
cafeteria [kæfɪ'tɪərɪə] *n* cafetería
caffein(e) ['kæfi:n] *n* cafeína
cage [keɪdʒ] *n* jaula
cagoule [kə'gu:l] *n* chubasquero
cake [keɪk] *n* (Culin: large) tarta; (: small) pastel *m*; (of soap) pastilla
calcium ['kælsɪəm] *n* calcio
calculate ['kælkjuleɪt] *vt* calcular;

calculation [-'leɪʃən] n cálculo, cómputo; **calculator** n calculadora

calendar ['kæləndə*] n calendario

calf [kɑːf] (pl **calves**) n (of cow) ternero, becerro; (of other animals) cría; (also: ~**skin**) piel f de becerro; (Anat) pantorrilla

calibre ['kælɪbə*] (Us **caliber**) n calibre m

call [kɔːl] vt llamar; (meeting) convocar ▷ vi (shout) llamar; (Tel) llamar (por teléfono); (visit: also: ~ **in**, ~ **round**) hacer una visita ▷ n llamada; (of bird) canto; **to be ~ed** llamarse; **on** ~ (on duty) de guardia; **call back** vi (return) volver; (Tel) volver a llamar; **call for** vt fus (demand) pedir, exigir; (fetch) pasar a recoger; **call in** vt (doctor, expert, police) llamar; **call off** vt (cancel: meeting, race) cancelar; (: deal) anular; (: strike) desconvocar; **call on** vt fus (visit) visitar; (turn to) acudir a; **call out** vi gritar; **call up** vt (Mil) llamar al servicio militar; (Tel) llamar; **callbox** (BRIT) n cabina telefónica; **call centre** (Us **call center**) n centro de atención al cliente; **caller** n visita; (Tel) usuario/a

callous ['kæləs] adj insensible, cruel

calm [kɑːm] adj tranquilo; (sea) liso, en calma ▷ n calma, tranquilidad f ▷ vt calmar, tranquilizar; **calm down** vi calmarse, tranquilizarse ▷ vt calmar, tranquilizar; **calmly** ['kɑːmlɪ] adv tranquilamente, con calma

Calor gas ['kælə*-] n butano

calorie ['kælərɪ] n caloría

calves [kɑːvz] npl of **calf**

camcorder ['kæmkɔːdə*] n videocámara

came [keɪm] pt of **come**

camel ['kæməl] n camello

camera ['kæmərə] n máquina fotográfica; (Cinema, TV) cámara; **in** ~ (Law) a puerta cerrada; **cameraman** (irreg) n cámara m; **camera phone** n teléfono con cámara

camouflage ['kæməflɑːʒ] n camuflaje m ▷ vt camuflar

camp [kæmp] n campamento, camping m; (Mil) campamento; (for prisoners) campo; (fig: faction) bando ▷ vi acampar ▷ adj afectado, afeminado

campaign [kæm'peɪn] n (Mil, Pol etc) campaña ▷ vi hacer campaña; **campaigner** n: **campaigner for** defensor(a) m/f de

camp: campbed (BRIT) n cama de campaña; **camper** n campista mf; (vehicle) caravana; **campground** (Us) n camping m, campamento; **camping** n camping m; **to go camping** hacer camping; **campsite** n camping m

campus ['kæmpəs] n ciudad f universitaria

can¹ n (of oil, water) bidón m; (tin) lata, bote m ▷ vt enlatar

○ **KEYWORD**

can² [kæn] (negative **cannot**, **can't**, conditional and pt **could**) aux vb **1** (be able to) poder; **you can do it if you try** puedes hacerlo si lo intentas; **I can't see you** no te veo

2 (know how to) saber; **I can swim/play tennis/drive** sé nadar/jugar al tenis/ conducir; **can you speak French?** ¿hablas or sabes hablar francés?

3 (may) poder; **can I use your phone?** ¿me dejas or puedo usar tu teléfono?

4 (expressing disbelief, puzzlement etc): **it can't be true!** ¡no puede ser (verdad)!; **what can he want?** ¿qué querrá?

5 (expressing possibility, suggestion etc): **he could be in the library** podría estar en la biblioteca; **she could have been delayed** pudo haberse retrasado

Canada ['kænədə] n Canadá; **Canadian** [kə'neɪdɪən] adj, n canadiense mf

canal [kə'næl] n canal m

canary [kə'nɛərɪ] n canario

Canary Islands [kə'nɛərɪ'aɪləndz]

npl: **the ~** las (Islas) Canarias

cancel ['kænsəl] *vt* cancelar; (*train*) suprimir; (*cross out*) tachar, borrar;
cancellation [-'leɪʃən] *n* cancelación *f*; supresión *f*

Cancer ['kænsə*] *n* (*Astrology*) Cáncer *m*

cancer ['kænsə*] *n* cáncer *m*

candidate ['kændɪdeɪt] *n* candidato/a

candle ['kændl] *n* vela; (*in church*) cirio; **candlestick** *n* (*single*) candelero; (*low*) palmatoria; (*bigger, ornate*) candelabro

candy ['kændɪ] *n* azúcar *m* cande; (*us*) caramelo; **candy bar** (*us*) *n* barrita (*dulce*); **candyfloss**(*BRIT*) *n* algodón (*azucarado*)

cane [keɪn] *n* (*Bot*) caña; (*stick*) vara, palmeta; (*for furniture*) mimbre *m* ▷ *vt* (*BRIT*: *Scol*) castigar (con vara)

canister ['kænɪstə*] *n* bote *m*, lata; (*of gas*) bombona

cannabis ['kænəbɪs] *n* marijuana

canned [kænd] *adj* en lata, de lata

cannon ['kænən] (*pl* ~ *or* ~**s**) *n* cañón *m*

cannot ['kænɔt] = **can not**

canoe [kə'nu:] *n* canoa; (*Sport*) piragua; **canoeing** *n* piragüismo

canon ['kænən] *n* (*clergyman*) canónigo; (*standard*) canon (*con vara*)

can-opener ['kænəupnə*] *n* abrelatas *m*

can't [kænt] = **can not**

canteen [kæn'ti:n] *n* (*eating place*) cantina; (*BRIT*: *of cutlery*) juego

canter ['kæntə*] *vi* ir a medio galope

canvas ['kænvəs] *n* (*material*) lona; (*painting*) lienzo; (*Naut*) velas *fpl*

canvass ['kænvəs] *vi* (*Pol*): **to ~ for** solicitar votos por ▷ *vt* (*Comm*) sondear

canyon ['kænjən] *n* cañón *m*

cap [kæp] *n* (*hat*) gorra; (*of pen*) capuchón *m*; (*of bottle*) tapa, tapón *m*; (*contraceptive*) diafragma *m*; (*for toy gun*) cápsula ▷ *vt* (*outdo*) superar; (*limit*)

recortar

capability [keɪpə'bɪlɪtɪ] *n* capacidad *f*

capable ['keɪpəbl] *adj* capaz

capacity [kə'pæsɪtɪ] *n* capacidad *f*; (*position*) calidad *f*

cape [keɪp] *n* capa; (*Geo*) cabo

caper ['keɪpə*] *n* (*Culin*: *gen pl*) alcaparra; (*prank*) broma

capital ['kæpɪtl] *n* (*city*) capital *f*; (*money*) capital *m*; (*also*: **~ letter**) mayúscula; **capitalism** *n* capitalismo; **capitalist** *adj*, *n* capitalista *mf*; **capital punishment** *n* pena de muerte

Capitol ['kæpɪtl] *n* ver recuadro

○ **CAPITOL**
○
○ El Capitolio (**Capitol**) es el edificio
○ del Congreso (**Congress**) de
○ los Estados Unidos, situado en
○ la ciudad de Washington. Por
○ extensión, también se suele llamar
○ así al edificio en el que tienen lugar
○ las sesiones parlamentarias de
○ la cámara de representantes de
○ muchos de los estados.

Capricorn ['kæprɪkɔ:n] *n* Capricornio

capsize [kæp'saɪz] *vt* volcar, hacer zozobrar ▷ *vi* volcarse, zozobrar

capsule ['kæpsju:l] *n* cápsula

captain ['kæptɪn] *n* capitán *m*

caption ['kæpʃən] *n* (*heading*) título; (*to picture*) leyenda

captivity [kæp'tɪvɪtɪ] *n* cautiverio

capture ['kæptʃə*] *vt* prender, apresar; (*animal, Comput*) capturar; (*place*) tomar; (*attention*) captar, llamar ▷ *n* apresamiento; captura; toma; (*data capture*) formulación de datos

car [ka:*] *n* coche *m*, carro (*LAM*), automóvil *m*; (*us Rail*) vagón *m*

carafe [kə'ræf] *n* jarra

caramel ['kærəməl] *n* caramelo

carat ['kærət] *n* quilate *m*

caravan ['kærəvæn] n (BRIT) caravana, rulof; (in desert) caravana; **caravan site** (BRIT) n camping m para caravanas

carbohydrate [kɑ:bəu'haɪdreɪt] n hidrato de carbono; (food) fécula

carbon ['kɑ:bən] n carbono; **carbon dioxide** n dióxido de carbono, anhídrido carbónico; **carbon monoxide** n monóxido de carbono

car boot sale n mercadillo organizado en un aparcamiento, en el que se exponen las mercancías en el maletero del coche

carburettor [kɑ:bju'retə*] (US **carburetor**) n carburador m

card [kɑ:d] n (material) cartulina; (index card etc) ficha; (playing card) carta, naipe m; (visiting card, greetings card etc) tarjeta; **cardboard** n cartón m; **card game** n juego de naipes or cartas

cardigan ['kɑ:dɪɡən] n rebeca

cardinal ['kɑ:dɪnl] adj cardinal; (importance, principal) esencial ▷ n cardenal m

cardphone [kɑ:dfəun] n cabina que funciona con tarjetas telefónicas

care [keə*] n cuidado; (worry) inquietud f; (charge) cargo, custodia ▷ vi: **to ~ about** (person, animal) tener cariño a; (thing, idea) preocuparse por; **~ of** en casa de, al cuidado de; **in sb's ~** a cargo de algn; **to take ~** cuidarse de, tener cuidado de; **to take ~ of** cuidar; (problem etc) ocuparse de; **I don't ~** no me importa; **I couldn't ~ less** eso me trae sin cuidado; **care for** vt fus cuidar a; (like) querer

career [kə'rɪə*] n profesión f; (in work, school) carrera ▷ vi (also: **~ along**) correr a toda velocidad

care: **carefree** adj despreocupado; **careful** adj cuidadoso; (cautious) cauteloso; **(be) careful!** ¡tenga cuidado!; **carefully** adv con cuidado, cuidadosamente; con cautela; **caregiver** (US) n (professional) enfermero/a m/f; (unpaid) persona que

cuida a un pariente o vecino; **careless** adj descuidado; (heedless) poco atento; **carelessness** n descuido, falta de atención; **carer** [kɛərə*] n (professional) enfermero/a m/f; (unpaid) persona que cuida a un pariente o vecino; **caretaker** n portero/a, conserje mf

car-ferry [kɑ:ferɪ] n transbordador m para coches

cargo [kɑ:gəu] (pl **-es**) n cargamento, carga

car hire n alquiler m de automóviles

Caribbean [kærɪ'bi:ən] n: **the ~ (Sea)** el (Mar) Caribe

caring [kɛərɪŋ] adj humanitario; (behaviour) afectuoso

carnation [kɑ:'neɪʃən] n clavel m

carnival [kɑ:nɪvəl] n carnaval m; (US: funfair) parque m de atracciones

carol [kærəl] n: **(Christmas) ~** villancico

carousel [kærə'sel] (US) n tiovivo, caballitos mpl

car park (BRIT) n aparcamiento, parking m

carpenter ['kɑ:pɪntə*] n carpintero/a

carpet [kɑ:pɪt] n alfombra; (fitted) moqueta ▷ vt alfombrar

car rental (US) n alquiler m de coches

carriage [kærɪdʒ] n (BRIT Rail) vagón m; (horse-drawn) coche m; (of goods) transporte m; (: cost) porte m, flete m; **carriageway** (BRIT) n (part of road) calzada

carrier [kæriə*] n (transport company) transportista, empresa de transportes; (Med) portador(a) m/f; **carrier bag** (BRIT) n bolsa de papel o plástico

carrot [kærət] n zanahoria

carry [kærɪ] vt (person) llevar; (transport) transportar; (involve: responsibilities etc) entrañar, implicar; (Med) ser portador de ▷ vi (sound) oírse; **to get carried away** (fig) entusiasmarse; **carry on** vi (continue) seguir (adelante), continuar ▷ vt proseguir, continuar; **carry out** vt (orders) cumplir; (investigation) llevar a cabo, realizar

cart [kɑːt] n carro, carreta ▷ vt (inf: transport) acarrear

carton ['kɑːtən] n (box) caja (de cartón); (of milk etc) bote m; (of yogurt) tarrina

cartoon [kɑː'tuːn] n (Press) caricatura; (comic strip) tira cómica; (film) dibujos mpl animados

cartridge ['kɑːtrɪdʒ] n cartucho; (of pen) recambio

car wash n lavado de coches

carve [kɑːv] vt (meat) trinchar; (wood, stone) cincelar, esculpir; (initials etc) grabar; **carving** n (object) escultura; (design) talla; (art) tallado

car wash n lavado de coches

case [keɪs] n (container) caja; (Med) caso; (for jewels etc) estuche m; (Law) causa, proceso; (BRIT: also: **suit~**) maleta; **in ~ of** en caso de; **in any ~** en todo caso; **just in ~** por si acaso

cash [kæʃ] n dinero en efectivo, dinero contante ▷ vt cobrar, hacer efectivo; **to pay (in) ~** pagar al contado; **~ on delivery** cóbrese al entregar; **cashback** n (discount) devolución f; (at supermarket etc) retirada de dinero en efectivo de un establecimiento donde se ha pagado con tarjeta; también dinero retirado; **cash card** n tarjeta f dinero; **cash desk** (BRIT) n caja; **cash dispenser** n cajero automático

cashew [kæ'ʃuː] n (also: **~ nut**) anacardo

cashier [kæ'ʃɪə*] n cajero/a

cashmere ['kæʃmɪə*] n cachemira

cash point n cajero automático

cash register n caja

casino [kə'siːnəu] n casino

casket ['kɑːskɪt] n cofre m, estuche m; (US: coffin) ataúd m

casserole ['kæsərəul] n (food, pot) cazuela

cassette [kæ'set] n casete f; **cassette player, cassette recorder** n casete m

cast [kɑːst] (pt, pp **~**) vt (throw) echar, arrojar, lanzar; (glance, eyes) dirigir;

(Theatre): **to ~ sb as Othello** dar a algn el papel de Otelo ▷ vi (Fishing) lanzar ▷ n (Theatre) reparto; (also: **plaster ~**) vaciado; **to ~ one's vote** votar; **to ~ doubt on** suscitar dudas acerca de; **cast off** vi (Naut) desamarrar; (Knitting) cerrar (los puntos)

castanets [kæstə'nets] npl castañuelas fpl

caster sugar ['kɑːstə*-] (BRIT) n azúcar m extrafino

Castile [kæs'tiːl] n Castilla; **Castilian** adj, n castellano/a m/f

cast-iron ['kɑːstaɪən] adj (lit) (hecho) de hierro fundido; (fig: case) irrebatible

castle ['kɑːsl] n castillo; (Chess) torre f

casual ['kæʒjul] adj fortuito; (irregular: work etc) eventual, temporero; (unconcerned) despreocupado; (clothes) informal

Be careful not to translate **casual** by the Spanish word casual.

casualty ['kæʒjultɪ] n víctima, herido/a; (dead) muerto/a; (Med: department) urgencias fpl

cat [kæt] n gato; (fig) felino

Catalan ['kætələn] adj, n catalán/ana m/f

catalogue ['kætələg] (US **catalog**) n catálogo ▷ vt catalogar

Catalonia [kætə'ləunɪə] n Cataluña

catalytic converter [kætə'lɪtɪkən'vəːtə*] n catalizador m

cataract ['kætərækt] n (Med) cataratas fpl

catarrh [kə'tɑː*] n catarro

catastrophe [kə'tæstrəfɪ] n catástrofe f

catch [kætʃ] (pt, pp **caught**) vt coger (SP), agarrar (LAM); (arrest) detener; (grasp) asir; (breath) contener; (surprise: person) sorprender; (attract: attention) captar; (hear) oír; (Med) contagiarse de, coger; **catch up** vi alcanzar ▷ vi (fire) encenderse; (in branches etc) enredarse ▷ n (fish etc) pesca; (act of catching) cogida; (hidden problem) dificultad f; (game)

pilla-pilla; (of lock) pestillo, cerradura;
to ~ fire encenderse; **to ~ sight of**
divisar; **catch up** vi (fig) ponerse al
día; **catching** ['kætʃɪŋ] adj (Med)
contagioso

category ['kætɪgərɪ] n categoría,
clase f

cater ['keɪtə*] vi: **to ~ for** (BRIT)
abastecer a; (needs) atender a;
(Comm: parties etc) proveer comida a

caterpillar ['kætəpɪlə*] n oruga,
gusano

cathedral [kə'θi:drəl] n catedral f

Catholic ['kæθəlɪk] adj, n (Rel)
católico/a m/f

Catseye® ['kæts'aɪ] (BRIT) n (Aut)
catafoto

cattle ['kætl] npl ganado

catwalk ['kætwɔːk] n pasarela

caught [kɔːt] pt, pp of **catch**

cauliflower ['kɒlɪflauə*] n coliflor f

cause [kɔːz] n causa, motivo, razón f;
(principle: also Pol) causa ▷ vt causar

caution ['kɔːʃən] n cautela,
prudencia; (warning) advertencia,
amonestación f ▷ vt amonestar;
cautious ['kɔːʃəs] adj cauteloso, prudente,
precavido

cave [keɪv] n cueva, caverna; **cave in**
vi (roof etc) derrumbarse, hundirse

caviar(e) ['kævɪɑː*] n caviar m

cavity ['kævɪtɪ] n hueco, cavidad f

cc abbr = **cubic centimetres**; c.c.; (= carbon
copy) copia hecha con papel del carbón

CCTV n abbr (= closed-circuit television)
circuito cerrado de televisión

CD n abbr (= compact disc) CD m; (player)
(reproductor m de) CD; **CD player** n
reproductor m de CD; **CD-ROM**
[siːdiː'rɒm] n abbr CD-ROM m; **CD**
writer n grabadora de CD

cease [siːs] vt, vi cesar; **ceasefire** n
alto m el fuego

cedar ['siːdə*] n cedro

ceilidh ['keɪlɪ] n baile con música y
danzas tradicionales escocesas o irlandesas

ceiling ['siːlɪŋ] n techo; (fig) límite m

celebrate ['selɪbreɪt] vt celebrar ▷ vi

divertirse; **celebration** [-'breɪʃən] n
fiesta, celebración f

celebrity [sɪ'lebrɪtɪ] n celebridad f

celery ['selərɪ] n apio

cell [sel] n celda; (Biol) célula; (Elec)
elemento

cellar ['selə*] n sótano; (for wine)
bodega

cello ['tʃeləu] n violoncelo

Cellophane® ['seləfeɪn] n celofán m

cellphone ['selfəun] n teléfono
celular

Celsius ['selsɪəs] adj centígrado

Celtic ['keltɪk] adj celta

cement [sə'ment] n cemento

cemetery ['semɪtrɪ] n cementerio

censor ['sensə*] n censor m ▷ vt (cut)
censurar; **censorship** n censura

census ['sensəs] n censo

cent [sent] n (unit of dollar) centavo,
céntimo; (unit of euro) céntimo; see
also **per**

centenary [sen'tiːnərɪ] n centenario

centennial [sen'tenɪəl] (US) n
centenario

center ['sentə*] (US) = **centre**

centi... ['sentɪ] prefix: **centigrade**
adj centígrado; **centimetre** (US
centimeter) n centímetro f; **centipede**
['sentɪpiːd] n ciempiés m inv

central ['sentrəl] adj central; (of
house etc) céntrico; **Central America**
n Centroamérica; **central heating**
n calefacción f central; **central**
reservation n (BRIT Aut) mediana

centre ['sentə*] (US **center**) n centro;
(fig) núcleo ▷ vt centrar; **centre-**
forward n (Sport) delantero centro;
centre-half n (Sport) medio centro

century ['sentjurɪ] n siglo; **20th ~**
siglo veinte

CEO n abbr = **chief executive officer**

ceramic [sɪ'ræmɪk] adj cerámico

cereal ['siːrɪəl] n cereal m

ceremony ['serɪmənɪ] n ceremonia;
to stand on ~ hacer ceremonias, estar
de cumplido

certain ['sə:tən] adj seguro;

(person): **a ~ Mr Smith** un tal Sr. Smith; (particular, some) cierto; **for ~ a** ciencia cierta; **certainly** adv (undoubtedly) ciertamente; (of course) desde luego, por supuesto; **certainty** n certeza, certidumbre f, seguridad f; (inevitability) certeza

certificate [sə'tɪfɪkɪt] n certificado

certify ['sɜːtɪfaɪ] vt certificar; (award diploma to) conceder un diploma a; (declare insane) declarar loco

cf. abbr (= compare) cfr

CFC n abbr (= chlorofluorocarbon) CFC m

chain [tʃeɪn] n cadena; f (of mountains) cordillera; (of events) sucesión f ▷ vt (also: ~ **up**) encadenar; **chain-smoke** vi fumar un cigarrillo tras otro

chair [tʃeə*] n silla; (armchair) sillón m, butaca; (of university) cátedra; (of meeting etc) presidencia ▷ vt (meeting) presidir; **chairlift** n telesilla; **chairman** (irreg) n presidente m; **chairperson** n presidente/a m/f; **chairwoman** (irreg) n presidenta

chalet ['ʃæleɪ] n chalet m (de madera)

chalk [tʃɔːk] n (Geo) creta; (for writing) tiza, gis m (MEX); **chalkboard** (US) n pizarrón (LAM), pizarra (SP)

challenge ['tʃælɪndʒ] n desafío, reto ▷ vt desafiar, retar; (statement, right) poner en duda; **to ~ sb to do sth** retar a algn a que haga algo; **challenging** adj (tone) de desafío

chamber ['tʃeɪmbə*] n cámara, sala; (Pol) cámara; (BRIT Law: gen pl) despacho; **~ of commerce** cámara de comercio; **chambermaid** n camarera

champagne [ʃæm'peɪn] n champaña m, champán m

champion ['tʃæmpɪən] n campeón/ona m/f; (of cause) defensor(a) m/f; **championship** n campeonato

chance [tʃɑːns] n (opportunity) ocasión f, oportunidad f; (likelihood) posibilidad f; (risk) riesgo ▷ vt arriesgar, probar ▷ adj fortuito, casual; **to ~ it** arriesgarse, intentarlo; **to take a ~** arriesgarse; **by ~** por casualidad

chancellor ['tʃɑːnsələ*] n canciller m; **Chancellor of the Exchequer** (BRIT) n Ministro de Hacienda

chandelier [ʃændə'lɪə*] n araña (de luces)

change [tʃeɪndʒ] vt cambiar; (replace) reemplazar; (gear, clothes, job) cambiar de; (transform) transformar ▷ vi cambiar(se); (change trains) hacer transbordo; (traffic lights) cambiar de color; (be transformed): **to ~ into** transformarse en ▷ n cambio; (alteration) modificación f; (transformation) transformación f; (of clothes) muda; (coins) suelto, sencillo; (money returned) vuelta; **to ~ gear** (Aut) cambiar de marcha; **to ~ one's mind** cambiar de opinión o idea; **for a ~** para variar; **change over** vi (from sth to sth) cambiar; (players etc) cambiar(se) ▷ vt cambiar; **changeable** adj (weather) cambiable; **change machine** n máquina de cambio; **changing room** (BRIT) n vestuario

channel ['tʃænl] n (TV) canal m; (of river) cauce m; (groove) conducto; (fig: medium) medio ▷ vt (river etc) encauzar; **the (English) C~** el Canal de la Mancha); **the C~ Islands** las Islas Normandas; **Channel Tunnel** n: **the Channel Tunnel** el túnel del Canal de la Mancha, el Eurotúnel

chant [tʃɑːnt] n (of crowd) gritos mpl; (Rel) canto ▷ vt (slogan, word) repetir a gritos

chaos ['keɪɒs] n caos m

chaotic [keɪ'ɒtɪk] adj caótico

chap [tʃæp] (BRIT: inf) n (man) tío, tipo

chapel ['tʃæpəl] n capilla

chapped [tʃæpt] adj agrietado

chapter ['tʃæptə*] n capítulo

character ['kærɪktə*] n carácter m, naturaleza, índole f; (moral strength, personality) carácter; (in novel, film) personaje m; **characteristic** ['rɪstɪk] adj característico ▷ n característica; **characterize** ['kærɪktəraɪz] vt caracterizar

charcoal ['tʃɑːkəʊl] n carbón m vegetal; *(Art)* carboncillo

charge [tʃɑːdʒ] n *(Law)* cargo, acusación f; *(cost)* precio, coste m; *(responsibility)* cargo ▷ vt *(Law)*: **to ~ (with)** acusar (de); *(battery)* cargar; *(price)* pedir; *(customer)* cobrar ▷ vi precipitarse; *(Mil)* cargar, atacar; **charge card** n tarjeta de cuenta; **charger** n *(also: **battery charger**)* cargador m (de baterías)

charismatic [kærɪzˈmætɪk] adj carismático

charity ['tʃærɪtɪ] n caridad f; *(organization)* sociedad f benéfica; *(money, gifts)* limosnas fpl; **charity shop** n *(BRIT)* tienda de artículos de segunda mano que dedica su recaudación a causas benéficas

charm [tʃɑːm] n encanto, atractivo; *(talisman)* hechizo; *(on bracelet)* dije m ▷ vt encantar; **charming** adj encantador(a)

chart [tʃɑːt] n *(diagram)* cuadro; *(graph)* gráfica; *(map)* carta de navegación ▷ vt *(course)* trazar; *(progress)* seguir; **charts** npl *(Top 40)*: **the ~s** los 40 principales *(SP)*

charter ['tʃɑːtə*] vt *(plane)* alquilar; *(ship)* fletar ▷ n *(of university, company)* estatutos mpl; **chartered accountant** *(BRIT)* n contable m/f diplomado/a; **charter flight** n vuelo chárter

chase [tʃeɪs] vt *(pursue)* perseguir; *(also: ~ away)* ahuyentar ▷ n persecución f

chat [tʃæt] vi *(also: **have a ~**)* charlar; *(on Internet)* chatear ▷ n charla; **chat up** vt *(inf: girl)* ligar con, enrollarse con; **chat room** n *(Internet)* chat m, canal m de charla; **chat show** *(BRIT)* n programa m de entrevistas

chatter ['tʃætə*] vi *(person)* charlar; *(teeth)* castañetear ▷ n *(of birds)* parloteo; *(of people)* charla, cháchara

chauffeur ['ʃəʊfə*] n chófer m

chauvinist ['ʃəʊvɪnɪst] n *(male chauvinist)* machista m; *(nationalist)* chovinista mf

cheap [tʃiːp] adj barato; *(joke)* de mal gusto; *(poor quality)* de mala calidad ▷ adv barato; **cheap day return** n billete de ida y vuelta el mismo día; **cheaply** adv barato, a bajo precio

cheat [tʃiːt] vi hacer trampa ▷ vt: **to ~ sb (out of sth)** estafar (algo) a algn ▷ n *(person)* tramposo/a; **cheat on** vt fus engañar

Chechnya ['tʃɪtʃnjɑː] n Chechenia

check [tʃɛk] vt *(examine)* controlar; *(facts)* comprobar; *(halt)* parar, detener; *(restrain)* refrenar, restringir ▷ n *(inspection)* control m, inspección f; *(curb)* freno; *(us: bill)* nota, cuenta; *(us)* = **cheque**; *(pattern: gen pl)* cuadro; **check in** vi *(at hotel)* firmar el registro; *(at airport)* facturar el equipaje ▷ vt *(luggage)* facturar; **check off** vt *(esp us: check)* comprobar; *(cross off)* tachar; **check out** vi *(of hotel)* marcharse; **check up** vi: **to check up on sth** comprobar algo; **to check up on sb** investigar a algn; **checkbook** *(us)* = **chequebook**; **checked** adj a cuadros; **checkers** *(us)* n juego de damas; **check-in** n *(also: **check-in desk**: at airport)* mostrador m de facturación; **checking account** *(us)* n cuenta corriente; **checklist** n lista (de control); **checkmate** n jaque m mate; **checkout** n caja; **checkpoint** n *(punto de)* control m; **checkroom** *(us)* n consigna; **checkup** n *(Med)* reconocimiento general

cheddar ['tʃɛdə*] n *(also: ~ cheese)* queso m cheddar

cheek [tʃiːk] n mejilla; *(impudence)* descaro; **what a ~!** ¡qué cara!; **cheekbone** n pómulo; **cheeky** adj fresco, descarado

cheer [tʃɪə*] vt vitorear, aplaudir; *(gladden)* alegrar, animar ▷ vi dar vivas ▷ n viva m; **cheer up** vi animarse ▷ vt alegrar, animar; **cheerful** adj alegre

cheerio [tʃɪərɪˈəʊ] (BRIT) excl ¡hasta luego!

cheerleader n [tʃiːliːdə*] n animador(a) m/f

cheese [tʃiːz] n queso; **cheeseburger** n hamburguesa con queso; **cheesecake** n pastel m de queso

chef [ʃef] n jefe/a m/f de cocina

chemical [ˈkemɪkəl] adj químico ▷ n producto químico

chemist [ˈkemɪst] n (BRIT: pharmacist) farmacéutico/a; (scientist) químico/a; **chemistry** n química; **chemist's (shop)**(BRIT) n farmacia

cheque [tʃek] (US **check**) n cheque m; **chequebook** n talonario de cheques (SP), chequera (LAM); **cheque card** n tarjeta de cheque

cherry [ˈtʃerɪ] n cereza; (also: ~ **tree**) cerezo

chess [tʃes] n ajedrez m

chest [tʃest] n (Anat) pecho; (box) cofre m, cajón m

chestnut [ˈtʃesnʌt] n castaña; (also: ~ **tree**) castaño

chest of drawers n cómoda

chew [tʃuː] vt mascar, masticar; **chewing gum** n chicle m

chic [ʃiːk] adj elegante

chick [tʃɪk] n pollito, polluelo*; (inf: girl) chica

chicken [ˈtʃɪkɪn] n gallina, pollo; (food) pollo; (inf: coward) gallina mf; **chicken out**(inf) vi rajarse; **chickenpox** n varicela

chickpea [ˈtʃɪkpiː] n garbanzo

chief [tʃiːf] n jefe/a m/f ▷ adj principal; **chief executive** (officer) n director(a) m/f general; **chiefly** adv principalmente

child [tʃaɪld] (pl **~ren**) n niño/a; (offspring) hijo/a m/f; **child abuse** n (with violence) malos tratos mpl a niños; (sexual) abuso m sexual de niños; **child benefit** n (BRIT) subsidio por cada hijo pequeño; **childbirth** n parto; **child-care** n cuidado de los niños; **childhood** n niñez f, infancia; **childish**

adj pueril, aniñado; **child minder** (BRIT) n madre f de día; **children** [ˈtʃɪldrən] npl of **child**

Chile [ˈtʃɪlɪ] n Chile m; **Chilean** adj, n chileno/a m/f

chill [tʃɪl] n frío; (Med) resfriado ▷ vt enfriar; (Culin) congelar; **chill out** vi (esp us: inf) tranquilizarse

chil(l)i [ˈtʃɪlɪ] (BRIT) n chile m, ají m (SC)

chilly [ˈtʃɪlɪ] adj frío

chimney [ˈtʃɪmnɪ] n chimenea

chimpanzee [tʃɪmpænˈziː] n chimpancé m

chin [tʃɪn] n mentón m, barbilla

China [ˈtʃaɪnə] n China

china [ˈtʃaɪnə] n porcelana; (crockery) loza

Chinese [tʃaɪˈniːz] adj chino ▷ n inv chino/a m/f; (Ling) chino

chip [tʃɪp] n (gen pl: Culin: BRIT) patata (SP) or papa (LAM) frita; (: US: also: **potato ~**) patata or papa frita; (of wood) astilla; (of glass, stone) lasca; (at poker) ficha; (Comput) chip m ▷ vt (cup, plate) desconchar; **chip shop** n pescadería (donde se vende principalmente pescado rebozado y patatas fritas)

chiropodist [kɪˈrɔpədɪst](BRIT) n pedicuro/a, callista m/f

chisel [ˈtʃɪzl] n (for wood) escoplo; (for stone) cincel m

chives [tʃaɪvz] npl cebollinos mpl

chlorine [ˈklɔːriːn] n cloro

choc-ice [ˈtʃɒkaɪs] n (BRIT) helado m cubierto de chocolate

chocolate [ˈtʃɒklɪt] n chocolate m; (sweet) bombón m

choice [tʃɔɪs] n elección f, selección f; (option) opción f; (preference) preferencia ▷ adj escogido

choir [ˈkwaɪə*] n coro

choke [tʃəʊk] vi ahogarse; (on food) atragantarse ▷ vt estrangular, ahogar; (block): **to be ~d with** estar atascado de ▷ n (Aut) estárter m

cholesterol [kəˈlestərɒl] n colesterol m

choose [tʃuːz] (pt **chose**, pp **chosen**)

vt escoger, elegir; (*team*) seleccionar;
to ~ to do sth optar por hacer algo

chop [tʃɔp] vt (*wood*) cortar, tajar;
(*Culin: also:* **~ up**) picar ▷ n (*Culin*)
chuleta; **chop down** vt (*tree*) talar;
chop off vt cortar (de un tajo);
chopsticks ['tʃɔpstiks] npl palillos
mpl

chord [kɔːd] n (*Mus*) acorde m

chore [tʃɔː*] n faena, tarea; (*routine
task*) trabajo rutinario

chorus ['kɔːrəs] n coro; (*repeated part
of song*) estribillo

chose [tʃəuz] pt of **choose**

chosen ['tʃəuzn] pp of **choose**

Christ [kraist] n Cristo

christen ['krisn] vt bautizar;
christening n bautizo

Christian ['kristiən] adj, n
cristiano/a m/f; **Christianity** [-'æniti]
n cristianismo; **Christian name** n
nombre m de pila

Christmas ['krisməs] n Navidad f;
Merry ~! ¡Felices Pascuas!; **Christmas
card** n crismas m inv, tarjeta de
Navidad; **Christmas carol** n villancico
m; **Christmas Day** n día m de Navidad;
Christmas Eve n Nochebuena;
Christmas pudding n (*esp BRIT*) pudin
m de Navidad; **Christmas tree** n árbol
m de Navidad

chrome [krəum] n cromo

chronic ['krɔnik] adj crónico

chrysanthemum [kri'sænθəməm]
n crisantemo

chubby ['tʃʌbi] adj regordete

chuck [tʃʌk] (*inf*) vt lanzar, arrojar;
(*BRIT: also:* **~ up**) abandonar; **chuck
out** vt (*person*) echar (fuera); (*rubbish
etc*) tirar

chuckle ['tʃʌkl] vi reírse entre dientes

chum [tʃʌm] n compañero/a

chunk [tʃʌŋk] n pedazo, trozo

church [tʃəːtʃ] n iglesia; **churchyard**
n cementerio

churn [tʃəːn] n (*for butter*)
mantequera; (*for milk*) lechera

chute [ʃuːt] n (*also:* **rubbish ~**)

vertedero; (*for coal etc*) rampa de caída

chutney ['tʃʌtni] n condimento a base
de frutas de la India

CIA (*us*) n abbr (= *Central Intelligence
Agency*) CIA f

CID (*BRIT*) n abbr (= *Criminal
Investigation Department*) ≈ B.I.C. f (*SP*)

cider ['saidə*] n sidra

cigar [si'gaː*] n puro

cigarette [sigə'rɛt] n cigarrillo;
cigarette lighter n mechero

cinema ['sinəmə] n cine m

cinnamon ['sinəmən] n canela

circle ['səːkl] n círculo; (*in theatre*)
anfiteatro ▷ vi dar vueltas ▷ vt
(*surround*) rodear, cercar; (*move round*)
dar la vuelta a

circuit ['səːkit] n circuito; (*tour*) gira;
(*track*) pista; (*lap*) vuelta

circular ['səːkjulə*] adj circular ▷ n
circular f

circulate ['səːkjuleit] vi circular;
(*person: at party etc*) hablar con los
invitados ▷ vt poner en circulación;
circulation [-'leiʃən] n circulación f;
(*of newspaper*) tirada

circumstances ['səːkəmstənsiz] npl
circunstancias fpl; (*financial condition*)
situación económica

circus ['səːkəs] n circo

cite [sait] vt citar

citizen ['sitizn] n (*Pol*) ciudadano/a;
(*of city*) vecino/a, habitante mf;
citizenship n ciudadanía f; (*BRIT: Scol*)
civismo

citrus fruits ['sitrəs-] npl agrios mpl

city ['siti] n ciudad f; **the C~** centro
financiero de Londres; **city centre** (*BRIT*)
n centro de la ciudad; **city technology
college** n centro de formación
profesional (*centro de enseñanza
secundaria que da especial importancia a la
ciencia y tecnología*.)

civic ['sivik] adj cívico; (*authorities*)
municipal

civil ['sivil] adj civil; (*polite*) atento,
cortés; **civilian** [si'viliən] adj civil (no
militar) ▷ n civil mf, paisano/a

civilization [sɪvɪlaɪˈzeɪʃən] n civilización f

civilized [ˈsɪvɪlaɪzd] adj civilizado

civil: civil law n derecho civil; **civil rights** npl derechos mpl civiles; **civil servant** n funcionario/a del Estado; **Civil Service** n administración f pública; **civil war** n guerra civil

CJD n abbr (= Creutzfeldt-Jakob disease) enfermedad de Creutzfeldt-Jakob

claim [kleɪm] vt exigir, reclamar; (rights etc) reivindicar; (assert) pretender ▷ vi (for insurance) reclamar ▷ n reclamación f; pretensión f; **claim form** n solicitud f

clam [klæm] n almeja

clamp [klæmp] n abrazadera, grapa ▷ vt (two things together) cerrar fuertemente; (one thing on another) afianzar (con abrazadera); (Aut: wheel) poner el cepo a

clan [klæn] n clan m

clap [klæp] vi aplaudir

claret [ˈklærət] n burdeos m inv

clarify [ˈklærɪfaɪ] vt aclarar

clarinet [klærɪˈnɛt] n clarinete m

clarity [ˈklærɪtɪ] n claridad f

clash [klæʃ] n enfrentamiento; choque m; desacuerdo; estruendo ▷ vi (fight) enfrentarse; (beliefs) chocar; (disagree) estar en desacuerdo; (colours) desentonar; (two events) coincidir

clasp [klɑːsp] n (hold) apretón m; (of necklace, bag) cierre m ▷ vt apretar; abrazar

class [klɑːs] n clase f ▷ vt clasificar

classic [ˈklæsɪk] adj, n clásico; **classical** adj clásico

classification [klæsɪfɪˈkeɪʃən] n clasificación f

classify [ˈklæsɪfaɪ] vt clasificar

classmate [ˈklɑːsmeɪt] n compañero/a de clase

classroom [ˈklɑːsrum] n aula; **classroom assistant** n profesor(a) m/f de apoyo

classy [ˈklɑːsɪ] adj (inf) elegante, con estilo

clatter [ˈklætə*] n estrépito ▷ vi hacer ruido or estrépito

clause [klɔːz] n cláusula; (Ling) oración f

claustrophobic [klɔːstrəˈfəubɪk] adj claustrofóbico; **I feel ~** me entra claustrofobia

claw [klɔː] n (of cat) uña; (of bird of prey) garra; (of lobster) pinza

clay [kleɪ] n arcilla

clean [kliːn] adj limpio; (record, reputation) bueno, intachable; (joke) decente ▷ vt limpiar; (hands etc) lavar; **clean up** vt limpiar, asear; **cleaner** n (person) asistenta; (substance) producto para la limpieza; **cleaner's** n tintorería; **cleaning** n limpieza

cleanser [ˈklɛnzə*] n (for face) crema limpiadora

clear [klɪə*] adj claro; (road, way) libre; (conscience) limpio, tranquilo; (skin) terso; (sky) despejado ▷ vt (space) despejar, limpiar; (Law: suspect) absolver; (obstacle) salvar, saltar por encima de; (cheque) aceptar ▷ vi (sky etc) despejarse ▷ adv: **~ of** a distancia de; **to ~ the table** recoger or levantar la mesa; **clear away** vt (things, clothes etc) quitar (de en medio); (dishes) retirar; **clear up** vt limpiar; (mystery) aclarar, resolver; **clearance** n (removal) despeje m; (permission) acreditación f; **clear-cut** adj bien definido, nítido; **clearing** n (in wood) claro; **clearly** adv claramente; (evidently) sin duda; **clearway** (BRIT) n carretera donde no se puede parar

clench [klɛntʃ] vt apretar, cerrar

clergy [ˈklɜːdʒɪ] n clero

clerk [klɑːk, (US) klɜːk] n (BRIT) oficinista mf; (US) dependiente/a m/f

clever [ˈklɛvə*] adj (intelligent) inteligente, listo; (skilful) hábil; (device, arrangement) ingenioso

cliché [ˈkliːʃeɪ] n cliché m, frase f hecha

click [klɪk] vt (tongue) chasquear; (heels) taconear ▷ vi (Comput) hacer clic; **to ~ on an icon** hacer clic en un icono

client ['klaɪənt] n cliente m/f

cliff [klɪf] n acantilado

climate ['klaɪmɪt] n clima m; **climate change** n cambio climático

climax ['klaɪmæks] n (of battle, career) apogeo; (of film, book) punto culminante; (sexual) orgasmo

climb [klaɪm] vi subir; (plant) trepar; (move with effort): **to ~ over a wall/into a car** trepar a una tapia/subir a un coche ▷ vt (stairs) subir; (tree) trepar a; (mountain) escalar ▷ n subida; **climb down** vi (fig) volverse atrás; **climber** n alpinista mf (SP, MEX), andinista mf (LAM); **climbing** n alpinismo (SP, MEX), andinismo (LAM)

clinch [klɪntʃ] vt (deal) cerrar; (argument) remachar

cling [klɪŋ] (pt, pp **clung**) vi: **to ~** agarrarse a; (clothes) pegarse a

Clingfilm® ['klɪŋfɪlm] n plástico adherente

clinic ['klɪnɪk] n clínica

clip [klɪp] n (for hair) horquilla; (also: **paper ~**) sujetapapeles m inv, clip m; (TV, Cinema) fragmento ▷ vt (cut) cortar; (also: **~ together**) unir; **clipping** n (newspaper) recorte m

cloak [kləʊk] n capa, manto ▷ vt (fig) encubrir, disimular; **cloakroom** n guardarropa; (BRIT: WC) lavabo (SP), aseos mpl (SP), baño (LAM)

clock [klɒk] n reloj m; **clock in** or **on** vi (with card) fichar, picar; (start work) entrar a trabajar; **clock off** or **out** vi (with card) fichar or picar la salida; (leave work) salir del trabajar; **clockwise** adv en el sentido de las agujas del reloj; **clockwork** n aparato de relojería ▷ adj (toy) de cuerda

clog [klɒg] n zueco, chanclo ▷ vt atascar ▷ vi (also: **~ up**) atascarse

clone [kləʊn] n clon m ▷ vt clonar

close¹ [kləʊs] adj (near): **~ (to)** cerca (de); (friend) íntimo; (connection) estrecho; (examination) detallado,

minucioso; (weather) bochornoso ▷ adv cerca; **~ by, ~ at hand** aquí cerca; **to have a ~ shave** (fig) escaparse por un pelo

close² [kləʊz] vt (shut) cerrar; (end) concluir, terminar ▷ vi (shop etc) cerrarse; (end) concluirse, terminarse ▷ n (end) fin m, final m, conclusión f; **close down** vi cerrarse definitivamente; **closed** adj (shop etc) cerrado

closely ['kləʊslɪ] adv (study) con detalle; (watch) de cerca; (resemble) estrechamente

closet ['klɒzɪt] n armario

close-up ['kləʊsʌp] n primer plano

closing time n hora de cierre

closure ['kləʊʒə*] n cierre m

clot [klɒt] n (gen) coágulo; (inf: idiot) imbécil m/f ▷ vi (blood) coagularse

cloth [klɒθ] n (material) tela, paño; (rag) trapo

clothes [kləʊðz] npl ropa; **clothes line** n cuerda (para tender la ropa); **clothes peg** (us **clothes pin**) n pinza

clothing ['kləʊðɪŋ] n = **clothes**

cloud [klaʊd] n nube f; **cloud over** vi (also fig) nublarse; **cloudy** adj nublado, nuboso; (liquid) turbio

clove [kləʊv] n clavo; **~ of garlic** diente m de ajo

clown [klaʊn] n payaso ▷ vi (also: **~ about, ~ around**) hacer el payaso

club [klʌb] n (society) club m; (weapon) porra, cachiporra; (also: **golf ~**) palo ▷ vt aporrear ▷ vi: **to ~ together** (for gift) comprar entre todos; **clubs** npl (Cards) tréboles mpl; **club class** n (Aviat) clase f preferente

clue [klu:] n pista; (in crosswords) indicación f; **I haven't a ~** no tengo ni idea

clump [klʌmp] n (of trees) grupo

clumsy ['klʌmzɪ] adj (person) torpe, desmañado; (tool) difícil de manejar; (movement) desgarbado

clung [klʌŋ] pt, pp of **cling**

cluster ['klʌstə*] n grupo ▷ vi

agruparse, apiñarse

clutch [klʌtʃ] *n* (Aut) embrague *m*; (grasp): **-es** garras *fpl* ▷ *vt* asir; agarrar

cm *abbr* (= centimetre) cm

Co. *abbr* = **county; company**

c/o *abbr* (= care of) c/a, a/c

coach [kəʊtʃ] *n* autocar *m* (SP), coche *m* de línea; (horse-drawn) coche *m*; (of train) vagón *m*, coche *m*; (Sport) entrenador/a *m/f*, instructor/a *m/f*; (tutor) profesor/a *m/f* particular ▷ *vt* (Sport) entrenar; (student) preparar, enseñar; **coach station** *n* estación *f* de autobuses *etc*; **coach trip** *n* excursión *f* en autocar

coal [kəʊl] *n* carbón *m*

coalition [kəʊəˈlɪʃən] *n* coalición *f*

coarse [kɔːs] *adj* basto, burdo; (vulgar) grosero, ordinario

coast [kəʊst] *n* costa, litoral *m* ▷ *vi* (Aut) ir en punto muerto; **coastal** *adj* costero, costanero; **coastguard** *n* guardacostas *m inv*; **coastline** *n* litoral *m*

coat [kəʊt] *n* abrigo; (of animal) pelaje *m*, lana; (of paint) mano *f*, capa ▷ *vt* cubrir, revestir; **coat hanger** *n* percha (SP), gancho (LAM); **coating** *n* capa, baño

coax [kəʊks] *vt* engatusar

cob [kɒb] *n see* **corn**

cobbled [ˈkɒbld] *adj*: **~ street** calle *f* empedrada, calle adoquinada

cobweb [ˈkɒbwɛb] *n* telaraña

cocaine [kəˈkeɪn] *n* cocaína

cock [kɒk] *n* (rooster) gallo; (male bird) macho *m*; (gun) amartillar; **cockerel** *n* gallito

cockney [ˈkɒknɪ] *n* habitante *m* de ciertos barrios de Londres

cockpit [ˈkɒkpɪt] *n* cabina

cockroach [ˈkɒkrəʊtʃ] *n* cucaracha

cocktail [ˈkɒkteɪl] *n* coctel *m*, cóctel *m*

cocoa [ˈkəʊkəʊ] *n* cacao; (drink) chocolate *m*

coconut [ˈkəʊkənʌt] *n* coco

cod [kɒd] *n* bacalao

C.O.D. *abbr* (= cash on delivery) C.A.E.

code [kəʊd] *n* código; (cipher) clave *f*; (dialling code) prefijo; (post code) código postal

coeducational [kəʊɛdjuˈkeɪʃənl] *adj* mixto

coffee [ˈkɒfɪ] *n* café *m*; **coffee bar** (BRIT) *n* cafetería; **coffee bean** *n* grano de café; **coffee break** *n* descanso (para tomar café); **coffee maker** *n* máquina de hacer café, cafetera; **coffeepot** *n* cafetera; **coffee shop** *n* café *m*; **coffee table** *n* mesita (para servir el café)

coffin [ˈkɒfɪn] *n* ataúd *m*

cog [kɒg] *n* (wheel) rueda dentada; (tooth) diente *m*

cognac [ˈkɒnjæk] *n* coñac *m*

coherent [kəʊˈhɪərənt] *adj* coherente

coil [kɔɪl] *n* rollo; (Elec) bobina, carrete *m*; (contraceptive) espiral *f* ▷ *vt* enrollar

coin [kɔɪn] *n* moneda ▷ *vt* (word) inventar, idear

coincide [kəʊɪnˈsaɪd] *vi* coincidir; (agree) estar de acuerdo; **coincidence** [kəʊˈɪnsɪdəns] *n* casualidad *f*

Coke® [kəʊk] *n* Coca-Cola®

coke [kəʊk] *n* (coal) coque *m*

colander [ˈkɒləndə*] *n* colador *m*, escurridor *m*

cold [kəʊld] *adj* frío ▷ *n* frío; (Med) resfriado; **it's ~** hace frío; **to be ~** (person) tener frío; **to catch (a) ~** resfriarse; **in ~ blood** a sangre fría; **cold sore** *n* herpes *mpl or fpl*

coleslaw [ˈkəʊlslɔː] *n* especie de ensalada de col

colic [ˈkɒlɪk] *n* cólico

collaborate [kəˈlæbəreɪt] *vi* colaborar

collapse [kəˈlæps] *vi* hundirse, derrumbarse; (Med) sufrir un colapso ▷ *n* hundimiento, derrumbamiento; (Med) colapso

collar [ˈkɒlə*] *n* (of coat, shirt) cuello; (of dog etc) collar; **collarbone** *n* clavícula

colleague [ˈkɔliːg] n colega mf; (at work) compañero/a

collect [kəˈlekt] vt (litter, mail etc) recoger; (as a hobby) coleccionar; (BRIT: call and pick up) recoger; (debts, subscriptions etc) recaudar ▷ vi reunirse; (dust) acumularse; **to call ~** (US Tel) llamar a cobro revertido;

collection [kəˈlekʃən] n colección f; (of mail, for charity) recogida f

collective [kəˈlektɪv] adj colectivo; **collector** n coleccionista mf

college [ˈkɔlɪdʒ] n colegio mayor; (of agriculture, technology) escuela universitaria

collide [kəˈlaɪd] vi chocar

collision [kəˈlɪʒən] n choque m

cologne [kəˈləun] n (also: **eau de ~**) (agua de) colonia

Colombia [kəˈlɔmbɪə] n Colombia; **Colombian** adj, n colombiano/a

colon [ˈkəulən] n (sign) dos puntos; (Med) colon m

colonel [ˈkəːnl] n coronel m

colonial [kəˈləunɪəl] adj colonial

colony [ˈkɔlənɪ] n colonia

colour etc [ˈkʌlə*] (US **color** etc) n color m ▷ vt color(e)ar; (dye) teñir; (fig: account) adornar; (: judgement) distorsionar ▷ vi (blush) sonrojarse; **colour in** vt colorear; **colour-blind** adj daltónico; **coloured** adj de color; (photo) en color; **colour film** n película en color; **colourful** adj lleno de color; (story) fantástico; (person) excéntrico; **colouring** n (complexion) tez f; (in food) colorante m; **colour television** n televisión f en color

column [ˈkɔləm] n columna

coma [ˈkəumə] n coma m

comb [kəum] n peine m; (ornamental) peineta ▷ vt (hair) peinar; (area) registrar a fondo

combat [ˈkɔmbæt] n combate m ▷ vt combatir

combination [kɔmbɪˈneɪʃən] n combinación f

combine [vb kəmˈbaɪn, n ˈkɔmbaɪn]

vt combinar; (qualities) reunir ▷ vi combinarse ▷ n (Econ) cartel m

○ KEYWORD

come [kʌm] (pt **came**, pp **come**) vi
1 (movement towards) venir; **to come running** venir corriendo
2 (arrive) llegar; **he's come here to work** ha venido aquí para trabajar; **to come home** volver a casa
3 (reach): **to come to** llegar a; **the bill came to £40** la cuenta ascendía a cuarenta libras
4 (occur): **an idea came to me** se me ocurrió una idea
5 (be, become): **to come loose/undone** etc aflojarse/desabrocharse/desatarse etc; **I've come to like him** por fin ha llegado a gustarme

come across vt fus (person) topar con; (thing) dar con

come along vi (BRIT: progress) ir

come back vi (return) volver

come down vi (price) bajar; (tree, building) ser derribado

come from vt fus (place, source) ser de

come in vi (visitor) entrar; (train, report) llegar; (fashion) ponerse de moda; (on deal etc) entrar

come off vi (button) soltarse, desprenderse; (attempt) salir bien

come on vi (pupil) progresar; (work, project) desarrollarse; (lights) encenderse; (electricity) volver; **come on!** ¡vamos!

come out vi (fact) salir a la luz; (book, sun) salir; (stain) quitarse

come round vi (after faint, operation) volver en sí

come to vi (wake) volver en sí

come up vi (sun) salir; (problem) surgir; (event) aproximarse; (in conversation) mencionarse

come up with vt fus (idea) sugerir; (money) conseguir

comeback [ˈkʌmbæk] n: **to make a ~**

(Theatre) volver a las tablas

comedian [kə'miːdɪən] n humorista mf

comedy ['kɒmɪdɪ] n comedia; (humour) comicidad f

comet ['kɒmɪt] n cometa m

comfort ['kʌmfət] n bienestar m; (relief) alivio m; vt consolar; **comfortable** adj cómodo; (financially) acomodado; (easy) fácil; **comfort station** (us) n servicios mpl

comic ['kɒmɪk] adj (also: **~al**) cómico ▷ n (comedian) cómico; (BRIT: for children) tebeo m; (BRIT: for adults) comic m; **comic book** n libro m de cómics; **comic strip** n tira cómica

comma ['kɒmə] n coma

command [kə'mɑːnd] n orden f, mandato; (Mil: authority) mando; (mastery) dominio ▷ vt (troops) mandar; (give orders to): **to ~ sb to do** mandar or ordenar a algn hacer; **commander** n (Mil) comandante mf, jefe/a m/f

commemorate [kə'meməreɪt] vt conmemorar

commence [kə'mens] vt, vi comenzar, empezar; **commencement** (us) n (Univ) (ceremonia de) graduación f

commend [kə'mend] vt elogiar, alabar; (recommend) recomendar

comment ['kɒment] n comentario ▷ vi: **to ~ on** hacer comentarios sobre; **"no ~"** (written) "sin comentarios"; (spoken) "no tengo nada que decir"; **commentary** ['kɒməntərɪ] n comentario; **commentator** ['kɒmənteɪtə*] n comentarista mf

commerce ['kɒməːs] n comercio

commercial [kə'məːʃəl] adj comercial ▷ n (TV, Radio) anuncio; **commercial break** n intermedio para publicidad

commission [kə'mɪʃən] n (committee, fee) comisión f ▷ vt (work of art) encargar; **out of ~** fuera de servicio; **commissioner** n (Police)

comisario de policía

commit [kə'mɪt] vt (act) cometer; (resources) dedicar; (to sb's care) entregar; **to ~** (to do) comprometerse (a hacer); **to ~ suicide** suicidarse; **commitment** n compromiso; (to ideology etc) entrega

committee [kə'mɪtɪ] n comité m

commodity [kə'mɒdɪtɪ] n mercancía

common ['kɒmən] adj común; (pej) ordinario ▷ n campo común; **commonly** adv comúnmente; **commonplace** adj de lo más común; **Commons** (BRIT) npl (Pol): **the Commons** (la Cámara de) los Comunes; **common sense** n sentido común; **Commonwealth** n: **the Commonwealth** la Commonwealth

communal [kə'mjuːnl] adj (property) comunal; (kitchen) común

commune n ['kɒmjuːn] (group) comuna f ▷ vi [kə'mjuːn]: **to ~ with** comulgar or conversar con

communicate [kə'mjuːnɪkeɪt] vt comunicar ▷ vi: **to ~ (with)** comunicarse (con); (in writing) estar en contacto (con)

communication [kəmjuːnɪ'keɪʃən] n comunicación f

communion [kə'mjuːnɪən] n (also: **Holy ~**) comunión f

communism ['kɒmjunɪzəm] n comunismo; **communist** adj, n comunista mf

community [kə'mjuːnɪtɪ] n comunidad f; (large group) colectividad f; **community centre** (us **community center**) n centro social; **community service** n trabajo m comunitario (prestado en lugar de cumplir una pena de prisión)

commute [kə'mjuːt] vi viajar a diario de la casa al trabajo ▷ vt conmutar; **commuter** n persona que viaja a diario de la casa al trabajo

compact [adj kəm'pækt, n 'kɒmpækt] adj compacto ▷ n (also: **powder ~**)

polvera; **compact disc** n compact
disc m; **compact disc player** n
reproductor m de disco compacto,
compact disc m

companion [kəmˈpænɪən] n
compañero/a

company [ˈkʌmpənɪ] n compañía;
(Comm) sociedad f, compañía; **to keep
sb ~** acompañar a algn; **company car**
n coche m de la empresa; **company
director** n director/a m/f de empresa

comparable [ˈkɒmpərəbl] adj
comparable

comparative [kəmˈpærətɪv]
adj relativo; (study) comparativo;
comparatively adv (relatively)
relativamente

compare [kəmˈpɛə*] vt: **to ~ sth/sb
with** or **to** comparar algo/a algn
con ▷ vi: **to ~ (with)** compararse
(con); **comparison** [-ˈpærɪsn] n
comparación f

compartment [kəmˈpɑːtmənt] n
(also: Rail) compartim(i)ento

compass [ˈkʌmpəs] n brújula;
compasses npl (Math) compás m

compassion [kəmˈpæʃən] n
compasión f

compatible [kəmˈpætɪbl] adj
compatible

compel [kəmˈpɛl] vt obligar;
compelling adj (fig: argument)
convincente

compensate [ˈkɒmpənseɪt] vt
compensar ▷ vi: **to ~ for** compensar;
compensation [-ˈseɪʃən] n (for loss)
indemnización f

compete [kəmˈpiːt] vi (take part)
tomar parte, concurrir; (vie with): **to ~
with** competir con, hacer competencia
a

competent [ˈkɒmpɪtənt] adj
competente, capaz

competition [kɒmpɪˈtɪʃ
n] n (contest) concurso; (rivalry)
competencia

competitive [kəmˈpetɪtɪv] adj (Econ,
Sport) competitivo

competitor [kəmˈpetɪtə*] n (rival)
competidor(a) m/f; (participant)
concursante mf

complacent [kəmˈpleɪsnt] adj
autocomplaciente

complain [kəmˈpleɪn] vi quejarse;
(Comm) reclamar; **complaint** n queja;
reclamación f; (Med) enfermedad f

complement [n ˈkɒmplɪmənt,
vb ˈkɒmplɪment] n complemento;
(esp of ship's crew) dotación
f ▷ vt (enhance) complementar;
complementary [kɒmplɪˈmentərɪ]
adj complementario

complete [kəmˈpliːt] adj (full)
completo; (finished) acabado ▷ vt
(fulfil) completar; (finish) acabar;
(a form) llenar; **completely** adv
completamente; **completion**
[-ˈpliːʃən] n terminación f; (of contract)
realización f

complex [ˈkɒmpleks] adj, n complejo

complexion [kəmˈplekʃən] n (of
face) tez f, cutis m

compliance [kəmˈplaɪəns] n
(submission) sumisión f; (agreement)
conformidad f; **in ~ with** de acuerdo
con

complicate [ˈkɒmplɪkeɪt] vt
complicar; **complicated** adj
complicado; **complication** [-ˈkeɪʃən]
n complicación f

compliment [ˈkɒmplɪmənt] n
(formal) cumplido ▷ vt felicitar;
complimentary [-ˈmentərɪ] adj
lisonjero; (free) de favor

comply [kəmˈplaɪ] vi: **to ~ with**
cumplir con

component [kəmˈpəunənt] adj
componente ▷ n (Tech) pieza

compose [kəmˈpəuz] vt: **to be ~d of**
componerse de; (music etc) componer;
to ~ o.s. tranquilizarse; **composer** n
(Mus) compositor(a) m/f; **composition**
[kɒmpəˈzɪʃən] n composición f

composure [kəmˈpəuʒə*] n
serenidad f, calma

compound [ˈkɒmpaund] n (Chem)

compuesto; (Ling) palabra compuesta;
(enclosure) recinto ▷ adj compuesto;
(fracture) complicado

comprehension [-'henʃən] n
comprensión f

comprehensive [kɒmprɪ'hensɪv]
adj exhaustivo; (Insurance) contra todo
riesgo; **comprehensive (school)** n
centro estatal de enseñanza secundaria ≈
Instituto Nacional de Bachillerato (SP)

compress [vb kəm'pres, n 'kɒmpres]
vt comprimir; (information) condensar
▷ n (Med) compresa

comprise [kəm'praɪz] vt (also: **be ~d
of**) comprender, constar de; (constitute)
constituir

compromise ['kɒmprəmaɪz] n
(agreement) arreglo ▷ vt comprometer
▷ vi transigir

compulsive [kəm'pʌlsɪv] adj
compulsivo; (viewing, reading) obligado

compulsory [kəm'pʌlsərɪ] adj
obligatorio

computer [kəm'pjuːtə*] n
ordenador m, computador m,
computadora f; **computer game** n
juego para ordenador; **computer-
generated** adj realizado por
ordenador, creado por ordenador;
computerize vt (data) computerizar;
(system) informatizar; **we're
computerized now** ya nos los
hemos informatizado; **computer
programmer** n programador(a)
m/f; **computer programming** n
programación f; **computer science** n
informática; **computer studies** npl
informática fsg, computación fsg (LAM)

computing [kəm'pjuːtɪŋ] n (activity,
science) informática

con [kɒn] vt (deceive) engañar; (cheat)
estafar ▷ n estafa

conceal [kən'siːl] vt ocultar

concede [kən'siːd] vt (point,
argument) reconocer; (territory) ceder;
to ~ (defeat) darse por vencido; **to ~
that** admitir que

conceited [kən'siːtɪd] adj presumido

conceive [kən'siːv] vt, vi concebir

concentrate ['kɒnsəntreɪt] vi
concentrarse ▷ vt concentrar

concentration [kɒnsən'treɪʃən] n
concentración f

concept ['kɒnsept] n concepto

concern [kən'səːn] n (matter)
asunto; (Comm) empresa; (anxiety)
preocupación f ▷ vt (worry) preocupar;
(involve) afectar; (relate to) tener que
ver con; **to be ~ed (about)** interesarse
(por), preocuparse (por); **concerning**
prep sobre, acerca de

concert ['kɒnsət] n concierto;
concert hall n sala de conciertos

concerto [kən'tʃəːtəu] n concierto

concession [kən'seʃən] n concesión
f; **tax ~** privilegio fiscal

concise [kən'saɪs] adj conciso

conclude [kən'kluːd] vt concluir;
(treaty etc) firmar; (agreement) llegar
a; (decide) llegar a la conclusión de;
conclusion [-'kluːʒən] n conclusión
f; firma

concrete ['kɒnkriːt] n hormigón m
▷ adj de hormigón; (fig) concreto

concussion [kən'kʌʃən] n
conmoción f cerebral

condemn [kən'dem] vt condenar;
(building) declarar en ruina

condensation [kɒndən'seɪʃən] n
condensación f

condense [kən'dens] vi condensarse
▷ vt condensar, abreviar

condition [kən'dɪʃən] n condición f,
estado; (requirement) condición f ▷ vt
condicionar; **on ~ that** a condición
(de) que; **conditional**
[kən'dɪʃənl] adj condicional;
conditioner n suavizante

condo ['kɒndəu] (us) n (inf) =
condominium

condom ['kɒndəm] n condón m

condominium [kɒndə'mɪnɪəm]
(us) n (building) bloque m de pisos or
apartamentos (propiedad de quienes lo
habitan), condominio (LAM); (apartment)
piso or apartamento (en propiedad),

condominio (LAM)

condone [kən'dəun] vt condonar

conduct [n 'kɔndʌkt, vb kən'dʌkt] n conducta, comportamiento m; (lead) conducir; (manage) llevar a cabo, dirigir; (Mus) dirigir; **to ~ o.s.** comportarse; **conducted tour** (BRIT) n visita acompañada; **conductor** n (of orchestra) director m; (US: on train) revisor/a m/f; (on bus) cobrador m; (Elec) conductor m

cone [kəun] n cono; (pine cone) piña; (on road) pivote m; (for ice-cream) cucurucho

confectionery [kən'fekʃənrɪ] n dulces mpl

confer [kən'fə:*] vt: **to ~ sth on** otorgar algo a ▷ vi conferenciar

conference ['kɔnfərns] n (meeting) reunión f; (convention) congreso

confess [kən'fes] vt confesar ▷ vi admitir; **confession** n [-'feʃən] n confesión f

confide [kən'faɪd] vi: **to ~ in** confiar en

confidence ['kɔnfɪdns] n (also: self-~) confianza; (secret) confidencia; **in ~** (speak, write) en confianza; **confident** adj seguro de sí mismo; (certain) seguro; **confidential** [kɔnfɪ'denʃəl] adj confidencial

confine [kən'faɪn] vt (limit) limitar; (shut up) encerrar; **confined** adj (space) reducido

confirm [kən'fə:m] vt confirmar; **confirmation** [kɔnfə'meɪʃən] n confirmación f

confiscate ['kɔnfɪskeɪt] vt confiscar

conflict [n 'kɔnflɪkt, vb kən'flɪkt] n conflicto ▷ vi (opinions) chocar

conform [kən'fɔ:m] vi conformarse; **to ~ to** ajustarse a

confront [kən'frʌnt] vt (problems) hacer frente a; (enemy, danger) enfrentarse con; **confrontation** [kɔnfrən'teɪʃən] n enfrentamiento

confuse [kən'fju:z] vt (perplex) aturdir, desconcertar; (mix up)

confundir; (complicate) complicar

confused adj confuso; (person) perplejo; **confusing** adj confuso; **confusion** [-'fju:ʒən] n confusión f

congestion [kən'dʒestʃən] n congestión f

congratulate [kən'grætjuleɪt] vt: **to ~ sb (on)** felicitar a algn (por); **congratulations** [-'leɪʃənz] npl felicitaciones fpl; **congratulations!** ¡enhorabuena!

congregation [-'geɪʃən] n (of a church) feligreses mpl

congress ['kɔngres] n congreso; (US): **C~** Congreso; **congressman** (irreg: US) n miembro del Congreso; **congresswoman** (irreg: US) n diputada, miembro del Congreso

conifer ['kɔnɪfə*] n conífera

conjugate ['kɔndʒugeɪt] vt conjugar; **conjugation** [kɔndʒə'geɪʃən] n conjugación f

conjunction [kən'dʒʌŋkʃən] n conjunción f; **in ~ with** junto con

conjure ['kʌndʒə*] vi hacer juegos de manos

connect [kə'nekt] vt juntar, unir; (Elec) conectar; (Tel: subscriber) poner; (: caller) poner al habla; (fig) relacionar, asociar ▷ vi: **to ~ with** (train) enlazar con; **to be ~ed with** (associated) estar relacionado con; **connecting flight** n vuelo m de enlace; **connection** [-ʃən] n juntura, unión f; (Elec) conexión f; (Rail) enlace m; (Tel) comunicación f; (fig) relación f

conquer ['kɔŋkə*] vt (territory) conquistar; (enemy, feelings) vencer

conquest ['kɔŋkwest] n conquista

cons [kɔnz] npl see **convenience; pro; mod**

conscience ['kɔnʃəns] n conciencia

conscientious [kɔnʃɪ'enʃəs] adj concienzudo; (objection) de conciencia

conscious ['kɔnʃəs] adj (deliberate) deliberado; (awake, aware) consciente; **consciousness** n conciencia; (Med) conocimiento

consecutive [kən'sɛkjutɪv] adj
consecutivo; **on 3 ~ occasions** en 3
ocasiones consecutivas

consensus [kən'sɛnsəs] n consenso

consent [kən'sɛnt] n
consentimiento ▷ vi: **to ~ (to)**
consentir (en)

consequence ['kɔnsɪkwəns]
n consecuencia; (significance)
importancia

consequently ['kɔnsɪkwəntlɪ] adv
por consiguiente

conservation [kɔnsə'veɪʃən] n
conservación f

conservative [kən'sə:vətɪv]
adj conservador(a); (estimate etc)
cauteloso; **Conservative** (BRIT) adj, n
(Pol) conservador(a) m/f

conservatory [kən'sə:vətrɪ] n
invernadero; (Mus) conservatorio

consider [kən'sɪdə*] vt considerar;
(take into account) tener en cuenta;
(study) estudiar, examinar; **to ~
doing sth** pensar en (la posibilidad
de) hacer algo; **considerable** adj
considerable; **considerably** adv
notablemente; **considerate** adj
considerado; **consideration** [-'reɪʃə
n] n consideración f; (factor) factor
m; **to give sth further consideration**
estudiar algo más a fondo;
considering prep teniendo en cuenta

consignment [kən'saɪnmənt]
n envío

consist [kən'sɪst] vi: **to ~ of** consistir
en

consistency [kən'sɪstənsɪ]
n (of argument etc) coherencia;
consecuencia; (thickness) consistencia

consistent [kən'sɪstənt] adj (person)
consecuente; (argument etc) coherente

consolation [kɔnsə'leɪʃən] n
consuelo

console¹ [kən'səul] vt consolar

console² ['kɔnsəul] n consola

consonant ['kɔnsənənt] n
consonante f

conspicuous [kən'spɪkjuəs] adj
(visible) visible

conspiracy [kən'spɪrəsɪ] n conjura,
complot m

constable ['kʌnstəbl] (BRIT) n policía
mf; **chief ~** = jefe m de policía

constant ['kɔnstənt] adj constante;
constantly adv constantemente

constipated ['kɔnstɪpeɪtəd] adj
estreñido

> Be careful not to translate
> **constipated** by the Spanish word
> constipado.

constipation [kɔnstɪ'peɪʃən] n
estreñimiento

constituency [kən'stɪtjuənsɪ] n
(Pol: area) distrito electoral; (: electors)
electorado

constitute ['kɔnstɪtju:t] vt
constituir

constitution [kɔnstɪ'tju:ʃən] n
constitución f

constraint [kən'streɪnt] n
obligación f; (limit) restricción f

construct [kən'strʌkt] vt construir;
construction [-ʃən] n construcción f;
constructive adj constructivo

consul ['kɔnsl] n cónsul mf;
consulate ['kɔnsjulɪt] n consulado

consult [kən'sʌlt] vt consultar;
consultant n (BRIT Med) especialista
mf; (other specialist) asesor(a)
m/f; **consultation** [kɔnsəl'teɪʃən] n
consulta; **consulting room** (BRIT) n
consultorio

consume [kən'sju:m] vt (eat)
comerse; (drink) beberse; (fire etc,
Comm) consumir; **consumer** n
consumidor(a) m/f

consumption [kən'sʌmpʃən] n
consumo

cont. abbr (= continued) sigue

contact ['kɔntækt] n contacto;
(person) contacto; (: pej) enchufe m ▷ vt
ponerse en contacto con; **contact
lenses** npl lentes fpl de contacto

contagious [kən'teɪdʒəs] adj
contagioso

contain [kən'teɪn] vt contener;

to ~ o.s. contenerse; **container**
n recipiente m; (for shipping etc)
contenedor m

contaminate [kən'tæmineɪt] vt
contaminar

cont'd abbr (= continued) sigue

contemplate ['kɒntəmpleɪt] vt
contemplar; (reflect upon) considerar

contemporary [kən'tempərərɪ] adj,
n contemporáneo/a m/f

contempt [kən'tempt] n desprecio;
~ of court (Law) desacato (a los
tribunales)

contend [kən'tend] vt (argue) afirmar
▷ vi: **to ~ with/for** luchar contra/por

content [adj, vb kən'tent, n
'kɒntent] adj (happy) contento;
(satisfied) satisfecho ▷ vt contentar;
satisfacer ▷ n contenido; **contents**
npl contenido; **(table of) ~s** índice m
de materias; **contented** adj contento;
satisfecho

contest [n 'kɒntest, vb kən'test] n
lucha; (competition) concurso m;
(dispute) impugnar; (Pol) presentarse
como candidato/a en

> Be careful not to translate **contest**
> by the Spanish word contestar.

contestant [kən'testənt] n
concursante mf; (in fight) contendiente
mf

context ['kɒntekst] n contexto

continent ['kɒntinənt] n continente
m; **the C~** (BRIT) el continente
europeo; **continental** [-'nentl] adj
continental; **continental breakfast** n
desayuno estilo europeo; **continental
quilt** (BRIT) n edredón m

continual [kən'tinjuəl] adj
continuo; **continually** adv
constantemente

continue [kən'tinju:] vi, vt seguir,
continuar

continuity [kɒnti'njuiti] n (also
Cine) continuidad f

continuous [kən'tinjuəs] adj
continuo; **continuous assessment**
(BRIT) n evaluación f continua;

continuously adv continuamente

contour [kɒn'tuə*] n contorno; (also:
~ line) curva de nivel

contraception [kɒntrə'sepʃən] n
contracepción f

contraceptive [kɒntrə'septiv] adj, n
anticonceptivo

contract [n 'kɒntrækt, vb kən'trækt]
n contrato ▷ vi (Comm): **to ~ to do
sth** comprometerse por contrato a
hacer algo; (become smaller) contraerse,
encogerse ▷ vt contraer; **contractor**
n contratista m

contradict [kɒntrə'dikt] vt
contradecir; **contradiction** [-ʃən] n
contradicción f

contrary¹ ['kɒntrərɪ] adj contrario
▷ n lo contrario; **on the ~** al contrario;
unless you hear to the ~ a no ser que
le digan lo contrario

contrary² [kən'treəri] adj (perverse)
terco

contrast [n 'kɒntrɑ:st, vt kən'trɑ:st]
n contraste m ▷ vt comparar; **in ~ to**
en contraste con

contribute [kən'tribju:t] vi
contribuir ▷ vt: **to ~ £10/an article** to
contribuir con 10 libras/un artículo
a; **to ~ to** (charity) donar a; (newspaper)
escribir para; (discussion) intervenir en;
contribution [kɒntri'bju:ʃən]
n (donation) donativo; (BRIT: for social
security) cotización f; (to debate)
intervención f; (to journal) colaboración
f; **contributor** n (to newspaper)
colaborador(a) m/f

control [kən'trəul] vt controlar;
(process etc) dirigir; (machinery)
manejar; (temper) dominar; (disease)
contener ▷ n control m; **controls** npl
(of vehicle) instrumentos mpl de mando;
(of radio) controles mpl; (governmental)
medidas fpl de control; **under ~** bajo
control; **to be in ~ of** tener el mando
de; **the car went out of ~** se perdió
el control del coche; **control tower** n
(Aviat) torre f de control

controversial [kɒntrə'və:ʃl] adj

polémico

controversy ['kɒntrəvə:sɪ] n
polémica

convenience [kən'vi:nɪəns] n
(easiness) comodidad f; (suitability)
idoneidad f; (advantage) ventaja; **at
your ~** cuando le sea conveniente;
all modern ~s, all mod cons (BRIT)
todo confort

convenient [kən'vi:nɪənt] adj
(useful) útil; (place, time) conveniente

convent ['kɒnvənt] n convento

convention [kən'vɛnʃən] n
convención f; (meeting) asamblea;
(agreement) convenio; **conventional**
adj convencional

conversation [kɒnvə'seɪʃən] n
conversación f

conversely [-'və:slɪ] adv a la inversa

conversion [kən'və:ʃən] n
conversión f

convert [vb kən'və:t, n 'kɒnvə:t] vt
(Rel, Comm) convertir; (alter): **to ~ sth
into/to** transformar algo en/convertir
algo a ▷ n converso/a; **convertible**
adj convertible ▷ n descapotable m

convey [kən'veɪ] vt llevar; (thanks)
comunicar; (idea) expresar; **conveyor
belt** n cinta transportadora

convict [vb kən'vɪkt, n 'kɒnvɪkt] vt
(find guilty) declarar culpable a ▷ n
presidiario/a; **conviction** [-ʃən] n
condena; (belief, certainty) convicción f

convince [kən'vɪns] vt convencer;
convinced adj: **convinced of/that**
convencido de/de que; **convincing** adj
convincente

convoy ['kɒnvɔɪ] n convoy m

cook [kuk] vt (stew etc) guisar; (meal)
preparar ▷ vi cocer; (person) cocinar
▷ n cocinero/a; **cook book** n libro de
cocina; **cooker** n cocina; **cookery** n
cocina; **cookery book** (BRIT) n =**cook
book; cookie** (US) n galleta; **cooking**
n cocina

cool [ku:l] adj fresco; (not afraid)
tranquilo; (unfriendly) frío ▷ vt enfriar
▷ vi enfriarse; **cool down** vt enfriar;

(fig: person, situation) calmarse; **cool
off** vi (become calmer) calmarse,
apaciguarse; (lose enthusiasm) perder
(el) interés, enfriarse

cop [kɒp] (inf) n poli mf(SP), tira
mf(MEX)

cope [kəup] vi: **to ~ with** (problem)
hacer frente a

copper ['kɒpə*] n (metal) cobre m;
(BRIT: inf) poli mf, tira mf(MEX)

copy ['kɒpɪ] n copia; (of book etc)
ejemplar m ▷ vt copiar; **copyright** n
derechos mpl de autor

coral ['kɒrəl] n coral m

cord [kɔ:d] n cuerda; (Elec) cable
m; (fabric) pana; **cords** npl (trousers)
pantalones mpl de pana; **cordless** adj
sin hilos

corduroy ['kɔ:dərɔɪ] n pana

core [kɔ:*] n centro, núcleo; (of fruit)
corazón m; (of problem) meollo ▷ vt
quitar el corazón de

coriander [kɒrɪ'ændə*] n culantro

cork [kɔ:k] n corcho; (tree) alcornoque
m; **corkscrew** n sacacorchos m inv

corn [kɔ:n] n (BRIT: cereal crop) trigo;
(US: maize) maíz m; (on foot) callo; **~ on
the cob** (Culin) mazorca, elote m (MEX),
choclo (SC)

corned beef [kɔ:nd-] n carne f
acecinada (en lata)

corner ['kɔ:nə*] n (outside) esquina;
(inside) rincón m; (in road) curva;
(Football: also: **~ kick**) córner m; (Boxing) esquina
▷ vt (trap) arrinconar; (Comm) acaparar
▷ vi (in car) tomar las curvas; **corner
shop** (BRIT) tienda de la esquina

cornflakes ['kɔ:nfleɪks] npl copos
mpl de maíz, cornflakes mpl

cornflour ['kɔ:nflauə*] (BRIT) n
harina de maíz

cornstarch ['kɔ:nstɑ:tʃ] (US) n =
cornflour

Cornwall ['kɔ:nwəl] n Cornualles m

coronary ['kɒrənrɪ] n (also: **~
thrombosis**) infarto

coronation [kɒrə'neɪʃən] n
coronación f

coroner ['kɒrənə*] n juez mf de instrucción

corporal ['kɔːpərl] n cabo ▷ adj: **~ punishment** castigo corporal

corporate ['kɔːpərɪt] adj (action, ownership) colectivo; (finance, image) corporativo

corporation [kɔːpə'reɪʃən] n (of town) ayuntamiento; (Comm) corporación f

corps [kɔː*, pl kɔːz] n inv cuerpo; **diplomatic ~** cuerpo diplomático; **press ~** gabinete m de prensa

corpse [kɔːps] n cadáver m

correct [kə'rɛkt] adj justo, exacto; (proper) correcto ▷ vt corregir; (exam) corregir, calificar; **correction** [-ʃən] n (act) corrección f; (instance) rectificación f

correspond [kɒrɪs'pɒnd] vi (write): **to ~ (with)** escribirse (con); (be equivalent to): **to ~ (to)** corresponder (a); (be in accordance): **to ~ (with)** corresponder (con); **correspondence** n correspondencia; **correspondent** n corresponsal mf; **corresponding** adj correspondiente

corridor ['kɒrɪdɔː*] n pasillo

corrode [kə'rəud] vt corroer ▷ vi corroerse

corrupt [kə'rʌpt] adj (person) corrupto; (Comput) corrompido ▷ vt corromper; (Comput) degradar; **corruption** n corrupción f; (of data) alteración f

Corsica ['kɔːsɪkə] n Córcega

cosmetic [kɒz'mɛtɪk] adj, n cosmético; **cosmetic surgery** n cirugía f estética

cosmopolitan [kɒzmə'pɒlɪtn] adj cosmopolita

cost [kɒst] (pt, pp ~) n (price) precio ▷ vi costar, valer ▷ vt preparar el presupuesto de; **how much does it ~?** ¿cuánto cuesta?; **to ~ sb time/effort** costarle a algn tiempo/esfuerzo; **it ~ him his life** le costó la vida; **at all ~s** cueste lo que cueste; **costs** npl (Comm)

costes mpl; (Law) costas fpl

co-star ['kəustɑː*] n coprotagonista mf

Costa Rica ['kɒstə'riːkə] n Costa Rica; **Costa Rican** adj, n costarriqueño/a

costly ['kɒstlɪ] adj costoso

cost of living n costo or coste m (Sp) de la vida

costume ['kɒstjuːm] n traje m; (BRIT: also: **swimming ~**) traje m de baño

cosy ['kəuzɪ] (US **cozy**) adj (person) cómodo; (room) acogedor(a)

cot [kɒt] n (BRIT: child's) cuna; (US: campbed) cama de campaña

cottage ['kɒtɪdʒ] n casita de campo; (rustic) barraca; **cottage cheese** n requesón m

cotton ['kɒtn] n algodón m; (thread) hilo; **cotton on** vi (inf): **to cotton on (to sth)** caer en la cuenta (de algo); **cotton bud** n (BRIT) bastoncillo de algodón; **cotton candy** (US) n algodón m (azucarado); **cotton wool** (BRIT) n algodón m (hidrófilo)

couch [kautʃ] n sofá m; (doctor's etc) diván m

cough [kɒf] vi toser ▷ n tos f; **cough mixture** n jarabe m para la tos

could [kud] pt of **can²**; **couldn't** = **could not**

council ['kaunsl] n consejo; **city** or **town ~** consejo municipal; **council estate** (BRIT) n urbanización de viviendas municipales de alquiler; **council house** (BRIT) n vivienda municipal de alquiler; **councillor** (US **councilor**) n concejal(a) m/f; **council tax** n (BRIT) contribución f municipal (dependiente del valor de la vivienda)

counsel ['kaunsl] n (advice) consejo; (lawyer) abogado/a ▷ vt aconsejar; **counselling** (US **counseling**) n (Psych) asistencia f psicológica; **counsellor** (US **counselor**) n consejero/a, abogado/a

count [kaunt] vt contar; (include) incluir ▷ vi contar ▷ n cuenta; (of votes) escrutinio; (level) nivel m;

(nobleman) conde m; **count in** (inf)
vt: **to count sb in on sth** contar con
algn para algo; **count on** vt fus contar
con; **countdown** n cuenta atrás

counter ['kauntə*] n (in shop)
mostrador m; (in games) ficha f ▷ vt
contrarrestar ▷ adv: **to run ~ to** ser
contrario a, ir en contra de; **counter
clockwise** (us) adv en sentido
contrario al de las agujas del reloj

counterfeit ['kauntəfɪt] n
falsificación f, simulación f ▷ vt
falsificar ▷ adj falso, falsificado

counterpart ['kauntəpɑːt] n
homólogo a

countess ['kauntɪs] n condesa

countless ['kauntlɪs] adj
innumerable

country ['kʌntrɪ] n país m; (native
land) patria f; (as opposed to town) campo;
(region) región f, tierra; **country and
western (music)** n música country;
country house n casa de campo;
countryside n campo

county ['kauntɪ] n condado

coup [kuː] (pl **~s**) n (also: **~ d'état**)
golpe m (de estado); (achievement) éxito

couple ['kʌpl] n (of things) par m;
(of people) pareja f; (married couple)
matrimonio; **a ~ of** un par de

coupon ['kuːpɒn] n cupón m;
(voucher) valé m

courage ['kʌrɪdʒ] n valor m, valentía f;
courageous [kəˈreɪdʒəs] adj valiente

courgette [kuəˈʒet] (BRIT) n
calabacín m, calabacita (MEX)

courier ['kurɪə*] n mensajero a; (for
tourists) guía mf (de turismo)

course [kɔːs] n (direction) dirección
f; (of river, Scol) curso; (process)
transcurso; (Med): **~ of treatment**
tratamiento; (of ship) rumbo; (part of
meal) plato; (Golf) campo; **of ~** desde
luego, naturalmente; **of ~!** ¡claro!

court [kɔːt] n (royal) corte f; (Law)
tribunal m, juzgado; (Tennis etc) pista,
cancha ▷ vt (woman) cortejar a; **to
take to ~** demandar

courtesy ['kɔːtəsɪ] n cortesía; **(by)
~ of** por cortesía de; **courtesy bus,
courtesy coach** n autobús m gratuito

court: **court-house** ['kɔːthaus] (us) n
palacio de justicia; **courtroom**
['kɔːtrum] n sala de justicia;
courtyard ['kɔːtjɑːd] n patio

cousin ['kʌzn] n primo a; **first ~**
primo a carnal, primo a hermano a

cover ['kʌvə*] vt cubrir; (feelings,
mistake) ocultar; (with lid) tapar; (book
etc) forrar; (distance) recorrer; (include)
abarcar; (protect: also: Insurance) cubrir;
(Press) investigar; (discuss) tratar
▷ n cubierta; (lid) tapa; (for chair etc)
funda; (envelope) sobre m; (for book)
forro; (of magazine) portada; (shelter)
abrigo; (Insurance) cobertura; (of spy)
cobertura; **covers** npl (on bed) sábanas,
mantas; **to take ~** (shelter) protegerse,
resguardarse; **under ~** (indoors) bajo
techo; **under ~ of darkness** al amparo
de la oscuridad; **under separate ~**
(Comm) por separado; **cover up** vi:
cover up for sb encubrir a algn;
coverage n (TV, Press) cobertura;
cover charge n precio del cubierto;
cover-up n encubrimiento

cow [kau] n vaca; (inf!: woman) bruja
▷ vt intimidar

coward ['kauəd] n cobarde mf;
cowardly adj cobarde

cowboy ['kaubɔɪ] n vaquero

cozy ['kəuzɪ] (us) adj = **cosy**

crab [kræb] n cangrejo

crack [kræk] n grieta; (noise) crujido;
(drug) crack m ▷ vt agrietar, romper;
(nut) cascar; (solve: problem) resolver;
(: code) descifrar; (whip etc) chasquear;
(knuckles) crujir; (joke) contar ▷ adj
(expert) de primera; **crack down on** vt
fus adoptar fuertes medidas contra;
cracked adj (cup, window) rajado;
(wall) resquebrajado; **cracker** n
(biscuit) crácker m; (Christmas cracker)
petardo sorpresa

crackle ['krækl] vi crepitar

cradle ['kreɪdl] n cuna

craft [krɑːft] n (skill) arte m; (trade) oficio; (cunning) astucia; (boat: pl inv) barco; (plane: pl inv) avión m; **craftsman** (irreg) n artesano; **craftsmanship** n (quality) destreza

cram [kræm] vt (fill): **to ~ sth with** llenar algo (a reventar) de; (put): **to ~ sth into** meter algo a la fuerza en ▷ vi (for exams) empollar

cramp [kræmp] n (Med) calambre m; **cramped** adj apretado, estrecho

cranberry ['krænbərɪ] n arándano agrio

crane [kreɪn] n (Tech) grúa; (bird) grulla

crap [kræp] n (inf!) mierda (!)

crash [kræʃ] n (noise) estrépito; (of cars etc) choque m; (of plane) accidente m de aviación; (Comm) quiebra ▷ vt (car, plane) estrellar ▷ vi (car, plane) estrellarse; (two cars) chocar; (Comm) quebrar; **crash course** n curso acelerado; **crash helmet** n casco (protector)

crate [kreɪt] n cajón m de embalaje; (for bottles) caja

crave [kreɪv] vt, vi: **to ~ (for)** ansiar, anhelar

crawl [krɔːl] vi (drag o.s.) arrastrarse; (child) andar a gatas, gatear; (vehicle) avanzar (lentamente) ▷ n (Swimming) crol m

crayfish ['kreɪfɪʃ] n inv (freshwater) cangrejo de río; (saltwater) langosta

crayon ['kreɪən] n lápiz m de color

craze [kreɪz] n (fashion) moda

crazy ['kreɪzɪ] adj (person) loco; (idea) disparatado; (inf: keen): **~ about sb/sth** loco por algn/algo

creak [kriːk] vi (floorboard) crujir; (hinge etc) chirriar, rechinar

cream [kriːm] n (of milk) nata, crema; (lotion) crema; (fig) flor f y nata de (colour) color crema; **cream cheese** n queso blanco; **creamy** adj cremoso; (colour) color crema

crease [kriːs] n (fold) pliegue m; (in trousers) raya; (wrinkle) arruga ▷ vt (wrinkle) arrugar ▷ vi (wrinkle up) arrugarse

create [kriː'eɪt] vt crear; **creation** [-ʃən] n creación f; **creative** adj creativo; **creator** n creador(a) m/f

creature ['kriːtʃə] n (animal) animal m, bicho; (person) criatura

crèche [krɛʃ] n guardería (infantil)

credentials [krɪ'dɛnʃlz] npl (references) referencias fpl; (identity papers) documentos mpl de identidad

credibility [krɛdɪ'bɪlɪtɪ] n credibilidad f

credible ['krɛdɪbl] adj creíble; (trustworthy) digno de confianza

credit ['krɛdɪt] n crédito; (Comm) honor m, mérito ▷ vt (Comm) abonar; (believe: also: **give ~ to**) creer, prestar fe a ▷ adj crediticio; **credits** npl (Cinema) fichas fpl técnicas; **to be in ~** (person) tener saldo a favor; **to ~ sb with** (fig) reconocer a algn el mérito de; **credit card** n tarjeta de crédito

creek [kriːk] n cala, ensenada; (US) riachuelo

creep [kriːp] (pt, pp **crept**) vi arrastrarse

cremate [krɪ'meɪt] vt incinerar

crematorium [krɛmə'tɔːrɪəm] (pl **crematoria**) n crematorio

crept [krɛpt] pt, pp of **creep**

crescent ['krɛsnt] n media luna; (street) calle f (en forma de semicírculo)

cress [krɛs] n berro

crest [krɛst] n (of bird) cresta; (of hill) cima, cumbre f; (of coat of arms) blasón m

crew [kruː] n (of ship etc) tripulación f; (TV, Cinema) equipo; **crew-neck** n cuello a la caja

crib [krɪb] n cuna ▷ vt (inf) plagiar

cricket ['krɪkɪt] n (insect) grillo; (game) críquet m; **cricketer** n jugador(a) m/f de críquet

crime [kraɪm] n (no pl: illegal activities) crimen m; (illegal action) delito; **criminal** ['krɪmɪnl] n criminal m ▷ adj delincuente mf ▷ adj (illegal)

delictivo) (law) penal
crimson ['krɪmzn] adj carmesí
cringe [krɪndʒ] vi agacharse,
encogerse
cripple ['krɪpl] n lisiado/a, cojo/a
▷ vt lisiar, mutilar
crisis ['kraɪsɪs] (pl **crises**) n crisis f inv
crisp [krɪsp] adj fresco; (vegetables
etc) crujiente; (manner) seco; **crispy**
adj crujiente
criterion [kraɪ'tɪərɪən] (pl **criteria**)
n criterio
critic ['krɪtɪk] n crítico/a; **critical**
adj crítico; (illness) grave; **criticism**
['krɪtɪsɪzm] n crítica; **criticize**
['krɪtɪsaɪz] vt criticar
Croat ['krəʊæt] adj, n = **Croatian**
Croatia [krəʊ'eɪʃə] n Croacia;
Croatian adj, n croata m/f ▷ n (Ling)
croata m
crockery ['krɒkərɪ] n loza, vajilla
crocodile ['krɒkədaɪl] n cocodrilo
crocus ['krəʊkəs] n croco, crocus m
croissant ['krwasɒŋ] n croissant m,
medialuna (esp LAM)
crook [krʊk] n ladrón/ona m/f; (of
shepherd) cayado; **crooked** ['krʊkɪd]
adj torcido; (dishonest) nada honrado
crop [krɒp] n (produce) cultivo;
(amount produced) cosecha; (riding crop)
látigo de montar ▷ vt cortar, recortar;
crop up vi surgir, presentarse
cross [krɒs] n cruz f; (hybrid) cruce
m ▷ vt cruzar, atravesar
▷ adj de mal humor, enojado; **cross
off** vt tachar; **cross out** vt tachar;
cross over vi cruzar; **cross-Channel
ferry** ['krɒs'tʃænl-] n transbordador
m que cruza el Canal de la Mancha;
crosscountry (race) n carrera a
campo traviesa, cross m; **crossing**
n (sea passage) travesía; (also:
pedestrian crossing) paso para
peatones; **crossing guard** (us) n
persona encargada de ayudar a los niños a
cruzar la calle; **crossroads** n cruce m,
encrucijada; **crosswalk** (us) n paso de
peatones; **crossword** n crucigrama m

crotch [krɒtʃ] n (Anat, of garment)
entrepierna
crouch [kraʊtʃ] vi agacharse,
acurrucarse
crouton ['kru:tɒn] n cubito de
pan frito
crow [krəʊ] n (bird) cuervo; (of cock)
canto, cacareo ▷ vi (cock) cantar
crowd [kraʊd] n muchedumbre
f, multitud f ▷ vt (fill) llenar ▷ vi
(gather): **to ~ round** reunirse en torno
a; (cram): **to ~ in** entrar en tropel;
crowded adj (full) atestado; (densely
populated) superpoblado
crown [kraʊn] n corona; (of head)
coronilla; (for tooth) funda; (of hill)
cumbre f ▷ vt coronar; (fig) completar,
rematar; **crown jewels** npl joyas
fpl reales
crucial ['kru:ʃl] adj decisivo
crucifix ['kru:sɪfɪks] n crucifijo
crude [kru:d] adj (materials) bruto;
(fig: basic) tosco; (: vulgar) ordinario;
crude (oil) n (petróleo) crudo
cruel ['krʊəl] adj cruel; **cruelty** n
crueldad f
cruise [kru:z] n crucero ▷ vi (ship)
hacer un crucero; (car) ir a velocidad
de crucero
crumb [krʌm] n miga, migaja
crumble ['krʌmbl] vt desmenuzar
▷ vi (building, also fig) desmoronarse
crumpet ['krʌmpɪt] n ≈ bollo para
tostar
crumple ['krʌmpl] vt (paper) estrujar;
(material) arrugar
crunch [krʌntʃ] vt (with teeth)
mascar; (underfoot) hacer crujir ▷ n
(fig) hora o momento de la verdad;
crunchy adj crujiente
crush [krʌʃ] n (crowd) aglomeración
f; (infatuation): **to have a ~ on sb**
estar loco por algn; (drink): **lemon
~** limonada ▷ vt aplastar; (paper)
estrujar; (cloth) arrugar; (fruit) exprimir;
(opposition) aplastar; (hopes) destruir
crust [krʌst] n corteza; (of snow, ice)
costra; **crusty** adj (bread) crujiente;

(person) de mal carácter

crutch [krʌtʃ] n muleta

cry [kraɪ] vi llorar ▷ n (shriek) chillido; (shout) grito; **cry out** vi (call out, shout) lanzar un grito, echar un grito ▷ vt gritar

crystal ['krɪstl] n cristal m

cub [kʌb] n cachorro; (also: ~ **scout**) niño explorador

Cuba ['kjuːbə] n Cuba; **Cuban** adj, n cubano/a m/f

cube [kjuːb] n cubo ▷ vt (Math) cubicar

cubicle ['kjuːbɪkl] n (at pool) caseta; (for bed) cubículo

cuckoo ['kukuː] n cuco

cucumber ['kjuːkʌmbə*] n pepino

cuddle ['kʌdl] vt abrazar ▷ vi abrazarse

cue [kjuː] n (snooker cue) taco; (Theatre etc) señal f

cuff [kʌf] n (of sleeve) puño; (us: of trousers) vuelta; (blow) bofetada ▷ **off the ~** adv de improviso; **cufflinks** npl gemelos mpl

cuisine [kwɪ'ziːn] n cocina

cul-de-sac ['kʌldəsæk] n callejón m sin salida

cull [kʌl] vt (idea) sacar ▷ n (of animals) matanza selectiva

culminate ['kʌlmɪneɪt] vi: **to ~ in** terminar en

culprit ['kʌlprɪt] n culpable mf

cult [kʌlt] n culto

cultivate ['kʌltɪveɪt] vt cultivar

cultural ['kʌltʃərəl] adj cultural

culture ['kʌltʃə*] n (also Biol) cultura; (Biol) cultivo

cumin ['kʌmɪn] n (spice) comino

cunning ['kʌnɪŋ] n astucia ▷ adj astuto

cup [kʌp] n taza; (as prize) copa

cupboard ['kʌbəd] n armario; (in kitchen) alacena

cup final n (Football) final f de copa

curator [kjuə'reɪtə*] n director(a) m/f

curb [kəːb] vt refrenar; (person)

reprimir ▷ n freno; (us) bordillo

curdle ['kəːdl] vi cuajarse

cure [kjuə*] vt curar ▷ n cura, curación f; (fig: solution) remedio

curfew ['kəːfjuː] n toque m de queda

curiosity [kjuərɪ'ɒsɪtɪ] n curiosidad f

curious ['kjuərɪəs] adj curioso; (person: interested): **to be ~** sentir curiosidad

curl [kəːl] n rizo ▷ vt (hair) rizar ▷ vi rizarse; **curl up** vi (person) hacerse un ovillo; **curler** n rulo; **curly** adj rizado

currant ['kʌrnt] n pasa (de Corinto); (blackcurrant, redcurrant) grosella

currency ['kʌrnsɪ] n moneda; **to gain ~** (fig) difundirse

current ['kʌrnt] n corriente f ▷ adj (accepted) corriente; (present) actual; **current account** (BRIT) n cuenta corriente; **current affairs** npl noticias fpl de actualidad; **currently** adv actualmente

curriculum [kə'rɪkjuləm] (pl ~**s** or **curricula**) n plan m de estudios; **curriculum vitae** n currículum m

curry ['kʌrɪ] n curry m ▷ vt: **to ~ favour with** buscar favores con; **curry powder** n curry en polvo

curse [kəːs] vi soltar tacos ▷ vt maldecir ▷ n maldición f; (swearword) palabrota, taco

cursor ['kəːsə*] n (Comput) cursor m

curt [kəːt] adj corto, seco

curtain ['kəːtn] n cortina; (Theatre) telón m

curve [kəːv] n curva ▷ vi (road) hacer una curva; (line etc) curvarse; **curved** adj curvo

cushion ['kuʃən] n cojín m; (of air) colchón m ▷ vt (shock) amortiguar

custard ['kʌstəd] n natillas fpl

custody ['kʌstədɪ] n custodia; **to take into ~** detener

custom ['kʌstəm] n costumbre f; (Comm) clientela

customer ['kʌstəmə*] n cliente m/f

customized ['kʌstəmaɪzd] adj (car etc) hecho a encargo

customs ['kʌstəmz] *npl* aduana;
customs officer *n* aduanero/a

cut [kʌt] (*pt, pp* **~**) *vt* cortar; (*price*)
rebajar; (*text, programme*) acortar;
(*reduce*) reducir ▷ *vi* cortar ▷ *n* (*of
garment*) corte *m*; (*in skin*) cortadura;
(*in salary etc*) rebaja; (*in spending*)
reducción *f*, recorte *m*; (*slice of meat*)
tajada; **to ~ a tooth** echar un diente;
to ~ and paste (*Comput*) cortar y pegar;
cut back *vt* (*plants*) podar; (*production,
expenditure*) reducir; **cut down**
vt (*tree*) derribar; (*reduce*) reducir; **cut
off** *vt* cortar; (*person, place*) aislar;
(*Tel*) desconectar; **cut out** *vt* (*shape*)
recortar; (*stop: activity etc*) dejar;
(*remove*) quitar; **cut up** *vt* cortar (en
pedazos); **cutback** *n* reducción *f*

cute [kjuːt] *adj* mono

cutlery ['kʌtləri] *n* cubiertos *mpl*

cutlet ['kʌtlɪt] *n* chuleta; (*nut etc
cutlet*) plato vegetariano hecho con nueces
y verdura en forma de chuleta

cut-price ['kʌtˈpraɪs] (*BRIT*) *adj* a
precio reducido

cut-rate ['kʌtˈreɪt] (*US*) *adj* =
cut-price

cutting ['kʌtɪŋ] *adj* (*remark*) mordaz
▷ *n* (*BRIT: from newspaper*) recorte *m*;
(*from plant*) esqueje *m*

CV *n abbr* = **curriculum vitae**

cwt *abbr* = **hundredweight(s)**

cybercafé ['saɪbəkæfeɪ] *n* cibercafé
m

cyberspace ['saɪbəspeɪs] *n*
ciberespacio

cycle ['saɪkl] *n* ciclo; (*bicycle*) bicicleta
▷ *vi* ir en bicicleta; **cycle hire** *n*
alquiler *m* de bicicletas; **cycle lane** *n*
carril-bici *m*; **cycle path** *n* carril-bici
m; **cycling** *n* ciclismo; **cyclist** *n*
ciclista *mf*

cyclone ['saɪkləun] *n* ciclón *m*

cylinder ['sɪlɪndə*] *n* cilindro; (*of gas*)
bombona

cymbal ['sɪmbl] *n* címbalo, platillo

cynical ['sɪnɪkl] *adj* cínico

Cypriot ['sɪprɪət] *adj, n* chipriota *m/f*

Cyprus ['saɪprəs] *n* Chipre *f*

cyst [sɪst] *n* quiste *m*; **cystitis**
[-'taɪtɪs] *n* cistitis *f*

czar [zɑː*] *n* zar *m*

Czech [tʃɛk] *adj, n* checo/a *m/f*; **Czech
Republic** *n*: **the Czech Republic** la
República Checa

d

D [di:] n (Mus) re m
dab [dæb] vt (eyes, wound) tocar (ligeramente); (paint, cream) poner un poco de
dad [dæd] n = **daddy**
daddy ['dædɪ] n papá m
daffodil ['dæfədɪl] n narciso
daft [dɑːft] adj tonto
dagger ['dægə*] n puñal m, daga
daily ['deɪlɪ] adj diario, cotidiano ▷ adv todos los días, cada día
dairy ['dɛərɪ] n (shop) lechería (on farm) vaquería; **dairy produce** n productos mpl lácteos
daisy ['deɪzɪ] n margarita
dam [dæm] n presa f ▷ vt construir una presa sobre, represar
damage ['dæmɪdʒ] n lesión f; daño; (dents etc) desperfectos mpl; (fig) perjuicio ▷ vt dañar, perjudicar; (spoil, break) estropear; **damages** npl (Law) daños mpl y perjuicios
damn [dæm] vt condenar; (curse) maldecir ▷ n (inf): **I don't give a ~** me importa un pito ▷ adj (inf: also: **~ed**)
maldito; **~ (it)!** ¡maldito sea!
damp [dæmp] adj húmedo, mojado ▷ n humedad f ▷ vt (also: **~en:** cloth, rag) mojar; (: enthusiasm) enfriar
dance [dɑːns] n baile m ▷ vi bailar; **dance floor** n pista f de baile; **dancer** n bailador(a) m/f; (professional) bailarín/ina m/f; **dancing** n baile m
dandelion ['dændɪlaɪən] n diente m de león
dandruff ['dændrəf] n caspa
Dane [deɪn] n danés/esa m/f
danger ['deɪndʒə*] n peligro; (risk) riesgo; **~!** (on sign) ¡peligro de muerte!; **to be in ~ of** correr riesgo de; **dangerous** adj peligroso
dangle ['dæŋgl] vt colgar ▷ vi pender, colgar
Danish ['deɪnɪʃ] adj danés/esa ▷ n (Ling) danés m
dare [dɛə*] vt: **to ~ sb to do** desafiar a algn a hacer ▷ vi: **to ~ (to) do sth** atreverse a hacer algo; **I ~ say** (I suppose) puede ser (que); **daring** adj atrevido, osado ▷ n atrevimiento, osadía
dark [dɑːk] adj oscuro; (hair, complexion) moreno ▷ n: **in the ~** a oscuras; **to be in the ~ about** (fig) no saber nada de; **after ~** después del anochecer; **darken** vt (colour) hacer más oscuro ▷ vi oscurecerse; **darkness** n oscuridad f; **darkroom** n cuarto oscuro
darling ['dɑːlɪŋ] adj, n querido/a m/f
dart [dɑːt] n dardo; (in sewing) pinza ▷ vi precipitarse; **dartboard** n diana; **darts** n (game) dardos mpl
dash [dæʃ] n (small quantity: of liquid) gota, chorrito; (sign) raya ▷ vt (throw) tirar; (hopes) defraudar ▷ vi precipitarse, ir de prisa
dashboard ['dæʃbɔːd] n (Aut) salpicadero
data ['deɪtə] npl datos mpl; **database** n base f de datos; **data processing** n proceso de datos
date [deɪt] n (day) fecha; (with

friend) cita f; (fruit) dátil m ▷ vt fechar; (person) salir con; **~ of birth** fecha de nacimiento; **to ~** adv hasta la fecha; **dated** adj anticuado

daughter ['dɔːtə*] n hija; **daughter-in-law** n nuera, hija política

daunting ['dɔːntɪŋ] adj desalentador(a)

dawn [dɔːn] n alba, amanecer m; (fig) nacimiento ▷ vi (day) amanecer; (fig): **it ~ed on him that ...** cayó en la cuenta de que ...

day [deɪ] n día m; (working day) jornada f; (heyday) tiempos mpl, días mpl; **the ~ before/after** el día anterior/ siguiente; **the ~ after tomorrow** pasado mañana; **the ~ before yesterday** anteayer; **the following ~** el día siguiente; **by ~** de día; **day-care centre** ['deɪkeə-] n centro de día; (for children) guardería f infantil; **daydream** vi soñar despierto; **daylight** n luz f (del día); **day return** (BRIT) n billete m de ida y vuelta (en un día); **daytime** n día m; **day-to-day** adj cotidiano; **day trip** n excursión f (de un día)

dazed [deɪzd] adj aturdido

dazzle ['dæzl] vt deslumbrar; **dazzling** adj (light, smile) deslumbrante; (colour) fuerte

DC abbr (= direct current) corriente f continua

dead [dɛd] adj muerto; (limb) dormido; (telephone) cortado; (battery) agotado ▷ adv (completely) totalmente; (exactly) exactamente; **to shoot sb ~** matar a algn a tiros; **~ tired** (de cansancio); **to stop ~** parar en seco; **dead end** n callejón m sin salida; **deadline** n fecha (or hora) tope; **deadly** adj mortal, fatal; **Dead Sea** n: **the Dead Sea** el Mar Muerto

deaf [dɛf] adj sordo; **deafen** vt ensordecer; **deafening** adj ensordecedor(a)

deal [diːl] (pt, pp ~t) n (agreement) pacto, convenio; (business deal) trato ▷ vt dar; (card) repartir; **a great ~**

(of) bastante, mucho; **deal with** vt fus (people) tratar con; (problem) ocuparse de; (subject) tratar de; **dealer** n comerciante m/f; (Cards) mano f; **dealings** npl (Comm) transacciones fpl; (relations) relaciones fpl

dealt [dɛlt] pt, pp of **deal**

dean [diːn] n (Rel) deán m; (Scol: BRIT) decano f; (: US) decano; rector m

dear [dɪə*] adj querido; (expensive) caro ▷ n: **my ~** mi querido f ▷ excl: **~ me!** ¡Dios mío!; **D~ Sir/Madam** (in letter) Muy Señor Mío, Estimado Señor/Estimada Señora; **D~ Mr/Mrs X** Estimado/a Señor(a) X; **dearly** adv (love) mucho; (pay) caro

death [dɛθ] n muerte f; **death penalty** n pena de muerte; **death sentence** n condena a muerte

debate [dɪ'beɪt] n debate m ▷ vt discutir

debit ['dɛbɪt] n debe m ▷ vt: **to ~ a sum to sb** or to sb's account cargar una suma en cuenta a algn; **debit card** n tarjeta f de débito

debris ['dɛbriː] n escombros mpl

debt [dɛt] n deuda; **to be in ~** tener deudas

debut ['deɪbjuː] n presentación f

Dec. abbr (= December) dic

decade ['dɛkeɪd] n decenio, década

decaffeinated [diː'kæfɪneɪtɪd] adj descafeinado

decay [dɪ'keɪ] n (of building) desmoronamiento; (of tooth) caries f inv ▷ vi (rot) pudrirse

deceased [dɪ'siːst] n: **the ~** el(la) difunto/a

deceit [dɪ'siːt] n engaño; **deceive** [dɪ'siːv] vt engañar

December [dɪ'sɛmbə*] n diciembre m

decency ['diːsənsɪ] n decencia

decent ['diːsənt] adj (proper) decente; (person; kind) amable, bueno

deception [dɪ'sɛpʃən] n engaño

deceptive [dɪ'sɛptɪv] adj engañoso

Be careful not to translate **deception** by the Spanish word *decepción*.

decide [dɪˈsaɪd] *vt* (*person*) decidir; (*question, argument*) resolver ▷ *vi* decidir; **to ~ to do/that** decidir hacer/que; **to ~ on sth** decidirse por algo

decimal [ˈdɛsɪməl] *adj* decimal ▷ *n* decimal *m*

decision [dɪˈsɪʒən] *n* decisión *f*

decisive [dɪˈsaɪsɪv] *adj* decisivo; (*person*) decidido

deck [dɛk] *n* (Naut) cubierta; (*of bus*) piso; (*record deck*) platina; (*of cards*) baraja; **deckchair** *n* tumbona

declaration [dɛkləˈreɪʃən] *n* declaración *f*

declare [dɪˈklɛə*] *vt* declarar

decline [dɪˈklaɪn] *n* disminución *f*, descenso ▷ *vt* rehusar ▷ *vi* (*person, business*) decaer; (*strength*) disminuir

decorate [ˈdɛkəreɪt] *vt* (*adorn*): **to ~ (with)** adornar (de), decorar (de); (*paint*) pintar; (*paper*) empapelar; **decoration** [-ˈreɪʃən] *n* adorno; (*act*) decoración *f*; (*medal*) condecoración *f*; **decorator** *n* (*workman*) pintor *m* (decorador)

decrease [*n* ˈdiːkriːs, *vb* dɪˈkriːs] *n*: **~ (in)** disminución *f* (de) ▷ *vt* disminuir, reducir ▷ *vi* reducirse

decree [dɪˈkriː] *n* decreto

dedicate [ˈdɛdɪkeɪt] *vt* dedicar; **dedicated** *adj* dedicado; (*Comput*) especializado; **dedicated word processor** procesador *m* de textos especializado *or* dedicado; **dedication** [-ˈkeɪʃən] *n* (*devotion*) dedicación *f*; (*in book*) dedicatoria

deduce [dɪˈdjuːs] *vt* deducir

deduct [dɪˈdʌkt] *vt* restar; descontar; **deduction** [dɪˈdʌkʃən] *n* (*amount deducted*) descuento; (*conclusion*) deducción *f*, conclusión *f*

deed [diːd] *n* hecho, acto; (*feat*) hazaña; (Law) escritura

deem [diːm] *vt* (*formal*) juzgar, considerar

deep [diːp] *adj* profundo; (*expressing measurements*) de profundidad; (*voice*) bajo; (*breath*) profundo; (*colour*) intenso ▷ *adv*: **the spectators stood 20 ~** los espectadores se formaron de 20 en fondo; **to be 4 metres ~** tener 4 metros de profundidad; **deep-fry** *vt* freír en aceite abundante; **deeply** *adv* (*breathe*) a pleno pulmón; (*interested, moved, grateful*) profundamente, hondamente

deer [dɪə*] *n inv* ciervo

default [dɪˈfɔːlt] *n*: **by ~** por incomparecencia ▷ *adj* (*Comput*) por defecto

defeat [dɪˈfiːt] *n* derrota ▷ *vt* derrotar, vencer

defect [*n* ˈdiːfɛkt, *vb* dɪˈfɛkt] *n* defecto ▷ *vi*: **to ~ to the enemy** pasarse al enemigo; **defective** [dɪˈfɛktɪv] *adj* defectuoso

defence [dɪˈfɛns] (*us* **defense**) *n* defensa

defend [dɪˈfɛnd] *vt* defender; **defendant** *n* acusado/a; (*in civil case*) demandado/a; **defender** *n* defensor/a *m/f*; (Sport) defensa *mf*

defense [dɪˈfɛns] (*us*) = **defence**

defensive [dɪˈfɛnsɪv] *adj* defensivo ▷ *n*: **on the ~** a la defensiva

defer [dɪˈfəː*] *vt* aplazar

defiance [dɪˈfaɪəns] *n* desafío; **in ~ of** en contra de; **defiant** [dɪˈfaɪənt] *adj* (*challenging*) desafiante, retador(a)

deficiency [dɪˈfɪʃənsɪ] *n* (*lack*) falta; (*defect*) defecto; **deficient** [dɪˈfɪʃənt] *adj* deficiente

deficit [ˈdɛfɪsɪt] *n* déficit *m*

define [dɪˈfaɪn] *vt* (*word etc*) definir; (*limits etc*) determinar

definite [ˈdɛfɪnɪt] *adj* (*fixed*) determinado; (*obvious*) claro; (*certain*) indudable; **he was ~ about it** no dejó lugar a dudas (sobre ello); **definitely** *adv* desde luego, por supuesto

definition [dɛfɪˈnɪʃən] *n* definición *f*; (*clearness*) nitidez *f*

deflate [diːˈfleɪt] *vt* desinflar

deflect [dɪˈflɛkt] *vt* desviar

defraud [dɪˈfrɔːd] *vt*: **to ~ sb of sth** estafar algo a algn

defrost [di:'frɔst] vt descongelar

defuse [di:'fju:z] vt desactivar; (situation) calmar

defy [dɪ'faɪ] vt (resist) oponerse a; (challenge) desafiar; (fig): **it defies description** resulta imposible describirlo

degree [dɪ'gri:] n grado; (Scol) título; **to have a ~ in maths** tener una licenciatura en matemáticas; **by ~s** (gradually) poco a poco, por etapas; **to some ~** hasta cierto punto

dehydrated [di:haɪ'dreɪtɪd] adj deshidratado; (milk) en polvo

de-icer [di:'aɪsə*] n descongelador m

delay [dɪ'leɪ] vt demorar, aplazar; (person) entretener; (train) retrasar ▷ vi tardar ▷ n demora, retraso; **to be ~ed** retrasarse; **without ~** en seguida, sin tardar

delegate [n 'dɛlɪgɪt, vb 'dɛlɪgeɪt] n delegado/a ▷ vt (person) delegar en; (task) delegar

delete [dɪ'li:t] vt suprimir, tachar

deli ['dɛlɪ] n = **delicatessen**

deliberate [adj dɪ'lɪbərɪt, vb dɪ'lɪbəreɪt] adj (intentional) intencionado; (slow) pausado, lento ▷ vi deliberar; **deliberately** adv (on purpose) a propósito

delicacy ['dɛlɪkəsɪ] n delicadeza; (choice food) manjar m

delicate ['dɛlɪkɪt] adj delicado; (fragile) frágil

delicatessen [dɛlɪkə'tɛsn] n ultramarinos mpl finos

delicious [dɪ'lɪʃəs] adj delicioso

delight [dɪ'laɪt] n (feeling) placer m, deleite m; (person, experience etc) encanto, delicia ▷ vt encantar, deleitar; **to take ~ in** deleitarse en; **delighted** adj: **delighted (at** or **with/to do)** encantado (con/de hacer); **delightful** adj encantador(a), delicioso

delinquent [dɪ'lɪŋkwənt] adj, n delincuente m

deliver [dɪ'lɪvə*] vt (distribute) repartir; (hand over) entregar; (message) comunicar; (speech) pronunciar; (Med) asistir al parto de; **delivery** n reparto; entrega; (of speaker) modo de expresarse; (Med) parto, alumbramiento; **to take delivery of** recibir

delusion [dɪ'lu:ʒən] n ilusión f, engaño

de luxe [də'lʌks] adj de lujo

delve [dɛlv] vi: **to ~ into** hurgar en

demand [dɪ'mɑ:nd] vt (gen) exigir; (rights) reclamar ▷ n exigencia; (claim) reclamación f; (Econ) demanda; **to be in ~** ser muy solicitado; **on ~** a solicitud; **demanding** adj (boss) exigente; (work) absorbente

demise [dɪ'maɪz] n (death) fallecimiento

demo ['dɛmən] (inf) n abbr (=demonstration) manifestación f

democracy [dɪ'mɔkrəsɪ] n democracia; **democrat** ['dɛməkræt] n demócrata mf; **democratic** [dɛmə'krætɪk] adj democrático; (us) demócrata

demolish [dɪ'mɔlɪʃ] vt derribar, demoler; (fig: argument) destruir

demolition [dɛmə'lɪʃən] n derribo, demolición f

demon ['di:mən] n (evil spirit) demonio

demonstrate ['dɛmənstreɪt] vt demostrar; (skill, appliance) mostrar ▷ vi manifestarse; **demonstration** [-'streɪʃən] n (Pol) manifestación f; (proof, exhibition) demostración f; **demonstrator** n (Pol) manifestante mf; (Comm) demostrador/a m/f; vendedor/a m/f

demote [dɪ'məut] vt degradar

den [dɛn] n (of animal) guarida; (room) habitación f

denial [dɪ'naɪəl] n (refusal) negativa; (of report etc) negación f

denim ['dɛnɪm] n tela vaquera; **denims** npl vaqueros mpl

Denmark ['dɛnmɑ:k] n Dinamarca

denomination [dɪnɒmɪˈneɪʃən] n
valor m; (Rel) confesión f
denounce [dɪˈnauns] vt denunciar
dense [dɛns] adj (crowd) denso; (thick)
espeso; (: foliage etc) tupido; (inf: stupid)
torpe
density [ˈdɛnsɪtɪ] n densidad f
  ▷**single/double-~ disk** n (Comput)
disco de densidad sencilla/de doble
densidad
dent [dɛnt] n abolladura ▷vt
(also: **make a ~ in**) abollar
dental [ˈdɛntl] adj dental; **dental
floss** [-flɒs] n seda dental; **dental
surgery** n clínica f dental, consultorio
m dental
dentist [ˈdɛntɪst] n dentista mf
dentures [ˈdɛntʃəz] npl dentadura
(postiza)
deny [dɪˈnaɪ] vt negar; (charge)
rechazar
deodorant [diːˈəudərənt] n
desodorante m
depart [dɪˈpɑːt] vi irse, marcharse;
(train) salir; **to ~ from** (fig: differ from)
apartarse de
department [dɪˈpɑːtmənt] n
(Comm) sección f; (Scol) departamento m;
(Pol) ministerio m; **department store** n
gran almacén m
departure [dɪˈpɑːtʃə*] n partida, ida;
(of train) salida; (of employee) marcha;
a new ~ un nuevo rumbo; **departure
lounge** n (at airport) sala de embarque
depend [dɪˈpɛnd] vi: **to ~ on** depender
de; (rely on) contar con; **it ~s** depende,
según; **~ing on the result** según el
resultado; **dependant** n dependiente
mf; **dependent** adj: **to be dependent
on** depender de ▷n = **dependant**
depict [dɪˈpɪkt] vt (in picture) pintar;
(describe) representar
deport [dɪˈpɔːt] vt deportar
deposit [dɪˈpɒzɪt] n depósito; (Chem)
sedimento; (of ore, oil) yacimiento m;
(gen) depositar; **deposit account** (BRIT)
n cuenta de ahorros
depot [ˈdɛpəu] n (storehouse)

depósito; (for vehicles) parque m; (us)
estación f
depreciate [dɪˈpriːʃɪeɪt] vi
depreciarse, perder valor
depress [dɪˈprɛs] vt deprimir; (wages
etc) hacer bajar; (press down) apretar;
depressed adj deprimido; **depressing**
adj deprimente; **depression**
[dɪˈprɛʃən] n depresión f
deprive [dɪˈpraɪv] vt: **to ~ sb** privar
a algn de; **deprived** adj necesitado
dept. abbr (= department) dto
depth [dɛpθ] n profundidad f; (of
cupboard) fondo; **to be in the ~s of
despair** sentir la mayor desesperación;
to be out of one's ~ (in water) no hacer
pie; (fig) sentirse totalmente perdido
deputy [ˈdɛpjutɪ] adj: **~ head**
subdirector(a) m/f ▷n sustituto/a,
suplente mf; (us Pol) diputado/a;
(us: also: **~ sheriff**) agente m del sheriff
derail [dɪˈreɪl] vt: **to be ~ed**
descarrilarse
derelict [ˈdɛrɪlɪkt] adj abandonado
derive [dɪˈraɪv] vt (benefit etc) obtener
  ▷vi: **to ~ from** derivarse de
descend [dɪˈsɛnd] vt, vi descender,
bajar; **to ~ from** descender de; **to
~ to** rebajarse a; **descendant** n
descendiente mf
descent [dɪˈsɛnt] n descenso; (origin)
descendencia
describe [dɪsˈkraɪb] vt describir;
description [-ˈkrɪpʃən] n descripción
f; (sort) clase f, género
desert [n ˈdɛzət, vb dɪˈzəːt] n desierto
  ▷vt abandonar ▷vi (Mil) desertar;
deserted [dɪˈzəːtɪd] adj desierto
deserve [dɪˈzəːv] vt merecer, ser
digno de
design [dɪˈzaɪn] n (sketch) bosquejo;
(layout, shape) diseño; (pattern) dibujo;
(intention) intención f ▷vt diseñar;
design and technology (BRIT: Scol) n
= dibujo y tecnología
designate [vb ˈdɛzɪgneɪt, adj
ˈdɛzɪgnɪt] vt (appoint) nombrar;
(destine) designar ▷adj designado

designer [dɪˈzaɪnə*] n diseñador(a) m/f; (fashion designer) modisto/a, diseñador(a) m/f de moda

desirable [dɪˈzaɪərəbl] adj (proper) deseable; (attractive) atractivo

desire [dɪˈzaɪə*] n deseo ▷ vt desear

desk [desk] n (in office) escritorio; (for pupil) pupitre m; (in hotel, at airport) recepción f; (BRIT: in shop, restaurant) caja; **desk-top publishing** [ˈdesktɒp-] n autoedición f

despair [dɪsˈpeə*] n desesperación f ▷ vi: **to ~ of** perder la esperanza de

despatch [dɪsˈpætʃ] n, vt = **dispatch**

desperate [ˈdespərɪt] adj desesperado; (fugitive) peligroso; **to be ~ for sth/to do** necesitar urgentemente algo/hacer; **desperately** adv desesperadamente; (very) terriblemente, gravemente

desperation [despəˈreɪʃən] n desesperación f; **in (sheer) ~** (absolutamente) desesperado

despise [dɪsˈpaɪz] vt despreciar

despite [dɪsˈpaɪt] prep a pesar de, pese a

dessert [dɪˈzɜːt] n postre m; **dessertspoon** n cuchara (de postre)

destination [destɪˈneɪʃən] n destino

destined [ˈdestɪnd] adj: **~ for London** con destino a Londres

destiny [ˈdestɪnɪ] n destino

destroy [dɪsˈtrɔɪ] vt destruir; (animal) sacrificar

destruction [dɪsˈtrʌkʃən] n destrucción f

destructive [dɪsˈtrʌktɪv] adj destructivo, destructor(a)

detach [dɪˈtætʃ] vt separar; (unstick) despegar; **detached** adj (attitude) objetivo, imparcial; **detached house** n ≈ chalé m, chalet m

detail [ˈdiːteɪl] n detalle m; (no pl: in picture etc) detalles mpl; (trifle) pequeñez f ▷ vt detallar; (MiL) destacar; **in ~** detalladamente; **detailed** adj detallado

detain [dɪˈteɪn] vt retener; (in captivity) detener

detect [dɪˈtekt] vt descubrir; (Med, Police) identificar; (MiL, Radar, Tech) detectar; **detection** [dɪˈtekʃən] n descubrimiento; identificación f; **detective** n detective mf; **detective story** n novela policíaca

detention [dɪˈtenʃən] n detención f, arresto; (Scol) castigo

deter [dɪˈtɜː*] vt (dissuade) disuadir

detergent [dɪˈtɜːdʒənt] n detergente m

deteriorate [dɪˈtɪərɪəreɪt] vi deteriorarse

determination [dɪtɜːmɪˈneɪʃən] n resolución f

determine [dɪˈtɜːmɪn] vt determinar; **determined** adj (person) resuelto, decidido; **determined to do** resuelto a hacer

deterrent [dɪˈterənt] n (MiL) fuerza de disuasión

detest [dɪˈtest] vt aborrecer

detour [ˈdiːtuə*] n (gen, us Aut) desviación f

detract [dɪˈtrækt] vt: **to ~ from** quitar mérito a, desvirtuar

detrimental [detrɪˈmentl] adj: **~ (to)** perjudicial (a)

devastating [ˈdevəsteɪtɪŋ] adj devastador(a); (fig) arrollador(a)

develop [dɪˈveləp] vt desarrollar; (Phot) revelar; (disease) coger; (habit) adquirir; (fault) empezar a tener ▷ vi desarrollarse; (advance) progresar; (facts, symptoms) aparecer; **developing country** n país m en (vías de) desarrollo; **development** n desarrollo; (advance) progreso; (of affair, case) desenvolvimiento; (of land) urbanización f

device [dɪˈvaɪs] n (apparatus) aparato, mecanismo

devil [ˈdevl] n diablo, demonio

devious [ˈdiːvɪəs] adj taimado

devise [dɪˈvaɪz] vt idear, inventar

devote [dɪˈvəut] vt: **to ~ sth to** dedicar algo a; **devoted** adj (loyal) leal, fiel; **to be devoted to sb** querer con devoción a algn; **the book is devoted to politics** el libro trata de la política; **devotion** n dedicación f; (Rel) devoción f

devour [dɪ'vaʊə*] vt devorar

devout [dɪ'vaʊt] adj devoto

dew [djuː] n rocío

diabetes [daɪə'biːtiːz] n diabetes f

diabetic [daɪə'bɛtɪk] adj, n diabético/a m/f

diagnose [daɪəgnəʊz] vt diagnosticar

diagnosis [daɪəg'nəʊsɪs] (pl -ses) n diagnóstico

diagonal [daɪ'ægənl] adj, n diagonal f

diagram [daɪəgræm] n diagrama m, esquema m

dial [daɪəl] n esfera (SP), cara (LAM); (on radio etc) dial m; (of phone) disco ▷ vt (number) marcar

dialect [daɪəlɛkt] n dialecto

dialling code [daɪəlɪŋ-] n prefijo

dialling tone(US **dial tone**) n (BRIT) señal f or tono de marcar

dialogue [daɪəlɒg](US **dialog**) n diálogo

diameter [daɪ'æmɪtə*] n diámetro

diamond [daɪəmənd] n diamante m; (shape) rombo; **diamonds** npl (Cards) diamantes mpl

diaper [daɪəpə*] (US) n pañal m

diarrhoea [daɪə'riːə] (US **diarrhea**) n diarrea

diary [daɪərɪ] n (daily account) diario; (book) agenda

dice [daɪs] n inv dados mpl ▷ vt (Culin) cortar en cuadritos

dictate [dɪk'teɪt] vt dictar; (conditions) imponer; **dictation** [-'teɪʃən] n dictado; (giving of orders) órdenes fpl

dictator [dɪk'teɪtə*] n dictador m

dictionary [dɪkʃənrɪ] n diccionario

did [dɪd] pt of **do**

didn't [dɪdnt] = **did not**

die [daɪ] vi morir; (fig: fade)

desvanecerse, desaparecer; **to be dying for sth/to do sth** morirse por algo/de ganas de hacer algo; **die down** vi apagarse; (wind) amainar; **die out** vi desaparecer

diesel [diːzəl] n vehículo con motor Diesel

diet [daɪət] n dieta; (restricted food) régimen m ▷ vi (also: **be on a ~**) estar a dieta, hacer régimen

differ [dɪfə*] vi: **to ~ (from)** (be different) ser distinto (a), diferenciarse (de); (disagree) discrepar (de); **difference** n diferencia f; (disagreement) desacuerdo; **different** adj diferente, distinto; **differentiate** [-'renʃieɪt] vi: **to differentiate (between)** distinguir (entre); **differently** adv de otro modo, en forma distinta

difficult [dɪfɪkəlt] adj difícil; **difficulty** n dificultad f

dig [dɪg] (pt, pp **dug**) vt (hole, ground) cavar ▷ n (prod) empujón m; (archaeological) excavación f; (remark) indirecta; **to ~ one's nails into** clavar las uñas en; **dig up** vt (information) desenterrar; (plant) desarraigar

digest [vb daɪ'dʒɛst, n daɪdʒɛst] vt (food) digerir; (facts) asimilar ▷ n resumen m; **digestion** [dɪ'dʒɛstʃən] n digestión f

digit [dɪdʒɪt] n (number) dígito; (finger) dedo; **digital** adj digital; **digital camera** n cámara digital; **digital TV** n televisión f digital

dignified [dɪgnɪfaɪd] adj grave, solemne

dignity [dɪgnɪtɪ] n dignidad f

digs [dɪgz] (BRIT) npl pensión f, alojamiento

dilemma [daɪ'lɛmə] n dilema m

dill [dɪl] n eneldo

dilute [daɪ'luːt] vt diluir

dim [dɪm] adj (light) débil; (outline) indistinto; (room) oscuro; (inf: stupid) lerdo ▷ vt (light) bajar

dime [daɪm] (US) n moneda de diez centavos

dimension [dɪ'mɛnʃən] n dimensión f

diminish [dɪ'mɪnɪʃ] vt, vi disminuir

din [dɪn] n estruendo, estrépito

dine [daɪn] vi cenar; **diner** n (person) comensal mf

dinghy ['dɪŋɡɪ] n bote m; (also: **rubber ~**) lancha (neumática)

dingy ['dɪndʒɪ] adj (room) sombrío; (colour) sucio

dining car ['daɪnɪŋ-] (BRIT) n (Rail) coche-comedor m

dining room ['daɪnɪŋ-] n comedor m

dining table n mesa f de comedor

dinner ['dɪnə*] n (evening meal) cena; (lunch) comida; (public) cena, banquete m; **dinner jacket** n smoking m; **dinner party** n cena; **dinner time** n (evening) hora de cenar; (midday) hora de comer

dinosaur ['daɪnəsɔː*] n dinosaurio m

dip [dɪp] n (slope) pendiente m; (in sea) baño; (Culin) salsa ▷ vt (in water) mojar; (ladle etc) meter; (BRIT Aut): **to ~ one's lights** poner luces de cruce ▷ vi (road etc) descender, bajar

diploma [dɪ'pləʊmə] n diploma m

diplomacy [dɪ'pləʊməsɪ] n diplomacia

diplomat ['dɪpləmæt] n diplomático/a; **diplomatic** [dɪplə'mætɪk] adj diplomático

dipstick ['dɪpstɪk] (BRIT) n (Aut) varilla de nivel (del aceite)

dire [daɪə*] adj calamitoso

direct [daɪ'rɛkt] adj directo; (challenge) claro; (person) franco ▷ vt dirigir; (order): **to ~ sb to do sth** mandar a algn hacer algo ▷ adv derecho; **can you ~ me to ...?** ¿puede indicarme dónde está ...?; **direct debit** (BRIT) n domiciliación f bancaria de recibos

direction [dɪ'rɛkʃən] n dirección f; **sense of ~** sentido de la dirección; **directions** npl (instructions) instrucciones fpl; **~s for use** modo de empleo

directly [dɪ'rɛktlɪ] adv (in straight line) directamente; (at once) en seguida

director [dɪ'rɛktə*] n director(a) m/f

directory [dɪ'rɛktərɪ] n (Tel) guía (telefónica); (Comput) directorio m; **directory enquiries** (US **directory assistance**) n (servicio de) información f

dirt [dɜːt] n suciedad f; (earth) tierra; **dirty** adj sucio; (joke) verde, colorado (MEX) ▷ vt ensuciar; (stain) manchar

disability [dɪsə'bɪlɪtɪ] n incapacidad f

disabled [dɪs'eɪbld] adj: **to be physically ~** ser minusválido/a; **to be mentally ~** ser deficiente mental

disadvantage [dɪsəd'vɑːntɪdʒ] n desventaja, inconveniente m

disagree [dɪsə'ɡriː] vi (differ) discrepar; **to ~ (with)** no estar de acuerdo (con); **disagreeable** adj desagradable; (person) antipático; **disagreement** n desacuerdo

disappear [dɪsə'pɪə*] vi desaparecer; **disappearance** n desaparición f

disappoint [dɪsə'pɔɪnt] vt decepcionar, defraudar; **disappointed** adj decepcionado; **disappointing** adj decepcionante; **disappointment** n decepción f

disapproval [dɪsə'pruːvəl] n desaprobación f

disapprove [dɪsə'pruːv] vi: **to ~ of** ver mal

disarm [dɪs'ɑːm] vt desarmar; **disarmament** [dɪs'ɑːməmənt] n desarme m

disaster [dɪ'zɑːstə*] n desastre m; **disastrous** [dɪ'zɑːstrəs] adj desastroso

disbelief [dɪsbə'liːf] n incredulidad f

disc [dɪsk] n disco; (Comput) = **disk**

discard [dɪs'kɑːd] vt (old things) tirar; (fig) descartar

discharge [vb dɪs'tʃɑːdʒ, n 'dɪstʃɑːdʒ] vt (task, duty) cumplir; (waste) verter; (patient) dar de alta; (employee) despedir; (soldier) licenciar; (defendant) poner en libertad ▷ n (Elec) descarga; (*Med*) supuración *f*; (*of duty*) desempeño; (*of debt*) pago, descargo

discipline ['dɪsɪplɪn] *n* disciplina ▷ *vt* disciplinar; (*punish*) castigar

disc jockey *n* pinchadiscos *mf inv*

disclose [dɪs'kləuz] *vt* revelar

disco ['dɪskəu] *n abbr* discoteca

discoloured [dɪs'kʌləd] (*us* **discolored**) *adj* descolorido

discomfort [dɪs'kʌmfət] *n* incomodidad *f*; (*unease*) inquietud *f*; (*physical*) malestar *m*

disconnect [dɪskə'nekt] *vt* separar; (*Elec etc*) desconectar

discontent [dɪskən'tent] *n* descontento

discontinue [dɪskən'tɪnjuː] *vt* interrumpir; (*payments*) suspender; **"-d"** (*Comm*) "ya no se fabrica"

discount [*n* 'dɪskaunt, *vb* dɪs'kaunt] *n* descuento ▷ *vt* descontar

discourage [dɪs'kʌrɪdʒ] *vt* desalentar; (*advise against*): **to ~ sb from doing** disuadir a algn de hacer

discover [dɪs'kʌvə*] *vt* descubrir; (*error*) darse cuenta de; **discovery** *n* descubrimiento

discredit [dɪs'kredɪt] *vt* desacreditar

discreet [dɪ'skriːt] *adj* (*tactful*) discreto; (*careful*) prudente

discrepancy [dɪ'skrepənsɪ] *n* diferencia

discretion [dɪ'skreʃən] *n* (*tact*) discreción *f*; **at the ~ of** a criterio de

discriminate [dɪ'skrɪmɪneɪt] *vi*: **to ~ between** distinguir entre; **to ~ against** discriminar contra; **discrimination** [-'neɪʃən] *n* (*discernment*) perspicacia; (*bias*) discriminación *f*

discuss [dɪ'skʌs] *vt* discutir; (*a theme*) tratar; **discussion** [dɪ'skʌʃən] *n* discusión *f*

disease [dɪ'ziːz] *n* enfermedad *f*

disembark [dɪsɪm'baːk] *vt*, *vi* desembarcar

disgrace [dɪs'greɪs] *n* ignominia;

(*shame*) vergüenza, escándalo ▷ *vt* deshonrar; **disgraceful** *adj* vergonzoso

disgruntled [dɪs'grʌntld] *adj* disgustado, descontento

disguise [dɪs'gaɪz] *n* disfraz *m* ▷ *vt* disfrazar; **in ~** disfrazado

disgust [dɪs'gʌst] *n* repugnancia ▷ *vt* repugnar, dar asco a

> Be careful not to translate **disgust** by the Spanish word *disgusto*.

disgusted [dɪs'gʌstɪd] *adj* indignado

> Be careful not to translate **disgusted** by the Spanish word *disgustado*.

disgusting [dɪs'gʌstɪŋ] *adj* repugnante, asqueroso; (*behaviour etc*) vergonzoso

dish [dɪʃ] *n* (*gen*) plato; **to do** or **wash the ~es** fregar los platos; **dishcloth** *n* estropajo

dishonest [dɪs'ɔnɪst] *adj* (*person*) poco honrado, tramposo; (*means*) fraudulento

dishtowel ['dɪʃtauəl] (*us*) *n* estropajo

dishwasher ['dɪʃwɔʃə*] *n* lavaplatos *m inv*

disillusion [dɪsɪ'luːʒən] *vt* desilusionar

disinfectant [dɪsɪn'fektənt] *n* desinfectante *m*

disintegrate [dɪs'ɪntɪgreɪt] *vi* disgregarse, desintegrarse

disk [dɪsk] *n* (*esp us*) = **disc**; (*Comput*) disco, disquete *m*; **single-/double-sided** ~ disco de una cara/dos caras; **disk drive** *n* disc drive *m*; **diskette** *n* = **disk**

dislike [dɪs'laɪk] *n* antipatía, aversión *f* ▷ *vt* tener antipatía a

dislocate ['dɪsləkeɪt] *vt* dislocar

disloyal [dɪs'lɔɪəl] *adj* desleal

dismal ['dɪzml] *adj* (*gloomy*) deprimente, triste; (*very bad*) malísimo, fatal

dismantle [dɪs'mæntl] *vt* desmontar, desarmar

dismay [dɪs'meɪ] n consternación f
▷ vt consternar

dismiss [dɪs'mɪs] vt (worker)
despedir; (pupils) dejar marchar;
(soldiers) dar permiso para irse; (idea,
Law) rechazar; (possibility) descartar;
dismissal n despido

disobedient [dɪsə'biːdɪənt] adj
desobediente

disobey [dɪsə'beɪ] vt desobedecer

disorder [dɪs'ɔːdə*] n desorden m;
(rioting) disturbios mpl; (Med) trastorno

disorganized [dɪs'ɔːgənaɪzd] adj
desorganizado

disown [dɪs'əun] vt (action) renegar
de; (person) negar cualquier tipo de
relación con

dispatch [dɪs'pætʃ] vt enviar ▷ n
(sending) envío; (Press) informe m; (Mil)
parte m

dispel [dɪs'pel] vt disipar

dispense [dɪs'pens] vt (medicines)
preparar; **dispense with** vt fus
prescindir de; **dispenser** n (container)
distribuidor automático

disperse [dɪs'pəːs] vt dispersar ▷ vi
dispersarse

display [dɪs'pleɪ] n (in shop window)
escaparate m; (exhibition) exposición
f; (Comput) visualización f; (of feeling)
manifestación f ▷ vt exponer;
manifestar; (ostentatiously) lucir

displease [dɪs'pliːz] vt (offend)
ofender; (annoy) fastidiar

disposable [dɪs'pəuzəbl] adj
desechable; (income) disponible

disposal [dɪs'pəuzl] n (of rubbish)
destrucción f; **at one's ~** a su
disposición

dispose [dɪs'pəuz] vi: **to ~ of**
(unwanted goods) deshacerse de;
(problem etc) resolver; **disposition**
[dɪspə'zɪʃən] n (nature)
temperamento; (inclination)
propensión f

disproportionate [dɪsprə'pɔːʃənət]
adj desproporcionado

dispute [dɪs'pjuːt] n disputa; (also:

industrial ~) conflicto (laboral)
▷ vt (argue) disputar, discutir; (question)
cuestionar

disqualify [dɪs'kwɒlɪfaɪ] vt (Sport)
desclasificar; **to ~ sb for sth/from
doing sth** incapacitar a algn para
algo/hacer algo

disregard [dɪsrɪ'gɑːd] vt (ignore) no
hacer caso de

disrupt [dɪs'rʌpt] vt (plans)
desbaratar, trastornar; (conversation)
interrumpir; **disruption**
[dɪs'rʌpʃən] n trastorno,
desbaratamiento; interrupción f

dissatisfaction [dɪssætɪs'fækʃən] n
disgusto, descontento

dissatisfied [dɪs'sætɪsfaɪd] adj
insatisfecho

dissect [dɪ'sekt] vt disecar

dissent [dɪ'sent] n disensión f

dissertation [dɪsə'teɪʃən] n tesina

dissolve [dɪ'zɒlv] vt disolver
▷ vi disolverse; **to ~ in(to) tears**
deshacerse en lágrimas

distance [ˈdɪstəns] n distancia; **in
the ~** a lo lejos

distant [ˈdɪstənt] adj lejano; (manner)
reservado, frío

distil [dɪs'tɪl] (US **distill**) vt destilar;
distillery n destilería

distinct [dɪs'tɪŋkt] adj (different)
distinto; (clear) claro; (unmistakeable)
inequívoco; **as ~ from** a diferencia
de; **distinction** f; (honour) honor m; (in
exam) sobresaliente m; **distinctive** adj
distintivo

distinguish [dɪs'tɪŋgwɪʃ] vt
distinguir; **to ~ o.s.** destacarse;
distinguished adj (eminent)
distinguido

distort [dɪs'tɔːt] vt distorsionar;
(shape, image) deformar

distract [dɪs'trækt] vt distraer;
distracted adj distraído; **distraction**
[dɪs'trækʃən] n distracción f;
(confusion) aturdimiento

distraught [dɪs'trɔːt] adj loco de

inquietud
distress [dɪsˈtrɛs] *n* (*anguish*)
angustia, aflicción *f* ▷ *vt* afligir;
distressing *adj* angustioso; doloroso
distribute [dɪsˈtrɪbjuːt] *vt* distribuir;
(*share out*) repartir; **distribution**
[-'bjuːʃən] *n* distribución *f*, reparto
m; **distributor** *n* (*Aut*) distribuidor *m*;
(*Comm*) distribuidora
district ['dɪstrɪkt] *n* (*of country*)
zona, región *f*; (*of town*) barrio; (*Admin*)
distrito; **district attorney** (*us*) *n*
fiscal *mf*
distrust [dɪsˈtrʌst] *n* desconfianza
▷ *vt* desconfiar de
disturb [dɪsˈtəːb] *vt* (*person: bother,
interrupt*) molestar; (*: upset*)
perturbar, inquietar; (*disorganize*)
alterar; **disturbance** *n* (*upheaval*)
perturbación *f*; (*political etc: gen
pl*) disturbio; (*of mind*) trastorno;
disturbed *adj* (*worried, upset*)
preocupado, angustiado; **emotionally
disturbed** trastornado; (*childhood*)
inseguro; **disturbing** *adj* inquietante,
perturbador(a)
ditch [dɪtʃ] *n* zanja; (*irrigation ditch*)
acequia ▷ *vt* (*inf: partner*) deshacerse
de; (*: plan, car etc*) abandonar
ditto ['dɪtəʊ] *adv* ídem, lo mismo
dive [daɪv] *n* (*from board*) salto;
(*underwater*) buceo; (*of submarine*)
sumersión *f* ▷ *vi* (*swimmer: into water*)
saltar; (*: under water*) zambullirse,
bucear; (*fish, submarine*) sumergirse;
(*bird*) lanzarse en picado; **~ into** (*bag
etc*) meter la mano en; (*place*) meterse
de prisa en; **diver** *n* (*underwater*) buzo
diverse [daɪˈvəːs] *adj* diversos/as,
varios/as
diversion [daɪˈvəːʃən] *n* (*BRIT Aut*)
desviación *f*; (*distraction, Mil*) diversión
f; (*of funds*) distracción *f*
diversity [daɪˈvəːsɪtɪ] *n* diversidad *f*
divert [daɪˈvəːt] *vt* (*turn aside*) desviar
divide [dɪˈvaɪd] *vt* dividir; (*separate*)
separar ▷ *vi* dividirse; (*road*)
bifurcarse; **divided highway** (*us*) *n*

carretera de doble calzada
divine [dɪˈvaɪn] *adj* (*also fig*) divino
diving [ˈdaɪvɪŋ] *n* (*Sport*) salto;
(*underwater*) buceo; **diving board** *n*
trampolín *m*
division [dɪˈvɪʒən] *n* división *f*;
(*sharing out*) reparto; (*disagreement*)
diferencias *fpl*; (*Comm*) sección *f*
divorce [dɪˈvɔːs] *n* divorcio
▷ *vt* divorciarse de; **divorced** *adj*
divorciado; **divorcee** [-'siː] *n*
divorciado/a
D.I.Y. (*BRIT*) *adj, n abbr* = **do-it-
yourself**
dizzy ['dɪzɪ] *adj* (*spell*) de mareo; **to
feel ~** marearse
DJ *n abbr* = **disc jockey**
DNA *n abbr* (= *deoxyribonucleic acid*)
ADN *m*

○ KEYWORD

do [duː] (*pt* **did**, *pp* **done**) *n* (*inf: party
etc*): **we're having a little do on
Saturday** damos una fiestecita el
sábado; **it was rather a grand do** fue
un acontecimiento a lo grande
▷ *aux vb* **1** (*in negative constructions: not
translated*): **I don't understand** no
entiendo
2 (*to form questions: not translated*):
didn't you know? ¿no lo sabías?; **what
do you think?** ¿qué opinas?
3 (*for emphasis, in polite expressions*):
**people do make mistakes
sometimes** sí que se cometen errores
a veces; **she does seem rather late**
a mí también me parece que se ha
retrasado; **do sit down/help yourself**
siéntate/sírvete por favor; **do take
care!** ¡ten cuidado!, ¡te pido!)
4 (*used to avoid repeating vb*): **she sings
better than I do** canta mejor que yo;
do you agree? – yes, I do/no, I don't
¿estás de acuerdo? – sí (lo estoy)/no
(lo estoy); **she lives in Glasgow – so
do I** vive en Glasgow – yo también; **he
didn't like it and neither did we** no

le gustó y a nosotros tampoco; **who made this mess? – I did** ¿quién hizo esta chapuza? – yo; **he asked me to help him and I did** me pidió que le ayudara y lo hice

5 (*in question tags*): **you like him, don't you?** te gusta, ¿verdad? *or* ¿no?; **I don't know him, do I?** creo que no le conozco

▷ vt 1 (*gen, carry out, perform etc*): **what are you doing tonight?** ¿qué haces esta noche?; **what can I do for you?** ¿en qué puedo servirle?; **to do the washing-up/cooking** fregar los platos/cocinar; **to do one's teeth/hair/nails** lavarse los dientes/ arreglarse el pelo/arreglarse las uñas 2 (*Aut etc*): **the car was doing 100** el coche iba a 100; **we've done 200 km already** ya hemos hecho 200 km; **he can do 100 in that car** puede ir a 100 en ese coche

▷ vi 1 (*act, behave*) hacer; **do as I do** haz como yo

2 (*get on, fare*): **he's doing well/badly at school** va bien/mal en la escuela; **the firm is doing well** la empresa anda or va bien; **how do you do?** mucho gusto; (*less formal*) ¿qué tal?

3 (*suit*): **will it do?** ¿sirve?, ¿está or va bien?

4 (*be sufficient*) bastar; **will £10 do?** ¿será bastante con £10?; **that'll do** así está bien; **that'll do!** (*in annoyance*) ¡ya está bien!, ¡basta ya!; **to make do (with)** arreglárselas (con)

do up vt (*laces*) atar; (*zip, dress, shirt*) abrochar; (*renovate: room, house*) renovar

do with vt fus (*need*): **I could do with a drink/some help** no me vendría mal un trago/un poco de ayuda; (*be connected*) tener que ver con: **what has it got to do with you?** ¿qué tiene que ver contigo?

do without vi pasar sin; **if you're late for tea then you'll do without** si llegas tarde tendrás que quedarte

sin cenar

▷ vt fus pasar sin; **I can do without a car** puedo pasar sin coche

dock [dɔk] n (*Naut*) muelle m; (*Law*) banquillo (de los acusados) m ▷ vi (*enter dock*) atracar (la) muelle; (*Space*) acoplarse; **docks** npl (*Naut*) muelles mpl, puerto sg

doctor ['dɔktə*] n médico/a; (*Ph. D. etc*) doctor(a) m/f ▷ vt (*drink etc*) adulterar; **Doctor of Philosophy** = Doctor en Filosofía y Letras

document ['dɔkjumənt] n documento; **documentary** [-'mɛntəri] adj documental ▷ n documental m; **documentation** [-mɛn'teɪʃən] n documentación f

dodge [dɔdʒ] n (*fig*) truco ▷ vt evadir; (*blow*) esquivar

dodgy ['dɔdʒi] adj (inf: *uncertain*) dudoso; (*suspicious*) sospechoso; (*risky*) arriesgado

does [dʌz] vb see **do**

doesn't ['dʌznt] = **does not**

dog [dɔg] n perro ▷ vt seguir los pasos de; (*bad luck*) perseguir; **doggy bag** ['dɔgi-] n bolsa para llevarse las sobras de la comida

do-it-yourself ['duːɪtjɔːˈsɛlf] n bricolaje m

dole [dəul] n (*BRIT*) (*payment*) subsidio de paro; **on the –** parado

doll [dɔl] n muñeca; (*us: inf: woman*) muñeca, gachí f

dollar ['dɔlə*] n dólar m

dolphin ['dɔlfin] n delfín m

dome [dəum] n (*Arch*) cúpula

domestic [də'mɛstik] adj (*animal, duty*) doméstico; (*flight, policy*) nacional; **domestic appliance** n aparato m doméstico, aparato m de uso doméstico

dominant ['dɔminənt] adj dominante

dominate ['dɔmineit] vt dominar

domino ['dɔminəu] (*pl* **-es**) n ficha de dominó; **dominoes** n (*game*) dominó

donate [dǝ'neɪt] vt donar; **donation** [dǝ'neɪʃən] n donativo

done [dʌn] pp of **do**

donkey ['dɒŋkɪ] n burro

donor ['dǝʊnǝ*] n , n donante mf; **donor card** n carta m de donante

don't [dǝʊnt] = **do not**

donut ['dǝʊnʌt] (us) n = **doughnut**

doodle ['duːdl] vi hacer dibujitos or garabatos

doom [duːm] n (fate) suerte f ▷ vt: **to be ~ed to failure** estar condenado al fracaso

door [dɔː*] n puerta; **doorbell** n timbre m; **door handle** n tirador m; (of car) manija; **doorknob** n pomo m de la puerta, manilla f (LAM); **doorstep** n peldaño; **doorway** n entrada, puerta

dope [dǝʊp] n (inf: illegal drug) droga; (: person) imbécil mf ▷ vt (horse etc) drogar

dormitory ['dɔːmɪtrɪ] n (BRIT) dormitorio; (us) colegio mayor

DOS n abbr (= disk operating system) DOS m

dosage ['dǝʊsɪdʒ] n dosis f inv

dose [dǝʊs] n dosis f inv

dot [dɒt] n punto ▷ vt: **~ted with** salpicado de; **on the ~** en punto; **dotcom** [dɒt'kɒm] n puntocom f inv; **dotted line** ['dɒtɪd-] n: **to sign on the dotted line** firmar

double ['dʌbl] adj doble ▷ adv (twice): **to cost ~** costar el doble ▷ n doble m ▷ vt doblar ▷ vi doblarse; **on the ~**, **at the ~** (BRIT) corriendo; **double back** vi (person) volver sobre sus pasos; **double bass** n contrabajo; **double bed** n cama de matrimonio; **double-check** vt volver a revisar ▷ vi: **I'll double-check** voy a revisarlo otra vez; **double-click** vi (Comput) hacer doble clic; **double-cross** vt (trick) engañar; (betray) traicionar; **doubledecker** n autobús m de dos pisos; **double glazing** (BRIT) n doble acristalamiento; **double room** n

habitación f doble; **doubles** n (Tennis) juego de dobles; **double yellow lines** npl (BRIT: Aut) línea doble amarilla de prohibido aparcar, ≈ línea f sg amarilla continua

doubt [daʊt] n duda ▷ vt dudar; (suspect) dudar de; **to ~ that** dudar que; **doubtful** adj dudoso; (person): **to be doubtful about sth** tener dudas sobre algo; **doubtless** adv sin duda

dough [dǝʊ] n masa, pasta; **doughnut** (us **donut**) n ≈ rosquilla

dove [dʌv] n paloma

down [daʊn] n (feathers) plumón m, flojel m ▷ adv (downwards) abajo, hacia abajo; (on the ground) por o en tierra ▷ prep abajo ▷ vt (inf: drink) beberse; **~ with X!** ¡abajo X!; **down-and-out** n vagabundo/a; **downfall** n caída, ruina; **downhill** adv: **to go downhill** (also fig) ir cuesta abajo

Downing Street ['daʊnɪŋ-] n (BRIT) Downing Street f

down: download vt (Comput) bajar; **downright** adj (nonsense, lie) manifiesto; (refusal) terminante.

Down's syndrome ['daʊnz-] n síndrome m de Down

down: downstairs adv (below) (en el piso de) abajo; (downwards) escaleras abajo; **down-to-earth** adj práctico; **downtown** adv en el centro de la ciudad; **down under** adv en Australia (or Nueva Zelanda); **downward** [-wǝd] adj, adv hacia abajo; **downwards** [-wǝdz] adv hacia abajo

doz. abbr = **dozen**

doze [dǝʊz] vi dormitar

dozen ['dʌzn] n docena; **a ~ books** una docena de libros; **~s of** cantidad de

Dr. abbr = **doctor; drive**

drab [dræb] adj gris, monótono

draft [drɑːft] n (first copy) borrador m; (Pol: of bill) anteproyecto; (us: call-up) quinta ▷ vt (plan) preparar; (write roughly) hacer un borrador de; see also **draught**

drag [dræg] vt arrastrar; (river) dragar,

rastrear ▷ vi (time) pasar despacio; (play, film etc) hacerse pesado ▷ n (inf) lata; (women's clothing): in ~ vestido de travestí; **to ~ and drop** (Comput) arrastrar y soltar

dragon ['drægən] n dragón m

dragonfly ['drægənflaɪ] n libélula

drain [dreɪn] n desaguadero; (in street) sumidero; (source of loss): **to be a ~ on** consumir, agotar ▷ vt (land, marshes) desaguar; (reservoir) desecar; (vegetables) escurrir ▷ vi escurrirse; **drainage** n (act) desagüe m; (Med, Agr) drenaje m; (sewage) alcantarillado; **drainpipe** n tubo de desagüe

drama ['drɑːmə] n (art) teatro; (play) drama m; (excitement) emoción f; **dramatic** [drə'mætɪk] adj dramático; (sudden, marked) espectacular

drank [dræŋk] pt of **drink**

drape [dreɪp] vt (cloth) colocar; (flag) colgar; **drapes** npl (us) cortinas fpl

drastic ['dræstɪk] adj (measure) severo; (change) radical, drástico

draught [drɑːft] (us **draft**) n (of air) corriente f de aire; (Naut) calado; **on ~** (beer) de barril; **draught beer** n cerveza de barril; **draughts** (BRIT) n (game) juego de damas

draw [drɔː] (pt drew, pp drawn) vt (picture) dibujar; (cart) tirar de; (curtain) correr; (take out) sacar; (attract) atraer; (money) retirar; (wages) cobrar ▷ vi (Sport) empatar ▷ n (Sport) empate m; (lottery) sorteo; **draw out** vi (lengthen) alargarse ▷ vt sacar; **draw up** vi (stop) pararse ▷ vt (chair) acercar; (document) redactar; **drawback** n inconveniente m, desventaja

drawer [drɔː*] n cajón m

drawing ['drɔːɪŋ] n dibujo; **drawing pin** (BRIT) n chincheta; **drawing room** n salón m

drawn [drɔːn] pp of **draw**

dread [dred] n pavor m, terror m ▷ vt temer, tener miedo or pavor a; **dreadful** adj horroroso

dream [driːm] (pt, pp ~ed or ~t) n

sueño ▷ vt, vi soñar; **dreamer** n soñador(a) m/f

dreamt [dremt] pt, pp of **dream**

dreary ['drɪərɪ] adj monótono

drench [drentʃ] vt empapar

dress [dres] n vestido; (clothing) ropa ▷ vt vestir; (wound) vendar ▷ vi vestirse; **to get ~ed** vestirse; **dress up** vi vestirse de etiqueta; (in fancy dress) disfrazarse; **dress circle** (BRIT) n principal m; **dresser** n (furniture) aparador m; (: us) cómoda (con espejo); **dressing** n (Med) vendaje m; (Culin) aliño; **dressing gown** (BRIT) n bata; **dressing room** n (Theatre) camarín m; (Sport) vestuario; **dressing table** n tocador m; **dressmaker** n modista, costurera

drew [druː] pt of **draw**

dribble ['drɪbl] vi (baby) babear ▷ vt (ball) regatear

dried [draɪd] adj (fruit) seco; (milk) en polvo

drier ['draɪə*] n = **dryer**

drift [drɪft] n (of current etc) flujo; (of snow) ventisquero; (meaning) significado ▷ vi (boat) ir a la deriva; (sand, snow) amontonarse

drill [drɪl] n (drill bit) broca; (tool for DIY etc) taladro; (of dentist) fresa; (for mining etc) perforadora, barrena; (Mil) instrucción f ▷ vt perforar, taladrar; (troops) enseñar la instrucción a ▷ vi (for oil) perforar

drink [drɪŋk] (pt drank, pp drunk) n bebida; (sip) trago ▷ vt, vi beber; **to have a ~** tomar algo; tomar una copa or un trago; **a ~ of water** un trago de agua; **drink-driving** n: **to be charged with drink-driving** ser acusado de conducir borracho or en estado de embriaguez; **drinker** n bebedor(a) m/f; **drinking water** n agua potable

drip [drɪp] n (act) goteo; (one drip) gota; (Med) gota a gota m ▷ vi gotear

drive [draɪv] (pt drove, pp driven) n (journey) viaje m (en coche); (also: **~way**) entrada; (energy) energía, vigor m; (Comput: also: **disk ~**) drive m ▷vt (car) conducir (SP), manejar (LAM); (nail) clavar; (push) empujar; (Tech: motor) impulsar ▷vi (Aut: at controls) conducir; (: travel) pasearse en coche; **left-/right-hand ~** conducción f a la izquierda/derecha; **to ~ sb mad** volverle loco a algn; **drive out** vt (force out) expulsar, echar; **drive-in** adj (esp US): **drive-in cinema** autocine m

driven ['drivn] pp of **drive**

driver ['draivə*] n conductor(a) m/f (SP), chofer m/f (LAM); (of taxi, bus) chófer m/f (SP), chofer m/f (LAM); **driver's license** (US) n carnet m de conducir

driveway ['draivwei] n entrada

driving ['draiviŋ] n el conducir (SP), el manejar (LAM); **driving instructor** n profesor(a) m/f de autoescuela (SP), instructor(a) m/f de manejo (LAM); **driving lesson** n clase f de conducir (SP) o manejar (LAM); **driving licence** (BRIT) n licencia de manejo (LAM), carnet m de conducir (SP); **driving test** n examen m de conducir (SP) o manejar (LAM)

drizzle ['drizl] n llovizna

droop [dru:p] vi (flower) marchitarse; (shoulders) encorvarse; (head) inclinarse

drop [drop] n (of water) gota; (lessening) baja; (fall) caída ▷vt dejar caer; (voice, eyes, price) bajar; (passenger) dejar; (omit) omitir ▷vi (object) caer; (wind) amainar; **drop in** vi (inf: visit): **to drop in (on)** pasar por casa de (algn); **drop off** vi (sleep) dormirse ▷vt (passenger) dejar; **drop out** vi (withdraw) retirarse

drought [draut] n sequía

drove [drəuv] pt of **drive**

drown [draun] vt ahogar ▷vi ahogarse

drowsy ['drauzi] adj soñoliento; **to be ~** tener sueño

drug [drʌg] n medicamento; (narcotic) droga ▷vt drogar; **to be on ~s** drogarse; **drug addict** n drogadicto/a; **drug dealer** n traficante m/f de drogas; **druggist** (US) n farmacéutico;

drugstore (US) n farmacia

drum [drʌm] n tambor m; (for oil, petrol) bidón m; **drums** npl batería; **drummer** n tambor m

drunk [drʌŋk] pp of **drink** ▷adj borracho ▷n (also: **-ard**) borracho/a; **drunken** adj borracho; (laughter, party) de borrachos

dry [drai] adj seco; (day) sin lluvia; (climate) árido, seco ▷vt secar; (tears) enjugarse ▷vi secarse; **dry off** vi secarse ▷vt secar; **dry up** vi (river) secarse; **dry-cleaner's** n tintorería; **dry-cleaning** n lavado en seco; **dryer** n (for hair) secador m; (US: for clothes) secadora

DSS n abbr = **Department of Social Security**

D & T (BRIT: Scol) n abbr (= design and technology) = dibujo y tecnología

DTP n abbr (= desk-top publishing) autoedición f

dual ['djuəl] adj doble; **dual carriageway** (BRIT) n carretera de doble calzada

dubious ['dju:biəs] adj indeciso; (reputation, company) sospechoso

duck [dʌk] n pato ▷vi agacharse

due [dju:] adj (owed): **he is ~ £10** se le deben 10 libras; (expected: event): **the meeting is ~ on Wednesday** la reunión tendrá que celebrarse el miércoles; (: arrival): **the train is ~ at 8am** el tren tiene su llegada para las 8; (proper) debido ▷n: **to give sb his (or her) ~** ser justo con algn ▷adv: **~ north** derecho al norte

duel ['djuəl] n duelo

duet [dju:'et] n dúo

dug [dʌg] pt, pp of **dig**

duke [dju:k] n duque m

dull [dʌl] adj (light) débil; (stupid) torpe; (boring) pesado; (sound, pain) sordo; (weather, day) gris ▷vt (pain, grief) aliviar; (mind, senses) entorpecer

dumb [dʌm] adj mudo; (pej: stupid) estúpido

dummy ['dʌmi] n (tailor's dummy)

maniquí m; (mock-up) maqueta;
(BRIT: for baby) chupete m ▷ adj falso,
postizo

dump [dʌmp] n (also: **rubbish ~**)
basurero, vertedero; (inf: place)
cuchitril m ▷ vt (put down) dejar; (get
rid of) deshacerse de; (Comput: data)
transferir

dumpling ['dʌmplɪŋ] n bola de masa
hervida

dune [djuːn] n duna

dungarees [dʌŋgə'riːz] npl mono

dungeon ['dʌndʒən] n calabozo

duplex ['djuːpleks] n dúplex m

duplicate [n 'djuːplɪkət, vb
'djuːplɪkeɪt] n duplicado ▷ vt
duplicar; (photocopy) fotocopiar;
(repeat) repetir; **in ~** por duplicado

durable ['djuərəbl] adj duradero

duration [djuə'reɪʃən] n duración f

during ['djuərɪŋ] prep durante

dusk [dʌsk] n crepúsculo, anochecer
m

dust [dʌst] n polvo ▷ vt quitar el
polvo a, desempolvar; (cake etc) **to ~
with** espolvorear de; **dustbin** (BRIT)
n cubo or bote m (MEX) or tacho (SC)
de la basura; **duster** n paño, trapo;
dustman (BRIT: irreg) n basurero;
dustpan n cogedor m; **dusty** adj
polvoriento

Dutch [dʌtʃ] adj holandés/esa ▷ n
(Ling) holandés m; **the Dutch** npl los
holandeses; **to go ~** (inf) pagar cada
uno lo suyo; **Dutchman** (irreg) n
holandés m; **Dutchwoman** (irreg) n
holandésa

duty ['djuːtɪ] n deber m; (tax) derechos
mpl de aduana; **on ~** de servicio; (at
night etc) de guardia; **off ~** libre (de
servicio); **duty-free** adj libre de
impuestos

duvet ['duːveɪ] (BRIT) n edredón m

DVD n abbr (= digital versatile or video
disc) DVD m; **DVD player** n lector m de
DVD; **DVD writer** n grabadora de DVD

dwarf [dwɔːf] (pl **dwarves**) n enano/
a ▷ vt empequeñecer

dwell [dwel] (pt, pp **dwelt**) vi morar;
dwell on vt fus explayarse en

dwelt [dwelt] pt, pp of **dwell**

dwindle ['dwɪndl] vi disminuir

dye [daɪ] n tinte m ▷ vt teñir

dying ['daɪɪŋ] adj moribundo

dynamic [daɪ'næmɪk] adj dinámico

dynamite ['daɪnəmaɪt] n dinamita

dyslexia [dɪs'leksɪə] n dislexia

dyslexic [dɪs'leksɪk] adj, n disléxico/
a m/f

E [iː] n (Mus) mi m

E111 n abbr (= Form E111) impreso E111

each [iːtʃ] adj cada inv ▷ pron cada uno; **~ other** el uno al otro; **they hate ~ other** se odian (entre ellos or mutuamente); **they have 2 books ~** tienen 2 libros por persona

eager ['iːgə*] adj (keen) entusiasmado; **to be ~ to do sth** tener muchas ganas de hacer algo, impacientarse por hacer algo; **to be ~ for** tener muchas ganas de

eagle ['iːgl] n águila

ear [ɪə*] n oreja; oído; (of corn) espiga; **earache** n dolor m de oídos; **eardrum** n tímpano

earl [əːl] n conde m

earlier ['əːlɪə*] adj anterior ▷ adv antes

early ['əːlɪ] adv temprano; (before time) con tiempo, con anticipación ▷ adj temprano; (settlers etc) primitivo; (death, departure) prematuro; (reply) pronto; **to have an ~ night** acostarse temprano; **in the ~ or ~ in the**

spring/19th century a principios de primavera/del siglo diecinueve; **early retirement** n jubilación f anticipada

earmark ['ɪəmɑːk] vt: **to ~ (for)** reservar (para), destinar (a)

earn [əːn] vt (salary) percibir; (interest) devengar; (praise) merecerse

earnest ['əːnɪst] adj (wish) fervoroso; (person) serio, formal; **in ~** en serio

earnings ['əːnɪŋz] npl (personal) sueldo, ingresos mpl; (company) ganancias fpl

ear: earphones npl auriculares mpl; **earplugs** npl tapones mpl para los oídos; **earring** n pendiente m, arete m

earth [əːθ] n tierra; (BRIT Elec) cable m de toma de tierra ▷ vt (BRIT Elec) conectar a tierra; **earthquake** n terremoto

ease [iːz] n facilidad f; (comfort) comodidad f ▷ vt (lessen: problem) mitigar; (: pain) aliviar; (: tension) reducir; **to ~ sth in/out** meter/sacar algo con cuidado; **at ~!** (Mil) ¡descansen!

easily ['iːzɪlɪ] adv fácilmente

east [iːst] n este m ▷ adj del este, oriental; (wind) este ▷ adv al este, hacia el este; **the E~** el Oriente; (Pol) los países del Este; **eastbound** adj en dirección este

Easter ['iːstə*] n Pascua (de Resurrección); **Easter egg** n huevo de Pascua

eastern ['iːstən] adj del este, oriental; (oriental) oriental

Easter Sunday n Domingo de Resurrección

easy ['iːzɪ] adj fácil; (simple) sencillo; (comfortable) holgado, cómodo; (relaxed) tranquilo ▷ adv: **to take it or things ~** (not hurry) tomarlo con calma; (rest) descansar; **easy-going** adj acomodadizo

eat [iːt] (pt ate, pp eaten) vt comer; **eat out** vi comer fuera

eavesdrop ['iːvzdrɔp] vi: **to ~ (on)** escuchar a escondidas

e-book ['i:buk] n libro electrónico

e-business ['i:bıznıs] n (company) negocio electrónico; (commerce) comercio electrónico

EC n abbr (= European Community) CE f

eccentric [ık'sentrık] adj, n excéntrico m/f

echo ['ɛkəʊ] (pl -es) n eco ⊳vt (sound) repetir ⊳vi resonar, hacer eco

eclipse [ı'klıps] n eclipse m

eco-friendly ['i:kəʊfrɛndlɪ] adj ecológico

ecological [i:kə'lɒdʒıkl] adj ecológico

ecology [ı'kɒlədʒı] n ecología; e-commerce n abbr comercio electrónico

economic [i:kə'nɒmık] adj económico; (business etc) rentable; economical adj económico; economics n (Scol) economía ⊳npl (of project etc) rentabilidad f

economist [ı'kɒnəmıst] n economista m/f

economize [ı'kɒnəmaız] vi economizar, ahorrar

economy [ı'kɒnəmı] n economía; economy class n (Aviat) clase f económica; economy class syndrome n síndrome m de la clase turista

ecstasy ['ɛkstəsı] n éxtasis m inv; (drug) éxtasis m inv; ecstatic [ɛks'tætık] adj extático

eczema ['ɛksımə] n eczema m

edge [ɛdʒ] n (of knife) filo; (of object) borde m; (of lake) orilla ⊳vt (Sewing) ribetear; on ~ (fig) = edgy; to ~ away from alejarse poco a poco de

edgy ['ɛdʒı] adj nervioso, inquieto

edible ['ɛdıbl] adj comestible

Edinburgh ['ɛdınbərə] n Edimburgo

edit ['ɛdıt] vt (be editor of) dirigir; (text, report) corregir, preparar; edition [ı'dıʃən] n edición f; editor n (of newspaper) director(a) m/f; (of column) foreign/political editor encargado de la sección de extranjero/ política; (of book) redactor(a) m/f;

editorial [-'tɔ:rıəl] adj editorial ⊳n editorial m

educate ['ɛdjukeıt] vt (gen) educar; (instruct) instruir; educated ['ɛdjukeıtıd] adj culto

education [ɛdju'keıʃən] n educación f; (schooling) enseñanza; (Scol) pedagogía; educational adj (policy etc) educacional; (experience) docente; (toy) educativo

eel [i:l] n anguila

eerie ['ıərı] adj misterioso

effect [ı'fɛkt] n efecto ⊳vt efectuar, llevar a cabo; to take ~ (law) entrar en vigor or vigencia; (drug) surtir efecto; in ~ en realidad; effects npl (property) efectos mpl; effective adj eficaz; (actual) verdadero; effectively adv eficazmente; (in reality) efectivamente

efficiency [ı'fıʃənsı] n eficiencia; rendimiento

efficient [ı'fıʃənt] adj eficiente; (machine) de buen rendimiento; efficiently adv eficientemente, de manera eficiente

effort ['ɛfət] n esfuerzo; effortless adj sin ningún esfuerzo; (style) natural

e.g. adv abbr (= exempli gratia) p. ej.

egg [ɛg] n huevo; hard-boiled/soft-boiled ~ huevo duro/pasado por agua; eggcup n huevera; eggplant (esp us) n berenjena; eggshell n cáscara de huevo; egg white n clara de huevo; egg yolk n yema de huevo

ego ['i:gəʊ] n ego

Egypt ['i:dʒıpt] n Egipto; Egyptian [ı'dʒıpʃən] adj, n egipcio/a m/f

eight [eıt] num ocho; eighteen num diez y ocho, dieciocho; eighteenth adj decimoctavo; the eighteenth floor la planta dieciocho; the eighteenth of August el dieciocho de agosto; eighth num octavo; eightieth ['eıtııθ] adj octogésimo

eighty ['eıtı] num ochenta

Eire ['ɛərə] n Eire m

either ['aıðə*] adj cualquiera de los dos; (both, each) cada ⊳pron: ~ (of

them) cualquiera (de los dos) ▷ *adv* tampoco ▷ *conj*: **~ yes or no** o sí o no; **on ~ side** en ambos lados; **I don't like ~** no me gusta ninguno/a de los(las) dos; **no, I don't ~** no, yo tampoco

eject [ɪ'dʒekt] *vt* echar, expulsar; (*tenant*) desahuciar

elaborate [*adj* ɪ'læbərɪt, *vb* ɪ'læbəreɪt] *adj* (*complex*) complejo ▷ *vt* (*expand*) ampliar; (*refine*) refinar ▷ *vi* explicar con más detalles

elastic [ɪ'læstɪk] *n* elástico ▷ *adj* elástico; (*fig*) flexible; **elastic band** (*BRIT*) *n* gomita

elbow ['elbəʊ] *n* codo

elder ['eldə*] *adj* mayor ▷ *n* (*tree*) saúco; (*person*) mayor; **elderly** *adj* de edad, mayor ▷ *npl*: **the elderly** los mayores

eldest ['eldɪst] *adj*, *n* el/la mayor

elect [ɪ'lekt] *vt* elegir ▷ *adj*: **the ~ president** el presidente electo; **to ~ to do** optar por hacer; **election** *n* elección *f*; **electoral** *adj* electoral; **electorate** *n* electorado

electric [ɪ'lektrɪk] *adj* eléctrico; **electrical** *adj* eléctrico; **electric blanket** *n* manta eléctrica; **electric fire** *n* estufa eléctrica; **electrician** [ɪlek'trɪʃən] *n* electricista *mf*; **electricity** [ɪlek'trɪsɪtɪ] *n* electricidad *f*; **electric shock** *n* electrochoque *m*; **electrify** [ɪ'lektrɪfaɪ] *vt* (*Rail*) electrificar; (*fig*: *audience*) electrizar

electronic [ɪlek'trɒnɪk] *adj* electrónico; **electronic mail** *n* correo electrónico; **electronics** *n* electrónica *f*

elegance ['elɪgəns] *n* elegancia

elegant ['elɪgənt] *adj* elegante

element ['elɪmənt] *n* elemento; (*of kettle etc*) resistencia

elementary [elɪ'mentərɪ] *adj* elemental; (*primitive*) rudimentario; **elementary school** (*US*) *n* escuela de enseñanza primaria

elephant ['elɪfənt] *n* elefante *m*

elevate ['elɪveɪt] *vt* (*gen*) elevar; (*in rank*) ascender

elevator ['elɪveɪtə*] (*US*) *n* ascensor *m*; (*in warehouse etc*) montacargas *m inv*

eleven [ɪ'levn] *num* once; **eleventh** *num* undécimo

eligible ['elɪdʒəbl] *adj*: **an ~ young man/woman** un buen partido; **to be ~ for sth** llenar los requisitos para algo

eliminate [ɪ'lɪmɪneɪt] *vt* (*suspect, possibility*) descartar

elm [elm] *n* olmo

eloquent ['eləkwənt] *adj* elocuente

else [els] *adv*: **something ~** otra cosa; **somewhere ~** en otra parte; **everywhere ~** en todas partes menos aquí; **where ~?** ¿dónde más?, ¿en qué otra parte?; **there was little ~ to do** apenas quedaba otra cosa que hacer; **nobody ~ spoke** no habló nadie más; **elsewhere** *adv* (*be*) en otra parte; (*go*) a otra parte

elusive [ɪ'luːsɪv] *adj* esquivo; (*quality*) difícil de encontrar

e-mail ['iːmeɪl] *n abbr* (= *electronic mail*) correo electrónico, e-mail *m*; **e-mail address** *n* dirección *f* electrónica, email *m*

embankment [ɪm'bæŋkmənt] *n* terraplén *m*

embargo [ɪm'bɑːgəʊ] (*pl* **~es**) *n* (*Comm, Naut*) embargo; (*prohibition*) prohibición *f*; **to put an ~ on sth** poner un embargo en algo

embark [ɪm'bɑːk] *vi* embarcarse ▷ *vt* embarcar; **to ~ on** (*journey*) emprender; (*course of action*) lanzarse a

embarrass [ɪm'bærəs] *vt* avergonzar; (*government etc*) dejar en mal lugar; **embarrassed** *adj* (*laugh, silence*) embarazoso

> Be careful not to translate **embarrassed** by the Spanish word *embarazada*.

embarrassing *adj* (*situation*) violento; (*question*) embarazoso; **embarrassment** *n* (*shame*) vergüenza; (*problem*): **to be an embarrassment for sb** poner en un aprieto a algn

embassy ['embəsɪ] n embajada

embrace [ɪm'breɪs] vt abrazar, dar un abrazo a; (include) abarcar ▷ vi abrazarse ▷ n abrazo

embroider [ɪm'brɔɪdə*] vt bordar; **embroidery** n bordado

embryo ['embrɪəʊ] n embrión m

emerald ['emərəld] n esmeralda

emerge [ɪ'mɜːdʒ] vi salir; (arise) surgir

emergency [ɪ'mɜːdʒənsɪ] n crisis f inv; **in an ~** en caso de urgencia; **state of ~** estado de emergencia; **emergency brake** (us) n freno de mano; **emergency exit** n salida de emergencia; **emergency landing** n aterrizaje m forzoso; **emergency room** (us: Med) n sala f de urgencias; **emergency services** npl (fire, police, ambulance) servicios mpl de urgencia or emergencia

emigrate ['emɪgreɪt] vi emigrar; **emigration** [emɪ'greɪʃən] n emigración f

eminent ['emɪnənt] adj eminente

emissions [ɪ'mɪʃənz] npl emisión f

emit [ɪ'mɪt] vt emitir; (smoke) arrojar; (smell) despedir; (sound) producir

emotion [ɪ'məʊʃən] n emoción f; **emotional** adj (needs) emocional; (person) sentimental; (scene) conmovedor(a), emocionante; (speech) emocionado

emperor ['empərə*] n emperador m

emphasis ['emfəsɪs] (pl -ses) n énfasis m inv

emphasize ['emfəsaɪz] vt (word, point) subrayar, recalcar; (feature) hacer resaltar

empire ['empaɪə*] n imperio

employ [ɪm'plɔɪ] vt emplear; **employee** [-'iː] n empleado/a; **employer** n patrón/ona m/f; empresario; **employment** n (work) trabajo; **employment agency** n agencia de colocaciones

empower [ɪm'paʊə*] vt: **to ~ sb to do sth** autorizar a algn para hacer algo

empress ['emprɪs] n emperatriz f

emptiness ['emptɪnɪs] n vacío; (of life etc) vaciedad f

empty ['emptɪ] adj vacío; (place) desierto; (house) desocupado; (threat) vano ▷ vt vaciar; (place) dejar vacío ▷ vi vaciarse; (house etc) quedar desocupado; **empty-handed** adj con las manos vacías

EMU n abbr (= European Monetary Union) UME f

emulsion [ɪ'mʌlʃən] n emulsión f; (also: ~ **paint**) pintura emulsión

enable [ɪ'neɪbl] vt: **to ~ sb to do sth** permitir a algn hacer algo

enamel [ɪ'næməl] n esmalte m; (also: ~ **paint**) pintura esmaltada

enchanting [ɪn'tʃɑːntɪŋ] adj encantador(a)

encl. abbr (= enclosed) adj

enclose [ɪn'kləʊz] vt (land) cercar; (letter etc) adjuntar; **please find ~d** le mandamos adjunto

enclosure [ɪn'kləʊʒə*] n cercado, recinto

encore [ɔŋ'kɔː*] excl ¡otra!, ¡bis! ▷ n bis m

encounter [ɪn'kaʊntə*] n encuentro ▷ vt encontrar, encontrarse con; (difficulty) tropezar con

encourage [ɪn'kʌrɪdʒ] vt alentar, animar; (activity) fomentar; (growth) estimular; **encouragement** n estímulo; (of industry) fomento

encouraging [ɪn'kʌrɪdʒɪŋ] adj alentador(a)

encyclop(a)edia [ensaɪkləʊ'piːdɪə] n enciclopedia

end [end] n fin m; (of table) extremo; (of street) final m; (Sport) lado ▷ vt terminar, acabar; (also: **bring to an ~**, **put an ~ to**) acabar con ▷ vi terminar, acabar; **in the ~** al fin; **on ~** (object) de punta, de cabeza; **to stand on ~** (hair) erizarse; **for hours on ~** hora tras hora; **end up** vi: **to end up in** terminar en; (place) ir a parar en

endanger [ɪn'deɪndʒə*] vt poner en peligro; **an ~ed species** una especie en peligro de extinción

endearing [ɪnˈdɪərɪŋ] adj simpático, atractivo

endeavour [ɪnˈdɛvə*] (US **endeavor**) n esfuerzo; (attempt) tentativa ▷ vi: **to ~ to do** esforzarse por hacer; (try) procurar hacer

ending [ˈɛndɪŋ] n (of book) desenlace m; (Ling) terminación f

endless [ˈɛndlɪs] adj interminable, inacabable

endorse [ɪnˈdɔːs] vt (cheque) endosar; (approve) aprobar; **endorsement** n (on driving licence) nota de inhabilitación

endurance [ɪnˈdjuərəns] n resistencia

endure [ɪnˈdjuə*] vt (bear) aguantar, soportar ▷ vi (last) durar

enemy [ˈɛnəmɪ] adj, n enemigo a m/f

energetic [ɛnəˈdʒɛtɪk] adj enérgico

energy [ˈɛnədʒɪ] n energía

enforce [ɪnˈfɔːs] vt (Law) hacer cumplir

engaged [ɪnˈgeɪdʒd] adj (BRIT: busy, in use) ocupado; (betrothed) prometido; **to get ~** prometerse; **engaged tone** (BRIT) (Tel) señal f de comunicado

engagement [ɪnˈgeɪdʒmənt] n (appointment) compromiso, cita; (booking) contratación f; (to marry) compromiso; (period) noviazgo; **engagement ring** n anillo de prometida

engaging [ɪnˈgeɪdʒɪŋ] adj atractivo

engine [ˈɛndʒɪn] n (Aut) motor m; (Rail) locomotora

engineer [ɛndʒɪˈnɪə*] n ingeniero; (BRIT: for repairs) mecánico; (on ship, US Rail) maquinista m; **engineering** n ingeniería

England [ˈɪŋglənd] n Inglaterra

English [ˈɪŋglɪʃ] adj inglés/esa ▷ n (Ling) inglés m; **the English** npl los ingleses mpl; **English Channel** n: **the English Channel** (el Canal de) la Mancha; **Englishman** (irreg) n inglés m; **Englishwoman** (irreg) n inglésa

engrave [ɪnˈgreɪv] vt grabar

engraving [ɪnˈgreɪvɪŋ] n grabado

enhance [ɪnˈhɑːns] vt (gen) aumentar; (beauty) realzar

enjoy [ɪnˈdʒɔɪ] vt (health, fortune) disfrutar de, gozar de; (like) gustarle a algn; **to ~ o.s.** divertirse; **enjoyable** adj agradable; (amusing) divertido

enjoyment n (joy) placer m; (activity) diversión f

enlarge [ɪnˈlɑːdʒ] vt aumentar; (broaden) extender; (Phot) ampliar ▷ vi: **to ~ on** (subject) tratar con más detalles; **enlargement** n (Phot) ampliación f

enlist [ɪnˈlɪst] vt alistar; (support) conseguir ▷ vi alistarse

enormous [ɪˈnɔːməs] adj enorme

enough [ɪˈnʌf] adj: **~ time/books** bastante tiempo/bastantes libros ▷ pron bastante(s) ▷ adv: **big ~** bastante grande; **he has not worked ~** no ha trabajado bastante; **have you got ~?** ¿tiene usted bastante(s)?; **~ to eat** (lo) suficiente de (o lo) bastante para comer; **~! ¡** basta ya!; **that's ~, thanks** con eso basta, gracias; **I've had ~ of him** estoy harto de él; **... which, funnily** o **oddly ~ ...** ... lo que, por extraño que parezca ...

enquire [ɪnˈkwaɪə*] vt, vi = **inquire**

enquiry [ɪnˈkwaɪərɪ] n (official investigation) investigación f

enrage [ɪnˈreɪdʒ] vt enfurecer

enrich [ɪnˈrɪtʃ] vt enriquecer

enrol [ɪnˈrəul] (US **enroll**) vt (members) inscribir; (Scol) matricular ▷ vi inscribirse; matricularse; **enrolment** (US **enrollment**) n inscripción f; matriculación f

en route [ɔnˈruːt] adv durante el viaje

en suite [ɔnˈswiːt] adj: **with ~ bathroom** con baño

ensure [ɪnˈʃuə*] vt asegurar

entail [ɪnˈteɪl] vt suponer

enter [ˈɛntə*] vt (room) entrar en; (club) hacerse socio de; (army) alistarse en; (sb for a competition) inscribir; (write

down) anotar, apuntar; (Comput) meter
▷ vi entrar

enterprise ['entəpraɪz] n
empresa; (spirit) iniciativa; **free
~** la libre empresa; **private ~** la
iniciativa privada; **enterprising** adj
emprendedor(a)

entertain [entə'teɪn] vt (amuse)
divertir; (invite: guest) invitar (a casa);
(idea) abrigar; **entertainer** n artista
mf; **entertaining** adj divertido,
entretenido; **entertainment** n
(amusement) diversión f; (show)
espectáculo

enthusiasm [ɪn'θuːzɪæzəm] n
entusiasmo

enthusiast [ɪn'θuːzɪæst] n
entusiasta mf; **enthusiastic** [-'æstɪk]
adj entusiasta; **to be enthusiastic
about** entusiasmarse por

entire [ɪn'taɪə*] adj entero; **entirely**
adv totalmente

entitle [ɪn'taɪtl] vt: **to ~ sb to sth** dar
a algn derecho a algo; **entitled**
(book) titulado; **to be entitled to do**
tener derecho a hacer

entrance [n 'entrəns, vb ɪn'trɑːns] n
entrada ▷ vt encantar, hechizar; **to
gain ~ to** (university etc) ingresar en;
entrance examination n examen
m de ingreso; **entrance fee** n cuota;
entrance ramp (us) n (Aut) rampa
de acceso

entrant ['entrənt] n (in race,
competition) participante mf; (in
examination) candidato/a

entrepreneur [ɔntrəprə'nəː] n
empresario

entrust [ɪn'trʌst] vt: **to ~ sth to sb**
confiar algo a algn

entry ['entrɪ] n entrada; (in
competition) participación f; (in
register) apunte m; (in account) partida;
(in reference book) artículo; **"no ~"**
"prohibido el paso"; (Aut) "dirección
prohibida"; **entry phone** n portero
automático

envelope ['envələup] n sobre m

envious ['envɪəs] adj envidioso; (look)
de envidia

environment [ɪn'vaɪərnmənt] n
(surroundings) entorno; (natural world):
the ~ el medio ambiente;
environmental [-'mentl] adj
ambiental; medioambiental;
environmentally [-'mentlɪ]
adv: **environmentally sound/friendly**
ecológico

envisage [ɪn'vɪzɪdʒ] vt prever

envoy ['envɔɪ] n enviado

envy ['envɪ] n envidia ▷ vt tener
envidia a; **to ~ sb sth** envidiar algo
a algn

epic ['epɪk] n épica ▷ adj épico

epidemic [epɪ'demɪk] n epidemia

epilepsy ['epɪlepsɪ] n epilepsia

epileptic ['epɪ'leptɪk] adj, n
epiléptico/a m/f; **epileptic fit**
['epɪ'leptɪk-] n ataque m de epilepsia,
acceso m epiléptico

episode ['epɪsəud] n episodio

equal ['iːkwl] adj igual; (treatment)
equitativo ▷ n igual mf ▷ vt ser igual
a; (fig) igualar; **to be ~ to** (task) estar
a la altura de; **equality** [iː'kwɔlɪtɪ]
n igualdad; **equalize** vi (Sport)
empatar; **equally** adv igualmente;
(share etc) a partes iguales

equation [ɪ'kweɪʒən] n (Math)
ecuación f

equator [ɪ'kweɪtə*] n ecuador m

equip [ɪ'kwɪp] vt equipar; (person)
proveer; **to be well ~ped** estar bien
equipado; **equipment** n equipo;
(tools) avíos mpl

equivalent [ɪ'kwɪvələnt] adj: **~ (to)**
equivalente (a) ▷ n equivalente m

ER abbr (BRIT: = Elizabeth Regina) la reina
Isabel; (us: Med) = **emergency room**

era ['ɪərə] n era, época

erase [ɪ'reɪz] vt borrar; **eraser** n
goma de borrar

erect [ɪ'rekt] adj erguido ▷ vt erigir,
levantar; (assemble) montar; **erection**
[-ʃən] n construcción f; (assembly)
montaje m; (Physiol) erección f

ERM n abbr (= Exchange Rate Mechanism) tipo de cambio europeo

erode [ɪ'rəʊd] vt (Geo) erosionar; (metal) corroer, desgastar; (fig) desgastar

erosion [ɪ'rəʊʒən] n erosión f; desgaste m

erotic [ɪ'rɒtɪk] adj erótico

errand ['ɛrnd] n recado (sp), mandado (LAM)

erratic [ɪ'rætɪk] adj desigual, poco uniforme

error ['ɛrə*] n error m, equivocación f

erupt [ɪ'rʌpt] vi entrar en erupción; (fig) estallar; **eruption** [ɪ'rʌpʃən] n erupción f; (of war) estallido

escalate ['ɛskəleɪt] vi extenderse, intensificarse

escalator ['ɛskəleɪtə*] n escalera móvil

escape [ɪ'skeɪp] n fuga ▷ vi escaparse; (flee) huir, evadirse; (leak) fugarse ▷ vt (responsibility etc) evitar, eludir; (consequences) escapar a; (elude): **his name ~s me** no me sale su nombre; **to ~ from** (place) escaparse de; (person) escaparse a

escort [n 'ɛskɔːt, vb ɪ'skɔːt] n acompañante mf; (Mil) escolta f ▷ vt acompañar

especially [ɪ'spɛʃlɪ] adv (above all) sobre todo; (particularly) en particular, especialmente

espionage ['ɛspɪɒnɑːʒ] n espionaje m

essay ['ɛseɪ] n (Literature) ensayo; (Scol: short) redacción f, (: long) trabajo

essence ['ɛsns] n esencia

essential [ɪ'sɛnʃl] adj (necessary) imprescindible; (basic) esencial; **essentially** adv esencialmente; **essentials** npl lo imprescindible, lo esencial

establish [ɪ'stæblɪʃ] vt establecer; (prove) demostrar; (relations) entablar; (reputation) ganarse; **establishment** n establecimiento; **the Establishment** la clase dirigente

estate [ɪ'steɪt] n (land) finca, hacienda; (inheritance) herencia f; (BRIT: also: **housing ~**) urbanización f; **estate agent** (BRIT) n agente mf inmobiliario/a; **estate car** (BRIT) n furgoneta

estimate [n 'ɛstɪmət, vb 'ɛstɪmeɪt] n estimación f, apreciación f; (assessment) tasa, cálculo; (Comm) presupuesto ▷ vt estimar, tasar; calcular

etc abbr (= et cetera) etc

eternal [ɪ'tɜːnl] adj eterno

eternity [ɪ'tɜːnɪtɪ] n eternidad f

ethical ['ɛθɪkl] adj ético; **ethics** ['ɛθɪks] n ética ▷ npl moralidad f

Ethiopia [iːθɪ'əʊpɪə] n Etiopía

ethnic ['ɛθnɪk] adj étnico; **ethnic minority** n minoría étnica

e-ticket ['iːtɪkɪt] n billete m electrónico (sp), boleto electrónico (LAM)

etiquette ['ɛtɪkɛt] n etiqueta

EU n abbr (= European Union) UE f

euro n euro

Europe ['jʊərəp] n Europa; **European** [-'pɪːən] n europeo a m/f; **European Community** n Comunidad f Europea; **European Union** n Unión f Europea

Eurostar® ['jʊərəʊstɑː*] n Eurostar® m

evacuate [ɪ'vækjʊeɪt] vt (people) evacuar; (place) desocupar

evade [ɪ'veɪd] vt evadir, eludir

evaluate [ɪ'væljʊeɪt] vt evaluar; (value) tasar; (evidence) interpretar

evaporate [ɪ'væpəreɪt] vi evaporarse; (fig) desvanecerse

eve [iːv] n: **on the ~ of** en vísperas de

even ['iːvn] adj (level) llano; (smooth) liso; (speed, temperature) uniforme; (number) par ▷ adv hasta, incluso; (introducing a comparison) aún, todavía; **~ if, ~ though** aunque +subjun; **~ more** aun más; **~ so** aun así; **not ~** ni siquiera; **~ he was there** hasta él estuvo allí; **~ on Sundays** incluso los domingos; **to get ~ with sb** ajustar cuentas con algn

evening ['iːvnɪŋ] *n* tarde *f*; (*late*) noche *f*; **in the ~** por la tarde; **evening class** *n* clase *f* nocturna; **evening dress** *n* (*no pl: formal clothes*) traje *m* de etiqueta; (*woman's*) traje *m* de noche

event [ɪ'vent] *n* suceso, acontecimiento *m*; (*Sport*) prueba; **in the ~ of** en caso de; **eventful** *adj* (*life*) activo; (*day*) ajetreado

eventual [ɪ'ventʃuəl] *adj* final

❗ Be careful not to translate **eventual** by the Spanish word **eventual**.

eventually *adv* (*finally*) finalmente; (*in time*) con el tiempo

ever ['evə*] *adv* (*at any time*) nunca, jamás; (*at all times*) siempre; (*in question*) **why ~ not?** ¿y por qué no?; **the best ~** lo nunca visto; **have you ~ seen it?** ¿lo ha visto usted alguna vez?; **better than ~** mejor que nunca; **~ since** *adv* desde entonces ▷ *conj* después de que; **evergreen** *n* árbol *m* de hoja perenne

○ KEYWORD

every ['evrɪ] *adj* **1** (*each*) cada; **every one of them** (*persons*) todos ellos/as; (*objects*) cada uno de ellos/as; **every shop in the town was closed** todas las tiendas de la ciudad estaban cerradas

2 (*all possible*) todo/a; **I gave you every assistance** te di toda la ayuda posible; **I have every confidence in him** tiene toda mi confianza; **we wish you every success** te deseamos toda suerte de éxitos

3 (*showing recurrence*) todo/a; **every day/week** todos los días/todas las semanas; **every other car had been broken into** habían forzado uno de cada dos coches; **she visits me every other/third day** me visita cada dos/tres días; **every now and then** de vez en cuando

every: everybody *pron* = **everyone**; **everyday** *adj* (*daily*) cotidiano, de todos los días; (*usual*) acostumbrado; **everyone** *pron* todos/as, todo el mundo; **everything** *pron* todo; **this shop sells everything** esta tienda vende de todo; **everywhere** *adv*: **I've been looking for you everywhere** te he estado buscando por todas partes; **everywhere you go you meet ...** en todas partes encuentras ...

evict [ɪ'vɪkt] *vt* desahuciar

evidence ['evɪdəns] *n* (*proof*) prueba; (*of witness*) testimonio; (*sign*) indicios *mpl*; **to give ~** prestar declaración, dar testimonio

evident ['evɪdənt] *adj* evidente, manifiesto; **evidently** *adv* por lo visto

evil ['iːvl] *adj* malo; (*influence*) funesto ▷ *n* mal *m*

evoke [ɪ'vəʊk] *vt* evocar

evolution [iːvə'luːʃən] *n* evolución *f*

evolve [ɪ'vɒlv] *vt* desarrollar ▷ *vi* evolucionar, desarrollarse

ewe [juː] *n* oveja

ex [eks] (*inf*) *n*: **my ~** mi ex

ex- [eks] *prefix* ex

exact [ɪg'zækt] *adj* exacto; (*person*) meticuloso ▷ *vt*: **to ~ sth (from)** exigir algo (de); **exactly** *adv* exactamente; (*indicating agreement*) exacto

exaggerate [ɪg'zædʒəreɪt] *vt*, *vi* exagerar; **exaggeration** [-'reɪʃən] *n* exageración *f*

exam [ɪg'zæm] *n abbr* (*Scol*) = **examination**

examination [ɪgzæmɪ'neɪʃən] *n* examen *m*; (*Med*) reconocimiento

examine [ɪg'zæmɪn] *vt* examinar; (*inspect*) inspeccionar, escudriñar; (*Med*) reconocer; **examiner** *n* examinador(a) *m/f*

example [ɪg'zɑːmpl] *n* ejemplo; **for ~** por ejemplo

exasperated [ɪg'zɑːspəreɪtɪd] *adj* exasperado

excavate ['ekskəveɪt] *vt* excavar

exceed [ɪk'siːd] *vt* (*amount*) exceder;

(*number*) pasar a; (*speed limit*)
sobrepasar; (*powers*) excederse en;
(*hopes*) superar; **exceedingly** *adv*
sumamente, sobremanera
excel [ɪk'sɛl] *vi* sobresalir; **to ~ o.s**
lucirse
excellence ['ɛksələns] *n* excelencia
excellent ['ɛksələnt] *adj* excelente
except [ɪk'sɛpt] *prep* (*also:* **~ for, ~ing**)
excepto, salvo ▷ *vt* exceptuar, excluir;
~ if/when excepto si/cuando; **~ that**
salvo que; **exception** [ɪk'sɛpʃən] *n*
excepción f; **to take exception to**
ofenderse por; **exceptional**
[ɪk'sɛpʃənl] *adj* excepcional;
exceptionally [ɪk'sɛpʃənəlɪ] *adv*
excepcionalmente, extraordinariamente
excerpt ['ɛksə:pt] *n* extracto
excess [ɪk'sɛs] *n* exceso; **excess
baggage** *n* exceso de equipaje;
excessive *adj* excesivo
exchange [ɪks'tʃeɪndʒ] *n*
intercambio; (*conversation*) diálogo;
(*also:* **telephone ~**) central f
(telefónica) ▷ *vt* **to ~ (for)** cambiar
(por); **exchange rate** *n* tipo de
cambio
excite [ɪk'saɪt] *vt* (*stimulate*)
estimular; (*arouse*) excitar; **excited**
adj: **to get excited** emocionarse;
excitement *n* (*agitation*) excitación
f; (*exhilaration*) emoción f; **exciting** *adj*
emocionante
exclaim [ɪk'skleɪm] *vi* exclamar;
exclamation [ɛksklə'meɪʃən] *n*
exclamación f; **exclamation mark** *n*
punto de admiración; **exclamation
point** (*us*)= **exclamation mark**
exclude [ɪk'sklu:d] *vt* excluir;
exceptuar
excluding [ɪk'sklu:dɪŋ] *prep*: **~ VAT**
IVA no incluido
exclusion [ɪk'sklu:ʒən] *n* exclusión f;
to the ~ of con exclusión de
exclusive [ɪk'sklu:sɪv] *adj* exclusivo;
(*club, district*) selecto; **~ of tax**
excluyendo impuestos; **exclusively**
adv únicamente

excruciating [ɪk'skru:ʃɪeɪtɪŋ]
adj (*pain*) agudísimo, atroz; (*noise,
embarrassment*) horrible
excursion [ɪk'skə:ʃən] *n* (*tourist
excursion*) excursión f
excuse [*n* ɪk'skju:s, *vb* ɪk'skju:z] *n*
disculpa, excusa; (*pretext*) pretexto ▷ *vt*
(*justify*) justificar; (*forgive*) disculpar,
perdonar; **to ~ sb from doing sth**
dispensar a algn de hacer algo; **~
me!** (*attracting attention*) ¡por favor!;
(*apologizing*) ¡perdón!; **if you will ~ me**
con su permiso
ex-directory ['ɛksdɪ'rɛktərɪ] (*BRIT*)
adj que no consta en la guía
execute ['ɛksɪkju:t] *vt* (*plan*) realizar;
(*order*) cumplir; (*person*) ajusticiar,
ejecutar; **execution** [-'kju:ʃən]
n realización f; cumplimiento;
ejecución f
executive [ɪg'zɛkjutɪv] *n* (*person,
committee*) ejecutivo; (*Pol: committee*)
poder *m* ejecutivo ▷ *adj* ejecutivo
exempt [ɪg'zɛmpt] *adj*: **~ from** exento
de ▷ *vt*: **to ~ sb from** eximir a algn de
exercise ['ɛksəsaɪz] *n* ejercicio ▷ *vt*
(*patience*) usar de; (*right*) valerse de;
(*dog*) llevar de paseo; (*mind*) preocupar
▷ *vi* (*also:* **to take ~**) hacer ejercicio(s);
exercise book *n* cuaderno
exert [ɪg'zə:t] *vt* ejercer; **to ~ o.s**
esforzarse; **exertion** [-ʃən] *n* esfuerzo
exhale [ɛks'heɪl] *vt* despedir ▷ *vi*
exhalar
exhaust [ɪg'zɔ:st] *n* (*Aut: also:* **~
pipe**) escape *m*; (*fumes*) gases *mpl* de
escape ▷ *vt* agotar; **exhausted** *adj*
agotado; **exhaustion** [ɪg'zɔ:stʃən] *n*
agotamiento; **nervous exhaustion**
postración f nerviosa
exhibit [ɪg'zɪbɪt] *n* (*Art*) obra
expuesta; (*Law*) objeto expuesto ▷ *vt*
(*show: emotions*) manifestar; (*: courage,
skill*) demostrar; (*paintings*) exponer;
exhibition [ɛksɪ'bɪʃən] *n* exposición f;
(*of talent etc*) demostración f
exhilarating [ɪg'zɪləreɪtɪŋ] *adj*
estimulante, tónico

exile ['ɛksaɪl] n exilio; (person) exiliado/a ▷ vt desterrar, exiliar

exist [ɪg'zɪst] vi existir; (live) vivir; **existence** n existencia; **existing** adj existente, actual

exit ['ɛksɪt] n salida ▷ vi (Theatre) hacer mutis; (Comput) salir (del sistema)

Be careful not to translate **exit** by the Spanish word **éxito**.

exit ramp (us) n (Aut) vía de acceso

exotic [ɪg'zɔtɪk] adj exótico

expand [ɪk'spænd] vt ampliar; (number) aumentar ▷ vi (population) aumentar; (trade etc) expandirse; (gas, metal) dilatarse

expansion [ɪk'spænʃən] n (of population) aumento; (of trade) expansión f

expect [ɪk'spɛkt] vt esperar; (require) contar con; (suppose) suponer ▷ vi: **to be ~ing** (pregnant woman) estar embarazada; **expectation** [ɛkspɛk'teɪʃən] n (hope) esperanza; (belief) expectativa

expedition [ɛkspə'dɪʃən] n expedición f

expel [ɪk'spɛl] vt arrojar; (from place) expulsar

expenditure [ɪks'pɛndɪtʃə*] n gastos mpl, desembolso; consumo

expense [ɪk'spɛns] n gasto, gastos mpl; (high cost) costa; **expenses** npl (Comm) gastos mpl; **at the ~ of** a costa de; **expense account** n cuenta de gastos

expensive [ɪk'spɛnsɪv] adj caro, costoso

experience [ɪk'spɪərɪəns] n experiencia ▷ vt experimentar; (suffer) sufrir; **experienced** adj experimentado

experiment [ɪk'spɛrɪmənt] n experimento ▷ vi hacer experimentos; **experimental** [-'mɛntl] adj experimental; **the process is still at the experimental stage** el proceso está todavía en prueba

expert ['ɛkspə:t] adj experto, perito ▷ n experto/a, perito/a; (specialist) especialista mf; **expertise** [-'ti:z] n pericia

expire [ɪk'spaɪə*] vi caducar, vencer; **expiry** n vencimiento; **expiry date** n (of medicine, food item) fecha de caducidad

explain [ɪk'spleɪn] vt explicar; **explanation** [ɛksplə'neɪʃən] n explicación f

explicit [ɪk'splɪsɪt] adj explícito

explode [ɪk'spləud] vi estallar, explotar; (population) crecer rápidamente; (with anger) reventar

exploit [n 'ɛksplɔɪt, vb ɪk'splɔɪt] n hazaña ▷ vt explotar; **exploitation** [-'teɪʃən] n explotación f

explore [ɪk'splɔ:*] vt explorar; (fig) examinar; investigar; **explorer** n explorador(a) m/f

explosion [ɪk'spləuʒən] n explosión f; **explosive** [ɪks'pləusɪv] adj, n explosivo

export [n ɛk'spɔ:t, n, cpd 'ɛkspɔ:t] vt exportar ▷ n (process) exportación f; (product) producto de exportación ▷ cpd de exportación; **exporter** n exportador m

expose [ɪk'spəuz] vt exponer; (unmask) desenmascarar; **exposed** adj expuesto

exposure [ɪk'spəuʒə*] n exposición f; (publicity) publicidad f; (Phot: speed) velocidad f de obturación; (: shot) fotografía f; **to die from ~** (Med) morir de frío

express [ɪk'sprɛs] adj (definite) expreso, explícito; (BRIT: letter etc) urgente ▷ n (train) rápido ▷ vt expresar; **expression** [ɪk'sprɛʃən] n expresión f; (of actor etc) sentimiento; **expressway** (us) n (urban motorway) autopista

exquisite [ɛk'skwɪzɪt] adj exquisito

extend [ɪk'stɛnd] vt (visit, street) prolongar; (building) ampliar; (invitation) ofrecer ▷ vt (land)

extenderse; *(period of time)* prolongarse
extension [ɪkˈstɛnʃən] n extensión
f; *(building)* ampliación f; *(of time)*
prolongación f; *(Tel: in private house)*
línea derivada; *(: in office)* extensión
f; **extension lead** n alargador m,
alargadera
extensive [ɪkˈstɛnsɪv] adj extenso;
(damage) importante; *(knowledge)*
amplio
extent [ɪkˈstɛnt] n *(breadth)*
extensión f; *(scope)* alcance m; **to some
~** hasta cierto punto; **to the ~ of ...**
hasta el punto de ...; **to such an ~ that
...** hasta tal punto que ...; **to what ~?**
¿hasta qué punto?
exterior [ɛkˈstɪərɪə*] adj exterior,
externo ▷ n exterior m
external [ɛkˈstə:nl] adj externo
extinct [ɪkˈstɪŋkt] adj *(volcano)*
extinguido; *(race)* extinto; **extinction**
n extinción f
extinguish [ɪkˈstɪŋgwɪʃ] vt
extinguir, apagar
extra [ˈɛkstrə] adj adicional ▷ adv *(in
addition)* de más ▷ n *(luxury, addition)*
extra m; *(Cinema, Theatre)* extra mf,
comparsa mf
extract [vb ɪkˈstrækt, n ˈɛkstrækt] vt
sacar; *(tooth)* extraer; *(money, promise)*
obtener ▷ n extracto
extradite [ˈɛkstrədaɪt] vt extraditar
extraordinary [ɪkˈstrɔ:dnrɪ] adj
extraordinario; *(odd)* raro
extravagance [ɪkˈstrævəgəns] n
derroche m, despilfarro; *(thing bought)*
extravagancia
extravagant [ɪkˈstrævəgənt]
adj *(lavish: person)* pródigo; *(: gift)*
(demasiado) caro; *(wasteful)*
despilfarrador(a)
extreme [ɪkˈstri:m] adj extremo,
extremado ▷ n extremo; **extremely**
adv sumamente, extremadamente
extremist [ɪkˈstri:mɪst] adj, n
extremista m/f
extrovert [ˈɛkstrəvə:t] n
extrovertido/a

eye [aɪ] n ojo ▷ vt mirar de soslayo,
ojear; **to keep an ~ on** vigilar; **eyeball**
n globo ocular; **eyebrow** n ceja;
eyedrops npl gotas fpl para los ojos,
colirio; **eyelash** n pestaña; **eyelid** n
párpado; **eyeliner** n delineador m (de
ojos); **eyeshadow** n sombreador m de
ojos; **eyesight** n vista; **eye witness** n
testigo mf presencial

f

F [ɛf] n (Mus) fa m

fabric ['fæbrɪk] n tejido, tela
> Be careful not to translate **fabric** by the Spanish word fábrica.

fabulous ['fæbjʊləs] adj fabuloso

face [feɪs] n (Anat) cara, rostro; (of clock) esfera (SP), cara (LAM); (of mountain) cara, ladera; (of building) fachada ▷ vt (direction) estar de cara a; (situation) hacer frente a; (facts) aceptar; **to lose ~** desprestigiarse; **to make o pull a ~** hacer muecas; **in the ~ of** (difficulties etc) ante; **on the ~ of it** a primera vista; **to ~** cara a cara; **face up to** vt fus hacer frente a, arrostrar; **face cloth** (BRIT) n manopla; **face pack** (BRIT) n mascarilla

facial ['feɪʃəl] adj de la cara ▷ n (also: **beauty ~**) tratamiento facial, limpieza

facilitate [fə'sɪlɪteɪt] vt facilitar

facilities [fə'sɪlɪtɪz] npl (buildings) instalaciones fpl; (equipment) servicios mpl; **credit ~** facilidades fpl de crédito

fact [fækt] n hecho; **in ~** en realidad

faction ['fækʃən] n facción f

factor ['fæktə*] n factor m

factory ['fæktərɪ] n fábrica

factual ['fæktjuəl] adj basado en los hechos

faculty ['fækəltɪ] n facultad f; (US: teaching staff) personal m docente

fad [fæd] n novedad f, moda

fade [feɪd] vi desteñirse; (sound, smile) desvanecerse; (light) apagarse; (flower) marchitarse; (hope, memory) perderse; **fade away** vi (sound) apagarse

fag [fæg] (BRIT: inf) n (cigarette) pitillo (SP), cigarro

Fahrenheit ['fɑːrənhaɪt] n Fahrenheit m

fail [feɪl] vt (candidate, test) suspender (SP), reprobar (LAM); (memory etc) fallar a ▷ vi suspender (SP), reprobar (LAM); (be unsuccessful) fracasar; (strength, brakes) fallar; (light) acabarse; **to ~ to do sth** (neglect) dejar de hacer algo; (be unable) no poder hacer algo; **without ~** sin falta; **failing** n falta, defecto ▷ prep a falta de; **failure** ['feɪljə*] n fracaso; (person) fracasado/a; (mechanical etc) fallo

faint [feɪnt] adj débil; (recollection) vago; (mark) apenas visible ▷ n desmayo ▷ vi desmayarse; **to feel ~** estar mareado, marearse; **faintest** adj: **I haven't the faintest idea** no tengo la más remota idea; **faintly** adv débilmente; (vaguely) vagamente

fair [fɛə*] adj justo; (hair, person) rubio; (weather) bueno; (good enough) regular; (considerable) considerable ▷ adv (play) limpio ▷ n feria; (BRIT: funfair) parque m de atracciones; **fairground** n recinto ferial; **fair-haired** adj (person) rubio; **fairly** adv (justly) con justicia, (quite) bastante; **fair trade** n comercio justo; **fairway** n (Golf) calle f

fairy ['fɛərɪ] n hada; **fairy tale** n cuento de hadas

faith [feɪθ] n fe f; (trust) confianza; (sect) religión f; **faithful** adj *(loyal: troops etc)* leal; *(spouse)* fiel; *(account)* exacto; **faithfully** *adv* fielmente; **yours faithfully** (BRIT: *in letters)* le saluda atentamente

fake [feɪk] *n (painting etc)* falsificación *f; (person)* impostor(a) *m/f* ▷ *adj* falso ▷ *vt* fingir; *(painting etc)* falsificar

falcon ['fɔːlkən] *n* halcón *m*

fall [fɔːl] *(pt* fell, *pp* fallen) *n* caída; *(in price etc)* descenso; *(US) (autumn)* caer(se); *(price)* bajar, descender; **falls** *npl (waterfall)* cascada, salto de agua; **to ~ flat** *(on one's face)* caerse (boca abajo); *(plan)* fracasar; *(joke, story)* no hacer gracia; **fall apart** *vi* deshacerse; **fall down** *vi (person)* caerse; *(building, hopes)* derrumbarse; **fall for** *vt fus (trick)* dejarse engañar por; *(person)* enamorarse de; **fall off** *vi* caerse; *(diminish)* disminuir; **fall out** *vi (friends etc)* reñir; *(hair, teeth)* caerse; **fall over** *vi* caer(se); **fall through** *vi (plan, project)* fracasar

fallen ['fɔːlən] *pp of* fall

fallout ['fɔːlaʊt] *n* lluvia radioactiva

false [fɔːls] *adj* falso; **under ~ pretences** con engaños; **false alarm** *n* falsa alarma; **false teeth** (BRIT) *npl* dentadura postiza

fame [feɪm] *n* fama

familiar [fə'mɪlɪə*] *adj* conocido, familiar; *(tone)* de confianza; **to be ~ with** *(subject)* conocer (bien); **familiarize** [fə'mɪlɪəraɪz] *vt*: **to familiarize o.s. with** familiarizarse con

family ['fæmɪlɪ] *n* familia; **family doctor** *n* médico/a de cabecera; **family planning** *n* planificación *f* familiar

famine ['fæmɪn] *n* hambre *f*, hambruna

famous ['feɪməs] *adj* famoso, célebre

fan [fæn] *n* abanico; *(Elec)* ventilador *m; (of pop star etc)* fan *mf; (Sport)* hincha *mf* ▷ *vt* abanicar; *(fire, quarrel)* atizar

fanatic [fə'nætɪk] *n* fanático/a

fan belt *n* correa del ventilador

fan club *n* club *m* de fans

fancy ['fænsɪ] *n (whim)* capricho, antojo; *(imagination)* imaginación *f* ▷ *adj (luxury)* lujoso, de lujo ▷ *vt (feel like, want)* tener ganas de; *(imagine)* imaginarse; *(think)* creer; **to take a ~ to sb** tomar cariño a algn; **he fancies her** *(inf)* le gusta (ella) mucho; **fancy dress** *n* disfraz *m*

fan heater *n* calefactor *m*

fantasize ['fæntəsaɪz] *vi* fantasear, hacerse ilusiones

fantastic [fæn'tæstɪk] *adj (enormous)* enorme; *(strange, wonderful)* fantástico

fantasy ['fæntəzɪ] *n (dream)* sueño; *(unreality)* fantasía

fanzine ['fænziːn] *n* fanzine *m*

FAQs *abbr (= frequently asked questions)* preguntas frecuentes

far [fɑː*] *adj (distant)* lejano ▷ *adv* lejos; *(much, greatly)* mucho; **~ away, ~ off** *(a)* lejos; **~ better** mucho mejor; **~ from** lejos de; **by ~** con mucho; **go as ~ as the farm** vaya hasta la granja; **as ~ as I know** que yo sepa; **how ~?** ¿hasta qué punto?; *(fig)* ¿hasta qué punto?

farce [fɑːs] *n* farsa

fare [fɛə*] *n (on trains, buses)* precio *(del billete); (in taxi: cost)* tarifa; *(food)* comida; **half ~** medio pasaje *m*; **full ~** pasaje completo

Far East *n*: **the ~** el Extremo Oriente

farewell [fɛə'wɛl] *excl, n* adiós *m*

farm [fɑːm] *n* cortijo (SP), hacienda (LAM), rancho (MEX), estancia (RPL) ▷ *vt* cultivar; **farmer** *n* granjero, hacendado (LAM), ranchero (MEX), estanciero (RPL); **farmhouse** *n* granja, casa del hacendado (LAM), rancho (MEX), casco de la estancia (RPL); **farming** *n* agricultura; *(of crops)* cultivo; *(of animals)* cría; **farmyard** *n* corral *m*

far-reaching [fɑːˈriːtʃɪŋ] *adj (reform, effect)* de gran alcance

fart [fɑːt] *(inf!)* *vi* tirarse un pedo (!)

farther ['fɑːðə*] *adv* más lejos, más allá ▷ *adj* más lejano

farthest ['fɑ:ðɪst] *superlative of* **far**

fascinate ['fæsɪneɪt] *vt* fascinar; **fascinated** *adj* fascinado

fascinating ['fæsɪneɪtɪŋ] *adj* fascinante

fascination [-'neɪʃən] *n* fascinación *f*

fascist ['fæʃɪst] *adj, n* fascista *m/f*

fashion ['fæʃən] *n* moda; (*fashion industry*) industria de la moda; (*manner*) manera *f* ▷ *vt* formar; **in ~** a la moda; **out of ~** pasado de moda; **fashionable** *adj* de moda; **fashion show** *n* desfile *m* de modelos

fast [fɑ:st] *adj* rápido; (*dye, colour*) resistente; (*clock*): **to be ~** estar adelantado ▷ *adv* rápidamente, de prisa; (*stuck, held*) firmemente ▷ *n* ayuno ▷ *vi* ayunar; **~ asleep** profundamente dormido

fasten ['fɑ:sn] *vt* atar, sujetar; (*coat, belt*) abrochar ▷ *vi* atarse; abrocharse

fast food *n* comida rápida, platos *mpl* preparados

fat [fæt] *adj* gordo; (*book*) grueso; (*profit*) grande, pingüe ▷ *n* grasa; (*on person*) carnes *fpl*; (*lard*) manteca

fatal ['feɪtl] *adj* (*mistake*) fatal; (*injury*) mortal; **fatality** [fə'tælɪtɪ] *n* (*road death etc*) víctima; **fatally** *adv* fatalmente; mortalmente

fate [feɪt] *n* destino; (*of person*) suerte *f*

father ['fɑ:ðə*] *n* padre *m*; **Father Christmas** *n* Papá *m* Noel; **father-in-law** *n* suegro

fatigue [fə'ti:g] *n* fatiga, cansancio

fattening ['fætnɪŋ] *adj* (*food*) que hace engordar

fatty ['fætɪ] *adj* (*food*) graso ▷ *n* (*inf*) gordito/a, gordinflón/ona *m/f*

faucet ['fɔ:sɪt] (*us*) *n* grifo (*sp*), llave *f*, canilla (*RPL*)

fault [fɔ:lt] *n* (*blame*) culpa; (*defect: in person, machine*) defecto; (*Geo*) falla ▷ *vt* criticar; **it's my ~** es culpa mía; **to find ~ with** criticar, poner peros a; **at ~** culpable; **faulty** *adj* defectuoso

fauna ['fɔ:nə] *n* fauna

favour *etc* ['feɪvə*] (*us* **favor** *etc*) *n* favor *m*; (*approval*) aprobación *f* ▷ *vt* (*proposition*) estar a favor de, aprobar; (*assist*) ser propicio a; **to do sb a ~** hacer un favor a algn; **to find ~ with sb** caer en gracia a algn; **in ~ of** a favor de; **favourable** *adj* favorable; **favourite** ['feɪvrɪt] *adj, n* favorito, preferido

fawn [fɔ:n] *n* cervato ▷ *adj* (*also*: **~-coloured**) color de cervato, leonado ▷ *vi*: **to ~ (up)on** adular

fax [fæks] *n* (*document*) fax *m*; (*machine*) telefax *m* ▷ *vt* mandar por telefax

FBI (*us*) *n abbr* (= *Federal Bureau of Investigation*) = BIC *f* (*sp*)

fear [fɪə*] *n* miedo, temor *m* ▷ *vt* tener miedo de, temer; **for ~ of** si; **fearful** *adj* temeroso, miedoso; (*awful*) terrible; **fearless** *adj* audaz

feasible ['fi:zəbl] *adj* factible

feast [fi:st] *n* banquete *m*; (*Rel: also*: **~day**) fiesta *f* ▷ *vi* festejar

feat [fi:t] *n* hazaña

feather ['feðə*] *n* pluma

feature ['fi:tʃə*] *n* característica; (*article*) artículo de fondo; (*in film*) presentar ▷ *vi*: **to ~ in** tener un papel destacado en; **features** *npl* (*of face*) facciones *fpl*; **feature film** *n* largometraje *m*

Feb. *abbr* (= *February*) feb

February ['februərɪ] *n* febrero

fed [fed] *pt, pp of* **feed**

federal ['fedərəl] *adj* federal

federation [fedə'reɪʃən] *n* federación *f*

fed up *adj*: **to be ~ (with)** estar harto (de)

fee [fi:] *n* pago; (*professional*) derechos *mpl*, honorarios *mpl*; (*of club*) cuota; **school ~s** matrícula

feeble ['fi:bl] *adj* débil; (*joke*) flojo

feed [fi:d] (*pt, pp* **fed**) *n* comida; (*of animal*) pienso; (*on printer*) dispositivo de alimentación *m* ▷ *vt* alimentar; (*BRIT: baby: breastfeed*) dar el pecho a; (*animal*) dar de comer a; (*data,*

information): **to ~ into** meter en;
feedback n reacción f, feedback m

feel [fiːl] (pt, pp **felt**) n (sensation)
sensación f; (sense of touch) tacto;
(impression): **to have the ~ of** parecerse
a ▷ vt tocar; (pain etc) sentir; (think,
believe) creer: **to ~ hungry/cold** tener
hambre/frío; **to ~ lonely/better**
sentirse solo/mejor; **I don't ~ well**
no me siento bien; **it ~s soft** es suave
al tacto; **to ~ like** (want) tener ganas
de; **feeling** n (physical) sensación f;
(foreboding) presentimiento; (emotion)
sentimiento

feet [fiːt] npl of **foot**

fell [fɛl] pt of **fall** ▷ vt (tree) talar

fellow ['fɛləu] n tipo, tío (sp);
(comrade) compañero; (of learned
society) socio/a; **fellow citizen** n
conciudadano/a; **fellow countryman**
(irreg) n compatriota m; **fellow men**
npl semejantes mpl; **fellowship** n
compañerismo; (grant) beca

felony ['fɛləni] n crimen m

felt [fɛlt] pt, pp of **feel** ▷ n fieltro;
felt-tip n (also: **felt-tip pen**)
rotulador m

female ['fiːmeɪl] n (pej: woman) mujer
f, tía; (Zool) hembra ▷ adj femenino;
hembra

feminine ['fɛmɪnɪn] adj femenino

feminist ['fɛmɪnɪst] n feminista

fence [fɛns] n valla, cerca ▷ vt (also: ~
in) cercar ▷ vi (Sport) hacer esgrima;
fencing n esgrima

fend [fɛnd] vi: **to ~ for o.s.** valerse por
sí mismo; **fend off** vt (attack) rechazar;
(questions) evadir

fender ['fɛndə*] (us) n guardafuego;
(Aut) parachoques m inv

fennel ['fɛnl] n hinojo

ferment [vb fə'mɛnt, n 'fəːmɛnt] vi
fermentar ▷ n (fig) agitación f

fern [fəːn] n helecho

ferocious [fə'rəuʃəs] adj feroz

ferret ['fɛrɪt] n hurón m

ferry ['fɛrɪ] n (small) barca (de pasaje),
balsa; (large: also: ~**boat**) transbordador

m, ferry m ▷ vt transportar

fertile ['fəːtaɪl] adj fértil; (Biol)
fecundo; **fertilize** ['fəːtɪlaɪz] vt (Biol)
fecundar; (Agr) abonar; **fertilizer** n
abono

festival ['fɛstɪvəl] n (Rel) fiesta; (Art,
Mus) festival m

festive ['fɛstɪv] adj festivo; **the ~
season** (BRIT: Christmas) las Navidades

fetch [fɛtʃ] vt ir a buscar; (sell for)
venderse por

fête [feɪt] n fiesta

fetus ['fiːtəs] (us) n = **foetus**

feud [fjuːd] n (hostility) enemistad f;
(quarrel) disputa

fever ['fiːvə*] n fiebre f; **feverish**
adj febril

few [fjuː] adj (not many) pocos ▷ pron
pocos; algunos; **a ~** adj unos pocos,
algunos; **fewer** adj menos; **fewest** adj
los(las) menos

fiancé [fɪ'ɑ̃ːŋseɪ] n novio, prometido;
fiancée n novia, prometida

fiasco [fɪ'æskəu] n fiasco

fib [fɪb] n mentirilla

fibre ['faɪbə*] (us fiber) n fibra;
fibreglass (us **Fiberglass**®) n fibra
de vidrio

fickle ['fɪkl] adj inconstante

fiction ['fɪkʃən] n ficción f; **fictional**
adj novelesco

fiddle ['fɪdl] n (Mus) violín m;
(cheating) trampa ▷ vt (BRIT: accounts)
falsificar; **fiddle with** vt fus juguetear
con

fidelity [fɪ'dɛlɪtɪ] n fidelidad f

field [fiːld] n campo; (fig) campo,
esfera; (Sport) campo (SP), cancha (LAM);
field marshal n mariscal m

fierce [fɪəs] adj feroz; (wind, heat)
fuerte; (fighting, enemy) encarnizado

fifteen [fɪf'tiːn] num quince;
fifteenth adj decimoquinto; **the
fifteenth floor** la planta quince;
the fifteenth of August el quince
de agosto

fifth [fɪfθ] num quinto

fiftieth ['fɪftɪθ] adj quincuagésimo

fifty ['fɪftɪ] *num* cincuenta; **fifty-fifty**
adj (deal, split) a medias ▷ *adv* a
medias, mitad por mitad

fig [fɪg] *n* higo

fight [faɪt] (*pt, pp* **fought**) *n* (gen)
pelea; (Mil) combate *m*; (struggle) lucha
▷ *vt* luchar contra; (cancer, alcoholism)
combatir; (election) intentar ganar;
(emotion) resistir ▷ *vi* pelear, luchar;
fight back *vi* defenderse; (after illness)
recuperarse ▷ *vt* (tears) contener;
fight off *vt* (attack, attacker) rechazar;
(disease, sleep, urge) luchar contra;
fighting *n* combate *m*, pelea

figure ['fɪgǝ*] *n* (Drawing, Geom)
figura, dibujo; (number, cipher) cifra;
(body, outline) tipo; (personality) figura
▷ *vt* (esp us) imaginar ▷ *vi* (appear)
figurar; **figure out** *vt* (work out)
resolver

file [faɪl] *n* (tool) lima; (dossier)
expediente *m*; (folder) carpeta;
(Comput) fichero; (row) fila ▷ *vt* limar;
(Law: claim) presentar; (store) archivar;
filing cabinet *n* fichero, archivador *m*

Filipino [fɪlɪ'pi:nǝu] *adj* filipino ▷ *n*
(person) filipino/a *m/f*; (Ling) tagalo

fill [fɪl] *vt* (space): **to ~ (with)** llenar
(de); (vacancy, need) cubrir ▷ *n*: **to eat
one's ~** llenarse; **fill in** *vt* rellenar; **fill
out** *vt* (form, receipt) rellenar; **fill up** *vt*
llenar (hasta el borde) ▷ *vi* (Aut) poner
gasolina

fillet ['fɪlɪt] *n* filete *m*; **fillet steak** *n*
filete *m* de ternera

filling ['fɪlɪŋ] *n* (Culin) relleno; (for
tooth) empaste *m*; **filling station** *n*
estación *f* de servicio

film [fɪlm] *n* película ▷ *vt* (scene)
filmar ▷ *vi* rodar (una película); **film
star** *n* astro, estrella de cine

filter ['fɪltǝ*] *n* filtro ▷ *vt* filtrar; **filter
lane** (BRIT) *n* carril *m* de selección

filth [fɪlθ] *n* suciedad *f*; **filthy** *adj*
sucio; (language) obsceno

fin [fɪn] *n* (gen) aleta

final ['faɪnl] *adj* (last) final, último;
(definitive) definitivo, terminante ▷ *n*

(BRIT Sport) final *f*; **finals** *npl* (Scol)
examen *m* final; (us Sport) final *f*

finale [fɪ'nɑ:lɪ] *n* final *m*

final: **finalist** *n* (Sport) finalista *mf*;
finalize *vt* concluir, completar; **finally**
adv (lastly) por último, finalmente;
(eventually) por fin

finance [faɪ'næns] *n* (money)
fondos *mpl* ▷ *vt* financiar; **finances**
npl finanzas *fpl*; (personal finances)
situación económica; **financial**
[-'nænfǝl] *adj* financiero; **financial
year** *n* ejercicio (financiero)

find [faɪnd] (*pt, pp* **found**) *vt*
encontrar, hallar; (come upon) descubrir
▷ *n* hallazgo; descubrimiento; **to ~ sb
guilty** (Law) declarar culpable a algn;
find out *vt* averiguar; (truth, secret)
descubrir; **to find out about** (subject)
informarse sobre; (by chance) enterarse
de; **findings** *npl* (Law) veredicto, fallo;
(of report) recomendaciones *fpl*

fine [faɪn] *adj* excelente; (thin) fino
▷ *adv* (well) bien ▷ *n* (Law) multa ▷ *vt*
(Law) multar; **to be ~** (person) estar
bien; (weather) hacer buen tiempo; **fine
arts** *npl* bellas artes *fpl*

finger ['fɪŋgǝ*] *n* dedo ▷ *vt* (touch)
manosear; **little/index ~** (dedo)
meñique *m*/índice *m*; **fingernail** *n*
uña; **fingerprint** *n* huella dactilar;
fingertip *n* yema del dedo

finish ['fɪnɪʃ] *n* (end) fin *m*; (Sport)
meta; (polish etc) acabado ▷ *vt, vi*
terminar; **to ~ doing sth** acabar de
hacer algo; **to ~ third** llegar el tercero;
finish off *vt* acabar, terminar; (kill)
acabar con; **finish up** *vt* acabar,
terminar ▷ *vi* ir a parar, terminar

Finland ['fɪnlǝnd] *n* Finlandia

Finn [fɪn] *n* finlandés/esa *m/f*;
Finnish *adj* finlandés/esa ▷ *n* (Ling)
finlandés *m*

fir [fǝ:*] *n* abeto

fire ['faɪǝ*] *n* fuego; (in hearth) lumbre
f; (accidental) incendio; (heater) estufa
▷ *vt* (gun) disparar; (interest) despertar;
(inf: dismiss) despedir ▷ *vi* (shoot)

disparar; **on ~** ardiendo, en llamas;
fire alarm n alarma de incendios;
firearm n arma de fuego; **fire brigade**
(us **fire department**) n (cuerpo de)
bomberos mpl; **fire engine** (BRIT) n
coche m de bomberos; **fire escape**
n escalera de incendios; **fire exit** n
salida de incendios; **fire extinguisher**
n extintor m (de incendios); **fireman**
(irreg) n bombero; **fireplace** n
chimenea; **fire station** n parque m
de bomberos; **firetruck** (us) n =**fire
engine**; **firewall** n (Internet) firewall
m; **firewood** n leña; **fireworks** npl
fuegos mpl artificiales

firm [fɜːm] adj firme; (look, voice)
resuelto ▷ n firma, empresa; **firmly**
adv firmemente; resueltamente

first [fɜːst] adj primero ▷ adv (before
others) primero; (when listing reasons
etc) en primer lugar, primera
▷ n (person: in race) primero/a; (Aut)
primera; (BRIT Scol) título de licenciado
con calificación de sobresaliente; **at ~** al
principio; **~ of all** ante todo; **first aid** n
primera ayuda, primeros auxilios mpl;
first-aid kit n botiquín m; **first-class**
adj (excellent) de primera (categoría);
(ticket etc) de primera clase; **first-hand**
adj de primera mano; **first lady** n
(esp us) primera dama; **firstly** adv en
primer lugar; **first name** n nombre m
(de pila); **first-rate** adj estupendo

fiscal ['fɪskəl] adj fiscal; **fiscal year** n
año fiscal, ejercicio

fish [fɪʃ] n (inv pez m; (food) pescado
▷ vt, vi pescar; **to go ~ing** ir de pesca;
~ and chips pescado frito con patatas
fritas; **fisherman** (irreg) n pescador
m; **fish fingers** (BRIT) npl croquetas
fpl de pescado; **fishing** n pesca;
fishing boat n barca de pesca; **fishing
line** n sedal m; **fishmonger** n (BRIT)
pescadero/a; **fishmonger's (shop)**
(BRIT) n pescadería; **fish sticks** (us)
npl = **fish fingers**; **fishy** (inf) adj
sospechoso

fist [fɪst] n puño

fit [fɪt] adj (healthy) en (buena)
forma; (proper) adecuado, apropiado
▷ vt (clothes) estar o sentar bien a;
(instal) poner; (equip) proveer, dotar;
(facts) cuadrar o corresponder con
▷ vi (clothes) sentar bien; (in space,
gap) caber; (facts) coincidir ▷ n (Med)
ataque m; **~ to** (ready) a punto de; **~ for**
apropiado para; **a ~ of anger/pride**
un arranque de cólera/orgullo; **this
dress is a good ~** este vestido me
sienta bien; **by ~s and starts** a rachas;
fit in vi (fig: person) llevarse bien
(con todos); **fitness** n (Med) salud
f; **fitted** adj (jacket, shirt) entallado;
(sheet) de cuatro picos; **fitted carpet**
n moqueta; **fitted kitchen** n cocina
amueblada; **fitting** adj apropiado ▷ n
(of dress) prueba; (of piece of equipment)
instalación f; **fitting room** n probador
m; **fittings** npl instalaciones fpl

five [faɪv] num cinco; **fiver** (inf) n
(BRIT) billete m de cinco libras; (us)
billete m de cinco dólares

fix [fɪks] vt (secure) fijar, asegurar;
(mend) arreglar; (prepare) preparar
▷ n: **to be in a ~** estar en un aprieto; **fix
up** vt (meeting) arreglar; **to fix sb up
with sth** proveer a algn de algo; **fixed**
adj (prices etc) fijo; **fixture** n (Sport)
encuentro

fizzy ['fɪzɪ] adj (drink) gaseoso

flag [flæg] n bandera; (stone) losa ▷ vi
decaer ▷ vt: **to ~ sb down** hacer señas
a algn para que se pare; **flagpole** n
asta de bandera

flair [fleə*] n aptitud f especial

flak [flæk] n (Mil) fuego antiaéreo;
(inf: criticism) lluvia de críticas

flake [fleɪk] n (of rust, paint) escama;
(of snow, soap powder) copo ▷ vi (also: ~
off) desconcharse

flamboyant [flæm'bɔɪənt] adj
(dress) vistoso; (person)
extravagante

flame [fleɪm] n llama

flamingo [flə'mɪŋɡəʊ] n flamenco

flammable ['flæməbl] adj

inflamable

flan [flæn] (BRIT) n tarta
▪ Be careful not to translate **flan** by the Spanish word *flan*.

flank [flæŋk] n (of animal) ijar m; (of army) flanco ▷ vt flanquear

flannel ['flænl] n (BRIT: also: **face ~**) manopla; (fabric) franela

flap [flæp] n (of pocket, envelope) solapa ▷ vt (wings, arms) agitar ▷ vi (sail, flag) ondear

flare [fleə*] n llamarada; (Mil) bengala; (in skirt etc) vuelo; **flares** npl (trousers) pantalones mpl de campana; **flare up** vi encenderse; (fig: person) encolerizarse; (: revolt) estallar

flash [flæʃ] n relámpago; (also: **news ~**) noticias fpl de última hora; (Phot) flash m ▷ vt (light, headlights) lanzar un destello con; (news, message) transmitir; (smile) lanzar ▷ vi brillar; (hazard light etc) lanzar destellos; **in a ~** en un instante; **he ~ed by** or **past** pasó como un rayo; **flashback** n (Cinema) flashback m; **flashbulb** n bombilla fusible; **flashlight** n linterna

flask [flɑːsk] n frasco; (also: **vacuum ~**) termo

flat [flæt] adj llano; (smooth) liso; (tyre) desinflado; (battery) descargado; (beer) muerto; (refusal etc) rotundo; (Mus) desafinado; (rate) fijo ▷ n (BRIT: apartment) piso (SP), departamento (LAM), apartamento (Aut) pinchazo; (Mus) bemol m; **to work ~ out** trabajar a toda mecha; **flatten** vt (also: **flatten out**) allanar; (smooth out) alisar; (building, plants) arrasar

flatter ['flætə*] vt adular, halagar; **flattering** adj halagüeño; (dress) que favorece

flaunt [flɔːnt] vt ostentar, lucir

flavour etc ['fleɪvə*] (US **flavor** etc) n sabor m, gusto ▷ vt sazonar, condimentar; **strawberry-flavoured** con sabor a fresa; **flavouring** n (in product) aromatizante m

flaw [flɔː] n defecto; **flawless** adj

flea [fliː] n pulga; **flea market** n rastro, mercadillo

flee [fliː] (pt, pp **fled**) vt huir de ▷ vi huir, fugarse

fleece [fliːs] n vellón m; (wool) lana; (top) forro polar ▷ vt (inf) desplumar

fleet [fliːt] n flota; (of lorries etc) escuadra

fleeting ['fliːtɪŋ] adj fugaz

Flemish ['flemɪʃ] adj flamenco

flesh [fleʃ] n carne f; (skin) piel f; (of fruit) pulpa

flew [fluː] pt of **fly**

flex [fleks] n cordón m ▷ vt (muscles) tensar; **flexibility** n flexibilidad f; **flexible** adj flexible; **flexitime** (US **flextime**) n horario flexible

flick [flɪk] n capirotazo; chasquido ▷ vt (with hand) dar un capirotazo a; (whip etc) chasquear; (switch) accionar; **flick through** vt fus hojear

flicker ['flɪkə*] vi (light) parpadear; (flame) vacilar

flies [flaɪz] npl of **fly**

flight [flaɪt] n vuelo; (escape) huida, fuga; (also: **~ of steps**) tramo (de escaleras); **flight attendant** n auxiliar mf de vuelo

flimsy ['flɪmzɪ] adj (thin) muy ligero; (building) endeble; (excuse) flojo

flinch [flɪntʃ] vi encogerse; **to ~ from** retroceder ante

fling [flɪŋ] (pt, pp **flung**) vt arrojar

flint [flɪnt] n pedernal m; (in lighter) piedra

flip [flɪp] vt dar la vuelta a; (switch: turn on) encender; (turn) apagar; (coin) echar a cara o cruz

flip-flops ['flɪpflɔps] npl (esp BRIT) chancletas fpl

flipper ['flɪpə*] n aleta

flirt [flɜːt] vi coquetear, flirtear ▷ n coqueta

float [fləʊt] n flotador m; (in procession) carroza; (money) reserva ▷ vi flotar; (swimmer) hacer la plancha

flock [flɔk] n (of sheep) rebaño; (of

birds) bandada ▷ vi: **to ~ to** acudir en tropel a

flood [flʌd] n inundación f; (of letters, imports etc) avalancha ▷ vt inundar ▷ vi (place) inundarse; (people): **to ~ into** inundar; **flooding** n inundaciones fpl; **floodlight** n foco

floor [flɔ:ʳ] n suelo; (storey) piso; (of sea) fondo ▷ vt (question) dejar sin respuesta; (: blow) derribar; **ground ~**, **first ~** (us) planta baja; **first ~**, **second ~** (us) primer piso; **floorboard** n tabla; **flooring** n suelo; (material) solería; **floor show** n cabaret m

flop [flɔp] n fracaso ▷ vi (fail) fracasar; (fall) derrumbarse; **floppy** adj flojo ▷ n (Comput: also: **floppy disk**) floppy m

flora ['flɔ:rə] n flora

floral ['flɔ:rl] adj (pattern) floreado

florist ['flɒrɪst] n florista mf; **florist's (shop)** n floristería

flotation [fləu'teɪʃən] n (of shares) emisión f; (of company) lanzamiento m

flour ['flauəʳ] n harina

flourish ['flʌrɪʃ] n florecer ▷ n ademán m, movimiento (ostentoso)

flow [fləu] n (movement) flujo; (of traffic) circulación f; (also: current) corriente f ▷ vi (river, blood) fluir; (traffic) circular

flower ['flauəʳ] n flor f ▷ vi florecer; **flower bed** n macizo; **flowerpot** n tiesto

flown [fləun] pp of **fly**

fl. oz. abbr (= fluid ounce)

flu [flu:] n: **to have ~** tener la gripe

fluctuate ['flʌktjueɪt] vi fluctuar

fluent ['flu:ənt] adj (linguist) que habla perfectamente; (speech) elocuente; **he speaks ~ French, he's ~ in French** domina el francés

fluff [flʌf] n pelusa; **fluffy** adj de pelo suave

fluid ['flu:ɪd] adj (movement) fluido, líquido; (situation) inestable ▷ n fluido, líquido; **fluid ounce** n onza f líquida

fluke [flu:k] (inf) n chiripa

flung [flʌŋ] pt, pp of **fling**

fluorescent [fluə'resnt] adj fluorescente

fluoride ['fluəraɪd] n fluoruro

flurry ['flʌrɪ] n (of snow) temporal m; **~ of activity** frenesí m de actividad

flush [flʌʃ] n rubor m; (fig: of youth etc) resplandor m ▷ vt limpiar con agua ▷ vi ruborizarse ▷ adj: **~ with** a ras de; **to ~ the toilet** hacer funcionar la cisterna

flute [flu:t] n flauta

flutter ['flʌtəʳ] n (of wings) revoloteo, aleteo; (fig): **a ~ of panic/excitement** una oleada de pánico/excitación ▷ vi revolotear

fly [flaɪ] (pt **flew**, pp **flown**) n (insect) mosca; (on trousers: also: **flies**) bragueta ▷ vt (plane) pilot(e)ar; (cargo) transportar (en avión); (distances) recorrer (en avión) ▷ vi volar; (passengers) ir en avión; (escape) evadirse; (flag) ondear; **fly away**, **fly off** vi emprender el vuelo; **fly-drive** n: **fly-drive holiday** vacaciones que incluyen vuelo y alquiler de coche; **flying** n (activity) (el) volar; (action) vuelo ▷ adj: **flying visit** visita relámpago; **with flying colours** con lucimiento; **flying saucer** n platillo volante; **flyover** (BRIT) n paso a desnivel o superior

FM abbr (Radio) (= frequency modulation) FM

foal [fəul] n potro

foam [fəum] n espuma ▷ vi hacer espuma

focus ['fəukəs] (pl **-es**) n foco; (centre) centro ▷ vt (field glasses etc) enfocar ▷ vi: **to ~ (on)** enfocar (a); (issue etc) centrarse en; **in/out of ~** enfocado/ desenfocado

foetus ['fi:təs] (us **fetus**) n feto

fog [fɒg] n niebla; **foggy** adj: **it's foggy** hay niebla, está brumoso; **fog lamp** (us **fog light**) n (Aut) faro de niebla

foil [fɔɪl] vt frustrar ▷ n hoja; (kitchen foil) papel m (de aluminio); (complement) complemento; (Fencing) florete m

fold [fəuld] n (*bend, crease*) pliegue m; (*Agr*) redil m ▷ vt doblar; (*arms*) cruzar; **fold up** vi plegarse, doblarse; (*business*) quebrar ▷ vt (*map etc*) doblar; **folder** n (*for papers*) carpeta (*Comput*) directorio; **folding** adj (*chair, bed*) plegable

foliage ['fəulɪɪdʒ] n follaje m

folk [fəuk] npl gente f ▷ adj popular, folklórico; **folks** npl (*family*) familia sg, parientes mpl; **folklore** ['fəuklɔ:*] n folklore m; **folk music** n música folk; **folk song** n canción f popular

follow ['fɒləu] vt seguir ▷ vi seguir; (*result*) resultar; **to ~ suit** hacer lo mismo; **follow up** vt (*letter, offer*) responder a; (*case*) investigar; **follower** n (*of person, belief*) partidario/a, **following** adj siguiente ▷ n afición f, partidarios mpl; **follow-up** n continuación f

fond [fɒnd] adj (*memory, smile etc*) cariñoso; (*hopes*) ilusorio; **to be ~ of** tener cariño a; (*pastime, food*) ser aficionado a

food [fu:d] n comida; **food mixer** n batidora; **food poisoning** n intoxicación f alimenticia; **food processor** n robot m de cocina; **food stamp**(*us*) n vale m para comida

fool [fu:l] n tonto/a; (*Culin*) puré m de frutas con nata ▷ vt engañar ▷ vi (*gen*) bromear; **fool about, fool around** vi hacer el tonto; **foolish** adj tonto; (*careless*) imprudente; **foolproof** adj (*plan etc*) infalible

foot [fut] (*pl* **feet**) n pie m; (*measure*) pie m (= 304 mm); (*of animal*) pata ▷ vt (*bill*) pagar; **on ~** a pie; **footage** n (*Cinema*) imágenes fpl; **foot-and-mouth (disease)** ['futənd'mauθ-] n fiebre f aftosa; **football** n balón m; (*game:* BRIT) fútbol m; (: *us*) fútbol m americano; **footballer** n (BRIT) = **football player**; **football match** n partido de fútbol; **football player** n (BRIT) futbolista mf; (*us*) jugador/a de fútbol americano; **footbridge** n

puente m para peatones; **foothills** npl estribaciones fpl; **foothold** n pie m firme; **footing** n (fig) posición f; **to lose one's footing** perder el pie; **footnote** n nota (al pie de la página); **footpath** n sendero; **footprint** n huella, pisada; **footstep** n paso; **footwear** n calzado

🔑 KEYWORD

for [fɔ:] prep 1(*indicating destination, intention*) para; **the train for London** el tren con destino a *or* de Londres; **he left for Rome** marchó para Roma; **he went for the paper** fue por el periódico; **is this for me?** ¿es esto para mí?; **it's time for lunch** es la hora de comer 2(*indicating purpose*) para; **what's it for?** ¿para qué (es)?; **to pray for peace** rezar por la paz 3(*on behalf of, representing*): **the MP for Hove** el diputado por Hove; **he works for the government/a local firm** trabaja para el gobierno/en una empresa local; **I'll ask him for you** se lo pediré por ti; **G for George** G de Gerona 4(*because of*) por esta razón; **for fear of being criticized** por temor a ser criticado 5(*with regard to*) para; **it's cold for July** hace frío para julio; **he has a gift for languages** tiene don de lenguas 6(*in exchange for*) por; **I sold it for £5** lo vendí por £5; **to pay 50 pence for a ticket** pagar 50 peniques por un billete 7(*in favour of*): **are you for or against us?** ¿estás con nosotros o contra nosotros?; **I'm all for it** estoy totalmente a favor; **vote for X** vote (a) X 8(*referring to distance*): **there are roadworks for 5 km** hay obras en 5 km; **we walked for miles** caminamos kilómetros y kilómetros 9(*referring to time*): **he was away for two years** estuvo fuera (durante) dos años; **it hasn't rained for 3 weeks** no ha llovido durante o en 3 semanas; **I have known her for years** la conozco desde hace años; **can you do it for tomorrow?** ¿lo podrás hacer para mañana?

10 (with infinitive clauses): **it is not for me to decide** la decisión no es cosa mía; **it would be best for you to leave** sería mejor que te fueras; **there is still time for you to do it** todavía te queda tiempo para hacerlo; **for this to be possible ...** para que esto sea posible ...

11 (in spite of) a pesar de: **for all his complaints** a pesar de sus quejas ▷ conj (since, as: rather formal) puesto que

forbid [fəˈbɪd] (pt **forbad(e)**, pp **forbidden**) vt prohibir; **to ~ sb to do sth** prohibir a algn hacer algo; **forbidden** pt of **forbid** ▷ adj (food, area) prohibido; (word, subject) tabú

force [fɔːs] n fuerza ▷ vt forzar; (push) meter a la fuerza; **to ~ o.s. to do** hacer un esfuerzo por hacer; **forced** adj forzado; **forceful** adj enérgico

ford [fɔːd] n vado

fore [fɔː*] n: **to come to the ~** empezar a destacar; **forearm** n antebrazo; **forecast** (pt, pp **forecast**) n pronóstico ▷ vt pronosticar; **forecourt** n patio; **forefinger** n (dedo) índice m; **forefront** n: **in the forefront of** en la vanguardia de; **foreground** n primer plano; **forehead** [ˈfɔrɪd] n frente f

foreign [ˈfɔrɪn] adj extranjero; (trade) exterior; (object) extraño; **foreign currency** n divisas fpl; **foreigner** n extranjero/a; **foreign exchange** n divisas fpl; **Foreign Office** (BRIT) n Ministerio de Asuntos Exteriores; **Foreign Secretary** (BRIT) n Ministro de Asuntos Exteriores

fore: **foreman** (irreg) n capataz m; (in construction) maestro de obras; **foremost** adj principal ▷ adv: **first**

and foremost ante todo; **forename** n nombre m (de pila)

forensic [fəˈrɛnsɪk] adj forense

foresee [fɔːˈsiː] (pt **foresaw**, pp **foreseen**) vt prever; **foreseeable** adj previsible

forest [ˈfɔrɪst] n bosque m; **forestry** n silvicultura

forever [fəˈrɛvə*] adv para siempre; (endlessly) constantemente

foreword [ˈfɔːwəd] n prefacio

forfeit [ˈfɔːfɪt] vt perder

forgave [fəˈgeɪv] pt of **forgive**

forge [fɔːdʒ] n herrería ▷ vt (signature, money) falsificar; (metal) forjar; **forger** n falsificador(a) m/f; **forgery** n falsificación f

forget [fəˈgɛt] (pt **forgot**, pp **forgotten**) vt olvidar ▷ vi olvidarse; **forgetful** adj despistado

forgive [fəˈgɪv] (pt **forgave**, pp **forgiven**) vt perdonar; **to ~ sb for sth** perdonar algo a algn

forgot [fəˈgɒt] pt of **forget**

forgotten [fəˈgɒtn] pp of **forget**

fork [fɔːk] n (for eating) tenedor m; (for gardening) horca; (of roads) bifurcación f ▷ vi (road) bifurcarse

forlorn [fəˈlɔːn] adj (person) triste, melancólico; (place) abandonado; (attempt, hope) desesperado

form [fɔːm] n forma; (BRIT Scol) clase f; (document) formulario ▷ vt formar; (idea) concebir; (habit) adquirir; **in top ~** en plena forma; **to ~ a queue** hacer cola

formal [ˈfɔːməl] adj (offer, receipt) por escrito; (person etc) correcto; (occasion, dinner) de etiqueta; (dress) correcto; (garden) de estilo) clásico; **formality** [-ˈmælɪtɪ] n (procedure) trámite m; corrección f; etiqueta

format [ˈfɔːmæt] n formato ▷ vt (Comput) formatear

formation [fɔːˈmeɪʃən] n formación f

former [ˈfɔːmə*] adj anterior; (earlier) antiguo; (ex) ex; **the ~ ... the latter ...** aquél ... éste ...; **formerly** adv antes

formidable ['fɔːmɪdəbl] adj formidable

formula ['fɔːmjulə] n fórmula

fort [fɔːt] n fuerte m

forthcoming [fɔːθ'kʌmɪŋ] adj próximo, venidero; (help, information) disponible; (character) comunicativo

fortieth ['fɔːtɪɪθ] adj cuadragésimo

fortify ['fɔːtɪfaɪ] vt (city) fortificar; (person) fortalecer

fortnight ['fɔːtnaɪt] (BRIT) n quince días mpl; quincena; **fortnightly** adj de cada quince días, quincenal ▷ adv cada quince días, quincenalmente

fortress ['fɔːtrɪs] n fortaleza

fortunate ['fɔːtʃənɪt] adj afortunado; **it is ~ that ...** (es una) suerte que ...; **fortunately** adv afortunadamente

fortune ['fɔːtʃən] n suerte f; (wealth) fortuna; **fortune-teller** n adivino/a

forty ['fɔːtɪ] num cuarenta

forum ['fɔːrəm] n foro

forward ['fɔːwəd] adj (movement, position) avanzado; (front) delantero; (in time) adelantado; (not shy) atrevido ▷ n (Sport) delantero ▷ vt (letter) remitir; (career) promocionar; **to move ~** avanzar; **forwarding address** n destinatario; **forward(s)** adv (hacia) adelante; **forward slash** n barra diagonal

fossil ['fɔsl] n fósil m

foster ['fɔstə*] vt (child) acoger en una familia; fomentar; **foster child** n hijo/a adoptivo/a; **foster mother** n madre f adoptiva

fought [fɔːt] pt, pp of **fight**

foul [faul] adj sucio, puerco; (weather, smell etc) asqueroso; (language) grosero; (temper) malísimo ▷ n (Sport) falta ▷ vt (dirty) ensuciar; **foul play** n (Law) muerte f violenta

found [faund] pt, pp of **find** ▷ vt fundar; **foundation** [-'deɪʃən] n (act) fundación f; (basis) base f; (also: **foundation cream**) crema base; **foundations** npl (of building)

cimientos mpl

founder ['faundə*] n fundador(a) m/f ▷ vi hundirse

fountain ['fauntɪn] n fuente f; **fountain pen** n (pluma) estilográfica (SP), pluma-fuente f (LAM)

four [fɔː*] num cuatro; **on all ~s** a gatas; **four-letter word** n taco; **four-poster** n (also: **four-poster bed**) cama de columnas; **fourteen** num catorce; **fourteenth** adj decimocuarto; **fourth** num cuarto; **four-wheel drive** n tracción f a las cuatro ruedas

fowl [faul] n ave f (de corral)

fox [fɔks] n zorro ▷ vt confundir

foyer ['fɔɪeɪ] n vestíbulo

fraction ['frækʃən] n fracción f

fracture ['fræktʃə*] n fractura

fragile ['frædʒaɪl] adj frágil

fragment ['frægmənt] n fragmento

fragrance ['freɪgrəns] n fragancia

frail [freɪl] adj frágil; (person) débil

frame [freɪm] n (Tech) armazón m; (of person) cuerpo; (of picture, door etc) marco; (of spectacles: also: **~s**) montura ▷ vt enmarcar; **framework** n marco

France [frɑːns] n Francia

franchise ['fræntʃaɪz] n (Pol) derecho de votar, sufragio; (Comm) licencia, concesión f

frank [fræŋk] adj franco ▷ vt (letter) franquear; **frankly** adv francamente

frantic ['fræntɪk] adj (distraught) desesperado; (hectic) frenético

fraud [frɔːd] n fraude m; (person) impostor/a m/f

fraught [frɔːt] adj: **~ with** lleno de

fray [freɪ] vi deshilacharse

freak [friːk] n (person) fenómeno; (event) suceso anormal

freckle ['frekl] n peca

free [friː] adj libre; (gratis) gratuito ▷ vt (prisoner etc) poner en libertad; (jammed object) soltar; **~ (of charge), for ~** gratis; **freedom** n libertad f; **Freefone ®** n número gratuito; **free gift** n prima; **free kick** n tiro libre; **freelance** adj independiente

▷ adv por cuenta propia; **freely** adv libremente; (*liberally*) generosamente; **Freepost®** n porte m pagado; **free-range** adj (hen, eggs) de granja; **freeway** (US) n autopista; **free will** n libre albedrío; **of one's own free will** por su propia voluntad

freeze [friːz] (pt **froze**, pp **frozen**) vi (weather) helar; (liquid, pipe, person) helarse, congelarse ▷ vt helar; (food, prices, salaries) congelar ▷ n helada; (on arms, wages) congelación f; **freezer** n congelador m, freezer m (SC)

freezing ['friːzɪŋ] adj helado; **three degrees below ~** tres grados bajo cero; **freezing point** n punto de congelación

freight [freit] n (goods) carga; (money charged) flete m; **freight train** n tren m de mercancías

French [frentʃ] adj francés/esa ▷ n (Ling) francés m; **the French** npl los franceses; **French bean** n judía verde; **French bread** n pan m francés; **French dressing** n (Culin) vinagreta; **French fried potatoes**, **French fries** (US) npl patatas fpl (SP) or papas fpl (LAM) fritas; **Frenchman** (irreg) n francés m; **Frenchwoman** (irreg) n francesa; **French stick** n barra de pan; **French window** n puerta de cristal

frenzy ['frenzɪ] n frenesí m

frequency ['friːkwənsɪ] n frecuencia f

frequent adj ['friːkwənt], vb fri'kwent] adj frecuente ▷ vt frecuentar; **frequently** [-əntlɪ] adv frecuentemente, a menudo

fresh [freʃ] adj fresco; (bread) tierno; (new) nuevo; **freshen** vi (wind, air) soplar más recio; **freshen up** vi (person) arreglarse, lavarse; **fresher** (BRIT: inf) n (Univ) estudiante mf de primer año; **freshly** adv (made, painted etc) recién; **freshman** (US: irreg) n = **fresher**; **freshwater** adj (fish) de agua dulce

fret [fret] vi inquietarse

Fri abbr (= Friday) vier

friction ['frɪkʃən] n fricción f

Friday ['fraɪdɪ] n viernes m inv

fridge [frɪdʒ] (BRIT) n frigorífico (SP), nevera (SP), refrigerador m (LAM), heladera (RPL)

fried [fraɪd] adj frito

friend [frend] n amigo/a; **friendly** adj simpático; (government) amigo; (place) acogedor/a; (match) amistoso; **friendship** n amistad f

fries [fraɪz] (esp US) npl = **French fried potatoes**

frigate ['frɪgɪt] n fragata f

fright [fraɪt] n (terror) terror m; (scare) susto; **to take ~** asustarse; **frighten** vt asustar; **frightened** adj asustado; **frightening** adj espantoso; **frightful** adj espantoso, horrible

frill [frɪl] n volante m

fringe [frɪndʒ] n (BRIT: of hair) flequillo; (on lampshade etc) flecos mpl; (of forest etc) borde m, margen m

Frisbee® ['frɪzbɪ] n frisbee® m

fritter ['frɪtə*] n buñuelo

frivolous ['frɪvələs] adj frívolo

fro [frəu] see **to**

frock [frɒk] n vestido

frog [frɒg] n rana; **frogman** (irreg) n hombre-rana m

KEYWORD

from [frɒm] prep **1** (indicating starting place) de, desde; **where do you come from?** ¿de dónde eres?; **from London to Glasgow** de Londres a Glasgow; **to escape from sth/sb** escaparse de algo/algn

2 (indicating origin etc) de; **a letter/ telephone call from my sister** una carta/llamada de mi hermana; **tell him from me that ...** dígale de mi parte que ...

3 (indicating time): **from one o'clock to or until or till two** de(sde) la una a or hasta las dos; **from January (on)** a partir de enero

4 (indicating distance) de; **the hotel is**

1 km from the beach el hotel está a 1 km de la playa
5 (*indicating price, number etc*) de; **prices range from £10 to £50** los precios van desde £10 a or hasta £50; **the interest rate was increased from 9% to 10%** el tipo de interés fue incrementado de un 9% a un 10%
6 (*indicating difference*) de; **he can't tell red from green** no sabe distinguir el rojo del verde; **to be different from sb/sth** ser diferente a algn/algo
7 (*because of, on the basis of*): **from what he says** por lo que dice; **weak from hunger** debilitado por el hambre

front [frʌnt] n (*foremost part*) parte f delantera; (*of house*) fachada; (*of dress*) delantero; (*promenade: also:* **sea ~**) paseo marítimo; (*Mil, Pol, Meteorology*) frente m; (*fig: appearances*) apariencias fpl ▷ adj (*wheel, leg*) delantero; (*row, line*) primero; **in ~** delante (de); **front door** n puerta principal; **frontier** ['frʌntɪə*] n frontera; **front page** n primera plana; **front-wheel drive** n tracción delantera

frost [frɒst] n helada; (*also:* **hoar~**) escarcha; **frostbite** n congelación f; **frosting** n (*esp us: icing*) glaseado; **frosty** adj (*weather*) de helada; (*welcome etc*) glacial

froth [frɒθ] n espuma

frown [fraun] vi fruncir el ceño

froze [frəuz] pt of **freeze**

frozen ['frəuzn] pp of **freeze**

fruit [fruːt] n inv fruta; fruto; (*fig*) fruto; resultados mpl; **fruit juice** n zumo (SP) or jugo (LAM) de fruta; **fruit machine** n (BRIT) máquina f tragaperras; **fruit salad** n macedonia (SP) or ensalada (LAM) de frutas

frustrate [frʌs'treɪt] vt frustrar; **frustrated** adj frustrado

fry [fraɪ] (*pt, pp* **fried**) vt freír; **small ~** gente f menuda; **frying pan** n sartén f

ft. abbr = **foot; feet**

fudge [fʌdʒ] n (*Culin*) caramelo blando

fuel [fjuəl] n (*for heating*) combustible m; (*coal*) carbón m; (*wood*) leña; (*for engine*) carburante m; **fuel tank** n depósito (de combustible)

fulfil [ful'fɪl] vt (*function*) cumplir con; (*condition*) satisfacer; (*wish, desire*) realizar

full [ful] adj lleno; (*fig*) pleno; (*complete*) completo; (*maximum*) máximo; (*information*) detallado; (*price*) íntegro; (*skirt*) amplio ▷ adv: **to know ~ well that** saber perfectamente que; **I'm ~ (up)** no puedo más; **~ employment** pleno empleo; **a ~ two hours** dos horas completas; **at ~ speed** a máxima velocidad; **in ~** (*reproduce, quote*) íntegramente; **full-length** adj (*novel etc*) entero; (*coat*) largo; (*portrait*) de cuerpo entero; **full moon** n luna llena; **full-scale** adj (*attack, war*) en gran escala; (*model*) de tamaño natural; **full stop** n punto; **full-time** adj (*work*) de tiempo completo ▷ adv: **to work full-time** trabajar a tiempo completo; **fully** adv completamente; (*at least*) por lo menos

fumble ['fʌmbl] vi: **to ~ with** manejar torpemente

fume [fjuːm] vi (*rage*) estar furioso; **fumes** npl humo, gases mpl

fun [fʌn] n (*amusement*) diversión f; **to have ~** divertirse; **for ~** en broma; **to make ~ of** burlarse de

function ['fʌŋkʃən] n función f ▷ vi funcionar

fund [fʌnd] n fondo; (*reserve*) reserva; **funds** npl (*money*) fondos mpl

fundamental [fʌndə'mentl] adj fundamental

funeral ['fjuːnərəl] n (*burial*) entierro; (*ceremony*) funerales mpl; **funeral director** n director(a) m/f de pompas fúnebres; **funeral parlour** (BRIT) n funeraria

funfair ['fʌnfɛə*] (BRIT) n parque m de atracciones

fungus ['fʌŋgəs] (*pl* **fungi**) n hongo; (*mould*) moho

funnel ['fʌnl] n embudo; (of ship) chimenea

funny ['fʌnɪ] adj gracioso, divertido; (strange) curioso, raro

fur [fə:*] n piel f; (BRIT: in kettle etc) sarro; **fur coat** n abrigo de pieles

furious ['fjʊərɪəs] adj furioso; (effort) violento

furnish ['fə:nɪʃ] vt amueblar; (supply) suministrar; (information) facilitar; **furnishings** npl muebles mpl

furniture ['fə:nɪtʃə*] n muebles mpl; **piece of ~** mueble m

furry ['fə:rɪ] adj peludo

further ['fə:ðə*] adj (new) nuevo, adicional ▷ adv más lejos; (more) más; (moreover) además ▷ vt promover, adelantar; **further education** n educación f superior; **furthermore** adv además

furthest ['fə:ðɪst] superlative of **far**

fury ['fjʊərɪ] n furia

fuse [fju:z] (US **fuze**) n fusible m; (for bomb etc) mecha ▷ vt (metal) fundir; (fig) fusionar ▷ vi fundirse; fusionarse; (BRIT Elec): **to ~ the lights** fundir los plomos; **fuse box** n caja de fusibles

fusion ['fju:ʒən] n fusión f

fuss [fʌs] n (excitement) conmoción f; (trouble) alboroto; **to make a ~** armar un lío or jaleo; **to make a ~ of sb** mimar a algn; **fussy** adj (person) exigente; (too ornate) recargado

future ['fju:tʃə*] adj futuro; (coming) venidero ▷ n futuro; (prospects) porvenir m; **in ~** de ahora en adelante; **futures** npl (Comm) operaciones fpl a término, futuros mpl

fuze [fju:z] (US) = **fuse**

fuzzy ['fʌzɪ] adj (Phot) borroso; (hair) muy rizado

g

G [dʒi:] n (Mus) sol m

g. abbr (= gram(s)) gr.

gadget ['gædʒɪt] n aparato

Gaelic ['geɪlɪk] adj, n (Ling) gaélico

gag [gæg] n (on mouth) mordaza; (joke) chiste m ▷ vt amordazar

gain [geɪn] n: **~ (in)** aumento (de); (profit) ganancia ▷ vt ganar ▷ vi (watch) adelantarse; **to ~ from/by sth** sacar provecho de algo; **to ~ on sb** ganar terreno a algn; **to ~ 3 lbs (in weight)** engordar 3 libras

gal. abbr = **gallon**

gala ['gɑ:lə] n fiesta

galaxy ['gæləksɪ] n galaxia

gale [geɪl] n (wind) vendaval m

gall bladder ['gɔ:l-] n vesícula biliar

gallery ['gælərɪ] n (also: **art ~: public**) pinacoteca; (: private) galería de arte; (for spectators) tribuna

gallon ['gælən] n galón m (BRIT = 4,546 litros, US = 3,785 litros)

gallop ['gæləp] n galope m ▷ vi galopar

gallstone ['gɔ:lstəun] n cálculo

biliario

gamble ['gæmbl] n (risk) riesgo ▷ vt jugar, apostar ▷ vi jugárselas; (bet) apostar: **to ~ on** apostar a; (success etc) contar con; **gambler** n jugador(a) m/f; **gambling** n juego

game [geɪm] n juego; (match) partido; (of cards) partida; (Hunting) caza ▷ adj (willing): **to be ~ for anything** atreverse a todo; **big ~** caza mayor (contest) juegos; (BRIT: Scol) deportes mpl; **games console** [geɪmz-] n consola de juegos; **game show** n programa m concurso m, concurso

gammon ['gæmən] n (bacon) tocino ahumado; (ham) jamón m ahumado

gang [gæŋ] n (of criminals) pandilla; (of friends etc) grupo; (of workmen) brigada

gangster ['gæŋstə*] n gángster m

gap [gæp] n vacío (SP), hueco (LAM); (in trees, traffic) claro; (in time) intervalo; (difference): **~ (between)** diferencia (entre)

gape [geɪp] vi mirar boquiabierto; (shirt etc) abrirse (completamente)

gap year n año sabático (antes de empezar a estudiar en la universidad)

garage ['gæra:ʒ] n garaje m; (for repairs) taller m; **garage sale** n venta de objetos usados (en el jardín de una casa particular)

garbage ['ga:bɪdʒ] (us) n basura; (inf: nonsense) tonterías fpl; **garbage can** n cubo o bote m (MEX) or tacho (SC) de la basura; **garbage collector** (us) n basurero/a

garden ['ga:dn] n jardín m; **gardens** npl (park) parque m; **garden centre** (BRIT) n centro de jardinería; **gardener** n jardinero/a; **gardening** n jardinería

garlic ['ga:lɪk] n ajo

garment ['ga:mənt] n prenda (de vestir)

garnish ['ga:nɪʃ] vt (Culin) aderezar

garrison ['gærɪsn] n guarnición f

gas [gæs] n gas m; (fuel) combustible m; (us: gasoline) gasolina ▷ vt asfixiar con gas; **gas cooker** (BRIT) n cocina de gas; **gas cylinder** n bombona de gas; **gas fire** n estufa de gas

gasket ['gæskɪt] n (Aut) junta de culata

gasoline ['gæsəli:n] (us) n gasolina

gasp [ga:sp] n boqueada; (of shock etc) grito sofocado ▷ vi (pant) jadear

gas: gas pedal n (esp us) acelerador m; **gas station** (us) n gasolinera; **gas tank** (us) n (Aut) depósito (de gasolina)

gate [geɪt] n puerta; (iron gate) verja

gateau ['gætəu] (pl **~x**) n tarta

gatecrash ['geɪtkræʃ] (BRIT) vt colarse en

gateway ['geɪtweɪ] n puerta

gather ['gæðə*] vt (flowers, fruit) coger (SP), recoger; (assemble) reunir; (pick up) recoger; (Sewing) fruncir; (understand) entender ▷ vi (assemble) reunirse; **to ~ speed** ganar velocidad; **gathering** n reunión f, asamblea

gauge [geɪdʒ] n (instrument) indicador m ▷ vt medir; (fig) juzgar

gave [geɪv] pt of **give**

gay [geɪ] adj (homosexual) gay; (joyful) alegre; (colour) vivo

gaze [geɪz] n mirada fija ▷ vi: **to ~ at sth** mirar algo fijamente

GB abbr = **Great Britain**

GCSE (BRIT) n abbr (= General Certificate of Secondary Education) examen de reválida que se hace a los 16 años

gear [gɪə*] n equipo, herramientas fpl; (Tech) engranaje m; (Aut) velocidad f, marcha m vt (fig: adapt): **to ~ sth to** adaptar o ajustar algo a; **top o high** (us)/**low ~** cuarta/primera velocidad; **in ~** en marcha; **gear up** vi prepararse; **gear box** n caja de cambios; **gear lever** n palanca de cambio; **gear shift** (us) n = **gear lever**; **gear stick** n (BRIT) palanca de cambios

geese [gi:s] npl of **goose**

gel [dʒɛl] n gel m
gem [dʒɛm] n piedra preciosa
Gemini ['dʒɛmɪnaɪ] n Géminis m, Gemelos mpl
gender ['dʒɛndə*] n género
gene [dʒiːn] n gen(e)m
general ['dʒɛnərəl] n general m ▷ adj general; **in ~** en general; **general anaesthetic** (us **general anesthetic**) n anestesia general; **general election** n elecciones fpl generales; **generalize** vi generalizar; **generally** adv generalmente, en general; **general practitioner** n médico general; **general store** n tienda (que vende de todo) (LAM, SP), almacén m (SC, SP)
generate ['dʒɛnəreɪt] vt (Elec) generar; (jobs, profits) producir
generation [dʒɛnə'reɪʃən] n generación f
generator ['dʒɛnəreɪtə*] n generador m
generosity [dʒɛnə'rɒsɪtɪ] n generosidad f
generous ['dʒɛnərəs] adj generoso
genetic [dʒɪ'nɛtɪk] adj: **~ engineering** ingeniería genética; **~ fingerprinting** identificación f genética; **genetically modified** adj transgénico; **genetics** n genética
genitals ['dʒɛnɪtlz] npl (órganos mpl) genitales mpl
genius ['dʒiːnɪəs] n genio
genome ['giːnəum] n genoma m
gent [dʒɛnt] n abbr (BRIT inf) = **gentleman**
gentle ['dʒɛntl] adj apacible, dulce; (animal) manso; (breeze, curve etc) suave
    Be careful not to translate **gentle** by the Spanish word gentil.
gentleman ['dʒɛntlmən] (irreg) n señor m; (well-bred man) caballero
gently ['dʒɛntlɪ] adv dulcemente, suavemente
gents [dʒɛnts] n aseos mpl (de caballeros)
genuine ['dʒɛnjuɪn] adj auténtico; (person) sincero; **genuinely** adv

sinceramente
geographic(al) [dʒɪə'græfɪk(l)] adj geográfico
geography [dʒɪ'ɒgrəfɪ] n geografía
geology [dʒɪ'ɒlədʒɪ] n geología
geometry [dʒɪ'ɒmətrɪ] n geometría
geranium [dʒɪ'reɪnjəm] n geranio
geriatric [dʒɛrɪ'ætrɪk] adj, n geriátrico m/f
germ [dʒɜːm] n (microbe) microbio, bacteria; (seed, fig) germen m
German ['dʒɜːmən] adj alemán/ana ▷ n alemán/ana m/f; (Ling) alemán m; **German measles** n rubéola
Germany ['dʒɜːmənɪ] n Alemania
gesture ['dʒɛstjə*] n gesto; (symbol) muestra

○ **KEYWORD**

get [gɛt] (pt, pp **got**, pp **gotten** (us)) vi
1 (become, be) ponerse, volverse; **to get old/tired** envejecer/cansarse; **to get drunk** emborracharse; **to get dirty** ensuciarse; **to get married** casarse; **when do I get paid?** ¿cuándo me pagan or se me paga?; **it's getting late** se está haciendo tarde
2 (go): **to get to/from** llegar a/de; **to get home** llegar a casa
3 (begin) empezar a; **to get to know sb** (llegar a) conocer a algn; **I'm getting to like him** me está empezando a gustar; **let's get going** or **started** ¡vamos (a empezar)!
4 (modal aux vb): **you've got to** do it tienes que hacerlo
▷ vt 1: **to get sth done** (finish) terminar algo; (have done) mandar hacer algo; **to get one's hair cut** cortarse el pelo; **to get the car going** or **to go** arrancar el coche; **to get sb to do sth** conseguir or hacer que algn haga algo; **to get sth/sb ready** preparar algo/a algn
2 (obtain: money, permission, results) conseguir; (find: job, flat) encontrar; (fetch: person, doctor) buscar; (object) ir a buscar, traer; **to get sth for sb**

conseguir algo para algn; **get me Mr Jones, please** (Tel) póngame (SP) or comuníqueme (LAM) con el Sr. Jones, por favor; **can I get you a drink?** ¿quieres algo de beber?
3 (receive: present, letter) recibir; (acquire: reputation) alcanzar; (: prize) ganar; **what did you get for your birthday?** ¿qué te regalaron por tu cumpleaños?; **how much did you get for the painting?** ¿cuánto sacaste por el cuadro?
4 (catch) coger (SP), agarrar (LAM); (hit: target etc) dar; **to get sb by the arm/throat** coger or agarrar a algn por el brazo/cuello; **get him!** ¡cógelo! (SP), ¡atrápalo! (LAM); **the bullet got him in the leg** la bala le dio en la pierna
5 (take, move) llevar; **to get sth to sb** hacer llegar algo a algn; **do you think we'll get it through the door?** ¿crees que lo podremos meter por la puerta?
6 (catch, take: plane, bus etc) coger (SP), tomar (LAM); **where do I get the train for Birmingham?** ¿dónde se coge or se toma el tren para Birmingham?
7 (understand) entender; (hear) oír; **I've got it!** ¡ya lo tengo!, ¡eureka!; **I don't get your meaning** no te entiendo; **I'm sorry, I didn't get your name** lo siento, no cogí su nombre
8 (have, possess): **to have got** tener
get away vi marcharse; (escape) escaparse
get away with vt fus hacer impunemente
get back vi (return) volver ▷ vt recobrar
get in vi entrar; (train) llegar; (arrive home) volver a casa, regresar
get into vt fus entrar en; (vehicle) subir a; **to get into a rage** enfadarse
get off vi (from train etc) bajar; (depart: person, car) marcharse ▷ vt (remove) quitar ▷ vt fus (train, bus) bajar de
get on vi (at exam etc): **how are you getting on?** ¿cómo te va?; (agree): **to**

get on (with) llevarse bien (con) ▷ vt fus subir a
get out vi salir; (of vehicle) bajar ▷ vt sacar
get out of vt fus salir de; (duty etc) escaparse de
get over vt fus (illness) recobrarse de
get through vi (Tel) (lograr) comunicarse
get up vi (rise) levantarse ▷ vt fus subir

getaway ['gɛtəweɪ] n fuga
Ghana ['gɑːnə] n Ghana
ghastly ['gɑːstlɪ] adj horrible
ghetto ['gɛtəu] n gueto
ghost [gəust] n fantasma m
giant ['dʒaɪənt] n gigante mf ▷ adj gigantesco, gigante
gift [gɪft] n regalo; (ability) talento; **gifted** adj dotado; **gift shop** (US **gift store**) n tienda de regalos; **gift token**, **gift voucher** n vale m canjeable por un regalo
gig [gɪg] n (inf: concert) actuación f
gigabyte ['dʒɪgəbaɪt] n gigabyte m
gigantic [dʒaɪ'gæntɪk] adj gigantesco
giggle ['gɪgl] vi reírse tontamente
gills [gɪlz] npl (of fish) branquias fpl, agallas fpl
gilt [gɪlt] adj, n dorado
gimmick ['gɪmɪk] n truco
gin [dʒɪn] n ginebra
ginger ['dʒɪndʒəʳ] n jengibre m
gipsy ['dʒɪpsɪ] n = **gypsy**
giraffe [dʒɪ'rɑːf] n jirafa
girl [gəːl] n (small) niña; (young woman) chica, joven f, muchacha; (daughter) hija; **an English ~** una chica inglesa; **girl band** n girl band m (grupo musical de chicas); **girlfriend** n (of girl) amiga; (of boy) novia; **Girl Scout** (US) n = **Girl Guide**
gist [dʒɪst] n lo esencial
give [gɪv] (pt **gave**, pp **given**) vt dar; (deliver) entregar; (as gift) regalar ▷ vi (break) romperse; (stretch: fabric) dar

de sí; **to ~ sb sth**, **~ sth to sb** dar algo a algn; **give away** vt (give free) regalar; (betray) traicionar; (disclose) revelar; **give back** vt devolver; **give in** vi ceder ▷ vt entregar; **give out** vt distribuir; **give up** vi rendirse, darse por vencido ▷ vt renunciar a; **to give up smoking** dejar de fumar; **to give o.s. up** entregarse

given ['gɪvn] pp of **give** ▷ adj (fixed: time, amount) determinado ▷ conj: **~ (that) ...** dado (que) ...; **~ the circumstances ...** dadas las circunstancias ...

glacier ['glæsɪə*] n glaciar m

glad [glæd] adj contento; **gladly** ['-lɪ] adv con mucho gusto

glamour ['glæmə*] (US **glamor**) n encanto, atractivo; **glamorous** adj encantador(a), atractivo

glance [glɑːns] n ojeada, mirada ▷ vi: **to ~ at** echar una ojeada a

gland [glænd] n glándula

glare [glɛə*] n (of anger) mirada feroz; (of light) deslumbramiento, brillo; **to be in the ~ of publicity** estar en el foco de la atención pública ▷ vi deslumbrar; **to ~ at** mirar con odio a; **glaring** adj (mistake) manifiesto

glass [glɑːs] n vidrio, cristal m; (for drinking) vaso; (: with stem) copa; **glasses** npl (spectacles) gafas fpl

glaze [gleɪz] vt (window) poner cristales a; (pottery) vidriar ▷ n vidriado

gleam [gliːm] vi brillar

glen [glɛn] n cañada

glide [glaɪd] vi deslizarse; (Aviat: birds) planear; **glider** n (Aviat) planeador m

glimmer ['glɪmə*] n luz f tenue; (of interest) muestra; (of hope) rayo

glimpse [glɪmps] n vislumbre m ▷ vt vislumbrar, entrever

glint [glɪnt] vi centellear

glisten ['glɪsn] vi relucir, brillar

glitter ['glɪtə*] vi relucir, brillar

global ['gləʊbl] adj mundial; **globalization** n globalización f;

global warming n (re)calentamiento global or de la tierra

globe [gləʊb] n globo; (model) globo terráqueo

gloom [gluːm] n oscuridad f; (sadness) tristeza; **gloomy** adj (dark) oscuro; (sad) triste; (pessimistic) pesimista

glorious ['glɔːrɪəs] adj glorioso; (weather etc) magnífico

glory ['glɔːrɪ] n gloria

gloss [glɒs] n (shine) brillo; (paint) pintura de aceite

glossary ['glɒsərɪ] n glosario

glossy ['glɒsɪ] adj lustroso; (magazine) de lujo

glove [glʌv] n guante m; **glove compartment** n (Aut) guantera

glow [gləʊ] vi brillar

glucose ['gluːkəʊs] n glucosa

glue [gluː] n goma (de pegar), cemento ▷ vt pegar

GM adj abbr (= genetically modified) transgénico

gm abbr (= gram) g

GMO n abbr (= genetically modified organism) organismo transgénico

GMT abbr (= Greenwich Mean Time) GMT

gnaw [nɔː] vt roer

go [gəʊ] (pt **went**, pp **gone**) ▷ vi (travel) viajar; (depart) irse, marcharse; (work) funcionar, marchar; (be sold) venderse; (time) pasar; (fit, suit): **to ~ with** hacer juego con; (become) ponerse; (break etc) estropearse, romperse ▷ n: **to have a ~ (at)** probar suerte (con); **to be on the ~** no parar; **whose ~ is it?** ¿a quién le toca?; **he's ~ing to do it** va a hacerlo; **to ~ for a walk** ir de paseo; **to ~ dancing** ir a bailar; **how did it ~?** ¿qué tal salió or resultó?, ¿cómo ha ido?; **to ~ round the back** pasar por detrás; **go ahead** vi seguir adelante; **go away** vi irse, marcharse; **go back** vi volver; **go by** vi (time) pasar ▷ vt fus seguirse por; **go down** vi bajar; (ship) hundirse; (sun) ponerse ▷ vt fus bajar; **go for** vt fus (fetch) ir por; (like) gustar; (attack) atacar; **go in** vi entrar; **go into** vt *fus* entrar en; (*investigate*) investigar; (*embark on*) dedicarse a; **go off** vi irse, marcharse; (*food*) pasarse; (*explode*) estallar; (*event*) realizarse ▷ vt *fus* dejar de gustar; **the idea** ya no me gusta tanto él/la idea; **go on** vi (*continue*) seguir, continuar; (*happen*) pasar, ocurrir; **to go on doing sth** seguir haciendo algo; **go out** vi salir; (*fire, light*) apagarse; **go over** vi (*ship*) zozobrar ▷ vt *fus* (*check*) revisar; **go past** vi, vt *fus* pasar; **go round** vi (*circulate: news, rumour*) correr; (*suffice*) alcanzar, bastar; (*revolve*) girar, dar vueltas; (*visit*): **to go round (to sb's)** pasar a ver (a algn); **to go round (by)** (*make a detour*) dar la vuelta (por); **go through** vt *fus* (*town etc*) atravesar; **go up** vi, vt *fus* subir; **go with** vt *fus* (*accompany*) ir con, acompañar a; **go without** vt *fus* pasarse sin

go-ahead ['gəʊəhɛd] *adj* (*person*) dinámico; (*firm*) innovador(a) ▷ n luz f verde

goal [gəʊl] *n* meta; (*score*) gol m
goalkeeper *n* portero; **goal-post** *n* poste m (de la portería)
goat [gəʊt] *n* cabra f
gobble ['gɔbl] vt (*also:* **~ down, ~ up**) tragarse, engullir
god [gɔd] *n* Dios m; **godchild** n ahijado/a; **goddaughter** n ahijada; **goddess** n diosa; **godfather** n padrino; **godmother** n madrina; **godson** n ahijado
goggles ['gɔglz] npl gafas fpl
going ['gəʊɪŋ] n (*conditions*) estado m del terreno ▷ *adj*: **the ~ rate** la tarifa corriente o en vigor
gold [gəʊld] n oro ▷ *adj* de oro; **golden** *adj* (*made of gold*) de oro; (*in colour*) dorado; (*fig*) n pez m de colores; **goldmine** n (*also fig*) mina de oro; **gold-plated** *adj* chapado en oro
golf [gɔlf] n golf m; **golf ball** n (*for game*) pelota de golf; (*on typewriter*) esfera; **golf club** n club m de golf;

(*stick*) palo (de golf); **golf course** n campo de golf; **golfer** n golfista mf
gone [gɔn] pp of **go**
gong [gɔŋ] n gong m
good [gʊd] *adj* bueno; (*pleasant*) agradable; (*kind*) bueno, amable; (*well-behaved*) educado ▷ n bien m, provecho; **goods** npl (*Comm*) mercancías fpl; **~!** ¡qué bien!; **to be ~ at** tener aptitud para; **to be ~ for** servir para; **it's ~ for you** te hace bien; **would you be ~ enough to ...?** ¿podría hacerme el favor de ...?; ¿sería tan amable de ...?; **a ~ deal (of)** mucho; **a ~ many** muchos; **to make ~** reparar; **it's no ~ complaining** no vale la pena de quejarse; **for ~** para siempre, definitivamente; **~ morning/afternoon!** ¡buenos días/buenas tardes!; **~ evening!** ¡buenas noches!; **~ night!** ¡buenas noches!
goodbye [gʊd'baɪ] excl ¡adiós!; **to say ~ (to)** (*person*) despedirse (de)
good: **Good Friday** n Viernes m Santo; **good-looking** *adj* guapo; **good-natured** *adj* amable, simpático; **goodness** n (*of person*) bondad f; **for goodness sake!** ¡por Dios!; **goodness gracious!** ¡Dios mío!; **goods train** (*BRIT*) n tren m de mercancías; **goodwill** n buena voluntad f
Google® ['gu:gəl] n Google ® ▷ vi hacer búsquedas en Internet ▷ vt buscar información en Internet sobre
goose [gu:s] (pl **geese**) n ganso, oca
gooseberry ['gʊzbərɪ] n grosella espinosa; **to play ~** hacer de carabina
goose bumps, goose pimples npl carne f de gallina
gorge [gɔːdʒ] n barranco ▷ vr: **to ~ o.s. (on)** atracarse (de)
gorgeous ['gɔːdʒəs] *adj* (*thing*) precioso; (*weather*) espléndido; (*person*) guapísimo
gorilla [gə'rɪlə] n gorila m
gosh [gɔʃ] (*inf*) excl ¡cielos!
gospel ['gɔspl] n evangelio
gossip ['gɔsɪp] n (*scandal*)

cotilleo, chismes *mpl*; (*chat*) charla; (*scandalmonger*) cotilla *m/f*, chismoso/a ▷ *vi* cotillear; **gossip column** *n* ecos *mpl* de sociedad

got [gɒt] *pt, pp of* **get**

gotten (*us*) ['gɒtn] *pp of* **get**

gourmet ['guəmeɪ] *n* gastrónomo/a *m/f*

govern ['gʌvən] *vt* gobernar; (*influence*) dominar; **government** *n* gobierno; **governor** *n* gobernador(a) *m/f*; (*of school etc*) miembro del consejo; (*of jail*) director(a) *m/f*

gown [gaʊn] *n* traje *m*; (*of teacher, BRIT: of judge*) toga

G.P. *n abbr* = **general practitioner**

grab [græb] *vt* coger (*sp*), agarrar (*LAM*), arrebatar ▷ *vi*: **to ~ at** intentar agarrar

grace [greɪs] *n* gracia ▷ *vt* honrar; (*adorn*) adornar; **5 days'** ~ un plazo de 5 días; **graceful** *adj* grácil, ágil; (*style, shape*) elegante, gracioso; **gracious** ['greɪʃəs] *adj* amable

grade [greɪd] *n* (*quality*) clase *f*, calidad *f*; (*in hierarchy*) grado; (*Scol: mark*) nota; (*us: school class*) curso ▷ *vt* clasificar; **grade crossing** (*us*) *n* paso a nivel; **grade school** (*us*) *n* escuela primaria

gradient ['greɪdɪənt] *n* pendiente *f*

gradual ['grædjuəl] *adj* paulatino; **gradually** *adv* paulatinamente

graduate [*n* 'grædjuət, *vb* 'grædjueɪt] *n* (*us: of high school*) graduado/a; (*of university*) licenciado/a ▷ *vi* graduarse; licenciarse; **graduation** [-'eɪʃən] *n* (*ceremony*) entrega del título

graffiti [grə'fiːtɪ] *n* pintadas *fpl*

graft [grɑːft] *n* (*Agr, Med*) injerto; (*BRIT: inf*) trabajo duro; (*bribery*) corrupción *f* ▷ *vt* injertar

grain [greɪn] *n* (*single particle*) grano; (*corn*) granos *mpl*, cereales *mpl*; (*of wood*) fibra

gram [græm] *n* gramo

grammar ['græmə*] *n* gramática; **grammar school** (*BRIT*) *n* = instituto

de segunda enseñanza, liceo (*sp*)

gramme [græm] *n* = **gram**

gran [græn] (*inf*) *n* (*BRIT*) abuelita

grand [grænd] *adj* magnífico, imponente; (*wonderful*) estupendo; (*gesture etc*) grandioso; **grandad** (*inf*) *n* = **granddad**; **grandchild** (*pl* **grandchildren**) *n* nieto/a *m/f*; **granddad** (*inf*) *n* yayo, abuelito; **granddaughter** *n* nieta; **grandfather** *n* abuelo; **grandma** (*inf*) *n* yaya, abuelita; **grandmother** *n* abuela; **grandpa** (*inf*) *n* = **granddad**; **grandparents** *npl* abuelos *mpl*; **grand piano** *n* piano de cola; **Grand Prix** ['grɑ̃ː'priː] *n* (*Aut*) gran premio, Grand Prix *m*; **grandson** *n* nieto

granite ['grænɪt] *n* granito

granny ['grænɪ] (*inf*) *n* abuelita, yaya

grant [grɑːnt] *vt* (*concede*) conceder; (*admit*) reconocer ▷ *n* (*Scol*) beca; (*Admin*) subvención *f*; **to take sth/sb for ~ed** dar algo por sentado/no hacer ningún caso a algn

grape [greɪp] *n* uva

grapefruit ['greɪpfruːt] *n* pomelo (*sp, sc*), toronja (*LAM*)

graph [grɑːf] *n* gráfica; **graphic** ['græfɪk] *adj* gráfico; **graphics** *n* artes *fpl* gráficas ▷ *npl* (*drawings*) dibujos *mpl*

grasp [grɑːsp] *vt* agarrar, asir; (*understand*) comprender ▷ *n* (*grip*) asimiento; (*understanding*) comprensión *f*

grass [grɑːs] *n* hierba; (*lawn*) césped (*sp*); **grasshopper** *n* saltamontes *m inv*

grate [greɪt] *n* parrilla de chimenea ▷ *vi*: **to ~ (on)** chirriar (sobre) ▷ *vt* (*Culin*) rallar

grateful ['greɪtful] *adj* agradecido

grater ['greɪtə*] *n* rallador *m*

gratitude ['grætɪtjuːd] *n* agradecimiento

grave [greɪv] *n* tumba ▷ *adj* serio, grave

gravel ['grævl] *n* grava

gravestone ['greɪvstəʊn] *n* lápida

graveyard ['greɪvjɑːd] n cementerio

gravity ['grævɪtɪ] n gravedad f

gravy ['greɪvɪ] n salsa de carne

gray [greɪ] adj = grey

graze [greɪz] vi pacer ▷ vt (touch lightly) rozar; (scrape) raspar ▷ n (Med) abrasión f

grease [griːs] n (fat) grasa; (lubricant) lubricante m ▷ vt engrasar; lubrificar; greasy adj grasiento

great [greɪt] adj grande; (inf) magnífico, estupendo; Great Britain n Gran Bretaña; great-grandfather n bisabuelo; great-grandmother n bisabuela; greatly adv muy; (with verb) mucho

Greece [griːs] n Grecia

greed [griːd] n (also: ~iness) codicia, avaricia; (for food) gula; (for power etc) avidez f; greedy adj avaro; (for food) glotón/ona

Greek [griːk] adj griego ▷ n griego/a; (Ling) griego

green [griːn] adj (also Pol) verde; (inexperienced) novato ▷ n verde m; (stretch of grass) césped m; (Golf) green; m greens npl (vegetables) verduras fpl; green card n (Aut) carta verde; (us: work permit) permiso de trabajo para los extranjeros en EE. UU.; greengage n (ciruela) claudia; greengrocer (BRIT) n verdulero/a; greenhouse n invernadero; greenhouse effect n efecto invernadero

Greenland ['griːnlənd] n Groenlandia

green salad n ensalada f (de lechuga, pepino, pimiento verde, etc)

greet [griːt] vt (welcome) dar la bienvenida a; (receive: news) recibir; greeting (welcome) bienvenida; greeting(s) card n tarjeta de felicitación

grew [gruː] pt of grow

grey [greɪ] (us gray) adj gris; (weather) sombrío; grey-haired adj canoso; greyhound n galgo

grid [grɪd] n reja; (Elec) red f; gridlock

n (traffic jam) retención f

grief [griːf] n dolor m, pena

grievance ['griːvəns] n motivo de queja, agravio

grieve [griːv] vi afligirse, acongojarse ▷ vt dar pena a; to ~ for llorar por

grill [grɪl] n (on cooker) parrilla; (also: mixed ~) parrillada ▷ vt (BRIT) asar a la parrilla; (inf: question) interrogar

grille [grɪl] n reja; (Aut) rejilla

grim [grɪm] adj (place) sombrío; (situation) triste; (person) ceñudo

grime [graɪm] n mugre f, suciedad f

grin [grɪn] n sonrisa abierta ▷ vi sonreír abiertamente

grind [graɪnd] (pt, pp ground) vt (coffee, pepper etc) moler; (us: meat) picar; (make sharp) afilar ▷ n (work) rutina

grip [grɪp] n (hold) asimiento; (control) control m, dominio; (of tyre etc) to have a good/bad ~ agarrarse bien/mal; (handle) asidero; (holdall) maletín m ▷ vt agarrar; (viewer, reader) fascinar; to get to ~s with enfrentarse con; gripping adj absorbente

grit [grɪt] n gravilla; (courage) valor m ▷ vt (road) poner gravilla en; to ~ one's teeth apretar los dientes

grits [grɪts] (us) npl maíz msg a medio moler

groan [grəun] n gemido; quejido ▷ vi gemir; quejarse

grocer ['grəusə*] n tendero (de ultramarinos (sp)); groceries npl comestibles mpl; grocer's (shop) n tienda de comestibles or (mex, cam) abarrotes, almacén (sc); grocery (shop) n tienda de ultramarinos

groin [grɔɪn] n ingle f

groom [gruːm] n mozo/a de cuadra; (also: bride~) novio ▷ vt (horse) almohazar; (fig): to ~ sb for preparar a algn para; well-~ed de buena presencia

groove [gruːv] n ranura, surco

grope [grəup] vi: to ~ for buscar a tientas

gross [grəus] adj (neglect, injustice) grave; (vulgar: behaviour) grosero;

(: *appearance*) de mal gusto; (*Comm*) bruto; **grossly** *adv* (*greatly*) enormemente

grotesque [grə'tesk] *adj* grotesco

ground [graund] *pt, pp of* **grind** ▷ *n* suelo, tierra *f*; (*Sport*) campo, terreno; (*reason: gen pl*) causa, razón *f*; (*US: also*: **~ wire**) tierra ▷ *vt* (*plane*) mantener en tierra; (*US Elec*) conectar con tierra; **grounds** *npl* (*of coffee etc*) poso; (*gardens etc*) jardines *mpl*, parque *m*; **on the ~** en el suelo; **to the ~** al suelo; **to gain/lose ~** ganar/perder terreno; **ground floor** *n* (*BRIT*) planta baja; **groundsheet** (*BRIT*) *n* tela impermeable; suelo; **groundwork** *n* preparación *f*

group [gru:p] *n* grupo; (*musical*) conjunto ▷ *vt* (*also*: **~ together**) agrupar ▷ *vi* (*also*: **~ together**) agruparse

grouse [graus] *n inv* (*bird*) urogallo ▷ *vi* (*complain*) quejarse

grovel ['grɔvl] *vi* (*fig*): **to ~ before** humillarse ante

grow [grəu] (*pt* **grew**, *pp* **grown**) *vi* crecer; (*increase*) aumentar; (*expand*) desarrollarse; (*become*) volverse; **to ~ rich/weak** enriquecerse/debilitarse ▷ *vt* cultivar; (*hair, beard*) dejar crecer; **grow on me** ese cuadro me gusta cada vez más; **grow up** *vi* crecer, hacerse hombre/mujer

growl [graul] *vi* gruñir

grown [grəun] *pp of* **grow**; **grown-up** *n* adulto/a, mayor *mf*

growth [grəuθ] *n* crecimiento, desarrollo; (*what has grown*) brote *m*; (*Med*) tumor *m*

grub [grʌb] *n* larva, gusano; (*inf: food*) comida

grubby ['grʌbɪ] *adj* sucio, mugriento

grudge [grʌdʒ] *n* (*motivo de*) rencor *m* ▷ *vt*: **to ~ sb sth** dar algo a algn de mala gana; **to bear sb a ~** guardar rencor a algn

gruelling ['gruəlɪŋ] (*US* **grueling**) *adj*

penoso, duro

gruesome ['gru:səm] *adj* horrible

grumble ['grʌmbl] *vi* refunfuñar, quejarse

grumpy ['grʌmpɪ] *adj* gruñón/ona

grunt [grʌnt] *vi* gruñir

guarantee [gærən'ti:] *n* garantía ▷ *vt* garantizar

guard [gɑ:d] *n* (*squad*) guardia; (*one man*) guardia *mf*; (*BRIT Rail*) jefe *m* de tren; (*on machine*) dispositivo de seguridad; (*also*: **fire~**) rejilla de protección ▷ *vt* guardar; (*prisoner*) vigilar; **to be on one's ~** estar alerta; **guardian** *n* guardián/ana *m/f*; (*of minor*) tutor(a) *m/f*

guerrilla [gə'rɪlə] *n* guerrillero/a

guess [ges] *vi* adivinar; (*US*) suponer ▷ *vt* adivinar; suponer ▷ *n* suposición *f*, conjetura; **to take** *or* **have a ~** tratar de adivinar

guest [gest] *n* invitado/a; (*in hotel*) huésped *mf*, guest *mf*; **guest house** *n* casa de huéspedes, pensión *f*; **guest room** *n* cuarto de huéspedes

guidance ['gaɪdəns] *n* (*advice*) consejos *mpl*

guide [gaɪd] *n* (*person*) guía *mf*; (*book, fig*) guía; (*also*: **Girl ~**) guía *f* ▷ *vt* (*round museum etc*) guiar; (*lead*) conducir; (*direct*) orientar; **guidebook** *n* guía; **guide dog** *n* perro *m* guía; **guided tour** *n* visita *f* con guía; **guidelines** *npl* (*advice*) directrices *fpl*

guild [gɪld] *n* gremio

guilt [gɪlt] *n* culpabilidad *f*; **guilty** *adj* culpable

guinea pig ['gɪnɪ-] *n* cobaya; (*fig*) conejillo de Indias

guitar [gɪ'tɑ:*] *n* guitarra; **guitarist** *n* guitarrista *m/f*

gulf [gʌlf] *n* golfo; (*abyss*) abismo

gull [gʌl] *n* gaviota

gulp [gʌlp] *vi* tragar saliva ▷ *vt* (*also*: **~ down**) tragarse

gum [gʌm] *n* (*Anat*) encía; (*glue*) goma, cemento; (*sweet*) caramelo de goma; (*also*: **chewing~**) chicle *m* ▷ *vt* pegar con goma

gun [gʌn] n (small) pistola, revólver m; (shotgun) escopeta; (rifle) fusil m; (cannon) cañón m; **gunfire** n disparos mpl; **gunman** (irreg) n pistolero; **gunpoint** n: **at gunpoint** a mano armada; **gunpowder** n pólvora; **gunshot** n escopetazo

gush [gʌʃ] vi salir a raudales; (person) deshacerse en efusiones

gust [gʌst] n (of wind) ráfaga

gut [gʌt] n intestino; **guts** npl (Anat) tripas fpl; (courage) valor m

gutter ['gʌtə*] n (of roof) canalón m; (in street) cuneta

guy [gaɪ] n (also: **~-rope**) cuerda; (inf: man) tío (sp), tipo; (figure) monigote m

Guy Fawkes' Night [gaɪˈfɔːks-] n ver recuadro

gym [dʒɪm] n gimnasio; **gymnasium** n gimnasio m/f; **gymnast** n gimnasta mf; **gymnastics** n gimnasia; **gym shoes** npl zapatillas fpl (de deporte)

gynaecologist [gaɪnɪˈkɒlədʒɪst] (us **gynecologist**) n ginecólogo/a

gypsy ['dʒɪpsɪ] n gitano/a

h

haberdashery [hæbəˈdæʃərɪ] (BRIT) n mercería

habit ['hæbɪt] n hábito, costumbre f; (drug habit) adicción f; (costume) hábito

habitat ['hæbɪtæt] n hábitat m

hack [hæk] vt (cut) cortar; (slice) tajar ▷ n (pej: writer) escritor(a) m/f a sueldo; **hacker** n (Comput) pirata mf informático/a

had [hæd] pt, pp of **have**

haddock ['hædək] (pl ~ or ~s) n especie de merluza

hadn't ['hædnt] = **had not**

haemorrhage ['hemərɪdʒ] (us **hemorrhage**) n hemorragia

haemorrhoids ['hemərɔɪdz] (us **hemorrhoids**) npl hemorroides fpl

haggle ['hægl] vi regatear

Hague [heɪg] n: **The ~** La Haya

hail [heɪl] n granizo; (fig) lluvia ▷ vt saludar; (taxi) llamar a; (acclaim) aclamar ▷ vi granizar; **hailstone** n (piedra de) granizo

hair [heə*] n pelo, cabellos mpl; (one hair) pelo, cabello; (on legs etc) vello;

to do one's ~ arreglarse el pelo; **to have grey ~** tener canas *fpl*; **hairband** *n* cinta; **hairbrush** *n* cepillo (para el pelo); **haircut** *n* corte *m* (de pelo); **hairdo** *n* peinado; **hairdresser** *n* peluquero/a; **hairdresser's** *n* peluquería; **hair dryer** *n* secador *m* de pelo; **hair gel** *n* fijador; **hair spray** *n* laca; **hairstyle** *n* peinado; **hairy** *adj* peludo; velludo; (*inf: frightening*) espeluznante

hake [heɪk] (*pl ~ or ~s*) *n* merluza

half [hɑːf] (*pl* **halves**) *n* mitad *f*; (*of beer*) = caña (sp), media pinta; (*Rail, Bus*) billete *m* de niño ▷ *adj* medio ▷ *adv* medio, a medias; **two and a ~** dos y media; **~ a dozen** media docena; **~ a pound** media libra; **to cut sth in ~** cortar algo por la mitad; **half board** *n* (*BRIT: in hotel*) media pensión; **half-brother** *n* hermanastro; **half day** *n* medio día *m*, media jornada; **half fare** *n* medio pasaje *m*; **half-hearted** *adj* indiferente, poco entusiasta; **half-hour** *n* media hora; **half-price** *adj, adv* a mitad de precio; **half term** (*BRIT*) *n* (*Scol*) vacaciones *fpl* de mediados del trimestre; **half-time** *n* descanso; **halfway** *adv* a medio camino; **halfway through** a mitad de

hall [hɔːl] *n* (*for concerts*) sala; (*entrance way*) hall *m*; vestíbulo

hallmark ['hɔːlmɑːk] *n* sello

hallo [həˈləu] *excl* = **hello**

hall of residence (*BRIT*) *n* residencia

Hallowe'en [hæləuˈiːn] *n* víspera de Todos los Santos

○ ● **HALLOWE'EN**
●
○ ● La tradición anglosajona dice
○ ● que en la noche del 31 de octubre,
○ ● **Hallowe'en**, víspera de Todos los
○ ● Santos, es posible ver a brujas y
○ ● fantasmas. En este día los niños
○ ● se disfrazan y van de puerta en
○ ● puerta llevando un farol hecho con
○ ● una calabaza en forma de cabeza

○ ● humana. Cuando se les abre la
○ ● puerta gritan "trick or treat",
○ ● amenazando con gastar una
○ ● broma a quien no les dé golosinas
○ ● o algo de calderilla.

hallucination [həluːsɪˈneɪʃən] *n* alucinación *f*

hallway ['hɔːlweɪ] *n* vestíbulo

halo ['heɪləu] *n* (*of saint*) halo, aureola

halt [hɔːlt] *n* (*stop*) alto, parada ▷ *vt* parar; interrumpir ▷ *vi* pararse

halve [hɑːv] *vt* partir por la mitad

halves [hɑːvz] *npl of* **half**

ham [hæm] *n* jamón *m* (cocido)

hamburger ['hæmbɜːgə*] *n* hamburguesa

hamlet ['hæmlɪt] *n* aldea

hammer ['hæmə*] *n* martillo ▷ *vt* (*nail*) clavar; (*force*): **to ~ an idea into sb/a message home** meter una idea en la cabeza a algn/machacar una idea ▷ *vi* dar golpes

hammock ['hæmək] *n* hamaca

hamper ['hæmpə*] *vt* estorbar ▷ *n* cesto

hamster ['hæmstə*] *n* hámster *m*

hamstring ['hæmstrɪŋ] *n* (*Anat*) tendón *m* de la corva

hand [hænd] *n* (*of clock*) aguja; (*writing*) letra; (*worker*) obrero ▷ *vt* dar, pasar; **to give or lend sb a ~** echar una mano a algn, ayudar a algn; **at ~** a mano; **in ~** (*time*) libre; (*job etc*) entre manos; **on ~** (*person, services*) a mano, al alcance; **to ~** (*information etc*) a mano; **on the one ~ ..., on the other ~ ...** por una parte ... por otra (parte) ...; **hand down** *vt* pasar, bajar; (*tradition*) transmitir; (*heirloom*) dejar en herencia (*us: sentence, verdict*) imponer; **hand in** *vt* entregar; **hand out** *vt* distribuir; **hand over** *vt* (*deliver*) entregar; **handbag** *n* bolso (sp), cartera (LAM), bolsa (MEX); **hand baggage** *n* = **hand luggage**; **handbook** *n* manual *m*; **handbrake** *n* freno de mano; **handcuffs** *npl* esposas *fpl*; **handful**

n puñado

handicap ['hændɪkæp] n minusvalía; (*disadvantage*) desventaja; (*Sport*) handicap m ▷ vt estorbar; **to be mentally ~ped** ser mentalmente m/f discapacitado; **to be physically ~ped** ser minusválido/a

handkerchief ['hæŋkətʃɪf] n pañuelo

handle ['hændl] n (*of door etc*) tirador m; (*of cup etc*) asa; (*of knife etc*) mango; (*for winding*) manivela ▷ vt (*touch*) tocar; (*deal with*) encargarse de; (*treat: people*) manejar; **"~ with care"** ("manéjese) con cuidado"; **to fly off the ~** perder los estribos; **handlebar(s)** n(pl) manillar m

hand: **hand luggage** n equipaje m de mano; **handmade** adj hecho a mano; **handout** n (*money etc*) limosna; (*leaflet*) folleto; **hands-free** adj (*phone*) manos libres m; **hands-free kit** n manos libres m inv

handsome ['hænsəm] adj guapo; (*building*) bello; (*fig: profit*) considerable

handwriting ['hændraɪtɪŋ] n letra

handy ['hændɪ] adj (*close at hand*) a la mano; (*tool etc*) práctico; (*skilful*) hábil, diestro

hang [hæŋ] (*pt, pp* **hung**) vt colgar; (*criminal: pt, pp* **hanged**) ahorcar ▷ vi (*painting, coat etc*) colgar; (*hair, drapery*) caer; **to get the ~ of sth** (*inf*) lograr dominar algo; **hang about or around** vi haraganear; **hang down** vi colgar, pender; **hang on** vi (*wait*) esperar; **hang out** vt (*washing*) tender, colgar ▷ vi (*inf: live*) vivir; (*spend time*) pasar el rato; **to hang out of sth** colgar fuera de algo; **hang round** vi = **hang around**; **hang up** vi (*Tel*) colgar ▷ vt colgar

hanger ['hæŋə*] n percha

hang-gliding ['-glaɪdɪŋ] n vuelo libre

hangover ['hæŋəuvə*] n (*after drinking*) resaca

hankie, hanky ['hæŋkɪ] n abbr =

handkerchief

happen ['hæpən] vi suceder, ocurrir; (*chance*): **he ~ed to hear/see** dió la casualidad de que oyó/vió; **as it ~s** da la casualidad de que

happily ['hæpɪlɪ] adv (*luckily*) afortunadamente; (*cheerfully*) alegremente

happiness ['hæpɪnɪs] n felicidad f; (*cheerfulness*) alegría

happy ['hæpɪ] adj feliz; (*cheerful*) alegre; **to be ~ (with)** estar contento (con); **to be ~ to do** estar encantado de hacer; **~ birthday!** ¡feliz cumpleaños!

harass ['hærəs] vt acosar, hostigar; **harassment** n persecución f

harbour ['hɑ:bə*] (*us* **harbor**) n puerto ▷ vt (*fugitive*) dar abrigo a; (*hope etc*) abrigar

hard [hɑ:d] adj duro; (*difficult*) difícil; (*work*) arduo; (*person*) severo; (*fact*) innegable ▷ adv (*work*) mucho, duro; (*think*) profundamente; **to look ~ at** clavar los ojos en; **to try ~** esforzarse; **no ~ feelings!** ¡sin rencor(es)!; **to be ~ of hearing** ser duro de oído; **to be ~ done by** ser tratado injustamente; **hardback** n libro en cartoné; **hardboard** n aglomerado m (*de madera*); **hard disk** n (*Comput*) disco duro o rígido; **harden** vt endurecer; (*fig*) curtir ▷ vi endurecerse; curtirse

hardly ['hɑ:dlɪ] adv apenas; **~ ever** casi nunca

hard: hardship n privación f; **hard shoulder** (*BRIT*) n (*Aut*) arcén m; **hard-up** (*inf*) adj sin un duro (*SP*), pelado, sin un centavo (*MEX*), pato (*SC*); **hardware** n ferretería; (*Comput*) hardware m; **hardware shop** (*US* **hardware store**) n ferretería; **hard-working** adj trabajador(a)

hardy ['hɑ:dɪ] adj fuerte; (*plant*) resistente

hare [hɛə*] n liebre f

harm [hɑ:m] n daño, mal m ▷ vt (*person*) hacer daño a; (*health, interests*) perjudicar; (*thing*) dañar; **out of ~'s**

way a salvo; **harmful** adj dañino;
harmless adj (person) inofensivo; (joke
etc) inocente

harmony ['hɑːmənɪ] n armonía

harness ['hɑːnɪs] n arreos mpl; (for
child) arneses m; (safety harness) arneses
mpl ▷ vt (horse) enjaezar; (resources)
aprovechar

harp [hɑːp] n arpa ▷ vi: **to ~ on
(about)** machacar (con)

harsh [hɑːʃ] adj (cruel) duro, cruel;
(severe) severo; (sound) áspero; (light)
deslumbrador(a)

harvest ['hɑːvɪst] n (harvest time)
siega; (of cereals etc) cosecha; (of grapes)
vendimia ▷ vt cosechar

has [hæz] vb see **have**

hasn't ['hæznt] = **has not**

hassle ['hæsl] (inf) n lata

haste [heɪst] n prisa; **hasten** ['heɪsn]
vt acelerar ▷ vi darse prisa; **hastily**
adv de prisa; precipitadamente; **hasty**
adj apresurado; (rash) precipitado

hat [hæt] n sombrero

hatch [hætʃ] n (Naut: also: **~way**)
escotilla; (also: **service ~**) ventanilla
▷ vi (bird) salir del cascarón ▷ vt
incubar; (plot) tramar; **5 eggs have ~ed**
han salido 5 pollos

hatchback ['hætʃbæk] n (Aut) tres or
cinco puertas m

hate [heɪt] vt odiar, aborrecer ▷ n
odio; **hatred** ['heɪtrɪd] n odio

haul [hɔːl] vt tirar ▷ n (of fish) redada;
(of stolen goods etc) botín m

haunt [hɔːnt] vt (ghost) aparecerse
en; (obsess) obsesionar ▷ n guarida;
haunted (house) (castle etc) embrujado;
(look) de angustia

○ KEYWORD

have [hæv] (pt, pp **had**) aux vb 1 (gen)
haber; **to have arrived/eaten** haber
llegado/comido; **having finished or
when he had finished, he left** cuando
hubo acabado, se fue

2 (in tag questions): **you've done it,**

haven't you? lo has hecho, ¿verdad?
or ¿no?

3 (in short answers and questions): **I
haven't** no; **so have I** sí, es verdad;
we haven't paid – yes we have!
no hemos pagado – ¡sí que hemos
pagado!; **I've been there before, have
you?** he estado allí antes, ¿y tú?

▷ modal aux vb (be obliged): **to have
(got) to do sth** tener que hacer algo;
you haven't to tell her no hay que or
no debes decírselo

▷ vt 1 (possess): **he has (got) blue
eyes/dark hair** tiene los ojos azules/el
pelo negro

2 (referring to meals etc): **to have
breakfast/lunch/dinner** desayunar/
comer/cenar; **to have a drink/a
cigarette** tomar algo/fumar un
cigarrillo

3 (receive): recibir; (obtain): obtener; **may
I have your address?** ¿puedes darme
tu dirección?; **you can have it for
£5** te lo puedes quedar por £5; **I must
have it by tomorrow** lo necesito para
mañana; **to have a baby** tener un
niño or bebé

4 (maintain, allow): **I won't have it/this
nonsense!** ¡no lo permitiré!/¡no
permitiré estas tonterías!; **we can't
have that** no podemos permitir eso

5 **to have sth done** hacer or mandar
hacer algo; **to have one's hair cut**
cortarse el pelo; **to have sb do sth**
hacer que algn haga algo

6 (experience, suffer): **to have a cold/flu**
tener un resfriado/la gripe; **she had
her bag stolen/her arm broken** le
robaron el bolso/se rompió un brazo;
to have an operation operarse

7 (+ noun): **to have a swim/walk/
bath/rest** nadar/dar un paseo/darse
un baño/descansar; **let's have a look**
vamos a ver; **to have a meeting/
party** celebrar una reunión/una fiesta;
let me have a try déjame intentarlo

haven ['heɪvn] n puerto; (fig) refugio

haven't ['hævnt] = **have not**

havoc ['hævək] n estragos mpl

Hawaii [hə'waɪi:] n (Islas fpl) Hawai fpl

hawk [hɔ:k] n halcón m

hawthorn ['hɔ:θɔ:n] n espino

hay [heɪ] n heno; **hay fever** n fiebre f del heno; **haystack** n almiar m

hazard ['hæzəd] n peligro ▷ vt aventurar; **hazardous** adj peligroso; **hazard warning lights** npl (Aut) señales fpl de emergencia

haze [heɪz] n neblina

hazel ['heɪzl] n (tree) avellano ▷ adj (eyes) color m de avellana; **hazelnut** n avellana

hazy ['heɪzɪ] adj brumoso; (idea) vago

he [hi:] pron él; **~ who ...** él que ..., quien ...

head [hɛd] n cabeza; (leader) jefe/a m/f; (of school) director(a) m/f ▷ vt (list) encabezar; (group) capitanear; (company) dirigir; **~s (or tails)** cara (o cruz); **~ first** de cabeza; **~ over heels** (in love) perdidamente; **to ~ the ball** cabecear (la pelota); **head for** vt fus dirigirse a; (disaster) ir camino de; **head off** vt (threat, danger) evitar; **headache** n dolor m de cabeza; **heading** n título; **headlamp** (BRIT) n = **headlight**; **headlight** n faro; **headline** n titular m; **head office** n oficina central, central f; **headphones** npl auriculares mpl; **headquarters** npl sede f central; (Mil) cuartel m general; **headroom** n (in car) altura interior; (under bridge) (límite m de) altura; **headscarf** n pañuelo; **headset** n cascos mpl; **headteacher** n director(directora); **head waiter** n maître m

heal [hi:l] vt curar ▷ vi cicatrizarse

health [hɛlθ] n salud f; **health care** n asistencia sanitaria; **health centre** (BRIT) n ambulatorio, centro médico; **health food** n alimentos mpl orgánicos; **Health Service** (BRIT) n el servicio de salud pública, = el Insalud (SP); **healthy** adj sano, saludable

heap [hi:p] n montón m ▷ vt: **to ~ (up)** amontonar; **to ~ sth with** llenar algo hasta arriba de; **~s of** un montón de

hear [hɪə*] (pt, pp ~d) vt (also Law) oír; (news) saber ▷ vi oír; **to ~ about** oír hablar de; **to ~ from sb** tener noticias de algn

heard [hɜ:d] pt, pp of **hear**

hearing ['hɪərɪŋ] n (sense) oído; (Law) vista; **hearing aid** n audífono

hearse [hɜ:s] n coche m fúnebre

heart [hɑ:t] n corazón m; (fig) valor m; (of lettuce) cogollo; **hearts** npl (Cards) corazones mpl; **to lose/take ~** descorazonarse/cobrar ánimo; **at ~** en el fondo; **by ~** (learn, know) de memoria; **heart attack** n infarto de miocardio); **heartbeat** n latido (del corazón); **heartbroken** adj: **she was heartbroken about it** esto le partió el corazón; **heartburn** n acedía; **heart disease** n enfermedad f cardíaca

hearth [hɑ:θ] n (fireplace) chimenea

heartless ['hɑ:tlɪs] adj despiadado

hearty ['hɑ:tɪ] adj (person) campechano; (laugh) sano; (dislike, support) absoluto

heat [hi:t] n calor m; (Sport: also: **qualifying ~**) prueba eliminatoria ▷ vt calentar; **heat up** vi calentarse ▷ vt calentar; **heated** adj caliente; (fig) acalorado; **heater** n estufa; (in car) calefacción f

heather ['hɛðə*] n brezo

heating ['hi:tɪŋ] n calefacción f

heatwave ['hi:tweɪv] n ola de calor

heaven ['hɛvn] n cielo; (fig) una maravilla; **heavenly** adj celestial; (fig) maravilloso

heavily ['hɛvɪlɪ] adv pesadamente; (drink, smoke) con exceso; (sleep, sigh) profundamente; (depend) mucho

heavy ['hɛvɪ] adj pesado; (work, blow) duro; (sea, rain, meal) fuerte; (drinker, smoker) grande; (responsibility) grave; (schedule) ocupado; (weather) bochornoso

Hebrew ['hi:bru:] adj, n (Ling) hebreo

hectare ['hɛktɑ:*] n (BRIT) hectárea

hectic ['hɛktɪk] adj agitado

he'd [hi:d] = **he would; he had**

hedge [hɛdʒ] n seto ▷ vi contestar con evasivas; **to ~ one's bets** (fig) cubrirse

hedgehog ['hɛdʒhɔg] n erizo

heed [hi:d] vt (also: **take ~**): **pay attention to**) hacer caso de

heel [hi:l] n talón m; (of shoe) tacón m ▷ vt (shoe) poner tacón a

hefty ['hɛftɪ] adj (person) fornido; (parcel, profit) gordo

height [haɪt] n (of person) estatura; (of building) altura; (high ground) cerro; (altitude) altitud f; (fig: of season): **at the ~ of summer** en los días más calurosos del verano; (: of power etc) cúspide f; (: of stupidity etc) colmo; **heighten** vt elevar; (fig) aumentar

heir [ɛə*] n heredero; **heiress** n heredera

held [hɛld] pt, pp of **hold**

helicopter ['hɛlɪkɔptə*] n helicóptero

hell [hɛl] n infierno; **~!** (inf) ¡demonios!

he'll [hi:l] = **he will; he shall**

hello [hə'ləu] excl ¡hola!; (to attract attention) ¡oiga!; (surprise) ¡caramba!

helmet ['hɛlmɪt] n casco

help [hɛlp] n ayuda; (cleaner etc) criada, asistenta ▷ vt ayudar; **~!** ¡socorro!; **~ yourself** sírvete; **he can't ~ it** no es culpa suya; **help out** vi ayudar, echar una mano ▷ vt: **to help sb out** ayudar a algn, echar una mano a algn; **helper** n ayudante mf; **helpful** adj útil; (person) servicial; (advice) útil; **helping** n ración f; **helpless** adj (incapable) incapaz; (defenceless) indefenso; **helpline** n teléfono de asistencia al público

hem [hɛm] n dobladillo ▷ vt poner or coser el dobladillo de

hemisphere ['hɛmɪsfɪə*] n hemisferio

hemorrhage ['hɛmərɪdʒ] (US) n = **haemorrhage**

hemorrhoids ['hɛmərɔɪdz] (US) npl = **haemorrhoids**

hen [hɛn] n gallina; (female bird) hembra

hence [hɛns] adv (therefore) por lo tanto; **2 years ~** de aquí a 2 años

hen night, hen party n (inf) despedida de soltera

hepatitis [hɛpə'taɪtɪs] n hepatitis f

her [hə:*] pron (direct) la; (indirect) le; (stressed, after prep) ella ▷ adj su; see also **me; my**

herb [hə:b] n hierba; **herbal** adj de hierbas; **herbal tea** n infusión f de hierbas

herd [hə:d] n rebaño

here [hɪə*] adv aquí; (at this point) en este punto; **~!** (present) ¡presente!; **~ is/are** aquí está/están; **~ she is** aquí está

hereditary [hɪ'rɛdɪtrɪ] adj hereditario

heritage ['hɛrɪtɪdʒ] n patrimonio

hernia ['hə:nɪə] n hernia

hero ['hɪərəu] (pl **~es**) n héroe m; (in book, film) protagonista m; **heroic** [hɪ'rəuɪk] adj heroico

heroin ['hɛrəuɪn] n heroína

heroine ['hɛrəuɪn] n heroína; (in book, film) protagonista

heron ['hɛrən] n garza

herring ['hɛrɪŋ] n arenque m

hers [hə:z] pron (el) suyo/(la) suya etc; see also **mine¹**

herself [hə:'sɛlf] pron (reflexive) se; (emphatic) ella misma; (after prep) sí (misma); see also **oneself**

he's [hi:z] = **he is; he has**

hesitant ['hɛzɪtənt] adj vacilante

hesitate ['hɛzɪteɪt] vi vacilar; (in speech) titubear; (be unwilling) resistirse a; **hesitation** ['-teɪʃən] n indecisión f; titubeo; dudas fpl

heterosexual [hɛtərəu'sɛksjuəl] adj heterosexual

hexagon ['hɛksəgən] n hexágono

hey [heɪ] *excl* ¡oye!, ¡oiga!

heyday ['heɪdeɪ] *n*: **the ~ of** el apogeo de

HGV *n abbr* (= *heavy goods vehicle*) vehículo pesado

hi [haɪ] *excl* ¡hola!; (*to attract attention*) ¡oiga!

hibernate ['haɪbəneɪt] *vi* invernar

hiccough ['hɪkʌp] = **hiccup**

hiccup ['hɪkʌp] *vi* hipar

HGV *n abbr* (= *heavy goods vehicle*) vehículo pesado

hid [hɪd] *pt of* **hide**

hidden ['hɪdn] *pp of* **hide** ▷ *adj*: **~ agenda** plan *m* encubierto

hide [haɪd] (*pt* **hid**, *pp* **hidden**) *n* (*skin*) piel *f* ▷ *vt* esconder, ocultar ▷ *vi*: **to ~ (from sb)** esconderse *or* ocultarse (de algn)

hideous ['hɪdɪəs] *adj* horrible

hiding ['haɪdɪŋ] *n* (*beating*) paliza; **to be in ~** (*concealed*) estar escondido

hi-fi ['haɪfaɪ] *n* estéreo, hifi *m* ▷ *adj* de alta fidelidad

high [haɪ] *adj* alto; (*speed, number*) grande; (*price*) elevado; (*wind*) fuerte; (*voice*) agudo ▷ *adv* alto, a gran altura; **it is 20 m ~** tiene 20 m de altura; **~ in the air** en las alturas; **highchair** *n* silla alta; **high-class** *adj* (*hotel*) de lujo; (*person*) distinguido, de categoría; (*food*) de alta categoría; **higher education** *n* educación *f or* enseñanza superior; **high heels** *npl* (*heels*) tacones *mpl* altos; (*shoes*) zapatos *mpl* de tacón; **high jump** *n* (*Sport*) salto de altura; **highlands** ['haɪləndz] *npl* tierras *fpl* altas; **the Highlands** (*in Scotland*) las Tierras Altas de Escocia; **highlight** *n* (*fig: of event*) punto culminante ▷ *vt* subrayar; **highlights** *npl* (*in hair*) reflejos *mpl*; **highlighter** *n* rotulador, marcador; **highly** *adv* sumamente; (*a lot*) muy bien; (*critical, confidential*) sumamente; **to speak/think highly of** hablar muy bien de/tener en mucho a; **highness** *n* altura; **Her/His Highness** Su Alteza; **high-rise** *n* (*also*: **high-rise block, high-rise building**) torre *f* de pisos; **high school**

n ≈ Instituto Nacional de Bachillerato (*SP*); **high season** (*BRIT*) *n* temporada alta; **high street** (*BRIT*) *n* calle *f* mayor; **high-tech** (*inf*) *adj* al-tec (*inf*), de alta tecnología; **highway** *n* carretera; (*US*) carretera nacional; autopista; **Highway Code** (*BRIT*) *n* código de la circulación

hijack ['haɪdʒæk] *vt* secuestrar; **hijacker** *n* secuestrador(a) *m/f*

hike [haɪk] *vi* (*go walking*) ir de excursión (a pie) ▷ *n* caminata; **hiker** *n* excursionista *mf*; **hiking** *n* senderismo

hilarious [hɪ'lɛərɪəs] *adj* divertidísimo

hill [hɪl] *n* colina; (*high*) montaña; (*slope*) cuesta; **hillside** *n* ladera; **hill walking** *n* senderismo (de montaña); **hilly** *adj* montañoso

him [hɪm] *pron* (*direct*) le, lo; (*indirect*) le; (*stressed, after prep*) él; *see also* **me**; **himself** *pron* (*reflexive*) se; (*emphatic*) él mismo; (*after prep*) sí (mismo); *see also* **oneself**

hind [haɪnd] *adj* posterior

hinder ['hɪndə*] *vt* estorbar, impedir

hindsight ['haɪndsaɪt] *n*: **with ~** en retrospectiva

Hindu ['hɪnduː] *n* hindú *mf*; **Hinduism** *n* (*Rel*) hinduismo

hinge [hɪndʒ] *n* bisagra, gozne *m* ▷ *vi* (*fig*): **to ~ on** depender de

hint [hɪnt] *n* indirecta; (*advice*) consejo; (*sign*) dejo ▷ *vt*: **to ~ that** insinuar que ▷ *vi*: **to ~ at** hacer alusión a

hip [hɪp] *n* cadera

hippie ['hɪpɪ] *n* hippie *m/f*, jipi *m/f*

hippo ['hɪpəʊ] (*pl* **~s**) *n* hipopótamo

hippopotamus [hɪpə'pɒtəməs] (*pl* **-es** *or* **hippopotami**) *n* hipopótamo

hippy ['hɪpɪ] *n* = **hippie**

hire [haɪə*] *vt* (*BRIT: car, equipment*) alquilar; (*worker*) contratar ▷ *n* alquiler *m*; **for ~** se alquila; (*taxi*) libre; **hire(d) car** (*BRIT*) *n* coche *m* de alquiler; **hire purchase** (*BRIT*) *n* compra a plazos

his | 412

his [hiz] *pron* (el) suyo/f(la) suya) *etc*
▷ *adj* su; *see also* **mine¹; my**
Hispanic [his'pænik] *adj* hispánico
hiss [his] *vi* silbar
historian [hi'stɔ:riən] *n*
historiador/a *m/f*
historic(al) [hi'stɔrik(l)] *adj*
histórico
history ['histəri] *n* historia
hit [hit] (*pt, pp* ~) *vt* (*strike*) golpear,
pegar; (*reach: target*) alcanzar; (*collide
with: car*) chocar contra; (*fig: affect*)
afectar ▷ *n* golpe *m*; (*success*) éxito;
(*on website*) visita; (*in web search*)
correspondencia; **to ~ it off with
sb** llevarse bien con algn; **hit back**
vi defenderse; (*fig*) devolver golpe
por golpe
hitch [hitʃ] *vt* (*fasten*) atar, amarrar;
(*also: ~ up*) remangar ▷ *n* (*difficulty*)
dificultad *f*; **to ~ a lift** hacer
autostop
hitch-hike ['hitʃhaik] *vi* hacer
autostop; **hitch-hiker** *n* autostopista
m/f; **hitch-hiking** *n* autostop *m*
hi-tech [hai'tek] *adj* de alta
tecnología
hitman ['hitmæn] (*irreg*) *n* asesino
a sueldo
HIV *n abbr* (= *human immunodeficiency
virus*) VIH *m*; **~-negative/positive**
VIH negativo/positivo
hive [haiv] *n* colmena
hoard [hɔ:d] *n* (*treasure*) tesoro;
(*stockpile*) provisión *f* ▷ *vt* acumular;
(*goods in short supply*) acaparar
hoarse [hɔ:s] *adj* ronco
hoax [həuks] *n* trampa
hob [hɔb] *n* quemador *m*
hobble ['hɔbl] *vi* cojear
hobby ['hɔbi] *n* pasatiempo, afición
f
hobo ['həubəu] (*us*) *n* vagabundo
hockey ['hɔki] *n* hockey *m*; **hockey
stick** *n* palo *m* de hockey
hog [hɔg] *n* cerdo, puerco ▷ *vt* (*fig*)
acaparar; **to go the whole ~** poner
toda la carne en el asador

Hogmanay [hɔgmə'nei] *n* ver
recuadro

hoist [hɔist] *n* (*crane*) grúa ▷ *vt*
levantar, alzar; (*flag, sail*) izar
hold [həuld] (*pt, pp* **held**) *vt* sostener;
(*contain*) contener; (*have: power,
qualification*) tener; (*keep back*) retener;
(*believe*) sostener; (*consider*) considerar;
(*keep in position*) mantener; **to ~
one's head up** mantener la cabeza alta; (*meeting*)
celebrar ▷ *vi* (*withstand pressure*)
resistir; (*be valid*) valer *n* (*grasp*)
asimiento; (*fig*) dominio; **~ the line!**
(*Tel*) ¡no cuelgue!; **to catch** or **get (a) ~ of**
agarrarse o asirse de; **hold back** *vt*
retener; (*secret*) ocultar; **hold on** *vi*
agarrarse bien; (*wait*) esperar; **hold
on!** (*Tel*) ¡(espere) un momento!; **hold
out** *vt* ofrecer ▷ *vi* (*resist*) resistir;
hold up *vt* (*raise*) levantar; (*support*)
apoyar; (*delay*) retrasar; (*rob*) asaltar;
holdall(BRIT) *n* bolsa; **holder** *n*
(*container*) receptáculo; (*of ticket, record*)
poseedor/a *m/f*; (*of office, title etc*)
titular *mf*
hole [həul] *n* agujero
holiday ['hɔlidei] *n* vacaciones
fpl; (*public holiday*) (día *m* de) fiesta,
día *m* feriado; **on ~** de vacaciones;
holiday camp *n* (BRIT: *also*: **holiday
centre**) centro de vacaciones; **holiday**

job n (BRIT) trabajillo extra para las vacaciones; **holiday-maker** (BRIT) n turista mf; **holiday resort** n centro turístico

Holland ['hɒlənd] n Holanda

hollow ['hɒləu] adj hueco; (claim) vacío; (eyes) hundido; (sound) sordo ▷ n hueco; (in ground) hoyo ▷ vt: **to ~ out** excavar

holly ['hɒlɪ] n acebo

Hollywood ['hɒlɪwud] n Hollywood m

holocaust ['hɒləkɔːst] n holocausto

holy ['həulɪ] adj santo, sagrado; (water) bendito

home [həum] n casa; (country) patria; (institution) asilo ▷ cpd (domestic) casero, de casa; (Econ, Pol) nacional etc) a fondo; **at ~** en casa; (in country) en el país; (fig) como pez en el agua; **to go/come ~** ir/volver a casa; **make yourself at ~** ¡estás en tu casa!; **home address** n domicilio; **homeland** n tierra natal; **homeless** adj sin hogar, sin casa; **homely** adj (simple) sencillo; **home-made** adj casero; **home match** n partido en casa; **Home Office** (BRIT) n Ministerio del Interior; **home owner** n propietario/a m/f de una casa; **home page** n página de inicio; **Home Secretary** (BRIT) n Ministro del Interior; **homesick** adj: **to be homesick** tener morriña, sentir nostalgia; **home town** n ciudad y natal; **homework** n deberes mpl

homicide ['hɒmɪsaɪd] (us) n homicidio

homoeopathic [həumɪə'pæθɪk] (us **homeopathic**) adj homeopático

homoeopathy [həumɪ'ɒpəθɪ] (us **homeopathy**) n homeopatía

homosexual [hɒməu'sɛksjuəl] adj, n homosexual mf

honest ['ɒnɪst] adj honrado; (sincere) franco, sincero; **honestly** adv honradamente; francamente; **honesty** n honradez f

honey ['hʌnɪ] n miel f; **honeymoon** n luna de miel; **honeysuckle** n madreselva

Hong Kong ['hɔŋ'kɔŋ] n Hong-Kong m

honorary ['ɒnərərɪ] adj (member, president) de honor; (title) honorífico; **~ degree** doctorado honoris causa

honour ['ɒnə*] (us **honor**) vt honrar; (commitment, promise) cumplir con ▷ n honor m, honra; **to graduate with ~s** ≈ licenciarse con matrícula (de honor); **honourable** (us **honorable**) adj honorable; **honours degree** n (Scol) título de licenciado con calificación alta

hood [hud] n capucha; (BRIT Aut) capota; (us Aut) capó m; (of cooker) campana de humos; **hoodie** n (top) jersey m con capucha

hoof [huːf] (pl **hooves**) n pezuña

hook [huk] n gancho; (on dress) corchete m, broche m; (for fishing) anzuelo ▷ vt enganchar; (fish) pescar

hooligan ['huːlɪgən] n gamberro

hoop [huːp] n aro

hooray [hu'reɪ] excl = **hurray**

hoot [huːt] (BRIT) vi (Aut) tocar el pito, pitar; (siren) (hacer) sonar; (owl) ulular

Hoover® ['huːvə*] (BRIT) n aspiradora ▷ vt: **to hoover** pasar la aspiradora por

hooves [huːvz] npl of **hoof**

hop [hɒp] vi saltar, brincar; (on one foot) saltar con un pie

hope [həup] vt, vi esperar ▷ n esperanza; **I ~ so/not** espero que sí/no; **hopeful** adj (person) optimista; (situation) prometedor(a); **hopefully** adv con esperanza; (one hopes): **hopefully he will recover** esperamos que se recupere; **hopeless** adj desesperado; (person): **to be hopeless** ser un desastre

hops [hɒps] npl lúpulo

horizon [hə'raɪzn] n horizonte m; **horizontal** [hɔrɪ'zɔntl] adj horizontal

hormone ['hɔːməun] n hormona

horn [hɔːn] n cuerno; (Mus: also:

French ~) trompa; (Aut) pito, claxon m

horoscope ['hɒrəskəʊp] n
horóscopo

horrendous [hɒ'rendəs] adj
horrendo

horrible ['hɒrɪbl] adj horrible

horrid ['hɒrɪd] adj horrible, horroroso

horrific [hɒ'rɪfɪk] adj (accident)
horroroso; (film) horripilante

horrifying ['hɒrɪfaɪɪŋ] adj horroroso

horror ['hɒrə*] n horror m; horror
film n película de horror

hors d'œuvre [ɔː'dəːvrə] n
entremeses mpl

horse [hɔːs] n caballo; **horseback**
n: **on horseback** a caballo; **horse
chestnut** n (tree) castaño de Indias;
(nut) castaña de Indias; **horsepower**
n caballo (de fuerza); **horse-racing** n
carreras fpl de caballos; **horseradish** n
rábano picante; **horse riding** n (BRIT)
equitación f

hose [həʊz] n manguera; **hosepipe**
n manguera

hospital ['hɒspɪtl] n hospital m

hospitality [hɒspɪ'tælɪtɪ] n
hospitalidad f

host [həʊst] n anfitrión m; (TV, Radio)
presentador m; (Rel) hostia; (large
number): **a ~ of** multitud de

hostage ['hɒstɪdʒ] n rehén m

hostel ['hɒstl] n hostal m; (youth) ~
albergue m juvenil

hostess ['həʊstɪs] n anfitriona;
(BRIT: air hostess) azafata; (TV, Radio)
presentadora

hostile ['hɒstaɪl] adj hostil

hostility [hɒ'stɪlɪtɪ] n hostilidad f

hot [hɒt] adj caliente; (weather)
caluroso, de calor; (as opposed to warm)
muy caliente; (spicy) picante; **to be
~** (person) tener calor; (object) estar
caliente; (weather) hacer calor; **hot dog**
n perro caliente

hotel [həʊ'tel] n hotel m

hot-water bottle [hɒt'wɔːtə*-] n
bolsa de agua caliente

hound [haʊnd] vt acosar ▷ n perro

(de caza)

hour ['aʊə*] n hora; **hourly** adj (de)
cada hora

house [n haʊs, pl 'haʊzɪz, vb haʊz] n
(gen, firm) casa; (Pol) cámara; (Theatre)
sala ▷ vt (person) alojar; (collection)
albergar; **on the ~** (fig) la casa invita;
household n familia; (home) casa;
householder n propietario/a; (head of
house) cabeza de familia; **housekeeper**
n ama de llaves; **housekeeping** n
(work) trabajos mpl domésticos; (money)
dinero m para gastos domésticos;
housewife (irreg) n ama de casa;
house wine n vino m de la casa;
housework n faenas fpl (de la casa)

housing ['haʊzɪŋ] n (act)
alojamiento; (houses) viviendas fpl;
**housing development, housing
estate** (BRIT) n urbanización f

hover ['hɒvə*] vi flotar (en el aire);
hovercraft n aerodeslizador m

how [haʊ] adv (in what way) cómo;
~ are you? ¿cómo estás?; **~ much milk,
many people?** ¿cuánta leche/gente?;
~ much does it cost? ¿cuánto cuesta?;
~ long have you been here? ¿cuánto
hace que estás aquí?; **~ old are you?**
¿cuántos años tienes?; **~ tall is he?**
¿cómo es de alto?; **~ is school?** ¿cómo
(te) va (en) la escuela?; **~ was the film?**
¿qué tal la película?; **~ lovely/awful!**
¡qué bonito/horror!

however [haʊ'evə*] adv: **~ I do it** lo
haga como lo haga; **~ cold it is** por
mucho frío que haga; **~ fast he runs**
por muy rápido que corra; **~ did you
do it?** ¿cómo lo hiciste? ▷ conj sin
embargo, no obstante

howl [haʊl] n aullido ▷ vi aullar;
(person) dar alaridos; (wind) ulular

H.P. n abbr = **hire purchase**

h.p. abbr = **horsepower**

HQ n abbr = **headquarters**

hr(s) abbr (= hour(s))

HTML n abbr (= hypertext markup
language) lenguaje m de hipertexto

hubcap ['hʌbkæp] n tapacubos m inv

huddle ['hʌdl] vi: **to ~ together**

acurrucarse

huff [hʌf] n: **in a ~** enojado

hug [hʌg] vt abrazar; (thing) apretar con los brazos

huge [hju:dʒ] adj enorme

hull [hʌl] n (of ship) casco

hum [hʌm] vt tararear, canturrear ▷ vi tararear, canturrear; (insect) zumbar

human ['hju:mən] adj, n humano

humane [hju:'meɪn] adj humano, humanitario

humanitarian [hju:mænɪ'teəriən] adj humanitario

humanity [hju:'mænɪti] n humanidad f

human rights npl derechos mpl humanos

humble ['hʌmbl] adj humilde

humid ['hju:mɪd] adj húmedo; **humidity** [-'mɪdɪti] n humedad f

humiliate [hju:'mɪlɪeɪt] vt humillar

humiliating [hju:'mɪlɪeɪtɪŋ] adj humillante, vergonzoso

humiliation [hju:mɪlɪ'eɪʃən] n humillación f

hummus ['hʊməs] n paté de garbanzos

humorous ['hju:mərəs] adj gracioso, divertido

humour ['hju:mə*] (us **humor**) n humorismo, sentido del humor; (mood) humor m ▷ vt (person) complacer

hump [hʌmp] n (in ground) montículo; (camel's) giba

hunch [hʌntʃ] n (premonition) presentimiento

hundred ['hʌndrəd] num ciento; (before n) cien; **~s of** centenares de; **hundredth** [-ɪdθ] adj centésimo

hung [hʌŋ] pt, pp of **hang**

Hungarian [hʌŋ'gɛəriən] adj, n húngaro/a m/f

Hungary ['hʌŋgəri] n Hungría

hunger ['hʌŋgə*] n hambre f ▷ vi: **to ~ for** (fig) tener hambre de, anhelar

hungry ['hʌŋgri] adj: **~ (for)** hambriento (de); **to be ~** tener hambre

hunt [hʌnt] vt (seek) buscar; (Sport) cazar ▷ vi (search): **to ~ (for)** buscar; (Sport) cazar ▷ n búsqueda; caza, cacería; **hunter** n cazador(a) m/f; **hunting** n caza

hurdle ['hə:dl] n (Sport) valla; (fig) obstáculo

hurl [hə:l] vt lanzar, arrojar

hurrah [hu'rɑ:] excl = **hurray**

hurray [hu'reɪ] excl ¡viva!

hurricane ['hʌrɪkən] n huracán m

hurry ['hʌri] n prisa ▷ vt (also: **~ up**: person) dar prisa a; (: work) apresurar, hacer de prisa; **to be in a ~** tener prisa; **hurry up** vi darse prisa, apurarse (LAM)

hurt [hə:t] (pt, pp **~**) vt hacer daño a ▷ vi doler ▷ adj lastimado

husband ['hʌzbənd] n marido

hush [hʌʃ] n silencio ▷ vt hacer callar; **~!** ¡chitón!, ¡cállate!

husky ['hʌski] adj ronco ▷ n perro esquimal

hut [hʌt] n cabaña; (shed) cobertizo

hyacinth ['haɪəsɪnθ] n jacinto

hydrangea [haɪ'dreɪndʒə] n hortensia

hydrofoil ['haɪdrəfɔɪl] n aerodeslizador m

hydrogen ['haɪdrədʒən] n hidrógeno

hygiene ['haɪdʒi:n] n higiene f; **hygienic** [-'dʒi:nɪk] adj higiénico

hymn [hɪm] n himno

hype [haɪp] (inf) n bombardeo publicitario

hyphen ['haɪfn] n guión m

hypnotize ['hɪpnətaɪz] vt hipnotizar

hypocrite ['hɪpəkrɪt] n hipócrita m/f

hypocritical [hɪpə'krɪtɪkl] adj hipócrita

hypothesis [haɪ'pɒθɪsɪs] (pl **hypotheses**) n hipótesis f inv

hysterical [hɪ'stɛrɪkl] adj histérico; (funny) para morirse de risa

hysterics [hɪ'stɛrɪks] npl histeria; **to be in ~** (fig) morirse de risa

I [aɪ] pron yo

ice [aɪs] n hielo; (ice cream) helado ▷ vt (cake) alcorzar ▷ vi (also: ~ over, ~ up) helarse; **iceberg** n iceberg m; **ice cream** n helado; **ice cube** n cubito de hielo; **ice hockey** n hockey m sobre hielo

Iceland ['aɪslənd] n Islandia; **Icelander** n islandés/esa m/f; **Icelandic** [aɪs'lændɪk] adj islandés/ esa ▷ n (Ling) islandés m

ice: ice lolly (BRIT) n polo; **ice rink** n pista de hielo; **ice skating** n patinaje m sobre hielo

icing ['aɪsɪŋ] n (Culin) alcorza; **icing sugar** n azúcar m glas(eado)

icon ['aɪkɔn] n icono

ICT (BRIT: Scol) n abbr (= information and communications technology) informática

icy ['aɪsɪ] adj helado

I'd [aɪd] = **I would**; **I had**

ID card n (identity card) DNI m

idea [aɪ'dɪə] n idea

ideal [aɪ'dɪəl] n ideal m ▷ adj ideal; **ideally** [-dɪəlɪ] adv idealmente;

they're ideally suited hacen una pareja ideal

identical [aɪ'dɛntɪkl] adj idéntico

identification [aɪdentɪfɪ'keɪʃə n] n identificación f; **(means of) ~**: documentos mpl personales

identify [aɪ'dentɪfaɪ] vt identificar

identity [aɪ'dentɪtɪ] n identidad f; **identity card** n carnet m de identidad; **identity theft** n robo de identidad

ideology [aɪdɪ'ɔlədʒɪ] n ideología

idiom ['ɪdɪəm] n modismo; (style of speaking) lenguaje m

> Be careful not to translate **idiom** by the Spanish word *idioma*.

idiot ['ɪdɪət] n idiota mf

idle ['aɪdl] adj (inactive) ocioso; (lazy) holgazán/ana; (unemployed) parado, desocupado; (machinery etc) parado; (talk etc) frívolo ▷ vi (machine) marchar en vacío

idol ['aɪdl] n ídolo

idyllic [ɪ'dɪlɪk] adj idílico

i.e. abbr (= that is) esto es

if [ɪf] conj si; **~ necessary** si fuera necesario, si hiciese falta; **~ I were you** yo en tu lugar; **~ so/not** de ser así/si no; **~ only I could!** ¡ojalá pudiera!; see also **as**; **even**

ignite [ɪg'naɪt] vt (set fire to) encender ▷ vi encenderse

ignition [ɪg'nɪʃən] n (Aut: process) ignición f; (: mechanism) encendido; **to switch on/off the ~** arrancar/apagar el motor

ignorance ['ɪgnərəns] n ignorancia

ignorant ['ɪgnərənt] adj ignorante; **to be ~ of** ignorar

ignore [ɪg'nɔː] vt (person, advice) no hacer caso de; (fact) pasar por alto

I'll [aɪl] = **I will**; **I shall**

ill [ɪl] adj enfermo, malo ▷ n mal m ▷ adv mal; **to be taken ~** ponerse enfermo

illegal [ɪ'liːgl] adj ilegal

illegible [ɪ'ledʒɪbl] adj ilegible

illegitimate [ɪlɪ'dʒɪtɪmət] adj

ilegítimo

ill health *n* mala salud *f*; **to be in ~** estar mal de salud

illiterate [ɪˈlɪtərət] *adj* analfabeto

illness [ˈɪlnɪs] *n* enfermedad *f*

illuminate [ɪˈluːmɪneɪt] *vt (room, street)* iluminar, alumbrar

illusion [ɪˈluːʒən] *n* ilusión *f*; *(trick)* truco

illustrate [ˈɪləstreɪt] *vt* ilustrar

illustration [ɪləˈstreɪʃən] *n (act of illustrating)* ilustración *f*; *(example)* ejemplo, ilustración *f*; *(in book)* lámina

I'm [aɪm] = **I am**

image [ˈɪmɪdʒ] *n* imagen *f*

imaginary [ɪˈmædʒɪnərɪ] *adj* imaginario

imagination [ɪmædʒɪˈneɪʃən] *n* imaginación *f*; *(inventiveness)* inventiva

imaginative [ɪˈmædʒɪnətɪv] *adj* imaginativo

imagine [ɪˈmædʒɪn] *vt* imaginarse

imbalance [ɪmˈbæləns] *n* desequilibrio

imitate [ˈɪmɪteɪt] *vt* imitar

imitation [ɪmɪˈteɪʃən] *n* imitación *f*; *(copy)* copia

immaculate [ɪˈmækjulət] *adj* inmaculado

immature [ɪməˈtjuə*] *adj (person)* inmaduro

immediate [ɪˈmiːdɪət] *adj* inmediato; *(pressing)* urgente, apremiante; *(nearest: family)* próximo; *(: neighbourhood)* inmediato;

immediately *adv (at once)* en seguida; *(directly)* inmediatamente; **immediately next to** muy junto a

immense [ɪˈmens] *adj* inmenso, enorme; *(importance)* enorme; **immensely** *adv* enormemente

immerse [ɪˈmɜːs] *vt (submerge)* sumergir; **to be ~d in** *(fig)* estar absorto en

immigrant [ˈɪmɪgrənt] *n* inmigrante *mf*; **immigration** [ɪmɪˈgreɪʃən] *n* inmigración *f*

imminent [ˈɪmɪnənt] *adj* inminente

immoral [ɪˈmɔrl] *adj* inmoral

immortal [ɪˈmɔːtl] *adj* inmortal

immune [ɪˈmjuːn] *adj*: **~ (to)** inmune (a); **immune system** *n* sistema *m* inmunitario

immunize [ˈɪmjunaɪz] *vt* inmunizar

impact [ˈɪmpækt] *n* impacto

impair [ɪmˈpeə*] *vt* perjudicar

impartial [ɪmˈpɑːʃl] *adj* imparcial

impatience [ɪmˈpeɪʃns] *n* impaciencia

impatient [ɪmˈpeɪʃnt] *adj* impaciente; **to get** or **grow ~** impacientarse

impeccable [ɪmˈpekəbl] *adj* impecable

impending [ɪmˈpendɪŋ] *adj* inminente

imperative [ɪmˈperətɪv] *adj (tone)* imperioso; *(need)* imprescindible

imperfect [ɪmˈpɜːfɪkt] *adj (goods etc)* defectuoso ⊳ *n (Ling: also: ~ tense)* imperfecto

imperial [ɪmˈpɪərɪəl] *adj* imperial

impersonal [ɪmˈpɜːsənl] *adj* impersonal

impersonate [ɪmˈpɜːsəneɪt] *vt* hacerse pasar por; *(Theatre)* imitar

impetus [ˈɪmpətəs] *n* ímpetu *m*; *(fig)* impulso

implant [ɪmˈplɑːnt] *vt (Med)* injertar, implantar; *(fig: idea, principle)* inculcar

implement [*n* ˈɪmplɪmənt, *vb* ˈɪmplɪment] *n* herramienta *f*; *(for cooking)* utensilio ⊳ *vt (regulation)* hacer efectivo; *(plan)* realizar

implicate [ˈɪmplɪkeɪt] *vt (compromise)* comprometer; **to ~ sb in sth** comprometer a algn en algo

implication [ɪmplɪˈkeɪʃən] *n* consecuencia; **by ~** indirectamente

implicit [ɪmˈplɪsɪt] *adj* implícito; *(belief, trust)* absoluto

imply [ɪmˈplaɪ] *vt (involve)* suponer; *(hint)* dar a entender que

impolite [ɪmpəˈlaɪt] *adj* mal educado

import [vb ɪm'pɔːt, n 'ɪmpɔːt] vt
importar ▷ n (Comm) importación
f; (: article) producto importado;
(meaning) significado, sentido

importance [ɪm'pɔːtəns] n
importancia

important [ɪm'pɔːtənt] adj
importante; **it's not ~** no importa, no
tiene importancia

importer [ɪm'pɔːtə*] n
importador(a) m/f

impose [ɪm'pəuz] vt imponer
▷ vi: **to ~ on sb** abusar de algn;
imposing adj imponente,
impresionante

impossible [ɪm'pɔsɪbl] adj
imposible; (person) insoportable

impotent [ɪm'pətənt] adj impotente

impoverished [ɪm'pɔvərɪʃt] adj
necesitado

impractical [ɪm'præktɪkl] adj
(person, plan) poco práctico

impress [ɪm'prɛs] vt impresionar;
(mark) estampar; **to ~ sth on sb** hacer
entender algo a algn

impression [ɪm'prɛʃən] n
impresión f; (imitation) imitación f; **to
be under the ~ that** tener la impresión
de que

impressive [ɪm'prɛsɪv] adj
impresionante

imprison [ɪm'prɪzn] vt encarcelar;
imprisonment n encarcelamiento;
(term of imprisonment) cárcel f

improbable [ɪm'prɔbəbl] adj
improbable, inverosímil

improper [ɪm'prɔpə*] adj
(unsuitable: conduct etc) incorrecto;
(: activities) deshonesto

improve [ɪm'pruːv] vt mejorar;
(foreign language) perfeccionar
▷ vi mejorarse; **improvement** n
mejoramiento; perfección f;
progreso

improvise ['ɪmprəvaɪz] vt, vi
improvisar

impulse ['ɪmpʌls] n impulso; **to act
on ~** obrar sin reflexión; **impulsive**

[ɪm'pʌlsɪv] adj irreflexivo

○ **KEYWORD**

in [ɪn] prep 1 (indicating place,
position, with place names) en; **in the
house/garden** en (la) casa/el jardín;
in here/there aquí/ahí or allí dentro;
in London/England en Londres/
Inglaterra

2 (indicating time) en; **in spring** en (la)
primavera; **in the afternoon** por la
tarde; **at 4 o'clock in the afternoon**
a las 4 de la tarde; **I did it in 3 hours/
days** lo hice en 3 horas/días; **I'll see
you in 2 weeks** or **in 2 weeks' time** te
veré dentro de 2 semanas

3 (indicating manner etc) en; **in a loud/
soft voice** en voz alta/baja; **in pencil/
ink** a lápiz/bolígrafo; **the boy in the
blue shirt** el chico de la camisa azul

4 (indicating circumstances): **in the sun/
shade/rain** al sol/a la sombra/bajo la
lluvia; **a change in policy** un cambio
de política

5 (indicating mood, state): **in tears** en
lágrimas, llorando; **in anger/despair**
enfadado/desesperado; **to live in
luxury** vivir lujosamente

6 (with ratios, numbers): **1 in 10
households, 1 household in 10** una
de cada 10 familias; **20 pence in the
pound** 20 peniques por libra; **they
lined up in twos** se alinearon de dos
en dos

7 (referring to people, works) en; entre;
the disease is common in children
la enfermedad es común entre los niños;
in (the works of) Dickens en (las
obras de) Dickens

8 (indicating profession etc): **to be in
teaching** estar en la enseñanza

9 (after superlative) de; **the best pupil
in the class** el(la) mejor alumno/a
de la clase

10 (with present participle): **in saying
this** al decir esto

▷ adv: **to be in** (person: at home) estar en

penalty ['penltı] n (gen) pena; (fine) multa

pence [pens] npl of **penny**

pencil ['pensl] n lápiz m; **pencil** in vt (appointment) apuntar con carácter provisional; **pencil case** n estuche m; **pencil sharpener** n sacapuntas m inv

pendant ['pendnt] n pendiente m

pending ['pendıŋ] prep antes de
▷ adj pendiente

penetrate ['penıtreıt] vt penetrar

penfriend ['penfrend] (BRIT) n amigo/a por carta

penguin ['peŋgwın] n pingüino

penicillin [penı'sılın] n penicilina

peninsula [pə'nınsjulə] n península

penis ['pi:nıs] n pene m

penitentiary [penı'tenʃərı] (US) n cárcel f, presidio

penknife ['pennaıf] n navaja

penniless ['penılıs] adj sin dinero

penny ['penı] (pl **pennies** or **pence**) (BRIT) n penique m; (US) centavo

penpal ['penpæl] n amigo/a por carta

pension ['penʃən] n (state benefit) jubilación f; **pensioner** (BRIT) n jubilado/a

pentagon ['pentəgən] (US) n: **the P~** (Pol) el Pentágono

PENTAGON

Se conoce como **Pentagon** al edificio de planta pentagonal que acoge las dependencias del Ministerio de Defensa estadounidense ("Department of Defense") en Arlington, Virginia. En lenguaje periodístico se aplica también a la dirección militar del país.

penthouse ['penthaus] n ático de lujo

penultimate [pe'nʌltımət] adj penúltimo

people ['pi:pl] npl gente f; (citizens)

pueblo, ciudadanos mpl; (Pol): **the ~** el pueblo ▷ n (nation, race) pueblo, nación f; **several ~ came** vinieron varias personas; **~ say that ...** dice la gente que ...

pepper ['pepə*] n (spice) pimienta; (vegetable) pimiento ▷ vt: **to ~ with** (fig) salpicar de; **peppermint** n (sweet) pastilla de menta

per [pə:*] prep por; **~ day/~son** por día/persona; **~ annum** al año

perceive [pə'si:v] vt percibir; (realize) darse cuenta de

per cent n por ciento

percentage [pə'sentıdʒ] n porcentaje m

perception [pə'sepʃən] n percepción f; (insight) perspicacia; (opinion etc) opinión f

perch [pə:tʃ] n (fish) perca; (for bird) percha ▷ vi: **to ~ (on)** (bird) posarse (en); (person) encaramarse (en)

percussion [pə'kʌʃən] n percusión f

perfect [adj, n 'pə:fıkt, vb pə'fekt] adj perfecto ▷ n (also: **~ tense**) perfecto ▷ vt perfeccionar; **perfection** [pə'fekʃən] n perfección f; **perfectly** ['pə:fıktlı] adv perfectamente

perform [pə'fɔ:m] vt (carry out) realizar, llevar a cabo; (Theatre) representar; (piece of music) interpretar ▷ vi (well, badly) funcionar; **performance** n (of a play) representación f; (of actor, athlete etc) actuación f; (of car, engine, company) rendimiento; (of economy) resultados mpl; **performer** n (actor) actor m, actriz f

perfume ['pə:fju:m] n perfume m

perhaps [pə'hæps] adv quizá(s), tal vez

perimeter [pə'rımıtə*] n perímetro

period ['pıərıəd] n período; (Scol) clase f; (full stop) punto; (Med) regla ▷ adj (costume, furniture) de época; **periodical** [pıərı'ɔdıkl] n periódico; **periodically** adv de vez en cuando, cada cierto tiempo

perish ['perɪʃ] vi perecer; (decay) echarse a perder

perjury ['pɜːdʒərɪ] n (Law) perjurio

perk [pɜːk] n extra m

perm [pɜːm] n permanente f

permanent ['pɜːmənənt] adj permanente; **permanently** adv (lastingly) para siempre, de modo definitivo; (all the time) permanentemente

permission [pə'mɪʃən] n permiso

permit [n 'pɜːmɪt, vt pə'mɪt] n permiso, licencia ▷ vt permitir

perplex [pə'pleks] vt dejar perplejo

persecute ['pɜːsɪkjuːt] vt perseguir

persecution [pɜːsɪ'kjuːʃən] n persecución f

persevere [pɜːsɪ'vɪə*] vi persistir

Persian ['pɜːʃən] adj, n persa mf; **the ~ Gulf** el Golfo Pérsico

persist [pə'sɪst] vi: **to ~ (in doing sth)** persistir (en hacer algo); **persistent** adj persistente; (determined) porfiado

person ['pɜːsn] n persona; **in ~** en persona; **personal** adj personal; individual; (visit) en persona; **personal assistant** n ayudante mf personal; **personal computer** n ordenador m personal; **personality** [-'nælɪtɪ] n personalidad f; **personally** adv personalmente; (in person) en persona; **to take sth personally** tomarse algo a mal; **personal organizer** n agenda; **personal stereo** n Walkman® m

personnel [pɜːsə'nel] n personal m

perspective [pə'spektɪv] n perspectiva

perspiration [pɜːspɪ'reɪʃən] n transpiración f

persuade [pə'sweɪd] vt: **to ~ sb to do sth** persuadir a algn para que haga algo

persuasion [pə'sweɪʒən] n persuasión f; (persuasiveness) persuasiva

persuasive [pə'sweɪsɪv] adj persuasivo

perverse [pə'vɜːs] adj perverso; (wayward) travieso

pervert [n 'pɜːvɜːt, vb pə'vɜːt] n pervertido/a ▷ vt pervertir; (truth, sb's words) tergiversar

pessimism ['pesɪmɪzəm] n pesimismo

pessimist ['pesɪmɪst] n pesimista mf; **pessimistic** [-'mɪstɪk] adj pesimista

pest [pest] n (insect) insecto nocivo; (fig) lata, molestia

pester ['pestə*] vt molestar, acosar

pesticide ['pestɪsaɪd] n pesticida m

pet [pet] n animal m doméstico ▷ cpd favorito ▷ vt acariciar; **teacher's ~** favorito/a (del profesor); **~ hate** manía

petal ['petl] n pétalo

petite [pə'tiːt] adj chiquita

petition [pə'tɪʃən] n petición f

petrified ['petrɪfaɪd] adj horrorizado

petrol ['petrəl] (BRIT) n gasolina

petroleum [pə'trəʊlɪəm] n petróleo

petrol: petrol pump(BRIT) n (in garage) surtidor m de gasolina; **petrol station**(BRIT) n gasolinera; **petrol tank**(BRIT) n depósito (de gasolina)

petticoat ['petɪkəʊt] n enaguas fpl

petty ['petɪ] adj (mean) mezquino; (unimportant) insignificante

pew [pjuː] n banco

pewter ['pjuːtə*] n peltre m

phantom ['fæntəm] n fantasma m

pharmacist ['fɑːməsɪst] n farmacéutico/a

pharmacy ['fɑːməsɪ] n farmacia

phase [feɪz] n fase f; **phase in** vt introducir progresivamente; **phase out** vt (machinery, product) retirar progresivamente; (job, subsidy) eliminar por etapas

Ph.D. abbr = **Doctor of Philosophy**

pheasant ['feznt] n faisán m

phenomena [fə'nɒmɪnə] npl of **phenomenon**

phenomenal [fɪ'nɒmɪnl] adj fenomenal, extraordinario

phenomenon [fə'nɒmɪnən] (pl **phenomena**) n fenómeno

Philippines ['fɪlɪpiːnz] npl: **the ~** las

casa; (*at work*) estar; (*train, ship, plane*) **haber llegado**; (*in fashion*) estar de moda; **she'll be in later today** llegará más tarde hoy; **to ask sb in** hacer pasar a algn; **to run/limp** *etc* **in** entrar corriendo/cojeando *etc* ▷ n: **the ins and outs** (*of proposal, situation etc*) los detalles

inability [ɪnə'bɪlɪtɪ] n: ~ **(to do)** incapacidad f (de hacer)

inaccurate [ɪn'ækjʊrət] *adj* inexacto, incorrecto

inadequate [ɪn'ædɪkwət] *adj* (*income, reply etc*) insuficiente; (*person*) incapaz

inadvertently [ɪnəd'vəːtntlɪ] *adv* por descuido

inappropriate [ɪnə'prəʊprɪət] *adj* inadecuado; (*improper*) poco oportuno

inaugurate [ɪ'nɔːgjʊreɪt] *vt* inaugurar; (*president, official*) investir

Inc. (*us*) *abbr* (= *incorporated*) S.A.

incapable [ɪn'keɪpəbl] *adj* incapaz

incense [n 'ɪnsɛns, vb ɪn'sɛns] n incienso ▷ vt (*anger*) indignar, encolerizar

incentive [ɪn'sɛntɪv] n incentivo, estímulo

inch [ɪntʃ] n pulgada; **to be within an ~ of** estar a dos dedos de; **he didn't give an ~** no dio concesión alguna

incidence ['ɪnsɪdns] n (*of crime, disease*) incidencia

incident ['ɪnsɪdnt] n incidente m

incidentally [ɪnsɪ'dɛntəlɪ] *adv* (*by the way*) a propósito

inclination [ɪnklɪ'neɪʃən] n (*tendency*) tendencia, inclinación f; (*desire*) deseo; (*disposition*) propensión f

incline [n 'ɪnklaɪn, vb ɪn'klaɪn] n pendiente m, cuesta ▷ vt (*head*) poner de lado ▷ vi inclinarse; **to be ~d to** (*tend*) tener tendencia a hacer algo

include [ɪn'kluːd] vt (*incorporate*) incluir; (*in letter*) adjuntar; **including** *prep* incluso, inclusive

inclusion [ɪn'kluːʒən] n inclusión f

inclusive [ɪn'kluːsɪv] *adj* inclusivo; ~ **of tax** incluidos los impuestos

income ['ɪnkʌm] n (*earned*) ingresos mpl; (*from property etc*) renta; (*from investment etc*) rédito; **income support** n (*BRIT*) ≈ ayuda familiar; **income tax** n impuesto sobre la renta

incoming ['ɪnkʌmɪŋ] *adj* (*flight, government etc*) entrante

incompatible [ɪnkəm'pætɪbl] *adj* incompatible

incompetence [ɪn'kɒmpɪtəns] n incompetencia

incompetent [ɪn'kɒmpɪtənt] *adj* incompetente

incomplete [ɪnkəm'pliːt] *adj* (*partial: achievement etc*) incompleto; (*unfinished: painting etc*) inacabado

inconsistent [ɪnkən'sɪstənt] *adj* inconsecuente; (*contradictory*) incongruente; ~ **with** (*que*) no concuerda con

inconvenience [ɪnkən'viːnjəns] n inconvenientes mpl; (*trouble*) molestia, incomodidad f ▷ vt incomodar

inconvenient [ɪnkən'viːnjənt] *adj* incómodo, poco práctico; (*time, place, visitor*) inoportuno

incorporate [ɪn'kɔːpəreɪt] vt incorporar; (*contain*) comprender; (*add*) agregar

incorrect [ɪnkə'rɛkt] *adj* incorrecto

increase [n 'ɪnkriːs, vb ɪn'kriːs] n aumento ▷ vi aumentar; (*grow*) crecer; (*price*) subir ▷ vt aumentar; (*price*) subir; **increasingly** *adv* cada vez más, más y más

incredible [ɪn'krɛdɪbl] *adj* increíble; **incredibly** *adv* increíblemente

incur [ɪn'kəː] vt (*expenditure*) incurrir; (*loss*) sufrir; (*anger, disapproval*) provocar

indecent [ɪn'diːsnt] *adj* indecente

indeed [ɪn'diːd] *adv* efectivamente, en realidad; (*in fact*) en efecto; (*furthermore*) es más; **yes ~!** ¡claro que sí!

indefinitely [ɪn'dɛfɪnɪtlɪ] adv (wait) indefinidamente

independence [ɪndɪ'pɛndns] n independencia; **Independence Day** (US) n Día m de la Independencia

○ **INDEPENDENCE DAY**

○ El cuatro de julio es **Independence**
○ **Day**, la fiesta nacional de Estados
○ Unidos, que se celebra en
○ conmemoración de la Declaración
○ de Independencia, escrita por
○ Thomas Jefferson y aprobada
○ en 1776. En ella se proclamaba
○ la independencia total de Gran
○ Bretaña de las trece colonias
○ americanas que serían el origen de
○ los Estados Unidos de América.

independent [ɪndɪ'pɛndnt] adj independiente; **independent school** n (BRIT) escuela f privada, colegio m privado

index ['ɪndɛks] (pl **-es**) n (in book) índice m; (: in library etc) catálogo; (pl **indices**: ratio, sign) exponente m

India ['ɪndɪə] n la India; **Indian** adj, n indio/a; **Red Indian** piel roja mf

indicate ['ɪndɪkeɪt] vt indicar; **indication** [-'keɪʃən] n indicio, señal f; **indicative** [ɪn'dɪkətɪv] adj: **to be indicative of** indicar; **indicator** n indicador m; (Aut) intermitente m

indices ['ɪndɪsiːz] npl of **index**

indict [ɪn'daɪt] vt acusar; **indictment** n acusación f

indifference [ɪn'dɪfrəns] n indiferencia

indifferent [ɪn'dɪfrənt] adj indiferente; (mediocre) regular

indigenous [ɪn'dɪdʒɪnəs] adj indígena

indigestion [ɪndɪ'dʒɛstʃən] n indigestión f

indignant [ɪn'dɪgnənt] adj: **to be ~ at sth/with sb** indignarse por

algo/con algn

indirect [ɪndɪ'rɛkt] adj indirecto

indispensable [ɪndɪ'spɛnsəbl] adj indispensable, imprescindible

individual [ɪndɪ'vɪdjuəl] n individuo ▷ adj individual; (personal) personal; (particular) particular; **individually** adv (singly) individualmente

Indonesia [ɪndə'niːzɪə] n Indonesia

indoor ['ɪndɔː*] adj (swimming pool) cubierto; (plant) de interior; (sport) bajo cubierta; **indoors** [ɪn'dɔːz] adv dentro

induce [ɪn'djuːs] vt inducir, persuadir; (bring about) producir; (labour) provocar

indulge [ɪn'dʌldʒ] vt (whim) satisfacer; (person) complacer; (child) mimar ▷ vi: **to ~ in** darse el gusto de; **indulgent** adj indulgente

industrial [ɪn'dʌstrɪəl] adj industrial; **industrial estate** (BRIT) n polígono (SP) or zona (LAM) industrial; **industrialist** n industrial mf; **industrial park** (US) n = **industrial estate**

industry ['ɪndəstrɪ] n industria; (diligence) aplicación f

inefficient [ɪnɪ'fɪʃənt] adj ineficaz, ineficiente

inequality [ɪnɪ'kwɔlɪtɪ] n desigualdad f

inevitable [ɪn'ɛvɪtəbl] adj inevitable; **inevitably** adv inevitablemente

inexpensive [ɪnɪk'spɛnsɪv] adj económico

inexperienced [ɪnɪk'spɪərɪənst] adj inexperto

inexplicable [ɪnɪk'splɪkəbl] adj inexplicable

infamous ['ɪnfəməs] adj infame

infant ['ɪnfənt] n niño/a; (baby) niño a pequeño/a, bebé mf; (pej) aniñado

infantry ['ɪnfəntrɪ] n infantería

infant school (BRIT) n parvulario

infect [ɪn'fɛkt] vt (wound) infectar; (food) contaminar; (person, animal) contagiar; **infection** [ɪn'fɛkʃən] n infección f; (fig) contagio; **infectious**

infekʃəs adj (also fig) contagioso

infer [ɪnˈfəː*] vt deducir, inferir

inferior [ɪnˈfɪərɪə*] adj, n inferior mf

infertile [ɪnˈfəːtaɪl] adj estéril; (person) infecundo

infertility [ɪnfəˈtɪlɪtɪ] n esterilidad f; fecundidad f

infested [ɪnˈfestɪd] adj: ~ with plagado de

infinite [ˈɪnfɪnɪt] adj infinito; **infinitely** adv infinitamente

infirmary [ɪnˈfəːmərɪ] n hospital m

inflamed [ɪnˈfleɪmd] adj: **to become ~** inflamarse

inflammation [ɪnfləˈmeɪʃən] n inflamación f

inflatable [ɪnˈfleɪtəbl] adj (ball, boat) inflable

inflate [ɪnˈfleɪt] vt (tyre, price etc) inflar; (fig) hinchar; **inflation** [ɪnˈfleɪʃən] n (Econ) inflación f

inflexible [ɪnˈfleksəbl] adj (rule) rígido; (person) inflexible

inflict [ɪnˈflɪkt] vt: **to ~ sth on sb** infligir algo en algn

influence [ˈɪnfluəns] n influencia ▷ vt influir en, influenciar; **under the of alcohol** en estado de embriaguez; **influential** [-ˈenʃl] adj influyente

influx [ˈɪnflʌks] n afluencia f

info (inf) [ˈɪnfəu] n =**information**

inform [ɪnˈfɔːm] vt: **to ~ sb of sth** informar a algn sobre or de algo ▷ vi: **to on sb** delatar a algn

informal [ɪnˈfɔːməl] adj (manner, tone) familiar; (dress, interview, occasion) informal; (visit, meeting) extraoficial

information [ɪnfəˈmeɪʃən] n información f; (knowledge) conocimientos mpl; **a piece of information** un dato; **information office** información f; **information technology** n informática

informative [ɪnˈfɔːmətɪv] adj informativo

infra-red [ɪnfrəˈred] adj infrarrojo

infrastructure [ˈɪnfrəstrʌktʃə*] n (of system etc) infraestructura

infrequent [ɪnˈfriːkwənt] adj infrecuente

infuriate [ɪnˈfjuərɪeɪt] vt: **to become ~d** ponerse furioso

infuriating [ɪnˈfjuərɪeɪtɪŋ] adj (habit, noise) enloquecedor(a)

ingenious [ɪnˈdʒiːnjəs] adj ingenioso

ingredient [ɪnˈɡriːdɪənt] n ingrediente m

inhabit [ɪnˈhæbɪt] vt vivir en; **inhabitant** n habitante mf

inhale [ɪnˈheɪl] vt inhalar ▷ vi (breathe in) aspirar; (in smoking) tragar; **inhaler** n inhalador m

inherent [ɪnˈhɪərənt] adj: ~ **in** or **to** inherente a

inherit [ɪnˈherɪt] vt heredar; **inheritance** n herencia; (fig) patrimonio

inhibit [ɪnˈhɪbɪt] vt inhibir, impedir; **inhibition** [-ˈbɪʃən] n cohibición f

initial [ɪˈnɪʃl] adj primero ▷ n inicial f ▷ vt firmar con las iniciales; **initials** npl (as signature) iniciales fpl; (abbreviation) siglas fpl; **initially** adv al principio

initiate [ɪˈnɪʃɪeɪt] vt iniciar; **to ~ proceedings against sb** (Law) entablar proceso contra algn

initiative [ɪˈnɪʃɪətɪv] n iniciativa f

inject [ɪnˈdʒekt] vt inyectar; **to ~ sb with sth** inyectar algo a algn; **injection** [ɪnˈdʒekʃən] n inyección f

injure [ˈɪndʒə*] vt (hurt) herir, lastimar; (fig: reputation etc) perjudicar; **injured** adj (person, arm) herido, lastimado; **injury** n herida, lesión f; (wrong) perjuicio, daño

> [!] Be careful not to translate **injury** by the Spanish word **injuria**.

injustice [ɪnˈdʒʌstɪs] n injusticia

ink [ɪŋk] n tinta; **ink-jet printer** [ˈɪŋkdʒet-] n impresora de chorro de tinta

inland [adj ˈɪnlənd, adv ɪnˈlænd] adj (waterway, port etc) interior ▷ adv tierra adentro; **Inland Revenue** (BRIT) n departamento de impuestos =

Hacienda f
in-laws ['ınlɔːz] npl suegros mpl
inmate ['ınmeıt] n (in prison) preso/a,
presidiario/a; (in asylum) internado/a
inn [ın] n posada, mesón m
inner ['ınə*] adj (courtyard, calm)
interior; (feelings) íntimo; **inner-city**
adj (schools, problems) de las zonas
céntricas pobres, de los barrios
céntricos pobres
inning ['ınıŋ] n (us: Baseball) inning
m, entrada; **~s** (Cricket) entrada, turno
innocence ['ınəsns] n inocencia f
innocent ['ınəsnt] adj inocente
innovation [ınəʊ'veıʃən] n
novedad f
innovative ['ınəʊ'veıtıv] adj
innovador
in-patient ['ınpeıʃənt] n paciente
m/f interno/a
input ['ınput] n entrada; (of resources)
inversión f; (Comput) entrada de datos
inquest ['ınkwest] n (coroner's)
encuesta judicial
inquire [ın'kwaıə*] vi preguntar
▷ vt: **to ~ whether** preguntar si; **to ~
about** (person) preguntar por; (fact)
informarse de; **inquiry** n pregunta;
(investigation) investigación, pesquisa;
"Inquiries" "Información"
ins. abbr = **inches**
insane [ın'seın] adj loco; (Med)
demente
insanity [ın'sænıtı] n demencia,
locura
insect ['ınsekt] n insecto; **insect
repellent** n loción f contra insectos
insecure [ınsı'kjuə*] adj inseguro
insecurity [ınsı'kjuərıtı] n
inseguridad f
insensitive [ın'sensıtıv] adj
insensible
insert [vb ın'sɜːt, n 'ınsɜːt] vt (into sth)
introducir ▷ n encarte m
inside ['ın'saıd] n interior m ▷ adj
interior, interno ▷ adv (be) (por)
dentro; (go) hacia dentro ▷ prep dentro
de; (of time): **~ 10 minutes** en menos

de 10 minutos; **inside lane** n (Aut: in
Britain) carril m izquierdo; (: in US,
Europe etc) carril m derecho; **inside out**
adv (turn) al revés; (know) a fondo
insight ['ınsaıt] n perspicacia
insignificant [ınsıg'nıfıknt] adj
insignificante
insincere [ınsın'sıə*] adj poco
sincero
insist [ın'sıst] vi insistir; **to ~ on**
insistir en; **to ~ that** insistir en que;
(claim) exigir que; **insistent** adj
insistente; (noise, action) persistente
insomnia [ın'sɒmnıə] n insomnio
inspect [ın'spekt] vt inspeccionar,
examinar; (troops) pasar revista a;
inspection [ın'spekʃən] n inspección
f, examen m; (of troops) revista;
inspector n inspector(a) m/f; (BRIT: o
buses, trains) revisor/a m/f
inspiration [ınspə'reıʃən] n
inspiración f; **inspire** [ın'spaıə*] vt
inspirar; **inspiring** adj inspirador(a)
instability [ınstə'bılıtı] n
inestabilidad f
install [ın'stɔːl] (us **instal**) vt instala
(official) nombrar; **installation**
[ınstə'leıʃən] n instalación f
instalment [ın'stɔːlmənt] (us
installment) n plazo; (of story)
entrega; (of TV serial etc) capítulo; **in ~
(pay, receive)** a plazos
instance ['ınstəns] n ejemplo, caso
for ~ por ejemplo; **in the first ~** en
primer lugar
instant ['ınstənt] n instante m,
momento ▷ adj inmediato; (coffee
etc) instantáneo; **instantly** adv en
seguida; **instant messaging** n
mensajería instantánea
instead [ın'sted] adv en cambio; **~ of**
en lugar de, en vez de
instinct ['ınstıŋkt] n instinto;
instinctive adj instintivo
institute ['ınstıtjuːt] n instituto;
(professional body) colegio ▷ vt (begin)
iniciar, empezar; (proceedings) entabla
(system, rule) establecer

institution [ɪnstɪ'tjuːʃən] n
institución f; (Med: home) asilo;
(: asylum) manicomio; (of system etc)
establecimiento; (of custom)
iniciación f

instruct [ɪn'strʌkt] vt: **to ~ sb in sth**
instruir a algn en o sobre algo; **to ~ sb
to do sth** dar instrucciones a algn de
hacer algo; **instruction** [ɪn'strʌkʃən] n
(teaching) instrucción f; **instructions**
npl (orders) órdenes fpl; **instructions
(for use)** modo de empleo; **instructor**
n instructor(a) m/f

instrument ['ɪnstrəmənt] n
instrumento; **instrumental** [-'mɛntl]
adj (Mus) instrumental; **to be
instrumental in** ser (el) artífice de

insufficient [ɪnsə'fɪʃənt] adj
insuficiente

insulate ['ɪnsjuleɪt] vt aislar;
insulation [-'leɪʃən] n aislamiento

insulin ['ɪnsjulɪn] n insulina

insult [n 'ɪnsʌlt, vb ɪn'sʌlt] n insulto
▷ vt insultar; **insulting** adj insultante

insurance [ɪn'ʃuərəns] n seguro;
fire/life ~ seguro contra incendios/
sobre la vida; **insurance company**
n compañía f de seguros; **insurance
policy** n póliza f de seguros; **insurance**

insure [ɪn'ʃuə*] vt asegurar

intact [ɪn'tækt] adj íntegro;
(unharmed) intacto

intake ['ɪnteɪk] n (of food) ingestión f;
(of air) consumo; (BRIT Scol): **an ~ of 200
a year** 200 matriculados al año

integral ['ɪntɪgrəl] adj (whole)
íntegro; (part) integrante

integrate ['ɪntɪgreɪt] vt integrar ▷ vi
integrarse

integrity [ɪn'tɛgrɪtɪ] n honradez f,
rectitud f

intellect ['ɪntəlɛkt] n intelecto;
intellectual [-'lɛktjuəl] adj, n
intelectual mf

intelligence [ɪn'tɛlɪdʒəns] n
inteligencia

intelligent [ɪn'tɛlɪdʒənt] adj
inteligente

intend [ɪn'tɛnd] vt (gift etc): **to ~ sth
for** destinar algo a; **to ~ to do sth** tener
intención de o pensar hacer algo

intense [ɪn'tɛns] adj intenso

intensify [ɪn'tɛnsɪfaɪ] vt intensificar;
(increase) aumentar

intensity [ɪn'tɛnsɪtɪ] n (gen)
intensidad f

intensive [ɪn'tɛnsɪv] adj intensivo;
intensive care n: **to be in intensive
care** estar bajo cuidados intensivos;
intensive care unit n unidad f de
vigilancia intensiva

intent [ɪn'tɛnt] n propósito; (Law)
premeditación f ▷ adj (absorbed)
absorto; (attentive) atento; **to all ~s
and purposes** prácticamente; **to
be ~ on doing sth** estar resuelto a
hacer algo

intention [ɪn'tɛnʃən] n intención f,
propósito; **intentional** adj deliberado

interact [ɪntər'ækt] vi influirse
mutuamente; **interaction**
[ɪntər'ækʃən] n interacción f, acción
recíproca; **interactive** adj (Comput)
interactivo

intercept [ɪntə'sɛpt] vt interceptar;
(stop) detener

interchange ['ɪntətʃeɪndʒ] n
intercambio; (on motorway)
intersección f

intercourse ['ɪntəkɔːs] n (sexual)
relaciones fpl sexuales

interest ['ɪntrɪst] n interés m ▷ vt interesar; **interested**
adj interesado; **to be interested
in** interesarse por; **interesting** adj
interesante; **interest rate** n tipo o
tasa de interés

interface ['ɪntəfeɪs] n (Comput)
junción f

interfere [ɪntə'fɪə*] vi: **to ~ in**
entrometerse en; **to ~ with** (hinder)
estorbar; (damage) estropear

interference [ɪntə'fɪərəns] n
intromisión f; (Radio, TV) interferencia

interim ['ɪntərɪm] n: **in the ~** en el
ínterin ▷ adj provisional

interior [ɪnˈtɪərɪə*] n interior m ▷ adj interior; **interior design** n interiorismo, decoración f de interiores

intermediate [ɪntəˈmiːdɪət] adj intermedio

intermission [ɪntəˈmɪʃən] n intermisión f; (Theatre) descanso

intern [vb ɪnˈtəːn, n ˈɪntəːn] (US) vt internar ▷ n interno/a

internal [ɪnˈtəːnl] adj (layout, pipes, security) interior; (injury, disease, memo) internal; **Internal Revenue Service** (US) n departamento de impuestos, ≈ Hacienda (SP)

international [ɪntəˈnæʃənl] adj internacional ▷ n (BRIT: match) partido internacional

Internet [ˈɪntənɛt] n: **the ~** Internet m or f; **Internet café** n cibercafé m; **Internet Service Provider** n proveedor m de (acceso a) Internet; **Internet user** n internauta mf

interpret [ɪnˈtəːprɪt] vt interpretar; (translate) traducir; (understand) entender ▷ vi hacer de intérprete; **interpretation** [ɪntəːprɪˈteɪʃən] n interpretación f; traducción f; **interpreter** n intérprete mf

interrogate [ɪnˈtɛrəugeɪt] vt interrogar; **interrogation** [-ˈgeɪʃən] n interrogatorio

interrogative [ɪntəˈrɔgətɪv] adj interrogativo

interrupt [ɪntəˈrʌpt] vt, vi interrumpir; **interruption** [-ˈrʌpʃən] n interrupción f

intersection [ɪntəˈsɛkʃən] n (of roads) cruce m

interstate [ˈɪntərsteɪt] (US) n carretera interestatal

interval [ˈɪntəvl] n intervalo; (BRIT Theatre, Sport) descanso; (Scol) recreo; **at ~s** a ratos, de vez en cuando

intervene [ɪntəˈviːn] vi intervenir; (event) interponerse; (time) transcurrir

interview [ˈɪntəvjuː] n entrevista ▷ vt entrevistarse con; **interviewer** n

entrevistador(a) m/f

intimate [adj ˈɪntɪmət, vb ˈɪntɪmeɪt] adj íntimo; (friendship) estrecho; (knowledge) profundo ▷ vt dar a entender

intimidate [ɪnˈtɪmɪdeɪt] vt intimidar, amedrentar

intimidating [ɪnˈtɪmɪdeɪtɪŋ] adj amedrentador, intimidante

into [ˈɪntuː] prep en; (towards) a; (inside) hacia el interior de; **~ 3 pieces/French** en 3 pedazos/al francés

intolerant [ɪnˈtɔlərənt] adj: **~ (of)** intolerante (con or para)

intranet [ˈɪntrænet] n intranet f

intransitive [ɪnˈtrænsɪtɪv] adj intransitivo

intricate [ˈɪntrɪkət] adj (design, pattern) intrincado

intrigue [ɪnˈtriːg] n intriga ▷ vt fascinar; **intriguing** adj fascinante

introduce [ɪntrəˈdjuːs] vt introducir, meter; (speaker, TV show etc) presentar; **to ~ sb (to sb)** presentar a algn (a algn); **to ~ sb to** (pastime, technique) introducir a algn a; **introduction** [-ˈdʌkʃən] n introducción f; (of person) presentación f; **introductory** [-ˈdʌktərɪ] adj introductorio; (lesson, offer) de introducción

intrude [ɪnˈtruːd] vi (person) entrometerse; **to ~ on** estorbar; **intruder** n intruso/a

intuition [ɪntjuːˈɪʃən] n intuición f

inundate [ˈɪnʌndeɪt] vt: **to ~ with** inundar de

invade [ɪnˈveɪd] vt invadir

invalid [n ˈɪnvælɪd, adj ɪnˈvælɪd] n (Med) minusválido/a ▷ adj (not valid) inválido, nulo

invaluable [ɪnˈvæljuəbl] adj inestimable

invariably [ɪnˈvɛərɪəblɪ] adv sin excepción, siempre; **she is ~ late** siempre llega tarde

invasion [ɪnˈveɪʒən] n invasión f

invent [ɪnˈvɛnt] vt inventar; **invention** [ɪnˈvɛnʃən] n invento;

(lie) ficción f, mentira; **inventor** n inventor(a) m/f

inventory ['ınvəntrı] n inventario

inverted commas [ın'vɜːtıd-] (BRIT) npl comillas fpl

invest [ın'vest] vt invertir ▷ vi: **to ~ in** (company etc) invertir dinero en; (fig: sth useful) comprar

investigate [ın'vestıgeıt] vt investigar; **investigation** [-'geıʃən] n investigación f, pesquisa

investigator [ın'vestıgeıtə*] n investigador(a) m/f; **private ~** investigador(a) m/f privado/a

investment [ın'vestmənt] n inversión f

investor [ın'vestə*] n inversionista mf

invisible [ın'vızıbl] adj invisible

invitation [ınvı'teıʃən] n invitación f

invite [ın'vaıt] vt invitar; (opinions etc) solicitar, pedir; **inviting** adj atractivo; (food) apetitoso

invoice ['ınvɔıs] n factura ▷ vt facturar

involve [ın'vɔlv] vt suponer, implicar; (concern, affect) corresponder; **to ~ sb (in sth)** comprometer a algn (con algo); **involved** adj complicado; **to be involved in** (take part) tomar parte en; (be engrossed) estar muy metido en; **involvement** n participación f, dedicación f

inward ['ınwəd] adj (movement) interior, interno; (thought, feeling) íntimo; **inward(s)** adv hacia dentro

iPod® ['aıpɔd] n iPod® m

IQ n abbr (= intelligence quotient) cociente m intelectual

IRA n abbr (= Irish Republican Army) IRA m

Iran [ı'rɑːn] n Irán m; **Iranian** [ı'reımıən] adj, n iraní mf

Iraq [ı'rɑːk] n Iraq; **Iraqi** adj, n iraquí mf

Ireland ['aıələnd] n Irlanda

iris ['aırıs] (pl **~es**) n (Anat) iris m;

(Bot) lirio

Irish ['aırıʃ] adj irlandés/esa ▷ npl: **the ~** los irlandeses; **Irishman** (irreg) n irlandés m; **Irishwoman** (irreg) n irlandesa

iron ['aıən] n hierro m; (for clothes) plancha f ▷ cpd de hierro ▷ vt (clothes) planchar

ironic(al) [aı'rɔnık(l)] adj irónico; **ironically** adv irónicamente

ironing ['aıənıŋ] n (activity) planchado; (clothes: ironed) ropa planchada; (: to be ironed) ropa por planchar; **ironing board** n tabla de planchar

irony ['aırənı] n ironía

irrational [ı'ræʃənl] adj irracional

irregular [ı'regjulə*] adj irregular; (surface) desigual; (action, event) anómalo; (behaviour) poco ortodoxo

irrelevant [ı'reləvənt] adj fuera de lugar, inoportuno

irresistible [ırı'zıstıbl] adj irresistible

irresponsible [ırı'spɔnsıbl] adj (act) irresponsable; (person) poco serio

irrigation [ırı'geıʃən] n riego

irritable ['ırıtəbl] adj (person) de mal humor

irritate ['ırıteıt] vt fastidiar; (Med) picar; **irritating** adj fastidioso; **irritation** [-'teıʃən] n fastidio; enfado; picazón f

IRS (us) n abbr = **Internal Revenue Service**

is [ız] vb see **be**

ISDN n abbr (= Integrated Services Digital Network) RDSI f

Islam ['ızlɑːm] n Islam m; **Islamic** [ız'læmık] adj islámico

island ['aılənd] n isla; **islander** n isleño/a

isle [aıl] n isla

isn't ['ıznt] = **is not**

isolated ['aısəleıtıd] adj aislado

isolation [aısə'leıʃən] n aislamiento

ISP n abbr = **Internet Service Provider**

Israel ['ızreıl] n Israel m; **Israeli**

[ɪz'reɪlɪ] adj, n israelí mf

issue ['ɪsjuː] n (problem, subject)
cuestión f; (outcome) resultado; (of
banknotes etc) emisión f; (of newspaper
etc) edición f ▷ vt (rations, equipment)
distribuir, repartir; (orders) dar;
(certificate, passport) expedir; (decree)
promulgar; (magazine) publicar;
(cheques) extender; (banknotes, stamps)
emitir; **at ~** en cuestión; **to take ~
with sb (over)** estar en desacuerdo
con algn (sobre); **to make an ~ of sth**
hacer una cuestión de algo

IT n abbr = **information technology**

○ KEYWORD

it [ɪt] pron 1 (specific subject: not generally
translated) él (ella); (: direct object) lo, la;
(: indirect object) le; (after prep) él (ella);
(abstract concept) ello; **it's on the table**
está en la mesa; **I can't find it** no lo (or
la) encuentro; **give it to me** dámelo
(or dámela); **I spoke to him about
it** le hablé del asunto; **what did you
learn from it?** ¿qué aprendiste de él (or
ella)?; **did you go to it?** (party, concert
etc) ¿fuiste?

2 (impersonal): **it's raining** llueve, está
lloviendo; **it's 6 o'clock/the 10th of
August** son las 6/es el 10 de agosto;
how far is it? – **it's 10 miles/2 hours
on the train** ¿a qué distancia está? – a
10 millas/2 horas en tren; **who is it?**
– **it's me** ¿quién es? – soy yo

Italian [ɪ'tæljən] adj italiano ▷ n
italiano/a; (Ling) italiano
italics [ɪ'tælɪks] npl cursiva
Italy ['ɪtəlɪ] n Italia
itch [ɪtʃ] n picazón f ▷ vi (part of body)
picar; **to ~ to do sth** rabiar por hacer
algo; **itchy** adj: **my hand is itchy** me
pica la mano
it'd ['ɪtd] = **it would; it had**
item ['aɪtəm] n artículo; (on agenda)
asunto (a tratar); (also: **news ~**) noticia
itinerary [aɪ'tɪnərərɪ] n itinerario

it'll ['ɪtl] = **it will; it shall**
its [ɪts] adj su; sus pl
it's [ɪts] = **it is; it has**
itself [ɪt'sɛlf] pron (reflexive) sí mismo/
a; (emphatic) él mismo(ella misma)
ITV n abbr (BRIT = Independent
Television) cadena de televisión comercial
independiente del Estado
I've [aɪv] = **I have**
ivory ['aɪvərɪ] n marfil m
ivy ['aɪvɪ] n (Bot) hiedra

j

jab [dʒæb] vt: **to ~ sth into sth** clavar algo en algo ▷ n (inf: Med) pinchazo

jack [dʒæk] n (Aut) gato; (Cards) sota

jacket [ˈdʒækɪt] n chaqueta, americana (SP), saco (LAM); (of book) sobrecubierta; **jacket potato** n patata asada (con piel)

jackpot [ˈdʒækpɒt] n premio gordo

Jacuzzi® [dʒəˈkuːzɪ] n jacuzzi®

jagged [ˈdʒægɪd] adj dentado

jail [dʒeɪl] n cárcel f ▷ vt encarcelar; **jail sentence** n pena f de cárcel

jam [dʒæm] n mermelada; (also: **traffic ~**) embotellamiento; (inf: difficulty) apuro ▷ vt (passage etc) obstruir; (mechanism, drawer etc) atascar; (Radio) interferir ▷ vi atascarse, trabarse; **to ~ sth into sth** meter algo a la fuerza en algo

Jamaica [dʒəˈmeɪkə] n Jamaica

jammed [dʒæmd] adj atascado

Jan abbr (=January) ene

janitor [ˈdʒænɪtə*] n (caretaker) portero, conserje m

January [ˈdʒænjuərɪ] n enero

Japan [dʒəˈpæn] n (el) Japón; **Japanese** [dʒæpəˈniːz] adj japonés/esa ▷ n inv japonés/esa m/f; (Ling) japonés m

jar [dʒɑː*] n tarro, bote m ▷ vi (sound) chirriar; (colours) desentonar

jargon [ˈdʒɑːgən] n jerga

javelin [ˈdʒævlɪn] n jabalina

jaw [dʒɔː] n mandíbula

jazz [dʒæz] n jazz m

jealous [ˈdʒeləs] adj celoso; (envious) envidioso; **jealousy** n celos mpl; envidia

jeans [dʒiːnz] npl vaqueros mpl, tejanos mpl

Jello® [ˈdʒeləu] (US) n gelatina

jelly [ˈdʒelɪ] n (jam) jalea; (dessert etc) gelatina; **jellyfish** n inv medusa, aguaviva (RPL)

jeopardize [ˈdʒepədaɪz] vt arriesgar, poner en peligro

jerk [dʒɜːk] n (jolt) sacudida; (wrench) tirón m; (inf) imbécil mf ▷ vt tirar bruscamente de ▷ vi (vehicle) traquetear

jersey [ˈdʒɜːzɪ] n jersey m

jersey [ˈdʒɜːzɪ] n jersey m; (fabric) (tejido de) punto

Jesus [ˈdʒiːzəs] n Jesús m

jet [dʒet] n (of gas, liquid) chorro; (Aviat) avión m a reacción; **jet lag** n desorientación f después de un largo vuelo; **jet-ski** vi practicar el motociclismo acuático

jetty [ˈdʒetɪ] n muelle m, embarcadero

Jew [dʒuː] n judío/a

jewel [ˈdʒuːəl] n joya; (in watch) rubí m; **jeweller** (US **jeweler**) n joyero/a; **jeweller's (shop)** (US **jewelry store**) n joyería; **jewellery** (US **jewelry**) n joyas fpl, alhajas fpl

Jewish [ˈdʒuːɪʃ] adj judío

jigsaw [ˈdʒɪgsɔː] n (also: **~ puzzle**) rompecabezas m inv, puzle m

job [dʒɒb] n (task) tarea; (post) empleo; **it's not my ~** no me incumbe a mí; **it's a good ~ that ...** menos mal que

...; **just the ~!** ¡estupendo!; **job centre** (BRIT) n oficina estatal de colocaciones; **jobless** adj sin trabajo

jockey ['dʒɔkɪ] n jockey mf ⊳ vi: **to ~ for position** maniobrar para conseguir una posición

jog [dʒɔg] vt empujar (ligeramente) ⊳ vi (run) hacer footing; **to ~ sb's memory** refrescar la memoria a algn; **jogging** n footing m

join [dʒɔɪn] vt (things) juntar, unir; (club) hacerse socio de; (Pol: party) afiliarse a; (queue) ponerse en; (meet: people) reunirse con ⊳ vi (roads) juntarse; (rivers) confluir ⊳ n juntura; **join in** vi tomar parte, participar ⊳ vt fus tomar parte or participar en; **join up** vi reunirse; (Mil) alistarse

joiner ['dʒɔɪnə*] (BRIT) n carpintero/a

joint [dʒɔɪnt] n (Tech) junta, unión f; (Anat) articulación f; (Culin) pieza de carne (para asar); (inf: place) tugurio; (: of cannabis) porro ⊳ adj (common) común; (combined) combinado; **joint account** n (with bank etc) cuenta común; **jointly** adv (gen) en común; (together) conjuntamente

joke [dʒəuk] n chiste m; (also: **practical ~**) broma ⊳ vi bromear; **to play a ~ on** gastar una broma a; **joker** n (Cards) comodín m

jolly ['dʒɔlɪ] adj (merry) alegre; (enjoyable) divertido ⊳ adv (BRIT: inf) muy, terriblemente

jolt [dʒəult] n (jerk) sacudida; (shock) susto ⊳ vt (physically) sacudir; (emotionally) asustar

Jordan ['dʒɔːdən] n (country) Jordania; (river) Jordán m

journal ['dʒəːnl] n (magazine) revista; (diary) periódico, diario; **journalism** n periodismo; **journalist** n periodista mf, reportero/a

journey ['dʒəːnɪ] n viaje m; (distance covered) trayecto

joy [dʒɔɪ] n alegría; **joyrider** n gamberro que roba un coche para dar una vuelta y luego abandonarlo; **joy stick** n

(Aviat) palanca de mando; (Comput) palanca de control

Jr abbr = **junior**

judge [dʒʌdʒ] n juez mf; (fig: expert) perito ⊳ vt juzgar; (consider) considerar

judo ['dʒuːdəu] n judo

jug [dʒʌg] n jarra

juggle ['dʒʌgl] vi hacer juegos malabares; **juggler** n malabarista mf

juice [dʒuːs] n zumo (SP), jugo (LAM); **juicy** adj jugoso

Jul abbr (= July) jul

July [dʒuːˈlaɪ] n julio

jumble ['dʒʌmbl] n revoltijo ⊳ vt (also: **~ up**) revolver; **jumble sale** (BRIT) n venta de objetos usados con fines benéficos

○ **JUMBLE SALE**

○ Los **jumble sales** son unos
○ mercadillos que se organizan con
○ fines benéficos en los locales de
○ un colegio, iglesia u otro centro
○ público. En ellos puede comprarse
○ todo tipo de artículos baratos de
○ segunda mano, sobre todo ropa,
○ juguetes, libros, vajillas o muebles.

jumbo ['dʒʌmbəu] n (also: **~ jet**) jumbo

jump [dʒʌmp] vi saltar, dar saltos; (with fear etc) pegar un bote; (increase) aumentar ⊳ vt saltar ⊳ n salto; aumento; **to ~ the queue** (BRIT) colarse

jumper ['dʒʌmpə*] n (BRIT: pullover) suéter m, jersey m; (US: dress) mandil m; **jumper cables** (US) npl = **jump leads**; **jump leads** (BRIT) npl cables mpl puente de batería

Jun. abbr = **junior**

junction ['dʒʌŋkʃən] n (BRIT: of roads) cruce m; (Rail) empalme m

June [dʒuːn] n junio

jungle ['dʒʌŋgl] n selva, jungla

junior ['dʒuːnɪə*] adj (in age) menor, más joven; (brother/sister etc): **seven**

years her ~ siete años menor que ella; *(position)* subalterno ▷ *n* menor *mf*, joven *mf*; **junior high school**(*US*) *n* centro de educación secundaria; *see also* **high school**; **junior school**(*BRIT*) *n* escuela primaria

junk [dʒʌŋk] *n (cheap goods)* baratijas *fpl*; *(rubbish)* basura; **junk food** *n* alimentos preparados y envasados de escaso valor nutritivo

junkie ['dʒʌŋkɪ] *(inf) n* drogadicto/a, yonqui *mf*

junk mail *n* propaganda de buzón

Jupiter ['dʒuːpɪtə*] *n (Mythology, Astrology)* Júpiter *m*

jurisdiction [dʒuərɪs'dɪkʃən] *n* jurisdicción *f*; **it falls** *or* **comes within/ outside our** ~ es/no es de nuestra competencia

jury ['dʒuərɪ] *n* jurado

just [dʒʌst] *adj* justo ▷ *adv (exactly)* exactamente; *(only)* sólo, solamente; **he's ~ done it/left** acaba de hacerlo/ irse; ~ **right** perfecto; ~ **two o'clock** las dos en punto; **she's ~ as clever as you** (ella) es tan lista como tú; ~ **as well that ...** menos mal que ...; ~ **as he was leaving** en el momento en que se marchaba; ~ **before/enough** justo antes/lo suficiente; ~ **here** aquí mismo; **he ~ missed** ha fallado por poco; ~ **listen to this** escucha esto un momento

justice ['dʒʌstɪs] *n* justicia; *(US: judge)* juez *mf*; **to do ~ to** *(fig)* hacer justicia a

justification [dʒʌstɪfɪ'keɪʃən] *n* justificación *f*

justify ['dʒʌstɪfaɪ] *vt* justificar; *(text)* alinear

jut [dʒʌt] *vi (also:* ~ **out)** sobresalir

juvenile ['dʒuːvənaɪl] *adj (court)* de menores; *(humour, mentality)* infantil ▷ *n* menor *m* de edad

K

K *abbr* (=*one thousand*) mil; (= *kilobyte*) kilobyte *m*, kilococteto

kangaroo [kæŋgə'ruː] *n* canguro

karaoke [kɑːrə'əʊkɪ] *n* karaoke

karate [kə'rɑːtɪ] *n* karate *m*

kebab [kə'bæb] *n* pincho moruno

keel [kiːl] *n* quilla; **on an even** ~ *(fig)* en equilibrio

keen [kiːn] *adj (interest, desire)* grande, vivo; *(eye, intelligence)* agudo; *(competition)* reñido; *(edge)* afilado; *(eager)* entusiasta; **to be ~ to do** *or* **on doing sth** tener muchas ganas de hacer algo; **to be ~ on sth/sb** interesarse por algo/algn

keep [kiːp] *(pt, pp* **kept)** *vt (preserve, store)* guardar; *(hold back)* quedarse con; *(maintain)* mantener; *(detain)* detener; *(shop)* ser propietario de; *(feed: family etc)* mantener; *(promise)* cumplir; *(chickens, bees etc)* criar; *(accounts)* llevar; *(diary)* escribir; *(prevent)*: **to ~ sb from doing sth** impedir a algn hacer algo ▷ *vi (food)* conservarse; *(remain)* seguir, continuar ▷ *n (of* castle) torreón m; (food etc) comida, subsistencia f; (inf): **for ~s** para siempre; **to ~ doing sth** seguir haciendo algo; **to ~ sb happy** tener a algn contento; **to ~ a place tidy** mantener un lugar limpio; **to ~ sth to o.s.** guardar algo para sí mismo; **to ~ sth (back) from sb** ocultar algo a algn; **to ~ time** (clock) mantener la hora exacta; **keep away** vt: **to keep sth/sb away from sb** mantener algo/a algn apartado de algn ▷ vi: **to keep away from** mantenerse apartado (de); **keep back** vt (crowd, tears) contener; (money) quedarse con; (conceal: information): **to keep sth back from sb** ocultar algo a algn ▷ vi hacerse a un lado; **keep off** vt (dog, person) mantener a distancia ▷ vi: **if the rain keeps off** si no llueve; **keep your hands off!** ¡no toques!; **"keep off the grass"** "prohibido pisar el césped"; **keep on** vi: **to keep on doing** seguir o continuar haciendo; **to keep on (about sth)** no parar de hablar (de algo); **keep out** vi (stay out) permanecer fuera; **"keep out"** "prohibida la entrada"; **keep up** vt mantener, conservar ▷ vi no retrasarse; **to keep up with** (pace) (level) mantenerse a la altura de; **keeper** n guardián/ana m/f; **keeping** n (care) cuidado; **in keeping with** de acuerdo con

kennel ['kɛnl] n perrera; **kennels** npl residencia canina

Kenya ['kɛnjə] n Kenia

kept [kɛpt] pt, pp of **keep**

kerb [kə:b] (BRIT) n bordillo

kerosene ['kɛrəsi:n] n keroseno

ketchup ['kɛtʃəp] n salsa de tomate, catsup M

kettle ['kɛtl] n hervidor m de agua

key [ki:] n llave f; (Mus) tono; (of piano, typewriter) tecla ▷ adj (issue etc) clave inv ▷ vt (also: ~ **in**) teclear; **keyboard** n teclado; **keyhole** n ojo (de la cerradura); **keyring** n llavero

kg abbr (= kilogram) kg

khaki ['kɑ:kɪ] n caqui

kick [kɪk] vt dar una patada o un puntapié a; (inf: habit) quitarse de ▷ vi (horse) dar coces ▷ n patada, puntapié m; (of animal) coz f; (thrill): **he does it for ~s** lo hace por pura diversión; **kick off** vi (Sport) hacer el saque inicial; **kick-off** n saque inicial; **the kick-off is at 10 o'clock** el partido empieza a las diez

kid [kɪd] n (inf: child) chiquillo/a; (animal) cabrito; (leather) cabritilla ▷ vi (inf) bromear

kidnap ['kɪdnæp] vt secuestrar; **kidnapping** n secuestro

kidney ['kɪdnɪ] n riñón m; **kidney bean** n judía, alubia

kill [kɪl] vt matar; (murder) asesinar ▷ n matanza; **to ~ time** matar el tiempo; **killer** n asesino/a; **killing** n (one) asesinato; (several) matanza; **to make a killing** (fig) hacer su agosto

kiln [kɪln] n horno

kilo ['ki:ləu] n kilo; **kilobyte** n (Comput) kilobyte m, kilooctecto; **kilogram(me)** n kilo, kilogramo; **kilometre** ['kɪləmi:tə*] (US **kilometer**) n kilómetro; **kilowatt** n kilovatio

kilt [kɪlt] n falda escocesa

kin [kɪn] n see **next-of-kin**

kind [kaɪnd] adj amable, atento ▷ n clase f, especie f; (species) género; **in ~** (Comm) en especie; **a ~ of** una especie de; **to be two of a ~** ser tal para cual

kindergarten ['kɪndəgɑ:tn] n jardín m de la infancia

kindly ['kaɪndlɪ] adj bondadoso; cariñoso ▷ adv bondadosamente, amablemente; **will you ~ ...** sea usted tan amable de ...

kindness ['kaɪndnɪs] n (quality) bondad f, amabilidad f; (act) favor m

king [kɪŋ] n rey m; **kingdom** n reino; **kingfisher** n martín m pescador; **king-size(d) bed** n cama de matrimonio extragrande

kiosk ['ki:ɔsk] n quiosco; (BRIT Tel) cabina

kipper ['kɪpə*] n arenque m ahumado

kiss [kɪs] *n* beso ▷ *vt* besar; **to ~ (each other)** besarse; **kiss of life** *n* respiración *f* boca a boca

kit [kɪt] *n* (*equipment*) equipo; (*tools etc*) (caja de) herramientas *fpl*; (*assembly kit*) juego de armar

kitchen ['kɪtʃɪn] *n* cocina

kite [kaɪt] *n* (*toy*) cometa

kitten ['kɪtn] *n* gatito/a

kiwi ['kiːwiː-] *n* (*also*: **~ fruit**) kiwi *m*

km *abbr* (*= kilometre*) km

km/h *abbr* (*= kilometres per hour*) km/h

knack [næk] *n*: **to have the ~ of doing sth** tener el don de hacer algo

knee [niː] *n* rodilla; **kneecap** *n* rótula

kneel [niːl] (*pt, pp* knelt) *vi* (*also*: **~ down**) arrodillarse

knelt [nɛlt] *pt, pp of* **kneel**

knew [njuː] *pt of* **know**

knickers ['nɪkəz] (BRIT) *npl* bragas *fpl*

knife [naɪf] (*pl* knives) *n* cuchillo ▷ *vt* acuchillar

knight [naɪt] *n* caballero; (*Chess*) caballo

knit [nɪt] *vt* tejer, tricotar ▷ *vi* hacer punto, tricotar; (*bones*) soldarse; **to ~ one's brows** fruncir el ceño; **knitting** *n* labor *f* de punto; **knitting needle** *n* aguja de hacer punto; **knitwear** *n* prendas *fpl* de punto

knives [naɪvz] *npl of* **knife**

knob [nɔb] *n* (*of door*) tirador *m*; (*of stick*) puño; (*on radio, TV*) botón *m*

knock [nɔk] *vt* (*strike*) golpear; (*bump into*) chocar contra; (*inf*) criticar ▷ *vi* (*at door etc*): **to ~ at/on** llamar a ▷ *n* golpe *m*; (*on door*) llamada; **knock down** *vt* atropellar; **knock off** (*inf*) *vi* (*finish*) salir del trabajo ▷ *vt* (*from price*) descontar; (*inf: steal*) birlar; **knock out** *vt* dejar sin sentido; (*Boxing*) poner fuera de combate, dejar K.O.; (*in competition*) eliminar; **knock over** *vt* (*object*) tirar; (*person*) atropellar; **knockout** *n* (*Boxing*) K.O. *m*, knockout *m* ▷ *cpd* (*competition etc*) eliminatorio

knot [nɔt] *n* nudo ▷ *vt* anudar

know [nəu] (*pt* knew, *pp* known)

vt (*facts*) saber; (*be acquainted with*) conocer; (*recognize*) reconocer, conocer; **to ~ how to swim** saber nadar; **to ~ about** *or* **of sb/sth** saber de algn/algo; **know-all** *n* sabelotodo *mf*; **know-how** *n* conocimientos *mpl*; **knowing** *adj* (*look*) de complicidad; **knowingly** *adv* (*purposely*) adrede; (*smile, look*) con complicidad; **know-it-all** (*us*) *n* = **know-all**

knowledge ['nɔlɪdʒ] *n* conocimiento; (*learning*) saber *m*, conocimientos *mpl*; **knowledgeable** *adj* entendido

known [nəun] *pp of* **know** ▷ *adj* (*thief, facts*) conocido; (*expert*) reconocido

knuckle ['nʌkl] *n* nudillo

koala [kəu'ɑːlə] *n* (*also*: **~ bear**) koala *m*

Koran [kɔ'rɑːn] *n* Corán *m*

Korea [kə'rɪə] *n* Corea; **Korean** *adj, n* coreano/a *m/f*

kosher ['kəuʃə*] *adj* autorizado por la ley judía

Kosovar ['kɔsəvɑː*], **Kosovan** ['kɔsəvən] *adj* kosovar

Kosovo ['kɔsəvəu] *n* Kosovo

Kremlin ['krɛmlɪn] *n*: **the ~** el Kremlin

Kuwait [ku'weɪt] *n* Kuwait *m*

I

L (BRIT) abbr = **learner driver**

l. abbr (= litre) l

lab [læb] n abbr = **laboratory**

label ['leɪbl] n etiqueta ▷ vt poner etiqueta a

labor etc ['leɪbə*] (US) = **labour** etc

laboratory [ləˈbɔrətərɪ] n laboratorio

Labor Day (US) n día m de los trabajadores (primer lunes de septiembre)

labor union (US) n sindicato

labour ['leɪbə*] (US **labor**) n (hard work) trabajo; (labour force) mano f de obra; (Med): **to be in ~** estar de parto ▷ vi: **to ~ (at sth)** trabajar (en algo) ▷ vt: **to ~ a point** insistir en un punto; **L~, the L~ party** (BRIT) el partido laborista, los laboristas mpl; **labourer** n peón m; **farm labourer** peón m; (day labourer) jornalero

lace [leɪs] n encaje m; (of shoe etc) cordón m ▷ vt (shoes: also: **~ up**) atarse (los zapatos)

lack [læk] n (absence) falta ▷ vt faltarle a algn, carecer de; **through** or

for ~ of por falta de; **to be ~ing** faltar, no haber; **to be ~ing in sth** faltarle a algn algo

lacquer ['lækə*] n laca

lacy ['leɪsɪ] adj (of lace) de encaje; (like lace) como de encaje

lad [læd] n muchacho, chico

ladder ['lædə*] n escalera (de mano); (BRIT: in tights) carrera

ladle ['leɪdl] n cucharón m

lady ['leɪdɪ] n señora; (dignified, graceful) dama; **"ladies and gentlemen ..."** "señoras y caballeros ..."; **young ~** señorita; **the ladies' (room)** los servicios de señoras; **ladybird** (US **ladybug**) n mariquita

lag [læg] n retraso ▷ vi (also: **~ behind**) retrasarse, quedarse atrás ▷ vt (pipes) revestir

lager ['lɑːgə*] n cerveza (rubia)

lagoon [ləˈguːn] n laguna

laid [leɪd] pt, pp of **lay**; **laid back** (inf) adj relajado

lain [leɪn] pp of **lie**

lake [leɪk] n lago

lamb [læm] n cordero; (meat) (carne f de) cordero

lame [leɪm] adj cojo; (excuse) poco convincente

lament [ləˈmɛnt] n quejo ▷ vt lamentarse de

lamp [læmp] n lámpara; **lamppost** (BRIT) n (poste m de) farol m; **lampshade** n pantalla

land [lænd] n tierra; (country) país m; (piece of land) terreno; (estate) tierras fpl, finca ▷ vi (of plane) aterrizar; (Aviat) aterrizar; (fig: fall) caer, terminar ▷ vt (passengers, goods) desembarcar; **to ~ sb with sth** (inf) hacer cargar a algn con algo; **landing** n aterrizaje m; (of staircase) rellano; **landing card** n tarjeta de desembarque; **landlady** n (of rented house, pub etc) dueña; **landlord** n propietario (of pub etc) patrón m; **landmark** n lugar m conocido; **to be a landmark** (fig) marcar un hito histórico; **landowner** n terrateniente *mf*; **landscape** *n* paisaje *m*; **landslide** *n* (Geo) corrimiento de tierras; (*fig*: Pol) victoria arrolladora

lane [leɪn] *n* (*in country*) camino; (Aut) carril *m*; (*in race*) calle *f*

language ['læŋgwɪdʒ] *n* lenguaje *m*; (*national tongue*) idioma *m*, lengua; **bad ~** palabrotas *fpl*; **language laboratory** *n* laboratorio de idiomas; **language school** *n* academia de idiomas

lantern ['læntn] *n* linterna, farol *m*

lap [læp] *n* (*of track*) vuelta; (*of body*) regazo ⊳ *vt* (*also*: **~ up**) beber a lengüetadas ⊳ *vi* (*waves*) chapotear; **to sit on sb's ~** sentarse en las rodillas de algn

lapel [lə'pɛl] *n* solapa

lapse [læps] *n* fallo; (*moral*) desliz *m*; (*of time*) intervalo ⊳ *vi* (*expire*) caducar; (*time*) pasar, transcurrir; **to ~ into bad habits** caer en malos hábitos

laptop (computer) ['læptɒp-] *n* (ordenador *m*) portátil *m*

lard [lɑːd] *n* manteca (de cerdo)

larder ['lɑːdə*] *n* despensa

large [lɑːdʒ] *adj* grande; **at ~** (*free*) en libertad; (*generally*) en general

> Be careful not to translate **large** by the Spanish word *largo*.

largely *adv* (*mostly*) en su mayor parte; (*introducing reason*) en gran parte;

large-scale *adj* (*map*) en gran escala; (*fig*) importante

lark [lɑːk] *n* (*bird*) alondra; (*joke*) broma

laryngitis [lærɪn'dʒaɪtɪs] *n* laringitis *f*

lasagne [lə'zænjə] *n* lasaña

laser ['leɪzə*] *n* láser *m*; **laser printer** *n* impresora (por) láser

lash [læʃ] *n* latigazo; (*tie*) pestaña ⊳ *vt* azotar; (*tie*) **to ~ to/ together** atar a/atar; **lash out** *vi*: **to lash out (at sb)** (*hit*) arremeter (contra algn); **to lash out against sb** lanzar invectivas contra algn

lass [læs] (BRIT) *n* chica

last [lɑːst] *adj* último; (*end: of series*

etc) final ⊳ *adv* (*most recently*) la última vez; (*finally*) por último ⊳ *vi* durar; (*continue*) continuar, seguir; **~ night** anoche; **~ week** la semana pasada; **at ~** por fin; **~ but one** penúltimo; **lastly** *adv* por último, finalmente; **last-minute** *adj* de última hora

latch [lætʃ] *n* pestillo; **latch onto** *vt fus* (*person, group*) pegarse a; (*idea*) agarrarse a

late [leɪt] *adj* (*far on: in time, process etc*) al final de; (*not on time*) tarde, atrasado; (*dead*) fallecido ⊳ *adv* tarde; (*behind time, schedule*) con retraso; **of ~** últimamente; **~ at night** a última hora de la noche; **in ~ May** hacia fines de mayo; **the ~ Mr X** el difunto Sr X; **latecomer** *n* recién llegado/a; **lately** *adv* últimamente; **later** *adj* (*date etc*) posterior; (*version etc*) más reciente ⊳ *adv* más tarde, después; **latest** ['leɪtɪst] *adj* último; **at the latest** más tardar

lather ['lɑːðə*] *n* espuma (de jabón) ⊳ *vt* enjabonar

Latin ['lætɪn] *n* latín *m* ⊳ *adj* latino; **Latin America** *n* América latina; **Latin American** *adj, n* latinoamericano/a *m/f*

latitude ['lætɪtjuːd] *n* latitud *f*; (*fig*) libertad *f*

latter ['lætə*] *adj* último; (*of two*) segundo ⊳ *n*: **the ~** el último, éste

laugh [lɑːf] *n* risa ⊳ *vi* reír(se); (**to do sth) for a ~** (*hacer algo*) en broma; **laugh at** *vt fus* reírse de; **laughter** *n* risa

launch [lɔːntʃ] *n* lanzamiento; (*boat*) lancha ⊳ *vt* (*ship*) botar; (*rocket etc*) lanzar; (*fig*) comenzar; **launch into** *vt fus* lanzarse a

launder ['lɔːndə*] *vt* lavar

Launderette® [lɔːn'drɛt] (BRIT) *n* lavandería (automática)

Laundromat® ['lɔːndrəmæt] (us) *n* **= Launderette**

laundry ['lɔːndrɪ] *n* (*dirty*) ropa sucia; (*clean*) colada; (*room*) lavadero

lava ['lɑːvə] n lava

lavatory ['lævətərɪ] n wáter m

lavender ['lævəndə*] n lavanda

lavish ['lævɪʃ] adj (amount) abundante; (person): **with** pródigo en; **to ~ sth on sb** colmar a algn de algo

law [lɔː] n ley f; (Scol) derecho; (a rule) regla; (professions connected with law) jurisprudencia; **lawful** adj legítimo, lícito; **lawless** adj (action) criminal

lawn [lɔːn] n césped m; **lawnmower** n cortacésped m

lawsuit ['lɔːsuːt] n pleito

lawyer ['lɔːjə*] n abogado/a; (for sales, wills etc) notario/a

lax [læks] adj laxo

laxative ['læksətɪv] n laxante m

lay [leɪ] (pt, pp **laid**) pt of **lie** ▷ adj laico; (not expert) lego ▷ vt (place) colocar; (eggs, table) poner; (cable) tender; (carpet) extender; **lay down** vt (pen etc) dejar; (rules etc) establecer; **to lay down the law** (pej) imponer las normas; **lay off** vt (workers) despedir; **lay on** vt (meal, facilities) proveer; **lay out** vt (spread out) disponer, exponer; **lay-by** n (BRIT Aut) área de aparcamiento

layer ['leɪə*] n capa

layman ['leɪmən] (irreg) n lego

layout ['leɪaut] n (design) plan m, trazado; (Press) composición f

lazy ['leɪzɪ] adj perezoso, vago; (movement) lento

lb. abbr = **pound** (weight)

lead¹ [liːd] pt, pp **led**) n (front position) delantera; (clue) pista; (Elec) cable m; (for dog) correa; (Theatre) papel m principal ▷ vt (walk etc in front) ir a la cabeza de; (guide): **to ~ sb somewhere** conducir a algn a algún sitio; (be leader) dirigir; (start, guide: activity) protagonizar ▷ vi (road, pipe etc) conducir a; (Sport) ir primero; **to be in the ~** (Sport) llevar la delantera; (fig) ir a la cabeza; **to ~ the way** llevar la delantera; **lead up to** vt fus (events)

conducir a; (in conversation) preparar el terreno para

lead² [lɛd] n (metal) plomo; (in pencil) mina

leader ['liːdə*] n jefe/a m/f, líder mf; (Sport) líder mf; **leadership** n dirección f; (position) mando; (quality) iniciativa

lead-free ['lɛdfriː] adj sin plomo

leading ['liːdɪŋ] adj (main) principal; (first) primero; (front) delantero

lead singer [liːd-] n cantante mf

leaf [liːf] (pl **leaves**) n hoja ▷ vi: **to ~ through** hojear; **to turn over a new ~** reformarse

leaflet ['liːflɪt] n folleto

league [liːg] n sociedad f; (Football) liga; **to be in ~ with** haberse confabulado con

leak [liːk] n (of liquid, gas) escape m, fuga; (in pipe) agujero; (in roof) gotera; (in security) filtración f ▷ vi (shoes, ship) hacer agua; (pipe) tener (un) escape; (roof) gotear; (liquid, gas) escaparse, fugarse; (fig) divulgarse ▷ vt (fig) filtrar

lean [liːn] (pt, pp **~ed** or **~t**) adj (thin) flaco; (meat) magro ▷ vt: **to ~ sth on sth** apoyar algo en algo ▷ vi (slope) inclinarse; **to ~ against** apoyarse contra; **to ~ on** apoyarse en; **lean forward** vi inclinarse hacia adelante; **lean over** vi inclinarse; **leaning** n: **leaning (towards)** inclinación f (hacia)

leant [lɛnt] pt, pp of **lean**

leap [liːp] (pt, pp **~ed** or **~t**) n salto ▷ vi saltar

leapt [lɛpt] pt, pp of **leap**

leap year n año bisiesto

learn [ləːn] (pt, pp **~ed** or **~t**) vt aprender ▷ vi aprender; **to ~ about sth** enterarse de algo; **to ~ to do sth** aprender a hacer algo; **learner** n (BRIT also: **learner driver**) principiante m; **learning** n el saber m, conocimientos mpl

learnt [ləːnt] pt, pp of **learn**

lease [liːs] n arriendo ▷ vt arrendar

leash [liːʃ] n correa

least [liːst] adj: **the ~** (slightest) el menor, el más pequeño; (smallest amount of) mínimo ▷ adv (+ vb) menos; (+ adj): **the ~ expensive** el (la) menos costoso/a; **the ~ possible effort** el menor esfuerzo posible; **at ~** por lo menos, al menos; **you could at ~ have written** por lo menos habrías podido escribir; **not in the ~** en absoluto

leather [ˈlɛðəʳ] n cuero

leave [liːv] (pt, pp **left**) vt dejar; (go away from) abandonar; (place etc: permanently) salir de ▷ vi (train etc) salir ▷ n permiso; **to ~ sth to sb** (money etc) legar algo a algn; (responsibility etc) encargar a algn de algo; **to be left** quedar, sobrar; **there's some milk left over** sobra or queda algo de leche; **on ~** de permiso; **leave behind** vt (on purpose) dejar; (accidentally) dejarse; **leave out** vt omitir

leaves [liːvz] npl of **leaf**

Lebanon [ˈlɛbənən] n: **the ~** el Líbano

lecture [ˈlɛktʃəʳ] n conferencia; (Scol) clase f ▷ vi dar una clase ▷ vt (scold): **to ~ sb on** or **about sth** echar una reprimenda a algn por algo; **to give a ~ on** dar una conferencia sobre; **lecture hall** n sala de conferencias; (Univ) aula f; **lecturer** n conferenciante mf; (BRIT: at university) profesor(a) m/f; **lecture theatre** n = **lecture hall**

led [lɛd] pt, pp of **lead¹**

ledge [lɛdʒ] n repisa; (of window) alféizar m; (of mountain) saliente m

leek [liːk] n puerro

left [lɛft] pt, pp of **leave** ▷ adj izquierdo; (remaining): **there are two ~** quedan dos ▷ n izquierda ▷ adv a la izquierda; **on** or **to the ~** a la izquierda; **the L~** (Pol) la izquierda; **left-hand** adj: **the left-hand side** la izquierda; **left-hand drive** adj: **a left-hand drive car** un coche con el volante a la izquierda; **left-handed** adj zurdo; **left-luggage locker** n (BRIT) consigna f automática; **left-luggage** (office)(BRIT) n consigna; **left-overs** npl sobras fpl; **left-wing** adj (Pol) de izquierdas, izquierdista

leg [lɛg] n (of person) pierna; (of animal, chair) pata; (trouser leg) pernera; (Culin: of lamb) pierna; (: of chicken) pata; (of journey) etapa

legacy [ˈlɛgəsɪ] n herencia

legal [ˈliːgl] adj (permitted by law) lícito; (of law) legal; **legal holiday**(US) n fiesta oficial; **legalize** vt legalizar; **legally** adv legalmente

legend [ˈlɛdʒənd] n (also fig: person) leyenda; **legendary** [-ərɪ] adj legendario

leggings [ˈlɛgɪŋz] npl mallas fpl, leggins mpl

legible [ˈlɛdʒəbl] adj legible

legislation [lɛdʒɪsˈleɪʃən] n legislación f

legislative [ˈlɛdʒɪslətɪv] adj legislativo

legitimate [lɪˈdʒɪtɪmət] adj legítimo

leisure [ˈlɛʒəʳ] n ocio, tiempo libre; **at ~** con tranquilidad; **leisure centre** (BRIT) n centro de recreo; **leisurely** adj sin prisa; lento

lemon [ˈlɛmən] n limón m; **lemonade** n (fizzy) gaseosa; **lemon tea** n té m con limón

lend [lɛnd] (pt, pp **lent**) vt: **to ~ sth to sb** prestar algo a algn

length [lɛŋθ] n (size) largo, longitud f; (distance): **the ~ of** todo lo largo de; (of swimming pool, cloth) largo; (of wood, string) trozo; (amount of time) duración f; **at ~** (at last) por fin, finalmente; (lengthily) largamente; **lengthen** vt alargar ▷ vi alargarse; **lengthways** adv a lo largo; **lengthy** adj largo, extenso

lens [lɛnz] n (of spectacles) lente f; (of camera) objetivo

Lent [lɛnt] n Cuaresma

lent [lɛnt] pt, pp of **lend**

lentil [ˈlɛntl] n lenteja

Leo [ˈliːəu] n Leo

leopard [ˈlɛpəd] n leopardo

leotard ['li:əta:d] n mallas fpl

leprosy ['leprəsi] n lepra

lesbian ['lezbiən] n lesbiana

less [les] adj (in size, degree etc) menor; (in quality) menos ▷ pron, adv menos ▷ prep: **~ tax/10% discount** menos impuestos/el 10 por ciento de descuento; **~ than half** menos de la mitad; **~ than ever** menos que nunca; **~ and ~** cada vez menos; **the ~ he works ...** cuanto menos trabaja ...; **lessen** vi disminuir, reducirse ▷ vt disminuir, reducir; **lesser** ['lesə*] adj menor; **to a lesser extent** en menor grado

lesson ['lesn] n clase f; (warning) lección f

let [let] (pt, pp ~) vt (allow) dejar, permitir; (BRIT: lease) alquilar; **to ~ sb do sth** dejar que algn haga algo; **to ~ sb know sth** comunicar algo a algn; **~'s go** ¡vamos!; **~ him come** que venga; **"to ~"** "se alquila"; **let down** vt (tyre) desinflar; (disappoint) defraudar; **let in** vt dejar entrar; (visitor etc) hacer pasar; **let off** vt (culprit) dejar escapar; (gun) disparar; (bomb) accionar; (firework) hacer estallar; **let out** vt dejar salir; (sound) soltar

lethal ['li:θl] adj (weapon) mortífero; (poison, wound) mortal

letter ['letə*] n (of alphabet) letra; (correspondence) carta; **letterbox** (BRIT) n buzón m

lettuce ['letɪs] n lechuga

leukaemia [lu:'ki:mɪə] (US **leukemia**) n leucemia

level ['levl] adj (flat) llano ▷ adv: **to draw ~ with** llegar a la altura de ▷ n nivel m; (height) altura ▷ vt nivelar; allanar; (destroy: building) derribar; (: forest) arrasar; **to be ~ with** estar a nivel de; **A ~s** (BRIT) = exámenes mpl de bachillerato superior, B.U.P. = AS = (BRIT) asignatura aprobada entre los "GCSEs" y los "A levels"; **on the ~** (fig: honest) serio; **level crossing** (BRIT) n paso a nivel

lever ['li:və*] n (also fig) palanca ▷ vt: **to ~ up** levantar con palanca; **leverage** n (using bar etc) apalancamiento; (fig: influence) influencia

levy ['levɪ] n impuesto ▷ vt exigir, recaudar

liability [laɪə'bɪlətɪ] n (pej: person, thing) estorbo, lastre m; (Jur: responsibility) responsabilidad f

liable ['laɪəbl] adj (subject): **to** sujeto a; (responsible): **~ for** responsable de; (likely): **~ to do** propenso a hacer

liaise [lɪ'eɪz] vi: **to ~ with** enlazar con

liar ['laɪə*] n mentiroso/a

liberal ['lɪbərəl] adj liberal; (offer, amount etc) generoso; **Liberal Democrat** n (BRIT) demócrata m/f liberal

liberate ['lɪbəreɪt] vt (people: from poverty etc) librar; (prisoner) libertar; (country) liberar

liberation [lɪbə'reɪʃən] n liberación f

liberty ['lɪbətɪ] n libertad f; **to be at ~** (criminal) estar en libertad; **to be at ~ to do** estar libre para hacer; **to take the ~ of doing sth** tomarse la libertad de hacer algo

Libra ['li:brə] n Libra

librarian [laɪ'brɛərɪən] n bibliotecario/a

library ['laɪbrərɪ] n biblioteca

> Be careful not to translate **library** by the Spanish word librería.

Libya ['lɪbɪə] n Libia

lice [laɪs] npl of **louse**

licence ['laɪsəns] (US **license**) n licencia; (permit) permiso; (also: **driving ~**) carnet m de conducir (SP), licencia de manejo (LAM)

license ['laɪsəns] n (US) = **licence** ▷ vt autorizar, dar permiso a; **licensed** adj (for alcohol) autorizado para vender bebidas alcohólicas; (car) matriculado; **license plate** n (US) placa (de matrícula); **licensing hours** (BRIT) npl horas durante las cuales se permite la venta y consumo de alcohol (en un bar etc)

lick [lɪk] vt lamer; (*inf: defeat*) dar una paliza a; **to ~ one's lips** relamerse

lid [lɪd] n (*of box, case*) tapa; (*of pan*) tapadera

lie [laɪ] (*pt* **lay**, *pp* **lain**) vi (*rest*) estar echado, estar acostado; (*of object: be situated*) estar, encontrarse; (*tell lies*) mentir ▷ n mentira; **to ~ low** (*fig*) mantenerse a escondidas; **lie about** or **around** vi (*things*) estar tirado; (*BRIT: people*) estar tumbado; **lie down** vi echarse, tumbarse

Liechtenstein ['lɪktənstaɪn] n Liechtenstein m

lie-in ['laɪɪn] (*BRIT*) n **to have a ~** quedarse en la cama

lieutenant [leftˈnənt, *us* luːˈtɛnənt] n (*Mil*) teniente mf

life [laɪf] (*pl* **lives**) n vida; **to come to ~** animarse; **life assurance** (*BRIT*) n seguro de vida; **lifeboat** n lancha de socorro; **lifeguard** n vigilante mf, socorrista mf; **life insurance** n = **life assurance**; **life jacket** n chaleco salvavidas; **lifelike** adj (*model etc*) que parece vivo; (*realistic*) realista; **life preserver** (*us*) n cinturón m/chaleco salvavidas; **life sentence** n cadena perpetua; **lifestyle** n estilo de vida; **lifetime** n (*of person*) vida; (*of thing*) período de vida

lift [lɪft] vt levantar; (*end: ban, rule*) levantar, suprimir ▷ vi (*fog*) disiparse ▷ n (*BRIT: machine*) ascensor m; **to give sb a ~** (*BRIT*) llevar a algn en el coche; **lift up** vt levantar; **lift-off** n despegue m

light [laɪt] (*pt, pp* **~ed** or **lit**) n luz f, (*lamp*) luz f, lámpara; (*Aut*) faro; (*for cigarette etc*) **have you got a ~?** ¿tienes fuego? ▷ vt (*candle, cigarette, fire*) encender (*SP*), prender (*LAM*); (*room*) alumbrar ▷ adj (*colour*) claro; (*not heavy, also fig*) ligero; (*room*) con mucha luz; (*gentle, graceful*) ágil; **lights** npl (*traffic lights*) semáforos mpl; **to come to ~** salir a luz; **in the ~ of** (*new evidence etc*) a la luz de; **light up** vi

(*smoke*) encender un cigarrillo; (*face*) iluminarse ▷ vt (*illuminate*) iluminar, alumbrar; (*set fire to*) encender; **light bulb** n bombilla (*SP*), foco (*MEX*), bujía (*CAM*), bombita (*RPL*); **lighten** vt (*make less heavy*) aligerar; **lighter** n (*also:* **cigarette lighter**) encendedor m, mechero; **light-hearted** adj (*person*) alegre; (*remark etc*) divertido; **lighthouse** n faro; **lighting** n (*system*) alumbrado; **lightly** adv ligeramente; (*not seriously*) con poca seriedad; **to get off lightly** ser castigado con poca severidad

lightning ['laɪtnɪŋ] n relámpago, rayo

lightweight ['laɪtweɪt] adj (*suit*) ligero ▷ n (*Boxing*) peso ligero

like [laɪk] vt gustarle a algn ▷ prep como ▷ adj parecido, semejante ▷ n: **and the ~** y otros por el estilo; **his ~s and dislikes** sus gustos y aversiones; **I would ~, I'd ~** me gustaría; (*for purchase*) quisiera; **would you ~ a coffee?** ¿te apetece un café?; **I ~ swimming** me gusta nadar; **she ~s apples** le gustan las manzanas; **to be** or **look ~ sb/sth** parecerse a algn/algo; **what does it look/taste/sound ~?** ¿cómo es/a qué sabe/cómo suena?; **that's just ~ him** es muy de él, es característico de él; **do it ~ this** hazlo así; **it is nothing ~ ...** no tiene parecido alguno con ...; **likeable** adj simpático, agradable

likelihood ['laɪklɪhud] n probabilidad f

likely ['laɪklɪ] adj probable; **he's ~ to leave** es probable que se vaya; **not ~!** ¡ni hablar!

likewise ['laɪkwaɪz] adv igualmente; **to do ~** hacer lo mismo

liking ['laɪkɪŋ] n: **~ (for)** (*person*) cariño (a); (*thing*) afición (a); **to be to sb's ~** ser del gusto de algn

lilac ['laɪlək] n (*tree*) lilo; (*flower*) lila

Lilo® ['laɪləu] n colchoneta inflable

lily ['lɪlɪ] n lirio, azucena; **~ of the**

valley lirio de los valles

limb [lɪm] n miembro

limbo ['lɪmbəu] n: **to be in ~** (fig) quedar a la expectativa

lime [laɪm] n (tree) limero; (fruit) lima; (Geo) cal f

limelight ['laɪmlaɪt] n: **to be in the ~** (fig) ser el centro de atención

limestone ['laɪmstəun] n piedra caliza

limit ['lɪmɪt] n límite m ▷ vt limitar; **limited** adj limitado; **to be limited to** limitarse a

limousine ['lɪməziːn] n limusina

limp [lɪmp] n: **to have a limp** tener cojera ▷ vi cojear ▷ adj flojo; (material) fláccido

line [laɪn] n línea; (rope) cuerda; (for fishing) sedal m; (wire) hilo; (row, series) fila, hilera; (of writing) renglón m, línea; (of song) verso; (on face) arruga; (Rail) vía m ▷ vt (road etc) llenar; (Sewing) forrar; **to ~ the streets** llenar las aceras; **in ~ with** alineado con; (according to) de acuerdo con; **line up** vi hacer cola ▷ vt alinear; (prepare) preparar; organizar

linear ['lɪnɪə*] adj lineal

linen ['lɪnɪn] n ropa blanca; (cloth) lino

liner ['laɪnə*] n vapor m de línea, transatlántico m; (for bin) bolsa de basura)

line-up ['laɪnʌp] n (us: queue) cola; (Sport) alineación f

linger ['lɪŋɡə*] vi retrasarse, tardar en marcharse; (smell, tradition) persistir

lingerie ['lænʒəriː] n lencería

linguist ['lɪŋɡwɪst] n lingüista mf; **linguistic** adj lingüístico

lining ['laɪnɪŋ] n forro; (Anat) (membrana) mucosa

link [lɪŋk] n (of a chain) eslabón m; (relationship) relación f, vínculo; (Internet) link m, enlace m ▷ vt vincular, unir; (associate): **to ~ with** o **to** relacionar con; **links** npl (Golf) campo de golf; **link up** vt acoplar ▷ vi unirse

lion ['laɪən] n león m; **lioness** n leona

lip [lɪp] n labio; **lipread** vi leer los labios; **lip salve** n crema protectora para labios; **lipstick** n lápiz m de labios, carmín m

liqueur [lɪ'kjuə*] n licor m

liquid ['lɪkwɪd] adj, n líquido; **liquidizer** [-aɪzə*] n licuadora

liquor ['lɪkə*] n licor m, bebidas fpl alcohólicas; **liquor store** (us) n bodega, tienda de vinos y bebidas alcohólicas

Lisbon ['lɪzbən] n Lisboa

lisp [lɪsp] n ceceo ▷ vi cecear

list [lɪst] n lista ▷ vt (mention) enumerar; (put on a list) poner en una lista

listen ['lɪsn] vi escuchar, oír; **to ~ to sb/sth** escuchar a algn/algo; **listener** n oyente mf; (Radio) radioyente mf

lit [lɪt] pt, pp of **light**

liter ['liːtə*] (us) n = **litre**

literacy ['lɪtərəsɪ] n capacidad f de leer y escribir

literal ['lɪtərl] adj literal; **literally** adv literalmente

literary ['lɪtərərɪ] adj literario

literate ['lɪtərət] adj que sabe leer y escribir; (educated) culto

literature ['lɪtərɪtʃə*] n literatura; (brochures etc) folletos mpl

litre ['liːtə*] (us **liter**) n litro

litter ['lɪtə*] n (rubbish) basura; (young animals) camada, cría; **litter bin** (BRIT) n papelera; **littered** adj: **littered with** (scattered) lleno de

little ['lɪtl] adj (small) pequeño; (not much) poco ▷ adv poco; **a ~** un poco (de); **~ house/bird** casita/pajarito; **a ~ bit** un poquito; **~ by ~** poco a poco; **little finger** n dedo meñique

live[1] [laɪv] adj (animal) vivo; (wire) conectado; (broadcast) en directo; (shell) cargado

live[2] [lɪv] vi vivir; **live together** vi vivir juntos; **live up to** vt fus (fulfil) cumplir con

livelihood ['laɪvlɪhud] n sustento

lively ['laɪvlɪ] adj vivo;

(interesting: place, book etc) animado

liven up ['laɪvn-] *vt* animar ▷ *vi* animarse

liver ['lɪvə*] *n* hígado

lives [laɪvz] *npl of* **life**

livestock ['laɪvstɔk] *n* ganado

living ['lɪvɪŋ] *adj (alive)* vivo ▷ *n*: **to earn** *or* **make a ~** ganarse la vida; **living room** *n* sala (de estar)

lizard ['lɪzəd] *n* lagarto; *(small)* lagartija

load [ləud] *n* carga; *(weight)* peso ▷ *vt (Comput)* cargar; *(also:* **~ up**): **to ~** cargar (con *or* de); **a ~ of rubbish** *(inf)* tonterías *fpl*; **a ~ of**, **~s of** *(fig)* (gran) cantidad *o*, montones de; **loaded** *adj (vehicle)*: **to be loaded with** estar cargado de

loaf [ləuf] *(pl* **loaves)** *n* (barra de) pan *m*

loan [ləun] *n* préstamo ▷ *vt* prestar; **on ~** prestado

loathe [ləuð] *vt* aborrecer; *(person)* odiar

loaves [ləuvz] *npl of* **loaf**

lobby ['lɔbɪ] *n* vestíbulo, sala de espera; *(Pol: pressure group)* grupo de presión ▷ *vt* presionar

lobster ['lɔbstə*] *n* langosta

local ['ləukl] *adj* local ▷ *n (pub)* bar *m*; **the locals** *npl* los vecinos, los del lugar; **local anaesthetic** *n (Med)* anestesia local; **local authority** *n* municipio, ayuntamiento *(sp)*; **local government** *n* gobierno municipal; **locally** [-kəlɪ] *adv* en la vecindad; por aquí

locate [ləu'keɪt] *vt (find)* localizar; *(situate)*: **to be ~d in** estar situado en

location [ləu'keɪʃən] *n* situación *f*; **on ~** *(Cinema)* en exteriores

loch [lɔx] *n* lago

lock [lɔk] *n (of door, box)* cerradura; *(of canal)* esclusa; *(of hair)* mechón *m* ▷ *vt (with key)* cerrar (con llave) ▷ *vi (door lock)* cerrarse (con llave); *(wheels)* trabarse; **lock in** *vt* encerrar; **lock out** *vt (person)* cerrar la puerta a; **lock up** *vt (criminal)* meter en la cárcel; *(mental*

patient) encerrar; *(house)* cerrar (con llave) ▷ *vi* echar la llave

locker ['lɔkə*] *n* casillero; **locker-room** *(us)* *n (Sport)* vestuario

locksmith ['lɔksmɪθ] *n* cerrajero *m*

locomotive [ləukə'məutɪv] *n* locomotora

lodge [lɔdʒ] *n* casita (del guarda) ▷ *vi (person)*: **to ~ (with)** alojarse (en casa de); *(bullet, bone)* incrustarse ▷ *vt* presentar; **lodger** *n* huésped *mf*

lodging ['lɔdʒɪŋ] *n* alojamiento, hospedaje *m*

loft [lɔft] *n* desván *m*

log [lɔg] *n (of wood)* leño, tronco; *(written account)* diario ▷ *vt* anotar; **log in**, **log on** *vi (Comput)* entrar en el sistema; **log off**, **log out** *vi (Comput)* salir del sistema

logic ['lɔdʒɪk] *n* lógica; **logical** *adj* lógico

logo ['ləugəu] *n* logotipo

lollipop ['lɔlɪpɔp] *n* pirulí *m*; **lollipop man/lady** *(BRIT: irreg)* *n* persona encargada de ayudar a los niños a cruzar la calle

lolly ['lɔlɪ] *n (inf: ice cream)* polo; *(: lollipop)* piruleta; *(: money)* guita

London ['lʌndən] *n* Londres; **Londoner** *n* londinense *mf*

lone [ləun] *adj* solitario

loneliness ['ləunlɪnɪs] *n* soledad *f*; aislamiento

lonely ['ləunlɪ] *adj (situation)* solitario; *(person)* solo; *(place)* aislado

long [lɔŋ] *adj* largo ▷ *adv* mucho tiempo, largamente ▷ *vi*: **to ~ for sth** anhelar algo; **so** *or* **as ~ as** mientras, con tal que; **don't be ~!** ¡no tardes!, ¡vuelve pronto!; **how ~ is the street?** ¿cuánto tiene la calle de largo?; **how ~ is the lesson?** ¿cuánto dura la clase?; **6 metres ~** que mide 6 metros, de 6 metros de largo; **6 months ~** que dura 6 meses, de 6 meses de duración; **all night ~** toda la noche; **he no ~er comes** ya no viene; **I can't stand it any ~er** ya no lo aguanto más; **~ before**

mucho antes; **before ~** (+*future*) dentro de poco; (+*past*) poco tiempo después; **at ~ last** al fin, por fin; **long-distance** *adj* (*race*) de larga distancia; (*call*) interurbano; **long-haul** *adj* (*flight*) de larga distancia; **longing** *n* anhelo, ansia; (*nostalgia*) nostalgia ▷ *adj* anhelante

longitude ['lɒŋgɪtjuːd] *n* longitud *f*

long: long jump *n* salto de longitud; **long-life** *adj* (*batteries*) de larga duración; (*milk*) uperizado; **long-sighted** (BRIT) *adj* présbita; **long-standing** *adj* de mucho tiempo; **long-term** *adj* a largo plazo

loo [luː] (BRIT: *inf*) *n* wáter *m*

look [luk] *vi* mirar; (*seem*) parecer; (*building etc*): **to ~ south/on to the sea** dar al sur/al mar ▷ *n* (*gen*): **to have a ~** mirar; (*glance*) mirada; (*appearance*) aire *m*, aspecto; **looks** *npl* (*good looks*) belleza; **~ (here)!** (*expressing annoyance etc*) ¡oye!; **~!** (*expressing surprise*) ¡mira!; **look after** *vt fus* (*care for*) cuidar a; (*deal with*) encargarse de; **look around** *vi* echar una mirada alrededor; **look at** *vt fus* mirar; (*read quickly*) echar un vistazo a; **look back** *vi* mirar hacia atrás; **look down on** *vt fus* (*fig*) despreciar, mirar con desprecio; **look for** *vt fus* buscar; **look forward to** *vt fus* esperar con ilusión; (*in letters*): **we look forward to hearing from you** quedamos a la espera de sus gratas noticias; **look into** *vt* investigar; **look out** *vi* (*beware*): **to look out (for)** tener cuidado (de); **look out for** *vt fus* (*seek*) buscar; (*await*) esperar; **look round** *vi* volver la cabeza; **look through** *vt fus* (*examine*) examinar; **look up** *vi* mirar hacia arriba; (*improve*) mejorar ▷ *vt* (*word*) buscar; **look up to** *vt fus* admirar; **lookout** *n* (*tower etc*) puesto de observación; (*person*) vigía *m/f*; **to be on the lookout for sth** estar al acecho de algo

loom [luːm] *vi*: **~ (up)** (*threaten*) surgir, amenazar; (*event: approach*) aproximarse

loony ['luːnɪ] (*inf*) *n*, *adj* loco/a *m/f*

loop [luːp] *n* lazo ▷ *vt*: **to ~ sth round sth** pasar algo alrededor de algo; **loophole** *n* escapatoria

loose [luːs] *adj* suelto; (*clothes*) ancho; (*morals, discipline*) relajado; **to be on the ~** estar en libertad; **to be at a ~ end** *or* **at ~ ends** (*us*) no saber qué hacer; **loosely** *adv* libremente, aproximadamente; **loosen** *vt* aflojar

loot [luːt] *n* botín *m* ▷ *vt* saquear

lop-sided ['lɔp'saɪdɪd] *adj* torcido

lord [lɔːd] *n* señor *m*; **L~ Smith** Lord Smith; **the L~** el Señor; **my ~** (*to bishop*) Ilustrísima; (*to noble etc*) Señor; **good L~!** ¡Dios mío!; **Lords** *npl* (BRIT: *Pol*): **the (House of) Lords** la Cámara de los Lores

lorry ['lɒrɪ] (BRIT) *n* camión *m*; **lorry driver** (BRIT) *n* camionero/a

lose [luːz] (*pt, pp* **lost**) *vt* perder ▷ *vi* perder, ser vencido; **to ~ (time)** (*clock*) atrasarse; **lose out** *vi* salir perdiendo; **loser** *n* perdedor(a) *m/f*

loss [lɒs] *n* pérdida; **heavy ~es** (*Mil*) grandes pérdidas; **to be at a ~** no saber qué hacer; **to ~** a sufrir pérdidas

lost [lɒst] *pt, pp* de **lose** ▷ *adj* perdido; **lost property** (*us* **lost and found**) *n* objetos *mpl* perdidos

lot [lɒt] *n* (*group: of things*) grupo; (*at auctions*) lote *m*; **the ~** el todo, todos; **a ~** (*large number: of books etc*) muchos; (*a great deal*) mucho, bastante; **a ~ of, ~s of** mucho(s) (*pl*); **I read a ~** leo bastante; **to draw ~s (for sth)** echar suertes (para decidir algo)

lotion ['ləʊʃən] *n* loción *f*

lottery ['lɒtərɪ] *n* lotería

loud [laud] *adj* (*voice, sound*) fuerte; (*laugh, shout*) estrepitoso; (*condemnation etc*) enérgico; (*gaudy*) chillón *m/f* ▷ *adv* (*speak etc*) fuerte; **out ~** en voz alta; **loudly** *adv* (*noisily*) fuerte; (*aloud*) en voz alta; **loudspeaker** *n* altavoz *m*

lounge [laundʒ] *n* salón *m*, sala (de

estar); (*at airport etc*) sala; (BRIT: *also*:
~-bar) salón-bar m ▷ vi (*also: ~ **about** or **around**) reposar, holgazanear

louse [laus] (*pl* **lice**) n piojo

lousy ['lauzɪ] (*inf*) *adj* (*bad quality*) malísimo, asqueroso; (*ill*) fatal

love [lʌv] n (*romantic, sexual*) amor m; (*kind, caring*) cariño n ▷ amar, querer; (*thing, activity*) encantarle a algn; "~ **from Anne**" (*on letter*) "un abrazo de Anne"; **to ~ to do** encantarle a algn hacer; **to be/fall in ~ with** estar enamorado/enamorarse de; **to make ~** hacer el amor; **for the ~ of** por amor de; **"15 ~"** (*Tennis*) "15 a cero"; **I ~ you** te quiero; **I ~ paella** me encanta la paella; **love affair** n aventura sentimental; **love life** n vida sentimental

lovely ['lʌvlɪ] *adj* (*delightful*) encantador(a); (*beautiful*) precioso

lover ['lʌvə*] n amante mf; (*person in love*) enamorado; (*amateur*): **a ~ of** un(a) aficionado/a o un(a) amante de

loving ['lʌvɪŋ] *adj* amoroso, cariñoso; (*action*) tierno

low [ləu] *adj, adv* bajo ▷ n (*Meteorology*) área de baja presión; **to be ~ on** (*supplies etc*) andar mal de; **to feel ~** sentirse deprimido; **to turn (down) ~** bajar; **low-alcohol** *adj* de bajo contenido en alcohol; **low-calorie** *adj* bajo en calorías

lower ['ləuə*] *adj* más bajo; (*less important*) menos importante ▷ vt bajar; (*reduce*) reducir ▷ vr: **to o.s. to** (*fig*) rebajarse a

low-fat *adj* (*milk, yoghurt*) desnatado; (*diet*) bajo en calorías

loyal ['lɔɪəl] *adj* leal; **loyalty** n lealtad f; **loyalty card** n tarjeta cliente

L.P. n *abbr* (= *long-playing record*) elepé m

L-plates ['el-] (BRIT) *npl* placas fpl de aprendiz de conductor

- **L-PLATES**
- En el Reino Unido las personas
- que están aprendiendo a conducir

deben llevar en la parte delantera
y trasera de su vehículo unas
placas blancas con una L en rojo
conocidas como **L-Plates** (de
learner). No es necesario que
asistan a clases teóricas sino que,
desde el principio, se le entrega
un carnet de conducir provisional
("provisional driving licence")
para que realicen sus prácticas,
aunque no pueden circular por
las autopistas y deben ir siempre
acompañados por un conductor
con carnet definitivo ("full driving
licence").

Lt *abbr* (= *lieutenant*) Tte.

Ltd *abbr* (= *limited company*) S.A.

luck [lʌk] n suerte f; **bad ~** mala suerte; **good ~!** ¡que tengas suerte!, ¡suerte!; **bad** *or* **hard** *or* **tough ~!** ¡qué pena!; **luckily** *adv* afortunadamente; **lucky** *adj* afortunado; (*at cards etc*) con suerte; (*object*) que trae suerte

lucrative ['lu:krətɪv] *adj* lucrativo

ludicrous ['lu:dɪkrəs] *adj* absurdo

luggage ['lʌgɪdʒ] n equipaje m; **luggage rack** n (*on car*) baca, portaequipajes m inv

lukewarm ['lu:kwɔ:m] *adj* tibio

lull [lʌl] n tregua ▷ vt: **to ~ sb to sleep** arrullar a algn; **to ~ sb into a false sense of security** dar a algn una falsa sensación de seguridad

lullaby ['lʌləbaɪ] n nana

lumber ['lʌmbə*] n (*junk*) trastos mpl viejos; (*wood*) maderos mpl

luminous ['lu:mɪnəs] *adj* luminoso

lump [lʌmp] n terrón m; (*fragment*) trozo; (*swelling*) bulto n (*also: ~ together*) juntar; **lump sum** n suma global; **lumpy** *adj* (*sauce*) lleno de grumos; (*mattress*) lleno de bultos

lunatic ['lu:nətɪk] *adj* loco

lunch [lʌntʃ] n almuerzo, comida ▷ vi almorzar; **lunch break**, **lunch hour** n hora del almuerzo; **lunch time** n hora de comer

lung [lʌŋ] n pulmón m
lure [luə*] n (attraction) atracción f
▷ vt tentar
lurk [ləːk] vi (person, animal) estar al
acecho; (fig) acechar
lush [lʌʃ] adj exuberante
lust [lʌst] n lujuria; (greed) codicia
Luxembourg ['lʌksəmbəːg] n
Luxemburgo
luxurious [lʌg'zjuəriəs] adj lujoso
luxury ['lʌkʃərɪ] n lujo ▷ cpd de lujo
Lycra® ['laɪkrə] n licra®
lying ['laɪɪŋ] n mentiras fpl ▷ adj
mentiroso
lyrics ['lɪrɪks] npl (of song) letra

m. abbr = **metre; mile; million**
M.A. abbr = **Master of Arts**
ma (inf) [mɑː] n mamá
mac [mæk] (BRIT) n impermeable m
macaroni [mækə'rəʊnɪ] n
macarrones mpl
Macedonia [mæsɪ'dəʊnɪə] n
Macedonia; **Macedonian** [-'dəʊnɪən]
adj macedonio ▷ n macedonio/a;
(Ling) macedonio
machine [mə'ʃiːn] n máquina
▷ vt (dress etc) coser a máquina;
(Tech) hacer a máquina; **machine
gun** n ametralladora; **machinery**
n maquinaria; (fig) mecanismo;
machine washable adj lavable a
máquina
macho ['mætʃəʊ] adj machista
mackerel ['mækrl] n inv caballa
mackintosh ['mækɪntɔʃ] (BRIT) n
impermeable m
mad [mæd] adj loco; (idea)
disparatado; (angry) furioso; (keen): **to
be ~ about sth** volverle loco a algn algo
Madagascar [mædə'gæskə*] n

Madagascar m

madam ['mædəm] n señora

mad cow disease n encefalopatía espongiforme bovina

made [meɪd] pt, pp of **make**;
made-to-measure (BRIT) adj hecho a la medida; **made-up** ['meɪdʌp] adj (story) ficticio

madly ['mædlɪ] adv locamente

madman ['mædmən] (irreg) n loco

madness ['mædnɪs] n locura

Madrid [mə'drɪd] n Madrid

Mafia ['mæfɪə] n Mafia

mag [mæg] n abbr (BRIT inf) = **magazine**

magazine [mægə'ziːn] n revista; (Radio, TV) programa m magazina

maggot ['mægət] n gusano

magic ['mædʒɪk] n magia ▷ adj mágico; **magical** adj mágico; **magician** [mə'dʒɪʃən] n mago/a; (conjurer) prestidigitador(a) m/f

magistrate ['mædʒɪstreɪt] n juez mf (municipal)

magnet ['mægnɪt] n imán m; **magnetic** [-'nɛtɪk] adj magnético; (personality) atrayente

magnificent [mæg'nɪfɪsənt] adj magnífico

magnify ['mægnɪfaɪ] vt (object) ampliar; (sound) aumentar; **magnifying glass** n lupa

magpie ['mægpaɪ] n urraca

mahogany [mə'hɔgənɪ] n caoba

maid [meɪd] n criada; **old ~** (pej) solterona

maiden name n nombre m de soltera

mail [meɪl] n correo; (letters) cartas fpl ▷ vt echar al correo; **mailbox** (US) n buzón m; **mailing list** n lista de direcciones; **mailman** (US: irreg) n cartero; **mail-order** n pedido postal

main [meɪn] adj principal; **main** ▷ n (pipe) cañería maestra; (US) red f eléctrica ▷ the **~s** npl (Elec) la red eléctrica; **in the ~** en general; **main course** n (Culin) plato principal; **mainland** n tierra firme; **mainly**

adv principalmente; **main road** n carretera; **mainstream** n corriente f principal; **main street** n calle f mayor

maintain [meɪn'teɪn] vt mantener; **maintenance** ['meɪntənəns] n mantenimiento; (Law) manutención f

maisonette [meɪzə'nɛt] n dúplex m

maize [meɪz] (BRIT) n maíz m, choclo (SC)

majesty ['mædʒɪstɪ] n majestad f; (title): **Your M~** Su Majestad

major ['meɪdʒə*] n (Mil) comandante mf ▷ adj (principal) (Mus) mayor

Majorca [mə'jɔːkə] n Mallorca

majority [mə'dʒɒrɪtɪ] n mayoría

make [meɪk] (pt, pp **made**) vt hacer; (manufacture) fabricar; (mistake) cometer; (speech) pronunciar; (cause to be): **to ~ sb sad** poner triste a algn; (force): **to ~ sb do sth** obligar a a hacer algo; (earn) ganar; (equal): **2 and 2 ~ 4** 2 y 2 son 4 ▷ n marca; **to ~ the bed** hacer la cama; **to ~ a fool of sb** poner a algn en ridículo; **to ~ a profit/loss** obtener ganancias/sufrir pérdidas; **to ~ it** (arrive) llegar; (achieve sth) tener éxito; **what time do you ~ it?** ¿qué hora tienes?; **to ~ do with** contentarse con; **make off** vi largarse; **make out** vt (decipher) descifrar; (understand) entender; (see) distinguir; (cheque) extender; **make up** vt (invent) inventar; (prepare) hacer; (constitute) constituir ▷ vi reconciliarse; (with cosmetics) maquillarse; **make up for** vt fus compensar; **makeover** ['meɪkəʊvə*] n (by beautician) sesión f de maquillaje y peluquería; (change of image) lavado de cara; **maker** n fabricante mf; (of film, programme) autor(a) m/f; **makeshift** adj improvisado; **make-up** n maquillaje m

making ['meɪkɪŋ] n (fig): **in the ~** en vías de formación; **to have the ~s of** (person) tener madera de

malaria [mə'lɛərɪə] n malaria

Malaysia [mə'leɪzɪə] n Malasia,

Malaysia

male [meɪl] n (Biol) macho ▷ adj (sex, attitude) masculino; (child etc) varón

malicious [mə'lɪʃəs] adj malicioso; rencoroso

malignant [mə'lɪgnənt] adj (Med) maligno

mall [mɔːl] (us) n (also: **shopping ~**) centro comercial

mallet ['mælɪt] n mazo

malnutrition [mælnju:'trɪʃən] n desnutrición f

malpractice [mæl'præktɪs] n negligencia profesional

malt [mɔːlt] n malta; (whisky) whisky m de malta

Malta ['mɔːltə] n Malta; **Maltese** [-'tiːz] adj, n inv maltés/esa m/f

mammal ['mæml] n mamífero

mammoth ['mæməθ] n mamut m ▷ adj gigantesco

man [mæn] (pl **men**) n hombre m; (mankind) el hombre m ▷ vt (Naut) tripular; (Mil) guarnecer; (operate: machine) manejar; **an old ~** un viejo; **~ and wife** marido y mujer

manage ['mænɪdʒ] vi arreglárselas, ir tirando ▷ vt (be in charge of) dirigir; (control: person) manejar; (: ship) gobernar; **manageable** adj manejable; **management** n dirección f; **manager** n director(a) m/f; (of pop star) mánager mf; (Sport) entrenador(a) m/f; **manageress** n directora, entrenadora; **managerial** [-ə'dʒɪərɪəl] adj directivo; **managing director** n director(a) m/f general

mandarin ['mændərɪn] n (also: **~ orange**) mandarina; (person) mandarín m

mandate ['mændeɪt] n mandato

mandatory ['mændətərɪ] adj obligatorio

mane [meɪn] n (of horse) crin f; (of lion) melena

maneuver [mə'nuːvə*] (us) = **manoeuvre**

mangetout [mɔnʒ'tuː] n tirabeque

mango ['mæŋgəu] (pl **-es**) n mango

man: manhole n agujero de acceso; **manhood** n edad f viril; (state) virilidad f

mania ['meɪnɪə] n manía; **maniac** ['meɪnɪæk] n maníaco/a; (fig) maníatico

manic ['mænɪk] adj frenético

manicure ['mænɪkjuə*] n manicura

manifest ['mænɪfest] vt manifestar, mostrar ▷ adj manifiesto

manifesto [mænɪ'festəu] n manifiesto

manipulate [mə'nɪpjuleɪt] vt manipular

man: mankind [mæn'kaɪnd] n humanidad f, género humano; **manly** adj varonil; **man-made** adj artificial

manner ['mænə*] n manera, modo; (behaviour) conducta, manera de ser; (type): **all ~ of things** toda clase de cosas; **manners** npl (behaviour) modales mpl; **bad ~s** mala educación

manoeuvre [mə'nuːvə*] vt, vi maniobrar ▷ n maniobra

manpower ['mænpauə*] n mano f de obra

mansion ['mænʃən] n palacio, casa grande

manslaughter ['mænslɔːtə*] n homicidio no premeditado

mantelpiece ['mæntlpiːs] n repisa, chimenea

manual ['mænjuəl] adj manual ▷ n manual m

manufacture [mænju'fæktʃə*] vt fabricar ▷ n fabricación f; **manufacturer** n fabricante mf

manure [mə'njuə*] n estiércol m

manuscript ['mænjuskrɪpt] n manuscrito

many ['menɪ] adj, pron muchos/as; **a great ~** muchísimos, un buen número de; **~ a time** muchas veces

map [mæp] n mapa m ▷ **to ~ out** vt proyectar

maple ['meɪpl] n arce m, maple m (LAM)

Mar abbr (= March) mar

mar [maː*] vt estropear

marathon ['mærəθən] n maratón m

marble ['maːbl] n mármol m; (toy) canica

March [maːtʃ] n marzo

march [maːtʃ] vi (Mil) marchar; (demonstrators) manifestarse ▷ n (Mil) marcha; (demonstration) manifestación f

mare [mɛə*] n yegua

margarine [maːdʒəˈriːn] n margarina

margin ['maːdʒɪn] n margen m; (Comm: profit margin) margen m de beneficios; **marginal** adj marginal; **marginally** adv ligeramente

marigold ['mærɪɡəʊld] n caléndula

marijuana [mærɪˈwaːnə] n marijuana

marina [məˈriːnə] n puerto deportivo

marinade [mærɪˈneɪd] n adobo

marinate ['mærɪneɪt] vt marinar

marine [məˈriːn] adj marino m; soldado de marina

marital ['mærɪtl] adj matrimonial; **marital status** n estado m civil

maritime ['mærɪtaɪm] adj marítimo

marjoram ['maːdʒərəm] n mejorana

mark [maːk] n marca, señal f; (in snow, mud etc) huella; (stain) mancha; (BRIT Scol) nota ▷ vt marcar; manchar; (damage: furniture) rayar; (indicate: place etc) señalar; (BRIT Scol) calificar, corregir; **to ~ time** marcar el paso; (fig) marcar(se) un ritmo; **marked** adj (obvious) marcado, acusado; **marker** n (sign) marcador m; (bookmark) señal f (de libro)

market ['maːkɪt] n mercado ▷ vt (Comm) comercializar; **marketing** n márketing m; **marketplace** n mercado; **market research** n análisis m inv de mercados

marmalade ['maːməleɪd] n mermelada de naranja

maroon [məˈruːn] vt: **to be ~ed** quedar aislado; (fig) quedar abandonado ▷ n (colour) granate m

marquee [maːˈkiː] n entoldado

marriage ['mærɪdʒ] n (relationship, institution) matrimonio; (wedding) boda; (act) casamiento; **marriage certificate** n partida de casamiento

married ['mærɪd] adj casado; (life, love) conyugal

marrow ['mærəʊ] n médula; (vegetable) calabacín m

marry ['mærɪ] vt casarse con; (father, priest etc) casar ▷ vi (also: **get married**) casarse

Mars [maːz] n Marte m

marsh [maːʃ] n pantano; (salt marsh) marisma

marshal ['maːʃl] n (Mil) mariscal m; (at sports meeting etc) oficial m; (us: of police, fire department) jefe/a m/f ▷ vt (thoughts etc) ordenar; (soldiers) formar

martyr ['maːtə*] n mártir mf

marvel ['maːvl] n maravilla, prodigio ▷ vi: **to ~ (at)** maravillarse (de); **marvellous** (us **marvelous**) adj maravilloso

Marxism ['maːksɪzəm] n marxismo

Marxist ['maːksɪst] adj, n marxista mf

marzipan ['maːzɪpæn] n mazapán m

mascara [mæsˈkaːrə] n rímel m

mascot ['mæskət] n mascota

masculine ['mæskjulɪn] adj masculino

mash [mæʃ] vt machacar; **mashed potato(es)** n(pl) puré m de patatas (SP) or papas (LAM)

mask [maːsk] n máscara ▷ vt (cover) enmascarar; (hide: feelings) esconder; **to ~ one's face** ocultarse la cara; (hide: feelings) esconder

mason ['meɪsn] n (also: **stone~**) albañil m; (also: **free~**) masón m; **masonry** n (in building) mampostería

mass [mæs] n (people) muchedumbre f; (of air, liquid etc) masa; (of detail, hair etc) gran cantidad f; (Rel) misa ▷ cpd

masivo ▷ vi reunirse; concentrarse;
the masses npl las masas; **~es of** (inf)
montones de

massacre ['mæsəkə*] n masacre f

massage ['mæsɑːʒ] n masaje m ▷ vt
dar masaje en

massive ['mæsɪv] adj enorme;
(support, changes) masivo

mass media npl medios mpl de
comunicación

mass-produce ['mæsprə'djuːs] vt
fabricar en serie

mast [mɑːst] n (Naut) mástil m; (Radio
etc) torre f

master ['mɑːstə*] n (of servant)
amo; (of situation) dueño, maestro;
(in primary school) maestro; (in
secondary school) profesor m; (title for
boys): **M~ X** Señorito X ▷ vt dominar;
mastermind n inteligencia superior
▷ vt dirigir, planear; **Master of
Arts/Science** n licenciado superior
en Letras/Ciencias; **masterpiece** n
obra maestra

masturbate ['mæstəbeɪt] vi
masturbarse

mat [mæt] n estera; (also: **door~**)
felpudo; (also: **table~**) salvamanteles m
inv, posavasos m inv ▷ adj = **matt**

match [mætʃ] n cerilla, fósforo;
(game) partido; (equal) igual m/f ▷ vt
(go well with) hacer juego con; (equal)
igualar; (correspond to) corresponderse
con; (pair: also: **~ up**) casar con ▷ vi
hacer juego; **to be a good ~** hacer
juego; **matchbox** n caja de cerillas;
matching adj que hace juego

mate [meɪt] n (workmate) colega mf;
(inf: friend) amigo/a; (animal) macho/
hembra; (in merchant navy) segundo
de a bordo ▷ vi acoplarse, aparearse
▷ vt aparear

material [mə'tɪərɪəl] n (substance)
materia; (information) material m;
(cloth) tejido, tela ▷ adj material;
(important) esencial; **materials** npl
materiales mpl

materialize [mə'tɪərɪəlaɪz] vi

materializarse

maternal [mə'təːnl] adj maternal

maternity [mə'təːnɪtɪ] n
maternidad f; **maternity hospital** n
hospital m de maternidad; **maternity
leave** n baja por maternidad

math [mæθ] (US) n = **mathematics**

mathematical [mæθə'mætɪkl] adj
matemático

mathematician [mæθəmə'tɪʃən] n
matemático/a

mathematics [mæθə'mætɪks] n
matemáticas fpl

maths [mæθs] (BRIT) n =
mathematics

matinée ['mætɪneɪ] n sesión f de
tarde

matron ['meɪtrən] n enfermera f jefe;
(in school) ama de llaves

matt [mæt] adj mate

matter ['mætə*] n cuestión f, asunto;
(Physics) sustancia, materia; (reading
matter) material m; (Med: pus) pus m
▷ vi importar; **what's the ~?** ¿qué pasa?;
no ~ what pase lo que pase; **as a ~
of course** por rutina; **as a ~ of fact**
de hecho

mattress ['mætrɪs] n colchón m

mature [mə'tjuə*] adj maduro
▷ vi madurar; **mature student** n
estudiante de más de 21 años; **maturity**
n madurez f

maul [mɔːl] vt magullar

mauve [məuv] adj de color malva (SP)
or guinda (LAM)

max abbr = **maximum**

maximize ['mæksɪmaɪz] vt (profits
etc) llevar al máximo; (chances)
maximizar

maximum ['mæksɪməm] (pl
maxima) adj máximo ▷ n máximo

May [meɪ] n mayo

may [meɪ] (conditional **might**) vi
(indicating possibility): **he ~ come** puede
que venga; (be allowed to): **~ I smoke?**
¿puedo fumar?; (wishes): **~ God bless**

you! ¡que Dios le bendiga!; **you ~ as
well go** bien puedes irte

maybe ['meɪbi] *adv* quizá(s)

May Day *n* el primero de Mayo

mayhem ['meɪhem] *n* caos *m* total

mayonnaise [meɪə'neɪz] *n*
mayonesa

mayor [meə*] *n* alcalde *m*; **mayoress**
n alcaldesa

maze [meɪz] *n* laberinto

MD *n abbr* = **managing director**

me [miː] *pron* (*direct*) me; (*stressed,
after pron*) mí; (*stressed,
after pron*) mí; ¿me
oyes?; **he heard ME** ¡me oyó a mí!; **it's
~ soy yo; **give them to ~** dámelos/las;
with/without ~ conmigo/sin mí

meadow ['medəʊ] *n* prado, pradera

meagre ['miːgə*] (*us* **meager**) *adj*
escaso, pobre

meal [miːl] *n* comida; (*flour*) harina;
mealtime *n* hora de comer

mean [miːn] (*pt, pp* ~**t**) *adj* (*with
money*) tacaño; (*unkind*) mezquino,
malo; (*shabby*) humilde; (*average*) medio
▷ *vt* (*signify*) querer decir, significar;
(*refer to*) referirse a; (*intend*): **to ~
do sth** pensar or pretender hacer algo
▷ *n* medio, término medio; **means**
npl (*way*) manera, modo; (*money*)
recursos *mpl*, medios *mpl*; **by ~s of**
mediante, por medio de; **by all ~s!**
¡naturalmente!, ¡claro que sí!; **do you ~
it?** ¿lo dices en serio?; **what do you ~?**
¿qué quiere decir?; **to be ~t for sb/sth**
ser para algn/algo

meaning ['miːnɪŋ] *n* significado,
sentido; (*purpose*) sentido, propósito;
meaningful *adj* significativo;
meaningless *adj* sin sentido

meant [ment] *pt, pp of* **mean**

meantime ['miːntaɪm] *adv* (*also:* **in
the ~**) mientras tanto

meanwhile ['miːnwaɪl] *adv* =
meantime

measles ['miːzlz] *n* sarampión *m*

measure ['meʒə*] *vt, vi* medir ▷ *n*
medida; (*ruler*) regla; **measurement**
['meʒəmənt] *n* (*measure*) medida;

(*act*) medición *f*; **to take sb's
measurements** tomar las medidas
a algn

meat [miːt] *n* carne *f*; **cold ~** fiambre
m; **meatball** *n* albóndiga

Mecca ['mekə] *n* La Meca

mechanic [mɪ'kænɪk] *n* mecánico/
a; **mechanical** *adj* mecánico

mechanism ['mekənɪzəm] *n*
mecanismo

medal ['medl] *n* medalla; **medallist**
(*us* **medalist**) *n* (*Sport*) medallista *mf*

meddle ['medl] *vi*: **to ~ in**
entrometerse en; **to ~ with sth**
manosear algo

media ['miːdɪə] *npl* medios *mpl* de
comunicación ▷ *npl of* **medium**

mediaeval [medɪ'iːvl] *adj* =
medieval

mediate ['miːdɪeɪt] *vi* mediar

medical ['medɪkl] *adj* médico ▷ *n*
reconocimiento médico; **medical
certificate** *n* certificado *m* médico

medicated ['medɪkeɪtɪd] *adj*
medicinal

medication [medɪ'keɪʃən] *n*
medicación *f*

medicine ['medsɪn] *n* medicina;
(*drug*) medicamento

medieval [medɪ'iːvl] *adj* medieval

mediocre [miːdɪ'əʊkə*] *adj*
mediocre

meditate ['medɪteɪt] *vi* meditar

meditation [medɪ'teɪʃən] *n*
meditación *f*

Mediterranean [medɪtə'reɪnɪən]
adj mediterráneo; **the ~ (Sea)** el (Mar)
Mediterráneo

medium ['miːdɪəm] (*pl* **media**)
adj mediano, regular ▷ *n* (*means*)
medio; (*pl* **mediums**: *person*) médium
mf; **medium-sized** *adj* de tamaño
mediano; (*clothes*) de (la) talla mediana;
medium wave *n* onda media

meek [miːk] *adj* manso, sumiso

meet [miːt] (*pt, pp* **met**) *vt* encontrar;
(*accidentally*) encontrarse con,
tropezar con; (*by arrangement*) reunirse

con; *(for the first time)* conocer; *(go and fetch)* ir a buscar; *(opponent)* enfrentarse con; *(obligations)* cumplir; *(encounter: problem)* hacer frente a; *(need)* satisfacer ▷ *vi* encontrarse; *(in session)* reunirse; *(join: objects)* unirse; *(for the first time)* conocerse; **meet up** *vi*: **to meet up with sb** reunirse con algn; **meet with** *vt fus (difficulty)* tropezar con; **to meet with success** tener éxito; **meeting** *n* encuentro; *(arranged)* cita, compromiso; *(business meeting)* reunión *f*; *(Pol)* mitin *m*; **meeting place** *n* lugar *m* de reunión or encuentro

megabyte ['mɛgəbait] *n* *(Comput)* megabyte *m*, megaocteto

megaphone ['mɛgəfəun] *n* megáfono

megapixel ['mɛgəpɪksl] *n* megapíxel *m*

melancholy ['mɛlənkəlɪ] *n* melancolía *f* ▷ *adj* melancólico

melody ['mɛlədɪ] *n* melodía *f*

melon ['mɛlən] *n* melón *m*

melt [mɛlt] *vi* *(metal)* fundirse; *(snow)* derretirse ▷ *vt* fundir

member ['mɛmbə*] *n* *(gen, Anat)* miembro *m*; *(of club)* socio/a; **Member of Congress** *(us)* *n* miembro *mf* del Congreso; **Member of Parliament** *n* *(BRIT)* diputado/a *m/f*, parlamentario/a *m/f*; **Member of the European Parliament** *n* diputado/a *m/f* del Parlamento Europeo, eurodiputado/a *m/f*; **Member of the Scottish Parliament** *(BRIT)* diputado/a del Parlamento escocés; **membership** *n* *(members)* número de miembros; *(state)* filiación *f*; **membership card** *n* carnet *m* de socio

memento [mə'mɛntəu] *n* recuerdo

memo ['mɛməu] *n* apunte *m*, nota

memorable ['mɛmərəbl] *adj* memorable

memorandum [mɛmə'rændəm] *(pl* **memoranda***)* *n* apunte *m*, nota; *(official note)* acta

memorial [mɪ'mɔːrɪəl] *n* monumento conmemorativo ▷ *adj* conmemorativo

memorize ['mɛməraɪz] *vt* aprender de memoria

memory ['mɛmərɪ] *n* *(also: Comput)* memoria; *(instance)* recuerdo; *(of dead person)*: **in ~ of** a la memoria de; **memory card** *n* *(for digital camera)* tarjeta de memoria

men [mɛn] *npl of* **man**

menace ['mɛnəs] *n* amenaza ▷ *vt* amenazar

mend [mɛnd] *vt* reparar, arreglar; *(darn)* zurcir ▷ *vi* reponerse ▷ *n*: **to be on the ~** ir mejorando; **to ~ one's ways** enmendarse

meningitis [mɛnɪn'dʒaɪtɪs] *n* meningitis *f*

menopause ['mɛnəupɔːz] *n* menopausia

men's room *(us)* *n*: **the ~** el servicio de caballeros

menstruation [mɛnstru'eɪʃən] *n* menstruación *f*

menswear ['mɛnzwɛə*] *n* confección *f* de caballero

mental ['mɛntl] *adj* mental; **mental hospital** *n* *(hospital m)* psiquiátrico; **mentality** [mɛn'tælɪtɪ] *n* mentalidad *f*; **mentally** *adv*: **to be mentally ill** tener una enfermedad mental

menthol ['mɛnθɒl] *n* mentol *m*

mention ['mɛnʃən] *n* mención *f* ▷ *vt* mencionar; *(speak)* hablar de; **don't ~ it!** ¡de nada!

menu ['mɛnjuː] *n* *(set menu)* menú *m*; *(printed)* carta; *(Comput)* menú *m*

MEP *n abbr* = **Member of the European Parliament**

mercenary ['məːsɪnərɪ] *adj, n* mercenario/a

merchandise ['məːtʃəndaɪz] *n* mercancías *fpl*

merchant ['məːtʃənt] *n* comerciante *mf*; **merchant navy** *(us)*, **merchant marine** *n* marina mercante

merciless ['mɜːsɪlɪs] *adj* despiadado
mercury ['mɜːkjʊrɪ] *n* mercurio
mercy ['mɜːsɪ] *n* compasión *f*; (*Rel*) misericordia; **at the ~ of** a la merced de
mere [mɪə*] *adj* simple, mero; **merely** *adv* simplemente, sólo
merge [mɜːdʒ] *vt* (*join*) unir ▷ *vi* unirse; (*Comm*) fusionarse; (*colours etc*) fundirse; **merger** *n* (*Comm*) fusión *f*
meringue [mə'ræŋ] *n* merengue *m*
merit ['merɪt] *n* mérito ▷ *vt* merecer
mermaid ['mɜːmeɪd] *n* sirena
merry ['merɪ] *adj* alegre; **M~ Christmas!** ¡Felices Pascuas!; **merry-go-round** *n* tiovivo
mesh [meʃ] *n* malla
mess [mes] *n* (*muddle: of situation*) confusión *f*; (*of room*) revoltijo *m*; (*dirt*) porquería; (*Mil*) comedor *m*; **mess about or around** (*inf*) *vi* perder el tiempo; (*pass the time*) entretenerse; **mess up** *vt* (*spoil*) estropear; (*dirty*) ensuciar; **mess with** (*inf*) *vt fus* (*challenge, confront*) meterse con (*inf*); (*interfere with*) interferir con
message ['mesɪdʒ] *n* recado, mensaje *m*
messenger ['mesɪndʒə*] *n* mensajero/a
Messrs *abbr* (*on letters*) (= *Messieurs*) Sres
messy ['mesɪ] *adj* (*dirty*) sucio; (*untidy*) desordenado
met [met] *pt, pp of* **meet**
metabolism [me'tæbəlɪzəm] *n* metabolismo
metal ['metl] *n* metal *m*; **metallic** [-'tælɪk] *adj* metálico
metaphor ['metəfə*] *n* metáfora
meteor ['miːtɪə*] *n* meteoro; **meteorite** [-aɪt] *n* meteorito
meteorology [miːtɪə'rɒlədʒɪ] *n* meteorología
meter ['miːtə*] *n* (*instrument*) contador *m*; (*US: unit*) = **metre** ▷ *vt* (*US Post*) franquear
method ['meθəd] *n* método; **methodical** [mɪ'θɒdɪkl] *adj* metódico

meths [meθs] *n* (*BRIT*) alcohol *m* metilado *or* desnaturalizado
meticulous [me'tɪkjʊləs] *adj* meticuloso
metre ['miːtə*] (*US* **meter**) *n* metro
metric ['metrɪk] *adj* métrico
metro ['metrəʊ] *n* metro
metropolitan [metrə'pɒlɪtən] *adj* metropolitano; **the M~ Police** (*BRIT*) la policía londinense
Mexican ['meksɪkən] *adj, n* mexicano/a, mejicano/a
Mexico ['meksɪkəʊ] *n* México, Méjico (*SP*)
mg *abbr* (= *milligram*) mg
mice [maɪs] *npl of* **mouse**
micro... [maɪkrəʊ] *prefix* micro...;
microchip *n* microplaqueta;
microphone *n* micrófono;
microscope *n* microscopio;
microwave *n* (*also:* **microwave oven**) horno microondas
mid [mɪd] *adj:* **in ~ May** a mediados de mayo; **in ~ afternoon** a media tarde; **in ~ air** en el aire; **midday** *n* mediodía *m*
middle ['mɪdl] *n* centro; (*half-way point*) medio; (*waist*) cintura ▷ *adj* de en medio; (*course, way*) intermedio;
in the ~ of the night en plena noche;
middle-aged *adj* de mediana edad;
Middle Ages *npl:* **the Middle Ages** la Edad Media; **middle-class** *adj* de clase media; **the middle class(es)** *npl* la clase media; **Middle East** *n* Oriente *m* Medio; **middle name** *n* segundo nombre; **middle school** *n* (*us*) colegio para niños de doce a catorce años; (*BRIT*) colegio para niños de ocho o nueve a doce o trece años
midge [mɪdʒ] *n* mosquito
midget ['mɪdʒɪt] *n* enano/a
midnight ['mɪdnaɪt] *n* medianoche *f*
midst [mɪdst] *n:* **in the ~ of** (*crowd*) en medio de; (*situation, action*) en mitad de
midsummer [mɪd'sʌmə*] *n:* **in ~** en pleno verano
midway [mɪd'weɪ] *adj, adv:* **~ (between)** a medio camino (entre); **~**

through a la mitad (de)
midweek [mɪd'wiːk] *adv* entre semana
midwife [mɪdwaɪf] (*irreg*) *n* comadrona, partera
midwinter [mɪd'wɪntə*] *n*: **in ~** en pleno invierno
might [maɪt] *vb see* **may** ▷ *n* fuerza, poder *m*; **mighty** *adj* fuerte, poderoso
migraine [miːgreɪn] *n* jaqueca
migrant [maɪgrənt] *n, adj* (*bird*) migratorio; (*worker*) emigrante
migrate [maɪ'greɪt] *vi* emigrar
migration [maɪ'greɪʃən] *n* emigración *f*
mike [maɪk] *n abbr* (= *microphone*) micro
mild [maɪld] *adj* (*person*) apacible; (*climate*) templado; (*slight*) ligero; (*taste*) suave; (*illness*) leve; **mildly** ['maɪldlɪ] *adv* ligeramente; suavemente; **to put it mildly** para no decir más
mile [maɪl] *n* milla; **mileage** *n* número de millas = kilometraje *m*; **mileometer** [maɪ'lɒmɪtə*] *n* = cuentakilómetros *m inv*; **milestone** *n* mojón *m*
military [mɪlɪtərɪ] *adj* militar
militia [mɪ'lɪʃə] *n* milicia
milk [mɪlk] *n* leche *f* ▷ *vt* (*cow*) ordeñar; (*fig*) chupar; **milk chocolate** *n* chocolate *m* con leche; **milkman** (*irreg*) *n* lechero; **milky** *adj* lechoso
mill [mɪl] *n* (*windmill etc*) molino; (*coffee mill*) molinillo; (*factory*) fábrica ▷ *vt* moler ▷ *vi* (*also*: **~ about**) arremolinarse
millennium [mɪ'lɛnɪəm] (*pl* **~s** or **millennia**) *n* milenio, milenario
milli... [mɪlɪ] *prefix*: **milligram(me)** *n* miligramo; **millilitre**(*us* **milliliter**) ['mɪlɪliːtə*] *n* mililitro; **millimetre**(*us* **millimeter**) *n* milímetro
million [mɪljən] *n* millón *m*; **a ~ times** un millón de veces; **millionaire** [-jə'nɛə*] *n* millonario/a; **millionth** [-θ] *adj* millonésimo
milometer [maɪ'lɒmɪtə*] (*BRIT*) *n* =

mileometer
mime [maɪm] *n* mímica; (*actor*) mimo/a ▷ *vt* remedar ▷ *vi* actuar de mimo
mimic [mɪmɪk] *n* imitador(a) *m/f* ▷ *adj* mímico ▷ *vt* remedar, imitar
min. *abbr* = **minimum; minute(s)**
mince [mɪns] *vt* picar ▷ *n* (*BRIT Culin*) carne *f* picada; **mincemeat** *n* conserva de fruta picada; (*us: meat*) carne *f* picada; **mince pie** *n* empanadilla rellena de fruta picada
mind [maɪnd] *n* mente *f*; (*intellect*) intelecto; (*contrasted with matter*) espíritu *m* ▷ *vt* (*attend to, look after*) ocuparse de, cuidar; (*be careful*) tener cuidado con; (*object to*): **I don't ~ the noise** no me molesta el ruido; **it is on my ~** me preocupa; **to bear sth in ~** tomar o tener algo en cuenta; **to make up one's ~** decidirse; **I don't ~** me es igual; **~ you ...** te advierto que ...; **never ~!** ¡es igual!, ¡no importal; (*don't worry*) ¡no te preocupes!; **"~ the step"** "cuidado con el escalón"; **mindless** *adj* (*crime*) sin motivo; (*work*) de autómata
mine¹ [maɪn] *pron* el mío/la mía etc; **a friend of ~** un(a) amigo/a mío/mía ▷ *adj*: **this book is ~** este libro es mío
mine² [maɪn] *n* mina ▷ *vt* (*coal*) extraer; (*bomb: beach etc*) minar; **minefield** *n* campo de minas; **miner** *n* minero/a
mineral [mɪnərəl] *adj* mineral ▷ *n* mineral *m*; **mineral water** *n* agua mineral
mingle [mɪŋgl] *vi*: **to ~ with** mezclarse con
miniature [mɪnətʃə*] *adj* (en) miniatura ▷ *n* miniatura
minibar [mɪnɪbɑː*] *n* minibar *m*
minibus [mɪnɪbʌs] *n* microbús *m*
minicab [mɪnɪkæb] *n* taxi *m* (*que sólo puede pedirse por teléfono*)
minimal [mɪnɪml] *adj* mínimo
minimize [mɪnɪmaɪz] *vt* minimizar; (*play down*) empequeñecer
minimum [mɪnɪməm] (*pl* **minima**

n, adj mínimo

mining ['maɪnɪŋ] n explotación f minera

miniskirt ['mɪnɪskə:t] n minifalda

minister ['mɪnɪstə*] n (BRIT Pol) ministro/a (SP), secretario/a (LAM); (Rel) pastor m ▷ vi: **to ~ to** atender a

ministry ['mɪnɪstrɪ] n (BRIT Pol) ministerio, secretaría (MEX); (Rel) sacerdocio

minor ['maɪnə*] adj (repairs, injuries) leve; (poet, planet) menor; (Mus) menor ▷ n (Law) menor m de edad

Minorca [mɪ'nɔ:kə] n Menorca

minority [maɪ'nɒrɪtɪ] n minoría

mint [mɪnt] n (plant) menta, hierbabuena; (sweet) caramelo de menta ▷ vt (coins) acuñar; **the (Royal) M~, the (US) M~** la Casa de la Moneda; **in ~ condition** en perfecto estado

minus ['maɪnəs] n (also: **~ sign**) signo de menos ▷ prep menos; **12 ~ 6 equals 6** 12 menos 6 son 6; **~ 24 °C** menos 24 grados

minute¹ ['mɪnɪt] n minuto; (fig) momento; **minutes** npl (of meeting) actas fpl; **at the last ~** a la última hora

minute² [maɪ'nju:t] adj diminuto; (search) minucioso

miracle ['mɪrəkl] n milagro

miraculous [mɪ'rækjuləs] adj milagroso

mirage ['mɪrɑ:ʒ] n espejismo

mirror ['mɪrə*] n espejo; (in car) retrovisor m

misbehave [mɪsbɪ'heɪv] vi portarse mal

misc. abbr = **miscellaneous**

miscarriage ['mɪskærɪdʒ] n (Med) aborto; **~ of justice** error m judicial

miscellaneous [mɪsɪ'leɪnɪəs] adj varios/as, diversos/as

mischief ['mɪstʃɪf] n travesuras fpl, diabluras fpl; (maliciousness) malicia; **mischievous** [-tʃɪvəs] adj travieso

misconception [mɪskən'sepʃən] n idea equivocada; equivocación f

---

451 | mission

misconduct [mɪs'kɒndʌkt] n mala conducta; **professional ~** falta profesional

miser ['maɪzə*] n avaro/a

miserable ['mɪzərəbl] adj (unhappy) triste, desgraciado; (unpleasant, contemptible) miserable

misery ['mɪzərɪ] n tristeza; (wretchedness) miseria, desdicha

misfortune [mɪs'fɔ:tʃən] n desgracia

misgiving [mɪs'gɪvɪŋ] n (apprehension) presentimiento; **to have ~s about sth** tener dudas acerca de algo

misguided [mɪs'gaɪdɪd] adj equivocado

mishap ['mɪshæp] n desgracia, contratiempo

misinterpret [mɪsɪn'tə:prɪt] vt interpretar mal

misjudge [mɪs'dʒʌdʒ] vt juzgar mal

mislay [mɪs'leɪ] vt extraviar, perder

mislead [mɪs'li:d] vt llevar a conclusiones erróneas; **misleading** adj engañoso

misplace [mɪs'pleɪs] vt extraviar

misprint ['mɪsprɪnt] n errata, error m de imprenta

misrepresent [mɪsreprɪ'zɛnt] vt falsificar

Miss [mɪs] n Señorita

miss [mɪs] vt (train etc) perder; (fail to hit: target) errar; (regret the absence of): **I ~ him** (yo) le echo de menos or a faltar; (fail to see): **you can't ~ it** no tiene pérdida ▷ vi fallar ▷ n (shot) tiro fallido or perdido; **miss out** (BRIT) vt omitir; **miss out on** vt fus (fun, party, opportunity) perderse

missile ['mɪsaɪl] n (Aviat) mísil m; (object thrown) proyectil m

missing ['mɪsɪŋ] adj (amy) ausente; (thing) perdido; (Mil): **~ in action** desaparecido en combate

mission ['mɪʃən] n misión f; (official representation) delegación f; **missionary** n misionero/a

misspell [mɪsˈspɛl] (pt, pp **misspelt** (BRIT) or **~ed**) vt escribir mal

mist [mɪst] n (light) neblina; (heavy) niebla; (at sea) bruma ▷ vi (eyes: also: **~ over, ~ up**) llenarse de lágrimas; (BRIT: windows: also: **~ over, ~ up**) empañarse

mistake [mɪsˈteɪk] (vt: irreg) n error m ▷ vt entender mal; **by ~** por equivocación; **to make a ~** equivocarse; **to ~ A for B** confundir A con B; **mistaken** pp of **mistake** ▷ adj equivocado; **to be mistaken** equivocarse, engañarse

mister [ˈmɪstə*] (inf) n señor m; see **Mr**

mistletoe [ˈmɪsltəʊ] n muérdago

mistook [mɪsˈtʊk] pt of **mistake**

mistress [ˈmɪstrɪs] n (lover) amante f; (of house) señora (de la casa); (BRIT: in primary school) maestra; (in secondary school) profesora; (of situation) dueña

mistrust [mɪsˈtrʌst] vt desconfiar de

misty [ˈmɪstɪ] adj (day) de niebla; (glasses etc) empañado

misunderstand [mɪsʌndəˈstænd] (irreg) vt, vi entender mal; **misunderstanding** n malentendido

misunderstood [mɪsʌndəˈstʊd] pt, pp of **misunderstand** ▷ adj (person) incomprendido

misuse [n mɪsˈjuːs, vb mɪsˈjuːz] n mal uso; (of power) abuso; (of funds) malversación f ▷ vt abusar de; malversar

mitt(en) [ˈmɪt(n)] n manopla

mix [mɪks] vt mezclar; (combine) unir ▷ vi mezclarse; (people) llevarse bien ▷ n mezcla; **mix up** vt mezclar; (confuse) confundir; **mixed** adj mixto; (feelings etc) encontrado; **mixed grill** n (BRIT) parrillada mixta; **mixed salad** n ensalada mixta; **mixed-up** adj (confused) confuso, revuelto; **mixer** n (for food) licuadora; (for drinks) coctelera; (person): **he's a good mixer** tiene don de gentes; **mixture** n mezcla; (also: **cough mixture**) jarabe

m; **mix-up** n confusión f

ml abbr (= millilitre(s)) ml

mm abbr (= millimetre) mm

moan [məʊn] n gemido ▷ vi gemir; (inf: complain): **to ~ (about)** quejarse (de)

moat [məʊt] n foso

mob [mɔb] n multitud f ▷ vt acosar

mobile [ˈməʊbaɪl] adj móvil ▷ n móvil m; **mobile home** n caravana; **mobile phone** n teléfono móvil

mobility [məʊˈbɪlɪtɪ] n movilidad f

mobilize [ˈməʊbɪlaɪz] vt movilizar

mock [mɔk] vt (ridicule) ridiculizar; (laugh at) burlarse de ▷ adj fingido; **~ exam** examen preparatorio antes de los exámenes oficiales" (BRIT: Scol: inf) exámenes mpl de prueba; **mockery** n burla

mod cons [ˈmɔdˈkɔnz] npl abbr (= modern conveniences) see **convenience**

mode [məʊd] n modo

model [ˈmɔdl] n modelo; (fashion model, artist's model) modelo mf ▷ adj modelo ▷ vt (clothes) modelar; (copy): **to ~ o.s. on** tomar como modelo a ▷ vi ser modelo; **to ~ clothes** pasar modelos, ser modelo

modem [ˈməʊdəm] n módem m

moderate [adj ˈmɔdərət, vb ˈmɔdəreɪt] adj moderado/a ▷ vi moderarse, calmarse ▷ vt moderar

moderation [mɔdəˈreɪʃən] n moderación f; **in ~** con moderación

modern [ˈmɔdən] adj moderno; **modernize** vt modernizar; **modern languages** npl lenguas fpl modernas

modest [ˈmɔdɪst] adj modesto; (small) módico; **modesty** n modestia

modification [mɔdɪfɪˈkeɪʃən] n modificación f

modify [ˈmɔdɪfaɪ] vt modificar

module [ˈmɔdjuːl] n (unit, component, Space) módulo

mohair [ˈməʊheə*] n mohair m

Mohammed [məˈhæmɛd] n Mahoma m

moist [mɔɪst] adj húmedo; **moisture** ['mɔɪstʃə*] n humedad f; **moisturizer** ['mɔɪstʃəraɪzə*] n crema hidratante

mold etc [məuld] (US) = **mould** etc

mole [məul] n (animal, spy) topo; (spot) lunar m

molecule ['mɒlɪkjuːl] n molécula

molest [məu'lest] vt importunar; (assault sexually) abusar sexualmente de

> Be careful not to translate **molest** by the Spanish word molestar.

molten ['məultən] adj fundido; (lava) líquido

mom [mɒm] (US) = **mum**

moment ['məumənt] n momento; **at the ~** de momento, por ahora; **momentarily** ['məuməntrɪlɪ] adv momentáneamente; (US: very soon) de un momento a otro; **momentary** adj momentáneo; **momentous** [-'mentəs] adj trascendental, importante

momentum [məu'mentəm] n momento; (fig) ímpetu m; **to gather ~** cobrar velocidad; (fig) ganar fuerza

mommy ['mɒmɪ] (US) = **mummy**

Mon abbr (= Monday) lun

Monaco ['mɒnəkəu] n Mónaco

monarch ['mɒnək] n monarca mf; **monarchy** n monarquía

monastery ['mɒnəstərɪ] n monasterio

Monday ['mʌndɪ] n lunes m inv

monetary ['mʌnɪtərɪ] adj monetario

money ['mʌnɪ] n dinero; (currency) moneda; **to make ~** ganar dinero; **money belt** n riñonera; **money order** n giro

mongrel ['mʌŋgrəl] n (dog) perro mestizo

monitor ['mɒnɪtə*] n (Scol) monitor m; (also: **television ~**) receptor m de control; (of computer) monitor m ▷ vt controlar

monk [mʌŋk] n monje m

monkey ['mʌŋkɪ] n mono

monologue ['mɒnəlɒg] n monólogo

monopoly [mə'nɒpəlɪ] n monopolio

monosodium glutamate [mɒnə'səudɪəm'gluː təmeɪt] n glutamato monosódico

monotonous [mə'nɒtənəs] adj monótono

monsoon [mɒn'suːn] n monzón m

monster ['mɒnstə*] n monstruo

month [mʌnθ] n mes m; **monthly** adj mensual ▷ adv mensualmente

monument ['mɒnjumənt] n monumento

mood [muːd] n humor m; (of crowd, group) clima m; **to be in a good/bad ~** estar de buen/mal humor; **moody** adj (changeable) de humor variable; (sullen) malhumorado

moon [muːn] n luna; **moonlight** n luz f de la luna

moor [muə*] n páramo ▷ vt (ship) amarrar ▷ vi echar las amarras

moose [muːs] n inv alce m

mop [mɒp] n fregona; (of hair) greña, melena ▷ vt fregar; **mop up** vt limpiar

mope [məup] vi estar or andar deprimido

moped ['məuped] n ciclomotor m

moral ['mɒrl] adj moral ▷ n moraleja; **morals** npl moralidad f, moral f

morale [mɔ'rɑːl] n moral f

morality [mə'rælɪtɪ] n moralidad f

morbid ['mɔːbɪd] adj (interest) morboso; (Med) mórbido

○ **KEYWORD**

more [mɔː*] adj 1 (greater in number etc) más; **more people/work than before** más gente/trabajo que antes

2 (additional) más; **do you want (some) more tea?** ¿quieres más té?; **is there any more wine?** ¿queda vino?; **it'll take a few more weeks** tardará unas semanas más; **it's 2 kms more to the house** faltan 2 kms para la casa; **more time/letters than we expected**

más tiempo del que/más cartas de las que esperábamos
▷ *pron* (*greater amount, additional amount*) más; **more than 10** más de 10; **it cost more than the other one/than we expected** costó más que el otro/de lo que esperábamos; **is there any more?** ¿hay más?; **many/much more** muchos(as)/mucho(a) más
▷ *adv* más; **more dangerous/easily (than)** más peligroso/fácilmente (que); **more and more expensive** cada vez más caro; **more or less** más o menos; **more than ever** más que nunca

moreover [mɔːˈrəʊvə*] *adv* además, por otra parte
morgue [mɔːg] *n* depósito de cadáveres
morning [ˈmɔːnɪŋ] *n* mañana; (*early morning*) madrugada ▷ *cpd* matutino, de la mañana; **in the ~** por la mañana; **7 o'clock in the ~** las 7 de la mañana; **morning sickness** *n* náuseas *fpl* matutinas
Moroccan [məˈrɒkən] *adj, n* marroquí *m/f*
Morocco [məˈrɒkəʊ] *n* Marruecos *m*
moron [ˈmɔːrɒn] (*inf*) *n* imbécil *mf*
morphine [ˈmɔːfiːn] *n* morfina
Morse [mɔːs] *n* (*also: ~ code*) (código) Morse
mortal [ˈmɔːtl] *adj, n* mortal *m*
mortar [ˈmɔːtə*] *n* argamasa
mortgage [ˈmɔːgɪdʒ] *n* hipoteca
▷ *vt* hipotecar
mortician [mɔːˈtɪʃən] (*us*) *n* director/a *m/f* de pompas fúnebres
mortified [ˈmɔːtɪfaɪd] *adj*: **I was ~ me** dio muchísima vergüenza
mortuary [ˈmɔːtjuərɪ] *n* depósito de cadáveres
mosaic [məʊˈzeɪɪk] *n* mosaico
Moslem [ˈmɒzləm] *adj, n* = **Muslim**
mosque [mɒsk] *n* mezquita
mosquito [mɒsˈkiːtəʊ] (*pl* **~es**) *n*

mosquito (*sp*), zancudo (*LAM*)
moss [mɒs] *n* musgo
most [məʊst] *adj* la mayor parte de, la mayoría de ▷ *pron* la mayor parte de, la mayoría ▷ *adv* el más; (*very*) muy; **the ~ (also: + adj)** el más; **~ of them** la mayor parte de ellos; **I saw the ~** yo vi el que más; **at the (very) ~** a lo sumo, todo lo más; **to make the ~ of** aprovechar (al máximo); **a ~ interesting book** un libro interesantísimo; **mostly** *adv* en su mayor parte, principalmente
MOT (*BRIT*) *n abbr* = **Ministry of Transport**; **the ~ (test)** inspección (*anual*) obligatoria de coches y camiones
motel [məʊˈtɛl] *n* motel *m*
moth [mɒθ] *n* mariposa nocturna; (*clothes moth*) polilla
mother [ˈmʌðə*] *n* madre *f* ▷ *adj* materno ▷ *vt* (*care for*) cuidar (como una madre); **motherhood** *n* maternidad *f*; **mother-in-law** *n* suegra; **mother-of-pearl** *n* nácar *m*; **Mother's Day** *n* Día *m* de la Madre; **mother-to-be** *n* futura madre *f*; **mother tongue** *n* lengua materna
motif [məʊˈtiːf] *n* motivo
motion [ˈməʊʃən] *n* movimiento; (*gesture*) ademán *m*, señal *f*; (*at meeting*) moción *f* ▷ *vt, vi*: **to ~ (to) sb to do sth** hacer señas a algn para que haga algo; **motionless** *adj* inmóvil; **motion picture** *n* película
motivate [ˈməʊtɪveɪt] *vt* motivar
motivation [məʊtɪˈveɪʃən] *n* motivación *f*
motive [ˈməʊtɪv] *n* motivo
motor [ˈməʊtə*] *n* motor *m*; (*BRIT: inf: vehicle*) coche *m* (*sp*), carro (*LAM*), automóvil *m* ▷ *adj* motor (*f: motora or motriz*); **motorbike** *n* moto *f*; **motorboat** *n* lancha motora; **motorcar** (*BRIT*) *n* coche *m*, carro, automóvil *m*; **motorcycle** *n* motocicleta; **motorcyclist** *n* motociclista *mf*; **motoring** (*BRIT*) *n* automovilismo; **motorist** *n* conductor(a) *m/f*, automovilista *mf*;

motor racing(BRIT) n carreras fpl de coches, automovilismo; **motorway** (BRIT) n autopista

motto ['mɔtəu] (pl **-es**) n lema m; (watchword) consigna

mould [məuld] (us **mold**) n molde m; (mildew) moho ▷ vt moldear; (fig) formar; **mouldy** adj enmohecido

mound [maund] n montón m, montículo

mount [maunt] n monte m ▷ vt montar, subir a; (jewel) engarzar; (picture) enmarcar; (exhibition etc) organizar ▷ vi (increase) aumentar; **mount up** vi aumentar

mountain ['mauntɪn] n montaña ▷ cpd de montaña; **mountain bike** n bicicleta de montaña; **mountaineer** n alpinista mf (SP, MEX), andinista mf (LAM); **mountaineering** n alpinismo m (SP, MEX), andinismo m (LAM); **mountainous** adj montañoso; **mountain range** n sierra

mourn [mɔːn] vt llorar, lamentar ▷ vi: **to ~ for** llorar la muerte de; **mourner** n doliente mf; dolorido/a; **mourning** n luto; **in mourning** de luto

mouse [maus] (pl **mice**) n (Zool, Comput) ratón m; **mouse mat** n (Comput) alfombrilla

moussaka [mu'saːkə] n musaca

mousse [muːs] n (Culin) crema batida; (for hair) espuma (moldeadora)

moustache [məs'taːʃ] (us **mustache**) n bigote m

mouth [mauθ, pl mauðz] n boca; (of river) desembocadura; **mouthful** n bocado; **mouth organ** n armónica; **mouthpiece** n (of musical instrument) boquilla; (spokesman) portavoz mf; **mouthwash** n enjuague m

move [muːv] n (movement) movimiento; (in game) jugada; (: turn to play) turno; (change: of house) mudanza; (: of job) cambio de trabajo ▷ vt mover; (emotionally) conmover; (Pol: resolution etc) proponer ▷ vi moverse; (traffic)

circular; (also: **~ house**) trasladarse, mudarse; **to ~ sb to do sth** mover a algn a hacer algo; **to get a ~ on** darse prisa; **move back** vi retroceder; **move in** vi (to a house) instalarse; (police, soldiers) intervenir; **move off** vi ponerse en camino; **move on** vi ponerse en camino; **move out** vi (of house) mudarse; **move over** vi apartarse, hacer sitio; **move up** vi (employee) ser ascendido; **movement** n movimiento

movie ['muːvɪ] n película; **to go to the ~s** ir al cine; **movie theater** (us) n cine m

moving ['muːvɪŋ] adj (emotional) conmovedor(a); (that moves) móvil

mow [məu] (pt **-ed**, pp **mowed** or **mown**) vt (grass, corn) cortar, segar; **mower** n (also: **lawnmower**) cortacéspedes m inv

Mozambique [məuzæm'biːk] n Mozambique m

MP n abbr = **Member of Parliament**

MP3 n MP3; **MP3 player** n reproductor m (de) MP3

mpg n abbr = **miles per gallon**

m.p.h. abbr = **miles per hour** (60 m.p.h. = 96 k.p.h.)

Mr ['mɪstə*] (us **Mr.**) n: **~ Smith** (el) Sr. Smith

Mrs ['mɪsɪz] (us **Mrs.**) n: **~ Smith** (la) Sra. Smith

Ms [mɪz] (us **Ms.**) n = **Miss** or **Mrs**; **~ Smith** (la) Sr(t)a. Smith

MSP n abbr = **Member of the Scottish Parliament**

Mt abbr (Geo) (= **mount**)

much [mʌtʃ] adj mucho ▷ adv mucho; (before pp) muy ▷ n or pron mucho; **how ~ is it?** ¿cuánto es?, ¿cuánto cuesta?; **too ~** demasiado; **it's not ~** no es mucho; **as ~ as** tanto como; **however ~ he tries** por mucho que se esfuerce

muck [mʌk] n suciedad f; **muck up** (inf) vt arruinar, estropear; **mucky** adj (dirty) sucio

mucus ['mjuːkəs] n mucosidad f, moco

mud [mʌd] n barro, lodo

muddle ['mʌdl] n desorden m, confusión f; (mix-up) embrollo, lío ▷ vt (also: ~ **up**) embrollar, confundir

muddy ['mʌdɪ] adj fangoso, cubierto de lodo

mudguard ['mʌdɡɑːd] n guardabarros m inv

muesli ['mjuːzlɪ] n muesli m

muffin ['mʌfɪn] n panecillo dulce

muffled ['mʌfld] adj (noise etc) amortiguado, apagado

muffler (US) ['mʌflə*] n (Aut) silenciador m

mug [mʌɡ] n taza grande (sin platillo); (for beer) jarra; (inf: face) jeta ▷ vt (assault) asaltar; **mugger** ['mʌɡə*] n atracador/a m/f; **mugging** n asalto

muggy ['mʌɡɪ] adj bochornoso

mule [mjuːl] n mula

multicoloured ['mʌltɪkʌləd] (US), **multicolored** adj multicolor

multimedia [mʌltɪ'miːdɪə] adj multimedia

multinational [mʌltɪ'næʃənl] n multinacional f ▷ adj multinacional

multiple ['mʌltɪpl] adj múltiple ▷ n múltiplo; **multiple choice (test)** n examen m de tipo test; **multiple sclerosis** n esclerosis f múltiple

multiplex cinema [mʌltɪpleks-] n multicines mpl

multiplication [mʌltɪplɪ'keɪʃən] n multiplicación f

multiply ['mʌltɪplaɪ] vt multiplicar ▷ vi multiplicarse

multistorey [mʌltɪ'stɔːrɪ] (BRIT) adj de muchos pisos

mum [mʌm] (BRIT: inf) n mamá ▷ adj: **to keep ~** mantener la boca cerrada

mumble ['mʌmbl] vt, vi hablar entre dientes, refunfuñar

mummy ['mʌmɪ] n (BRIT: mother) mamá; (embalmed) momia

mumps [mʌmps] n paperas fpl

munch [mʌntʃ] vt, vi mascar

municipal [mjuː'nɪsɪpl] adj municipal

mural ['mjuərl] n (pintura) mural m

murder ['mɜːdə*] n asesinato; (in law) homicidio ▷ vt asesinar, matar; **murderer** n asesino

murky ['mɜːkɪ] adj (water) turbio; (street, night) lóbrego

murmur ['mɜːmə*] n murmullo ▷ vt, vi murmurar

muscle ['mʌsl] n músculo; (fig: strength) garra, fuerza; **muscular** ['mʌskjulə*] adj muscular; (person) musculoso

museum [mjuː'zɪəm] n museo

mushroom ['mʌʃrum] n seta, hongo; (Culin) champiñón m ▷ vi crecer de la noche a la mañana

music ['mjuːzɪk] n música; **musical** adj musical; (sound) melodioso; (person) con talento musical ▷ n (show) comedia musical; **musical instrument** n instrumento musical; **musician** [-'zɪʃən] n músico/a

Muslim ['mʌzlɪm] adj, n musulmán/ ana m/f

muslin ['mʌzlɪn] n muselina

mussel ['mʌsl] n mejillón m

must [mʌst] aux vb (obligation): **I ~ do it** debo hacerlo, tengo que hacerlo; (probability): **he ~ be there by now** ya debe (de) estar allí ▷ n: **it's a ~** es imprescindible

mustache ['mʌstæʃ] (US) n = **moustache**

mustard ['mʌstəd] n mostaza

mustn't ['mʌsnt] = **must not**

mute [mjuːt] adj, n mudo/a m/f

mutilate ['mjuːtɪleɪt] vt mutilar

mutiny ['mjuːtɪnɪ] n motín m ▷ vi amotinarse

mutter ['mʌtə*] vt, vi hablar entre dientes, refunfuñar

mutton ['mʌtn] n carne f de cordero

mutual ['mjuːtʃuəl] adj mutuo; (interest) común

muzzle ['mʌzl] n hocico; (for dog) bozal m; (of gun) boca ▷ vt (dog) poner

un bozal a

my [maɪ] *adj* mi(s); **~ house/brother/ sisters** mi casa/mi hermano/mis hermanas; **I've washed ~ hair/cut ~ finger** me he lavado el pelo/cortado un dedo; **is this ~ pen or yours?** ¿es este bolígrafo mío o tuyo?

myself [maɪˈsɛlf] *pron* (*reflexive*) me; (*emphatic*) yo mismo; (*after prep*) mí (mismo); *see also* **oneself**

mysterious [mɪsˈtɪərɪəs] *adj* misterioso

mystery [ˈmɪstərɪ] *n* misterio

mystical [ˈmɪstɪkl] *adj* místico

mystify [ˈmɪstɪfaɪ] *vt* (*perplex*) dejar perplejo

myth [mɪθ] *n* mito; **mythology** [mɪˈθɔlədʒɪ] *n* mitología

n/a *abbr* (= *not applicable*) no interesa

nag [næg] *vt* (*scold*) regañar

nail [neɪl] *n* (*human*) uña; (*metal*) clavo ▷ *vt* clavar; **to ~ sth to sth** clavar algo en algo; **to ~ sb down to doing sth** comprometer a algn a que haga algo; **nailbrush** *n* cepillo para las uñas; **nailfile** *n* lima para las uñas; **nail polish** *n* esmalte *m* or laca para las uñas; **nail polish remover** *n* quitaesmalte *m*; **nail scissors** *npl* tijeras *fpl* para las uñas; **nail varnish** (*BRIT*) *n* = **nail polish**

naïve [naɪˈiːv] *adj* ingenuo

naked [ˈneɪkɪd] *adj* (*nude*) desnudo; (*flame*) expuesto al aire

name [neɪm] *n* nombre *m*; (*surname*) apellido; (*reputation*) fama, renombre *m* ▷ *vt* (*child*) poner nombre a; (*criminal*) identificar; (*price, date etc*) fijar; **what's your ~?** ¿cómo se llama?; **by ~** de nombre; **in the ~ of** en nombre de; **to give one's ~ and address** dar sus señas; **namely** *adv* a saber

nanny [ˈnænɪ] *n* niñera

nap [næp] n (sleep) sueñecito, siesta

napkin ['næpkɪn] n (also: **table ~**) servilleta

nappy ['næpɪ] (BRIT) n pañal m

narcotics npl (illegal drugs) estupefacientes mpl, narcóticos mpl

narrative ['nærətɪv] n narrativa ▷ adj narrativo

narrator [nə'reɪtə*] n narrador(a) m/f

narrow ['nærəʊ] adj estrecho, angosto; (fig: majority etc) corto; (: ideas etc) estrecho ▷ vi (road) estrecharse; (diminish) reducirse; **to have a ~ escape** escaparse por los pelos; **narrow down** vt (search, investigation, possibilities) restringir, limitar; (list) reducir; **narrowly** adv (miss) por poco; **narrow-minded** adj de miras estrechas

nasal ['neɪzl] adj nasal

nasty ['nɑːstɪ] adj (remark) feo; (person) antipático; (revolting: taste, smell) asqueroso; (wound, disease etc) peligroso, grave

nation ['neɪʃən] n nación f

national ['næʃənl] adj, n nacional m/f; **national anthem** n himno nacional; **national dress** n vestido nacional; **National Health Service** (BRIT) n servicio nacional de salud pública ≈ Insalud m (SP); **National Insurance** (BRIT) n seguro social nacional; **nationalist** adj, n nacionalista mf; **nationality** [-'nælɪtɪ] n nacionalidad f; **nationalize** vt nacionalizar; **national park** (BRIT) n parque m nacional; **National Trust** n (BRIT) organización encargada de preservar el patrimonio histórico británico

nationwide ['neɪʃənwaɪd] adj en escala o a nivel nacional

native ['neɪtɪv] n (local inhabitant) natural mf, nacional mf ▷ adj (indigenous) indígena; (country) natal; (innate) natural, innato; **a ~ of Russia** un(a) natural mf de Rusia; **Native American** adj, n americano/a

indígena, amerindio/a; **native speaker** n hablante mf nativo/a

NATO ['neɪtəʊ] n abbr (= North Atlantic Treaty Organization) OTAN f

natural ['nætʃrəl] adj natural; **natural gas** n gas m natural; **natural history** n historia natural; **naturally** adv naturalmente; (of course) desde luego, por supuesto; **natural resources** npl recursos mpl naturales

nature ['neɪtʃə*] n (also: **N~**) naturaleza; (group, sort) género, clase f; (character) carácter m, genio; **by ~** por or de naturaleza; **nature reserve** n reserva natural

naughty ['nɔːtɪ] adj (child) travieso

nausea ['nɔːsɪə] n náuseas fpl

naval ['neɪvl] adj naval, de marina

navel ['neɪvl] n ombligo

navigate ['nævɪgeɪt] vt gobernar ▷ vi navegar; (Aut) ir de copiloto; **navigation** [-'geɪʃən] n (action) navegación f; (science) náutica

navy ['neɪvɪ] n marina de guerra; (ships) armada, flota

Nazi ['nɑːtsɪ] n nazi m

NB abbr (= nota bene) nótese

near [nɪə*] adj (place, relation) cercano; (time) próximo ▷ adv cerca ▷ prep (also: **~ to**: space) cerca de, junto a; (: time) cerca de ▷ vt acercarse a, aproximarse a; **nearby** [nɪə'baɪ] adj cercano, próximo ▷ adv cerca; **nearly** adv casi, por poco; **I nearly fell** por poco me caigo; **near-sighted** adj miope, corto de vista

neat [niːt] adj (place) ordenado, bien cuidado; (person) pulcro; (plan) ingenioso; (spirits) solo; **neatly** adv (tidily) con esmero; (skilfully) ingeniosamente

necessarily ['nɛsɪsrɪlɪ] adv necesariamente

necessary ['nɛsɪsrɪ] adj necesario, preciso

necessity [nɪ'sɛsɪtɪ] n necesidad f

neck [nɛk] n (of person, garment, bottle) cuello; (of animal) pescuezo ▷ vi

(inf**)** besuquearse; **~ and ~** parejos;

necklace ['nɛklɪs] n collar m; **necktie** ['nɛktaɪ] n corbata

nectarine ['nɛktərɪn] n nectarina

need [niːd] n (lack) escasez f, falta; (necessity) necesidad f ▷ vt (require) necesitar; **I ~ to do it** tengo que o debo hacerlo; **you don't ~ to go** no hace falta que (te) vayas

needle ['niːdl] n aguja ▷ vt (fig: inf) picar, fastidiar

needless ['niːdlɪs] adj innecesario; **~ to say** huelga decir que

needlework ['niːdlwəːk] n (activity) costura, labor f de aguja

needn't ['niːdnt] = **need not**

needy ['niːdɪ] adj necesitado

negative ['nɛɡətɪv] n (Phot) negativo; (Ling) negación f ▷ adj negativo

neglect [nɪ'ɡlɛkt] vt (one's duty) faltar a, no cumplir con; (child) descuidar, desatender ▷ n (of house, garden etc) abandono; (of child) desatención f; (of duty) incumplimiento

negotiate [nɪ'ɡəuʃɪeɪt] vt (treaty, loan) negociar; (obstacle) franquear; (bend in road) tomar ▷ vi: **to ~ (with)** negociar (con)

negotiations [nɪɡəuʃɪ'eɪʃənz] n pl n negociaciones

negotiator [nɪ'ɡəuʃɪeɪtə*] n negociador(a) m/f

neighbour ['neɪbə*] (us **neighbor** etc) n vecino/a; **neighbourhood** n (place) vecindad f, barrio; (people) vecindario; **neighbouring** adj vecino

neither ['naɪðə*] adj vi ▷ conj: **I didn't move and ~ did John** no me he movido, ni Juan tampoco ▷ pron ninguno ▷ adv: **~ good nor bad** ni bueno ni malo; **~ is true** ninguno/a de los/las dos es cierto/a

neon ['niːɔn] n neón m

Nepal [nɪ'pɔːl] n Nepal m

nephew ['nɛvjuː] n sobrino

nerve [nəːv] n (Anat) nervio; (courage) valor m; (impudence) descaro, frescura

(nervousness) nerviosismo msg, nervios mpl; **a fit of ~s** un ataque de nervios

nervous ['nəːvəs] adj (anxious, Anat) nervioso; (timid) tímido, miedoso; **nervous breakdown** n crisis f nerviosa

nest [nɛst] n (of bird) nido; (wasps' nest) avispero ▷ vi anidar

net [nɛt] n (gen) red f; (fabric) tul m ▷ adj (Comm) neto, líquido ▷ vt (fish) coger (sp) o agarrar (LAM) con red; (Sport) marcar; **netball** n básquet m

Netherlands ['nɛðələndz] npl: **the ~** los Países Bajos

nett [nɛt] adj = **net**

nettle ['nɛtl] n ortiga

network ['nɛtwəːk] n red f

neurotic [njuə'rɔtɪk] adj neurótico/a

neuter ['njuːtə*] adj (Ling) neutro ▷ vt castrar, capar

neutral ['njuːtrəl] adj (person) neutral; (colour etc, Elec) neutro ▷ n (Aut) punto muerto

never ['nɛvə*] adv nunca, jamás; **I ~ went** no fui nunca; **~ in my life** jamás en su vida; see also **mind**; **never-ending** adj interminable, sin fin; **nevertheless** [nɛvəðə'lɛs] adv sin embargo, no obstante

new [njuː] adj nuevo; (brand new) a estrenar; (recent) reciente; **New Age** n Nueva Era; **newborn** adj recién nacido; **newcomer** ['njuːkʌmə*] n recién venido/a o llegado/a; **newly** adv nuevamente, recién

news [njuːz] n noticias fpl; **a piece of ~** una noticia; **the ~** (Radio, TV) las noticias fpl; **news agency** n agencia de noticias; **newsagent** (BRIT) n vendedor(a) m/f de periódicos; **newscaster** n presentador(a) m/f, locutor(a) m/f; **news dealer** (us) n = **newsagent**; **newsletter** n hoja informativa, boletín m; **newspaper** n periódico, diario; **newsreader** n = **newscaster**

newt [njuːt] n tritón m

New Year n Año Nuevo; **New Year's**

Day n Día m de Año Nuevo; New
Year's Eve n Nochevieja
New Zealand [njuːˈziːlənd] n
Nueva Zelanda f; New Zealander n
neozelandés/esa m/f
next [nekst] adj (house, room)
vecino; (bus stop, meeting) próximo;
(following: page etc) siguiente ▷ adv
después; **the ~ day** el día siguiente;
~ time la próxima vez; **~ year** el año
próximo or que viene; **~ to** junto a,
al lado de; **~ to nothing** casi nada;
please! ¡el siguiente!; next door adv
en la casa de al lado ▷ adj vecino, de
al lado; next-of-kin n pariente m
más cercano
NHS n abbr = National Health Service
nibble [ˈnɪbl] vt mordisquear,
mordisca
nice [naɪs] adj (likeable) simpático;
(kind) amable; (pleasant) agradable;
(attractive) bonito, lindo (LAM); nicely
adv amablemente; bien
niche [niːʃ] n (Arch) nicho, hornacina
nick [nɪk] n (wound) rasguño; (cut,
indentation) mella, muesca ▷ vt (inf)
birlar, robar; **in the ~ of time** justo
a tiempo
nickel [ˈnɪkl] n níquel m; (US) moneda
de 5 centavos
nickname [ˈnɪkneɪm] n apodo, mote
m ▷ vt apodar
nicotine [ˈnɪkətiːn] n nicotina
niece [niːs] n sobrina
Nigeria [naɪˈdʒɪərɪə] n Nigeria
night [naɪt] n noche f; (evening)
tarde f; **the ~ before last** anteanoche;
at ~, by ~ de noche, por la noche;
night club n cabaret m; nightdress
(BRIT) n camisón m; nightie [ˈnaɪtɪ]
n = nightdress; nightlife n vida
nocturna; nightly adj de todas las
noches ▷ adv todas las noches, cada
noche; nightmare n pesadilla; night
school n clase(s) f(pl) nocturna(s);
night shift n turno nocturno or de
noche; night-time n noche f
nil [nɪl] (BRIT) n (Sport) cero, nada

nine [naɪn] num nueve; nineteen
num diecinueve, diez y nueve;
nineteenth [naɪnˈtiːnθ] adj
decimonoveno, decimonono;
ninetieth [ˈnaɪntɪθ] adj
nonagésimo; ninety num noventa
ninth [naɪnθ] adj noveno
nip [nɪp] vt (pinch) pellizcar; (bite)
morder
nipple [ˈnɪpl] n (Anat) pezón m
nitrogen [ˈnaɪtrədʒən] n nitrógeno

○ KEYWORD

no [nəʊ] (pl noes) adv (opposite of "yes")
no; **are you coming? ~ no (I'm not)**
¿vienes? – no (no voy); **would you like some
more? ~ no thank you** ¿quieres más?
– no gracias ▷ adj (not any): **I have no
money/time/books** no tengo dinero/
tiempo/libros; **no other man would
have done it** ningún otro lo hubiera
hecho; **"no entry"** "prohibido el paso";
"no smoking" "prohibido fumar"
▷ n no m

nobility [nəʊˈbɪlɪtɪ] n nobleza
noble [ˈnəʊbl] adj noble
nobody [ˈnəʊbədɪ] pron nadie
nod [nɒd] vi saludar con la cabeza;
(in agreement) decir que sí con la
cabeza; (doze) dar cabezadas ▷ vt: **to
~ one's head** inclinar la cabeza ▷ n
inclinación f de cabeza; nod off vi dar
cabezadas
noise [nɔɪz] n ruido; (din) escándalo,
estrépito; noisy adj ruidoso; (child)
escandaloso
nominal [ˈnɒmɪnl] adj nominal
nominate [ˈnɒmɪneɪt] vt (propose)
proponer; (appoint) nombrar;
nomination [nɒmɪˈneɪʃən] n
propuesta; nombramiento; nominee
[-ˈniː] n candidato/a
none [nʌn] pron ninguno/a ▷ adv de
ninguna manera; **~ of you** ninguno
de vosotros; **I've ~ left** no me queda
ninguno/a; **he's ~ the worse for it** no

le ha hecho ningún mal

nonetheless [nʌnðə'les] *adv* sin embargo, no obstante

non-fiction [nɒn'fɪkʃən] *n* literatura no novelesca

nonsense ['nɒnsəns] *n* tonterías *fpl*, disparates *fpl*; ~! ¡qué tonterías!

non: non-smoker *n* no fumador(a) *m/f*; **non-smoking** *adj* (de) no fumador; **non-stick** *adj* (pan, surface) antiadherente

noodles ['nu:dlz] *npl* tallarines *mpl*

noon [nu:n] *n* mediodía *m*

no-one ['nəʊwʌn] *pron* = **nobody**

nor [nɔ:*] *conj* = **neither** ▷ *adv* see **neither**

norm [nɔ:m] *n* norma

normal ['nɔ:ml] *adj* normal; **normally** *adv* normalmente

north [nɔ:θ] *n* norte *m* ▷ *adj* del norte, norteño ▷ *adv* al or hacia el norte; **North America** *n* América del Norte; **North American** *adj, n* norteamericano/a *m/f*; **northbound** ['nɔ:θbaʊnd] *adj* (traffic) que se dirige al norte; (carriageway) de dirección norte; **north-east** *n* nor(d)este *m*; **northeastern** *adj* nor(d)este, nor(d)este; **northern** ['nɔ:ðən] *adj* norteño, del norte; **Northern Ireland** *n* Irlanda del Norte; **North Korea** *n* Corea del Norte; **North Pole** *n* Polo Norte; **North Sea** *n* Mar del Norte; **north-west** *n* nor(d)oeste *m*; **northwestern** ['nɔ:θ'westən] *adj* noroeste, del noroeste

Norway ['nɔ:weɪ] *n* Noruega; **Norwegian** [-'wi:dʒən] *adj* noruego/a ▷ *n* noruego/a; (Ling) noruego

nose [nəʊz] *n* (Anat) nariz *f*; (Zool) hocico; (sense of smell) olfato ▷ *vi*: **to ~ about** curiosear; **nosebleed** *n* hemorragia nasal; **nosey** (inf) *adj* curioso, fisgón/ona

nostalgia [nɒs'tældʒɪə] *n* nostalgia

nostalgic [nɒs'tældʒɪk] *adj* nostálgico

nostril ['nɒstrɪl] *n* ventana de la nariz

nosy ['nəʊzɪ] (inf) *adj* = **nosey**

not [nɒt] *adv* no; **~ that** ... no es que ...; **it's too late, isn't it?** es demasiado tarde, ¿verdad or no?; **~ yet/now** todavía/ahora no; **why ~?** ¿por qué no?; see also **all; only**

notable ['nəʊtəbl] *adj* notable; **notably** *adv* especialmente

notch [nɒtʃ] *n* muesca, corte *m*

note [nəʊt] *n* (Mus, record, letter) nota; (banknote) billete *m*; (tone) tono ▷ *vt* (observe) notar, observar; (write down) apuntar, anotar; **notebook** *n* libreta, cuaderno; **noted** ['nəʊtɪd] *adj* célebre, conocido; **notepad** *n* bloc *m*; **notepaper** *n* papel *m* para cartas

nothing ['nʌθɪŋ] *n* nada; (zero) cero; **he does ~** no hace nada; **~ new** nada nuevo; **~ much** no mucho; **for ~** (free) gratis, sin pago; (in vain) en balde

notice ['nəʊtɪs] *n* (announcement) anuncio; (warning) aviso; (dismissal) despido; (resignation) dimisión *f*; (period of time) plazo ▷ *vt* (observe) notar, observar; **to bring sth to sb's ~** (attention) llamar la atención de algn sobre algo; **to take ~ of** tomar nota de, prestar atención a; **at short ~** con poca anticipación; **until further ~** hasta nuevo aviso; **to hand in one's ~** dimitir

> Be careful not to translate **notice** by the Spanish word *noticia*.

noticeable *adj* evidente, obvio

notify ['nəʊtɪfaɪ] *vt*: **to ~ sb (of sth)** comunicar (algo) a algn

notion ['nəʊʃən] *n* idea; (opinion) opinión *f*; **notions** *npl* (us) mercería

notorious [nəʊ'tɔ:rɪəs] *adj* notorio

notwithstanding [nɒtwɪθ'stændɪŋ] *adv* no obstante, sin embargo; **~ this** a pesar de esto

nought [nɔ:t] *n* cero

noun [naʊn] *n* nombre *m*, sustantivo

nourish ['nʌrɪʃ] *vt* nutrir; (fig) alimentar; **nourishment** *n* alimento, sustento

Nov. *abbr* (= November) nov

novel ['nɒvl] *n* novela ▷ *adj* (new)

nuevo, original; (*unexpected*) insólito;
novelist n novelista mf; **novelty** n
novedad f

November [nəʊˈvɛmbə*] n
noviembre m

novice [ˈnɒvɪs] n (*Rel*) novicio/a

now [naʊ] adv (*at the present time*)
ahora; (*these days*) actualmente, hoy
día ▷ conj: **~ (that)** ya que, ahora que;
right ~ ahora mismo; **by ~** ya; **just
~** ahora mismo; **~ and then, ~ and
again** de vez en cuando; **from ~ on** de
ahora en adelante; **nowadays** [ˈnaʊə
deɪz] adv hoy (en) día, actualmente

nowhere [ˈnəʊwɛə*] adv (*direction*)
a ninguna parte; (*location*) en ninguna
parte

nozzle [ˈnɒzl] n boquilla

nr abbr (*BRIT*) **= near**

nuclear [ˈnjuːklɪə*] adj nuclear

nucleus [ˈnjuːklɪəs] (*pl* **nuclei**) n
núcleo

nude [njuːd] adj, n desnudo/a m/f; **in
the ~** desnudo

nudge [nʌdʒ] vt dar un codazo a

nudist [ˈnjuːdɪst] n nudista mf

nudity [ˈnjuːdɪtɪ] n desnudez f

nuisance [ˈnjuːsns] n molestia,
fastidio; (*person*) pesado, latoso; **what
a ~!** ¡qué lata!

numb [nʌm] adj: **~ with cold/fear**
entumecido por el frío/paralizado
de miedo

number [ˈnʌmbə*] n número;
(*quantity*) cantidad f ▷ vt (*pages etc*)
numerar, poner número a; (*amount to*)
sumar, ascender a; **to be ~ed among**
figurar entre; **a ~ of** varios, algunos;
they were ten in ~ eran diez; **number
plate** (*BRIT*) n matrícula, placa;
Number Ten (*BRIT*: 10 *Downing
Street*) residencia del primer ministro

numerical [njuːˈmɛrɪkl] adj
numérico

numerous [ˈnjuːmərəs] adj
numeroso

nun [nʌn] n monja, religiosa

nurse [nəːs] n enfermero/a; (*also*:

~maid) niñera ▷ vt (*patient*) cuidar,
atender

nursery [ˈnəːsərɪ] n (*institution*)
guardería infantil; (*room*) cuarto de los
niños; (*for plants*) criadero, semillero;
nursery rhyme n canción f infantil;
nursery school n parvulario, escuela
de párvulos; **nursery slope** (*BRIT*) n
(*Ski*) cuesta para principiantes

nursing [ˈnəːsɪŋ] n (*profession*)
profesión f de enfermera; (*care*)
asistencia, cuidado; **nursing home** n
clínica de reposo

nurture [ˈnəːtʃə*] vt (*child, plant*)
alimentar, nutrir

nut [nʌt] n (*Tech*) tuerca; (*Bot*) nuez f

nutmeg [ˈnʌtmɛg] n nuez f moscada

nutrient [ˈnjuːtrɪənt] adj nutritivo
▷ n elemento nutritivo

nutrition [njuːˈtrɪʃən] n nutrición f,
alimentación f

nutritious [njuːˈtrɪʃəs] adj
alimenticio

nuts [nʌts] (*inf*) adj loco

NVQ n abbr (*BRIT*) **= National
Vocational Qualification**

nylon [ˈnaɪlɒn] n nilón m ▷ adj de
nilón

O

oath [əʊθ] n juramento; (swear word) palabrota; **on** (BRIT) or **under** ~ bajo juramento

oak [əʊk] n roble m ▷ adj de roble

O.A.P. (BRIT) n, abbr = **old-age pensioner**

oar [ɔ:ʳ] n remo

oasis [əʊˈeɪsɪs] (pl **oases**) n oasis m inv

oath [əʊθ] n juramento; (swear word) palabrota; **on** (BRIT) or **under** ~ bajo juramento

oatmeal [ˈəʊtmiːl] n harina de avena

oats [əʊts] npl avena

obedience [əˈbiːdɪəns] n obediencia

obedient [əˈbiːdɪənt] adj obediente

obese [əʊˈbiːs] adj obeso

obesity [əʊˈbiːsɪtɪ] n obesidad f

obey [əˈbeɪ] vt obedecer; (instructions, regulations) cumplir

obituary [əˈbɪtjʊərɪ] n necrología

object [n ˈɒbdʒɪkt, vb əbˈdʒɛkt] n objeto; (purpose) objeto, propósito; (Ling) complemento ▷ vi: **to ~ to** estar en contra de; (proposal) oponerse a; **to ~ that** objetar que; **expense is no**

~ no importa cuánto cuesta; **I ~!** ¡yo protesto!; **objection** [əbˈdʒɛkʃən] n protesta; **I have no objection to ...** no tengo inconveniente en que ...; **objective** adj, n objetivo

obligation [ɒblɪˈgeɪʃən] n obligación f; (debt) deber m; **without ~** sin compromiso

obligatory [əˈblɪgətərɪ] adj obligatorio

oblige [əˈblaɪdʒ] vt (do a favour for) complacer, hacer un favor a; **to ~ sb to do sth** forzar or obligar a algn a hacer algo; **to be ~d to sb for sth** estarle agradecido a algn por algo

oblique [əˈbliːk] adj oblicuo; (allusion) indirecto

obliterate [əˈblɪtəreɪt] vt borrar

oblivious [əˈblɪvɪəs] adj: **~ of** inconsciente de

oblong [ˈɒblɒŋ] adj rectangular ▷ n rectángulo

obnoxious [əbˈnɒkʃəs] adj odioso, detestable; (smell) nauseabundo

oboe [ˈəʊbəʊ] n oboe m

obscene [əbˈsiːn] adj obsceno

obscure [əbˈskjʊəʳ] adj oscuro ▷ vt oscurecer; (hide) esconder

observant [əbˈzɜːvnt] adj observador(a)

observation [ɒbzəˈveɪʃən] n observación f; (Med) examen m

observatory [əbˈzɜːvətrɪ] n observatorio

observe [əbˈzɜːv] vt observar; (rule) cumplir; **observer** n observador(a) m/f

obsess [əbˈsɛs] vt obsesionar; **obsession** [əbˈsɛʃən] n obsesión f; **obsessive** adj obsesivo; obsesionada

obsolete [ˈɒbsəliːt] adj: **to be ~** estar en desuso

obstacle [ˈɒbstəkl] n obstáculo; (nuisance) estorbo

obstinate [ˈɒbstɪnɪt] adj terco, porfiado; (determined) obstinado

obstruct [əbˈstrʌkt] vt obstruir; (hinder) estorbar, obstaculizar; **obstruction** [əbˈstrʌkʃən] n (action)

obstrucción f; (object) estorbo, obstáculo
obtain [əb'teɪn] vt obtener; (achieve) conseguir

obvious ['ɒbvɪəs] adj obvio, evidente; **obviously** adv evidentemente, naturalmente; **obviously not** por supuesto que no

occasion [ə'keɪʒən] n oportunidad f, ocasión f; (event) acontecimiento; **occasional** adj ocasional, esporádico; **occasionally** adv de vez en cuando

occult [ɒ'kʌlt] adj (gen) oculto

occupant ['ɒkjupənt] n (of house) inquilino/a; (of car) ocupante mf

occupation [ɒkju'peɪʃən] n ocupación f; (job) trabajo; (pastime) ocupaciones fpl

occupy ['ɒkjupaɪ] vt (seat, post, time) ocupar; (house) habitar; **to ~ o.s. in doing** pasar el tiempo haciendo

occur [ə'kə:*] vi pasar, suceder; **to sb** ocurrírsele a algn; **occurrence** [ə'kʌrəns] n acontecimiento; (existence) existencia

ocean ['əuʃən] n océano

o'clock [ə'klɒk] adv: **it is 5** ~ son las 5

Oct. abbr (= October) oct

October [ɒk'təubə*] n octubre m

octopus ['ɒktəpəs] n pulpo

odd [ɒd] adj extraño, raro; (number) impar; (sock, shoe etc) suelto; **60-~** 60 y pico; **at ~ times** de vez en cuando; **to be the ~ one out** estar de más; **oddly** adv curiosamente, extrañamente; see also **enough**; **odds** npl (in betting) puntos mpl de ventaja; **it makes no odds** da lo mismo; **at odds** reñidos/as; **odds and ends** minucias fpl

odometer [ɒ'dɒmɪtə*] (us) n cuentakilómetros m inv

odour ['əudə*] (us **odor**) n olor m; (unpleasant) hedor m

🔘 **KEYWORD**

of [ɒv, əv] prep **1** (gen) de; **a friend of ours** un amigo nuestro; **a boy of 10** un

chico de 10 años; **that was kind of you** eso fue muy amable por or de tu parte

2 (expressing quantity, amount, dates etc) de; **a kilo of flour** un kilo de harina; **there were three of them** había tres; **three of us went** tres de nosotros fuimos; **the 5th of July** el 5 de julio

3 (from, out of) de; **made of wood** (hecho) de madera

off [ɒf] adj, adv (engine) desconectado; (light) apagado; (tap) cerrado; (BRIT: food: bad) pasado, malo; (: milk) cortado; (cancelled) cancelado ▷ prep de; **to be** ~ (to leave) irse, marcharse; **to be ~ sick** estar enfermo or de baja; **a day** ~ un día libre or sin trabajar; **to have an ~ day** tener un día malo; **he had his coat** ~ se había quitado el abrigo; **10%** ~ (Comm) (con el) 10% de descuento; **5 km** ~ **(the road)** a 5 km (de la carretera); ~ **the coast** frente a la costa; **I'm** ~ **meat** (no longer eat/like it) paso de la carne; **on the** ~ **chance** por si acaso; ~ **and on** de vez en cuando

offence [ə'fɛns] (us **offense**) n (crime, delito; **to take** ~ **at** ofenderse por

offend [ə'fɛnd] vt (person) ofender; **offender** n delincuente mf

offense [ə'fɛns] (us) n = **offence**

offensive [ə'fɛnsɪv] adj ofensivo; (smell etc) repugnante ▷ n (Mil) ofensiva

offer ['ɒfə*] n oferta, ofrecimiento; (proposal) propuesta ▷ vt ofrecer; (opportunity) facilitar; **"on** ~" (Comm) "en oferta"

offhand [ɒf'hænd] adj informal ▷ adv de improviso

office ['ɒfɪs] n (place) oficina; (room) despacho; (position) carga, oficio; **doctor's** ~ (us) consultorio; **to take** ~ entrar en funciones; **office block** (us), **office building** n bloque m de oficinas; **office hours** npl horas fpl de oficina; (us Med) horas fpl de consulta

officer ['ɒfɪsə*] n (Mil etc) oficial mf;

(also: **police ~**) agente mf de policía; (of organization) director(a) m/f

ffice worker n oficinista mf

fficial [əˈfɪʃl] adj oficial, autorizado
▷ n funcionario/a, oficial m/f

ff: off-licence(BRIT) n (shop) bodega
tienda de vinos y bebidas alcohólicas;
off-line adj, adv (Comput) fuera de
línea; **off-peak** adj (electricity) de
banda económica; (ticket) billete de
precio reducido por viajar fuera de las horas
punta; **off-putting**(BRIT) adj (person)
asqueroso; (remark) desalentador(a);
off-season adj, adv fuera de
temporada

○ OFF-LICENCE

- En el Reino Unido la venta
- de bebidas alcohólicas está
- estrictamente regulada
- y se necesita una licencia
- especial, con la que cuentan
- los bares, restaurantes y los
- establecimientos de **off-licence**,
- los únicos lugares en donde
- se pueden adquirir bebidas
- alcohólicas para su consumo
- fuera del local, de donde viene
- su nombre. También venden
- bebidas no alcohólicas, tabaco,
- chocolatinas, patatas fritas, etc.
- y a menudo forman parte de una
- cadena nacional.

ffset [ˈɔfsɛt] vt contrarrestar,
compensar

ffshore [ɔfˈʃɔːʳ] adj (breeze, island)
costera; (fishing) de bajura

ffside [ˈɔfˈsaɪd] adj (Sport) fuera de
juego; (Aut: in UK) del lado derecho,
; in US, Europe etc) del lado
izquierdo

ffspring [ˈɔfsprɪŋ] n inv
descendencia

ften [ˈɔfn] adv a menudo, con
frecuencia; **how ~ do you go?** ¿cada
cuánto vas?

oh [əʊ] excl ¡ah!

oil [ɔɪl] n aceite m; (petroleum)
petróleo; (for heating) aceite m
combustible ▷ vt engrasar; **oil filter**
n (Aut) filtro de aceite; **oil painting**
n pintura al óleo; **oil refinery** n
refinería de petróleo; **oil rig** n torre
f de perforación; **oil slick** n marea
negra; **oil tanker** n petrolero; (truck)
camión m cisterna; **oil well** n pozo
(de petróleo); **oily** adj aceitoso; (food)
grasiento

ointment [ˈɔɪntmənt] n ungüento

O.K., okay [ˈəʊˈkeɪ] excl ¡O.K.!, ¡está
bien!, ¡vale! (SP) ▷ adj bien ▷ vt dar el
visto bueno a

old [əʊld] adj viejo; (former) antiguo;
how ~ are you? ¿cuántos años
tienes?, ¿qué edad tienes?; **he's 10
years ~** tiene 10 años; **~er brother**
hermano mayor; **old age** n vejez f;
old-age pension n (BRIT) jubilación
f, pensión f; **old-age pensioner**
(BRIT) n jubilado/a; **old-fashioned**
adj anticuado, pasado de moda; **old
people's home** n (esp BRIT) residencia
f de ancianos

olive [ˈɔlɪv] n (fruit) aceituna; (tree)
olivo ▷ adj (also: **~-green**) verde oliva;
olive oil n aceite m de oliva

Olympic [əʊˈlɪmpɪk] adj olímpico;
the ~ Games, the ~s las
Olimpiadas

omelet(te) [ˈɔmlɪt] n tortilla
francesa (SP), omelette f (LAM)

omen [ˈəʊmən] n presagio

ominous [ˈɔmɪnəs] adj de mal
agüero, amenazador(a)

omit [əʊˈmɪt] vt omitir

○ KEYWORD

on [ɔn] prep 1 (indicating position) en;
sobre; **on the wall** en la pared; **it's on
the table** está sobre or en la mesa; **on
the left** a la izquierda
2 (indicating means, method, condition
etc): **on foot** a pie; **on the train/**

plane (go) en tren/avión; (be) en el tren/el avión; **on the radio/television/telephone** por o en la radio/televisión/al teléfono; **to be on drugs** drogarse; (Med) estar a tratamiento; **to be on holiday/business** estar de vacaciones/en viaje de negocios

3 (referring to time): **on Friday** el viernes; **on Fridays** los viernes; **on June 20th** el 20 de junio; **a week on Friday** del viernes en una semana; **on arrival** al llegar; **on seeing this** al ver esto

4 (about, concerning) sobre, acerca de; **a book on physics** un libro de o sobre física

▷ adv 1 (referring to dress): **to have one's coat on** tener or llevar el abrigo puesto; **she put her gloves on** se puso los guantes

2 (referring to covering): **"screw the lid on tightly"** "cerrar bien la tapa"

3 (further, continuously): **to walk etc on** seguir caminando etc

▷ adj 1 (functioning, in operation: machine, radio, TV, light) encendido/a (SP), prendido/a (LAM); (: tap) abierto/a; (: brakes) echado/a, puesto/a; **is the meeting still on?** (in progress) ¿todavía continúa la reunión?; (not cancelled) ¿va a haber reunión al fin?; **there's a good film on at the cinema** ponen una buena película en el cine

2 **that's not on!** (inf: not possible) ¡eso ni hablar!; (: not acceptable) ¡eso no se hace!

once [wʌns] adv una vez; (formerly) antiguamente ▷ conj una vez que; **~ he had left/it was done** una vez que se había marchado/se hizo; **at ~** en seguida, inmediatamente; (simultaneously) a la vez; **~ a week** una vez por semana; **~ more** otra vez; **~ and for all** de una vez por todas; **~ upon a time** érase una vez

oncoming ['ɒnkʌmɪŋ] adj (traffic) que viene de frente

○ **KEYWORD**

one [wʌn] num un(o)/una; **one hundred and fifty** ciento cincuenta; **one by one** uno a uno

▷ adj 1 (sole) único; **the one book which** el único libro que; **the one man who** el único que

2 (same) mismo/a; **they came in the one car** vinieron en un solo coche

▷ pron 1 **this one** éste(ésta); **that one** ése(ésa); (more remote) aquél(aquella); **I've already got (a red) one** ya tengo uno/a rojo/a; **one by one** uno/a por uno/a

2 **one another** os (SP), se (+ el uno al otro, unos a otros etc); **do you two ever see one another?** ¿vosotros dos os veis alguna vez? (SP), ¿se ven ustedes dos alguna vez?; **the boys didn't dare look at one another** los chicos no se atrevieron a mirarse (el uno al otro); **they all kissed one another** se besaron unos a otros

3 (impers): **one never knows** nunca se sabe; **to cut one's finger** cortarse el dedo; **one needs to eat** hay que comer

one-off [wʌn'ɒf] (BRIT: inf) n (event) acontecimiento único

oneself [wʌn'sɛlf] pron (reflexive) se; (after prep) sí; (emphatic) uno/a mismo/a; **to hurt ~** hacerse daño; **to keep sth for ~** guardarse algo; **to talk to ~** hablar solo

one: **one-shot** [wʌn'ʃɒt] (US) n = **one-off**; **one-sided** adj (argument) parcial; **one-to-one** adj (relationship) de dos; **one-way** adj (street) de sentido único

ongoing ['ɒngəʊɪŋ] adj continuo

onion ['ʌnjən] n cebolla

on-line ['ɒnlaɪn] adj, adv (Comput) en línea

onlooker ['ɒnlʊkə*] n espectador(a) m/f

nly ['əʊnlɪ] *adv* solamente, sólo ▷ *adj* único, solo ▷ *conj* solamente que, pero; **an ~ child** un hijo único; **not ~ ... but also ...** no sólo ... sino también ...

n-screen [ɒn'skriːn] *adj* (Comput etc) en pantalla; (romance, kiss) cinematográfico

nset ['ɒnset] *n* comienzo

nto ['ɒntuː] *prep* = **on to**

nward(s) ['ɒnwəd(z)] *adv* (move) (hacia) adelante; **from that time ~** desde entonces en adelante

ops [ʊps] *excl* (also: **~-a-daisy!**) ¡huy!

oze [uːz] *vi* rezumar

paque [əʊ'peɪk] *adj* opaco

pen ['əʊpn] *adj* abierto; (car) descubierto; (road, view) despejado; (meeting) público; (admiration) manifiesto ▷ *vt* abrir ▷ *vi* abrirse; (book etc: commence) comenzar; **in the ~ (air)** al aire libre; **open up** *vt* abrir; (blocked road) despejar ▷ *vi* abrirse, empezar; **open-air** *adj* al aire libre; **opening** *n* abertura; (start) comienzo; (opportunity) oportunidad f; **opening hours** *npl* horario de apertura; **open learning** *n* enseñanza flexible a tiempo parcial; **openly** *adv* abiertamente; **open-minded** *adj* imparcial; **open-necked** *adj* (shirt) desabrochado; sin corbata; **open-plan** *adj*: **open-plan office** gran oficina sin particiones; **Open University** *n* (BRIT) ≈ Universidad f Nacional de Enseñanza a Distancia, UNED f

presentación de unos trabajos y la asistencia a los cursos de verano.

opera ['ɒpərə] *n* ópera; **opera house** *n* teatro de la ópera; **opera singer** *n* cantante m/f de ópera

operate ['ɒpəreɪt] *vt* (machine) hacer funcionar; (company) dirigir ▷ *vi* funcionar; **to ~ on sb** (Med) operar a algn

operating room ['ɒpəreɪtɪŋ-] *(US)* quirófano, sala de operaciones

operating theatre (BRIT) *n* sala de operaciones

operation [ɒpə'reɪʃən] *n* operación f; (of machine) funcionamiento; **to be in ~** estar funcionando o en funcionamiento; **to have an ~** (Med) ser operado; **operational** *adj* operacional, en buen estado

operative ['ɒpərətɪv] *adj* en vigor

operator ['ɒpəreɪtə*] *n* (of machine) maquinista m/f; (Tel) operador(a) m/f, telefonista mf

opinion [ə'pɪnɪən] *n* opinión f; **in my ~** en mi opinión, a mi juicio; **opinion poll** *n* encuesta, sondeo

opponent [ə'pəʊnənt] *n* adversario/a, contrincante m/f

opportunity [ɒpə'tjuːnɪtɪ] *n* oportunidad f; **to take the ~ of doing** aprovechar la ocasión para hacer

oppose [ə'pəʊz] *vt* oponerse a; **to be ~d to sth** oponerse a algo; **as ~d to** a la diferencia de

opposite ['ɒpəzɪt] *adj* opuesto, contrario a; (house etc) de enfrente ▷ *adv* en frente ▷ *prep* en frente de, frente a ▷ *n* lo contrario

opposition [ɒpə'zɪʃən] *n* oposición f

oppress [ə'pres] *vt* oprimir

opt [ɒpt] *vi*: **to ~ for** optar por; **to ~ to do** optar por hacer; **opt out** *vi*: **to opt out of** optar por no hacer

optician [ɒp'tɪʃən] *n* óptico m/f

optimism ['ɒptɪmɪzəm] *n* optimismo

optimist ['ɒptɪmɪst] *n* optimista mf;

optimistic [-'mɪstɪk] adj optimista

optimum ['ɔptɪməm] adj óptimo

option ['ɔpʃən] n opción f; optional adj facultativo, discrecional

or [ɔː*] conj o; (before o, ho) u; (with negative): he hasn't seen ~ heard anything no ha visto ni oído nada; ~ else si no

oral ['ɔːrəl] adj oral ▷n examen m oral

orange ['ɔrɪndʒ] n (fruit) naranja ▷ adj color naranja; orange juice n jugo m de naranja, zumo m de naranja (sp); orange squash n naranjada

orbit ['ɔːbɪt] n órbita ▷vt, vi orbitar

orchard ['ɔːtʃəd] n huerto

orchestra ['ɔːkɪstrə] n orquesta; (us: seating) platea

orchid ['ɔːkɪd] n orquídea

ordeal [ɔː'diːl] n experiencia horrorosa

order ['ɔːdə*] n orden m; (command) orden f; (good order) buen estado; (Comm) pedido ▷vt (also: put in ~) arreglar, poner en orden; (Comm) pedir; (command) mandar, ordenar; in ~ en orden; (of document) en regla; in ~ to do/that para hacer/que; in ~ to do/that para hacer/que; in ~ to do/that para hacer/que; on ~ (Comm) pedido; to be out of ~ estar desordenado; (not working) no funcionar; to ~ sb to do sth mandar a algn hacer algo; order form n hoja de pedido; orderly n (Mil) ordenanza m; (Med) enfermero/a (auxiliar) ▷ adj ordenado

ordinary ['ɔːdnrɪ] adj corriente, normal; (pej) ordinario y corriente; out of the ~ fuera de lo común

ore [ɔː*] n mineral m

oregano [ɔrɪ'gɑːnəu] n orégano

organ ['ɔːgən] n órgano; organic [ɔː'gænɪk] adj orgánico; organism n organismo

organization [ɔːgənaɪ'zeɪʃən] n organización f

organize ['ɔːgənaɪz] vt organizar; organized ['ɔːgənaɪzd] adj organizado; organizer n

organizador(a) m/f

orgasm ['ɔːgæzəm] n orgasmo

orgy ['ɔːdʒɪ] n orgía

oriental [ɔːrɪ'entl] adj oriental

orientation [ɔːrɪen'teɪʃən] n orientación f

origin ['ɔrɪdʒɪn] n origen m

original [ə'rɪdʒɪnl] adj original; (first) primero; (earlier) primitivo ▷n original m; originally adv al principio

originate [ə'rɪdʒɪneɪt] vi: to ~ from, to ~ in surgir de, tener su origen en

Orkneys ['ɔːknɪz] npl: the ~ (also: the Orkney Islands) las Orcadas

ornament ['ɔːnəmənt] n adorno; (trinket) chuchería; ornamental [-'mentl] adj decorativo, de adorno

ornate [ɔː'neɪt] adj muy ornado, vistoso

orphan ['ɔːfn] n huérfano/a

orthodox ['ɔːθədɔks] adj ortodoxo

orthopaedic [ɔːθə'piːdɪk] (us orthopedic) adj ortopédico

osteopath ['ɔstɪəpæθ] n osteópata mf

ostrich ['ɔstrɪtʃ] n avestruz m

other ['ʌðə*] adj otro ▷ pron: the ~ (one) el(la) otro/a ▷ adv: ~ than aparte de; otherwise adv de otra manera ▷ conj (if not) si no

otter ['ɔtə*] n nutria

ouch [autʃ] excl ¡ay!

ought [ɔːt] (pt ~) aux vb: I ~ to do it debería hacerlo; this ~ to have been corrected esto debiera haberse corregido; he ~ to win (probability) debe o debiera ganar

ounce [auns] n onza (28.35g)

our [auə*] adj nuestro; see also my; ours pron (el) nuestro/(la) nuestra etc; see also mine[1]; ourselves pron pl (reflexive, after prep) nosotros; (emphatic) nosotros mismos; see also oneself

oust [aust] vt desalojar

out [aut] adv fuera, afuera; (not at home) fuera (de casa); (light, fire) apagado; ~ there allí (fuera); he's ~ (absent) no está, ha salido; to be ~ in

one's calculations equivocarse (en sus cálculos); **to run ~** salir corriendo; **~ loud** en alta voz; **~ of** (outside) fuera de (because of: anger etc) por; **~ of petrol** sin gasolina; **"~ of order"** "no funciona"; **outback** n interior m; (of flight) de salida; (flight: not return) de ida; **outbreak** n (of war) comienzo; (of disease) epidemia; (of violence etc) ola; **outburst** n explosión f, arranque m; **outcast** n paria mf; **outcome** n resultado; **outcry** n protestas fpl; **outdated** adj anticuado, fuera de moda; **outdoor** adj exterior, de aire libre; (clothes) de calle; **outdoors** adv al aire libre

outer ['autə*] adj exterior, externo; **outer space** n espacio exterior
outfit ['autfɪt] n (clothes) conjunto m; **out:**
outgoing adj (character) extrovertido; (retiring: president etc) saliente; **outgoings** (BRIT) npl gastos mpl; **outhouse** n dependencia
outing ['autɪŋ] n excursión f, paseo m; **out:**
outlaw n proscrito ▷ vt proscribir; **outlay** n inversión f;
outlet n salida; (of pipe) desagüe m; (US Elec) toma de corriente; (also:
retail outlet) punto de venta; **outline** n (shape) contorno, perfil m; (sketch, plan) esbozo ▷ vt (plan etc) esbozar; **in outline** (fig) a grandes rasgos; **outlook** n (fig: prospects) perspectivas fpl; (: for weather) pronóstico; **outnumber** vt superar en número; **out-of-date** adj (passport) caducado; (clothes) pasado de moda; **out-of-doors** adv al aire libre; **out-of-the-way** adj apartado; **out-of-town** adj (shopping centre etc) en las afueras; **outpatient** n paciente mf externo/a; **outpost** n puesto avanzado; **output** n (volumen m de) producción m, rendimiento; (Comput) salida

outrage ['autreɪdʒ] n escándalo; (atrocity) atrocidad f ▷ vt ultrajar; **outrageous** [-'reɪdʒəs] adj monstruoso

outright [adv aut'raɪt, adj 'autraɪt] adv (ask, deny) francamente; (refuse) rotundamente; (win) de manera absoluta; (be killed) en el acto ▷ adj franco; rotundo
outset ['autset] n principio
outside [aut'saɪd] n exterior m ▷ adj exterior, externo ▷ adv fuera ▷ prep fuera de; (beyond) más allá de; **at the ~** (fig) a lo sumo; **outside lane** n (Aut: in Britain) carril m de la derecha; (: in US, Europe etc) carril m de la izquierda; **outside line** n (Tel) línea exterior; **outsider** n (stranger) extraño, forastero
out: outsize adj (clothes) de talla grande; **outskirts** npl alrededores mpl, afueras fpl; **outspoken** adj muy franco; **outstanding** adj excepcional, destacado; (remaining) pendiente
outward ['autwəd] adj (sign) externo; (journey) de ida; **outwards** adv (esp BRIT)= **outward**
outweigh [aut'weɪ] vt pesar más que
oval ['əuvl] adj ovalado ▷ n óvalo
ovary ['əuvərɪ] n ovario
oven ['ʌvn] n horno; **oven glove** n guante m para el horno, manopla para el horno; **ovenproof** adj resistente al horno; **oven-ready** adj listo para el horno
over ['əuvə*] adv encima, por encima ▷ adj or adv (finished) terminado; (surplus) de sobra ▷ prep (on) encima de; (above) sobre; (on the other side of) al otro lado de; (more than) más de; (during) durante; **~ here** (por) aquí; **~ there** (por) allí o allá; **~ all** (everywhere) por todas partes; **~ and ~ (again)** una y otra vez; **~ and above** además de; **to ask sb ~** invitar a algn a casa; **to bend ~** = inclinarse

overall [adj, n 'əuvərɔːl, adv əuvər'ɔːl] adj (length etc) total; (study) de conjunto ▷ adv en conjunto ▷ n (BRIT) guardapolvo; **overalls** npl (boiler suit) mono (SP) or overol m (LAM) (de trabajo)
overboard adv (Naut) por la borda

overcame [əuvəˈkeɪm] pt of **overcome**

overcast [ˈəuvəkɑːst] adj encapotado

overcharge [əuvəˈtʃɑːdʒ] vt: **to ~ sb** cobrar un precio excesivo a algn

overcoat [ˈəuvəkəut] n abrigo, sobretodo

overcome [əuvəˈkʌm] vt vencer; (difficulty) superar

over: overcrowded adj atestado de gente; (city, country) superpoblado; **overdo** (irreg) vt exagerar; (overcook) cocer demasiado; **to overdo it** (work etc) pasarse; **overdone** [əuvəˈdʌn] adj (vegetables) recocido; (steak) demasiado hecho; **overdose** n sobredosis f inv; **overdraft** n saldo deudor; **overdrawn** adj (account) en descubierto; **overdue** adj retrasado; **overestimate** vt sobreestimar

overflow [vb əuvəˈfləu, n ˈəuvəfləu] vi desbordarse ▷ n (also: ~ **pipe**) (cañería de) desagüe m

overgrown [əuvəˈgrəun] adj (garden) invadido por la vegetación

overhaul [vb əuvəˈhɔːl, n ˈəuvəhɔːl] vt revisar, repasar ▷ n revisión f

overhead [adv əuvəˈhed, adj, n ˈəuvəhed] adv por arriba or encima ▷ adj (cable) aéreo n (us) **overheads**; **overhead projector** n retroproyector; **overheads** npl (expenses) gastos mpl generales

over: overhear vt oír por casualidad; **overheat** vi (engine) recalentarse; **overland** adj, adv por tierra; **overlap** [əuvəˈlæp] vi traslaparse; **overleaf** adv al dorso; **overload** vt sobrecargar; **overlook** vt (have view of) dar a, tener vistas a; (miss: by mistake) pasar por alto; (excuse) perdonar

overnight [əuvəˈnaɪt] adv durante la noche, (fig) de la noche a la mañana ▷ adj de noche; **to stay ~** pasar la noche; **overnight bag** n fin m de semana, neceser m de viaje

overpass (us) [ˈəuvəpɑːs] n paso superior

overpower [əuvəˈpauə*] vt dominar; (fig) embargar; **overpowering** adj (heat) agobiante; (smell) penetrante

over: overreact [əuvərɪˈækt] vi reaccionar de manera exagerada; **overrule** vt (decision) anular; (claim) denegar; **overrun** (irreg) vt (country) invadir; (time limit) rebasar, exceder

overseas [əuvəˈsiːz] adv (abroad: live) en el extranjero; (travel) al extranjero ▷ adj (trade) exterior; (visitor) extranjero

oversee [əuvəˈsiː] (irreg) vt supervisa

overshadow [əuvəˈʃædəu] vt: **to be ~ed by** estar a la sombra de

oversight [ˈəuvəsaɪt] n descuido

oversleep [əuvəˈsliːp] (irreg) vi quedarse dormido

overspend [əuvəˈspend] (irreg) vi gastar más de la cuenta; **we have overspent by 5 pounds** hemos excedido el presupuesto en 5 libras

overt [əuˈvɜːt] adj abierto

overtake [əuvəˈteɪk] (irreg) vt sobrepasar; (BRIT Aut) adelantar

over: overthrow (irreg) vt (government) derrocar; **overtime** n horas fpl extraordinarias

overtook [əuvəˈtuk] pt of **overtake**

over: overturn vt volcar; (fig: plan) desbaratar; (: government) derrocar ▷ vi volcar; **overweight** adj demasiado gordo or pesado; **overwhelm** vt aplastar; (emotion) sobrecoger; **overwhelming** adj (victory, defeat) arrollador(a); (feeling) irresistible

ow [au] excl ¡ay!

owe [əu] vt: **to ~ sb sth, to ~ sth to sb** deber algo a algn; **owing to** prep debido a, por causa de

owl [aul] n búho, lechuza

own [əun] vt tener, poseer ▷ adj propio; **a room of my ~** una habitación propia; **to get one's ~ back** tomar revancha; **on one's ~** solo, a solas; **own up** vi confesar; **owner** n dueño/a;

ownership n posesión f
ox [ɔks] (pl **~en**) n buey m
Oxbridge [ˈɔksbrɪdʒ] n universidades
de Oxford y Cambridge
oxen [ˈɔksən] npl of **ox**
oxygen [ˈɔksɪdʒən] n oxígeno m
oyster [ˈɔɪstə*] n ostra f
oz. abbr = **ounce(s)**
ozone [ˈəʊzəʊn] n ozono; **ozone
friendly** adj que no daña la capa de
ozono; **ozone layer** n capa f de ozono

p [piː] abbr = **penny; pence**
P.A. n abbr = **personal assistant;
public address system**
p.a. abbr = **per annum**
pace [peɪs] n paso ⊳ vi: **to ~ up and
down** pasearse de un lado a otro; **to
keep ~ with** llevar el mismo paso que;
pacemaker n (Med) regulador m
cardíaco, marcapasos m inv; (Sport: also:
pacesetter) liebre f
Pacific [pəˈsɪfɪk] n: **the ~ (Ocean)** el
(Océano) Pacífico
pacifier [ˈpæsɪfaɪə*] (us) n (dummy)
chupete m
pack [pæk] n (packet) paquete m;
(of hounds) jauría; (of people) manada,
bando; (of cards) baraja; (bundle) fardo;
(us: of cigarettes) paquete m; (back pack)
mochila ⊳ vt (fill) llenar; (in suitcase etc)
meter, poner; (cram) llenar, atestar; **to
~ (one's bags)** hacerse la maleta; **to
~ sb off** despachar a algn; **pack in** vi
(watch, car) estropearse ⊳ vt (inf) dejar;
pack it in! ¡para!, ¡basta ya!; **pack up** vi
(inf: machine) estropearse; (person) irse

▷vt (belongings, clothes) recoger; (goods, presents) empaquetar, envolver

package ['pækɪdʒ] n paquete m; (bulky) bulto; (also: ~ **deal**) acuerdo global; **package holiday** n vacaciones fpl organizadas; **package tour** n viaje m organizado

packaging ['pækɪdʒɪŋ] n envase m

packed [pækt] adj abarrotado; **packed lunch** n almuerzo m frío

packet ['pækɪt] n paquete m

packing ['pækɪŋ] n embalaje m

pact [pækt] n pacto m

pad [pæd] n (of paper) bloc m; (cushion) cojinete m; (inf: home) casa ▷vt rellenar; **padded** adj (jacket) acolchado; (bra) reforzado

paddle ['pædl] n (oar) canalete m; (us: for table tennis) paleta f ▷vt impulsar con canalete ▷vi (with feet) chapotear; **paddling pool** (BRIT) n estanque m de juegos

paddock ['pædək] n corral m

padlock ['pædlɔk] n candado

paedophile ['piːdəʊfaɪl] (us **pedophile**) adj de pedófilos ▷n pedófilo/a

page [peɪdʒ] n (of book) página; (of newspaper) botones m; (also: ~ **boy**) paje m ▷vt (in hotel etc) llamar por altavoz a

pager ['peɪdʒə*] n (Tel) busca m

paid [peɪd] pt, pp of **pay** ▷adj (work) remunerado; (holiday) pagado; (official etc) a sueldo; **to put ~ to** (BRIT) acabar con

pain [peɪn] n dolor m; **to be in ~** sufrir; **to take ~s to do sth** tomarse grandes molestias en hacer algo; **painful** adj doloroso; (difficult) penoso; (disagreeable) desagradable; **painkiller** n analgésico; **painstaking** ['peɪnzteɪkɪŋ] adj (person) concienzudo, esmerado

paint [peɪnt] n pintura ▷vt pintar; **to ~ the door blue** pintar la puerta de azul; **paintbrush** n (of artist) pincel m; (of decorator) brocha; **painter** n pintor(a) m/f; **painting** n pintura

pair [peə*] n (of shoes, gloves etc) par m; (of people) pareja; **a ~ of scissors** unas tijeras; **a ~ of trousers** unos pantalones, un pantalón

pajamas [pə'dʒɑːməz] (us) npl pijama m

Pakistan [pɑːkɪ'stɑːn] n Paquistán m; **Pakistani** adj, n paquistaní mf

pal [pæl] (inf) n compinche mf, compañero/a

palace ['pæləs] n palacio

pale [peɪl] adj (gen) pálido; (colour) claro ▷n; **to be beyond the ~** pasarse de la raya

Palestine ['pælɪstaɪn] n Palestina; **Palestinian** [-'tɪnɪən] adj, n palestino/a m/f

palm [pɑːm] n (Anat) palma; (also: ~ **tree**) palmera, palma ▷vt; **to ~ sth off on sb** (inf) encajar algo a algn

pamper ['pæmpə*] vt mimar

pamphlet ['pæmflət] n folleto

pan [pæn] n (also: **sauce~**) cacerola, cazuela, olla; (also: **frying ~**) sartén f

pancake ['pænkeɪk] n crepe f

panda ['pændə] n panda m

pane [peɪn] n cristal m

panel ['pænl] n (of wood etc) panel m; (Radio, TV) panel m de invitados

panhandler ['pænhændlə*] (us) n (inf) mendigo/a

panic ['pænɪk] n terror m pánico ▷vi dejarse llevar por el pánico

panorama [pænə'rɑːmə] n panorama m

pansy ['pænzɪ] n (Bot) pensamiento; (inf, pej) maricón m

pant [pænt] vi jadear

panther ['pænθə*] n pantera

panties ['pæntɪz] npl bragas fpl, pantis mpl

pantomime ['pæntəmaɪm] (BRIT) n revista musical representada en Navidad, basada en cuentos de hadas

● **PANTOMIME**

● En época navideña se ponen en

escena en los teatros británicos las llamadas **pantomimes**, que son versiones libres de cuentos tradicionales como Aladino o El gato con botas. En ella nunca faltan personajes como la dama ("dame"), que siempre interpreta un actor, el protagonista joven ("principal boy"), normalmente interpretado por una actriz, y el malvado ("villain"). Es un espectáculo familiar en el que se anima al público a participar y aunque va dirigido principalmente a los niños, cuenta con grandes dosis de humor para adultos.

pants [pænts] n (BRIT: underwear: woman's) bragas fpl; (: man's) calzoncillos mpl; (US: trousers) pantalones mpl

paper ['peɪpə*] n papel m; (also: **news~**) periódico, diario; (academic essay) ensayo; (exam) examen m ▷ adj de papel ▷ vt empapelar, tapizar (MEX); **papers** npl (also: **identity ~s**) papeles mpl, documentos mpl; **paperback** n libro en rústica; **paper bag** n bolsa de papel; **paper clip** n clip m; **paper shop** (BRIT) n tienda de periódicos; **paperwork** n trabajo administrativo

paprika ['pæprɪkə] n pimentón m

par [pɑː*] n par f; (Golf) par m; **to be on a ~ with** estar a la par con

paracetamol [pærə'siːtəmɒl] (BRIT) n paracetamol m

parachute ['pærəʃuːt] n paracaídas m inv

parade [pə'reɪd] n desfile m ▷ vt (show) hacer alarde de ▷ vi desfilar; (Mil) pasar revista

paradise ['pærədaɪs] n paraíso

paradox ['pærədɒks] n paradoja

paraffin ['pærəfɪn] (BRIT) n (also: ~ oil) parafina

paragraph ['pærəɡrɑːf] n párrafo

parallel ['pærəlel] adj en paralelo;

(fig) semejante ▷ n (line) paralela; (fig, Geo) paralelo

paralysed ['pærəlaɪzd] adj paralizado

paralysis [pə'rælɪsɪs] n parálisis f inv

paramedic [pærə'medɪk] n auxiliar m/f sanitario/a

paranoid ['pærənɔɪd] adj (person, feeling) paranoico/a

parasite ['pærəsaɪt] n parásito/a

parcel ['pɑːsl] n paquete m ▷ vt (also: ~ **up**) empaquetar, embalar

pardon ['pɑːdn] n (Law) indulto ▷ vt perdonar; **~ me!, I beg your ~!** (I'm sorry!) ¡perdone usted!; **(I beg your) ~, ~ me?** (US: what did you say?) ¿cómo?

parent ['peərənt] n (mother) madre f; (father) padre m; **parents** npl padres mpl

> Be careful not to translate **parent** by the Spanish word *pariente*.

parental [pə'rentl] adj paternal/maternal

Paris ['pærɪs] n París

parish ['pærɪʃ] n parroquia

Parisian [pə'rɪzɪən] adj, n parisiense mf

park [pɑːk] n parque m ▷ vt aparcar, estacionar ▷ vi aparcar, estacionarse

parking ['pɑːkɪŋ] n aparcamiento, estacionamiento; **"no ~"** "prohibido estacionarse"; **parking lot** (US) n parking m; **parking meter** n parquímetro; **parking ticket** n multa de aparcamiento

parkway ['pɑːkweɪ] (US) n alameda

parliament ['pɑːləmənt] n parlamento; (Spanish) Cortes fpl; **parliamentary** [-'mentərɪ] adj parlamentario

El Parlamento británico (**Parliament**) tiene como sede el palacio de Westminster, también llamado "Houses of Parliament" y consta de dos cámaras. La Cámara de los Comunes ("House of Commons"), compuesta por 650 diputados (**Members of Parliament**) elegidos por sufragio universal en su respectiva circunscripción electoral (constituency), se reúne 175 días al año y sus sesiones son moderadas por el Presidente de la Cámara (**Speaker**). La cámara alta es la Cámara de los Lores ("House of Lords") y está formada por miembros que han sido nombrados por el monarca o que han heredado su escaño. Su poder es limitado, aunque actúa como tribunal supremo de apelación, excepto en Escocia.

Parmesan [pɑːmɪˈzæn] n (also: ~ **cheese**) queso parmesano

parole [pəˈrəʊl] n: **on ~** libre bajo palabra

parrot [ˈpærət] n loro, papagayo

parsley [ˈpɑːslɪ] n perejil m

parsnip [ˈpɑːsnɪp] n chirivía

parson [ˈpɑːsn] n cura m

part [pɑːt] n (gen, Mus) parte f; (bit) trozo; (of machine) pieza; (Theatre etc) papel m; (of serial) entrega; (us: in hair) raya ▷ adv **partly** ▷ vt separar ▷ vi (people) separarse; (crowd) apartarse; **to take ~ in** tomar parte or participar en; **to take sth in good ~** tomar algo en buena parte; **to take sb's ~** defender a algn; **for my ~** por mi parte; **for the most ~** en su mayor parte; **to ~ one's hair** hacerse la raya; **part with** vt fus ceder, entregar; (money) pagar; **part of speech** n parte f de la oración, categoría f gramatical

partial [ˈpɑːʃl] adj parcial; **to be ~ to** ser aficionado a

participant [pɑːˈtɪsɪpənt] n (in competition) concursante mf; (in campaign etc) participante mf

participate [pɑːˈtɪsɪpeɪt] vi: **to ~ in** participar en

particle [ˈpɑːtɪkl] n partícula; (of dust) grano

particular [pɑːˈtɪkjʊləʳ] adj (special) particular; (concrete) concreto; (given) determinado; (fussy) quisquilloso; (demanding) exigente; **in ~** en particular; **particularly** adv (in particular) sobre todo; (difficult, good etc) especialmente; **particulars** npl (information) datos mpl; (details) pormenores mpl

parting [ˈpɑːtɪŋ] n (act) separación f; (farewell) despedida; (BRIT: in hair) raya ▷ adj de despedida

partition [pɑːˈtɪʃən] n (Pol) división f; (wall) tabique m

partly [ˈpɑːtlɪ] adv en parte

partner [ˈpɑːtnəʳ] n (Comm) socio/a; (Sport, at dance) pareja; (spouse) cónyuge mf; (lover) compañero/a; **partnership** n asociación f; (Comm) sociedad f

partridge [ˈpɑːtrɪdʒ] n perdiz f

part-time [ˈpɑːtˈtaɪm] adj, adv a tiempo parcial

party [ˈpɑːtɪ] n (Pol) partido; (celebration) fiesta; (group) grupo; (Law) parte f interesada ▷ cpd (Pol) de partido

pass [pɑːs] vt (time, object) pasar; (place) pasar por; (overtake) rebasar; (exam) aprobar; (approve) aprobar ▷ vi pasar; (Scol) aprobar, ser aprobado ▷ n (permit) permiso; (membership card) carnet m; (in mountains) puerto, desfiladero; (Sport) pase m; (Scol: also: ~ **mark**) **to get a ~** aprobar en; **to ~ sth through sth** pasar algo por algo; **to make a ~ at sb** (inf) hacer proposiciones a algn; **pass away** vi fallecer; **pass by** vi pasar ▷ vt (ignore) pasar por alto; **pass on** vt transmitir; **pass out** vi desmayarse; **pass over** vi, vt omitir, pasar por alto; **pass up** vt (opportunity) renunciar a; **passable** adj (road) transitable; (tolerable) pasable

passage [ˈpæsɪdʒ] n (also: **~way**) pasillo; (act of passing) tránsito; (fare,

in book) pasaje m; (by boat) travesía; (Anat) tubo

passenger ['pæsɪndʒə*] n pasajero/ a, viajero/a

passer-by [pɑːsə'baɪ] n transeúnte mf

passing place n (Aut) apartadero

passion ['pæʃən] n pasión f; **passionate** adj apasionado; **passion fruit** n fruta de la pasión, granadilla

passive ['pæsɪv] adj (gen, also Ling) pasivo

passport ['pɑːspɔːt] n pasaporte m; **passport control** n control m de pasaporte; **passport office** n oficina de pasaportes

password ['pɑːswɜːd] n contraseña

past [pɑːst] prep (in front of) por delante de; (further than) más allá de; (later than) después de ▷ adj pasado; (president etc) antiguo ▷ n (time) pasado; (of person) antecedentes mpl; **he's ~ forty** tiene más de cuarenta años; **ten/quarter ~ eight** las ocho y diez/cuarto; **for the ~ few/3 days** durante los últimos días/últimos 3 días; **to run ~ sb** pasar a algn corriendo

pasta ['pæstə] n pasta

paste [peɪst] n pasta; (glue) engrudo ▷ vt pegar

pastel ['pæstl] adj pastel; (painting) al pastel

pasteurized ['pæstəraɪzd] adj pasteurizado

pastime ['pɑːstaɪm] n pasatiempo

pastor ['pɑːstə*] n pastor m

past participle [-'pɑːtɪsɪpl] n (Ling) participio m (de) pasado or (de) pretérito or pasivo

pastry ['peɪstrɪ] n (dough) pasta; (cake) pastel m

pasture ['pɑːstʃə*] n pasto

pasty¹ ['pæstɪ] n empanada

pasty² ['peɪstɪ] adj (complexion) pálido

pat [pæt] vt dar una palmadita a; (dog etc) acariciar

patch [pætʃ] n (of material, : eye patch) parche m; (mended part) remiendo; (of

land) terreno ▷ vt remendar; **(to go through) a bad ~** (pasar por) una mala racha; **patchy** adj desigual

pâté ['pæteɪ] n paté m

patent ['peɪtnt] n patente f ▷ vt patentar ▷ adj patente, evidente

paternal [pə'tɜːnl] adj paternal; (relation) paterno

paternity leave [pə'tɜːnɪtɪ-] n permiso m por paternidad, licencia por paternidad

path [pɑːθ] n camino, sendero; (trail, track) pista; (of missile) trayectoria

pathetic [pə'θetɪk] adj patético, lastimoso; (very bad) malísimo

pathway ['pɑːθweɪ] n sendero, vereda

patience ['peɪʃns] n paciencia; (BRIT Cards) solitario

patient ['peɪʃnt] n paciente mf ▷ adj paciente, sufrido

patio ['pætɪəu] n patio

patriotic [pætrɪ'ɔtɪk] adj patriótico

patrol [pə'trəul] n patrulla ▷ vt patrullar por; **patrol car** n coche m patrulla

patron ['peɪtrən] n (in shop) cliente mf; (of charity) patrocinador/a m/f; **~ of the arts** mecenas m

patronizing ['pætrənaɪzɪŋ] adj condescendiente

pattern ['pætən] n (Sewing) patrón m; (design) dibujo; **patterned** adj (material) estampado

pause [pɔːz] n pausa ▷ vi hacer una pausa

pave [peɪv] vt pavimentar; **to ~ the way for** preparar el terreno para

pavement ['peɪvmənt] n (BRIT) acera, banqueta (MEX), andén m (CAM), vereda (SC)

pavilion [pə'vɪlɪən] n (Sport) caseta

paving ['peɪvɪŋ] n pavimento, enlosado

paw [pɔː] n pata

pawn [pɔːn] n (Chess) peón m; (fig) instrumento ▷ vt empeñar; **pawn broker** n prestamista mf

pay [peɪ] (pt, pp **paid**) n (wage etc)
sueldo, salario ▷ vt pagar ▷ vi (be
profitable) rendir; **to ~ attention
(to)** prestar atención (a); **to ~ sb a
visit** hacer una visita a algn; **to ~
one's respects to sb** presentar sus
respetos a algn; **pay back** vt (money)
reembolsar; (person) pagar; **pay for** vt
fus pagar; **pay in** vt ingresar; **pay off**
vt saldar ▷ vi (scheme, decision) dar
resultado; **pay out** vt (money) gastar,
desembolsar; **pay up** vt pagar (de
mala gana); **payable** adj: **payable to**
pagadero a; **pay day** n día m de paga;
pay envelope (us) n = **pay packet**;
payment n pago; **monthly payment**
mensualidad f; **payout** n pago; (in
competition) premio en metálico; **pay
packet** (BRIT) n sobre m (de paga); **pay
phone** n teléfono público; **payroll** n
nómina; **pay slip** n recibo de sueldo;
pay television n televisión f de pago

PC n abbr = **personal computer**; (BRIT)
(= police constable) policía mf ▷ adv abbr
= **politically correct**

p.c. abbr = **per cent**

PDA n abbr (= personal digital assistant)
agenda electrónica

PE n abbr (= physical education) ed. física

pea [pi:] n guisante m (SP), arveja
(LAM), chícharo (MEX, CAM)

peace [pi:s] n paz f; (calm) paz f,
tranquilidad f; **peaceful** adj (gentle)
pacífico; (calm) tranquilo, sosegado

peach [pi:tʃ] n melocotón m (SP),
durazno (LAM)

peacock ['pi:kɔk] n pavo real

peak [pi:k] n (of mountain) cumbre
f, cima; (of cap) visera f; (fig) cumbre f;
peak hours npl horas fpl punta

peanut ['pi:nʌt] n cacahuete m
(SP), maní m (LAM), cacahuate m
(MEX); **peanut butter** n manteca de
cacahuete o maní

pear [peə*] n pera

pearl [pə:l] n perla

peasant ['peznt] n campesino/a

peat [pi:t] n turba

pebble ['pebl] n guijarro

peck [pek] vt (also: **~ at**) picotear
▷ n picotazo; (kiss) besito; **peckish**
(BRIT: inf) adj: **I feel peckish** tengo
ganas de picar algo

peculiar [pɪ'kju:lɪə*] adj (odd)
extraño, raro; (typical) propio,
característico; **~ to** propio de

pedal ['pedl] n pedal m ▷ vi pedalear

pedalo ['pedələu] n patín m a pedal

pedestal ['pedəstl] n pedestal m

pedestrian [pɪ'destrɪən] n peatón/
ona m/f ▷ adj pedestre; **pedestrian
crossing** (BRIT) n paso de peatones;
pedestrianized adj: **a pedestrianized
street** una calle peatonal; **pedestrian
precinct** (us **pedestrian zone**) n zona
peatonal

pedigree ['pedɪgri:] n genealogía; (of
animal) raza, pedigrí m ▷ cpd (animal)
de raza, de casta

pedophile ['pi:dəufaɪl] (us) n =
paedophile

pee [pi:] (inf) vi mear

peek [pi:k] vi mirar a hurtadillas

peel [pi:l] n piel f; (of orange, lemon)
cáscara; (: removed) peladuras fpl ▷ vt
pelar ▷ vi (paint etc) desconcharse;
(wallpaper) despegarse, desprenderse;
(skin) pelar

peep [pi:p] n (BRIT: look) mirada
furtiva; (sound) pío ▷ vi (BRIT: look)
mirar furtivamente

peer [pɪə*] vi: **to ~ at** escudriñar
▷ n (noble) par m; (equal) igual m;
(contemporary) contemporáneo m

peg [peg] n (for coat etc) gancho,
colgadero; (BRIT: also: **clothes ~**) pinza

pelican ['pelɪkən] n pelícano;
pelican crossing (BRIT) n (Aut) paso de
peatones señalizado

pelt [pelt] vt: **~ sb with sth** arrojarle
algo a algn ▷ vi (rain) llover a cántaros;
(inf: run) correr ▷ n piel f

pelvis ['pelvɪs] n pelvis f

pen [pen] n (fountain pen) pluma;
(ballpoint pen) bolígrafo; (for sheep)
redil m

Filipinas

philosopher [fɪ'lɔsəfə*] n filósofo/a

philosophical [fɪlə'sɔfɪkl] adj filosófico

philosophy [fɪ'lɔsəfɪ] n filosofía

phlegm [flɛm] n flema

phobia [ˈfəubjə] n fobia

phone [fəun] n teléfono, llamar por teléfono; **to be on the ~** tener teléfono; (be calling) estar hablando por teléfono; **phone back** vt, vi volver a llamar; **phone up** vt, vi llamar por teléfono; **phone book** n guía telefónica; **phone booth** n cabina telefónica; **phone box** (BRIT) n = **phone booth**; **phone call** n llamada (telefónica); **phonecard** n tarjeta; **phone number** n número de teléfono

phonetics [fəˈnɛtɪks] n fonética

phoney [ˈfəunɪ] adj falso

photo [ˈfəutəu] n foto f; **photo album** n álbum m de fotos; **photocopier** n fotocopiadora; **photocopy** n fotocopia ▷ vt fotocopiar

photograph [ˈfəutəɡrɑːf] n fotografía ▷ vt fotografiar; **photographer** [fəˈtɔɡrəfə*] n fotógrafo; **photography** [fəˈtɔɡrəfɪ] n fotografía

phrase [freɪz] n frase f ▷ vt expresar; **phrase book** n libro de frases

physical [ˈfɪzɪkl] adj físico; **physical education** n educación f física; **physically** adv físicamente

physician [fɪˈzɪʃən] n médico,a

physicist [ˈfɪzɪsɪst] n físico,a

physics [ˈfɪzɪks] n física

physiotherapist [fɪzɪəuˈθɛrəpɪst] n fisioterapeuta

physiotherapy [fɪzɪəuˈθɛrəpɪ] n fisioterapia

physique [fɪˈziːk] n físico

pianist [ˈpiːənɪst] n pianista mf

piano [pɪˈænəu] n piano

pick [pɪk] n (tool: also: **-axe**) pico, piqueta ▷ vt (select) elegir, escoger; (gather) coger (SP), recoger; (remove, take out) sacar, quitar; (lock) abrir con

ganzúa; **take your ~** escoja lo que quiera; **the ~ of** lo mejor de; **to ~ one's nose/teeth** hurgarse las narices/ limpiarse los dientes; **to ~ a quarrel with sb** meterse con algn; **pick on** vt fus (person) meterse con; **pick out** vt escoger; (distinguish) identificar; **pick up** vi (improve: sales) ir mejor; (: patient) reponerse; (Finance) recobrarse ▷ vt recoger; (learn) aprender; (Police: arrest) detener; (person: for sex) ligar; (Radio) captar; **to pick up speed** acelerarse; **to pick o.s. up** levantarse

pickle [ˈpɪkl] n (also: **~s**: as condiment) escabeche m; (fig: mess) apuro ▷ vt encurtir

pickpocket [ˈpɪkpɔkɪt] n carterista mf

pick-up [ˈpɪkʌp] n (also: **~ truck**) furgoneta, camioneta

picnic [ˈpɪknɪk] n merienda ▷ vi de merienda; **picnic area** n zona de picnic; (Aut) área de descanso

picture [ˈpɪktʃə*] n cuadro; (painting) pintura; (photograph) fotografía; (TV) imagen f; (film) película, film; (fig: description) descripción f; (: situation) situación f ▷ vt (imagine) imaginar; **pictures** npl: **the ~s** (BRIT) el cine; **picture frame** n marco; **picture messaging** n (envío de) mensajes con imágenes

picturesque [pɪktʃəˈrɛsk] adj pintoresco

pie [paɪ] n pastel m; (open) tarta; (small: of meat) empanada

piece [piːs] n pedazo, trozo; (of cake) trozo; (item) pieza; **a ~ of clothing/ furniture/advice** una prenda (de vestir)/un mueble/un consejo ▷ vt: **to ~ together** juntar; (Tech) armar; **to take to ~s** desmontar

pie chart n gráfico de sectores o tarta

pier [pɪə*] n muelle m, embarcadero

pierce [pɪəs] vt perforar; **pierced** adj: **I've got pierced ears** tengo los agujeros hechos en las orejas

pig [pɪɡ] n cerdo, chancho (LAM);

(pej: unkind person) asqueroso; *(: greedy person)* glotón/ona *m/f*

pigeon ['pɪdʒən] *n* paloma; *(as food)* pichón *m*

piggy bank ['pɪgɪ-] *n* hucha *(en forma de cerdito)*

pigsty ['pɪgstaɪ] *n* pocilga

pigtail *n (girl's)* trenza

pike [paɪk] *n (fish)* lucio

pilchard ['pɪltʃəd] *n* sardina

pile [paɪl] *n* montón *m*; *(of carpet, cloth)* pelo; **pile up** *vi +adv (accumulate: work)* amontonarse, acumularse *vt +adv (put in a heap: books, clothes)* apilar, amontonar; *(accumulate)* acumular; **piles** *npl (Med)* almorranas *fpl*, hemorroides *mpl*; **pile-up** *n (Aut)* accidente *m* múltiple

pilgrimage ['pɪlgrɪmɪdʒ] *n* peregrinación *f*, romería

pill [pɪl] *n* píldora; **the ~** la píldora

pillar ['pɪlə*] *n* pilar *m*

pillow ['pɪləu] *n* almohada; **pillowcase** *n* funda

pilot ['paɪlət] *n* piloto *cpd (scheme etc)* piloto *vt* pilotar; **pilot light** *n* piloto

pimple ['pɪmpl] *n* grano

PIN *n abbr (= personal identification number)* número personal

pin [pɪn] *n* alfiler *m* *vt* prender *(con alfiler)*; **~s and needles** hormigueo; **to ~ sb down** *(fig)* hacer que algn concrete; **to ~ sth on sb** *(fig)* colgarle a algn el sambenito de algo

pinafore ['pɪnəfɔ:*] *n* delantal *m*

pinch [pɪntʃ] *n (of salt etc)* pizca *vt* pellizcar; *(inf: steal)* birlar; **at a ~** en caso de apuro

pine [paɪn] *n (also: ~ tree)* pino *vi:* **to ~** *vi* por suspirar por

pineapple ['paɪnæpl] *n* piña, ananás *m*

ping [pɪŋ] *n (noise)* sonido agudo; **ping-pong®** *n* pingpong® *m*

pink [pɪŋk] *adj* rosado, *(color de)* rosa *n (colour)* rosa; *(Bot)* clavel *m*, clavellina

pinpoint ['pɪnpɔɪnt] *vt* precisar

pint [paɪnt] *n* pinta *(BRIT = 568cc, US = 473cc)*; *(BRIT: inf: of beer)* pinta de cerveza *jarra (SP)*

pioneer [paɪə'nɪə*] *n* pionero/a

pious ['paɪəs] *adj* piadoso, devoto

pip [pɪp] *n (seed)* pepita; **the ~s** *(BRIT)* la señal

pipe [paɪp] *n* tubo, caño; *(for smoking)* pipa *vt* conducir en cañerías; **pipeline** *n (for oil)* oleoducto; *(for gas)* gasoducto; **piper** *n* gaitero/a

pirate ['paɪərət] *n* pirata *mf* *vt (cassette, book)* piratear

Pisces ['paɪsi:z] *n* Piscis *m*

piss [pɪs] *(infl)* *vi* mear; **pissed** *(infl) adj (drunk)* borracho

pistol ['pɪstl] *n* pistola

piston ['pɪstən] *n* pistón *m*, émbolo

pit [pɪt] *n* hoyo; *(also: coal ~)* mina; *(in garage)* foso de inspección; *(also: orchestra~)* platea *vt:* **to ~ one's wits against sb** medir fuerzas con algn

pitch [pɪtʃ] *n (Mus)* tono; *(BRIT Sport)* campo, terreno; *(fig)* punto; *(tar)* brea *vt (throw)* arrojar, lanzar *vi (fall)* caer(se); **to ~ a tent** montar una tienda *(de campaña)*; **pitch-black** *adj* negro como boca de lobo

pitfall ['pɪtfɔ:l] *n* riesgo

pith [pɪθ] *n (of orange)* médula

pitiful ['pɪtɪful] *adj (touching)* lastimoso, conmovedor/a

pity ['pɪtɪ] *n* compasión *f*, piedad *f* *vt* compadecer(se de); **what a ~!** ¡qué pena!

pizza ['pi:tsə] *n* pizza

placard ['plækɑ:d] *n* letrero; *(in march etc)* pancarta

place [pleɪs] *n* lugar *m*, sitio; *(seat)* plaza, asiento; *(post)* puesto; *(home):* **at/to his ~** en/a su casa; *(role: in society etc)* papel *m* *vt (object)* poner, colocar; *(identify)* reconocer; **to take ~** tener lugar; **to be ~d** *(in race, exam)* colocarse; **out of ~** *(not suitable)* fuera de lugar; **in the first ~** en primer lugar; **to change ~s with sb** cambiar de sitio con algn; **~ of birth** lugar m de nacimiento; **place mat** n (wooden etc) salvamanteles m inv; (linen etc) mantel m individual; **placement** n (positioning) colocación f; (at work) emplazamiento f

placid ['plæsɪd] adj apacible

plague [pleɪg] n plaga; (Med) peste f ▷ vt (fig) acosar, atormentar

plaice [pleɪs] n inv platija

plain [pleɪn] adj (unpatterned) liso; (clear) claro, evidente; (simple) sencillo; (not handsome) poco atractivo ▷ adv claramente ▷ n llano, llanura; **plain chocolate** n chocolate m amargo; **plainly** adv claramente

plaintiff ['pleɪntɪf] n demandante mf

plait [plæt] n trenza

plan [plæn] n (drawing) plano; (scheme) plan m, proyecto ▷ vt proyectar, planificar ▷ vi hacer proyectos; **to ~ to do** pensar hacer

plane [pleɪn] n (Aviat) avión m; (Math, fig) plano; (also: **~ tree**) plátano; (tool) cepillo

planet ['plænɪt] n planeta m

plank [plæŋk] n tabla

planning ['plænɪŋ] n planificación f; **family ~** planificación familiar

plant [plɑːnt] n planta; (machinery) maquinaria; (factory) fábrica ▷ vt plantar; (field: seed/bomb) colocar

plantation [plæn'teɪʃən] n plantación f; (estate) hacienda

plaque [plæk] n placa

plaster ['plɑːstə*] n (for walls) yeso; (also: **~ of Paris**) yeso mate, escayola (sp); (BRIT: also: **sticking ~**) tirita (sp), curita (LAM) ▷ vt enyesar; (cover): **to ~ with** llenar o cubrir de; **plaster cast** n (Med) escayola; (model, statue) vaciado m de yeso

plastic ['plæstɪk] n plástico ▷ adj de plástico; **plastic bag** n bolsa de plástico; **plastic surgery** n cirujía plástica

plate [pleɪt] n (dish) plato; (metal, in book) lámina; (dental plate) placa de

dentadura postiza

plateau ['plætəʊ] (pl **~s** or **~x**) n meseta, altiplanicie f

platform ['plætfɔːm] n (Rail) andén m; (stage, BRIT: on bus) plataforma; (at meeting) tribuna; (Pol) programa m (electoral)

platinum ['plætɪnəm], adj, n platino

platoon [plə'tuːn] n pelotón m

platter ['plætə*] n fuente f

plausible ['plɔːzɪbl] adj verosímil; (person) convincente

play [pleɪ] n (Theatre) obra, comedia ▷ vt (game) jugar; (compete against) jugar contra; (instrument) tocar; (part: in play etc) hacer el papel de; (tape, record) poner ▷ vi jugar; (band) tocar; (tape, record) sonar; **to ~ safe** ir a lo seguro; **play back** vt (tape) poner; **play up** vi (cause trouble to) dar guerra; **player** n jugador/a m/f; (Theatre) actor(actriz) m/f; (Mus) músico/a; **playful** adj juguetón/ona; **playground** n (in school) patio de recreo; (in park) parque m infantil; **playgroup** n jardín m de niños; **playing card** n naipe m, carta; **playing field** n campo de deportes; **playschool** n = **playgroup**; **playtime** n (Scol) recreo; **playwright** n dramaturgo/a

plc abbr (= public limited company) ≈ S.A.

plea [pliː] n súplica, petición f; (Law) alegato, defensa

plead [pliːd] vt (Law): **to ~ sb's case** defender a algn; (give as excuse) poner como pretexto ▷ vi (Law) declararse; (beg): **to ~ with sb** suplicar o rogar a algn

pleasant ['plɛznt] adj agradable

please [pliːz] excl ¡por favor! ▷ vt (give pleasure to) dar gusto a, agradar ▷ vi (think fit): **do as you ~** haz lo que quieras; **~ yourself!** (inf) ¡haz lo que quieras!, ¡como quieras!; **pleased** adj (happy) alegre, contento; **pleased (with)** satisfecho (de); **pleased to meet you** ¡encantado!, ¡tanto gusto!

pleasure ['plɛʒə*] n placer m, gusto;

"it's a ~" el gusto es mío"

pleat [pli:t] n pliegue m

pledge [plɛdʒ] n (promise) promesa, voto ▷ vt prometer

plentiful ['plɛntɪful] adj copioso, abundante

plenty ['plɛntɪ] n: **~ of** mucho(s)/a(s)

pliers ['plaɪəz] npl alicates mpl, tenazas fpl

plight [plaɪt] n situación f difícil

plod [plɔd] vi caminar con paso pesado; (fig) trabajar laboriosamente

plonk [plɔŋk] (inf) n (BRIT: wine) vino peleón ▷ vt: **to ~ sth down** dejar caer algo

plot [plɔt] n (scheme) complot m, conjura; (of story, play) argumento; (of land) terreno ▷ vt (mark out) trazar; (conspire) tramar, urdir ▷ vi conspirar

plough (us **plow**) [plau] n arado ▷ vt (earth) arar; **to ~ money into** invertir dinero en; **ploughman's**(BRIT) n almuerzo de pub a base de pan, queso y encurtidos

plow [plau] (us) = **plough**

ploy [plɔɪ] n truco, estratagema

pluck [plʌk] vt (fruit) coger (SP), recoger (LAM); (musical instrument) puntear; (bird) desplumar; (eyebrows) depilar; **to ~ up courage** hacer de tripas corazón

plug [plʌg] n tapón m; (Elec) enchufe m, clavija; (Aut: also: **spark(ing) ~**) bujía ▷ vt (hole) tapar; (inf: advertise) dar publicidad a; **plug in** vt (Elec) enchufar; **plughole** n desagüe m

plum [plʌm] n (fruit) ciruela

plumber ['plʌmə*] n fontanero/a (SP, CAM), plomero/a (LAM)

plumbing ['plʌmɪŋ] n (trade) fontanería, plomería; (piping) cañería

plummet ['plʌmɪt] vi: **to ~ (down)** caer a plomo

plump [plʌmp] adj rechoncho, rollizo ▷ vi: **to ~ for** (inf: choose) optar por

plunge [plʌndʒ] n zambullida ▷ vt sumergir, hundir ▷ vi (fall) caer; (dive) saltar; (person) arrojarse; **to take the**

~ lanzarse

plural ['pluərəl] adj plural ▷ n plural m

plus [plʌs] n (also: **~ sign**) signo más ▷ prep más, y, además de; **ten/twenty ~** más de diez/veinte

ply [plaɪ] vt (a trade) ejercer ▷ n (ship) ir y venir ▷ n (of wool, rope) cabo; **to ~ sb with drink** insistir en ofrecer a algn muchas copas; **plywood** n madera contrachapada

P.M. n abbr = **Prime Minister**

p.m. adv abbr (= post meridiem) de la tarde or noche

PMS n abbr (= premenstrual syndrome) SPM m

PMT n abbr (= premenstrual tension) SPM m

pneumatic drill [nju:'mætɪk-] n martillo neumático

pneumonia [nju:'məunɪə] n pulmonía

poach [pəutʃ] vt (cook) escalfar; (steal) cazar (or pescar) en vedado ▷ vi cazar (or pescar) en vedado; **poached** adj escalfado

P.O. Box n abbr (= Post Office Box) apdo., aptdo.

pocket ['pɔkɪt] n bolsillo; (fig: small area) bolsa ▷ vt meter en el bolsillo; (steal) embolsar; **to be out of ~** (BRIT) salir perdiendo; **pocketbook**(us) n cartera; **pocket money** n asignación

pod [pɔd] n vaina

podiatrist [pɔ'di:ətrɪst] (us) n pedicuro/a

podium ['pəudɪəm] n podio

poem ['pəuɪm] n poema m

poet ['pəuɪt] n poeta m/f; **poetic** [-'ɛtɪk] adj poético; **poetry** n poesía

poignant ['pɔɪnjənt] adj conmovedor(a)

point [pɔɪnt] n punto; (tip) punta; (purpose) fin m, propósito; (use) utilidad f; (significant part) lo significativo; (moment) momento; (Elec) toma (de corriente); (also: **decimal ~**): **2 ~ 3** (**2.3**) dos coma tres (2,3) ▷ vt señalar; (gun etc): **to ~ sth at sb** apuntar algo a algn ▷ vi: **to ~ at** señalar; **points** npl (Aut) contactos mpl; (Rail) agujas fpl; **to be on the ~ of doing sth** estar a punto de hacer algo; **to make a ~ of** poner empeño en; **to get/miss the ~ come to the ~** ir al meollo; **there's no ~ (in doing)** no tiene sentido (hacer); **point out** vt señalar; **point-blank** adv (say, refuse) sin más hablar; (also: **at point-blank range**) a quemarropa; **pointed** adj (shape) puntiagudo, afilado; (remark) intencionado; **pointer** n (needle) aguja, indicador m; **pointless** adj sin sentido; **point of view** n punto de vista

poison ['pɔɪzn] n veneno ▷ vt envenenar; **poisonous** adj venenoso; (fumes etc) tóxico

poke [pəuk] vt (jab with finger, stick etc) empujar; (put: **to put sth in(to)** introducir algo en; **poke about or around** vi fisgonear; **poke out** vi (stick out) salir

poker ['pəukə*] n atizador m; (Cards) póker m

Poland ['pəulənd] n Polonia

polar ['pəulə*] adj polar; **polar bear** n oso polar

pole [pəul] n palo; (fixed) poste m; (Geo) polo; **pole bean** (us) n = judía verde; **pole vault** n salto con pértiga

police [pə'li:s] n policía ▷ vt vigilar; **police car** n coche-patrulla m; **police constable** (BRIT) n guardia m, policía m; **police force** n cuerpo de policía; **policeman** (irreg) n policía m, guardia m; **police officer** n guardia m, policía m; **police station** n comisaría; **policewoman** (irreg) n mujer f policía

policy ['pɔlɪsɪ] n política; (also: **insurance ~**) póliza

polio ['pəulɪəu] n polio f

polish ['pɔlɪʃ] adj polaco ▷ n (Ling) polaco

polish ['pɔlɪʃ] n (for shoes) betún m; (for floor) cera (de lustrar); (shine) brillo,

lustre m; (fig: refinement) educación f ▷ vt limpiar; (make shiny) pulir, sacar brillo a; **polish off** vt (food) despachar; **polished** adj (fig: person) elegante

polite [pə'laɪt] adj cortés, atento; **politeness** n cortesía

political [pə'lɪtɪkl] adj político; **politically** adv políticamente; **politically correct** políticamente correcto

politician [pɔlɪ'tɪʃən] n político/a

politics ['pɔlɪtɪks] n política

poll [pəul] n (election) votación f; (also: **opinion ~**) sondeo, encuesta ▷ vt (votes) obtener

pollen ['pɔlən] n polen m

polling station ['pəulɪŋ-] n centro electoral

pollute [pə'lu:t] vt contaminar

pollution [pə'lu:ʃən] n polución f, contaminación f del medio ambiente

polo ['pəuləu] n (sport) polo; **polo-neck** adj de cuello vuelto ▷ n (sweater) suéter m de cuello vuelto; **polo shirt** n polo, niqui m

polyester [pɔlɪ'estə*] n poliéster m

polystyrene [pɔlɪ'staɪri:n] n poliestireno

polythene ['pɔlɪθi:n] (BRIT) n politeno; **polythene bag** n bolsa de plástico

pomegranate ['pɔmɪɡrænɪt] n granada

pompous ['pɔmpəs] adj pomposo

pond [pɔnd] n (natural) charca; (artificial) estanque m

ponder ['pɔndə*] vt meditar

pony ['pəunɪ] n poni m; **ponytail** n coleta; **pony trekking** (BRIT) n excursión f a caballo

poodle ['pu:dl] n caniche m

pool [pu:l] n (natural) charca; (also: **swimming ~**) piscina, alberca (MEX), pileta (RPL); (fig: of light etc) charco; (Sport) chapolín m ▷ vt juntar; **pools** npl quinielas fpl

poor [puə*] adj pobre; (bad) de mala

calidad ▷ npl: **the ~** los pobres; **poorly**
adj mal, enfermo ▷ adv mal
pop [pɒp] n (sound) ruido seco; (Mus)
(música) pop m; (inf: father) papá m;
(drink) gaseosa ▷ vt (put quickly) meter
(de prisa) ▷ vi reventar; (cork) saltar;
pop in vi entrar un momento; **pop
out** vi salir un momento; **popcorn** n
palomitas fpl
poplar ['pɒplə*] n álamo
popper ['pɒpə*] (BRIT) n automático
poppy ['pɒpɪ] n amapola
Popsicle® ['pɒpsɪkl] (US) n polo
pop star n estrella del pop
popular ['pɒpjulə*] adj popular;
popularity [pɒpju'lærɪtɪ] n
popularidad f
population [pɒpju'leɪʃən] n
población f
pop-up ['pɒpʌp] (Comput) adj (menu,
window) emergente ▷ n ventana
emergente, (ventana f) pop-up f
porcelain ['pɔ:slɪn] n porcelana
porch [pɔ:tʃ] n pórtico, entrada; (US)
veranda
pore [pɔ:*] n poro ▷ vi: **to ~ over**
engolfarse en
pork [pɔ:k] n carne f de cerdo or
(LAM) chancho; **pork chop** n chuleta
de cerdo; **pork pie** n (BRIT Culin)
empanada de carne de cerdo
porn [pɔ:n] n (inf) porno inv ▷ n
porno; **pornographic** [pɔ:nə'græfɪk]
adj pornográfico; **pornography**
[pɔ:'nɒgrəfɪ] n pornografía
porridge ['pɒrɪdʒ] n gachas fpl de
avena
port [pɔ:t] n puerto; (Naut: left side)
babor m; (wine) vino de Oporto; **~ of
call** puerto de escala
portable ['pɔ:təbl] adj portátil
porter ['pɔ:tə*] n (for luggage)
maletero; (doorkeeper) portero/a,
conserje m/f
portfolio [pɔ:t'fəuliəu] n cartera
portion ['pɔ:ʃən] n porción f; (of food)
ración f
portrait ['pɔ:treɪt] n retrato

portray [pɔ:'treɪ] vt retratar; (actor)
representar
Portugal ['pɔ:tjugl] n Portugal m
Portuguese [pɔ:tju'gi:z] adj
portugués/esa ▷ n inv portugués/esa
m/f; (Ling) portugués m
pose [pəuz] n postura, actitud f ▷ vi
(pretend): **to ~ as** hacerse pasar por ▷ vt
(question) plantear; **to ~ for** posar para
posh [pɒʃ] (inf) adj elegante, de lujo
position [pə'zɪʃən] n posición f;
(job) puesto; (situation) situación f
▷ vt colocar
positive ['pɒzɪtɪv] adj positivo;
(certain) seguro; (definite) definitivo;
positively adv (affirmatively,
enthusiastically) de forma positiva;
(inf: really) absolutamente
possess [pə'zes] vt poseer;
possession [pə'zeʃən] n posesión
f; **possessions** fpl (belongings)
pertenencias fpl; **possessive** adj
posesivo
possibility [pɒsɪ'bɪlɪtɪ] n posibilidad
f
possible ['pɒsɪbl] adj posible; **as big
as ~** lo más grande posible; **possibly**
adv (conceivably); **I cannot possibly
come** me es imposible venir
post [pəust] n (BRIT: system) correos
mpl; (BRIT: letters, delivery) correo;
(job, situation) puesto; (pole) poste
m ▷ vt (BRIT: send by post) echar al
correo; (BRIT: appoint): **to ~ to** enviar a;
postage n porte m, franqueo; **postal**
adj postal, de correos; **postal order** n
giro postal; **postbox**(BRIT) n buzón m;
postcard n tarjeta postal; **postcode**
(BRIT) n código postal
poster ['pəustə*] n cartel m
postgraduate ['pəust'grædjuət] n
posgraduado/a
postman ['pəustmən] (BRIT: irreg) n
cartero
postmark ['pəustmɑ:k] n
matasellos m inv
post-mortem [-'mɔ:təm] n
autopsia

post office n (building) (oficina de) correos m; (organization): **the Post Office** Correos m inv (SP), Dirección f General de Correos (LAM)

postpone [pəsˈpəun] vt aplazar

posture ['postʃə*] n postura, actitud f

postwoman ['pəustwumən] (BRIT: irreg) n cartera

pot [pot] n (for cooking) olla; (teapot) tetera; (coffeepot) cafetera; (for flowers) maceta; (for jam) tarro, pote m; (inf: marijuana) chocolate m ▷ vt (plant) poner en tiesto; **to go to ~** (inf) irse al traste

potato [pəˈteitəu] (pl **~es**) n patata (SP), papa (LAM); **potato peeler** n pelapatatas m inv

potent ['pəutnt] adj potente, poderoso; (drink) fuerte

potential [pəˈtɛnʃl] adj potencial, posible ▷ n potencial m

pothole ['pothəul] n (in road) bache m; (BRIT: underground) gruta

pot plant ['potpla:nt] n planta de interior

potter ['potə*] n alfarero/a ▷ vi: **to ~ around** or **about** (BRIT) hacer trabajitos; **pottery** n cerámica; (factory) alfarería

potty ['poti] n orinal m de niño

pouch [pautʃ] n (Zool) bolsa; (for tobacco) petaca

poultry ['pəultri] n aves fpl de corral; (meat) pollo

pounce [pauns] vi: **to ~ on** precipitarse sobre

pound [paund] n libra (weight = 453g or 16oz; money = 100 pence) ▷ vt (beat) golpear; (crush) machacar ▷ vi (heart) latir; **pound sterling** n libra esterlina

pour [po:*] vt echar; (tea etc) servir ▷ vi correr, fluir; **to ~ sb a drink** servirle a algn una copa; **pour in** vi (people) entrar en tropel; **pour out** vi salir en tropel ▷ vt (drink) echar, servir; (fig): **to pour out one's feelings** desahogarse; **pouring** adj: **pouring rain** lluvia torrencial

pout [paut] vi hacer pucheros

poverty ['povəti] n pobreza, miseria

powder ['paudə*] n polvo; (also: **face ~**) polvos mpl ▷ vt (colognise): **to ~ one's face** empolvarse la cara; **powdered milk** n leche f en polvo

power ['pauə*] n poder m; (strength) fuerza; (nation, Tech) potencia; (drive) empuje m; (Elec) fuerza, energía ▷ vt impulsar; **to be in ~** (Pol) estar en el poder; **power cut** n apagón m; **power failure** n = **power cut**; **powerful** adj poderoso; (engine) potente; (speech etc) convincente; **powerless** adj: **powerless (to do)** incapaz (de hacer); **power point** (BRIT) n enchufe m; **power station** n central f eléctrica

p.p. abbr (= per procurationem): **p.p. J. Smith** p.p. (por poder de) J. Smith; (= pages) págs

PR n abbr = **public relations**

practical ['præktikl] adj práctico; **practical joke** n broma pesada; **practically** adv (almost) casi

practice ['præktis] n (habit) costumbre f; (exercise) práctica, ejercicio; (training) adiestramiento; (Med: of profession) práctica, ejercicio; (Med, Law: business) consulta ▷ vt, vi (US) = **practise**; **in ~** (in reality) en la práctica; **out of ~** desentrenado

practise ['præktis] (US **practice**) vt (carry out) practicar; (profession) ejercer; (train at) practicar ▷ vi ejercer; (train) practicar; **practising** adj (Christian etc) practicante; (lawyer) en ejercicio

practitioner [præk'tiʃənə*] n (Med) médico/a

pragmatic [præg'mætik] adj pragmático/a

prairie ['prɛəri] n pampa

praise [preiz] n alabanza(s) f(pl), elogio(s) m(pl) ▷ vt alabar, elogiar

pram [præm] (BRIT) n cochecito de niño

prank [præŋk] n travesura

prawn [prɔːn] n gamba; prawn

cocktail n cóctel m de gambas

pray [preɪ] vi rezar; **prayer** [prɛə*] n oración f, rezo; (entreaty) ruego, súplica

preach [pri:tʃ] vi predicar; **preacher** n predicador(a) m/f

precarious [prɪˈkɛərɪəs] adj precario

precaution [prɪˈkɔ:ʃən] n precaución f

precede [prɪˈsi:d] vt, vi preceder; **precedent** [ˈpresɪdənt] n precedente m; **preceding** [prɪˈsi:dɪŋ] adj anterior

precinct [ˈpri:sɪŋkt] n recinto

precious [ˈprɛʃəs] adj precioso

precise [prɪˈsaɪs] adj preciso, exacto; **precisely** adv precisamente, exactamente

precision [prɪˈsɪʒən] n precisión f

predator [ˈprɛdətə*] n depredador m

predecessor [ˈpri:dɪsɛsə*] n antecesor(a) m/f

predicament [prɪˈdɪkəmənt] n apuro

predict [prɪˈdɪkt] vt pronosticar; **predictable** adj previsible; **prediction** [-ˈdɪkʃən] n predicción f

predominantly [prɪˈdɔmɪnəntlɪ] adv en su mayoría

preface [ˈprefəs] n prefacio

prefect [ˈpri:fɛkt] (BRIT) n (in school) monitor(a) m/f

prefer [prɪˈfə:*] vt preferir; **to ~ doing** or **to do** preferir hacer; **preferable** [ˈprefrəbl] adj preferible; **preferably** [ˈprefrəblɪ] adv de preferencia; **preference** [ˈprefrəns] n preferencia; (priority) prioridad f

prefix [ˈpri:fɪks] n prefijo

pregnancy [ˈprɛgnənsɪ] n (of woman) embarazo; (of animal) preñez f

pregnant [ˈprɛgnənt] adj (woman) embarazada; (animal) preñada

prehistoric [ˈpri:hɪsˈtɔrɪk] adj prehistórico

prejudice [ˈprɛdʒudɪs] n prejuicio; **prejudiced** adj (person) predispuesto

preliminary [prɪˈlɪmɪnərɪ] adj preliminar

prelude [ˈprɛlju:d] n preludio

premature [ˈprɛmətʃuə*] adj prematuro

premier [ˈprɛmɪə*] adj primero, principal ⊳ n (Pol) primer(a) ministro/a

première [ˈprɛmɪɛə*] n estreno

Premier League [ˈprɛmɪə'li:g] n primera división

premises [ˈprɛmɪsɪz] npl (of business etc) local m; **on the ~** en el lugar mismo

premium [ˈpri:mɪəm] n premio; (insurance) prima; **to be at a ~** ser muy solicitado

premonition [prɛməˈnɪʃən] n presentimiento

preoccupied [pri:ˈɔkjupaɪd] adj ensimismado

prepaid [pri:ˈpeɪd] adj porte pagado

preparation [prɛpəˈreɪʃən] n preparación f; **preparations** npl preparativos mpl

preparatory school [prɪˈpærətərɪ-] n escuela preparatoria

prepare [prɪˈpɛə*] vt preparar, disponer; (Culin) preparar ⊳ vi: **to ~ for** (action) prepararse or disponerse para; (event) hacer preparativos para; **~d to** dispuesto a; **~d for** listo para

preposition [prɛpəˈzɪʃən] n preposición f

prep school [prɛp-] n = **preparatory school**

prerequisite [pri:ˈrɛkwɪzɪt] n requisito

preschool [ˈpri:sku:l] adj preescolar

prescribe [prɪˈskraɪb] vt (Med) recetar

prescription [prɪˈskrɪpʃən] n (Med) receta

presence [ˈprɛzns] n presencia; in **sb's ~** en presencia de algn; **~ of mind** aplomo

present [adj, n ˈprɛznt, vb prɪˈzɛnt] (in attendance) presente; (current) actual ⊳ n (gift) regalo; (actuality): **the ~** la actualidad, el presente ⊳ vt (introduce, describe) presentar; (expound) exponer; (give) presentar, dar, ofrecer; (Theatre) representar; **to give sb a ~** regalar algo a algn; **at ~** actualmente; **presentable** [prɪˈzɛntəbl] adj: **to make o.s. presentable** arreglarse; **presentation** [-ˈteɪʃən] n presentación f; (of report etc) exposición f; (formal ceremony) entrega de un regalo; **present-day** adj actual; **presenter** [prɪˈzɛntə*] n (Radio, TV) locutor(a) m/f; **presently** adv (soon) dentro de poco; (now) ahora; **present participle** n participio (de) presente

reservation [rɛzəˈveɪʃən] n conservación f

reservative [prɪˈzəːvətɪv] n conservante m

reserve [prɪˈzəːv] vt (keep safe) preservar, proteger; (maintain) mantener; (food) conservar ▷ n (for game) coto, vedado; (often pl: jam) conserva, confitura

reside [prɪˈzaɪd] vi presidir

resident [ˈprɛzɪdənt] n presidente m/f; **presidential** [-ˈdɛnʃl] adj presidencial

ress [prɛs] n (newspapers): **the P~** la prensa; (printer's) imprenta; (of button) pulsación f ▷ vt empujar; (button etc) apretar; (clothes: iron) planchar; (put pressure on: person) presionar; (insist): **to ~ sth on sb** insistir en que algn acepte algo ▷ vi (squeeze) apretar; (pressurize): **to ~ for** presionar por; **we are ~ed for time/money** estamos apurados de tiempo/dinero; **press conference** n rueda de prensa; **pressing** adj apremiante; **press stud** (BRIT) n botón m de presión; **press-up** (BRIT) n plancha

ressure [ˈprɛʃə*] n presión f; **to put ~ on sb** presionar a algn; **pressure cooker** n olla a presión; **pressure group** n grupo de presión

restige [prɛsˈtiːʒ] n prestigio

restigious [prɛsˈtɪdʒəs] adj prestigioso

resumably [prɪˈzjuːməblɪ] adv es de suponer que, cabe presumir que

presume [prɪˈzjuːm] vt: **to ~ (that)** presumir (que), suponer (que)

pretence [prɪˈtɛns] (US **pretense**) n fingimiento; **under false ~s** con engaños

pretend [prɪˈtɛnd] vt, vi (feign) fingir

> Be careful not to translate **pretend** by the Spanish word **pretender**.

pretense [prɪˈtɛns] (US) n =**pretence**

pretentious [prɪˈtɛnʃəs] adj presumido; (ostentatious) ostentoso, aparatoso

pretext [ˈpriːtɛkst] n pretexto

pretty [ˈprɪtɪ] adj bonito, lindo (LAM) ▷ adv bastante

prevail [prɪˈveɪl] vi (gain mastery) prevalecer; (be current) predominar; **prevailing** adj (dominant) predominante

prevalent [ˈprɛvələnt] adj (widespread) extendido

prevent [prɪˈvɛnt] vt: **to ~ sb from doing sth** impedir a algn hacer algo; **to ~ sth from happening** evitar que ocurra algo; **prevention** [prɪˈvɛnʃən] n prevención f; **preventive** adj preventivo

preview [ˈpriːvjuː] n (of film) preestreno

previous [ˈpriːvɪəs] adj previo, anterior; **previously** adv antes

prey [preɪ] n presa ▷ vi: **to ~ on** (feed on) alimentarse de; **it was ~ing on his mind** le preocupaba, le obsesionaba

price [praɪs] n precio ▷ vt (goods) fijar el precio de; **priceless** adj que no tiene precio; **price list** n tarifa

prick [prɪk] n (sting) picadura ▷ vt pinchar; (hurt) picar; **to ~ up one's ears** aguzar el oído

prickly [ˈprɪklɪ] adj espinoso; (fig: person) enojadizo

pride [praɪd] n orgullo; (pej) soberbia ▷ vt: **to ~ o.s. on** enorgullecerse de

priest [priːst] n sacerdote m

primarily [ˈpraɪmərɪlɪ] adv ante todo

primary [ˈpraɪmərɪ] adj (first in importance) principal ▷ n (US Pol)

elección f primaria; **primary school**
(BRIT) n escuela primaria
prime [praɪm] adj primero, principal;
(excellent) selecto, de primera clase
▷ n: **in the ~ of life** en la flor de la vida
▷ vt (wood: fig) preparar; **~ example**
ejemplo típico; **Prime Minister** n
primer(a) ministro/a
primitive ['prɪmɪtɪv] adj primitivo;
(crude) rudimentario
primrose ['prɪmrəuz] n primavera,
prímula
prince [prɪns] n príncipe m
princess [prɪn'ses] n princesa
principal ['prɪnsɪpl] adj principal,
mayor ▷ n director(a) m/f; **principally**
adv principalmente
principle ['prɪnsɪpl] n principio; **in ~**
en principio; **on ~** por principio
print [prɪnt] n (footprint) huella;
(fingerprint) huella dactilar; (letters)
letra de molde; (fabric) estampado;
(Art) grabado; (Phot) impresión
f ▷ vt imprimir; (cloth) estampar;
(write in capitals) escribir en letras de
molde; **out of ~** agotado; **print out** vt
(Comput) imprimir; **printer** n (person)
impresor/a m/f; (machine) impresora;
printout n (Comput) impresión f
prior ['praɪə*] adj anterior, previo;
(more important) más importante; **~
to** antes de
priority [praɪ'ɔrɪtɪ] n prioridad f; **to
have ~ (over)** tener prioridad (sobre)
prison ['prɪzn] n cárcel f, prisión f
▷ cpd carcelario; **prisoner** n (in prison)
preso/a; (captured person) prisionero/a;
prisoner-of-war n prisionero de
guerra
pristine ['prɪstiːn] adj prístino
privacy ['prɪvəsɪ] n intimidad f
private ['praɪvɪt] adj (personal)
particular; (property, industry, discussion
etc) privado; (person) reservado; (place)
tranquilo ▷ n soldado raso; **"~"** (on
envelope) "confidencial"; (on door)
"prohibido el paso"; **in ~** en privado;
privately adv en privado; (in o.s.)

en secreto; **private property** n
propiedad f privada; **private school** n
colegio particular
privatize ['praɪvɪtaɪz] vt privatizar
privilege ['prɪvɪlɪdʒ] n privilegio;
(prerogative) prerrogativa
prize [praɪz] n premio ▷ adj de
primera clase ▷ vt apreciar, estimar;
prize-giving n distribución f de
premios; **prizewinner** n premiado/a
pro [prəu] n (Sport) profesional mf
▷ prep a favor de; **the ~s and cons** los
pros y los contras
probability [prɔbə'bɪlɪtɪ] n
probabilidad f; **in all ~** con toda
probabilidad
probable ['prɔbəbl] adj probable
probably ['prɔbəblɪ] adv
probablemente
probation [prə'beɪʃən] n: **on ~**
(employee) a prueba; (Law) en libertad
condicional
probe [prəub] n (Med, Space) sonda;
(enquiry) encuesta, investigación f ▷ vt
sondar; (investigate) investigar
problem ['prɔbləm] n problema m
procedure [prə'siːdʒə*] n
procedimiento; (bureaucratic) trámites
mpl
proceed [prə'siːd] vi (do
afterwards): **to ~ to do sth** proceder
a hacer algo; (continue): **to ~ (with)**
continuar o seguir (con); **proceedings**
npl acto(s) pl; (Law) proceso;
proceeds ['prəusiːdz] npl (money)
ganancias fpl, ingresos mpl
process ['prəuses] n proceso ▷ vt
tratar, elaborar
procession [prə'seʃən] n desfile m;
funeral ~ cortejo fúnebre
proclaim [prə'kleɪm] vt (announce)
anunciar
prod [prɔd] vt empujar ▷ n empujón
m
produce [n 'prɔdjuːs, vt prə'djuːs]
n (Agr) productos mpl agrícolas ▷ vt
producir; (play, film, programme)
presentar; **producer** n productor(a)

product ['prɒdʌkt] n producto;
production f; [prə'dʌkʃən] n
producción f; (Theatre) presentación
f; **productive** [prə'dʌktɪv]
adj productivo; **productivity**
[prɒdʌk'tɪvɪtɪ] n productividad f
Prof. [prɒf] abbr (= professor) Prof
profession [prə'feʃən] n profesión
f; **professional** adj profesional ▷ n
profesional mf; (skilled person) perito
professor [prə'fesə*] n (BRIT)
catedrático/a; (US, CANADA) profesor(a)
m/f
profile ['prəufaɪl] n perfil m
profit ['prɒfɪt] n (Comm) ganancia
f ▷ vi: **to ~ by** or **from** aprovechar or sacar
provecho de; **profitable** adj (Econ)
rentable
profound [prə'faund] adj profundo
programme ['prəugræm] (US
program) n programa m ▷ vt
programar; **programmer** (US
programer) n programador(a) m/f;
programming (US **programing**) n
programación f
progress [n 'prəugres, vi prə'gres]
n progreso; (development) desarrollo
▷ vi progresar, avanzar; **in ~** en curso;
progressive [-'gresɪv] adj progresivo;
(person) progresista
prohibit [prə'hɪbɪt] vt prohibir; **to
~ sb from doing sth** prohibir a algn
hacer algo
project [n 'prɒdʒekt, vb
prə'dʒekt] n proyecto ▷ vt
proyectar ▷ vi (stick out) salir,
sobresalir; **projection**
[prə'dʒekʃən] n proyección f;
(overhang) saliente m; **projector**
[prə'dʒektə*] n proyector m
prolific [prə'lɪfɪk] adj prolífico
prolong [prə'lɒŋ] vt prolongar,
extender
prom [prɒm] n abbr = **promenade**
(US: ball) baile m de gala; **the P~s** ver

recuadro

promenade [prɒmə'nɑːd] n (by sea)
paseo marítimo
prominent ['prɒmɪnənt] adj
(standing out) saliente; (important)
eminente, importante
promiscuous [prə'mɪskjuəs] adj
(sexually) promiscuo
promise ['prɒmɪs] n promesa
▷ vt, vi prometer; **promising** adj
prometedor(a)
promote [prə'məut] vt (employee)
ascender; (product, pop star) hacer
propaganda por; (ideas) fomentar;
promotion [-'məuʃən] n (advertising
campaign) campaña f de promoción; (in
rank) ascenso
prompt [prɒmpt] adj rápido ▷ adv: **at
6 o'clock ~** a las seis en punto ▷ n
(Comput) aviso ▷ vt (urge) mover,
incitar; (when talking) instar; (Theatre)
apuntar; **to ~ sb to do sth** instar
a algn a hacer algo; **promptly** adv
rápidamente; (exactly) puntualmente
prone [prəun] adj (lying) postrado; **~
to** propenso a
prong [prɒŋ] n diente m, punta
pronoun ['prəunaun] n pronombre

m
pronounce [prə'nauns] vt
pronunciar
pronunciation [prənʌnsɪ'eɪʃən] n
pronunciación f
proof [pruːf] n prueba ⊳ adj: ~
against a prueba de
prop [prɔp] n apoyo m; (fig) sostén m
accesorios mpl, at(t)rezzo msg; **prop up**
vt (roof, structure) apuntalar; (economy)
respaldar
propaganda [prɔpə'gændə] n
propaganda
propeller [prə'pelə*] n hélice f
proper ['prɔpə*] adj (suited, right)
propio; (exact) justo; (seemly) correcto,
decente; (authentic) verdadero;
(referring to place): **the village ~**
el pueblo mismo; **properly** adv
(adequately) correctamente; (decently)
decentemente; **proper noun** n
nombre m propio
property ['prɔpətɪ] n propiedad f;
(personal) bienes mpl muebles
prophecy ['prɔfɪsɪ] n profecía f
prophet ['prɔfɪt] n profeta m
proportion [prə'pɔːʃən] n
proporción f; (share) parte f;
proportions npl (size) dimensiones fpl;
proportional adj: **proportional (to)**
en proporción (con)
proposal [prə'pəuzl] n (offer of
marriage) oferta f de matrimonio; (plan)
proyecto
propose [prə'pəuz] vt proponer ⊳ vi
declararse; **to ~ to do** tener intención
de hacer
proposition [prɔpə'zɪʃən] n
propuesta
proprietor [prə'praɪətə*] n
propietario/a, dueño/a
prose [prəuz] n prosa
prosecute ['prɔsɪkjuːt] vt (Law)
procesar; **prosecution** [-'kjuːʃən]
n proceso, causa; (accusing
side) acusación f; **prosecutor** n
acusador(a) m/f; (also: **public
prosecutor**) fiscal mf

prospect [n 'prɔspekt, vb
prə'spekt] n (possibility) posibilidad
f; (outlook) perspectiva ⊳ vi: **to ~
for** buscar; **prospects** npl (for work
etc) perspectivas fpl; **prospective**
[prə'spektɪv] adj futuro
prospectus [prə'spektəs] n
prospecto
prosper ['prɔspə*] vi prosperar;
prosperity [-'sperɪtɪ] n prosperidad f;
prosperous adj próspero
prostitute ['prɔstɪtjuːt] n
prostituta; (male) hombre que se dedica a
la prostitución
protect [prə'tekt] vt proteger;
protection [-'tekʃən] n protección f;
protective adj protector(a)
protein ['prəutiːn] n proteína
protest [n 'prəutest, vb prə'test] n
protesta ⊳ vi: **to ~ about** or **at/against**
protestar de/contra ⊳ vt (insist): **to ~
(that)** insistir en (que)
Protestant ['prɔtɪstənt] adj, n
protestante m f
protester [prə'testə*] n
manifestante mf
protractor [prə'træktə*] n (Geom)
transportador m
proud [praud] adj orgulloso; (pej)
soberbio, altanero
prove [pruːv] vt probar; (show)
demostrar ⊳ vi: **to ~ (to be) correct**
resultar correcto; **to ~ o.s.** probar
su valía
proverb ['prɔvɜːb] n refrán m
provide [prə'vaɪd] vt proporcionar,
dar; **to ~ sb with sth** proveer a algn
de algo; **provide for** vt fus (person)
mantener a; (problem etc) tener en
cuenta; **provided conj: provided
(that)** con tal de que, a condición
de que; **providing** [prə'vaɪdɪŋ]
conj: **providing (that)** a condición de
que, con tal de que
province ['prɔvɪns] n provincia; (fig)
esfera; **provincial** [prə'vɪnʃəl] adj
provincial; (pej) provinciano
provision [prə'vɪʒən] n (supplying)

suministro, abastecimiento; (of contract etc) disposición f; **provisions** npl (food) comestibles mpl; **provisional** adj provisional

provocative [prə'vɔkətɪv] adj provocativo

provoke [prə'vəuk] vt (cause) provocar, incitar; (anger) enojar

prowl [praul] vi (also: ~ **about**, ~ **around**) merodear ▷ n: **on the ~** de merodeo

proximity [prɔk'sɪmɪtɪ] n proximidad f

proxy ['prɔksɪ] n: **by ~** por poderes

prudent ['pru:dənt] adj prudente

prune [pru:n] n ciruela pasa ▷ vt podar

pry [praɪ] vi: **to ~ (into)** entrometerse (en)

PS n abbr (= postscript) P.D.

pseudonym ['sju:dənɪm] n seudónimo

PSHE (BRIT: Scol) n abbr (= personal, social and health education) formación social y sanitaria

psychiatric [saɪkɪ'ætrɪk] adj psiquiátrico

psychiatrist [saɪ'kaɪətrɪst] n psiquiatra mf

psychic ['saɪkɪk] adj (also: ~**al**) psíquico

psychoanalysis [saɪkəuə'nælɪsɪs] n psicoanálisis m inv

psychological [saɪkə'lɔdʒɪkl] adj psicológico

psychologist [saɪ'kɔlədʒɪst] n psicólogo/a

psychology [saɪ'kɔlədʒɪ] n psicología

psychotherapy [saɪkəu'θerəpɪ] n psicoterapia

pt abbr = **pint(s); point(s)**

PTO abbr (= please turn over) sigue

pub [pʌb] n abbr (= public house) pub m, bar m

puberty ['pju:bətɪ] n pubertad f

public ['pʌblɪk] adj público ▷ n: **the ~** el público; **in ~** en público; **to make ~** hacer público

publication [pʌblɪ'keɪʃən] n publicación f

public: public company n sociedad f anónima; **public convenience**(BRIT) n aseos mpl públicos (SP); sanitarios mpl (LAM); **public holiday** (día m de) fiesta (SP), (día m) feriado (LAM); **public house**(BRIT) n bar m, pub m

publicity [pʌb'lɪsɪtɪ] n publicidad f

publicize ['pʌblɪsaɪz] vt publicitar

public: public limited company n sociedad f anónima (S.A.); **publicly** adv públicamente, en público; **public opinion** n opinión f pública; **public relations** n relaciones fpl públicas; **public school** n (BRIT) escuela privada; (US) instituto; **public transport** n transporte m público

publish ['pʌblɪʃ] vt publicar; **publisher** n (person) editor(a) m/f; (firm) editorial f; **publishing** n (industry) industria del libro

pub lunch n almuerzo que se sirve en un pub; **to go for a ~** almorzar o comer en un pub

pudding ['pudɪŋ] n pudín m; (BRIT: dessert) postre m; **black ~** morcilla

puddle ['pʌdl] n charco

Puerto Rico [pwe:təu'ri:kəu] n Puerto Rico

puff [pʌf] n soplo; (of smoke, air) bocanada f; (of breathing) resoplido ▷ vt: **to ~ one's pipe** chupar la pipa ▷ vi (pant) jadear; **puff pastry** n hojaldre m

pull [pul] n (tug): **to give sth a ~** dar un tirón a algo ▷ vt tirar de; (press: trigger) apretar; (haul) tirar, arrastrar; (close: curtain) echar ▷ vi tirar; **to ~ to pieces** hacer pedazos; **not to ~ one's punches** no andarse con bromas; **to ~ one's weight** hacer su parte; **to ~ o.s. together** sobreponerse; **to ~ sb's leg** tomar el pelo a algn; **pull apart** vt (break) romper; **pull away** vi (vehicle: move off) salir, arrancar; (draw back) apartarse bruscamente; **pull back** vi (lever etc)

tirar hacia sí; (curtains) descorrer ▷ vi
(refrain) contenerse; (Mil: withdraw)
retirarse; **pull down** vt (building)
derribar; **pull in** vi (car etc) parar
(junto a la acera); (train) llegar a la
estación; **pull off** vt (deal etc) cerrar;
pull out vi (car, train etc) salir ▷ vt
sacar, arrancar; **pull over** vi (Aut)
hacerse a un lado; **pull up** vi (stop)
parar ▷ vt (raise) levantar; (uproot)
arrancar, desarraigar

pulley ['pulɪ] n polea

pullover ['puləʊvə*] n jersey m,
suéter m

pulp [pʌlp] n (of fruit) pulpa

pulpit ['pulpɪt] n púlpito

pulse [pʌls] n (Anat) pulso; (rhythm)
pulsación f; (Bot) legumbre f; **pulses**
n legumbres

puma ['pjuːmə] n puma m

pump [pʌmp] n bomba; (shoe)
zapatilla ▷ vt sacar con una bomba;
pump up vt inflar

pumpkin ['pʌmpkɪn] n calabaza

pun [pʌn] n juego de palabras

punch [pʌntʃ] n (blow) golpe m,
puñetazo; (tool) punzón m; (drink)
ponche m ▷ vt (hit): **to ~ sb/sth** dar
un puñetazo o golpear a algn/algo;
punch-up (BRIT: inf) n riña

punctual ['pʌŋktjuəl] adj puntual

punctuation [pʌŋktjuˈeɪʃən] n
puntuación f

puncture ['pʌŋktʃə*] (BRIT) n
pinchazo ▷ vt pinchar

punish ['pʌnɪʃ] vt castigar;
punishment n castigo

punk [pʌŋk] n (also: ~ **rocker**)
punki m/f; (also: ~ **rock**) música punk;
(us: inf: hoodlum) rufián m

pup [pʌp] n cachorro

pupil ['pjuːpl] n alumno/a; (of eye)
pupila

puppet ['pʌpɪt] n títere m

puppy ['pʌpɪ] n cachorro, perrito

purchase ['pəːtʃɪs] n compra ▷ vt
comprar

pure [pjuə*] adj puro; **purely** adv

puramente

purify ['pjuərɪfaɪ] vt purificar,
depurar

purity ['pjuərɪtɪ] n pureza

purple ['pəːpl] adj purpúreo; morado

purpose ['pəːpəs] n propósito; **on ~** a
propósito, adrede

purr [pəː*] vi ronronear

purse [pəːs] n monedero;
(us: handbag) bolso sf; cartera (LAM),
bolsa (MEX) ▷ vt fruncir

pursue [pəˈsjuː] vt seguir

pursuit [pəˈsjuːt] n (chase) caza;
(occupation) actividad f

pus [pʌs] n pus m

push [puʃ] n empuje m, empujón
m; (of button) presión f; (drive) empuje
m ▷ vt empujar; (button) apretar;
(promote) promover ▷ vi empujar;
(demand): **to ~ for** luchar por; **push in**
vi colarse; **push off** (inf) vi largarse;
push on vi seguir adelante; **push over**
vt (cause to fall) hacer caer, derribar;
(knock over) volcar; **push through** vt
(crowd) abrirse paso a empujones ▷ vt
(measure) despachar; **pushchair** (BRIT)
n sillita de ruedas; **pusher** n (drug
pusher) traficante m/f de drogas; **push-
up** (us) n plancha

pussy(-cat) ['pusɪ-] (inf) n minino
(inf)

put [put] (pt, pp ~) vt (place) poner,
colocar; (put into) meter; (say) expresar;
(a question) hacer; (estimate) estimar;
put aside vt (lay down: book etc) dejar
o poner a un lado; (save) ahorrar; (in
shop) guardar; **put away** vt (store)
guardar; **put back** vt (replace) devolver
a su lugar; (postpone) aplazar; **put by**
vt (money) guardar; **put down** vt (on
ground) poner en el suelo; (animal)
sacrificar; (in writing) anotar; (revolt
etc) sofocar; (attribute): **to put sth
down to** atribuir algo a; **put forward**
vt (ideas) presentar, proponer; **put
in** vt (complaint) presentar; (time)
dedicar; **put off** vt (postpone) aplazar;
(discourage) desanimar; **put on** vt

ponerse; (light etc) encender; (play etc) presentar; (gain): **to put on weight** engordar; (brake) echar; (record, kettle etc) poner; (assume) adoptar; **put out** vt (fire, light) apagar; (rubbish etc) sacar; (cat etc) echar; (one's hand) alargar; (inf: person): **to be put out** alterarse; **put through** vt (Tel) poner; (plan etc) hacer aprobar; **put together** vt unir, reunir; (assemble: furniture) armar, montar; (meal) preparar; **put up** vt (raise) levantar, alzar; (hang) colgar; (build) construir; (increase) aumentar; (accommodate) alojar; **put up with** vt fus aguantar

putt [pʌt] n putt m, golpe m corto; **putting green** n green m; minigolf m

puzzle ['pʌzl] n rompecabezas m inv; (also: **crossword ~**) crucigrama m; (mystery) misterio ▷ vt dejar perplejo, confundir ▷ vi: **to ~ over sth** devanarse los sesos con algo; **puzzled** adj perplejo; **puzzling** adj misterioso, extraño

pyjamas [pɪˈdʒɑːməz] (BRIT) npl pijama m

pylon ['paɪlən] n torre f de conducción eléctrica

pyramid ['pɪrəmɪd] n pirámide f

q

quack [kwæk] n graznido; (pej: doctor) curandero/a

quadruple [kwɒˈdrupl] vt, vi cuadruplicar

quail [kweɪl] n codorniz f ▷ vi: **to ~ at** or **before** amedrentarse ante

quaint [kweɪnt] adj extraño; (picturesque) pintoresco

quake [kweɪk] vi temblar ▷ n abbr = **earthquake**

qualification [kwɒlɪfɪˈkeɪʃən] n (ability) capacidad f; (often pl: diploma etc) título; (reservation) salvedad f

qualified ['kwɒlɪfaɪd] adj capacitado; (professionally) titulado; (limited) limitado

qualify ['kwɒlɪfaɪ] vt (make competent) capacitar; (modify) modificar ▷ vi (in competition): **to ~ (for)** calificarse (para); (pass examination(s): **to ~ (as)** calificarse (de), graduarse (en); (be eligible): **to ~ (for)** reunir los requisitos (para)

quality ['kwɒlɪtɪ] n calidad f; (of person) cualidad f

qualm [kwɑːm] n escrúpulo
quantify ['kwɒntɪfaɪ] vt cuantificar
quantity ['kwɒntɪtɪ] n cantidad f; **in ~** en grandes cantidades
quarantine ['kwɒrəntiːn] n cuarentena
quarrel ['kwɒrl] n riña, pelea ▷ vi reñir, pelearse
quarry ['kwɒrɪ] n cantera
quart [kwɔːt] n ≈ litro
quarter ['kwɔːtə*] n cuarto, cuarta parte f; (us: coin) moneda de 25 centavos; (of year) trimestre m; (district) barrio ▷ vt dividir en cuartos; (Mil: lodge) alojar; **quarters** npl (barracks) cuartel m; (living quarters) alojamiento; **a ~ of an hour** un cuarto de hora; **quarter final** n cuarto de final; **quarterly** adj trimestral ▷ adv cada 3 meses, trimestralmente
quartet(te) [kwɔː'tɛt] n cuarteto
quartz [kwɔːts] n cuarzo
quay [kiː] n (also: **~side**) muelle m
queasy ['kwiːzɪ] adj: **to feel ~** tener náuseas
queen [kwiːn] n reina; (Cards etc) dama
queer [kwɪə*] adj raro, extraño ▷ n (inf: highly offensive) maricón m
quench [kwɛntʃ] vt: **to ~ one's thirst** apagar la sed
query ['kwɪərɪ] n (question) pregunta ▷ vt dudar de
quest [kwɛst] n busca, búsqueda
question ['kwɛstʃən] n pregunta; (doubt) duda; (matter) asunto, cuestión f ▷ vt (doubt) dudar de; (interrogate) interrogar, hacer preguntas a; **beyond ~** fuera de toda duda; **out of the ~** imposible; ni hablar; **questionable** adj dudoso; **question mark** n punto de interrogación; **questionnaire** [-'nɛə*] n cuestionario
queue [kjuː] (BRIT) n cola ▷ vi (also: **~ up**) hacer cola
quiche [kiːʃ] n quiche m
quick [kwɪk] adj rápido; (agile) ágil; (mind) listo ▷ n: **cut to the ~** (fig) herido en lo vivo; **be ~!** ¡date prisa!; **quickly** adv rápidamente, de prisa
quid [kwɪd] (BRIT) n inv libra
quiet ['kwaɪət] adj (voice, music etc) bajo; (person, place) tranquilo; (ceremony) íntimo ▷ n silencio; (calm) tranquilidad f ▷ vt, vi (US)=**quieten**

┃ Be careful not to translate **quiet** by the Spanish word *quieto*.

quietly adv tranquilamente; (silently) silenciosamente
quilt [kwɪlt] n edredón m
quirky ['kwɜːkɪ] adj raro, estrafalario
quit [kwɪt] (pt, pp ~ or ~**ted**) vt dejar, abandonar; (premises) desocupar ▷ vi (give up) renunciar; (resign) dimitir
quite [kwaɪt] adv (rather) bastante; (entirely) completamente; **that's not ~ big enough** no acaba de ser lo bastante grande; **~ a few of them** un buen número de ellos; **~ (so)!** ¡así es!, ¡exactamente!
quits [kwɪts] adj: **~ (with)** en paz (con); **let's call it ~** dejémoslo en tablas
quiver ['kwɪvə*] vi estremecerse
quiz [kwɪz] n concurso ▷ vt interrogar
quota ['kwəʊtə] n cuota
quotation [kwəʊ'teɪʃən] n cita; (estimate) presupuesto; **quotation marks** npl comillas fpl
quote [kwəʊt] n cita; (estimate) presupuesto ▷ vt citar; (price) cotizar ▷ vi: **to ~ from** citar de; **quotes** npl (inverted commas) comillas fpl

r

rabbi ['ræbaɪ] n rabino
rabbit ['ræbɪt] n conejo
rabies ['reɪbiːz] n rabia
RAC (BRIT) n abbr (= Royal Automobile Club) = RACE m
rac(c)oon [rə'kuːn] n mapache m
race [reɪs] n carrera; (species) raza ▷ vt (horse) hacer correr; (engine) acelerar ▷ vi (compete) competir; (run) correr; (pulse) latir a ritmo acelerado; **race car** (US) n = **racing car**; **racecourse** n hipódromo; **racehorse** n caballo de carreras; **racetrack** n pista; (for cars) autódromo
racial ['reɪʃl] adj racial
racing ['reɪsɪŋ] n carreras fpl; **racing car** (BRIT) n coche m de carreras; **racing driver** (BRIT) n piloto m de carreras
racism ['reɪsɪzəm] n racismo; **racist** [-sɪst] adj, n racista mf
rack [ræk] n (also: **luggage ~**) rejilla; (shelf) estante m; (also: **roof ~**) baca, portaequipajes m inv; (dish rack) escurreplatos m inv; (clothes rack)

percha ▷ vt atormentar; **to ~ one's brains** devanarse los sesos
racket ['rækɪt] n (for tennis) raqueta; (noise) ruido, estrépito; (swindle) estafa, timo
racquet ['rækɪt] n raqueta
radar ['reɪdɑː*] n radar m
radiation [reɪdɪ'eɪʃən] n radiación f
radiator ['reɪdɪeɪtə*] n radiador m
radical ['rædɪkl] adj radical
radio ['reɪdɪəu] n radio f; **on the ~** por radio; **radioactive** adj radioactivo; **radio station** n emisora
radish ['rædɪʃ] n rábano
RAF n abbr (= Royal Air Force) las Fuerzas Aéreas Británicas
raffle ['ræfl] n rifa, sorteo
raft [rɑːft] n balsa; (also: **life ~**) balsa salvavidas
rag [ræg] n (piece of cloth) trapo; (torn material) harapo; (pej: newspaper) periodicucho; (for charity) actividades estudiantiles benéficas; **rags** npl (torn clothes) harapos mpl
rage [reɪdʒ] n rabia, furor m ▷ vi (person) rabiar, estar furioso; (storm) bramar; **it's all the ~** (very fashionable) está muy de moda
ragged ['rægɪd] adj (edge) desigual, mellado; (appearance) andrajoso, harapiento
raid [reɪd] n (Mil) incursión f; (criminal) asalto; (by police) redada ▷ vt invadir, atacar; asaltar
rail [reɪl] n (on stair) barandilla, pasamanos m inv; (on bridge, balcony) pretil m; (of ship) barandilla; (also: **towel ~**) toallero; **railcard** n (BRIT) tarjeta para obtener descuentos en el tren; **railing(s)** n(pl) vallado; **railroad** (US) n = **railway**; **railway** (BRIT) n ferrocarril m, vía férrea; **railway line** (BRIT) n línea (de ferrocarril); **railway station** (BRIT) n estación f de ferrocarril
rain [reɪn] n lluvia ▷ vi llover; **in the ~** bajo la lluvia; **it's ~ing** llueve, está lloviendo; **rainbow** n arco iris;

raincoat n impermeable m; **raindrop** n gota de lluvia; **rainfall** n lluvia; **rainforest** n selvas fpl tropicales; **rainy** adj lluvioso

raise [reɪz] n aumento ▷ vt levantar; (increase) aumentar; (improve: morale) subir; (: standards) mejorar; (doubts) suscitar; (a question) plantear; (cattle, family) criar; (crop) cultivar; (army) reclutar; (loan) obtener; **to ~ one's voice** alzar la voz

raisin ['reɪzn] n pasa de Corinto

rake [reɪk] n (tool) rastrillo; (person) libertino ▷ vt (garden) rastrillar

rally ['rælɪ] n (Pol etc) reunión f, mitin m; (Aut) rallye m; (Tennis) peloteo ▷ vt reunir ▷ vi recuperarse

RAM [ræm] n abbr (= random access memory) RAM f

ram [ræm] n carnero; (also: **battering ~**) ariete m ▷ vt (crash into) dar contra, chocar con; (push: fist etc) empujar con fuerza

Ramadan [ræmə'dæn] n ramadán m

ramble ['ræmbl] n caminata, excursión f en el campo ▷ vi (pej: also: ~ **on**) divagar; **rambler** n excursionista mf; **rambling** adj (speech) inconexo; (house) laberíntico; (Bot) trepador(a)

ramp [ræmp] n rampa; **on/off ~** (us Aut) vía de acceso/salida

rampage [ræm'peɪdʒ] n: **to be on the ~** desmandarse ▷ vi: **they went rampaging through the town** recorrieron la ciudad armando alboroto

ran [ræn] pt of **run**

ranch [rɑːntʃ] n hacienda, estancia

random ['rændəm] adj fortuito, sin orden; (Comput, Math) aleatorio ▷ n: **at ~** al azar

rang [ræŋ] pt of **ring**

range [reɪndʒ] n (of mountains) cadena de montañas, cordillera; (of missile) alcance m; (of voice) registro; (series) serie f; (of products) surtido; (Mil: also: **shooting ~**) campo de tiro;

(also: **kitchen ~**) fogón m ▷ vt (place) colocar; (arrange) arreglar ▷ vi: **to ~ over** (extend) extenderse por; **to ~ from ... to ...** oscilar entre ... y ...

ranger [reɪndʒə*] n guardabosques mf inv

rank [ræŋk] n (row) fila; (Mil) rango; (status) categoría, clase f; (BRIT: also: **taxi ~**) parada de taxis ▷ vi: **to ~ among** figurar entre ▷ adj fétido, rancio; **the ~ and file** (fig) la base

ransom ['rænsəm] n rescate m; **to hold to ~** (fig) hacer chantaje a

rant [rænt] vi divagar, desvariar

rap [ræp] n golpe m, dar un golpecito en ▷ n (music) rap m

rape [reɪp] n violación f; (Bot) colza ▷ vt violar

rapid ['ræpɪd] adj rápido; **rapidly** adv rápidamente; **rapids** npl (Geo) rápidos mpl

rapist ['reɪpɪst] n violador m

rapport [ræ'pɔː*] n simpatía

rare [reə*] adj raro, poco común; (Culin: steak) poco hecho; **rarely** adv pocas veces

rash [ræʃ] adj imprudente, precipitado ▷ n (Med) sarpullido, erupción f (cutánea); (of events) serie f

rasher ['ræʃə*] n lonja

raspberry ['rɑːzbərɪ] n frambuesa

rat [ræt] n rata

rate [reɪt] n (ratio) razón f; (price) precio; (: of hotel etc) tarifa; (of interest) tipo; (speed) velocidad f ▷ vt (value) tasar; (estimate) estimar; **rates** npl (BRIT: property tax) impuesto municipal; (fees) tarifa; **to ~ sth/sb as** considerar algo/a algn como

rather ['rɑːðə*] adv: **it's ~ expensive** es algo caro; (too much) es demasiado caro; (to some extent) más bien; **there's a lot too** hay bastante; **I would** or **I'd ~ go** preferiría ir; **or ~** mejor dicho

rating ['reɪtɪŋ] n tasación f; (score) índice m; (of ship) clase f; **ratings** npl (Radio, TV) niveles mpl de audiencia

ratio ['reɪʃɪəu] n razón f; **in the ~ of**

100 to 1 a razón de 100 a 1

ration ['ræʃən] n ración f ▷ vt racionar; **rations** npl víveres mpl

rational ['ræʃənl] adj (solution, reasoning) lógico, razonable; (person) cuerdo, sensato

rattle ['rætl] n golpeteo; (of train etc) traqueteo; (for baby) sonaja, sonajero ▷ vi castañetear; (car, bus): **to ~ along** traquetear ▷ vt hacer sonar agitando

rave [reɪv] vi (in anger) encolerizarse; (with enthusiasm) entusiasmarse; (Med) delirar, desvariar ▷ n (inf: party) rave m

raven ['reɪvən] n cuervo

ravine [rə'vi:n] n barranco

raw [rɔ:] adj crudo; (not processed) bruto; (sore) vivo; (inexperienced) novato, inexperto; **~ materials** materias primas

ray [reɪ] n rayo; **~ of hope** (rayo de) esperanza

razor ['reɪzə*] n (open) navaja; (safety razor) máquina de afeitar; (electric razor) máquina (eléctrica) de afeitar; **razor blade** n hoja de afeitar

Rd abbr = **road**

RE n abbr (BRIT) = **religious education**

re [ri:] prep con referencia a

reach [ri:tʃ] n alcance m; (of river etc) extensión f entre dos recodos ▷ vt alcanzar, llegar a; (achieve) lograr ▷ vi extenderse; **within ~** al alcance (de la mano); **out of ~** fuera del alcance; **reach out** vt (hand) tender ▷ vi: **to reach out for sth** alargar or tender la mano para tomar algo

react [ri:'ækt] vi reaccionar; **reaction** [-'ækʃən] n reacción f; **reactor** [ri:'æktə*] n (also: **nuclear reactor**) reactor m (nuclear)

read [ri:d, pt, pp **red**] (pt, pp **~**) vi leer ▷ vt leer; (understand) entender; (study) estudiar; **read out** vt leer en alta voz; **reader** n lector(a) m/f; (BRIT: at university) profesor(a) m/f adjunto/a

readily ['rɛdɪlɪ] adv (willingly) de buena gana; (easily) fácilmente; (quickly) en seguida

reading ['ri:dɪŋ] n lectura; (on instrument) indicación f

ready ['rɛdɪ] adj listo, preparado; (willing) dispuesto; (available) disponible ▷ adv: **~-cooked** listo para comer ▷ n: **at the ~** (Mil) listo para tirar ▷ **to get ~** vi prepararse ▷ **to get ~** vt preparar; **ready-made** adj confeccionado

real ['rɪəl] adj verdadero, auténtico; **in ~ terms** en términos reales; **real ale** n cerveza elaborada tradicionalmente; **real estate** n bienes mpl raíces; **realistic** [-'lɪstɪk] adj realista; **reality** [ri:'ælɪtɪ] n realidad f; **reality TV** n telerrealidad f

realization [rɪəlaɪ'zeɪʃən] n comprensión f; (fulfilment, Comm) realización f

realize ['rɪəlaɪz] vt (understand) darse cuenta de

really ['rɪəlɪ] adv realmente; (for emphasis) verdaderamente; (actually): **what ~ happened** lo que pasó en realidad; **~? ¿de veras?; ~!** (annoyance) ¡vamos!, ¡por favor!

realm [rɛlm] n reino; (fig) esfera

realtor ['rɪəltɔ:*](us) n agente mf inmobiliario/a

reappear [ri:ə'pɪə*] vi reaparecer

rear [rɪə*] adj trasero ▷ n parte f trasera ▷ vt (cattle, family) criar ▷ vi (also: **~ up**) (animal) encabritarse

rearrange [ri:ə'reɪndʒ] vt ordenar or arreglar de nuevo

rear: **rear-view mirror** n (Aut) (espejo) retrovisor m; **rear-wheel drive** n tracción f trasera

reason ['ri:zn] n razón f ▷ vi: **to ~ with sb** tratar de que algn entre en razón; **it stands to ~ that ...** es lógico que ...; **reasonable** adj razonable; (sensible) sensato; **reasonably** adv razonablemente; **reasoning** n razonamiento, argumentos mpl

reassurance [ri:ə'ʃuərəns] n consuelo

reassure [ri:ə'ʃuə*] vt tranquilizar,

alentar; **to ~ sb that** ... tranquilizar a algn asegurando que ...

rebate ['ri:beɪt] n (on tax etc) desgravación f

rebel [n 'rebl, vi rɪ'bel] n rebelde mf ▷ vi rebelarse, sublevarse; **rebellion** [rɪ'beljən] n rebelión f, sublevación f; **rebellious** [rɪ'beljəs] adj rebelde; (child) revoltoso

rebuild [vb riː'bɪld] vt reconstruir

recall [vb rɪ'kɔːl, n 'riːkɔːl] vt (remember) recordar; (ambassador etc) retirar ▷ n recuerdo; retirada

rec'd abbr (= received) rbdo

receipt [rɪ'siːt] n (document) recibo; (for parcel etc) acuse m de recibo; (act of receiving) recepción f; **receipts** npl (Comm) ingresos mpl

> Be careful not to translate **receipt** by the Spanish word **receta**.

receive [rɪ'siːv] vt recibir; (guest) acoger; (wound) sufrir; **receiver** n (Tel) auricular m; (Radio) receptor m; (of stolen goods) perista mf; (Comm) administrador m jurídico

recent ['riːsnt] adj reciente; **recently** adv recientemente; **recently arrived** recién llegado

reception [rɪ'sepʃən] n recepción f; (welcome) acogida; **reception desk** n recepción f; **receptionist** n recepcionista m

recession [rɪ'seʃən] n recesión f

recharge [riː'tʃɑːdʒ] vt (battery) recargar

recipe ['resɪpɪ] n receta; (for disaster, success) fórmula

recipient [rɪ'sɪpɪənt] n recibidor(a) m/f; (of letter) destinatario/a

recital [rɪ'saɪtl] n recital m

recite [rɪ'saɪt] vt (poem) recitar

reckless ['rekləs] adj temerario, imprudente; (driving, driver) peligroso

reckon ['rekən] vt calcular; (consider) considerar; (think): **I ~ that** ... me parece que ...

reclaim [rɪ'kleɪm] vt (land, waste) recuperar; (land: from sea) rescatar;

(demand back) reclamar

recline [rɪ'klaɪn] vi reclinarse

recognition [rekəg'nɪʃən] n reconocimiento; **transformed beyond ~** irreconocible

recognize ['rekəgnaɪz] vt: **to ~ (by/as)** reconocer (por/como)

recollection [rekə'lekʃən] n recuerdo

recommend vt recomendar; **recommendation** [rekəmen'deɪʃən] n recomendación f

reconcile ['rekənsaɪl] vt (two people) reconciliar; (two facts) compaginar; **to ~ o.s. to sth** conformarse a algo

reconsider [riːkən'sɪdə*] vt repensar

reconstruct [riːkən'strʌkt] vt reconstruir

record [n, adj 'rekɔːd, vt rɪ'kɔːd] n (Mus) disco; (of meeting etc) acta; (register) registro, partida; (file) archivo; (also: **criminal ~**) antecedentes mpl; (written) expediente m; (Sport, Comput) récord m ▷ adj récord, sin precedentes ▷ vt registrar; (Mus: song etc) grabar; **in ~ time** en un tiempo récord; **off the ~** adj no oficial ▷ adv confidencialmente; **recorded delivery** (BRIT) n (Post) entrega con acuse de recibo; **recorder** n (Mus) flauta de pico; **recording** n (Mus) grabación f; **record player** n tocadiscos m inv

recount [rɪ'kaunt] vt contar

recover [rɪ'kʌvə*] vt recuperar ▷ vi (from illness, shock) recuperarse; **recovery** n recuperación f

recreate [riːkrɪ'eɪt] vt recrear

recreation [rekrɪ'eɪʃən] n recreo; **recreational vehicle** (us) n caravan or rulota pequeña; **recreational drug** n droga recreativa

recruit [rɪ'kruːt] n recluta mf ▷ vt reclutar; (staff) contratar; **recruitment** n reclutamiento

rectangle ['rektæŋgl] n rectángulo; **rectangular** [-'tæŋgjulə*] adj rectangular

rectify ['rektɪfaɪ] vt rectificar

rector ['rɛktə*] n (Rel) párroco

recur [rɪ'kə:*] vi repetirse; (pain, illness) producirse de nuevo; **recurring** adj (problem) repetido, constante

recyclable [ri:'saɪkləbl] adj reciclable

recycle [ri:'saɪkl] vt reciclar

recycling [ri:'saɪklɪŋ] n reciclaje

red [rɛd] n rojo ▷ adj rojo; (hair) pelirrojo; (wine) tinto; **to be in the ~** (account) estar en números rojos; (business) tener un saldo negativo; **to give sb the ~ carpet treatment** recibir a algn con todos los honores; **Red Cross** n Cruz f Roja; **redcurrant** n grosella roja

redeem [rɪ'di:m] vt redimir; (promises) cumplir; (sth in pawn) desempeñar; (fig, also Rel) rescatar

red-haired adj pelirrojo; **redhead** n pelirrojo/a; **red-hot** adj candente; **red light** n: **to go through a red light** (Aut) pasar la luz roja; **red-light district** n barrio chino

red meat n carne f roja

reduce [rɪ'dju:s] vt reducir; **to ~ sb to tears** hacer llorar a algn; **"~ speed now"** (Aut) "reduzca la velocidad"; **reduced** adj (decreased) reducido, rebajado; **at a reduced price** con rebaja o descuento; **"greatly reduced prices"** "grandes rebajas"; **reduction** [rɪ'dʌkʃən] n reducción f; (of price) rebaja, (discount) descuento; (smaller-scale copy) copia reducida

redundancy [rɪ'dʌndənsɪ] n (dismissal) despido; (unemployment) desempleo

redundant [rɪ'dʌndnt] adj (BRIT: worker) parado, sin trabajo; (detail, object) superfluo; **to be made ~** quedar(se) sin trabajo

reed [ri:d] n (Bot) junco, caña; (Mus) lengüeta

reef [ri:f] n (at sea) arrecife m

reel [ri:l] n carrete m, bobina; (of film) rollo; (dance) baile escocés ▷ vt (also: ~ up) devanar; (also: ~ in) sacar ▷ vi

(sway) tambalear(se)

ref [rɛf] (inf) n abbr = **referee**

refectory [rɪ'fɛktərɪ] n comedor m

refer [rɪ'fə:*] vt (send: patient) referir; (: matter) remitir ▷ vi: **to ~ to** (allude to) referirse a, aludir a; (apply to) relacionarse con; (consult) consultar

referee [rɛfə'ri:] n árbitro; (BRIT: for job application): **to be a ~ for sb** proporcionar referencias a algn ▷ vt (match) arbitrar en

reference ['rɛfrəns] n referencia; (for job application: letter) carta de recomendación; **with ~ to** (Comm: in letter) me remito a, ... ; **reference number** n número de referencia

refill [vt ri:'fɪl, n 'ri:fɪl] vt rellenar ▷ n repuesto, recambio

refine [rɪ'faɪn] vt refinar; **refined** adj (person) fino; **refinery** n refinería

reflect [rɪ'flɛkt] vt reflejar ▷ vi (think) reflexionar, pensar; **it ~s badly/well on him** le perjudica/le hace honor; **reflection** [-'flɛkʃən] n (act) reflexión f; (image) reflejo; (criticism) crítica; **on reflection** pensándolo bien

reflex ['ri:flɛks] adj, n reflejo

reform [rɪ'fɔ:m] n reforma ▷ vt reformar

refrain [rɪ'freɪn] vi: **to ~ from doing** abstenerse de hacer ▷ n estribillo

refresh [rɪ'frɛʃ] vt refrescar; **refreshing** adj refrescante; **refreshments** npl refrescos mpl

refrigerator [rɪ'frɪdʒəreɪtə*] n frigorífico (sp), nevera (sp), refrigerador m (LAM), heladera (RPL)

refuel [ri:'fjuəl] vi repostar (combustible)

refuge ['rɛfju:dʒ] n refugio, asilo; **to take ~ in** refugiarse en; **refugee** [rɛfju'dʒi:] n refugiado/a

refund [n 'ri:fʌnd, vb rɪ'fʌnd] n reembolso ▷ vt devolver, reembolsar

refurbish [ri:'fə:bɪʃ] vt restaurar, renovar

refusal [rɪ'fju:zəl] n negativa; **to have first ~ on** tener la primera

opción f
refuse¹ ['refju:s] n basura
refuse² [rɪ'fju:z] vt rechazar; (invitation) declinar; (permission) denegar ▷ vi: **to ~ to do** sth negarse a hacer algo; (horse) rehusar
regain [rɪ'ɡeɪn] vt recobrar, recuperar
regard [rɪ'ɡɑ:d] n mirada; (esteem) respeto; (attention) consideración f ▷ vt (consider) considerar; **to give one's ~s to** saludar de su parte a; **"with kindest ~s"** "con muchos recuerdos"; **as ~s, with ~ to** con respecto a, en cuanto a; **regarding** prep con respecto a, en cuanto a; **regardless** adv a pesar de todo; **regardless of** sin reparar en
regenerate [rɪ'dʒenəreɪt] vt regenerar
reggae ['reɡeɪ] n reggae m
regiment ['redʒɪmənt] n regimiento
region ['ri:dʒən] n región f; **in the ~ of** (fig) alrededor de; **regional** adj regional
register ['redʒɪstə*] n registro ▷ vt registrar; (birth) declarar; (car) matricular; (letter) certificar; (instrument) marcar, indicar ▷ vi (at hotel) registrarse; (as student) matricularse; (make impression) producir impresión; **registered** adj (letter, parcel) certificado
registrar ['redʒɪstrɑ:*] n secretario/a (del registro civil)
registration [redʒɪs'treɪʃən] n (act) declaración f; (Aut: also: ~ number) matrícula
registry office ['redʒɪstrɪ-] (BRIT) n registro civil; **to get married in a ~** casarse por lo civil
regret [rɪ'ɡret] n sentimiento, pesar m ▷ vt sentir, lamentar; **regrettable** adj lamentable
regular ['reɡjulə*] adj regular; (soldier) profesional; (usual) habitual; (: doctor) de cabecera ▷ n (: client etc) cliente a m/f habitual; **regularly** adv con regularidad; (often) repetidas veces
regulate ['reɡjuleɪt] vt controlar;

regulation [-'leɪʃən] n (rule) regla, reglamento
rehabilitation ['ri:əbɪlɪ'teɪʃən] n rehabilitación f
rehearsal [rɪ'hə:səl] n ensayo
rehearse [rɪ'hə:s] vt ensayar
reign [reɪn] n reinado; (fig) predominio ▷ vi reinar; (fig) imperar
reimburse [ri:ɪm'bə:s] vt reembolsar
rein [reɪn] n (for horse) rienda
reincarnation [ri:ɪnkɑ:'neɪʃən] n reencarnación f
reindeer ['reɪndɪə*] n inv reno
reinforce [ri:ɪn'fɔ:s] vt reforzar; **reinforcements** npl (Mil) refuerzos mpl
reinstate [ri:ɪn'steɪt] vt reintegrar; (tax, law) reinstaurar
reject [n 'ri:dʒekt, vb rɪ'dʒekt] n (thing) desecho ▷ vt rechazar; (suggestion) descartar; (coin) expulsar; **rejection** [rɪ'dʒekʃən] n rechazo
rejoice [rɪ'dʒɔɪs] vi: **to ~ at o over** regocijarse o alegrarse de
relate [rɪ'leɪt] vt (tell) contar, relatar; (connect) relacionar ▷ vi relacionarse; **related** adj afín; (person) emparentado; **related to** (subject) relacionado con; **relating to** prep referente a
relation [rɪ'leɪʃən] n (person) familiar mf, pariente mf; (link) relación f; **relations** npl (relatives) familiares mpl; **relationship** n relación f; (personal) relaciones fpl; (also: **family relationship**) parentesco
relative ['relətɪv] n pariente mf, familiar mf ▷ adj relativo; **relatively** adv (comparatively) relativamente
relax [rɪ'læks] vi descansar; (unwind) relajarse ▷ vt (one's grip) soltar, aflojar; (control) relajar; (mind, person) descansar; **relaxation** [ri:læk'seɪʃən] n descanso; (of rule, control) relajamiento; (entertainment) diversión f; **relaxed** adj relajado; (tranquil) tranquilo; **relaxing** adj relajante
relay ['ri:leɪ] n (race) carrera de relevos

▷vt (Radio, TV) retransmitir
release [rɪˈliːs] n (liberation) liberación f; (from prison) puesta en libertad; (of gas etc) escape m; (of film etc) estreno; (of record) lanzamiento ▷vt (prisoner) poner en libertad; (gas) despedir, arrojar; (from wreckage) soltar; (catch, spring etc) desenganchar; (film) estrenar; (book) publicar; (news) difundir
relegate [ˈrɛləgeɪt] vt relegar; (BRIT Sport) **to be ~d to** bajar a
relent [rɪˈlɛnt] vi ablandarse; **relentless** adj implacable
relevant [ˈrɛləvənt] adj (fact) pertinente; **~ to** relacionado con
reliable [rɪˈlaɪəbl] adj (person, firm) de confianza, de fiar; (method, machine) seguro; (source) fidedigno
relic [ˈrɛlɪk] n (Rel) reliquia f; (of the past) vestigio
relief [rɪˈliːf] n (from pain, anxiety) alivio; (help, supplies) socorro, ayuda; (Art, Geo) relieve m
relieve [rɪˈliːv] vt (pain) aliviar; (bring help to) ayudar, socorrer; (take over from) sustituir; (~ guard) relevar; **to ~ sb of sth** quitar algo a algn; **to ~ o.s.** hacer sus necesidades; **relieved** adj: **to be relieved** sentir un gran alivio
religion [rɪˈlɪdʒən] n religión f
religious [rɪˈlɪdʒəs] adj religioso; **religious education** n educación f religiosa
relish [ˈrɛlɪʃ] n (Culin) salsa; (enjoyment) entusiasmo m ▷vt (food etc) saborear; (enjoy): **to ~ sth** hacerle mucha ilusión a algo algo
relocate [riːləʊˈkeɪt] vt cambiar de lugar, mudar ▷vi mudarse
reluctance [rɪˈlʌktəns] n renuencia
reluctant [rɪˈlʌktənt] adj renuente; **reluctantly** adv de mala gana
rely on [rɪˈlaɪ-] vt fus depender de; (trust) contar con
remain [rɪˈmeɪn] vi (survive) quedar; (be left) sobrar; (continue) quedar(se), permanecer; **remainder** n resto;

remaining adj que queda(n); (surviving) restante(s); **remains** npl restos mpl
remand [rɪˈmɑːnd] n: **on ~** detenido (bajo custodia) ▷vt: **to be ~ed in custody** quedar detenido bajo custodia
remark [rɪˈmɑːk] n comentario ▷vt comentar; **remarkable** adj (outstanding) extraordinario
remarry [riːˈmærɪ] vi volver a casarse
remedy [ˈrɛmədɪ] n remedio ▷vt remediar, curar
remember [rɪˈmɛmbə*] vt recordar, acordarse de; (bear in mind) tener presente; (send greetings to): **~ me to him** dale recuerdos de mi parte; **Remembrance Day** n = día en el que se recuerda a los caídos en las dos guerrasmundiales

○ **REMEMBRANCE DAY**
○
○ En el Reino Unido el domingo
○ más próximo al 11 de noviembre
○ se conoce como Remembrance
○ **Sunday** o Remembrance
○ **Day**, aniversario de la firma del
○ armisticio de 1918 que puso fin a
○ la Primera Guerra Mundial. Ese
○ día, a las once de la mañana (hora
○ en que se firmó el armisticio), se
○ recuerda a los que murieron en
○ las dos guerras mundiales con
○ dos minutos de silencio ante los
○ monumentos a los caídos. Allí se
○ colocan coronas de amapolas,
○ flor que también se suele llevar
○ prendida en el pecho tras pagar un
○ donativo destinado a los inválidos
○ de guerra.

remind [rɪˈmaɪnd] vt: **to ~ sb to do sth** recordar a algn que haga algo; **to ~ sb of sth** (of fact) recordar a algn algo; **she ~s me of her mother** me recuerda a su madre; **reminder** n notificación f; (memento) recuerdo

reminiscent [remɪˈnɪsnt] adj: **to be ~ of sth** recordar algo

remnant [ˈremnənt] n resto; (of cloth) retal m

remorse [rɪˈmɔːs] n remordimientos mpl

remote [rɪˈməut] adj (distant) lejano; (person) distante; **remote control** n telecontrol m; **remotely** adv remotamente; (slightly) levemente

removal [rɪˈmuːvəl] n (taking away) el quitar; (BRIT: from house) mudanza; (from office: dismissal) destitución f; (Med) extirpación f; **removal man** (irreg) n (BRIT) mozo de mudanzas; **removal van** (BRIT) n camión m de mudanzas

remove [rɪˈmuːv] vt quitar; (employee) destituir; (name: from list) tachar, borrar; (doubt) disipar; (abuse) suprimir, acabar con; (Med) extirpar

Renaissance [rɪˈneɪsɑ̃s] n: **the ~** el Renacimiento

rename [riːˈneɪm] vt poner nuevo nombre a

render [ˈrendə*] vt (thanks) dar; (aid) proporcionar, prestar; (make): **to ~ sth useless** hacer algo inútil

rendezvous [ˈrɒndɪvuː] n cita

renew [rɪˈnjuː] vt renovar; (resume) reanudar; (loan etc) prorrogar

renovate [ˈrenəveɪt] vt renovar

renowned [rɪˈnaund] adj renombrado

rent [rent] n (for house) arriendo, renta ▷ vt alquilar; **rental** n (for television, car) alquiler m

reorganize [riːˈɔːɡənaɪz] vt reorganizar

rep [rep] n abbr = **representative**

repair [rɪˈpeə*] n reparación f, compostura f ▷ vt reparar, componer; (shoes) remendar; **in good/bad ~** en buen/mal estado; **repair kit** n caja de herramientas

repay [riːˈpeɪ] vt (money) devolver, reembolsar; (person) pagar; (debt) liquidar; (sb's efforts) devolver,

corresponder a; **repayment** n reembolso, devolución f; (sum of money) recompensa

repeat [rɪˈpiːt] n (Radio, TV) reposición f ▷ vt repetir ▷ vi repetirse; **repeatedly** adv repetidas veces; **repeat prescription** n (BRIT) receta renovada

repellent [rɪˈpelənt] adj repugnante ▷ n: **insect ~** crema o loción f anti-insectos

repercussions [riːpəˈkʌʃənz] npl consecuencias fpl

repetition [repɪˈtɪʃən] n repetición f

repetitive [rɪˈpetɪtɪv] adj repetitivo

replace [rɪˈpleɪs] vt (put back) devolver a su sitio; (take the place) reemplazar, sustituir; **replacement** n (act) reposición f; (thing) recambio; (person) suplente mf

replay [ˈriːpleɪ] n (Sport) desempate m; (of tape, film) repetición f

replica [ˈreplɪkə] n copia, reproducción f (exacta)

reply [rɪˈplaɪ] n respuesta, contestación f ▷ vi contestar, responder

report [rɪˈpɔːt] n informe m; (Press etc) reportaje m; (BRIT: also: **school ~**) boletín m escolar; (of gun) estallido ▷ vt informar de; (Press etc) hacer un reportaje sobre; (notify: accident, culprit) denunciar ▷ vi (make a report) presentar un informe; (present o.s.): **to ~ (to sb)** presentarse (ante algn); **report card** n (US, SCOTTISH) cartilla escolar; **reportedly** adv según se dice; **reporter** n periodista mf

represent [reprɪˈzent] vt representar; (Comm) ser agente de; (describe): **to ~ sth as** describir algo como; **representation** [-ˈteɪʃən] n representación f; **representative** n representante mf; (US Pol) diputado/a m/f ▷ adj representativo

repress [rɪˈpres] vt reprimir; **repression** [-ˈpreʃən] n represión f

reprimand [ˈreprɪmɑːnd] n

reprimenda ▷vt reprender

reproduce [ri:prə'dju:s] vt reproducir ▷vi reproducirse; **reproduction** [-'dʌkʃən] n reproducción f

reptile ['reptail] n reptil m

republic [ri'pʌblɪk] n república; **republican** adj, n republicano/a m/f

reputable ['repjutəbl] adj (make etc) de renombre

reputation [repju'teɪʃən] n reputación f

request [ri'kwest] n petición f; (formal) solicitud f ▷ vt **to ~ sth of** or **from sb** solicitar algo a algn; **request stop** (BRIT) n parada discrecional

require [ri'kwaɪə*] vt (need: person) necesitar, tener necesidad de; (: thing, situation) exigir; (want) pedir; **to ~ sb to do sth** pedir a algn que haga algo; **requirement** n requisito; (need) necesidad f

resat [ri:'sæt] pt, pp of **resit**

rescue ['reskju:] n rescate m ▷ vt rescatar

research [ri'sə:tʃ] n investigaciones fpl ▷ vt investigar

resemblance [ri'zembləns] n parecido m

resemble [ri'zembl] vt parecerse a

resent [ri'zent] vt tomar a mal; **resentful** adj resentido; **resentment** n resentimiento

reservation [rezə'veɪʃən] n reserva; **reservation desk** (US) n (in hotel) recepción f

reserve [ri'zə:v] n reserva; (Sport) suplente mf ▷ vt (seats etc) reservar; **reserved** adj reservado

reservoir ['rezəvwa:*] n (artificial lake) embalse m, tank; (small) depósito

residence ['rezidəns] n (formal: home) domicilio; (length of stay) permanencia; **residence permit** (BRIT) n permiso de permanencia

resident ['rezidənt] n (of area) vecino/a; (in hotel) huésped mf ▷ adj (population) permanente; (doctor)

residente; **residential** [-'denʃəl] adj residencial

residue ['rezidju:] n resto

resign [ri'zain] vt renunciar a ▷ vi dimitir; **to ~ o.s. to** (situation) resignarse a; **resignation** [rezig'neɪʃən] n dimisión f; (state of mind) resignación f

resin ['rezin] n resina

resist [ri'zist] vt resistir, oponerse a; **resistance** n resistencia

resit [ri:'sit] (BRIT) (pt, pp **resat**) vt (exam) volver a presentarse a; (subject) recuperar, volver a examinarse de (SP)

resolution [rezə'lu:ʃən] n resolución f

resolve [ri'zolv] n resolución f ▷ vt resolver ▷ vi: **to ~ to do** resolver hacer

resort [ri'zo:t] n (town) centro turístico; (recourse) recurso ▷ vi: **to ~ to** recurrir a; **in the last ~** como último recurso

resource [ri'so:s] n recurso; **resourceful** adj despabilado, ingenioso

respect [ris'pekt] n respeto ▷ vt respetar; **respectable** adj respetable; (large: amount) apreciable; (passable) tolerable; **respectful** adj respetuoso; **respective** adj respectivo; **respectively** adv respectivamente

respite ['respait] n respiro

respond [ris'pond] vi responder; (react) reaccionar; **response** [-'pons] n respuesta; reacción f

responsibility [risponsi'biliti] n responsabilidad f

responsible [ris'ponsibl] adj (character) serio, formal; (job) de confianza; (liable): **~ (for)** responsable (de); **responsibly** adv con seriedad

responsive [ris'ponsiv] adj sensible

rest [rest] n descanso, reposo; (Mus, pause) pausa, silencio; (support) apoyo; (remainder) resto ▷ vi descansar; (be supported): **to ~ on** descansar sobre ▷ vt: **to ~ sth on/against** apoyar algo en or sobre/contra: **the ~ of them** (people, objects) los demás; **it ~s with him to ...** depende de él el que ...

restaurant ['restərɒŋ] n restaurante m; **restaurant car** (BRIT) n (Rail) coche-comedor m

restless ['restlɪs] adj inquieto

restoration [restə'reɪʃən] n restauración f; devolución f

restore [rɪ'stɔː*] vt (building) restaurar; (sth stolen) devolver; (health) restablecer; (to power) volver a poner a

restrain [rɪs'treɪn] vt (feeling) contener, refrenar; (person): **to ~ (from doing)** disuadir (de hacer); **restraint** n (restriction) restricción f; (moderation) moderación f; (of manner) reserva

restrict [rɪs'trɪkt] vt restringir, limitar; **restriction** [-kʃən] n restricción f, limitación f

rest room (US) n aseos mpl

restructure [riː'strʌktʃə*] n reestructurar

result [rɪ'zʌlt] n resultado ▷ vi: **to ~ in** terminar en, tener por resultado; **as a ~ of** a consecuencia de

resume [rɪ'zjuːm] vt reanudar ▷ vi comenzar de nuevo

▌ Be careful not to translate **resume** by the Spanish word resumir.

résumé ['reɪzjuːmeɪ] n resumen m; (US) curriculum m

resuscitate [rɪ'sʌsɪteɪt] vt (Med) resucitar

retail ['riːteɪl] adj, adv al por menor; **retailer** n detallista mf

retain [rɪ'teɪn] vt (keep) retener, conservar

retaliation [rɪtælɪ'eɪʃən] n represalias fpl

retarded [rɪ'taːdɪd] adj retrasado

retire [rɪ'taɪə*] vi (give up work) jubilarse; (withdraw) retirarse; (go to bed) acostarse; **retired** adj (person) jubilado; **retirement** n (giving up work; state) retiro, (: act) jubilación f

retort [rɪ'tɔːt] vi contestar

retreat [rɪ'triːt] n (place) retiro; (Mil)

retirada ▷ vi retirarse

retrieve [rɪ'triːv] vt recobrar; (situation, honour) salvar; (Comput) recuperar; (error) reparar

retrospect ['retrəspekt] n: **in ~** retrospectivamente; **retrospective** [-'spektɪv] adj retrospectivo; (law) retroactivo

return [rɪ'təːn] n (going or coming back) vuelta, regreso; (of sth stolen etc) devolución f; (Finance: from land, shares) ganancia, ingresos mpl ▷ cpd (journey) de regreso; (BRIT: ticket) de ida y vuelta; (match) de vuelta ▷ vi (person etc: come or go back) volver, regresar; (symptoms etc) reaparecer; (regain): **to ~ to** recuperar ▷ vt devolver; (favour, love etc) corresponder a; (verdict) pronunciar; (Pol: candidate) elegir; **returns** npl (Comm) ingresos mpl; **in ~ (for)** a cambio (de); **by ~ of post** a vuelta de correo; **many happy ~s (of the day)!** ¡feliz cumpleaños!; **return ticket** n (esp BRIT) billete m (SP) or boleto m (LAM) de ida y vuelta, billete m redondo (MEX)

reunion [riː'juːnɪən] n (of family) reunión f; (of two people, school) reencuentro

reunite [riːjuː'naɪt] vt reunir; (reconcile) reconciliar

revamp [riː'væmp] vt renovar

reveal [rɪ'viːl] vt revelar; **revealing** adj revelador(a)

revel ['revl] vi: **to ~ in sth/in doing sth** gozar de algo/con hacer algo

revelation [revə'leɪʃən] n revelación f

revenge [rɪ'vendʒ] n venganza; **to take ~ on** vengarse de

revenue ['revənjuː] n ingresos mpl, rentas fpl

Reverend ['revərənd] adj (in titles): **the ~ John Smith** (Anglican) el Reverendo John Smith; (Catholic) el Padre John Smith; (Protestant) el Pastor John Smith

reversal [rɪ'vəːsl] n (of order)

inversión f; (of direction, policy) cambio; (of decision) revocación f

reverse [rɪˈvəːs] n (opposite) contrario; (back: of cloth) revés m; (: of coin) reverso; (: of paper) dorso; (Aut: also: ~ **gear**) marcha atrás, revés m ▷ adj (order) inverso; (direction) contrario; (process) opuesto ▷ vt (decision, Aut) dar marcha atrás a; (position, function) invertir ▷ vi (BRIT Aut) dar marcha atrás; **reverse-charge call** (BRIT) n llamada a cobro revertido; **reversing lights** (BRIT) npl (Aut) luces fpl de retroceso

revert [rɪˈvəːt] vi: **to ~ to** volver a

review [rɪˈvjuː] n (magazine, Mil) revista; (of book, film) reseña; (US: examination) repaso, examen m ▷ vt repasar, examinar; (Mil) pasar revista a; (book, film) reseñar

revise [rɪˈvaɪz] vt (manuscript) corregir; (opinion) modificar; (price, procedure) revisar ▷ vi (study) repasar; **revision** [rɪˈvɪʒən] n corrección f; modificación f; (for exam) repaso

revival [rɪˈvaɪvəl] n (recovery) reanimación f; (of interest) renacimiento m; (Theatre) reestreno; (of faith) despertar m

revive [rɪˈvaɪv] vt resucitar; (custom) restablecer; (hope) despertar; (play) reestrenar ▷ vi (person) volver en sí; (business) reactivarse

revolt [rɪˈvəult] n rebelión f ▷ vi rebelarse, sublevarse ▷ vt dar asco a, repugnar; **revolting** adj asqueroso, repugnante

revolution [rɛvəˈluːʃən] n revolución f; **revolutionary** adj, n revolucionario/a m/f

revolve [rɪˈvɔlv] vi dar vueltas, girar; (life, discussion): **to ~ (a)round** girar en torno a

revolver [rɪˈvɔlvə*] n revólver m

reward [rɪˈwɔːd] n premio, recompensa f ▷ vt: **to ~ (for)** recompensar or premiar (por); **rewarding** adj (fig) valioso

rewind [riːˈwaɪnd] vt rebobinar

rewritable [riːˈraɪtəbl] adj (CD, DVD) reescribible

rewrite [riːˈraɪt] (pt rewrote, pp **rewritten**) vt reescribir

rheumatism [ˈruːmətɪzəm] n reumatismo, reúma m

rhinoceros [raɪˈnɔsərəs] n rinoceronte m

rhubarb [ˈruːbɑːb] n ruibarbo

rhyme [raɪm] n rima; (verse) poesía

rhythm [ˈrɪðm] n ritmo

rib [rɪb] n (Anat) costilla ▷ vt (mock) tomar el pelo a

ribbon [ˈrɪbən] n cinta; **in ~s** (torn) hecho trizas

rice [raɪs] n arroz m; **rice pudding** n arroz m con leche

rich [rɪtʃ] adj rico; (soil) fértil; (food) pesado; (: sweet) empalagoso; (abundant): **~ in** (minerals etc) rico en

rid [rɪd] (pt, pp ~) vt: **to ~ sb of sth** librar a algn de algo; **to get ~ of** deshacerse or desembarazarse de

riddle [ˈrɪdl] n (puzzle) acertijo; (mystery) enigma m, misterio ▷ vt: **to be ~d with** ser lleno o plagado de

ride [raɪd] (pt rode, pp **ridden**) n paseo; (distance covered) viaje m, recorrido ▷ vi (as sport) montar; (go somewhere) on horse, bicycle) dar un paseo, pasearse; (travel: on horse, motorcycle, bus) viajar ▷ vt (a horse) montar a; (a bicycle, motorcycle) andar en; (distance) recorrer; **to take sb for a ~** (fig) engañar a algn; **rider** n (on horse) jinete mf; (on bicycle) ciclista mf; (on motorcycle) motociclista mf

ridge [rɪdʒ] n (of hill) cresta; (of roof) caballete m; (wrinkle) arruga

ridicule [ˈrɪdɪkjuːl] n irrisión f, burla ▷ vt poner en ridículo, burlarse de; **ridiculous** [rɪˈdɪkjuləs] adj ridículo

riding [ˈraɪdɪŋ] n equitación f; **I like ~** me gusta montar a caballo; **riding school** n escuela de equitación

rife [raɪf] adj: **to be ~** ser muy común; **to be ~ with** abundar en

rifle ['raɪfl] *n* rifle *m*, fusil *m* ▷ *vt* saquear

rift [rɪft] *n* (*in clouds*) claro; (*fig: disagreement*) desavenencia

rig [rɪg] *n* (*also:* **oil ~**: *at sea*) plataforma petrolera ▷ *vt* (*election etc*) amañar

right [raɪt] *adj* (*correct*) correcto, exacto; (*suitable*) indicado, debido; (*proper*) apropiado; (*just*) justo; (*morally good*) bueno; (*not left*) derecho ▷ *n* bueno; (*title, claim*) derecho ▷ *n* derecha ▷ *adv* bien, correctamente; (*not left*) a la derecha; (*exactly*): ~ **now** ahora mismo ▷ *vt* enderezar; (*correct*) corregir ▷ *excl* ¡bueno!, ¡está bien!; **to be ~** (*person*) tener razón; (*answer*) ser correcto; **is that the ~ time?** (*of clock*) ¿es esa la hora buena?; **by ~s** en justicia; **on the ~** a la derecha; **to be in the ~** tener razón; **~ away** en seguida; **~ in the middle** exactamente en el centro; **right angle** *n* ángulo recto; **rightful** *adj* legítimo; **right-hand** *adj*: **right-hand drive** conducción *f* por la derecha; **the right-hand side** derecha; **right-handed** *adj* diestro; **rightly** *adv* correctamente, debidamente; (*with reason*) con razón; **right of way** *n* (*on path etc*) derecho de paso; (*Aut*) prioridad *f*; **right-wing** *adj* (*Pol*) derechista

rigid ['rɪdʒɪd] *adj* rígido; (*person, ideas*) inflexible

rigorous ['rɪgərəs] *adj* riguroso

rim [rɪm] *n* borde *m*; (*of spectacles*) aro; (*of wheel*) llanta

rind [raɪnd] *n* (*of bacon*) corteza; (*of lemon etc*) cáscara; (*of cheese*) costra

ring [rɪŋ] (*pt* **rang**, *pp* **rung**) *n* (*of metal*) aro; (*on finger*) anillo; (*of people*) corro; (*of objects*) círculo; (*gang*) banda; (*for boxing*) cuadrilátero; (*of circus*) pista; (*bull ring*) ruedo, plaza; (*sound of bell*) toque *m* ▷ *vi* (*on telephone*) llamar por teléfono; (*bell*) repicar; (*doorbell, phone*) sonar; (*also:* **~ out**) sonar; (*ears*) zumbar ▷ *vt* (BRIT Tel) llamar, telefonear; (*bell etc*) hacer sonar;

(*doorbell*) tocar; **to give sb a ~** (BRIT Tel) llamar or telefonear a algn; **ring back** (BRIT) *vt, vi* (Tel) devolver la llamada; **ring off** (BRIT) *vi* (Tel) colgar, cortar la comunicación; **ring up** (BRIT) *vt* (Tel) llamar, telefonear; **ringing tone** *n* (Tel) tono de llamada; **ringleader** *n* (*of gang*) cabecilla *m*; **ring road** *n* (BRIT) carretera periférica or de circunvalación; **ringtone** *n* (*on mobile*) tono de llamada

rink [rɪŋk] *n* (*also:* **ice ~**) pista de hielo

rinse [rɪns] *n* aclarado; (*dye*) tinte *m* ▷ *vt* aclarar; (*mouth*) enjuagar

riot ['raɪət] *n* motín *m*, disturbio ▷ *vi* amotinarse; **to run ~** desmandarse

rip [rɪp] *n* rasgón *m*, rasgadura ▷ *vt* rasgar, desgarrar ▷ *vi* rasgarse, desgarrarse; **rip off** *vt* (*inf: cheat*) estafar; **rip up** *vt* hacer pedazos

ripe [raɪp] *adj* maduro

rip-off ['rɪpɔf] *n* (*inf*): **it's a ~!** ¡es una estafa!, ¡es un timo!

ripple ['rɪpl] *n* onda, rizo; (*sound*) murmullo ▷ *vi* rizarse

rise [raɪz] (*pt* **rose**, *pp* **risen**) *n* (*slope*) cuesta, pendiente *f*; (*hill*) altura; (BRIT: *in wages*) aumento; (*in prices, temperature*) subida; (*fig: to power etc*) ascenso ▷ *vi* subir; (*waters*) crecer; (*sun, moon*) salir; (*person: from bed etc*) levantarse; (*also:* **~ up**: *rebel*) sublevarse; (*in rank*) ascender; **to give ~ to** dar lugar or origen a; **to ~ to the occasion** ponerse a la altura de las circunstancias; **risen** ['rɪzn] *pp of* **rise**; **rising** *adj* (*increasing: number*) creciente; (*: prices*) en aumento or alza; (*tide*) creciente; (*sun, moon*) naciente

risk [rɪsk] *n* riesgo, peligro ▷ *vt* arriesgar; (*run the risk of*) exponerse a; **to take** or **run the ~ of doing** correr el riesgo de hacer; **at ~** en peligro; **at one's own ~** bajo su propia responsabilidad; **risky** *adj* arriesgado, peligroso

rite [raɪt] *n* rito; **last ~s** exequias *f pl*

ritual ['rɪtjuəl] *adj* ritual ▷ *n* ritual

m, rito

rival ['raɪvl] n rival mf; (in business) competidor(a) m/f ▷ adj rival, opuesto ▷ vt competir con; **rivalry** n competencia

river ['rɪvə*] n río ▷ cpd (port) de río; (traffic) fluvial; **up/down** ~ río arriba/abajo; **riverbank** n orilla f (del río)

rivet ['rɪvɪt] n roblón m, remache m ▷ vt (fig) captar

road [rəud] n camino; (motorway etc) carretera; (in town) calle f ▷ cpd (accident) de tráfico; **major/minor** ~ carretera principal/secundaria; **roadblock** n barricada; **road map** n mapa m de carreteras; **road rage** n agresividad al volante; **road safety** n seguridad f vial; **roadside** n borde m (del camino); **roadsign** n señal f de tráfico; **road tax** n (BRIT) impuesto m de rodaje; **roadworks** npl obras fpl

roam [rəum] vi vagar

roar [rɔː*] n rugido; (of vehicle, storm) estruendo; (of laughter) carcajada ▷ vi rugir; hacer estruendo; **to ~ with laughter** reírse a carcajadas; **to do a ~ing trade** hacer buen negocio

roast [rəust] n carne f asada, asado ▷ vt asar; (coffee) tostar; **roast beef** n rosbif m

rob [rɔb] vt robar; **to ~ sb of sth** robar algo a algn; (fig: deprive) quitar algo a algn; **robber** n ladrón/ona m/f; **robbery** n robo

robe [rəub] n (for ceremony etc) toga; (also: **bath~**) albornoz m

robin ['rɔbɪn] n petirrojo

robot ['rəubɔt] n robot m

robust [rəu'bʌst] adj robusto, fuerte

rock [rɔk] n roca; (boulder) peña, peñasco; (us: small stone) piedrecita; (BRIT: sweet) ~ pirulí ▷ vt (swing gently: cradle) balancear, mecer; (: child) arrullar; (shake) sacudir ▷ vi mecerse, balancearse; sacudirse; **on the ~s** (drink) con hielo; (marriage etc) en ruinas; **rock and roll** n rocanrol m; **rock climbing** n (Sport) escalada

rocket ['rɔkɪt] n cohete m; **rocking chair** ['rɔkɪŋ-] n mecedora

rocky ['rɔkɪ] adj rocoso

rod [rɔd] n vara, varilla; (also: **fishing ~**) caña

rode [rəud] pt of **ride**

rodent ['rəudnt] n roedor m

rogue [rəug] n pícaro, pillo

role [rəul] n papel m; **role-model** n modelo a imitar

roll [rəul] n rollo; (of bank notes) fajo; (also: **bread~**) panecillo; (register, list) lista, nómina; (sound of drums etc) redoble m ▷ vt hacer rodar; (also: **~ up**: string) enrollar; (cigarette) liar; (also: **~ out**: pastry) aplanar; (flatten: road, lawn) apisonar ▷ vi rodar; (drum) redoblar; (ship) balancearse; **roll over** vi dar una vuelta; **roll up** vi (inf: arrive) aparecer; (carpet) arrollar; (: sleeves) arremangar; **roller** n rodillo; (wheel) rueda; (for road) apisonadora; (for hair) rulo; **Rollerblades®** npl patines mpl en línea; **roller coaster** n montaña rusa; **roller skates** npl patines mpl de rueda; **roller-skating** n patinaje sobre ruedas; **to go roller-skating** ir a patinar (sobre ruedas); **rolling pin** n rodillo (de cocina)

ROM [rɔm] n abbr (Comput: = read only memory) ROM f

Roman ['rəumən] (irreg) adj romano/a; **Roman Catholic** (irreg) adj, n católico/a m/f (romano/a)

romance [rə'mæns] n (love affair) amor m; (charm) lo romántico; (novel) novela de amor

Romania etc [ruː'meɪnɪə] n = **Rumania** etc

Roman numeral n número romano

romantic [rə'mæntɪk] adj romántico

Rome [rəum] n Roma

roof [ruːf] (pl ~s) n techo; (of house) techo, tejado ▷ vt techar, poner techo a; **the ~ of the mouth** el paladar; **roof rack** n (Aut) baca, portaequipajes m inv

rook [ruk] n (bird) graja; (Chess) torre f

room [ruːm] n cuarto, habitación
f; (also: **bed-**) dormitorio, recámara
(MEX), pieza (SC); (in school etc) sala;
(space, scope) sitio, cabida; **roommate**
n compañero/a de cuarto; **room
service** n servicio de habitaciones;
roomy adj espacioso, (garment)
amplio

rooster ['ruːstə'] n gallo

root [ruːt] n raíz f ▷ vi arraigarse

rope [rəup] n cuerda; (Naut) cable
m ▷ vt (tie) atar o amarrar con (una)
cuerda; (climbers: also: **- together**)
encordarse; (an area: also: **- off**)
acordonar; **to know the -s** (fig)
conocer los trucos (del oficio)

rose [rəuz] pt of **rise** ▷ n rosa; (shrub)
rosal m; (on watering can) roseta

rosé ['rəuzeɪ] n vino rosado

rosemary ['rəuzməri] n romero

rosy ['rəuzɪ] adj rosado, sonrosado; **a
- future** un futuro prometedor

rot [rɒt] n podredumbre f; (fig: pej)
tonterías fpl ▷ vt pudrir ▷ vi pudrirse

rota ['rəutə] n (sistema m de)
turnos m

rotate [rəu'teɪt] vt (revolve) hacer
girar, dar vueltas a; (jobs) alternar ▷ vi
girar, dar vueltas

rotten ['rɒtn] adj (decayed) podrido,
corrompido; (inf: bad) pocho; **to feel -**
(ill) sentirse fatal

rough [rʌf] adj (skin, surface) áspero;
(terrain) quebrado; (road) desigual,
(voice) bronco; (person, manner)
tosco, grosero; (weather) borrascoso;
(treatment) brutal; (sea) picado; (town,
area) peligroso; (cloth) basto; (plan)
preliminar; (guess) aproximado ▷ n
(Golf): **in the -** en las hierbas altas; **to
- it** vivir sin comodidades; **to sleep -**
(BRIT) pasar la noche al raso; **roughly**
adv (handle) torpemente; (make)
toscamente; (speak) groseramente;
(approximately) aproximadamente

roulette [ruː'let] n ruleta

round [raund] adj redondo ▷ n
círculo; (BRIT: of toast) rebanada;

(of policeman) ronda; (of milkman)
recorrido; (of doctor) visitas fpl; (game: of
cards, in competition) partida; (of
ammunition) cartucho; (Boxing) asalto;
(of talks) ronda ▷ vt (corner) doblar
▷ prep alrededor de; (surrounding): **- his
neck/the table** en su cuello/alrededor
de la mesa; (in a circular movement): **to
move - the room/sail - the world**
dar una vuelta a la habitación/
circunnavegar el mundo; (in various
directions): **to move - a room/house**
moverse por toda la habitación/casa;
(approximately) alrededor de; **all -**
por todos lados; **the long way -** por
el camino menos directo; **all (the)
year -** durante todo el año; **it's just
- the corner** (fig) está a la vuelta de la
esquina; **- the clock** adv las 24 horas;
to go - to sb's (house) ir a casa de
algn; **to go - the back** pasar por atrás;
enough to go - bastante (para todos);
a - of applause una salva de aplausos;
a - of drinks/sandwiches una ronda
de bebidas/bocadillos; **round off** vt
(speech etc) acabar, poner término a;
round up vt (cattle) acorralar; (people)
reunir; (price) redondear; **roundabout**
(BRIT) n (Aut) isleta; (at fair) tiovivo
▷ adj (route, means) indirecto; **round
trip** n viaje m de ida y vuelta; **roundup**
n rodeo; (of criminals) redada; (of news)
resumen m

rouse [rauz] vt (wake up) despertar;
(stir up) suscitar

route [ruːt] n ruta, camino; (of bus)
recorrido; (of shipping) derrota

routine [ruː'tiːn] adj rutinario ▷ n
rutina; (Theatre) número

row[1] [rəu] n (line) fila, hilera; (Knitting)
pasada ▷ vi (in boat) remar ▷ vt
conducir remando; **4 days in a -** 4 días
seguidos

row[2] [rau] n (racket) escándalo;
(dispute) bronca, pelea; (scolding)
regaño ▷ vi pelear(se)

rowboat ['rəubəut] (US) = **rowing
boat**

rowing ['rəʊɪŋ] n remo; **rowing boat** (BRIT) n bote m de remos

royal ['rɔɪəl] adj real; **royalty** n (royal persons) familia real; (payment to author) derechos mpl de autor

rpm abbr (= revs per minute) r.p.m.

R.S.V.P. abbr (= répondez s'il vous plaôt) SRC

Rt. Hon. abbr (BRIT) (= Right Honourable) título honorífico de diputado

rub [rʌb] vt frotar; (scrub) restregar ▷ n: **to give sth a ~** frotar algo; **to ~ sb up** or **~ sb** (us) **the wrong way** entrañe algn por mal ojo; **rub in** vt (ointment) aplicar frotando; **rub off** vi borrarse; **rub out** vt borrar

rubber ['rʌbə*] n caucho, goma; (BRIT: eraser) goma de borrar; **rubber band** n gomita; **rubber gloves** npl guantes mpl de goma

rubbish ['rʌbɪʃ] n basura; (waste) desperdicios mpl; (fig: pej) tonterías fpl; (junk) pacotilla; **rubbish bin** (BRIT) n cubo or bote m (MEX) or tacho (sc) de la basura; **rubbish dump** (BRIT) n vertedero, basurero

rubble ['rʌbl] n escombros mpl

ruby ['ru:bɪ] n rubí m

rucksack ['rʌksæk] n mochila

rudder ['rʌdə*] n timón m

rude [ru:d] adj (impolite: person) mal educado; (: word, manners) grosero; (crude) crudo; (indecent) indecente

ruffle ['rʌfl] vt (hair) despeinar; (clothes) arrugar; **to get ~d** (fig: person) alterarse

rug [rʌg] n alfombra; (BRIT: blanket) manta

rugby ['rʌgbɪ] n rugby m

rugged ['rʌgɪd] adj (landscape) accidentado; (features) robusto

ruin ['ru:ɪn] n ruina ▷ vt arruinar; (spoil) estropear; **ruins** npl ruinas fpl, restos mpl

rule [ru:l] n (norm) norma, costumbre f; (regulation, ruler) regla; (government) dominio ▷ vt (country, person) gobernar ▷ vi gobernar; (Law) fallar;

as a ~ por regla general; **rule out** vt excluir; **ruler** n (sovereign) soberano; (for measuring) regla; **ruling** adj (party) gobernante; (class) dirigente ▷ n (Law) fallo, decisión f

rum [rʌm] n ron m

Rumania [ru:'meɪnɪə] n Rumania; **Rumanian** adj rumano/a m/f; (Ling) rumano

rumble ['rʌmbl] n (noise) ruido sordo ▷ vi retumbar, hacer un ruido sordo; (stomach, pipe) sonar

rumour ['ru:mə*] (US **rumor**) n rumor m ▷ vt: **it is ~ed that** ... se rumorea que ...

rump steak n filete m de lomo

run [rʌn] (pt **ran**, pp **run**) n (fast pace): **at a ~** corriendo; (Sport, in tights) carrera; (outing) paseo, excursión f; (distance travelled) trayecto; (series) serie f; (Theatre) temporada; (Ski) pista ▷ vt correr; (operate: business) dirigir; (: competition, course) organizar; (: hotel, house) administrar, llevar; (Comput) ejecutar; (pass: hand) pasar; (Press: feature) publicar ▷ vi correr; (work: machine) funcionar, marchar; (bus, train: operate) circular, ir; (: travel) ir; (continue: play) seguir; (contract) ser válido; (flow: river) fluir; (colours, washing) desteñirse; (in election) ser candidato; **there was a ~ on** (meat, tickets) hubo mucha demanda de; **in the long ~** a la larga; **on the ~** en fuga; **I'll ~ you to the station** te llevaré a la estación (en coche); **to ~ a risk** correr un riesgo; **to ~ a bath** llenar la bañera; **run after** vt fus (to catch up) correr tras; (chase) perseguir; **run away** vi huir; **run down** vt (production) ir reduciendo; (factory) ir restringiendo la producción en; (car) atropellar; (criticize) criticar; **to be run down** (person: tired) estar debilitado; **run into** vt fus (meet: person, trouble) tropezar con; (collide with) chocar con; **run off** vt (water) dejar correr; (copies) sacar ▷ vi huir corriendo; **run out** vi (person) salir corriendo; (*liquid*) irse; (*lease*) caducar, vencer; (*money etc*) acabarse; **run out of** *vt fus* quedarse sin; **run over** *vt* (*Aut*) atropellar ▷ *vt fus* (*revise*) repasar; **run through** *vt fus* (*instructions*) repasar; **run up** *vt* (*debt*) contraer; **to run up against** (*difficulties*) tropezar con;

runaway *adj* (*horse*) desbocado; (*truck*) sin frenos; (*child*) escapado de casa

rung [rʌŋ] *pp of* **ring** ▷ *n* (*of ladder*) escalón *m*, peldaño

runner ['rʌnə*] *n* (*in race: person*) corredor(a) *m/f*; (*: horse*) caballo; (*on sledge*) patín *m*; **runner bean** (*BRIT*) *n* = judía verde; **runner-up** *n* subcampeón/ona *m/f*

running ['rʌnɪŋ] *n* (*sport*) atletismo; (*of business*) administración *f* ▷ *adj* (*water, costs*) corriente; (*commentary*) continuo; **to be in/out of the ~ for sth** tener/no tener posibilidades de ganar algo; **6 days** ~ 6 días seguidos

runny ['rʌnɪ] *adj* fluido; (*nose, eyes*) gastante

run-up ['rʌnʌp] *n*: **~ to** (*election etc*) período previo a

runway ['rʌnweɪ] *n* (*Aviat*) pista de aterrizaje

rupture ['rʌptʃə*] *n* (*Med*) hernia ▷ *vt*: **to ~ o.s.** causarse una hernia

rural ['ruərl] *adj* rural

rush [rʌʃ] *n* ímpetu *m*; (*hurry*) prisa; (*Comm*) demanda repentina; (*current*) corriente fluerte; (*of feeling*) torrente *m*; (*Bot*) junco ▷ *vt* apresurar; (*work*) hacer de prisa ▷ *vi* correr, precipitarse; **rush hour** *n* horas *fpl* punta

Russia ['rʌʃə] *n* Rusia; **Russian** *adj* ruso/a ▷ *n* ruso/a *m/f*; (*Ling*) ruso

rust [rʌst] *n* herrumbre *f*, moho ▷ *vi* oxidarse

rusty ['rʌstɪ] *adj* oxidado

ruthless ['ruːθlɪs] *adj* despiadado

RV (*us*) *n abbr* = **recreational vehicle**

rye [raɪ] *n* centeno

S

Sabbath ['sæbəθ] *n* domingo; (*Jewish*) sábado

sabotage ['sæbətɑːʒ] *n* sabotaje *m* ▷ *vt* sabotear

saccharin(e) ['sækərɪn] *n* sacarina

sachet ['sæʃeɪ] *n* sobrecito

sack [sæk] *n* (*bag*) saco, costal *m* ▷ *vt* (*dismiss*) despedir; (*plunder*) saquear; **to get the ~** ser despedido

sacred ['seɪkrɪd] *adj* sagrado, santo

sacrifice ['sækrɪfaɪs] *n* sacrificio ▷ *vt* sacrificar

sad [sæd] *adj* (*unhappy*) triste; (*deplorable*) lamentable

saddle ['sædl] *n* silla (de montar); (*of cycle*) sillín *m* ▷ *vt* (*horse*) ensillar; **to be ~d with sth** (*inf*) quedar cargado con algo

sadistic [sə'dɪstɪk] *adj* sádico

sadly ['sædlɪ] *adv* lamentablemente; **to be ~ lacking in** estar por desgracia carente de

sadness ['sædnɪs] *n* tristeza

s.a.e. *abbr* (= *stamped addressed envelope*) sobre con las propias señas de uno y con sello

safari [səˈfɑːrɪ] n safari m

safe [seɪf] adj (out of danger) fuera de peligro; (not dangerous, sure) seguro; (unharmed) ileso ▷ n caja de caudales, caja fuerte; **~ and sound** sano y salvo; **(just) to be on the ~ side** para mayor seguridad; **safely** adv seguramente, con seguridad; **to arrive safely** llegar bien; **safe sex** n sexo seguro or sin riesgo

safety [ˈseɪftɪ] n seguridad f; **safety belt** n cinturón m (de seguridad); **safety pin** n imperdible m, seguro (MEX); alfiler m de gancho (SC)

saffron [ˈsæfrən] n azafrán m

sag [sæg] vi aflojarse

sage [seɪdʒ] n (herb) salvia; (man) sabio

Sagittarius [sædʒɪˈtɛərɪəs] n Sagitario

Sahara [səˈhɑːrə] n: **the ~ (Desert)** (el desierto del) Sáhara

said [sɛd] pt, pp of **say**

sail [seɪl] n (on boat) vela; (trip): **to go for a ~** dar un paseo en barco ▷ vt (boat) gobernar ▷ vi (travel: ship) navegar; (Sport) hacer vela; (begin voyage) salir; **they ~ed into Copenhagen** arribaron a Copenhague; **sailboat** (US) n = **sailing boat**; **sailing** n (Sport) vela; **to go sailing** hacer vela; **sailing boat** n barco de vela; **sailor** n marinero, marino

saint [seɪnt] n santo

sake [seɪk] n: **for the ~ of** por; por el (la) mismo/a, los(las) mismos/as; **the ~ book as** el mismo libro que; **at the ~ time** (at the same moment) al mismo tiempo; (yet) sin embargo; **just the ~** sin embargo, aun así; **to do the ~ (as sb)** hacer lo mismo (que algn); **the ~ to you!** ¡igualmente!

salad [ˈsæləd] n ensalada; **salad cream** (BRIT) n (especie f de) mayonesa; **salad dressing** n aliño

salami [səˈlɑːmɪ] n salami m, salchichón m

salary [ˈsælərɪ] n sueldo

sale [seɪl] n venta; (at reduced prices) liquidación f, saldo; (auction) subasta; **sales** npl (total amount sold) ventas fpl, facturación f; **"for ~"** "se vende"; **on ~** en venta; **on ~ or return** (goods) venta por reposición; **sales assistant** (US),

sales clerk n dependiente/a m/f;

salesman/woman (irreg) n (in shop) dependiente/a m/f; **salesperson** (irreg) n vendedor(a) m/f, dependiente/a m/f; **sales rep** n representante mf, agente mf comercial

saline [ˈseɪlaɪn] adj salino

saliva [səˈlaɪvə] n saliva

salmon [ˈsæmən] n inv salmón m

salon [ˈsælɒn] n (hairdressing salon) peluquería; (beauty salon) salón m de belleza

saloon [səˈluːn] n (US) bar m, taberna; (BRIT Aut) coche m (de) turismo; (ship's lounge) cámara, salón m

salt [sɔlt] n sal f ▷ vt salar; (put salt on) poner sal en; **saltwater** adj de agua salada; **salty** adj salado

salute [səˈluːt] n saludo; (of guns) salva ▷ vt saludar

salvage [ˈsælvɪdʒ] n (saving) salvamento, recuperación f; (things saved) objetos mpl salvados ▷ vt salvar

Salvation Army [sælˈveɪʃən-] n Ejército de Salvación

same [seɪm] adj mismo ▷ pron: **the ~** el(la) mismo/a, los(las) mismos/as; **the ~ book as** el mismo libro que; **at the ~ time** (at the same moment) al mismo tiempo; (yet) sin embargo; **just the ~** sin embargo, aun así; **to do the ~ (as sb)** hacer lo mismo (que algn); **the ~ to you!** ¡igualmente!

sample [ˈsɑːmpl] n muestra ▷ vt (food) probar; (wine) catar

sanction [ˈsæŋkʃən] n aprobación f ▷ vt sancionar; aprobar; **sanctions** npl (Pol) sanciones fpl

sanctuary [ˈsæŋktjuərɪ] n santuario; (refuge) asilo, refugio; (for wildlife) reserva

sand [sænd] n arena; (beach) playa ▷ vt (also: **~ down**) lijar

sandal [ˈsændl] n sandalia

sand: **sandbox** (US) n = **sandpit**; **sandcastle** n castillo de arena; **sand dune** n duna; **sandpaper** n papel m de lija; **sandpit** n (for children) cajón m

de arena; **sands** *npl* playa *sg* de arena;
sandstone ['sændstəʊn] *n* piedra
arenisca
sandwich ['sændwɪtʃ] *n* sandwich
m ▷ *vt* intercalar; **~ed between**
apretujado entre; **cheese/ham ~**
sandwich de queso/jamón
sandy ['sændɪ] *adj* arenoso; *(colour)*
rojizo
sane [seɪn] *adj* cuerdo; *(sensible)*
sensato

Be careful not to translate **sane** by
the Spanish word *sano*.

sang [sæŋ] *pt of* **sing**
sanitary towel (*us* **sanitary napkin**)
n paño higiénico, compresa
sanity ['sænɪtɪ] *n* cordura; *(of
judgment)* sensatez *f*
sank [sæŋk] *pt of* **sink**
Santa Claus [sæntə'klɔːz] *n* San
Nicolás, Papá Noel
sap [sæp] *n* *(of plants)* savia ▷ *vt*
(strength) minar, agotar
sapphire ['sæfaɪə*] *n* zafiro
sarcasm ['sɑːkæzm] *n* sarcasmo
sarcastic [sɑː'kæstɪk] *adj* sarcástico
sardine [sɑː'diːn] *n* sardina
SASE (*us*) *n abbr* (= *self-addressed
stamped envelope*) *sobre con las propias
señas de uno y con sello*
Sat. *abbr* (= *Saturday*) sáb
sat [sæt] *pt, pp of* **sit**
satchel ['sætʃl] *n* *(child's)* mochila,
cartera (*sp*)
satellite ['sætəlaɪt] *n* satélite *m*;
satellite dish *n* antena de televisión
por satélite; **satellite television** *n*
televisión *f* vía satélite
satin ['sætɪn] *n* raso ▷ *adj* de raso
satire ['sætaɪə*] *n* sátira
satisfaction [sætɪs'fækʃən] *n*
satisfacción *f*
satisfactory [sætɪs'fæktərɪ] *adj*
satisfactorio
satisfied ['sætɪsfaɪd] *adj* satisfecho;
to be ~ (with sth) estar satisfecho
(de algo)
satisfy ['sætɪsfaɪ] *vt* satisfacer;

(convince) convencer
Saturday ['sætədeɪ] *n* sábado
sauce [sɔːs] *n* salsa; *(sweet)* crema;
jarabe *m*; **saucepan** *n* cacerola, olla
saucer ['sɔːsə*] *n* platillo; **Saudi
Arabia** *n* Arabia Saudí or Saudita
sauna ['sɔːnə] *n* sauna
sausage ['sɔsɪdʒ] *n* salchicha;
sausage roll *n* empanada de
salchicha
sautéed ['səʊteɪd] *adj* salteado
savage ['sævɪdʒ] *adj* *(cruel, fierce)*
feroz, furioso; *(primitive)* salvaje ▷ *n*
salvaje *m/f* ▷ *vt* *(attack)* embestir
save [seɪv] *vt* *(rescue)* salvar, rescatar;
(money, time) ahorrar; *(put by, keep: seat)*
guardar; *(Comput)* salvar (y guardar);
(avoid: trouble) evitar; *(Sport)* parar ▷ *vi*
(also: ~ up) ahorrar ▷ *n* *(Sport)* parada
▷ *prep* salvo, excepto
savings ['seɪvɪŋz] *npl* ahorros *mpl*;
savings account *n* cuenta de ahorros;
savings and loan association (*us*) *n*
sociedad *f* de ahorro y préstamo
savoury ['seɪvərɪ] (*us* **savory**) *adj*
sabroso; *(dish: not sweet)* salado
saw [sɔː] *(pt* **-ed***, pp* **-ed** *or* **-n**) *pt
of* **see** *n* *(tool)* sierra ▷ *vt* serrar;
sawdust *n* (a)serrín *m*
sawn [sɔːn] *pp of* **saw**
saxophone ['sæksəfəʊn] *n* saxófono
say [seɪ] (*pt, pp* **said**) *n*: **to have one's
~** expresar su opinión ▷ *vt* decir; **to
have a** *or* **some ~ in sth** tener voz or
tener que ver en algo; **to ~ yes/no** decir
que sí/no; **could you ~ that again?**
¿podría repetir eso?; **that is to ~** es
decir; **that goes without ~ing** ni que
decir tiene; **saying** *n* dicho, refrán *m*
scab [skæb] *n* costra; *(pej)* esquirol *m*
scaffolding ['skæfəldɪŋ] *n* andamio,
andamiaje *m*
scald [skɔːld] *n* escaldadura ▷ *vt*
escaldar
scale [skeɪl] *n* *(gen, Mus)* escala;
(of fish) escama; *(of salaries, fees
etc)* escalafón *m* ▷ *vt* *(mountain)*
escalar; *(tree)* trepar; **scales** *npl* *(for*

weighing: *small*) balanza; (; *large*) báscula; **on a large ~** en gran escala; **~ of charges** tarifa, lista de precios

scallion ['skæljən] (*us*) *n* cebolleta

scallop ['skɔləp] *n* (*Zool*) venera; (*Sewing*) festón *m*

scalp [skælp] *n* cabellera ▷ *vt* escalpar

scalpel ['skælpl] *n* bisturí *m*

scam [skæm] *n* (*inf*) estafa, timo

scampi ['skæmpɪ] *npl* gambas *fpl*

scan [skæn] *vt* (*examine*) escudriñar; (*glance at quickly*) dar un vistazo a; (*TV, Radar*) explorar, registrar ▷ *n* (*Med*): **to have a ~** pasar por el escáner

scandal ['skændl] *n* escándalo; (*gossip*) chismes *mpl*

Scandinavia [skændɪ'neɪvɪə] *n* Escandinavia; **Scandinavian** *adj, n* escandinavo/a *m/f*

scanner ['skænə*] *n* (*Radar, Med*) escáner *m*

scapegoat ['skeɪpgəut] *n* cabeza de turco, chivo expiatorio

scar [skɑ:] *n* cicatriz *f*; (*fig*) señal *f* ▷ *vt* dejar señales en

scarce [skɛəs] *adj* escaso; **to make o.s. ~** (*inf*) esfumarse; **scarcely** *adv* apenas

scare [skɛə*] *n* susto, sobresalto; (*panic*) pánico ▷ *vt* asustar, espantar; **to ~ sb stiff** dar a algn un susto de muerte; **bomb ~** amenaza de bomba; **scarecrow** *n* espantapájaros *m inv*; **scared** *adj*: **to be scared** estar asustado

scarf [skɑ:f] (*pl* **~s** *or* **scarves**) *n* (*long*) bufanda; (*square*) pañuelo

scarlet ['skɑ:lɪt] *adj* escarlata

scarves [skɑ:vz] *npl of* **scarf**

scary ['skɛərɪ] (*inf*) *adj* espeluznante

scatter ['skætə*] *vt* (*spread*) esparcir, desparramar; (*put to flight*) dispersar ▷ *vi* desparramarse; dispersarse

scenario [sɪ'nɑ:rɪəu] *n* (*Theatre*) argumento; (*Cinema*) guión *m*; (*fig*) escenario

scene [si:n] *n* (*Theatre, fig etc*)

escena; (*of crime etc*) escenario; (*view*) panorama *m*; (*fuss*) escándalo; **scenery** *n* (*Theatre*) decorado; (*landscape*) paisaje *m*

▌ Be careful not to translate **scenery** by the Spanish word *escenario*.

scenic *adj* pintoresco

scent [sɛnt] *n* perfume *m*, olor *m*; (*fig: track*) rastro, pista

sceptical ['skɛptɪkl] *adj* escéptico

schedule ['ʃɛdju:l] (*us*) ['skɛdju:l] *n* (*timetable*) horario; (*of events*) programa *m*; (*list*) lista ▷ *vt* (*visit*) fijar la hora de; **to arrive on ~** llegar a la hora debida; **to be ahead of/behind ~** estar adelantado/en retraso; **scheduled flight** *n* vuelo regular

scheme [ski:m] *n* (*plan*) plan *m*, proyecto; (*plot*) intriga; (*arrangement*) disposición *f*; (*pension scheme etc*) sistema *m* ▷ *vi* (*intrigue*) intrigar

schizophrenic [skɪtzə'frɛnɪk] *adj* esquizofrénico

scholar ['skɔlə*] *n* (*pupil*) alumno/a; (*learned person*) sabio *m*, erudito/a; **scholarship** *n* erudición *f*; (*grant*) beca

school [sku:l] *n* escuela, colegio; (*in university*) facultad *f* ▷ *cpd* escolar; **schoolbook** *n* libro de texto; **schoolboy** *n* alumno; **school children** *npl* alumnos *mpl*; **schoolgirl** *n* alumna; **schooling** *n* enseñanza; **schoolteacher** *n* (*primary*) maestro/a; (*secondary*) profesor/a *m/f*

science ['saɪəns] *n* ciencia; **science fiction** *n* ciencia-ficción *f*; **scientific** [-'tɪfɪk] *adj* científico; **scientist** *n* científico/a

sci-fi ['saɪfaɪ] *n abbr* (*inf*) = **science fiction**

scissors ['sɪzəz] *npl* tijeras *fpl*; **a pair of ~** unas tijeras

scold [skəuld] *vt* regañar

scone [skɔn] *n* pastel de pan

scoop [sku:p] *n* (*for flour etc*) pala; (*Press*) exclusiva

scooter ['sku:tə*] *n* moto *f*; (*toy*) patinete *m*

scope [skəʊp] *n* (of plan) ámbito; (of person) competencia; (opportunity) libertad *f* (de acción)

scorching ['skɔːtʃɪŋ] *adj* (heat, sun) abrasador(a)

score [skɔː*] *n* (points etc) puntuación *f*; (Mus) partitura; (twenty) veintena ▷ *vt* (goal, point) ganar; (mark) rayar; (achieve: success) conseguir ▷ *vi* marcar un tanto; (Football) marcar (un) gol; (keep score) llevar el tanteo; **~s of** (lots of) decenas de; **on that ~** en lo que se refiere a eso; **to ~ 6 out of 10** obtener una puntuación de 6 sobre 10; **score out** *vt* tachar; **scoreboard** *n* marcador *m*; **scorer** *n* marcador *m*; (keeping score) encargado/a del marcador

scorn [skɔːn] *n* desprecio

Scorpio ['skɔːpɪəʊ] *n* Escorpión *m*

scorpion ['skɔːpɪən] *n* alacrán *m*

Scot [skɒt] *n* escocés/esa *m/f*

Scotch tape® (us) *n* cinta adhesiva, celo, scotch® *f*

Scotland ['skɒtlənd] *n* Escocia

Scots [skɒts] *adj* escocés/esa; **Scotsman** (*irreg*) *n* escocés; **Scotswoman** (*irreg*) *n* escocesa; **Scottish** ['skɒtɪʃ] *adj* escocés/esa; **Scottish Parliament** *n* Parlamento escocés

scout [skaʊt] *n* (Mil: also: **boy ~**) explorador *m*; **girl ~** (us) niña exploradora

scowl [skaʊl] *vi* fruncir el ceño; **to ~ at sb** mirar con ceño a algn

scramble ['skræmbl] *n* (climb) subida (difícil); (struggle) pelea ▷ *vi*: **to ~ through/out** abrirse paso/salir con dificultad; **to ~ for** pelear por; **scrambled eggs** *npl* huevos *mpl* revueltos

scrap [skræp] *n* (bit) pedacito *m*; (fig) pizca; (fight) riña, bronca; (also: **~ iron**) chatarra, hierro viejo ▷ *vt* (discard) desechar, descartar ▷ *vi* reñir, armar una bronca; **scraps** *npl* (waste) sobras *fpl*, desperdicios *mpl*; **scrapbook** *n*

álbum *m* de recortes

scrape [skreɪp] *n*: **to get into a ~** meterse en un lío ▷ *vt* (skin etc) rasguñar; (scrape against) rozar ▷ *vi*: **to ~ through** (exam) aprobar por los pelos; **scrap paper** *n* pedazos *mpl* de papel

scratch [skrætʃ] *n* rasguño; (from claw) arañazo ▷ *vt* (paint, car) rayar; (with claw, nail) rasguñar, arañar; (rub: nose etc) rascarse ▷ *vi* rascarse; **to start from ~** partir de cero; **to be up to ~** cumplir con los requisitos; **scratch card** (BRIT) tarjeta *f* de "rasque y gane"

scream [skriːm] *n* chillido ▷ *vi* chillar

screen [skriːn] *n* (Cinema, TV) pantalla; (movable barrier) biombo ▷ *vt* (conceal) tapar; (from the wind etc) proteger; (film) proyectar; (candidates etc) investigar a; **screening** *n* (Med) investigación *f* médica; **screenplay** *n* guión *m*; **screen saver** *n* (Comput) protector *m* de pantalla

screw [skruː] *n* tornillo ▷ *vt* (also: **~ in**) atornillar; **screw up** *vt* (paper etc) arrugar; **to screw up one's eyes** arrugar el entrecejo; **screwdriver** *n* destornillador *m*

scribble ['skrɪbl] *n* garabatos *mpl* ▷ *vt, vi* garabatear

script [skrɪpt] *n* (Cinema etc) guión *m*; (writing) escritura, letra

scroll [skrəʊl] *n* rollo

scrub [skrʌb] *n* (land) maleza ▷ *vt* fregar, restregar; (inf: reject) cancelar, anular

scruffy ['skrʌfɪ] *adj* desaliñado, piojoso

scrum(mage) ['skrʌm(ɪdʒ)] *n* (Rugby) melée *f*

scrutiny ['skruːtɪnɪ] *n* escrutinio, examen *m*

scuba diving ['skuːbə'daɪvɪŋ] *n* submarinismo

sculptor ['skʌlptə*] *n* escultor(a) *m/f*

sculpture ['skʌlptʃə*] *n* escultura

scum [skʌm] *n* (on liquid) espuma;

(pej: people) escoria
scurry ['skʌrɪ] *vi* correr; **to ~ off**
escabullirse
sea [si:] *n* mar *m* ▷ *cpd* de mar,
marítimo; **by ~** *(travel)* en barco; **on the
~** *(boat)* en el mar; *(town)* junto al mar;
to be all at ~ *(fig)* estar despistado;
out to ~, at ~ en alta mar; **seafood**
n mariscos *mpl*; **sea front** *n* paseo
marítimo; **seagull** *n* gaviota
seal [si:l] *n (animal)* foca; *(stamp)* sello
▷ *vt (close)* cerrar; **seal off** *vt (area)*
acordonar
sea level *n* nivel del mar
seam [si:m] *n* costura; *(of metal)*
juntura; *(of coal)* veta, filón *m*
search [sɜ:tʃ] *n (for person, thing)*
busca, búsqueda; *(Comput)* búsqueda;
(inspection: of sb's home) registro ▷ *vt
(look in)* buscar en; *(examine)* examinar;
(person, place) registrar ▷ *vi:* **to ~ for**
buscar; **in ~ of** en busca de; **search
engine** *n (Comput)* buscador *m*; **search
party** *n* pelotón *m* de salvamento
sea: **seashore** *n* playa, orilla del mar;
seasick *adj* mareado; **seaside**
n playa, orilla del mar; **seaside resort** *n*
centro turístico costero
season ['si:zn] *n (of year)* estación
f; *(sporting etc)* temporada; *(of films
etc)* ciclo ▷ *vt (food)* sazonar; **in/out
of ~** en sazón/fuera de temporada;
seasonal *adj* estacional; **seasoning**
n condimento, aderezo; **season ticket**
n abono
seat [si:t] *n (in bus, train)* asiento;
(chair) silla; *(Parliament)* escaño *m*;
(buttocks) culo, trasero; *(of trousers)*
culera ▷ *vt* sentar; *(have room for)*
tener cabida para; **to be ~ed** sentarse;
seat belt *n* cinturón *m* de seguridad;
seating *n* asientos *mpl*
sea: **sea water** *n* agua del mar;
seaweed *n* alga marina
sec. *abbr* =**second(s)**
secluded [sɪ'klu:dɪd] *adj* retirado
second ['sɛkənd] *adj* segundo ▷ *adv*
en segundo lugar ▷ *n* segundo;

(Aut: also: **~ gear)** segunda; *(Comm)*
artículo con algún desperfecto; *(BRIT
Scol: degree)* título de licenciado con
calificación de notable ▷ *vt (motion)*
apoyar; **secondary** *adj* secundario;
secondary school *n* escuela
secundaria; **second-class** *adj* de
segunda clase ▷ *adv* en segunda; *(Rail)* en segundo;
secondhand *adj* de segunda mano,
usado; **secondly** *adv* en segundo
lugar; **second-rate** *adj* de segunda
categoría; **second thoughts:** **to have
second thoughts** cambiar de opinión;
on second thoughts *or* **thought** *(us)*
pensándolo bien
secrecy ['si:krəsɪ] *n* secreto
secret ['si:krɪt] *adj, n* secreto; **in ~**
en secreto
secretary ['sɛkrətərɪ] *n* secretario/a;
S~ of State (for) *(BRIT Pol)* Ministro
(de)
secretive ['si:krətɪv] *adj* reservado,
sigiloso
secret service *n* servicio secreto
sect [sɛkt] *n* secta
section ['sɛkʃən] *n (gen)* sección *f*; *(part)*
parte *f*; *(of document)* artículo; *(of
opinion)* sector *m*; *(cross-section)* corte
m transversal
sector ['sɛktə*] *n* sector *m*
secular ['sɛkjulə*] *adj* secular, seglar
secure [sɪ'kjuə*] *adj (firmly
fixed)* firme, fijo ▷ *vt (fix)* asegurar,
afianzar; *(get)* conseguir
security [sɪ'kjuərɪtɪ] *n* seguridad
f; *(for loan)* fianza; *(: object)* prenda;
securities *npl (Comm)* valores *mpl*,
títulos *mpl*; **security guard** *n* guardia
m/f de seguridad
sedan [sɪ'dæn] *(us)* *n (Aut)* sedán *m*
sedate [sɪ'deɪt] *adj* tranquilo ▷ *vt*
tratar con sedantes
sedative ['sɛdɪtɪv] *n* sedante *m*,
sedativo
seduce [sɪ'dju:s] *vt* seducir;
seductive [-'dʌktɪv] *adj* seductor(a)
see [si:] *(pt* **saw**, *pp* **seen)** *vt* ver;
(accompany): **to ~ sb to the door**

acompañar a algn a la puerta; (*understand*) ver, comprender ▷ vi ver ▷ n (*arz*)obispado; **to ~ that** (*ensure*) asegurar que; **~ you soon!** ¡hasta pronto!; **see off** vt despedir; **see out** vt (*take to the door*)acompañar hasta la puerta; **see through** vt fus (*fig*) calar ▷ vt (*plan*) llevar a cabo; **see to** vt fus atender a, encargarse de

seed [siːd] n semilla; (*in fruit*) pepita; (*fig: gen pl*) germen m; (*Tennis etc*) preseleccionado/a; **to go to ~** (*plant*) granar; (*fig*) descuajarse

seeing [ˈsiːɪŋ] conj: **~ (that)** visto que, en vista de que

seek [siːk] (*pt, pp* **sought**) vt buscar; (*post*) solicitar

seem [siːm] vi parecer; **there ~s to be ...** parece que hay ...; **seemingly** adv aparentemente, según parece

seen [siːn] pp *of* **see**

seesaw [ˈsiːsɔː] n subibaja

segment [ˈsegmənt] n (*part*) sección f; (*of orange*) gajo

segregate [ˈsegrigeit] vt segregar

seize [siːz] vt (*grasp*) agarrar, asir; (*take possession of*) secuestrar; (: *territory*) apoderarse de; (*opportunity*) aprovecharse de

seizure [ˈsiːʒəʳ] n (*Med*) ataque m; (*Law, of power*) incautación f

seldom [ˈseldəm] adv rara vez

select [sɪˈlekt] adj selecto, escogido ▷ vt escoger, elegir; (*Sport*) seleccionar; **selection** n selección f, elección f; (*Comm*) surtido; **selective** adj selectivo

self [self] (*pl* **selves**) n uno mismo; **the ~** el yo ▷ prefix auto...; **self-assured** adj seguro de sí mismo; **self-catering** adj (*flat etc*) con cocina; **self-centred** (*us* **self-centered**) adj egocéntrico; **self-confidence** n confianza en sí mismo; **self-confident** adj seguro de sí (mismo), lleno de confianza en sí mismo; **self-conscious** adj cohibido; **self-contained** (*brit*) adj (*flat*) con

entrada particular; **self-control** n autodominio; **self-defence** (*us* **self-defense**) n defensa propia; **self-drive** adj (*brit*) choche or (*sp*) chófer; **self-employed** adj que trabaja por cuenta propia; **self-esteem** n amor m propio; **self-indulgent** adj autocomplaciente; **self-interest** n egoísmo; **selfish** adj egoísta; **self-pity** n lástima de sí mismo; **self-raising** [selfˈreɪzɪŋ] (*us* **self-rising**) adj: **self-raising flour** harina con levadura; **self-respect** n amor m propio; **self-service** adj de autoservicio

sell [sel] (*pt, pp* **sold**) vt vender ▷ vi venderse; **to ~ at** or **for £10** venderse a 10 libras; **sell off** vt liquidar; **sell out** vi: **to sell out of tickets/milk** vender todas las entradas/toda la leche; **sell-by date** n fecha de caducidad; **seller** n vendedor(a) m/f

Sellotape® [ˈseləuteɪp] (*brit*) n celo (*sp*), cinta Scotch® (*lam*) or Dúrex® (*mex, arg*)

selves [selvz] npl *of* **self**

semester [sɪˈmestəʳ] (*us*) n semestre m

semi... [semi] prefix semi..., medio...; **semicircle** n semicírculo; **semidetached (house)** n (*casa*) semiseparada; **semi-final** n semifinal m

seminar [ˈseminɑːʳ] n seminario

semi-skimmed [semiˈskimd] adj semidesnatado; **semi-skimmed (milk)** n leche semidesnatada

senate [ˈsenɪt] n senado; **the S~** (*us*) el Senado; **senator** n senador(a) m/f

send [send] (*pt, pp* **sent**) vt mandar, enviar; (*signal*) transmitir; **send back** vt devolver; **send for** vt fus mandar traer; **send in** vt (*report, application, resignation*) mandar; **send off** vt (*goods*) despachar; (*brit Sport: player*) expulsar; **send on** vt (*letter, luggage*) remitir; (*person*) mandar; **send out** vt (*invitation*) mandar; (*signal*) emitir; **send up** vt (*person, price*) hacer subir;

(BRIT: parody) parodiar; **sender** n remitente mf; **send-off** n: **a good send-off** una buena despedida

senile ['si:naɪl] adj senil

senior ['si:nɪə*] adj (older) mayor, más viejo; (: on staff) de más antigüedad; (of higher rank) superior; **senior citizen** n persona de la tercera edad; **senior high school** (us) ≈ instituto de enseñanza media; see also **high school**

sensation [sen'seɪʃən] n sensación f; **sensational** adj sensacional

sense [sens] n (faculty, meaning) sentido; (feeling) sensación f; (good sense) sentido común, juicio ▷ vt sentir, percibir; **it makes ~** tiene sentido; **senseless** adj estúpido, insensato; (unconscious) sin conocimiento; **sense of humour** (BRIT) n sentido del humor

sensible ['sensɪbl] adj sensato; (reasonable) razonable, lógico

Be careful not to translate **sensible** by the Spanish word **sensible**.

sensitive ['sensɪtɪv] adj sensible; (touchy) susceptible

sensual ['sensjʊəl] adj sensual

sensuous ['sensjʊəs] adj sensual

sent [sent] pt, pp of **send**

sentence ['sentns] n (Ling) oración f; (Law) sentencia, fallo ▷ vt: **to ~ sb to death/to 5 years (in prison)** condenar a algn a muerte/a 5 años de cárcel

sentiment ['sentɪmənt] n sentimiento; (opinion) opinión f; **sentimental** [-'mentl] adj sentimental

Sep. abbr (= September) sep., set.

separate [adj 'seprɪt, vb 'sepəreɪt] adj separado; (distinct) distinto ▷ vt separar; (part) dividir ▷ vi separarse; **separately** adv por separado; **separates** npl (clothes) coordinados mpl; **separation** [-'reɪʃən] n separación f

September [sep'tembə*] n se(p)tiembre m

septic ['septɪk] adj séptico; **septic**

tank n fosa séptica

sequel ['si:kwl] n consecuencia, resultado; (of story) continuación f

sequence ['si:kwəns] n sucesión f, serie f; (Cinema) secuencia

sequin ['si:kwɪn] n lentejuela

Serb [sə:b] adj, n = **Serbian**

Serbian ['sə:bɪən] adj serbio ▷ n serbio/a; (Ling) serbio

sergeant ['sɑ:dʒənt] n sargento

serial ['sɪərɪəl] n (TV) telenovela, serie f televisiva; (Book) serie f; **serial killer** n asesino/a múltiple; **serial number** n número de serie

series ['sɪərɪz] n inv serie f

serious ['sɪərɪəs] adj serio; (grave) grave; **seriously** adv en serio; (ill, wounded etc) gravemente

sermon ['sə:mən] n sermón m

servant ['sə:vənt] n servidor(a) m/f; (house servant) criado/a

serve [sə:v] vt servir; (customer) atender; (train) pasar por; (apprenticeship) hacer; (prison term) cumplir ▷ vi servir; (at table) servir; (Tennis) sacar; **to ~ as/for/to do** servir de/para/para hacer ▷ n (Tennis) saque m; **it ~ s him right** se lo tiene merecido; **server** n (Comput) servidor m

service ['sə:vɪs] n servicio; (Rel) misa; (Aut) mantenimiento; (dishes etc) juego ▷ vt (car etc) revisar; (: repair) reparar; **to be of ~ to sb** ser útil a algn; **~ included/not included** servicio incluido/no incluido (Econ: tertiary sector) sector m terciario or de servicios; (BRIT: on motorway) área de servicios; (Mil): **the S~s** las fuerzas armadas; **service area** n (on motorway) área de servicio; **service charge** (BRIT) n servicio; **serviceman** (irreg) n militar m; **service station** n estación f de servicio

serviette [sə:vɪ'et] (BRIT) n servilleta

session ['seʃən] n sesión f; **to be in ~** estar en sesión

set [set] (pt, pp ~) n juego; (Radio) aparato; (TV) televisor m; (of utensils)

batería; (of cutlery) cubierto; (of books)
colección f; (Tennis) set m; (group
of people) grupo; (Cinema) plató m;
(Theatre) decorado; (Hairdressing)
marcado ▷ adj (fixed) fijo; (ready) listo
▷ vt (place) poner, colocar; (fix) fijar;
(adjust) ajustar, arreglar; (decide: rules
etc) establecer, decidir ▷ vi sun
ponerse; (jam, jelly) cuajarse; (concrete)
fraguar; (bone) componerse; **to be ~ on
doing sth** estar empeñado en hacer
algo; **to ~ to music** poner música a;
to ~ on fire incendiar, poner fuego a;
to ~ free poner en libertad; **to ~ sth
going** poner algo en marcha; **to ~ sail**
zarpar, hacerse a la vela; **set aside** vt
poner aparte, dejar de lado; (money,
time) reservar; **set down** vt (bus, train)
dejar; **set in** vi (infection) declararse;
(complications) comenzar; **the rain
has set in for the day** parece que va a
llover todo el día; **set off** vi partir ▷ vt
(bomb) hacer estallar; (events) poner en
marcha; (show up well) hacer resaltar;
set out vi partir ▷ vt (arrange)
disponer; (state) exponer; **to set out
to do sth** proponerse hacer algo; **set
up** vt establecer; **setback** n revés m,
contratiempo; **set menu** n menú m
settee [se'tiː] n sofá m
setting ['setɪŋ] n (scenery) marco;
(position) disposición f; (of sun) puesta;
(of jewel) engaste m, montadura
settle ['setl] vt (argument) resolver;
(accounts) ajustar, liquidar; (Med: calm)
calmar, sosegar ▷ vi (dust etc)
depositarse; (weather) serenarse; **to
~ for sth** convenir en aceptar algo;
to ~ on sth decidirse por algo; **settle
down** vi (get comfortable) ponerse
cómodo, acomodarse; (calm down)
calmarse, tranquilizarse; (live quietly)
echar raíces; **settle in** vi instalarse;
settle up vi: **to settle up with sb**
ajustar cuentas con algn; **settlement**
n (payment) liquidación f; (agreement)
acuerdo, convenio; (village etc) pueblo
setup ['setʌp] n sistema m; (situation)

situación f
seven ['sevn] num siete; **seventeen**
num diez y siete, diecisiete;
seventeenth [sevn'tiːnθ] adj
decimoséptimo; **seventh** num
séptimo; **seventieth** ['sevntɪɪθ] adj
septuagésimo; **seventy** num setenta
sever ['sevə*] vt cortar; (relations)
romper
several ['sevrəl] adj, pron varios/as
m/fpl, algunos/as m/fpl; **~ of us** varios
de nosotros
severe [sɪ'vɪə*] adj severo; (serious)
grave; (hard) duro; (pain) intenso
sew [səu] (pt **~ed**, pp **~n**) vt, vi coser
sewage ['suːɪdʒ] n aguas fpl
residuales
sewer ['suːə*] n alcantarilla, cloaca
sewing ['səuɪŋ] n costura; **sewing
machine** n máquina de coser
sewn [səun] pp of **sew**
sex [seks] n sexo; (lovemaking): **to
have ~** hacer el amor; **sexism** ['seksɪzə
m] n sexismo; **sexist** adj, n sexista
mf; **sexual** ['seksjuəl] adj sexual;
sexual intercourse n relaciones fpl
sexuales; **sexuality** [seksju'ælɪtɪ] n
sexualidad f; **sexy** adj sexy
shabby ['ʃæbɪ] adj (person)
desharrapado; (clothes) raído, gastado;
(behaviour) ruin inv
shack [ʃæk] n choza, chabola
shade [ʃeɪd] n sombra; (for lamp)
pantalla; (for eyes) visera; (of colour)
matiz m, tonalidad f; (small quantity): **a
~ (too big/more)** un poquitín
(grande/más) ▷ vt dar sombra a; (eyes)
proteger del sol; **in the ~** en la sombra;
shades npl (sunglasses) gafas fpl de sol
shadow ['ʃædəu] n sombra ▷ vt
(follow) seguir y vigilar; **shadow
cabinet** (BRIT) n (Pol) gabinete paralelo
formado por el partido de oposición
shady ['ʃeɪdɪ] adj sombreado;
(fig: dishonest) sospechoso; (: deal)
turbio
shaft [ʃɑːft] n (of arrow, spear) astil m;
(Aut, Tech) eje m, árbol m; (of mine) pozo;

(of lift) hueco, caja; (of light) rayo

shake [ʃeɪk] (pt **shook**, pp **shaken**) vt sacudir; (building) hacer temblar; (bottle, cocktail) agitar ▷ vi (tremble) temblar; **to ~ one's head** (in refusal) negar con la cabeza; (in dismay) mover or menear la cabeza, incrédulo; **to ~ hands with sb** estrechar la mano a algn; **shake off** vt sacudirse; (fig) deshacerse de; **shake up** vt agitar; (fig) reorganizar; **shaky** adj (hand, voice) trémulo; (building) inestable

shall [ʃæl] aux vb: **~ I help you?** ¿quieres que te ayude?; **I'll buy three, ~ I?** compro tres, ¿no te parece?

shallow ['ʃæləu] adj poco profundo; (fig) superficial

sham [ʃæm] n fraude m, engaño

shambles ['ʃæmblz] n confusión f

shame [ʃeɪm] n vergüenza ▷ vt avergonzar; **it is a ~ that/to do es** una lástima que/hacer; **what a ~!** ¡qué lástima!; **shameful** adj vergonzoso; **shameless** adj desvergonzado

shampoo [ʃæm'puː] n champú m ▷ vt lavar con champú

shandy ['ʃændɪ] n mezcla de cerveza con gaseosa

shan't [ʃɑːnt] = **shall not**

shape [ʃeɪp] n forma ▷ vt formar, dar forma a; (sb's ideas) formar; (sb's life) determinar; **to take ~** tomar forma

share [ʃɛə*] n (part) parte f, porción f; (contribution) cuota; (Comm) acción f ▷ vt dividir; (have in common) compartir; **to ~ out (among** or **between)** repartir (entre); **shareholder** (BRIT) n accionista mf

shark [ʃɑːk] n tiburón m

sharp [ʃɑːp] adj (blade, nose) afilado; (point) puntiagudo; (outline) definido; (pain) intenso; (Mus) desafinado; (contrast) marcado; (voice) agudo; (person: quick-witted) astuto; (: dishonest) poco escrupuloso ▷ n (Mus) sostenido ▷ adv: **at 2 o'clock** ~ a las 2 en punto; **sharpen** vt afilar; (pencil) sacar punta a; (fig) agudizar;

sharpener n (also: **pencil sharpener**) sacapuntas m inv; **sharply** adv (turn, stop) bruscamente; (stand out, contrast) claramente; (criticize, retort) severamente

shatter ['ʃætə*] vt hacer añicos or pedazos; (fig: ruin) destruir, acabar con ▷ vi hacerse añicos; **shattered** (grief-stricken) destrozado, deshecho; (exhausted) agotado, hecho polvo

shave [ʃeɪv] vt afeitar, rasurar ▷ vi afeitarse, rasurarse ▷ n: **to have a ~** afeitarse; **shaver** n (also: **electric shaver**) máquina de afeitar (eléctrica)

shavings ['ʃeɪvɪŋz] npl (of wood etc) virutas fpl

shaving cream ['ʃeɪvɪŋ-] n crema de afeitar

shaving foam n espuma de afeitar

shawl [ʃɔːl] n chal m

she [ʃiː] pron ella

sheath [ʃiːθ] n vaina; (contraceptive) preservativo

shed [ʃed] (pt, pp ~) n cobertizo ▷ vt (skin) mudar; (tears, blood) derramar; (load) derramar; (workers) despedir

she'd [ʃiːd] = **she had**; **she would**

sheep [ʃiːp] n inv oveja; **sheepdog** n perro pastor; **sheepskin** n piel f de carnero

sheer [ʃɪə*] adj (utter) puro, completo; (steep) escarpado; (material) diáfano ▷ adv verticalmente

sheet [ʃiːt] n (on bed) sábana; (of paper) hoja; (of glass, metal) lámina; (of ice) capa

sheik(h) [ʃeɪk] n jeque m

shelf [ʃelf] (pl **shelves**) n estante m

shell [ʃel] n (on beach) concha; (of egg, nut etc) cáscara; (explosive) proyectil m, obús m; (of building) armazón f ▷ vt (peas) desenvainar; (Mil) bombardear

she'll [ʃiːl] = **she will**; **she shall**

shellfish ['ʃelfɪʃ] n inv crustáceo; (as food) mariscos mpl

shelter ['ʃeltə*] n abrigo, refugio ▷ vt (aid) amparar, proteger; (give lodging to) abrigar ▷ vi abrigarse, refugiarse;

sheltered adj (life) protegido; (spot) abrigado

shelves [ʃɛlvz] npl of **shelf**

shelving [ˈʃɛlvɪŋ] n estantería

shepherd [ˈʃɛpəd] n pastor m ▷ vt (guide) guiar, conducir; **shepherd's pie** (BRIT) n pastel de carne y patatas

sheriff [ˈʃɛrɪf] (US) n sheriff m

sherry [ˈʃɛrɪ] n jerez m

she's [ʃiːz] = **she is; she has**

Shetland [ˈʃɛtlənd] n (also: **the ~s, the ~ Isles**) las Islas de Zetlandia

shield [ʃiːld] n escudo; (protection) blindaje m ▷ vt: **to ~ (from)** proteger (de)

shift [ʃɪft] n (change) cambio; (at work) turno ▷ vt trasladar; (remove) quitar ▷ vi moverse

shin [ʃɪn] n espinilla

shine [ʃaɪn] (pt, pp **shone**) n brillo, lustre m ▷ vi brillar, relucir ▷ vt (shoes) lustrar, sacar brillo a; **to ~ a torch on sth** dirigir una linterna hacia algo

shingles [ˈʃɪŋglz] n (Med) herpes mpl o fpl

shiny [ˈʃaɪnɪ] adj brillante, lustroso

ship [ʃɪp] n buque m, barco ▷ vt (goods) embarcar; (send) transportar o enviar por vía marítima; **shipment** n (act) embarque m; (traffic) buques mpl; **shipwreck** n naufragio ▷ vt: **to be shipwrecked** naufragar; **shipyard** n astillero

shirt [ʃəːt] n camisa; **in (one's) ~ sleeves** en mangas de camisa

shit [ʃɪt] (infl) excl ¡mierda! (!)

shiver [ˈʃɪvə*] n escalofrío ▷ vi temblar, estremecerse; (with cold) tiritar

shock [ʃɔk] n (impact) choque m; (Elec) descarga (eléctrica); (emotional) conmoción f; (start) sobresalto, susto; (Med) postración f nerviosa ▷ vt dar un susto a; (offend) escandalizar; **shocking** adj (awful) espantoso; (outrageous) escandaloso

shoe [ʃuː] n (pt, pp **shod**) n zapato; (for horse) herradura ▷ vt (horse) herrar; **shoelace** n cordón m; **shoe polish** n betún m; **shoeshop** n zapatería

shone [ʃɔn] pt, pp of **shine**

shook [ʃuk] pt of **shake**

shoot [ʃuːt] (pt, pp **shot**) n (on branch, seedling) retoño, vástago ▷ vt disparar; (kill) matar a tiros; (wound) pegar un tiro; (execute) fusilar; (film) rodar, filmar ▷ vi (Football) chutar; **shoot down** vt (plane) derribar; **shoot up** vi (prices) dispararse; **shooting** n (shots) tiros mpl; (Hunting) caza con escopeta

shop [ʃɔp] n tienda; (workshop) taller m ▷ vi (also: **go ~ping**) ir de compras; **shop assistant** (BRIT) n dependiente/a m/f; **shopkeeper** n tendero/a; **shoplifting** n mechería; **shopping** n (goods) compras fpl; **shopping bag** n bolsa (de compras); **shopping centre** (US **shopping center**) n centro comercial; **shopping mall** n centro comercial; **shopping trolley** n (BRIT) carrito de la compra; **shop window** n escaparate m (SP), vidriera (LAM)

shore [ʃɔː*] n orilla ▷ vt: **to ~ (up)** reforzar; **on ~** en tierra

short [ʃɔːt] adj corto; (in time) breve, de corta duración; (person) bajo; (curt) brusco, seco; (insufficient) insuficiente; **(a pair of) ~s** (unos) pantalones mpl cortos; **to be ~ of sth** estar falto de algo; **in ~** en pocas palabras; **~ of doing ...** fuera de que ...; **it is ~ for** es la forma abreviada de; **to cut ~** (speech, visit) interrumpir, terminar inesperadamente; **everything ~ of ...** todo menos ...; **to fall ~ of** no alcanzar; **to run ~ of** quedarle a algn poco; **to stop ~** parar en seco; **to stop ~ of** detenerse antes de; **shortage** n: **a ~ of** una falta de; **shortbread** n especie de mantecada; **shortcoming** n defecto, deficiencia; **short(crust) pastry** (BRIT) n pasta quebradiza; **shortcut** n atajo; **shorten** vt acortar; (visit) interrumpir; **shortfall** n déficit m; **shorthand** (BRIT) n taquigrafía; **short-lived** adj efímero; **shortly** adv en breve, dentro de poco; **shorts** npl pantalones mpl cortos; (US) calzoncillos mpl; **short-sighted** (BRIT) adj miope; (fig) imprudente; **short-sleeved** adj de manga corta; **short story** n cuento; **short-tempered** adj enojadizo; **short-term** adj (effect) a corto plazo

shot [ʃɔt] pt, pp of **shoot** ▷ n (sound) tiro, disparo; (try) tentativa; (injection) inyección f; (Phot) toma, fotografía; **to be a good/poor ~** (person) tener buena/mala puntería; **like a ~** (without any delay) como un rayo; **shotgun** n escopeta

should [ʃud] aux vb: **I ~ go now** debo irme ahora; **he ~ be there now** debe de haber llegado (ya); **I ~ go if I were you** yo en tu lugar me iría; **I ~ like to** me gustaría

shoulder ['ʃəuldə*] n hombro ▷ vt (fig) cargar con; **shoulder blade** n omóplato

shouldn't ['ʃudnt] = **should not**

shout [ʃaut] n grito ▷ vt gritar ▷ vi gritar, dar voces

shove [ʃʌv] n empujón m ▷ vt empujar; (inf: put) **to ~ sth in** meter algo a empellones

shovel ['ʃʌvl] n pala; (mechanical) excavadora ▷ vt mover con pala

show [ʃəu] (pt **~ed**, pp **~n**) n (of emotion) demostración f; (semblance) apariencia; (exhibition) exposición f; (Theatre) función f, espectáculo; (TV) show m ▷ vt mostrar, enseñar; (courage etc) mostrar, manifestar; (exhibit) exponer; (film) proyectar ▷ vi mostrarse; (appear) aparecer; **for ~** para impresionar; **on ~** (exhibits etc) expuesto; **show in** vt (person) hacer pasar; **show off** vi (pej) presumir ▷ vt (display) lucir; **show out** vt **to show sb out** acompañar a algn a la puerta; **show up** vi (stand out) destacar; (inf: turn up) aparecer ▷ vt (unmask) desenmascarar; **show business** n

mundo del espectáculo

shower ['ʃauə*] n (rain) chaparrón m, chubasco; (of stones etc) lluvia; (for bathing) ducha, regadera (MEX) ▷ vi llover ▷ vt (fig): **to ~ sb with sth** colmar a algn de algo; **to have a ~** ducharse; **shower cap** n gorro de baño; **shower gel** n gel m de ducha

showing ['ʃəuɪŋ] n (of film) proyección f

show jumping n hípica

shown [ʃəun] pp of **show**

show: **show-off** (inf) n (person) presumido/a; **showroom** n sala de muestras

shrank [ʃræŋk] pt of **shrink**

shred [ʃred] n (gen pl) triza, jirón m ▷ vt hacer trizas; (Culin) desmenuzar

shrewd [ʃru:d] adj astuto

shriek [ʃri:k] n chillido ▷ vi chillar

shrimp [ʃrɪmp] n camarón m

shrine [ʃraɪn] n santuario, sepulcro

shrink [ʃrɪŋk] (pt **shrank**, pp **shrunk**) vi encogerse; (be reduced) reducirse; (also: **~ away**) retroceder ▷ vt encoger ▷ n (inf, pej) loquero/a; **to ~ from (doing) sth** no atreverse a hacer algo

shrivel ['ʃrɪvl] (also: **~ up**) vt (dry) secar ▷ vi secarse

shroud [ʃraud] n sudario ▷ vt: **~ed in mystery** envuelto en el misterio

Shrove Tuesday ['ʃrəuv-] n martes m de carnaval

shrub [ʃrʌb] n arbusto

shrug [ʃrʌg] n encogimiento de hombros ▷ vt, vi: **to ~ (one's shoulders)** encogerse de hombros; **shrug off** vt negar importancia a

shrunk [ʃrʌŋk] pp of **shrink**

shudder ['ʃʌdə*] n estremecimiento, escalofrío ▷ vi estremecerse

shuffle ['ʃʌfl] vt (cards) barajar ▷ vi: **to ~ (one's feet)** arrastrar los pies

shun [ʃʌn] vt rehuir, esquivar

shut [ʃʌt] (pt, pp **~**) vt cerrar ▷ vi cerrarse; **shut down** vt, vi cerrar; **shut up** vi (inf: keep quiet) callarse ▷ vt (close) cerrar; (silence) hacer callar;

shutter n contraventana; (Phot) obturador m

shuttle ['ʃʌtl] n lanzadera; (also: ~ **service**) servicio rápido y continuo entre dos puntos; (Aviat) puente m aéreo; **shuttlecock** n volante m

shy [ʃaɪ] adj tímido

sibling ['sɪblɪŋ] n (formal) hermano/a

Sicily ['sɪsɪlɪ] n Sicilia

sick [sɪk] adj (ill) enfermo; (nauseated) mareado; (humour) negro; (vomiting): **to be ~** (BRIT) vomitar; **to feel ~** tener náuseas; **to be ~ of** (fig) estar harto de; **sickening** adj (fig) asqueroso; **sick leave** n baja por enfermedad; **sickly** adj enfermizo; (smell) nauseabundo; **sickness** n enfermedad f, mal m; (vomiting) náuseas fpl

side [saɪd] n (gen) lado; (of body) costado; (of lake) orilla; (of hill) ladera; (team) equipo ▷ adj (door, entrance) lateral ▷ vi: **to ~ with sb** tomar el partido de algn; **by the ~ of** al lado de; **~ by ~** juntos/as; **from ~ to ~** de un lado para otro; **from all ~s** de todos lados; **to take ~s (with)** tomar partido (con); **sideboard** n aparador m; **sideboards** (BRIT) npl = **sideburns**; **sideburns** npl patillas fpl; **sidelight** n (Aut) luz flateral; **sideline** n (Sport) línea de banda; (fig) empleo suplementario; **side order** n plato de acompañamiento; **side road** n (BRIT) calle f lateral; **side street** n calle f lateral; **sidetrack** vt (fig) desviar (de su propósito); **sidewalk** (US) n acera; **sideways** adv de lado

siege [siːdʒ] n cerco, sitio

sieve [sɪv] n colador m ▷ vt cribar

sift [sɪft] vt cribar; (fig: information) escudriñar

sigh [saɪ] n suspiro ▷ vi suspirar

sight [saɪt] n (faculty) vista; (spectacle) espectáculo; (on gun) mira, alza ▷ vt divisar; **in ~** a la vista; **out of ~** fuera de (la) vista; **on ~** sin previo aviso; **sightseeing** n excursionismo, turismo; **to go sightseeing** hacer turismo

sign [saɪn] n (with hand) señal f, seña; (trace) huella, rastro; (notice) letrero; (written) signo ▷ vt firmar; (Sport) fichar; **to ~ sth over to sb** firmar el traspaso de algo a algn; **sign for** vt fus (item) firmar el recibo de; **sign in** vi firmar el registro (al entrar); **sign on** vi (BRIT: as unemployed) registrarse como desempleado; (for course) inscribirse ▷ vt (Mil) alistar; (employee) contratar; **sign up** vi (Mil) alistarse; (for course) inscribirse ▷ vt (player) fichar

signal ['sɪgnl] n señal f ▷ vi señalizar ▷ vt (person) hacer señas a; (message) comunicar por señales

signature ['sɪgnətʃəʳ] n firma

significance [sɪg'nɪfɪkəns] n (importance) trascendencia

significant [sɪg'nɪfɪkənt] adj significativo; (important) trascendente

signify ['sɪgnɪfaɪ] vt significar

sign language n lenguaje m para sordomudos

signpost ['saɪnpəust] n indicador m

Sikh [siːk] adj, n sij mf

silence ['saɪləns] n silencio ▷ vt acallar; (guns) reducir al silencio

silent ['saɪlnt] adj silencioso; (not speaking) callado; (film) mudo; **to remain ~** guardar silencio

silhouette [sɪlu:'et] n silueta

silicon chip ['sɪlɪkən-] n plaqueta de silicio

silk [sɪlk] n seda ▷ adj de seda

silly ['sɪlɪ] adj (person) tonto; (idea) absurdo

silver ['sɪlvəʳ] n plata; (money) moneda suelta ▷ adj de plata; (colour) plateado; **silver-plated** adj plateado

similar ['sɪmɪləʳ] adj: **~ (to)** parecido or semejante (a); **similarity** [-'lærɪtɪ] n semejanza; **similarly** adv del mismo modo

simmer ['sɪməʳ] vi hervir a fuego lento

simple ['sɪmpl] adj (easy) sencillo; (foolish, Comm: interest) simple;

simplicity [-'plɪsɪtɪ] n sencillez f;
simplify ['sɪmplɪfaɪ] vt simplificar;
simply adv (live, talk) sencillamente;
(just, merely) sólo
simulate ['sɪmjʊleɪt] vt fingir,
simular
simultaneous [sɪməl'teɪnɪəs] adj
simultáneo; **simultaneously** adv
simultáneamente
sin [sɪn] n pecado ▷ vi pecar
since [sɪns] adv desde entonces,
después ▷ prep desde ▷ conj (time)
desde que; (because) ya que, puesto
que; **~ then, ever ~** desde entonces
sincere [sɪn'sɪə*] adj sincero;
sincerely adv: **yours sincerely** (in
letters) le saluda atentamente
sing [sɪŋ] (pt **sang**, pp **sung**) vt, vi
cantar
Singapore [sɪŋə'pɔ:*] n Singapur m
singer ['sɪŋə*] n cantante mf
singing ['sɪŋɪŋ] n canto
single ['sɪŋgl] adj único, solo;
(unmarried) soltero; (not double) simple,
sencillo ▷ n (BRIT: also: **~ ticket**) billete
m sencillo; (record) sencillo, single
m; **singles** npl (Tennis) individual
m; **single out** vt (choose) escoger;
single bed n cama individual; **single
file** n: **in single file** en fila de uno;
single-handed adj sin ayuda; **single-
minded** adj resuelto, firme; **single
parent** n padre m soltero, madre f
soltera (o divorciado etc); **single parent
family** familia monoparental; **single
room** n cuarto individual
singular ['sɪŋgjʊlə*] adj (odd) raro,
extraño; (outstanding) excepcional ▷ n
(Ling) singular m
sinister ['sɪnɪstə*] adj siniestro
sink [sɪŋk] (pt **sank**, pp **sunk**) n
fregadero ▷ vt (ship) hundir, echar
a pique; (foundations) excavar ▷ vi
hundirse; **to ~ sth into** hundir algo en;
sink in vi (fig) penetrar, calar
sinus ['saɪnəs] n (Anat) seno
sip [sɪp] n sorbo ▷ vt sorber, beber
a sorbitos

sir [sə*] n señor m; **S~ John Smith** Sir
John Smith; **yes ~** sí, señor
siren ['saɪərn] n sirena
sirloin ['sə:lɔɪn] n (also: **~ steak**)
solomillo
sister ['sɪstə*] n hermana;
(BRIT: nurse) enfermera jefe; **sister-in-
law** n cuñada
sit [sɪt] (pt, pp **sat**) vi sentarse; (be
sitting) estar sentado; (assembly)
reunirse; (for painter) posar ▷ vt (exam)
presentarse a, sufrir; **sit back** vi (in seat)
recostarse; **sit down** vi sentarse;
sit on vt fus (jury, committee) ser
miembro de, formar parte de; **sit up** vi
incorporarse; (not go to bed) velar
sitcom ['sɪtkɔm] n abbr (= situation
comedy) comedia de situación
site [saɪt] n sitio; (also: **building ~**)
solar m ▷ vt situar
sitting ['sɪtɪŋ] n (of assembly etc)
sesión f; (in canteen) turno; **sitting
room** n sala de estar
situated ['sɪtjʊeɪtɪd] adj situado
situation [sɪtjʊ'eɪʃən] n situación f;
"~s vacant" (BRIT) "ofrecen trabajo"
six [sɪks] num seis; **sixteen** num diez
y seis, dieciséis; **sixteenth** [sɪks'ti:nθ]
adj decimosexto; **sixth** [sɪksθ] num
sexto; **sixth form** n (BRIT) clase f de
alumnos del sexto año (de 16 a 18 años de
edad); **sixth-form college** n instituto
m para alumnos de 16 a 18 años;
sixtieth ['sɪkstɪɪθ] adj sexagésimo;
sixty num sesenta
size [saɪz] n tamaño; (extent)
extensión f; (of clothing) talla; (of shoes)
número; **sizeable** adj importante,
considerable
sizzle ['sɪzl] vi crepitar
skate [skeɪt] n patín m; (fish: pl
inv) raya f ▷ vi patinar; **skateboard**
n monopatín m; **skateboarding** n
monopatín m; **skater** n patinador(a)
m/f; **skating** n patinaje m; **skating
rink** n pista de patinaje
skeleton ['skelɪtn] n esqueleto;
(Tech) armazón f; (outline) esquema m

skeptical ['skeptɪkl] (us) = **sceptical**

sketch [sketʃ] n (drawing) dibujo; (outline) esbozo, bosquejo; (Theatre) sketch m ▷ vt dibujar; (plan etc: also: ~ **out**) esbozar

skewer ['skjuːə*] n broqueta

ski [skiː] n esquí m ▷ vi esquiar; **ski boot** n bota de esquí

skid [skɪd] n patinazo ▷ vi patinar

ski: skier n esquiador(a) m/f; **skiing** n esquí m

skilful ['skɪlful] (us **skillful**) adj diestro, experto

ski lift n telesilla m, telesquí m

skill [skɪl] n destreza, pericia; técnica; **skilled** adj hábil, diestro; (worker) cualificado

skim [skɪm] vt (milk) desnatar; (glide over) rozar, rasar ▷ vi **to ~ through** (book) hojear; **skimmed milk** (us **skim milk**) n leche f desnatada

skin [skɪn] n piel f; (complexion) cutis m ▷ vt (fruit etc) pelar; (animal) despellejar; **skinhead** n cabeza m/f rapada, skin(head) m/f; **skinny** adj flaco

skip [skɪp] n brinco, salto; (BRIT: container) contenedor m ▷ vi brincar; (with rope) saltar a la comba ▷ vt saltarse

ski: ski pass n forfait m (de esquí); **ski pole** n bastón m de esquiar

skipper ['skɪpə*] n (Naut, Sport) capitán m

skipping rope ['skɪpɪŋ-] (us **skip rope**) n comba

skirt [skɜːt] n falda, pollera (sc) ▷ vt (go round) ladear

skirting board ['skɜːtɪŋ-] (BRIT) n rodapié m

ski slope n pista de esquí

ski suit n traje m de esquiar

skull [skʌl] n calavera; (Anat) cráneo

skunk [skʌŋk] n mofeta

sky [skaɪ] n cielo; **skyscraper** n rascacielos m inv

slab [slæb] n (stone) bloque m; (flat) losa; (of cake) trozo

slack [slæk] adj (loose) flojo; (slow) de poca actividad; (careless) descuidado; **slacks** npl pantalones mpl

slain [sleɪn] pp of **slay**

slam [slæm] vt (throw) arrojar (violentamente); (criticize) criticar duramente ▷ vi (door) cerrarse de golpe; **to ~ the door** dar un portazo

slander ['slɑːndə*] n calumnia, difamación f

slang [slæŋ] n argot m; (jargon) jerga

slant [slɑːnt] n sesgo, inclinación f; (fig) interpretación f

slap [slæp] n palmada; (in face) bofetada ▷ vt dar una palmada or bofetada a; (paint etc): **to ~ sth on sth** embadurnar algo con algo ▷ adv (directly) exactamente, directamente

slash [slæʃ] vt acuchillar; (fig: prices) fulminar

slate [sleɪt] n pizarra ▷ vt (fig: criticize) criticar duramente

slaughter ['slɔːtə*] n (of animals) matanza; (of people) carnicería ▷ vt matar; **slaughterhouse** n matadero

Slav [slɑːv] adj eslavo

slave [sleɪv] n esclavo/a ▷ vi (also: ~ **away**) sudar tinta; **slavery** n esclavitud f

sley [sleɪ] (pt **slew**, pp **slain**) vt matar

sleazy ['sliːzɪ] adj de mala fama

sled [sled] (us) = **sledge**

sledge [sledʒ] n trineo

sleek [sliːk] adj (shiny) lustroso; (car etc) elegante

sleep [sliːp] (pt, pp **slept**) n sueño ▷ vi dormir; **to go to ~** quedarse dormido; **sleep in** vi (oversleep) quedarse dormido; **sleep together** vi (have sex) acostarse juntos; **sleeper** n (person) durmiente mf; (BRIT Rail: on track) traviesa; (: train) coche-cama m; **sleeping bag** n saco de dormir; **sleeping car** n coche-cama m; **sleeping pill** n somnífero; **sleepover** n: **we're having a sleepover at Jo's** nos vamos a quedar a dormir en casa de Jo; **sleepwalk** vi caminar dormido;

(habitually) ser sonámbulo; **sleepy** adj soñoliento; (place) soporífero

sleet [sli:t] n aguanieve f

sleeve [sli:v] n manga; (Tech) manguito; (of record) portada; **sleeveless** adj sin mangas

sleigh [sleɪ] n trineo

slender ['slɛndə*] adj delgado; (means) escaso

slept [slɛpt] pt, pp of **sleep**

slew [slu:] pt of **slay** ▷ vi (BRIT: veer) torcerse

slice [slaɪs] n (of meat) tajada; (of bread) rebanada; (of lemon) rodaja; (utensil) pala ▷ vt cortar (en tajos), rebanar

slick [slɪk] adj (skilful) hábil, diestro; (clever) astuto ▷ n (also: **oil ~**) marea negra

slide [slaɪd] (pt, pp **slid**) n (movement) descenso, desprendimiento; (in playground) tobogán m; (Phot) diapositiva; (BRIT: also: **hair ~**) pasador m ▷ vt correr, deslizar ▷ vi (slip) resbalarse; (glide) deslizarse; **sliding** adj (door) corredizo

slight [slaɪt] adj (slim) delgado; (frail) delicado; (pain etc) leve; (trivial) insignificante; (small) pequeño ▷ n desaire m ▷ vt (insult) ofender, desairar; **not in the ~est** en absoluto; **slightly** adv ligeramente, un poco

slim [slɪm] adj delgado, esbelto; (fig: chance) remoto ▷ vi adelgazar; **slimming** n adelgazamiento

slimy ['slaɪmɪ] adj cenagoso

sling [slɪŋ] (pt, pp **slung**) n (Med) cabestrillo; (weapon) honda ▷ vt tirar, arrojar

slip [slɪp] n (slide) resbalón m; (mistake) descuido; (underskirt) combinación f; (of paper) papelito ▷ vt (slide) deslizar ▷ vi deslizarse; (stumble) resbalar(se); (decline) decaer; (move smoothly): **to ~ into/out of** (room etc) entrar en/salirse de; **to give sb the ~** eludir a algn; **a ~ of the tongue** un lapsus; **to ~ sth on/off** ponerse/quitarse algo;

slip up vi (make mistake) equivocarse; meter la pata

slipper ['slɪpə*] n zapatilla, pantufla

slippery ['slɪpərɪ] adj resbaladizo;

slip road (BRIT) n carretera de acceso

slit [slɪt] (pt, pp ~) n raja; (cut) corte m ▷ vt rajar; cortar

slog [slɒg] (BRIT) n sudar tinta; **it was a ~** costó trabajo (hacerlo)

slogan ['sləʊgən] n eslogan m, lema m

slope [sləʊp] n (up) cuesta, pendiente f; (down) declive m; (side of mountain) falda, vertiente m ▷ vi: **to ~ down** estar en declive; **to ~ up** inclinarse; **sloping** adj en pendiente; en declive; (writing) inclinado

sloppy ['slɒpɪ] adj (work) descuidado; (appearance) desaliñado

slot [slɒt] n ranura ▷ vt: **to ~ into** encajar en; **slot machine** n (BRIT: vending machine) distribuidor m automático; (for gambling) tragaperras m inv

Slovakia [sləʊˈvækɪə] n Eslovaquia

Slovene [sləʊˈviːn] adj esloveno ▷ n esloveno/a; (Ling) esloveno; **Slovenia** [sləʊˈviːnɪə] n Eslovenia; **Slovenian** adj, n = **Slovene**

slow [sləʊ] adj lento; (not clever) lerdo; (watch): **to be ~** atrasar ▷ adv lentamente, despacio ▷ vt, vi retardar; "**~**" (road sign) "disminuir velocidad"; **slow down** vi reducir la marcha; **slowly** adv lentamente, despacio; **slow motion**: **in slow motion** a cámara lenta

slug [slʌg] n babosa; (bullet) posta; **sluggish** adj lento; (person) depresión

slum [slʌm] n casucha

slump [slʌmp] n (economic) depresión f ▷ vi hundirse; (prices) caer en picado

slung [slʌŋ] pt, pp of **sling**

slur [slɜ:*] n: **to cast a ~ on** insultar ▷ vt (speech) pronunciar mal

sly [slaɪ] adj astuto; (smile) taimado

smack [smæk] n bofetada ▷ vt dar con la mano a; (child, on face) abofetear

▷ vi: **to ~ of** saber a, oler a

small [smɔːl] adj pequeño; **small ads** (BRIT) npl anuncios mpl por palabras; **small change** n suelto, cambio

smart [smɑːt] adj elegante; (clever) listo, inteligente; (quick) rápido, vivo ▷ vi escocer, picar; **smartcard** n tarjeta inteligente

smash [smæʃ] n (also: **~-up**) choque m; (Mus) exitazo ▷ vt (break) hacer pedazos; (car etc) estrellar; (Sport: record) batir ▷ vi hacerse pedazos; (against wall etc) estrellarse; **smashing** (inf) adj estupendo

smear [smɪə*] n mancha; (Med) frotis m inv ▷ vt untar; **smear test** n (Med) citología, frotis m inv (cervical)

smell [smel] (pt, pp **smelt** or **~ed**) n olor m; (sense) olfato ▷ vt, vi oler; **smelly** adj maloliente

smelt [smelt] pt, pp of **smell**

smile [smaɪl] n sonrisa ▷ vi sonreír

smirk [smɜːk] n sonrisa falsa or afectada

smog [smɔg] n esmog m

smoke [sməuk] n humo ▷ vi fumar; (chimney) echar humo ▷ vt (cigarettes) fumar; **smoke alarm** n detector m de humo, alarma contra incendios; **smoked** adj (bacon, glass) ahumado; **smoker** n fumador(a) m/f; (Rail) coche m fumador; **smoking** n: **"no smoking"** "prohibido fumar"

Be careful not to translate **smoking** by the Spanish word *smoking*.

smoky adj (room) lleno de humo; (taste) ahumado

smooth [smuːð] adj liso; (sea) tranquilo; (flavour, movement) suave; (sauce) fino; (person: pej) meloso ▷ vt (also: **~ out**) alisar; (creases, difficulties) allanar

smother ['smʌðə*] vt sofocar; (repress) contener

SMS n abbr (= short message service) (servicio) SMS; **SMS message** n (mensaje m) SMS

smudge [smʌdʒ] n mancha ▷ vt

manchar

smug [smʌg] adj presumido; orondo

smuggle ['smʌgl] vt pasar de contrabando; **smuggling** n contrabando

snack [snæk] n bocado; **snack bar** n cafetería

snag [snæg] n problema m

snail [sneɪl] n caracol m

snake [sneɪk] n serpiente f

snap [snæp] n (sound) chasquido; (photograph) foto f ▷ adj (decision) instantáneo ▷ vt (break) quebrar; (fingers) castañetear ▷ vi quebrarse; (fig: speak sharply) contestar bruscamente; **to ~ shut** cerrarse de golpe; **snap at** vt fus (dog) intentar morder; **snap up** vt agarrar; **snapshot** n foto f (instantánea)

snarl [snɑːl] vi gruñir

snatch [snætʃ] n (small piece) fragmento ▷ vt (snatch away) arrebatar; (fig) agarrar; **to ~ some sleep** encontrar tiempo para dormir

sneak [sniːk] (pt (US) **snuck**) vi: **to ~ in/out** entrar/salir a hurtadillas ▷ n (inf) soplón/ona m/f; **to ~ up on sb** aparecérsele de improviso a algn; **sneakers** npl zapatos mpl de lona

sneer [snɪə*] vi reír con sarcasmo; (mock): **to ~ at** burlarse de

sneeze [sniːz] vi estornudar

sniff [snɪf] vi sollozar ▷ vt husmear, oler; (drugs) esnifar

snigger ['snɪgə*] vi reírse con disimulo

snip [snɪp] n tijeretazo; (BRIT: inf: bargain) ganga ▷ vt tijeretear

sniper ['snaɪpə*] n francotirador(a) m/f

snob [snɔb] n (e)snob mf

snooker ['snuːkə*] n especie de billar

snoop [snuːp] vi: **to ~ about** fisgonear

snooze [snuːz] n siesta ▷ vi echar una siesta

snore [snɔː*] n ronquido ▷ vi roncar

snorkel ['snɔːkl] n (tubo) respirador m

snort [snɔːt] n bufido ▷ vi bufar

snow [snəʊ] n nieve f ▷ vi nevar; **snowball** n bola de nieve ▷ vi (fig) agrandarse, ampliarse; **snowstorm** n nevada, nevasca

snub [snʌb] vt (person) desairar ▷ n desaire m, repulsa

snug [snʌg] adj (cosy) cómodo m; (fitted) ajustado

○ **KEYWORD**

so [səʊ] adv **1** (thus, likewise) así, de este modo; **if so** de ser así; **I like swimming – so do I** a mí me gusta nadar – a mí también; **I've got work to do – so has Paul** tengo trabajo que hacer – Paul también; **it's 5 o'clock – so it is!** son las cinco – ¡pues es verdad!; **I hope/think so** espero/creo que sí; **so far** hasta ahora; (in past) hasta este momento
2 (in comparisons etc: to such a degree) tan; **so quickly (that)** tan rápido (que); **so big (that)** tan grande (que); **she's not so clever as her brother** no es tan lista como su hermano; **we were so worried** estábamos preocupadísimos
3: **so much** adj, adv tanto; **so many** tantos/as
4 (phrases): **10 or so** unos 10, 10 o así; **so long!** (inf: goodbye) ¡hasta luego!

▷ conj **1** (expressing purpose): **so as to do** para hacer; **so (that)** para que +subjun
2 (expressing result) así que; **so you see, I could have gone** así que ya ves, (yo) podría haber ido

soak [səʊk] vt (drench) empapar; (steep in water) remojar ▷ vi remojarse, estar a remojo; **soak up** vt absorber; **soaking** adj (also: **soaking wet**) calado or empapado (hasta los huesos or el tuétano)

so-and-so [ˈsəʊənsəʊ] n (somebody) fulano/a de tal

soap [səʊp] n jabón m; **soap opera** n telenovela; **soap powder** n jabón

m en polvo

soar [sɔː*] vi (on wings) remontarse; (rocket: prices) dispararse; (building etc) elevarse

sob [sɔb] n sollozo ▷ vi sollozar

sober [ˈsəʊbə*] adj (serious) serio; (not drunk) sobrio; (colour, style) discreto; **sober up** vt quitar la borrachera

soccer [ˈsɔkə*] n fútbol m

sociable [ˈsəʊʃəbl] adj sociable

social [ˈsəʊʃl] adj social ▷ n velada, fiesta; **socialism** n socialismo; **socialist** adj, n socialista mf; **socialize** vi: **to socialize (with)** alternar (con); **social life** n vida social; **socially** adv socialmente; **social security** n seguridad f social; **social services** npl servicios mpl sociales; **social work** n asistencia f social; **social worker** n asistente/a m/f social

society [səˈsaɪətɪ] n sociedad f; (club) asociación f; (also: **high ~**) alta sociedad

sociology [səʊsɪˈɔlədʒɪ] n sociología

sock [sɔk] n calcetín m

socket [ˈsɔkɪt] n cavidad f; (BRIT Elec) enchufe m

soda [ˈsəʊdə] n (Chem) sosa; (also: ~ **water**) soda; (us: also: ~ **pop**) gaseosa

sodium [ˈsəʊdɪəm] n sodio

sofa [ˈsəʊfə] n sofá m; **sofa bed** n sofá-cama m

soft [sɔft] adj (lenient, not hard) blando; (gentle, not bright) suave; **soft drink** n bebida no alcohólica; **soft drugs** npl drogas fpl blandas; **soften** [ˈsɔfn] vt ablandar; suavizar; (effect) amortiguar ▷ vi ablandarse; suavizarse; **softly** adv suavemente; (gently) delicadamente, con delicadeza; **software** n (Comput) software m

soggy [ˈsɔgɪ] adj empapado

soil [sɔɪl] n (earth) tierra, suelo ▷ vt ensuciar

solar [ˈsəʊlə*] adj solar; **solar power** n energía solar; **solar system** n sistema m solar

sold [səʊld] pt, pp of **sell**
soldier ['səʊldʒə*] n soldado; (army man) militar m
sold out adj (Comm) agotado
sole [səʊl] n (of foot) planta; (of shoe) suela; (fish: pl inv) lenguado ▷ adj único; **solely** adv únicamente, sólo, solamente; **I will hold you solely responsible** le consideraré el único responsable
solemn ['sɒləm] adj solemne
solicitor [sə'lɪsɪtə*] (BRIT) n (for wills etc) = notario/a; (in court) = abogado/a m/f
solid ['sɒlɪd] adj sólido; (gold etc) macizo ▷ n sólido
solitary ['sɒlɪtərɪ] adj solitario, solo
solitude ['sɒlɪtjuːd] n soledad f
solo ['səʊləʊ] n solo ▷ adv (fly) en solitario; **soloist** n solista m/f
soluble ['sɒljʊbl] adj soluble
solution [sə'luːʃən] n solución f
solve [sɒlv] vt resolver, solucionar
solvent ['sɒlvənt] adj (Comm) solvente ▷ n (Chem) solvente m
sombre ['sɒmbə*] (us **somber**) adj sombrío

○ **KEYWORD**

some [sʌm] adj **1** (a certain amount or number): **some tea/water/biscuits** té/agua/(unas) galletas; **there's some milk in the fridge** hay leche en el frigo; **there were some people outside** había algunas personas fuera; **I've got some money, but not much** tengo algo de dinero, pero no mucho
2 (certain: in contrasts) algunos/as; **some people say that ...** hay quien dice que ...; **some films were excellent, but most were mediocre** hubo películas excelentes, pero la mayoría fueron mediocres
3 (unspecified): **some woman was asking for you** una mujer estuvo preguntando por ti; **he was asking for some book (or other)** pedía un libro;

some day algún día; **some day next week** un día de la semana que viene
▷ pron **1** (a certain number): **I've got some** (books etc) tengo algunos/as
2 (a certain amount) algo; **I've got some** (money, milk) tengo algo; **could I have some of that cheese?** ¿me puede dar un poco de ese queso?; **I've read some of the book** he leído parte del libro
▷ adv: **some 10 people** unas 10 personas, una decena de personas

some: somebody ['sʌmbədɪ] pron = **someone; somehow** adv de alguna manera; (for some reason) por una u otra razón; **someone** pron alguien; **someplace** (us) adv = **somewhere; something** pron algo; **would you like something to eat/drink?** ¿te gustaría cenar/tomar algo?; **sometime** adv (in future) algún día, en algún momento; (in past): **sometime last month** durante el mes pasado; **sometimes** adv a veces; **somewhat** adv algo; **somewhere** adv (be) en alguna parte; (go) a alguna parte; **somewhere else** (be) en otra parte; (go) a otra parte
son [sʌn] n hijo
song [sɒŋ] n canción f
son-in-law ['sʌnɪnlɔː] n yerno
soon [suːn] adv pronto, dentro de poco; **~ afterwards** poco después; see also **sooner; sooner** adv (time) antes, más temprano; (preference: rather): **I would sooner do that** preferiría hacer eso; **sooner or later** tarde o temprano
soothe [suːð] vt tranquilizar; (pain) aliviar
sophisticated [sə'fɪstɪkeɪtɪd] adj sofisticado
sophomore ['sɒfəmɔː*] (us) n estudiante m/f de segundo año
soprano [sə'prɑːnəʊ] n soprano f
sorbet ['sɔːbeɪ] n sorbete m
sordid ['sɔːdɪd] adj (place etc) sórdido; (motive etc) mezquino
sore [sɔː*] adj (painful) doloroso, que duele ▷ n llaga

sorrow ['sɒrəu] n pena, dolor m
sorry ['sɒrɪ] adj (regretful) arrepentido; (condition, excuse) lastimoso; **~!** ¡perdón!, ¡perdone!; **~?** ¿cómo?; **to feel ~ for sb** tener lástima a algn; **I feel ~** me da lástima
sort [sɔ:t] n clase f, género, tipo; **sort out** vt (papers) clasificar; (organize) ordenar, organizar; (resolve: problem, situation etc) arreglar, solucionar
SOS n SOS m
so-so ['səusəu] adv regular, así así
sought [sɔ:t] pt, pp of **seek**
soul [səul] n alma
sound [saund] n (noise) sonido, ruido; (volume: on TV etc) volumen m; (Geo) estrecho ▷ adj (healthy) sano; (safe, not damaged) en buen estado; (reliable: person) digno de confianza; (sensible) sensato, razonable; (secure: investment) seguro ▷ adv: **~ asleep** profundamente dormido ▷ vt (alarm) sonar ▷ vi sonar, resonar; (fig: seem) parecer; **to ~ like** sonar a; **soundtrack** n (of film) banda sonora
soup [su:p] n (thick) sopa; (thin) caldo
sour ['sauə*] adj agrio; (milk) cortado; **it's ~ grapes** (fig) están verdes
source [sɔ:s] n fuente f
south [sauθ] n sur m ▷ adj del sur, sureño ▷ adv al sur, hacia el sur; **South Africa** n África del Sur; **South African** adj, n sudafricano/a m/f; **South America** n América del Sur, Sudamérica; **South American** adj, n sudamericano/a m/f; **southbound** adj (con) rumbo al sur; **southeastern** [sauθi:'istən] adj sureste, del sureste; **southern** ['sʌðən] adj del sur, meridional; **South Korea** n Corea del Sur; **South Pole** n Polo Sur; **southward(s)** adv hacia el sur; **southwest** n suroeste m; **southwestern** [sauθ'westən] adj suroeste
souvenir [su:və'nɪə*] n recuerdo
sovereign ['sɒvrɪn] adj, n soberano/a m/f
sow¹ [səu] (pt ~**ed**, pp **sown**) vt

sembrar
sow² [sau] n cerda, puerca
soya ['sɔɪə] (BRIT) n soja
spa [spa:] n balneario
space [speɪs] n espacio; (room) sitio ▷ cpd espacial ▷ vt (also: **~ out**) espaciar; **spacecraft** n nave f espacial; **spaceship** n **= spacecraft**
spacious ['speɪʃəs] adj amplio
spade [speɪd] n (tool) pala, laya; **spades** npl (Cards: British) picas fpl; (: Spanish) espadas fpl
spaghetti [spə'getɪ] n espaguetis mpl, fideos mpl
Spain [speɪn] n España
spam [spæm] n (junk e-mail) spam m
span [spæn] n (of bird, plane) envergadura; (of arch) luz f; (in time) lapso ▷ vt extenderse sobre, cruzar; (fig) abarcar
Spaniard ['spænjəd] n español(a) m/f
Spanish ['spænɪʃ] adj español(a) ▷ n (Ling) español m, castellano; **the Spanish** npl los españoles
spank [spæŋk] vt zurrar
spanner ['spænə*] (BRIT) n llave f (inglesa)
spare [spea*] adj de reserva; (surplus) sobrante, de más ▷ n = **spare part** ▷ vt (do without) pasarse sin; (refrain from hurting) perdonar; **to ~** (surplus) sobrante, de sobra; **spare part** n pieza de repuesto; **spare room** n cuarto de los invitados; **spare time** n tiempo libre; **spare tyre** (US **spare tire**) n (Aut) neumático or llanta (LAM) de recambio; **spare wheel** n (Aut) rueda de recambio
spark [spa:k] n chispa; (fig) chispazo; **spark(ing) plug** n bujía
sparkle ['spa:kl] n centelleo, destello ▷ vi (shine) relucir, brillar
sparrow ['spærəu] n gorrión m
sparse [spa:s] adj esparcido, escaso
spasm ['spæzəm] n (Med) espasmo
spat [spæt] pt, pp of **spit**
spate [speɪt] n (fig): **a ~ of** un

torrente de

spatula ['spætjələ] n espátula

speak [spi:k] (pt **spoke**, pp **spoken**) vt (language) hablar; (truth) decir ▷ vi hablar; (make a speech) intervenir ▷ to ~ **to sb/of** or **about sth** hablar con algn/de o sobre algo; **~ up!** ¡habla fuerte!; **speaker** n (in public) orador(a) m/f; (also: **loudspeaker**) altavoz m; (for stereo etc) bafle m; (Pol): **the Speaker** (BRIT) el Presidente de la Cámara de los Comunes; (US) el Presidente del Congreso

spear [spɪə*] n lanza ▷ vt alancear

special ['speʃl] adj especial; (edition etc) extraordinario; (delivery) urgente; **special delivery** (Post): **by special delivery** por entrega urgente; **special effects** npl (Cine) efectos mpl especiales; **specialist** n especialista mf; **speciality** [speʃɪ'ælɪtɪ] (BRIT) n especialidad f; **specialize** vi: **to specialize (in)** especializarse (en); **specially** adv sobre todo, en particular; **special needs** npl (BRIT): **children with special needs** niños que requieren una atención diferenciada; **special offer** n (Comm) oferta especial; **special school** n (BRIT) colegio m de educación especial; **specialty** (US) n = **speciality**

species ['spi:ʃi:z] n inv especie f

specific [spə'sɪfɪk] adj específico; **specifically** adv específicamente; **specify** ['spesɪfaɪ] vt, vi especificar, precisar

specimen ['spesɪmən] n ejemplar m; (Med: of urine) espécimen m; (: of blood) muestra

speck [spek] n grano, mota

spectacle ['spektəkl] n espectáculo; **spectacles** npl (BRIT: glasses) gafas fpl (SP), anteojos mpl; **spectacular** [-'tækjulə*] adj espectacular; (success) impresionante

spectator [spek'teɪtə*] n espectador(a) m/f

spectrum ['spektrəm] (pl **spectra**) n espectro

speculate ['spekjuleɪt] vi: **to ~ (on)** especular (en)

sped [sped] pt, pp of **speed**

speech [spi:tʃ] n (faculty) habla; (formal talk) discurso; (spoken language) lenguaje m; **speechless** adj mudo, estupefacto

speed [spi:d] n velocidad f; (haste) prisa; (promptness) rapidez f; **at full** or **top ~** a máxima velocidad; **speed up** vi acelerarse ▷ vt acelerar; **speedboat** n lancha motora; **speeding** n (Aut) exceso de velocidad; **speed limit** n límite m de velocidad, velocidad f máxima; **speedometer** [spɪ'dɔmɪtə*] n velocímetro; **speedy** adj (fast) veloz, rápido; (prompt) pronto

spell [spel] (pt, pp **spelt** (BRIT) or **~ed**) n (also: **magic ~**) encanto, hechizo; (period of time) rato, período ▷ vt deletrear; (fig) anunciar, presagiar; **to cast a ~ on sb** hechizar a algn; **he can't ~** pone faltas de ortografía; **spell out** vt (explain): **to spell sth out for sb** explicar algo a algn en detalle; **spellchecker** ['speltʃekə*] n corrector m ortográfico; **spelling** n ortografía

spelt [spelt] pt, pp of **spell**

spend [spend] (pt, pp **spent**) vt (money) gastar; (time) pasar; (life) dedicar; **spending** n: **government spending** gastos mpl del gobierno

spent [spent] pt, pp of **spend** ▷ adj (cartridge, bullets, match) usado

sperm [spɜ:m] n esperma

sphere [sfɪə*] n esfera

spice [spaɪs] n especia ▷ vt condimentar

spicy ['spaɪsɪ] adj picante

spider ['spaɪdə*] n araña

spike [spaɪk] n (point) punta; (Bot) espiga

spill [spɪl] (pt, pp **spilt** or **~ed**) vt derramar, verter ▷ vi derramarse; **to ~ over** desbordarse

spin [spɪn] (pt, pp **spun**) n (Aviat) barrena; (trip in car) paseo (en coche); (on ball) efecto ▷ vt (wool etc) hilar; (ball

etc) hacer girar ▷ vi girar, dar vueltas
spinach ['spɪnɪtʃ] n espinaca; (*as food*) espinacas *fpl*
spinal ['spaɪnl] *adj* espinal
spin doctor n informador(a) parcial al servicio de un partido político etc
spin-dryer(BRIT) n secador m centrífugo
spine [spaɪn] n espinazo, columna vertebral; (*thorn*) espina
spiral ['spaɪərəl] n espiral f ▷ vi (*fig: prices*) subir desorbitadamente
spire ['spaɪə*] n aguja, chapitel m
spirit ['spɪrɪt] n (*soul*) alma; (*ghost*) fantasma m; (*attitude, sense*) espíritu m; (*courage*) valor m, ánimo; **spirits** *npl* (*drink*) licor(es) m(pl); **in good ~s** alegre, de buen ánimo
spiritual ['spɪrɪtjuəl] *adj* espiritual ▷ n espiritual m
spit [spɪt] (*pt, pp* **spat**) n (*for roasting*) asador m, espetón m; (*saliva*) saliva ▷ vi escupir; (*sound*) chisporrotear; (*rain*) lloviznar
spite [spaɪt] n rencor m, ojeriza ▷ vt causar pena a, mortificar; **in ~ of** a pesar de, pese a; **spiteful** *adj* rencoroso, malévolo
splash [splæʃ] n (*sound*) chapoteo; (*of colour*) mancha ▷ vt salpicar ▷ vi (*also: ~ about*) chapotear; **splash out** (*inf*) vi (BRIT) derrochar dinero
splendid ['splendɪd] *adj* espléndido
splinter ['splɪntə*] n (*of wood etc*) astilla; (*in finger*) espigón m ▷ vi astillarse, hacer astillas
split [splɪt] (*pt, pp* **~**) n hendedura, raja; (*fig*) división f; (*Pol*) escisión f ▷ vt partir, rajar; (*party*) dividir; (*share*) repartir ▷ vi dividirse, escindirse; **split up** vi (*couple*) separarse; (*meeting*) acabarse
spoil [spɔɪl] (*pt, pp* **~t** *or* **~ed**) *vt* (*damage*) dañar; (*mar*) estropear; (*child*) mimar, consentir
spoilt [spɔɪlt] *pt, pp of* **spoil** ▷ *adj* (*child*) mimado, consentido; (*ballot paper*) invalidado

spoke [spəʊk] *pt of* **speak** ▷ n rayo, radio
spoken ['spəʊkn] *pp of* **speak**
spokesman ['spəʊksmən] (*irreg*) n portavoz m
spokesperson ['spəʊkspɜːsn] (*irreg*) n portavoz m/f, vocero/a (LAM)
spokeswoman ['spəʊkswʊmən] (*irreg*) n portavoz f
sponge [spʌndʒ] n esponja; (*also: ~ cake*) bizcocho ▷ vt (*wash*) lavar con esponja ▷ vi: **to ~ off** *or* **on sb** vivir a costa de algn; **sponge bag**(BRIT) n esponjera
sponsor ['spɒnsə*] n patrocinador(a) m/f ▷ vt (*applicant, proposal etc*) proponer; **sponsorship** n patrocinio
spontaneous [spɒn'teɪnɪəs] *adj* espontáneo
spooky ['spuːkɪ] (*inf*) *adj* espeluznante, horripilante
spoon [spuːn] n cuchara; **spoonful** n cucharada
sport [spɔːt] n deporte m; (*person*): **to be a good ~** ser muy majo ▷ vt (*wear*) lucir, ostentar; **sport jacket**(us) n = **sports jacket**; **sports car** n coche m deportivo; **sports centre**(BRIT) n polideportivo; **sports jacket**(BRIT) n chaqueta deportiva; **sportsman**(*irreg*) n deportista m; **sports utility vehicle** n todoterreno m *inv*; **sportswear** n trajes *mpl* de deporte *or* sport; **sportswoman**(*irreg*) n deportista f; **sporty** *adj* deportista
spot [spɒt] n sitio, lugar m; (*dot: on pattern*) punto, mancha; (*pimple*) grano; (*Radio*) cuña publicitaria; (*TV*) espacio publicitario; (*small amount*): **a ~ of** un poquito de ▷ vt (*notice*) notar, observar; **on the ~** allí mismo; **spotless** *adj* perfectamente limpio; **spotlight** n foco, reflector m; (*Aut*) faro auxiliar
spouse [spauz] n cónyuge mf
sprain [spreɪn] n torcedura ▷ vt: **to ~ one's ankle/wrist** torcerse el tobillo/la muñeca
sprang [spræŋ] *pt of* **spring**

sprawl | 532

sprawl [sprɔːl] *vi* tumbarse

spray [spreɪ] *n* rociada; (*of sea*) espuma; (*container*) atomizador *m*; (*for paint etc*) pistola rociadora; (*of flowers*) ramita ▷ *vt* rociar; (*crops*) regar

spread [sprɛd] (*pt, pp* ~) *n* extensión *f*; (*for bread etc*) pasta para untar; (*inf: food*) comilona ▷ *vt* extender; (*butter*) untar; (*wings, sails*) desplegar; (*work, wealth*) repartir; (*scatter*) esparcir ▷ *vi* (*also:* ~ **out**: *stain*) extenderse; (*news*) diseminarse; **spread out** *vi* (*move apart*) separarse; **spreadsheet** *n* hoja electrónica *or* de cálculo

spree [spriː] *n*: **to go on a** ~ ir de juerga

spring [sprɪŋ] (*pt* **sprang**, *pp* **sprung**) *n* (*season*) primavera *f*; (*leap*) salto, brinco; (*coiled metal*) resorte *m*; (*of water*) fuente *f*, manantial *m* ▷ *vi* saltar, brincar; **spring up** *vi* (*fig: appear*) aparecer; (*problem*) surgir; **spring onion** *n* cebolleta

sprinkle [ˈsprɪŋkl] *vt* (*pour: liquid*) rociar; (*: salt, sugar*) espolvorear; **to** ~ **water etc on, ~ with water** *etc* rociar *or* salpicar de agua *etc*

sprint [sprɪnt] *n* esprint *m* ▷ *vi* esprintar

sprung [sprʌŋ] *pp of* **spring**

spun [spʌn] *pt, pp of* **spin**

spur [spəː*] *n* espuela; (*fig*) estímulo, aguijón *m* ▷ *vt* (*also:* ~ **on**) estimular, incitar; **on the** ~ **of the moment** de improviso

spurt [spəːt] *n* (*of energy*) chorro; (*of energy*) arrebato ▷ *vi* chorrear

spy [spaɪ] *n* espía *mf* ▷ *vi*: **to** ~ **on** espiar a ▷ *vt* (*see*) divisar, lograr ver

sq. *abbr* = **square**

squabble [ˈskwɔbl] *vi* reñir, pelear

squad [skwɔd] *n* (*Mil*) pelotón *m*; (*Police*) brigada; (*Sport*) equipo

squadron [ˈskwɔdrn] *n* (*Mil*) escuadrón *m*; (*Aviat, Naut*) escuadra

squander [ˈskwɔndə*] *vt* (*money*) derrochar, despilfarrar; (*chances*) desperdiciar

square [skwɛə*] *n* cuadro; (*in town*) plaza; (*inf: person*) carca *m/f* ▷ *adj* cuadrado; (*inf: ideas, tastes*) trasnochado ▷ *vt* (*arrange*) arreglar; (*Math*) cuadrar; (*reconcile*) compaginar; **all** ~ igual(es); (*in game*) en paz; **to have a** ~ **meal** comer caliente; **2 metres** ~ 2 metros en cuadro; **2** ~ **metres** 2 metros cuadrados; **square root** *n* raíz *f* cuadrada

squash [skwɔʃ] *n* (*BRIT: drink*): **lemon/orange** ~ zumo (*SP*) *or* jugo (*LAM*) de limón/naranja; (*US Bot*) calabacín *m*; (*Sport*) squash *m* ▷ *vt* aplastar

squat [skwɔt] *adj* achaparrado ▷ *vi* (*also:* ~ **down**) agacharse, sentarse en cuclillas; **squatter** *n* okupa *mf* (*SP*)

squeak [skwiːk] *vi* (*hinge*) chirriar, rechinar; (*mouse*) chillar

squeal [skwiːl] *vi* chillar, dar gritos agudos

squeeze [skwiːz] *n* presión *f*; (*of hand*) apretón *m*; (*Comm*) restricción *f* ▷ *vt* (*hand, arm*) apretar

squid [skwɪd] *n inv* calamar *m*; (*Culin*) calamares *mpl*

squint [skwɪnt] *vi* bizquear, ser bizco ▷ *n* (*Med*) estrabismo

squirm [skwəːm] *vi* retorcerse, revolverse

squirrel [ˈskwɪrəl] *n* ardilla

squirt [skwəːt] *vi* salir a chorros ▷ *vt* chiscar

Sr *abbr* = **senior**

Sri Lanka [sriːˈlæŋkə] *n* Sri Lanka *m*

St *abbr* = **saint**; **street**

stab [stæb] *n* (*with knife*) puñalada; (*of pain*) pinchazo; (*inf: try*): **to have a** ~ **at (doing) sth** intentar (hacer) algo ▷ *vt* apuñalar

stability [stəˈbɪlɪtɪ] *n* estabilidad *f*

stable [ˈsteɪbl] *adj* estable ▷ *n* cuadra, caballeriza

stack [stæk] *n* montón *m*, pila *f* ▷ *vt* amontonar, apilar

stadium [ˈsteɪdɪəm] *n* estadio

staff [stɑːf] *n* (*work force*) personal *m*,

plantilla; (BRIT Scol) cuerpo docente ▷ vt proveer de personal

stag [stæg] n ciervo, venado

stage [steɪdʒ] n escena; (point) etapa; (platform) plataforma; (profession): **the ~** el teatro ▷ vt (play) poner en escena, representar; (organize) montar, organizar; **in ~s** por etapas

stagger ['stægə*] vi tambalearse ▷ vt (amaze) asombrar; (hours, holidays) escalonar; **staggering** adj asombroso

stagnant ['stægnənt] adj estancado

stag night, stag party n despedida de soltero

stain [steɪn] n mancha; (colouring) tintura ▷ vt manchar; (wood) teñir; **stained glass** n vidrio m de color; **stainless steel** n acero inoxidable

staircase ['steəkeɪs] n = **stairway**

stairs [steəz] npl escaleras fpl

stairway ['steəweɪ] n escalera

stake [steɪk] n estaca, poste m; (Comm) interés m; (Betting) apuesta f ▷ vt (money) apostar; (life) arriesgar; (reputation) poner en juego; (claim) presentar una reclamación; **to be at ~** estar en juego

stale [steɪl] adj (bread) duro; (food) pasado; (smell) rancio; (beer) agrio

stalk [stɔːk] n tallo, caña ▷ vt acechar, cazar al acecho

stall [stɔːl] n (in market) puesto; (in stable) casilla (de establo) ▷ vt (Aut) calar; (fig) dar largas a ▷ vi (Aut) calarse; (fig) andarse con rodeos

stamina ['stæmɪnə] n resistencia

stammer ['stæmə*] n tartamudeo ▷ vi tartamudear

stamp [stæmp] n sello (SP), estampilla (LAM), timbre m (MEX); (mark) marca, huella; (on document) timbre m ▷ vi (also: **~ one's foot**) patear ▷ vt (mark) marcar; (letter) franquear; (with rubber stamp) sellar; **stamp out** vt (fire) apagar con el pie; (crime, opposition) acabar con; **stamped addressed envelope** n (BRIT) sobre m sellado con las señas propias

stampede [stæm'piːd] n estampida

stance [stæns] n postura

stand [stænd] (pt, pp **stood**) n (position) posición f, postura; (for taxis) parada; (hall stand) perchero; (music stand) atril m; (Sport) tribuna; (at exhibition) stand m ▷ vi (be) estar, encontrarse; (be on foot) estar de pie; (rise) levantarse; (remain) quedar en pie; (in election) presentar candidatura ▷ vt (place) poner, colocar; (withstand) aguantar, soportar; (invite to) invitar; **to make a ~** (fig) mantener una postura firme; **to ~ for parliament** (BRIT) presentarse (como candidato) a las elecciones; **stand back** vi retirarse; **stand by** vi (be ready) estar listo ▷ vt fus (opinion) aferrarse a; (person) apoyar; **stand down** vi (withdraw) ceder el puesto; **stand for** vt fus (signify) significar; (tolerate) aguantar, permitir; **stand in for** vt fus suplir a; **stand out** vi destacarse; **stand up** vi levantarse, ponerse de pie; **stand up for** vt fus defender; **stand up to** vt fus hacer frente a

standard ['stændəd] n patrón m, norma; (level) nivel m; (flag) estandarte m ▷ adj (size etc) normal, corriente; (text) básico; **standards** npl (morals) valores mpl morales; **standard of living** n nivel m de vida

standing ['stændɪŋ] adj (on foot) de pie, en pie; (permanent) permanente ▷ n reputación f; **of many years' ~** que lleva muchos años; **standing order** (BRIT) n (at bank) orden f de pago permanente

stand: **standpoint** n punto de vista; **standstill** n: **at a standstill** (industry, traffic) paralizado; (car) parado; **to come to a standstill** quedar paralizado; pararse

stank [stæŋk] pt of **stink**

staple ['steɪpl] n (for papers) grapa ▷ adj (food etc) básico ▷ vt grapar

star [stɑː*] n estrella; (celebrity) estrella, astro ▷ vt (Theatre, Cinema)

ser el/la protagonista de; **the stars** npl
(Astrology) el horóscopo

starboard ['stɑ:bəd] n estribor m

starch [stɑ:tʃ] n almidón m

stardom ['stɑ:dəm] n estrellato

stare [steə*] n mirada fija ▷ vi: **to ~
at** mirar fijo

stark [stɑ:k] adj (bleak) severo,
escueto ▷ adv: **~ naked** en cueros

start [stɑ:t] n principio, comienzo;
(departure) salida; (sudden movement)
salto, sobresalto; (advantage) ventaja
▷ vt empezar, comenzar; (cause)
causar; (found) fundar; (engine) poner
en marcha ▷ vi comenzar, empezar;
(with fright) asustarse, sobresaltarse;
(train etc) salir; **to ~ doing or to do
sth** empezar a hacer algo; **start off**
vi empezar, comenzar; (leave) salir,
ponerse en camino; **start out** vi
(begin) empezar; (set out) partir, salir;
start up vi comenzar; (car) ponerse
en marcha ▷ vt comenzar; poner en
marcha; **starter** n (Aut) botón m de
arranque; (Sport: official) juez mf de
salida; (BRIT Culin) entrante m; **starting
point** n punto de partida

startle ['stɑ:tl] vt asustar,
sobrecoger; **startling** adj alarmante

starvation [stɑ:'veɪʃən] n hambre f

starve [stɑ:v] vi tener mucha
hambre; (to death) morir de hambre
▷ vt hacer pasar hambre

state [steɪt] n estado ▷ vt (say,
declare) afirmar; **the S-s** los Estados
Unidos; **to be in a ~** estar agitado;
statement n afirmación f; **state
school** n escuela or colegio estatal;
statesman (irreg) n estadista m

static ['stætɪk] n (Radio) parásitos mpl
▷ adj estático

station ['steɪʃən] n estación f; (Radio)
emisora; (rank) posición f social ▷ vt
colocar, situar; (Mil) apostar

stationary ['steɪʃnərɪ] adj
estacionario, fijo

stationer's (shop) (BRIT) n
papelería

stationery [-nərɪ] n papel m de
escribir, artículos mpl de escritorio

station wagon (US) n ranchera

statistic [stə'tɪstɪk] n estadística;
statistics n (science) estadística

statue ['stætjuː] n estatua

stature ['stætʃə*] n estatura; (fig)
talla

status ['steɪtəs] n estado; (reputation)
estatus m; **status quo** n (e)statu
quo m

statutory ['stætjutrɪ] adj
estatutorio

staunch [stɔ:ntʃ] adj leal,
incondicional

stay [steɪ] n estancia ▷ vi quedar(se);
(as guest) hospedarse; **to ~ put** seguir
en el mismo sitio; **to ~ the night/5
days** pasar la noche/estar 5 días;
stay away vi (from person, building)
no acercarse; (from event) no acudir;
stay behind vi quedar atrás; **stay
in** vi quedarse en casa; **stay on** vi
quedarse; **stay out** vi (of house) no
volver a casa; (on strike) permanecer
en huelga; **stay up** vi (at night) velar,
no acostarse

steadily ['stedɪlɪ] adv
constantemente; (firmly) firmemente;
(work, walk) sin parar; (gaze) fijamente

steady ['stedɪ] adj (firm) firme;
(regular) regular; (person, character)
sensato, juicioso; (boyfriend) formal;
(look, voice) tranquilo ▷ vt (stabilize)
estabilizar; (nerves) calmar

steak [steɪk] n filete m; (beef) bistec m

steal [sti:l] (pt **stole**, pp **stolen**) vt
robar ▷ vi robar; (move secretly) andar
a hurtadillas

steam [sti:m] n vapor m; (mist) vaho,
humo ▷ vt (Culin) cocer al vapor ▷ vi
echar vapor; **steam up** vi (window)
empañarse; **to get steamed up
about sth** (fig) ponerse negro por algo;
steamy adj (room) lleno de vapor;
(window) empañado; (heat, atmosphere)
bochornoso

steel [sti:l] n acero ▷ adj de acero

steep [stiːp] *adj* escarpado, abrupto; (*stair*) empinado; (*price*) exhorbitante, excesivo ▷ *vt* empapar, remojar

steeple ['stiːpl] *n* aguja

steer [stɪə] *vt* (*car*) conducir (SP), manejar (LAM); (*person*) dirigir ▷ *vi* conducir, manejar; **steering** *n* (*Aut*) dirección *f*; **steering wheel** *n* volante *m*

stem [stɛm] *n* (*of plant*) tallo; (*of glass*) pie *m* ▷ *vt* detener; (*blood*) restañar

step [stɛp] *n* paso; (*on stair*) peldaño, escalón *m* ▷ *vi*: **to ~ forward/back** dar un paso adelante/hacia atrás; **steps** *npl* (BRIT) = **stepladder**; **in/out of ~ (with)** acorde/en disonancia (con); **step down** *vi* (*fig*) retirarse; **step in** *vi* entrar; (*fig*) intervenir; **step up** *vt* (*increase*) aumentar; **stepbrother** *n* hermanastro; **stepchild** (*pl* **stepchildren**) *n* hijastro/a *m/f*; **stepdaughter** *n* hijastra; **stepfather** *n* padrastro; **stepladder** *n* escalera doble o de tijera; **stepmother** *n* madrastra; **stepsister** *n* hermanastra; **stepson** *n* hijastro

stereo ['stɛrɪəu] *n* estéreo ▷ *adj* (*also:* **~phonic**) estéreo, estereofónico

stereotype ['stɪərɪətaɪp] *n* estereotipo *m* ▷ *vt* estereotipar

sterile ['stɛraɪl] *adj* estéril; **sterilize** ['stɛrɪlaɪz] *vt* esterilizar

sterling ['stəːlɪŋ] *adj* (*silver*) de ley ▷ *n* (*Econ*) libras *fpl* esterlinas *fpl*; **one pound ~** una libra esterlina

stern [stəːn] *adj* severo, austero ▷ *n* (*Naut*) popa

steroid ['stɪərɔɪd] *n* esteroide *m*

stew [stjuː] *n* estofado, guiso ▷ *vt* estofar, guisar; (*fruit*) cocer

steward ['stjuːəd] *n* camarero; **stewardess** *n* (*esp on plane*) azafata

stick [stɪk] (*pt*, *pp* **stuck**) *n* palo; (*of dynamite*) barreno; (*as weapon*) porra; (*also:* **walking ~**) bastón *m* ▷ *vt* (*glue*) pegar; (*inf: put*) meter; (*: tolerate*) aguantar, soportar; (*thrust*): **to ~ sth into** clavar or hincar algo en ▷ *vi*

pegarse; (*be unmoveable*) quedarse parado; (*in mind*) quedarse grabado; **stick out** *vi* sobresalir; **stick up** *vi* sobresalir; **stick up for** *vt fus* defender; **sticker** *n* (*label*) etiqueta engomada; (*with slogan*) pegatina; **sticking plaster** *n* esparadrapo; **stick shift** (US) *n* (Aut) palanca de cambios

sticky ['stɪkɪ] *adj* pegajoso; (*label*) engomado; (*fig*) difícil

stiff [stɪf] *adj* rígido, tieso; (*hard*) duro; (*manner*) estirado; (*difficult*) difícil; (*person*) inflexible; (*price*) exhorbitante ▷ *adv*: **scared/bored ~** muerto de miedo/aburrimiento

stifling ['staɪflɪŋ] *adj* (*heat*) sofocante, bochornoso

stigma ['stɪgmə] *n* (*fig*) estigma *m*

stiletto [stɪ'lɛtəu] (BRIT) *n* (*also:* **~ heel**) tacón *m* de aguja

still [stɪl] *adj* inmóvil, quieto ▷ *adv* todavía; (*even now*) todavía; (*nonetheless*) sin embargo, aun así

stimulate ['stɪmjuleɪt] *vt* estimular

stimulus ['stɪmjuləs] (*pl* **stimuli**) *n* estímulo, incentivo

sting [stɪŋ] (*pt*, *pp* **stung**) *n* picadura; (*pain*) escozor *m*, picazón *f*; (*organ*) aguijón *m* ▷ *vt*, *vi* picar

stink [stɪŋk] (*pt* **stank**, *pp* **stunk**) *n* hedor *m*, tufo ▷ *vi* heder, apestar

stir [stəː*] *n* (*fig: agitation*) conmoción *f* ▷ *vt* (*tea etc*) remover; (*fig: emotions*) provocar ▷ *vi* moverse; **stir up** *vt* (*trouble*) fomentar; **stir-fry** *vt* sofreír removiendo ▷ *n* plato preparado sofriendo y removiendo sus ingredientes

stitch [stɪtʃ] *n* (*Sewing*) puntada; (*Knitting*) punto; (*Med*) punto de sutura; (*pain*) punzada ▷ *vt* coser; (*Med*) suturar

stock [stɔk] *n* (*Comm: reserves*) existencias *fpl*, stock *m*; (*: selection*) surtido; (*Agr*) ganado, ganadería; (*Culin*) caldo; (*descent*) raza, estirpe *f*; (*Finance*) capital *m* ▷ *adj* (*fig: reply etc*) clásico ▷ *vt* (*have in stock*) tener existencias de; **~s and shares** acciones y valores: **in ~** en existencia or almacén; **out of ~** = agotado; **to take ~ of** (fig) asesorar, examinar; **stockbroker** ['stɔkbrəukə*] n agente mf or corredor mf de bolsa(s); **stock cube** (BRIT) n pastilla de caldo; **stock exchange** n bolsa; **stockholder** ['stɔkhəuldə*] (US) n accionista m/f

stocking ['stɔkɪŋ] n media
stock market n bolsa (de valores)
stole [stəul] pt of **steal** ▷ n estola
stolen ['stəuln] pp of **steal**
stomach ['stʌmək] n (Anat) estómago m; (belly) vientre m ▷ vt tragar, aguantar; **stomachache** n dolor m de estómago
stone [stəun] n piedra; (in fruit) hueso (= 6.348 kg; 14 libras) ▷ adj de piedra ▷ vt apedrear; (fruit) deshuesar
stood [stud] pt, pp of **stand**
stool [stu:l] n taburete m
stoop [stu:p] vi (also: ~ **down**) doblarse, agacharse; (also: **have a ~**) ser cargado de espaldas
stop [stɔp] n parada; (in punctuation) punto ▷ vt parar, detener; (cease) suspender; (block: pay) suspender; (: cheque) invalidar; (also: **put a ~ to**) poner término a ▷ vi pararse, detenerse; (end) acabarse; **to ~ doing sth** dejar de hacer algo; **stop by** vi pasar por; **stop off** vi interrumpir el viaje; **stop over** n parada; (Aviat) escala; **stoppage** n (strike) paro; (blockage) obstrucción f
storage ['stɔ:rɪdʒ] n almacenaje m
store [stɔ:*] n (stock) provisión f; (depot: BRIT: large shop) almacén m; (reserve) reserva, repuesto ▷ vt almacenar; **stores** npl víveres mpl; **to be in ~ for sb** (fig) esperarle a algn; **storekeeper** n (US) tendero/a
storey ['stɔ:rɪ] (US **story**) n piso
storm [stɔ:m] n tormenta; (fig: of applause) salva; (: of criticism) nube f ▷ vi (fig) rabiar ▷ vt tomar por asalto; **stormy** adj tempestuoso
story ['stɔ:rɪ] n historia; (lie) mentira;

(US) = **storey**
stout [staut] adj (strong) sólido; (fat) gordo, corpulento; (resolute) resuelto ▷ n cerveza negra
stove [stəuv] n (for cooking) cocina; (for heating) estufa
straight [streɪt] adj recto, derecho; (frank) franco, directo; (simple) sencillo ▷ adv derecho, directamente; (drink) sin mezcla; **to put** or **get sth ~** dejar algo en claro; ~ **away**, ~ **off** en seguida; **straighten** vt (also: **straighten out**) enderezar, poner derecho ▷ vi (also: **straighten up**) enderezarse, ponerse derecho; **straightforward** adj (simple) sencillo; (honest) honrado, franco
strain [streɪn] n tensión f; (Tech) presión f; (Med) torcedura; (breed) tipo, variedad f ▷ vt (back etc) torcerse; (resources) agotar; (stretch) estirar; (food, tea) colar; **strained** adj (muscle) torcido; (laugh) forzado; (relations) tenso; **strainer** n colador m
strait [streɪt] n (Geo) estrecho (fig): **to be in dire ~s** estar en un gran apuro
strand [strænd] n (of thread) hebra; (of hair) trenza; (of rope) ramal m; **stranded** adj (person: without money) desamparado; (: without transport) colgado
strange [streɪndʒ] adj (not known) desconocido; (odd) extraño, raro; **strangely** adv de un modo raro; **stranger** n desconocido/a; (from another area) forastero/a

▌ Be careful not to translate **stranger** by the Spanish word extranjero.

strangle ['stræŋgl] vt estrangular
strap [stræp] n correa; (of slip, dress) tirante m
strategic [strə'ti:dʒɪk] adj estratégico
strategy ['strætɪdʒɪ] n estrategia
straw [strɔ:] n paja; (drinking straw) caña, pajita; **that's the last ~!** ¡eso es el colmo!
strawberry ['strɔ:bərɪ] n fresa,

frutilla (sc)

stray [streɪ] adj (animal) extraviado; (bullet) perdido; (scattered) disperso ▷ vi extraviarse, perderse

streak [striːk] n raya; (in hair) raya ▷ vt rayar ▷ vi: **to ~ past** pasar como un rayo

stream [striːm] n riachuelo, arroyo; (of people, vehicles) riada, caravana; (of smoke, insults etc) chorro ▷ vt (Scol) dividir en grupos por habilidad ▷ vi correr, fluir; **to ~ in/out** (people) entrar/salir en tropel

street [striːt] n calle f; **streetcar** (US) n tranvía m; **street light** n farol m (LAM), farola (SP); **street map** n plano (de la ciudad); **street plan** n plano

strength [streŋθ] n fuerza; (of girder, knot etc) resistencia; (fig: power) poder m; **strengthen** vt fortalecer, reforzar

strenuous ['strenjuəs] adj (energetic, determined) enérgico

stress [stres] n presión f; (mental strain) estrés m; (accent) acento ▷ vt subrayar, recalcar; (syllable) acentuar; **stressed** adj (tense) estresado, agobiado; (syllable) acentuado; **stressful** adj (job) estresante

stretch [stretʃ] n (of sand etc) trecho ▷ vi estirarse; (extend): **to ~ to** o **as far as** extenderse hasta ▷ vt extender, estirar; (make demands) exigir el máximo esfuerzo a; **stretch out** vi tenderse ▷ vt (arm etc) extender; (spread) estirar

stretcher ['stretʃə*] n camilla

strict [strɪkt] adj severo; (exact) estricto; **strictly** adv severamente, estrictamente

stride [straɪd] (pt **strode**, pp **stridden**) n zancada, tranco ▷ vi dar zancadas, andar a trancos

strike [straɪk] (pt, pp **struck**) n huelga; (of oil etc) descubrimiento; (attack) ataque m ▷ vt golpear, pegar; (oil etc) descubrir; (bargain, deal) cerrar ▷ vi declararse en huelga; (attack) atacar; (clock) dar la hora; **on ~** (workers)

en huelga; **to ~ a match** encender un fósforo; **striker** n huelguista mf; (Sport) delantero; **striking** adj llamativo

string [strɪŋ] (pt, pp **strung**) n cuerda; (row) hilera ▷ vt: **to ~ together** ensartar; **to ~ out** extenderse; **the strings** npl (Mus) los instrumentos de cuerda; **to pull ~s** (fig) mover palancas

strip [strɪp] n tira; (of land) franja; (of metal) cinta, lámina ▷ vt desnudar; (paint) quitar; (also: **~ down**: machine) desmontar ▷ vi desnudarse; **strip off** vt (paint etc) quitar ▷ vi (person) desnudarse

stripe [straɪp] n raya; (Mil) galón m; **striped** adj a rayas, rayado

stripper ['strɪpə*] n artista mf de striptease

strip-search ['strɪpsɜːtʃ] vt: **to ~ sb** desnudar y registrar a algn

strive [straɪv] (pt **strove**, pp **striven**) vi: **to ~ for sth/to do sth** luchar por conseguir/hacer algo

strode [strəʊd] pt of **stride**

stroke [strəʊk] n (blow) golpe m; (Swimming) brazada; (Med) apoplejía; (of paintbrush) toque m ▷ vt acariciar; **at a ~** de un solo golpe

stroll [strəʊl] n paseo, vuelta ▷ vi dar un paseo o una vuelta; **stroller** (US) n (for child) sillita de ruedas

strong [strɒŋ] adj fuerte; **they are 50 ~** son 50 y basta; **stronghold** n fortaleza; (fig) baluarte m; **strongly** adv fuertemente, con fuerza; (believe) firmemente

strove [strəʊv] pt of **strive**

struck [strʌk] pt, pp of **strike**

structure ['strʌktʃə*] n estructura; (building) construcción f

struggle ['strʌgl] n lucha ▷ vi luchar

strung [strʌŋ] pt, pp of **string**

stub [stʌb] n (of ticket etc) talón m; (of cigarette) colilla; **to ~ one's toe on** sth dar con el dedo (del pie) contra algo; **stub out** vt apagar

stubble ['stʌbl] n rastrojo; (on chin)

barba (incipiente)

stubborn ['stʌbən] adj terco, testarudo

stuck [stʌk] pt, pp of **stick** ▷ adj (jammed) atascado

stud [stʌd] n (shirt stud) corchete m; (of boot) taco; (earring) pendiente m (de bolita); (also: ~ **farm**) caballeriza; (also: ~ **horse**) caballo semental ▷ vt (fig): ~**ded with** salpicado de

student ['stjuːdənt] n estudiante mf ▷ adj estudiantil; **student driver** (us) n conductor(a) m/f en prácticas; **students' union** n (building) centro de estudiantes; (BRIT: association) federación f de estudiantes

studio ['stjuːdɪəʊ] n estudio; (artist's) taller m; **studio flat** n estudio

study ['stʌdɪ] n estudio ▷ vt estudiar; (examine) examinar, investigar ▷ vi estudiar

stuff [stʌf] n materia; (substance) material m, sustancia; (things) cosas fpl ▷ vt llenar; (Culin) rellenar; (animals) disecar; (inf: push) meter; **stuffing** n relleno; **stuffy** adj (room) mal ventilado; (person) de miras estrechas

stumble ['stʌmbl] vi tropezar, dar un traspié; ~ **across**, ~ **on** (fig) tropezar con

stump [stʌmp] n (of tree) tocón m; (of limb) muñón m ▷ vt: **to be ~ed for an answer** no saber qué contestar

stun [stʌn] vt dejar sin sentido

stung [stʌŋ] pt, pp of **sting**

stunk [stʌŋk] pp of **stink**

stunned [stʌnd] adj (dazed) aturdido, atontado; (amazed) pasmado; (shocked) anonadado

stunning ['stʌnɪŋ] adj (fig: news) pasmoso; (: outfit etc) sensacional

stunt [stʌnt] n (in film) escena peligrosa; (publicity stunt) truco publicitario

stupid ['stjuːpɪd] adj estúpido, tonto; **stupidity** [-'pɪdɪtɪ] n estupidez f

sturdy ['stɜːdɪ] adj robusto, fuerte

stutter ['stʌtə*] n tartamudeo ▷ vi

tartamudear

style [staɪl] n estilo; **stylish** adj elegante, a la moda; **stylist** n (hair stylist) peluquero/a

sub... [sʌb] prefix sub...; **subconscious** adj subconsciente

subdued [səb'djuːd] adj (light) tenue; (person) sumiso, manso

subject [n 'sʌbdʒɪkt, vb səb'dʒɛkt] n súbdito; (Scol) asignatura; (matter) tema m; (Grammar) sujeto ▷ vt: **to ~ sb to sth** someter a, algn a algo; **to be ~ to** (law) estar sujeto a; (person) ser propenso a; **subjective** [-'dʒɛktɪv] adj subjetivo; **subject matter** n (content) contenido

subjunctive [səb'dʒʌŋktɪv] adj, n subjuntivo

submarine [sʌbmə'riːn] n submarino

submission [səb'mɪʃən] n sumisión

submit [səb'mɪt] vt someter ▷ vi: **to ~ to sth** someterse a algo

subordinate [sə'bɔːdɪnət] adj, n subordinado/a m/f

subscribe [səb'skraɪb] vi suscribir; **to ~ to** (opinion, fund) suscribir, aprobar; (newspaper) suscribirse a

subscription [səb'skrɪpʃən] n abono; (to magazine) suscripción f

subsequent ['sʌbsɪkwənt] adj subsiguiente, posterior; **subsequently** adv posteriormente, más tarde

subside [səb'saɪd] vi hundirse; (flood) bajar; (wind) amainar

subsidiary [səb'sɪdɪərɪ] adj secundario ▷ n sucursal f, filial f

subsidize ['sʌbsɪdaɪz] vt subvencionar

subsidy ['sʌbsɪdɪ] n subvención f

substance ['sʌbstəns] n sustancia

substantial [səb'stænʃl] adj sustancial, sustancioso; (fig) importante

substitute ['sʌbstɪtjuːt] n (person) suplente mf; (thing) sustituto ▷ vt: **to ~ A for B** sustituir A por B, reemplazar B por A; **substitution** n sustitución f

subtle ['sʌtl] *adj* sutil

subtract [səb'trækt] *vt* restar, sustraer

suburb ['sʌbɜːb] *n* barrio residencial; **the ~s** las afueras (de la ciudad); **suburban** [sə'bɜːbən] *adj* suburbano; (*train etc*) de cercanías

subway ['sʌbweɪ] *n* (BRIT) paso subterráneo or inferior; (US) metro

succeed [sək'siːd] *vi* (*person*) tener éxito; (*plan*) salir bien ▷ *vt* suceder a; **to ~ in doing** lograr hacer

success [sək'ses] *n* éxito

> Be careful not to translate **success** by the Spanish word *suceso*.

successful *adj* exitoso; (*business*) próspero; **to be successful (in doing)** lograr (hacer); **successfully** *adv* con éxito

succession [sək'seʃən] *n* sucesión *f*, serie *f*

successive [sək'sesɪv] *adj* sucesivo, consecutivo

successor [sək'sesə*] *n* sucesor(a) *m/f*

succumb [sə'kʌm] *vi* sucumbir

such [sʌtʃ] *adj* tal, semejante; (*of that kind*): **~ a book** tal libro; (*so much*): **~ courage** tanto valor ▷ *adv* tan; **~ a long trip** un viaje tan largo; **~ a lot of** tanto(s)/a(s); **~ as** (*like*) tal como; **as ~** como tal; **such-and-such** *adj* tal o cual

suck [sʌk] *vt* chupar; (*bottle*) sorber; (*breast*) mamar

Sudan [su'dæn] *n* Sudán *m*

sudden ['sʌdn] *adj* (*rapid*) repentino, súbito; (*unexpected*) imprevisto; **all of a ~** de repente; **suddenly** *adv* de repente

sue [suː] *vt* demandar

suede [sweɪd] *n* ante *m*, gamuza

suffer ['sʌfə*] *vt* sufrir, padecer; (*tolerate*) aguantar, soportar ▷ *vi* sufrir; **to ~ from** (*illness etc*) padecer; **suffering** *n* sufrimiento

suffice [sə'faɪs] *vi* bastar, ser suficiente

sufficient [sə'fɪʃənt] *adj* suficiente,

bastante

suffocate ['sʌfəkeɪt] *vi* ahogarse, asfixiarse

sugar ['ʃugə*] *n* azúcar *m* ▷ *vt* echar azúcar a, azucarar

suggest [sə'dʒest] *vt* sugerir; **suggestion** [-'dʒestʃən] *n* sugerencia

suicide ['suːɪsaɪd] *n* suicidio; (*person*) suicida *mf*; *see also* **commit**; **suicide attack** *n* atentado suicida; **suicide bomber** *n* terrorista *mf* suicida; **suicide bombing** *n* atentado suicida

suit [suːt] *n* (*man's*) traje *m*; (*woman's*) conjunto; (*Law*) pleito; (*Cards*) palo ▷ *vt* convenir; (*clothes*) sentar a, ir bien a; (*adapt*): **to ~ sth to** adaptar algo a; **well ~ed** (*well matched: couple*) hecho el uno para el otro; **suitable** *adj* conveniente; (*apt*) indicado; **suitcase** *n* maleta, valija (RPL)

suite [swiːt] *n* (*of rooms, Mus*) suite *f*; (*furniture*): **bedroom/dining room ~** (juego de) dormitorio/comedor; *see also* **three-piece suite**

sulfur ['sʌlfə*] (US) *n* = **sulphur**

sulk [sʌlk] *vi* estar de mal humor

sulphur ['sʌlfə*] (US **sulfur**) *n* azufre *m*

sultana [sʌl'tɑːnə] *n* (*fruit*) pasa de Esmirna

sum [sʌm] *n* suma; (*total*) total *m*; **sum up** *vt* resumir ▷ *vi* hacer un resumen

summarize ['sʌməraɪz] *vt* resumir

summary ['sʌmərɪ] *n* resumen *m* ▷ *adj* (*justice*) sumario

summer ['sʌmə*] *n* verano ▷ *cpd* de verano; **in ~** en verano; **summer holidays** *npl* vacaciones *fpl* de verano; **summertime** *n* (*season*) verano

summit ['sʌmɪt] *n* cima, cumbre *f*, (*also*: **~ conference**, **~ meeting**) (conferencia) cumbre *f*

summon ['sʌmən] *vt* (*person*) llamar; (*meeting*) convocar; (*Law*) citar

Sun. *abbr* (=*Sunday*) dom

sun [sʌn] *n* sol *m*; **sunbathe** *vi* tomar el sol; **sunbed** *n* cama solar;

sunblock n filtro solar; **sunburn** (*painful*) quemadura; (*tan*) bronceado; **sunburned, sunburnt** adj (*painfully*) quemado por el sol; (*tanned*) bronceado
Sunday ['sʌndɪ] n domingo
sunflower ['sʌnflauə*] n girasol m
sung [sʌŋ] pp of **sing**
sunglasses ['sʌŋglɑːsɪz] npl gafas fpl (SP) or anteojos fpl (LAM) de sol
sunk [sʌŋk] pp of **sink**
sun: sunlight n luz f del sol; **sun lounger** n tumbona, perezosa (LAM); **sunny** adj soleado; (*day*) de sol; (*fig*) alegre; **sunrise** n salida del sol; **sun roof** n (Aut) techo corredizo; **sunscreen** n protector m solar; **sunset** n puesta del sol; **sunshade** n (*over table*) sombrilla; **sunshine** n sol m; **sunstroke** n insolación f; **suntan** n bronceado m; **suntan lotion** n bronceador m; **suntan oil** n aceite m bronceador
super ['suːpə*] (inf) adj genial
superb [suːˈpəːb] adj magnífico, espléndido
superficial [suːpəˈfɪʃəl] adj superficial
superintendent [suːpərɪnˈtɛndənt] n director(a) m/f; (Police) subjefe/a m/f
superior [suˈpɪərɪə*] adj superior; (*smug*) desdeñoso ▷ n superior m
superlative [suˈpəːlətɪv] n superlativo
supermarket ['suːpəmɑːkɪt] n supermercado
supernatural [suːpəˈnætʃərəl] adj sobrenatural ▷ n: **the ~** lo sobrenatural
superpower ['suːpəpauə*] n (Pol) superpotencia
superstition [suːpəˈstɪʃən] n superstición f
superstitious [suːpəˈstɪʃəs] adj supersticioso
superstore ['suːpəstɔː*] n (BRIT) hipermercado
supervise ['suːpəvaɪz] vt supervisar; **supervision** [-ˈvɪʒən] n supervisión f; **supervisor** n supervisor(a) m/f

supper ['sʌpə*] n cena
supple ['sʌpl] adj flexible
supplement [n 'sʌplɪmənt, vb sʌplɪˈmɛnt] n suplemento ▷ vt suplir
supplier [səˈplaɪə*] n (Comm) distribuidor(a) m/f
supply [səˈplaɪ] vt (*provide*) suministrar; (*equip*): **to ~ (with)** proveer (de) ▷ n provisión f; (*of gas, water etc*) suministro; **supplies** npl (*food*) víveres mpl; (Mil) pertrechos mpl
support [səˈpɔːt] n apoyo; (Tech) soporte m ▷ vt apoyar; (*financially*) mantener; (*uphold, Tech*) sostener

> Be careful not to translate **support** by the Spanish word *soportar*.

supporter n (Pol etc) partidario/a; (Sport) aficionado/a
suppose [səˈpəuz] vt suponer; (*imagine*) imaginarse; (*duty*): **to be ~d to do sth** deber hacer algo; **supposedly** [səˈpəuzɪdlɪ] adv según cabe suponer; **supposing** conj en caso de que
suppress [səˈprɛs] vt suprimir; (*yawn*) ahogar
supreme [suˈpriːm] adj supremo
surcharge ['səːtʃɑːdʒ] n sobretasa, recargo
sure [ʃuə*] adj seguro; (*definite, convinced*) cierto; **to make ~ of sth/that** asegurarse de algo/asegurar que; **~!** (*of course*) ¡claro!, ¡por supuesto!; **~ enough** efectivamente; **surely** adv (*certainly*) seguramente
surf [səːf] n olas fpl ▷ vt: **to ~ the Net** navegar por Internet
surface ['səːfɪs] n superficie f ▷ vt (*road*) revestir ▷ vi salir a la superficie; **by ~ mail** por vía terrestre
surfboard ['səːfbɔːd] n tabla (de surf)
surfer ['səːfə*] n (*in sea*) surfista m/f; **web** or **net ~** internauta m/f
surfing ['səːfɪŋ] n surf m
surge [səːdʒ] n oleada, oleaje m ▷ vi (*wave*) romper; (*people*) avanzar en tropel
surgeon ['səːdʒən] n cirujano/a

urgery ['sə:dʒərɪ] n cirugía; (BRIT: room) consultorio

urname ['sə:neɪm] n apellido

urpass [sə:'pɑ:s] vt superar, exceder

urplus ['sə:pləs] n excedente m; (Comm) superávit m ▷ adj excedente, sobrante

urprise [sə'praɪz] n sorpresa ▷ vt sorprender; **surprised** adj (look, smile) de sorpresa; **to be surprised** sorprenderse; **surprising** adj sorprendente; **surprisingly** adv: **it was surprisingly easy** me etc sorprendió lo fácil que fue

surrender [sə'rɛndə*] n rendición f, entrega f ▷ vi rendirse, entregarse

surround [sə'raʊnd] vt rodear, circundar; (Mil etc) cercar; **surrounding** adj circundante; **surroundings** npl alrededores mpl, cercanías fpl

surveillance [sə:'veɪləns] n vigilancia

survey [n 'sə:veɪ, vb sə:'veɪ] n inspección f, reconocimiento m; (inquiry) encuesta ▷ vt examinar, inspeccionar; (look at) mirar, contemplar; **surveyor** n agrimensor(a) m/f

survival [sə'vaɪvl] n supervivencia

survive [sə'vaɪv] vi sobrevivir; (custom etc) perdurar ▷ vt sobrevivir a; **survivor** n superviviente mf

suspect [adj, n 'sʌspɛkt, vb səs'pɛkt] adj, n sospechoso/a m/f ▷ vt (person) sospechar de; (think) sospechar

suspend [səs'pɛnd] vt suspender; **suspended sentence** n (Law) libertad f condicional; **suspenders** npl (BRIT) ligas fpl; (US) tirantes mpl

suspense [səs'pɛns] n incertidumbre f, duda; (in film etc) suspense m; **to keep sb in ~** mantener a algn en suspense

suspension [səs'pɛnʃən] n (gen, Aut) suspensión f; (of driving licence) privación f; **suspension bridge** n puente m colgante

suspicion [səs'pɪʃən] n sospecha; (distrust) recelo; **suspicious** adj

receloso; (causing suspicion) sospechoso

sustain [səs'teɪn] vt sostener, apoyar; (suffer) sufrir, padecer

SUV (esp US) n abbr (= sports utility vehicle) todoterreno m inv, 4X4 m

swallow ['swɔləʊ] n (bird) golondrina ▷ vt tragar; (fig.: pride) tragarse

swam [swæm] pt of **swim**

swamp [swɔmp] n pantano, ciénaga ▷ vt (with water etc) inundar; (fig) abrumar, agobiar

swan [swɔn] n cisne m

swap [swɔp] n canje m, intercambio ▷ vt: **to ~ (for)** cambiar (por)

swarm [swɔ:m] n (of bees) enjambre m; (fig) multitud f ▷ vi (bees) formar un enjambre; (people) pulular; **to be ~ing with** ser un hervidero de

sway [sweɪ] vi mecerse, balancearse ▷ vt (influence) mover, influir en

swear [swɛə*] (pt **swore**, pp **sworn**) vi (curse) maldecir; (promise) jurar ▷ vt jurar; **swear in** vt: **to be sworn in** prestar juramento; **swearword** n taco, palabrota

sweat [swɛt] n sudor m ▷ vi sudar

sweater ['swɛtə*] n suéter m

sweatshirt ['swɛtʃə:t] n suéter m

sweaty ['swɛtɪ] adj sudoroso

Swede [swi:d] n sueco/a

swede [swi:d] (BRIT) n nabo

Sweden ['swi:dn] n Suecia; **Swedish** ['swi:dɪʃ] adj sueco ▷ n (Ling) sueco

sweep [swi:p] (pt, pp **swept**) n (act) barrido; (also: **chimney ~**) deshollinador(a) m/f ▷ vt barrer; (with arm) empujar; (current) arrastrar ▷ vi barrer; (arm etc) moverse rápidamente ▷ vt (wind) soplar con violencia

sweet [swi:t] n (candy) dulce m, caramelo; (BRIT: pudding) postre m ▷ adj dulce; (fig: kind) dulce, amable; (: attractive) mono; **sweetcorn** n maíz m; **sweetener** ['swi:tnə*] n (Culin) edulcorante m; **sweetheart** n novio/a; **sweetshop** n (BRIT) confitería f, bombonería

swell [swɛl] (pt **~ed**, pp **swollen** or **~ed**)

n (*of sea*) marejada, oleaje *m* ▷ *adj* (*us: inf: excellent*) estupendo, fenomenal ▷ *vt* hinchar, inflar ▷ *vi* (*also:* **~ up**) hincharse; (*numbers*) aumentar; (*sound, feeling*) ir aumentando; **swelling** *n* (*Med*) hinchazón *f*

swept [swɛpt] *pt, pp of* **sweep**

swerve [swɜːv] *vi* desviarse bruscamente

swift [swɪft] *n* (*bird*) vencejo ▷ *adj* rápido, veloz

swim [swɪm] (*pt* **swam**, *pp* **swum**) *n*: **to go for a ~** ir a nadar o a bañarse ▷ *vi* nadar; (*head, room*) dar vueltas ▷ *vt* nadar; (*the Channel etc*) cruzar a nado; **swimmer** *n* nadador(a) *m/f*; **swimming** *n* natación *f*; **swimming costume** (BRIT) *n* bañador *m*, traje *m* de baño; **swimming pool** *n* piscina, alberca (MEX), pileta (RPL); **swimming trunks** *npl* bañador *m* (de hombre); **swimsuit** *n* = **swimming costume**

swing [swɪŋ] (*pt, pp* **swung**) *n* (*in playground*) columpio; (*movement*) balanceo, vaivén *m*; (*change of direction*) viraje *m*; (*rhythm etc*) ritmo ▷ *vt* balancear; (*also:* **~ round**) voltear, girar ▷ *vi* balancearse, columpiarse; (*also:* **~ round**) dar media vuelta; **to be in full ~** estar en plena marcha

swipe card [swaɪp-] *n* tarjeta magnética deslizante, tarjeta swipe

swirl [swɜːl] *vi* arremolinarse

Swiss [swɪs] *adj, n inv* suizo/a *m/f*

switch [swɪtʃ] *n* (*for light etc*) interruptor *m*; (*change*) cambio ▷ *vt* (*change*) cambiar de; **switch off** *vt* apagar; (*engine*) parar; **switch on** *vt* encender (SP), prender (LAM); (*engine, machine*) arrancar; **switchboard** *n* (*Tel*) centralita (SP), conmutador *m* (LAM)

Switzerland ['swɪtsələnd] *n* Suiza

swivel ['swɪvl] *vi* (*also:* **~ round**) girar

swollen ['swəulən] *pp of* **swell**

swoop [swuːp] *n* (*by police etc*) redada ▷ *vi* (*also:* **~ down**) calarse

swop [swɔp] = **swap**

sword [sɔːd] *n* espada; **swordfish** *n*

pez *m* espada

swore [swɔːˀ] *pt of* **swear**

sworn [swɔːn] *pp of* **swear** ▷ *adj* (*statement*) bajo juramento; (*enemy*) implacable

swum [swʌm] *pp of* **swim**

swung [swʌŋ] *pt, pp of* **swing**

syllable ['sɪləbl] *n* sílaba

syllabus ['sɪləbəs] *n* programa *m* de estudios

symbol ['sɪmbl] *n* símbolo; **symbolic(al)** [sɪm'bɒlɪk(l)] *adj* simbólico; **to be symbolic(al) of sth** simbolizar algo

symmetrical [sɪ'mɛtrɪkl] *adj* simétrico

symmetry ['sɪmɪtrɪ] *n* simetría

sympathetic [sɪmpə'θɛtɪk] *adj* (*understanding*) comprensivo; (*showing support*): **~ to(wards)** bien dispuesto hacia

> Be careful not to translate **sympathetic** by the Spanish word *simpático*.

sympathize ['sɪmpəθaɪz] *vi*: **to ~ with** (*person*) compadecerse de; (*feelings*) comprender; (*cause*) apoyar

sympathy ['sɪmpəθɪ] *n* (*pity*) compasión *f*

symphony ['sɪmfənɪ] *n* sinfonía

symptom ['sɪmptəm] *n* síntoma *m*, indicio

synagogue ['sɪnəgɒg] *n* sinagoga

syndicate ['sɪndɪkɪt] *n* sindicato; (*of newspapers*) agencia *f* de noticias

syndrome ['sɪndrəum] *n* síndrome *m*

synonym ['sɪnənɪm] *n* sinónimo

synthetic [sɪn'θɛtɪk] *adj* sintético

Syria ['sɪrɪə] *n* Siria

syringe [sɪ'rɪndʒ] *n* jeringa

syrup ['sɪrəp] *n* jarabe *m*; (*also:* **golden ~**) almíbar *m*

system ['sɪstəm] *n* sistema *m*; (*Anat*) organismo; **systematic** [-'mætɪk] *adj* sistemático, metódico; **systems analyst** *n* analista *mf* de sistemas

t

a [tɑː] (BRIT: inf) excl ¡gracias!

tab [tæb] n lengüeta; (label) etiqueta;
to keep ~s on (fig) vigilar

able ['teɪbl] n mesa; (of statistics etc)
cuadro, tabla ▷ vt (BRIT: motion etc)
presentar; **to lay** or **set the ~** poner la
mesa; **tablecloth** n mantel m; **table
d'hôte** [tɑːbl'dəut] adj del menú;
table lamp n lámpara de mesa;
tablemat n (for plate) posaplatos
m inv; (for hot dish) salvamantel m;
tablespoon n cuchara de servir;
(also: **tablespoonful**: as measurement)
cucharada

ablet ['tæblɪt] n (Med) pastilla,
comprimido; (of stone) lápida

able tennis n ping-pong m, tenis
m de mesa

abloid ['tæblɔɪd] n periódico
popular sensacionalista

taboo [tə'buː] adj, n tabú m

tack [tæk] n (nail) tachuela; (fig)
rumbo ▷ vt (nail) clavar con tachuelas;
(stitch) hilvanar ▷ vi virar

tackle ['tækl] n (fishing tackle)
aparejo (de pescar); (for lifting)
aparejo ▷ vt (difficulty) enfrentarse
con; (challenge: person) hacer frente a;
(grapple with) agarrar; (Football) cargar;
(Rugby) placar

tacky ['tækɪ] adj pegajoso; (pej) cutre

tact [tækt] n tacto, discreción f;
tactful adj discreto, diplomático

tactics ['tæktɪks] npl táctica

tactless ['tæktlɪs] adj indiscreto

tadpole ['tædpəʊl] n renacuajo

taffy ['tæfɪ] (us) n melcocha

tag [tæg] n (label) etiqueta

tail [teɪl] n cola; (of shirt, coat) faldón m
▷ vt (follow) vigilar a; **tails** npl (formal
suit) levita

tailor ['teɪlə*] n sastre m

Taiwan [taɪ'wɑːn] n Taiwán m;
Taiwanese [taɪwə'niːz] adj, n
taiwanés/esa m/f

take [teɪk] (pt **took**, pp **taken**) vt
tomar; (grab) coger (SP), agarrar (LAM);
(gain: prize) ganar; (require: effort,
courage) exigir; (tolerate: pain etc)
aguantar; (hold: passengers etc) tener
cabida para; (accompany, bring, carry)
llevar; (exam) presentarse a; **to ~ sth
from** (drawer etc) sacar algo de; (person)
quitar algo a; **I ~ it that ...** supongo

talc [tælk] *n* (*also*: **~um powder**) (polvos de) talco

tale [teɪl] *n* (*story*) cuento; (*account*) relación *f*; **to tell ~s** (*fig*) chivarse

talent ['tælnt] *n* talento; **talented** *adj* de talento

talk [tɔːk] *n* charla; (*conversation*) conversación *f*; (*gossip*) habladurías *fpl*, chismes *mpl* ▷ *vi* hablar; **talks** *npl* (*Pol etc*) conversaciones *fpl*; **to ~ about** hablar de; **to ~ sb into doing sth** convencer a algn para que haga algo; **to ~ sb out of doing sth** disuadir a algn de que haga algo; **to ~ shop** hablar del trabajo; **talk over** *vt* discutir; **talk show** *n* programa *m* de entrevistas

tall [tɔːl] *adj* alto; (*object*) grande; **to be 6 feet ~** (*person*) = medir 1 metro 80

tambourine [tæmbə'riːn] *n* pandereta

tame [teɪm] *adj* domesticado; (*fig*) mediocre

tamper ['tæmpə*] *vi*: **to ~ with** tocar, andar con

tampon ['tæmpən] *n* tampón *m*

tan [tæn] *n* (*also*: **sun~**) bronceado ▷ *vi* ponerse moreno ▷ *adj* (*colour*) marrón

tandem ['tændəm] *n* tándem *m*

tangerine [tændʒə'riːn] *n* mandarina

tangle ['tæŋgl] *n* enredo; **to get in(to) a ~** enredarse

tank [tæŋk] *n* (*water tank*) depósito, tanque *m*; (*for fish*) acuario; (*Mil*) tanque *m*

tanker ['tæŋkə*] *n* (*ship*) buque *m*, cisterna; (*truck*) camión *m* cisterna

tanned [tænd] *adj* (*skin*) moreno

tantrum ['tæntrəm] *n* rabieta

Tanzania [tænzə'nɪə] *n* Tanzania

tap [tæp] *n* (*BRIT*: *on sink etc*) grifo (*SP*), llave *f*, canilla (*US*); (*gas tap*) llave *f*; (*gentle blow*) golpecito ▷ *vt* (*hit gently*) dar golpecitos en; (*resources*) utilizar, explotar; (*telephone*) intervenir; **on ~** (*fig*: *resources*) a mano; **tap dancing** *n* claqué *m*

tape [teɪp] *n* (*also*: **magnetic ~**) cinta magnética; (*cassette*) cassette *f*, cinta; (*sticky tape*) cinta adhesiva; (*for tying*) cinta ▷ *vt* (*record*) grabar (en cinta); (*stick with tape*) pegar con cinta adhesiva; **tape measure** *n* cinta métrica, metro; **tape recorder** *n* grabadora

tapestry ['tæpɪstrɪ] *n* (*object*) tapiz *m*; (*art*) tapicería

tar [tɑː] *n* alquitrán *m*, brea

target ['tɑːgɪt] *n* blanco

tariff ['tærɪf] *n* (*on goods*) arancel *m*; (*BRIT*: *in hotels etc*) tarifa

tarmac ['tɑːmæk] *n* (*BRIT*: *on road*) asfaltado; (*Aviat*) pista (de aterrizaje)

tarpaulin [tɑː'pɔːlɪn] *n* lona impermeabilizada

tarragon ['tærəgən] *n* estragón *m*

tart [tɑːt] *n* (*Culin*) tarta; (*BRIT*: *inf*: *prostitute*) puta ▷ *adj* agrio, ácido

tartan ['tɑːtn] n tejido escocés m

tartar(e) sauce ['tɑːtə-] n salsa tártara

task [tɑːsk] n tarea; **to take to ~** reprender

taste [teɪst] n (sense) gusto; (flavour) sabor m; (sample): **have a ~** prueba un poquito!; (fig) muestra, idea ▷ vt probar ▷ vi: **to ~ of** or **like** (fish, garlic etc) saber a; **you can ~ the garlic (in it)** se nota el sabor a ajo; **in good/bad ~** de buen/mal gusto; **tasteful** adj de buen gusto; **tasteless** adj (food) soso; (remark etc) de mal gusto; **tasty** adj sabroso, rico

tatters ['tætəz] npl: **in ~** hecho jirones

tattoo [tə'tuː] n tatuaje m; (spectacle) espectáculo militar ▷ vt tatuar

taught [tɔːt] pt, pp of **teach**

taunt [tɔːnt] n burla ▷ vt burlarse de

Taurus ['tɔːrəs] n Tauro

taut [tɔːt] adj tirante, tenso

tax [tæks] n impuesto m ▷ vt gravar (con un impuesto); (fig: memory) poner a prueba; (: patience) agotar; **tax-free** adj libre de impuestos

taxi ['tæksɪ] n taxi m ▷ vi (Aviat) rodar por la pista; **taxi driver** n taxista mf; **taxi rank** (BRIT) n = **taxi stand**; **taxi stand** n parada de taxis

tax payer n contribuyente mf

TB n abbr = **tuberculosis**

tea [tiː] n té m; (BRIT: meal) = merienda (SP); cena; **high ~** (BRIT) merienda-cena (SP); **tea bag** n bolsita de té; **tea break** (BRIT) n descanso para el té

teach [tiːtʃ] (pt, pp taught) vt: **to ~ sb sth, ~ sth to sb** enseñar algo a algn ▷ vi (be a teacher) ser profesor(a), enseñar; **teacher** n (in secondary school) profesor(a) m/f; (in primary school) maestro/a, profesor(a) de EGB; **teaching** n enseñanza

tea: tea cloth n (BRIT) paño de cocina, trapo de cocina (LAM); **teacup** n taza para el té

tea leaves npl hojas de té

team [tiːm] n equipo; (of horses) tiro m;

team up vi asociarse

teapot ['tiːpɒt] n tetera

tear¹ [tɪə*] n lágrima; **in ~s** llorando

tear² [tɛə*] (pt tore, pp torn) n rasgón m, desgarrón m ▷ vt romper, rasgar ▷ vi rasgarse; **tear apart** vt (also fig) hacer pedazos; **tear down** vt +adv (building, statue) derribar; (poster, flag) arrancar; **tear off** vt (sheet of paper etc) arrancar; (one's clothes) quitarse a tirones; **tear up** vt (sheet of paper etc) romper

tearful ['tɪəful] adj lloroso

tear gas ['tɪə-] n gas m lacrimógeno

tearoom ['tiːruːm] n salón m de té

tease [tiːz] vt tomar el pelo a

tea: teaspoon n cucharita; (also: **teaspoonful**: as measurement) cucharadita; **teatime** n hora del té; **tea towel** (BRIT) n paño de cocina

technical ['tɛknɪkl] adj técnico

technician [tɛk'nɪʃn] n técnico/a

technique [tɛk'niːk] n técnica

technology [tɛk'nɒlədʒɪ] n tecnología

teddy (bear) ['tɛdɪ-] n osito de felpa

tedious ['tiːdɪəs] adj pesado, aburrido

tee [tiː] n (Golf) tee m

teen [tiːn] adj = **teenage** ▷ n (US) = teenager

teenage ['tiːneɪdʒ] adj (fashions etc) juvenil; (children) quinceañero; **teenager** n adolescente mf

teens [tiːnz] npl: **to be in one's ~** ser adolescente

teeth [tiːθ] npl of **tooth**

teetotal ['tiː'təutl] adj abstemio

telecommunications [telɪkəmjuː-nɪ'keɪʃənz] n telecomunicaciones fpl

telegram ['telɪgræm] n telegrama m

telegraph pole ['telɪgrɑːf-] n poste m telegráfico

telephone ['telɪfəun] n teléfono ▷ vt llamar por teléfono, telefonear; (message) dar por teléfono; **to be on the ~** (talking) hablar por teléfono; (possessing telephone) tener teléfono;

telephone book n guía f telefónica;
telephone booth, **telephone box**
(BRIT) n cabina telefónica; **telephone
call** n llamada f telefónica; **telephone
directory** n guía (telefónica);
telephone number n número de
teléfono

telesales ['telɪseɪlz] npl televenta(s)
(f(pl))

telescope ['telɪskəʊp] n telescopio

televise ['telɪvaɪz] vt televisar

television ['telɪvɪʒən] n televisión
f; **on ~** en la televisión; **television
programme** n programa m de
televisión

tell [tel] (pt, pp **told**) vt decir;
(relate: story) contar; (distinguish): **to
~ sth from** distinguir algo de ▷ vi
(talk): **to ~ (of)** contar; (have effect)
tener efecto; **to ~ sb to do** mandar
a algn hacer algo; **tell off** vt: **to tell sb
off** regañar a algn; **teller** n (in bank)
cajero/a

telly ['telɪ] (BRIT: inf) n abbr
(= television) tele f

temp [temp] n abbr (BRIT)
(= temporary) temporero/a

temper ['tempə*] n (nature) carácter
m; (mood) humor m; (bad temper) (mal)
genio; (fit of anger) acceso de ira ▷ vt
(moderate) moderar; **to be in a ~** estar
furioso; **to lose one's ~** enfadarse,
enojarse

temperament ['temprəmə
nt] n (nature) temperamento;
temperamental [temprə'mentl] adj
temperamental

temperature ['temprətʃə*] n
temperatura; **to have** o **run a ~**
tener fiebre

temple ['templ] n (building) templo;
(Anat) sien f

temporary ['tempərərɪ] adj
provisional; (passing) transitorio;
(worker) temporero; (job) temporal

tempt [tempt] vt tentar; **to ~ sb into
doing sth** tentar or inducir a algn a
hacer algo; **temptation** n tentación

f; **tempting** adj tentador(a); (food)
apetitoso/a

ten [ten] num diez

tenant ['tenənt] n inquilino/a

tend [tend] vt cuidar ▷ vi: **to ~ to
do sth** tener tendencia a hacer algo;
tendency ['tendənsɪ] n tendencia

tender ['tendə*] adj (person, care)
tierno, cariñoso; (meat) tierno; (sore)
sensible ▷ n (Comm: offer) oferta;
(money): **legal ~** moneda de curso legal
▷ vt ofrecer

tendon ['tendən] n tendón m

tenner ['tenə*] n (inf) (billete m de)
diez libras m

tennis ['tenɪs] n tenis m; **tennis
ball** n pelota de tenis; **tennis court**
n cancha de tenis; **tennis match** n
partido de tenis; **tennis player** n
tenista mf; **tennis racket** n raqueta
de tenis

tenor ['tenə*] n (Mus) tenor m

tenpin bowling ['tenpɪn-] n (juego
de los) bolos

tense [tens] adj (person) nervioso;
(moment, atmosphere) tenso; (muscle)
tenso, en tensión ▷ n (Ling) tiempo

tension ['tenʃən] n tensión f

tent [tent] n tienda (de campaña
(SP), carpa (LAM)

tentative ['tentətɪv] adj (person,
smile) indeciso; (conclusion, plans)
provisional

tenth [tenθ] num décimo

tent: tent peg n clavija, estaca; **tent
pole** n mástil m

tepid ['tepɪd] adj tibio

term [tə:m] n (word) término;
(period) período; (Scol) trimestre m ▷ vt
llamar; **terms** npl (conditions, Comm)
condiciones fpl; **in the short/long ~**
a corto/largo plazo; **to be on good
~s with sb** llevarse bien con algn; **to
come to ~s with** (problem) aceptar

terminal ['tə:mɪnl] adj (disease)
mortal; (patient) terminal ▷ n (Elec)
borne m; (Comput) terminal m; (also:
air ~) terminal f; (BRIT: also: **coach ~**)

estación f **terminal** f
erminate ['tɜːmɪneɪt] vt terminar
ermini ['tɜːmɪnaɪ] npl of **terminus**
erminology [tɜːmɪ'nɒlədʒɪ] n terminología
terminus ['tɜːmɪnəs] (pl **termini**) n término, (estación f) terminal f
errace ['tɛrəs] n terraza; (BRIT: row of houses) hilera de casas adosadas; **the ~s** (BRIT Sport) las gradas fpl; **terraced** adj (garden) en terrazas; (house) adosado
errain [tɛ'reɪn] n terreno
errestrial [tɪ'restrɪəl] adj (life) terrestre; (BRIT: channel) de transmisión (por) vía terrestre
errible ['tɛrɪbl] adj terrible, horrible; (inf) atroz; **terribly** adv terriblemente; (very badly) malísimamente
errier ['tɛrɪə] n terrier m
errific [tə'rɪfɪk] adj (very great) tremendo; (wonderful) fantástico, fenomenal
errified ['tɛrɪfaɪd] adj aterrorizado
errify ['tɛrɪfaɪ] vt aterrorizar; **terrifying** adj aterrador(a)
territorial [tɛrɪ'tɔːrɪəl] adj territorial
territory ['tɛrɪtərɪ] n territorio
error ['tɛrə] n terror m; **terrorism** n terrorismo; **terrorist** n terrorista mf; **terrorist attack** n atentado (terrorista)
est [tɛst] n (gen, Chem) prueba; (Med) examen m; (Scol) examen m, test m; (also: **driving ~**) examen m de conducir ▷ vt probar, poner a prueba; (Med, Scol) examinar
esticle ['tɛstɪkl] n testículo
estify ['tɛstɪfaɪ] vi (Law) prestar declaración; **to ~ to sth** atestiguar algo
estimony ['tɛstɪmənɪ] n (Law) testimonio
est: test match n (Cricket, Rugby) partido internacional; **test tube** n probeta
etanus ['tɛtənəs] n tétano
ext [tɛkst] n texto; (on mobile phone)

mensaje m de texto ▷ vt: **to ~ sb** (inf) enviar un mensaje (de texto) or un SMS a algn; **textbook** n libro de texto
textile ['tɛkstaɪl] n textil m, tejido
text message n mensaje m de texto
text messaging [-'mesɪdʒɪŋ] n (envío de) mensajes mpl de texto
texture ['tɛkstʃə*] n textura
Thai [taɪ] adj, n tailandés/esa m/f
Thailand ['taɪlænd] n Tailandia
than [ðæn] conj (in comparisons): **more ~ 10/once** más de 10/una vez; **I have more/less ~ you/Paul** tengo más/menos que tú/Paul; **she is older ~ you think** es mayor de lo que piensas
thank [θæŋk] vt dar las gracias a, agradecer; **~ you (very much)** muchas gracias; **~ God!** ¡gracias a Dios! ▷ excl (also: **many ~s, ~s a lot**) ¡gracias! ▷ **~s to** prep gracias a; **thanks** npl gracias fpl; **thankfully** adv (fortunately) afortunadamente; **Thanksgiving (Day)** n día m de Acción de Gracias

⬤ **THANKSGIVING (DAY)**

⬤ En Estados Unidos el cuarto jueves
⬤ de noviembre es **Thanksgiving**
⬤ **Day**, fiesta oficial en la que se
⬤ recuerda la celebración que
⬤ hicieron los primeros colonos
⬤ norteamericanos ("Pilgrims"
⬤ o "Pilgrim Fathers") tras la
⬤ estupenda cosecha de 1621, por
⬤ la que se dan gracias a Dios. En
⬤ Canadá se celebra una fiesta
⬤ semejante el segundo lunes
⬤ de octubre, aunque no está
⬤ relacionada con dicha fecha
⬤ histórica.

◯ **KEYWORD**

that [ðæt] (pl **those**) adj (demonstrative) ese/a; (pl) esos/as; (more remote) aquel(aquella); (pl) aquellos/as; **leave those books on the table** deja

esos libros sobre la mesa; **that one** ése(ésa); *(more remote)* aquél(aquélla); **that one over there** ése(ésa) de ahí; aquél(aquélla) de allí
▷ *pron* **1** *(demonstrative)* ése/a; *(pl)* ésos/as; *(neuter)* eso; *(more remote)* aquél/aquélla; *(pl)* aquéllos/as; *(neuter)* aquello; **what's that?** ¿qué es eso (or aquello)?; **who's that?** ¿quién es ése (or aquélla))?; **is that you?** ¿eres tú?; **will you eat all that?** ¿vas a comer todo eso?; **that's my house** ésa es mi casa; **that's what he said** eso es lo que dijo; **that is (to say)** es decir
2 *(relative: subject, object)* que; *(with preposition)* (el (la)) que etc, el(la) cual etc; **the book (that) I read** el libro que leí; **the books that are in the library** los libros que están en la biblioteca; **all (that) I have** todo lo que tengo; **the box (that) I put it in** la caja en la que *or* donde lo puse; **the people (that) I spoke to** la gente con la que hablé
3 *(relative: of time)* que; **the day (that) he came** el día (en) que vino
▷ *conj* que; **he thought that I was ill** creyó que yo estaba enfermo
▷ *adv* *(demonstrative)*: **I can't work that much** no puedo trabajar tanto; **I didn't realise it was that bad** no creí que fuera tan malo; **that high** así de alto

thatched [ˈθætʃt] *adj* *(roof)* de paja; *(cottage)* con tejado de paja

thaw [θɔː] *n* deshielo ▷ *vi* *(ice)* derretirse; *(food)* descongelarse ▷ *vt* *(food)* descongelar

the [ðiː, ðə] *def art* **1** *(gen)* el *f*, la *pl*, los *fpl*, las (NB *'el' immediately before f n beginning with stressed (h)a; a+ el =al; de + el =del)*: **the boy/girl** el chico/la chica; **the books/flowers** los libros/las flores; **to the postman/from the drawer** al cartero/del cajón; **I haven't the time/money** no tengo

tiempo/dinero
2 *(+adj to form n)* los; lo; **the rich and the poor** los ricos y los pobres; **to attempt the impossible** intentar lo imposible
3 *(in titles)*: **Elizabeth the First** Isabel primera; **Peter the Great** Pedro el Grande
4 *(in comparisons)*: **the more he works the more he earns** cuanto más trabaja más gana

theatre [ˈθɪətə*] (*us* **theater**) *n* teatro; *(also:* **lecture ~**) aula; *(Med: also:* **operating ~**) quirófano

theft [θɛft] *n* robo

their [ðɛə*] *adj* su; **theirs** *pron* (el) suyo/(la) suya etc); *see also* **my; mine**[1]

them [ðɛm, ðəm] *pron* *(direct)* los/las; *(indirect)* les; *(stressed, after prep)* ellos(ellas); *see also* **me**

theme [θiːm] *n* tema *m*; **theme park** *n* parque de atracciones *(en torno a un tema central)*

themselves [ðəmˈsɛlvz] *pl pron* *(subject)* ellos mismos(ellas mismas); *(complement)* se; *(after prep)* sí (mismos(as)); *see also* **oneself**

then [ðɛn] *adv* *(at that time)* entonces; *(next)* después; *(later)* luego, después; *(and also)* además ▷ *conj* *(therefore)* en ese caso, entonces ▷ *adj*: **the ~ president** el entonces presidente; **by ~** para entonces; **from ~ on** desde entonces

theology [θɪˈɒlədʒɪ] *n* teología

theory [ˈθɪərɪ] *n* teoría

therapist [ˈθɛrəpɪst] *n* terapeuta *mf*

therapy [ˈθɛrəpɪ] *n* terapia

there [ðɛə*] *adv* **1** **there is, there are** hay; **there is no-one here/no bread left** no hay nadie aquí/no queda pan; **there has been an accident** ha habido un accidente
2 *(referring to place)* ahí; *(distant)* allí; **it's**

there está ahí; **put it in/on/up/down there** ponlo ahí dentro/encima/arriba/abajo; **I want that book there** quiero ese libro de ahí; **there he is!** ¡ahí está!

3 there, there (esp to child) ea, ea

here: thereabouts adv por ahí; **thereafter** adv después; **thereby** adv así, de ese modo; **therefore** adv por lo tanto; **there's = there is; there has**

thermal ['θə:ml] adj termal; (paper) térmico

thermometer [θə'mɔmitə*] n termómetro

thermostat ['θə:məustæt] n termostato

these [ði:z] pl adj estos/as ▷ pl pron éstos/as

thesis ['θi:sis] (pl **theses**) n tesis f inv

they [ðei] pl pron ellos (ellas); (stressed) ellos (mismos) (ellas (mismas)); ~ **say that** ... (it is said that) se dice que ...; **they'd = they had; they would; they'll = they shall; they will; they're = they are; they've = they have**

thick [θik] adj (in consistency) espeso; (in size) grueso; (stupid) torpe ▷ n: **in the ~ of the battle** en lo más reñido de la batalla; **it's 20 cm ~** tiene 20 cm de espesor; **thicken** vi espesarse ▷ vt (sauce etc) espesar; **thickness** n espesor m; grueso

thief [θi:f] (pl **thieves**) n ladrón/ona m/f

thigh [θai] n muslo

thin [θin] adj (person, animal) flaco; (in size) delgado; (in consistency) poco espeso; (hair, crowd) escaso ▷ vt: **to ~ (down)** diluir

thing [θiŋ] n cosa; (object) objeto, artículo; (matter) asunto; (mania): **to have a ~ about sb/sth** estar obsesionado con algn/algo; **things** npl (belongings) efectos mpl (personales); **the best ~ would be to ...** lo mejor sería ...; **how are ~s?** ¿qué tal?

think [θiŋk] (pt, pp **thought**) vi

pensar ▷ vt pensar, creer; **what did you ~ of them?** ¿qué te parecieron?; **to ~ about sth/sb** pensar en algo/algn; **I'll ~ about it** lo pensaré; **to ~ of doing sth** pensar en hacer algo; **I ~ so/not** creo que sí/no; **to ~ well of sb** tener buen concepto de algn; **think over** vt reflexionar sobre, meditar; **think up** vt (plan etc) idear

third [θə:d] adj (before n) tercer(a); (following n) tercero/a ▷ n tercero/a; (fraction) tercio; (BRIT Scol: degree) título de licenciado con calificación de aprobado; **thirdly** adv en tercer lugar; **third party insurance** (BRIT) n seguro contra terceros; **Third World** n Tercer Mundo

thirst [θə:st] n sed f; **thirsty** adj (person, animal) sediento; (work) que da sed; **to be thirsty** tener sed

thirteen ['θə:'ti:n] num trece; **thirteenth** [-'ti:nθ] adj decimotercero

thirtieth ['θə:tiəθ] adj trigésimo

thirty ['θə:ti] num treinta

○ KEYWORD

this [ðis] (pl **these**) adj (demonstrative) este/a pl; estos/as; (neuter) esto; **this man/woman** este hombre (esta mujer); **these children/flowers** estos chicos/estas flores; **this one** (here) éste/a, esto (de aquí) ▷ pron (demonstrative) éste/a pl, éstos/as; (neuter) esto; **who is this?** ¿quién es éste/ésta?; **what is this?** ¿qué es esto?; **this is where I live** aquí vivo; **this is what he said** esto es lo que dijo; **this is Mr Brown** (in introductions) le presento al Sr. Brown; (photo) éste es el Sr. Brown; (on telephone) habla el Sr. Brown
▷ adv (demonstrative): **this high/long** etc así de alto/largo etc; **this far** hasta aquí

thistle ['θisl] n cardo

thorn [θɔːn] n espina

thorough ['θʌrə] adj (search) minucioso; (wash) a fondo; (knowledge, research) profundo; (person) meticuloso; **thoroughly** adv (search) minuciosamente; (study) profundamente; (wash) a fondo; (utterly: bad, wet etc) completamente, totalmente

those [ðəuz] pl adj esos(esas); (more remote) aquellos/as

though [ðəu] conj aunque ▷ adv sin embargo

thought [θɔːt] pt, pp of **think** ▷ n pensamiento; (opinion) opinión f; **thoughtful** adj pensativo; (serious) serio; (considerate) atento; **thoughtless** adj desconsiderado

thousand ['θauzənd] num mil; **two ~** dos mil; **~s of** miles de; **thousandth** num milésimo

thrash [θræʃ] vt azotar; (defeat) derrotar

thread [θred] n hilo; (of screw) rosca ▷ vt (needle) enhebrar

threat [θret] n amenaza; **threaten** vi amenazar ▷ vt: **to threaten sb with/to do** amenazar a algn con/con hacer; **threatening** adj amenazador(a), amenazante

three [θriː] num tres; **three-dimensional** adj tridimensional; **three-piece suite** n tresillo; **three-quarters** npl tres cuartas partes; **three-quarters full** tres cuartas partes lleno

threshold ['θreʃhəuld] n umbral m

threw [θruː] pt of **throw**

thrill [θrɪl] n (excitement) emoción f; (shudder) estremecimiento ▷ vt emocionar; **to be ~ed** (with gift etc) estar encantado; **thrilled** adj: **I was thrilled** Estaba emocionada; **thriller** n novela (or obra or película) de suspense; **thrilling** adj emocionante

thriving ['θraɪvɪŋ] adj próspero

throat [θrəut] n garganta; **to have a sore ~** tener dolor de garganta

throb [θrɔb] vi latir; dar punzadas; vibrar

throne [θrəun] n trono

through [θruː] prep por, a través de; (time) durante; (by means of) por medio de, mediante; (owing to) gracias a ▷ adj (ticket, train) directo ▷ adv completamente, de parte a parte; de principio a fin; **to put sb ~ to sb** (Tel) poner or pasar a algn con algn; **to be ~** (Tel) tener comunicación; (have finished) haber terminado; **"no ~ road"** (BRIT) "calle sin salida"; **throughout** prep (place) por todas partes de, por todo; (time) durante todo ▷ adv por or en todas partes

throw [θrəu] (pt **threw**, pp **thrown**) n tiro; (Sport) lanzamiento ▷ vt tirar, echar; (Sport) lanzar; (rider) derribar; (fig) desconcertar; **to ~ a party** dar una fiesta; **throw away** vt tirar; (money) derrochar; **throw in** vt (Sport: ball) sacar; (include) incluir; **throw off** vt deshacerse de; **throw out** vt tirar; (person) echar; expulsar; **throw up** vi vomitar

thru [θruː] (US) = **through**

thrush [θrʌʃ] n zorzal m, tordo

thrust [θrʌst] (pt, pp **~**) vt empujar con fuerza

thud [θʌd] n golpe m sordo

thug [θʌg] n gamberro/a

thumb [θʌm] n (Anat) pulgar m; **to ~ a lift** hacer autostop; **thumbtack** (US) n chincheta (SP)

thump [θʌmp] n golpe m; (sound) ruido seco or sordo ▷ vt golpear ▷ vi (heart etc) palpitar

thunder ['θʌndə*] n trueno ▷ vi tronar; (train etc): **to ~ past** pasar como un trueno; **thunderstorm** n tormenta

Thur(s). abbr (= Thursday) juev

Thursday ['θɜːzdɪ] n jueves m inv

thus [ðʌs] adv así, de este modo

thwart [θwɔːt] vt frustrar

thyme [taɪm] n tomillo

Tibet [tɪ'bet] n el Tíbet

tick [tɪk] n (sound: of clock) tictac m;

mark) palomita; (Zool) garrapata; (BRIT: inf): **in a ~** en un instante ▷vi hacer tictac ▷vt marcar; **tick off** vt marcar; (person) reñir

cket ['tɪkɪt] n billete m (SP), boleto (LAM); (for cinema etc) entrada; (in shop: on goods) etiqueta; (for raffle) papeleta; (for library) tarjeta; (parking ticket) multa de aparcamiento (SP) or por estacionamiento (LAM); **ticket barrier** n (BRIT: Rail) barrera más allá de la cual se necesita billete/boleto; **ticket collector** n revisor(a) m/f; **ticket inspector** n revisor(a) m/f, inspector(a) m/f de boletos (LAM); **ticket machine** n máquina de billetes (SP) or boletos (LAM); **ticket office** n (Theatre) taquilla (SP), boletería (LAM); (Rail) mostrador m de billetes (SP) or boletos (LAM)

ickle ['tɪkl] vt hacer cosquillas a ▷vi hacer cosquillas; **ticklish** adj (person) cosquilloso; (problem) delicado

ide [taɪd] n marea; (fig: of events etc) curso, marcha

idy ['taɪdɪ] adj (room etc) ordenado; (dress, work) limpio; (person) (bien) arreglado ▷vt (also: **~ up**) poner en orden

ie [taɪ] n (string etc) atadura; (BRIT: also: **neck~**) corbata; (fig: link) vínculo, lazo; (Sport etc: draw) empate m ▷vt atar ▷vi (Sport etc) empatar; **to ~ in a bow** atar con un lazo; **to ~a knot in sth** hacer un nudo en algo; **tie down** vt (fig: person: restrict) atar; (: to price, date etc) obligar a; **tie up** vt (dog, person) atar; (arrangements) concluir; **to be tied up** (busy) estar ocupado

iger ['taɪgə*] n tigre m

ight [taɪt] adj (rope) tirante; (money) escaso; (clothes) ajustado; (bend) cerrado; (shoes, schedule) apretado; (budget) ajustado; (control) estricto; (inf: drunk) borracho ▷adv (squeeze) muy fuerte; (shut) bien; **tighten** vt (rope) estirar; (screw, grip) apretar;

(security) reforzar ▷vi estirarse; apretarse; **tightly** adv (grasp) muy fuerte; **tights** (BRIT) npl panti mpl

tile [taɪl] n (on roof) teja; (on floor) baldosa; (on wall) azulejo

till [tɪl] n caja (registradora) ▷vt (land) cultivar ▷prep, conj = **until**

tilt [tɪlt] vt inclinar ▷vi inclinarse

timber ['tɪmbə*] n (material) madera

time [taɪm] n tiempo; (epoch: often pl) época; (by clock) hora; (moment) momento; (occasion) vez f; (Mus) compás m ▷vt calcular or medir el tiempo de; (race) cronometrar; (remark, visit etc) elegir el momento para; **a long ~** mucho tiempo; **4 at a ~** de 4 en 4; **4 a la vez**; **for the ~ being** de momento, por ahora; **from ~ to ~** de vez en cuando; **at ~s** a veces; **in ~** (soon enough) a tiempo; (after some time) con el tiempo; (Mus) al compás; **in a week's ~** dentro de una semana; **in no ~** en un abrir y cerrar de ojos; **any ~** cuando sea; **on ~** a la hora; **5 5 5 por 5**; **what ~ is it?** ¿qué hora es?; **to have a good ~** pasarlo bien, divertirse; **time limit** n plazo; **timely** adj oportuno; **timer** n (in kitchen etc) programador m horario; **time-share** n apartamento (or casa) a tiempo compartido; **timetable** n horario; **time zone** n huso horario

timid ['tɪmɪd] adj tímido

timing ['taɪmɪŋ] n (Sport) cronometraje m; **the ~ of his resignation** el momento que eligió para dimitir

tin [tɪn] n estaño; (also: **~ plate**) hojalata; (BRIT: can) lata; **tinfoil** n papel m de estaño

tingle ['tɪŋgl] vi (person): **to ~ (with)** estremecerse (de); (hands etc) hormiguear

tinker ['tɪŋkə*]: **~ with** vt fus jugar con, tocar

tinned [tɪnd] (BRIT) adj (food) en lata, en conserva

tin opener [-əupnə*] (BRIT) n abrelatas m inv

tint [tɪnt] n matiz m; (for hair) tinte m; **tinted** adj (hair) teñido; (glass, spectacles) ahumado

tiny ['taɪnɪ] adj minúsculo, pequeñito

tip [tɪp] n (end) punta; (gratuity) propina; (BRIT: for rubbish) vertedero; (advice) consejo ▷ vt (waiter) dar una propina a; (tilt) inclinar; (empty: also: ~ **out**) vaciar, echar; (overturn: also: ~ **over**) volcar; **tip off** vt avisar, poner sobre aviso a

tiptoe ['tɪptəʊ] n: **on ~** de puntillas

tire ['taɪə*] n (us) = **tyre** ▷ vt cansar ▷ vi cansarse; (become bored) aburrirse; **tired** adj cansado; **to be tired of sth** estar harto de algo; **tire pressure** (us) = **tyre pressure**; **tiring** adj cansado

tissue ['tɪʃu:] n tejido; (paper handkerchief) pañuelo de papel, kleenex® m; **tissue paper** n papel m de seda

tit [tɪt] n (bird) herrerillo común; **to give ~ for tat** dar ojo por ojo

title ['taɪtl] n título

T-junction ['ti:dʒʌŋkʃən] n cruce m en T

TM abbr = **trademark**

○ **KEYWORD**

to [tu:, tə] prep 1 (direction) a; **to go to France/London/school/the station** ir a Francia/Londres/al colegio/a la estación; **to go to Claude's/the doctor's** ir a casa de Claude/al médico; **the road to Edinburgh** la carretera de Edimburgo

2 (as far as) hasta, a; **from here to London** de aquí a or hasta Londres; **to count to 10** contar hasta 10; **from 40 to 50 people** entre 40 y 50 personas

3 (with expressions of time): **a quarter/ twenty to 5** las 5 menos cuarto/veinte

4 (for, of): **the key to the front door** la llave de la puerta principal; **she is secretary to the director** es la secretaria del director; **a letter to his wife** una carta a or para su mujer

5 (expressing indirect object) a; **to give sth to sb** darle algo a algn; **to talk to sb** hablar con algn; **to be a danger to sb** ser un peligro para algn; **to carry out repairs to sth** hacer reparaciones en algo

6 (in relation to): **3 goals to 2** 3 goles a 2; **30 miles to the gallon** ≈ 94 litros a los cien (kms)

7 (purpose, result): **to come to sb's aid** venir en auxilio or ayuda de algn; **to sentence sb to death** condenar a algn a muerte; **to my great surprise** con gran sorpresa mía

▷ with vb 1 (simple infin): **to go/eat** ir/comer

2 (following another vb): **to want/try/ start to do** querer/intentar/empezar a hacer

3 (with vb omitted): **I don't want to** no quiero

4 (purpose, result) para; **I did it to help you** lo hice para ayudarte; **he came to see you** vino a verte

5 (equivalent to relative clause): **I have things to do** tengo cosas que hacer; **the main thing is to try** lo principal es intentarlo

6 (after adj etc): **ready to go** listo para irse; **too old to ...** demasiado viejo (como) para ...

▷ adv: **pull/push the door to** tirar de/empujar la puerta

toad [təʊd] n sapo; **toadstool** n hongo venenoso

toast [təʊst] n (Culin) tostada; (drink, speech) brindis m ▷ vt (Culin) tostar; (drink to) brindar por; **toaster** n tostador m

tobacco [tə'bækəʊ] n tabaco

toboggan [tə'bɒgən] n tobogán m

today [tə'deɪ] adv, n (also fig) hoy m

toddler ['tɒdlə*] n niño/a (que empieza a andar)

toe [təʊ] n dedo (del pie); (of shoe) punta; **to ~ the line** (fig) conformarse:

toenail n uña del pie

toffee ['tɒfɪ] n toffee m

together [tə'geðə*] adv juntos; (at same time) al mismo tiempo, a la vez; **~ with** junto con

toilet ['tɔɪlət] n inodoro; (BRIT: room) (cuarto de) baño, servicio ▷ cpd (soap etc) de aseo; **toilet bag** n neceser m, bolsa de aseo; **toilet paper** n papel m higiénico; **toiletries** npl artículos mpl de tocador; **toilet roll** n rollo de papel higiénico

token ['təukən] n (sign) señal f, muestra; (souvenir) recuerdo; (disc) ficha ▷ adj (strike, payment etc) simbólico; **book/record ~** (BRIT) vale m para comprar libros/discos; **gift ~** (BRIT) vale-regalo

Tokyo ['təukjəu] n Tokio, Tokío

told [təuld] pt, pp of **tell**

tolerant ['tɔlərnt] adj: **~ of** tolerante con

tolerate ['tɔləreɪt] vt tolerar

toll [təul] n (of casualties) número de víctimas; (tax, charge) peaje m ▷ vi (bell) doblar; **toll call** n (us Tel) conferencia, llamada interurbana; **toll-free** (us) adj, adv gratis

tomato [tə'mɑːtəu] (pl **~es**) n tomate m; **tomato sauce** n salsa de tomate

tomb [tuːm] n tumba; **tombstone** n lápida

tomorrow [tə'mɔrəu] adv, n (also: fig) mañana; **the day after ~** pasado mañana; **~ morning** mañana por la mañana

ton [tʌn] n tonelada (BRIT = 1016 kg; US = 907 kg); (metric ton) tonelada métrica; **~s of** (inf) montones de

tone [təun] n tono ▷ vi (also: **~ in**) armonizar; **tone down** vt (criticism) suavizar; (colour) atenuar

tongs [tɒnz] npl (for coal) tenazas fpl; (curling tongs) tenacillas fpl

tongue [tʌn] n lengua; **~ in cheek** irónicamente

tonic ['tɒnɪk] n (Med) tónico; (also: **~ water**) (agua) tónica

tonight [tə'naɪt] adv, n esta noche; esta tarde

tonne [tʌn] n tonelada (métrica) (1.000kg)

tonsil ['tɒnsl] n amígdala; **tonsillitis** [-'laɪtɪs] n amigdalitis f

too [tuː] adv (excessively) demasiado; (also) también; **~ much** demasiado; **~ many** demasiados/as

took [tuk] pt of **take**

tool [tuːl] n herramienta; **tool box** n caja de herramientas; **tool kit** n juego de herramientas

tooth [tuːθ] (pl **teeth**) n (Anat, Tech) diente m; (molar) muela; **toothache** n dolor m de muelas; **toothbrush** n cepillo de dientes; **toothpaste** n pasta de dientes; **toothpick** n palillo

top [tɒp] n (of mountain) cumbre f, cima; (of tree) copa; (of head) coronilla; (of ladder, page) lo alto; (of table) superficie f; (of cupboard) parte f de arriba; (lid: of box) tapa; (: of bottle, jar) tapón m; (of list etc) cabeza; (toy) peonza; (garment) blusa; camiseta ▷ adj de arriba; (in rank) principal, primero; (best) mejor ▷ vt (exceed) exceder; (be first in) encabezar; **on ~ of** (above) sobre, encima de; (in addition to) además de; **from ~ to bottom** de pies a cabeza; **top up** vt llenar; (mobile phone) recargar (el saldo de); **top floor** n último piso; **top hat** n sombrero de copa

topic ['tɒpɪk] n tema m; **topical** adj actual

topless ['tɒplɪs] adj (bather, bikini) topless inv

topping ['tɒpɪŋ] n (Culin): **with a ~ of cream** con nata por encima

topple ['tɒpl] vt derribar ▷ vi caerse

top-up card n (for mobile phone) tarjeta prepago

torch [tɔːtʃ] n (BRIT) antorcha; (BRIT: electric) linterna

tore [tɔː*] pt of **tear²**

torment [n 'tɔːment, vt tɔːment] n tormento ▷ vt atormentar; (fig: annoy) fastidiar

torn [tɔːn] *pp of* **tear²**

tornado [tɔːˈneɪdəu] (*pl* -es) *n* tornado

torpedo [tɔːˈpiːdəu] (*pl* -es) *n* torpedo

torrent [ˈtɒrnt] *n* torrente *m*; **torrential** [tɒˈrɛnʃl] *adj* torrencial

tortoise [ˈtɔːtəs] *n* tortuga

torture [ˈtɔːtʃə*] *n* tortura ▷ *vt* torturar; (*fig*) atormentar

Tory [ˈtɔːrɪ] (*BRIT*) *adj*, *n* (*Pol*) conservador(a) *m/f*

toss [tɒs] *vt* tirar, echar; (*one's head*) sacudir; **to ~ a coin** echar a cara o cruz; **to ~ up for sth** jugar a cara o cruz algo; **to ~ and turn** (*in bed*) dar vueltas

total [ˈtəutl] *adj* todo, entero; (*emphatic: failure etc*) completo, total ▷ *n* total *m*, suma ▷ *vt* (*add up*) sumar; (*amount to*) ascender a

totalitarian [təutælɪˈtɛərɪən] *adj* totalitario

totally [ˈtəutəlɪ] *adv* totalmente

touch [tʌtʃ] *n* tacto; (*contact*) contacto ▷ *vt* tocar; (*emotionally*) conmover; **a ~ of** (*fig*) un poquito de; **to get in ~ with sb** ponerse en contacto con algn; **to lose ~** (*friends*) perder contacto; **touch down** *vi* (*on land*) aterrizar; (*on water*) amerizar *m*; (*us Football*) ensayo; **touched** *adj* (*moved*) conmovido; **touching** *adj* (*moving*) conmovedor(a); **touchline** *n* (*Sport*) línea de banda; **touch-sensitive** *adj* sensible al tacto

tough [tʌf] *adj* (*material*) resistente; (*meat*) duro; (*problem etc*) difícil; (*policy, stance*) inflexible; (*person*) fuerte

tour [tuə*] *n* viaje *m*, vuelta; (*also:* **package ~**) viaje *m* todo comprendido; (*of town, museum*) visita; (*by band etc*) gira ▷ *vt* recorrer, visitar; **tour guide** *n* guía *m/f* turístico/a

tourism [ˈtuərɪzm] *n* turismo

tourist [ˈtuərɪst] *n* turista *mf* ▷ *cpd* turístico; **tourist office** *n* oficina de turismo

tournament [ˈtuənəmənt] *n* torneo

tour operator *n* touroperador(a) *m/f*, operador(a) *m/f* turístico/a

tow [təu] *vt* remolcar; **"on or in** (*us*) **~"** (*Aut*) "a remolque"; **tow away** *vt* llevarse a remolque

toward(s) [təˈwɔːd(z)] *prep* hacia; (*attitude*) respecto a, con; (*purpose*) para

towel [ˈtauəl] *n* toalla; **towelling** *n* (*fabric*) felpa

tower [ˈtauə*] *n* torre *f*; **tower block** (*BRIT*) *n* torre *f* (de pisos)

town [taun] *n* ciudad *f*; **to go to ~** ir a la ciudad; (*fig*) echar la casa por la ventana; **town centre** (*BRIT*) *n* centro de la ciudad; **town hall** *n* ayuntamiento

tow truck (*us*) *n* camión *m* grúa

toxic [ˈtɒksɪk] *adj* tóxico

toy [tɔɪ] *n* juguete *m*; **toy with** *vt fus* jugar con; (*idea*) acariciar; **toyshop** *n* juguetería

trace [treɪs] *n* rastro ▷ *vt* (*draw*) trazar, delinear; (*locate*) encontrar; (*follow*) seguir la pista de

track [træk] *n* (*mark*) huella, pista; (*path: gen*) camino, senda; (: *of bullet etc*) trayectoria; (: *of suspect, animal*) pista, rastro; (*Rail*) vía; (*Sport*) pista; (*on tape, record*) canción *f* ▷ *vt* seguir la pista de; **to keep ~ of** mantenerse al tanto de, seguir; **track down** *vt* (*prey*) seguir el rastro de; (*sth lost*) encontrar; **tracksuit** *n* chándal *m*

tractor [ˈtræktə*] *n* tractor *m*

trade [treɪd] *n* comercio; (*skill, job*) oficio ▷ *vi* negociar, comerciar ▷ *vt* (*exchange*) cambiar; **to ~ sth (for sth)** cambiar algo (por algo); **trade in** (*old car etc*) ofrecer como parte del pago; **trademark** *n* marca de fábrica; **trader** *n* comerciante *mf*; **tradesman** (*irreg*) *n* (*shopkeeper*) tendero; **trade union** *n* sindicato

trading [ˈtreɪdɪŋ] *n* comercio

tradition [trəˈdɪʃən] *n* tradición *f*; **traditional** *adj* tradicional

traffic [ˈtræfɪk] *n* (*gen, Aut*) tráfico,

circulación f ▷ vi: **to ~ in** (pej: liquor, drugs) traficar en; **traffic circle** (us) n isleta; **traffic island** n refugio, isleta; **traffic jam** n embotellamiento; **traffic lights** npl semáforo; **traffic warden** n guardia mf de tráfico

tragedy ['trædʒədɪ] n tragedia

tragic ['trædʒɪk] adj trágico

trail [treɪl] n (tracks) rastro, pista; (path) camino, sendero; (dust, smoke) estela ▷ vt (drag) arrastrar; (follow) seguir la pista de ▷ vi arrastrar; (in contest etc) ir perdiendo; **trailer** n (Aut) remolque m; (caravan) caravana f; (Cinema) trailer m, avance m

train [treɪn] n tren m; (of dress) cola; (series) serie f ▷ vt (educate, teach skills to) formar; (sportsman) entrenar; (dog) adiestrar; (point: gun etc): **to ~ on** apuntar a ▷ vi (Sport) entrenarse; (learn a skill): **to ~ as a teacher** etc estudiar para profesor etc; **one's ~ of thought** el razonamiento de algn; **trainee** [treɪ'niː] n aprendiz(a) m/f; **trainer** n (Sport: coach) entrenador(a) m/f; (of animals) domador(a) m/f; **trainers** npl (shoes) zapatillas fpl (de deporte); **training** n formación f; entrenamiento; **to be in training** (Sport) estar entrenando; **training course** n curso de formación; **training shoes** npl zapatillas fpl (de deporte)

trait [treɪt] n rasgo

traitor ['treɪtə*] n traidor(a) m/f

tram [træm] (BRIT) n (also: **~car**) tranvía m

tramp [træmp] n (person) vagabundo/a; (inf: pej: woman) puta

trample ['træmpl] vt: **to ~ (underfoot)** pisotear

trampoline ['træmpəliːn] n trampolín m

tranquil ['træŋkwɪl] adj tranquilo; **tranquillizer** (us **tranquilizer**) n (Med) tranquilizante m

transaction [træn'zækʃən] n transacción f, operación f

transatlantic ['trænzət'læntɪk] adj transatlántico

transcript ['trænskrɪpt] n copia

transfer [n 'trænsfə:*, vb træns'fə:*] n (of employees) traslado; (of money, power) transferencia; (Sport) traspaso; (picture, design) calcomanía ▷ vt trasladar; transferir; **to ~ the charges** (BRIT Tel) llamar a cobro revertido

transform [træns'fɔːm] vt transformar; **transformation** n transformación f

transfusion [træns'fjuːʒən] n transfusión f

transit ['trænzɪt] n: **in ~** en tránsito

transition [træn'zɪʃən] n transición f

transitive ['trænzɪtɪv] adj (Ling) transitivo

translate [trænz'leɪt] vt traducir; **translation** [-'leɪʃən] n traducción f; **translator** n traductor(a) m/f

transmission [trænz'mɪʃən] n transmisión f

transmit [trænz'mɪt] vt transmitir; **transmitter** n transmisor m

transparent [træns'pærnt] adj transparente

transplant [træns'plɑːnt] n (Med) transplante m

transport [n 'trænspɔːt, vt træns'pɔːt] n transporte m; (car) coche m (SP), carro (LAM), automóvil m ▷ vt transportar; **transportation** [-'teɪʃən] n transporte m

transvestite [trænz'vestaɪt] n travestí mf

trap [træp] n (snare, trick) trampa; (carriage) cabriolé m ▷ vt coger (SP) or agarrar (LAM) (en una trampa); (trick) engañar; (confine) atrapar

trash [træʃ] n (rubbish) basura; (nonsense) tonterías fpl; (pej): **the book/film is ~** el libro/la película no vale nada; **trash can** (us) n cubo or bote m (MEX) or tacho (SC) de la basura

trauma ['trɔːmə] n trauma m; **traumatic** [trɔː'mætɪk] adj traumático

travel ['trævl] n el viajar ▷ vi viajar
▷ vt (distance) recorrer; **travel agency**
n agencia de viajes; **travel agent** n
agente mf de viajes; **travel insurance**
n seguro de viaje; **traveller**(us
traveler) n viajero/a; **traveller's**
cheque(us **traveler's check**) n
cheque m de viaje; **travelling**(us
traveling) n los viajes, el viajar;
travel-sick adj: **to get travel-sick**
marearse al viajar; **travel sickness**
n mareo

tray [treɪ] n bandeja; (on desk) cajón m

treacherous ['tretʃərəs] adj traidor,
traicionero; (dangerous) peligroso

treacle ['triːkl] (BRIT) n melaza

tread [tred] (pt **trod**, pp **trodden**)
n (step) paso, pisada; (sound) ruido
de pasos; (of stair) escalón m; (of tyre)
banda de rodadura ▷ vi pisar; **tread**
on vt fus pisar

treasure ['treʒə*] n tesoro ▷ vt
(value: object, friendship) apreciar;
(: memory) guardar; **treasurer** n
tesorero/a

treasury ['treʒərɪ] n: **the T~** el
Ministerio de Hacienda

treat [triːt] n (present) regalo ▷ vt
tratar; **to ~ sb to sth** invitar a algn a
algo; **treatment** n tratamiento

treaty ['triːtɪ] n tratado

treble ['trebl] adj triple ▷ vt triplicar
▷ vi triplicarse

tree [triː] n árbol m; **~ trunk** tronco
(de árbol)

trek [trek] n (long journey) viaje m
largo y difícil; (tiring walk) caminata

tremble ['trembl] vi temblar

tremendous [trɪ'mendəs] adj
tremendo, enorme; (excellent)
estupendo

trench [trentʃ] n zanja

trend [trend] n (tendency) tendencia;
(of events) curso; (fashion) moda; **trendy**
adj de moda

trespass ['trespəs] vi: **to ~ on** entrar
sin permiso en; **"no ~ing"** prohibido
el paso"

trial ['traɪəl] n (Law) juicio, proceso;
(test: of machine etc) prueba; **trial**
period n periodo de prueba

triangle ['traɪæŋgl] n (Math, Mus)
triángulo

triangular [traɪ'æŋgjulə*] adj
triangular

tribe [traɪb] n tribu f

tribunal [traɪ'bjuːnl] n tribunal m

tribute ['trɪbjuːt] n homenaje m,
tributo; **to pay ~ to** rendir homenaje a

trick [trɪk] n (skill, knack) tino, truco;
(conjuring trick) truco; (joke) broma;
(Cards) baza ▷ vt engañar; **to play a**
~ on sb gastar una broma a algn; **that**
should do the ~ a ver si funciona así

trickle ['trɪkl] n (of water etc) goteo
▷ vi gotear

tricky ['trɪkɪ] adj difícil; delicado

tricycle ['traɪsɪkl] n triciclo

trifle ['traɪfl] n bagatela; (Culin) dulce
de bizcocho borracho, gelatina, fruta y
natillas ▷ adv: **a ~ long** un poquito largo

trigger ['trɪgə*] n (of gun) gatillo

trim [trɪm] adj (house, garden) en
buen estado; (person, figure) esbelto
▷ n (haircut etc) recorte m; (on car)
guarnición f; (neaten) arreglar; (cut)
recortar; (decorate) adornar; (Naut: a
sail) orientar

trio ['triːəʊ] n trío

trip [trɪp] n viaje m; (excursion)
excursión f; (stumble) traspié m ▷ vi
(stumble) tropezar; (go lightly) andar a
paso ligero; **on a ~** de viaje; **trip up** vi
tropezar, caerse ▷ vt hacer tropezar
or caer

triple ['trɪpl] adj triple

triplets ['trɪplɪts] npl trillizos/as
mpl/fpl

tripod ['traɪpɒd] n trípode m

triumph ['traɪʌmf] n triunfo
▷ vi: **to ~ (over)** vencer; **triumphant**
[traɪ'ʌmfənt] adj (team etc) triunfal;
(wave, return) triunfal

trivial ['trɪvɪəl] adj insignificante;
(commonplace) banal

trod [trɒd] pt of **tread**

trodden ['trɒdn] pp of **tread**

trolley ['trɒlɪ] n carrito; (also: ~ **bus**) trolebús m

trombone [trɒm'bəun] n trombón m

troop [tru:p] n grupo, banda; **troops** npl (Mil) tropas fpl

trophy ['trəufɪ] n trofeo

tropical ['trɒpɪkl] adj tropical

trot [trɒt] n trote m ▷ vi trotar; **on the ~** (BRIT: fig) seguidos/as

trouble ['trʌbl] n problema m, dificultad f; (worry) preocupación f; (bother, effort) molestia, esfuerzo; (unrest) inquietud f; (Med): **stomach** etc ~ problemas mpl gástricos etc ▷ vt (disturb) molestar; (worry) preocupar, inquietar ▷ vi: **to ~ to do sth** molestarse en hacer algo; **troubles** npl (Pol etc) conflictos mpl; (personal) problemas mpl; **to be in ~** estar en un apuro; **it's no ~!** ¡no es molestia (ninguna)!; **what's the ~?** (with broken TV etc) ¿cuál es el problema?; (doctor to patient) ¿qué pasa?; **troubled** adj (person) preocupado; (country, epoch, life) agitado; **troublemaker** n agitador(a) m/f; (child) alborotador m; **troublesome** adj molesto

trough [trɒf] n (also: **drinking ~**) abrevadero; (also: **feeding ~**) comedero; (depression) depresión f

trousers ['trauzəz] npl pantalones mpl; **short ~** pantalones mpl cortos

trout [traut] n inv trucha

trowel ['trauəl] n (of gardener) palita; (of builder) paleta

truant ['truənt] n: **to play ~** (BRIT) hacer novillos

truce [tru:s] n tregua

truck [trʌk] n (lorry) camión m; (Rail) vagón m; **truck driver** n camionero

true [tru:] adj verdadero; (accurate) exacto; (genuine) auténtico; (faithful) fiel; **to come ~** realizarse

truly ['tru:lɪ] adv (really) realmente; (truthfully) verdaderamente; (faithfully): **yours ~** (in letter) le saluda atentamente

trumpet ['trʌmpɪt] n trompeta

trunk [trʌŋk] n (of tree, person) tronco; (of elephant) trompa; (case) baúl m; (US Aut) maletero; **trunks** npl (also: **swimming ~s**) bañador m (de hombre)

trust [trʌst] n confianza; (responsibility) responsabilidad f; (Law) fideicomiso ▷ vt (rely on) tener confianza en; (hope) esperar; (entrust): **to ~ sth to sb** confiar algo a algn; **to take sth on ~** fiarse de algo; **trusted** adj de confianza; **trustworthy** adj digno de confianza

truth [tru:θ, pl tru:ðz] n verdad f; **truthful** adj veraz

try [traɪ] n tentativa, intento; (Rugby) ensayo ▷ vt (attempt) intentar; (test: also: ~ **out**) probar, someter a prueba; (Law) juzgar, procesar; (strain: patience) hacer perder ▷ vi probar; **to have a ~** probar suerte; **to ~ to do sth** intentar hacer algo; ~ **again!** ¡vuelve a probar!; ~ **harder!** ¡esfuérzate más!; **well, I tried** al menos lo intenté; **try on** vt (clothes) probarse; **trying** adj (experience) cansado; (person) pesado

T-shirt ['ti:ʃə:t] n camiseta

tub [tʌb] n cubo (SP), cubeta (SP, MEX), balde m (LAM); (bath) bañera (SP), tina (LAM), bañadera (RPL)

tube [tju:b] n tubo; (BRIT: underground) metro; (for tyre) cámara de aire

tuberculosis [tjubə:kju'ləusɪs] n tuberculosis f inv

tube station (BRIT) n estación f de metro

tuck [tʌk] vt (put) poner; **tuck away** vt (money) guardar; (building): **to be tucked away** esconderse, ocultarse; **tuck in** vt meter dentro; (child) arropar ▷ vi (eat) comer con apetito; **tuck shop** n (Scol) tienda ~ bar m (del colegio) (SP)

Tue(s). abbr (= Tuesday) mart

Tuesday ['tju:zdɪ] n martes m inv

tug [tʌg] n (ship) remolcador m ▷ vt tirar de

tuition [tju:'ɪʃən] n (BRIT) enseñanza;

(: *private tuition*) clases *fpl* particulares; (*us*: *school fees*) matrícula

tulip ['tjuːlɪp] *n* tulipán *m*

tumble ['tʌmbl] *n* (*fall*) caída ▷ *vi* caer; **to ~ to sth** (*inf*) caer en la cuenta de algo; **tumble dryer**(BRIT) *n* secadora

tumbler ['tʌmblə*] *n* (*glass*) vaso

tummy ['tʌmɪ] (*inf*) *n* barriga, tripa

tumour ['tjuːmə*] (*us* **tumor**) *n* tumor *m*

tuna ['tjuːnə] *n inv* (*also*: **~ fish**) atún *m*

tune [tjuːn] *n* melodía *f* (*Mus*) afinar; (*Radio, TV, Aut*) sintonizar; **to be in/out of ~** (*instrument*) estar afinado/desafinado; (*singer*) cantar afinadamente/desafinar; **to be in/out of ~ with** (*fig*) estar de acuerdo/en desacuerdo con; **tune in** *vi*: **to tune in (to)** (*Radio, TV*) sintonizar (con); **tune up** *vi* (*musician*) afinar (su instrumento)

tunic ['tjuːnɪk] *n* túnica

Tunisia [tjuː'nɪzɪə] *n* Túnez *m*

tunnel ['tʌnl] *n* túnel *m*; (*in mine*) galería ▷ *vi* construir un túnel/una galería

turf [təːf] *n* césped *m*; (*clod*) tepe *m* ▷ *vt* cubrir con césped

Turk [təːk] *n* turco/a

Turkey ['təːkɪ] *n* Turquía

turkey ['təːkɪ] *n* pavo

Turkish ['təːkɪʃ] *adj, n* turco; (*Ling*) turco

turmoil ['təːmɔɪl] *n*: **in ~** revuelto

turn [təːn] *n* turno; (*in road*) curva; (*of mind, events*) rumbo; (*Theatre*) número; (*Med*) ataque *m* ▷ *vt* girar, volver; (*collar, steak*) dar la vuelta a; (*page*) pasar; (*change*): **to ~ sth into** convertir algo en ▷ *vi* volver; (*person: look back*) volverse; (*reverse direction*) dar la vuelta; (*milk*) cortarse; (*become*): **to ~ nasty/forty** ponerse feo/cumplir los cuarenta; **a good ~** un favor; **it gave**

me quite a ~ me dio un susto; **"no left ~"** (*Aut*) "prohibido girar a la izquierda"; **it's your ~** te toca a ti; **in ~** por turnos; **to take ~s (at)** turnarse (en); **turn around** *vi* (*person*) volverse, darse la vuelta ▷ *vt* (*object*) dar la vuelta a, voltear (LAM); **turn away** *vi* apartar la vista ▷ *vt* rechazar; **turn back** *vi* volverse atrás ▷ *vt* hacer retroceder; (*clock*) retrasar; **turn down** *vt* (*refuse*) rechazar; (*reduce*) bajar; (*fold*) doblar; **turn in** *vi* (*inf: go to bed*) acostarse ▷ *vt* (*fold*) doblar hacia dentro; **turn off** *vi* (*from road*) desviarse ▷ *vt* (*light, radio etc*) apagar; (*tap*) cerrar; (*engine*) parar; **turn on** *vt* (*light, radio etc*) encender (SP), prender (LAM); (*tap*) abrir; (*engine*) poner en marcha; **turn out** *vt* (*light, gas*) apagar; (*produce*) producir ▷ *vi* (*voters*) concurrir; **to turn out to be ...** resultar ser ...; **turn over** *vi* (*person*) volverse ▷ *vt* (*object*) dar la vuelta a; (*page*) volver; **turn round** *vi* volverse; (*rotate*) girar; **turn to** *vt fus*: **to turn to sb** acudir a algn; **turn up** *vi* (*person*) llegar, presentarse; (*lost object*) aparecer ▷ *vt* (*gen*) subir; **turning** *n* (*in road*) vuelta; **turning point** *n* (*fig*) momento decisivo

turnip ['təːnɪp] *n* nabo

turn: turnout *n* concurrencia; **turnover** *n* (*Comm: amount of money*) volumen *m* de ventas; (: *of goods*) movimiento; **turnstile** *n* torniquete *m*; **turn-up**(BRIT) (*on trousers*) vuelta

turquoise ['təːkwɔɪz] *n* (*stone*) turquesa ▷ *adj* color turquesa

turtle ['təːtl] *n* galápago; **turtleneck (sweater)** *n* jersey *m* de cuello vuelto

tusk [tʌsk] *n* colmillo

tutor ['tjuːtə*] *n* profesor(a) *m/f*; **tutorial** [-'tɔːrɪəl] *n* (*Scol*) seminario

tuxedo [tʌk'siːdəu] (*us*) *n* smóking *m*, esmoquin *m*

TV [tiː'viː] *n abbr* (=*television*) tele *f*

tweed [twiːd] *n* tweed *m*

tweezers ['twiːzəz] *npl* pinzas *fpl* (de depilar)

twelfth [twɛlfθ] num duodécimo

twelve [twɛlv] num doce; **at ~ o'clock** (midday) a mediodía; (midnight) a medianoche

twentieth ['twɛntɪɪθ] adj vigésimo

twenty ['twɛntɪ] num veinte

twice [twaɪs] adv dos veces; **~ as much** dos veces más

twig [twɪg] n ramita

twilight ['twaɪlaɪt] n crepúsculo

twin [twɪn] adj, n gemelo/a m/f ▷ vt hermanar; **twin(-bedded) room** n habitación f doble; **twin beds** npl camas fpl gemelas

twinkle ['twɪŋkl] vi centellear; (eyes) brillar

twist [twɪst] n (action) torsión f; (in road, coil) vuelta; (in wire, flex) doblez f; (in story) giro ▷ vt torcer; (weave) trenzar; (roll around) enrollar; (fig) deformar ▷ vi serpentear

twit [twɪt] (inf) n tonto

twitch [twɪtʃ] n (pull) tirón m; (nervous) tic m ▷ vi crisparse

two [tu:] num dos; **to put ~ and ~ together** (fig) atar cabos

type [taɪp] n (category) tipo, género; (model) tipo; (Typ) tipo, letra ▷ vt (letter etc) escribir a máquina; **typewriter** n máquina de escribir

typhoid ['taɪfɔɪd] n tifoidea

typhoon [taɪˈfuːn] n tifón m

typical ['tɪpɪkl] adj típico; **typically** adv típicamente

typing ['taɪpɪŋ] n mecanografía

typist ['taɪpɪst] n mecanógrafo/a

tyre ['taɪə*] (us **tire**) n neumático, llanta (LAM); **tyre pressure** (BRIT) n presión f de los neumáticos

U

UFO ['juːfəu] n abbr (= unidentified flying object) OVNI m

Uganda [juːˈgændə] n Uganda

ugly ['ʌglɪ] adj feo; (dangerous) peligroso

UHT abbr (= UHT milk) leche f UHT, leche f uperizada

UK n abbr = **United Kingdom**

ulcer ['ʌlsə*] n úlcera; (mouth ulcer) llaga

ultimate ['ʌltɪmət] adj último, final; (greatest) máximo; **ultimately** adv (in the end) por último, al final; (fundamentally) a or en fin de cuentas

ultimatum [ʌltɪˈmeɪtəm] (pl **~s** or **ultimata**) n ultimátum m

ultrasound ['ʌltrəsaund] n (Med) ultrasonido

ultraviolet ['ʌltrəˈvaɪəlɪt] adj ultravioleta

umbrella [ʌmˈbrɛlə] n paraguas m inv; (for sun) sombrilla

umpire ['ʌmpaɪə*] n árbitro

UN n abbr (= United Nations) NN. UU.

unable [ʌnˈeɪbl] adj: **to be ~ to do sth**

no poder hacer algo

unacceptable [ʌnək'septəbl] adj (proposal, behaviour, price) inaceptable; **it's ~ that** no se puede aceptar que

unanimous [juː'nænɪməs] adj unánime

unarmed [ʌn'ɑːmd] adj (defenceless) inerme; (without weapon) desarmado

unattended [ʌnə'tendɪd] adj desatendido

unattractive [ʌnə'træktɪv] adj poco atractivo

unavailable [ʌnə'veɪləbl] adj (article, room, book) no disponible; (person) ocupado

unavoidable [ʌnə'vɔɪdəbl] adj inevitable

unaware [ʌnə'weə*] adj: **to be ~ of** ignorar; **unawares** adv: **to catch sb unawares** pillar a algn desprevenido

unbearable [ʌn'bɛərəbl] adj insoportable

unbeatable [ʌn'biːtəbl] adj (team) invencible; (price) inmejorable; (quality) insuperable

unbelievable [ʌnbɪ'liːvəbl] adj increíble

unborn [ʌn'bɔːn] adj que va a nacer

unbutton [ʌn'bʌtn] vt desabrochar

uncalled-for [ʌn'kɔːldfɔː*] adj gratuito, inmerecido

uncanny [ʌn'kænɪ] adj extraño

uncertain [ʌn'sɜːtn] adj incierto; (indecisive) indeciso; **uncertainty** n incertidumbre f

unchanged [ʌn'tʃeɪndʒd] adj igual, sin cambios

uncle ['ʌŋkl] n tío

unclear [ʌn'klɪə*] adj poco claro; **I'm still ~ about what I'm supposed to do** todavía no tengo muy claro lo que tengo que hacer

uncomfortable [ʌn'kʌmfətəbl] adj incómodo; (uneasy) inquieto

uncommon [ʌn'kɒmən] adj poco común, raro

unconditional [ʌnkən'dɪʃənl] adj incondicional

unconscious [ʌn'kɒnʃəs] adj sin sentido; (unaware) **to be ~ of** no darse cuenta de ▷ n: **the ~** el inconsciente

uncontrollable [ʌnkən'trəuləbl] adj (child etc) incontrolable; (temper) indomable; (laughter) incontenible

unconventional [ʌnkən'venʃənl] adj poco convencional

uncover [ʌn'kʌvə*] vt descubrir; (take lid off) destapar

undecided [ʌndɪ'saɪdɪd] adj (character) indeciso; (question) no resuelto

undeniable [ʌndɪ'naɪəbl] adj innegable

under ['ʌndə*] prep debajo de; (less than) menos de; (according to) según, de acuerdo con; (sb's leadership) bajo ▷ adv debajo, abajo; **~ there** allí abajo; **~ repair** en reparación; **undercover** adj clandestino; **underdone** adj (Culin) poco hecho; **underestimate** vt subestimar; **undergo** (irreg) vt sufrir; (treatment) recibir; **undergraduate** n estudiante mf; **underground** n (BRIT: railway) metro; (Pol) movimiento clandestino ▷ adj (car park) subterráneo ▷ adv (work) en la clandestinidad; **undergrowth** n maleza; **underline** vt subrayar; **undermine** vt socavar, minar; **underneath** [ʌndə'niːθ] adv debajo ▷ prep debajo de, bajo; **underpants** npl calzoncillos mpl; **underpass** (BRIT) n paso subterráneo; **underprivileged** adj desposeído; **underscore** vt subrayar; **undershirt** (US) n camiseta; **underskirt** (BRIT) n enagua fpl

understand [ʌndə'stænd] vt, vi entender, comprender; (assume) tener entendido; **understandable** adj comprensible; **understanding** adj comprensivo ▷ n comprensión f, entendimiento; (agreement) acuerdo

understatement [ʌndəsteɪtmənt] n modestia (excesiva); **that's an ~!** ¡eso es decir poco!

understood [ʌndə'stud] pt, pp of

understand ⊳ *adj* (*agreed*) acordado; (*implied*): **it is ~ that** se sobreentiende que

undertake [ʌndəˈteɪk] (*irreg*) *vt* emprender; **to ~ to do sth** comprometerse a hacer algo

undertaker [ˈʌndəteɪkə*] *n* director(a) *m/f* de pompas fúnebres

undertaking [ˈʌndəteɪkɪŋ] *n* empresa; (*promise*) promesa

under: **underwater** *adv* bajo el agua ⊳ *adj* submarino; **underway** *adj*: **to be underway** (*meeting*) estar en marcha; (*investigation*) estar llevándose a cabo; **underwear** *n* ropa interior; **underwent** *vb see* **undergo**; **underworld** *n* (*of crime*) hampa, inframundo

undesirable [ʌndɪˈzaɪərəbl] *adj* (*person*) indeseable; (*thing*) poco aconsejable

undisputed [ʌndɪˈspjuːtɪd] *adj* incontestable

undo [ʌnˈduː] (*irreg*) *vt* (*laces*) desatar; (*button etc*) desabrochar; (*spoil*) deshacer

undone [ʌnˈdʌn] *pp of* **undo** ⊳ *adj*: **to come** ~ (*clothes*) desabrocharse; (*parcel*) desatarse

undoubtedly [ʌnˈdaʊtɪdlɪ] *adv* indudablemente, sin duda

undress [ʌnˈdrɛs] *vi* desnudarse

unearth [ʌnˈəːθ] *vt* desenterrar

uneasy [ʌnˈiːzɪ] *adj* intranquilo, preocupado; (*feeling*) desagradable; (*peace*) inseguro

unemployed [ʌnɪmˈplɔɪd] *adj* parado, sin trabajo ⊳ *npl*: **the ~** los parados

unemployment [ʌnɪmˈplɔɪmənt] *n* paro, desempleo; **unemployment benefit** *n* (BRIT) subsidio de desempleo o paro

unequal [ʌnˈiːkwəl] *adj* (*unfair*) desigual; (*size, length*) distinto

uneven [ʌnˈiːvn] *adj* desigual; (*road etc*) lleno de baches

unexpected [ʌnɪkˈspɛktɪd] *adj* inesperado; **unexpectedly** *adv* inesperadamente

unfair [ʌnˈfɛə*] *adj*: **~ (to sb)** injusto (con algn)

unfaithful [ʌnˈfeɪθful] *adj* infiel

unfamiliar [ʌnfəˈmɪlɪə*] *adj* extraño, desconocido; **to be ~ with** desconocer

unfashionable [ʌnˈfæʃnəbl] *adj* pasado o fuera de moda

unfasten [ʌnˈfɑːsn] *vt* (*knot*) desatar; (*dress*) desabrochar; (*open*) abrir

unfavourable [ʌnˈfeɪvərəbl] (*us* **unfavorable**) *adj* desfavorable

unfinished [ʌnˈfɪnɪʃt] *adj* inacabado, sin terminar

unfit [ʌnˈfɪt] *adj* bajo de forma; (*incompetent*): **~ (for)** incapaz (de); **~ for work** no apto para trabajar

unfold [ʌnˈfəuld] *vt* desdoblar ⊳ *vi* abrirse

unforgettable [ʌnfəˈɡɛtəbl] *adj* inolvidable

unfortunate [ʌnˈfɔːtʃnət] *adj* desgraciado; (*event, remark*) inoportuno; **unfortunately** *adv* desgraciadamente

unfriendly [ʌnˈfrɛndlɪ] *adj* antipático; (*behaviour, remark*) hostil, poco amigable

unfurnished [ʌnˈfəːnɪʃt] *adj* sin amueblar

unhappiness [ʌnˈhæpɪnɪs] *n* tristeza, desdicha

unhappy [ʌnˈhæpɪ] *adj* (*sad*) triste; (*unfortunate*) desgraciado; (*childhood*) infeliz; **~ about/with** (*arrangements etc*) poco contento con, descontento de

unhealthy [ʌnˈhɛlθɪ] *adj* (*place*) malsano; (*person*) enfermizo; (*fig: interest*) morboso

unheard-of [ʌnˈhəːdɔv] *adj* inaudito, sin precedente

unhelpful [ʌnˈhɛlpful] *adj* (*person*) poco servicial; (*advice*) inútil

unhurt [ʌnˈhəːt] *adj* ileso

unidentified [ʌnaɪˈdɛntɪfaɪd] *adj* no identificado, sin identificar; *see* *also* **UFO**

uniform ['ju:nɪfɔ:m] *n* uniforme *m*
▷ *adj* uniforme

unify ['ju:nɪfaɪ] *vt* unificar, unir

unimportant [ʌnɪm'pɔ:tənt] *adj* sin
importancia

uninhabited [ʌnɪn'hæbɪtɪd] *adj*
desierto

unintentional [ʌnɪn'tɛnʃənəl] *adj*
involuntario

union ['ju:njən] *n* unión *f*; (*also:* **trade
~**) sindicato ▷ *cpd* sindical; **Union Jack**
n bandera del Reino Unido

unique [ju:'ni:k] *adj* único

unisex ['ju:nɪsɛks] *adj* unisex

unit ['ju:nɪt] *n* unidad *f*; (*section: of
furniture etc*) elemento; (*team*) grupo;
kitchen ~ módulo de cocina

unite [ju:'naɪt] *vt* unir ▷ *vi* unirse;
united *adj* unido; (*effort*) conjunto;
United Kingdom *n* Reino Unido;
United Nations (Organization) *n*
Naciones *fpl* Unidas; **United States (of
America)** *n* Estados Unidos

unity ['ju:nɪtɪ] *n* unidad *f*

universal [ju:nɪ'və:sl] *adj* universal

universe ['ju:nɪvə:s] *n* universo

university [ju:nɪ'və:sɪtɪ] *n*
universidad *f*

unjust [ʌn'dʒʌst] *adj* injusto

unkind [ʌn'kaɪnd] *adj* poco amable;
(*behaviour, comment*) cruel

unknown [ʌn'nəun] *adj*
desconocido

unlawful [ʌn'lɔ:ful] *adj* ilegal, ilícito

unleaded [ʌn'lɛdɪd] *adj* (*petrol, fuel*)
sin plombo

unleash [ʌn'li:ʃ] *vt* desatar

unless [ʌn'lɛs] *conj* a menos que;
~ he comes a menos que venga; **~
otherwise stated** salvo indicación
contraria

unlike [ʌn'laɪk] *adj* (*not alike*) distinto
de *or* a; (*not like*) poco propio de ▷ *prep*
a diferencia de

unlikely [ʌn'laɪklɪ] *adj* improbable;
(*unexpected*) inverosímil

unlimited [ʌn'lɪmɪtɪd] *adj* ilimitado

unlisted [ʌn'lɪstɪd] (*us*) *adj* (*Tel*) que
no consta en la guía

unload [ʌn'ləud] *vt* descargar

unlock [ʌn'lɔk] *vt* abrir (con llave)

unlucky [ʌn'lʌkɪ] *adj* desgraciado;
(*object, number*) que da mala suerte; **to
be ~** tener mala suerte

unmarried [ʌn'mærɪd] *adj* soltero

unmistak(e)able [ʌnmɪs'teɪkəbl] *adj*
inconfundible

unnatural [ʌn'nætʃrəl] *adj* (*gen*)
antinatural; (*manner*) afectado; (*habit*)
perverso

unnecessary [ʌn'nɛsəsərɪ] *adj*
innecesario, inútil

UNO ['ju:nəu] *n abbr* (= *United Nations
Organization*) ONU *f*

unofficial [ʌnə'fɪʃl] *adj* no oficial;
(*news*) sin confirmar

unpack [ʌn'pæk] *vi* deshacer las
maletas ▷ *vt* deshacer

unpaid [ʌn'peɪd] *adj* (*bill, debt*) sin
pagar, impagado; (*Comm*) pendiente;
(*holiday*) sin sueldo; (*work*) sin pago,
voluntario

unpleasant [ʌn'plɛznt] *adj*
(*disagreeable*) desagradable; (*person,
manner*) antipático

unplug [ʌn'plʌg] *vt* desenchufar,
desconectar

unpopular [ʌn'pɔpjulə*] *adj*
impopular, poco popular

unprecedented [ʌn'prɛsɪdəntɪd]
adj sin precedentes

unpredictable [ʌnprɪ'dɪktəbl] *adj*
imprevisible

unprotected ['ʌnprə'tɛktɪd] *adj* (*sex*)
sin protección

unqualified [ʌn'kwɔlɪfaɪd] *adj* sin
título, no cualificado; (*success*) total

unravel [ʌn'rævl] *vt* desenmarañar

unreal [ʌn'rɪəl] *adj* irreal;
(*extraordinary*) increíble

unrealistic [ʌnrɪə'lɪstɪk] *adj* poco
realista

unreasonable [ʌn'ri:znəbl] *adj*
irrazonable; (*demand*) excesivo

unrelated [ʌnrɪ'leɪtɪd] *adj* sin

relación; (family) no emparentado
unreliable [ʌnrɪˈlaɪəbl] adj (person) informal; (machine) poco fiable
unrest [ʌnˈrest] n inquietud f, malestar m; (Pol) disturbios mpl
unroll [ʌnˈrəʊl] vt desenrollar
unruly [ʌnˈruːlɪ] adj indisciplinado
unsafe [ʌnˈseɪf] adj peligroso
unsatisfactory ['ʌnsætɪsˈfæktərɪ] adj poco satisfactorio
unscrew [ʌnˈskruː] vt destornillar
unsettled [ʌnˈsetld] adj inquieto, intranquilo; (weather) variable
unsettling [ʌnˈsetlɪŋ] adj perturbador(a), inquietante
unsightly [ʌnˈsaɪtlɪ] adj feo
unskilled [ʌnˈskɪld] adj (work) no especializado; (worker) no cualificado
unspoiled ['ʌnˈspɔɪld], **unspoilt** ['ʌnˈspɔɪlt] adj (place) que no ha perdido su belleza natural
unstable [ʌnˈsteɪbl] adj inestable
unsteady [ʌnˈstedɪ] adj inestable
unsuccessful [ʌnsəkˈsesful] adj (attempt) infructuoso; (writer, proposal) sin éxito; **to be ~** (in attempting sth) no tener éxito, fracasar
unsuitable [ʌnˈsuːtəbl] adj inapropiado; (time) inoportuno
unsure [ʌnˈʃʊə*] adj inseguro, poco seguro
untidy [ʌnˈtaɪdɪ] adj (room) desordenado; (appearance) desaliñado
untie [ʌnˈtaɪ] vt desatar
until [ənˈtɪl] prep hasta ▷ conj hasta que; **~ he comes** hasta que venga; **~ now** hasta ahora; **~ then** hasta entonces
untrue [ʌnˈtruː] adj (statement) falso
unused [ʌnˈjuːzd] adj sin usar
unusual [ʌnˈjuːʒʊəl] adj insólito, poco común; (exceptional) inusitado
unusually adv (exceptionally) excepcionalmente; **he arrived unusually early** llegó más temprano que de costumbre
unveil [ʌnˈveɪl] vt descubrir
unwanted [ʌnˈwɒntɪd] adj (clothing)

viejo; (pregnancy) no deseado
unwell [ʌnˈwel] adj: **to be/feel ~** estar indispuesto/sentirse mal
unwilling [ʌnˈwɪlɪŋ] adj: **to be ~ to do sth** estar poco dispuesto a hacer algo
unwind [ʌnˈwaɪnd] (irreg) vt desenvolver ▷ vi (relax) relajarse
unwise [ʌnˈwaɪz] adj imprudente
unwittingly [ʌnˈwɪtɪŋlɪ] adv inconscientemente, sin darse cuenta
unwrap [ʌnˈræp] vt desenvolver
unzip [ʌnˈzɪp] vt abrir la cremallera de; (Comput) descomprimir

○ **KEYWORD**

up [ʌp] prep: **to go/be up sth** subir/ estar subido en algo; **he went up the stairs/the hill** subió las escaleras/la colina; **we walked/climbed up the hill** subimos la colina; **they live further up the street** viven más arriba en la calle; **go up that road and turn left** sigue por esa calle y gira a la izquierda
▷ adv **1** (upwards, higher) más arriba; **up in the mountains** en lo alto (de la montaña); **put it a bit higher up** ponlo un poco más arriba or alto; **up there** ahí or allí arriba; **up above** en lo alto, por encima, arriba
2: **to be up** (out of bed) estar levantado; (prices, level) haber subido
3: **up to** (as far as) hasta; **up to now** hasta ahora or la fecha
4: **to be up to** (depending on): **it's up to you** (depending on) depende de ti; **he's not up to it** (job, task etc) no es capaz de hacerlo; **his work is not up to the required standard** su trabajo no da la talla; (inf: be doing): **what is he up to?** ¿qué estará tramando?
▷ n: **ups and downs** altibajos mpl

up-and-coming [ʌpəndˈkʌmɪŋ] adj prometedor(a)
upbringing ['ʌpbrɪŋɪŋ] n educación

f

update [ʌp'deɪt] vt poner al día

upfront [ʌp'frʌnt] adj claro, directo
▷ adv a las claras; (pay) por adelantado;
to be ~ about sth admitir algo
claramente

upgrade [ʌp'greɪd] vt (house)
modernizar; (employee) ascender

upheaval [ʌp'hiːvl] n trastornos mpl;
(Pol) agitación f

uphill [ʌp'hɪl] adj cuesta arriba;
(fig: task) penoso, difícil ▷ adv: **to go ~**
ir cuesta arriba

uphold [ʌp'həʊld] vt (irreg: like **hold**)
sostener

upholstery [ʌp'həʊlstərɪ] n
tapicería

upmarket [ʌp'mɑːkɪt] adj (product)
de categoría

upon [ə'pɒn] prep sobre

upper ['ʌpə*] adj superior, de arriba
▷ n (of shoe: also: **~s**) empeine m; **upper-
class** adj de clase alta

upright ['ʌpraɪt] adj derecho;
(vertical) vertical; (fig) honrado

uprising ['ʌpraɪzɪŋ] n sublevación f

uproar ['ʌprɔː*] n escándalo

upset [n 'ʌpset, vb, adj ʌp'set] n (to
plan etc) revés n, contratiempo; (Med)
trastorno ▷ vt irreg (glass etc) volcar;
(plan) alterar; (person) molestar,
disgustar ▷ adj molesto, disgustado;
(stomach) revuelto

upside-down [ʌpsaɪd'daʊn] adv al
revés; **to turn a place ~** (fig) revolverlo
todo

upstairs [ʌp'steəz] adv arriba ▷ adj
(room) de arriba ▷ n el piso superior

up-to-date [ʌptə'deɪt] adj al día

uptown ['ʌptaʊn] (us) adv hacia las
afueras ▷ adj exterior, de las afueras

upward ['ʌpwəd] adj ascendente;
upward(s) adv hacia arriba; (more
than): **upward(s) of** más de

uranium [juə'reɪnɪəm] n uranio

Uranus [juə'reɪnəs] n Urano

urban ['əːbən] adj urbano

urge [əːdʒ] n (desire) deseo ▷ vt: **to ~
sb to do sth** animar a algn a hacer algo

urgency ['əːdʒənsɪ] n urgencia

urgent ['əːdʒənt] adj urgente; (voice)
perentorio

urinal ['juərɪnl] n (building) urinario;
(vessel) orinal m

urinate ['juərɪneɪt] vi orinar

urine ['juərɪn] n orina, orines mpl

US n abbr (= United States) EE. UU.

us [ʌs] pron nos; (after prep) nosotros/
as; see also **me**

USA n abbr (= United States (of America))
EE.UU.

use [n juːs, vb juːz] n uso, empleo;
(usefulness) utilidad f ▷ vt usar,
emplear; **she ~d to do it** (ella) solía or
acostumbraba hacerlo; **in ~** en uso; **out
of ~** en desuso; **to be of ~** servir; **it's
no ~** (pointless) es inútil; (not useful) no
sirve; **to be ~d to** estar acostumbrado
a, acostumbrar; **use up** vt (food)
consumir; (money) gastar; **used** [juːzd]
adj (car) usado; **useful** adj útil;
useless adj (unusable) inservible;
(pointless) inútil; (person) incapaz;
user n usuario/a; **user-friendly** adj
(computer) amistoso

usual ['juːʒʊəl] adj normal, corriente;
as ~ como de costumbre; **usually** adv
normalmente

utensil [juː'tensl] n utensilio;
kitchen ~s batería de cocina

utility [juː'tɪlɪtɪ] n utilidad f; (public
utility) (empresa de) servicio público

utilize ['juːtɪlaɪz] vt utilizar

utmost ['ʌtməʊst] adj mayor ▷ n: **to
do one's ~** hacer todo lo posible

utter ['ʌtə*] adj total, completo
▷ vt pronunciar, proferir; **utterly** adv
completamente, totalmente

U-turn ['juː'təːn] n viraje m en
redondo

V

v. _abbr_ = **verse; versus;** (= volt) v;
(= vide) véase

vacancy ['veɪkənsɪ] n (BRIT: job)
vacante f; (room) habitación f libre;
(= vide) "**no vacancies**" "completo"

vacant ['veɪkənt] adj desocupado,
libre; (expression) distraído

vacate [və'keɪt] vt (house, room)
desocupar; (job) dejar (vacante)

vacation [və'keɪʃən] n vacaciones
fpl; **vacationer** (us **vacationist**) n
turista m/f

vaccination [væksɪ'neɪʃən] n
vacunación f

vaccine ['væksiːn] n vacuna

vacuum ['vækjum] n vacío; **vacuum
cleaner** n aspiradora

vagina [və'dʒaɪnə] n vagina

vague [veɪg] adj vago; (memory)
borroso; (ambiguous) impreciso;
(person: absent-minded) distraído;
(: evasive): **to be ~** no decir las cosas
claramente

vain [veɪn] adj (conceited) presumido;
(useless) vano, inútil; **in ~** en vano

Valentine's Day ['væləntaɪnzdeɪ] n
día de los enamorados

valid ['vælɪd] adj válido; (ticket)
valedero; (law) vigente

valley ['vælɪ] n valle m

valuable ['væljuəbl] adj (jewel) de
valor; (time) valioso; **valuables** npl
objetos mpl de valor

value ['væljuː] n valor m; (importance)
importancia ▷ vt (fix price of) tasar,
valorar; (esteem) apreciar; **values** npl
(principles) principios mpl

valve [vælv] n válvula

vampire ['væmpaɪə*] n vampiro

van [væn] n (Aut) furgoneta,
camioneta

vandal ['vændl] n vándalo/a;
vandalism n vandalismo; **vandalize**
vt dañar, destruir

vanilla [və'nɪlə] n vainilla

vanish ['vænɪʃ] vi desaparecer

vanity ['vænɪtɪ] n vanidad f

vapour ['veɪpə*] (us **vapor**) n vapor
m; (on breath, window) vaho

variable ['veərɪəbl] adj variable

variant ['veərɪənt] n variante f

variation [veərɪ'eɪʃən] n variación f

varied ['veərɪd] adj variado

variety [və'raɪətɪ] n (diversity)
diversidad f; (type) variedad f

various ['veərɪəs] adj (several: people)
varios/as; (reasons) diversos/as

varnish ['vɑːnɪʃ] n barniz m; (nail
varnish) esmalte m ▷ vt barnizar; (nails)
pintar (con esmalte)

vary ['veərɪ] vt variar; (change)
cambiar ▷ vi variar

vase [vɑːz] n jarrón m

 Be careful not to translate **vase** by
the Spanish word _vaso_.

Vaseline® ['væsɪliːn] n vaselina®

vast [vɑːst] adj enorme

VAT [væt] (BRIT) n abbr (= value added
tax) IVA m

vault [vɔːlt] n (of roof) bóveda;
(tomb) panteón m; (in bank) cámara
acorazada ▷ vt (also: **~ over**) saltar
(por encima de)

VCR n abbr = **video cassette recorder**

VDU n abbr (= visual display unit) UPV f

veal [viːl] n ternera

veer [vɪə*] vi (vehicle) virar; (wind) girar

vegan ['viːɡən] n vegetariano/a estricto/a, vegetaliano/a

vegetable ['vedʒtəbl] n (Bot) vegetal m; (edible plant) legumbre f, hortaliza ▷ adj vegetal

vegetarian [vedʒɪ'tɛərɪən] adj, n vegetariano/a m/f

vegetation [vedʒɪ'teɪʃən] n vegetación f

vehicle ['viːɪkl] n vehículo; (fig) medio

veil [veɪl] n velo ▷ vt velar

vein [veɪn] n vena; (of ore etc) veta

Velcro® ['vɛlkrəʊ] n velcro® m

velvet ['vɛlvɪt] n terciopelo

vending machine ['vɛndɪŋ-] n distribuidor m automático

vendor ['vɛndə*] n vendedor(a) m/f; **street ~** vendedor(a) m/f callejero/a

vengeance ['vɛndʒəns] n venganza; **with a ~** (fig) con creces

venison ['vɛnɪsn] n carne f de venado

venom ['vɛnəm] n veneno; (bitterness) odio

vent [vɛnt] n (in jacket) respiradero; (in wall) rejilla (de ventilación) ▷ vt (fig: feelings) desahogar

ventilation [vɛntɪ'leɪʃən] n ventilación f

venture ['vɛntʃə*] n empresa ▷ vt (opinion) ofrecer ▷ vi arriesgarse, lanzarse; **business ~** empresa comercial

venue ['vɛnjuː] n lugar m

Venus ['viːnəs] n Venus m

verb [vəːb] n verbo; **verbal** adj verbal

verdict ['vəːdɪkt] n veredicto, fallo; (fig) opinión f, juicio

verge [vəːdʒ] (BRIT) n borde m; **"soft ~s"** (Aut) "arcén m no asfaltado"; **to be on the ~ of doing sth** estar a punto de hacer algo

verify ['vɛrɪfaɪ] vt comprobar, verificar

versatile ['vəːsətaɪl] adj (person) polifacético; (machine, tool etc) versátil

verse [vəːs] n poesía; (stanza) estrofa; (in bible) versículo

version ['vəːʃən] n versión f

versus ['vəːsəs] prep contra

vertical ['vəːtɪkl] adj vertical

very ['vɛrɪ] adv muy ▷ adj: **the ~ book which** el mismo libro que; **the ~ last** el último de todos; **at the ~ least** al menos; **~ much** muchísimo

vessel ['vɛsl] n (ship) barco; (container) vasija; see **blood**

vest [vɛst] n (BRIT) camiseta; (US: waistcoat) chaleco

vet [vɛt] vt (candidate) investigar ▷ n abbr (BRIT) = **veterinary surgeon**

veteran ['vɛtərn] n excombatiente mf, veterano/a

veterinary surgeon ['vɛtrɪnərɪ-] (US **veterinarian**) n veterinario/a m/f

veto ['viːtəʊ] (pl **-es**) n veto ▷ vt prohibir, poner el veto a

via ['vaɪə] prep por, por medio de

viable ['vaɪəbl] adj viable

vibrate [vaɪ'breɪt] vi vibrar

vibration [vaɪ'breɪʃən] n vibración f

vicar ['vɪkə*] n párroco (de la Iglesia Anglicana)

vice [vaɪs] n (evil) vicio; (Tech) torno de banco; **vice-chairman** (irreg) n vicepresidente m

vice versa [vaɪsɪ'vəːsə] adv viceversa

vicinity [vɪ'sɪnɪtɪ] n: **in the ~ (of)** cercano/a

vicious ['vɪʃəs] adj (attack) violento; (words) cruel; (horse, dog) resabido

victim ['vɪktɪm] n víctima

victor ['vɪktə*] n vencedor(a) m/f

Victorian [vɪk'tɔːrɪən] adj victoriano

victorious [vɪk'tɔːrɪəs] adj vencedor(a)

victory ['vɪktərɪ] n victoria

video ['vɪdɪəʊ] n vídeo (SP), video (LAM); **video call** n videollamada; **video camera** n videocámara, cámara de vídeo; **video (cassette) recorder** n vídeo (SP), video

(LAM): video game n videojuego;
videophone n videoteléfono; **video
shop** n videoclub m; **video
tape** n cinta de vídeo

vie [vaɪ] vi: **to ~ (with sb for sth)**
competir (con algn por algo)

Vienna [vɪˈenə] n Viena

Vietnam [vjetˈnæm] n Vietnam
m; **Vietnamese** [-nəˈmiːz] n inv, adj
vietnamita mf

view [vjuː] n vista; (outlook)
perspectiva; (opinion) opinión f, criterio
▷ vt (look at) mirar; (fig) considerar;
on ~ (in museum etc) expuesto; **in full
~ (of)** en plena vista (de); **in ~ of the
weather/the fact that** en vista del
tiempo/del hecho de que; **in my ~** en
mi opinión; **viewer** n espectador(a)
m/f; (TV) telespectador(a) m/f;
viewpoint n (attitude) punto de vista;
(place) mirador m

vigilant ['vɪdʒɪlənt] adj vigilante
vigorous ['vɪgərəs] adj enérgico,
vigoroso

vile [vaɪl] adj vil, infame; (smell)
asqueroso; (temper) endemoniado

villa ['vɪlə] n (country house) casa de
campo; (suburban house) chalet m

village ['vɪlɪdʒ] n aldea; **villager** n
aldeano/a

villain ['vɪlən] n (scoundrel) malvado/
a; (in novel) malo; (BRIT: criminal)
maleante mf

vinaigrette [vɪneɪˈgrɛt] n vinagreta
vine [vaɪn] n vid f
vinegar ['vɪnɪgə*] n vinagre m
vineyard ['vɪnjɑːd] n viña, viñedo
vintage ['vɪntɪdʒ] n (year) vendimia,
cosecha ▷ cpd de época
vinyl ['vaɪnl] n vinilo
viola [vɪˈəʊlə] n (Mus) viola
violate ['vaɪəleɪt] vt violar
violation [vaɪəˈleɪʃən] n violación f;
in ~ of sth en violación de algo
violence ['vaɪələns] n violencia
violent ['vaɪələnt] adj violento;
(intense) intenso
violet ['vaɪələt] adj violado, violeta

▷ n (plant) violeta

violin [vaɪəˈlɪn] n violín m
VIP n abbr (= very important person) VIP m
virgin ['vɜːdʒɪn] n virgen f
Virgo ['vɜːgəʊ] n Virgo
virtual ['vɜːtjuəl] adj virtual;
virtually adv prácticamente; **virtual
reality** n (Comput) mundo or realidad
f virtual

virtue ['vɜːtjuː] n virtud f; (advantage)
ventaja; **by ~ of** en virtud de
virus ['vaɪərəs] n (also Comput)
virus m inv

visa ['viːzə] n visado (SP), visa (LAM)
vise [vaɪs] (US) n (Tech) = **vice**
visibility [vɪzɪˈbɪlɪtɪ] n visibilidad f
visible ['vɪzəbl] adj visible
vision ['vɪʒən] n (sight) vista;
(foresight, in dream) visión f

visit ['vɪzɪt] n visita ▷ vt (person
(US: also: **~ with**) visitar, hacer una
visita a; (place) ir a, (ir a) conocer;
visiting hours npl (in hospital etc)
horas fpl de visita; **visitor** n (in
museum) visitante mf; (invited to house)
visita; (tourist) turista mf; **visitor
centre** (US **visitor center**) n centro m
de información

visual ['vɪzjuəl] adj visual; **visualize**
vt imaginarse

vital ['vaɪtl] adj (essential) esencial,
imprescindible; (dynamic) dinámico;
(organ) vital

vitality [vaɪˈtælɪtɪ] n energía,
vitalidad f

vitamin ['vɪtəmɪn] n vitamina
vivid ['vɪvɪd] adj (account) gráfico;
(light) intenso; (imagination, memory)
vivo

V-neck [ˈviːnɛk] n cuello de pico
vocabulary [vəʊˈkæbjʊlərɪ] n
vocabulario
vocal ['vəʊkl] adj vocal; (articulate)
elocuente
vocational [vəʊˈkeɪʃənl] adj
profesional
vodka ['vɒdkə] n vodka m
vogue [vəʊg] n: **in ~** en boga

voice [vɔɪs] n voz f ▷ vt expresar;
voice mail n fonobuzón m
void [vɔɪd] n vacío; (hole) hueco ▷ adj
(invalid) nulo, inválido; (empty): **~ of**
carente or desprovisto de
volatile ['vɔlətaɪl] adj (situation)
inestable; (person) voluble; (liquid)
volátil
volcano [vɔl'keɪnəu] (pl **~es**) n
volcán m
volleyball ['vɔlɪbɔːl] n vol(e)ibol m
volt [vəult] n voltio; **voltage** n
voltaje m
volume ['vɔljuːm] n (gen) volumen
m; (book) tomo
voluntarily ['vɔləntrɪlɪ] adv
libremente, voluntariamente
voluntary ['vɔləntərɪ] adj voluntario
volunteer [vɔlən'tɪə*] n voluntario/
a ▷ vt (information) ofrecer ▷ vi
ofrecerse (de voluntario); **to ~ to do**
ofrecerse a hacer
vomit ['vɔmɪt] n vómito ▷ vt, vi
vomitar
vote [vəut] n voto; (votes cast)
votación f; (right to vote) derecho
de votar; (franchise) sufragio ▷ vt
(chairman) elegir; (propose): **to ~ that**
proponer que ▷ vi votar, ir a votar; **~
of thanks** voto de gracias; **voter** n
votante mf; **voting** n votación f
voucher ['vautʃə*] n (for meal, petrol)
vale m
vow [vau] n voto ▷ vt: **to ~ to do/
that** jurar hacer/que
vowel ['vauəl] n vocal f
voyage ['vɔɪɪdʒ] n viaje m
vulgar ['vʌlgə*] adj (rude) ordinario,
grosero; (in bad taste) de mal gusto
vulnerable ['vʌlnərəbl] adj
vulnerable
vulture ['vʌltʃə*] n buitre m

W

waddle ['wɔdl] vi anadear
wade [weɪd] vi: **to ~ through** (water)
vadear; (fig: book) leer con dificultad
wafer ['weɪfə*] n galleta, barquillo
waffle ['wɔfl] n (Culin) gofre m ▷ vi
dar el rollo
wag [wæg] vt menear, agitar ▷ vi
moverse, menearse
wage [weɪdʒ] n (also: **~s**) sueldo,
salario ▷ vt: **to ~ war** hacer la guerra
wag(g)on ['wægən] n (horse-drawn)
carro; (BRIT Rail) vagón m
wail [weɪl] n gemido ▷ vi gemir
waist [weɪst] n cintura, talle m;
waistcoat (BRIT) n chaleco
wait [weɪt] n (interval) pausa ▷ vi
esperar; **to lie in ~ for** acechar a; **I
can't ~ to** (fig) estoy deseando; **to ~
for** esperar (a); **wait on** vt fus servir
a; **waiter** n camarero; **waiting list**
n lista de espera; **waiting room** n
sala de espera; **waitress** ['weɪtrɪs] n
camarera
waive [weɪv] vt suspender
wake [weɪk] (pt **woke** or **~d**, pp **woken**

or **~d**) vt (also: **~ up**) despertar ▷ vi (also: **~ up**) despertarse ▷ n (for dead person) vela, velatorio; (Naut) estela
Wales [weɪlz] n País m de Gales; **the Prince of ~** el príncipe de Gales
walk [wɔːk] n (stroll) paseo; (hike) excursión f a pie, caminata; (gait) paso, andar m; (in park etc) paseo, alameda ▷ vi andar, caminar; (for pleasure, exercise) pasear ▷ vt (dog) pasear; **'10 minutes' ~ from here** a 10 minutos de aquí andando; **people from all ~s of life** gente de todas las esferas; **walk out** vi (audience) salir; (workers) declararse en huelga; **walker** n (person) paseante mf, caminante m f; **walkie-talkie** [ˈwɔːkɪˈtɔːkɪ] n walkie-talkie m; **walking** n el andar; **walking shoes** npl zapatos mpl para andar; **walking stick** n bastón m; **Walkman®** n Walkman® m; **walkway** n paseo
wall [wɔːl] n pared f; (exterior) muro; (city wall etc) muralla
wallet [ˈwɔlɪt] n cartera, billetera
wallpaper [ˈwɔːlpeɪpə*] n papel m pintado ▷ vt empapelar
walnut [ˈwɔːlnʌt] n nuez f; (tree) nogal m
walrus [ˈwɔːlrəs] (pl **~** or **~es**) n morsa
waltz [wɔːlts] n vals m ▷ vi bailar el vals
wand [wɔnd] n (also: **magic ~**) varita (mágica)
wander [ˈwɔndə*] vi (person) vagar; deambular; (thoughts) divagar ▷ vt recorrer, vagar por
want [wɔnt] vt querer, desear; (need) necesitar ▷ n: **for ~ of** por falta de; **wanted** adj (criminal) buscado; **"wanted"** (in advertisements) "se busca"
war [wɔː*] n guerra; **to make ~ (on)** declarar la guerra (a)
ward [wɔːd] n (in hospital) sala; (Pol) distrito electoral; (Law: child: also: **~ of court**) pupilo/a
warden [ˈwɔːdn] n (BRIT: of institution) director(a) m/f; (of park, game reserve)

guardián/ana m/f; (BRIT: also: **traffic ~**) guardia mf
wardrobe [ˈwɔːdrəub] n armario, ropero; (clothes) vestuario
warehouse [ˈwɛəhaus] n almacén m, depósito
warfare [ˈwɔːfɛə*] n guerra
warhead [ˈwɔːhɛd] n cabeza armada
warm [wɔːm] adj caliente; (thanks) efusivo; (clothes etc) abrigado; (welcome, day) caluroso; **it's ~** hace calor; **I'm ~** tengo calor; **warm up** vi (room) calentarse; (person) entrar en calor; (athlete) hacer ejercicios de calentamiento ▷ vt calentar; **warmly** adv afectuosamente; **warmth** n calor m
warn [wɔːn] vt avisar, advertir; **warning** n aviso, advertencia; **warning light** n luz f de advertencia
warrant [ˈwɔrnt] n autorización f; (Law: to arrest) orden f de detención; (: to search) mandamiento de registro
warranty [ˈwɔrənti] n garantía
warrior [ˈwɔriə*] n guerrero/a
Warsaw [ˈwɔːsɔː] n Varsovia
warship [ˈwɔːʃip] n buque m o barco de guerra
wart [wɔːt] n verruga
wartime [ˈwɔːtaim] n: **in ~** en tiempos de guerra, en la guerra
wary [ˈwɛəri] adj cauteloso
was [wɔz] pt of **be**
wash [wɔʃ] vt lavar ▷ vi lavarse; (sea etc): **to ~ against/over sth** llegar hasta/cubrir algo ▷ n (clothes etc) lavado; (of ship) estela; **to have a ~** lavarse; **wash up** vi (BRIT) fregar los platos; (US) lavarse; **washbasin** (US) n lavabo; **wash cloth** (US) n manopla; **washer** n (Tech) arandela; **washing** n (dirty) ropa sucia; (clean) colada; **washing line** n cuerda de (colgar) la ropa; **washing machine** n lavadora; **washing powder** (BRIT) n detergente m (en polvo)
Washington [ˈwɔʃintən] n Washington m

wash: washing-up (BRIT) n fregado, platos mpl (para fregar); **washing-up liquid** (BRIT) n líquido lavavajillas; **washroom** (US) n servicios mpl

wasn't ['wɒznt] = **was not**

wasp [wɒsp] n avispa

waste [weɪst] n derroche m, despilfarro; (of time) pérdida; (food) sobras fpl; (rubbish) basura, desperdicios mpl ▷ adj (material) de desecho; (left over) sobrante; (land) baldío, descampado ▷ vt malgastar, derrochar; (time) perder; (opportunity) desperdiciar; **waste ground** (BRIT) n terreno baldío; **wastepaper basket** n papelera

watch [wɒtʃ] n (also: **wrist ~**) reloj m; (Mil: group of guards) centinela m; (act) vigilancia; (Naut: spell of duty) guardia ▷ vt (look at) mirar, observar; (: match, programme) ver; (spy on, guard) vigilar; (be careful of) cuidarse de, tener cuidado de ▷ vi ver, mirar; (keep guard) montar guardia; **watch out** vi cuidarse, tener cuidado; **watchdog** n perro guardián; (fig) persona u organismo encargado de asegurarse de que las empresas actúan dentro de la legalidad; **watch strap** n pulsera (de reloj)

water ['wɔ:tə*] n agua ▷ vt (plant) regar ▷ vi (eyes) llorar; (mouth) hacerse la boca agua; **water down** vt (milk etc) aguar; (fig: story) dulcificar, diluir; **watercolour** (US **watercolor**) n acuarela; **watercress** n berro; **waterfall** n cascada, salto de agua; **watering can** n regadera; **watermelon** n sandía; **waterproof** adj impermeable; **water-skiing** n esquí m acuático

watt [wɒt] n vatio

wave [weɪv] n (of hand) señal f con la mano; (on water) ola; (Radio, in hair) onda; (fig) oleada ▷ vi agitar la mano; (flag etc) ondear ▷ vt (handkerchief, gun) agitar; **wavelength** n longitud f de onda

waver ['weɪvə*] vi (voice, love etc)

flaquear; (person) vacilar

wavy ['weɪvɪ] adj ondulado

wax [wæks] n cera ▷ vt encerar ▷ vi (moon) crecer

way [weɪ] n camino; (distance) trayecto, recorrido; (direction) dirección f, sentido; (manner) modo, manera; (habit) costumbre f; **which ~? - this ~** ¿por dónde? or ¿en qué dirección? - por aquí; **on the ~** (en route) en (el) camino; **to be on one's ~** estar en camino; **to be in the ~** bloquear el camino; (fig) estorbar; **to go out of one's ~ to do sth** desvivirse por hacer algo; **under ~** en marcha; **to lose one's ~** extraviarse; **in a ~** en cierto modo or sentido; **no ~!** (inf) ¡de eso nada!; **by the ~ ...** a propósito ...; **"~ in"** (BRIT) "entrada"; **"~ out"** (BRIT) "salida"; **the ~ back** el camino de vuelta; **"give ~"** (BRIT Aut) "ceda el paso"

W.C. n (BRIT) wáter m

we [wi:] pl pron nosotros/as

weak [wi:k] adj débil, flojo; (tea etc) claro; **weaken** vi debilitarse; (give way) ceder ▷ vt debilitar; **weakness** n debilidad f; (fault) punto débil; **to have a weakness for** tener debilidad por

wealth [welθ] n riqueza; (of details) abundancia; **wealthy** adj rico

weapon ['wepən] n arma; **~s of mass destruction** armas de destrucción masiva

wear [weə*] (pt **wore**, pp **worn**) n (use) uso; (deterioration through use) desgaste m ▷ vt (clothes) llevar; (shoes) calzar; (damage: through use) gastar, usar ▷ vi (last) durar; (rub through etc) desgastarse; **evening ~** ropa de etiqueta; **sports-/baby-~** ropa de deportes/de niños; **wear off** vi (pain etc) pasar, desaparecer; **wear out** vt desgastar; (person, strength) agotar

weary ['wɪərɪ] adj cansado; (dispirited) abatido ▷ vi **to ~** cansarse de

weasel ['wi:zl] n (Zool) comadreja

weather ['weðə*] n tiempo ▷ vt (storm, crisis) hacer frente a; **under**

the ~ (fig: ill) indispuesto, pachucho; **weather forecast** n boletín m meteorológico

weave [wiːv] (pt **wove**, pp **woven**) vt (cloth) tejer; (fig) entretejer

web [wɛb] n (of spider) telaraña f; (on duck's foot) membrana f; (network) red f; **the (World Wide) W~** la Red; **web address** n dirección f de Internet; **webcam** n webcam f; **web page** n (página) web m or f; **website** n sitio web

Wed. abbr (= Wednesday) miérc

wed [wɛd] (pt, pp ~**ded**) vt casar ▷ vi casarse

we'd [wiːd] = **we had**; **we would**

wedding ['wɛdɪŋ] n boda, casamiento; **silver/golden ~ (anniversary)** bodas fpl de plata/de oro; **wedding anniversary** n aniversario de boda; **wedding day** n día m de la boda; **wedding dress** n traje m de novia; **wedding ring** n alianza

wedge [wɛdʒ] n (of wood etc) cuña; (of cake) trozo ▷ vt acuñar; (push) apretar

Wednesday ['wɛdnzdɪ] n miércoles m inv

wee [wiː] (SCOTTISH) adj pequeñito

weed [wiːd] n mala hierba, maleza ▷ vt escardar, desherbar; **weedkiller** n herbicida m

week [wiːk] n semana; **a ~ today/on Friday** de hoy/del viernes en ocho días; **weekday** n día m laborable; **weekend** n fin m de semana; **weekly** adv semanalmente, cada semana ▷ adj semanal ▷ n semanario

weep [wiːp] (pt, pp **wept**) vi, vt llorar

weigh [weɪ] vt, vi pesar; **to ~ anchor** levar anclas; **weigh up** vt sopesar

weight [weɪt] n peso; (metal weight) pesa; **to lose/put on ~** adelgazar/engordar; **weightlifting** n levantamiento de pesas

weir [wɪə*] n presa

weird [wɪəd] adj raro, extraño

welcome ['wɛlkəm] adj bienvenido

▷ n bienvenida ▷ vt dar la bienvenida a; (be glad of) alegrarse de; **thank you - you're ~** gracias - de nada

weld [wɛld] n soldadura ▷ vt soldar

welfare ['wɛlfɛə*] n bienestar m; (social aid) asistencia social; **welfare state** n estado del bienestar

well [wɛl] n fuente f, pozo ▷ adv bien ▷ adj: **to be ~** estar bien (de salud) ▷ excl ¡vaya!, ¡bueno!; **as ~** también; **as ~ as** además de; **~ done!** ¡bien hecho!; **get ~ soon!** ¡que te mejores pronto!; **to do ~** (business) ir bien; (person) tener éxito

we'll [wiːl] = **we will**; **we shall**

well: well-behaved adj bueno; **well-built** adj (person) fornido; **well-dressed** adj bien vestido

wellies ['wɛlɪz] (inf) npl (BRIT) botas de goma

well: well-known adj (person) conocido; **well-off** adj acomodado; **well-paid** [wɛl'peɪd] adj bien pagado, bien retribuido

Welsh [wɛlʃ] adj galés/esa ▷ n (Ling) galés m; **Welshman** (irreg) n galés m; **Welshwoman** (irreg) n galesa

went [wɛnt] pt of **go**

wept [wɛpt] pt, pp of **weep**

were [wəː*] pt of **be**

we're [wɪə*] = **we are**

weren't [wəːnt] = **were not**

west [wɛst] n oeste m ▷ adj occidental, del oeste ▷ adv al or hacia el oeste; **the W~** el Oeste, el Occidente; **westbound** ['wɛstbaund] adj (traffic, carriageway) con rumbo al oeste; **western** adj occidental ▷ n (Cinema) película del oeste; **West Indian** adj, n antillano/a m/f

wet [wɛt] adj (damp) húmedo; (soaked) mojado; (rainy) lluvioso ▷ n (BRIT: Pol) conservador(a) m/f moderado/a; **to get ~** mojarse; **"~ paint"** "recién pintado"; **wetsuit** n traje m térmico

we've [wiːv] = **we have**

whack [wæk] vt dar un buen golpe a

whale [weɪl] n (Zool) ballena

wharf [wɔːf] (pl **wharves**) n muelle m

○ KEYWORD

what [wɒt] adj 1 (in direct/indirect questions) qué; **what size is he?** ¿qué talla usa?; **what colour/shape is it?** ¿de qué color/forma es?
2 (in exclamations): **what a mess!** ¡qué desastre!; **what a fool I am!** ¡qué tonto soy!
▷ pron 1 (interrogative) qué; **what are you doing?** ¿qué haces or estás haciendo?; **what is happening?** ¿qué pasa or está pasando?; **what is it called?** ¿cómo se llama?; **what about me?** ¿y yo qué?; **what about doing ...?** ¿qué tal si hacemos ...?
2 (relative) lo que; **I saw what you did/was on the table** vi lo que hiciste/había en la mesa
▷ pron (disbelieving) ¡cómo!; **what, no coffee!** ¡que no hay café!

whatever [wɒt'evə*] adj: **~ book you choose** cualquier libro que elijas
▷ pron: **do ~ is necessary** haga lo que sea necesario; **~ happens** pase lo que pase; **no reason ~** no hay razón alguna or ninguna razón sea la que sea; **nothing ~** nada en absoluto

whatsoever [wɒtsəu'evə*] adj see **whatever**

wheat [wiːt] n trigo

wheel [wiːl] n rueda; (Aut: also: **steering ~**) volante m; (Naut) timón m ▷ vt (pram etc) empujar ▷ vi (also: **~ round**) dar la vuelta, girar; **wheelbarrow** n carretilla; **wheelchair** n silla de ruedas; **wheel clamp** n (Aut) cepo

wheeze [wiːz] vi resollar

○ KEYWORD

when [wɛn] adv cuando; **when did it happen?** ¿cuándo ocurrió?; **I know**

when it happened sé cuándo ocurrió
▷ conj 1 (at, during, after the time that) cuando; **be careful when you cross the road** ten cuidado al cruzar la calle; **that was when I needed you** fue entonces que te necesité
2 (on, at which): **on the day when I met him** el día en qué lo conocí
3 (whereas) cuando

whenever [wɛn'evə*] conj cuando; (every time that) cada vez que ▷ adv cuando sea

where [wɛə*] adv dónde ▷ conj donde; **this is ~** aquí es donde; **whereabouts** adv dónde ▷ n: **nobody knows his whereabouts** nadie conoce su paradero; **whereas** conj visto que, mientras; **whereby** pron por lo cual; **wherever** conj dondequiera que; (interrogative) dónde

whether [ˈwɛðə*] conj si; **I don't know ~ to accept or not** no sé si aceptar o no; **~ you go or not** vayas o no vayas

○ KEYWORD

which [wɪtʃ] adj 1 (interrogative: direct, indirect) qué; **which picture(s) do you want?** ¿qué cuadro(s) quieres?; **which one?** ¿cuál?
2 **in which case**: **we got there at 8 pm, by which time the cinema was full** llegamos allí a las 8, cuando el cine estaba lleno
▷ pron 1 (interrogative) cuál; **I don't mind which** el/la que sea
2 (relative: replacing noun) que; (: replacing clause) lo que; (: after preposition) (el)(la)(los)(las) que etc/el/la cual etc; **the apple which you ate/which is on the table** la manzana que comiste/que está en la mesa; **the chair on which you are sitting** la silla en la que estás sentado; **he said he knew, which is true/I feared** dijo que lo sabía, lo cual or lo

que es cierto/me temía

whichever [wɪtʃ'evə*] *adj*: **take ~ book you prefer** coja (sp) el libro que prefiera; **~ book you take** cualquier libro que coja

while [waɪl] *n* rato, momento ▷ *conj* mientras; (*although*) aunque; **for a ~** durante algún tiempo

whilst [waɪlst] *conj* = **while**

whim [wɪm] *n* capricho

whine [waɪn] *n* (*of pain*) gemido; (*of engine*) zumbido; (*of siren*) aullido ▷ *vi* gemir; zumbar; (*fig: complain*) gimotear

whip [wɪp] *n* látigo; (*Pol: person*) encargado de la disciplina partidaria en el parlamento ▷ *vt* azotar; (*Culin*) batir; (*move quickly*): **to ~ sth out/off** sacar/quitar algo de un tirón; **whipped cream** *n* nata or crema montada

whirl [wə:l] *vt* hacer girar, dar vueltas a ▷ *vi* girar, dar vueltas; (*leaves etc*) arremolinarse

whisk [wɪsk] *n* (*Culin*) batidor *m* ▷ *vt* (*Culin*) batir; **to ~ sb away** *or* **off** llevar volando a algn

whiskers ['wɪskəz] *npl* (*of animal*) bigotes *mpl*; (*of man*) patillas *fpl*

whisky [wɪskɪ] (US, IRELAND) *n* = **whisky**

whisky [wɪskɪ] *n* whisky *m*

whisper ['wɪspə*] *n* susurro ▷ *vi*, *vt* susurrar

whistle [wɪsl] *n* (*sound*) silbido; (*object*) silbato ▷ *vi* silbar

white [waɪt] *adj* blanco; (*pale*) pálido ▷ *n* blanco; (*of egg*) clara; **whiteboard** *n* pizarra blanca; **interactive whiteboard** pizarra interactiva; **White House** (US) *n* Casa Blanca; **whitewash** *n* (*paint*) jalbegue *m*, cal *f* ▷ *vt* blanquear

whiting ['waɪtɪŋ] *n inv* (*fish*) pescadilla

Whitsun ['wɪtsn] *n* pentecostés *m*

whittle [wɪtl] *vt*: **to ~ away**, **~ down** ir reduciendo

whizz [wɪz] *vi*: **to ~ past** *or* **by** pasar a toda velocidad

○ **KEYWORD**

who [hu:] *pron* 1 (*interrogative*) quién; **who is it?**, **who's there?** ¿quién es?; **who are you looking for?** ¿a quién buscas?; **I told her who I was** le dije quién era yo
2 (*relative*) que; **the man/woman who spoke to me** el hombre/la mujer que habló conmigo; **those who can swim** los que saben *or* sepan nadar

whoever [hu:'evə*] *pron*: **~ finds it** cualquiera or quienquiera que lo encuentre; **ask ~ you like** pregunta a quien quieras; **~ he marries** no importa con quién se case

whole [həʊl] *adj* (*entire*) todo, entero; (*not broken*) intacto ▷ *n* todo; (*all*): **the ~ of the town** toda la ciudad, la ciudad entera *m*; (*total*) total *m*; (*sum*) conjunto; **on the ~**, **as a ~** en general; **wholefood(s)** *n(pl)* alimento(s) *m(pl)* integral(es); **wholeheartedly** [həʊl'hɑːtɪdlɪ] *adv* con entusiasmo; **wholemeal** *adj* integral; **wholesale** *n* venta al por mayor ▷ *adj* al por mayor; (*fig: destruction*) sistemático; **wholewheat** *adj* = **wholemeal**; **wholly** *adv* totalmente, enteramente

○ **KEYWORD**

whom [hu:m] *pron* 1 (*interrogative*): **whom did you see?** ¿a quién viste?; **to whom did you give it?** ¿a quién se lo diste?; **tell me from whom you received it** dígame de quién lo recibió
2 (*relative*) que; (*to whom*): **of whom** de quien(es), del/de la que *etc*; **the man whom I saw/to whom I wrote** el hombre que vi/a quien escribí; **the lady about/with whom I was talking** la señora de (la) que/con

quien o (la) que hablaba

whore [hɔː*] (inf, pej) n puta

○ **KEYWORD**

whose [huːz] adj 1 (possessive: interrogative): **whose book is this?, whose is this book?** ¿de quién es este libro?; **whose pencil have you taken?** ¿de quién es el lápiz que has cogido?; **whose daughter are you?** ¿de quién eres hija?

2 (possessive: relative) cuyo/a, pl cuyos/ as; **the man whose son you rescued** el hombre cuyo hijo rescataste; **those whose passports I have** aquellas personas cuyos pasaportes tengo; **the woman whose car was stolen** la mujer a quien le robaron el coche

▷ pron (possessive; **whose is this?** ¿de quién es esto?; **I know whose it is** sé de quién es

○ **KEYWORD**

why [waɪ] adv por qué; **why not?** ¿por qué no?; **why not do it now?** ¿por qué no lo haces (or hacemos etc) ahora?

▷ conj: **I wonder why he said that me** pregunto por qué dijo eso; **that's not why I'm here** no es por eso por (lo) que estoy aquí; **the reason why** la razón por la que

▷ excl (expressing surprise, shock, annoyance) ¡hombre!, ¡vaya!; (explaining): **why, it's you!** ¡hombre, eres tú!; **why, that's impossible** ¡pero sí eso es imposible!

wicked [ˈwɪkɪd] adj malvado, cruel
wicket [ˈwɪkɪt] n (Cricket: stumps) palos mpl; (: grass area) terreno de juego
wide [waɪd] adj ancho; (area, knowledge) vasto, grande; (choice) amplio ▷ adv: **to open ~** abrir de par en par; **to shoot ~** errar el tiro; **widely**

adv (travelled) mucho; (spaced) muy; **it is widely believed/known that ...** mucha gente piensa/sabe que ...; **widen** vt ensanchar; (experience) ampliar ▷ vi ensancharse; **wide open** adj abierto de par en par; **widespread** adj extendido, general
widow [ˈwɪdəʊ] n viuda; **widower** n viudo
width [wɪdθ] n anchura; (of cloth) ancho
wield [wiːld] vt (sword) blandir; (power) ejercer
wife [waɪf] (pl **wives**) n mujer f, esposa
wig [wɪg] n peluca
wild [waɪld] adj (animal) salvaje; (plant) silvestre; (person) furioso, violento; (idea) descabellado; (rough: sea) bravo; (: land) agreste; (: weather) muy revuelto; **wilderness** [ˈwɪldənɪs] n desierto; **wildlife** n fauna; **wildly** adv (behave) locamente; (lash out) a diestro y siniestro; (guess) a lo loco; (happy) a más no poder

○ **KEYWORD**

will [wɪl] aux vb 1 (forming future tense): **I will finish it tomorrow** lo terminaré o voy a terminar mañana; **I will have finished it by tomorrow** lo habré terminado para mañana; **will you do it?** – **yes I will/no I won't** ¿lo harás? – sí/no

2 (in conjectures, predictions): **he will** or **he'll be there by now** ya habrá o debe (de) haber llegado; **that will be the postman** será o debe ser el cartero

3 (in commands, requests, offers): **will you be quiet!** ¿quieres callarte?; **will you help me?** ¿quieres ayudarme?; **will you have a cup of tea?** ¿te apetece un té?; **I won't put up with it!** ¡no lo soporto!

▷ vt (pt, pp **willed**): **to will sb to do sth** desear que algn haga algo; **he willed himself to go on** con gran fuerza de voluntad, continuó

▷ *n* voluntad *f*; (*testament*) testamento

willing ['wɪlɪŋ] *adj* (*with goodwill*) de buena voluntad; (*enthusiastic*) entusiasta; **he's ~ to do it** está dispuesto a hacerlo; **willingly** *adv* con mucho gusto

willow ['wɪləʊ] *n* sauce *m*

willpower ['wɪlpaʊə*] *n* fuerza de voluntad

wilt [wɪlt] *vi* marchitarse

win [wɪn] (*pt, pp* **won**) *n* victoria, triunfo ▷ *vt* ganar; (*obtain*) conseguir, lograr ▷ *vi* ganar; **win over** *vt* convencer a

wince [wɪns] *vi* encogerse

wind[1] [wɪnd] *n* viento; (*Med*) gases *mpl* ▷ *vt* (*take breath away from*) dejar sin aliento a

wind[2] [waɪnd] (*pt, pp* **wound**) *vt* enrollar; (*wrap*) envolver; (*clock, toy*) dar cuerda a ▷ *vi* (*road, river*) serpentear; **wind down** *vt* (*car window*) bajar; (*fig: production, business*) disminuir; **wind up** *vt* (*clock*) dar cuerda a; (*debate, meeting*) concluir, terminar

windfall ['wɪndfɔ:l] *n* golpe *m* de suerte

winding ['waɪndɪŋ] *adj* (*road*) tortuoso; (*staircase*) de caracol

windmill ['wɪndmɪl] *n* molino de viento

window ['wɪndəʊ] *n* ventana; (*in car, train*) ventanilla; (*in shop etc*) escaparate *m* (*SP*), vidriera (*LAM*); **window box** *n* jardinera de ventana; **window cleaner** *n* (*person*) limpiacristales *mf inv*; **window pane** *n* cristal *m*; **window seat** *n* asiento junto a la ventana; **windowsill** *n* alféizar *m*, repisa

windscreen ['wɪndskri:n] (*US* **windshield**) *n* parabrisas *m inv*; **windscreen wiper** (*US* **windshield wiper**) *n* limpiaparabrisas *m inv*

windsurfing ['wɪndsə:fɪŋ] *n* windsurf *m*

windy ['wɪndɪ] *adj* de mucho viento; **it's ~** hace viento

wine [waɪn] *n* vino; **wine bar** *n* enoteca; **wine glass** *n* copa (para vino); **wine list** *n* lista de vinos; **wine tasting** *n* degustación *f* de vinos

wing [wɪŋ] *n* ala; (*Aut*) aleta; **wing mirror** *n* (espejo) retrovisor *m*

wink [wɪŋk] *n* guiño, pestañeo ▷ *vi* guiñar, pestañear

winner ['wɪnə*] *n* ganador(a) *m/f*

winning ['wɪnɪŋ] *adj* (*team*) ganador(a); (*goal*) decisivo; (*smile*) encantador/a

winter ['wɪntə*] *n* invierno ▷ *vi* invernar; **winter sports** *npl* deportes *mpl* de invierno; **wintertime** *n* invierno

wipe [waɪp] *n*: **to give sth a ~** pasar un trapo sobre algo ▷ *vt* (*clean*); (*tape*) borrar; **wipe out** *vt* (*debt*) liquidar; (*memory*) borrar; (*destroy*) destruir; **wipe up** *vt* limpiar

wire ['waɪə*] *n* alambre *m*; (*Elec*) cable *m* (eléctrico); (*Tel*) telegrama *m* ▷ *vt* (*house*) poner la instalación eléctrica en; (*also*: **~ up**) conectar; (*person: telegram*) telegrafiar

wiring ['waɪərɪŋ] *n* instalación *f* eléctrica

wisdom ['wɪzdəm] *n* sabiduría, saber *m*; (*good sense*) cordura; **wisdom tooth** *n* muela del juicio

wise [waɪz] *adj* sabio; (*sensible*) juicioso

wish [wɪʃ] *n* deseo ▷ *vt* desear; **best ~es** (*on birthday etc*) felicidades *fpl*; **with best ~es** (*in letter*) saludos *mpl*, recuerdos *mpl*; **to ~ sb goodbye** despedirse de algn; **he ~ed me well** me deseó mucha suerte; **to ~ to do/sb to do sth** querer hacer/que algn haga algo; **to ~ for** desear

wistful ['wɪstful] *adj* pensativo

wit [wɪt] *n* ingenio, gracia; (*also*: **~s**) inteligencia; (*person*) chistoso/a

witch [wɪtʃ] *n* bruja

○ **KEYWORD**

with [wɪð, wɪθ] *prep* **1** (*accompanying, in the company of*) con (con +*mí, ti, sí* =

conmigo, contigo, consigo); **I was with him** estaba con él; **we stayed with friends** nos quedamos en casa de unos amigos; **I'm (not) with you** (*don't understand*) (no) te entiendo; **to be with it** (*inf: person: up-to-date*) estar al tanto; (*: alert*) ser despabilado **2** (*descriptive, indicating manner etc*) con; de; **a room with a view** una habitación con vistas; **the man with the grey hair/blue eyes** el hombre del sombrero gris/de los ojos azules; **red with anger** rojo de ira; **to shake with fear** temblar de miedo; **to fill sth with water** llenar algo de agua

withdraw [wɪθ'drɔ:] *vt* retirar, sacar ▷ *vi* retirarse; **to ~ money (from the bank)** retirar fondos (del banco); **withdrawal** *n* retirada; (*of money*) reintegro; **withdrawn** *pp of* **withdraw** ▷ *adj* (*person*) reservado, introvertido

withdrew [wɪθ'dru:] *pt of* **withdraw**

wither ['wɪðə*] *vi* marchitarse

withhold [wɪθ'həʊld] *vt* (*money*) retener; (*decision*) aplazar; (*permission*) negar; (*information*) ocultar

within [wɪð'ɪn] *prep* dentro de ▷ *adv* dentro; **~ reach (of)** al alcance (de); **~ sight (of)** a la vista (de); **~ the week** antes de acabar la semana; **~ a mile (of)** a menos de una milla (de)

without [wɪð'aʊt] *prep* sin; **to go ~ sth** pasar sin algo

withstand [wɪθ'stænd] *vt* resistir a

witness ['wɪtnɪs] *n* testigo *mf* ▷ *vt* (*event*) presenciar; (*document*) atestiguar la veracidad de; **to bear ~ to** (*fig*) ser testimonio de

witty ['wɪtɪ] *adj* ingenioso

wives [waɪvz] *npl of* **wife**

wizard ['wɪzəd] *n* hechicero

wk *abbr* = **week**

wobble ['wɒbl] *vi* temblar; (*chair*) cojear

woe [wəʊ] *n* desgracia

woke [wəʊk] *pt of* **wake**

woken ['wəʊkən] *pp of* **wake**

wolf [wʊlf] *n* lobo

woman ['wʊmən] *n* (*pl* **women**) mujer *f*

womb [wu:m] *n* matriz *f*, útero

women ['wɪmɪn] *npl of* **woman**

won [wʌn] *pt, pp of* **win**

wonder ['wʌndə*] *n* maravilla, prodigio; (*feeling*) asombro ▷ *vi*: **to ~ whether/why** preguntarse si/por qué; **to ~ at** asombrarse de; **to ~ about** pensar sobre o en; **it's no ~ (that)** no es de extrañarse (que *+subjun*); **wonderful** *adj* maravilloso

won't [wəʊnt] = **will not**

wood [wʊd] *n* (*timber*) madera; (*forest*) bosque *m*; **wooden** *adj* de madera; (*fig*) inexpresivo; **woodwind** *n* (*Mus*) instrumentos *mpl* de viento de madera; **woodwork** *n* carpintería

wool [wʊl] *n* lana; **to pull the wool over sb's eyes** (*fig*) engatusar a algn; **woollen** (*US* **woolen**) *adj* de lana; **woolly** (*US* **wooly**) *adj* lanudo, de lana; (*fig: ideas*) confuso

word [wɜ:d] *n* palabra; (*news*) noticia; (*promise*) palabra de honor ▷ *vt* redactar; **in other ~s** en otras palabras; **to break/keep one's ~** faltar a la palabra/cumplir la promesa; **to have ~s with sb** reñir con algn; **wording** *n* redacción *f*; **word processing** *n* proceso de textos; **word processor** *n* procesador *m* de textos

wore [wɔ:*] *pt of* **wear**

work [wɜ:k] *n* trabajo; (*job*) empleo, trabajo; (*Art, Literature*) obra ▷ *vi* trabajar; (*mechanism*) funcionar, marchar; (*medicine*) ser eficaz, surtir efecto ▷ *vt* (*shape*) trabajar; (*stone etc*) tallar; (*mine etc*) explotar; (*machine*) manejar, hacer funcionar ▷ *npl* (*of clock, machine*) mecanismo; **to be out of ~** estar parado, no tener trabajo; **to ~ loose** (*part*) desprenderse; (*knot*) aflojarse; **works** *n* (*BRIT: factory*) fábrica; **work out** *vi* (*plans etc*) salir bien, funcionar; **works** vt (problem) resolver; (plan) elaborar; **it works out at £100** suma 100 libras; **worker** n trabajador(a) m/f, obrero/a; **work experience** n: **I'm going to do my work experience in a factory** voy a hacer las prácticas en una fábrica; **workforce** n mano de obra; **working class** n clase f obrera ▷ adj: **working-class** obrero; **working week** n semana laboral; **workman** (irreg) n obrero; **work of art** n obra de arte; **workout** n (Sport) sesión f de ejercicios; **work permit** n permiso de trabajo; **workplace** n lugar m de trabajo; **worksheet** n (Scol) hoja de ejercicios; **workshop** n taller m; **work station** n puesto or estación f de trabajo; **work surface** n encimera; **worktop** n encimera

world [wəːld] n mundo ▷ cpd (champion) del mundo; (power, war) mundial; **to think the ~ of sb** (fig) tener un concepto muy alto de algn; **World Cup** n (Football): **the World Cup** el Mundial, los Mundiales; **world-wide** adj mundial, universal; **World-Wide Web** n: **the World-Wide Web** el World Wide Web

worm [wəːm] n (also: **earth ~**) lombriz f

worn [wɔːn] pp of **wear** ▷ adj usado; **worn-out** adj (object) gastado; (person) rendido, agotado

worried ['wʌrɪd] adj preocupado

worry ['wʌrɪ] n preocupación f ▷ vt preocupar, inquietar ▷ vi preocuparse; **worrying** adj inquietante

worse [wəːs] adj, adv peor ▷ n lo peor; **a change for the ~** un empeoramiento; **worsen** vt, vi empeorar; **worse off** adj (financially): **to be worse off** tener menos dinero; (fig): **you'll be worse off this way** de esta forma estarás peor que nunca

alcalde; (: to judge) señor juez

worst [wəːst] adj, adv peor ▷ n lo peor; **at ~** en lo peor de los casos

worth [wəːθ] n valor m ▷ adj: **to be ~** valer; **it's ~ it** vale or merece la pena; **to be ~ one's while (to do)** merecer la pena (hacer); **worthless** adj sin valor; (useless) inútil; **worthwhile** adj (activity) que merece la pena; (cause) loable

worthy ['wəːðɪ] adj respetable; (motive) honesto; **~ of** digno de

○ KEYWORD

would [wud] aux vb **1** (conditional tense): **if you asked him he would do it** si se lo pidieras, lo haría; **if you had asked him he would have done it** si se lo hubieras pedido, lo habría or hubiera hecho

2 (in offers, invitations, requests): **would you like a biscuit?** ¿quieres una galleta?; (formal) ¿querría una galleta?; **would you ask him to come in?** ¿quiere hacerle pasar?; **would you open the window please?** ¿quiere or podría abrir la ventana, por favor?

3 (in indirect speech): **I said I would do it** dije que lo haría

4 (emphatic): **it would have to snow today!** ¡tenía que nevar precisamente hoy!

5 (insistence): **she wouldn't behave** no quiso comportarse bien

6 (conjecture): **it would have been midnight** sería medianoche; **it would seem so** parece ser que sí

7 (indicating habit): **he would go there on Mondays** iba allí los lunes

wouldn't ['wudnt] = **would not**

wound¹ [wuːnd] n herida ▷ vt herir

wound² [waund] pt, pp of **wind²**

wove [wəuv] pt of **weave**

woven ['wəuvən] pp of **weave**

wrap [ræp] vt (also: **~ up**) envolver; (gift) envolver, abrigar ▷ vi (dress

warmly) abrigarse; **wrapper** n (*on chocolate*) papel m; (BRIT: *of book*) sobrecubierta; **wrapping** n envoltura, envase m; **wrapping paper** n papel m de envolver; (*fancy*) papel m de regalo
wreath [riːð, pl riːðz] n (*funeral wreath*) corona
wreck [rɛk] n (*ship: destruction*) naufragio; (: *remains*) restos mpl del barco; (*pej: person*) ruina f ▷ vt (*car etc*) destrozar; (*chances*) arruinar; **wreckage** n restos mpl; (*of building*) escombros mpl
wren [rɛn] n (Zool) reyezuelo
wrench [rɛntʃ] n (Tech) llave f inglesa; (*tug*) tirón m; (*fig*) dolor m ▷ vt arrancar; **to ~ sth from sb** arrebatar algo violentamente a algn
wrestle ['rɛsl] vi: **to ~ (with sb)** luchar (con *or* contra algn); **wrestler** n luchador(a) m/f (de lucha libre); **wrestling** n lucha libre
wretched ['rɛtʃɪd] adj miserable
wriggle ['rɪgl] vi (*also*: **~ about**) menearse, retorcerse
wring [rɪŋ] (*pt, pp* **wrung**) vt retorcer; (*wet clothes*) escurrir; (*fig*): **to ~ sth out of sb** sacar algo por la fuerza a algn
wrinkle ['rɪŋkl] n arruga ▷ vt arrugar ▷ vi arrugarse
wrist [rɪst] n muñeca
writable ['raɪtəbl] adj (CD, DVD) escribible
write [raɪt] (*pt* **wrote**, *pp* **written**) vt escribir; (*cheque*) extender ▷ vi escribir; **write down** vt escribir; (*note*) apuntar; **write off** vt (*debt*) borrar (como incobrable); (*fig*) desechar por inútil; **write out** vt escribir; **write-off** n siniestro total; **writer** n escritor(a) m/f
writing ['raɪtɪŋ] n escritura; (*handwriting*) letra; (*of author*) obras fpl; **in ~** por escrito; **writing paper** n papel m de escribir
written ['rɪtn] *pp* of **write**
wrong [rɒŋ] adj (*wicked*) malo; (*unfair*) injusto; (*incorrect*) equivocado,

incorrecto; (*not suitable*) inoportuno, inconveniente; (*reverse*) del revés ▷ adv equivocadamente ▷ n injusticia ▷ vt ser injusto con; **you are ~ to do it** haces mal en hacerlo; **you are ~ about that, you've got it ~** en eso estás equivocado; **to be in the ~** no tener razón, tener la culpa; **what's ~?** ¿qué pasa?; **to go ~** (*person*) equivocarse; (*plan*) salir mal; (*machine*) estropearse; **wrongly** adv mal, incorrectamente; (*by mistake*) por error; **wrong number** n (Tel): **you've got the wrong number** se ha equivocado de número
wrote [rəut] *pt* of **write**
wrung [rʌŋ] *pt, pp* of **wring**
WWW n abbr (= *World Wide Web*) WWW m

XL abbr = **extra large**

Xmas ['ɛksməs] n abbr = **Christmas**

X-ray ['ɛksreɪ] n radiografía ▷ vt radiografiar, sacar radiografías de

xylophone ['zaɪləfəun] n xilófono

yacht [jɔt] n yate m; **yachting** n (sport) balandrismo

yard [jɑːd] n patio; (measure) yarda; **yard sale** (us) n venta de objetos usados (en el jardín de una casa particular)

yarn [jɑːn] n hilo; (tale) cuento, historia

yawn [jɔːn] n bostezo ▷ vi bostezar

yd. abbr (=yard) yda

yeah [jɛə] (inf) adv sí

year [jɪə*] n año; **to be 8 ~s old** tener 8 años; **an eight-~-old child** un niño de ocho años (de edad); **yearly** adj anual ▷ adv anualmente, cada año

yearn [jəːn] vi: **to ~ for sth** añorar algo, suspirar por algo

yeast [jiːst] n levadura

yell [jɛl] n grito, alarido ▷ vi gritar

yellow ['jɛləu] adj amarillo; **Yellow Pages®** npl páginas fpl amarillas

yes [jɛs] adv sí ▷ n sí m; **to say/ answer** ~ decir/contestar que sí

yesterday ['jɛstədɪ] adv ayer ▷ n ayer m; ~ **morning/evening** ayer por la mañana/tarde; **all day** ~ todo el día de ayer

yet [jet] *adv* ya; *(negative)* todavía
▷ *conj* sin embargo, a pesar de todo;
it is not finished ~ todavía no está
acabado; **the best ~** el/la mejor hasta
ahora; **as ~** hasta ahora, todavía

yew [juː] *n* tejo

Yiddish ['jɪdɪʃ] *n* yiddish *m*

yield [jiːld] *n (Agr)* cosecha; *(Comm)*
rendimiento ▷ *vt* ceder; *(results)*
producir, dar; *(profit)* rendir ▷ *vi*
rendirse, ceder; *(US Aut)* ceder el paso

yob(bo) ['jɔb(bəʊ)] *n (BRIT inf)*
gamberro

yoga ['jəʊɡə] *n* yoga *m*

yog(h)ourt ['jəʊɡət] *n* yogur *m*

yog(h)urt ['jəʊɡət] *n* = **yog(h)ourt**

yolk [jəʊk] *n* yema (de huevo)

KEYWORD

you [juː] *pron* **1** *(subject: familiar)* tú;
(pl) vosotros/as (SP), ustedes (LAM);
(polite) usted; *(pl)* ustedes; **you are
very kind** eres, es *etc* muy amable; **you
Spanish enjoy your food** a vosotros
(or ustedes) los españoles os *(or* les)
gusta la comida; **you and I will go**
iremos tú y yo

2 *(object: direct: familiar)* te; *(pl)* os (SP),
les (LAM); *(polite)* le; *(pl)* les; *(f)* la; *(pl)* las;
I know you te/le *etc* conozco

3 *(object: indirect: familiar)* te; *(pl)* os (SP),
les (LAM); *(polite)* le; *(pl)* les; **I gave the
letter to you yesterday** te/os *etc* di
la carta ayer

4 *(stressed)* **I told you to do it** te dije a
ti que lo hicieras, es a ti a quien dije que
lo hicieras; *see also* **3**; **5**

5 *(after prep: NB: con +ti =
contigo: familiar)* ti; *(pl)* vosotros/as
(SP), ustedes (LAM); *(: polite)* usted;
(pl) ustedes; **it's for you** es para
ti/vosotros *etc*

6 *(comparisons: familiar)* tú; *(pl)*
vosotros/as (SP), ustedes (LAM);
(: polite) usted; *(pl)* ustedes; **she's
younger than you** es más joven que

tú/vosotros *etc*

7 *(impersonal one)*: **fresh air does you
good** el aire puro (te) hace bien; **you
never know** nunca se sabe; **you can't
do that!** ¡eso no se hace!

you'd [juːd] = **you had; you would**

you'll [juːl] = **you will; you shall**

young [jʌŋ] *adj* joven ▷ *npl (of
animal)* cría; *(people)*: **the ~** los jóvenes,
la juventud; **youngster** *n* joven *mf*

your [jɔː*] *adj* tu; *(pl)* vuestro; *(formal)*
su; *see also* **my**

you're [juə*] = **you are**

yours [jɔːz] *pron* tuyo *(pl)*, vuestro;
(formal) suyo; *see also* **faithfully; mine¹**
see also **sincerely**

yourself [jɔːˈself] *pron* tú mismo;
(complement) te; *(after prep)* ti (mismo);
(formal) usted mismo; *(: complement)*
se; *(after prep)* sí (mismo); **yourselves**
pl pron vosotros mismos; *(after prep)*
vosotros (mismos); *(formal)* ustedes
(mismos); *(: complement)* se; *(: after prep)*
sí mismos; *see also* **oneself**

youth [*pl* juːðz *n*] juventud *f*; *(young
man)* joven *m*; **youth club** *n* club *m*
juvenil; **youthful** *adj* juvenil; **youth
hostel** *n* albergue *m* de juventud

you've [juːv] = **you have**

Z

zeal [ziːl] n celo, entusiasmo
zebra ['ziːbrə] n cebra; **zebra crossing** (BRIT) n paso de peatones
zero ['zɪərəʊ] n cero
zest [zɛst] n ánimo, vivacidad f; (of orange) piel f
zigzag ['zɪgzæg] n zigzag m ▷ vi zigzaguear, hacer eses
Zimbabwe [zɪm'bɑːbwɪ] n Zimbabue m
zinc [zɪŋk] n cinc m, zinc m
zip [zɪp] n (also: ~ **fastener**, (US) **~per**) cremallera (SP), cierre (AM) m, zíper m (MEX, CAM) ▷ vt (also: ~ **up**) cerrar la cremallera de; (file) comprimir; **zip code** (US) n código postal; **zip file** n (Comput) archivo comprimido; **zipper** (US) n cremallera
zit [zɪt] n grano
zodiac ['zəʊdɪæk] n zodíaco
zone [zəʊn] n zona
zoo [zuː] n (jardín m) zoo m
zoology [zuː'ɒlədʒɪ] n zoología
zoom [zuːm] vi: **to ~ past** pasar zumbando; **zoom lens** n zoom m
zucchini [zuː'kiːnɪ] (US) n(pl) calabacín(ines) m(pl)

Phrasefinder

Guía del viajero

TOPICS		TEMAS

TOPICS | TEMAS

MEETING PEOPLE | CONOCER A GENTE

Hello!	¡Buenos días!
Good evening!	¡Buenas tardes!
Good night!	¡Buenas noches!
Goodbye!	¡Adiós!
What's your name?	¿Cómo se llama usted?
My name is ...	Me llamo ...
This is ...	Le presento a ...
my wife.	*mi mujer.*
my husband.	*mi marido.*
my partner.	*mi pareja.*
Where are you from?	¿De dónde es usted?
I come from ...	Soy de ...
How are you?	¿Cómo está usted?
Fine, thanks.	Bien, gracias.
And you?	¿Y usted?
Do you speak English?	¿Habla usted inglés?
I don't understand Spanish.	No entiendo el español.
Thanks very much!	¡Muchas gracias!

Asking the Way | ¿Cómo ir hasta …?

Where is the nearest …?	¿Dónde está el/la … más próximo(-a)?
How do I get there?	¿Cómo voy hasta allí?
How do I get to …?	¿Cómo voy hasta el/la …?
Is it far?	¿Está muy lejos?
How far is it to there?	¿Qué distancia hay hasta allí?
Is this the right way to …?	¿Es éste el camino correcto para ir al/a la/a …?
I'm lost.	Me he perdido.
Can you show me on the map?	¿Me lo puede señalar en el mapa?
Which signs should I follow?	¿Qué indicadores tengo que seguir?
You have to turn round.	Tiene que dar la vuelta.
Go straight on.	Siga todo recto.
Turn left/right.	Tuerza a la izquierda/ a la derecha.
Take the second street on the left/right.	Tome la segunda calle a la izquierda/a la derecha.

Car Hire | Alquiler de coches

I want to hire …	Quisiera alquilar …
a car.	un coche.
a moped.	una motocicleta.
a motorbike.	una moto.
A small car, please.	Un coche pequeño, por favor.
An automatic, please.	Un coche con cambio automático, por favor.

GETTING AROUND | TRASLADOS

How much is it for ...?	¿Cuánto cuesta por ...?
one day	*un día*
a week	*una semana*
I'd like to leave the car in ...	Quisiera entregar el coche en ...
Is there a kilometre charge?	¿Hay que pagar kilometraje?
How much is the kilometre charge?	¿Cuánto hay que pagar por kilómetro?
What is included in the price?	¿Qué se incluye en el precio?
I'd like to arrange ...	Quisiera contratar ...
collision damage waiver.	*un seguro con limitación de responsabilidad.*
personal accident insurance.	*un seguro de ocupantes.*
I'd like a child seat for a ...-year-old child.	Quisiera un asiento infantil para un niño de ... años.
Please show me the controls.	¿Puede explicarme las funciones de los interruptores?
What do I do if I have an accident/if I break down?	¿Qué debo hacer en caso de accidente/de avería?

Breakdowns | Averías

My car has broken down.	Tengo una avería.
Call the breakdown service, please.	Por favor, llame al servicio de auxilio en carretera.
I'm a member of a rescue service.	Soy socio(-a) de un club del automóvil.
I'm on my own.	Estoy solo(-a).
I have children in the car.	Llevo niños conmigo.

Can you tow me to the next garage, please?	Por favor, remólqueme hasta el taller más próximo.
Where is the next garage?	¿Dónde está el taller más próximo?
... is broken.	... está roto.
The exhaust	El escape
The gearbox	El cambio
The windscreen	El parabrisas
... are not working.	... no funcionan.
The brakes	Los frenos
The headlights	Las luces
The windscreen wipers	Los limpiaparabrisas
The battery is flat.	La batería está descargada.
The car won't start.	El motor no arranca.
The engine is overheating.	El motor se recalienta.
The oil warning light won't go off.	El piloto del aceite no se apaga.
The oil/petrol tank is leaking.	El cárter de aceite/el depósito de combustible tiene una fuga.
I have a flat tyre.	He tenido un pinchazo.
Can you repair it?	¿Puede repararlo?
When will the car be ready?	¿Cuándo estará listo el coche?
Do you have the parts for ...?	¿Tienen recambios para ...?
The car is still under warranty.	El coche aún tiene garantía.

Parking | Aparcamiento

Can I park here?	¿Puedo aparcar aquí?
How long can I park here?	¿Cuánto tiempo puedo dejar aparcado el coche aquí?

GETTING AROUND | TRASLADOS

Do I need to buy a (car- parking) ticket?	¿Tengo que sacar un ticket de estacionamiento?
Where is the ticket machine?	¿Dónde está el expendedor de tickets de estacionamiento?
The ticket machine isn't working.	El expendedor de tickets de estacionamiento no funciona.
Where do I pay the fine?	¿Dónde puedo pagar la multa?

Petrol Station | Gasolinera

Where is the nearest petrol station?	¿Dónde está la gasolinera más próxima?
Fill it up, please.	Lleno, por favor.
30 euros' worth of ..., please.	30 euros de ...
diesel	*diesel.*
(unleaded) economy petrol	*gasolina normal.*
premium unleaded	*súper.*
Pump number ... please.	Número ..., por favor.
Please check ...	Por favor, compruebe ...
the tyre pressure.	*la presión de los neumáticos.*
the oil.	*el aceite.*
the water.	*el agua.*
A token for the car wash, please.	Deme una ficha para el túnel de lavado.

Accident | Accidentes

Please call ...	Por favor, llame ...
the police.	*a la policía.*
the emergency doctor.	*al médico de urgencia.*
Here are my insurance details.	Éstos son los datos de mi seguro.

GETTING AROUND | TRASLADOS

Give me your insurance details, please.	Por favor, deme los datos de su seguro.
Can you be a witness for me?	¿Puede ser usted mi testigo?
You were driving too fast.	Usted conducía muy rápido.
It wasn't your right of way.	Usted no tenía preferencia.

Travelling by Car | Viajando en coche

What's the best route to ...?	¿Cuál es el mejor camino para ir a ...?
Where can I pay the toll?	¿Dónde puedo pagar el peaje?
I'd like a motorway tax sticker ...	Quisiera un indicativo de pago de peaje ...
for a week.	*para una semana.*
for a month.	*para un mes.*
for a year.	*para un año.*
Do you have a road map of this area?	¿Tiene un mapa de carreteras de esta zona?

Cycling | En bicicleta

Is there a cycle map of this area?	¿Hay mapas de esta zona con carril-bici?
Where is the cycle path to ...?	¿Dónde está el carril-bici para ir a ...?
How far is it now to ...?	¿Cuánto queda para llegar a ...?
Can I keep my bike here?	¿Puedo dejar aquí mi bicicleta?
Please lock my bike in a secure place.	Por favor, deje la bicicleta con cadena en un lugar seguro.
My bike has been stolen.	Me han robado la bicicleta.
Where is the nearest bike repair shop?	¿Dónde hay por aquí un taller de bicicletas?

x

GETTING AROUND | TRASLADOS

The frame is twisted.	El cuadro de la bicicleta se ha torcido.
The brake isn't/the gears aren't working.	El freno/el cambio de marchas no funciona.
The chain is broken.	La cadena se ha roto.
I've got a flat tyre.	He tenido un pinchazo.
I need a puncture repair kit.	Necesito una caja de parches.

Train	Ferrocarril
A single to ..., please.	Un billete sencillo para ..., por favor.
I would like to travel first/second class.	Me gustaría viajar en primera/segunda clase.
Two returns to ..., please.	Dos billetes de ida y vuelta para ..., por favor.
Is there a reduction ...?	¿Hay descuento ...?
for students	*para estudiantes*
for pensioners	*para pensionistas*
for children	*para niños*
with this pass	*con este carnet*
I'd like to reserve a seat on the train to ... please.	Una reserva para el tren que va a ..., por favor.
Non smoking/smoking, please.	No fumadores/fumadores, por favor.
Facing the front, please.	Mirando hacia adelante, por favor.
I want to book a couchette/a berth to ...	Quisiera reservar una litera/coche-cama para ...
When is the next train to ...?	¿Cuándo sale el próximo tren para ...?

GETTING AROUND	TRASLADOS
s there a supplement to pay?	¿Tengo que pagar suplemento?
Do I need to change?	¿Hay que hacer transbordo?
Where do I change?	¿Dónde tengo que hacer transbordo?
Will my connecting train wait?	¿El tren de enlace esperará?
Is this the train for ...?	¿Es éste el tren que va a ...?
Excuse me, that's my seat.	Perdone, éste es mi asiento.
I have a reservation.	Tengo una reserva.
Is this seat free?	¿Está libre este asiento?
Please let me know when we get to ...	¿Por favor, avíseme cuando lleguemos a ...?
Where is the buffet car?	¿Dónde está el coche restaurante?
Where is coach number ...?	¿Cuál es el vagón número ...?

Ferry	Transbordador
Is there a ferry to ...?	¿Sale algún transbordador para ...?
When is the next ferry to ...?	¿Cuándo sale el próximo transbordador para ...?
When is the first/last ferry to ...?	¿Cuándo sale el primer/ último transbordador para ...?
How much is ...?	¿Cuánto cuesta ...?
a single	*el billete sencillo*
a return	*el billete de ida y vuelta*
How much is it for a car/camper with ... people?	¿Cuánto cuesta transportar el coche/coche caravana con ... personas?

GETTING AROUND	TRASLADOS
Where does the boat leave from?	¿De dónde zarpa el barco?
How long does the crossing take?	¿Cuánto dura la travesía?
Do they serve food on board?	¿Sirven comida en el barco?
Where is ...?	¿Dónde está ...?
the restaurant	el restaurante
the bar	el bar
the duty-free shop	la tienda de duty-free
How do I get to the car deck?	¿Cómo llego a la cubierta donde están los coches?
Where is cabin number ...?	¿Dónde está la cabina número ...?
Do you have anything for seasickness?	¿Tienen algo para el mareo?

Plane	Avión
Where is the luggage for the flight from ...?	¿Dónde está el equipaje procedente de...?
Where can I change some money?	¿Dónde puedo cambiar dinero?
How do I get to ... from here?	¿Cómo se va desde aquí a ...?
Where is ...?	¿Dónde está ...?
the taxi rank	la parada de taxis
the bus stop	la parada del bus
the information office	la oficina de información
I'd like to speak to a representative of British Airways.	Quisiera hablar con un representante de British Airways.
My luggage hasn't arrived.	Mi equipaje no ha llegado.
Can you page ...?	¿Puede llamar por el altavoz a ...?

GETTING AROUND | TRASLADOS

Where do I check in for the flight to ...?	¿Dónde hay que facturar para el vuelo a ...?
Which gate for the flight to ...?	¿Cuál es la puerta de embarque del vuelo para ...?
When is the latest I can check in?	¿Hasta qué hora como máximo se puede facturar?
When does boarding begin?	¿Cuándo es el embarque?
Window/aisle, please.	Ventanilla/pasillo, por favor.
I've lost my boarding pass/ my ticket.	He perdido la tarjeta de embarque/el billete.
I'd like to change/ cancel my flight.	Quisiera cambiar la reserva de vuelo/anular la reserva.

Local Public Transport | Transporte público de cercanías

How do I get to ...?	¿Cómo se llega al/a la/ hasta ...?
Which number goes to ...?	¿Qué línea va hasta ...?
Where is the nearest ...?	¿Dónde está la próxima ...?
bus stop	*parada del bus*
tram stop	*parada de tranvía*
underground station	*estación de metro*
suburban railway station	*estación de cercanías*
Where is the bus station?	¿Dónde está la estación de autobuses?
A ticket, please.	Un billete, por favor.
To ...	A ...
For ... zones.	Para ... zonas.
Is there a reduction ...?	¿Hay descuento ...?
for students	*para estudiantes*
for pensioners	*para pensionistas*

GETTING AROUND | TRASLADOS

for children	*para niños*
for the unemployed	*para desempleados*
with this card	*con este carnet*
Do you have multi-journey tickets/day tickets?	¿Hay tarjetas multiviaje/ billetes para todo un día?
How does the (ticket) machine work?	¿Cómo funciona la máquina (de billetes)?
Do you have a map of the rail network?	¿Tiene un plano de la red de trenes?
Please tell me when to get off.	¿Puede decirme cuándo tengo que bajar?
What is the next stop?	¿Cuál es la próxima parada?
Can I get past, please?	¿Me deja pasar?

Taxi | Taxi

Where can I get a taxi?	¿Dónde puedo coger un taxi?
Call me a taxi, please.	¿Puede llamar a un taxi?
Please order me a taxi for ... o'clock.	Por favor, pídame un taxi para las ...
To the airport/station, please.	Al aeropuerto/a la estación, por favor.
To the ... hotel, please.	Al hotel ..., por favor.
To this address, please.	A esta dirección, por favor.
I'm in a hurry.	Tengo mucha prisa.
How much is it?	¿Cuánto cuesta el trayecto?
I need a receipt.	Necesito un recibo.
I don't have anything smaller.	No tengo moneda más pequeña.
Keep the change.	Quédese con el cambio.
Stop here, please.	Pare aquí, por favor.

Camping | Camping

Is there a campsite here?	¿Hay un camping por aquí?
We'd like a site for ...	Quisiéramos un lugar para ...
a tent.	*una tienda de campaña.*
a camper van.	*un coche caravana.*
a caravan.	*una caravana.*
We'd like to stay one night/ ... nights.	Queremos quedarnos una noche/... noches.
How much is it per night?	¿Cuánto es por noche?
Where are ...?	¿Dónde están ...?
the toilets	*los lavabos*
the showers	*las duchas*
the dustbins	*los contenedores de basura*
Where is ...?	¿Dónde está ...?
the shop	*la tienda*
the site office	*la oficina de administración*
the restaurant	*el restaurante*
Can we camp here overnight?	¿Podemos acampar aquí esta noche?
Can we park our camper van/caravan here overnight?	¿Podemos aparcar aquí esta noche el coche caravana/ la caravana?

Self-Catering | Vivienda para las vacaciones

Where do we get the key for the apartment/house?	¿Dónde nos dan la llave para el piso/la casa?
Which is the key for this door?	¿Qué llave es la de esta puerta?
Do we have to pay extra for electricity/gas?	¿Hay que pagar aparte la luz/ el gas?

GETTING AROUND	ALOJAMIENTO
Where are the fuses?	¿Dónde están los fusibles?
Where is the electricity meter?	¿Dónde está el contador de la luz?
Where is the gas meter?	¿Dónde está el contador del gas?
How does ... work?	¿Cómo funciona ...?
the washing maching	*la lavadora*
the cooker	*la cocina*
the heating	*la calefacción*
the water heater	*el calentador de agua*
Please show us how this works.	¿Puede mostrar cómo funciona por favor?
Whom do I contact if there are any problems?	¿Con quién debo hablar si hubiera algún problema?
We need ...	Necesitamos ...
a second key.	*otra copia de la llave.*
more sheets.	*más sábanas.*
more crockery.	*más vajilla.*
The gas has run out.	Ya no queda gas.
There is no electricity.	No hay corriente.
Where do we hand in the key when we're leaving?	¿Dónde hay que entregar la llave cuando nos vayamos?
Do we have to clean the apartment/the house before we leave?	¿Hay que limpiar el piso/ la casa antes de marcharnos?

Hotel	Hotel
Do you have a ... for tonight?	¿Tienen una ... para esta noche
single room	*habitación individual*
double room	*habitación doble*
room for ... people	*habitación para ... personas*

with bath	con baño
with shower	con ducha
I want to stay for one night/ ... nights.	Quisiera pasar una noche/ ... noches.
I booked a room in the name of ...	Tengo reservada una habitación a nombre de ...
I'd like another room.	Quisiera otra habitación.
What time is breakfast?	¿Cuándo sirven el desayuno?
Where is breakfast served?	¿Dónde sirven el desayuno?
Can I have breakfast in my room?	¿Podrían traerme el desayuno a la habitación?
Where is ...?	¿Dónde está ...?
the restaurant	*el restaurante*
the bar	*el bar*
the gym	*el gimnasio*
the swimming pool	*la piscina*
Put that in the safe, please.	Por favor, póngalo en la caja fuerte.
I'd like an alarm call for tomorrow morning at ...	Por favor, despiértenme mañana a las ...
I'd like to get these things washed/cleaned.	¿Puede lavarme/limpiarme esto?
Please bring me ...	Por favor, tráigame ...
... doesn't work.	... no funciona.
The key, please.	La llave, por favor.
Room number ...	Número de habitación ...
Are there any messages for me?	¿Hay mensajes para mí?
Please prepare the bill.	Por favor, prepare la cuenta.

SHOPPING | DE COMPRAS

I'm looking for ...	Estoy buscando ...
I'd like ...	Quisiera ...
Do you have ...?	¿Tienen ...?
Can you show me ..., please?	¿Podría mostrarme ...?
Where is the nearest shop which sells ...?	¿Dónde hay por aquí una tienda de ...?
photographic equipment	*fotografía*
shoes	*zapatos*
souvenirs	*recuerdos*
Do you have this ...?	¿Lo tiene ...?
in another size	*en otra talla*
in another colour	*en otro color*
I take size ...	Mi talla es la ...
What shoe size are you?	¿Qué número calza?
I'm a size 5½.	Calzo un cuarenta.
I'll take it.	Me lo quedo.
Do you have anything else?	¿Tienen alguna otra cosa distinta?
That's too expensive.	Es demasiado caro.
I'm just looking.	Sólo estaba mirando.
Do you take ...?	¿Aceptan ...?
credit cards	*tarjetas de crédito*
eurocheques	*eurocheques*

Food Shopping | Alimentos

Where is the nearest ...?	¿Dónde hay por aquí cerca ...?
supermarket	*un supermercado*
baker's	*una panadería*
butcher's	*una carnicería*
greengrocer's	*una frutería y verdulería*

SHOPPING | DE COMPRAS

Where can you buy groceries?	¿Dónde se puede comprar comida?
Where is the market?	¿Dónde está el mercado?
When is the market on?	¿Cuándo hay mercado?
a kilo of ...	un kilo de ...
a pound of ...	medio kilo de ...
200 grams of ...	doscientos gramos de ...
... slices of ...	... lonchas de ...
a litre of ...	un litro de ...
a bottle of ...	una botella de ...
a packet of ...	un paquete de ...

Post Office | Correos

Where is the nearest post office?	¿Dónde queda la oficina de Correos más cercana?
When does the post office open?	¿Cuándo abre Correos?
Where can I buy stamps?	¿Dónde puedo comprar sellos?
I'd like ... stamps for postcards/letters to Britain/the United States.	Quisiera ... sellos para postales/cartas a Gran Bretaña/Estados Unidos.
I'd like to post/send ...	Quisiera entregar ...
this letter.	esta carta.
this small packet.	este pequeño paquete.
this parcel.	este paquete.
By airmail/express mail/registered mail.	Por avión/por correo urgente/certificado.
I'd like to send a telegram.	Quisiera mandar un telegrama.
Here is the text.	Aquí tiene el texto.

SHOPPING | DE COMPRAS

Is there any mail for me?	¿Tengo correo?
Where is the nearest postbox?	¿Dónde hay un buzón de correos por aquí cerca?

Photos and Videos | Vídeo y fotografía

A colour film/slide film, please.	Un carrete en color/un carrete para diapositivas, por favor.
With twenty-four/thirty-six exposures.	De veinticuatro/treinta y seis fotos.
Can I have a tape for this video camera, please?	Quisiera una cinta para esta cámara.
Can I have batteries for this camera, please?	Quisiera pilas para esta cámara, por favor.
The camera is sticking.	La cámara se atasca.
Can you take the film out, please.	Por favor, saque el carrete.
Can you develop this film, please?	Quisiera revelar este carrete.
I'd like the photos …	Las fotos las quiero …
matt.	*en mate.*
glossy.	*en brillo.*
ten by fifteen centimetres.	*en formato de diez por quince.*
When will the photos be ready?	¿Cuándo puedo pasar a recoger las fotos?
How much do the photos cost?	¿Cuánto cuesta el revelado?
Are you allowed to take photos here?	¿Aquí se pueden sacar fotos?
Could you take a photo of us, please?	¿Podría sacarnos una foto?

Sightseeing | Visitas turísticas

Where is the tourist office?	¿Dónde está la oficina de turismo?
Do you have any leaflets about ...?	¿Tienen folletos sobre ...?
What sights can you visit here?	¿Qué se puede visitar aquí?
Are there any sightseeing tours of the town?	¿Se organizan visitas por la ciudad?
When is ... open?	¿Cuándo está abierto(-a) ...?
the museum	*el museo*
the church	*la iglesia*
the castle	*el palacio*
How much does it cost to get in?	¿Cuánto cuesta la entrada?
Are there any reductions ...?	¿Hay descuento ...?
for students	*para estudiantes*
for children	*para niños*
for pensioners	*para pensionistas*
for the unemployed	*para desempleados*
Is there a guided tour in English?	¿Hay alguna visita guiada en inglés?
I'd like a catalogue.	Quisiera un catálogo.
Can I take photos here?	¿Puedo sacar fotos?
Can I film here?	¿Puedo filmar?

Entertainment | Ocio

What is there to do here?	¿Qué se puede hacer por aquí?
Do you have a list of events?	¿Tiene una guía de ocio?

LEISURE | OCIO

Where can we ...?	**¿Dónde se puede ...?**
go dancing	*bailar*
hear live music	*escuchar música en directo*
Where is there ...?	**¿Dónde hay ... ?**
a nice bar	*un buen bar*
a good club	*una buena discoteca*
What's on tonight ...?	**¿Qué dan esta noche ...?**
at the cinema	*en el cine*
at the theatre	*en el teatro*
at the opera	*en la ópera*
at the concert hall	*en la sala de conciertos*
Where can I buy tickets for ...?	**¿Dónde puedo comprar entradas para ...?**
the theatre	*el teatro*
the concert	*el concierto*
the opera	*la ópera*
the ballet	*el ballet*
How much is it to get in?	**¿Cuánto cuesta la entrada?**
I'd like a ticket/... tickets for ...	**Quisiera una entrada/... entradas para ...**
Are there any reductions for ...?	**¿Hay descuento para ...?**
children	*niños*
pensioners	*pensionistas*
students	*estudiantes*
the unemployed	*desempleados*

At the Beach	En la playa
Can you swim here/ in this lake?	**¿Se puede uno bañar aquí/ en este lago?**

LEISURE | OCIO

Where is the nearest quiet beach?	¿Dónde hay una playa tranquila por aquí cerca?
How deep is the water?	¿Qué profundidad tiene el agua?
What is the water temperature?	¿Qué temperatura tiene el agua?
Are there currents?	¿Hay corrientes?
Is it safe to swim here?	¿Se puede nadar aquí sin peligro?
Is there a lifeguard?	¿Hay socorrista?
Where can you ...?	¿Dónde se puede ... por aquí?
go surfing	hacer surf
go waterskiing	practicar esquí acuático
go diving	bucear
go paragliding	hacer parapente
I'd like to hire ...	Quisiera alquilar ...
a beach chair.	un sillón de playa.
a deckchair.	una tumbona.
a sunshade.	una sombrilla.
a surfboard.	una tabla de surf.
a jet-ski.	una moto acuática.
a rowing boat.	un bote de remos.
a pedal boat.	un patín a pedales.

Sport | Deporte

Where can we ...?	¿Dónde se puede ...?
play tennis/golf	jugar a tenis/golf
go swimming	ir a nadar
go riding	montar a caballo
go fishing	ir a pescar
go rowing	hacer remo

LEISURE | OCIO

How much is it per hour?	¿Cuánto cuesta la hora?
Where can I book a court?	¿Dónde puedo reservar una pista?
Where can I hire rackets?	¿Dónde puedo alquilar raquetas de tenis?
Where can I hire a rowing boat/a pedal boat?	¿Dónde puedo alquilar un bote de remos/ un patín a pedales?
Do you need a fishing permit?	¿Se necesita un permiso de pesca?
Where will I get a fishing permit?	¿Dónde me pueden dar un permiso de pesca?
Which sporting events can we go to?	¿Qué actividades deportivas se pueden ver por aquí?
I'd like to see ...	Quisiera ver ...
a football match.	un partido de fútbol.
a horse race.	carreras de caballos.

Skiing | Esquí

Where can I hire skiing equipment?	¿Dónde puedo alquilar un equipo de esquí?
I'd like to hire ...	Quisiera alquilar ...
downhill skis.	unos esquís (de descenso).
cross-country skis.	unos esquís de fondo.
ski boots.	unas botas de esquí.
ski poles.	unos bastones de esquí.
Can you tighten my bindings, please?	¿Podría ajustarme la fijación, por favor?
Where can I buy a ski pass?	¿Dónde puedo comprar el forfait?

I'd like a ski pass ...	Quisiera un forfait ...
for a day.	*para un día.*
for five days.	*para cinco días.*
for a week.	*para una semana.*
How much is a ski pass?	¿Cuánto cuesta el forfait?
When does the first/ last chair-lift leave?	¿Cuándo sale el primer/ el úlitmo telesilla?
Do you have a map of the ski runs?	¿Tiene un mapa de las pistas?
Where are the beginners' slopes?	¿Dónde están las pistas para principiantes?
How difficult is this slope?	¿Cuál es la dificultad de esta pista?
Is there a ski school?	¿Hay una escuela de esquí?
Where is the nearest mountain rescue service post?	¿Dónde se encuentra la unidad más próxima de servicio de salvamento?
Where is the nearest mountain hut?	¿Dónde se encuentra el refugio más próximo?
What's the weather forecast?	¿Cuál es el pronóstico del tiempo?
What is the snow like?	¿Cómo es el estado de la nieve?
Is there a danger of avalanches?	¿Hay peligro de aludes?

FOOD AND DRINK | COMIDA Y BEBIDA

A table for ... people, please.	Una mesa para ... personas, por favor.
The ... please.	Por favor, ...
menu	*la carta.*
wine list	*la carta de vinos.*
What do you recommend?	¿Qué me recomienda?
Do you have ...?	¿Sirven ...?
any vegetarian dishes	*platos vegetarianos*
children's portions	*raciones para niños*
Does that contain ...?	¿Tiene esto ...?
peanuts	*cacahuetes*
alcohol	*alcohol*
Can you bring (more) ... please?	Por favor, traiga (más) ...
I'll have ...	Para mí ...
The bill, please.	La cuenta, por favor.
All together, please.	Cóbrelo todo junto.
Separate bills, please.	Haga cuentas separadas, por favor.
Keep the change.	Quédese con el cambio.
I didn't order this.	Yo no he pedido esto.
The bill is wrong.	La cuenta está mal.
The food is cold/too salty.	La comida está fría/ demasiado salada.

Where can I make a phone call?	¿Dónde puedo hacer una llamada por aquí cerca?
Where is the nearest card phone?	¿Dónde hay un teléfono de tarjetas cerca de aquí?
Where is the nearest coin box?	¿Dónde hay un teléfono de monedas cerca de aquí?
I'd like a twenty-five euro phone card.	Quisiera una tarjeta de teléfono de veinticinco euros.
I'd like some coins for the phone, please.	Necesito monedas para llamar por teléfono.
I'd like to make a reverse charge call.	Quisiera hacer una llamada a cobro revertido.
Hello.	Hola.
This is ...	Soy ...
Who's speaking, please?	¿Con quién hablo?
Can I speak to Mr/Ms ..., please?	¿Puedo hablar con el señor/ la señora ...?
Extension ..., please.	Por favor, póngame con el número ...
I'll phone back later.	Volveré a llamar más tarde.
Can you text me your answer?	¿Puede contestarme con mensaje de móvil?
Where can I charge my mobile phone?	¿Dónde puedo cargar la batería del móvil?
I need a new battery.	Necesito una batería nueva.
Where can I buy a top-up card?	¿Dónde venden tarjetas para móviles?
I can't get a network.	No hay cobertura.

PRACTICALITIES | DATOS PRÁCTICOS

Passport/Customs | Pasaporte/Aduana

Here is ...	Aquí tiene ...
my passport.	mi pasaporte.
my identity card.	mi documento de identidad.
my driving licence.	mi permiso de conducir.
my green card.	mi carta verde.
Here are my vehicle documents.	Aquí tiene la documentación de mi vehículo.
The children are on this passport.	Los niños están incluidos en este pasaporte.
Do I have to pay duty on this?	¿Tengo que declararlo?
This is ...	Esto es ...
a present.	un regalo.
a sample.	una muestra.
This is for my own personal use.	Es para consumo propio.
I'm on my way to ...	Estoy de paso para ir a ...

At the bank | En el banco

Where can I change money?	¿Dónde puedo cambiar diner
Is there a bank/bureau de change here?	¿Hay por aquí un banco/ una casa de cambio?
When is the bank/bureau de change open?	¿Cuándo está abierto el banc abierta la casa de cambio?
I'd like ... euros.	Quisiera ... euros.
I'd like to cash these traveller's cheques/ eurocheques.	Quisiera cobrar estos cheque de viaje/eurocheques.

PRACTICALITIES | DATOS PRÁCTICOS

What's the commission?	¿Cuánto cobran de comisión?
Can I use my credit card to get cash?	¿Puedo sacar dinero en efectivo con mi tarjeta de crédito?
Where is the nearest cash machine?	¿Dónde hay por aquí un cajero automático?
The cash machine swallowed my card.	El cajero automático no me ha devuelto la tarjeta.
Can you give me some change, please.	Deme cambio en monedas, por favor.

Repairs — Reparaciones

Where can I get this repaired?	¿Dónde pueden repararme esto?
Can you repair ...?	¿Puede reparar ...?
these shoes	*estos zapatos*
this watch	*este reloj*
this jacket	*esta chaqueta*
Is it worth repairing?	¿Vale la pena repararlo?
How much will the repairs cost?	¿Cuánto cuesta la reparación?
Where can I have my shoes reheeled?	¿Dónde me pueden poner tacones nuevos?
When will it be ready?	¿Cuándo estará listo?
Can you do it straight away?	¿Puede hacerlo ahora mismo?

PRACTICALITIES | DATOS PRÁCTICOS

Emergency Services	Servicios de urgencia
Help!	¡Socorro!
Fire!	¡Fuego!
Please call ...	Por favor, llame a ...
the emergency doctor.	*un médico de urgencia.*
the fire brigade.	*los bomberos.*
the police.	*la policía.*
I need to make an urgent phone call.	Tengo que hacer una llamada urgente.
I need an interpreter.	Necesito un intérprete.
Where is the police station?	¿Dónde está la comisaría?
Where is the nearest hospital?	¿Dónde está el hospital más cercano?
I want to report a theft.	Quisiera denunciar un robo.
... has been stolen.	Han robado ...
There's been an accident.	Ha habido un accidente.
There are ... people injured.	Hay ... heridos.
My location is ...	Estoy en ...
I've been ...	Me han ...
robbed.	*robado.*
attacked.	*atracado.*
raped.	*violado.*
I'd like to phone my embassy.	Quisiera hablar con mi embajada.

Pharmacy | Farmacia

Where is the nearest pharmacy?	¿Dónde hay por aquí una farmacia?
Which pharmacy provides emergency service?	¿Qué farmacia está de guardia?
I'd like something for ...	Quisiera algo para ...
diarrhoea.	la diarrea.
a temperature.	la fiebre.
travel sickness.	el mareo.
a headache.	el dolor de cabeza.
a cold.	el resfriado.
I'd like ...	Quisiera ...
plasters.	tiritas.
a bandage.	un vendaje.
some paracetamol.	paracetamol.
I can't take ...	Soy alérgico(-a) a la ...
aspirin.	aspirina.
penicillin.	penicilina.
Is is safe to give to children?	¿Pueden tomarlo los niños?
How should I take it?	¿Cómo tengo que tomarlo?

At the Doctor's | En la consulta médica

I need a doctor.	Necesito que me atienda un médico.
Where is casualty?	¿Dónde está Urgencias?
I have a pain here.	Me duele aquí.
I feel ...	Tengo ...
hot.	mucho calor.
cold.	frío.
I feel sick.	Me siento mal.
I feel dizzy.	Tengo mareos.

HEALTH | SALUD

I'm allergic to ...	Tengo alergia a ...
I am ...	Yo ...
pregnant.	*estoy embarazada.*
diabetic.	*soy diabético(-a).*
HIV-positive.	*soy seropositivo(-a).*
I'm on this medication.	Estoy tomando este medicamento.
My blood group is ...	Mi grupo sanguíneo es ...

At the Hospital | En el hospital

Which ward is ... in?	¿En qué unidad está ...?
When are visiting hours?	¿Cuándo son las horas de visita?
I'd like to speak to ...	Quisiera hablar con ...
a doctor.	*un médico.*
a nurse.	*una enfermera.*
When will I be discharged?	¿Cuándo me van a dar de alta

At the Dentist's | En el dentista

I need a dentist.	Tengo que ir al dentista.
This tooth hurts.	Me duele este diente.
One of my fillings has fallen out.	Se me ha caído un empaste.
I have an abscess.	Tengo un absceso.
I want/don't want an injection for the pain.	Quiero/no quiero que me ponga una inyección para calmar el dolor.
Can you repair my dentures?	¿Me puede reparar la dentadura?
I need a receipt for the insurance.	Necesito un recibo para mi seguro.

Business Travel	Viajes de negocios
I'd like to arrange a meeting with ...	Quisiera concertar hora para una reunión con ...
I have an appointment with Mr/Ms ...	Tengo una cita con el señor/ la señora ...
Here is my card.	Aquí tiene mi tarjeta.
I work for ...	Trabajo para ...
How do I get to ...?	¿Cómo se llega ...?
your office	*a su despacho*
I need an interpreter.	Necesito un intérprete.
Can you copy that for me, please?	Por favor, hágame una copia de eso.
May I use ...?	¿Puedo usar ...?
your phone	*su teléfono*
your computer	*su ordenador*

Disabled Travellers	Minusválidos
Is it possible to visit ... with a wheelchair?	¿La visita a ... es posible también para personas en silla de ruedas?
Where is the wheelchair-accessible entrance?	¿Por dónde se puede entrar con la silla de ruedas?
Is your hotel accessible to wheelchairs?	¿Tiene su hotel acceso para minusválidos?
I need a room ...	Necesito una habitación ...
on the ground floor.	*en la planta baja.*
with wheelchair access.	*con acceso para minusválidos.*
Do you have a lift for wheelchairs?	¿Tienen ascensor para minusválidos?
Do you have wheelchairs?	¿Tienen sillas de ruedas?

TRAVELLERS | VIAJEROS

Where is the disabled toilet?	¿Dónde está el lavabo para minusválidos?
Can you help me get on/ off please?	¿Podría ayudarme a subir/ bajar, por favor?
A tyre has burst.	Se ha reventado un neumático.
The battery is flat.	La batería está descargada.
The wheels lock.	Las ruedas se bloquean.

Travelling with children | Viajando con niños

Are children allowed in too?	¿Pueden entrar niños?
Is there a reduction for children?	¿Hay descuento para niños?
Do you have children's portions?	¿Sirven raciones para niños?
Do you have ...?	¿Tienen ...?
a high chair	*una sillita*
a cot	*una cama infantil*
a child's seat	*un asiento infantil*
a baby's changing table	*una mesa para cambiar al bebé*
Where can I change the baby?	¿Dónde puedo cambiar al bebé?
Where can I breast-feed the baby?	¿Dónde puedo dar el pecho al niño?
Can you warm this up, please?	¿Puede calentarlo, por favor?
What is there for children to do?	¿Qué pueden hacer aquí los niños?
Is there a child-minding service?	¿Hay aquí un servicio de guardería?
My son/daughter is ill.	Mi hijo/mi hija está enfermo(-a).